//Welcome to the Armored Core VI: Fires of Rubicon Official Pilot's Manual.

This is a game that shows off the very best action combat its too-long dormant genre has to offer; seeing Armored Core VI played well can't help but inspire a desire to master it. Marking the return of a much-loved franchise with a long and complex history, it presents an unusual proposition for those new to the series. It tells an entirely new story that—while built on the series' narrative foundations—maintains a degree of separation from (almost) all that has come before.

This means that newcomers to Armored Core needn't worry about their lack of grounding in the series' lore. The same can't be said, however, of jumping into Armored Core VI with no experience of the combat and assembly flow that has been the series' cornerstone since its inception. This can be a very challenging game, especially to those unfamiliar with its brand of fast-paced mecha action, and there hasn't been anything else quite like it in far too long.

Despite the game's focus on the deeply rewarding AC assembly process, our goal with this book was not to provide an encyclopedia of stats and build possibilities. We've tried to impart the necessary knowledge to make every part of that process easy to understand, without intruding on its inherent creativity. We placed most of our focus, however, on the 59 missions (and 41 virtual Arena battles) in which all of the game's action takes place.

Most of this book's pages are dedicated to ensuring that anyone who wants to master these challenges and experience the game's entire story can comfortably do so. It'll be an experience to savor—good luck, 621.

Team Future Press//

CHAPTER OVERVIEW

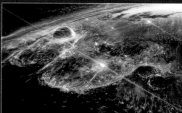

TABLE OF CONTENTS

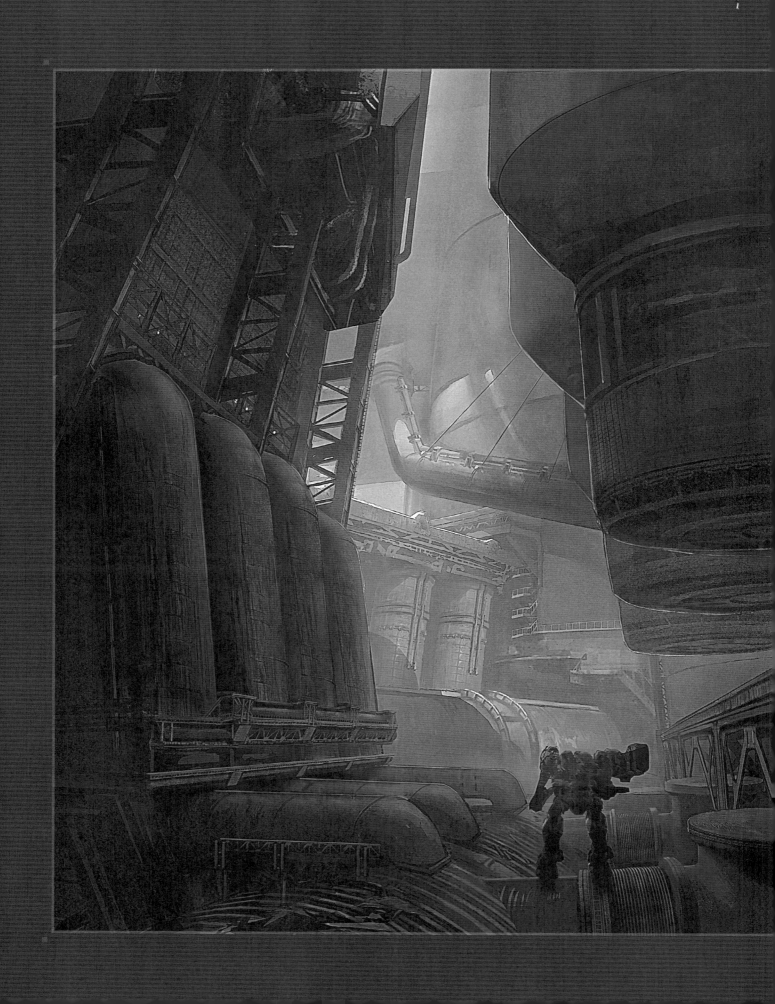

CHAPTER 1 SYSTEM GUIDE

Landing on Rubicon plunges you into a fight for survival. You'll need to learn how to pilot your Armored Core while navigating the immediate threats posed by the established factional forces. This chapter will bring you up to speed as a pilot, detailing key mechanics and introducing you to the depths of Armored Core VI's combat systems.

GETTING STARTED

As the latest entry in a long-running series that first made its debut in 1997, Armored Core VI can best be described as a third-person mech action game with a heavy emphasis on shooting, vertical mobility, and customization. Many of its elements might feel familiar, but in typical FromSoftware fashion, the gameplay has been carefully crafted and refined to offer a degree of depth and flexibility that sets it apart from other titles. This section will cover some of the basics you should know before getting started with the game.

CONTROLS

The first step to forging your reputation as an independent mercenary is to become familiar with your AC's basic controls. Regardless of which platform you're playing on, Armored Core VI is primarily designed to be played using a gamepad, so all control explanations in this guide will use the default gamepad control scheme (Type A). If you're playing on PC, that version also supports full mouse & keyboard controls that you can customize to your liking from the Input Device Settings tab in the System Menu. When using a gamepad, the Control Settings tab in the System Menu offers the choice between three control type presets. Here's a brief overview of each type:

- **Type A**
  All weapon functionality is assigned to triggers and shoulder buttons, prioritizing ease of use of your AC's arsenal. Jump and Quick Boost controls are relegated to the face buttons, which can potentially limit your ability to move the camera with the Right Stick while performing these actions.

- **Type B**
  Jump and Quick Boost controls are assigned to the triggers, prioritizing the ability to evade or remain airborne without letting go of the Right Stick. Shoulder weapons are moved to the face buttons, which can make it more challenging to use charge attacks without first using Target Assist to lock on to an enemy.

- **Type C**
  Similar to Type B, but hand weapons are assigned to the face buttons instead.

If none of these preset control types are quite to your liking, it's also possible to create up to three custom control layouts. To do so, pick one of the custom presets in Control Assignments and then use the Edit button to select a base configuration; you'll then be able to fully edit the function of each button. Changes you make are saved to the selected custom preset.

DIFFICULTY

Armored Core VI is designed to be a challenging experience and doesn't feature traditional difficulty settings. However, how difficult a particular mission or opponent will be can vary wildly depending on how you've customized your AC. Gaining knowledge of the systems and mechanics as you play, as well as learning enemy attacks, will also contribute greatly to your success. Veteran pilots looking for more of a challenge should aim to unlock S-Rank ratings when replaying missions.

Game progress is tied to a single save file per profile, so always use the Continue option unless you're sure you want to delete all of your progress.

LEXICON OF TERMS

Armored Core VI features a lot of unique terminology and introduces many intricate concepts early on, and keeping track of it all might feel overwhelming when you first start playing. To help make things easier, this brief lexicon covers essential specs and gameplay systems.

AP

Armor Points—equivalent to health points in other games. Once this value reaches zero, your AC or the enemy craft is destroyed.

EN

Energy—amount of power generated/consumed by AC parts and a stamina-like resource required to perform specific high-mobility actions during gameplay.

FCS

Fire Control System—inner AC part that affects target tracking and missile lock capabilities.

ACS

Attitude Control System—standard on-board system that governs the stability of a craft and its capacity to withstand impacts from attacks before being staggered.

HUD

Heads-up Display—on-screen interface that appears when controlling your AC.

Specs

Performance specifications of AC parts and overall assembly; equivalent of stats in other games.

Assembly/Build

AC configuration—influences functionality and performance of AC based on parts installed. Both terms are used interchangeably.

COAM

Universal currency on Rubicon—credits/money received as payment for completing jobs and exchanged for new AC parts.

OS Tuning

Operating System Tuning—feature that allows you to upgrade and expand your AC's combat potential by spending OST Chips.

OST Chips

Operating System Tuning Chips—special currency acquired by defeating Arena opponents and used to perform OS upgrades.

Hunter Class

Rank based on how many combat logs you have collected; each new class rank awards a new AC part.

Combat Log

Collectibles acquired through defeating specially marked enemies that contribute to raising your Hunter Class.

Data Log

Pieces of lore unlocked by accessing wrecks found by exploring during missions.

HUD OVERVIEW

The first step to becoming a skilled AC pilot is to familiarize yourself with the heads-up display that appears once you enter the cockpit. This interface conveys vital information about your operational status and enemy threats. Taking the time to review the various on-screen elements and gauges will ensure you always know what's going on once the action heats up.

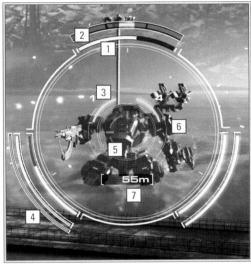

MAIN HUD

1 AP

AP remaining; AP is displayed as both a gauge and precise numerical value to help track the amount of damage sustained. Red damage numbers appear above the AP gauge when enemy attacks hit you.

2 Repair

Repair kits remaining; the small gauge below represents the cooldown period between uses.

3 Scan

Readiness of scanning ability; the small gauge below represents the period between uses.

4 Expansion

Core expansion uses remaining. Following activation, the indicator blinks red until the cooldown period is complete.

5 ACS Gauge

Amount of strain accumulated on the ACS. This gauge fills up based on the impact of enemy attacks and blinks red when your ACS is overloaded.

6 EN Gauge

Amount of EN currently available. This gauge depletes whenever you perform EN-consuming actions and blinks red when empty. EN supply then begins replenishing after a short delay.

7 Compass

Compass that displays navigational coordinates based on the direction the camera is facing; also tracks objective markers and threats.

8 Boost Movement Indicator

Indicates when boost movement is toggled on.

9 System Abnormality Gauge

Displays the level of shock or heat buildup when hit by attacks with those properties, resulting in an electrical discharge or ACS anomaly when the gauge is full.

10 Overburdened Status Indicators

Indicates when leg or arm units have exceeded their load limit, resulting in impaired mobility or target tracking.

11 Ammo Status

Ammo remaining for individual arm and shoulder units. The top value displays ammo currently loaded, and the bottom value displays the total ammo supply. When the bottom value reaches zero, the corresponding weapon can no longer be used until you resupply.

12 Targeting Reticle

Highlights the current lock-on target and displays combat information about the target's status and your AC's arm and shoulder units.

13 Attack Indicators

Warning signals that appear near the center of the HUD to help anticipate the direction and severity of incoming attacks. Weaker attacks are signaled by small orange indicators, whereas stronger attacks are signaled by large red indicators and a distinct audio cue.

14 Current Objective

Displays the next mission objective that you must complete in order to progress.

15 Speed Meter

Displays the speed at which your AC is moving.

16 Altitude Meter

Displays the current altitude level of your AC.

17 Access Prompt

Highlights objects that you can interact with during missions; objects with higher levels of security take longer to access.

TARGETING SYSTEM ELEMENT

1 Target AP

Target's AP. Damage numbers are briefly visible below this gauge when you land a hit.

2 Target ACS Gauge

Target's ACS gauge. This gauge gradually fills up based on the impact of attacks and blinks red when target's ACS is overloaded.

3 Homing Missile Lock

Readiness of homing missile lock for units installed on your AC. The yellow gauges represent each of your arm and back units and begin filling up after acquiring a target, with a full gauge indicating that missile lock is ready. The adjacent value represents the number of homing shots aimed at the target, which can be spread across multiple targets with multi-lock.

4 Weapon Status

Displays how much ammo is available for each arm or back unit installed on your AC. Depending on the reload type, these gauges represent either the amount of ammo loaded in the active magazine or the total supply remaining, with a red overlapping gauge indicating reload time or weapon heat buildup. Some weapons also feature an adjacent gauge that fills up when readying a charge attack.

5 Reticle

The reticle will sway and attempt to center on the current target during engagements, turning red to indicate when target tracking is active. Recoil is represented by reticle bloom when firing.

6 Target Assist Indicator

When Target Assist is engaged, white brackets will close to form a circle around the reticle.

7 Distance to Target

Displays the current distance in meters between your AC and the target.

GAME FLOW

This section aims to shed some light on the game's overall structure by taking a high level view of some of the concepts that will be introduced as you progress. As is traditionally the case in the Armored Core series, this a game of two halves: assembly and combat. Each of these aspects feeds into the other, and mastering only one of them will lead to a much less balanced play experience.

THE GARAGE

Serving as your central hub and base of operations throughout the game, the Garage menu is your starting point for customizing your AC, shopping for new parts, viewing your mercenary license, participating in VR simulations, and taking on requests from clients. You'll automatically return to the Garage menu after each deployment and will unlock access to more of its features as you progress through the storyline. This section provides a brief overview of each option found in the Garage.

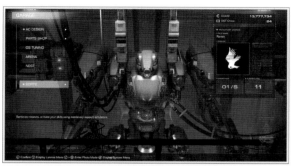

A small teal-colored icon next to a Garage menu entry highlights that a new option, mission, or part has been unlocked in that section.

AC Design — P.28

Access granted:
Complete Prologue "Illegal Entry"

Selecting AC Design opens a host of sub-menus that allow you to customize every aspect of your AC, from its parts and overall performance to its paint scheme and other cosmetic details. The following options are available:

Assembly
Analyze your AC's specs and modify both its design and performance by installing parts from the available selection.

Paint
Change your AC's color scheme, including the material properties and degree of weathering on individual parts.

Decals
Further personalize the appearance of your AC by applying preset emblems or user-created images onto its frame.

Image Editor
Combine multiple layers of preset shapes to create custom images. These can be saved as decals and applied to any part of your AC.

AC Data
Allows you to save your current assembly or instantly load into a different AC build (including data unlocked by defeating Arena opponents) without needing to access the Assembly menu.

Parts Shop — P.50

Access granted:
Complete Missions "Destroy Artillery Installations" or "Grid 135 Cleanup"

Operated by ALLMIND and accessible to all mercenaries, the Parts Shop is a support service that you can access in order to buy additional AC parts from an ever-expanding catalog. You can also sell any parts you own here in exchange for COAM.

Buy
View the current selection of parts available for purchase and compare specs with currently installed parts.

Sell
Sell any obtained parts to earn back their full COAM value. Any parts you've sold immediately become available to repurchase in the Buy menu.

OS Tuning — P.32

Access granted:
Complete Mission "Retrieve Combat Logs" or "Investigate BAWS Arsenal No. 2"

The OS Tuning menu is where you can spend OST Chips earned in the Arena to install OS upgrades to your AC, unlocking new abilities and permanent performance boosts.

Arena — P.348

Access granted:
Complete Mission "Retrieve Combat Logs" or "Investigate BAWS Arsenal No. 2"

This option lets you participate in the Arena, a combat aptitude evaluation program in which you can face off against simulations of all registered mercenaries operating on Rubicon to climb the ranks and earn rewards.

Nest — P.25

Access granted:
Complete Mission "Ocean Crossing"

Here you can enter the Nest, an online battle simulator that lets you team up and fight against other players in various game modes. This feature requires an active internet connection on all platforms and an active subscription to PlayStation Plus or Xbox Game Pass Core on consoles.

Sortie — P.96

Access granted: Complete Prologue "Illegal Entry"

Here you'll find multiple sub-menus from which you can head out on new missions, replay those you've previously completed or hone your skills using mercenary support simulators. The following options are available in the Sortie menu:

Missions
View requests received from clients and sortie on new missions. Completing available missions will progress the story and unlock more missions.

Replay Mission
Revisit missions that you have already completed to earn additional COAM, recover missing logs, or improve your mission rating.

Training
Access mercenary training programs to learn how to control your AC and gain an understanding of basic tactics. You will earn new parts each time you complete a training program.

AC Test
Deploy your AC in a testing simulation to evaluate its performance and tweak your assembly before heading out on the battlefield.

Mercenary License

Access granted:
Complete Prologue "Illegal Entry"

Another service offered by ALLMIND, the Mercenary License program tracks your progress on Rubicon and archives the data logs you've salvaged from wrecks.

Edit Name
Change the pilot name that you entered at the beginning of the game.

Edit Emblem
Swap to a different mercenary emblem by choosing from any available preset design or user-created image.

Archives
Consult all archived data logs you've collected in the field.

Tips
Review all of the gameplay tips you've been shown so far while playing.

MISSIONS & PROGRESSION

Progressing through the game requires you to complete missions, and doing so will often unlock new features and rewards. The game begins with the "Illegal Entry" prologue mission, the completion of which unlocks access to the Garage. New features will unlock in the Garage as you finish more missions and advance the story—you can take on new mission requests or access VR training programs in the Arena by selecting the "Sortie" option.

CHAPTERS

The game's story is divided into five chapters, with each one culminating in events that alter the state of affairs on Rubicon. Each chapter features a different number of missions, with some being much shorter than others. The Mission Intel chapter of this book, starting on P.94, provides a detailed walkthrough of all the missions organized in the order you'll first encounter them as you progress.

THE ARENA

ALLMIND will register you to the Arena near the end of Chapter 1, and you'll regularly unlock new tiers of Arena battles from then on. The ideal progression consists of alternating between completing missions and climbing the Arena's ranks, as this approach quickly unlocks more OST Chips to upgrade your AC. For tips on how to vanquish each opponent, head to the Arena chapter starting on P.346.

THE BENEFITS OF TRAINING

It's essential to run through new training programs the moment they become available. Not only do these brief tutorials introduce you to important gameplay concepts, but finishing one always unlocks unique AC parts that will open up more options when assembling your AC. There are seven training programs in total, and you'll earn the "Advanced Mercenary" certification and emblems after finishing the entire series. See P.394 for the list of parts you'll unlock by completing training missions.

REPLAYING MISSIONS

After completing a mission for the first time, you'll unlock the option to replay it again from the Replay Mission menu. Replaying a mission will allow you to earn more COAM, find missing collectibles, or aim for a better mission rating. You'll have the option to repeat briefings when replaying a mission, but won't be able to watch any cutscene or conversation that may have taken place after first completing it—you also won't be able to affect the course of events for that playthrough by making decisions that differ from your original choices. When starting a New Game+ cycle, you'll keep access to the full list of missions you've completed; once a mission is unlocked, it's available to replay whenever you choose.

NEW GAME+ CYCLES

Once you've completed a playthrough, your progression and rank in the Arena will carry over to the next cycle of the game, saving you the trouble of having to climb up the ranks or acquire parts all over again. The difficulty of the game does not change on subsequent playthroughs, and since you'll have a much wider selection of parts available and a better grasp of AC assembly, many of the key battles are likely to be easier to deal with. Make sure to pay attention to the Arena in New Game+ and New Game++, because even though there are no more ranks to climb, ALLMIND may have further uses for your combat data (see P.349 for more info).

New Game+ cycles are also home to Alt missions, in which you can take part in the same events from a different perspective. Accessing these mission is based on your choices, and completing them can lead to different endings to the game. Everything that awaits you in these Alt missions is covered in the Mission Intel chapter, starting on P.94. If you aren't sensitive to spoilers, you can also follow our recommended mission order across three play cycles in the Progression Guide section on P.398.

EARNING COAM

COAM is the universal currency used in the game and your main reward for completing missions. How much COAM you earn from a mission will depend on its base reward, in addition to other factors such as bonus pay—which you can earn for eliminating optional targets—with expenses incurred from repair and ammo costs being deducted from your total. You'll receive a breakdown of your total income and expenses at the end of each mission, and you can press $\bigcirc$/$\bigtriangleup$ to expand this into an itemized statement. While you can rack up enough expenses during a mission for your rewards to be a negative value, it's not possible for your total COAM to be negative, which means you can't ever go into debt.

PHOTO MODE

Pressing the Options/Touchpad button during regular gameplay will enter Photo Mode. Here you can take creatve screenshots with a host of controls and effects to tweak, in order to get the image exactly as you want it. All effects will be removed once you resume play. Screens will be saved using your PC or console's system menus, which requires pressing the Share/Create button. Note that Photo Mode also works in the Garage, and allows you to see more of the area than you usually otherwise could.

After crash-landing on Rubicon, you'll need to complete the prologue to earn your license to operate as a registered mercenary and take on jobs from various factions.

Tutorial tips appear as you progress to explain the fundamentals of movement and combat. These can be accessed at any time from the Mercenary License menu and are well worth digesting.

The alternate path of the "Attack the Dam Complex" mission sees you fighting the Redguns, who were your allies in the standard version of the mission. Betraying them will have ramifications that will be felt throughout the rest of that playthrough.

Completing bonus objectives, minimizing damage to your AC, and conserving ammo can all contribute to raising your final COAM income at the end of a mission.

COMBAT ZONE

Each mission takes place within a specific section of the region you're operating in—this combat zone is defined with a red boundary line at its edges. The exact position of a combat zone's boundary can change from one mission to another, and can even shift within a mission as you complete objectives and the area of operation is updated. If you're aiming to fully explore during a mission, boosting in a direction until you hit the edge of the combat zone and following it around can be a good way to make sure you've covered the entire perimeter.

Red holographic borders signify the boundary of the mission's combat zone and can't be crossed. Combat zones also feature vertical boundaries, preventing you from ascending too high and damaging you if you fall below the limit.

Reaching a checkpoint is signaled by an on-screen message in the lower-right corner of your HUD.

CHECKPOINTS

Some lengthier missions feature checkpoints that are automatically triggered upon reaching a certain location or completing specific objectives. In the event that your AC is destroyed, you can resume the mission from the most recent checkpoint instead of restarting from the beginning. The number of checkpoints varies per mission, with some sorties including none at all and forcing you to always restart from the beginning. While using checkpoints will prevent you from earning an S-Rank rating when replaying missions, they can be an invaluable aid when simply attempting to get through a challenging section.

Resuming from a checkpoint fully replenishes your AP, ammunition, repair kits, and core expansion uses, giving you a much better chance of getting through the section that just bested you. Before instantly restarting from a checkpoint, it's important to remember that you have access to the Assembly menu on the Mission Failed screen. If you're having trouble with a section and the simple resupply that comes with using a checkpoint isn't sufficient, you can always tinker with your build before heading back into the fray.

ACCESS PROMPTS

While most situations in the game can be solved through combat, there are instances where you'll need to make use of your AC's less lethal systems to access objects in the environment. Icons showing an available system access point can pop up on anything from sealed doorways, wrecks containing secure data logs, and part containers with encrypted locks. These icons typically appear when you're 300m away from an accessible object, but you'll need to have direct line of sight to see them, and not everything that can be accessed will show up with a scan.

Accessible objects can have differing levels of security—from level one to three—and the object's level dictates how long it will take your systems to access it, with one being the fastest and three the slowest. Once you're within 50m you'll see a prompt telling you to press Ⓨ/△ to begin accessing the system. As long as you stay within 100m of the object you're trying to access, you'll be free to move around or fire at enemies. However, if you move out of range, the connection will be lost and you'll have to start again. Note that an OS Tuning upgrade can decrease how long it takes to access an object in the environment; see P.32 for more details.

SUPPLY SHERPAS

Supply sherpas are remotely deployed support units that restore your AP and fully restock your resources when accessed, including repair kits, ammo, and core expansion uses. You won't encounter supply sherpas in every mission, but they generally appear before a challenging boss fight during lengthier sorties. You'll occasionally receive a message from your handler letting you know that you can summon a sherpa nearby, but in most instances, you'll need to look out for the hexagonal resupply icon to let you know that one is available. Supply sherpas are a one-time-use unit, so it's best to deplete your resources as much as possible by taking out any nearby enemies before resupplying. There's rarely more than a single sherpa in the missions that offer them and there's no penalty for resupplying, so we recommend taking advantage of these helpful support units whenever they appear.

PART CONTAINERS

Part containers are unique objects in the environment that hold new parts that you can permanently unlock to further customize your AC. They're often hidden away or guarded by enemies that you'll need to defeat before you can safely retrieve their contents. Doing so is always worthwhile, however, since there's no other way to obtain the parts contained within them. Part containers don't start showing up until the first mission of Chapter 2, but from that point onward you should be diligently scanning the environment in the hopes of revealing a hidden container, because unlike wrecks, your scanner will actually detect them. For a full list of part containers and their contents, head over to P.394 in the Archive section of the Extra Intel chapter.

Part containers feature a flashing orange light that makes them stand out from other objects in the environment and easier to find while you're boosting through missions.

MISSION GAMEPLAY LOOP

Every aspect of Armored Core VI revolves around your AC and its configuration. Your choice of parts, as well as your ability to make effective use of these parts, will play an integral role in determining the outcome of each mission. As you progress, it's best to think of each mission as its own self-contained challenge that influences the optimal types of AC assembly. As you can see in the diagram here, your choices in the Assembly will feed into the mission you tackle, which will then lead you back to Assembly again after observing the threats and reassessing your AC's build.

Mission briefings can provide valuable intel about the threats you'll be facing, and may help to reveal what you'll be up against.

GAMEPLAY LOOP

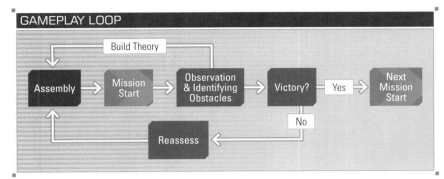

Inspiration can often be found just browsing through the Parts Shop. Look carefully at each part's specs, and find what best fits the task before you.

INITIAL ASSEMBLY

You can't tailor your build to a particular mission until you've at least been through it once and seen the challenges it presents. You can, however, view the mission's briefing to gain some insight and then head back to the Assembly if the clues suggest a particular build will be beneficial. You should consider your first trip out on a mission to be a learning experience during which you put together a plan about how to tackle the threats and obstacles you encounter within it, rather than going in with the assumption that you'll be able to clear it on your first attempt.

This means your initial assembly should be something you think will suit your desired playstyle, while also not being too specialized in a single area—if you have the parts available, try to equip a mix of damage types, for example. It's worth reminding yourself that just because a weapon isn't viable for a particular mission, this doesn't mean it won't prove useful later on.

OBSERVING

During a mission, it's important to observe and take note of the kinds of threats you're facing and how well your AC build was able to deal with them. Of particular importance are the effects that the damage types of your weapons have on certain enemies; kinetic weapons may be more or less effective compared to energy weapons against particular enemies, for example.

It's also crucial to pay attention to your ammunition and note whether the total number of rounds your desired weapon comes with is enough to sustain you throughout the mission. The type of weapon may be useful in the mission you're planning for, but its total ammunition count may not be appropriate for either the length of the mission, or the number of specific enemies you intend to use it against. Remember that being able to equip four weapons at once doesn't mean you should be using all four weapons during every encounter. Some weapons shine at the start of a fight when you're trying to strain your opponent's ACS, whereas others are better used against staggered enemies. Using weapons at the appropriate time will help significantly with your ammunition management. Your AP is another resource that you need to keep in mind; not having enough to last you to the end of a mission is one of the clearest signs that you may want to adjust your build or consider a different approach.

REASSESSING

If you're struggling because your AC isn't performing adequately when faced against the challenges presented in the mission, it's time to head back to the Assembly and re-evaluate your build. Questioning what caused you to fail the mission and identifying which aspects of your AC you can alter based on the parts available will give you a better chance at victory. Try asking yourself some of the following questions to help determine which areas of your build need to be adjusted:

Q: Am I dealing enough damage?

A: Experiment with different damage types to figure out the enemy's weaknesses or focus on staggering before following up with direct hits to increase your damage output.

Q: Is my AC getting staggered or destroyed too easily?

A: Equip sturdier frame parts that increase your AP and attitude stability. Identify the most dangerous attacks used by enemies and raise your defensive specs against that damage type.

Q: Do I run out of EN too quickly when maneuvering my AC?

A: Try lowering your total weight and switching to a different generator or booster with specs that better support your heavy use of EN-consuming actions.

Q: Is there an easier way to avoid this attack that keeps hitting me?

A: Adopting a different approach, such as focusing on aerial evasion with tetrapod legs, increasing Quick Boost distance with reverse-joint legs, or equipping a shield to mitigate damage, can often make all the difference.

Q: Could fighting at long range or focusing on close range combat make things easier in this scenario?

A: Trying out weapons that are more effective at different ranges can often make difficult battles much easier.

You'll find yourself in a multitude of different combat scenarios both in terms of terrain and enemy configuration, so varying your AC's frame and inner parts to suit the task at hand will be just as important as the weapons you choose to equip. For example, in one mission you may find yourself in a large, open space combating a single enemy AC. Contrast this with another mission in which you cover great distances while battling dozens of enemies in sustained aerial combat. What you choose to enter these missions with may look entirely different when you factor in different playstyles, movement options, or the ammunition you'll need. To learn everything there is to know about designing your AC, turn to P.26.

COLLECTIBLES AND RANKING

While the critical path through most missions is clearly indicated by objective markers, venturing off course and exploring every nook and cranny of the environment can often be rewarding. What form that reward takes can be anything from additional information that you recover from a wreck to increase your understanding of the world around you and the motivations of characters, or simply an additional part that could slot into your AC build. This section covers the various types of collectibles or bonus objectives that you can encounter during missions.

MISSION RANKS

Mission ranks are grades used to evaluate your performance when opting to play through a mission multiple times via Mission Replay; you will never be graded during regular story progression. Your rank at the end is based on numerous factors relating to your performance—including the amount of damage taken, your total clear time, ammo consumed and enemies defeated, and whether you've used a checkpoint. The highest rank is an S, while the lowest you can achieve is a D. Achieving an S-Rank rating on a mission has no tangible benefit, other than higher payout on the mission result screen due to how well you're likely to have performed. There is, however, an associated Trophy/Achievement and unique emblem for achieving an S-Rank rating on all missions. This is one of the toughest challenges Armored Core VI has to offer, as it will require mastery of both combat and build crafting. Turn to P.401 for our full S-Rank guide, including tips and builds for every mission.

The Mission Replay menu shows the highest ratings earned.

DATA LOGS

Data logs are encrypted messages and intel stored inside the wreckage of downed crafts that you can view—and permanently add to your archives—by moving close enough until an access prompt appears. Your scanner cannot highlight wrecks, so you'll need to scour every corner of the environment while looking out for the telltale sparks emanating from machine carcasses, indicating that a data log is hidden within it. There are multiple types of data logs, though there is no difference in how you obtain them, and unlike combat logs, acquiring data logs won't unlock new AC parts. However, Rubicon is brimming with mysteries and veiled motives, and finding data logs helps pull back the curtain on various facets of the story. For more on the archives and a full list of data logs, head to P.396.

Make sure to investigate wrecks with an access prompt.

COMBAT LOGS

After completing the "Destroy Artillery Installations" and "Grid 135 Cleanup" missions, you'll gain access to the Loghunt Program. From this point onward you'll begin encountering enemies that reward you with combat logs when destroyed. Special or more dangerous enemies—such as hostile ACs and heavy MTs—will typically contain these logs, and you'll acquire many of them through natural progression as you destroy key opponents while moving between objectives. Occasionally, however, combat logs can be found on regular enemies in optional areas, far away from any objective, and only by fully exploring the mission will you be able to collect them all.

COMBAT LOG TIERS			
Bronze	Silver	Gold	Platinum

If you pay close attention while targeting enemies, any that have a combat log can be easily identified by the small combat log icon near their AP gauge. They'll also have green optical sensors, rather than the typical red ones. If you follow the Mission Intel chapter's walkthroughs (starting on P.94) while playing, you'll find each combat log highlighted on the maps.

Note the combat log icon to left of this Heavy MT's AP gauge.

HUNTER CLASS & COMBAT LOG TIERS

Combat logs won't reward you with COAM, but will be added to the overall combat log tally used to determine your Hunter Class rank (00–15) whenever you complete a mission in which you've acquired one. There are four ranks of combat logs: bronze, silver, gold, and platinum, with bronze providing the smallest increase to your Hunter Class and platinum offering the highest. Tougher enemies, such as ACs, generally carry higher-tier logs, thus providing the greatest increase to your Hunter Class. Reaching a new Hunter Class rank always rewards you with a unique part that cannot be obtained through any other means. If you want to acquire every part, you'll need to seek out as many combat logs as possible. Head to P.394 for an overview of all combat logs and a complete list of Hunter Class rewards.

This Loghunt Program progress screen appears after completing a mission to highlight the combat logs you've collected during that sortie.

GAMEPLAY & COMBAT

From infiltrating an enemy excavation site deep underground to tackling a massive, two-kilometer tall weaponized mining fortress, you'll be thrown into a wide variety of scenarios that will test your mettle as you battle your way across Rubicon. In this section, we'll lift the veil on key gameplay systems to help get you started on the journey toward mastering them and becoming an elite mercenary.

REPAIR KITS

Repair kits are a major new addition to the Armored Core series, making it possible to recover some of the AP lost after sustaining damage on the field. You'll begin every mission with a limited supply of three repair kits, which you can use by pressing ⇧ on the directional pad. Using a repair kit instantly restores some AP without interrupting your movement or actions, so there's no downside to repairing while under attack. However, remember that you won't be able to use repair kits when your AC is in specific states, like during melee attack animations or during the brief stagger resulting from an ACS overload. There's also a short cooldown period of roughly two seconds between repair kit uses, represented by the repair gauge on your HUD. You'll have to wait until this gauge fills up again before recovering another chunk of AP.

Each repair kit recovers a fixed 4,000 AP by default, which can be increased to a maximum of 6,000 via OS Tuning upgrades. Because you only have access to three repair kits per mission, it's generally best to wait until you've taken significant damage before using one. Always keep an eye on your AP gauge whenever you get staggered, however, and get ready to use a repair kit the moment you regain control since direct hits while your ACS is overloaded can quickly deplete AP.

Although your allotment of repair kits is limited, you can sometimes restock at supply sherpas during lengthier missions. Failing a mission and restarting from a checkpoint also refills your repair kits, so don't be afraid to use them when retrying a tricky section. You'll receive a warning from your on-board computer letting you know how many repair kits are left each time you use one.

REPAIR RESTRICTIONS

You won't be able to use repair kits under the following conditions:

- Your AP is full
- During the initial stagger following ACS overload
- Using melee attacks (including Boost Kick)
- Firing charge attacks
- Activating Core Expansions
- Grabbed by enemies
- Fighting in the Arena or Nest battle simulators

COMPASS

The compass at the bottom of the HUD can be an invaluable tool for navigation, as well as for identifying the relative position of enemies or objectives. The marker in the center displays a 360-degree numerical coordinate based on the current orientation of the camera, which you can use to keep your bearings when navigating the game's complex environments. Compass coordinates are occasionally referenced in this book to point you in a precise direction, so it's a good idea to familiarize yourself with how they work.

| Allied Units | Coordinate | Current Lock-on Target | Enemy (Above) |

Enemies will appear as red markers on the compass as soon as they've detected you, even if you've never looked in their direction. The same is true of hostiles that are visible and within lock-on range, and the target you've locked onto will be highlighted with a square around its icon on the compass. In addition, arrows that point upward or downward will inform you if the enemy is above or below you, which can be especially useful in aerial battles against strong opponents. Enemies you've scanned will appear on the compass for the entire duration of the scan, and mission objectives are shown as blue dots. When dealing with enemies that are difficult to track, the compass can allow you to quickly adjust your view in their direction.

SCANNING

Every AC's head is equipped with a scanner that you can activate by pressing ⇩ on the directional pad. This sends out a scanning pulse that sweeps across the environment to detect enemies and part containers. Scanning can give you an edge on the battlefield by temporarily highlighting enemies concealed behind walls or cover. Scanned threats will appear as a glowing orange model when obscured from view, allowing your FCS to achieve lock on without direct line of sight. Depending on the firing trajectory of your weapons, scanning can be used to hit previously hidden enemies without giving them a chance to retaliate. For example, you can use vertical missile launchers to rain destruction from above after scanning an enemy that's taking cover behind a barricade.

Scanning can also be an essential tool when facing cloaked enemies that make use of monitor display jamming technology. Any target that's in direct view when picked up by your scanner will be highlighted with a faint orange outline even if it would otherwise be invisible. Listen for high-pitched pinging sounds when scanning, as this reveals the number of targets or objects that have been detected. Part containers picked up by your scanner are signaled with a lower-pitched ping.

While the scanning pulse appears to be an outwardly expanding sphere, it can only detect threats in a tall and wide, cone-shaped area in front of your AC. Always remember to turn the camera in the direction you wish to survey before scanning. Threats or part containers at higher or lower altitudes can often be detected, but your scanner will never pick up signals from behind or at the edges of your periphery.

Your scanner provides many tactical advantages, but remember that there's a significant cooldown period before you can use it again. Equipping different head parts can either increase or decrease the time between scanner uses, as well as affect the scanning distance and duration for which targets remain highlighted.

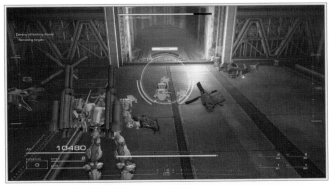

Scanning through walls or obstacles can detect enemies and part containers, though it won't reveal data logs.

ATTACK INDICATORS

Whenever an enemy fires at you, regardless of how potentially dangerous that attack is, you'll be warned by blinking attack indicators around the edges of your reticle. The cardinal direction of the indicator is relative to the camera, and corresponds to the approximate direction in which that attack originates. This functionality works even if the assailant is off-screen, allowing you to quickly locate threats and neutralize them. Depending on the type of attack, the indicators can vary in intensity and color and are grouped into two main responses:

1. Small orange indicators that signal weakly damaging attacks, like machine gun fire. This mostly serves as a helpful aid for mopping up weaker enemies.

2. Large red indicators accompanied by a high-pitched warning sound that signal highly damaging attacks, such as bazookas and charged laser blasts. These attacks are also accompanied by a red square-shaped indicator overlaid on the weapon firing at you. You will even notice multiple square indicators appearing if the weapon fires in quick succession.

Don't take this second category of attacks with audio cues lightly—they're typically the ones that strip off large chunks of your AP, or deal large amounts of strain to your ACS. Evading or using a shield to block these attacks should be your highest priority during any engagement, and failure to do so will rapidly take you toward the mission fail screen.

The timing of when you should evade each of these strong attacks varies wildly depending on both distance and weapon type. Charged linear rifle or laser rifle shots hit extremely quickly, while grenades and bazooka shells tend to travel slower, and if you use a Quick Boost as soon as you hear the audio cue signaling such an attack, you'll likely be hit before you can boost again. Use this visual warning in tandem with the loud audio cue to figure out the optimal timing for dodging or shielding against dangerous attacks. With a bit of practice, attack indicators can even allow you to evade attacks originating from off-screen.

Attack indicators are valuable tools in combat, but remember that melee attacks won't trigger them. Because of how dangerous these can be, you'll have to stay vigilant when engaging enemies with melee capabilities at close range, such as tetrapod MTs wielding laser blades. Don't simply expect an attack indicator to always warn you of imminent danger.

In the screen above, the orange attack indicator warns of incoming missiles from an off-screen enemy, while both the red indicator and square-shaped overlay on the artillery's cannon alert you of the deadly laser blast its about to fire.

MOVEMENT

The fully 3D, omni-directional movement system in Armored Core VI offers an exceptional degree of freedom when navigating environments and engaging in combat. While movement in most action games is often restricted to a flat circle on the X-axis with limited verticality, movement in Armored Core VI can best be visualized as a sphere, with your AC's boosters making it possible to ascend on the Y-axis at any point while simultaneously moving in any other direction. As an AC pilot, you'll be traversing combat zones at high velocity, boosting on the ground or in the air to reach your objective or close the gap with enemies. How you approach each situation is limited only by your skill and imagination, and this section will teach you everything you need to know to master the art of moving with an AC.

EN MANAGEMENT

Before diving into the core movement mechanics, it's important to go over EN management. This stamina-like resource is needed to power all of your AC's advanced movement options, like Quick Boosts, and managing it poorly can lead to disastrous results, especially if you run out while engaged in combat. You can still rely on boost movement when no EN is available, but you won't be able to perform any EN-consuming actions until your EN gauge has at least partially recharged. EN recovers exponentially faster while your legs are in contact with a surface, so a key part of EN management is learning how to shift between boosting in the air and briefly landing to replenish EN before the gauge is empty. Once your EN gauge is below 25%, it will turn red and a distinct audio cue will trigger to warn you that you're about to run out.

Whenever you're running low on EN, it's generally better to stop using EN-consuming actions and allow your gauge to quickly recharge rather than letting it fully deplete. This is to avoid the lengthier cooldown period before your generator can begin to resupply EN after completely running out. If you do run out, your on-board systems will inform you via a chime-like audio cue that repeats until resupply kicks

EN only drains while you're ascending, so if used in short bursts, you can greatly prolong the amount of time you can spend in the air, allowing you to cross large gaps.

in. Running out of EN while airborne will force your AC to descend; it's possible to recover EN in the air, but this happens at a much slower rate than on the ground.

In many ways, your improvement as an AC pilot will hinge on how efficiently you manage your EN gauge. It's possible to maximize your total EN capacity and minimize the EN consumption of actions like Quick Boosts by customizing your AC in the Assembly (see P.35 for a detailed analysis of all specs), but effective use of EN will largely come down to your piloting skills.

EN CONSUMING ACTIONS

All of the following actions consume EN and will drain your EN gauge:

- Ascending
- Quick Boost
- Assault Boost
- Melee weapon attacks (initial thrust)
- Hovering (Tetrapod legs only)

BOOST MOVEMENT

Pressing Ⓑ/〇 while moving toggles boost movement, a faster mode of loco-motion that utilizes the thrust from your AC's boosters to increase its overall speed. Since boost movement doesn't consume EN and remains active until you let go of the Left Stick, it should serve as your default movement option in most situations. It's especially important to activate boost movement when engaging enemies, as the increase in speed makes your AC more difficult to accurately track and hit. It's worth noting that boost movement also works when airborne to increase your horizontal mobility and slightly slow down the rate of descent as you fall.

Instead of toggling it on with a button press, It's also possible to smoothly transition into boost movement by performing a Quick Boost—look for jets emanating from your AC's boosters and a "boost on" indicator to the right of your EN gauge to confirm that boost movement is active. Boosting while moving sideways with Target Assist enabled is sometimes referred to as "boost strafing," and can be the optimal way to fight against some opponents in one-on-one scenarios. How fast your AC can go during boost movement is determined by its Boost Speed spec.

VERTICALITY

Exploiting your AC's vertical mobility is extremely important—many missions require you to scale tall structures, cross expansive divides, or explore underground facilities. Outside of navigation, shifting to aerial combat and making full use of ver-ticality can give you an overwhelming tactical advantage in many combat scenarios.

You'll quickly notice how difficult it can be to hit enemies that are soaring above you, so securing the high ground is always a good strategy. Attacking enemies while above them not only makes it easier to keep track of their movements, but weapons with a large blast radius, such as grenade launchers or plasma rifles, become noticeably more potent when fired from this vantage point. Even if the shot initially misses the mark, enemies will often get caught in the explosion caused by it hitting the ground near them.

EN management comes into play once again, however, as staying airborne will be a continuous drain on your reserves, especially if you Quick Boost in the air. Take note of the environment you find yourself in and look for elevated surfaces that you can perch on and continue fighting from while your EN resupplies. Vantage points will rarely be far away, as the combat zones you engage in are designed to reward you for thinking tactically and being aware of your surroundings.

An aerial approach can often give you the offensive and defensive edge in battle.

FALL DAMAGE

As you approach the lower bounds of a combat zone, a red "lower area limit" warning will flash in the center of the screen. If you continue to descend beyond this point, your AC's autopilot will activate, and you'll reappear nearby a moment later. Falling outside the combat zone always deals damage equivalent to 35% of your maximum AP. Be particularly cautious when navigating treacherous environments if your AP is below this threshold, as the next fall will outright destroy your AC and result in mission failure.

VERTICAL CATAPULTS

Environments that emphasize vertical traversal often feature vertical catapults placed near sheer cliffs or other structures that would otherwise be challenging to scale. As their name implies, these small launch pads can be used to catapult your AC in a straight vertical trajectory at high velocity without draining your EN. To per-form a Vertical Launch, simply step on the flat platform delineated by orange lights and press Ⓐ/Ⓧ. Despite being intended to assist with traversal, you can also use nearby Vertical Catapults to quickly gain air superiority in battle.

Keep an eye out for vertical catapults to help you rapidly gain a lot of altitude and reach objectives.

QUICK BOOSTS

Quick Boosts are fast horizontal dashes ideal for dodging incoming attacks or swiftly repositioning your AC on the battlefield. You can perform a Quick Boost in any direc-tion along the X-axis, even when airborne, by tilting the Left Stick before pressing Ⓧ/▢. However, it's crucial to remember that your AC won't be invincible at any point during a Quick Boost, forcing you to fully clear the radius of incoming attacks to avoid taking damage.

Quick Boost effectiveness depends on various factors, like your AC's total weight along with its booster and legs. Some leg types, like those that are reverse-joint, can perform Quick Boosts that cover larger distances due to their spring-like design. Conversely, the heavier tank or tetrapod legs can't cover as much ground with a single Quick Boost. The booster installed on your AC influences how fast and how far it can Quick Boost, how much EN it consumes, and even the cooldown period between Quick Boost activations. Pay close attention to your booster's specs in the Assembly if you feel like you aren't able to Quick Boost effectively. Lastly, note that depending on the Jump Distance spec of your legs, Quick Boosts performed while on the ground are often slightly faster and cover more distance, as the AC can use its legs to propel itself horizontally by jumping at the start.

Performing well-timed Quick Boosts is often the best defensive tactic for evading high-velocity projectiles. Just remember to keep an eye on your EN; if you run out, you won't be able to Quick Boost until it recharges.

JUMPING OUT OF HARM'S WAY

While Quick Boosts are generally your best option for avoiding damage, some attacks with a wide, horizontal area of effect or large blast radius are almost guaranteed to hit you if you try to evade them with a Quick Boost. When facing attacks that feel impossible to dodge from the ground, try jumping and boosting upward instead. Jumping itself doesn't cost any EN, but remember that how high your AC can jump is primarily influenced by the Jump Height spec on your assembly's leg units.

Jumping over attacks can be just as viable as a Quick Boost in certain situations.

ASSAULT BOOST

Pressing in the Left Stick revs up your boosters and initiates an Assault Boost, a versatile high-velocity flying maneuver used to rush toward a target or rapidly move in the direction the camera is facing. Assault Boost is primarily designed to reward aggressive battlefield tactics, allowing you to close the gap with an enemy much faster than normally possible while overwhelming their ACS in the process.

Combat Applications

It's possible to open fire without stopping during an Assault Boost if you attack with firearms that don't cause enough kickback to interrupt your movement. This is important to remember, since attacking mid-boost with the weapons held in your hands inflicts 20% greater impact. Use this additional impact bonus to quickly stagger an enemy before following up with direct hits. Although very few of the shoulder weapons benefit from the Assault Boost impact bonus, if you have missile launchers equipped, it's often still worth firing volleys of missiles while closing the distance with stronger opponents.

If you're locked on to an enemy using Target Assist, performing an Assault Boost will cause your AC to fly directly toward this target. Though this linear approach can put you in their direct line of fire, enemy attacks that hit you during an Assault Boost will be more easily deflected, reducing their impact by 30%. This defensive perk makes it more difficult for enemies to stagger you as you rush toward them, but be aware that you'll still take full AP damage from each shot. Moving the Left

Stick to either side during an Assault Boost will cause your AC to quickly evade in the corresponding direction at the cost of some EN. When timed perfectly, this technique makes it possible to avoid attacks anticipated by your systems, such as explosive shells or sniper lasers that travel in a straight line. Pay attention to attack indicators, and dodge at the last second to juke out of the way while continuing to approach your target. Learning to pressure opponents using Assault Boosts is an essential skill to master, since it allows you to quickly overload their ACS and set them up for devastating direct hits with melee weapons or similarly powerful attacks while they're staggered.

Blunt Force Trauma

Ramming directly into an enemy during an Assault Boost will inflict 50 kinetic damage and 111 impact regardless of your total weight. While this brazen tactic won't put much of a dent in stronger targets, it can be effective at knocking smaller opponents like guard mechs or light MTs off balance. You can then combo with a heavy impact Boost Kick by pressing in the Left Stick the instant you hear the crunch of your AC ramming into the target.

Traversal Applications

Outside of its usefulness in combat scenarios, Assault Boost also doubles as an excellent traversal tool that's ideal for cruising across long stretches of terrain or flying over obstacles. Whenever you aren't locked on to an enemy with Target Assist, initiating an Assault Boost will cause your AC to fly toward the direction in which the camera is currently facing. You can then use the Right Stick to adjust your horizontal or vertical trajectory while flying.

The turning radius is limited as a result of the high-speed thrust from your boosters, but you retain enough control to steer yourself onto platforms or away from obstacles. It's worth noting that evading left or right will change which side of the screen your AC occupies, which can be useful to avoid obstacles during traversal.

Pointing the camera above your current position before activating an Assault Boost allows you to quickly ascend at a diagonal angle while continuing to move forward. This useful trick works when grounded, after jumping to initially gain more altitude, or while already in the air. You can even trigger an Assault Boost to quickly change trajectory while airborne by rotating the camera in the desired direction and pressing in the Left Stick. With the Quick Turn ability unlocked, you can also perform 90-degree snap turns to the left or right during an Assault Boost, making it even more versatile as a traversal option.

Infinite Airtime

By equipping a generator with a high Supply Recovery spec, such as the DF-GN-02 LING TAI, it becomes possible to chain multiple Assault Boosts and use them to stay airborne indefinitely. Just point the camera up and continue boosting until you run out of EN, then activate another Assault Boost as soon as your generator's supply recovery kicks in. This is even more effective if you equip a booster with superior AB Thrust and AB EN Consumption specs, as these two values determine the speed and EN consumption rate of your Assault Boosts.

During an Assault Boost, your reticle will lock on to the closest visible target within range if Target Assist is disabled, allowing you to fire at them while flying along a separate trajectory.

"Double Trigger" style builds benefit greatly from aggressive use of Assault Boost, since opening fire with two firearms at the same time allows you to take full advantage of the impact bonus while rapidly closing in on targets.

LEG TYPES & MOBILITY

Your AC's legs will have the most dramatic influence on its mobility. There are four different types of leg units, each with their own movement style, and learning which leg type is best for your desired playstyle is vital; you won't fully appreciate the impact each type can have on your tactical possibilities until you experiment with them. Here we'll provide a quick overview of each type's strengths:

- **Bipedal** legs are the "default" leg type. They're well-rounded and come in a large variety of models that can support everything from lightweight to heavyweight assemblies. They function as you might anticipate, and are the most multi-purpose leg type, having no particular strengths or weaknesses.

- **Reverse Joint** legs are designed to maximize jumping capabilities. These spring-like legs enable ACs to hop over greater distances during Quick Boosts and have the highest jump height of any leg type, making them ideal for quickly shifting into aerial combat at no EN cost. They suffer from low attitude stability, however, so pilots favoring reverse-joint legs will need to put this additional mobility to good use to avoid getting staggered.

- **Tetrapod** legs are built to maximize the amount of time you spend airborne. While less nimble on the ground than other leg types, tapping Ⓐ/Ⓧ again while in the air will activate hover mode, allowing you to maintain the current altitude until you run out of EN. You can sustain an aerial position with these legs for far longer than any other type, especially when paired with a generator with a high EN capacity. Tetrapod legs can also support enough load to outfit your AC with heavier weaponry, letting you become a mobile flying fortress; a key advantage of hover mode is that you won't need to stop moving to absorb the recoil normally associated with firing heavier weapons or unleashing charge attacks.

Hover Mode

Sustaining hover mode consumes 65 EN per second while active. This is a fixed value that isn't influenced by anything else, such as your booster or total weight. The only way to extend your hover time is to equip a generator with a higher EN Capacity spec, since that increases your EN gauge.

- **Tank** legs excel at ground-based warfare, trading aerial mobility for the highest available defense and load limit. While all other leg types are compatible with the full range of booster parts, tank legs come with their own internal boosters that can't be swapped out. To offset this drawback, the high stability of tank legs makes it possible to fire heavy weaponry with lots of recoil, like laser cannons, while moving at full speed on the ground. Tank legs can also perform drifts after a Quick Boost, which more advanced pilots can use to outmaneuver targets and make themselves more difficult to hit. Although limited to only three models, each of the tank legs have distinct pros and cons; one of them might have an extremely high boost speed, for example, while another might feature an aerodynamic design, making aerial combat feasible while still benefiting from some of the other advantages inherent to tank legs.

The Art of Drifting

By holding the Left Stick in a different direction than your current trajectory when falling or after using a Quick Boost, you can cause your AC to drift in that direction the instant it touches the ground. Drifting tightens your turning radius when changing directions with tank legs, conserving speed and making you harder track as you continue pummeling the target. Once you've started drifting, it's then possible to keep the momentum going indefinitely by moving the Left Stick in a circular pattern. Remembering to drift in combat can be tricky, so it's a good idea to practice in the AC Test simulation. If you're struggling to get your AC to drift, make sure to hold the Left Stick in the desired direction before its legs touch the ground.

BOOSTERS

EN plays a crucial role in determining how mobile your AC can be, so it's essential to carefully consider which booster to install. Boosters have a significant influence on your overall boost movement and upward thrust potential, as well as EN consumption when ascending and performing maneuvers like Quick Boosts and Assault Boosts. Depending on your playstyle and overall assembly, being able to perform EN-consuming actions with greater frequency can be more important than how fast your AC moves when boosting around the battlefield. It's also important to pay attention to the QB Reload Ideal Weight spec when choosing boosters; if the total weight of your assembly rises above this value, you will incur a progressively more severe penalty to Quick Boost reload time based on how far above this ideal weight your current total weight is.

Boosters also influence how much EN is consumed and how far your AC can thrust forward to chase the locked-on target after initiating a melee attack.

BOOST KICKS

Unlocked via OS tuning, Boost Kick is a powerful melee strike that you can perform by pressing in the Left Stick during an Assault Boost, and is useful for throwing opponents off balance after closing the gap. While a Boost Kick can deal enough damage to destroy weaker targets, the main strength of this maneuver is the high level of ACS strain it inflicts. Going for a Boost Kick is a high-risk, high-reward tactic, as rushing directly into melee range can put you in a vulnerable position. However, using Boost Kicks when enemies are wide open can completely change how you approach combat, allowing you to press your advantage by following up with other close-range weapons after the kick connects.

The damage inflicted by a Boost Kick is classified as kinetic and varies based on your AC's total weight, with heavier builds generating more powerful kicks. Reverse-joint legs also gain a significant bonus to Boost Kick damage. To learn more about Boost Kicks, including specific damage and impact values, turn to P.34.

Equipping different leg types alters the animation, range, and impact power of your Boost Kicks.

Combat in Armored Core VI isn't strictly a point-and-shoot affair; it's deeply multifaceted, and can require you to consider many factors, even before a fight actually begins. This section will teach you some of the key concepts involved.

FIRING WEAPONS

AC assemblies offer a total of four weapon slots: R-Arm, L-Arm, R-Back, and L-Back units. Each weapon installed on your AC has a dedicated input on your controller and can either be fired independently or in a combined fashion to overwhelm the opposition with a simultaneous barrage of attacks. This signature ability of ACs to fire up to four weapons at once is a key differentiating factor compared to most other action games, and requires a bit of practice to fully master.

When fighting enemies, take a moment to ask yourself if you're making optimal use of all the weapons at your disposal instead of primarily attacking with only a fraction of your destructive potential. For example, weapons like back-mounted missile launchers can be used to build up strain on the enemy's ACS while you simultaneously fire with a pair of machine guns held in both hands. Some heavy-duty ordinance can't be fired in tandem with other weapons, however, so it's essential to keep these factors in mind when assembling your AC and piloting it in combat.

It can take some time to get accustomed to firing all four weapons while also moving around and aiming, but reaching the point where that becomes second nature is a goal well worth working toward.

DOUBLE TRIGGER BUILDS

"Double Trigger" style builds are ACs that wield the same ranged weapon, such as a pair of fast-firing machine guns or heavy-hitting shotguns, in both hands. This streamlined approach to AC design enables you to output a sustained and predictable stream of damage very quickly, and works well with aggressive use of Assault Boosts to take advantage of the extra impact damage gained by both weapons.

The ability to constantly track your opponent with a torrent of bullets—especially while you strafe around them during boost movement—can make Double Trigger builds very tricky to counter and a good starting point for less experienced AC pilots.

RELOAD TYPES

Another important element to consider when engaging in combat is the current reload status of each weapon, which you can track using the four curved gauges that surround the bottom half of your reticle. Each weapon class is assigned one of the following three reload types, which influences how they should be managed in battle:

Single Shot

 This straightforward reload type occurs automatically after firing a single shot and is generally associated with powerful explosive weapons like bazookas or missile launchers.

Magazine

 Many kinetic weapons use magazines that must be reloaded when empty. The reloading process happens automatically whenever a magazine runs dry, but you also have the option to manually reload at any time by pressing ⓨ/△ + the corresponding weapon input. Always make sure weapon magazines are reloaded between skirmishes, and do your best to reload before an enemy staggers to maximize your damage output.

Overheat

Some weapons generate heat with each shot and will overheat once their heat tolerance is exceeded, becoming unable to fire until they finish cooling down. Pay attention to the red bar that fills up on the corresponding weapon gauge and stop firing before it reaches the top to allow the weapon to gradually cool down instead of overheating. The amount of heat generated per shot varies by weapon, with stronger charge attacks or melee weapons often overheating in a single shot.

ACS STRAIN & STAGGERS

The ACS (Attitude Control System) of a craft governs how much accumulated strain it can withstand from the impact of repeated attacks, before being thrown off balance and becoming exposed to highly damaging direct hits. Both your AC and the majority of enemies you'll face off against feature an ACS gauge that gradually builds up each time an attack hits, and will begin to regenerate after a short period of no damage being taken. The gauge is segmented into three identical sections, with the central part filling up first. An ACS overload occurs once this ACS gauge reaches its limit, causing the afflicted craft to briefly lose all motor control and enter a vulnerable state known as a "stagger."

The ACS gauge is absolutely central to gameplay in Armored Core VI and dictates the pace of combat by fostering a dynamic back-and-forth flow to the action—aim to pressure your opponent with repeated attacks until you stagger them, and switch to a more defensive playstyle when your ACS gauge nears its limit to avoid getting staggered yourself.

STAGGER KNOCKBACK

Entering a staggered state knocks the afflicted craft backward while interrupting its actions and preventing it from moving for a short duration. This brief stagger animation can be exploited even further by using a Boost Kick to knock the enemy back a much greater distance, extending the window during which it's unable to fight back. Melee weapons capable of dealing multiple consecutive hits are also able to trigger additional stagger animations and keep the target locked in place while you deal severe direct hit damage.

DIRECT HITS

While an enemy is staggered immediately following an ACS overload, you'll have a brief window within which your next attacks will gain an additional damage modifier: these are called direct hits. Every weapon has its own Direct Hit Adjustment spec, and the higher that value, the greater the damage modifier will be when using it against a staggered enemy—though its base damage is still the primary factor in determining the resulting damage. Weapons with both high base attack power and a high Direct Hit Adjustment spec will deal immense damage to staggered enemies. It can often help to have a well-rounded set of weaponry; utilize weapons with high impact specs to strain the enemy's ACS, and then keep weapons with high attack power and direct hit adjustment reloaded and ready to fire once they're staggered.

Keeping weapons with a high direct hit potential primed and ready to take advantage of an ACS overload can cause devastating amounts of damage.

IMPACT

In addition to dealing AP damage, each attack in the game also inflicts a certain amount of ACS strain on the target, determined by the Impact and Accumulative Impact specs of the part utilized as a weapon. The following is a brief explanation to help you understand the crucial distinction between immediate impact and accumulative impact:

Impact

This immediate impact type corresponds to the ACS strain inflicted the moment an attack hits and is instantly visible on the target's ACS gauge. Standard impact is always higher than accumulative impact, but quickly resets after a short period of roughly one second.

Accumulative Impact

This sustained impact corresponds to the ACS strain that lingers for a longer period after the immediate strain has reset. Pay attention to the target's ACS gauge after landing a hit and you will notice that a portion of the impact quickly dissipates; accumulative impact is the portion of the initial impact that remains visible on the ACS gauge after the immediate impact is reset. Accumulative impact is always less potent than immediate impact, but lasts for roughly five seconds before the target's ACS begins to recover.

To overload an opponent's ACS and trigger a stagger, you'll need to keep up the pressure by landing multiple hits in quick succession. The most important thing to focus on is ensuring that you don't give the target's ACS gauge enough time to recover between each hit, particularly when attacking with weapons that deal high amounts of immediate impact but low accumulative impact. Always keep the interplay between immediate impact and accumulative impact in mind when designing your AC and when aiming to stagger opponents.

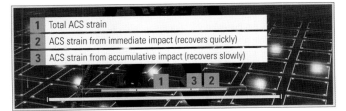

1	Total ACS strain
2	ACS strain from immediate impact (recovers quickly)
3	ACS strain from accumulative impact (recovers slowly)

RICOCHET

Ricochet is a mechanic that can cause kinetic or energy rounds to bounce off the target's armor, losing all but a fraction of their attack power and impact. The range at which this can happen is determined by a combination of the target's defensive specs and both the Ideal Range and Effective Range specs of the attacker's weapons. Remember that you're essentially wasting ammo whenever ricocheting occurs, so identifying the ranges at which your weapons lose their potency against different types of enemies is key to improving your damage output. On the other hand, learning the ranges at which you're safe against specific attacks based on your current defensive specs can allow you to greatly minimize the damage taken.

Note the "ricochet" notification above your AP gauge when a shot bounces off your AC. A similar prompt also appears below the enemy's AP gauge when your rounds ricochet.

CORE EXPANSIONS

Occupying the bottom slot in the Assembly menu, Core Expansions are a special type of parts that must be unlocked via OST Chips and then equipped to your AC. Core Expansions enable the use of powerful offensive or defensive abilities that can be activated by pressing in the Left Stick + Ⓨ/△ to instantly turn the tides of battle. These range from the devastating Assault Armor that generates a massive explosive blast capable of damaging nearby enemies and canceling enemy projectiles, to the life-saving Terminal Armor that automatically activates upon receiving otherwise fatal damage, encasing you in a temporary pulse barrier while your AC carries on fighting with a single AP.

To balance out their usefulness and prevent them from being too powerful, Core Expansions can only be activated a limited number of times per sortie. The number of activations starts at one, but it's usually possible to increase available Core Expansion activations by investing additional OST Chips into them, with Terminal Armor being the only outlier. If multiple activations are available when you use a Core Expansion, it will enter a cooldown period before it can be used again (indicated by the HUD icon blinking red and your AC's generator emanating heat). For a detailed analysis of the four available Core Expansion types, head to P.93.

You aren't the only AC user on Rubicon with access to Core Expansions; some of the tougher enemy ACs will make liberal use of them, both aggressively and as a last-ditch effort to claw back from defeat.

The targeting reticle is the main HUD element that helps you decide when or if you should fire on an enemy, and can even govern how your AC moves in relation to the target in an encounter. Like many systems in the game, it presents you with a wealth of information that you need to quickly process in the heat of combat. Coming to grips with exactly what the targeting reticle is showing and how you can manipulate it on the fly is another aspect of combat that you'll need to master during your career as a mercenary. This section will walk you through the key principles related to acquiring and successfully hitting targets.

RANGE CATEGORIES

The range at which you engage targets is broken down into three distinct range categories based on your distance to the enemy:

▮ **Close-range** (within 130 meters)
▮ **Medium-range** (130–260 meters)
▮ **Long-range** (beyond 260 meters)

This terminology appears throughout both the game and this guide, so it's important to familiarize yourself with all three range categories and pay attention to how far you are from targets when playing. Always keep optimal range in mind when thinking about which weapons and FCS to install, as a mismatch between your playstyle and your AC's capabilities can drastically reduce its effectiveness in battle. Consult P.40 in the AC Design section to learn about how the Ideal Range and Effective Range specs of weapons influence their behavior depending on your distance to the target. The diagram here helps to visualize these three distinct ranges.

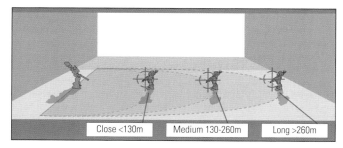

| Close <130m | Medium 130-260m | Long >260m |

FCS PARTS AND COMBAT RANGE

Your FCS part is responsible for improving the aim of your weapons at specific ranges and modifying how quickly your missiles lock on to their target. Each FCS features aiming assist specs that focus on one or more of the combat ranges defined earlier: close-range, medium-range, or long-range. If you find it challenging to consistently hit agile enemies capable of fast evasive maneuvers, like Quick Boosts, make sure to equip an FCS designed to assist your aim at the range you're fighting at relative to the enemy.

Your choice of FCS won't matter much when fighting slower enemies, but those capable of accelerating and dodging at high speeds will prove difficult to track, causing your reticle to sway erratically and your shots to miss. The higher your FCS assist spec for a specific combat range, the faster your reticle will center on the current lock-on target when fighting within that range, indicating that your next shots will hit the mark. Each FCS also has Missile Lock Correction and Multi-Lock Correction specs (P.46), which are important to consider if your build relies heavily on missiles or other homing weapons. Whether you're intent on fighting at a fixed combat range regardless of the scenario, or trying to adapt your playstyle to the unique challenges that each mission presents, picking the right FCS to complement your choice of weaponry is of utmost importance.

LOCK-ON

Once you move within 450m of an enemy, your reticle will snap to and automatically lock on to the target closest to the center of the screen, at which point it will continue tracking it for as long as this target remains within the boundaries of the camera. The target's AP and ACS gauges become visible above the reticle whenever you're locked on. If you have any missiles equipped, you'll also notice the yellow missile lock gauges start to automatically fill around the targeting crosshairs in the center of your reticle, with each of them representing one of your weapon slots. Any potential lock-on target that is visible and within 450m will be highlighted with a small gray circle; to lock-on to a different target, simply move the camera until that enemy is closest to the center of the screen. You will also hear a short high-pitched beep whenever you acquire a lock-on target or switch to a different one.

The reticle will continue to appear white when within 391m–450m of the target, meaning that while you've acquired a lock-on and the reticle will automatically follow that enemy's movements, any non-homing shots you fire will not yet benefit from target tracking to assist in hitting moving targets.

MULTI-LOCK

Multi-lock offers a way to take out a group of weaker enemies in a single volley. Holding down the corresponding input with multi-lock capable weapons will begin filling the multi-lock gauge. Once it's full, releasing the button will split the weapon's payload between a number of visible targets within lock-on range. The maximum number of multi-lock targets is determined by the weapon's Maximum Lock Count spec. If fewer than the max targets are acquired by multi-lock, the payload gets divided evenly across the number of targets. Pressing Ⓨ/△ will cancel a multi-lock, locking onto a single target instead.

TARGET TRACKING

Moving within 390m of an enemy will cause your reticle to turn red, informing you that target tracking is now active. Any non-homing weapon you open fire with at this point will benefit from the predictive firing capabilities of your AC, ensuring that your shots compensate for enemy movements. Whenever this red reticle is squarely on the target, your shots will hit the mark unless the enemy performs an evasive maneuver to temporarily throw off your target tracking. How quickly this red reticle can snap to targets depends on various factors, such as the Firearm Specialization spec of the AC's arms, the assist specs of its FCS, and whether Target Assist is currently engaged.

TARGET ASSIST

Target Assist is an optional feature of the targeting reticle that you can toggle on or off by pressing the Right Stick. When Target Assist is active, your reticle and camera will stay focused on the current lock-on target, eliminating the need to manually adjust your view with the Right Stick during combat. Enabling Target Assist also causes your AC to consistently face the current target, with all horizontal movements now strafing around the enemy. This makes it easier to dodge incoming attacks while simultaneously firing your own shots.

However, it's important to understand that while Target Assist keeps an enemy in your sights, enabling it will also reduce your AC's target tracking performance. This reduction in target tracking accuracy is generally not very noticeable in most situations but can significantly affect your ability to land shots against fast-moving enemies that Quick Boost often, like LCs or rival ACs. More advanced players or those aiming to master the game should try to gradually reduce their reliance on Target Assist in most scenarios, but remember that there are advantages to this feature, and it's perfectly fine to rely on it if you find that it suits your playstyle better. You can choose whether Target Assist remains enabled after you've destroyed your current target by toggling the Maintain Target Assist option in the Game Settings menu. The following page includes an overview of pros and cons to help you judge when or why it might be advantageous to enable Target Assist.

» Makes it easy to focus all of your attention on a single target while keeping it in the center of the screen, removing the need to manually rotate the camera when fighting. Very useful when fighting against agile targets that boost all over the place, and a must if you're having difficulty manually tracking targets.

» Your AC always faces the target when Target Assist is active. Because your movement becomes relative to the target, Target Assist can allow you to strafe boost around an opponent and perform complex maneuvers like jumping over it without losing lock on at any point.

» You can still switch targets by moving the Right Stick even when Target Assist is engaged, allowing you to change your focus to high-priority enemies as the situation evolves.

» Very helpful in one-on-one duels against tougher opponents, like bosses, since it makes it much easier to observe their behavior and learn how they telegraph attacks. Your Quick Boosts being relative to the enemy can also make it easier to avoid certain attacks, like vertical slashes or high-velocity sniper shots aimed directly at you.

» Being focused on a single target makes it more likely you'll lose track of what's happening during encounters involving groups of multiple enemies. Although you can switch targets while Target Assist is active, it's easier and quicker to do so with it disabled.

» You have a much greater degree of control over your AC's movements when Target Assist is disabled, since your AC won't automatically move relative to the target's current position. This means that you don't have to fly directly at an enemy during an Assault Boost; you can still fire at it as long as it remains visible and within lock-on range. The enemy could be at the very edge of your screen and your FCS would still lock on to it without the need to engage Target Assist, giving you maximum control of your movement during encounters.

» There's a significant penalty to target tracking when Target Assist is active, which translates to your red predictive fire reticle taking longer to center on the target. The more you practice manually keeping the camera trained on the enemy, the better you'll get at hitting fast-moving opponents that otherwise prove difficult for your AC's target tracking to zero in on while Target Assist is enabled.

With Target Assist enabled, your AC will only lock on to enemies once they're within the bounding box represented by the four curved lines surrounding the reticle.

The closer the enemy is to the center of the camera when Target Assist is disabled, the quicker the red predictive fire reticle will snap to the target, so there's a tangible benefit to mastering the art of manually tracking targets.

WEAPONS & DAMAGE TYPES

Weapons are capable of dealing three main types of damage: kinetic, energy, and explosive. Each of these damage types has its own properties, and the defensive performance of your AC against each type is determined by the combined defensive specs of its frame parts. In addition to a large selection of ranged weapon classes, you will also have access to specialized melee weapons that can only be equipped in an AC's L-Arm Unit slot, and defensive pulse shields that can only be equipped in an L-Back Unit slot. Many weapons can also perform charge attacks by holding the input, increasing your build's versatility by giving you multiple ways to deal damage with a single weapon.

MELEE WEAPONS

Melee weapons are a unique class of weapons that specialize in delivering extremely high attack power and impact, but can only be equipped in the L-Arm Unit slot and require you to get up close and personal with your target to land a hit. Your introduction to melee weapons in the prologue teaches you that they can also break the physical shields found on some MTs, and likewise have high PA Interference specs, making them ideal at disrupting pulse shields and barriers.

Almost all melee weapons overheat after a single use, and many exhibit substantial cooldown times before they can be used again. Except for the explosive thrower, none of the melee weapons use ammo, which makes them ideal for conserving the ammo of other weapons and keeping costs low during missions. Depending on the weapon, initiating a melee attack when locked on to a target may automatically activate your boosters and cause your AC to rush toward the enemy in an attempt

to close the gap. Both the range of this short dash and the EN it consumes are influenced by the booster part outfitted on your AC.

All melee weapons feature a unique charge attack that can drastically alter their functionality, such as the laser blade performing circular spinning slashes with a massive area of effect instead of its standard horizontal slash. Many of them can also perform combo strings if you repeatedly press the input—you can find out exactly how many times each weapon can attack by looking at their Consecutive Hits spec. While melee weapons are risky to use, their high attack power and direct hit adjustment make them the absolute best weapons for taking advantage of an enemy's ACS overload window.

By quickly switching targets between hits, it's possible to eliminate multiple enemies in a single melee combo if they're closely grouped together.

MELEE ATTACK CANCELING

At any time between the point where you initiate a melee attack and when your AC actually swings the weapon, it's possible to cancel a melee attack by performing a Quick Boost or Assault Boost. While this technique will consume EN from both the thrust associated with closing in on the target and the Quick Boost or Assault Boost itself, it won't cause the melee weapon to overheat. As a result, it's possible to cancel melee attacks in this manner as long as you have enough EN.

This type of canceling is primarily useful to avoid committing to lengthy melee attack animations if the situation changes while you rush toward the target or to fake out opponents in online battles. However, a more advanced application consists of equipping the AB-J-137 KIKAKU booster to increase the speed of your AC well beyond what it can otherwise reach while it rushes at a target after starting a melee attack. By Quick Boost canceling just before your AC swings and immediately initiating another melee attack, you can close in on targets significantly faster than otherwise possible with any other method.

KINETIC WEAPONS

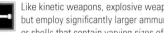

Kinetic weapons inflict physical damage using bullet-like rounds or blunt force. They're often most powerful at close or medium range and offer a balanced mix of attack power and impact. They generally fire much faster than the other weapons, both in terms of number of rounds and projectile velocity, making them reliable and easy to handle. On average, kinetic weapons also have the highest direct hit adjustment of all the weapon types, allowing them to quickly output a lot of damage once the target is staggered. With a few exceptions, kinetic weapon types are less likely to be effective at long range than other categories of weaponry, and their rounds are prone to ricocheting unless you're fighting within the weapon's ideal range.

ENERGY WEAPONS

As their name implies, these weapons utilize energy beams to inflict damage. They typically fire slower, but have more range, maximizing attack power at the cost of lower impact. Many can also be charged to concentrate their firepower and unleash an even more devastating attack. This focus on raw damage output means that energy weapons excel at reducing a target's AP with each shot, but their low impact and direct hit adjustment specs makes them less effective at building up strain and dealing damage to staggered enemies. Energy weapons are further divided into multiple "sub-categories," each with different properties:

▐ **Laser** weapons fire standard blue beams that travel in a straight trajectory. Many of the melee weapons also use this same laser technology to emit blue energy beams.

▐ **Plasma** weapons fire purple beams that are immune to ricocheting and create a medium-sized plasma explosion upon colliding with the target or environment. This explosion deals multiple hits to enemies caught within it.

▐ **Pulse** weapons fire green orb-shaped projectiles and are specifically designed to break down pulse armor or shielding. Your default HI-32: BU-TT/A pulse blade also relies on this technology to disrupt barriers.

Though not exclusively found on energy-based weaponry, the yellow shock damage type always inflicts energy damage in addition to shock buildup capable of triggering devastating electrical discharges.

Rather than needing to be reloaded like most kinetic weapons, energy weapons are managed through an overheating system. Firing them builds up heat, and if they're used too frequently in quick succession, they'll overheat and need to go through a lengthy cooldown period before they can be used again. To avoid that scenario, keep an eye on the gauges around your reticle as they'll let you know how hot your energy weapons are getting, and be sure to stop firing them before they overheat.

EXPLOSIVE WEAPONS

Like kinetic weapons, explosive weapons also fire physical projectiles, but employ significantly larger ammunition such as missiles, grenades, or shells that contain varying sizes of explosive payload. They have the highest attack power and impact values of all weapons, but they're heavy, have a slow rate of fire, and often feature high recoil that requires most ACs to come to a stop and brace themselves before firing while on the ground, leaving you briefly vulnerable. Their slow rate of fire also makes them a fairly high risk option, because most attack windows are only large enough to get a single shot off, so the resulting damage loss if you miss that shot is huge.

If you can master their weakness and take advantage of their strengths, however, explosive weapons can be excellent for dealing huge amounts of damage while an enemy is staggered. The large area that some of these weapons impacts across also makes them ideal for taking out groups of weaker enemies in a single shot, or for catching mobile enemies when firing down on them from above. In addition, explosive weapons are immune to ricochet and will lose none of their effectiveness at longer ranges. Missiles may lose targeting eventually and explode prematurely, and grenades and shells may miss, but any explosive that connects will deal full damage, no matter how far away the target is. Like energy weapons, they tend to have "sub-categories," but can be generally classified in three ways:

▐ **Missiles** generally fire multiple smaller projectiles with homing properties. If you have missiles with multi-lock capabilities equipped, you can hold the corresponding weapon input while locked on to a single target to split the payload and hit multiple targets in a single volley.

▐ **Bazookas** and **grenades** fire a single, high-velocity explosive, often causing a large explosion once it makes contact with either an enemy or the terrain, dealing splash damage to everything in the vicinity. Due to their high recoil, you'll often have to sacrifice mobility in order to utilize the full power of bazookas and grenade cannons.

▐ **Incendiary weapons**, like the flamethrower and napalm bomb launcher, also deal explosive damage, though with the addition of heat buildup that can inflict a debilitating ACS anomaly.

Explosive weapons are the most effective weapon type for building up accumulative strain on an opponent's ACS, making them ideal for staggering opponents during protracted encounters against tougher enemies.

CORAL WARFARE

As you progress, you will begin encountering enemy attacks and AC parts that inflict Coral-based damage. This fourth damage type is unique in the sense that it ignores all defensive specs and ricochet, allowing it to deal its full attack power against any target within the weapon's effective range. Coral attacks can be easily identified by their distinct crimson color, so do your best to avoid getting hit when fighting foes who have access to this type of advanced weaponry.

CHARGE ATTACKS

Certain weapons can perform charge attacks that exhibit special properties and behavior distinct from their regular attacks, such as firing a triple-burst shot instead of single rounds. Beyond simply dealing more damage, charge attacks often open up new tactical possibilities, so you'll want to experiment with each compatible weapon category to discover what their charge attack can do. Learning to use charge attacks will help increase your performance in a wide variety of combat scenarios.

Holding down the button assigned to a compatible weapon will begin charging it up, which is indicated by a yellow bar filling up on the corresponding gauge around the reticle. Once this yellow bar is full, you'll hear a faint beeping sound and the weapon will glow or animate to indicate that the charge is ready; you can continue holding the button and release it when ready to fire the charge shot. It's worth noting that some melee weapons, like the default HI-32: BU-TT/A pulse blade, only require you to hold down the assigned button for a second to use a charge attack.

Full-Charge Attacks
A small selection of weapons you will acquire later in the game also feature the ability to charge past their initial limit if you continue to hold the button. An orange bar will slowly fill over the yellow bar until it's full, at which point you can release the button to unleash a devastating full-charge attack. Weapons capable of performing full-charge attacks have three distinct firing modes, making them some of the most versatile in your arsenal.

Firing Stance
Firing heavy ordinance like bazookas or performing charge attacks can cause your AC to stop and assume a firing stance to counteract the heavy recoil, impeding mobility and leaving you briefly vulnerable. Depending on the weapon, you might also experience some degree of kickback that pushes your AC backward. Equipping tetrapod or tank legs can help to mitigate or outright eliminate the temporary loss of mobility that comes from entering a firing stance. The kickback associated with firing high-recoil weapons like grenade cannons isn't always a negative, however, as it can be used to briefly halt your descent when airborne and potentially keep your AC in the air long enough for its EN to replenish.

CANCELING CHARGES
Pressing the Ⓨ/△ button at any point while charging weapons or using multi-lock will instantly cancel the action and reset your weapons to their neutral state. Canceling charges can be useful when the situation changes and you no longer want to risk firing a charge attack or if you want to avoid wasting ammo after defeating enemies with other weapons.

RECOIL

All non-homing ranged weapons, such as assault rifles, laser shotguns, and even pulse guns, generate some degree of recoil when fired. You can observe this by paying close attention to the crosshairs on your reticle as you fire these weapons. The more the lines on the crosshair bloom, the less accurate the shots are likely to be. The severity of the accuracy penalty associated with recoil depends on multiple factors, like the weapon's Recoil spec, the Recoil Control spec of your arms, along with how your handling of the weapon itself.

Sustained fire with weapons like machine guns will lead to a progressive degradation in accuracy, which is worsened even further when opening fire with multiple weapons simultaneously, as is typical in Double Trigger builds. The reticle will quickly tighten up again if you pause firing for a second, however, which can be a better alternative to continuing to fire and failing to hit the target. The farther away from the target you are, the more likely recoil is to be a factor, so experiment with equipping arms with higher levels of recoil control and pause when firing if necessary to prevent a severe loss of accuracy. Lastly, while it might seem counterintuitive, it's important to note that the Recoil Control spec of your arms also influences the degree of recoil experienced when firing shoulder units.

PULSE SHIELDS & GUARDING

Pulse shields are another specialized weapon type, and can only be equipped in the L-Back slot. Upon deploying them, they'll mitigate the damage and impact of incoming attacks within a 180-degree radius in front of you. Their Damage Mitigation and Impact Dampening specs correlate to the percentage of each attack's damage that they'll reduce: a shield with 63 damage mitigation spec will reduce incoming damage by 63%, for example. Shields also have an "Initial Guard" mechanic that functions similar to a parry. This offers different—and usually much higher—reduction values, which can be found under the IG Damage Mitigation and IG Impact Dampening specs.

The Initial Guard window is the brief period immediately following deployment of the shield—the amount of time it's active is shown in the IG Duration spec and varies from shield to shield. As an example, if a shield has an IG duration spec of 0.2, you'll have 0.2 seconds of Initial Guard when deploying it. Shields build up heat whenever you deploy them (shown via the Deploy Heat Buildup spec); doing so in quick succession either when trying to block incoming attacks with Initial Guards or just deploying the shield again after movement will cause it to overheat and result in a lengthy cooldown before it can be used again.

While your shield may absorb much of the incoming impact, it's still possible for you to be staggered with it deployed. If that happens, your shield will immediately be canceled and go on cooldown, which is indicated by visible heat and an orange glow emanating from the part. When using shields, you'll need to be especially mindful of enemies using pulse and melee weapons, as they'll be able to break your shield easily.

Some shields are better suited to being deployed for longer periods to mitigate incoming damage and impact, while others can almost entirely nullify attacks with an Initial Guard if timed correctly.

PULSE BARRIERS
Pulse armors are protective energy shields that certain enemies can generate. These spherical barriers encase the enemy in a bubble of shimmering energy, and will prevent all attacks from hitting them until disrupted. The AP gauge of targets with pulse armor turns blue to indicate the status of their barrier, and a "shield" prompt appears above your reticle whenever a hit connects. Dealing enough damage to cancel an enemy's pulse armor will immediately overload its ACS and leave it vulnerable to direct hits. Melee and pulse weapons with a high PA Interference spec will manage this feat much more easily than others. You'll need to act quickly at that point, however, since these more advanced adversaries can often regenerate a new barrier after a brief moment of vulnerability.

In addition, you'll also occasionally encounter standard enemies, like quad drones, outfitted with pulse protection generators that produce a larger barrier. Don't bother wasting ammo on these static barriers, since they're impervious to all damage. The only way to disable them is to enter inside the barrier and take out the enemy generating it.

PURGING WEAPONS

With the "Automatically Purge Weapon" option set to on in the Game Settings section of the System menu, your AC will automatically purge any of its weapons when their respective ammunition supply has been fully depleted. Jettisoning useless weapons has the benefit of reducing your AC's total weight, which slightly improves its overall speed and maneuverability based on how heavy the part was. Don't worry about permanently losing purged parts or paying extra to retrieve them; there's zero drawback associated with this, and all purged weapons are automatically replenished upon resupplying at a sherpa or any time you restart a checkpoint or complete a mission. It's also possible to unlock the ability to manually purge weapons via the Weight Control OS Tuning function, which you can learn more about on P.34.

SYSTEM ABNORMALITIES

System abnormalities encompass a wide range of secondary effects caused by exposure to environmental hazards, like searing heat, or damage from special weaponry, like shock-inducing stun bomb launchers. System abnormalities are negative in nature, and meant to impair your performance or further debilitate you during a combat scenario; they're rarely capable of winning a battle themselves, but can complement the rest of an arsenal quite potently and should be respected.

These debilitating conditions can occur in two forms depending on the exact status abnormality. The first involves gradual heat or shock buildup; the initial hit of an attack capable of inflicting either type of buildup will cause a small red ACS Anomaly or yellow Electrical Discharge gauge to appear above your ACS gauge. These small gauges will then continue to fill with every attack that deals buildup of the same type, until the gauge is full and the system abnormality is inflicted. If you manage to avoid any subsequent buildup, the gauge will gradually deplete to zero (at a fixed rate of five points per second) and no status abnormality will occur. The second type of system abnormality is much more straightforward, consisting of localized jamming rounds that can instantly impair your lock-on capabilities when within their radius or line of sight.

Your AC has a variable amount of resistance to heat and shock buildup based on the System Recovery spec of its head part; the higher this spec, the more repeated exposure or hits it takes to fill the gauge and trigger an ACS anomaly or electrical discharge. Independent of its head or overall build, every AC has a hidden ACS anomaly and electrical discharge tolerance that's equivalent to a fixed 490 points worth of buildup, with higher System Recovery specs increasing the AC's buildup resistance instead of raising its tolerance limit. It's also worth noting that pulse shields can be deployed to negate heat and shock buildup, making these defensive shoulder units extremely useful against opponents capable of inflicting status abnormalities. Unfortunately, repair kits can't be used to remove system abnormalities and their associated buildup, so be sure not to waste them for this purpose.

Your AC isn't the only craft with a vulnerability to system abnormalities; you can also outfit it with weaponry capable of inflicting system abnormalities against enemies. Much like that of your AC, each enemy type has a hidden heat or shock tolerance that generally amounts to 500 points for standard enemies and up to 999 points for certain bosses. As a result, you'll typically need to deal 500 points of either heat or shock buildup to trigger the effect. Regular enemies have no individual resistances to these effects, which would otherwise influence how much is inflicted by each attack. Stronger enemies, bosses, and rival ACs often have such resistances, however, with bosses in particular occasionally benefiting from high enough resistances to make them effectively immune.

ACS Anomaly

 ACS anomaly occurs when a craft is exposed to sufficient amounts of heat buildup, either from environmental hazards like lava or fire, or weapons like flamethrowers and napalm bombs. When triggered, ACS anomaly will interfere with the craft's ACS and greatly reduce its stability, causing it to receive an additional 50% impact from incoming attacks for the next 10 seconds. ACS anomaly makes attacks that naturally inflict a lot of ACS strain essentially guaranteed to cause a stagger and those with low impact much more dangerous than usual. Steer clear of heat-inducing hazards and attacks, and use flamethrowers or napalm bomb

launchers to inflict ACS anomaly on tougher opponents before staggering them with high-impact weapons. Since there's no way to visually confirm if you've triggered an ACS anomaly on an enemy, you'll have to estimate when you've dealt enough buildup before switching to other weapons that strain their ACS.

The heat buildup caused by flamethrowers can quickly result in ACS anomaly. Your priority when facing enemies that wield these weapons should always be to retreat to a safe distance, even at the expense of attacking.

Electrical Discharge

 Electrical discharge is triggered when a craft is exposed to sufficient shock buildup from sources like the stun smog produced by PCA repair mechs or advanced weaponry like stun needle launchers. Once the gauge is filled, a single burst of 1600 damage occurs along with a brief stagger that interrupts the target's actions and leaves it vulnerable. Damage dealt by an electrical discharge is always fixed 1600, regardless of the target's resistances, defensive specs, or maximum AP, and is instantly inflicted the moment the status abnormality triggers.

While this damage value might not appear impressive at first glance, the true potential of shock-inducing weapons lies in the fact that you can begin buildup up to another electrical discharge the instant the previous one occurs. With a loadout that focuses on shock-based weaponry, like dual stun guns and stun needle launchers, it's possible to completely decimate the AP gauge of some tougher enemies by triggering back-to-back electrical discharge, particularly if their resistances make them susceptible to shock buildup.

Camera Disruption

Camera disruption is exclusive to the BAWS jamming bomb launcher and hinders the lock-on capabilities of crafts that are within the radius or line of sight of its special chaff rounds. If you step into one of these spherical chaff clouds, your AC's instruments will become jammed, disabling your compass and rendering you unable to lock on to anything outside the cloud. The abnormality dissipates immediately upon exiting the cloud, but although it appears transparent, the chaff cloud can prevent lock-on if its located between you and enemies. This goes both ways, hindering enemies from effectively targeting you while also disrupting your ability to lock on to them. Some weapons that pass through the chaff cloud can also suffer from impaired effectiveness. For more details on the jamming bomb launcher and how to use it, turn to P.57.

Outside of fighting other ACs in the Nest, your opponents won't have access to jamming rounds.

NEST

Once you've completed the "Ocean Crossing" mission at the end of Chapter 2, you'll be able to access the Nest, an online battle simulator that lets you team up and fight against other players in various game modes. This requires an internet connection on all platforms, and an active subscription to either PlayStation Plus or Xbox Game Pass Core if playing on consoles.

All of your parts and AC data carry over into the Nest, and many players entering this mode will have their own ACs designed exclusively for battling other players. It's a good idea to create Nest-specific builds and save them in your AC Data slots. The Nest also offers an opportunity to truly express yourself, as your customization options beyond your AC are presented here, such as your emblem, and AC name.

Game Updates

Occasionally, the game will receive updates that can alter the balance of specific weapons or parts, which can have a significant impact on your online experience. If you're enjoying online play, then it's worth keeping track of the official Armored Core VI website, where detailed update notes are published whenever the game is updated. Because the game evolves over time, the available options and modes are almost certain to change; this section covers the basic options available in the period after the game's launch.

Both your pilot name and emblem will be visible to other players in the Nest; you can edit both by opening the License menu in the Garage.

CUSTOM MATCH

Matches in Armored Core VI's Nest are all organized via lobbies, which are known as "rooms," and all game modes focus on eliminating other players. You can battle with or against your friends as well as random players to see who the dominant pilot is. Custom matches allow you to create or search for rooms, in which you'll be matched with other players who are searching for the same room settings. The maximum amount of players in a single room is nine, but only up to six of these can be combatants; the other members who are present in the room will be assigned as spectators. Depending on how the room is configured, spectators may have the option to rotate in as players.

MATCH LOG

Match Log is where you can see the results of the matches you've played. All matches, private or public, are cached here for you to review. You'll see the match results and the names and emblems of the players involved.

MATCH SETTINGS

You can either search for or create rooms in the Nest by selecting your desired match specifications. In either case, the options you'll be able to select from are all detailed here.

Room Search Settings	
Capacity	2 players
Match Format	Single
Time Limit	2 minutes
Map	Grid 086
Member Rotation	Losers Rotate
Keywords	---
Search	

MATCH FORMAT

Single
- 1-vs-1. The first player to secure a two-phase lead wins.
- Win phase or draw to earn 1 point. First player to score 2 points wins.
- Capacity in Single play is up to nine players, so if you want to be sure you'll be playing and not spectating, set the capacity to two when searching.

Team
- 3-vs-3. Two teams compete in an endurance match.
- Destroy enemy ACs to score team points. The highest-scoring team when time is called wins.
- The player with the most kills will be marked as a priority target. Destroy them to earn extra points.
- Capacity is again up to nine players, which includes three spectating players.

MEMBER ROTATION

Locked
- No automatic rotation. Members are locked in for subsequent sorties.

Losers Rotate
- Losers of previous match spectate, changing places with reserves who did not sortie.

Winners Rotate
- Winners of previous match spectate, changing places with reserves who did not sortie.

AVAILABLE COMBAT ZONES
- Bona Dea Dunes
- Wall Sector
- Jorgen Refueling Base
- Old Bertram Spaceport
- Grid 086
- Upper Grid 086, Outer Shell
- Grid 012
- Watchpoint Delta
- Xylem, the Floating City

TIME LIMITS
- 2 minutes
- 3 minutes
- 5 minutes
- 7 minutes
- 10 minutes

ACCESS

Open
- Players can join via room search.

Private
- Room will not appear in room search.

KEYWORDS

If you're looking to match with specific people, you can create matches with a "keyword," which is effectively a lobby password. You can also search for that specific keyword if it was given to you by a friend.

Allies and adversaries are each assigned a number in multiplayer; allies have green HUD marking, while opponents are purple.

The current match's time limit is always present on your HUD.

CHAPTER 2 ASSEMBLY

Assembling an Armored Core is a process that rewards those who dig deep into the systems that hold an AC together. Every spec has its intricacies, and every part has synergies and surprises for expert assemblers to uncover. This chapter will take you through the building process, explain the specs, and showcase every single part you can acquire.

ASSEMBLY & SPECS

Due to the highly customizable nature of ACs, putting one together with your own selection of parts and expressing your personal style through its visual appearance is a major component in making your experience with the game feel unique. You can decide which weapons, head, core, arms, legs, booster, FCS, generator, and expansion parts to equip in order to truly fine-tune your playstyle; every choice you make will have a significant impact on your AC's specs and how it controls. In this section we'll cover the Assembly, briefly look at cosmetic customization, and provide detailed explanations for each spec.

PARTS SHOP

Accessible to all registered mercenaries operating on Rubicon, the Parts Shop is where you'll trade your hard-earned COAM in exchange for new parts to expand your customization potential. If you're ever unhappy with a purchase or simply need some extra COAM, remember that you can always sell parts back to the shop at full market value and buy them again later.

BUYING PARTS

Parts available for purchase come in various categories, including arm and shoulder weapons, frame parts, and inner parts. If you're curious about a weapon or leg part and want to learn more before buying it, you can press ⓧ/▢ on the selected part to play a short video that showcases its basic functions. Make sure to watch these to the end, because many weapons have multiple functions that will be shown one after the other. Most weapons can be equipped to either both arm or both back unit slots, but if you want to equip a matching pair of the same weapon, you'll need to own a duplicate for each slot. If you acquire a weapon from a parts container or mission reward, you'll only be given either the left or right version of it; the opposite version will appear for purchase in the Parts Shop after the mission.

MANUFACTURERS

There are many corporations and factions operating on Rubicon, and as an independent mercenary you'll have access to parts manufactured by most of them. Some manufacturers specialize in specific systems or damage types, whereas others are more generalized. Once you become familiar with what they typically produce, you'll know which manufacturer to look out for when testing or selecting new parts.

ALLMIND
The mercenary support system. AC parts developed by ALLMIND all consist of experimental frame parts and energy weapons.

Arquebus ADD
The "Advanced Development Division" of Arquebus is a subsidiary that handles the design and manufacturing of cutting-edge AC parts.

Arquebus Corporation
One of main extraplanetary corporations involved in the Coral war, Arquebus specializes in the development of laser-based weaponry.

Balam Industries
The other major extraplanetary corporation drawn to Rubicon by the stirring embers, Balam's designs favor kinetic ammunition and overall mobility.

BAWS
Native to the Belius region, "Belius Applied Weapon Systems" capitalizes on the conflict by selling its mass-produced weapons and parts to any faction.

Dafeng Core Industries
Owned by Balam, Dafeng manufactures highly destructive explosive weapons along with frame parts sturdy enough to withstand their impact.

Elcano Foundry
Elcano Foundry focuses primarily on lightweight parts, making them a go-to manufacturer for pilots who prefer fast and nimble AC builds.

Furlong Dynamics
A seemingly neutral player in the war, Furlong specializes in missile launchers and FCS parts designed to optimize missile lock time.

Melinite
With a focus on raw explosive power and attention to detail, Melinite offers a small but potent lineup of bazookas and grenade launchers.

RaD
Led by the brilliant "Cinder" Carla, RaD produces a range of unique weapons and parts featuring eccentric designs that reflect their creator's personality.

Rubicon Research Institute
Lost in the Fires of Ibis centuries ago, the Rubicon Research Institute developed experimental weapons and AC technology capable of harnessing Coral to enhance output and performance.

Schneider
Part of the Arquebus Group, Schneider specializes in high-mobility AC parts and unconventional weaponry designed to fill specialized roles in combat.

Takigawa Harmonics

Takigawa's expertise is in the field of high-frequency pulse technology, producing both offensive and defensive weaponry such as the default pulse blade and various types of pulse shields.

VCPL

True to its name, the "Vice and Cohen Plasma Laboratory" focuses most of its R&D efforts on plasma-based weapon systems.

SELLING PARTS

All of your parts can be sold back at market value, which means that buying and trying out new parts is a 100% risk-free investment. If a new purchase doesn't end up being to your liking, you can always sell the part back and recoup all of its cost before investing that amount into something else. Experimentation is encouraged, since you won't lose any of your valuable COAM. Keep in mind, however, that only parts you currently own will be available when accessing the Assembly from the Mission Failed menu, so building up a large selection of parts will give you more options for pushing through a difficult section if your current build is struggling.

FRESH STOCK

Completing certain missions will cause new parts to become available through Parts Shop updates. The first updates happen frequently throughout Chapter 1, but subsequent updates will be spread out as rewards for finishing chapters, with the final two unlocking well into a second playthrough. ALLMIND will alert you whenever there's fresh stock in the Parts Shop, and you'll also notice a small blue icon next to the Parts Shop option to signal that there are parts you haven't browsed through and examined already. The exact conditions for unlocking each Parts Shop update are listed in the chart below.

Parts Shop Updates	
Shop Update 1	Complete "Destroy Artillery Installations" or "Grid 135 Cleanup"
Shop Update 2	Complete "Destroy the Weaponized Mining Ship" and "Attack the Dam Complex"
Shop Update 3	Complete "Operation Wallclimber"
Shop Update 4	Complete "Attack the Watchpoint"
Shop Update 5	Complete "Ocean Crossing"
Shop Update 6	Complete "Destroy the Ice Worm"
Shop Update 7	Complete "Escape"
Shop Update 8	Complete "Ocean Crossing" in NG+
Shop Update 9	Complete "Destroy the Ice Worm" in NG+

ASSEMBLY

After your first mission as a licensed mercenary, you'll be able to access the Assembly from the AC Design menu in the Garage. While your initial AC gives you a small sample of some of the potential options, you'll need to experiment with the weapons and parts currently available to start formulating a build.

SWAPPING PARTS

The Assembly is where you'll choose from the various parts you own to put together your custom AC build. The parts available to you in the Assembly are acquired from either Hunter Class rewards, parts containers, training programs, or from buying them in the Parts Shop. If you fail a mission, you'll be able to directly access the Assembly without having to return to the Garage menu, allowing you to adjust your build before making another attempt; take some time to familiarize yourself with the Assembly, because you'll likely be spending a lot of time there.

Upon first entering the Assembly, you'll be shown an overview of your current AC and what's equipped in each slot. Selecting any of those parts slots will take you to a new menu that allows you to cycle through each available part for that slot, or you can use the LB/L1 and RB/R1 buttons to move between slots. Just like in the Parts Shop, you'll be able to preview weapons and leg parts by pressing X/□ when a part is highlighted in the Assembly.

PART CATEGORIES

An AC's parts are divided into three major categories: weapons, frame parts, and inner parts. The weapon category is divided into four slots for weapon units, while the frame features one slot each for a head, core, arm, and leg part. Finally, the inner category allows one slot each to install a booster, FCS, and a generator. When building your AC in the Assembly, try to evaluate each part's unique advantages and drawbacks as it relates to the mission at hand. For example, not every mission requires a melee weapon, so swapping it for another gun may be the best option. How weapons synergize with one another is a major factor in how effective your offense can be, and there are countless effective combinations to discover.

Previewing weapons before purchasing them can help you decide if they might be a good fit for your loadout on the next sortie.

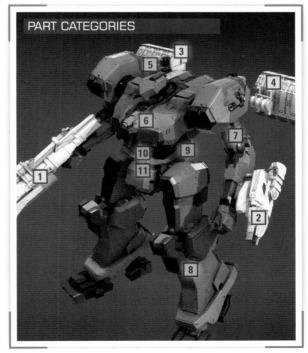

PART CATEGORIES

WEAPONS

1	R-ARM UNIT
2	L-ARM UNIT
3	R-BACK UNIT
4	L-BACK UNIT

FRAME PARTS

5	HEAD
6	CORE
7	ARMS
8	LEGS

INNER PARTS

9	BOOSTER
10	FCS
11	GENERATOR

AC TEST

AC Test is a virtual testing environment accessible either from the Sortie menu or the Assembly, and is easily overlooked despite being highly useful for evaluating your build's overall capabilities and how each part's specs affect your AC's performance. It places you in a flat, box-shaped room with the option to choose which enemy type to practice against via the enemy settings option, either with or without their AI active. It also offers a supply option, which will replenish your AP and ammo, as well as instant access to the Assembly. Any changes that you make within the AC Test program are applied to your Assembly when you exit.

EXPANSIONS

The expansion slot is occupied by a unique category of parts that only become available once you've unlocked a Core Expansion using OST Chips obtained from defeating Arena opponents. After unlocking a Core Expansion via OS Tuning, you'll need to equip it in the Assembly before it becomes available in a mission. See P.92 for a full analysis of all the Core Expansions and tips on how to exploit their full defensive and offensive potential.

OVERBURDENING

AC WEIGHT CLASSES

The total weight of your AC determines which of the three weight classes it fits within: lightweight, mediumweight, or heavyweight. While weight classes aren't a strict measure of overall performance, you can use the total weight ranges listed here to figure out which class your AC belongs to based on its current total weight load.

Class	Total Weight
Lightweight	35,000–59,999
Mediumweight	60,000–79,999
Heavyweight	80,000+

The Load Limit spec specifies the weight that equipped legs can support before becoming overburdened. Once surpassed, an AC cannot deploy at all without equipping lighter parts or making use of the Weight Control OS Tuning function. Overburdening the AC impacts thrust speed, Quick Boost speed, Quick Boost reload time, and EN recovery rate—all of which are visible in AC specs and scale negatively as your AC takes on additional weight.

If Weight Control is unlocked and you opt to deploy while overburdened, a few additional drawbacks not reflected in your specs can also be felt on the battlefield. Walking speed is impacted significantly, with even slight overburden slowing basic locomotion to a crawl. Additionally, jump height is significantly reduced, and only gets worse as your AC gets heavier. Lastly, falls to the ground—be it from jumps or descents from tall heights—stall the AC's movement for around half a second, regardless of how overburdened it is. Manually purging weapons can be used to offload some of the weight of your AC and improve its mobility.

ARMS OVERBURDENED

The Arms Load Limit spec determines the total weight both arms can bear before becoming overburdened. Once that limit is surpassed, the AC won't be stopped from

Pay attention to any bright red indicators when designing your AC, as these conditions can either prevent you from deploying or severely reduce your overall performance.

deploying into missions, but will face severe penalties in combat, as both recoil control and target tracking will be significantly affected and impact your ability to land shots on distant or moving targets. The answer to this problem is to either equip arms with higher load capacity or swap to lighter weapons while crafting your assembly.

EN SHORTFALL

This crippling condition occurs whenever your AC's Total EN Load spec exceeds its EN Output spec, and prevents you from deploying due to lack of available power required to support all equipped parts. The only way to prevent EN shortfall is to either equip parts with a lower EN load or a generator and core combo capable of producing a high enough EN output to support the current assembly's EN requirements.

COSMETIC CUSTOMIZATION

In addition to outfitting your AC with parts that determine its overall performance, Armored Core VI also offers an extensive suite of visual customization options accessible via the AC Design menu. There, you can select from a range of preset color schemes and emblems, or create your own entirely original designs to conquer the battlefield in style.

PAINT

You can customize your AC's paint job by changing the color of the entire frame all at once, or by choosing a custom color for each individual part, including arm and back units. Each part can be painted with preset color sets and patterns, or you can individually paint the main, sub, support, optional, other, and device portions of each individual part of your AC. In addition, you can change its reflectiveness and luster, giving you immense control over the look of your mech. Finally, you can also pick the kind of weathering your AC displays, regardless of combat damage, all of which give you near-endless customization options.

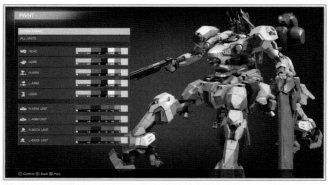

The Paint menu offers editable color palettes for each individual frame part and weapon.

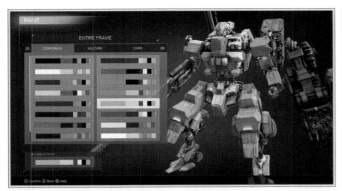

It's quick and easy to apply a paint job to your entire AC using either the existing color set or one you've put together yourself.

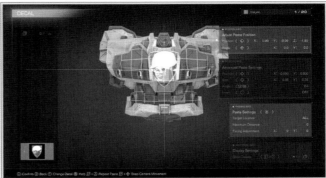

You can use the "Custom Decals" option in the Decals menu to adjust the position of an emblem on each part of your frame.

DECALS & EMBLEMS

Much like with a paint job, you can choose from a collection of preset images that are acquired as you proceed through the game, each of which can be equipped to any of your frame parts as a decal in the Decals menu, or onto your Mercenary License as an emblem in the License menu.

IMAGE EDITOR

If you're feeling particularly creative, you can design your own custom image by accessing the Image Editor menu. This custom editor provides you with a 41x41 square grid where you can insert either basic or preset images to use as building blocks for creating your image. Even though you're given what initially feels like a limited 41x41 square grid to work in, your image is not limited to 41x41 pixels—these are merely gridlines to help guide you. You also have access to 23 pages' worth of preset "pieces" to choose from, which you can freely alter in terms of dimensions and colors. With the ability to stack up to 128 layers on top of one another, your imagination is the only limit. Once you're satisfied with a custom image, you can save it, then apply it to either your AC as a decal or your Mercenary License as an emblem. You can also download images other players have created. To do so, open the Image Editor, then select the Download tab and you'll get a box pop up in which you can put the unique Share ID of the item you want to download. Once you have it, it can be equipped in the same manner as the normal versions.

You can also upload your own creations by going to the image in the Image Editor, pressing $(Y)/(\triangle)$, then selecting Upload. Once that process is complete, you'll be given the Share ID for your item and other people will be able to download and use it.

AC DATA

Once you've settled on a build you like or found one that's proven particularly useful, you won't have to abandon it if you want to experiment with new designs. Instead, you can save it in the AC Data section of the AC Design menu, which enables you to save and load up to 160 AC assemblies split across four different user presets that can hold 40 ACs each. These custom user ACs even carry across saves, so if you were to start an entirely new game, your AC designs would still be accessible in AC Data.

A red ! warning will appear next to any saved AC design whenever you sell some of the parts that it's built from, signifying that parts are missing from your collection to complete the assembly. If you try to load an old design that's missing parts, you'll have the option to buy the parts from the shop, provided you have the COAM available. The Preset tab of the AC Data menu is reserved for the ACs of other pilots

you'll meet across Rubicon. You can obtain their data by defeating their ACs in the Arena, which will then unlock the option to load their data in the Preset tab and use their AC for yourself. Unlike rebuilding an old AC of your own design, the red ! warning on a Preset denotes more than just parts you've sold. These ACs might include parts you haven't even acquired yet, such as those earned as rewards for later Hunter Class rankings, or from parts containers in missions. In this case, the Load option will be unavailable to select.

DATA UPLOAD

You can also upload your saved ACs for others to use. Doing so will provide you with a code that you can share, which can then be entered by players on the same platform as you, allowing them to load up your AC. As usual, they will need to own all of the necessary parts in order to deploy the AC.

The color of your booster jets is determined by your choice of generator manufacturer, ranging from orange to blue and even red based on the technology used.

After selling a lot of parts, you might find that a number of your saved builds become unusable without spending large sums of COAM.

Build choices in Armored Core VI aren't limited to which parts you equip; it's also possible to apply OS upgrades to your AC via OS Tuning, which lets you enhance its general performance or unlock new features and abilities at the system OS level. The OS Tuning menu becomes accessible from the Garage after completing either the "Retrieve Combat Logs" or "Investigate BAWS Arsenal No.2" missions in Chapter 1.

Applying OS upgrades requires a finite resource called OST Chips, with each upgrade costing a specific amount to install. The only way to earn OST Chips is to defeat an opponent in the Arena for the first time, with higher-ranked pilots rewarding you with progressively more OST Chips. There are 197 OST Chips to earn in total, which corresponds to the precise amount needed to unlock all upgrades. If you aren't satisfied with your current OS upgrades or want to reconfigure them to better suit a mission, you can refund all your OST Chips by pressing Ⓨ/△ in the OS Tuning menu. Be aware that resetting OS upgrades will cost you a fixed amount of COAM based on the number of OST Chips being reset; this process won't be expensive at first, but becomes significantly more costly as you earn and invest more OST Chips into upgrading your AC.

Many OS upgrades feature a series of incremental updates. You begin by installing the initial upgrade, which provides some benefits, and can then purchase additional updates using more OST Chips to further enhance performance. For example, the base version of an upgrade might offer a 3% damage increase to your ranged energy weaponry for two OST Chips, while the final update of the same upgrade provides a larger 15% damage increase, though at a steeper OST Chip cost.

ATTACK & DAMAGE CONTROL

While the other OS Tuning categories allow you to unlock new abilities and parts to expand your tactical options, the Attack Control and Damage Control categories serve as a means through which you can passively improve the general offensive and defensive performance of your AC, regardless of your build. Generally speaking, it's worth investing your initial OST Chips into some of the System Unlocks or Core Expansions, since they're so fundamental and help round out your AC's abilities. Once you're happy with what you have there, you should start investing into Attack Control and Damage Control upgrades to raise your AC's performance.

If you like swapping weapons often to capitalize on enemy weaknesses, then you can take a broad approach by improving the damage type increases evenly. If you favor specific weapons or damage types, then you can just as easily put all of your chips into maximizing the damage increase for those types. Given the breadth of weapons you have access to, you might also not yet know what you want to settle on. In these instances, you can't go wrong with investing chips into **Direct Hit Modifier - Damage Tuning**, because of how universally helpful it is for all weapons. This can then have a knock-on effect on your weapon selection, because weapons with higher direct hit modifiers will see even more benefit, which helps illustrate how interlinked these systems are with the parts you equip, even in ways that are not immediately apparent.

Melee Weapons - Drive Control Tuning also affects the damage dealt by Boost Kicks, so consider upgrading it if you're a Boost Kick aficionado.

Your progress through the game can influence which passive upgrades you choose to invest OST Chips into, as you'll need to factor in the weapons currently available. Kinetic and explosive ranged weapons are commonplace during the early chapters of the game, so putting chips into **Kinetic Weapons – Fire Control Tuning** or **Explosive Weapons – Fuse Control Tuning** could provide a benefit to a larger selection of weapons. As more and more energy-based weapons become available, you can reset your OS upgrades and refocus in a different area if you find yourself gravitating more toward them.

The same can be said for **Melee Weapons – Drive Control Tuning**, since even though you start with a melee weapon, by the time you've installed all the System Unlocks and Core Expansions, putting chips into the more general damage types will likely provide a bigger benefit. It should also be noted that regardless of what type of damage a melee weapon deals, you won't see any increase in its damage by investing in the three damage-type upgrades. Only the **Melee Weapons – Drive Control Tuning** or **Direct Hit Modifier – Damage Tuning** can increase the damage these weapons deal.

Damage Control upgrades are also important early on, especially **ACS – Dynamic Deflection Control Tuning**. The additional defense against all sources of damage can give you some breathing room if you're feeling overwhelmed while learning to pilot your AC, and the updates allow this upgrade to scale well into later missions and remain relevant on any build. A substantial 15% of all incoming damage will be negated once you unlock the final upgrade, which makes each level of **ACS – Dynamic Deflection Control Tuning** extremely valuable and worth periodically investing in as you progress through the game.

Keep in mind that ACS - Dynamic Deflection Control Tuning does not mitigate the amount of impact you take from attacks, only the actual damage they deal, so it won't help prevent you from getting staggered.

ACCESS SPEED – OPTIMIZATION

Access Speed – Optimization increases the speed at which your AC's system can decrypt access codes on interactable objects, such as doors and wrecks, reducing the time this takes by 50% at its highest level. Every object with an access prompt is affected by this upgrade, but higher security decryption will still be relatively slow. This upgrade does not affect your offensive or defensive capabilities, and is at best a tertiary asset to combat. Unless you need a few extra seconds when going for an S-Rank rating, this upgrade should be low priority.

Although on the lower end in terms of priority, repair kits are your lifeblood on the battle-field, and as such being able to increase their potency by up to an additional 2000 AP can often be the difference between making it through a battle with a tough opponent or being reduced to a pile of scrap. Repair Kits – Optimization is important, but should probably be considered after some investment in ACS – Dynamic Deflection Control Tuning. In a tense combat scenario, if you use a repair kit with too much AP remaining, the additional AP will be wasted, so you'll need to be very mindful of when you use repair kits after installing the upgrades. Additionally, against challenging bosses, an extra 2000 AP restored won't benefit you as much as a 15% decrease to all damage, and repair kits are unusable in any of the Arena battles, so this upgrade will not make obtaining more OST Chips any easier.

Use pulse protection barriers to create temporary bubbles of safety on the battlefield.

Kinetic Weapons – Fire Control Tuning

>> INSTALL	Kinetic Damage: +3%	2	
>> UPDATE . 1	Kinetic Damage: +6%	3	
>> UPDATE . 2	Kinetic Damage: +9%	4	
>> UPDATE . 3	Kinetic Damage: +12%	5	
>> UPDATE . 4	Kinetic Damage: +15%	7	

Explosive Weapons – Fuse Control Tuning

>> INSTALL	Explosive Damage: +3%	2	
>> UPDATE . 1	Explosive Damage: +6%	3	
>> UPDATE . 2	Explosive Damage: +9%	4	
>> UPDATE . 3	Explosive Damage: +12%	5	
>> UPDATE . 4	Explosive Damage: +15%	7	

Energy Weapons – Output Control Tuning

>> INSTALL	Energy Damage: +3%	2	
>> UPDATE . 1	Energy Damage: +6%	3	
>> UPDATE . 2	Energy Damage: +9%	4	
>> UPDATE . 3	Energy Damage: +12%	5	
>> UPDATE . 4	Energy Damage: +15%	7	

Melee Weapons – Drive Control Tuning

>> INSTALL	Melee Weapon Damage: +5%	3	
>> UPDATE . 1	Melee Weapon Damage: +10%	5	
>> UPDATE . 2	Melee Weapon Damage: +15%	7	

Direct Hit Modifier – Damage Tuning

>> INSTALL	Direct Hit Damage: +5%	4	
>> UPDATE . 1	Direct Hit Damage: +10%	6	
>> UPDATE . 2	Direct Hit Damage: +15%	8	

Access Speed – Optimization

>> INSTALL	Access Speed: +50%	2	
>> UPDATE . 1	Access Speed: +100%	4	

ACS – Dynamic Deflection Control Tuning

>> INSTALL	Damage Mitigation: 3%	2	
>> UPDATE . 1	Damage Mitigation: 6%	4	
>> UPDATE . 2	Damage Mitigation: 9%	6	
>> UPDATE . 3	Damage Mitigation: 12%	8	
>> UPDATE . 4	Damage Mitigation: 15%	10	

Repair Kits – Optimization

>> INSTALL	Repair Kit Effectiveness: +500	3	
>> UPDATE . 1	Repair Kit Effectiveness: +1000	5	
>> UPDATE . 2	Repair Kit Effectiveness: +1500	7	
>> UPDATE . 3	Repair Kit Effectiveness: +2000	10	

CORE EXPANSIONS

Core Expansions are a key AC component that grants you access to unique defensive or offensive capabilities. When used under the right circumstances, these can dramatically alter the flow of an encounter. Whether it's a last-second reprieve from failure, or an expanding shockwave that can clear the sky of missiles, the situations in which these abilities can be used are almost endless, and although you can only equip a single Core Expansion at a time, you should always have one in your arsenal. For more details on expansions, see P.92 in the Parts Catalog.

Assault Armor

>> INSTALL	Unlocks: Assault Armor	1	
>> UPDATE . 1	Additional Charges: Assault Armor	3	
>> UPDATE . 2	Additional Charges: Assault Armor	5	

Assault Armor creates an area-of-effect pulse shockwave that expands outwardly from your AC, canceling out incoming projectiles and dealing severe damage and impact to all nearby targets. Assault armor is the only Core Expansion that prioritizes offense.

Pulse Armor

>> INSTALL	Unlocks: Pulse Armor	3	
>> UPDATE . 1	Additional Charges: Pulse Armor	5	

Pulse Armor generates a small spherical barrier that surrounds and follows your AC, temporarily shielding it from incoming attacks. The barrier only lasts a maximum of 10 seconds and will dissipate after absorbing enough damage, so you'll have to pick the right moment to activate this defensive Core Expansion.

Pulse Protection

>> INSTALL	Unlocks: Pulse Protection	2	
>> UPDATE . 1	Additional Charges: Pulse Protection	3	
>> UPDATE . 2	Additional Charges: Pulse Protection	4	

Pulse Protection creates a large bubble-like barrier that remains in a fixed location to provide temporary cover from all angles. Enemy projectiles are absorbed by the protective barrier for up to 25 seconds, while your weapons are attuned to its frequency and can pass through unimpeded to hit targets on the other side.

Terminal Armor

>> INSTALL	Unlocks: Terminal Armor	5	

Terminal Armor automatically triggers once your AC's AP reaches zero, encasing it in a life-saving pulse barrier that absorbs incoming damage for a few seconds. This temporary shield won't last long, but is sturdy enough to practically make you invincible while you focus on finding cover or fighting back.

Terminal armor can give you a second chance to make it out of difficult situations alive.

SYSTEM UNLOCKS

Unlike the passive enhancements found in the other OS Tuning categories, System Unlocks each grant access to unique abilities that can alter your playstyle and open up new build possibilities. It's worth taking some time to learn about these unlockable OS functions, since installing them will augment your AC's capabilities in various ways that can make designing and piloting it even more interesting.

Boost Kick

» INSTALL	Unlocks: Boost Kick	1 🖭

One of the first OS Tuning upgrades you should install, Boost Kick unlocks the ability to cap off an Assault Boost with a swift kinetic kick designed to throw your target off balance. Damage and impact varies based on your assembly, but a Boost Kick typically hits hard enough to instantly stagger or outright destroy any generic

Leg Type	Impact
Bipedal	480
Reverse-Joint	700
Tetrapod	360
Tank	600

weaponry or light MT. Since Boost Kicks are fast and don't consume ammo or extra EN, they're ideal for chasing down targets once you've closed the gap with an Assault Boost. The type of legs you have equipped determines the range, motion, and impact of a Boost Kick. Tetrapod legs have a wider area of effect but lower impact, while reverse-joint legs deliver the most impact but in a narrower area. Boost Kicks have significant forward momentum, causing your AC to surge toward the target. Once again, the distance traveled depends on your leg type, so practice in AC Test to get a feel for how close you should be to a target before triggering a Boost Kick.

While Boost Kicks are good at staggering enemies, their high direct hit adjustment also makes them excel at hammering vulnerable opponents following an ACS overload. The amount of base kinetic damage each Boost Kick inflicts ranges anywhere between 350 to 700 based on your AC's total weight, with heftier builds capable of delivering stronger kicks. Triggering a stagger will cause enemies to briefly lose balance; if you hit them with a Boost Kick at that point, they'll be sent reeling backward and will remain vulnerable to direct hits for longer. You can even use Quick Boosts to cancel the recovery of a Boost Kick, allowing you to keep up the pressure with multiple Boost Kicks in quick succession. Target Assist can help you line up Boost Kicks, but turning it off provides greater flexibility in terms of angle of approach if you're skilled enough to manually aim them. It's possible to alter the trajectory of the Boost Kick after initiating it by moving the camera. Your AC always aims its kicks in the center of the screen where the reticle sits; advanced pilots can use this to catch agile foes off guard, instead of relying on a linear approach using Target Assist.

Light MTs can be easily dispatched with Boost Kicks.

Weapon Bay

» INSTALL	Unlocks: Weapon Bay	2 🖭

For those interested in unlocking even more build possibilities and freedom in combat, the Weapon Bay function allows your AC to equip arm unit weapons onto its back unit slots and switch to them on the fly by pressing (LB)/(L1) and (RB)/(R1). Once this feature is unlocked, both back unit slots in the Assembly will feature a secondary tab, indicated by a white dot, where you can select any available arm weapons to equip. Switching to different weapons when piloting your AC is extremely fast and snappy, making it possible to keep backups on standby and instantly grab them when the situation requires it.

Weapons that are in the process of being reloaded or cooling down after overheating can be stored on your weapon bays, allowing you to use another weapon until they're ready to fire again. This ability to switch arm units on the fly can mitigate the drawbacks of some incredibly powerful weapons, such as a lengthy reload or cooldown time. If you enjoy using shotguns for instance, this feature lets you equip two pairs of different models and focus exclusively on that weapon category, swapping to one model as the other reloads. Weapon bays also make it possible to outfit your AC with two melee weapons at a time, opening up the potential for lengthy melee combos by switching to the bayed weapon while the other cools down. Considering its usefulness and low OST Chip cost, Weapon Bay should be considered a high priority OS upgrade.

Weight Control

» INSTALL	Unlocks: Weight Control	3 🖭

Installing Weight Control unlocks the ability to sortie when your AC is overburdened, as well as to manually purge any equipped weapons to lighten weight load and improve mobility. With this ability unlocked, you can deploy in a lumbering AC carrying an extremely heavy arsenal that increases its destructive potential, and gradually purge weapons to lower its weight burden and increase movement speed once you deem that specific weapons have outlived their usefulness for the current situation.

The simplest use case for the ability to manually purge weapons is shedding them as their ammunition depletes, (or when they've run dry if you've opted to disable the Automatically Purge Weapon option in the Game Settings menu). This includes scenarios like mid-mission boss fights or other challenging foes, where you may want to purge a weapon to increase your speed to better evade attacks during a certain phase of the fight. Weight Control opens up a variety of interesting build possibilities by allowing you to more readily ignore weight restrictions of your AC, but be mindful of its relatively high installation cost. While you should aim to unlock it sooner rather than later, there are more essential upgrades to invest your OST Chips in early on.

Manual Aiming

» INSTALL	Unlocks: Manual Aiming	2 🖭

The Manual Aiming ability is an upgrade geared toward advanced pilots. It allows you to take full control of the targeting reticle, rather than making use of your AC's standard auto-targeting systems. If you're confident in your aiming abilities, or just want an easier time singling out specific targets that you want to hit, enabling this functionality might be what you're looking for. Chances are you'll find yourself quickly switching to Target Assist instead of Manual Aiming in most combat situations. However, an example of a situation where Manual Aiming can prove useful is when attempting to fire weapons with a large blast radius at a group of enemies from above; your lock-on system would normally prioritize firing directly at a single target, while switching to Manual Aiming can let you aim the shot squarely in the center of the pack to ensure you catch them all in the explosion.

Quick Turn

» INSTALL	Unlocks: Quick Turn	1 🖭

If you're using a speedy AC, or just want an easier time keeping enemies in your crosshairs, unlocking Quick Turn might help. To use it, hold down (B)/(◎) and move the Left Stick in the direction you want your AC to quickly turn. It instantly positions the camera behind your AC, and can be used as either a very fast 90- or 180-degree turn. Performing a Quick Turn doesn't consume EN, and the way it repositions the camera allows for a faster perspective switch than even maximum sensitivity settings can provide.

While the majority of targets you face do not move fast enough to require using this ability to keep them in your sights, Quick Turn is very cheap to install and increases your AC's mobility options in interesting ways. Most notably, using 90-degree Quick Turns during an Assault Boost will cause your AC to make a sharp turn without interrupting the Assault Boost. This consumes a bit of EN, but allows you to navigate complex environments at faster speeds and confuse enemies by quickly shifting angles. You can also end an Assault Boost with a 180-degree Quick Turn to instantly face a target after boosting past it, which can be useful in AC duels or to attack the weak spot of bosses with frontal armor like the JUGGERNAUT.

You can perform a Quick Turn mid Quick Boost, which can be useful in high-speed duels, since your AC needs to face the target before firing its weapons.

SPECS

Specs are at the heart of everything related to customizing your AC's behavior and performance. This section is designed to advance your understanding of how your AC truly works by going over each spec and their individual effects on your overall assembly. Specs are presented according to their in-game order for ease of reference while tinkering with your build in the Assembly, with each spec's header displaying the in-game icons for the parts it's either affected by (in the case of AC specs) or found on (in the case of part specs). We've also included minimum and maximum values for each spec wherever it makes sense, but keep in mind that not all specs are included in those tables due to too many variables sometimes influencing the range of possible values.

ANALYZING SPECS

When inspecting part specs, paying attention to the gauges next to each spec allows you to easily keep track of how the part you're viewing performs in relation to the minimum and maximum values of a given spec. For example, the MA-J-201 RANSETSU-AR has a Direct Hit Adjustment spec of 185, with the gauge next to that spec sitting at roughly the 50% mark, indicating that this weapon's performance when landing direct hits is average relative to the entire catalog of weapon parts. If a gauge is completely full, it means you're looking at the best part for the spec in question.

While browsing unequipped parts in the Assembly, you'll also notice both the gauges and numbers accompanying them changing colors. Blue notes improvements in a spec compared to your currently equipped part, while red notes a loss in performance. White is neutral, meaning that the spec does not change. In simple terms, blue is an upgrade and red is a downgrade. Based on your goals, a red spec for heavier parts might not be a bad thing, but be aware that there will always be trade-offs when equipping a new part.

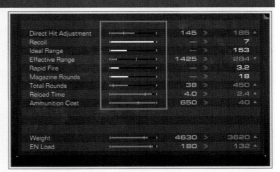

AC SPECS

Before focusing on the individual specs associated with each part, it's important to first learn about AC specs, which collectively provide an overview of your AC's performance. This group of specs serves as a summary of statistics vital to your AC and will fluctuate in value based on its equipped parts. By default, only six essential AC specs are visible, including defensive performance—a unique spec that displays your average rating against the three main damage types. Pressing ⓨ/△ will bring up the full list of 24 specs that make the entirety of your overall AC specs.

Min/Max Values		
Spec	Min	Max
AP	5720	18680
Anti-Kinetic Defense	950	1421
Anti-Energy Defense	935	1415
Anti-Explosive Defense	938	1353
Attitude Stability	1190	2807

AP

Overall durability of the AC.

Once AP reaches zero, your AC will explode, resulting in mission failure. The total AP value displayed in the AC specs is calculated by adding up the individual AP value of each frame part currently equipped, with the core and legs providing the largest boost. As a general rule, lighter frame assemblies feature less AP but better agility, while heavier builds are slower but benefit from drastically higher AP. If you find that your AC gets destroyed too quickly, consider swapping to sturdier frame parts to raise its total AP.

Anti-Kinetic Defense

Defense rating against kinetic damage.

The total Anti-Kinetic Defense spec of an AC is calculated by adding up the individual anti-kinetic defense value of each equipped frame part. In addition to reducing the amount of AP lost when hit by kinetic attacks, this spec also influences the range at which kinetic projectiles will ricochet and begin to deal drastically lower damage. The higher the Anti-Kinetic Defense spec of an AC, the closer the enemy will have to be before its ranged kinetic attacks can reliably deal their maximum damage potential.

DEFENSE SPECS

The baseline value for any of the three defense specs is 1000; going below results in more damage taken, while going above will decrease the potency of attacks. Every 10 points above or below is equal to a 1% reduction/increase in damage taken of that type.

Anti-Energy Defense

Defense rating against energy damage.

This spec functions identically to Anti-Kinetic Defense, with an AC's total Anti-Energy Defense spec being calculated by adding up each frame part's corresponding value. Anti-Energy Defense will influence both the damage taken when hit by any type of energy attacks, along with the distance at which ranged lasers will ricochet off your armor. As a result, swapping in parts with a higher Anti-Energy Defense spec can greatly increase your survivability when facing enemies that rely on energy-based weaponry, such as PCA LCs outfitted with sniper rifles.

Anti-Explosive Defense

Defense rating against explosive/incendiary damage.

Like the other main defensive specs, an AC's total Anti-Explosive Defense spec is calculated by adding up all its frame parts' anti-explosive defense values. However, because explosive- and incendiary-based attacks can never ricochet, a higher Anti-Explosive Defense spec only reduces damage taken from both of these damage types without influencing their effective range against your AC. It's also worth pointing out that while raising this spec will help mitigate incendiary damage, it won't increase your resistance to heat buildup.

Attitude Stability

The maximum load the ACS (Attitude Control System) can support.

Your total Attitude Stability spec is calculated by adding up the Attitude Stability of your head, core, and leg parts. A greater overall attitude stability rating means that your AC can handle significantly more strain from the impact of enemy attacks before it staggers and becomes vulnerable to direct hits. The gap between an assembly with the lowest possible Attitude Stability spec and the highest is dramatic, so it's important to consider this spec if you find yourself getting staggered too quickly when engaging in combat.

Attitude Recovery

The ability of the ACS to manage strain.

The Attitude Recovery spec is exclusively determined by an AC's total weight, with lighter assemblies being able to recover from accumulative impact significantly faster than heavier ones. The advantage of a higher attitude recovery rating becomes more noticeable after avoiding damage for roughly five seconds during combat, as this is when the ACS begins to recover from accumulative impact at an exponential rate. Better attitude recovery helps counteract lightweight builds by speeding up the accumulative impact recovery process. Heavier builds, on the other hand, have better stability but may struggle with slower attitude recovery during intense battles.

Attitude Recovery Rating Based on Total Weight		
Total Weight	Attitude Recovery	Base Accumulative Impact Recovery Speed
39,999 or lower	150	15/sec
40,000–49,999	149–135	14.9–13.5/sec
50,00–69,999	134–105	13.4–10.5/sec
70,000–79,999	104–90	10.4–9.0/sec
80,000–125,000+	89–57	8.9–5.7/sec

Min/Max Values		
Spec	Min	Max
Attitude Recovery	57	150
Target Tracking	41	104
QB EN Consumption	355	917
EN Capacity	2000	4420
EN Recharge Delay	0.44	4.66
Total Arms Load	960	20240
Arms Load Limit	10520	21300
Load Limit	47820	100300
EN Output	1942	5581

Target Tracking

Target tracking performance during lock-on.

This spec influences how accurately your reticle can track agile targets once it turns red to signify that target tracking is active during lock-on. The higher this value, the better your AC will be at predicting the movements of enemies and landing shots against mobile targets. Your Target Tracking spec is exclusively determined by the Firearm Specialization spec on your AC's arms. While a higher target tracking rating is always preferable, it's important to keep in mind that other factors, such as the specs of your FCS and whether Target Assist is activated, also play an important role in influencing your AC's ability to accurately land shots against fast-moving targets.

Boost Speed

Maximum speed of the AC during boost movement.

The Boost Speed spec serves as a gauge of your AC's overall velocity during boost movement and directly correlates to the max speed shown on the left side of the HUD while boosting on the ground. This value is determined by both the Thrust spec of your booster part and the AC's total weight, so pay attention to these factors when looking to increase your boost movement speed.

QB Speed

Initial velocity at which the AC travels when performing a Quick Boost.

The Quick Boost speed of an AC is influenced by the QB Thrust spec of its booster part along with its total weight, with lighter builds capable of performing faster Quick Boosts that improve their ability to successfully dodge incoming attacks. The higher this value, the faster your AC will travel during a Quick Boost. ▶ A

QB EN Consumption

Amount of EN consumed when using Quick Boost.

The lower the QB EN Consumption spec, the more consecutive Quick Boosts you'll be able to use before exhausting your EN supply. The value displayed in AC specs is based on the QB EN Consumption spec of your equipped booster part, which is then multiplied by your core's Booster Efficiency Adjustment spec to determine the exact amount of EN consumed during each Quick Boost.

QB Reload Time

Reload time for Quick Boost.

A lower QB Reload Time spec enables your AC to perform multiple consecutive Quick Boosts with minimal downtime between each use. The value displayed in your AC specs is exclusively determined by the QB Reload Time spec of your equipped booster. However, keep in mind that exceeding the booster's QB Reload Ideal Weight spec will gradually increase the reload time between Quick Boosts. If your goal is to be as agile as possible, you'll need to keep your AC's total weight below the QB reload ideal weight shown in its booster's specs.

EN Capacity

Total amount of EN available for use.

The higher this value is, the more EN-consuming actions you can perform before running out of EN and having to wait for your generator to replenish its supply. EN capacity is determined exclusively by your AC's generator, which means the only way to raise this spec is to swap to a higher-capacity generator. Unlike many other AC specs, your build's total weight has no influence on its EN Capacity. ▶ B

EN Supply Efficiency

Rate at which EN is supplied to the AC.

The higher your EN Supply Efficiency spec, the more EN your generator will supply per second once the EN gauge begins to refill. An assembly's EN Supply Efficiency spec is calculated based on the difference between its EN Output and Total EN Load specs. A larger surplus of EN output compared to total EN load will greatly increase your AC's EN Supply Efficiency spec, offering a tangible performance boost to EN recovery speed when opting for parts with a lower overall EN load burden.

EN Recharge Delay

Duration of the delay before EN is recharged.

The lower the EN Recharge Delay spec, the shorter the downtime (in seconds) before the EN gauge begins to recover after being partially depleted. This spec is primarily influenced by the generator's EN Recharge spec, which is then multiplied by the core's Generator Supply Adjustment spec to determine the final value. Don't overlook the EN Recharge Delay spec when designing your AC, since a lengthy delay before your EN gauge begins to recover after performing EN-consuming actions can drastically influence how it performs during sorties. ▶ C

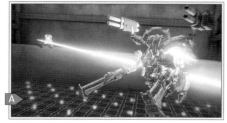

Total Weight

Total weight of all AC parts.

This straightforward spec is calculated by adding up the weight of all individual parts that make up your AC assembly, including its legs. Equipping heavier parts increases total weight, which has the downside of lowering attitude recovery, boost speed, and Quick Boost performance when compared to lighter AC builds. Always keep your Total Weight spec in mind before swapping to heavier parts or equipping additional weapons to your AC, as this is another important factor that can drastically influence how it feels to control.

Total Arms Load

Arm load weight.

The Total Arms Load spec represents the combined weight of both weapons currently equipped on your arms. Be careful that this value doesn't exceed the Arms Load Limit spec shown directly below in your AC specs, as going beyond that limit will result in deploying with overburdened arms. Shoulder-mounted weapons don't add to the Total Arms Load spec, but swapping to different R-Arm or L-Arm units carried in weapon bays will transfer their weight to the arms.

Arms Load Limit

Maximum weight arms can carry without compromising on stable operating performance.

All arm parts feature an Arms Load Limit spec that dictates how much weight your AC can carry in the R-Arm and L-Arm Unit slots before becoming overburdened. Higher values make it possible to equip heavier weapons without suffering from significant degradation in recoil control and target tracking performance when firing weapons held in either hand. Overburdened arms won't stop you from deploying, but it's much better to switch to arms that can handle the added weight if you find your preferred loadout creates too great a burden.

Total Load

Body load weight.

Total load corresponds to the sum of all equipped parts on your AC minus its legs, which are what supports the rest of the body. Make sure this value doesn't exceed the Load Limit spec that the currently installed legs can handle, or your AC will be overburdened and unable to sortie until you reduce its weight or swap to legs capable of supporting a greater load limit. Unlocking the Weight Control function in the OS Tuning menu can allow you to deploy even when overburdened. However, keep in mind that this will negatively affect mobility to a degree proportionate with the amount of extra weight loaded onto the AC.

Load Limit

Maximum weight legs can support.

This value is critical when selecting which legs to equip, as it determines how much combined weight the assembly can support from all its other parts. Heavier legs tend to have a higher load limit, but at the cost of reduced mobility compared to lighter legs. The Load Limit spec is one of the foundational specs of any AC; always pay attention to this value when considering changing to a different leg unit, as it's likely that you'll also need to swap out other parts in order to fit within or take advantage of the new load limit.

Increasing your AC's total weight will lower your movement speed, even when still below your load limit.

Total EN Load

EN load of the AC.

The Total EN Load spec represents the sum of EN load values from all equipped parts. Make sure this value doesn't exceed the EN Output spec directly below it, or your AC will go into EN shortfall and won't be able to sortie until you either lighten your EN Load, or swap to a generator and core combo capable of producing a higher EN output. Unlike total load, there's no way to bypass this EN shortfall sortie restriction, forcing you to reduce your total EN load before you're allowed to deploy.

EN Output

EN output of the AC.

The EN Output spec is best described as identical to an AC's load limit, but for EN load instead of weight. Except for your Expansion slot, all parts require a portion of the EN that your generator is able to output. A higher EN output allows you to equip more EN-intensive parts before entering EN shortfall, but bear in mind that keeping a larger surplus between your total EN load and EN output increases your EN Supply Efficiency spec, meaning that your EN gauge will refill more quickly. Two components determine the final EN output value: each generator features its own raw EN Output spec, which is then multiplied by your core's Generator Output Adjustment spec.

It might be tempting to push the limits of your EN output by equipping parts with a high EN load, but you should keep the bonus to EN supply efficiency that comes from having a surplus in mind.

CURRENT LOAD SPECS

The Current Load, Current Arms Load, and Current EN Load specs are all reference gauges added to the AC specs menu to help you visualize the AC's current burden in proportion to its related Load Limit, Arms Load Limit, and EN Output specs. Basically, each gauge shows you whether you're over or under the respective limit. When installing new parts, the gauge turning blue indicates a lighter load, while red indicates additional burden to load. White means there's no change. Remaining below the various load limits prevents serious drawbacks and can also offer performance benefits, so use these gauges to get an overview of your AC's overall equipment load.

The small arrow above each gauge indicates the current load limit your AC can support for that spec.

WEAPON & PART SPECS

Now that you've learned about your AC's overall specs, it's time to dig d eeper by going into the individual specs that appear on the various parts in each of the slot types. For ease of use, we've sorted all part specs by slot types they can appear in while also respecting the in-game order visible when inspecting part specs.

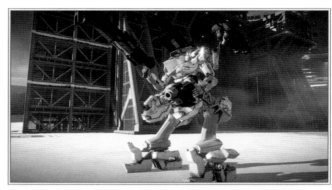

UNIVERSAL PART SPECS

With the sole exception of generators not featuring an EN load value, both specs covered in this small section are universally found on every part in the game, so it's a good idea to familiarize yourself with how they work before moving on to the other categories.

Higher weight and EN load from certain parts will sometimes limit your ability to equip other parts.

Weight

Weight of an individual part equipped to the AC.

The weight of a part determines the exact burden added to your AC's Total Load or Total Arms Load specs after installing it. While heavier parts tend to have better overall specs, remember that adding more weight to your assembly comes at the cost of decreased speed and agility. How heavy a part is should always be one of the main factors to consider when deciding whether or not it fits your overall design goals. ▶ A

EN Load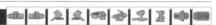

EN load of the part.

Similar to weight, each part also features an EN Load spec that determines how much it contributes to your AC's Total EN Load spec. It's important to pay attention to each part's EN load, since there isn't always a clear relationship between the weight of a part and its EN output requirements. In general, energy- and explosive-based weaponry tends to have higher EN Load specs than kinetic weapons, but this isn't always the case.

As with reducing your AC's overall weight, there are also significant benefits to lowering your total EN load in relation to your EN Output spec. Any residual EN is put toward improving your EN Supply Efficiency spec while providing a surplus that can be used to charge energy-based weapons without any penalty to EN recovery. As a result, it can be worth installing parts with a smaller EN load footprint even if your total EN load is already below the value shown on your EN Output spec. ▶ B

ARM & BACK UNIT WEAPON SPECS

Attack Power

Damage-dealing performance.

The Attack Power spec of a weapon represents its damage potential per attack against a target with standard defenses to that damage type. In practice, the final damage output can increase or decrease depending on various factors, like the target's defensive specs or if ricocheting occurs. While attack power doesn't always translate to exact damage dealt, it still serves as a valuable metric to gauge damage potential. It's worth remembering that lower Attack Power specs don't always correlate to a lower damage output per second, however, since rate of fire and other properties all contribute to a weapon's overall performance in battle.

Impact

ACS overload performance.

This spec corresponds to the amount of strain added to the opponent's ACS gauge per attack. Except when Assault Boost, ricochet, or pulse shields are involved, this value translates to the precise amount of impact inflicted with each projectile or attack. Keep in mind that this standard type of impact resets within a short period of time, so you'll need to keep attacking without pausing to overload your target's ACS.

Accumulative Impact

Accumulative ACS overload performance.

Complementary to the Impact spec, this value represents the amount of accumulative strain added to the opponent's ACS gauge per hit. Weapons with a higher Accumulative Impact spec are particularly effective at staggering more resilient enemies, since each hit inflicts strain that takes longer to recover from and progressively builds up as you continue fighting.

Min/Max Values		
Spec	Min	Max
Attack Power	25	2133
Impact	3	2040
Accumulative Impact	1	1638
Blast Radius	7	90
ATK Heat Buildup	9	700
Consecutive Hits	1	3
Chg. Attack Power	672	4630
Chg. Impact	198	4050
Chg. Accum. Impact	132	4050
Chg. Blast Radius	20	70
Chg. Heat Buildup	90	1000
Full Chg. Attack Power	2522	2835
Full Chg. Impact	1930	4050
Full Chg. Accum. Impact	1033	4050
Direct Hit Adjustment	100	270
PA Interference	112	550
Recoil	3	100

Blast Radius

Size of the explosions generated by the weapon's ammo.

Blast radius values correspond to the dimension of spherical explosions generated by the weapon in meters. The larger the attack's blast radius, the more effective the resulting explosion will be at dealing splash damage to clustered groups of targets, with all enemies caught in the blast receiving full damage.

ATK Heat Buildup

Heat buildup when attacking.

The ATK Heat Buildup spec is primarily found on energy-based weaponry and indicates exactly how much heat is added to a weapon's overheat gauge with each standard attack. Overheat occurs when the amount of weapon heat generated exceeds the maximum tolerance value of 1000, so this spec allows you to roughly gauge how many attacks you can use in quick succession before overheating occurs.

Consecutive Hits

Number of chain attacks possible with additional inputs.

Exclusive to melee weapons, the Consecutive Hits spec corresponds to the maximum number of consecutive inputs possible with each melee weapon before the weapon overheats. It's worth pointing out that this value doesn't always translate to the maximum number of hits dealt as part of a melee weapon's full combo string, since some weapons, like the VP-67EB stun baton, can strike the enemy multiple times with a single button press depending on the attack animation.

Chg. Attack Power

Damage-dealing performance for charge attacks.

Behaving identically to standard attack power, the Charge Attack Power spec corresponds to a weapon's damage potential when unleashing a charge attack. All the same factors involved in determining the final damage output still apply here, which makes this spec a useful indicator of how much stronger a weapon's charge attack will be compared with its standard attacks..

Chg. Impact

ACS overload performance for charge attacks.

This value corresponds to the exact amount of immediate ACS strain inflicted by the impact of a charge attack. To compensate for the slower nature of these attacks, a weapon's Charge Impact spec is typically multiple times greater than its regular Impact spec, which can often allow you to stagger most standard enemies in a single hit.

Chg. Accum. Impact

Accumulative ACS overload performance for charge attacks.

The Charge Accumulative Impact spec of a weapon corresponds to the exact amount of accumulative ACS strain dealt with a charge attack. The higher this value, the better the charge attack will be at building up sustained ACS strain when hitting targets..

Chg. Blast Radius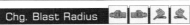

Size of explosions resulting from charge attacks.

Like the standard version of this spec, the charge blast radius value of a weapon corresponds to the dimensions of the spherical explosions generated by its charge attack. In general, you can expect explosions resulting from charge attacks to be significantly bigger than those caused by standard attacks..

Chg. Heat Buildup

Heat buildup when using charge attacks.

The Charge Heat Buildup spec indicates exactly how much weapon heat is generated when using a charge attack. This value is always significantly higher than the amount of weapon heat buildup caused by standard attacks, so it's an important factor to consider during combat. Remember that any weapon with a Charge Heat Buildup spec of 1000 is guaranteed to instantly overheat after performing a charge attack, forcing you to rely on other weapons until it's ready to use again.

Full Chg. Attack Power

Damage dealing performance for full-charge attacks.

Only found on experimental rifles capable of charging up beyond the standard limits of more conventional weaponry, the Full Charge Attack Power spec displays how much attack power these weapons will deliver when unleashing a full-charge attack.

Full Chg. Impact

ACS overload performance for full-charge attacks.

The Full Charge Impact spec represents the maximum amount of immediate ACS strain that can be inflicted with a full-charge attack if all hits connect.

Full Chg. Accum. Impact

Accumulative ACS overload performance for full-charge attacks.

This spec corresponds to the maximum amount of sustained ACS strain that can be inflicted with a full-charge attack if all hits connect.

Full Chg. Blast Radius

Size of explosions resulting from full-charge attacks.

Exclusive to the 44-142 KRSV multi energy rifle, the Full Charge Blast Radius spec corresponds to the dimension of the explosions generated by a full-charge attack with this weapon in meters.

Full Chg. Heat Buildup

Heat buildup when using full-charge attacks.

This spec corresponds to the amount of heat buildup generated by a full-charge attack. Both weapons capable of performing full-charge attacks share a Full Charge Heat Buildup spec of 1000, which means they will instantly overheat after firing one of these devastating attacks.

Direct Hit Adjustment

Damage multiplier when attacking a staggered enemy.

The higher the Direct Hit Adjustment spec, the more damage the weapon will inflict when landing direct hits against staggered opponents. This value corresponds to the exact percentage increase in damage dealt with direct hits. For example, the default RF-024 TURNER assault rifle has an attack power of 105 and a direct hit adjustment value of 185. If we multiply 105 attack power by 1.85, we'll arrive at 194, which translates to the damage this weapon deals with direct hits. As always, keep in mind that other factors, such as the enemy's defenses against the weapon's damage type, can influence the outcome.

PA Interference

Ability to interfere with enemy pulse barriers.

While all types of attacks can eventually disrupt an enemy's pulse barriers, those with a PA Interference spec gain a bonus to their effectiveness against this type of shielding. When it comes to ranged options, you will mostly encounter this spec on high-frequency pulse guns and Coral-based weaponry, but almost all melee weapons also excel at canceling out pulse barriers.

Recoil

Recoil that occurs when firing.

Recoil is exclusively found on ranged weaponry and is an indicator of how much kickback will be generated when firing a weapon. The higher the Recoil spec, the more the reticle blooms each time you fire, and the less accurate your shots become. This behavior is most obvious during continuous fire with full-auto weapons, but recoil also applies to other types of non-homing weaponry, such as bazookas and laser rifles. Equipping arms with a high Recoil Control spec can help to absorb the recoil and minimize the accuracy penalty. Finally, It's worth pointing out that weapons with a very high Recoil spec will also typically cause your AC to briefly stop moving and enter a firing stance when fired, which is a drawback that's independent of the reticle bloom and can only be mitigated by equipping either tetrapod or tank legs.

Min/Max Values		
Spec	Min	Max
Guidance	110	480
Ideal Range	76	310
Effective Range	62	2500
Homing Lock Time	0.3	5.0
Max. Lock Count	1	12
Rapid Fire	0.4	2.0
Chg. EN Load	435	1440
Charge Time	0.5	5.0
Chg. Ammo Consumption	1.0	12.0
Full Chg. Time	4.3	4.5
Full Chg. Ammo Consump.	10	12.0
Magazine Rounds	3	45.0
Total Rounds	12	1300
Reload Time	1.3	12.0
Cooling	95	1308
Ammunition Cost	20	1600

Guidance

Tracking performance of missiles and other homing weapons.

Only applicable to missile launchers and other homing weapons, the Guidance spec represents the accuracy of homing projectiles when tracking moving targets. The higher the value, the better the turning speed and precision of guided projectiles, making this spec a useful indicator of the overall ability of homing weapons to adjust their trajectory mid-flight and successfully hit evasive opponents.

Ideal Range

Range at which attack power is guaranteed without ricocheting.

The ideal range of a weapon corresponds to the range (in meters) within which your shots are guaranteed not to ricochet, regardless of the target's defense values against that damage type. This spec applies to most ranged kinetic- and energy-based weapons, and is crucial to consider when wielding weapons like laser rifles, gatling guns, and shotguns. While firing at an enemy within your weapon's ideal range will prevent your shots from ricocheting off its armor, keep in mind that depending on the target's defense, the final damage output can still be lower or higher than your weapon's base Attack Power spec.

Effective Range

Range at which attacks are effective.

A weapon's Effective Range spec corresponds to an average range (in meters) at which shots can deliver their full attack power against a target. In practice, the effective range of non-explosive weapons can vary significantly based on each enemy's defensive specs. For example, when fighting an AC with a baseline Anti-Kinetic Defense spec, the MG-014 LUDOW machine gun, with an effective range of 236, won't ricochet up to a distance of roughly 280 meters. Against an enemy with higher anti-kinetic defense, however, the same LUDLOW machine gun may begin to suffer from ricochet even within its effective range of 236 meters, forcing you to draw closer to the weapon's ideal range before shots no longer ricochet. As mentioned before, the lower the enemy's defense against your weapon type, the further you can pull back—even beyond the limit of effective range—without suffering from ricochet.

For weapons that aren't affected by ricocheting, like pulse guns, bazookas, and missile launchers, the Effective Range spec indicates the maximum range at which their projectiles can travel before disappearing and losing all ability to deal damage.

Homing Lock Time

Time it takes to acquire lock-on for missiles and other homing weapons.

The Homing Lock Time spec corresponds to the number of seconds required for missiles and homing weapons to fully lock-on to a target, which is represented by a small yellow gauge in the center of your reticle that begins to fill the instant you target an enemy. Once this gauge is full, the projectiles you launch with that weapon will track the target. Firing homing weapons before acquiring a full lock-on will severely impair or outright disable the tracking ability of its projectiles. While the Homing Lock Time spec of a homing weapon determines its base lock-on duration, the Missile Lock Correction spec of your FCS also works as an adjustment value, and can either positively or negatively influence your actual lock-on Extra period.

Max. Lock Count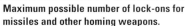

Maximum possible number of lock-ons for missiles and other homing weapons.

Missile launchers and other homing weapons with a Maximum Lock Count spec of two or higher allow you to engage multi-lock by holding down the corresponding input whenever multiple enemies are visible and within lock-on range. This value directly translates to the number of enemies that can be simultaneously targeted, making weapons with a high Maximum Lock Count spec ideal for quickly dispatching large groups of weaker enemies.

Rapid Fire

Speed of rapid fire.

The Rapid Fire spec directly translates to the average number of rounds that a weapon can fire within a second. For example, the RF-024 TURNER assault rifle has a rapid fire value of 3.4, which means that it will average out to 3.4 rounds per second if fired long enough, while the MG-014 LUDLOW machine gun will average out to 10 rounds within the same window.

Chg. EN Load

EN load when charging.

Think of the Charge EN Load spec as a secondary EN load requirement that only takes effect whenever you hold down the input to ready a charge attack with certain energy- or Coral-based weapons. Because a weapon's Charge EN Load spec is always higher than its standard EN Load spec, readying a charge attack with weapons that carry this spec will temporarily raise your total EN load. If this transient increase in EN load causes your total EN load to surpass your AC's EN Output spec, you'll suffer from a severe reduction in EN recovery speed whenever the weapon is charging. The penalty to EN recovery instantly goes away the moment you either cancel or fire the charge attack. It's important to keep in mind that charging up multiple energy- or Coral-based weapons simultaneously can easily raise your total EN load well beyond your EN Output spec unless your build has a large enough surplus to prevent this from happening.

Homing projectiles with a high Guidance spec are perfect for handling fast-moving enemies like ACs.

Missiles with a high Maximum Lock Count spec excel at dispatching hordes of weak enemies, which would take longer to defeat with single-target weaponry.

Charge Time

The time it takes to complete charging.

The Charge Time spec corresponds to the number of seconds it takes to ready a charge attack with the weapon. While this value directly translates to the time required to charge most weapons, keep in mind that depending on the Energy Firearm Specialization spec of the currently equipped generator, some energy-based weaponry, like laser rifles, can exhibit slower or faster charging rates than those displayed on their Charge Time spec.

Chg. Ammo Consumption

Ammunition consumed by charge attacks.

This value corresponds to the precise number of rounds consumed when performing a charge attack with some energy- and Coral-based weapons. More powerful weapons tend to require a larger amount of ammunition per charge attack. Pay attention to this spec in relation to the weapon's total rounds value, since heavy use of charge attacks can often quickly deplete your ammo supply.

Full Chg. Time

The time it takes to reach full charge.

Functioning just like the standard Charging Time spec, this value translates to the number of seconds needed to ready a full-charge attack when starting the charging process from zero. ▶ A

Full Chg. Ammo Consump.

Ammunition consumed by full-charge attacks.

This value corresponds to the number of rounds consumed by the weapon when firing a full-charge attack. It's worth noting that in the case of the IB-C03W1: WLT 011 Coral rifle, the Full Charge Ammo Consumption. spec refers to the maximum ammo expended if you allow the full-charge attack to continue firing for its maximum duration.

Magazine Rounds

Number of rounds loaded per magazine.

This spec displays the number of rounds that can be fired with the weapon before you need to reload. Larger magazines are always preferable, but how long the weapon is able to fire before reloading also heavily depends on its rate of fire. After reloading, the magazine's rounds will be fully replenished as long as you have a sufficient ammunition remaining in reserve.

Total Rounds

Total number of rounds that can be fired.

This value corresponds to the total number of rounds available when deploying with a weapon. Once this number hits zero, the weapon can no longer be used during the current sortie unless you resupply at a sherpa or restart from a checkpoint. While the number of total rounds available is usually high enough to avoid running out with balanced use of your AC's arsenal, it's an important factor to consider if you plan on relying more heavily on one or two weapons during lengthier missions.

Reload Time

Time from start to completion of reload.

The reload time value corresponds to the number of seconds needed to ready your weapon for its next set of rounds, missiles, or shells. Stronger weapons tend to feature higher Reload Time specs, making it essential to keep reload times in mind during combat to ensure you can always continue attacking with another weapon. Remember that you can manually reload kinetic weapons at any time to keep their magazines full ahead of the next encounter or in preparation to capitalize on enemy stagger. ▶ B

Cooling

Speed at which heat buildup is reduced when cooling weapon.

The Cooling spec determines how quickly accumulated heat is dissipated after firing a weapon that generates heat when attacking. This value translates to the precise rate at which the red weapon heat gauge cools off per second, with a full heat gauge being equivalent to a value of 1000. By understanding this, it's possible to deduce that a weapon with a cooling value of 250 would take roughly four seconds to fully cool down after overheating. However, keep in mind that there's always a short pause before cooling begins and the red gauge begins to visibly deplete after firing or overheating, and the example above does not take this pause into account. ▶ C

Ammunition Cost

Cost per round fired.

This value corresponds to the exact cost per round that will added to your operational expenses at the end of a mission when firing this weapon. For weapons that fire multiple rounds with a single input, such as the BML-G1/P20MLT-04 missile launcher, each projectile in the volley is counted individually. Ammunition cost may influence your weapon selection for a particular mission if, for example, you're attempting to achieve an S-Rank rating and want to minimize the penalty associated with higher total ammunition costs.

Magazine Rounds and Total Rounds specs tend to go hand-in-hand; large magazines equate to large reserve ammunition, and vice versa.

The repercussions of Charge Ammo Consumption and Full Charge Ammo Consumption specs mean you can't aimlessly charge up every shot of your weapons, or you'll burn through rounds in record time.

Contrary to previous titles in the series, laser weapons now have an associated Ammunition Cost to consider.

L-BACK UNIT SHIELD SPECS

Damage Mitigation

Ability to mitigate incoming damage while performing a regular guard.

This value corresponds to the percentage of damage blocked by a shield outside of its Initial Guard window. The higher this value, the better suited a shield will be at reducing the amount of incoming damage when used as a general damage-mitigation tool deployed for longer durations without focusing on timing Initial Guards in sync with enemy attacks.

Impact Dampening

Ability to mitigate incoming ACS burden while performing a regular guard.

The Impact Dampening spec corresponds to the percentage of impact that will be blocked by a shield deployed outside of its Initial Guard window. Shields are one of the only ways to mitigate incoming impact, so those with higher impact dampening values can offer a significant degree of protection against ACS overload while active.

IG Damage Mitigation

Ability to mitigate incoming damage while performing an Initial Guard.

This spec is the Initial Guard equivalent of a shield's basic Damage Mitigation spec, and represents the percentage of damage blocked during the Initial Guard window. As a reward for successfully timing your guard just before an enemy attack hits, the Initial Guard damage mitigation of a shield is generally much greater than during a regular guard.

IG Impact Dampening

Ability to mitigate ACS strain while performing an Initial Guard.

A shield's IG Impact Dampening spec corresponds to the percentage of impact blocked during the Initial Guard window. These values are always quite high, so it's possible to use Initial Guards to mitigate the vast majority of ACS strain inflicted if your reflexes are good enough to deploy the shield just before a powerful attack hits.

IG Duration

Total duration window of Initial Guard damage reduction.

Timed in seconds, Initial Guard duration corresponds to the exact time window during which a shield is considered to be in its Initial Guard state. Being aware of the IG Duration spec of your equipped shield is essential when aiming to capitalize on the benefits of Initial Guard. Some shields offer more lenient Initial Guard windows, but you'll always need relatively good timing since this value never extends beyond roughly a second and a half.

Idle Damage Mitigation

Damage mitigation for attacks caught by guard while shield is in an idle state.

Only found on the VE-61PSA pulse scutum, this spec corresponds to the greatly reduced percentage of incoming damage that will be mitigated by this shield until it's been deployed long enough to exit its idle state and reach its full damage-mitigation potential.

Idle Impact Mitigation

ACS strain mitigation for attacks caught by guard while shield is in an idle state.

Also exclusive to the VE-61PSA pulse scutum, this value corresponds to the drastically lower percentage of ACS strain that will be mitigated by this shield until it's been deployed long enough to exit its idle state and fully deploy.

Idle Time

Time until idle state ends.

The final exclusive spec for the VE-61PSA pulse scutum, the Idle Time spec represents the exact amount of time this shield has to remain deployed before transitioning from its weak idle mode to its high-performance mode. Once this happens, all mitigation will be based on the much higher Damage Mitigation and Impact Dampening specs until the shield is canceled.

Min/Max Values		
Spec	Min	Max
Damage Mitigation	30	86
Impact Dampening	25	70
IG Damage Mitigation	21	96
IG Impact Dampening	18	95
IG Duration	0.2	1.6
Dply. Heat Buildup	140	670
Deployment Range	180	360

Dply. Heat Buildup

Heat buildup when deploying shield.

This value corresponds to the amount of heat buildup generated each time the shield is deployed. Just like with weapons, the maximum tolerance of a shield's heat gauge is equivalent to 1000 heat buildup. This spec is an important factor to consider when using shields, as it dictates how many times you can deploy a particular shield within a short window of time before it overheats and temporarily becomes unusable. If a shield has a Deploy Heat Buildup spec of 480, for example, it can only be deployed twice in quick succession without overheating, as doing so will generate a combined total of 960 heat and almost completely fill the heat gauge. A shield's Cooling spec determines the speed at which heat buildup is reduced when cooling, but keep in mind that even the fastest-cooling shields will be disabled for upward of seven seconds after overheating.

Deployment Range

Area in which shield is capable of blocking attacks.

A shield's Deployment Range spec determines the range of protection offered to the AC when guarding. The easiest way to understand how this spec works is to visualize the value in degrees; a Deployment Range spec of 180 allows you to successfully guard incoming attacks from the front, while a deployment range of 360 protects you from all angles. Except for the IB-C03W4: NGI 028 prototype Coral shield, all other available shields feature a standard deployment range of 180 degrees.

FRAME UNIT SPECS

These defense-oriented specs are present on every frame part, except for the Attitude Stability spec not being applicable to arms. The individual values for each of these specs are combined to determine your AC's total values, which can be viewed in your overall AC specs. A more detailed analysis of how these specs work is available earlier in this chapter, so flip back to P.35 for additional info on the topic.

AP

Resilience of the part.

This spec corresponds to the amount of AP the individual frame part contributes to the total AP of the assembly. Equipping frame parts with higher AP values will improve the overall resilience of your AC.

Anti-Kinetic Defense

Defense rating against kinetic damage.

Total anti-kinetic defense is calculated by adding up the individual anti-kinetic defense value of each equipped frame part. In addition to reducing the amount of AP lost when hit by kinetic attacks, anti-kinetic defense also influences the range at which kinetic projectiles will ricochet and deal less damage.

Your choice of leg and core parts contributes the most to your overall AP. Your arms come in third place, with the head part only providing a small percentage of your total AP.

Anti-Energy Defense

Defense rating against energy damage.

This spec functions identically to anti-kinetic defense, with an AC's total anti-energy defense being calculated by adding up each equipped frame part's defensive value against this damage type.

Anti-Explosive Defense

Defense rating against explosive damage.

Like other defense spec, an AC's total anti-explosive defense is calculated by adding up the anti-explosive defense values of all its frame parts. Equipping parts that raise this spec will lower damage taken from explosive weaponry as well as incendiary damage from flamethrowers and napalm bombs.

Attitude Stability

The maximum load the ACS can support.

This spec corresponds to the amount of attitude stability the individual frame part contributes to the AC's total. Equipping frame parts with a higher Attitude Stability spec will increase the amount of ACS strain the AC can withstand.

HEAD PART ONLY SPECS

Min/Max Values		
Spec	Min	Max
System Recovery	84	154
Scan Distance	340	700
Scan Effect Duration	3.0	18.0
Scan Standby Time	3.6	12.0

System Recovery

Ability to detect system abnormalities and recover.

The System Recovery spec of a head part is entirely responsible for determining the AC's ability to withstand shock and heat exposure before the buildup of these effects triggers an electrical discharge or ACS anomaly. A system recovery value of 100 is the baseline, with every point below or above reducing or increasing your shock and heat buildup resistance by 1%. The difference in resistance between equipping head parts with the lowest and highest possible System Recovery spec is quite dramatic, making this spec an important factor to consider when facing elemental hazards or enemies that rely on incendiary or shock-based weaponry. It's worth noting that, once triggered, the time it takes to recover from an ACS anomaly caused by heat buildup will always be roughly 5 seconds regardless of your AC's System Recovery spec.

Scan Distance

Range within which scanning can detect enemies or part containers.

This value corresponds to the range, in meters, at which the head's built-in scanner can detect and highlight enemies or part containers when sending out a pulse. For example, a head part with a Scan Distance spec of 300 will uncover a detectable entity within a range of up to 300 meters. In addition to determining the maximum scan distance on the Z-axis, this spec also influences the range at which your scanner can detect targets above or below its position on the Y-axis. Equipping a head part with a high Scan Distance spec is both helpful when surveying areas for threats and when hunting for hidden combat logs or part containers.

If you're struggling with system abnormalities, examine your choice of head part and consider equipping one with a higher System Recovery spec to increase your resistances to heat and shock buildup.

Scan Effect Duration

Scan visibility duration after having detected enemies or part containers.

Scan effect duration represents the number of seconds during which scanned targets will remain visibly highlighted after detection. Higher values mean that enemies and parts containers remain easy to keep track of for a longer duration, which can be particularly useful during encounters against agile opponents that make use of environmental cover to break line of sight.

When replaying missions, it's a good idea to install a head part with a high Scan Distance spec to help reveal any part containers you might have missed on your first run.

Scan Standby Time

Wait time between scan usages.

The Scan Standby Time spec indicates exactly how many seconds the scanner function will take to cool down and become ready again after use. The lower the value, the more often you'll be able to scan the environment for concealed threats or part containers during sorties. The gap between the lowest and highest values is quite large, which can drastically alter the feel of different head parts if your playstyle involves a lot of scanning.

CORE PART ONLY SPECS

Min/Max Values		
Spec	Min	Max
Booster Efficiency Adj.	76	126
Generator Output Adj.	83	126
Generator Supply Adj.	89	112

Booster Efficiency Adj.

Adjustment to booster EN efficiency.

The booster efficiency adjustment value of an AC's core is a percentage-based multiplier applied to the QB EN Consumption spec of the booster to determine the actual amount of EN consumed with each Quick Boost. A higher Booster Efficiency Adjustment spec results in a lower final QB EN consumption rating in the AC specs. It's essential to consider this spec when choosing a core, as it can significantly affect EN consumption when using Quick Boosts

Generator Output Adj.

Adjustment to generator EN output.

The Generator Output Adjustment spec is a percentage-based multiplier applied to the EN Output spec of the equipped generator to determine the final EN Output displayed under AC specs. This is another crucial spec to consider when choosing which core to equip on your AC, as it can either decrease or increase the maximum EN load that the assembly can handle before going into EN shortfall. The higher the Generator Output Adjustment spec, the greater the actual EN output of a generator will be.

Generator Supply Adj.

Adjustment to generator EN supply performance.

The last of the adjustment specs found on core parts, the Generator Supply Adjustment spec is a percentage-based multiplier applied to the generator's EN Recharge spec to determine the assembly's final EN Recharge Delay—an AC spec that corresponds to the number of seconds before EN recovery begins after an EN-consuming action. The higher a core's Generator Supply Adjustment spec, the less time it will take to start recovering EN, even when using the same generator.

ARMS PART ONLY SPECS

Arms Load Limit

Maximum weight arms can carry without compromising on stable operating performance.

This spec is identical to the Arms Load Limit AC spec, and corresponds to the combined maximum weight that the arms can support when equipping weapons in the R-Arm and L-Arm Unit slots before becoming overburdened and suffering from compromised recoil and target tracking performance. ▶ A

Recoil Control

Ability to absorb recoil.

The Recoil Control spec of your arms influences their ability to manage the recoil of ranged weaponry and minimize the associated reduction in accuracy. Arms with superior recoil control are well-suited to builds that depend on continuous firing with ranged weapons, like dual machine guns wielded in a Double Trigger style. The higher the Recoil Control spec, the more likely the shot is to land closer to the center of the reticle, which is essential for hitting targets at long ranges, especially with weapons like bazookas that suffer from heavy recoil.

Firearm Specialization

Suitability for using firearms.

The degree of firearm specialization of an AC's arms determines the performance of its Target Tracking spec, which is visible in the AC specs. The higher the Firearm Specialization spec of its arms, the better the AC will be at predicting the movement of evasive targets when the reticle turns red and target tracking is active. Although arm parts are the only factor that influence an AC's Target Tracking spec, it's important to remember that other factors, such as the choice of FCS and whether Target Assist is engaged, also play a significant role in determining the final accuracy of predictive fire against fast-moving enemies. ▶ B

Melee Specialization

Suitability for using melee weapons.

The Melee Specialization spec is a modifier applied to all melee weapons equipped on your arms, including punches with the AC's fists. The higher the value, the greater your damage output with arm-based melee attacks. Starting from a baseline value

Min/Max Values		
Spec	Min	Max
Arms Load Limit	10520	21300
Recoil Control	45	232
Firearm Specialization	26	160
Melee Specialization	13	158

of 100 melee specialization, each point above or below will increase or decrease the damage output of arm-based melee attacks by 2%. This spec can significantly influence the effectiveness of melee weapons, so choosing a pair of arms with a high degree of melee specialization is a critical factor to consider when favoring this type of close-quarters fighting.

LEG PART ONLY SPECS

Load Limit

Maximum weight legs can support.

The Load Limit spec assigned to leg units serves as the foundation of every build, since this value single-handedly determines the maximum amount of weight that the rest of the assembly can support before becoming overburdened. Legs are the only factor influencing the load limit of an AC, so the Load Limit spec of equipped leg parts is always identical to the Load Limit spec visible in your AC specs.

Jump Distance

Horizontal jumping performance.

Jump distance influences the horizontal distance traveled when using Quick Boosts from the ground. The higher the value, the more ground the AC will cover when using its legs to propel itself during a Quick Boost, with reverse-joint legs excelling in this spec. However, keep in mind that other factors can also influence the distance covered with a Quick Boost, such as the QB Thrust and QB Jet Duration specs of the equipped booster. Due to their lack of actual legs, this spec is absent on tank-style leg units.

Jump Height

Vertical jumping performance.

The Jump Height spec of your legs corresponds to the maximum height traveled in meters when jumping directly upward from the ground. The higher the value, the more vertical distance your AC will cover with a jump, which can make traversing environments and transitioning to aerial combat easier since jumping doesn't consume EN. Your AC's jump height is solely determined by this value and isn't affected by its total weight or booster. Similar to jump distance, this spec is not applicable to tank legs.

Travel Speed

Speed while boost is disengaged.

This tank-exclusive spec corresponds to the speed at which the AC travels when not using boost movement. The value directly translates to the maximum basic locomotion speed with these legs equipped, and isn't influenced by other factors like boosters or the total weight of the assembly. ▶ C

Min/Max Values		
Spec	Min	Max
Load Limit	47820	100300
Jump Distance	56	386
Jump Height	14	80
Travel Speed	136	194
High-Speed Perf.	316	430

High-Speed Perf.

Speed while boost is engaged.

Exclusive to tank legs, the High-Speed Performance spec influences the speed of the AC when using boost movement. It's best to think of this value as the theoretical top speed for a particular set of tank legs, which is then adjusted lower based on the total weight of the AC to determine its actual Boost Speed in the AC specs.

The specs covered in this section are all related to the various facets of your AC's overall mobility, such as boost movement, Quick Boost, and Assault Boost. Although technically exclusive to boosters, you will also encounter most of these specs when inspecting tanks legs, as these unique leg units all feature built-in boosters that cannot be swapped out for another model.

Thrust

Thrust of boost movement.

The Thrust spec of your booster plays a large role in determining your Boost Speed spec, which corresponds to the maximum speed of the AC while boost movement is active. Since boost movement doesn't consume EN and is your primary mode of locomotion, this spec is particularly important to consider when designing your AC as it can greatly influence how it feels to control and its ability to outmaneuver opponents in combat. However, it's important to remember that the assembly's Total Weight spec also influences its max boost speed, with lighter builds being significantly faster than those burdened with heavier parts.

Upward Thrust

Vertical thrust of boost movement.

The Upward Thrust spec determines how quickly your AC can ascend while consuming EN with its booster after jumping. Equipping a booster with superior upward thrust capabilities is essential when designing an AC that prioritizes vertical mobility and aerial combat, such as builds outfitted with tetrapod legs that depend on rapidly ascending and hovering above the battlefield while raining down overwhelming firepower from above.

Upward EN Consumption

EN consumed by ascending boost movement.

This value corresponds to the EN burned per second while ascending with your booster, which together with your generator's EN Capacity spec will determine how long you can continue boosting vertically before running out of EN. The lower the Upward EN Consumption spec of your booster, the more slowly your EN gauge will deplete each second while ascending. Keep in mind that air time can be extended by tapping the jump button to maintain your current altitude, which is a useful technique to master when crossing large gaps or engaging in aerial combat.

QB Thrust

Initial thrust of Quick Boost movement.

The QB Thrust spec of your booster represents the initial velocity of Quick Boosts, and is the most influential spec when it comes to determining the final QB Speed spec of your AC. If your goal is to design an AC that's able to swiftly dodge enemy attacks just before they hit, make sure to pay attention to this spec when choosing a booster.

Depending on the overall design of your AC, you might prioritize upward thrust over thrust. Tetrapod ACs naturally tend to be airborne and favor higher Upward Thrust specs.

QB Jet Duration

Duration of Quick Boost jets.

This spec corresponds to the time window, in seconds, during which your booster jets are active when performing a Quick Boost. The higher the number, the farther your AC will be propelled when using a Quick Boost. Though the boosters with the highest QB jet duration values cap out at roughly half a second, the extra dodge distance they provide can mean the difference between successfully getting out of harm's way or getting caught in the blast radius of an exploding grenade shell.

QB EN Consumption

EN consumed by Quick Boost.

A booster's QB EN Consumption spec corresponds to the base amount of EN consumed by a Quick Boost. Unlike the seemingly identical spec seen in your AC specs, this raw value strictly represents the booster's efficiency before its been multiplied by your core's Booster Efficiency Adjustment spec to determine the final amount of EN consumed when using a Quick Boost. If your playstyle relies on heavy Quick Boost usage, it's essential to equip a booster with a low QB EN Consumption spec.

QB Reload Time

Reload time for Quick Boost.

The QB Reload Time spec of your booster corresponds to the cooldown window, in seconds, required before it becomes possible to Quick Boost again after use. Shorter intervals enable you to perform multiple successive Quick Boosts with very little downtime in between activations. Keep in mind that the value shown here represents the optimal performance of the booster, which can only be achieved if your AC's total weight remains below the booster's QB Reload Ideal Weight spec.

Min/Max Values		
Spec	Min	Max
Thrust	5417	6801
Upward Thrust	4767	6334
Upward EN Consumption	405	800
QB Thrust	17500	22200
QB Jet Duration	0.26	0.54
QB EN Consumption	480	740
QB Reload Time	0.30	0.91
QB Reload Ideal Weight	60900	100600
AB Thrust	7584	10085
AB EN Consumption	320	435

QB Reload Ideal Weight

Maximum tolerable AC weight before Quick Boost reload time is compromised.

This value determines exactly how much total weight your AC can carry before its Quick Boost reload time is compromised. The QB Reload Ideal Weight spec of boosters are generally high enough to fit within the total weight values of lighter midweight builds, but heavier ACs will require boosters with higher values to avoid suffering from a penalty to Quick Boost reload time. Going slightly over the ideal weight of your booster won't have much of a negative impact, but the drawbacks will gradually become more severe if you continue to add weight without swapping to a more appropriate booster for your AC's weight class.

AB Thrust

Thrust of Assault Boost movement.

This value influences the maximum speed at which your AC travels during an Assault Boost. Boosters with a Higher AB Thrust spec significantly increase how fast you can close the gap using an Assault Boost, which makes it easier to pressure opponents or capitalize on the short stagger window with devastating melee attacks after overloading their ACS. The total weight of your assembly is also a factor when determining how fast your AC moves during an Assault Boost, so consider shedding some weight in addition to equipping a booster with a superior AB Thrust spec if your goal is to maximize speed. ▶ D

AB EN Consumption

EN consumed by Assault Boost.

The AB EN Consumption spec corresponds to your EN burn per second during an Assault Boost. Lower values will extend your Assault Boost duration by slowing down the rate at which your EN gauge drains. For example, a booster with an AB EN consumption value of 300 paired with a generator with an EN capacity of 3000 will afford you roughly 10 seconds of maximum Assault Boost duration from a full EN gauge. Being able to Assault Boost for longer is especially useful during traversal since it can allow you to more easily reach elevated locations or bypass heavily defended areas by flying directly above the enemy forces guarding them.

Melee Atk. Thrust

Thrust when homing in on enemies using melee weapons.

This booster spec influences the speed and distance at which your AC homes in on a target after initiating a melee attack. Higher values extend the range at which you can successfully chase down a target with melee attacks, while also making it possible to close the gap more quickly. Builds incorporating melee weapons will benefit greatly from equipping a booster with a high Melee Attack Thrust spec due to how short the window to capitalize on enemy stagger can often be. Lowering your AC's total weight can also increase the speed at which it moves toward the target after initiating a melee attack; by combining a lightweight build outfitted with a booster that excels in melee attack thrust performance, like the AB-J-137 KIKAKU, it's even possible to temporarily achieve speeds that go beyond any other movement option.

Melee Atk. EN Consump.

EN consumed by movement resulting from use of melee weapon.

Like most other booster actions, thrusting toward a target after initiating a melee attack consumes a portion of your EN gauge. The Melee Attack EN Consumption spec corresponds to the exact EN burn rate per second of your AC while it boosts within striking distance of the enemy. Because the distance traveled is always relatively short, the effects of this spec won't be as keenly felt as some others, but it's another factor to consider if your build focuses heavily on melee weapons. It's worth pointing out that running out of EN after initiating a melee attack won't cancel it—although this is liable to leave you in a disadvantageous position and unable to quickly dodge or escape until your EN resupplies.

Melee attack thrust can be thought of as a light form of tracking. The faster you close the distance to a target, the less chance they'll evade your melee strike.

The Close-Range Assist spec not apply to melee weaponry, so don't be too concerned about the efficacy of these armaments when choosing your FCS.

The Melee Attack EN Consumption spec is important for avoiding getting caught at close range with a depleted EN gauge, which is almost certainly a death sentence.

FCS PART SPECS

Close-Range Assist

Aiming assistance performance at close range.

This spec influences the accuracy of predictive fire when engaging targets within a close range of 130 meters or less. Equipping an FCS with a higher Close-Range Assist spec prevents your reticle from swinging as far away from an enemy whenever it performs fast evasive maneuvers like Quick Boosts, which has the benefit of reducing the time it takes for your AC's target tracking to re-center the reticle on the target. If your build uses weapons designed for close-range combat, such as handguns or shotguns, make sure to equip an FCS with a high Close-Range Assist spec to maximize your ability to hit moving targets when fighting up close and personal.

Medium-Range Assist

Aiming assistance performance at medium range.

The Medium-Range Assist spec functions identically to its close-range counterpart, but is optimized for combat at ranges between 130–260 meters. Many weapon categories, like assault rifles or laser shotguns, are most effective when engaging targets within those distances, so equipping an FCS with superior medium-range assist values can improve your overall performance when focusing on this type of loadout.

Long-Range Assist

Aiming assistance performance at long range.

Last of the FCS assist spec trio, the Long-Range Assist spec provides the same benefits as the others but is instead tuned to maximize predictive fire performance at distances beyond 260 meters. If you prefer to hang back and engage targets from farther away with long-range weaponry like plasma rifles or laser cannons, equipping an FCS that excels at this spec should be a priority to improve the odds of hitting your mark.

Min/Max Values		
Spec	Min	Max
Close-Range Assist	10	90
Medium-Range Assist	12	80
Long-Range Assist	3	92
Missile Lock Correction	65	150
Multi-Lock Correction	40	120

Missile Lock Correction

Modifier for the time it takes to acquire lock-on for missiles and other homing weapons.

Missile lock correction is a percentage-based multiplier applied to the Homing Lock Time spec of a weapon to determine the final time needed to lock-on to a single target with missiles and other homing weapons. The baseline value is 100, with every point below or above either increasing or decreasing lock-on time by 1%. The higher the Missile Lock Correction spec of your FCS, the faster you can lock-on to a single target, while lower values will result in more sluggish lock-on times. As a result, AC builds that focus on missiles to deal damage and inflict ACS strain will want to pay attention to this spec.

Multi-Lock Correction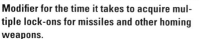

Modifier for the time it takes to acquire multiple lock-ons for missiles and other homing weapons.

The Multi-Lock Correction spec functions identically to its missile lock counterpart, but instead focuses on modifying the time needed to ready a multi-lock attack on a group of targets. The higher the value, the less time needed to acquire multiple lock-ons when holding down the weapon input. An FCS with a high Multi-Lock Correction spec can significantly improve your combat effectiveness if your AC is outfitted with weapons capable of splitting their payload to hit multiple targets, like plasma missile launchers.

Although the effects of FCS assist specs are negligible when fighting less agile targets, they can easily make the difference between victory and defeat when facing off against faster bosses or ACs.

Using an FCS with poor missile lock and multi-lock corrections will find you frustrated with how long you need to target foes, significantly hampering your ordinance.

GENERATOR ONLY PART SPECS

EN Capacity

Total amount of EN available for use.

A generator's EN Capacity spec corresponds to the exact amount of EN that will be available for use in the AC's EN gauge. While the gauge itself doesn't visually grow larger to reflect this change, equipping generators with higher EN capacity values translates to a bigger EN pool that you can use to perform EN-consuming actions like Quick Boosts. The difference between the minimum and maximum values is more than double, so it's important to consider how this spec fits into your overall AC design relative to other factors that affect EN consumption.

EN Recharge

The ability of the generator to initiate EN recharge.

This generator spec influences the EN Recharge Delay spec of your AC—a value that corresponds to the length of the delay before EN recovery kicks in after a portion of the EN gauge has been depleted by the use of EN-consuming actions. The higher the generator's EN Recharge spec, the lower the AC's EN Recharge Delay spec will be, resulting in less downtime before a partially depleted EN gauge begins to recharge. Keep in mind that while the EN Recharge spec of your generator is the main contributing factor to reducing the EN recharge delay value displayed in the AC specs, it will also be modified by your core's Generator Supply Adjustment spec to arrive at the final duration of the delay.

Supply Recovery

The ability of the generator to recover after interruption of EN supply.

The supply recovery rating of a generator affects how long it will take to cool down and begin recovering EN again whenever you fully deplete the EN gauge. The Supply Recovery spec doesn't interact with other specs at all, and is the only factor used to determine the length of this cooldown period. The higher a generator's Supple Recovery spec, the more quickly you'll replenish EN after running out and be able to use actions like Quick Boosts again. With this in mind, It's a value that you should pay special consideration to if you find yourself running out of EN often when piloting your AC.

Post-Recovery EN Supply

Amount of EN that is immediately recharged after generator EN supply has been restored.

This value corresponds to the exact amount of EN that becomes available the moment the generator recovers from complete EN depletion, with higher values making it possible to immediately use multiple EN-consuming actions when supply resumes. For example, the VP-20S generator, carrying a Post-Recovery EN Supply spec of 1200, will instantly supply 1200 EN to your EN gauge after it recovers from complete EN depletion. Remember to keep the relationship between Supply Recovery and Post-Recovery EN Supply specs in mind, since there's always a trade-off to make. You can either opt for a generator with a fast supply recovery time but low amount of immediate EN after full depletion, or a slower recovery time but with much more EN immediately available once the generator recovers.

Energy Firearm Spec.

Efficiency of EN output diverted to ranged energy weapons.

In contrast with the other generator specs that all revolve around the EN gauge, the Energy Firearm Specialization spec instead works as a multiplier that scales the Attack Power and Charging Time specs of compatible energy firearms. A value of 100 represents the baseline, with each point above or below this value either increasing or decreasing the damage output and charging speed of most ranged energy weapons by 0.5% and 1% respectively. The highest possible Energy Firearm Specialization spec increases damage by 25% and reduces charging times by 50% compared to baseline, so equipping a generator with a high value in this spec—or at the very least avoiding one with a value that's significantly below 100—should be a priority if your AC's loadout primarily consists of energy firearms like laser shotguns or plasma cannons. Remember that not all energy-based weapons are affected by this spec, however, with the list of exceptions including all melee weapons, stun bomb launchers, plasma missile launchers, laser orbits, laser turrets, and laser drones.

EN Output

Generator EN output.

The EN Output spec represents the raw output capability of the generator before it's modified by your core's Generator Output Adjustment spec, which then results in the final EN output value displayed in the AC specs. When designing an AC build, it's crucial to select a combination of generator and core that can provide a sufficiently high EN output to accommodate the total EN load requirements of the parts and weapons you plan to equip.

Min/Max Values		
Spec	Min	Max
EN Capacity	2000	4420
EN Recharge	238	2000
Supply Recovery	312 (4s Delay)	833 (1.8s Delay)
Post-Recovery EN Supply	280	3300
Energy Firearm Spec	61	150
EN Output	3860	11030

EXPANSION ONLY PART SPECS

Effect Range

Range corresponding to the furthest reach of explosions.

This spec represents the maximum reach in meters of the explosive blast unleashed when activating assault armor. Attack power and impact are reduced at this range, but incoming projectiles are still canceled by the blast. ▶ A

Resilience

Resilience of the barrier produced.

The Resilience spec determines the durability of pulse barriers generated when activating defensive expansion parts. The higher this value, the more damage the barrier can absorb before breaking. ▶ B

Duration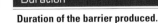

Duration of the barrier produced.

This value corresponds to the maximum number of seconds that a pulse barrier generated by a Core Expansion can last before dissipating. The barrier's durability will gradually deplete as this invisible timer counts down, making it progressively weaker as it gets closer to expiring.

Min/Max Values		
Spec	Min	Max
Resilience	3300	20000
Duration	5	25

BUILD SHOWCASE

Now that you're accustomed to the basic fundamental aspects of AC design, here are a few examples of custom assemblies designed to give you a taste of what's possible when tapping into the creative freedom supported by Armored Core VI's multi-layered and interlocking systems.

The four AC builds presented here are diverse in parts and playstyle, suitable for a range of skill levels from novice to advanced pilots. Unlock and equip the parts listed here to recreate each build, and if you want to know more, follow the page references to the Parts Catalog for information on how to best use them.

BERSERKER

The Berserker gets up close, personal, and aims to stay there with two melee weapons on deck owing to the Weapons Bay installation. ▶ A

Pros

❚ Agile enough to easily get in and out of close quarters thanks to its reverse-jointed legs.

❚ Weapons cool down even when stowed, with cooldown times that complement each other.

❚ A heavy-hitting melee attack will always be available whether the enemy is in or out of stagger.

Cons

❚ Low total AP makes this the easiest of the four showcased builds to destroy.

❚ Poor attitude stability means this build easily staggers if caught off guard by a powerful attack.

❚ Being forced to fight at close range means that you'll need sharp reflexes to avoid incoming attacks.

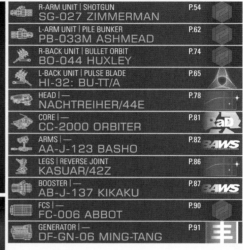

R-ARM UNIT | SHOTGUN	SG-027 ZIMMERMAN	P.54
L-ARM UNIT | PILE BUNKER	PB-033M ASHMEAD	P.62
R-BACK UNIT | BULLET ORBIT	BO-044 HUXLEY	P.74
L-BACK UNIT | PULSE BLADE	HI-32: BU-TT/A	P.65
HEAD | —	NACHTREIHER/44E	P.78
CORE | —	CC-2000 ORBITER	P.81
ARMS | —	AA-J-123 BASHO	P.82
LEGS | REVERSE JOINT	KASUAR/42Z	P.86
BOOSTER | —	AB-J-137 KIKAKU	P.87
FCS | —	FC-006 ABBOT	P.90
GENERATOR | —	DF-GN-06 MING-TANG	P.91

FLARE

This AC lights up the battlefield, maintaining pressure at all angles with a pure plasma loadout effective against a variety of enemy types. ▶ B

Pros

❚ The blast radius from the Vvc-760PR plasma rifles is sizeable enough to catch even some of the most agile foes if shot at the ground from above.

❚ Dual shoulder-mounted Vvc-70VPM vertical plasma missile launchers fire projectiles that easily penetrate frontal defenses.

❚ Utterly decimates enemies with low anti-energy defenses.

Cons

❚ However, hyper-specialization means that it struggles against opponents with high anti-energy defense.

❚ Doesn't deliver much of an extra punch to staggered opponents due to the loadout's low direct hit adjustment values.

❚ Features relatively poor mobility compared to other builds available.

R-ARM UNIT | PLASMA RIFLE	Vvc-760PR	P.60
L-ARM UNIT | PLASMA RIFLE	Vvc-760PR	P.60
R-BACK UNIT | PLASMA MISSILE LAUNCHER	Vvc-70VPM	P.73
L-BACK UNIT | PLASMA MISSILE LAUNCHER	Vvc-70VPM	P.73
HEAD | —	HD-011 MELANDER	P.77
CORE | —	DF-BD-08 TIAN-QIANG	P.80
ARMS | —	VP-46D	P.83
LEGS | BIPEDAL	DF-LG-08 TIAN-QIANG	P.85
BOOSTER | —	BUERZEL/21D	P.88
FCS | —	FCS-G2/P05	P.89
GENERATOR | —	VE-20C	P.92

A

B

C

REVOLVER

The trigger-happy Revolver goes akimbo with dual VIENTOs, needling enemies ever closer to ACS overload with each shot.

Pros

▌ EL-PW-00 VIENTO needle guns excel at building ACS strain, with fast reload speeds designed to beat out enemy impact recovery windows.

▌ Powerful dual laser cannons annihilate opponents during stagger, especially if charged beforehand.

▌ Tank legs negate firing stance from charge attacks, allowing you to remain mobile and within optimal range at all times.

Cons

▌ Doesn't output high amounts of immediate impact compared to other builds, and may need an extra reload cycle from the VIENTOs to overload tougher opponents.

▌ Charged laser cannon shots can potentially miss the mark if fired at staggered enemies while moving.

▌ Must remain within short ideal range window for needle guns to be effective and struggles when shifting to aerial combat.

R-ARM UNIT | NEEDLE GUN EL-PW-00 VIENTO	P.55	
L-ARM UNIT | NEEDLE GUN EL-PW-00 VIENTO	P.55	
R-BACK UNIT | LASER CANNON VE-60LCA	P.67	
L-BACK UNIT | LASER CANNON VP-60LCS	P.67	
HEAD | — HC-3000 WRECKER	P.79	
CORE | — DF-BD-08 TIAN-QIANG	P.80	
ARMS | — NACHTREIHER/46E	P.83	
LEGS | TANK EL-TL-11 FORTALEZA	P.87	
BOOSTER | —		
FCS | — FC-008 TALBOT	P.90	
GENERATOR | — VE-20C	P.92	

KAMI

The Kami is the god of the skies, maintaining altitude indefinitely thanks to the firing stance imposed by the SONGBIRDS during descent.
► C

Pros

▌ Permanent airtime as long as the SONGBIRDS are fired upon full depletion of EN, giving enough time for EN recovery to kick in.

▌ Heavy explosive ordinance safely deals damage and impact from above.

▌ Excellent attitude stability makes the build difficult to stagger.

Cons

▌ Struggles to maintain altitude if the SONGBIRDS are on cooldown when EN runs out, though dual bazookas can buy you enough time if fired carefully.

▌ Suffers against opponents with high anti-explosive defense.

▌ Not great at ground combat where its projectiles are more easily avoided.

R-ARM UNIT | BAZOOKA DF-BA-06 XUAN-GE	P.56	
L-ARM UNIT | BAZOOKA DF-BA-06 XUAN-GE	P.56	
R-BACK UNIT | GRENADE CANNON SONGBIRDS	P.66	
L-BACK UNIT | GRENADE CANNON SONGBIRDS	P.66	
HEAD | — AH-J-124 BASHO	P.77	
CORE | — VP-40S	P.80	
ARMS | — AR-011 MELANDER	P.82	
LEGS | TETRAPOD VP-424	P.86	
BOOSTER | — BC-0400 MULE	P.89	
FCS | — IB-C03F: WLT 001	P.9	
GENERATOR | — VE-20D	P.92	

PARTS CATALOG

Welcome to the Parts Catalog. This comprehensive section documents all the weapons and parts you can obtain and equip when building your AC, organized by category based on the in-game order for an optimal browsing experience. Each part's entry is filled with useful information, such as full specs, in-game descriptions, and unlock conditions. For every weapon category, like burst rifles, we'll also offer insights into their use cases and provide recommendations for specs to consider during the assembly process.

USING THIS SECTION

A lot of information is presented for each weapon and part, and though most of it is self-explanatory, we'll begin by breaking down each element here. For detailed explanations of particular specs, you should refer to the Assembly & Specs section, starting on P.28; even specs that may seem innocuously simple can often have intricacies that affect a part's ideal use and the type of assembly it's best suited for.

1 Weapon/Part Category

Weapons and parts are covered by category. For weapons, the text that accompanies each category provides info and tips about that weapon type, with categories featuring multiple weapon choices also including comparisons of strengths and weaknesses for all models. AC parts are covered in a slightly different format, with each major category, like heads, featuring its own analysis of the available roster, along with use cases for a few standout models.

2 Weapon/Part ID

Here, you'll see the part's name, its manufacturer's logo, and an image of its in-game model. For a list of all parts manufacturers, see P.28.

3 Part Info

This is the official in-game description for the weapon, which provides a summary of its characteristics and can often include lore or story-related details.

4 Unlock Condition

The text here explains how to acquire the weapon. Unlock conditions are often shared for right and left slot versions. In some cases, each slot will have its own unique conditions.

5 Buy/Sell Value

Shows the value in COAM that the weapon or part can be purchased or sold for in the Parts Shop.

6 Part Specs

Here is where you'll find the part's ratings for each of the specs that affect its performance. For an explanation of each individual spec, consult the Weapons & Part Specs section, starting on P.38.

7 Weapon Attributes

These icons represent the weapon's key attributes, such as damage type, attack type, reload type, and also highlight any additional effects it can apply. The full legend for these icons is shown directly below.

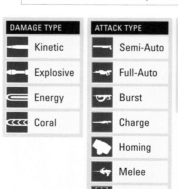

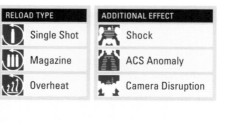

DAMAGE TYPE		ATTACK TYPE		RELOAD TYPE		ADDITIONAL EFFECT	
	Kinetic		Semi-Auto		Single Shot		Shock
	Explosive		Full-Auto		Magazine		ACS Anomaly
	Energy		Burst		Overheat		Camera Disruption
	Coral		Charge				
			Homing				
			Melee				
			Shield				

R-ARM UNIT/L-ARM UNIT

Parts listed here are all weapons that can be installed on either L-Arm and R-Arm Unit slots. You can acquire or purchase both a left- and right-arm version of each one, making it possible to wield two of any of these weapons simultaneously.

BURST RIFLE

The **MA-J-200 RANSETSU-RF** is a unique and versatile kinetic rifle with two distinct firing modes —standard single-round shots, and charged triple-round bursts—both of which maintain consistency of attack power and impact per round. While sporting a noticeably lower rate of rapid fire compared to the MA-J-201 RANSETSU-AR, it offers superior accumulative impact per shot and faster reload times. Its high impact and direct hit adjustment values make it a versatile choice to either induce stagger, or land charged burst shots after staggering.

The MA-J-200 RANSETSU-RF's generous effective range and low recoil means it can be used to take out weaker targets, such as light MTs, from the edge of your lock-on range without ricocheting. Although this weapon boasts a fast charge time, keep in mind that firing burst shots will force your AC to stop unless you're using tetrapod or tank legs.

MA-J-200 RANSETSU-RF

■ PART INFO Burst rifle developed by BAWS. Consumes kinetic ammunition to deliver on reliable offensive potential, both in terms of damage and impact. Can be charged to fire burst shots.

■ UNLOCK CONDITION (RIGHT/LEFT ARM) Parts Shop Update 1: Complete either "Destroy Artillery Installations" or "Grid 135 Cleanup"

■ PART SPECS		€ 105,000	
Attack Power	224	Rapid Fire	1.5
Impact	245	Charge Time	0.7
Accumulative Impact	91	Magazine Rounds	15
Chg. Attack Power	224x3	Total Rounds	375
Chg. Impact	245x3	Reload Time	1.8
Chg. Accum. Impact	91x3	Ammunition Cost	100
Direct Hit Adjustment	220	Weight	4210
Recoil	12	EN Load	158
Ideal Range	180	Interrupts Assault Boost	Chg. Atk
Effective Range	321	Assault Boost Impact Bonus	Yes

A Double Trigger MA-J-200 RANSETSU-RF loadout can deliver sufficient impact to reliably stagger most targets with enough rounds left in both magazines to capitalize on its high direct hit potential.

LINEAR RIFLE

Regular shots from linear rifles pack a solid punch, and charge shots accelerate the round even further, allowing you to deliver a much more powerful blow capable of crippling opponents from a distance. These potent charge attacks make linear rifles ideal for instantly taking out targets or quickly overloading their ACS, especially with the element of surprise. While the **LR-036 CURTIS** isn't capable of fully automatic fire, repeatedly pressing the trigger lets you fire a barrage of shots without any risk of overheating. Firing more than two charged shots in quick succession will cause the rifle to overheat, however, leaving you reliant on other weapons while it cools down. Consider equipping arms with better recoil control to prevent your shots from veering off target when using this linear rifle from a distance, especially if you plan to wield two of them in a Double Trigger configuration.

The **LR-037 HARRIS** is a high-firepower model that boasts greatly increased attack power and impact along with a longer effective range when compared to the LR-036 CURTIS. This model makes numerous sacrifices for single-shot damage potential, namely reduced performance in rate of fire, weight, EN load, magazine size, reload time, and a doubling of ammo cost per round. Charge attacks with the LR-037 HARRIS are devastating, but will instantly cause the rifle to overheat. While the cooldown period is shorter than the LR-036 CURTIS, you'll want to bring other weapons to deliver follow-up direct hits against staggered opponents.

LR-036 CURTIS

■ PART INFO High-speed linear rifle developed by Balam. A special type of rifle that accelerates rounds using electromagnetic propulsion. Charging the weapon further increases round velocity, in turn increasing damage.

■ UNLOCK CONDITION (RIGHT/LEFT ARM) Reward/Parts Shop: Complete "Beginner Training 2: Combat Fundamentals"

■ PART SPECS		€ 65,000	
Attack Power	142	Rapid Fire	2.5
Impact	135	Charge Time	0.5
Accumulative Impact	52	Magazine Rounds	12
Chg. Attack Power	689	Total Rounds	420
Chg. Impact	850	Reload Time	2.2
Chg. Accum. Impact	260	Cooling	155
Chg. Heat Buildup	550	Ammunition Cost	100
Direct Hit Adjustment	220	Weight	4150
Recoil	24	EN Load	289
Ideal Range	190	Interrupts Assault Boost	Chg. Atk
Effective Range	337	Assault Boost Impact Bonus	Yes

LR-037 HARRIS

■ PART INFO High-firepower linear rifle developed by Balam. The lengthened barrel provides extra distance for rounds to accelerate, allowing for high damage at long range. However, this comes at the cost of rapid-fire potential.

■ UNLOCK CONDITION (RIGHT/LEFT ARM) Parts Shop Update 6: Complete "Destroy the Ice Worm"

■ PART SPECS		€ 135,000	
Attack Power	239	Rapid Fire	1.3
Impact	285	Charge Time	0.8
Accumulative Impact	109	Magazine Rounds	10
Chg. Attack Power	977	Total Rounds	360
Chg. Impact	1250	Reload Time	3.0
Chg. Accum. Impact	380	Cooling	350
Chg. Heat Buildup	1000	Ammunition Cost	200
Direct Hit Adjustment	220	Weight	4840
Recoil	35	EN Load	441
Ideal Range	195	Interrupts Assault Boost	Chg. Atk
Effective Range	376	Assault Boost Impact Bonus	Yes

ASSAULT RIFLE

Assault rifles are balanced kinetic weapons that don't require much finesse to use and come with enough ammo to last throughout most sorties, making them a perfect choice for novice AC pilots. The **RF-024 TURNER** doesn't excel in any specialized role, but offers solid performance against early threats. When paired with the AC-2000 TOOL ARM unit installed on your starter AC, you won't have to worry about actively managing recoil during fully automatic fire, except when attacking smaller targets at long range. Once within effective range, it's best to hold down the trigger and overwhelm your targets with sustained fire. The **RF-025 SCUDDER** is a high-firepower variant focused on damage and impact in exchange for a slower rate of fire and smaller magazine. It's tuned for precision and can be slightly unwieldy during fully automatic fire; you'll need to pay attention to the spread of your rounds when holding down the trigger, and briefly stop firing when accuracy wanes.

RF-024 TURNER

■ PART INFO Standard assault rifle developed by Balam. Balances rapid-fire performance and firepower, making it easy to use on full auto. A long-selling classic popular with anyone from new corporate recruits to veteran mercenaries.

■ UNLOCK CONDITION (RIGHT/LEFT ARM) Default/Parts Shop Update 1: Complete either "Destroy Artillery Installations" or "Grid 135 Cleanup"

■ PART SPECS		€ 55,000	
Attack Power	105	Magazine Rounds	18
Impact	65	Total Rounds	540
Accumulative Impact	25	Reload Time	2.2
Direct Hit Adjustment	185	Ammunition Cost	40
Recoil	17	Weight	3560
Ideal Range	160	EN Load	102
Effective Range	296	Interrupts Assault Boost	No
Rapid Fire	3.4	Assault Boost Impact Bonus	Yes

RF-025 SCUDDER

■ PART INFO High-firepower assault rifle developed by Balam. This variation has been adjusted to focus on the offensive performance of individual shots. However, the longer firing cycle demands more precise aiming.

■ UNLOCK CONDITION (RIGHT/LEFT ARM) Parts Shop Update 5: Complete "Ocean Crossing"

■ PART SPECS		€ 205,000	
Attack Power	135	Magazine Rounds	15
Impact	82	Total Rounds	450
Accumulative Impact	35	Reload Time	2.4
Direct Hit Adjustment	185	Ammunition Cost	50
Recoil	19	Weight	3830
Ideal Range	162	EN Load	153
Effective Range	304	Interrupts Assault Boost	No
Rapid Fire	2.9	Assault Boost Impact Bonus	Yes

Using a Double Trigger configuration doesn't mean that it's always appropriate to hold down both triggers simultaneously. Emptying the magazine of your first MG-014 LUDLOW before firing the second can close gaps in your offense that are otherwise exposed during reload times.

BURST ASSAULT RIFLE

The **MA-J-201 RANSETSU-AR** is a unique assault rifle with a burst-oriented design, enabling it to fire precise triple-shot volleys from a distance. Unlike the MA-J-200 RANSETSU-RF, this weapon foregoes the ability to fire individual rounds, firing exclusively in three-round bursts instead. Its extremely low recoil makes it accurate at longer ranges, but the small magazine size means frequent reloading.

While each burst is less powerful than the MA-J-200 RANSETSU-RF's charge attacks, it can output damage at a more consistent rhythm if you hold down the trigger. You'll need to make sure all three shots from each burst connect to maximize this rifle's potential. Equipping an FCS that specializes in medium- or long-range targeting along with arms with a high degree of firearm specialization can help ensure more of the burst shots hit their mark. The MA-J-201 RANSETSU-AR isn't ideal for building up ACS strain against faster or more evasive opponents like rival ACs. However, pairing it with other weapons that focus on dealing accumulative impact can make up for this shortcoming.

MA-J-201 RANSETSU-AR

■ PART INFO Burst assault rifle developed by BAWS. This weapon offers high accuracy and spontaneous firepower thanks to its burst-oriented design, leading to its mass production for use by new recruits to the Rubicon Liberation Front.

■ UNLOCK CONDITION (RIGHT/LEFT ARM) Parts Shop Update 4: Complete "Attack the Watchpoint"

■ PART SPECS		€ 111,000	
Attack Power	77×3	Magazine Rounds	18
Impact	64×3	Total Rounds	450
Accumulative Impact	17×3	Reload Time	1.9
Direct Hit Adjustment	185	Ammunition Cost	40
Recoil	7	Weight	3620
Ideal Range	153	EN Load	132
Effective Range	284	Interrupts Assault Boost	No
Rapid Fire	3.2	Assault Boost Impact Bonus	Yes

MACHINE GUN

Machine guns have excellent rapid-fire capabilities, making them ideal weapons for suppressing enemies at medium or close range. Each individual round has limited attack power and impact, but sustained fire can quickly overload an opponent's ACS. These weapons reveal their true potential when used in Double Trigger builds, either in identical pairs or in combination with a different weapon type. Just remember to keep an eye on your ammo supply, as an over reliance on machine guns can often leave you empty before the mission is complete.

Wielding two **MG-014 LUDLOW** machine guns won't require high EN load, and allows you to dance around opponents while unleashing a barrage of bullets. Reload time is short, but you'll only be able to keep up sustained fire for three seconds before emptying a magazine. It's a good idea to balance the use of these machine guns with back-mounted weapons like homing missiles, making it possible to eliminate smaller threats from a distance or continue pressuring opponents during reloads. The MG-014 LUDLOW quickly loses effectiveness as you move further away from a target, so make sure that you're within range before opening fire. Letting loose with a pair of these machines guns while closing the gap with an Assault Boost can often deal enough impact to stagger your opponent, especially if followed with a Boost Kick at close range.

A heavier machine gun optimized for sustained fully automatic fire, the **DF-MG-02 CHANG-CHEN** features a 50% larger magazine size than the MG-014 LUDLOW, making it possible to fire continuously for just under five seconds. Its reloading process is slower, though, so remember to ready a fresh magazine before entering combat. This model's focus on sustained output comes at the cost of slight reductions in firepower and effective range, while the oversized magazine increases its weight and EN load. The DF-MG-02 CHANG-CHEN can be a powerhouse when used in Double Trigger builds, though you'll need to equip arms with high recoil control.

MG-014 LUDLOW

■ PART INFO Machine gun developed by Balam. Has excellent rapid-fire output, but somewhat lacking in firepower when used alone. Shines in Double Trigger builds, whether using two of this weapon or in combination with another.

■ UNLOCK CONDITION (RIGHT/LEFT ARM) Reward/Parts Shop: Complete "Beginner Training 1: Basic Controls"

■ PART SPECS   € 45,000

Attack Power	42	Magazine Rounds	30
Impact	41	Total Rounds	720
Accumulative Impact	19	Reload Time	1.5
Direct Hit Adjustment	195	Ammunition Cost	20
Recoil	4	Weight	2450
Ideal Range	115	EN Load	82
Effective Range	236	Interrupts Assault Boost	No
Rapid Fire	10.0	Assault Boost Impact Bonus	Yes

DF-MG-02 CHANG-CHEN

■ PART INFO Machine gun developed by Dafeng Core Industry. This weapon was designed for sustained combat potential, and uses oversize ammunition magazines. Minimal need for reloading makes it well suited for suppressive fire.

■ UNLOCK CONDITION (RIGHT/LEFT ARM) Parts Shop Update 6: Complete "Destroy the Ice Worm"

■ PART SPECS   € 120,000

Attack Power	39	Magazine Rounds	45
Impact	40	Total Rounds	990
Accumulative Impact	18	Reload Time	2.2
Direct Hit Adjustment	195	Ammunition Cost	20
Recoil	6	Weight	3280
Ideal Range	100	EN Load	143
Effective Range	220	Interrupts Assault Boost	No
Rapid Fire	10.0	Assault Boost Impact Bonus	Yes

BURST MACHINE GUN

Combining the ease of use of a machine gun with highly accurate burst-fire capabilities, the **MA-E-210 ETSUJIN** is a good kinetic option when assembling a fast, lightweight AC. Its precise four-shot bursts are powerful enough to dispatch most light MTs in just a few volleys. You'll be reloading often when holding down the trigger, but thanks to the quick reload time, this won't result in lengthy gaps in your offense. The MA-E-210 ETSUJIN's accuracy means that it can reliably hit targets even when installed on lightweight arms that don't excel at recoil control. This advantage combined with a balanced mix of firepower and impact can make the burst machine gun particularly effective at staggering rival ACs when engaging at mid-range or closer. Like other machine guns, the MA-E-210 ETSUJIN can quickly run out of ammo during longer missions if you rely on it exclusively. This is a good support weapon for complementing larger artillery, or for keeping as backup stored in weapon bays.

MA-E-210 ETSUJIN

■ PART INFO Burst machine gun developed by BAWS. The burst-oriented design of this weapon makes it both easy to use and highly accurate. A strong candidate for use as a sub-weapon in lightweight builds.

■ UNLOCK CONDITION (RIGHT/LEFT ARM) Parts Shop Update 5: Complete "Ocean Crossing"

■ PART SPECS   € 74,000

Attack Power	46×4	Magazine Rounds	24
Impact	48×4	Total Rounds	600
Accumulative Impact	22×4	Reload Time	1.5
Direct Hit Adjustment	195	Ammunition Cost	30
Recoil	3	Weight	2810
Ideal Range	106	EN Load	98
Effective Range	224	Interrupts Assault Boost	No
Rapid Fire	8.1	Assault Boost Impact Bonus	Yes

Opening fire during an Assault Boost once you're within the effective range of the DF-GA-08 HU-BEN gatling gun can tear through a target's ACS gauge at lightning speeds.

GATLING GUN

When you need to overpower the opposition with superior rapid-fire performance, look no further than the **DF-GA-08 HU-BEN**. This behemoth features six rotating barrels that can output a sustained barrage of bullets without the need to reload. Firing the gatling gun generates considerable amounts of heat, however; listen for a high-pitched sound effect that warns you once the heat buildup reaches roughly 80% and stop firing at this point to let the weapon cool down. While the DF-GA-08 HU-BEN can bring immense amounts of firepower to bear on a single target, it's a poor fit for builds that prioritize speed. The high rate of fire also comes at the detriment of accuracy, meaning that you'll have to get fairly close to targets. Its main advantage is its ability to output sustained damage that even the most evasive enemies will find difficult to consistently avoid at medium to close range. The combined impact of each round can quickly overwhelm most opponent's ACS, particularly when wielding two of these weapons at once.

DF-GA-08 HU-BEN

■ PART INFO Gatling gun developed by Dafeng Core Industry. Equipped with overwhelming rapid-fire performance and sustained firepower, it embodies the "domination through material superiority" mantra of Dafeng's parent company, Balam.

■ UNLOCK CONDITION (RIGHT/LEFT ARM) Parts Shop Update 4: Complete "Attack the Watchpoint"

■ PART SPECS   € 170,000

Attack Power	25	Rapid Fire	20.0
Impact	25	Total Rounds	1300
Accumulative Impact	11	Cooling	220
ATK Heat Buildup	9	Ammunition Cost	30
Direct Hit Adjustment	215	Weight	5800
Recoil	5	EN Load	425
Ideal Range	130	Interrupts Assault Boost	No
Effective Range	226	Assault Boost Impact Bonus	Yes

SHOTGUN

Shotguns are ideal for building ACS strain and dealing heavy damage, and their respectable direct hit adjustment values make them a solid choice to exploit enemy stagger. Given their high spread and high recoil, your best bet is to forgo recoil control entirely in favor of firearm specialization to ensure shots connect with their intended target. Equip a close-range FCS when using shotguns, since their poor effective range values will have you meeting the enemy in close quarters.

The **SG-026 HALDEMAN** has the highest rate of fire, and is the most EN efficient among shotguns, pairing well with builds that need to conserve EN output. Short reload times make it easy to leverage this nimble shotgun's punchy direct hits during staggers. Inferior range values to the SG-07 ZIMMERMAN mean that you'll need to get closer to enemies with high anti-kinetic defense in order to mitigate ricochet. This weapon is a balanced choice for builds seeking the raw power of a shotgun, while maintaining a brisk firing rate. The **SG-07 ZIMMERMAN**, meanwhile, offers increased range and larger bullet spread, making it effective at medium range when fighting bulky enemies like BAWS tetrapod MTs. It's particularly powerful directly next to a target, however, as each of the projectiles will connect. Its high impact can stagger enemies quickly, especially if you open fire during an Assault Boost. Try to ensure you're close enough to reduce wasted shots, though, since missing the mark can put a large dent in your damage output due to lengthier reload times.

A blast from the unconventional **HM-0777 SWEET SIXTEEN** can deliver serious damage and ACS strain at point blank. With the lowest weight in the shotgun category, this special RaD design is a good pick for lightweight builds that can handle the extra EN Load, though its low range and recoil values mean you'll need to pull as close as possible to the enemy to avoid ricochet and lost accuracy. An FCS specializing in close-range combat is especially important with this shotgun. The SWEET SIXTEEN's sluggish reload speed and limited reach make it a risky option, but its devastating impact and direct hit potential rewards you for staying up close and personal during engagements.

SG-026 HALDEMAN

■ **PART INFO** Close-range shotgun developed by Balam. Fires in a spread, resulting in excellent impact albeit with a short range. Regardless, this weapon offers unparalleled potency in close-range engagements.

■ **UNLOCK CONDITION (RIGHT/LEFT ARM)** Parts Shop Update 2: Complete both "Destroy the Weaponized Mining Ship" and "Attack the Dam Complex"

■ PART SPECS		€ 75,000	
Attack Power	576	Total Rounds	66
Impact	360	Reload Time	1.3
Accumulative Impact	280	Ammunition Cost	200
Direct Hit Adjustment	190	Weight	3660
Recoil	90	EN Load	185
Ideal Range	88	Interrupts Assault Boost	No
Effective Range	169	Assault Boost Impact Bonus	Yes

SG-027 ZIMMERMAN

■ **PART INFO** Long-range shotgun developed by Balam. Uses specialized large shells to improve shot density, extending effective range but reducing the firing cycle.

■ **UNLOCK CONDITION (RIGHT/LEFT ARM)** Parts Shop Update 5: Complete "Ocean Crossing"

■ PART SPECS		€ 115,000	
Attack Power	800	Total Rounds	53
Impact	620	Reload Time	2.0
Accumulative Impact	360	Ammunition Cost	350
Direct Hit Adjustment	180	Weight	4400
Recoil	90	EN Load	242
Ideal Range	102	Interrupts Assault Boost	No
Effective Range	184	Assault Boost Impact Bonus	Yes

WR-0777 SWEET SIXTEEN

■ **PART INFO** Special shotgun developed by RaD. Strictly speaking, this unique weapon is not a true shotgun, as its area attacks are enabled by firing individual projectiles from multiple barrels simultaneously.

■ **UNLOCK CONDITION (RIGHT/LEFT ARM)** Parts Shop Update 5: Complete "Ocean Crossing"

■ PART SPECS		€ 49,000	
Attack Power	85×13	Total Rounds	546
Impact	61×13	Reload Time	3.0
Accumulative Impact	41×13	Ammunition Cost	30
Direct Hit Adjustment	205	Weight	1640
Recoil	100	EN Load	268
Ideal Range	76	Interrupts Assault Boost	No
Effective Range	155	Assault Boost Impact Bonus	Yes

HANDGUN

Delivering serious stopping power with each pull of the trigger, handguns are all about rapidly pounding the target's ACS with high-impact rounds at close range. Their lightweight design makes them excel as support firearms used to stagger enemies, setting up direct hit opportunities that you can capitalize on with highly damaging melee weapons like the pile bunker. Handguns quickly become ineffective at medium range, so always pair them with an FCS that specializes in close-range combat.

The **HG-003 COQUILLETT** features a high rate of fire, but short reload times balance out how often this gun will empty its magazine. Double Trigger builds should use Boost Kicks or back weapons with high attack power or direct hit ratings to capitalize on enemy ACS overload windows, with both the EARSHOT grenade cannon and the VP-60LCS laser cannon being strong candidates. The **HG-004 DUCKETT** packs even more of a punch than its shorter-barreled counterpart but suffers in rate of fire and reload time. You'll need to make sure each shot counts against agile targets, baiting them to dodge with other weapons before letting loose a punishing shot from this destructive handgun.

HG-003 COQUILLETT

■ **PART INFO** Large-caliber handgun developed by Balam. The rise of Core Theory introduced a new kind of close-quarters combat and with it a reappraisal of handguns, which demonstrate stopping power with tremendous impact potential.

■ **UNLOCK CONDITION (RIGHT/LEFT ARM)** Parts Shop Update 1: Complete either "Destroy Artillery Installations" or "Grid 135 Cleanup"

■ PART SPECS		€ 35,000	
Attack Power	166	Magazine Rounds	7
Impact	235	Total Rounds	196
Accumulative Impact	149	Reload Time	2.1
Direct Hit Adjustment	125	Ammunition Cost	100
Recoil	32	Weight	1200
Ideal Range	85	EN Load	122
Effective Range	167	Interrupts Assault Boost	No
Rapid Fire	2.5	Assault Boost Impact Bonus	Yes

HG-004 DUCKETT

■ **PART INFO** Long-barreled handgun developed by Balam. This model increases firepower while retaining the impact potential of its predecessor. Still, taking advantage of this weapon in a large-scale engagement demands skill and experience.

■ **UNLOCK CONDITION (RIGHT/LEFT ARM)** Parts Shop Update 6: Complete "Destroy the Ice Worm"

■ PART SPECS		€ 112,000	
Attack Power	235	Magazine Rounds	7
Impact	300	Total Rounds	182
Accumulative Impact	151	Reload Time	2.5
Direct Hit Adjustment	125	Ammunition Cost	120
Recoil	30	Weight	1650
Ideal Range	90	EN Load	158
Effective Range	178	Interrupts Assault Boost	No
Rapid Fire	1.7	Assault Boost Impact Bonus	Yes

BURST HANDGUN

The compact **MA-E-211 SAMPU** burst handgun is custom engineered to inflict maximum ACS strain on the target while minimizing the weight and EN load of the weapon. Compared to other handguns, it trades raw damage for snappier reload times and more balanced recoil. Two shots fired for each pull of the trigger make it easy to maintain pressure on an opponent as you draw it closer to ACS overload. Effective range is comparable to other handguns, so this unique burst model is still only truly effective at close range when fighting anything beyond light MTs. Since you'll primarily use it in close quarters, it's best to prioritize firearm specialization over recoil control.

The SG-07 ZIMMERMAN is a good addition to most builds, with few weapons rivaling its ability to build ACS strain.

Needle guns excel at opening up direct hit windows to dish out punishment.

The VP-66EG stun gun can quickly build up enough shock to trigger crippling electrical discharges.

With the lowest weight of all firearms in the game, the MA-E-211 SAMPU can prove to be an excellent sub-weapon for lightweight assemblies aiming to keep overall burden low, by allowing that type of build to equip a particularly heavy weapon, such as the IB-C03W1: WLT011 Coral rifle, in the opposite hand without overburdening the arms.

MA-E-211 SAMPU

 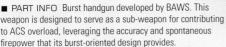

■ PART INFO Burst handgun developed by BAWS. This weapon is designed to serve as a sub-weapon for contributing to ACS overload, leveraging the accuracy and spontaneous firepower that its burst-oriented design provides.

■ UNLOCK CONDITION (RIGHT/LEFT ARM) Parts Shop Update 6: Complete "Destroy the Ice Worm"

■ PART SPECS		€ 73,000	
Attack Power	87×2	Magazine Rounds	12
Impact	105×2	Total Rounds	300
Accumulative Impact	64×2	Reload Time	1.9
Direct Hit Adjustment	125	Ammunition Cost	40
Recoil	15	Weight	960
Ideal Range	80	EN Load	62
Effective Range	165	Interrupts Assault Boost	No
Rapid Fire	5.1	Assault Boost Impact Bonus	Yes

NEEDLE GUN

The **EL-PW-00 VIENTO**'s needle-sharp rounds quickly build impact with a nimble, semi-automatic firing rate. Functionally, the needle gun handles similarly to handguns, but with a design focused on balancing overall power and recoil. The EL-PW-00 VIENTO's primary duty will be to nudge opponents toward ACS overload with a barrage of manually fired rounds. Increased range compared to the handgun family allows more flexible play at medium ranges, but you'll need to be close to enemies with high anti-kinetic defense to avoid ricochet. Focus on firearm specialization to synergize with this weapon's low recoil, and center your FCS choice on close and medium ranges. Heavy-hitting back weapons will pair well to take advantage of stagger windows, and boosters with superior AB thrust can help to close gaps against distant opponents while racking up extra impact from needle shots.

EL-PW-00 VIENTO

■ PART INFO Needle gun developed by Elcano. A semi-auto weapon that fires special needle-shaped ammunition. Provides a good balance of attack power and impact.

■ UNLOCK CONDITION (RIGHT/LEFT ARM) Parts Shop Update 7: Complete "Escape"

■ PART SPECS		€ 148,000	
Attack Power	181	Magazine Rounds	5
Impact	195	Total Rounds	160
Accumulative Impact	127	Reload Time	1.9
Direct Hit Adjustment	130	Ammunition Cost	80
Recoil	15	Weight	1180
Ideal Range	105	EN Load	215
Effective Range	192	Interrupts Assault Boost	No
Rapid Fire	4.0	Assault Boost Impact Bonus	Yes

STUN GUN

The unassuming **VP-66EG** stun gun can come as a shocking revelation to targets with inadequate shock resistance. Electrified probes launched into enemies build up shock, eventually triggering a highly damaging electrical discharge that also causes a brief loss of control. The lower the opponent's shock resistance, the sooner they succumb to the effects. Despite its poor impact values, damage builds up quickly if shots consistently connect. The stun gun is a specialized weapon that's best wielded in pairs against high AP targets, since its high rate of fire means the magazine can be emptied quickly to trigger back-to-back electrical discharges. Probes deal damage three times: an initial kinetic hit, followed by another two bursts of shock damage. The secondary bursts each inflict 25 points of shock buildup, though your probes won't cause any buildup if the initial hit ricochets.

VP-66EG

■ PART INFO Stun gun developed by Arquebus. Fires electrified probes, the effects of which build up to induce a forced discharge of electricity in the afflicted craft. Frequently used to immobilize and seize hardware from enemies and rivals.

■ UNLOCK CONDITION (RIGHT/LEFT ARM) Parts Shop Update 9: Complete "Destroy the Ice Worm" in NG+

■ PART SPECS		€ 129,000	
Attack Power	104	Magazine Rounds	7
Impact	54	Total Rounds	133
Accumulative Impact	32	Reload Time	1.8
Direct Hit Adjustment	195	Ammunition Cost	150
Recoil	14	Weight	980
Ideal Range	100	EN Load	247
Effective Range	159	Interrupts Assault Boost	No
Rapid Fire	6.7	Assault Boost Impact Bonus	No

BAZOOKA

Bazookas are large-barreled explosive weapons that fire a massive, explosive shell. Firing them causes significant recoil and enters a firing stance that ceases all mobility, unless they're used with tetrapod or tank legs. The **DF-BA-06 XUAN-GE** is the most well-rounded of the three bazookas, and one of the most balanced explosive weapons in general. It features a deep ammo reserve with respectable reload times, has high attack and impact values, and its accumulative impact is enough to progress toward ACS overload between reload times. Double Trigger builds with this bazooka are a powerful option—especially in the early game. Choosing arms with good recoil control will help balance out the understandably high recoil, but be aware that firing back-to-back shots against a moving enemy will reduce your accuracy.

The **MAJESTIC** features longer reload times and lower round count in exchange for improved attack and impact values. It hits hard, builds huge impact, and deals slightly better direct hit damage than the DF-BA-06 XUAN-GE. Boost Kicks offer one way to keep up pressure between shots, and back weapons with shorter reload windows are another. You can rush the opponent with Boost Kicks and missiles until it staggers—at which point you unload with a shot or two from the MAJESTIC.

Intended as the bazooka option for lightweight builds, the **LITTLE GEM** trades some proficiency in every spec in exchange for a significantly lighter weight and EN load. Just like the bulkier alternatives, this smaller model's high recoil also induces a firing stance, but with the added downside of much more limited ammo reserves. Despite its drawbacks, the LITTLE GEM is still unmistakably a bazooka, delivering the welcome punch of attack and impact that you seek from this category.

DF-BA-06 XUAN-GE

- **PART INFO** Bazooka developed by Dafeng Core Industry. Rounds explode on contact, guaranteeing heavy impact damage without ricocheting. With more rounds than most competing models, Dafeng bazookas deliver on sustained firepower.

- **UNLOCK CONDITION (RIGHT/LEFT ARM)** Parts Shop Update 1: Complete either "Destroy Artillery Installations" or "Grid 135 Cleanup"

- **PART SPECS**　　€ 70,000

Attack Power	895	Total Rounds	78
Impact	980	Reload Time	3.4
Accumulative Impact	765	Ammunition Cost	450
Blast Radius	15	Weight	5480
Direct Hit Adjustment	185	EN Load	240
Recoil	90	Interrupts Assault Boost	Yes
Effective Range	740	Assault Boost Impact Bonus	No

MAJESTIC

- **PART INFO** Medium-sized bazooka developed by Melinite. Known for their attention to detail, even down to the composition of the explosive charges, Melinite's engineers designed this weapon for efficiency and ease of use from the ground up.

- **UNLOCK CONDITION (RIGHT/LEFT ARM)** Parts Shop Update 5: Complete "Ocean Crossing"

- **PART SPECS**　　€ 121,000

Attack Power	1109	Total Rounds	52
Impact	1090	Reload Time	4.2
Accumulative Impact	850	Ammunition Cost	600
Blast Radius	15	Weight	4660
Direct Hit Adjustment	190	EN Load	178
Recoil	85	Interrupts Assault Boost	Yes
Effective Range	800	Assault Boost Impact Bonus	No

LITTLE GEM

- **PART INFO** Compact bazooka developed by Melinite. Designed for lightweight builds and indoor engagements. Compromises have been made on the number and precision of rounds, but it amply retains Melinite's trademark explosive power.

- **UNLOCK CONDITION (RIGHT/LEFT ARM)** Parts Shop Update 6: Complete "Destroy the Ice Worm"

- **PART SPECS**　　€ 163,000

Attack Power	819	Total Rounds	36
Impact	910	Reload Time	4.4
Accumulative Impact	670	Ammunition Cost	450
Blast Radius	15	Weight	3100
Direct Hit Adjustment	180	EN Load	192
Recoil	80	Interrupts Assault Boost	Yes
Effective Range	690	Assault Boost Impact Bonus	No

DETONATING BAZOOKA

The **44-141 JVLN ALPHA** delivers explosive shells that create a rippling chain of explosions. This detonating bazooka makes its mark in two areas: impact, and direct hit damage. Colossal impact is inflicted immediately, with a great chunk of accumulative impact lingering afterward, and its high direct hit adjustment modifier makes it an amazing choice during stagger. It's best paired with options that are geared toward building impact—shotguns, missiles, or Boost Kicks—to unleash a shell from the JVLN ALPHA when the moment is right. High reload times and low ammunition count can make it difficult to use as your main weapon in longer sorties, but it's possible if you pick your shots carefully.

44-141 JVLN ALPHA

- **PART INFO** Special bazooka developed by ALLMIND. Creates a chain of explosions on contact that layer on impact damage. Compared to standard explosive weapons, this weapon has notably high direct hit damage.

- **UNLOCK CONDITION (RIGHT/LEFT ARM)** Reward/Parts Shop: Hunter Class 2

- **PART SPECS**　　€ 210,000

Attack Power	1075	Total Rounds	44
Impact	1390	Reload Time	4.3
Accumulative Impact	905	Ammunition Cost	750
Blast Radius	15	Weight	7420
Direct Hit Adjustment	220	EN Load	299
Recoil	80	Interrupts Assault Boost	Yes
Effective Range	760	Assault Boost Impact Bonus	No

GRENADE LAUNCHER

This category of explosives is all about blast radius; even grenades that miss their target create a wide area of effect, all but guaranteeing at least some damage. Strategic use on groups and cornered opponents is recommended, and fans of tetrapod legs will likely find this weapon category one of the most effective for their build. Grenade launchers have noticeably more recoil than bazookas, making arms with high recoil control an important choice. The range on most models is also much more limited, with grenades automatically detonating in mid-air after reaching the end of their effective range.

The **DF-GR-07 GOU-CHEN** is an excellent well-rounded grenade launcher, offering respectable direct hit damage and blast radius against balanced reload time and recoil. The splash damage from two rounds will bring most opponents to stagger, or very close to it. **DIZZY**, meanwhile, sports higher damage, impact, and blast radius, but with the added downsides of dramatically shorter range and a significantly longer reload time. The ability to effectively fill the reload time gap is even more critical when using the DIZZY, but its significantly wider blast radius can make it worth the risk. Be aware, however, of this weapon's dizzying weight and EN load burdens. **IRIDIUM** offers a compact grenade launcher option for lighter builds; both weight and EN load are significantly lower, and even the recoil and reload times are the best in the category. Though still capable of delivering a potent payload, IRIDIUM's blast radius and effective range are the lowest in the category. As expected of the load-conscious model, its attack and impact stats are the lowest of all grenade launchers. Used with the appropriate build, however, that won't matter; ACS strain still builds quickly with a point-blank shot.

All bazooka shells feature a 15m blast radius, allowing them to blow away tightly clustered groups of enemies.

The MA-T-222 KYORAI is great for bullying enemy ACs from medium range, as they'll likely circle into the flames while you stand unaffected.

The DIZZY's incredible blast radius is especially efficient when paired with the tetrapod's aerial supremacy.

DF-GR-07 GOU-CHEN

■ PART INFO Grenade launcher developed by Dafeng Core Industry. Grenades create sphere-shaped explosions centered on the point of impact, allowing each shot to deal significant damage to multiple targets in a wide area.

■ UNLOCK CONDITION (RIGHT/LEFT ARM) Parts Shop/Reward: Complete "Intermediate Support 3: Tetrapod ACs"

■ PART SPECS		€ 140,000	
Attack Power	1450	Total Rounds	40
Impact	1197	Reload Time	5.9
Accumulative Impact	906	Ammunition Cost	1200
Blast Radius	70	Weight	5460
Direct Hit Adjustment	140	EN Load	385
Recoil	100	Interrupts Assault Boost	Yes
Effective Range	625	Assault Boost Impact Bonus	No

DIZZY

■ PART INFO Heavy grenade launcher developed by Melinite. A handheld weapon painstakingly designed—from the composition of its explosive charges to the specifications of its barrel—to maximize firepower. Greatest blast radius in its class.

■ UNLOCK CONDITION (RIGHT/LEFT ARM) Parts Shop Update 7: Complete "Escape"

■ PART SPECS		€ 260,000	
Attack Power	1650	Total Rounds	38
Impact	1278	Reload Time	7.1
Accumulative Impact	1003	Ammunition Cost	1500
Blast Radius	90	Weight	6420
Direct Hit Adjustment	145	EN Load	455
Recoil	100	Interrupts Assault Boost	Yes
Effective Range	285	Assault Boost Impact Bonus	No

IRIDIUM

■ PART INFO Compact grenade launcher developed by Melinite. Defies conventional wisdom that lightweight craft are forced to rely on repeated weak attacks. Limited number of rounds, but its blast radius and power are nothing to sneer at.

■ UNLOCK CONDITION (RIGHT/LEFT ARM) Parts Shop Update 4: Complete "Attack the Watchpoint"

■ PART SPECS		€ 214,000	
Attack Power	1090	Total Rounds	32
Impact	991	Reload Time	4.5
Accumulative Impact	845	Ammunition Cost	800
Blast Radius	60	Weight	2020
Direct Hit Adjustment	140	EN Load	290
Recoil	88	Interrupts Assault Boost	Yes
Effective Range	245	Assault Boost Impact Bonus	No

NAPALM BOMB LAUNCHER

The **MA-T-222 KYORAI** lobs three incendiary rounds, covering the immediate area in fire. With its modest weight and extremely low EN load, this weapon is easily slotted into most builds to cripple tougher opponents with ACS anomaly, making them much easier to stagger by receiving 50% extra impact for the next five seconds. Your own flames cannot harm you, but enemies will suffer 100 heat buildup for each round that hits, with an additional 50 each time the flames deal damage. The KYORAI's normal shots release three rounds along the same angle, leading to a vertical column of flames; if you charge the shot, these rounds will split apart, allowing you to cover a wider horizontal area. With its wide and continuous radius, tetrapod users will find great utility from the KYORAI's napalm; circling the enemy while airborne makes it easier to bait them into your flames. Be aware that this weapon is almost entirely useless against aerial opponents, since enemies that never make contact with the flames below won't take damage from them.

MA-T-222 KYORAI

■ PART INFO Napalm bomb launcher developed by BAWS. Launches ultra-hot incendiary rounds that scorch the area around the point of impact, limiting the maneuverability of ground-based enemies.

■ UNLOCK CONDITION (RIGHT/LEFT ARM) Parts Shop Update 4: Complete "Attack the Watchpoint"

■ PART SPECS		€ 91,000	
Attack Power	366×3	Total Rounds	63
Impact	149×3	Reload Time	2.3
Accumulative Impact	80×3	Ammunition Cost	200
Blast Radius	20	Weight	2890
Direct Hit Adjustment	170	EN Load	60
Recoil	50	Interrupts Assault Boost	No
Charge Time	0.8	Assault Boost Impact Bonus	Yes

JAMMING BOMB LAUNCHER

The **MA-T-223 KYORIKU**'s jamming rounds cause an effect known as camera disruption; a temporary state preventing lock-on of any targeting system passing through the jamming particle cloud—be it yours or the enemy's. The lifespan of a jamming particle cloud is approximately eight seconds, and can affect the guidance of missiles and other projectiles. Charging the launcher discharges the round directly in front of you, making it strategically useful in temporarily mitigating ranged fire. The combined reload and charge times fall just short of the eight-second duration of a jamming round chaff cloud, meaning that you can stack the effect almost indefinitely—or at least long enough to prepare your next move. You may find it more productive to incorporate weaponry that works well with manual aiming, so that you effectively fire at your target while their systems are debilitated.

MA-T-223 KYORIKU

■ PART INFO Jamming round launcher developed by BAWS. Craft caught in the blast will suffer from compromised lock-on capabilities. However, exploiting this trick calls for considerable tactical finesse.

■ UNLOCK CONDITION (RIGHT/LEFT ARM) Parts Shop Update 6: Complete "Destroy the Ice Worm"

■ PART SPECS		€ 103,000	
Attack Power	0	Total Rounds	40
Impact	45	Reload Time	5.5
Accumulative Impact	4	Ammunition Cost	100
Blast Radius	60	Weight	2600
Direct Hit Adjustment	100	EN Load	52
Recoil	40	Interrupts Assault Boost	No
Charge Time	0.8	Assault Boost Impact Bonus	No

The MA-T-223 KYORIKU excels at disrupting the accuracy of sniper rounds fired by GHOST units.

STUN BOMB LAUNCHER

The **WS-1200 THERAPIST** fires three rounds that explode into an electrified field upon impact, embedding shards into enemies that deal little damage but deliver 55 shock buildup with each hit to quickly trigger electrical discharges. Outside of its regular arcing shots effective at longer ranges, the THERAPIST can also be charged to fire its three rounds sideways, enabling a wider area of effect, making it similar in usage to the MA-T-222 KYORAI. Charged shots must be used at close range, however, because they do not travel far before detonating. Unlike the VP-66EG, the THERAPIST only gets three rounds off before reload kicks in, and since you have to be close, there's a high emphasis on shot placement and timing with this weapon since every miss can prove costly. Due to its decreased rate of fire, it's recommended you slot it into a support role to build up damage over time, with more powerful weapons as your primary damage source. Minimal damage and impact make this launcher ineffective against enemies with high shock resistance; the longer it takes to trigger electrical discharges, the better other options will be.

WS-1200 THERAPIST

■ PART INFO Stun round launcher developed by RaD. Fires special projectiles that scatter electrified metallic shards, the effects of which build up to induce a forced electrical discharge in the afflicted craft.

■ UNLOCK CONDITION (RIGHT/LEFT ARM) Parts Shop Update 5: Complete "Ocean Crossing"

■ PART SPECS		€ 138,000	
Attack Power	92×3	Total Rounds	57
Impact	107×3	Reload Time	2.8
Accumulative Impact	46×3	Ammunition Cost	150
Blast Radius	20	Weight	3180
Direct Hit Adjustment	130	EN Load	82
Recoil	40	Interrupts Assault Boost	No
Charge Time	0.8	Assault Boost Impact Bonus	No

FLAMETHROWER

The **HB-0000 BAD COOK** unleashes a sustained stream of searing flames that cause severe AP loss per second to anything caught in their path. Prolonged contact with flames inflicts 30 heat buildup per hit, which amounts to roughly 250 heat buildup per second. Effective use of the BAD COOK means weakening an enemy with ACS anomaly before comboing into a high-impact strike, preferably with a back weapon so that you can continue burning them. BAD COOK has deceptive range and remains effective at medium range, so you don't have to get right next to the target to drench them in flames. However, the closer you are, the more difficult it will be for agile opponents to move out of the flames, especially if you use this flamethrower as an ambush weapon by storing it in a weapon bay and swapping to it at the right moment.

WB-0000 BAD COOK

■ PART INFO Flamethrower developed by RaD. A weaponized form of a tool used to melt down scrap at ultra-high temperatures. Continued use at point-blank range is enough to outstrip an AC's antithermal defenses.

■ UNLOCK CONDITION (RIGHT/LEFT ARM) Part Container: "Eliminate 'Honest' Brute"/Parts Shop

■ PART SPECS		€ 49,000	
Attack Power	85	Total Rounds	1200
Impact	3	Cooling	250
Accumulative Impact	1	Ammunition Cost	40
ATK Heat Buildup	15	Weight	6210
Direct Hit Adjustment	115	EN Load	403
Recoil	10	Interrupts Assault Boost	No
Effective Range	200	Assault Boost Impact Bonus	No
Rapid Fire	8.4		

LASER RIFLE

In similar fashion to linear rifles, laser rifles fire long-range shots that can be charged for extra power. Compared to kinetic weapons, energy weapons like laser rifles lack the raw impact for ACS strain, and lean toward reliable damage. The **VP-66LR** is light, has a moderate EN Load, and is optimized for close-to-medium range engagements, firing a single beam at a time. It can fire almost two shots per second in quick succession, complemented by a large total round count. It's far and away the weakest of the laser rifles, but its charged shot deals over four times the damage while consuming only three rounds, helping offset the VP-66LR's lack of power.

The **VE-66LRA** hits harder from longer ranges, ideal for sniping targets but suffering from an increase in heat generated and overall weight burden. While this weapon can be fired six times before needing to cool down, the moderate ammo count and high cooling time means it shouldn't be fired rapidly. It features an extremely high effective range, however, and shines when you need powerful, precise shots. The **VE-66LRB** offers a power increase over the VE-66LRA, which it accomplishes by firing two tightly-packed energy beams at once. It doubles down on all of the VE-66LRA's strengths, but also its weaknesses. It can only fire four regular shots or a single charged shot before overheating, and suffers from an extremely lengthy cooling period.

VP-66LR

■ PART INFO Laser rifle developed by Arquebus. One of the most commonly-used laser weapons on the battlefield, this is a flagship product for the corporation. Can be charged to amplify its power.

■ UNLOCK CONDITION (RIGHT/LEFT ARM) Parts Shop Update 2: Complete both "Destroy the Weaponized Mining Ship" and "Attack the Dam Complex"

■ PART SPECS		€ 98,000	
Attack Power	256	Rapid Fire	1.7
Impact	105	Chg. EN Load	538
Accumulative Impact	46	Charge Time	1.6
ATK Heat Buildup	160	Chg. Ammo Consumption	3
Chg. Attack Power	1222	Total Rounds	280
Chg. Impact	500	Cooling	413
Chg. Accum. Impact	180	Ammunition Cost	150
Chg. Heat Buildup	660	Weight	3560
Direct Hit Adjustment	140	EN Load	480
Recoil	18	Interrupts Assault Boost	Chg. Atk
Ideal Range	200	Assault Boost Impact Bonus	Yes
Effective Range	263		

VE-66LRA
 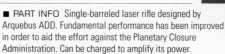

■ PART INFO Single-barreled laser rifle designed by Arquebus ADD. Fundamental performance has been improved in order to aid the effort against the Planetary Closure Administration. Can be charged to amplify its power.

■ UNLOCK CONDITION (RIGHT/LEFT ARM) Parts Shop Update 6: Complete "Destroy the Ice Worm"

■ PART SPECS		€ 180,000	
Attack Power	466	Rapid Fire	1.1
Impact	194	Chg. EN Load	628
Accumulative Impact	81	Charge Time	2.8
ATK Heat Buildup	180	Chg. Ammo Consumption	3
Chg. Attack Power	1677	Total Rounds	90
Chg. Impact	535	Cooling	335
Chg. Accum. Impact	230	Ammunition Cost	250
Chg. Heat Buildup	730	Weight	4940
Direct Hit Adjustment	140	EN Load	532
Recoil	30	Interrupts Assault Boost	Chg. Atk
Ideal Range	220	Assault Boost Impact Bonus	Yes
Effective Range	382		

VE-66LRB

■ PART INFO Double-barreled laser rifle designed by Arquebus ADD. This is a power-hungry, high-performance variant that features two barrels in a vertical juxtaposition. Can be charged to amplify its power.

■ UNLOCK CONDITION (RIGHT/LEFT ARM) Parts Shop Update 7: Complete "Escape"

■ PART SPECS   € 235,000

Attack Power	778	Rapid Fire	0.7
Impact	288	Chg. EN Load	737
Accumulative Impact	134	Charge Time	2.3
ATK Heat Buildup	280	Chg. Ammo Consumption	3
Chg. Attack Power	2352	Total Rounds	108
Chg. Impact	690	Cooling	246
Chg. Accum. Impact	330	Ammunition Cost	400
Chg. Heat Buildup	1000	Weight	7760
Direct Hit Adjustment	145	EN Load	604
Recoil	20	Interrupts Assault Boost	Chg. Atk
Ideal Range	206	Assault Boost Impact Bonus	Yes
Effective Range	324		

VP-66LS

■ PART INFO Laser shotgun developed by Arquebus. True to style, this weapon remains reliable at medium range. Charge to concentrate the laser, producing an energy explosion.

■ UNLOCK CONDITION (RIGHT/LEFT ARM) Parts Shop Update 4: Complete "Attack the Watchpoint"

■ PART SPECS   € 105,000

Attack Power	560	Effective Range	259
Impact	304	Rapid Fire	0.8
Accumulative Impact	88	Chg. EN Load	582
ATK Heat Buildup	190	Charge Time	0.9
Chg. Attack Power	1307	Chg. Ammo Consumption	4
Chg. Impact	950	Total Rounds	60
Chg. Accum. Impact	460	Cooling	203
Chg. Blast Radius	45	Ammunition Cost	300
Chg. Heat Buildup	650	Weight	3540
Direct Hit Adjustment	145	EN Load	510
Recoil	20	Interrupts Assault Boost	Chg. Atk
Ideal Range	130	Assault Boost Impact Bonus	Yes

LASER SHOTGUN

Laser shotguns are exactly what their names suggest: laser weapons that fire a small cluster of energy beams in a single shot. Energy shotguns generally lack the stopping power and direct hit adjustment of their kinetic counterparts. However, due to the nature of energy weapons, they can fire multiple times without needing to reload after each shot. The **WUERGER/66E** has a substantial spread, and most shots will miss at medium-to-long range. It's capable of firing six shots before needing to cool, but the low cooling means you'll be waiting for a lengthy period once it overheats, so you'll need to plan your offense around that. The WUERGER/66E has a unique charged attack, producing an 85m energy spike at the end of the shotgun that effectively gives it a powerful melee attack. Pair it with a melee weapon, and charge the WUERGER while you attack with your left hand, following-up with a quick, powerful punch with your right hand.

The **VP-66LS** has a much tighter spread than the WUERGER/66E, and rather than firing in a square, the VP-66LS fires eight beams in a rhombus. It lacks the width to catch enemies, but is far more reliable when used at medium range. In comparison to the WUERGER/66E, the VP-66LS trades slightly higher attack power for lower impact and accumulative impact. The VP-66LS can still get six shots off before overheating, but takes longer to cool down and fires slower. The VP-66LS's charged attack is a large, explosive energy beam, functioning similarly to a plasma attack. Once the beam makes contact with an enemy, it causes a large explosion, giving this weapon a lot of mix-up potential, especially when fired from above.

WUERGER/66E

■ PART INFO Laser shotgun developed by Schneider. Dominates at close range with diffuse laser beams. Charge the weapon to concentrate the beams and produce a thrusting "spike" of energy.

■ UNLOCK CONDITION (RIGHT/LEFT ARM) Parts Shop Update 6: Complete "Destroy the Ice Worm"

■ PART SPECS   € 147,000

Attack Power	504	Rapid Fire	1.1
Impact	405	Chg. EN Load	484
Accumulative Impact	144	Charge Time	0.6
ATK Heat Buildup	180	Chg. Ammo Consumption	3
Chg. Attack Power	1459	Total Rounds	66
Chg. Impact	950	Cooling	244
Chg. Accum. Impact	360	Ammunition Cost	200
Chg. Heat Buildup	1000	Weight	2880
Direct Hit Adjustment	145	EN Load	440
Recoil	20	Interrupts Assault Boost	Chg. Atk
Ideal Range	130	Assault Boost Impact Bonus	Yes
Effective Range	235		

LASER HANDGUN

The laser handgun is a miniaturized laser rifle, and in almost every facet, operates like a weakened VE-66LRA laser rifle, making it more of a complementary weapon. This is a sidearm, and while it can struggle to carry an assembly on its own, it makes a great companion to many weapons in a Double Trigger loadout, especially another laser handgun, giving your AC extremely high attack speed.

The **VP-66LH** has one of the highest rates of fire among the energy weapons, trailing only pulse guns. Combined with its high ammo count and the fact that you can get 12 shots off before it overheats, this gun can pack a punch. When charged, the VP-66LH rapid-fires six full power shots in the span of about 1 second without additional ammo cost or overheating the weapon, making it a very reliable option. As this laser handgun retains the respectable direct hit adjustment of other laser weapons, it can deal surprisingly solid damage when paired with a weapon that deals high impact. It won't beat the VE-66LRB or VE-66LRA in this regard, but with its light weight and low EN load, the VP-66LH can still find its place in plenty of assemblies.

VP-66LH

■ PART INFO Laser handgun developed by Arquebus. Essentially a miniaturized laser rifle, this energy weapon offers unparalleled ease of use. Fires in bursts when charged.

■ UNLOCK CONDITION (RIGHT/LEFT ARM) Reward/Parts Shop: Complete "Intermediate Support 2: Reverse-Jointed ACs"

■ PART SPECS   € 92,000

Attack Power	175	Effective Range	247
Impact	95	Rapid Fire	2.5
Accumulative Impact	39	Chg. EN Load	435
ATK Heat Buildup	90	Charge Time	1.2
Chg. Attack Power	175×6	Total Rounds	380
Chg. Impact	95×6	Cooling	315
Chg. Accum. Impact	39×6	Ammunition Cost	80
Chg. Heat Buildup	90	Weight	2800
Direct Hit Adjustment	140	EN Load	395
Recoil	17	Interrupts Assault Boost	Chg. Atk
Ideal Range	190	Assault Boost Impact Bonus	Yes

PLASMA RIFLE

When a plasma rifle round connects with an object, it explodes into a plasma sphere that deals continuous damage for as long as it persists. In conjunction with the fact that plasma shots don't ricochet, these properties make plasma weapons similar to explosives. The **Vvc-760PR** strikes seven times after the initial hit, and as a plasma weapon's attack power and impact values correspond to a sum of all hits, its high attack power won't be reflected if a target escapes the plasma explosion. Thanks to its generous 30m explosion radius, however, the likelihood of something escaping unscathed is low, especially if you fire from above. Its charged shot fires three powered-up plasma beams that spread out the further they travel, with each causing their own plasma explosion with a 60m radius, though overlapping beams don't cause additional damage

Compared to the Vvc-760PR, the **IA-C01W1: NEBULA** is a slightly lighter weapon, designed for sustained fire. It has lower attack and impact, a smaller blast radius, and only hits for a total of six times per round rather than eight. Lower power comes with lower heat buildup, which allows the IA-C01W1: NEBULA to fire six shots before overheating. Additionally, it has over twice the rate of fire, giving the rifle much greater damage potential than the Vvc-760PR. The caveat being that the IA-C01W1: NEBULA only comes with 58 rounds, which won't last during long missions. It's with its charged shot that the rifle truly shines, however, creating a powerful plasma blast with a radius of 70m and can be fired repeatedly.

VVC-760PR

■ PART INFO Plasma rifle developed by VCPL. Plasma explosions create a damage-inflicting area that remains active for a brief period of time. Charging the weapon causes the plasma fire to scatter, producing multiple explosions.

■ UNLOCK CONDITION (RIGHT/LEFT ARM) Parts Shop Update 2: Complete both "Destroy the Weaponized Mining Ship" and "Attack the Dam Complex"

■ PART SPECS		€ 202,000	
Attack Power	936	Effective Range	430
Impact	384	Rapid Fire	0.7
Accumulative Impact	248	Chg. EN Load	593
Blast Radius	30	Charge Time	1.5
ATK Heat Buildup	300	Chg. Ammo Consumption	3
Chg. Attack Power	1368	Total Rounds	90
Chg. Impact	712	Cooling	254
Chg. Accum. Impact	368	Ammunition Cost	360
Chg. Blast Radius	60	Weight	3330
Chg. Heat Buildup	1000	EN Load	490
Direct Hit Adjustment	125	Interrupts Assault Boost	Chg. Atk
Recoil	15	Assault Boost Impact Bonus	Yes

IA-C01W1: NEBULA

■ PART INFO Plasma rifle developed long ago by the Rubicon Research Institute. Focuses on suppressive potential, prioritizing rapid-fire performance over explosive power. Can be charged to increase output and expand blast radius.

■ UNLOCK CONDITION (RIGHT/LEFT ARM) Part Container: "Tunnel Sabotage"/Parts Shop: Obtain R-Arm Unit Version

■ PART SPECS		€ 185,000	
Attack Power	528	Effective Range	460
Impact	198	Rapid Fire	1.5
Accumulative Impact	132	Chg. EN Load	737
Blast Radius	20	Charge Time	2.7
ATK Heat Buildup	175	Chg. Ammo Consumption	3
Chg. Attack Power	1716	Total Rounds	58
Chg. Impact	840	Cooling	238
Chg. Accum. Impact	432	Ammunition Cost	600
Chg. Blast Radius	70	Weight	3890
Chg. Heat Buildup	625	EN Load	609
Direct Hit Adjustment	125	Interrupts Assault Boost	Chg. Atk
Recoil	15	Assault Boost Impact Bonus	No

CORAL RIFLE

Coral is a unique damage type that bypasses all defenses, and Coral rifles feature an additional benefit of passive PA interference, making them effective against shields and barriers. Their heavy EN load makes them some of the most expensive arms weapons to add to your assembly, but the triple-hit explosive blast radius produced from one shot of the **IA-C01W6: NB-REDSHIFT** is worth the cost of entry—even more so with the damage and impact achieved from a full-charge attack. The REDSHIFT gets off around five shots before it needs to cool, so shots must be taken carefully, but used strategically, it will be the hardest hitter in your loadout.

At first glance, the **IB-C03W1: WLT 011** may seem like a terrible prospect compared to the REDSHIFT with its inferior attack, blast radius, and increased EN load. It makes up for those shortcomings, however, with its unique multi-stage charge attacks. The first state, similar to the REDSHIFT, fires off an attack with comparable characteristics. The WLT 011's second level fires off a massive, swirling energy beam for a three second duration, the impact of which surpasses even explosive weaponry—instantly staggering most foes. Additionally, the beam can be freely moved, cleaving the area ahead of your AC. While Target Assist is lost and firing stance is mandatory—even for tank legs—it's hard to beat the WLT 011's upsides for those up to the task of manually aiming.

IA-C01W6: NB-REDSHIFT

■ PART INFO Experimental weapon developed long ago by the Rubicon Research Institute. Manipulates Coral swarm intelligence using energy to produce chain explosions. Charging the weapon increases the number of these explosions.

■ UNLOCK CONDITION (RIGHT/LEFT ARM) Arena/Parts Shop: Defeat δ-3 Classified Subject

■ PART SPECS		€ 312,000	
Attack Power	765	Effective Range	580
Impact	188	Rapid Fire	0.7
Accumulative Impact	188	Chg. EN Load	808
Blast Radius	24	Charge Time	1.7
ATK Heat Buildup	280	Chg. Ammo Consumption	2
Chg. Attack Power	1718	Total Rounds	52
Chg. Impact	936	Cooling	186
Chg. Accum. Impact	936	Ammunition Cost	500
Chg. Blast Radius	42	Weight	4040
Chg. Heat Buildup	450	EN Load	667
Direct Hit Adjustment	190	Interrupts Assault Boost	Chg. Atk
PA Interference	122	Assault Boost Impact Bonus	No
Recoil	15		

IB-C03W1: WLT 011

■ PART INFO Prototype Coral beam weapon developed long ago by the the Rubicon Research Institute. Manipulates Coral swarm intelligence using energy to adjust shape/directionality of beam. Two-stage charge allows for fine-tuned control.

■ UNLOCK CONDITION (RIGHT/LEFT ARM) Arena/Parts Shop: Defeat δ-2 Subject 51-201 W

■ PART SPECS		€ 335,000	
Attack Power	405	Effective Range	940
Impact	152	Rapid Fire	1.1
Accumulative Impact	152	Chg. EN Load	1020
Blast Radius	7	Full Chg. Time	4.3
ATK Heat Buildup	200	Full Chg. Ammo Consumption	12
Full Chg. Attack Power	2835	Total Rounds	180
Full Chg. Impact	4050	Cooling	180
Full Chg. Accum. Impact	4050	Ammunition Cost	400
Full Chg. Heat Buildup	1000	Weight	9030
Direct Hit Adjustment	190	EN Load	850
PA Interference	120	Interrupts Assault Boost	Chg. Atk
Recoil	15	Assault Boost Impact Bonus	Yes

MULTI ENERGY RIFLE

Another weapon with a two-step charge, the multi energy rifle can fire plasma blasts, focus its energy into a more powerful laser attack, or combine both into a devastating amplified energy beam. The **44-142 KRSV**'s default fire is similar to a plasma rifle, albeit slightly weaker. To make up for this, it has an incredible rate of fire, which keeps it competitive with plasma rifles in damage per second. Due to the KRSV's total round count of 80, and a smaller blast radius than either plasma rifle, this is not the most efficient way to use this weapon. Any laser rifle's charged attack will outpace the KRSV's initial charge in damage, but it charges quickly enough to remain comparable, and can be used multiple times before overheating. The second charge state is a hyper-powered plasma explosion. Like Coral rifles, the initial hit will deal the bulk of the damage, with another three consecutive hits dealing additional damage. The second stage has a considerable charge time, and each shot consumes an eight of your weapon's total rounds. Should you attempt to use its second stage shot, it deals nearly unrivaled impact and damage for an energy weapon.

44-142 KRSV

- **PART INFO** Multi energy rifle developed by ALLMIND. Capable of laser, plasma, or combined fire, this weapon is equipped with a two-stage charge system that provides a choice of firing modes.

- **UNLOCK CONDITION (RIGHT/LEFT ARM)** Reward/Parts Shop: Hunter Class 12

PART SPECS — € 377,000

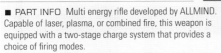

Attack Power	312	Effective Range	620
Impact	112	Rapid Fire	3.4
Accumulative Impact	76	Chg. EN Load	955
Blast Radius	20	Full Chg. Time	4.5
ATK Heat Buildup	120	Full Chg. Ammo Consumption	10
Full Chg. Attack Power	2522	Total Rounds	80
Full Chg. Impact	1930	Cooling	167
Full Chg. Accum. Impact	1033	Ammunition Cost	600
Full Chg. Blast Radius	30	Weight	10120
Full Chg. Heat Buildup	1000	EN Load	707
Direct Hit Adjustment	125	Interrupts Assault Boost	Chg. Atk
Recoil	40	Assault Boost Impact Bonus	No

PULSE GUN

Pulse guns are a fully-automatic class of energy weapon, firing pulse blasts almost as fast as gatling guns. They're primarily used for disrupting pulse shields and armor, rapidly building ACS strain on any enemy attempting to deploy pulse defenses. When up against such an enemy, it's best to pair a pulse gun with a weapon with high direct hit adjustment, though pulse guns can deal surprising damage when two are used in a Double Trigger configuration. Sustained fire will inflict extreme PA interference, along with proportional heat buildup; the **HI-16: GU-Q1** can only sustain fire for less than 1.5 seconds before reaching its heat threshold. While it has a moderate cooling period that won't drastically impact combat, it's still a good idea to feather the trigger to avoid overheating.

Compared to the HI-16: GU-Q1, the **HI-18: GU-A2** is a solid weapon for dealing with small-to-medium enemies. The extra area covered by each pulse blast, and its longer effective range, means that this is ultimately a more accurate pulse gun, and can be used from further away, or against more evasive enemies. The HI-18: GU-A2 also deals greater PA Interference, making it better for disrupting pulse shields and barriers. All-around, the HI-18: GU-A2 outshines the HI-16: GU-Q1; though do note its increased cooling period.

HI-16: GU-Q1

- **PART INFO** Rapid-fire pulse gun developed by Takigawa Harmonics. Destroys targets with sustained high-frequency oscillation, making it especially suited for canceling out pulse defenses, which use the same technology.

- **UNLOCK CONDITION (RIGHT/LEFT ARM)** Parts Shop Update 3: Complete "Operation Wallclimber"

PART SPECS — € 90,000

Attack Power	36	Rapid Fire	20.0
Impact	11	Total Rounds	560
Accumulative Impact	6	Cooling	623
ATK Heat Buildup	35	Ammunition Cost	30
Direct Hit Adjustment	140	Weight	2110
PA Interference	527	EN Load	368
Recoil	5	Interrupts Assault Boost	No
Effective Range	250	Assault Boost Impact Bonus	Yes

HI-18: GU-A2

- **PART INFO** Spread pulse gun developed by Takigawa Harmonics. This weapon features a larger oscillator to further improve firepower and effective range, as well as enhance its ability to cancel out pulse defenses.

- **UNLOCK CONDITION (RIGHT/LEFT ARM)** Parts Shop Update 5: Complete "Ocean Crossing"

PART SPECS — € 159,000

Attack Power	68	Rapid Fire	10.0
Impact	24	Total Rounds	380
Accumulative Impact	12	Cooling	295
ATK Heat Buildup	55	Ammunition Cost	60
Direct Hit Adjustment	150	Weight	2650
PA Interference	537	EN Load	446
Recoil	5	Interrupts Assault Boost	No
Effective Range	310	Assault Boost Impact Bonus	Yes

MISSILE LAUNCHER

Missile launchers offer an excellent way to strain the ACS of single targets, or eliminate entire groups of weaker enemies in a single salvo. Each **HML-G2/P19M-LT-04** has the capacity of shooting four missiles at a time, making them especially dangerous when equipped on both arm units. The maximum amount of targets they can lock onto is four, but it's worth noting that you're unable to only fire off a single missile, and instead will be emitting all four missiles simultaneously. While this isn't necessarily a bad thing, it does mean that you're only able to fire it 45 times

Like bazookas and grenade launchers, the VVc-760PR plasma rifle is often best fired from above to benefit from its blast radius.

HI-18: GU-A2 pulse guns eat through the pulse shielding of bosses such as BALTEUS. They can even be paired with pulse cannons to stack the effect.

HML-G2/P19MLT-04 missile launchers are a great foundation for full-missile builds—a fun and effective way to deal explosive damage from afar.

before you run out of ammunition. Though these missiles release faster than a lot of other explosive weaponry, they'll still struggle with incredibly mobile targets. Handheld missile launchers may not be ideally suited against the most agile opponents, but they remain an excellent choice against everything else.

HML-G2/P19MLT-04

■ PART INFO Handheld multi-missile launcher developed by Furlong Dynamics. A masterpiece of Furlong's second-gen lineup, this weapon is capable of multi-locking up to four targets.

■ UNLOCK CONDITION (RIGHT/LEFT ARM) Parts Shop Update 4: Complete "Attack the Watchpoint"

■ PART SPECS		€ 80,000	
Attack Power	216×4	Total Rounds	180
Impact	175×4	Reload Time	3.0
Accumulative Impact	123×4	Ammunition Cost	150
Direct Hit Adjustment	155	Weight	3250
Guidance	180	EN Load	165
Effective Range	2500	Interrupts Assault Boost	No
Homing Lock Time	0.4	Assault Boost Impact Bonus	No
Max. Lock Count	4		

SPLIT MISSILE LAUNCHER

The **HML-G3/P08SPL-06** is an explosive weapon that fires individual missiles with no multi-lock capability, which makes it best suited for single target use. Each missile fired splits into six sub-missiles, and since you carry 38 shots, you can effectively fire up to 228 missiles at a single target. The missiles can reach their target very quickly, but without the multi-lock offered by other hand missiles, this split missile launcher isn't recommended for use against mobile or multiple targets. With that said, it remains highly effective against slower foes like heavy MTs. The HML-G3/P08SPL-06 is heavier compared to other hand missiles, as well as being less efficient with impact and accumulative impact. It does have high attack power on its side, though, which makes it a decent option to use against a target that is already staggered.

HML-G3/P08SPL-06

■ PART INFO Handheld split missile launcher developed by Furlong Dynamics. An ambitious entry in Furlong's third-gen lineup, this weapon improves accuracy with missile payloads that split as they approach their target.

■ UNLOCK CONDITION (RIGHT/LEFT ARM) Parts Shop Update 7: Complete "Escape"

■ PART SPECS		€ 127,000	
Attack Power	1056	Total Rounds	38
Impact	600	Reload Time	4.0
Accumulative Impact	420	Ammunition Cost	650
Direct Hit Adjustment	145	Weight	4630
Guidance	180	EN Load	180
Effective Range	1425	Interrupts Assault Boost	No
Homing Lock Time	0.6	Assault Boost Impact Bonus	No
Max. Lock Count	1		

SIEGE MISSILE LAUNCHER

The siege missile launcher is an explosive weapon that fires homing missiles that have a delayed homing sequence. The 13 missiles fired from the **WS-5000 APERITIF** will hover in the air before heading off toward their designated target in rapid succession; there is no multi-lock available for this weapon, and only a single enemy can be targeted. Even mobile targets may struggle evading this weapon, as the missiles launch quickly once they begin their homing sequence.

WS-5000 APERITIF

■ PART INFO Handheld siege missile launcher developed by RaD. The missiles linger for a short while after launch before propelling themselves toward the target, allowing the user to effectively surround their target single-handedly.

■ UNLOCK CONDITION (RIGHT/LEFT ARM) Parts Shop Update 8: Complete "Ocean Crossing" in NG+

■ PART SPECS		€ 168,000	
Attack Power	78×13	Total Rounds	338
Impact	78×13	Reload Time	6.5
Accumulative Impact	47×13	Ammunition Cost	70
Direct Hit Adjustment	155	Weight	4600
Guidance	180	EN Load	165
Effective Range	1200	Interrupts Assault Boost	No
Homing Lock Time	0.5	Assault Boost Impact Bonus	No
Max. Lock Count	1		

L-ARM UNIT

The parts listed here can only be installed on your AC's left arm. All of them are melee weapons, with the technical exception of the explosive thrower.

PILE BUNKER

The PB-033M ASHMEAD pile bunker aims to deconstruct opposing forces with a direct blow of its massive steel pile. Attacks with the pile bunker thrust the AC forward to meet the enemy with a swift, frontal attack, and with some of the best attack and impact values in the melee category, the ASHMEAD deals incredible damage and ACS strain to anything unfortunate enough to be in its direct path. Charge attacks with this weapon are some of the most potent in the entire game. There is a catch, however, as these attacks only activate after a brief wind-up period. Using it against an enemy that's already staggered mitigates the risk from the wind-up period, but keep in mind that it has limited range so you'll want to pair the pile bunker with a booster that has a high Melee Attack Thrust spec.

PB-033M ASHMEAD

■ PART INFO Pile bunker developed by Balam. This weapon gores the target with a massive steel pile, obliterating it through sheer physical force. Charge to prime the firing hammer, enabling attacks that are enhanced by explosive damage.

■ UNLOCK CONDITION (LEFT ARM) Parts Shop Update 4: Complete "Attack the Watchpoint"

■ PART SPECS		€ 185,000	
Attack Power	1688	Direct Hit Adjustment	150
Impact	1150	PA Interference	135
Accumulative Impact	850	Cooling	284
Consecutive Hits	1	Weight	4180
Chg. Attack Power	4630	EN Load	225
Chg. Impact	1800	Interrupts Assault Boost	Yes
Chg. Accum. Impact	1100		

EXPLOSIVE THROWER

Scattering a sprinkling of miniature explosives to decimate the immediate area, the **DF-ET-09 TAI-YANG-SHOU** explosive thrower is a unique fusion of melee and ranged weaponry. The default swing produces a horizontal sweep that deals equal damage and impact to anything in the contact radius, and by charging the attack, it's even possible to release explosives in a rising diagonal pattern capable of hitting elevated targets.

While the explosive thrower is still best used from close range, there's a bit more room for error thanks to its effective range—which extends as far as 125 meters before you risk missing your attack. Unlike most melee weapons, it's slightly limited by its total round count, and should be used sparingly in longer missions. Being one of the few melee options with ranged capability, tetrapod users will get good mileage out of the TAIYANG-SHOU while hovering because the standard sweep will paint a 180-degree area below the AC with explosives.

DF-ET-09 TAI-YANG-SHOU

■ PART INFO Explosive launcher developed by Dafeng Core Industry. Scatters a spray of compact explosives to devastate the area ahead of the user. Charge to arrange the spray of projectiles into a vertical spread.

■ UNLOCK CONDITION (LEFT ARM) Parts Shop Update 6: Complete "Destroy the Ice Worm"

■ PART SPECS		€ 215,000	
Attack Power	1142	Direct Hit Adjustment	190
Impact	830	Effective Range	125
Accumulative Impact	650	Total Rounds	48
Blast Radius	20	Reload Time	3.1
Chg. Attack Power	1142	Ammunition Cost	600
Chg. Impact	830	Weight	3790
Chg. Accum. Impact	650	EN Load	160
Chg. Blast Radius	25	Interrupts Assault Boost	Yes

CHAINSAW

With hefty attack values and the best direct hit damage in the game, the **WB-0010 DOUBLE TROUBLE** is capable of rapidly shredding anything caught in its teeth. Its attacks temporarily immobilize the enemy as they're pulled in and scraped by each blade on the chain. Standard swipes hit twice in a row for moderate damage and impact, but charge attacks are where the trouble really starts. Priming the charge attack deals continuous AP damage and impact to anything it touches, and upon release, the target is caught in a continuous cutting cycle that staggers even the burliest opponents. Particularly long cooling times mean that use should be considered carefully, however; using the chainsaw to build impact could mean that it's not ready once you've staggered the enemy. Getting the most damage out of DOUBLE TROUBLE's extended charge attack animation is a must, so pay close attention to your booster's Melee Attack Thrust spec, which influences the speed at which you move when you release the button to engage the enemy.

WB-0010 DOUBLE TROUBLE

■ PART INFO Chainsaw developed by RaD. Originally a tool used by industrial demolition craft, now repurposed as a weapon. Charge to deploy the blades, which can be pushed into a target to rapidly accumulate damage.

■ UNLOCK CONDITION (LEFT ARM) Part Container: Eliminate "Honest" Brute

■ PART SPECS		€ 69,000	
Attack Power	1025	Direct Hit Adjustment	270
Impact	750	PA Interference	119
Accumulative Impact	375	Cooling	302
Consecutive Hits	2	Weight	5090
Chg. Attack Power	2970	EN Load	108
Chg. Impact	2380	Interrupts Assault Boost	Yes
Chg. Accum. Impact	840		

STUN BATON

A shockingly capable melee option, the **VP-67EB** stun baton acts like a melee version of the VP-66EG stun gun—short cooldowns, speedy damage output, and ample buildup of shock throughout the six hits of its regular attack combo. Charging the stun baton unleashes an electrified melee thrust that plants a delayed shock "bomb," which explodes roughly two seconds later into a secondary shock blast for considerable impact and severe shock buildup.

Like other weapons that build shock, this stun baton becomes less useful the more resistant the enemy is to shock. Despite that, the damage is solid, and the cooldowns are brief enough that you may still opt to keep this baton handy if it fits your agile, close-ranged brawler playstyle. The VP-67EB also carries an unexpectedly potent direct hit adjustment rating, making it likely to be the best damage dealer in your loadout against staggered foes. Enemies in ACS overload can remain locked in place and unable to act for the entirety of the lengthy combo animation, while enough shock continues to build up to eventually force an electrical discharge.

VP-67EB

■ PART INFO Stun baton developed by Arquebus. Repeated attacks induce a forced electrical discharge effect on afflicted craft. Charge to expose the core rod of the baton and attack with a brutal electrified thrust.

■ UNLOCK CONDITION (LEFT ARM) Parts Shop Update 5: Complete "Ocean Crossing"

■ PART SPECS		€ 94,000	
Attack Power	229	Direct Hit Adjustment	215
Impact	215	PA Interference	140
Accumulative Impact	85	Cooling	1156
Consecutive Hits	3	Weight	1720
Chg. Attack Power	1461	EN Load	198
Chg. Impact	1360	Interrupts Assault Boost	Yes
Chg. Accum. Impact	590		

LASER DAGGER

The **VP-67LD** laser dagger shares a lot of similarities with the stun baton, but its lower weight and EN load make it adaptable to nearly any build. Its superior cooling times make it even easier to use repeatedly in combat. Three consecutive strikes make up its normal attack, building up decent damage and impact. Its charged attack is a broad horizontal swipe, cleaving the area in front of the AC, and is capable of dealing huge impact if you successfully corner your foe. Its direct hit damage is inferior to the VP-66EG, but employing this dagger as your primary damage source during stagger is still possible. Fast cooldown speeds make it possible to connect up to six standard hits or two charged hits before the direct hit window closes. During stagger, standard hits are recommended against agile opponents, while charged hits are safe to capitalize upon for slower-moving enemies.

VP-67LD

■ PART INFO Laser dagger developed by Arquebus. Designed for close-range combat using lightweight craft, this energy weapon is built to deliver agile slashing attacks. Charge to blitz the area with an instantaneous sweep attack.

■ UNLOCK CONDITION (LEFT ARM) Parts Shop Update 7: Complete "Escape"

■ PART SPECS		€ 135,000	
Attack Power	752	Direct Hit Adjustment	175
Impact	310	PA Interference	118
Accumulative Impact	120	Cooling	1308
Consecutive Hits	3	Weight	1350
Chg. Attack Power	1688	EN Load	150
Chg. Impact	1100	Interrupts Assault Boost	Yes
Chg. Accum. Impact	375		

LASER BLADE

The **Vvc-770LB** laser blade offers a slower but more powerful energy-based melee option, delivering a single crescent slash with a wide horizontal arc. Charge attacks reveal a three-pronged blade that sweeps twice in a circular motion for even greater damage and impact, covering a large enough radius to reach distant targets or instantly demolish squads of weaker foes.

Compared to the VP-67 laser dagger, the Vvc-770LB 's cooldown periods are naturally much longer, though this laser blade makes up for it in markedly improved damage and impact output, delivered within the same time frame. With its direct hit adjustment value, it does well enough against staggered opponents, but you may find its best use in building ACS strain—especially with charged strikes. If you have another weapon in your loadout with superior direct hit modifiers, put the Vvc-770LB on stagger duty while your off-hand weapon takes care of the rest.

VVC-770LB

■ PART INFO Laser blade developed by VCPL. Stable laser control enables powerful, energy-based slashing attacks. Charge the weapon to increase laser output, enabling combo attacks that sweep through the surrounding area.

■ UNLOCK CONDITION (LEFT ARM) Parts Shop Update 3: Complete "Operation Wallclimber"

■ PART SPECS		€ 210,000	
Attack Power	1630	Direct Hit Adjustment	195
Impact	1100	PA Interference	127
Accumulative Impact	330	Cooling	317
Consecutive Hits	1	Weight	2680
Chg. Attack Power	1170×2	EN Load	365
Chg. Impact	750×2	Interrupts Assault Boost	Yes
Chg. Accum. Impact	280×2		

LASER SLICER

The **Vvc-774LS** is a dual-bladed rotating energy weapon that unleashes a series of whirling slashes capable of slicing through enemy frames with strong stagger potential. This laser slicer can be charged and used as a spinning shield while advancing forward to deliver a powerful slash. As a bonus, incoming fire during a charge attack can be deflected, minimizing damage and ACS strain.

This is a potent weapon, and its charge attacks can build up as much impact as the Vvc-770LB laser blade. Its direct hit damage is inferior, however, making it a less attractive choice for hitting staggered opponents. Your choice between this and the Vvc-774LS will likely come down to how important you find its defensive bullet deflecting property to be, or possibly its aesthetic in relation to your build's theme.

VVC-774LS

■ PART INFO Laser slicer developed by VCPL. This double-bladed weapon is equipped with a rotation system to carve through targets. Charge to increase rotation speed and advance aggressively while slashing through incoming fire.

■ UNLOCK CONDITION (LEFT ARM) Parts Shop Update 9: Complete "Destroy the Ice Worm" in NG+

■ PART SPECS		€ 339,000	
Attack Power	1615	Direct Hit Adjustment	185
Impact	900	PA Interference	122
Accumulative Impact	225	Cooling	267
Consecutive Hits	2	Weight	3260
Chg. Attack Power	2612	EN Load	328
Chg. Impact	1500	Interrupts Assault Boost	Yes
Chg. Accum. Impact	375		

LASER LANCE

Functioning like an energy-based version of the pile bunker, the **VE-67LLA** laser lance thrusts your AC forwards with its own internal booster to impale the enemy with a piercing attack. Unlike the pile bunker, however, the internal booster covers a lot of ground very quickly, allowing you to initiate it from long range and rapidly close the gap. The charged attacks rev up the internal booster to travel even further and faster than before, allowing it to hit targets up to 200m away. Charged attacks also hit multiple times, dealing enough combined impact to stagger most enemies, or deal massive direct hit damage to one that's already staggered. On paper, the specs for this weapon may seem lackluster compared to other melee weapons, but the range at which you can use it—along with the closing speed and the charge attack's multiple hits—more than make up for any apparent shortcomings.

VE-67LLA

■ PART INFO Laser lance designed by Arquebus ADD. Uses the thrust of its internal booster to launch into energy-based piercing attacks. Booster thrust can be increased by charging the weapon, allowing high-speed, long-distance rushes.

■ UNLOCK CONDITION (LEFT ARM) Parts Shop Update 6: Complete "Destroy the Ice Worm"

■ PART SPECS		€ 270,000	
Attack Power	1151	Direct Hit Adjustment	195
Impact	800	PA Interference	131
Accumulative Impact	400	Cooling	263
Consecutive Hits	1	Weight	4520
Chg. Attack Power	2381	EN Load	460
Chg. Impact	1800	Interrupts Assault Boost	Yes
Chg. Accum. Impact	900		

The 44-143 HMMR plasma thrower deflects incoming fire in the most stylish manner.

PLASMA THROWER

The **44-143 HMMR** plasma thrower is an interesting weapon with unique capabilities, once it starts whipping around. Standard attacks lash the enemy up to twice with consecutive cracks of the whip, each dealing high damage and impact. Like the laser lance, however, the charged attack is where a lot of this weapon's utility stems from. Charging the weapon will spin the plasma whip indefinitely, dealing damage and impact to anything up close, as well as deflecting a portion of incoming fire, making it an effective tool to use while approaching an enemy. Assault Boost is disabled while it's spinning, but you can still fire other weapons while closing the gap. Once you're within range, you can maintain pressure on larger and less agile opponents by circling them with a spinning whip. When you eventually release the button, you'll whip the thrower forward to plant a series of plasma bombs that will damage anything in their horizontal radius, giving you another option to catch enemies, or to create a barrier while you move away.

44-143 HMMR

■ PART INFO Plasma mine launcher developed by ALLMIND. Launches a rotating unit that uses centrifugal force and thrust support to strike targets. Charge the weapon to scatter mines as the weapon swings, causing plasma explosions.

■ UNLOCK CONDITION (LEFT ARM) Reward: Hunter Class 6

■ PART SPECS		€ 172,000	
Attack Power	1381	Direct Hit Adjustment	165
Impact	810	PA Interference	142
Accumulative Impact	520	Effective Range	78
Consecutive Hits	2	Cooling	366
Chg. Attack Power	265×6	Weight	2410
Chg. Impact	33×6	EN Load	311
Chg. Accum. Impact	22×6	Interrupts Assault Boost	Yes
Chg. Blast Radius	20		

PULSE BLADE

Available from the moment you set foot on Rubicon, the **HI-32: BU-TT/A** pulse blade remains a reliable option throughout the game. Standard attacks hit up to two times, dishing out great damage and impact, while effectively breaking down pulse barriers on opponents that wield them. Charged attacks thrust the AC forward for a cleaving swipe, hitting a wider horizontal area more likely to catch foes attempting to make a getaway.

You can assign this blade to almost any role—whether it's to build up to stagger, or exploit it. With their high direct hit damage, pulse blades are strong options during enemy stagger, and their low weight and EN values make them easy to equip on both light and heavyweight builds.

HI-32: BU-TT/A

■ PART INFO Pulse blade developed by Takigawa Harmonics. Delivers slashing attacks with high-frequency oscillation that are ideal for canceling out pulse defenses. Charge to increase output and pound targets with more powerful oscillation.

■ UNLOCK CONDITION (/LEFT ARM) Default

■ PART SPECS   € –

Attack Power	963	Direct Hit Adjustment	230
Impact	710	PA Interference	147
Accumulative Impact	450	Cooling	282
Consecutive Hits	2	Weight	1800
Chg. Attack Power	1586	EN Load	213
Chg. Impact	1200	Interrupts Assault Boost	Yes
Chg. Accu. Impact	650		

LIGHT WAVE BLADE

Slashing forward with high-powered waves of light, the **IA-C01W2: MOONLIGHT** light wave blade takes the concept of the BU-TT/A pulse blade, and adds ranged capability. While weaker in nearly every area, the MOONLIGHT does allow you to strike from rather long distances. Its basic attacks hit twice, while charge attacks hit once in a much wider area—more easily pinning enemies attempting to pull back or away. Holding in place while your enemy expends their own EN reserve can be advantageous; at least one of your attacks is likely to connect, while you get to preserve EN for evasive action afterward. Despite being a melee weapon, light waves discharged have long travel distances: default attacks have a maximum distance of around 300m, while charge attacks move up to 200m.

IA-C01W2: MOONLIGHT

■ PART INFO Light-wave blade developed long ago by the Rubicon Research Institute. Fuses laser and pulse technology to accompany slashing attacks with waves of light. Charge to increase output, emitting larger waves of light.

■ UNLOCK CONDITION (LEFT ARM) Part Container: "Reach the Coral Convergence"

■ PART SPECS   € 270,000

Attack Power	615	Direct Hit Adjustment	175
Impact	495	PA Interference	112
Accumulative Impact	495	Effective Range	280
Consecutive Hits	2	Cooling	209
Chg. Attack Power	2010	Weight	2200
Chg. Impact	910	EN Load	544
Chg. Accu. Impact	910	Interrupts Assault Boost	Yes

CORAL OSCILLATOR

Manipulating Coral to produce supercharged waves of light, the **IA-C01W7: ML-REDSHIFT** is a Coral melee weapon capable of ranged damage, much like the IA-C01W2: MOONLIGHT. Comparatively, the REDSHIFT outputs higher damage and impact with standard attacks, but takes a hit in charge attack stats. Similarly, standard attacks hit up to two times up to a range of 280m, while charge attacks cleave an area 200m ahead horizontally, more likely to hit fleeing foes.

The **IB-C03W2: WLT 101** trades the ranged capabilities of the REDSHIFT and MOONLIGHT for cleaving swipes. Its standard attacks hit once for heavy damage and impact. Charge attacks hit a wide horizontal area in front of your AC, and are particularly potent, nearly maxing out the ACS gauge on ACs with lower attitude stability. While there are superior options for exploiting staggered opponents, its higher direct hit adjustment rating compared to the REDSHIFT and MOONLIGHT make it a viable option. Generally, the WLT 101 is best used to build ACS strain against a cornered opponent—one that has exhausted its EN—but this Coral oscillator is versatile enough to serve many purposes.

IA-C01W7: ML-REDSHIFT

■ PART INFO Experimental weapon developed long ago by the Rubicon Research Institute. Manipulates Coral swarm intelligence using energy to accompany slashing attacks with waves of light. Charge to increase output and produce larger waves.

■ UNLOCK CONDITION (LEFT ARM) Arena: Defeat δ-3 Classified Subject

■ PART SPECS   € 343,000

Attack Power	727	Direct Hit Adjustment	190
Impact	530	PA Interference	126
Accumulative Impact	530	Effective Range	280
Consecutive Hits	2	Cooling	209
Chg. Attack Power	1614	Weight	2200
Chg. Impact	820	EN Load	544
Chg. Accu. Impact	820	Interrupts Assault Boost	Yes

IB-C03W2: WLT 101

■ PART INFO Prototype Coral oscillator developed long ago by the Rubicon Research Institute. Manipulates Coral swarm intelligence using energy to create a blade-like beam. Charge the weapon to perform sweeping area attacks.

■ UNLOCK CONDITION (LEFT ARM) Reward: Hunter Class 15

■ PART SPECS   € 368,000

Attack Power	1350	Direct Hit Adjustment	210
Impact	960	PA Interference	140
Accumulative Impact	960	Cooling	199
Consecutive Hits	1	Weight	2030
Chg. Attack Power	1950	EN Load	642
Chg. Impact	1450	Interrupts Assault Boost	Yes
Chg. Accu. Impact	1450		

Try pairing the IA-C01W2: MOONLIGHT with high impact weapons like the DF-BA-06 XUAN-GE for a combo that baits the opponent to expend their EN before your final attack.

R-BACK UNIT/L-BACK UNIT

These parts feature both a right shoulder and left shoulder version that you'll need to purchase or acquire separately. You can equip two at the same time.

SPREAD BAZOOKA

The spread bazooka is an explosive back unit that launches multiple rockets in a shotgun-like spread. Charges within a cluster drift apart during travel, meaning some damage may be lost in the spread.

The **SB-033M MORLEY** launches off a five charge spread, dealing more damage as more of the charges hit your target. A great option to blast entire groups of enemies such as light MTs and generic weaponry, but the spread distance can be a drawback against mobile ACs unless you stick very close to them. The MORLEY is an excellent choice for stationary boss encounters and catching close-range ACs, as long as you pay mind to its 20 round reserve and slow rate of fire. Bipedal and reverse joint builds are locked into firing stance once you fire.

SB-033M MORLEY

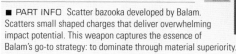

■ PART INFO Scatter bazooka developed by Balam. Scatters small shaped charges that deliver overwhelming impact potential. This weapon captures the essence of Balam's go-to strategy: to dominate through material superiority.

■ UNLOCK CONDITION (RIGHT/LEFT BACK) Parts Shop Update 6: Complete "Destroy the Ice Worm"

■ PART SPECS		€ 255,000	
Attack Power	1360	Total Rounds	20
Impact	1450	Reload Time	5.0
Accumulative Impact	860	Ammunition Cost	800
Blast Radius	15	Weight	8480
Direct Hit Adjustment	190	EN Load	465
Recoil	70	Interrupts Assault Boost	Yes
Effective Range	510	Assault Boost Impact Bonus	No

GRENADE CANNON

Grenade cannons fire grenades that detonate on impact with either an enemy, the environment, or upon reaching the edge of their effective range. These weapons can deal extreme damage as well as impact, making them some of the strongest explosive weapons available.

The **EARSHOT** only fires a single grenade, but has the strongest attack power and largest blast radius in its class, making it very effective when dealing with groups of enemies. Though powerful, this weapon is slow to reload, and can't be fired in rapid succession. You also only get a total of 16 grenades to fire with this unit, so while it's imperative that you make each shot count, it can be an excellent choice when used in a pair for specific boss fights. Firing two at once can also instantly stagger or outright destroy some enemy ACs.

SONGBIRDS fires two grenades in rapid succession from its 42 round reserve, and although it loses out to the EARSHOT in terms of raw damage, it has significant

advantages in other areas. Its vastly increased ammo count makes it more of a general purpose weapon rather than the situational powerhouse that is the EARSHOT, something that's further reinforced by its faster reload time. Its lower weight and EN load also means you'll have to make fewer compromises when trying to equip them on light -or medium-weight builds.

EARSHOT

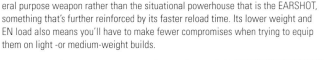

■ PART INFO Heavy grenade cannon developed by Melinite. A high-end model, its raw power and blast radius verge on excessive and make it hard to handle, yet still it enchants mercenaries with its considerable destructive force.

■ UNLOCK CONDITION (RIGHT/LEFT BACK) Parts Shop Update 7: Complete "Escape"

■ PART SPECS		€ 303,000	
Attack Power	2098	Total Rounds	16
Impact	1455	Reload Time	9.3
Accumulative Impact	1101	Ammunition Cost	1600
Blast Radius	90	Weight	7230
Direct Hit Adjustment	145	EN Load	386
Recoil	70	Interrupts Assault Boost	Yes
Effective Range	720	Assault Boost Impact Bonus	No

SONGBIRDS

■ PART INFO Compact double-barreled grenade cannon developed by Melinite. Commissioned for medium-weight ACs, its compact size reduces its explosive power, but the double-barreled format makes strides toward resolving the issue.

■ UNLOCK CONDITION (RIGHT/LEFT BACK) Parts Shop Update 4: Complete "Attack the Watchpoint"

■ PART SPECS		€ 182,000	
Attack Power	655x2	Total Rounds	42
Impact	635x2	Reload Time	6.4
Accumulative Impact	494x2	Ammunition Cost	600
Blast Radius	60	Weight	5500
Direct Hit Adjustment	140	EN Load	285
Recoil	60	Interrupts Assault Boost	Yes
Effective Range	625	Assault Boost Impact Bonus	No

STUN NEEDLE LAUNCHER

The **VE-60SNA** fires a single bolt with great accuracy, and is a powerful kinetic weapon for back slots that's all but essential for the battle against the ICE WORM. Outside of that encounter—where a single launcher serves its purpose—the VE-60SNA is a strong performer in Double Trigger setups. Its high reload times are made up for in part by its ammo efficiency, with enough in reserve to see you through nearly every mission. Stun needle rounds initially deal kinetic damage, shortly followed by two explosions, dealing 200 shock buildup each. As a result, the VE-60SNA excels in multiple scenarios: it can instantly trigger electrical discharges against opponents susceptible to shock, cause severe ACS strain in a single burst, or exploit direct hit windows from afar due to its massive effective range.

Outside of the ICE WORM encounter, stun needle launchers are among the most potent weapons for direct hit damage during enemy AC stagger.

With the right build, SONGBIRDS can be used to grant tetrapods infinite airtime if fired after running out of EN while hovering.

VP-60LCD diffuse laser cannons are one of your best choices for direct hit damage with an energy weapon. Optimal use is to begin charging ahead of the enemy entering ACS overload.

VE-60SNA

■ **PART INFO** Anti-Ice Worm weapon designed by Arquebus ADD. Neutralizes Coral shielding with electrical interference, by firing a massive electrified needle to create a powerful discharge at the point of impact.

■ **UNLOCK CONDITION (RIGHT/LEFT BACK)** Prototype Issued: Unlock "Destroy the Ice Worm"/Parts Shop: Complete "Destroy the Ice Worm"

■ PART SPECS		€ 283,000	
Attack Power	1088	Total Rounds	30
Impact	641	Reload Time	5.0
Accumulative Impact	339	Ammunition Cost	800
Blast Radius	30	Weight	6150
Direct Hit Adjustment	195	EN Load	825
Recoil	70	Interrupts Assault Boost	Yes
Ideal Range	280	Assault Boost Impact Bonus	No
Effective Range	490		

LASER CANNON

Laser cannons are back-mounted variants of laser rifles. The extra support from their rear mounting gives laser cannons a higher EN output, and an appropriate boost to power and impact when compared to their arm-mounted cousins. Their long range, high power, and respectable direct hit adjustments makes them great options for builds focusing on exploiting ACS overload windows.

An adaptation of a laser rifle, the **VP-60LCS** looses a single, high powered round, dealing more damage than even the VE-66LRB. This will be a stable source of damage that can be used on assemblies with moderate weight and EN load limits. The VP-60LCS can fire four times before overheating, and while it does get a respectable increase to both damage and impact from charging, this weapon is most effective when using consecutive normal shots. The damage you can inflict by using it in this manner can make it an incredible early-game boss killer.

The **VE-60LCA** is a triple barreled laser cannon that deals incredible damage and impact; it's far and away the most powerful energy weapon at your disposal, and properly timed hits against staggered opponents will deal unparalleled damage for a ranged weapon. Overwhelming power comes with overwhelming drawbacks, however. The VE-60LCA has only 24 total rounds, a crippling cooling rate, the longest charge time of any weapon and is ludicrously demanding on even the heaviest ACs. Despite all of this, its charge attack still shines, and a single charge shot can easily remove a quarter of even the hardiest AC's AP when overloaded. Missing such a shot will mean losing a quarter of your total ammo, though.

VP-60LCS

■ **PART INFO** Laser cannon developed by Arquebus. This is an enlarged version of the standard laser rifle, reimagined as a back- mounted weapon. Charge the weapon to amplify its power.

■ **UNLOCK CONDITION (RIGHT/LEFT BACK)** Parts Shop Update 2: Complete both "Destroy the Weaponized Mining Ship" and "Attack the Dam Complex"

■ PART SPECS		€ 147,000	
Attack Power	925	Rapid Fire	0.7
Impact	500	Chg. EN Load	759
Accumulative Impact	180	Charge Time	1.6
ATK Heat Buildup	320	Chg. Ammo Consumption	3
Chg. Attack Power	1621	Total Rounds	57
Chg. Impact	750	Cooling	210
Chg. Accu. Impact	280	Ammunition Cost	450
Chg. Heat Buildup	1000	Weight	5190
Direct Hit Adjustment	145	EN Load	683
Recoil	70	Interrupts Assault Boost	Yes
Ideal Range	230	Assault Boost Impact Bonus	No
Effective Range	359		

VE-60LCA

■ **PART INFO** Triple-barreled laser cannon designed by Arquebus ADD. Simultaneous fire from all barrels provides overwhelming offensive potential at the cost of a hefty EN burden. Charge to amplify firepower.

■ **UNLOCK CONDITION (RIGHT/LEFT BACK)** Parts Shop Update 9: Complete "Destroy the Ice Worm" in NG+

■ PART SPECS		€ 333,000	
Attack Power	633×3	Rapid Fire	0.4
Impact	199×3	Chg. EN Load	1440
Accumulative Impact	76×3	Charge Time	5.0
ATK Heat Buildup	700	Chg. Ammo Consumption	6
Chg. Attack Power	1015×3	Total Rounds	24
Chg. Impact	330×3	Cooling	155
Chg. Accu. Impact	185×3	Ammunition Cost	450
Chg. Heat Buildup	1000	Weight	14820
Direct Hit Adjustment	145	EN Load	1200
Recoil	70	Interrupts Assault Boost	Yes
Ideal Range	240	Assault Boost Impact Bonus	No
Effective Range	402		

DIFFUSE LASER CANNON

A back-mounted laser shotgun, the **VP-60LCD** is similar to its smaller cousins, but its increased reliability at slightly longer ranges makes it generally more useful in combat. Overall, this is an offensive upgrade over a laser shotgun, with a minor trade-off in general speed, losing rapid fire and having a longer charge time. A normal shot fires 12 powerful beams at once in a loose, vertical oval shape, or you can charge it to release a single, focused beam of energy. The individual beams in the normal shot still deal great damage and impact, making glancing shots more effective when compared with laser shotguns. Despite having similar effective range and greater ideal range to the VP-66LS, the way the shots spread mean that you'll still be better off firing normal shots at close range, switching to charged shots at medium range or further.

VP-60LCD

■ **PART INFO** Spread laser cannon developed by Arquebus. This is an enlarged version of the standard laser shotgun, reimagined as a back-mounted weapon. Charge to concentrate the laser, producing an energy explosion.

■ **UNLOCK CONDITION (RIGHT/LEFT BACK)** Parts Shop Update 6: Complete "Destroy the Ice Worm"

■ PART SPECS		€ 215,000	
Attack Power	1308	Effective Range	252
Impact	648	Rapid Fire	0.6
Accumulative Impact	204	Chg. EN Load	902
ATK Heat Buildup	440	Charge Time	2.0
Chg. Attack Power	1782	Chg. Ammo Consumption	3
Chg. Impact	980	Total Rounds	54
Chg. Accu. Impact	439	Cooling	232
Chg. Blast Radius	45	Ammunition Cost	650
Chg. Heat Buildup	1000	Weight	7620
Direct Hit Adjustment	145	EN Load	784
Recoil	45	Interrupts Assault Boost	Yes
Ideal Range	180	Assault Boost Impact Bonus	No

PLASMA CANNON

Continuing the trend, plasma cannons are plasma rifles designed for auxiliary fire from an AC's back. Rather than being a direct upgrade to either the Vvc-760PR or IA-C01W1: NEBULA, the **FASAN/60E** takes characteristics of both. Its plasma rifle lineage is clear, so don't expect anything other than a respectably powerful and versatile backup weapon. Its standard fire resembles the Vvc-760PR, firing a single, powerful plasma round that leaves a large plasma explosion. The FASAN/60E fires slower and builds up heat much quicker, but it will outpace the competition in damage quite handily. Comparatively, its charged shot is more in line with the IA-C01W1: NEBULA, firing a single, dominating round. Where Double Trigger plasma rifles can be effectively used throughout entire missions and deal respectable damage in their own right, if you need a hit of raw, unbridled power to deliver a single devastating blow, the FASAN/60E is a strong option.

FASAN/60E

■ PART INFO Plasma cannon developed by Schneider. The internals of this weapon feature plasma technology provided by VCPL. Charge to ramp up output and expand blast radius.

■ UNLOCK CONDITION (RIGHT/LEFT BACK) Parts Shop Update 7: Complete "Escape"

■ PART SPECS		€ 217,000	
Attack Power	1560	Effective Range	440
Impact	840	Rapid Fire	0.5
Accumulative Impact	570	Chg. EN Load	944
Blast Radius	30	Charge Time	2.0
ATK Heat Buildup	465	Chg. Ammo Consumption	3
Chg. Attack Power	2412	Total Rounds	39
Chg. Impact	1272	Cooling	196
Chg. Accu. Impact	792	Ammunition Cost	540
Chg. Blast Radius	60	Weight	6270
Chg. Heat Buildup	1000	EN Load	882
Direct Hit Adjustment	125	Interrupts Assault Boost	Yes
Recoil	70	Assault Boost Impact Bonus	No

PULSE CANNON

The **KRANICH/60Z** pulse cannon is a back-mounted energy weapon that makes the effectiveness of the pulse gun available to the back slot. Like pulse guns, holding the trigger continuously fires pulse blasts until you cease fire or overheat the weapon. Rounds that make contact disrupt the enemy's shielding and build up ACS strain, so it's a good idea to pair the pulse cannon with weapons that deal high direct hit damage to exploit stagger windows. PA interference and effective range are superior to the HI-18 GU-A2 and HI-16 GU-Q1, but it loses out to the GU-Q1 in fire rate and cooling. Using a pair of KRANICHs does free up your arm slots to wield other high-impact weapons, however, which can be a particularly effective combo given the potential damage they can inflict on staggered enemies. The heavy EN load of these weapons will mean that you'll need a suitably beefy generator to go with them, which can make it difficult to incorporate on lighter builds.

KRANICH/60Z

■ PART INFO Pulse cannon developed by Schneider. Powerful, continuous high-frequency oscillation cancels out pulse defenses with ease. Features a distinctive spec that creates oscillations from a "string."

■ UNLOCK CONDITION (RIGHT/LEFT BACK) Parts Shop Update 9: Complete "Destroy the Ice Worm" in NG+

■ PART SPECS		€ 177,000	
Attack Power	85	Rapid Fire	10.0
Impact	20	Total Rounds	560
Accumulative Impact	10	Cooling	225
ATK Heat Buildup	65	Ammunition Cost	40
Direct Hit Adjustment	145	Weight	2100
PA Interference	550	EN Load	652
Recoil	10	Interrupts Assault Boost	No
Effective Range	490	Assault Boost Impact Bonus	Yes

PULSE SHIELD LAUNCHER

The **EULE/60D** pulse shield launcher combines defensive properties with a bit of disruptive offense. This back unit launcher deploys circular pulse barriers that slowly encroach forward and temporarily absorb all incoming fire—from the enemy and yourself—until the shield breaks or expires. Pulse barriers that aren't destroyed last for seven seconds before collapsing inward and exploding, inflicting damage and straining the ACS of nearby enemies.

Though untouched barriers will eventually explode, they lack the resilience to hold up long enough in most combat scenarios. Pulse barriers fired in too close a range will not fully deploy and instead hit the enemy for a tiny amount of damage, but significant ACS strain. Pull back to at least medium range for the shield to set up properly. Combo potential with the MA-T-223 KYORIKU—to jam the enemy's lock on—exists, if you're looking to expand upon the theme of disrupting the opponent.

EULE/60D

■ PART INFO Pulse shield launcher developed by Schneider. Deploys pulse barriers that cancel out incoming fire. Craft that come into contact with these barriers suffer major ACS strain due to resulting sensor interference.

■ UNLOCK CONDITION (RIGHT/LEFT BACK) Parts Shop Update 6: Complete "Destroy the Ice Worm"

■ PART SPECS		€ 243,000	
Attack Power	455	Magazine Rounds	3
Impact	640	Total Rounds	45
Accumulative Impact	461	Reload Time	6.0
Blast Radius	15	Ammunition Cost	400
Direct Hit Adjustment	155	Weight	2760
PA Interference	175	EN Load	382
Recoil	4	Interrupts Assault Boost	No
Effective Range	62	Assault Boost Impact Bonus	Yes
Rapid Fire	3.4		

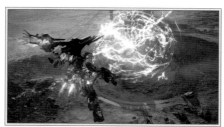

Charged shots from the FASAN/60E plasma cannon expel a blast radius that rivals explosive rounds.

The KRANICH/60Z can serve as your back-mounted option for disrupting pulse defenses, or even stacked with pulse guns to multiply the effect.

Though unlikely in most cases, rounds launched by the EULE/60D will eventually detonate on the opponent and build ACS strain if left unchecked.

LIGHT WAVE CANNON

The **IA-C01W3: AURORA** light wave cannon fires four waves of projectiles that can multi-lock to strike up to four enemies at once with energy-based damage. The AURORA takes the homing capabilities of missile launchers, and the high energy damage of laser cannons, and meets the two in the middle. Compared to missile launchers, the AURORA's homing lock times are notably higher, but its damage is higher than the BML-G1/P20MLT-04—which also fires four missiles. However, it's lower than that of laser cannons. High effective range makes the AURORA deadly from very long distances, but make sure your choice of FCS is appropriate for the range you intend to use this cannon from.

IA-C01W3: AURORA

■ PART INFO Light-wave cannon developed long ago by the Rubicon Research Institute. This fusion of laser and pulse technology fires energy projectiles accompanied by distinctive fluctuations.

■ UNLOCK CONDITION (RIGHT/LEFT BACK) Part Container: "Reach the Coral Convergence"/Parts Shop

■ PART SPECS		€ 340,000	
Attack Power	134×4	Max. Lock Count	4
Impact	102×4	Total Rounds	100
Accumulative Impact	102×4	Reload Time	5.5
Direct Hit Adjustment	175	Ammunition Cost	80
PA Interference	117	Weight	3330
Guidance	240	EN Load	390
Effective Range	930	Interrupts Assault Boost	No
Homing Lock Time	3.3	Assault Boost Impact Bonus	No

MISSILE LAUNCHER

Missile launchers deploy explosive projectiles with homing capabilities that allow them to seek out enemies and deliver an explosive payload. The more cells available to a launcher, the more missiles available to fire in a single volley. With their excellent ability to build ACS strain, they are best paired with weapons that have high direct hit adjustment values to inflict the most damage possible on staggered opponents.

The **BML-G1/P20MLT-04** is a lightweight pick that fits on nearly any build, capable of multi-lock on up to four targets. Upgraded models **BML-G2/P03MLT-06** and **BML-G2/P05MLT-10** make concessions in homing lock time and reload time, but fire extra missiles—six and ten, respectively—in exchange, making them significantly more powerful per volley fired. Generally, if you can afford the increased weight and EN load burden, go for the higher missile count, since their primary use case is in pressuring opponents with endless swarms of projectiles.

BML-G1/P20MLT-04

■ PART INFO Four-cell missile launcher developed by Furlong Dynamics. Missiles track targets and explode on hit, contributing greatly to build-up of ACS strain. Compact model for lightweight builds. Capable of multi-lock.

■ UNLOCK CONDITION (RIGHT/LEFT BACK) Default/Parts Shop Update 1: Complete either "Destroy Artillery Installations" or "Grid 135 Cleanup"

■ PART SPECS		€ 74,000	
Attack Power	103×4	Total Rounds	140
Impact	72×4	Reload Time	4.0
Accumulative Impact	43×4	Ammunition Cost	80
Direct Hit Adjustment	145	Weight	2120
Guidance	180	EN Load	154
Effective Range	2500	Interrupts Assault Boost	No
Homing Lock Time	0.3	Assault Boost Impact Bonus	No
Max. Lock Count	4		

BML-G2/P03MLT-06

■ PART INFO Six-cell missile launcher developed by Furlong Dynamics. Missiles track targets and explode on hit, contributing greatly to build-up of ACS strain. Standard model for medium-weight builds. Capable of multi-lock.

■ UNLOCK CONDITION (RIGHT/LEFT BACK) Parts Shop Update 6: Complete "Destroy the Ice Worm"

■ PART SPECS		€ 111,000	
Attack Power	103×6	Total Rounds	228
Impact	72×6	Reload Time	5.0
Accumulative Impact	43×6	Ammunition Cost	80
Direct Hit Adjustment	145	Weight	3840
Guidance	180	EN Load	241
Effective Range	2500	Interrupts Assault Boost	No
Homing Lock Time	0.4	Assault Boost Impact Bonus	No
Max. Lock Count	6		

BML-G2/P05MLT-10

■ PART INFO Ten-cell missile launcher developed by Furlong Dynamics. Missiles track targets and explode on hit, contributing greatly to build-up of ACS strain. Oversize model for heavyweight builds. Capable of multi-lock.

■ UNLOCK CONDITION (RIGHT/LEFT BACK) Parts Shop Update 4: Complete "Attack the Watchpoint"

■ PART SPECS		€ 165,000	
Attack Power	103×10	Total Rounds	300
Impact	72×10	Reload Time	6.4
Accumulative Impact	43×10	Ammunition Cost	80
Direct Hit Adjustment	145	Weight	5220
Guidance	180	EN Load	320
Effective Range	2500	Interrupts Assault Boost	No
Homing Lock Time	0.8	Assault Boost Impact Bonus	No
Max. Lock Count	10		

SPLIT MISSILE LAUNCHER

Split missile launchers are like standard missile launchers, but with a twist. Deployed missiles split apart once they're in close proximity to their target, leading to numerous sub-missiles that close in on them from all angles. Generally intended to put targets into a sticky situation that they cannot easily get out of, especially if paired with vertical missiles to truly close all gaps.

As the entry level model, the The **BML-G2/P16SPL-08** launches a single cell that lacks multi-lock capabilities and is designed to put pressure on single targets with a large number of sub-missiles. Compared to the standard **BML-G2/P03MLT-06** missile launcher, it has lower attack and impact values, but is superior in every

The BML-G2/P17SPL-16 split missile launcher provides useful distraction to enemies that may not see your next attack coming, like a strike from the plasma thrower.

other spec. Advancing to the **BML-G2/P19SPL-12**, you'll gain an additional cell, which means you can multi-lock with this launcher if you choose. Each cell releases less sub-missiles than the BML-G2/P16SPL-08 so you'll be dealing less damage to each individual target, but your overall damage will be much higher. Finally, the BML-G2/P17SPL-16 takes the best of both split missile launchers to fire off two cells that split into an eight-way missile volley with homing capability. Since this version also retains the multi-lock capabilities of the of the BML-G2/P19SPL-12, if your build can handle the increased EN load, and your playstyle can handle the longer reload times, the additional damage and versatility it provides is worth those trade offs.

BML-G2/P19SPL-12

■ PART INFO Two-cell, six-way split missile launcher developed by Furlong Dynamics. Missiles split before contact and surround target with homing sub-missiles. This model focuses on flexibility at the cost of sub-missile count.

■ UNLOCK CONDITION (RIGHT/LEFT BACK) Parts Shop Update 7: Complete "Escape"

■ PART SPECS		€ 123,000	
Attack Power	600×2	Total Rounds	80
Impact	402×2	Reload Time	6.0
Accumulative Impact	240×2	Ammunition Cost	400
Direct Hit Adjustment	140	Weight	3580
Guidance	135	EN Load	325
Effective Range	1425	Interrupts Assault Boost	No
Homing Lock Time	1.5	Assault Boost Impact Bonus	No
Max. Lock Count	2		

BML-G2/P16SPL-08

■ PART INFO Launcher for 8-way split missiles developed by Furlong Dynamics. Missiles split before contact and surround target with homing sub-missiles. Suited for aggressive solo tactics against one or multiple targets.

■ UNLOCK CONDITION (RIGHT/LEFT BACK) Parts Shop Update 4: Complete "Attack the Watchpoint"

■ PART SPECS		€ 85,000	
Attack Power	688	Total Rounds	40
Impact	536	Reload Time	5.1
Accumulative Impact	320	Ammunition Cost	500
Direct Hit Adjustment	140	Weight	2800
Guidance	135	EN Load	228
Effective Range	1425	Interrupts Assault Boost	No
Homing Lock Time	1.5	Assault Boost Impact Bonus	No
Max. Lock Count	1		

BML-G2/P17SPL-16

■ PART INFO Two-cell, 8-way split missile launcher developed by Furlong Dynamics. Missiles split before contact and surround target with homing sub-missiles. A simple evolution that uses two batteries instead of one.

■ UNLOCK CONDITION (RIGHT/LEFT BACK) Parts Shop Update 6: Complete "Destroy the Ice Worm"

■ PART SPECS		€ 160,000	
Attack Power	688×2	Total Rounds	72
Impact	536×2	Reload Time	7.7
Accumulative Impact	320×2	Ammunition Cost	500
Direct Hit Adjustment	140	Weight	5010
Guidance	135	EN Load	510
Effective Range	1425	Interrupts Assault Boost	No
Homing Lock Time	2.0	Assault Boost Impact Bonus	No
Max. Lock Count	2		

DUAL MISSILE LAUNCHER

Cells on a dual missile launcher contain a single missile each and are arranged in a mirrored configuration, meaning a two-cell launcher like the **BML-G1/P31DUO-02** fires a total of four missiles. Like split missile launchers, dual missiles also deploy in pincer formation, but they do so straight away rather than following a delay. Dual missile launchers can pair well with vertical missile launchers to pin the enemy from all angles, but be aware that missiles fired in too close of a range will wrap around the back of the target and miss.

The number of mirrored cells are also what dictates the amount of targets the unit can lock onto for most of these units rather than the total number of missiles that are fired. That means although the BML-G1/P31DUO-02 releases four missiles, you can only multi-lock two targets with it, and while it has the lowest offensive specs in the category, its fast reload times and low weight and EN load means it can be used quickly and often on nearly any build. By virtue of being able to fire additional missiles and lock onto an extra target, the **BML-G1/ P32DUO-03** will allow you to dispatch multiple targets at a faster rate, and even if the offensive specs haven't increased, you'll be dealing more damage overall to single targets. Operating slightly differently, the **BML-G2/P08DUO-03** is the only dual missile launcher that can lock onto as many targets as it has cells, for a total of six. The increased weight and EN load of this unit are worth building around if your focus is multiple enemies, but for single targets, the strain on your EN and weight might make the other units better options.

BML-G1/P31DUO-02

■ PART INFO Compact, two-cell dual missile launcher developed by Furlong Dynamics. Traps targets in pincer trajectory, limiting evasive options. This model is suitable for use with lightweight builds, and is capable of multi-lock.

■ UNLOCK CONDITION (RIGHT/LEFT BACK) Parts Shop Update 1: Complete either "Destroy Artillery Installations" or "Grid 135 Cleanup"

■ PART SPECS		€ 144,000	
Attack Power	148×4	Total Rounds	124
Impact	94×4	Reload Time	3.5
Accumulative Impact	62×4	Ammunition Cost	70
Direct Hit Adjustment	150	Weight	1900
Guidance	145	EN Load	182
Effective Range	500	Interrupts Assault Boost	No
Homing Lock Time	0.4	Assault Boost Impact Bonus	No
Max. Lock Count	2		

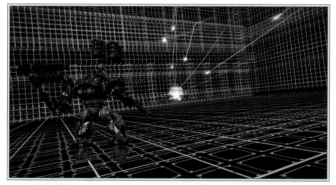

The BML-G1/P31DUO-02 dual missile launcher pairs well with any vertical missile launcher to pinch the enemy with a volley from all angles.

BML-G1/P32DUO-03

■ PART INFO Compact, three-cell dual missile launcher developed by Furlong Dynamics. Traps targets in pincer trajectory, limiting evasive options. This is a simple revision of an existing weapon for coaxial use. Capable of multi-lock.

■ UNLOCK CONDITION (RIGHT/LEFT BACK) Parts Shop Update 5: Complete "Ocean Crossing"

■ PART SPECS		€ 180,000	
Attack Power	148×6	Total Rounds	180
Impact	94×6	Reload Time	4.3
Accumulative Impact	62×6	Ammunition Cost	70
Direct Hit Adjustment	150	Weight	3450
Guidance	145	EN Load	262
Effective Range	500	Interrupts Assault Boost	No
Homing Lock Time	0.4	Assault Boost Impact Bonus	No
Max. Lock Count	3		

BML-G2/P08DUO-03

■ PART INFO Medium-sized, three-cell dual missile launcher developed by Furlong Dynamics. Traps targets in pincer trajectory, limiting evasive options. A coaxial version of an existing Furlong multi-missile launcher, capable of multi-lock.

■ UNLOCK CONDITION (RIGHT/LEFT BACK) Parts Shop Update 7: Complete "Escape"

■ PART SPECS		€ 228,000	
Attack Power	177×6	Total Rounds	156
Impact	111×6	Reload Time	5.8
Accumulative Impact	72×6	Ammunition Cost	100
Direct Hit Adjustment	150	Weight	4020
Guidance	145	EN Load	332
Effective Range	500	Interrupts Assault Boost	No
Homing Lock Time	0.7	Assault Boost Impact Bonus	No
Max. Lock Count	6		

VERTICAL MISSILE LAUNCHER

As the name states, vertical missile launchers deploy explosive homing projectiles with a vertical trajectory, bypassing enemy cover and frontal shielding. Missiles launched will then descend upon the target, delivering damage and impact from above. As with other missile types, vertical missiles are great for building ACS strain, and are best coupled with either high direct hit damage weapons, or other types of missile launcher if you're trying to overwhelm the enemy from all angles.

Keeping in line with other variations of missile delivery units, as you progress up through the iterations, each subsequent model fires an additional number of missiles. More missiles means you'll be able to inflict both additional single target damage, and be able to lock onto and destroy larger groups of enemies. Weight and EN burdens on your AC also increase in tandem with the damage output, so while the **BML-G2/P01VTC-04** can easily be used on nearly any build without compromising movement speed or agility, once you start considering the **BML-G1/P07VTC-12**, you'll likely need to move to heavier assemblies that can deal with the increased load. Don't rule out the BML-G2/P01VTC-04 or **BML-G1/P03VTC-08** even on heavier assemblies though, because their much lower lock on and reload times can still make them a viable option when time is of the essence.

BML-G1/P01VTC-04

■ PART INFO Four-cell vertical missile launcher developed by Furlong Dynamics. High vertical trajectory allows missiles to deny enemies cover and circumvent such defenses. This is the lightweight AC model, and is also capable of multi-lock.

■ UNLOCK CONDITION (RIGHT/LEFT BACK) Reward: Complete "Intermediate Support 4: Tank ACs"/Parts Shop

■ PART SPECS		€ 85,000	
Attack Power	124×4	Total Rounds	108
Impact	89×4	Reload Time	4.8
Accumulative Impact	55×4	Ammunition Cost	120
Direct Hit Adjustment	150	Weight	2240
Guidance	480	EN Load	258
Effective Range	1000	Interrupts Assault Boost	No
Homing Lock Time	0.4	Assault Boost Impact Bonus	No
Max. Lock Count	4		

BML-G1/P03VTC-08

■ PART INFO Eight-cell vertical missile launcher developed by Furlong Dynamics. High vertical trajectory allows missiles to deny enemies cover and circumvent such defenses. This is the medium-weight AC model, and is also capable of multi-lock.

■ UNLOCK CONDITION (RIGHT/LEFT BACK) Parts Shop Update 2: Complete both "Destroy the Weaponized Mining Ship" and "Attack the Dam Complex"

■ PART SPECS		€ 112,000	
Attack Power	124×8	Total Rounds	224
Impact	89×8	Reload Time	6.0
Accumulative Impact	55×8	Ammunition Cost	120
Direct Hit Adjustment	150	Weight	3920
Guidance	480	EN Load	380
Effective Range	1000	Interrupts Assault Boost	No
Homing Lock Time	0.8	Assault Boost Impact Bonus	No
Max. Lock Count	8		

BML-G1/P07VTC-12

■ PART INFO Twelve-cell vertical missile launcher developed by Furlong Dynamics. High vertical trajectory allows missiles to deny enemies cover and circumvent such defenses. This is the heavyweight AC model, and is also capable of multi-lock.

■ UNLOCK CONDITION (RIGHT/LEFT BACK) Parts Shop Update 7: Complete "Escape"

■ PART SPECS		€ 188,000	
Attack Power	124×12	Total Rounds	360
Impact	89×12	Reload Time	7.5
Accumulative Impact	55×12	Ammunition Cost	120
Direct Hit Adjustment	150	Weight	5010
Guidance	480	EN Load	525
Effective Range	1000	Interrupts Assault Boost	No
Homing Lock Time	1.4	Assault Boost Impact Bonus	No
Max. Lock Count	12		

BML-G1/P07VTC-12 vertical missile launcher fires a volley that easily navigates around stubborn frontal defenses, including the RLF's JUGGERNAUT.

The BML-G3/P05ACT-02 active homing missile launcher is useful to pressure agile units, and also performs well against slower tetrapod MTs and bosses.

WS-5001 SOUP's manually staggered rate of fire is great at keeping enemy ACs on the defensive, making them expend EN while you conserve your own.

EL-PW-01 TRUENO is one of the best options for direct hit damage. With its projectile velocity, even the shortest stagger windows can be exploited.

ACTIVE HOMING MISSILE LAUNCHER

Active homing missile launchers deploy projectiles that gradually follow the target until they either find their mark or run out of fuel and disengage. Highly mobile enemies capable of dodging for extended periods of time can have an easier time evading this type of missiles than others, but the fact that they will have to contend with it for so long opens them up to other forms of attack while they're distracted. Where these weapons truly shine, however, is against slower or stationary targets where they can deliver their payload as quickly as possible. The additional missile you gain when moving from the **BML-G3/P04ACT-01** to the **BML-G3/P05ACT-02** greatly increases the damage you can inflict, and you gain the ability to muli-lock, so if your build can support the additional weight and EN load, it will be the better option under nearly all circumstances.

BML-G3/P04ACT-01

■ PART INFO Homing missile launcher developed by Furlong Dynamics. Features high-powered payloads with propulsion systems deliberately slowed down. Missiles hound targets during lengthy airborne time, enabling heavy pressure tactics.

■ UNLOCK CONDITION (RIGHT/LEFT BACK) Parts Shop Update 3: Complete "Operation Wallclimber"

■ PART SPECS		€ 98,000	
Attack Power	486	Max. Lock Count	1
Impact	540	Total Rounds	45
Accumulative Impact	378	Reload Time	2.4
Blast Radius	12	Ammunition Cost	450
Direct Hit Adjustment	165	Weight	2680
Guidance	115	EN Load	213
Effective Range	1000	Interrupts Assault Boost	No
Homing Lock Time	2.0	Assault Boost Impact Bonus	No

BML-G3/P05ACT-02

■ PART INFO Twin-cell homing missile launcher developed by Furlong Dynamics. Features high-powered payloads with propulsion systems deliberately slowed down. The twin-cell format adds to pressure potential and enables multi-lock.

■ UNLOCK CONDITION (RIGHT/LEFT BACK) Parts Shop Update 6: Complete "Destroy the Ice Worm"

■ PART SPECS		€ 145,000	
Attack Power	486×2	Max. Lock Count	2
Impact	540×2	Total Rounds	72
Accumulative Impact	378×2	Reload Time	4.2
Blast Radius	12	Ammunition Cost	450
Direct Hit Adjustment	165	Weight	4320
Guidance	115	EN Load	424
Effective Range	1000	Interrupts Assault Boost	No
Homing Lock Time	2.8	Assault Boost Impact Bonus	No

CONTAINER MISSILE LAUNCHER

The **BML-G1/P29CNT** fires a container that deploys multiple homing missiles. Fired volleys tend to be inaccurate, so it's recommended to pull at least 190m from the target, as firing from too close a distance can result in the container sailing past the target or even hitting the ground in some cases, with damage lost either way. With a paltry 12 rounds and volatile accuracy, container missiles are largely best reserved for pressure tactics in multiplayer.

BML-G1/P29CNT

■ PART INFO Container missile launcher developed by Furlong Dynamics. Fires a container that flies in a forward trajectory and is loaded with a large number of micro-missiles, which scatter explosions during the container's flight.

■ UNLOCK CONDITION (RIGHT/LEFT BACK) Parts Shop Update 7: Complete "Escape"

■ PART SPECS		€ 250,000	
Attack Power	1422	Reload Time	12.0
Impact	1278	Ammunition Cost	800
Accumulative Impact	828	Weight	6370
Direct Hit Adjustment	140	EN Load	150
Guidance	120	Interrupts Assault Boost	Yes
Effective Range	700	Assault Boost Impact Bonus	No
Total Rounds	12		

CLUSTER MISSILE LAUNCHER

The **WR-0999 DELIVERY BOY** fires a singular missile above a target that releases up to three waves of smaller explosive rounds aimed at the enemy like a bombing run, with the missile circling back around two additional times. 20 total rounds may seem low, but since each of those releases so many additional rounds, they can still go a long way in a fight. Being heavy and slow to unleash its damage, this type of missile launcher isn't well suited for trying to stagger enemies, especially evasive ones, but a pair of them against a more static target can be very formidable.

WR-0999 DELIVERY BOY

■ PART INFO Cluster missile launcher developed by RaD. Packed with a large number of compact explosives to carpet-bomb the area. Apparently, this design came from the feverish mind of a Coral-addled engineer.

■ UNLOCK CONDITION (RIGHT/LEFT BACK) Parts Shop Update 8: Complete "Ocean Crossing" in NG+

■ PART SPECS		€ 298,000	
Attack Power	2133	Max. Lock Count	1
Impact	2040	Total Rounds	20
Accumulative Impact	1638	Reload Time	9.0
Blast Radius	24	Ammunition Cost	600
Direct Hit Adjustment	175	Weight	6890
Guidance	200	EN Load	499
Effective Range	1049	Interrupts Assault Boost	Yes
Homing Lock Time	5.0	Assault Boost Impact Bonus	No

SCATTER MISSILE LAUNCHER

Unlike traditional missile launchers that fire off their entire loaded salvo at once, the scatter missile launcher lets you fire off 10 missiles three times in a row before it needs to reload. The deep ammo reserves let you use this weapon very liberally, and since it retains the excellent ACS straining capabilities of other types of missile launcher, the end result will be a lot of staggered enemies. The **WS-5001 SOUP**'s pitfall is that its missiles can struggle against agile targets, especially at close range where they'll often miss their mark, but if you can keep your distance and play to its strengths, it can be a solid option for many builds.

WS-5001 SOUP

■ PART INFO Scatter missile launcher developed by RaD. Features a unique construction that allows it to fire 10-missile salvos in three consecutive stages for sustained overwhelming force.

■ UNLOCK CONDITION (RIGHT/LEFT BACK) Parts Shop Update 8: Complete "Ocean Crossing" in NG+

■ PART SPECS		€ 326,000	
Attack Power	78×10	Total Rounds	420
Impact	77×10	Reload Time	8.0
Accumulative Impact	55×10	Ammunition Cost	50
Direct Hit Adjustment	145	Weight	5620
Guidance	180	EN Load	680
Effective Range	2500	Interrupts Assault Boost	No
Homing Lock Time	0.5	Assault Boost Impact Bonus	No
Max. Lock Count	1		

DETONATING MISSILE LAUNCHER

The **45-091 JVLN BETA** fires a unique warhead that leaves a trail of volatile fuel along its trajectory, which ignites in a series of rapid chain explosions once the missile detonates. This detonating missile excels at catching evasive targets like ACs in the delayed explosions, particularly those that are eager to retaliate after dodging the initial projectile. Because of its speed, guidance, and the chain explosions it creates, this unconventional missile launcher is also well suited to taking out clusters of enemies like light MTs in chaotic battlefield scenarios.

45-091 JVLN BETA

■ PART INFO Special missile launcher developed by ALLMIND. Creates a chain of delayed explosions along the missile's trajectory, allowing for sustained suppressive fire even against targets that manage to evade the initial missile.

■ UNLOCK CONDITION (RIGHT/LEFT BACK) Reward/Parts Shop: Hunter Class 4

■ PART SPECS		€ 210,000	
Attack Power	791	Max. Lock Count	1
Impact	717	Total Rounds	32
Accumulative Impact	563	Reload Time	3.6
Blast Radius	20	Ammunition Cost	450
Direct Hit Adjustment	165	Weight	4250
Guidance	360	EN Load	425
Effective Range	360	Interrupts Assault Boost	No
Homing Lock Time	2.4	Assault Boost Impact Bonus	No

NEEDLE MISSILE LAUNCHER

The **EL-PW-01 TRUENO** needle missile launcher fires stake projectiles that tear through the enemy's armor with blunt kinetic power. They deploy at an incredible rate, making some of the hardest projectiles to evade and a great choice against evasive enemies or other players. It builds moderate impact, but its high direct hit adjustment value makes it a phenomenal option once you've staggered an enemy. Its direct competition is arguably the SONGBIRDS grenade cannon, a launcher that the TRUENO beats in raw speed, but loses to it in damage and impact. Both weapons are best used when the opponent has exhausted their EN

or overloaded their ACS, with the TRUENO serving as a kinetic alternative against enemies with high anti-explosive defenses.

EL-PW-01 TRUENO

■ PART INFO Needle missile launcher developed by Elcano. Fires stake-shaped projectiles at high velocity that bore through the target's armor. These are non-explosive missiles that rely on raw physical power.

■ UNLOCK CONDITION (RIGHT/LEFT BACK) Arena/Parts Shop: Defeat Classified Subject 51-101 R in NG++

■ PART SPECS		€ 271,000	
Attack Power	415×2	Max. Lock Count	1
Impact	385×2	Total Rounds	62
Accumulative Impact	215×2	Reload Time	4.2
Direct Hit Adjustment	215	Ammunition Cost	300
Guidance	110	Weight	3100
Ideal Range	310	EN Load	420
Effective Range	410	Interrupts Assault Boost	Yes
Homing Lock Time	4.2	Assault Boost Impact Bonus	No

PLASMA MISSILE LAUNCHER

The plasma missile launchers fire volleys of plasma missiles either horizontally or vertically, depending on the model. Functionally, the missiles behave similar to their explosive cousins and can serve as a direct alternative if you're looking to exploit an enemy's energy damage weakness. These missiles do travel slower than traditional ones, but create large plasma explosions upon impact, making them much harder to cleanly evade. This is especially true of the **Vvc-70VPM**, which rains down the missiles from above and can cover large areas in plasma explosions. Coupled with their large ammo reserves, these properties make plasma missile launchers highly dependable back units.

VVC-703PM

■ PART INFO Three-cell plasma missile launcher developed by VCPL. Proximity fuses trigger plasma explosions, creating a damage area. A light, compact weapon suitable for a wide range of builds and capable of multi-lock.

■ UNLOCK CONDITION (RIGHT/LEFT BACK) Parts Shop Update 4: Complete "Attack the Watchpoint"

■ PART SPECS		€ 202,000	
Attack Power	760	Max. Lock Count	3
Impact	384	Total Rounds	120
Accumulative Impact	248	Reload Time	4.0
Blast Radius	26	Ammunition Cost	100
Direct Hit Adjustment	125	Weight	2720
Guidance	180	EN Load	245
Effective Range	1500	Interrupts Assault Boost	No
Homing Lock Time	0.3	Assault Boost Impact Bonus	No

VVC-706PM

■ PART INFO Six-cell plasma missile launcher developed by VCPL. Proximity fuses trigger plasma explosions, creating a damage area. This coaxial arrangement of twin three-cell launchers is capable of multi-lock.

■ UNLOCK CONDITION (RIGHT/LEFT BACK) Parts Shop Update 6: Complete "Destroy the Ice Worm"

■ PART SPECS		€ 310,000	
Attack Power	760	Max. Lock Count	6
Impact	384	Total Rounds	210
Accumulative Impact	248	Reload Time	6.0
Blast Radius	26	Ammunition Cost	100
Direct Hit Adjustment	125	Weight	4800
Guidance	180	EN Load	342
Effective Range	1500	Interrupts Assault Boost	No
Homing Lock Time	0.3	Assault Boost Impact Bonus	No

VVC-70VPM's vertical volley deals well with impenetrable frontal defenses, but is also a great way to diversify your damage output from an explosive missile loadout.

VVC-70VPM

■ PART INFO Vertical plasma missile launcher developed by VCPL. Overhead plasma explosions help to circumvent cover or similar defenses. The vertical trajectory of the missiles further hinders enemy evasion. Capable of multi-lock.

■ UNLOCK CONDITION (RIGHT/LEFT BACK) Parts Shop Update 2: Complete both "Destroy the Weaponized Mining Ship" and "Attack the Dam Complex"

■ PART SPECS   € 96,000

Attack Power	760	Max. Lock Count	5
Impact	384	Total Rounds	240
Accumulative Impact	248	Reload Time	6.2
Blast Radius	26	Ammunition Cost	150
Direct Hit Adjustment	125	Weight	3760
Guidance	180	EN Load	268
Effective Range	750	Interrupts Assault Boost	No
Homing Lock Time	0.5	Assault Boost Impact Bonus	No

CORAL MISSILE LAUNCHER

The **IB-C03W3: NGI 006** is the only missile launcher capable of inflicting Coral damage, which means its missiles outright ignore the target's defensive specs. Uniquely, this Coral missile launcher can also be charged to break off into a swarm of missiles that can collectively deal more than quadruple the damage of a regular warhead. Since charged missiles don't consume any additional ammo, it's usually better to rely on them as your primary firing mode when using this Coral launcher. Your playstyle should then revolve around having a missile charged and ready so that you can release it at the most opportune time.

IB-C03W3: NGI 006

■ PART INFO Prototype Coral missile launcher developed long ago by the Rubicon Research Institute. Energy interference applied to swarm intelligence enables Coral-based tracking/detonation control. Charge to dramatically increase damage potential.

■ UNLOCK CONDITION (RIGHT/LEFT BACK) Part Container: "Regain Control of the Xylem"/Parts Shop: Obtain R-Arm Unit Version

■ PART SPECS   € 380,000

Attack Power	827	Max. Lock Count	1
Impact	720	Chg. EN Load	932
Accumulative Impact	720	Charge Time	3.5
Blast Radius	36	Chg. Ammo Consumption	1
Chg. Attack Power	4087	Total Rounds	24
Chg. Impact	2496	Reload Time	8.6
Chg. Accu. Impact	2496	Ammunition Cost	650
Chg. Blast Radius	56	Weight	4200
Direct Hit Adjustment	185	EN Load	783
Guidance	110	Interrupts Assault Boost	No
Effective Range	1000	Assault Boost Impact Bonus	No
Homing Lock Time	4.9		

BULLET ORBIT

Once deployed, the **BO-044 HUXLEY** bullet orbit hovers above your AC for 10 seconds, automatically firing eight-shot bursts of kinetic rounds at a single target until it's manually recalled or overheats. The damage output of an orbit might not seem impressive on paper and there's a lengthy cooldown between uses, but this weapon's strength comes from the fact that orbits operate autonomously, allowing them to passively deal damage to your current lock-on target. This lets you focus on handling other weapons or evading attacks while dealing continuous damage, since orbit fire isn't interrupted when using Quick Boosts or Assault Boost.

Bullet orbits are especially effective at maintaining pressure on enemy ACs, making them an ideal complement for most close-to-medium range loadouts. If two BO-044 HUXLEYs are equipped, they can be alternated for near-continuous fire, or deployed simultaneously for greater impact buildup. Regardless of your playstyle, bullet orbits are invaluable for their ability to postpone the decay of accumulative impact and induce stagger when facing fast and agile targets.

BO-044 HUXLEY

■ PART INFO Kinetic-ammo orbits developed by Balam. These orbits follow the user's AC and automatically fire at any enemy craft they detect. The control components of the orbits incorporate the technology of an Arquebus affiliate.

■ UNLOCK CONDITION (RIGHT/LEFT BACK) Parts Shop Update 9: Complete "Destroy the Ice Worm" in NG+

■ PART SPECS   € 305,000

Attack Power	28x8	Total Rounds	240
Impact	39x8	Cooling	95
Accumulative Impact	15x8	Ammunition Cost	50
Direct Hit Adjustment	175	Weight	2230
Ideal Range	130	EN Load	435
Effective Range	205	Interrupts Assault Boost	No
Rapid Fire	5.6	Assault Boost Impact Bonus	No

LASER ORBIT

Laser orbits are the energy equivalent of the kinetic bullet orbit. The **45-091 ORBT** attacks in bursts of three laser shots before briefly pausing, and unlike its kinetic counterpart that excels at inflicting ACS strain, this energy-based model focuses on raw damage output at longer effective ranges. Light assemblies with an open back slot can make use of this weapon to bolster their energy damage output with few drawbacks; this laser orbit comes with a large ammo reserve, so you'll get plenty of uptime out of it if you remember to recall it before it overheats. It's important to keep in mind that the damage of laser orbits isn't affected by your generator's Energy Firearm Specialization spec, which makes them a strong energy damage option when using generators that suffer in this department.

45-091 ORBT

■ PART INFO Laser orbits developed by ALLMIND. These orbits follow the user's AC and automatically fire at any enemy craft they detect. The technology used to control the orbits was implemented by ALLMIND's neuroengineering division.

■ UNLOCK CONDITION (RIGHT/LEFT BACK) Reward/Parts Shop: Hunter Class 8

■ PART SPECS   € 280,000

Attack Power	135x3	Total Rounds	165
Impact	70x3	Cooling	116
Accumulative Impact	39x3	Ammunition Cost	100
Direct Hit Adjustment	135	Weight	2010
Ideal Range	198	EN Load	446
Effective Range	262	Interrupts Assault Boost	No
Rapid Fire	1.0	Assault Boost Impact Bonus	No

LASER TURRET

Unlike orbits, laser turrets cover a fixed area once deployed, continuously firing at targets within their extensive effective range for up to 10 shots per turret. The **VP-60LT** operates using magazines loaded with three turrets and each can remain active for 20 seconds, allowing you to exert temporary control over a large area by strategically placing multiple active turrets. This weapon is a versatile back unit, equally useful for defending crucial combat zone positions against waves of enemies as it is for pressuring rival AC pilots by forcing them to dodge a swarm of lasers during heated duels.

VP-60LT

■ PART INFO Laser turret developed by Arquebus. When launched, it hovers in place to provide supporting laser fire. The turret is stationary and does not follow the user like orbits, calling for some planning for optimal placement.

■ UNLOCK CONDITION (RIGHT/LEFT BACK) Parts Shop Update 6: Complete "Destroy the Ice Worm"

■ PART SPECS		€ 194,000	
Attack Power	146×10	Total Rounds	52
Impact	81×10	Reload Time	5.0
Accumulative Impact	39×10	Ammunition Cost	500
Direct Hit Adjustment	135	Weight	2800
Ideal Range	250	EN Load	560
Effective Range	304	Interrupts Assault Boost	No
Rapid Fire	0.9	Assault Boost Impact Bonus	No
Magazine Rounds	3		

LASER DRONE

Vvc-700LD laser drones function similarly to orbits and turrets, autonomously firing at enemies within their range once deployed. Rather than staying in a fixed location or following you, however, these drones independently pursue a single target, positioning themselves overhead before shooting three lasers each in a fixed rhythm. Six drones are released upon activation, forcing the enemy to either dodge multiple times or take damage. The Vvc-700LD can also be charged, causing drones to merge into two enhanced drones that attack in tandem to deal increased damage. A pair of charged drones can deal severe damage to staggered opponents, so line up their release with an ACS overload to maximize potential direct hit damage.

VVC-700LD

■ PART INFO Laser drones developed by VCPL. When launched, these drones surround enemy machines and provide supporting laser fire. The drones also pursue enemies, allowing the user to effectively outnumber their target.

■ UNLOCK CONDITION (RIGHT/LEFT BACK) Parts Shop/Arena: Defeat 01/S V.I Freud

■ PART SPECS		€ 247,000	
Attack Power	288×6	Max. Lock Count	1
Impact	105×6	Charge Time	0.8
Accumulative Impact	63×6	Total Rounds	120
Chg. Attack Power	1370×2	Reload Time	10.0
Chg. Impact	480×2	Ammunition Cost	150
Chg. Accu. Impact	244×2	Weight	3800
Direct Hit Adjustment	135	EN Load	570
Guidance	360	Interrupts Assault Boost	No
Effective Range	400	Assault Boost Impact Bonus	No
Homing Lock Time	0.3		

L-BACK UNIT

The parts exclusive to this slot are focused on increasing your AC's defensive capabilities by allowing it to deploy various types of shields and barriers to mitigate incoming damage and ACS strain.

PULSE SHIELD

Pulse shields deploy full-sized, defensive barriers that offer a balanced focus between regular guarding and Initial Guards. Like most shield types, pulse shields only protect from frontal attacks and can negate system abnormality buildup from flames or shock. Out of all defensive pulse barriers, pulse shields generate the least amount of heat when deployed, making them reliable choices for most assemblies.

The **VP-61PS** is a curved, rectangular shield with the most well-rounded design of the pulse shield category. Possessing excellent protection during regular guards and Initial Guards, the main drawback to this shield is its comparatively higher heat buildup. The **SI-24: SU-Q5** deploys a rectangular shield with curved edges. What it lacks in defensive performance and cooling is mitigated by invitingly low weight and EN load, as well as a lengthy Initial Guard duration.

For pilots who depend more on regular guarding than on timing-based Initial Guards, the **SI-27: SU-R8** offers best-in-class standard damage mitigation and impact dampening ratings. This shield's Initial Guard specs are poor, however, so it's better to avoid any attempts at deploying it in sync with enemy attacks. It compensates for this drawback with remarkable cooling and low heat buildup, allowing for more frequent activation during combat.

VP-61PS

■ PART INFO Pulse shield developed by Arquebus. Used by the Vespers, this shield boasts excellent damage mitigation. Has a window of heightened output immediately after deploying the shield that is capable of canceling out incoming fire.

■ UNLOCK CONDITION (LEFT BACK) Parts Shop Update 4: Complete "Attack the Watchpoint"

■ PART SPECS		€ 123,000	
Damage Mitigation	58	Deployment Range	180
Impact Dampening	40	Cooling	144
IG Damage Mitigation	78	Weight	2700
IG Impact Dampening	80	EN Load	310
IG Duration	0.6	Interrupts Assault Boost	N/A
Dply. Heat Buildup	190		

SI-24: SU-Q5

■ PART INFO Standard pulse shield developed by Takigawa Harmonics. Generally unremarkable in terms of performance, but is well balanced for its low EN footprint. It also offers a relatively long Initial Guard duration for ease of use.

■ UNLOCK CONDITION (LEFT BACK) Parts Shop Update 1: Complete either "Destroy Artillery Installations" or "Grid 135 Cleanup"

■ PART SPECS		€ 43,000	
Damage Mitigation	45	Deployment Range	180
Impact Dampening	25	Cooling	88
IG Damage Mitigation	65	Weight	2010
IG Impact Dampening	75	EN Load	220
IG Duration	1.0	Interrupts Assault Boost	N/A
Dply. Heat Buildup	160		

SI-27: SU-R8

■ PART INFO Circular pulse shield developed by Takigawa Harmonics. Concave design improves efficiency of fire interception. The shield is optimized for standard deflection, resulting in a relatively brief Initial Guard duration.

■ UNLOCK CONDITION (LEFT BACK) Parts Shop Update 5: Complete "Ocean Crossing"

■ PART SPECS		€ 100,000	
Damage Mitigation	63	Deployment Range	180
Impact Dampening	48	Cooling	110
IG Damage Mitigation	67	Weight	3150
IG Impact Dampening	79	EN Load	323
IG Duration	0.2	Interrupts Assault Boost	N/A
Dply. Heat Buildup	140		

PULSE BUCKLER

Pulse bucklers deploy smaller defensive barriers than pulse shields, providing less protection during regular guarding and instead focusing on superior Initial Guard specs to defend against especially threatening attacks. Pulse bucklers are a skill-intensive category ready to reward those that put in the time to perfect Initial Guard timing. The **VP-61PB** deploys a diamond-shaped buckler with poor damage and impact mitigation, but incredible Initial Guard specs that almost completely negate damage and impact if activated a split second before a single, powerful attack connects. Its unforgiving Initial Guard duration does make it a high-risk, high-reward option, but if you master the timing, the VP-61PB can be used to turn the tides of battle in your favor.

Although the **SI-29: SU TT/C** provides noticeably less impressive mitigation during Initial Guards, its massive Initial Guard duration window makes it excel at significantly reducing the damage and strain caused by multi-hit attacks like volleys of missiles that hammer your AC in quick succession. It does also generate more heat with each use than the VP-61PB, requiring you to monitor possible overheating with each successive use.

VP-61PB

■ PART INFO Pulse buckler developed by Arquebus. Has high Initial Guard output, but only deploys for a short duration, requiring the user to predictively deploy in anticipation of when enemy attacks will land.

■ UNLOCK CONDITION (LEFT BACK) Parts Shop Update 4: Complete "Attack the Watchpoint"

■ PART SPECS		€ 76,000	
Damage Mitigation	35	Deployment Range	180
Impact Dampening	35	Cooling	132
IG Damage Mitigation	96	Weight	1920
IG Impact Dampening	95	EN Load	285
IG Duration	0.3	Interrupts Assault Boost	N/A
Dply. Heat Buildup	480		

SI-29: SU-TT/C

■ PART INFO Pulse buckler developed by Takigawa Harmonics. Features a relatively long Initial Guard duration and reliably cancels out enemy fire. However, reduced output during regular guarding hinders sustained defense potential.

■ UNLOCK CONDITION (LEFT BACK) Parts Shop Update 3: Complete "Operation Wallclimber"

■ PART SPECS		€ 62,000	
Damage Mitigation	30	Deployment Range	180
Impact Dampening	56	Cooling	142
IG Damage Mitigation	82	Weight	3380
IG Impact Dampening	76	EN Load	385
IG Duration	1.6	Interrupts Assault Boost	N/A
Dply. Heat Buildup	670		

PULSE SCUTUM

The **VE-61PSA** pulse scutum deploys a large, towering defensive barrier with a unique design that eschews the ability to perform Initial Guards. Unlike other types of pulse barriers, the scutum initially deploys in an idle mode that exhibits extremely weak damage mitigation and impact dampening. However, keeping the pulse scutum deployed for four seconds will activate its high-performance mode and impart the full benefits of its damage mitigation and impact reduction capabilities. In exchange for its lengthy idle mode duration that makes it poor at quickly defending in a reactive manner, the VE-61PSA offers the best regular guarding capabilities of any shield once in high-performance mode. This shield should be deployed preemptively and kept active for long periods, ideal for slower heavyweight builds that depend less on evasion than on raw defensive capabilities, such as mobile fortresses outfitted with tank or tetrapod legs.

VE-61PSA

■ PART INFO Pulse scutum designed by Arquebus ADD. Unlike other models, this shield must remain idle for a short time after deployment to exhibit its true potential. Regular guarding provides higher damage mitigation than IG.

■ UNLOCK CONDITION (LEFT BACK) Parts Shop Update 9: Complete "Destroy the Ice Worm" in NG+

■ PART SPECS		€ 197,000	
Damage Mitigation	86	Deployment Range	180
Impact Dampening	70	Cooling	113
Idle Damage Mitigation	21	Weight	4100
Idle Impact Mitigation	18	EN Load	480
Idle Time	4.0	Interrupts Assault Boost	N/A
Dply. Heat Buildup	270		

CORAL SHIELD

The special **IB-C03W4: NGI 028** shield uses Coral technology to project a 360-degree barrier that completely surrounds your AC, protecting it from all angles when deployed. This Coral shield works well in chaotic scenarios where you're surrounded by enemies and can't keep track of all incoming attacks, even offering protection against hard-to-evade attacks like vertical missiles raining down from above. These powerful defensive advantages don't come without an associated cost, however, as evidenced by a prohibitively high EN load that makes this Coral shield challenging to incorporate on most builds without careful planning.

IB-C03W4: NGI 028

■ PART INFO Prototype Coral shield developed long ago by the Rubicon Research Institute. Application of energy interference to the Coral's swarm intelligence manipulates the arrangement of Coral particles, creating a 360-degree defense.

■ UNLOCK CONDITION (LEFT BACK) Part Container: "Regain Control of the Xylem"

■ PART SPECS		€ 255,000	
Damage Mitigation	55	Deployment Range	360
Impact Dampening	50	Cooling	100
IG Damage Mitigation	88	Weight	2170
IG Impact Dampening	77	EN Load	800
IG Duration	0.8	Interrupts Assault Boost	N/A
Dply. Heat Buildup	450		

FRAME PARTS

HEAD

Your frame's head will have the smallest impact on your AC's defenses and total AP. Additionally, between your head, core and legs, it will add the least to your attitude stability. While its defensive contributions shouldn't be ignored, it'll set itself apart in support abilities. Your head will have a massive impact on your scan distance and the scan effect duration, making it a vital piece of your frame if you scan often.

Heads also also feature a System Recovery spec, which is the sole factor determining your AC's resistance against heat and shock buildup that can result in ACS anomaly or electrical discharges. The higher this value, the more exposure you can withstand. Be careful not to equip a head with system recovery below 100 in scenarios where you'll be facing lots of flames or shock-inducing attacks. Scan distance, however, works just as its name implies. The **AH-J-124 BASHO**, for example, has a scan distance of 400, meaning your systems will detect objects and enemies within 400m. Similarly, the

scan effect duration corresponds to how many seconds your scan lasts. Heads have a range from 3.0-18.0, which means your scan can keep an object highlighted from anywhere between 3 and 18 seconds. Finally, heads have a scan standby time spec, which affects how long your scan takes, in seconds, to cool down.

Unlike most other frame parts, head parts will be highly situational. You'll really want to consider heads like the **VE-44B** for missions with cloaked enemies, or large, vertical areas with walls, where scanning can make things easier for you. The VE-44B will again be a standout option if you have reason to believe you'll need protection from electrical discharge or ACS anomaly. Another consideration is complementing your assembly's defensive or weight profile. Options include the **HC-3000 WRECKER** for when you need added defense, or **DF-HD-08 TIAN-QIANG** for light builds that want the lowest weight possible. Both of these heads eschew the unique support values that heads provide, but will fit in with most combat situations due to how little your head piece demands from your AC.

AH-J-124 BASHO

- **PART INFO** Head part developed by BAWS for an old-generation AC. Said AC was one of the earliest models, developed to succeed MT-class machines, and modern fans of such classic hardware are fond of its characteristic bulk.

- **UNLOCK CONDITION** Parts Shop Update 5: Complete "Ocean Crossing"

■ PART SPECS			€ 61,000
AP	1250	Scan Distance	340
Anti-Kinetic Defense	191	Scan Effect Duration	14.4
Anti-Energy Defense	169	Scan Standby Time	10.8
Anti-Explosive Defense	192	Weight	4600
Attitude Stability	370	EN Load	95
System Recovery	84		

AH-J-124/RC JAILBREAK

- **PART INFO** Junk. Originally a head part for an old-generation AC developed by BAWS. RaD engineers infiltrated Institute City to make field repairs—just enough to make this part operable, but not enough to fix its weathered armor.

- **UNLOCK CONDITION** Reward: Complete "Escape"

■ PART SPECS			€ –
AP	1000	Scan Distance	400
Anti-Kinetic Defense	181	Scan Effect Duration	6.0
Anti-Energy Defense	159	Scan Standby Time	10.8
Anti-Explosive Defense	182	Weight	4250
Attitude Stability	302	EN Load	95
System Recovery	60		

HD-011 MELANDER

- **PART INFO** Medium-weight head part developed by Balam. The simple design and solid performance of this model make it suited for mass production—reflecting Balam's strategy of overwhelming its enemies with its material superiority.

- **UNLOCK CONDITION** Parts Shop Update 1: Complete either "Destroy Artillery Installations" or "Grid 135 Cleanup"

■ PART SPECS			€ 75,000
AP	910	Scan Distance	310
Anti-Kinetic Defense	173	Scan Effect Duration	4.8
Anti-Energy Defense	168	Scan Standby Time	4.2
Anti-Explosive Defense	170	Weight	3160
Attitude Stability	430	EN Load	135
System Recovery	115		

HD-033M VERRILL

- **PART INFO** Retrofitted head part developed by Balam. This high-end model is a strong performer with a hefty energy footprint, and features an intimidating spider-eye design chosen to suit the tastes of the Redguns' commander.

- **UNLOCK CONDITION** Parts Shop Update 6: Complete "Destroy the Ice Worm"

■ PART SPECS			€ 205,000
AP	1080	Scan Distance	510
Anti-Kinetic Defense	188	Scan Effect Duration	7.8
Anti-Energy Defense	185	Scan Standby Time	5.4
Anti-Explosive Defense	185	Weight	3830
Attitude Stability	469	EN Load	240
System Recovery	112		

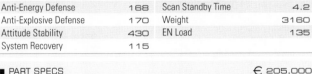

HD-012 MELANDER C3

- **PART INFO** Custom head part developed by Balam. Altered to improve combat suitability, the revisions to this model include partial armor plating and the addition of a scanner module.

- **UNLOCK CONDITION** Complete "Underground Exploration - Depth 2" OR Complete "Illegal Entry" (Pre-order Bonus only)

■ PART SPECS			€ –
AP	970	Scan Distance	580
Anti-Kinetic Defense	175	Scan Effect Duration	12.0
Anti-Energy Defense	177	Scan Standby Time	10.8
Anti-Explosive Defense	169	Weight	3300
Attitude Stability	436	EN Load	165
System Recovery	106		

DF-HD-08 TIAN-QIANG

- **PART INFO** Head part developed by Dafeng Core Industries for the heavyweight TIAN-QIANG AC. Incorporates only the most essential functionality with a minimalist build in keeping with Dafeng's "stout tree, slender branches" philosophy.

- **UNLOCK CONDITION** Parts Shop Update 1: Complete either "Destroy Artillery Installations" or "Grid 135 Cleanup"

■ PART SPECS			€ 58,000
AP	320	Scan Distance	250
Anti-Kinetic Defense	142	Scan Effect Duration	7.0
Anti-Energy Defense	140	Scan Standby Time	11.4
Anti-Explosive Defense	184	Weight	1230
Attitude Stability	207	EN Load	88
System Recovery	73		

VP-44S

■ PART INFO Mass-produced head part developed by Arquebus. A number of refinements and updates have been made to the strong foundation laid by the preceding model, creating a masterpiece in the realm of second-generation AC parts.

■ UNLOCK CONDITION Parts Shop Update 1: Complete either "Destroy Artillery Installations" or "Grid 135 Cleanup"

■ PART SPECS			€ 124,000
AP	850	Scan Distance	520
Anti-Kinetic Defense	170	Scan Effect Duration	7.2
Anti-Energy Defense	172	Scan Standby Time	5.1
Anti-Explosive Defense	168	Weight	3080
Attitude Stability	408	EN Load	148
System Recovery	117		

VP-44D

■ PART INFO Head part developed by Arquebus, derived from an existing model. Engineered in anticipation of regular use by the Vespers, this model features further improvements to stability.

■ UNLOCK CONDITION Parts Shop Update 7: Complete "Escape"

■ PART SPECS			€ 231,000
AP	880	Scan Distance	530
Anti-Kinetic Defense	150	Scan Effect Duration	14.4
Anti-Energy Defense	183	Scan Standby Time	10.2
Anti-Explosive Defense	172	Weight	3260
Attitude Stability	496	EN Load	177
System Recovery	100		

NACHTREIHER/44E

■ PART INFO Lightweight head part developed by Schneider. Schneider is a specialist in aerodynamic research, and this model reflects their experience with a light but highly stable build.

■ UNLOCK CONDITION Parts Shop Update 1: Complete either "Destroy Artillery Installations" or "Grid 135 Cleanup"

■ PART SPECS			€ 84,000
AP	590	Scan Distance	280
Anti-Kinetic Defense	153	Scan Effect Duration	13.2
Anti-Energy Defense	155	Scan Standby Time	9.6
Anti-Explosive Defense	152	Weight	2320
Attitude Stability	422	EN Load	210
System Recovery	92		

KASUAR/44Z

■ PART INFO Expanded head part developed by Schneider. This model further improves on stability but with a higher energy burden, resulting in excellent performance in aerial combat.

■ UNLOCK CONDITION Parts Shop Update 4: Complete "Attack the Watchpoint"

■ PART SPECS			€ 210,000
AP	400	Scan Distance	620
Anti-Kinetic Defense	149	Scan Effect Duration	5.4
Anti-Energy Defense	157	Scan Standby Time	3.6
Anti-Explosive Defense	151	Weight	2590
Attitude Stability	498	EN Load	254
System Recovery	128		

VE-44A

■ PART INFO Heavyweight head part designed by Arquebus ADD. Incorporates cutting-edge technology to enable defiance of the PCA. This model's distinctive curved armor plating provides solid defense against damage of all kinds.

■ UNLOCK CONDITION Parts Shop Update 6: Complete "Destroy the Ice Worm"

■ PART SPECS			€ 275,000
AP	1060	Scan Distance	490
Anti-Kinetic Defense	179	Scan Effect Duration	12.6
Anti-Energy Defense	188	Scan Standby Time	9.9
Anti-Explosive Defense	178	Weight	3640
Attitude Stability	413	EN Load	182
System Recovery	110		

VE-44B

■ PART INFO Special head part designed by Arquebus ADD. Engineered to accommodate a proposal from V.VII, this model maximizes scanning performance, positioning its overall performance close to that of a surveillance-oriented concept model.

■ UNLOCK CONDITION Parts Shop Update 7: Complete "Escape"

■ PART SPECS			€ 306,000
AP	1040	Scan Distance	700
Anti-Kinetic Defense	167	Scan Effect Duration	18.0
Anti-Energy Defense	181	Scan Standby Time	4.8
Anti-Explosive Defense	166	Weight	4320
Attitude Stability	435	EN Load	265
System Recovery	154		

HC-2000 FINDER EYE

■ PART INFO Head part for scout ACs developed by RaD. Originally specced for surveying terrain, this model makes up for what it lacks in combat performance with a light energy footprint and commendable ease of use.

■ UNLOCK CONDITION Default

■ PART SPECS			€ –
AP	660	Scan Distance	290
Anti-Kinetic Defense	157	Scan Effect Duration	4.2
Anti-Energy Defense	142	Scan Standby Time	3.6
Anti-Explosive Defense	153	Weight	2670
Attitude Stability	346	EN Load	125
System Recovery	102		

HC-2000/BC SHADE EYE

■ PART INFO Custom part derived from the scout AC head developed by RaD. Comprehensively rebuilt for combat by an anonymous independent mercenary group, this model takes some steps forward but sacrifices the minimalism of its predecessor.

■ UNLOCK CONDITION Reward: Defeat Classified Subject 51-016 GA (Arena)

■ PART SPECS			€ 147,000
AP	770	Scan Distance	450
Anti-Kinetic Defense	174	Scan Effect Duration	10.8
Anti-Energy Defense	167	Scan Standby Time	9.0
Anti-Explosive Defense	181	Weight	3090
Attitude Stability	448	EN Load	163
System Recovery	120		

HC-3000 WRECKER

- **PART INFO** Head part for construction ACs developed by RaD. Specced for demolition work, this model makes up for combat performance shortcomings with its sturdiness and outstanding defensive performance.
- **UNLOCK CONDITION** Part Container: "Infiltrate Grid 086"

■ PART SPECS			€ 59,000
AP	1130	Scan Distance	270
Anti-Kinetic Defense	200	Scan Effect Duration	3.0
Anti-Energy Defense	170	Scan Standby Time	12.0
Anti-Explosive Defense	187	Weight	3800
Attitude Stability	322	EN Load	102
System Recovery	75		

HS-5000 APPETIZER

- **PART INFO** Head part for a combat AC developed by RaD. Though it was assembled from a patchwork of reclaimed resources, RaD mobilized its entire engineering team to fine-tune its design for formidable performance.
- **UNLOCK CONDITION** Parts Shop Update 8: Complete "Ocean Crossing" in NG+

■ PART SPECS			€ 199,000
AP	760	Scan Distance	610
Anti-Kinetic Defense	176	Scan Effect Duration	6.0
Anti-Energy Defense	180	Scan Standby Time	4.8
Anti-Explosive Defense	176	Weight	3000
Attitude Stability	376	EN Load	103
System Recovery	93		

EL-TH-10 FIRMEZA

- **PART INFO** Lightweight head part developed by Elcano. In keeping with Elcano's roots in producing and forging steel, this model exhibits craftsman-like flair, being light while providing reliable defenses.
- **UNLOCK CONDITION** Parts Shop Update 4: Complete "Attack the Watchpoint"

■ PART SPECS			€ 177,000
AP	480	Scan Distance	330
Anti-Kinetic Defense	156	Scan Effect Duration	15.0
Anti-Energy Defense	158	Scan Standby Time	9.6
Anti-Explosive Defense	154	Weight	2570
Attitude Stability	398	EN Load	134
System Recovery	99		

EL-PH-00 ALBA

- **PART INFO** A new head part developed by Elcano. This model utilizes technology received from Furlong Dynamics to achieve improved overall balance and precise AC control.
- **UNLOCK CONDITION** Reward: Complete "Breach the Kármán Line"

■ PART SPECS			€ 208,000
AP	600	Scan Distance	500
Anti-Kinetic Defense	171	Scan Effect Duration	3.6
Anti-Energy Defense	171	Scan Standby Time	5.4
Anti-Explosive Defense	171	Weight	2800
Attitude Stability	414	EN Load	205
System Recovery	111		

20-081 MIND ALPHA

- **PART INFO** Head part developed by ALLMIND for model ACs. Designed as part of a research project to extend human sensory capabilities, with numerous optimizations to create an AC that, to the pilot, feels like an extension of the body.
- **UNLOCK CONDITION** Reward: Hunter Class 10

■ PART SPECS			€ 223,000
AP	820	Scan Distance	320
Anti-Kinetic Defense	178	Scan Effect Duration	6.0
Anti-Energy Defense	186	Scan Standby Time	4.8
Anti-Explosive Defense	173	Weight	3350
Attitude Stability	395	EN Load	142
System Recovery	109		

20-082 MIND BETA

- **PART INFO** Model head part developed by ALLMIND. In line with a change in approach, this part maximizes stability at the expense of armor robustness.
- **UNLOCK CONDITION** Reward: Hunter Class 14

■ PART SPECS			€ 261,000
AP	520	Scan Distance	540
Anti-Kinetic Defense	158	Scan Effect Duration	12.0
Anti-Energy Defense	164	Scan Standby Time	9.0
Anti-Explosive Defense	150	Weight	3460
Attitude Stability	536	EN Load	128
System Recovery	96		

IA-C01H: EPHEMERA

- **PART INFO** Head part for the EPHEMERA unpiloted ACs, developed long ago by the Rubicon Research Institute. An old development quirk allows for piloted operation, but one should not expect any concessions for the limits of human sight.
- **UNLOCK CONDITION** Part Container: "Unknown Territory Survey".

■ PART SPECS			€ 237,000
AP	990	Scan Distance	550
Anti-Kinetic Defense	160	Scan Effect Duration	4.8
Anti-Energy Defense	189	Scan Standby Time	6.0
Anti-Explosive Defense	186	Weight	4330
Attitude Stability	480	EN Load	233
System Recovery	132		

IB-C03H: HAL 826

- **PART INFO** Head part for the HAL 826 piloted AC, developed long ago by the Rubicon Research Institute. The last of the Ibis Series and the only piloted Ibis craft, it was built to be the final safety valve to prevent a Coral Collapse.
- **UNLOCK CONDITION** Reward: Complete "Bring Down the Xylem"

■ PART SPECS			€ 254,000
AP	930	Scan Distance	600
Anti-Kinetic Defense	169	Scan Effect Duration	16.8
Anti-Energy Defense	182	Scan Standby Time	11.4
Anti-Explosive Defense	180	Weight	3760
Attitude Stability	451	EN Load	215
System Recovery	125		

Your core is the biggest determining factor when it comes to your AC's defenses. In general, the bulk of your durability will come from your core, with only your legs having a bigger impact on your AP and attitude stability. Cores also have several percentage-based adjustment values that are tied to booster and generator specs. Booster efficiency adjustment, generator output adjustment, and generator supply adjustment respectively augment your booster's Quick Boost EN consumption rate, the efficiency of your generator's EN output, and the time it takes for your EN to begin recovering.

Heavy core pieces will typically have greater defenses, AP, and attitude stability, while lighter ones will often have better booster efficiency adjustment, generator output, and generator supply adjustment values, but this is not an absolute rule. To make the most out of your core choice, you'll need to pair it with appropriate boosters and generators, as adjustment values act as multipliers to several specs provided by those parts. If you choose to ignore these values and the impact they can have on other parts of your AC, you may notice a change in how your AC handles without understanding why.

As mentioned, heavy cores like the **VE-40A** will excel defensively, but lag behind in efficiently utilizing your booster, while the lighter **IA-C01C: EPHEMERA** will make better use of auxiliary parts, but will sacrifice raw bulk. There is a lot you need to consider when picking an appropriate core, as every one is unique. Even the aforementioned VE-40A will come with one of the best generator output adjustment values, while the similarly bulky **CS-5000 MAIN DISH**'s will be fairly mediocre in this regard, instead focusing on a higher generator supply adjustment.

AC-J-120 BASHO

■ PART INFO Core part developed by BAWS for an old-generation AC. Said AC was one of the earliest models, developed to succeed MT-class machines, and modern fans of such classic hardware are fond of its characteristic bulk.

■ UNLOCK CONDITION Parts Shop Update 5: Complete "Ocean Crossing"

■ PART SPECS			€ 166,000
AP	3580	Booster Efficiency Adj.	119
Anti-Kinetic Defense	435	Generator Output Adj.	83
Anti-Energy Defense	398	Generator Supply Adj.	94
Anti-Explosive Defense	460	Weight	16100
Attitude Stability	476	EN Load	300

AC-J-120/RC JAILBREAK

■ PART INFO Junk. Originally a core part for an old-generation AC developed by BAWS. RaD engineers infiltrated Institute City to make field repairs—just enough to make this part operable, but not enough to fix its weathered armor.

■ UNLOCK CONDITION Reward: Complete "Escape"

■ PART SPECS			€ −
AP	2400	Booster Efficiency Adj.	119
Anti-Kinetic Defense	405	Generator Output Adj.	83
Anti-Energy Defense	368	Generator Supply Adj.	94
Anti-Explosive Defense	420	Weight	12350
Attitude Stability	403	EN Load	300

BD-011 MELANDER

■ PART INFO Medium-weight core part developed by Balam. The simple design and solid performance of this model make it suited for mass production—reflecting Balam's strategy of overwhelming its enemies with its material superiority.

■ UNLOCK CONDITION Parts Shop Update 1: Complete either "Destroy Artillery Installations" or "Grid 135 Cleanup"

■ PART SPECS			€ 195,000
AP	3230	Booster Efficiency Adj.	98
Anti-Kinetic Defense	438	Generator Output Adj.	105
Anti-Energy Defense	380	Generator Supply Adj.	97
Anti-Explosive Defense	429	Weight	15800
Attitude Stability	458	EN Load	304

BD-012 MELANDER C3

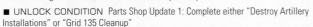

■ PART INFO Custom core part developed by Balam. Altered to improve combat suitability, this model features a lighter basic frame enhanced with partial armor plating to maintain a modest weight.

■ UNLOCK CONDITION Complete "Underground Exploration - Depth 2" OR Complete "Illegal Entry" (Pre-order Bonus only)

■ PART SPECS			€ −
AP	2830	Booster Efficiency Adj.	103
Anti-Kinetic Defense	425	Generator Output Adj.	102
Anti-Energy Defense	377	Generator Supply Adj.	103
Anti-Explosive Defense	428	Weight	14050
Attitude Stability	433	EN Load	322

DF-BD-08 TIAN-QIANG

■ PART INFO Core part developed by Dafeng Core Industries for the heavyweight TIAN-QIANG AC. This is the "trunk" in Dafeng's "stout tree, slender branches" philosophy; a defensive foundation with extremely heavy, sturdy armor.

■ UNLOCK CONDITION Parts Shop Update 1: Complete either "Destroy Artillery Installations" or "Grid 135 Cleanup"

■ PART SPECS			€ 390,000
AP	4100	Booster Efficiency Adj.	76
Anti-Kinetic Defense	473	Generator Output Adj.	114
Anti-Energy Defense	438	Generator Supply Adj.	90
Anti-Explosive Defense	478	Weight	20650
Attitude Stability	629	EN Load	388

VP-40S

■ PART INFO Mass-produced core part developed by Arquebus. A number of refinements and updates have been made to the strong foundation laid by the preceding model, creating a masterpiece in the realm of second-generation AC parts.

■ UNLOCK CONDITION Parts Shop Update 1: Complete either "Destroy Artillery Installations" or "Grid 135 Cleanup"

■ PART SPECS			€ 354,000
AP	3160	Booster Efficiency Adj.	102
Anti-Kinetic Defense	427	Generator Output Adj.	106
Anti-Energy Defense	436	Generator Supply Adj.	102
Anti-Explosive Defense	389	Weight	15030
Attitude Stability	446	EN Load	337

NACHTREIHER/40E

■ PART INFO Lightweight core part developed by Schneider. Schneider is a specialist in aerodynamic research, and this model reflects their experience with a light and highly agile build.

■ UNLOCK CONDITION Parts Shop Update 1: Complete either "Destroy Artillery Installations" or "Grid 135 Cleanup"

■ PART SPECS			€ 275,000
AP	2630	Booster Efficiency Adj.	126
Anti-Kinetic Defense	349	Generator Output Adj.	91
Anti-Energy Defense	359	Generator Supply Adj.	109
Anti-Explosive Defense	331	Weight	9820
Attitude Stability	366	EN Load	330

VE-40A

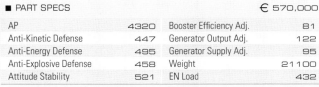

- **PART INFO** Heavyweight core part designed by Arquebus ADD. Incorporates cutting-edge technology to enable defiance of the PCA. This model features excellent generator output adjustment and solid defense against damage of all kinds.
- **UNLOCK CONDITION** Parts Shop Update 6: Complete "Destroy the Ice Worm"

■ PART SPECS			€ 570,000
AP	4320	Booster Efficiency Adj.	81
Anti-Kinetic Defense	447	Generator Output Adj.	122
Anti-Energy Defense	495	Generator Supply Adj.	95
Anti-Explosive Defense	458	Weight	21100
Attitude Stability	521	EN Load	432

CC-2000 ORBITER

- **PART INFO** Core part for scout ACs developed by RaD. Originally specced for extravehicular activity in space, this model makes up for what it lacks in combat performance with a light energy footprint and commendable ease of use.
- **UNLOCK CONDITION** Default

■ PART SPECS			€ –
AP	2780	Booster Efficiency Adj.	100
Anti-Kinetic Defense	393	Generator Output Adj.	103
Anti-Energy Defense	366	Generator Supply Adj.	93
Anti-Explosive Defense	374	Weight	12650
Attitude Stability	407	EN Load	267

CC-3000 WRECKER

- **PART INFO** Core part for construction ACs developed by RaD. Specced for demolition work, this model makes up for combat performance shortcomings with its sturdiness and outstanding physical defenses.
- **UNLOCK CONDITION** Part Container: "Infiltrate Grid 086"

■ PART SPECS			€ 158,000
AP	3940	Booster Efficiency Adj.	80
Anti-Kinetic Defense	468	Generator Output Adj.	96
Anti-Energy Defense	434	Generator Supply Adj.	100
Anti-Explosive Defense	461	Weight	19000
Attitude Stability	532	EN Load	310

CS-5000 MAIN DISH

- **PART INFO** Core part for a combat AC developed by RaD. Though it was assembled from a patchwork of reclaimed resources, RaD mobilized its entire engineering team to fine-tune its design for formidable performance.
- **UNLOCK CONDITION** Parts Shop Update 8: Complete "Ocean Crossing" in NG+

■ PART SPECS			€ 519,000
AP	3890	Booster Efficiency Adj.	79
Anti-Kinetic Defense	476	Generator Output Adj.	97
Anti-Energy Defense	489	Generator Supply Adj.	112
Anti-Explosive Defense	469	Weight	23600
Attitude Stability	641	EN Load	413

EL-TC-10 FIRMEZA

- **PART INFO** Lightweight core part developed by Elcano. In keeping with Elcano's roots in producing and forging steel, this model exhibits craftsman-like flair, being light while providing reliable defenses.
- **UNLOCK CONDITION** Parts Shop Update 4: Complete "Attack the Watchpoint"

■ PART SPECS			€ 452,000
AP	2500	Booster Efficiency Adj.	111
Anti-Kinetic Defense	384	Generator Output Adj.	104
Anti-Energy Defense	360	Generator Supply Adj.	89
Anti-Explosive Defense	375	Weight	10890
Attitude Stability	410	EN Load	351

EL-PC-00 ALBA

- **PART INFO** A new core part developed by Elcano. This model utilizes technological insights derived from analyzing Schneider ACs to achieve improved overall balance and high suitability for aerial combat.
- **UNLOCK CONDITION** Reward: Complete "Breach the Kármán Line"

■ PART SPECS			€ 531,000
AP	2850	Booster Efficiency Adj.	115
Anti-Kinetic Defense	370	Generator Output Adj.	101
Anti-Energy Defense	370	Generator Supply Adj.	105
Anti-Explosive Defense	370	Weight	12000
Attitude Stability	368	EN Load	315

07-061 MIND ALPHA

- **PART INFO** Core part developed by ALLMIND for model ACs. Designed as part of a research project to extend human sensory capabilities, with numerous optimizations to create an AC that, to the pilot, feels like an extension of the body.
- **UNLOCK CONDITION** Reward: Hunter Class 5

■ PART SPECS			€ 553,000
AP	3520	Booster Efficiency Adj.	95
Anti-Kinetic Defense	440	Generator Output Adj.	112
Anti-Energy Defense	455	Generator Supply Adj.	104
Anti-Explosive Defense	445	Weight	16510
Attitude Stability	455	EN Load	364

IA-C01C: EPHEMERA

- **PART INFO** Core part for the EPHEMERA unpiloted ACs, developed long ago by the Rubicon Research Institute. An old development quirk allows for piloted operation, but the core box makes only perfunctory concessions for a human occupant.
- **UNLOCK CONDITION** Part Container: "Underground Exploration – Depth 3"

■ PART SPECS			€ 590,000
AP	2710	Booster Efficiency Adj.	101
Anti-Kinetic Defense	335	Generator Output Adj.	126
Anti-Energy Defense	382	Generator Supply Adj.	96
Anti-Explosive Defense	350	Weight	13200
Attitude Stability	353	EN Load	412

IB-C03C: HAL 826

- **PART INFO** Core part for the HAL 826 piloted AC, developed long ago by the Rubicon Research Institute. The last of the Ibis Series and the only piloted Ibis craft, it was built to be the final safety valve to prevent a Coral Collapse.
- **UNLOCK CONDITION** Reward: Complete "Bring Down the Xylem"

■ PART SPECS			€ 663,000
AP	3670	Booster Efficiency Adj.	96
Anti-Kinetic Defense	451	Generator Output Adj.	120
Anti-Energy Defense	469	Generator Supply Adj.	108
Anti-Explosive Defense	463	Weight	18520
Attitude Stability	385	EN Load	366

Each arm part has its own AP defense values that contribute to your AC's defensive capability, displayed under AC Specs. More importantly, each arm part has a unique arms load limit value that, once surpassed, reduces the predictive fire accuracy and recoil control of equipped weapons until the arms are no longer overburdened. An arm's recoil control influences its ability to tame the natural inaccuracy and spread of projectiles introduced by sustained fire. Weapons with high recoil demand arms with high recoil control to balance out the effect. Firearm specialization influences the accuracy of predictive fire, meaning your likelihood to land shots on moving targets. In the case where your AC is equipped with a low recoil weapon, you can safely tip your spec balance in favor of firearm specialization—which will be reflected as target tracking in AC Specs. Lastly, melee specialization correlates to increased damage output from melee weaponry, with differences becoming very noticeable as the value increases; don't overlook this spec on a build that prefers to get up close.

Like other frame parts, your choice of arm should fit your build—and in the case of arms, should complement your chosen weaponry. For builds interested in supporting as heavy a set of weaponry as possible: the **VE-46A** will get you there. Be weary of the heavy burden the VE-46A puts on your legs, however. The **AC-3000 WRECKER** successfully tames weapons with high recoil, but suffers when it comes to target tracking. It's recommended to bring weapons held by the WRECKER into close range

to make up for the loss of firearm specialization. On the other hand, the **NACHTREI-HER/46E** features excellent firearm specialization—meaning great target tracking—but is inferior at dealing with recoil, making it the better choice for low recoil weapons. Lastly, the **AA-J-120 BASHO** gives the largest boost to melee specialization, meaning more melee damage output. In exchange for the extra damage, the BASHO takes a big hit in both recoil control and firearm specialization, but that will largely be made up for by fighting at close range to capitalize on the extra melee damage.

ENTER THE FIST

If you deploy with empty R-Arm or L-Arm Unit slots or purge weapons from your hands, your AC's unarmed fists can be turned into melee weapons used to bludgeon opponents with metal-crunching left or right hooks—an unexpectedly effective option that advanced pilots can exploit in creative ways. Each punch costs EN and generates some heat buildup, dealing a fixed 600 impact along with a variable amount of kinetic damage based on the Melee Specialization of your arms. Fists can be used to combo into other melee weapons, like the pile bunker. For example, when equipped with the AB-J-137 KIKAKU booster, you can engage your melee thrust by throwing a high-impact punch, setting up colossal direct hit damage on a freshly staggered enemy with a fully charged pile bunker strike.

AA-J-123 BASHO

■ PART INFO Arm parts developed by BAWS for an old-generation AC. Said AC was one of the earliest models, developed to succeed MT-class machines, and modern fans of such classic hardware are fond of its characteristic bulk.

■ UNLOCK CONDITION Parts Shop Update 5: Complete "Ocean Crossing"

■ PART SPECS			€ 81,000
AP	2430	Recoil Control	66
Anti-Kinetic Defense	208	Firearm Specialization	53
Anti-Energy Defense	191	Melee Specialization	158
Anti-Explosive Defense	225	Weight	10480
Arms Load Limit	10520	EN Load	210

AA-J-123/RC JAILBREAK

■ PART INFO Junk. Originally arm parts for an old-generation AC developed by BAWS. RaD engineers infiltrated Institute City to make field repairs—just enough to make this part operable, but not enough to fix its weathered armor.

■ UNLOCK CONDITION Reward: Complete "Escape"

■ PART SPECS			€ –
AP	1000	Recoil Control	45
Anti-Kinetic Defense	180	Firearm Specialization	45
Anti-Energy Defense	190	Melee Specialization	112
Anti-Explosive Defense	215	Weight	8480
Arms Load Limit	10520	EN Load	210

AR-011 MELANDER

■ PART INFO Medium-weight arm parts developed by Balam. The simple design and solid performance of this model make it suited for mass production—reflecting Balam's strategy of overwhelming its enemies with its material superiority.

■ UNLOCK CONDITION Parts Shop Update 1: Complete either "Destroy Artillery Installations" or "Grid 135 Cleanup"

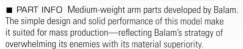

■ PART SPECS			€ 95,000
AP	2260	Recoil Control	120
Anti-Kinetic Defense	247	Firearm Specialization	100
Anti-Energy Defense	217	Melee Specialization	96
Anti-Explosive Defense	234	Weight	13650
Arms Load Limit	15100	EN Load	265

AR-012 MELANDER C3

■ PART INFO Custom arm parts developed by Balam. Altered to improve combat suitability, this model features a lighter basic frame while also enhancing arm maneuverability.

■ UNLOCK CONDITION Complete "Underground Exploration - Depth 2" OR Complete "Illegal Entry" (Pre-order Bonus only)

■ PART SPECS			€ –
AP	2010	Recoil Control	102
Anti-Kinetic Defense	239	Firearm Specialization	128
Anti-Energy Defense	212	Melee Specialization	102
Anti-Explosive Defense	233	Weight	12300
Arms Load Limit	12000	EN Load	232

DF-AR-08 TIAN-QIANG

■ PART INFO Arm parts developed by Dafeng Core Industries for the heavyweight TIAN-QIANG AC. Built to embody Dafeng's "stout tree, slender branches" philosophy, their weight is balanced by heavy upper arms and lighter forearms.

■ UNLOCK CONDITION Parts Shop Update 1: Complete either "Destroy Artillery Installations" or "Grid 135 Cleanup"

■ PART SPECS			€ 200,000
AP	2480	Recoil Control	155
Anti-Kinetic Defense	260	Firearm Specialization	92
Anti-Energy Defense	250	Melee Specialization	84
Anti-Explosive Defense	251	Weight	20020
Arms Load Limit	19500	EN Load	295

DF-AR-09 TIAN-LAO

■ PART INFO Revised arm parts developed by Dafeng Core Industries. This model attempts to further refine Dafeng's "stout tree, slender branches" philosophy by enhancing the durability of the armor plating around the shoulders.

■ UNLOCK CONDITION Parts Shop Update 4: Complete "Attack the Watchpoint"

■ PART SPECS			€ 310,000
AP	3070	Recoil Control	145
Anti-Kinetic Defense	305	Firearm Specialization	95
Anti-Energy Defense	251	Melee Specialization	68
Anti-Explosive Defense	277	Weight	26740
Arms Load Limit	17200	EN Load	266

VP-46S

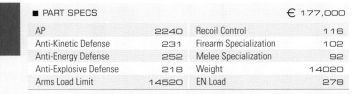

■ PART INFO Mass-produced arm parts developed by Arquebus. A number of refinements and updates have been made to the strong foundation laid by the preceding model, creating a masterpiece in the realm of second-generation AC parts.

■ UNLOCK CONDITION Parts Shop Update 1: Complete either "Destroy Artillery Installations" or "Grid 135 Cleanup"

■ PART SPECS   € 177,000

AP	2240	Recoil Control	116
Anti-Kinetic Defense	231	Firearm Specialization	102
Anti-Energy Defense	252	Melee Specialization	92
Anti-Explosive Defense	218	Weight	14020
Arms Load Limit	14520	EN Load	278

VP-46D

■ PART INFO Arm parts developed by Arquebus, derived from an existing model. Engineered in anticipation of regular use by the Vespers, this model features further improvements to performance.

■ UNLOCK CONDITION Parts Shop Update 7: Complete "Escape"

■ PART SPECS   € 258,000

AP	1620	Recoil Control	105
Anti-Kinetic Defense	196	Firearm Specialization	133
Anti-Energy Defense	230	Melee Specialization	117
Anti-Explosive Defense	190	Weight	10990
Arms Load Limit	11800	EN Load	248

NACHTREIHER/46E

■ PART INFO Lightweight arm parts developed by Schneider. Schneider is a specialist in aerodynamic research, and this model reflects their experience with a light and highly agile build.

■ UNLOCK CONDITION Parts Shop Update 1: Complete either "Destroy Artillery Installations" or "Grid 135 Cleanup"

■ PART SPECS   € 138,000

AP	1860	Recoil Control	87
Anti-Kinetic Defense	204	Firearm Specialization	160
Anti-Energy Defense	213	Melee Specialization	95
Anti-Explosive Defense	195	Weight	11420
Arms Load Limit	12730	EN Load	302

VE-46A

■ PART INFO Heavyweight arm parts designed by Arquebus ADD. Incorporates cutting-edge technology to enable defiance of the PCA. This model's distinctive curved armor plating provides solid defense against damage of all kinds.

■ UNLOCK CONDITION Parts Shop Update 6: Complete "Destroy the Ice Worm"

■ PART SPECS   € 286,000

AP	2660	Recoil Control	170
Anti-Kinetic Defense	262	Firearm Specialization	80
Anti-Energy Defense	270	Melee Specialization	76
Anti-Explosive Defense	257	Weight	22210
Arms Load Limit	21300	EN Load	380

AC-2000 TOOL ARM

■ PART INFO Arm parts for scout ACs developed by RaD. Originally specced for recovering scrap, this model makes up for what it lacks in combat performance with a light energy footprint and commendable ease of use.

■ UNLOCK CONDITION Default

■ PART SPECS   € –

AP	1990	Recoil Control	110
Anti-Kinetic Defense	207	Firearm Specialization	96
Anti-Energy Defense	204	Melee Specialization	100
Anti-Explosive Defense	209	Weight	11300
Arms Load Limit	13300	EN Load	216

AC-3000 WRECKER

■ PART INFO Arm parts for construction ACs developed by RaD. Specced for demolition work, this model makes up for combat performance shortcomings with its sturdiness and excellent recoil control.

■ UNLOCK CONDITION Part Container: "Infiltrate Grid 086"

■ PART SPECS   € 79,000

AP	2030	Recoil Control	232
Anti-Kinetic Defense	232	Firearm Specialization	26
Anti-Energy Defense	170	Melee Specialization	13
Anti-Explosive Defense	237	Weight	14650
Arms Load Limit	15800	EN Load	220

AS-5000 SALAD

■ PART INFO Arm parts for a combat AC developed by RaD. Though it was assembled from a patchwork of reclaimed resources, RaD mobilized its entire engineering team to fine-tune its design for formidable performance.

■ UNLOCK CONDITION Parts Shop Update 8: Complete "Ocean Crossing" in NG+

■ PART SPECS   € 249,000

AP	2600	Recoil Control	140
Anti-Kinetic Defense	258	Firearm Specialization	88
Anti-Energy Defense	271	Melee Specialization	80
Anti-Explosive Defense	255	Weight	20940
Arms Load Limit	18700	EN Load	356

EL-TA-10 FIRMEZA

■ PART INFO Lightweight arm parts developed by Elcano. In keeping with Elcano's roots in producing and forging steel, this model exhibits craftsman-like flair, being light while providing dependable carrying capacity.

■ UNLOCK CONDITION Parts Shop Update 4: Complete "Attack the Watchpoint"

■ PART SPECS   € 227,000

AP	1900	Recoil Control	111
Anti-Kinetic Defense	210	Firearm Specialization	122
Anti-Energy Defense	214	Melee Specialization	110
Anti-Explosive Defense	187	Weight	11220
Arms Load Limit	13540	EN Load	270

EL-PA-00 ALBA

■ PART INFO New arm parts developed by Elcano. This model utilizes technology received from Furlong Dynamics to achieve improved overall balance and precise AC control.

■ UNLOCK CONDITION Reward: Complete "Breach the Kármán Line"

■ PART SPECS   € 266,000

AP	1750	Recoil Control	101
Anti-Kinetic Defense	205	Firearm Specialization	136
Anti-Energy Defense	205	Melee Specialization	85
Anti-Explosive Defense	205	Weight	9810
Arms Load Limit	11350	EN Load	315

04-101 MIND ALPHA

- **PART INFO** Arm parts developed by ALLMIND for model ACs. Designed as part of a research project to extend human sensory capabilities, with numerous optimizations to create an AC that, to the pilot, feels like an extension of the body.
- **UNLOCK CONDITION** Reward: Hunter Class 1

PART SPECS			€ 272,000
AP	2300	Recoil Control	142
Anti-Kinetic Defense	245	Firearm Specialization	103
Anti-Energy Defense	260	Melee Specialization	79
Anti-Explosive Defense	246	Weight	16960
Arms Load Limit	15550	EN Load	358

IA-C01A: EPHEMERA

- **PART INFO** Arm parts for the EPHEMERA unpiloted ACs, developed long ago by the Rubicon Research Institute. An old development quirk allows for piloted operation, albeit with actuation translation that outstrips the capability of human nerves.
- **UNLOCK CONDITION** Part Container: "Underground Exploration – Depth 2"

PART SPECS			€ 296,000
AP	2380	Recoil Control	108
Anti-Kinetic Defense	219	Firearm Specialization	104
Anti-Energy Defense	263	Melee Specialization	106
Anti-Explosive Defense	256	Weight	12700
Arms Load Limit	12680	EN Load	312

IB-C03A: HAL 826

- **PART INFO** Arm parts for the HAL 826 piloted AC, developed long ago by the Rubicon Research Institute. The last of the Ibis Series and the only piloted Ibis craft, it was built to be the final safety valve to prevent a Coral Collapse.
- **UNLOCK CONDITION** Reward: Complete "Bring Down the Xylem"

PART SPECS			€ 322,000
AP	2210	Recoil Control	125
Anti-Kinetic Defense	225	Firearm Specialization	123
Anti-Energy Defense	248	Melee Specialization	104
Anti-Explosive Defense	236	Weight	14160
Arms Load Limit	14000	EN Load	300

LEGS

Legs make up a large part of your AC's overall defense. Each leg part has its own AP and anti-kinetic/energy/explosive defense values that contribute to the totals shown under AC Specs. Legs share attitude stability—a spec that determines the AC's ability to resist stagger—with the core, but also feature three unique specs that determine both its mobility, and ability to sortie at all. Load limit—set entirely by the legs—determines the total weight tolerated by the legs before becoming overburdened and unable to deploy. Jump distance and jump height determine the distance of Quick Boosts, and the maximum distance of vertical jumps, respectively.

Leg parts come in four varieties, all unique enough in use that they are almost new categories in themselves. Bipedal legs attempt to strike a balance between load limit, mobility, and defense. That doesn't mean that all of them cut right down the middle spec-wise, however; some allow a deficiency in one spec to allow another to shine. For example, the **VE-42A** legs support high load limits, but suffer in mobility, as made evident by their poor jump distance and jump height specs.

Reverse-joint legs trade proficiencies in defense and load limit for high jump distance and jump height values. ACs set up with a pair of these cover a lot of ground quickly when using Quick Boost, and easily cover gaps when jumping, leading to high mobility in combat, and easy traversal of terrain. This mobility comes at a cost,

though; attitude stability is at its lowest with reverse-joint legs, and you'll stagger more easily. A great example of this is the **KASUAR/42Z**: a pair of legs with incredible mobility, but lacking in load limit and attitude stability.

Tetrapod legs combine high load limits with a unique mode of mobility. Toggling vertical thrust after jumping allows your AC to hover until the AC either runs out of EN, or is staggered by the opponent. This airborne mobility allows ACs to avoid dangers they would otherwise have to engage on the ground, with the ability to rain down upon enemies with ranged weaponry. Tetrapods lack mobility during Quick Boosts or when leaping off of the ground, and their defensive maneuvering capability is only fully realized in mid-air. **The LG-033M VERRILL** supports higher load limits, while the **VP-424** is lighter and is designed for higher mobility.

Finally, tank legs are the foundation for sturdy, heavyweight builds with high load limits, defensive specs and attitude stability. They make some concessions in mobility, and while some speed and agility is offered by the tank's internal boosters and ability to drift, they're still a far cry from bipedal and reverse-joint legs. The **LG-022T BORNEMISSZA** is capable of carrying the heaviest weaponry, while the other two focus on specific terrains; the **VE-42B** performs exceptionally in aerial combat, and the **EL-TL-11 FORTALEZA** has incredible ground speed.

AL-J-121 BASHO

- **PART INFO** Bipedal legs developed by BAWS for an old-generation AC. Said AC was one of the earliest models, developed to succeed MT-class machines, and modern fans of such classic hardware are fond of its characteristic bulk.
- **UNLOCK CONDITION** Parts Shop Update 5: Complete "Ocean Crossing"

PART SPECS			€ 141,000
AP	4160	Load Limit	62600
Anti-Kinetic Defense	362	Jump Distance	132
Anti-Energy Defense	325	Jump Height	25
Anti-Explosive Defense	398	Weight	20520
Attitude Stability	824	EN Load	300

AL-J-121/RC JAILBREAK

- **PART INFO** Junk. Originally bipedal leg parts for an old-generation AC developed by BAWS. RaD engineers infiltrated Institute City to make field repairs—just enough to make this part operable, but not enough to fix its weathered armor.
- **UNLOCK CONDITION** Reward: Complete "Escape"

PART SPECS			€ –
AP	2000	Load Limit	62600
Anti-Kinetic Defense	351	Jump Distance	132
Anti-Energy Defense	315	Jump Height	25
Anti-Explosive Defense	388	Weight	18560
Attitude Stability	658	EN Load	300

LG-011 MELANDER

- **PART INFO** Medium-weight bipedal leg parts developed by Balam. The simple design and solid performance of this model make it suited for mass production—reflecting Balam's strategy of overwhelming its enemies with its material superiority.
- **UNLOCK CONDITION** Parts Shop Update 1: Complete either "Destroy Artillery Installations" or "Grid 135 Cleanup"

PART SPECS			€ 175,000
AP	4150	Load Limit	60520
Anti-Kinetic Defense	369	Jump Distance	107
Anti-Energy Defense	340	Jump Height	22
Anti-Explosive Defense	361	Weight	18700
Attitude Stability	843	EN Load	365

LG-012 MELANDER C3

■ PART INFO Custom bipedal leg parts developed by Balam. Altered to improve combat suitability, this model features a lighter basic frame enhanced with partial armor plating to maintain a modest weight.

■ UNLOCK CONDITION Complete "Underground Exploration - Depth 2" OR Complete "Illegal Entry" (Pre-order Bonus only)

■ PART SPECS			€ –
AP	3880	Load Limit	55400
Anti-Kinetic Defense	363	Jump Distance	118
Anti-Energy Defense	339	Jump Height	26
Anti-Explosive Defense	357	Weight	17210
Attitude Stability	835	EN Load	355

DF-LG-08 TIAN-QIANG

■ PART INFO Bipedal legs developed by Dafeng Core Industries for the heavyweight TIAN-QIANG AC. Built to embody Dafeng's "stout tree, slender branches" philosophy, their weight is balanced by heavy upper legs and lighter lower legs.

■ UNLOCK CONDITION Parts Shop Update 1: Complete either "Destroy Artillery Installations" or "Grid 135 Cleanup"

■ PART SPECS			€ 350,000
AP	5300	Load Limit	82600
Anti-Kinetic Defense	414	Jump Distance	90
Anti-Energy Defense	382	Jump Height	20
Anti-Explosive Defense	395	Weight	23600
Attitude Stability	925	EN Load	400

VP-422

■ PART INFO Mass-produced bipedal leg parts developed by Arquebus. A number of refinements and updates have been made to the strong foundation laid by the preceding model, creating a masterpiece in the realm of second-generation AC parts.

■ UNLOCK CONDITION Parts Shop Update 1: Complete either "Destroy Artillery Installations" or "Grid 135 Cleanup"

■ PART SPECS			€ 313,000
AP	3960	Load Limit	58620
Anti-Kinetic Defense	352	Jump Distance	112
Anti-Energy Defense	379	Jump Height	23
Anti-Explosive Defense	334	Weight	17900
Attitude Stability	830	EN Load	387

NACHTREIHER/42E

■ PART INFO Lightweight bipedal leg parts developed by Schneider. Schneider is a specialist in aerodynamic research, and this model reflects their experience with a light and highly agile build.

■ UNLOCK CONDITION Parts Shop Update 1: Complete either "Destroy Artillery Installations" or "Grid 135 Cleanup"

■ PART SPECS			€ 243,000
AP	3500	Load Limit	48650
Anti-Kinetic Defense	295	Jump Distance	228
Anti-Energy Defense	330	Jump Height	52
Anti-Explosive Defense	298	Weight	14030
Attitude Stability	711	EN Load	462

VE-42A

■ PART INFO Heavyweight bipedal leg parts designed by Arquebus ADD. Incorporates cutting-edge technology to enable defiance of the PCA. This model utilizes hover movement for increased loading capacity and greatly improved stability.

■ UNLOCK CONDITION Parts Shop Update 6: Complete "Destroy the Ice Worm"

■ PART SPECS			€ 504,000
AP	6000	Load Limit	85700
Anti-Kinetic Defense	397	Jump Distance	56
Anti-Energy Defense	453	Jump Height	14
Anti-Explosive Defense	394	Weight	28950
Attitude Stability	977	EN Load	465

2C-2000 CRAWLER

■ PART INFO Bipedal legs for scout ACs developed by RaD. Originally specced for surface surveys of astronomical objects, this model makes up for what it lacks in combat performance with a light energy footprint and commendable ease of use.

■ UNLOCK CONDITION Default

■ PART SPECS			€ –
AP	3650	Load Limit	53700
Anti-Kinetic Defense	326	Jump Distance	100
Anti-Energy Defense	322	Jump Height	24
Anti-Explosive Defense	337	Weight	16300
Attitude Stability	799	EN Load	280

2C-3000 WRECKER

■ PART INFO Bipedal leg parts for construction ACs developed by RaD. Specced for demolition work, this model makes up for combat performance shortcomings with its sturdiness and outstanding loading capacity.

■ UNLOCK CONDITION Part Container: "Infiltrate Grid 086"

■ PART SPECS			€ 139,000
AP	5220	Load Limit	68900
Anti-Kinetic Defense	350	Jump Distance	86
Anti-Energy Defense	312	Jump Height	17
Anti-Explosive Defense	383	Weight	21680
Attitude Stability	1003	EN Load	680

2S-5000 DESSERT

■ PART INFO Bipedal leg parts for a combat AC developed by RaD. Though it was assembled from a patchwork of reclaimed resources, RaD mobilized its entire engineering team to fine-tune its design for formidable performance.

■ UNLOCK CONDITION Parts Shop Update 8: Complete "Ocean Crossing" in NG+

■ PART SPECS			€ 439,000
AP	5450	Load Limit	77100
Anti-Kinetic Defense	396	Jump Distance	80
Anti-Energy Defense	408	Jump Height	19
Anti-Explosive Defense	382	Weight	25880
Attitude Stability	997	EN Load	420

EL-TL-10 FIRMEZA

■ PART INFO Lightweight bipedal leg parts developed by Elcano. In keeping with Elcano's roots in producing and forging steel, this model exhibits craftsman-like flair, being light yet retaining high load capacity.

■ UNLOCK CONDITION Parts Shop Update 4: Complete "Attack the Watchpoint"

■ PART SPECS			€ 400,000
AP	3600	Load Limit	52100
Anti-Kinetic Defense	328	Jump Distance	120
Anti-Energy Defense	266	Jump Height	28
Anti-Explosive Defense	270	Weight	11200
Attitude Stability	737	EN Load	378

EL-PL-OO ALBA

■ PART INFO New bipedal leg parts developed by Elcano. This model utilizes technological insights derived from analyzing Schneider ACs to achieve improved overall balance and high suitability for aerial combat.

■ UNLOCK CONDITION Reward: Complete "Breach the Kármán Line"

■ PART SPECS			€ 469,000
AP	3850	Load Limit	50100
Anti-Kinetic Defense	316	Jump Distance	95
Anti-Energy Defense	316	Jump Height	33
Anti-Explosive Defense	316	Weight	13150
Attitude Stability	809	EN Load	360

06-041 MIND ALPHA

■ PART INFO Bipedal legs developed by ALLMIND for model ACs. Designed as part of a research project to extend human sensory capabilities, with numerous optimizations to create an AC that, to the pilot, feels like an extension of the body.

■ UNLOCK CONDITION Reward: Hunter Class 3

■ PART SPECS			€ 482,000
AP	4360	Load Limit	63810
Anti-Kinetic Defense	370	Jump Distance	103
Anti-Energy Defense	390	Jump Height	22
Anti-Explosive Defense	356	Weight	22100
Attitude Stability	894	EN Load	432

IA-C01L: EPHEMERA

■ PART INFO Bipedal legs for EPHEMERA unpiloted ACs, developed long ago by the Rubicon Research Institute. An old development quirk allows for piloted operation, albeit with actuation translation that outstrips the capability of human nerves.

■ UNLOCK CONDITION Part Container: "Underground Exploration – Depth 1"

■ PART SPECS			€ 521,000
AP	3800	Load Limit	55050
Anti-Kinetic Defense	297	Jump Distance	109
Anti-Energy Defense	352	Jump Height	27
Anti-Explosive Defense	352	Weight	15200
Attitude Stability	805	EN Load	398

IB-C03L: HAL 826

■ PART INFO Bipedal legs for the HAL 826 piloted AC, developed long ago by the Rubicon Research Institute. The last of the Ibis Series and the only piloted Ibis craft, it was built to be the final safety valve to prevent a Coral Collapse.

■ UNLOCK CONDITION Reward: Complete "Bring Down the Xylem"

■ PART SPECS			€ 563,000
AP	4000	Load Limit	64900
Anti-Kinetic Defense	359	Jump Distance	115
Anti-Energy Defense	380	Jump Height	27
Anti-Explosive Defense	351	Weight	20890
Attitude Stability	906	EN Load	385

KASUAR/42Z

■ PART INFO Lightweight reverse-joint legs developed by Schneider. These legs sacrifice stability and defensive performance to provide exceptional jumping performance, enabling agile transitions to aerial combat—as is Schneider's forte.

■ UNLOCK CONDITION Parts Shop Update 2: Complete both "Destroy the Weaponized Mining Ship" and "Attack the Dam Complex"

■ PART SPECS			€ 192,000
AP	3400	Load Limit	47820
Anti-Kinetic Defense	293	Jump Distance	386
Anti-Energy Defense	328	Jump Height	80
Anti-Explosive Defense	290	Weight	19060
Attitude Stability	630	EN Load	388

06-042 MIND BETA

■ PART INFO Alternative reverse-joint legs developed by ALLMIND. Marking a new approach, this part explores changes in human sensory perception through introduction of alien elements; in this case, animal-like digitigrade legs.

■ UNLOCK CONDITION Reward: Hunter Class 7

■ PART SPECS			€ 521,000
AP	3920	Load Limit	61600
Anti-Kinetic Defense	340	Jump Distance	334
Anti-Energy Defense	360	Jump Height	60
Anti-Explosive Defense	364	Weight	22000
Attitude Stability	675	EN Load	426

RC-2000 SPRING CHICKEN

■ PART INFO Heavyweight reverse-joint legs for scout ACs developed by RaD. Originally specced for resource transportation rather than combat, these legs are capable of leaping up to high positions while supporting a significant weight burden.

■ UNLOCK CONDITION Parts Shop Update 5: Complete "Ocean Crossing"

■ PART SPECS			€ 419,000
AP	4080	Load Limit	68360
Anti-Kinetic Defense	357	Jump Distance	317
Anti-Energy Defense	334	Jump Height	70
Anti-Explosive Defense	360	Weight	25890
Attitude Stability	686	EN Load	402

LG-033M VERRILL

■ PART INFO Tetrapod leg option developed by Balam. The design division was all but held at gunpoint to produce a model that satisfied the Redguns' demand for a highly mobile AC platform also capable of supporting heavy weaponry.

■ UNLOCK CONDITION Parts Shop Update 6: Complete "Destroy the Ice Worm"

■ PART SPECS			€ 465,000
AP	5250	Load Limit	76200
Anti-Kinetic Defense	402	Jump Distance	82
Anti-Energy Defense	357	Jump Height	15
Anti-Explosive Defense	372	Weight	36200
Attitude Stability	1413	EN Load	675

VP-424

■ PART INFO Tetrapod leg parts developed by Arquebus, derived from an existing model. Intended for tetrapods deployed along-side Arquebus's bipedal and reverse-joint ACs, this model focuses on mobility to enable hovering-based fire support.

■ UNLOCK CONDITION Parts Shop Update 3: Complete "Operation Wallclimber"

■ PART SPECS			€ 313,000
AP	4100	Load Limit	69800
Anti-Kinetic Defense	366	Jump Distance	103
Anti-Energy Defense	384	Jump Height	18
Anti-Explosive Defense	386	Weight	31600
Attitude Stability	1366	EN Load	760

LG-022T BORNEMISSZA

■ PART INFO Heavyweight tank parts developed by Balam. Designed with the simple goal of turning ACs into tanks capable of carrying the heavy weaponry manufactured by Dafeng Core Industries.

■ UNLOCK CONDITION Parts Shop Update 3: Complete "Operation Wallclimber"

■ PART SPECS   € 280,000

AP	10040	Upward EN Consumption	700
Anti-Kinetic Defense	440	QB Thrust	22150
Anti-Energy Defense	336	QB Jet Duration	0.34
Anti-Explosive Defense	399	QB EN Consumption	810
Attitude Stability	1630	QB Reload Time	0.80
Load Limit	100300	QB Reload Ideal Weight	100300
Travel Speed	150	AB Thrust	8001
High-Speed Perf.	376	AB EN Consumption	360
Thrust	4667	Weight	49800
Upward Thrust	3667	EN Load	455

VE-42B

■ PART INFO Special tank parts designed by Arquebus ADD. Prioritizes hovering performance and forward propulsion to focus on aerial combat. During development, the specs were stolen and leaked by an independent mercenary.

■ UNLOCK CONDITION Parts Shop Update 7: Complete "Escape"

■ PART SPECS   € 490,000

AP	8600	Upward EN Consumption	912
Anti-Kinetic Defense	379	QB Thrust	21500
Anti-Energy Defense	460	QB Jet Duration	0.40
Anti-Explosive Defense	406	QB EN Consumption	880
Attitude Stability	924	QB Reload Time	0.70
Load Limit	91000	QB Reload Ideal Weight	91000
Travel Speed	136	AB Thrust	10502
High-Speed Perf.	316	AB EN Consumption	430
Thrust	5984	Weight	46600
Upward Thrust	5001	EN Load	824

EL-TL-11 FORTALEZA

■ PART INFO Lightweight tank parts developed by Elcano. Inspired by wheelchairs made for competitive sports, this product was an instant success with soldiers who had lost the use of their legs in combat but still pined for the battlefield.

■ UNLOCK CONDITION Parts Shop Update 5: Complete "Ocean Crossing"

■ PART SPECS   € 385,000

AP	5860	Upward EN Consumption	780
Anti-Kinetic Defense	345	QB Thrust	25000
Anti-Energy Defense	311	QB Jet Duration	0.26
Anti-Explosive Defense	314	QB EN Consumption	720
Attitude Stability	822	QB Reload Time	0.50
Load Limit	69300	QB Reload Ideal Weight	69300
Travel Speed	194	AB Thrust	8835
High-Speed Perf.	430	AB EN Consumption	378
Thrust	5334	Weight	24650
Upward Thrust	4667	EN Load	620

INNER PARTS

BOOSTER

Boosters are the driving force behind all forms of thrust-based movement. Once engaged, ACs travel at increased speeds based on the booster's thrust value, much faster than what is possible with basic unassisted locomotion. Vertical thrust—based on the booster's upward thrust—is also possible, allowing easy ascension to higher ground, or safety from dangers at ground level. Beyond that, boosters also enable tactical thrust movements. Quick Boost, the speed of which is determined by QB thrust, allows quick evasive reaction to incoming attacks to more easily relocate to a position of safety. On the offensive end, Assault Boosts—with speed determined by the booster's AB thrust—are an excellent aid for both traversal and closing the gap between you and the opponent. Similarly, melee attacks engage their own thrust movement, the speed determined by the booster's melee attack thrust, to quickly catch an enemy in close quarters to prepare an assault.

Your booster choices are numerous, and should be carefully selected to fit your build and battle plan, but standouts parts are available for particular situations. For pure thrust movement speed, the **BST-G2/P06SPD** achieves the fastest travel without consuming EN. Similarly, the **BUERZEL/21D** supports the fastest AB thrust values, though it comes at an EN cost. For tetrapod leg builds, the **BC-0400 MULE** is a great companion, with its minimal upward EN consumption value leaving you with plenty of EN to hover following your initial ascension. For pure Quick Boost speed, the **IB-C03B: NGI 001** achieves the highest velocity during evasive maneuvers. Keep in mind that lighter builds will more easily achieve greater Quick Boost distances, however, and are less likely to surpass a booster's QB reload ideal weight, allowing for rapid Quick Boosts. Lastly, builds set up for close-range melee damage will benefit greatly from the **AB-J-137 KIKAKU**'s incredible melee attack thrust.

AB-J-137 KIKAKU

■ PART INFO Booster developed by BAWS for an old-generation AC. An early AC model, it marked an attempt to faithfully represent Core Theory, and so its booster's specs were tweaked for melee performance—such was the trend.

■ UNLOCK CONDITION Parts Shop Update 4: Complete "Attack the Watchpoint"

■ PART SPECS   € 53,000

Thrust	5667	QB Reload Ideal Weight	75800
Upward Thrust	4917	AB Thrust	8218
Upward EN Consumption	656	AB EN Consumption	320
QB Thrust	19150	Melee Attack Thrust	14019
QB Jet Duration	0.31	Melee Atk. EN Consump.	425
QB EN Consumption	550	Weight	1820
QB Reload Time	0.55	EN Load	266

BST-G2/P04

■ PART INFO Second-generation booster developed by Furlong Dynamics. Designed to counteract the inevitable weight increases that result from improving AC performance. Performs well in a variety of assemblies including medium-weight builds.

■ UNLOCK CONDITION Parts Shop Update 1: Complete either "Destroy Artillery Installations" or "Grid 135 Cleanup"

■ PART SPECS			€ 72,000
Thrust	6001	QB Reload Ideal Weight	82000
Upward Thrust	5400	AB Thrust	8501
Upward EN Consumption	650	AB EN Consumption	353
QB Thrust	20600	Melee Attack Thrust	9668
QB Jet Duration	0.38	Melee Atk. EN Consump.	470
QB EN Consumption	560	Weight	1710
QB Reload Time	0.56	EN Load	250

BST-G1/P10

■ PART INFO First-generation booster developed by Furlong Dynamics. Though inferior to current models, this booster remains a viable choice, especially for lightweight assemblies, due to its modest energy burden and ease of use.

■ UNLOCK CONDITION Default

■ PART SPECS			€ −
Thrust	5734	QB Reload Ideal Weight	65200
Upward Thrust	5084	AB Thrust	8735
Upward EN Consumption	630	AB EN Consumption	377
QB Thrust	17600	Melee Attack Thrust	8218
QB Jet Duration	0.39	Melee Atk. EN Consump.	529
QB EN Consumption	480	Weight	1300
QB Reload Time	0.60	EN Load	130

BST-G2/P06SPD

■ PART INFO Second-generation booster developed by Furlong Dynamics. This model prizes movement speed over Quick Boost thrust, making it a good fit for assemblies that are designed for endurance.

■ UNLOCK CONDITION Parts Shop Update 6: Complete "Destroy the Ice Worm"

■ PART SPECS			€ 133,000
Thrust	6801	QB Reload Ideal Weight	76000
Upward Thrust	5217	AB Thrust	8685
Upward EN Consumption	672	AB EN Consumption	381
QB Thrust	18600	Melee Attack Thrust	10652
QB Jet Duration	0.36	Melee Atk. EN Consump.	507
QB EN Consumption	700	Weight	1420
QB Reload Time	0.50	EN Load	390

ALULA/21E

■ PART INFO Booster specialized for initial thrust, developed by Schneider. Intended for use with Schneider frames, it allows for extremely high evasive performance when used as part of a lightweight assembly.

■ UNLOCK CONDITION Reward: Complete "Intermediate Support 1: Assembling an AC"

■ PART SPECS			€ 60,000
Thrust	6668	QB Reload Ideal Weight	62400
Upward Thrust	5067	AB Thrust	9085
Upward EN Consumption	760	AB EN Consumption	435
QB Thrust	21650	Melee Attack Thrust	10868
QB Jet Duration	0.30	Melee Atk. EN Consump.	575
QB EN Consumption	690	Weight	1900
QB Reload Time	0.35	EN Load	410

FLUEGEL/21Z

■ PART INFO Booster specialized for high mobility, developed by Schneider. Commissioned by Arquebus, this part is well balanced and offers stable performance even when used as part of a medium-weight assembly.

■ UNLOCK CONDITION Parts Shop Update 5: Complete "Ocean Crossing"

■ PART SPECS			€ 202,000
Thrust	6101	QB Reload Ideal Weight	73800
Upward Thrust	5634	AB Thrust	8668
Upward EN Consumption	680	AB EN Consumption	398
QB Thrust	20000	Melee Attack Thrust	9918
QB Jet Duration	0.40	Melee Atk. EN Consump.	543
QB EN Consumption	600	Weight	1980
QB Reload Time	0.50	EN Load	282

BUERZEL/21D

■ PART INFO Booster specialized for long-distance cruising, developed by Schneider. Maximizes Assault Boost thrust and energy efficiency to provide excellent performance when rapidly closing in on a target from long range.

■ UNLOCK CONDITION Parts Shop Update 3: Complete "Operation Wallclimber"

■ PART SPECS			€ 151,000
Thrust	6167	QB Reload Ideal Weight	100600
Upward Thrust	4834	AB Thrust	10085
Upward EN Consumption	710	AB EN Consumption	378
QB Thrust	18050	Melee Attack Thrust	10402
QB Jet Duration	0.26	Melee Atk. EN Consump.	588
QB EN Consumption	536	Weight	2240
QB Reload Time	0.91	EN Load	480

BC-0600 12345

■ PART INFO Booster developed by RaD for heavy combat machines. Extended Quick Boost jet duration allows for reliable thrust regardless of weight. The eccentric model number suggests development under intoxicating influences.

■ UNLOCK CONDITION Part Container: "Eliminate "Honest" Brute"

■ PART SPECS			€ 84,000
Thrust	5801	QB Reload Ideal Weight	97000
Upward Thrust	5200	AB Thrust	8084
Upward EN Consumption	800	AB EN Consumption	372
QB Thrust	18900	Melee Attack Thrust	8118
QB Jet Duration	0.54	Melee Atk. EN Consump.	496
QB EN Consumption	520	Weight	1360
QB Reload Time	0.80	EN Load	180

BC-0400 MULE

■ PART INFO Booster developed by RaD for heavyweight machines. Designed for heavy-industry ACs primarily working on the ground, it suffers from a slow vertical boost but boasts excellent energy efficiency.

■ UNLOCK CONDITION Parts Shop Update 5: Complete "Ocean Crossing"

■ PART SPECS			€ 88,000
Thrust	5417	QB Reload Ideal Weight	80000
Upward Thrust	4767	AB Thrust	7584
Upward EN Consumption	405	AB EN Consumption	381
QB Thrust	17500	Melee Attack Thrust	7018
QB Jet Duration	0.46	Melee Atk. EN Consump.	390
QB EN Consumption	670	Weight	970
QB Reload Time	0.58	EN Load	200

BC-0200 GRIDWALKER

■ PART INFO Booster developed by RaD for lightweight machines. A design subcontracted by Elcano, this model was built for transport operations in the Grid and on other complex terrain, with only a modest EN requirement when in midair.

■ UNLOCK CONDITION Parts Shop Update 8: Complete "Ocean Crossing" in NG+

■ PART SPECS			€ 169,000
Thrust	6401	QB Reload Ideal Weight	60900
Upward Thrust	6334	AB Thrust	8585
Upward EN Consumption	660	AB EN Consumption	387
QB Thrust	19000	Melee Attack Thrust	11468
QB Jet Duration	0.33	Melee Atk. EN Consump.	520
QB EN Consumption	660	Weight	2010
QB Reload Time	0.70	EN Load	244

IA-C01B: GILLS

■ PART INFO Booster for unpiloted ACs, developed long ago by the Rubicon Research Institute. No consideration has been given to the g-force tolerance of human pilots, enabling uncompromising performance and rapid-fire Quick Boosts.

■ UNLOCK CONDITION Part Container: "Underground Exploration – Depth 2"

■ PART SPECS			€ 296,000
Thrust	6317	QB Reload Ideal Weight	68300
Upward Thrust	5334	AB Thrust	8335
Upward EN Consumption	580	AB EN Consumption	391
QB Thrust	18850	Melee Attack Thrust	6184
QB Jet Duration	0.28	Melee Atk. EN Consump.	630
QB EN Consumption	620	Weight	1590
QB Reload Time	0.30	EN Load	400

IB-C03B: NGI 001

■ PART INFO Prototype booster for piloted ACs, developed long ago by the Rubicon Research Institute. This model's design makes allowances for exoatmospheric operation, with a particular focus on enhanced Quick Boost-related specs.

■ UNLOCK CONDITION Reward: Hunter Class 13

■ PART SPECS			€ 323,000
Thrust	6467	QB Reload Ideal Weight	90200
Upward Thrust	6001	AB Thrust	8835
Upward EN Consumption	750	AB EN Consumption	405
QB Thrust	22200	Melee Attack Thrust	10535
QB Jet Duration	0.43	Melee Atk. EN Consump.	558
QB EN Consumption	740	Weight	1930
QB Reload Time	0.63	EN Load	342

FCS

The FCS, or Fire Control System, is responsible for all things related to target acquisition. The FCS influences the time required to acquire targets via missile lock and multi-lock, which is especially important for assemblies reliant on missile-based weaponry. All FCS models begin target acquisition at 450m. What varies across models is the range at which predictive fire becomes active (when the reticle turns red), and the accuracy at which your shots track targets at close, medium, and long distances.

Which FCS you choose to install is an important decision that can dramatically influence your AC's performance in combat. For example, pairing an FCS model designed to accurately track targets at long range—like the **VE-21A**—with an AC otherwise outfitted for close-combat scenarios creates a fundamental mismatch that will degrade its ability to accurately hit agile targets at close range. Instead, you should favor an FCS that offers better predictive fire assist performance based on the effective ranges of the weapons you have equipped, such as the **FC-006 ABBOT** or **IA-C01F: OCELLUS**, in a case where you need close-range assistance.

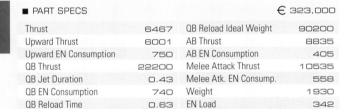

FCS-G1/P01

■ PART INFO First-generation FCS developed by Furlong Dynamics. This model dates from a time before Furlong specialized in missile development, but it remains in production due to its balanced performance and low energy burden.

■ UNLOCK CONDITION Default

■ PART SPECS			€ –
Close-Range Assist	38	Multi-Lock Correction	40
Medium-Range Assist	27	Weight	80
Long-Range Assist	20	EN Load	198
Missile Lock Correction	79		

FCS-G2/P05

■ PART INFO Second-generation FCS developed by Furlong Dynamics. This model was developed just as Furlong transitioned to its specialization in missiles, and improves on the first gen's specs while retaining its balanced performance.

■ UNLOCK CONDITION Parts Shop Update 3: Complete "Operation Wallclimber"

■ PART SPECS			€ 67,000
Close-Range Assist	42	Multi-Lock Correction	60
Medium-Range Assist	80	Weight	100
Long-Range Assist	26	EN Load	232
Missile Lock Correction	105		

FCS-G2/P10SLT

■ PART INFO Second-generation FCS developed by Furlong Dynamics. This model was developed after Furlong had established itself as a true missile specialist, and is principally designed to reduce missile lock time.

■ UNLOCK CONDITION Parts Shop Update 1: Complete either "Destroy Artillery Installations" or "Grid 135 Cleanup"

■ PART SPECS			€ 96,000
Close-Range Assist	40	Multi-Lock Correction	90
Medium-Range Assist	41	Weight	120
Long-Range Assist	29	EN Load	209
Missile Lock Correction	150		

FCS-G2/P12SML

■ PART INFO Second-generation FCS developed by Furlong Dynamics. This model was developed after Furlong had established itself as a true missile specialist, and is principally designed to improve multi-lock performance.

■ UNLOCK CONDITION Parts Shop Update 5: Complete "Ocean Crossing"

■ PART SPECS			€ 141,000
Close-Range Assist	28	Multi-Lock Correction	120
Medium-Range Assist	52	Weight	130
Long-Range Assist	30	EN Load	278
Missile Lock Correction	132		

FC-006 ABBOT

■ PART INFO Close-range combat FCS developed by Balam. In order to achieve overwhelming superiority in close-range firearms combat, Balam made compromises in missile performance to instead focus on precise targeting assistance.

■ UNLOCK CONDITION Reward: Complete "Intermediate Support 1: Assembling an AC"

■ PART SPECS			€ 135,000
Close-Range Assist	70	Multi-Lock Correction	46
Medium-Range Assist	32	Weight	90
Long-Range Assist	5	EN Load	266
Missile Lock Correction	74		

FC-008 TALBOT

■ PART INFO FCS for assault operations developed by Balam. Taking lessons from the Jupiter War, Balam improved the missile performance of their FCS products, leading to the creation of this long-seller with excellent overall balance.

■ UNLOCK CONDITION Parts Shop Update 4: Complete "Attack the Watchpoint"

■ PART SPECS			€ 155,000
Close-Range Assist	63	Multi-Lock Correction	62
Medium-Range Assist	54	Weight	140
Long-Range Assist	11	EN Load	312
Missile Lock Correction	103		

VE-21A

■ PART INFO Long-range combat FCS designed by Arquebus ADD. A concept model designed for obliterating targets well before contact—in many respects, a move away from Core Theory toward earlier visions of mechanized warfare.

■ UNLOCK CONDITION Parts Shop Update 6: Complete "Destroy the Ice Worm"

■ PART SPECS			€ 228,000
Close-Range Assist	10	Multi-Lock Correction	79
Medium-Range Assist	36	Weight	85
Long-Range Assist	92	EN Load	364
Missile Lock Correction	65		

VE-21B

■ PART INFO Long-range combat FCS designed by Arquebus ADD. Retains ADD's earlier focus on obliterating targets at range, while also improving missile performance across the board to enable a "walking fortress" style of AC.

■ UNLOCK CONDITION Parts Shop Update 7: Complete "Escape"

■ PART SPECS			€ 315,000
Close-Range Assist	15	Multi-Lock Correction	70
Medium-Range Assist	50	Weight	160
Long-Range Assist	80	EN Load	388
Missile Lock Correction	97		

IA-C01F: OCELLUS

■ PART INFO FCS for unpiloted ACs, developed long ago by the Rubicon Research Institute. Capable of exceptionally high-resolution capture in close-range engagements, making no concessions for the human brain's limitations in processing visuals.

■ UNLOCK CONDITION Part Container: "Underground Exploration - Depth 3"

■ PART SPECS			€ 367,000
Close-Range Assist	90	Multi-Lock Correction	50
Medium-Range Assist	12	Weight	130
Long-Range Assist	3	EN Load	292
Missile Lock Correction	85		

IB-C03F: WLT 001

■ PART INFO FCS for piloted ACs, developed long ago by the Rubicon Research Institute. Adapted for Coral data conductors while still faithful to Core Theory. Excellent processing capabilities that virtually extend the pilot's senses.

■ UNLOCK CONDITION Reward: Hunter Class 11

■ PART SPECS			€ 400,000
Close-Range Assist	50	Multi-Lock Correction	66
Medium-Range Assist	72	Weight	150
Long-Range Assist	48	EN Load	486
Missile Lock Correction	102		

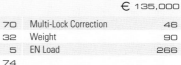

GENERATOR

If legs are the foundation of an AC's physical frame, the generator is the foundation of its internal functionality. The generator creates and supplies energy—known as EN—to an AC's components, allowing equipped parts to function, and enabling a number of energy consuming actions to be performed. EN output—the total energy available for supply to equipped parts—can be likened to the load limit found on leg parts. Where load limit supports the burden of the external, EN output supports the internal. The equipped generator, along with a bit of help from your core's Generator Output Adjustment spec, determines the final EN output value found under AC Specs. If the EN load of equipped parts surpass the displayed EN output, the AC goes into EN shortfall and cannot sortie until action is taken.

Generators govern key specs that impact combat efficiency and mobility. EN capacity determines the total EN made available for EN-consuming actions largely invoked by the equipped booster—vertical thrust, Quick Boost, Assault Boost, and melee attack thrust—and is visualized by the bar in the bottom center of the heads-up display. Spent EN is eventually replenished by the generator based on its EN recharge and supply recovery specs, which determine the time necessary

to initiate recovery following partial and complete EN depletion. Post-recovery EN supply provides a set amount of immediately usable EN following full depletion of EN, and is made available as soon as EN recovery initiates. Finally, the energy firearm specialization value provides noticeable improvements to energy weaponry, in both attack power and charge time.

Care will need to be taken when choosing a generator, as there will always be trade-offs to make when choosing one over another. The **VP-20D** supports the highest EN load of any generator, and easily carries the EN burden of the most intensive builds. **DF-GN-08 SAN-TAI** offers a very high EN capacity, which combined with low EN consumption values from your equipped booster can allow an AC to perform EN-consuming actions repeatedly before full depletion. The **DF-GN-02 LING-TAI** excels in EN recharge, performing the most efficiently at restoring partial EN depletion during combat. Special mention goes to the **VE-20B**, which has the highest energy firearm specialization, and will halve the charge time of energy weapons, with its primary drawback being low EN output, making it difficult to fully utilize without planning.

AG-J-098 JOSO

■ PART INFO Internal combustion generator developed by BAWS for an old-generation AC. Performance is not dissimilar to generic labor MT models, making it an unreliable choice for combat use in a modern AC build.

■ UNLOCK CONDITION Default

■ PART SPECS			€ –
EN Capacity	2300	Energy Firearm Spec.	72
EN Recharge	769	Weight	3420
Supply Recovery	500	EN Output	2600
Post-Recovery EN Supply	400		

AG-E-013 YABA

■ PART INFO Internal combustion generator developed by BAWS for modern ACs. A balanced model capable of withstanding the demands of modern combat, its development was aimed at narrowing Rubicon's post-closure technological gap.

■ UNLOCK CONDITION Parts Shop Update 4: Complete "Attack the Watchpoint"

■ PART SPECS			€ 240,000
EN Capacity	2850	Energy Firearm Spec.	95
EN Recharge	1000	Weight	5080
Supply Recovery	555	EN Output	3000
Post-Recovery EN Supply	1000		

AG-T-005 HOKUSHI

■ PART INFO BAWS internal combustion generator developed in tandem with Elcano. Improved output allows for use of high-burden parts, but emergency cooling speed leaves much to be desired, calling for a degree of EN management finesse.

■ UNLOCK CONDITION Parts Shop Update 7: Complete "Escape"

■ PART SPECS			€ 312,000
EN Capacity	3160	Energy Firearm Spec.	90
EN Recharge	952	Weight	7080
Supply Recovery	370	EN Output	3810
Post-Recovery EN Supply	850		

DF-GN-02 LING-TAI

■ PART INFO Internal combustion generator developed by Dafeng Core Industries. Commissioned by Balam, the specifications for this model demanded lightweight construction matched with excellent cooling performance.

■ UNLOCK CONDITION Parts Shop Update 1: Complete either "Destroy Artillery Installations" or "Grid 135 Cleanup"

■ PART SPECS			€ 90,000
EN Capacity	2000	Energy Firearm Spec.	61
EN Recharge	2000	Weight	3860
Supply Recovery	833	EN Output	2340
Post-Recovery EN Supply	280		

DF-GN-06 MING-TANG

■ PART INFO Internal combustion generator developed by Dafeng Core Industries. A joint development with Balam, this model focuses on ensuring both good cooling performance and a high EN capacity.

■ UNLOCK CONDITION Parts Shop Update 3: Complete "Operation Wallclimber"

■ PART SPECS			€ 170,000
EN Capacity	2900	Energy Firearm Spec.	76
EN Recharge	1250	Weight	6320
Supply Recovery	666	EN Output	3160
Post-Recovery EN Supply	440		

DF-GN-08 SAN-TAI

■ PART INFO Internal combustion generator developed by Dafeng Core Industries. This model was designed for use with the corporation's independently-manufactured heavyweight ACs, and features outstanding EN capacity.

■ UNLOCK CONDITION Parts Shop Update 6: Complete "Destroy the Ice Worm"

■ PART SPECS			€ 300,000
EN Capacity	4420	Energy Firearm Spec.	88
EN Recharge	1176	Weight	10060
Supply Recovery	625	EN Output	3210
Post-Recovery EN Supply	810		

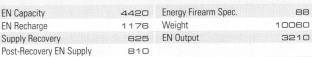

VP-20S

■ PART INFO Circulating-current generator developed by Arquebus. Tailored to lightweight ACs, such as those built by Schneider, efforts were made to keep its weight modest while providing capable output for its size.

■ UNLOCK CONDITION Reward: Complete "Intermediate Support 1: Assembling an AC"

■ PART SPECS			€ 126,000
EN Capacity	2500	Energy Firearm Spec.	94
EN Recharge	833	Weight	3800
Supply Recovery	434	EN Output	3200
Post-Recovery EN Supply	1200		

VP-20C

■ PART INFO Circulating-current generator developed by Arquebus. The design goal for this model was to create a generator with no drawbacks, resulting in a product that provides stable performance in any AC assembly.

■ UNLOCK CONDITION Parts Shop Update 5: Complete "Ocean Crossing"

■ PART SPECS			€ 229,000
EN Capacity	2720	Energy Firearm Spec.	100
EN Recharge	909	Weight	5320
Supply Recovery	454	EN Output	3670
Post-Recovery EN Supply	1100		

VP-20D

■ PART INFO Circulating-current generator developed by Arquebus. Designed with a focus on EN capacity and output to support Arquebus energy weapons, it supplies more raw power than any other corporate product on the market.

■ UNLOCK CONDITION Parts Shop Update 3: Complete "Operation Wallclimber"

■ PART SPECS			€ 416,000
EN Capacity	3250	Energy Firearm Spec.	98
EN Recharge	714	Weight	11030
Supply Recovery	384	EN Output	4430
Post-Recovery EN Supply	1400		

VE-20A

■ PART INFO Circulating-current generator designed by Arquebus ADD. Engineered to support high-spec energy weapon prototypes, it maximizes EN output at the expense of sacrificing performance in other regards.

■ UNLOCK CONDITION Parts Shop Update 6: Complete "Destroy the Ice Worm"

■ PART SPECS			€ 206,000
EN Capacity	2460	Energy Firearm Spec.	116
EN Recharge	740	Weight	3590
Supply Recovery	416	EN Output	3120
Post-Recovery EN Supply	600		

VE-20B

■ PART INFO Circulating-current generator designed by Arquebus ADD. Engineered to maximize energy weapon specialization, this model even sacrifices EN output to a degree, positioning its performance somewhere close to a concept model.

■ UNLOCK CONDITION Parts Shop Update 9: Complete "Destroy the Ice Worm" in NG+

■ PART SPECS			€ 324,000
EN Capacity	3300	Energy Firearm Spec.	150
EN Recharge	763	Weight	5860
Supply Recovery	392	EN Output	2890
Post-Recovery EN Supply	800		

VE-20C

■ PART INFO Circulating-current generator designed by Arquebus ADD. Features improved EN capacity and output while retaining a focus on energy weapon specialization. However, it suffers from a heavy weight burden and cooling difficulties.

■ UNLOCK CONDITION Parts Shop Update 7: Complete "Escape"

■ PART SPECS			€ 405,000
EN Capacity	3690	Energy Firearm Spec.	128
EN Recharge	555	Weight	10130
Supply Recovery	377	EN Output	4090
Post-Recovery EN Supply	720		

IA-C01G: AORTA

■ PART INFO Coral-based internal combustion generator developed long ago by the Rubicon Research Institute. This model takes advantage of the Coral's biological traits, enabling rapid recovery by pushing combustion to its limit.

■ UNLOCK CONDITION Part Container: "Survey the Uninhabited Floating City"

■ PART SPECS			€ 460,000
EN Capacity	3000	Energy Firearm Spec.	105
EN Recharge	238	Weight	4330
Supply Recovery	333	EN Output	3500
Post-Recovery EN Supply	2000		

IB-C03G: NGI 000

■ PART INFO Prototype Coral-based internal combustion generator developed long ago by the Rubicon Research Institute. Optimized for power-hungry Coral weapons, with rapid EN recovery enabled by maximized combustion.

■ UNLOCK CONDITION Reward: Hunter Class 9

■ PART SPECS			€ 510,000
EN Capacity	4400	Energy Firearm Spec.	110
EN Recharge	250	Weight	8950
Supply Recovery	312	EN Output	4340
Post-Recovery EN Supply	3300		

EXPANSION

Expansions are unlocked through OS Tuning, and are the final piece of the assembly puzzle. When used correctly, they give you access to a myriad of new tactical opportunities. With no associated weight or EN cost, you're free to pick and choose between those you've unlocked, regardless of what the rest of your build is comprised of. Most Expansions have both offensive and defensive applications, though some may lean more one way than the other. They can be used either strategically to help you execute a plan of attack, or reactively to help you get out of trouble. All Core Expansions employ pulse technology to create spherical barriers with varying effects, ranging from debilitating blast waves to protective barriers.

Understanding the unique specs found on these parts will help you make a more informed decision about which to equip. Resilience and duration specs are both found on defensive-orientated expansion parts, and describe the barrier's AP and its lifespan in seconds. On expansions geared more toward offense, blast radius lets you know the range in meters of the most impactful part of the attack, and the effect range is the maximum distance at which it will hit a target. For a more detailed breakdown of these specs, see P.39 and P.47.

Assault Armor creates an expanding pulse energy explosion around your AC. It takes a second to prime after you input the command, leaving your AC briefly immobile and vulnerable. You'll need to activate it pre-emptively, when you anticipate that an enemy will launch an attack, rather than when you're just about to be hit. The explosion deals full damage to anything within 60m, and a reduced amount at up to 199m, which is the limit of its effective range. The huge impact damage it deals is enough to stagger most standard or strong enemies. Against bosses, it's an effective tool for staggering them, and its high direct hit adjustment makes using it as a final attack just before the boss recovers from a stagger equally effective. It can also intercept and negate any projectiles it comes into contact with, regardless of how many or how strong they are. Many bosses have projectile attacks that can be exceptionally difficult to evade, especially when you're still learning the encounter and are often out of the optimal position for evasion. With assault armor, you can essentially ignore any projectile attack, be they large salvos of missiles, or highly-focused energy beams.

ASSAULT ARMOR

- PART INFO Core Expansion: Assault Armor. Creates a pulse explosion centered on the AC, canceling out incoming enemy fire and creating a damaging area-of-effect shockwave.

- UNLOCK CONDITION OS Tuning

- PART SPECS   € −

Attack Power	1500	Blast Radius	60
Impact	2000	Effect Range	200
Accumulative Impact	1380	Direct Hit Adjustment	230

Pulse Protection establishes a defensive barrier around your AC that stays in the exact position in which you activate it. This barrier is much larger than the one generated by pulse armor, has greater resilience, and lasts for longer, making it an excellent choice if you know you're going to stay in a particular location. Unlike pulse armor, which has some offensive applications, pulse protection is almost entirely defensive. The barrier's radius is substantial, but staying within it will limit your movement options. The barrier negates incoming projectiles, but you can still fire through it to hit enemies outside; enemies themselves can still safely pass through it, however. While outside the barrier, you can rotate and move around it as needed, to ensure it's always providing you with the best protection and allowing you to track your opponent's movement. Using this method, even if an enemy passes through one side of the barrier, they'd still have to get through the other side before they could fire on you, giving you more time to react.

PULSE PROTECTION

- PART INFO Core Expansion: Pulse Protection. Creates a pulse barrier in a fixed position, providing cover from enemy fire until the barrier reaches its durability or time limit. The barrier is not permanent and will disappear after time has passed.

- UNLOCK CONDITION OS Tuning

- PART SPECS   € −

| Resilience | 4000 | Duration | 25 |

Pulse Armor forms a defensive barrier around your AC that stays with you while you move and absorbs both the damage and impact of incoming attacks. The barrier does not last indefinitely, however, and it can only be maintained for the length of its duration spec. Similarly, it cannot withstand sustained heavy attacks, because it has finite resilience, and once its AP threshold has been met, the barrier will dissipate. Given both of those limitations, the correct timing is crucial to getting the most out of this expansion, and you also need to keep in mind the strength of the attacks you're thinking of using it against.

Unlike assault armor, if you use this to protect yourself against an incoming projectile attack and that attack deals more damage than the resilience of the barrier, you'll still take some damage. However, you can use this to defend against hard-to-evade melee attacks to reduce their lethality. Using it in anticipation of a dangerous attack is the most obvious use case for this expansion, but it can also be used offensively. If, for example, you know you're about to trade blows with an enemy, preemptively activating pulse armor will give you a defensive cushion to absorb some of their attacks. It's also an excellent tool for close-range builds, letting them rush toward an enemy safely, as they'll either have to escape or try to destroy your pulse armor quickly to thwart your assault.

PULSE ARMOR

- PART INFO Core Expansion: Pulse Armor. Creates a pulse barrier that trails the AC, dramatically increasing defensive performance until it exceeds its durability or time limit.

- UNLOCK CONDITION OS Tuning

- PART SPECS   € −

| Resilience | 3300 | Duration | 10 |

Equipping a Coral-based generator will change the color of your Core Expansion abilities to a crimson red. These generators also increase the effectiveness of assault armor, allowing it to bypass enemy defenses by changing the damage type to Coral instead of energy.

Terminal Armor, unlike other expansions, does not require manual activation. Instead, it gets deployed automatically upon your AC receiving lethal damage. Once active, it creates a barrier similar to pulse armor that follows you around, negating incoming damage, though with much higher resilience and much shorter duration. The barrier has such high resilience that it effectively provides temporary invulnerability; practically nothing can break through it during its short lifespan. While it's active, you'll need to quickly gauge the situation and take stock of your options; if you were out of repair kits, your best choice is try to defeat the opponent before the barrier dissipates. If you have repair kits, however, then you might be better off using the time to create some separation, heal up, and reset the encounter.

It's best suited for use against bosses or other tough enemies that have the potential to crush your AC in a few swift attacks. Against such foes, it not only serves as a savior if you take an untimely hit, but also as a powerful learning tool that allows you to stay in the fight longer to learn more about the enemy you're facing. This is a very important thing to keep in mind, because, while the other expansions have more strategic uses, they require some foreknowledge of the opponent or attacks you'll be going up against. If you do not yet have that knowledge, terminal armor is a neutral option that will help you regardless of the opponent you're facing.

TERMINAL ARMOR

- PART INFO Core Expansion: Terminal Armor. An emergency variant of Pulse Armor that trails the AC, activating when the AC has reached critical AP damage.

- UNLOCK CONDITION OS Tuning

- PART SPECS   € −

| Resilience | 20000 | Duration | 5 |

CHAPTER 3 MISSION INTEL

Finding yourself on Rubicon, a planet obviously ravaged by a long history of conflict and hubris, you'll need to stay alive long enough to forge your own path. Your prowess as an AC pilot will draw the interest of almost every faction, and many will react by sending their strongest forces to wipe you out. This chapter takes you through the entire game, mission by mission, providing the navigation and combat intel you need to complete your objectives, regardless of who you side with.

USING THIS CHAPTER

Welcome to the Mission Intel chapter: here every mission in the game is covered with a step-by-step walkthrough that follows a specific route, which we've highlighted on the accompanying maps. Any ACs or bosses you'll encounter in these missions are also covered here, with full strategies and detailed breakdowns of their potential attacks.

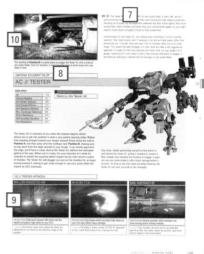

We'll explain each element here to ensure that the format used across the following pages is clear:

1 Mission Objectives

These are the key objectives that will change as you proceed through the mission. When the objective changes, you'll see the new objective listed before the relevant Step Point in the mission's text.

2 Mission Summary

This text provides a summary of the mission and introduces you to its major features and threats.

3 Mission Overview

Here you'll find the mission's key details, such as the name of the combat zone, the amount of COAM awarded and any features unlocked upon completion.

4 Enemy Data

This table shows the details of each enemy type you'll encounter in the mission. The colored dot to the left indicates which type they will appear as on the maps, based on the map legend shown above right.

5 Map

Each mission's map shows the locations of all enemies and features our suggested route, as well as the Step Point markers that make orienting yourself while reading the text easy.

6 Assembly

Here we provide a recommended build that should be affordable at the current point in the game, and will help to make certain threats in the mission easier to handle.

7 Step Points

Step Points link the main walkthrough text to the maps, while breaking the text into smaller chunks to make it easier to follow. To know where the current Step Point begins in the combat zone, simply find its corresponding number on the map.

8 Boss/AC Entry

For each boss and AC you'll encounter, we've provided their specs and outlined a strategy to defeat them. If an enemy AC can use repair kits, then amount they have available will be listed with their specs.

9 Boss/AC Attacks ▽

Here you'll find a list of the attacks that the boss or AC can use in battle. We describe each attack and how to evade it, and those that prompt an audible system alert are marked with a red triangle symbol. Attack phases are marked if they appear only in specific phases; those that don't identify the phase they're used in apply to the entire fight.

10 Screenshots

Screenshots are always connected back to the relevant text via matching red letters; an A, for example, will appear both in the lower left of the screenshot and at the end of the related paragraph of text. Standalone screenshots with captions will not be linked to the text in this way.

MAP LEGEND

Here you'll see the full set of icons used on the maps throughout this chapter. Enemies are marked on the maps according to their starting locations. To make enemies easier to identify, they are categorized into Weak, Medium and Strong types.

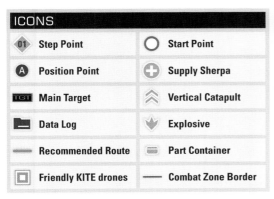

ICONS		
01 Step Point		◯ Start Point
A Position Point		⊕ Supply Sherpa
TGT Main Target		≫ Vertical Catapult
Data Log		⌄ Explosive
Recommended Route		⊟ Part Container
▢ Friendly KITE drones		Combat Zone Border

ENEMIES	
◯ Weak Enemy	◆ Medium Sniper
◯ Medium Enemy	◆ Strong Sniper
● Strong Enemy	◆ Artillery Sniper
◯ Artillery	■ Mission Target
◯ AC	● Boss/Warship

COMBAT LOG MODIFIERS

◆ Enemy icons can be modified to indicate that they carry combat logs. The example shown here is a strong enemy sniper with a silver combat log.

COMBAT LOG COLORS	
◆ Bronze	◆ Gold
◆ Silver	◆ Platinum

MISSION HUD ELEMENTS

Some elements appear on your HUD during missions to make progression easier. Paying attention to these will ensure that you're aware of your key objectives and targets.

Objective Markers
Objective markers will point you toward the next important mission location, which can sometimes be multiple locations that you can choose to tackle in any order. Objective markers appear as small blue dots on your compass.

Target Markers
Critical targets for elimination during a mission are identified by this HUD element, and will also appear on your compass as a small red square with "TGT" above it.

Warning Updates
These small yellow triangles appear on your HUD to alert you when new enemies or threats enter the immediate area.

MISSION BRIEFINGS

A short briefing will play out before each mission, usually given by Handler Walter or the mission's primary client. These briefings provide some background on the area you're entering and the objectives to be completed, and will occasionally include some clues as to what you'll encounter and—for those trying to piece together the events occurring on Rubicon—your client's motivations.

CHAPTERS

The game's story is split into five separate chapters, punctuated by key developments as your journey on Rubicon progresses. The length of each chapter isn't equal; some feature a lot more missions than others. Each mission that concludes a chapter is marked on the Missions menu with a small orange chevron symbol. These missions are invariably home to the game's toughest boss battles and most critical events.

REWARDS & BONUS PAY

In addition to potentially unlocking new training programs, features or Parts Shop updates, each completed mission will reward you with some of the game's currency, COAM. The costs of the ammo you expend and any repairs from damage taken are always subtracted from the mission's base payout. Missions can also sometimes offer opportunities for bonus pay, either for destroying specific enemy units or by taking out additional targets such as fuel tanks; taking advantage of these situations when they arise is crucial to ensure you're never short on currency. Whenever bonus pay is available, the Enemy Data chart for the mission will display the amount each enemy awards.

Here three different objective locations are available at once, and you're free to choose which order to tackle them in.

DECISIONS

As you progress through the campaign and complete missions, new job offers from clients are unlocked in small groups that you can complete in any order. However, you'll occasionally come across multiple missions in a group that are all labeled as a "Decision." Decisions indicate missions that conflict with each other due to your potential clients having opposing goals. You can look at the overview for each mission, watch its briefing, and play through a portion of it, but as soon as you finish any mission marked as a decision, the others will become unavailable on your current playthrough. In order to complete all missions, you'll need to play through the game multiple times while choosing a different set of decisions along the way. For more on this, and our recommended route through three full playthroughs, head to P.398.

Some mission scenarios conflict with each other, which is known as a "Decision" point; see P.398 to learn which missions lead to certain alternate missions and endings.

> ### "'Raven.' That's your new name here on Rubicon."
> —Handler Walter

Having made your way to the surface of Rubicon, your first mission is to assume the identity of a fallen pilot—this will let you register as a mercenary and accept contracts from the planet's active factions. You'll spend the introductory section learning the basic controls and getting a feel for piloting your AC, and must then head to the contaminated city to find your new license. You can approach the potential locations in any order you like; however, there are numerous enemies patrolling the city that will engage you on sight. You don't have to destroy any enemies other than in the mission's final encounter, but it's worth familiarizing yourself with the game's combat by engaging targets along the way.

The basic enemies here provide a sample of what combat will be like moving forward, and the mission's boss, an AH12: HC HELICOPTER, will pose a challenge to new players. Keep in mind that it's best to avoid being overly reliant on your missile launcher to dispatch bipedal MTs while exploring the city, or you'll run the risk of depleting its ammo reserves before the final encounter; your pulse blade has no ammunition constraints, so using it whenever possible is a good ammo-saving option.

MISSION OBJECTIVES
- Reach the Catapult
- Obtain a Mercenary License
- Destroy the PCA Heavy Combat Helicopter

MISSION INFO

Combat Zone	Southern Belius—Grid 135/Contaminated City
Client	Handler Walter
Reward	170,000
Max Bonus Pay	—
Completion Unlocks	Sortie Menu, AC Design Menu, and Beginner Training 1: Basic Controls
Combat Logs	—
Data Logs	4
Part Containers	—

ENEMY DATA

	No.	AP	AS	Bonus Pay	Analysis
MT-T-026 Guard Mech (Rifle)	26	102	121	—	P.310
CD-E-086 Aerial Defense Drones (Mini Gatling Gun)	22	40	—	—	P.308
MT-E-104 Bipedal MT (Machine Gun)	26	470	364	—	P.315
MT-E-104 Bipedal MT (Dual Machine Gun)	4	470	364	—	P.316
MT-E-104 Bipedal MT (Machine Gun & Shield)	4	470	364	—	P.315
MT-E-104 Bipedal MT (Missile Launcher)	8	470	364	—	P.316
AH12: HC HELICOPTER	1	23875	2400	—	—

BOSS

License Code: Raven

08

07

x3

x6

License Code: Monkey Gordo

D

x2

x4

x4

x4

C

x2

x3

License Code: G7 Hakra

06

x4

x2

x3

x2

x3

x2

License Code: Thomas Kirk

05

x4

x2

x2

B

04

x3

03

ASSEMBLY

You're provided with only a base AC for this mission, and its capabilities are average, both defensively and offensively. Your RF-024 TURNER is a solid mid-range weapon that can dispatch most enemies in this mission with just a few shots, but if you come across a group, the multi-lock capabilities of the BML-G1/P20MLT-04 will serve you better. Nothing in your current equipment can match the pure power of your pulse blade, however, and taking some time early in the mission to get used to the ranges at which it can hit enemies will make things much easier for you toward the end.

01	R-ARM UNIT | ASSAULT RIFLE RF-024 TURNER	P.52
02	L-ARM UNIT | PULSE BLADE HI-32: BU-TT/A	P.65
03	R-BACK UNIT | MISSILE LAUNCHER BML-G1/P20MLT-04	P.69
04	L-BACK UNIT | —	—
05	HEAD | — HC-2000 FINDER EYE	P.78
06	CORE | — CC-2000 ORBITER	P.81
07	ARMS | — AC-2000 TOOL ARM	P.83
08	LEGS | BIPEDAL 2C-2000 CRAWLER	P.85
09	BOOSTER | — BST-G1/P10	P.88
10	FCS | — FCS-G1/P01	P.89
11	GENERATOR | — AG-J-098 JOSO	P.91

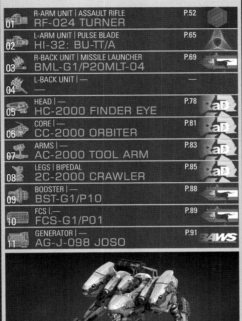

OBJECTIVE

Reach the Catapult

01 ◆ You'll begin inside the facility into which you unceremoniously crashed, and since it's far away from your intended landing zone, you'll need to make your way out and get back on target. At the far end of the room you're in, you'll need to ascend up a series of ledges to reach the maintenance tunnel that leads to the next section of the facility.

02 ◆ Once you reach this location, you'll have an excellent vantage point from which to survey the large room ahead of you, where a number of hostile units await. The enemies should be unaware of your presence at this point (marked with an "unaware" indicator above them when you target them), and that means your first shot will deal additional impact, putting greater ACS strain on that enemy than hits during regular combat would, and giving you a head start toward staggering them. Directly below you is a group of four patrolling enemies, and from this vantage point, you can use your missiles to multi-lock and destroy them with a single barrage. Drop down and push further into the room once the initial group has been dealt with, and then use your assault rifle to quickly dispatch the two bipedal MTs when they're within range.

A number of tutorials will pop up throughout this mission, and since this game has a lot of unique controls and systems, it's worth paying attention to all of them.

Using the environment to your advantage can make encounters significantly easier, so always survey new areas before initiating combat.

Continue along the left-hand side of the tracks until you're within range of the next enemy group, and once again use your assault rifle while boosting toward the container they're standing near. While engaging those enemies, a bipedal MT located near the door you need to access will likely spot you and begin firing missiles; either use Quick Boosts to evade them, or take cover behind the container if you're close enough. Wait for an opening, then Assault Boost toward it and finish it off with a pulse blade slash. Now that the area is clear, access the door and proceed to **Position A**, where you'll find a catapult that you can use to reach the city below.

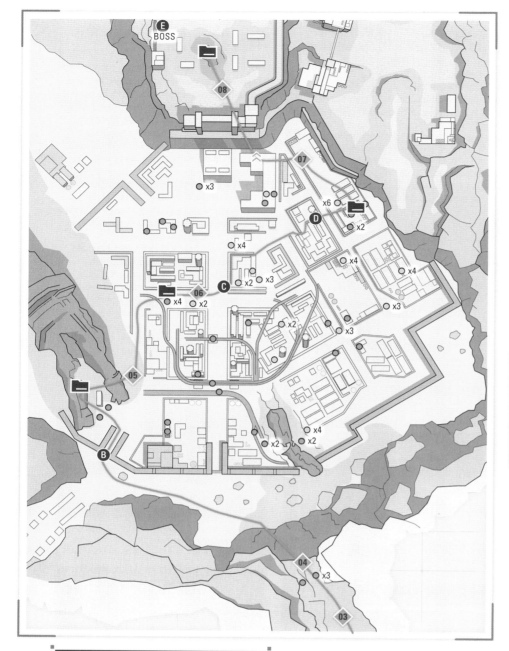

You can go to the objective locations in any order you like, but since the one near **Position B** is closest, that's the most obvious first choice.

It can be difficult to spot the enemies among the debris, so make sure to use your scanner to pinpoint their locations.

As you approach this area, a PCA Subject Guard heavy combat helicopter will swoop in and begin raining down heavy missiles on the RLF bipedal MTs stationed near the next objective. You can't damage it yet, and the blasts from its missiles pack quite a punch, so keep your distance until it flies away.

ting them with your weapons can be quite difficult. Thankfully, it's possible to remain undetected and get quite close to them by entering the city this way, allowing you to rapidly close the remaining distance with an Assault Boost and dispatch them with pulse blade combos. Once they're defeated, access the wreckage at the objective location to get the license. It's expired, however, so you'll need to investigate the next wreck.

05 ◈ Instead of heading directly toward the next objective, follow the city wall from here. When you reach the opening, use the wall and the destroyed highway in the area for cover while you take out any enemies that may have survived the attack from the HC Helicopter. The license you obtain from scanning this wreck doesn't meet your requirements either, so you'll need to check the final location.

06 ◈ You'll need to move through the city to reach the next wreck, so avoiding combat won't be easy. Since this wreck is quite heavily guarded, a cautious approach is prudent. A downed chopper has created a hole in the wall at **Position C**, and if you pass through it, you can weave between the walls and buildings to arrive relatively unscathed at another hole in a wall at **Position D**. From there, you have

CHECKPOINTS

Landing after using the catapult will automatically trigger your first checkpoint; this is where you'll restart from if you're destroyed or otherwise fail the mission. Restarting from a checkpoint fully resupplies all of your ammunition and repair kits, and once you've unlocked the Assembly, you'll be able to access it from the Mission Failed menu and adjust your loadout.

OBJECTIVE

Obtain a Mercenary License

03 ◈ A short distance ahead of your landing point you'll see a group of bipedal MTs; these, along with all future enemies, have a lot more AP than the ones you've encountered previously. Use this group to familiarize yourself with how many shots it takes to destroy them with each of your weapons, so that

you don't waste any ammunition when you face them again later in this mission.

Stop at the top of the cliff just beyond those enemies—from here, you can see the contaminated city below, as well as the three wrecks that Walter marks as worth investigating for a potential license. There are no enemies outside of the city walls, and it's possible to avoid a lot of those within the city by skirting around the boundary of the combat zone. You won't benefit from taking out additional enemies, and since there's a difficult encounter at the end of the mission, it's best to conserve your missile ammunition.

04 ◈ Drop down from the cliffs and start heading toward the opening in the city wall at **Position B**, then use your scanner to reveal the location of the two bipedal MTs guarding the wreck you need to access. These enemies are carrying shields, so hit-a clear line of sight over the enemies surrounding the wreck and can use a combination of multi-lock missiles and assault rifle fire to dispatch them, while using the wall and nearby building for cover. Once the area is clear, boost over and access the final wreck.

07 ◈ After retrieving the first three license codes and finding none of them suitable, Walter discovers one final wreck and marks its location for you. However, a group of enemies guard the area just in front of the vertical catapult you need to use to reach the wreck. If you stay low while approaching this point, you can cut across behind them and use the vertical catapult without engaging in combat.

08 ◈ Shortly after you retrieve the license from the wreck, the AH12: HC HELICOPTER that you encountered earlier will return, ready to engage you. This means it's a good idea to accustom yourself with the layout of this area before accessing the wreck, because you'll want to know where all of the potential cover is located. Once you're prepared, access the final wreck and get into position to fight the boss.

Investigating objects that stand out in the environment during missions, such as this downed transport helicopter, can often point you toward useful traversal routes or even hidden parts or collectibles.

AH12

HC HELICOPTER

The AH12: HC HELICOPTER is equipped with powerful munitions that it can use frequently, and depending on your positioning, this can make evading its attacks quite difficult. There are buildings scattered around the arena that can provide useful cover, but you can never hide for long as the AH12: HC HELICOPTER will often reposition itself. Try to only take cover against a single incoming attack, and then move to a different position. If you lose track of the boss due to your proximity to a building, remember that you can scan to highlight it.

BASIC SPECS

AP	23875
Attitude Stability	2400
Anti-Kinetic Defense	1210
Anti-Energy Defense	700
Anti-Explosive Defense	1145
Elec. Discharge Tolerance	—
Shock Resistance	—
ACS Anomaly Tolerance	—
Heat Resistance	—

OBJECTIVE

Destroy the PCA Heavy Combat Helicopter

The AH12: HC HELICOPTER approaches the arena from **Position E**. As soon as you've accessed the final wreck, move in that direction so that you can get underneath it straight away; this boss is most dangerous at medium- to long-range, so staying close as much as possible will improve your odds of success. You can start damaging the boss before its AP gauge appears on your HUD—use this time to land as many strikes as possible, especially from your pulse blade, since it deals far more damage and impact than anything else in your current arsenal. If this initial strike goes well, you can deplete a large portion of the boss's AP gauge before it even becomes a threat.

Staggering the HC HELICOPTER should be your primary goal, in order to capitalize on the additional damage from direct hits. Whenever possible, Assault Boost toward it while firing, and then use your pulse blade once you're within range to inflict as much ACS strain as possible. Pay close attention to the boss's ACS gauge while doing this, to ensure that your pulse blade is available for use once it staggers. With good timing and positioning, you can land a pulse blade combo the instant it staggers, and then get a second one in just before it recovers for a huge chunk of damage. Keep up the pressure by constantly using Assault Boosts to close the gap while firing whenever the boss repositions. Be sure to listen out for attack indicators warning you of incoming grenades, so you know when to seek cover or take to the air to avoid the ensuing blasts. As soon as you bring the chopper down, the mission will be complete.

Staying underneath the HC HELICOPTER will allow you to avoid many of its attacks, while also placing you in a good position from which to retaliate.

AH12 HC HELICOPTER ATTACKS

GRENADE CANNON ▼	MULTI MISSILE LAUNCHER	GATLING GUN
DESCRIPTION Head-on volley of high-impact grenades launched from underside grenade cannon. No homing capabilities, but large blast radius upon detonation.	**DESCRIPTION** Releases a high volume of low-impact missiles with strong homing capability. Can be fired either from one side, or both sides simultaneously.	**DESCRIPTION** Deals heavy AP damage at effective range and inflicts severe strain on your ACS. Can either fire from one side, or both sides simultaneously.
EVASION Take cover behind buildings or ascend and keep moving while airborne.	**EVASION** Quick Boost to either side of the salvo, or jump and ascend into the air.	**EVASION** Quickly take cover behind a building or position yourself underneath the boss.

DESTROY ARTILLERY INSTALLATIONS

"Show that interloper what makes the Liberation Front strong!"

—RLF Soldier

The Rubicon Liberation Front has positioned a number of artillery installations around the contaminated city that you ventured into in the previous mission. Balam Industries have hired you to destroy these installations, so that they can safely proceed with their efforts to survey the area for Coral. You'll encounter a high volume of enemies in this mission and each one, including the artillery, will award

bonus pay, making it potentially quite lucrative. It's possible to largely avoid the enemies that are spread throughout the city if you want a safe and quiet approach, but destroying those near the artillery will make things a bit easier.

It can be worth hunting down as many enemies as possible for bonus pay, but you may want to leave doing so until after you've destroyed most of the artillery installations, as this will reduce the amount of incoming fire you'll need to contend with. If this is your first mission after finishing the prologue, then completing it will unlock access to the Parts Shop in the Garage.

MISSION INFO

Combat Zone	Southern Belius—Contaminated City
Client	Balam Industries
Reward	100,000
Max Bonus Pay	106,800
Completion Unlocks	Parts Shop, Beginner Training 2: Combat Fundamentals (If completed before "Grid 135 Cleanup"), Loghunt Program (If completed after "Grid 135 Cleanup")
Combat Logs	—
Data Logs	—
Part Containers	—

MISSION OBJECTIVE

Destroy All Artillery Installations

ENEMY DATA

	No.	AP	AS	Bonus Pay	Analysis
Shielded Artillery (Grenade Cannon)	7	470	—	2000	P.326
Shielded Artillery (Sniper Cannon)	2	437	—	2000	P.327
MT-T-026 Guard Mech (Rifle)	18	102	121	800	P.310
CH-T-025 Attack Helicopter (Anti-Tank Cannon)	15	28	—	800	P.309
MT-E-104 Bipedal MT (Machine Gun)	4	470	364	2400	P.315
MT-E-104 Bipedal MT (Dual Machine Gun)	9	470	364	2400	P.316
MT-E-104 Bipedal MT (Grenade Cannon)	7	470	364	2400	P.316
MT-E-104 Bipedal MT (Missile Launcher)	6	470	364	2400	P.316

ASSEMBLY

You're provided with the same AC for this mission as you used to get through the prologue, and since you're already familiar with its offensive and defensive capabilities, you should feel right at home when starting this mission.

01	R-ARM UNIT | ASSAULT RIFLE **RF-024 TURNER**	P.52
02	L-ARM UNIT | PULSE BLADE **HI-32: BU-TT/A**	P.65
03	R-BACK UNIT | MISSILE LAUNCHER **BML-G1/P20MLT-04**	P.69
04	L-BACK UNIT | —	—
05	HEAD | — **HC-2000 FINDER EYE**	P.78
06	CORE | — **CC-2000 ORBITER**	P.81
07	ARMS | — **AC-2000 TOOL ARM**	P.83
08	LEGS | BIPEDAL **2C-2000 CRAWLER**	P.85
09	BOOSTER | — **BST-G1/P10**	P.88
10	FCS | — **FCS-G1/P01**	P.89
11	GENERATOR | — **AG-J-098 JOSO**	P.91

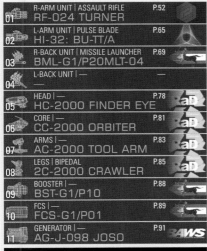

HIGHWAY THROUGH THE DANGER ZONE

The artillery installations now present in the city are incredibly dangerous and have extremely long range. Their firing angles are limited, however, so staying out of their line of sight will make things much easier. The recommended route through this mission has been planned with that in mind, and if followed, will prevent the artillery from ever being able to target you.

This second set of artillery near **Position B** could easily fire on you if you head directly for them; moving back out of the city and flanking around behind the artillery lets you destroy them in relative safety.

Although the bipedal MTs on the road in front of the artillery near Position A can fire at you, you're outside of their effective range so their shots will deal negligible damage even if they hit you.

OBJECTIVE

Destroy All Artillery Installations

01 On your way here from the starting point, you'll encounter two groups of enemies; use the multi-lock on your missile launcher to dispatch the first group quickly. After progressing a bit further, Assault Boost toward the second group while using your assault rifle to destroy one enemy, before slashing the other with your pulse blade when you're close enough. Continuing through the opening in the wall—much like in the previous mission—will place you in the direct line of sight of two artillery emplacements. To avoid this, ascend over the corner of the wall and enter the debris field instead.

Use your scanner while moving through the debris to reveal the locations of the enemies hidden within it. After defeating them, head to **Position A** and go through the opening in the debris to emerge behind the first set of artillery; they can't shoot you from here, so boost over and take out the enemies behind them. The artillery has a frontal layer of plating that makes hitting them from the front futile, so always attack them from behind. Once they're destroyed, finish off the other bipedal MTs on the road in front of them.

02 The next set of artillery is located almost directly opposite the ones you just destroyed, but heading straight toward them will place you in their

sights. Instead, head back to the opening in the city wall and flank around the outskirts until you reach **Position B**. From there, you can safely target all of the helicopters protecting the artillery. If you boost upward, you can also get line of sight on the bipedal MT on the rooftop next to them—destroy that before once again dismantling the artillery installations.

MAXIMUM PAYOUT

The mission will end shortly after the final artillery installation is destroyed, so if you want to sweep the area for enemies to gain more bonus pay rewards, be sure to leave one intact until you're ready to complete the mission. Be careful when moving around the interior of the city, however, because even without the artillery, the numerous grenade-cannon wielding bipedal MTs can still pose a threat.

03 Given the danger of a direct approach on the next artillery, it's recommended to take a detour around the outskirts of the city instead. Continue around the wall until you reach **Position C**, and then ascend over it and take out the artillery directly on the rooftop ahead of you. You can use the base of the artillery installation and the rooftop you're on to block any incoming missiles from the MTs on the adjacent rooftops, and then pop out between their volleys to pick them off. After destroying everything within range, Assault Boost toward **Position D** and finish off the remaining enemies before taking out both of the artillery installations there. The immediate area should be relatively clear at this point, so you can either continue racking up bonus pay or head straight for the final artillery installation and destroy it to complete the mission.

Among the artillery installations near **Position D** are a pair of especially lethal sniper cannon variants that have significantly more range, fire much higher velocity shells and inflict more damage than regular artillery. This means that staying behind them is essential.

//01-B
GRID 135 CLEANUP

"You've got ID. Now you need a rep. Get their attention, 621."

—Handler Walter

The competition between Balam and Arquebus to control the survey efforts within the contaminated city has moved to one of the surrounding grids: Grid 135. Arquebus would have you enter the area and eliminate a squad of Dafeng bipedal MTs, guard mechs, attack helicopters, and quad drones. This is a straightforward job, taking place entirely within a single large room that contains all of your designated targets. The combat zone is broken up into three lengthy walkways separated by gaps in the floor; if you fall into these gaps and cannot boost back out, you'll take AP damage as you reappear on the walkways again, so be mindful of your footing and manage your EN carefully.

MISSION INFO

Combat Zone	Southern Belius — Grid 135
Client	Arquebus Corporation
Reward	68,000
Max Bonus Pay	—
Completion Unlocks	Parts Shop, Beginner Training 2: Combat Fundamentals (If completed before "Destroy Artillery Installations"), Loghunt Program (If completed after "Destroy Artillery Installations")
Combat Logs	—
Data Logs	—
Part Containers	—

MISSION OBJECTIVE

Annihilate the Dafeng MT Squad

ENEMY DATA

	No.	AP	AS	Bonus Pay	Analysis
● MT-T-026 Guard Mech (Rifle)	6	102	121	—	P.310
● CH-T-025 Attack Helicopter (Anti-Tank Cannon)	13	28	—	—	P.309
● CD-J-098 Quad Drone (Cluster Missile Launcher)	2	302	310	—	P.312
● MT-E-104 BAWS Bipedal MT (Machine Gun & Shield)	5	470	364	—	P.315
● MT-E-104 BAWS Bipedal MT (Missile Launcher)	3	470	364	—	P.316
○ IA-27: GHOST (Melee Type)	1	3820	1066	—	P.343

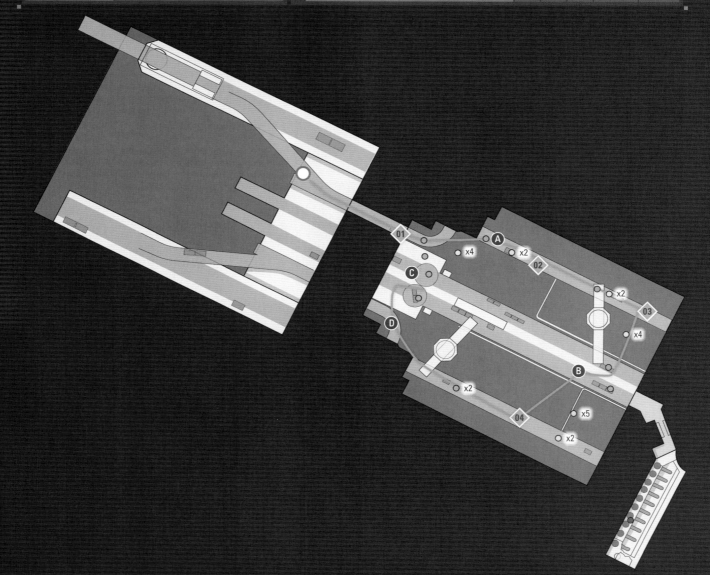

Near **Position B** is a small aperture leading back to your crash site, and the GHOST that ambushes you there offers a considerable optional challenge.

If you keep back from the edge of the tracks here, you'll be able to avoid most of the incoming missiles from the bipedal MTs on the adjacent tracks.

ASSEMBLY

For this mission, you'll primarily be sticking with the same base AC you started with in the prologue. If you've already completed the "Destroy Artillery Instillations" mission and have access to the Parts Shop, however, there's one additional unit that might serve you well in this sortie: the L-Back version of the BML-G1/P20MLT-04 missile launcher. Given that you're forced to engage with a lot of enemies in this combat zone, the extra firepower and ability to multi-lock onto more enemies will be very handy.

01	R-ARM UNIT | ASSAULT RIFLE RF-024 TURNER	P.52
02	L-ARM UNIT | PULSE BLADE HI-32: BU-TT/A	P.65
03	R-BACK UNIT | MISSILE LAUNCHER BML-G1/P20MLT-04	P.69
04	L-BACK UNIT | —	
05	HEAD | — HC-2000 FINDER EYE	P.78
06	CORE | — CC-2000 ORBITER	P.81
07	ARMS | — AC-2000 TOOL ARM	P.83
08	LEGS | BIPEDAL 2C-2000 CRAWLER	P.85
09	BOOSTER | — BST-G1/P10	P.88
10	FCS | — FCS-G1/P01	P.89
11	GENERATOR | — AG-J-098 JOSO	P.91

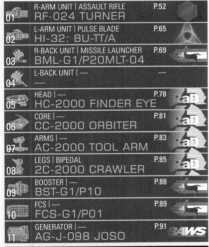

OBJECTIVE   Annihilate the Dafeng MT Squad

01 ◈ Continue along the tracks and scan the doorway to gain access to the room you need to clear. Don't enter it straight away, however; instead, use your missile launcher to take out the helicopters directly ahead of you. After taking a few steps into the room, you'll be detected by the enemies near **Position A**—the bipedal MT there has a shield, so shooting at it from a distance isn't going to work. Move forward until it comes into view, then Assault Boost directly toward it and use your pulse blade to destroy it before unloading your assault rifle into the other nearby enemies.

02 ◈ Carefully approach the container on which the two guard mechs were standing. This will place you just within lock-on range of the bipedal MT perched on the crane further ahead, without it detecting you—fire a single missile salvo to destroy it. Once that enemy is destroyed, boost along the tracks and defeat the two guard mechs that were standing below it.

03 ◈ Near the end of those same tracks, you'll spot a group of helicopters off to the side, so use your multi-lock missiles again to take them all out quickly. You can also destroy one of the bipedal MTs on the adjacent tracks from here, but to reach the other one, you'll need to Assault Boost across the gap to get into range. As soon as the last bipedal MT is destroyed, move up the central tracks to **Position B**. From here, you'll be able to target another group of helicopters as well as a pair of guard mechs toward the opposite side of the room. At this point, you should see "TGT" markers appear on the last remaining targets, and you'll also receive a comms message letting you know that a squad of enemy reinforcements has entered the room; these will begin to group up near **Position C**.

04 ◈ The two bipedal MTs remaining from the initial group of targets both have shields, so jump across to the tracks here and Assault Boost toward them to get within your pulse blade's range. When you're ready to take on the reinforcements, boost along the tracks and then jump across to **Position D**. The reinforcement group consists of a pair of bipedal MTs with shields, and a pair of quad drones utilizing cluster missiles that drop additional payloads as they travel, making them by far the bigger threat. From this position, you have a clear line of sight on both of them, and any incoming fire from the bipedal MTs should be blocked by either the tracks or the support structure they're standing near. Once the drones are down, jump over and use your pulse blade to mop up those bipedal MTs and complete the mission.

If you're having trouble targeting the attack helicopters and guard mechs, you can try jumping above the pipes to get a clearer shot.

//02-A
DESTROY THE TRANSPORT HELICOPTERS

"...Now they're asking for you by name."

—Handler Walter

Balam's subsidiary, Dafeng, has taken a combat role against the RLF in this region and Balam wants to recruit you to lend them some much-needed support. The area of operation contains three transport helicopter sites, each of which is defended by higher volumes of enemies than you may have previously encountered, consisting of bipedal MTs, artillery, armored combat vehicles, and a single tetrapod MT. The area is mostly open with some structures and buildings allowing for cover, but the variable heights of these structures as well as a wooded section at the beginning of the mission will have an impact on your ability to spot threats, so scanning often is recommended. Although not required for the mission, if you want to maximize your bonus pay, it's worth taking a trip back down into the city to destroy the enemies still patrolling within its walls.

MISSION OBJECTIVE
Destroy All Transport Helicopters

MISSION INFO

Combat Zone	Southern Belius—Contaminated City
Client	Balam Industries
Reward	80,000
Max Bonus Pay	99,200
Completion Unlocks	—
Combat Logs	Silver x1
Data Logs	—
Part Containers	—

ENEMY DATA

	No.	AP	AS	Bonus Pay	Analysis
● TH-E-012 Transport Helicopter	6	750	—	—	P.314
● CV-T-020 Armored Combat Vehicle	4	73	—	800	P.313
○ MT-T-026 Guard Mech (Rifle)	2	102	121	800	P.310
○ Artillery (Horizontal Missile Launcher)	2	202	—	4000	P.328
● MT-E-104 Bipedal MT (Machine Gun)	12	470	364	2400	P.315
● MT-E-104 Bipedal MT (Hand Rocket Launcher)	6	470	364	2400	P.317
● MT-E-104 Bipedal MT (Shotgun)	1	470	364	2400	P.317
● MT-E-104 Bipedal MT (Missile Launcher)	7	470	364	2400	P.316
○ MT-J-048 Tetrapod MT (Laser Blade)	1	13370	2200	24000	P.322

ASSEMBLY

Given the amount and difficulty of the enemies you encounter in this mission, it's worth spending some of your hard-earned COAM to purchase a few upgrades for your AC before you tackle it. The extra damage you'll gain by equipping a DF-BA-06 XUAN-GE and additional BML-G1/P20MLT-04 will help deal with the increased number of enemies, and provide a hard-hitting option to use against more robust foes.

Some MTs in this mission are armed with shields, so stick with your HI-32: BU-TT/A to make dispatching them easy, while also giving you a strong close-range option against the tougher enemies. If you prefer to stay at medium range, then you could swap out the HI-32: BU-TT/A for the MG-014 LUDLOW that you can unlock by completing the first set of training programs, but you'd need to purchase the L-Arm version of it from the Parts Shop. Since you'll be using a lot of missiles with this build, the large reduction in lock-on times that you get from the FCS-G2/P10SLT will come in very handy. Finally, the DF-GN-02 LING-TAI Generator vastly improves your EN recharge and supply recovery specs for only a minor EN capacity reduction, making the overall trade-off more than worthwhile.

01	R-ARM UNIT | BAZOOKA **DF-BA-06 XUAN GE**	P.56
02	L-ARM UNIT | PULSE BLADE **HI-32: BU-TT/A**	P.65
03	R-BACK UNIT | MISSILE LAUNCHER **BML-G1/P20MLT-04**	P.69
04	L-BACK UNIT | MISSILE LAUNCHER **BML-G1/P20MLT-04**	P.69
05	HEAD | — **HC-2000 FINDER EYE**	P.78
06	CORE | — **CC-2000 ORBITER**	P.81
07	ARMS | — **AC-2000 TOOL ARM**	P.83
08	LEGS | BIPEDAL **2C-2000 CRAWLER**	P.85
09	BOOSTER | — **BST-G1/P10**	P.88
10	FCS | — **FCS-G2/P10SLT**	P.90
11	GENERATOR | — **DF-GN-02 LING-TAI**	P.91

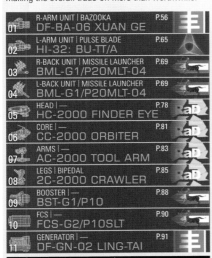

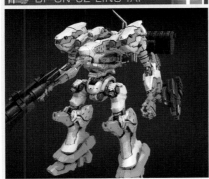

The buildings around the crater can provide excellent cover from the tetrapod MT's attacks if you decide to take it head on.

01 From your starting point atop a cliff, you can see a squad of bipedal MTs patrolling near the first helicopter you need to destroy; they're too far away to engage from here, but if you Assault Boost to the rooftops above the helicopter at **Position A**, you'll have an excellent vantage point from which to destroy them all. The bipedal MTs will sometimes try to jump up to your rooftop, so use your scanner to keep an eye on them and destroy them before they can get a clear shot at you.

02 From your position on the rooftop, you can see across the area to where the next helicopter is located. You should notice a blockade in front of it, consisting of numerous bipedal MTs and support units, along with a pair of artillery missile arrays. The artillery's presence will make a direct approach highly dangerous, so a much safer option is to flank around the area by following the road to **Position B**, and then cut across the cliffs and jump up to the rooftops of the building near the blockade at **Position C**.

Similarly to the previous encounter, your elevated position gives you a commanding advantage over both the enemies and artillery installations below, allowing you to fire down on them almost unchallenged. The height difference also allows you to bypass the shields of the units carrying them. It's possible they'll jump up and block your shots; if this occurs, simply boost over and finish them off with your pulse blade. If you move from the front of these buildings to the opposite side, you can also destroy a pair of bipedal MTs that are perched on the cliffs between you and the final group of helicopters.

03 Those final helicopters are located in the same area where you faced the AH12: HC HELICOPTER in the prologue, but if you were to Assault Boost directly over there, you'd immediately come under fire from the bipedal MTs guarding the helicopters. Instead, jump across to the rooftop here and destroy the nearby bipedal MTs, then Assault Boost toward the vertical catapult at **Position D** and use it to reach the top of the structure at **Position E**.

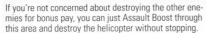

If you're not concerned about destroying the other enemies for bonus pay, you can just Assault Boost through this area and destroy the helicopter without stopping.

Use the vertical catapult at **Position D** to reach the helicopters waiting at **Position E**.

BONUS PAY

If you're going for maximum bonus pay, you should venture out into the city before using the vertical catapult, and destroy the enemies there if you haven't already done so.

04 The enemies in the area will become alerted to your presence when you land, but the tetrapod MT in the middle won't move—as long as you stay away from the edge, it wont have an angle to hit you from where it is. The group of bipedal MTs in the middle will start moving toward you, so approach the edge and—in between the tetrapod MT's attacks—pick them off as they approach.

At this point, you can focus on destroying the remaining helicopter targets to complete the mission as Walter suggests. Destroying the tetrapod MT, however, yields a high amount of bonus pay and a combat log, so engaging it is worth the effort. The safest way to defeat it is to hold your position here, because even though it's too far away for your systems to lock onto, you can manually aim and fire your bazooka. Doing so will inflict full damage regardless of range, so move backward to dodge its shots, and then move in again to fire your own back at it. It will move around intermittently; wait for it to stop again and you can resume fire. If you don't have an angle, you can simply move along the top of the structure until you do.

Dropping down into the area and engaging the tetrapod MT directly is a faster, but significantly more dangerous option, that forces you to contend with its shotgun and pulse blade. The sniper cannon is still its deadliest attack—always be on the lookout for the alert indicators, so you know when to Quick Boost out of the way. Jumping up and over the tetrapod MT can help avoid its melee attacks while allowing you to fire down on it when you're close. From further away, be aware that despite its size, it can cover large distances very quickly by leaping toward you. The remaining bipedal MTs might also enter the fray if you're moving around a lot. If this happens, make sure to take cover form the tetrapod MT and finish them off first, to avoid contending with attacks from multiple enemies.

//02-B
DESTROY THE TESTER AC

"I... just... I just wanted a callsign of my own"

—Dafeng Student Pilot

Arquebus has received intel that a new AC is being transported out of the contaminated city to Balam HQ. They're hiring any available mercenaries to make sure that doesn't happen, which provides an opportunity for you to earn some reward money. The Tester AC is the only hostile enemy in this mission, and defeating it is your sole objective. You'll encounter it atop a small compound that features plenty of buildings surrounded by a significant amount of open space; bring the battle into this open area if you prefer freely moving around without having to worry about contending with obstacles.

MISSION OBJECTIVE
Destroy the Tester AC

MISSION INFO

Combat Zone	Southern Belius—Contaminated City
Client	Arquebus Corporation
Reward	95,000
Max Bonus Pay	—
Completion Unlocks	—
Combat Logs	Silver x1
Data Logs	—
Part Containers	—

ENEMY DATA

	No.	AP	AS	Bonus Pay	Analysis
◎ TESTER AC / Dafeng Student Pilot	1	11100	1551	—	—

ASSEMBLY

The same build that you used for the "Destroy the Transport Helicopters" mission will serve you just as well in this one-on-one duel. ACs provide some of the toughest battles in the game, so don't expect a quick kill, and place great emphasis on straining your opponent's ACS. The dual missile launchers combined with the bazooka will let you inflict significant amounts of both impact and accumulative impact from medium range. The pulse blade, as usual, is your heavy hitter—make sure to position yourself such that you're close enough to use it the instant you stagger the Tester AC.

01	R-ARM UNIT | BAZOOKA **DF-BA-06 XUAN GE**	P.56
02	L-ARM UNIT | PULSE BLADE **HI-32: BU-TT/A**	P.65
03	R-BACK UNIT | MISSILE LAUNCHER **BML-G1/P20MLT-04**	P.69
04	L-BACK UNIT | MISSILE LAUNCHER **BML-G1/P20MLT-04**	P.69
05	HEAD | — **HC-2000 FINDER EYE**	P.78
06	CORE | — **CC-2000 ORBITER**	P.81
07	ARMS | — **AC-2000 TOOL ARM**	P.83
08	LEGS | BIPEDAL **2C-2000 CRAWLER**	P.85
09	BOOSTER | — **BST-G1/P10**	P.88
10	FCS | — **FCS-G2/P10SLT**	P.90
11	GENERATOR | — **DF-GN-02 LING-TAI**	P.91

This building at **Position B** is a great place to stagger the Tester AC with a strike of your pulse blade. Even if it recovers, it won't have the room to boost away from your blade in time.

DAFENG STUDENT PILOT

AC // TESTER

BASIC SPECS

AP	11100
Attitude Stability	1551
Anti-Kinetic Defense	1289
Anti-Energy Defense	1210
Anti-Explosive Defense	1308
Elec. Discharge Tolerance	490
Shock Resistance	-50%
ACS Anomaly Tolerance	490
Heat Resistance	-50%

OBJECTIVE

Destroy the Tester AC

01 ◈ The Tester AC is outfitted with its own pulse blade, a burst rifle, and an active homing missile launcher that fires slow-moving but high impact projectiles. Avoiding its missiles can be especially awkward due their travel speed; they move slower than other missiles, but faster than your normal boost speed, so you might need to Quick Boost a couple of times to fully evade them.

Unfortunately for the Tester AC, the Dafeng pilot controlling it is not a trained operator; they react slowly, won't maneuver a lot and will back away rather than pressuring you. Crucially, they also won't fire its missiles when you're at close range. This means the best strategy is to stay close and take a very aggressive approach. A single hit from your bazooka will nearly max out your target's ACS gauge, meaning you'll only need to land a few missiles afterward to stagger it, providing an opening to unleash the full damage of your pulse blade.

The Tester AC is unaware of you when the mission begins, which allows you to get into position to deal a very potent opening strike. Rather than heading straight toward your target, Assault Boost along the wall to **Position A**, and then jump onto the rooftops near **Position B**, making sure to stay back from the edge nearest to your target. If you slowly approach the edge, you'll have a clean shot at the Tester AC without the helicopter getting in the way. When you're ready, fire your bazooka at it while it's unaware to exploit the surprise attack impact bonus, then launch a salvo of missiles. The Tester AC will stagger as soon as the missiles hit, so begin moving toward it, aiming to get close enough to use your pulse blade the instant its ACS overloads.

Stay close, ideally positioning yourself so that there's a wall behind the Tester AC, giving it nowhere to retreat to. Now unleash your bazooka and missiles to stagger it again, and use your pulse blade to inflict major damage before it recovers. As long as you stay close and keep attacking, the Tester AC will soon succumb to the onslaught.

AC // TESTER ATTACKS

MA-J 201 RANSETSU-AR	HI-32 BU-TT/A	BML-G3/P05ACT-02

DESCRIPTION Triple-burst assault rifle which can fire rapidly and places high strain on your ACS.	**DESCRIPTION** Pulse blade which can place high strain on your ACS and inflicts heavy damage.	**DESCRIPTION** Missile launcher which releases two slow-moving active homing missiles.
EVASION Quick Boost away from where the shots are being fired or out-distance the effective range of the weapon.	**EVASION** The blade is drawn as the TESTER AC approaches you. Quick Boost away from it during this time.	**EVASION** The missiles can track you for an extended period as they will rarely impact the ground. Lead them into an object in the environment.

ATTACK THE DAM COMPLEX

> *"Why don't you start a sewing club together...*
> *and stitch that damn mouth of yours shut!"*
>
> —G1 Michigan

Balam has chosen you to take part in an operation against the RLF. Heading to the Gallia Dam Complex, you'll join up with two in-house pilots from the Balam Redguns: G4 Volta and G5 Iguazu. Together you must destroy a series of generators in the area that are supplying the RLF with energy. The enemies you'll encounter use a combination of explosive and kinetic damage, including the enemy AC defending one of the final targets. There's also an optional encounter with a tetrapod MT that uses an energy-based laser blade.

The mission takes place in an open area with increasing levels of elevation as you progress through the complex. Your allies will often take the lead and openly engage enemies as they reach them, so you can use them to take some of the heat off you—since the enemies are already in established elevated positions, the extra breathing room they give you is more than welcome. This is especially important since this is a long mission with no checkpoints to rely on.

MISSION OBJECTIVES

Annihilate enemy MT squad / Destroy target facilities

Destroy remaining target facilities

MISSION INFO

Combat Zone	Southern Belius—Gallia Dam Complex
Client	Balam Industries
Reward	190,000
Max Bonus Pay	—
Completion Unlocks	Training Exercise: Intermediate Support 1 & 2, Parts Shop Update 2 (If completed after "Destroy the Weaponized Mining Ship")
Combat Logs	Silver x1, Gold x1
Data Logs	—
Part Containers	—

ENEMY DATA

		No.	AP	AS	Bonus Pay	Analysis
■	Power Generator	4	650	—	—	—
●	MT-T-026 Guard Mech (Rifle)	6	102	121	—	P.310
●	CV-T-020 Armored Combat Vehicle	14	73	—	—	P.313
○	Artillery (Bazooka)	4	269	—	—	P.327
○	Artillery (Multi Missile Launcher)	2	202	—	—	P.328
●	MT-E-104 Bipedal MT (Machine Gun)	13	470	364	—	P.315
●	MT-E-104 Bipedal MT (Dual Machine Gun)	5	470	364	—	P.316
●	MT-E-104 Bipedal MT (Hand Rocket Launcher)	2	470	364	—	P.317
●	MT-E-104 Bipedal MT (Cluster Gun)	5	470	364	—	P.317
●	MT-E-104 Bipedal MT (Grenade Cannon)	7	470	364	—	P.316
○	MT-J-048 Tetrapod MT (Laser Blade)	1	13370	2200	—	P.322
◎	AC BURN PICKAXE / Index Dunham	1	11420	1620	—	—

ASSEMBLY

Since the ally ACs you sortie with on this mission take the role of front-line assaults, swapping out the usual HI-32: BU-TT/A for something with a bit more range—such as the MG-014 LUDLOW—is a good option. Its high rate of fire lets you quickly finish off any enemies that have been weakened by either your allies or your own missiles, and it still packs enough of a punch to easily take out smaller enemies on its own. The rest of the loadout remains much the same, with the dual missile launchers providing excellent range and ability to take out multiple targets, and the bazooka for inflicting high damage when you need it—such as for quickly destroying the generators.

01	R-ARM UNIT | BAZOOKA DF-BA-06 XUAN GE	P.56
02	L-ARM UNIT | MACHINE GUN MG-014 LUDLOW	P.53
03	R-BACK UNIT | MISSILE LAUNCHER BML-G1/P20MLT-04	P.69
04	L-BACK UNIT | MISSILE LAUNCHER BML-G1/P20MLT-04	P.69
05	HEAD | — HC-2000 FINDER EYE	P.78
06	CORE | — CC-2000 ORBITER	P.81
07	ARMS | — AC-2000 TOOL ARM	P.83
08	LEGS | BIPEDAL 2C-2000 CRAWLER	P.85
09	BOOSTER | — BST-G1/P10	P.88
10	FCS | — FCS-G1/P01	P.89
11	GENERATOR | — DF-GN-02 LING-TAI	P.91

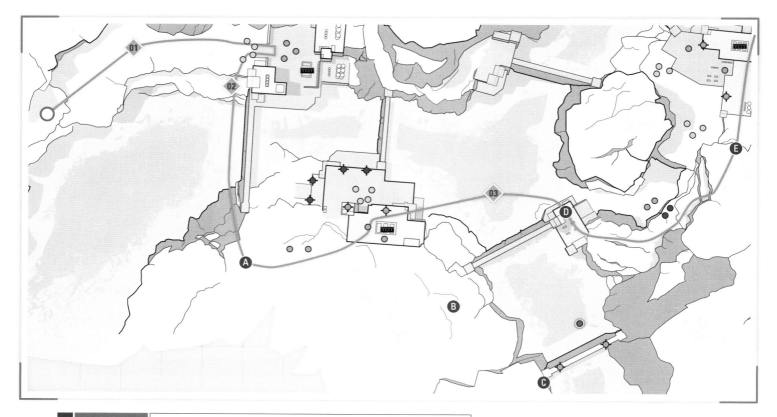

OBJECTIVE | Annihilate enemy MT squad / Destroy target facilities

01 You'll begin alongside Volta and Iguazu, and your initial target is just ahead of you, guarded by group of bipedal MTs and few combat vehicles in support. Your allies don't wait for you and will begin their assault shortly after the mission begins, so follow behind them and use your missile launchers to multi-lock onto the smaller vehicles and destroy them as soon as they're within range. Taking those enemies out allows your allies to pull the focus of the bipedal MTs rather than dealing with the small fry, which in turn should enable you to use your bazooka to pick them off while they're distracted. Volta and Iguazu won't destroy the target generator for you, so once all of the surrounding enemies have been dealt with, destroy the generator and get ready to move on the next one.

02 Volta and Iguazu will begin heading for the next objective location as soon as the first generator has been destroyed, but that area is defended by a significant number of artillery installations and bipedal MTs outfitted with grenade cannons; even with your allies drawing fire, it can be a dangerous direct approach. A more tactically sound option is to drop down the front side of the nearby dam wall and follow it along to the adjacent cliffs. You can then ascend those cliffs and emerge behind all of the enemies and artillery at **Position A**, surprising them while Volta and Iguazu are engaging them from the front. As long as you stay on the ground here, the artillery can't get a clear shot at you—focus your fire on the bipedal MTs, since they pose the greatest threat. As before, when the area is clear, destroy the generator to get the location of your next target.

03 Shortly after the objective updates, Volta and Iguazu will split up and approach it in a pincer maneuver, with one following a ravine and the other going up and over a dam wall. The dam route has fewer initial threats to deal with, but puts you in an unfavorable position to approach the generator, while heading straight up the ravine forces you to contend with direct fire from both enemies and artillery. With a bit of maneuvering and use of the environment, however, the ravine can actually be the safest approach.

Scale the building at **Position D**, and then use the cliffs beyond it to flank behind the artillery and destroy it easily while your ally deals with the bipedal MTs below. From there, ascend the nearby cliffs to reach the vantage point at **Position E** from which you can easily destroy most of the enemies in the area and the generator. You don't need to destroy

Silver Combat Log
TETRAPOD MT

To retrieve this combat log, you'll need to destroy a nearby tetrapod MT that's equipped with the same weapons as the one you faced in the "Destroy the Transport Helicopters" mission. To make matters more complicated, there are two bipedal MTs with grenade cannons overlooking the area. Though these MTs might not pose much of a threat on their own, you can quickly get into trouble if you try to deal with the tetrapod MT while also dodging their shells.

Your best option is to flank around them using the cliffs at **Position B** and head to **Position C** just behind the dam wall they're standing on. From there, you can quickly and easily destroy them without having to worry about the tetrapod MT. You can then move toward the roof of the small tower in the corner and start firing down at the tetrapod MT below you with your missiles and bazooka until it's destroyed. It cannot boost itself up to you, and although it will fire at you, its shots will hit the wall, so moving backwards slightly will allow you to avoid getting caught in the blast.

When assaulting the first generator, try to keep the fight near the front of this area. Moving too close to the generator will cause the artillery and bipedal MTs defending the second target to open fire on you.

All enemies and the generators at both sites have to be destroyed before you'll get your next targets, so you can't just destroy the generator and move on.

all of the enemies in order to progress at this stage of the mission, but doing so will ensure that Volta and Iguazu don't remain behind in combat, and you'll want them with you for an upcoming fight.

04 ◈ When you begin to approach the next objective, the pilot of the AC BURN PICKAXE, Index Dunham, announces himself and enters the fight in an effort to protect the final generator. This battle is totally optional, but since destroying BURN PICKAXE yields a combat log, it's recommended that you dispose of it before heading to the final generator. The group of bipedal MTs at the base of the complex can tie up your allies for quite some time if you don't get involved; having them free to help you against BURN PICKAXE will make that fight much easier, so destroying that initial group should be your first goal.

Your allies take a direct approach toward the MTs' location, so if you follow the top of the dam wall and then come in from the side, you can destroy the bipedal MTs while they're distracted. At this point, if you simply want to complete the mission, you can jump up to the catapult and use it to reach the top of the complex where the final generator is located. Destroy the generator and the mission will end.

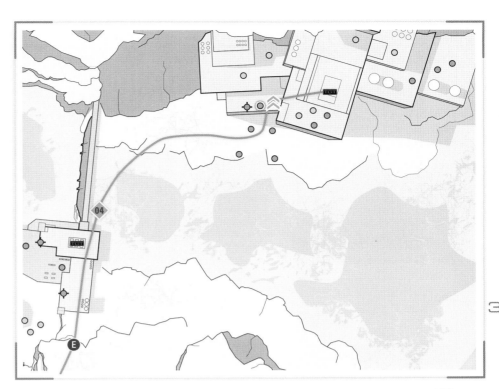

Even though numerous enemies surround the final generator, you can jump up to it and destroy it quickly to bring the mission to an end.

G4 and G5 are valuable allies against BURN PICKAXE, so stall for a moment while you allow them to catch up.

INDEX DURHAM

AC // BURN PICKAXE

If you've already taken out the group of bipedal MTs at the base of the complex and are still in that area, BURN PICKAXE will drop down and immediately attack you. Let your allies land the first attacks so that its focus switches to them, and try to keep them between you and the enemy AC at all times so that they can act as shields for you. Keeping the fight in this area or on the ice field gives you plenty of room to move around and keep your distance from BURN PICKAXE. Maintaining your distance is key to an easy fight here, because if you draw the attention of the enemy AC by firing overly aggressively, the extra space will let you easily back off a bit until your allies draw its fire once again.

The Redguns won't deal a lot of damage, but the impact from their combined fire will help toward staggering BURN PICKAXE so that you can land high-damage shots with your bazooka. If you've acquired all combat logs up to this point, upon completing this mission, you'll unlock the 04-101 MIND ALPHA arm unit, which offers a nice defensive upgrade over the default arms, albeit with a slight reduction in melee specialization.

BASIC SPECS

AP	11420
Attitude Stability	1620
Anti-Kinetic Defense	1228
Anti-Energy Defense	1083
Anti-Explosive Defense	1310
Elec. Discharge Tolerance	490
Shock Resistance	-32%
ACS Anomaly Tolerance	490
Heat Resistance	-32%

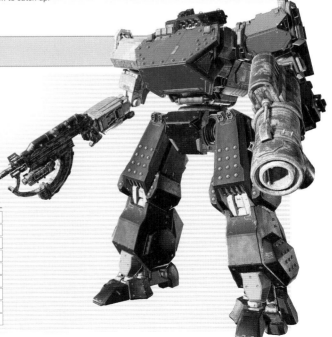

//03-B
DESTROY THE WEAPONIZED MINING SHIP

"A fitting end for something built to fail."

—Handler Walter

Arquebus, on behalf of their affiliate Schneider, is tasking you with reaching and destroying a special RLF vessel: the weaponized mining ship STRIDER. This mining-ship-turned-mobile-weapon platform is hindering Arquebus's Coral efforts, and they will not allow the RLF to have their way with the dunes. While the STRIDER is technically a boss enemy, tackling it requires destroying a series of targets until you reach its core: the Eye. Defending the ship are a number of bipedal MTs and guard mechs that you'll either need to fight your way through or bypass, and since both the area and the ship itself are so expansive, the mission will encompass a great deal of movement and verticallity. Though unlikely, it's possible to fail the mission by taking too long, as the STRIDER eventually moves outside the combat zone.

MISSION OBJECTIVES

Approach the Weaponized Mining Ship STRIDER

Destroy the STRIDER's Leg Unit

Destroy All Sub-Generators

Destroy the Eye

Withdraw From the Deck

MISSION INFO

Combat Zone	Western Belius—Bona Dea Dunes
Client	Arquebus Corporation
Reward	270,000
Max Bonus Pay	—
Completion Unlocks	Training Exercise: Intermediate Support 1 & 2, Parts Shop Update 2 (If completed after "Attack the Dam Complex")
Combat Logs	—
Data Logs	—
Part Containers	—

ENEMY DATA

	No.	AP	AS	Bonus Pay	Analysis
● MT-T-026 Guard Mech (Rifle)	3	102	121	—	P.310
● MT-E-104 Bipedal MT (Hand Rocket Launcher)	9	470	364	—	P.317
● EB-0309 STRIDER (Turrets)	19	90	—	—	—
● EB-0309 STRIDER (Missile Launchers)	6	202	—	—	—
● EB-0309 STRIDER (Sub-Generators)	4	650	—	—	—
● EB-0309 STRIDER (Eye)	1	8980	—	—	—

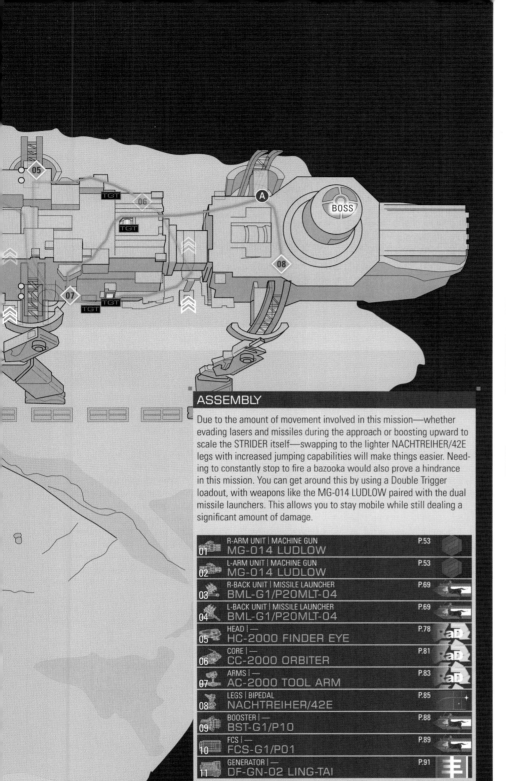

ASSEMBLY

Due to the amount of movement involved in this mission—whether evading lasers and missiles during the approach or boosting upward to scale the STRIDER itself—swapping to the lighter NACHTREIHER/42E legs with increased jumping capabilities will make things easier. Needing to constantly stop to fire a bazooka would also prove a hindrance in this mission. You can get around this by using a Double Trigger loadout, with weapons like the MG-014 LUDLOW paired with the dual missile launchers. This allows you to stay mobile while still dealing a significant amount of damage.

01	R-ARM UNIT | MACHINE GUN MG-014 LUDLOW	P.53	
02	L-ARM UNIT | MACHINE GUN MG-014 LUDLOW	P.53	
03	R-BACK UNIT | MISSILE LAUNCHER BML-G1/P20MLT-04	P.69	
04	L-BACK UNIT | MISSILE LAUNCHER BML-G1/P20MLT-04	P.69	
05	HEAD | — HC-2000 FINDER EYE	P.78	
06	CORE | — CC-2000 ORBITER	P.81	
07	ARMS | — AC-2000 TOOL ARM	P.83	
08	LEGS | BIPEDAL NACHTREIHER/42E	P.85	
09	BOOSTER | — BST-G1/P10	P.88	
10	FCS | — FCS-G1/P01	P.89	
11	GENERATOR | — DF-GN-02 LING-TAI	P.91	

Approach the Weaponized Mining Ship STRIDER

01 ◈ Not only does heading straight toward the STRIDER force you to constantly contend with the Variable High-Power Laser it fires in various forms, but there are numerous other enemies scattered along the way that will do their best to ensure that the laser hits you. A quicker and safer option is turn your heading to roughly 170 on your compass and Assault Boost in that general direction until you're almost directly behind the STRIDER. Taking this route will keep you out of its range until you're behind it, at which point it won't have a clear angle to fire on you and you can safely start approaching.

Once you get closer, the STRIDER will begin firing a concentrated laser beam in addition to salvos of homing missiles. Use Quick Boosts or cover to evade its attacks.

■ OBJECTIVE

Destroy the STRIDER's leg unit

02 ◈ Upon reaching the back of the STRIDER, Walter tells you to take out one of its legs to slow it down and possibly create a way to board it. To get into position to fire on the leg joint, you'll need to boost around the side of the STRIDER and head to the top of a nearby dune. While you'll still be safe from the laser as long as you don't go too far out, it will begin firing missiles at you; wait until you've dodged a missile salvo, and only then attack the leg joint.

Destroying the joint causes the rear portion of the ship to decouple and come crashing down to the ground. Some targets mounted on the STRIDER come into view while this is happening, so keep an eye out for them and destroy them once they're within range. It's possible to get caught in the destruction if you get too close to the edge of the cliff at this point, and if that happens your AC will be instantly destroyed. Make sure to keep your distance until the dust settles before beginning your ascent.

Destroying the bipedal MT in the area before turning your attention to the leg unit will ensure that it doesn't sneak up and attack you.

MOVING TARGET

Once the ship's captain decouples the body from the portion of the STRIDER that you destroyed, the rest of the STRIDER continues to walk along its path. This means that if you don't make the jump onto its body by the time it distances itself about 2,500 meters from the destroyed section, you'll hear Walter tell you there's no way aboard and you'll fail the mission.

OBJECTIVE	Destroy All Sub-Generators

03 ◇ Time is of the essence now, because you need to scale the crashed section of the STRIDER and make it over to the rest of the body before it can walk too far away. Now on its side, the part of the STRIDER's rear section that's directly facing you features numerous areas of support structures that form a series of platforms you can use to jump up to the top of it. The top section forms a makeshift runway leading straight toward the body of the STRIDER, so line yourself up and Assault Boost over to it before it gets too far away.

04 ◇ You can destroy the sub-generators in any order you like, but our recommended order not only gives you an efficient route, but also allows you to stay mostly out of harm's way. The first sub-generator is underneath the STRIDER, and the easiest way to reach it is to start by heading upward. From the platform you landed on, set your heading to 180 and scale the series of platforms directly ahead of you, then follow the walkway around once you reach the top. Look directly down over the edge from there and you should see a platform with a vertical catapult on it; drop down onto that, and then look back under the STRIDER and jump over to the rotating platform to get a clear shot on the sub-generator. Once it's destroyed, Assault Boost back over to the vertical catapult you just passed and use it to reach a platform near the top of the ship.

05 ◇ Upon landing on this platform, the Eye will once again resume firing at you, but as long as you stay close to the body of the STRIDER, it won't be able to hit you. Next, jump across to the platform ahead of you that's near the next sub-generator. Unfortunately, you can't get a clear shot on it from here and will need to use some careful maneuvering to find an angle. Wait for the Eye to fire, and then jump out and around the outside of the sub-generator so that you can shoot between its outer casings, and then land safely on the walkway on the other side of it. If you missed some shots and didn't quite destroy it, just repeat the process.

06 ◇ The next sub-generator is located on the opposite side of the STRIDER, but taking a route over its topside would expose you to its laser fire. Instead, follow the walkway around until you can see the platform beneath the neck joint of the STRIDER, jump across to it, then ascend to the platform you can see above you on the opposite side. From there you can follow the platform around until you're near the next sub-generator and use the same tactic of jumping out and around it while firing to destroy it.

Use your machine guns to quickly take out the STRIDER's turrets without slowing down as you jump past them.

You can jump back to the vertical catapult, but given that the STRIDER is moving, it's quite easy to run out of EN while you compensate, making Assault Boost the much safer option.

07 ◇ The final sub-generator is on top of the ship, so you'll need to venture within firing range of the Eye. You can use a series of platforms on the side to reach the top, but don't start ascending until after the Eye has fired so that you have some room to move. Upon reaching the top, you can quickly get behind some containers near the edge and use them to block the laser. Wait there again until after it has fired, and then quickly boost out and destroy the nearby sub-generator. Now the time has come to turn your sights on the Eye to finally cripple this behemoth for good.

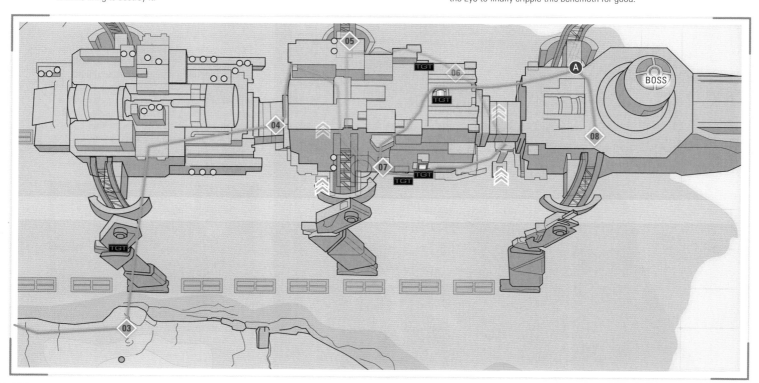

A single salvo from both of your missile launchers will easily destroy the generator, so you can just fire them and then concentrate on landing safely.

You have enough EN to make it to this platform by jumping, but you can Assault Boost to make it easier.

EB-0309

STRIDER

The immense power unleashed by the Eye can make for a very dangerous direct assault, and while you can use a series of Quick Boosts to keep circling around it and avoid the lasers, there's a much simpler and safer option. Wait behind the final sub-generator until after the Eye has fired, and then quickly boost over to the front section of the ship where the Eye is located, and drop over the side to a platform just below the top at **Position A**. While you're on that platform, the Eye cannot hit you, so simply wait until it fires, then jump up and unload your weapons, making sure to land before it fires again.

BASIC SPECS	
AP	8980
Attitude Stability	—
Anti-Kinetic Defense	1000
Anti-Energy Defense	1000
Anti-Explosive Defense	1000
Elec. Discharge Tolerance	500
Shock Resistance	0%
ACS Anomaly Tolerance	500
Heat Resistance	0%

OBJECTIVE

Destroy the Eye

EB-0309 STRIDER ATTACKS

DIFFUSE LASER ▼

DESCRIPTION Sustained Variable High-Power diffuse fire from variable high-power laser consisting of a large volume of small bolts.

EVASION Position yourself on a platform that blocks the Eye's direct line of sight.

CONCENTRATED LASER ▼

DESCRIPTION Uses its variable high-power laser to output a concentrated laser beam that sweeps horizontally regardless of your position.

EVASION Position yourself on a platform that blocks the Eye's direct line of sight.

HEAVY MISSILE LAUNCHER SALVO

DESCRIPTION Releases a large volume of high-impact missiles in a pincer trajectory.

EVASION Place yourself on a platform which blocks the Eye's direct line of sight.

PULSE ARMOR

DESCRIPTION The Eye charges energy and releases a spherical pulse shockwave to overload your ACS and damage your AC; used at close range.

EVASION Quick Boost away from the Eye as it charges the pulse.

OBJECTIVE   Withdraw From the Deck

08 ◈ Repeat the process described above a few times and the Eye will soon be destroyed. This job isn't quite over yet, though; destroying the Eye triggers a chain reaction in the rest of the STRIDER that will cause it to explode,

so you need to clear the area as soon as possible. Jump back up to the top of the STRIDER and Walter will soon update your objective to a location in the dunes that you need to reach in order to clear the blast radius. Turn your sights toward it and Assault Boost in that direction—simply keep flying until you reach it to complete the mission.

"You ready to climb the Wall?"

—V.IV Rusty

In Operation Wallclimber, your mission is to clear out a pair of gatling gun emplacements and a tetrapod MT along the approach to the Wall, then scale the fortress from the inside and eliminate the JUGGERNAUT heavy mobile artillery platform that's bombarding the area from atop it. Most enemies you'll encounter primarily rely on explosive weaponry, but you'll also have to contend with some potent kinetic ordinance from the more dangerous foes such as the sniper cannon artillery, the tetrapod MT and the JUGGERNAUT, so prepare accordingly. There are a number of opportunities to obtain combat and data logs as you proceed, and they can all be acquired with only a minimal amount of deviation from the mission objectives.

MISSION OBJECTIVES

Destroy the City Gatling Cannon and Tetrapod MT

Penetrate the Wall and Reach the Top

Destroy JUGGERNAUT Heavy Mobile Artillery Platform

MISSION INFO

Combat Zone	Central Belius—Liberation Front Fortress "The Wall"
Client	Arquebus Corporation
Reward	330,000
Max Bonus Pay	193,600
Completion Unlocks	Training Exercise: "Intermediate Support 3: Tetrapod ACs", Training Exercise: "Intermediate Support 4: Tank ACs", Parts Shop Update 3
Combat Logs	Bronze x3
Data Logs	2
Part Containers	—

ENEMY DATA

	No.	AP	AS	Bonus Pay	Analysis
MT-T-026 Guard Mech (Rifle)	4	102	121	800	P.310
MT-E-104 Bipedal MT (Machine Gun)	7	470	364	2400	P.315
MT-E-104 Bipedal MT (Dual Machine Guns)	5	470	364	2400	P.316
MT-E-104 Bipedal MT (Hand Rocket Launcher)	6	470	364	2400	P.317
MT-E-104 Bipedal MT (Grenade Cannon)	9	470	364	2400	P.316
MT-E-104 Bipedal MT (Shotgun)	1	470	364	2400	P.317
MT-E-104 Bipedal MT (Missile Launcher)	3	470	364	2400	P.316
Artillery (Gatling Gun)	2	403	—	8000	P.328
Artillery (Bazooka)	5	269	—	4000	P.327
Artillery (Sniper Cannon)	14	437	—	4000	P.327
MT-J-048 Tetrapod MT (9-Shot Bazooka)	1	13370	2200	24000	P.323
HA-T-102 JUGGERNAUT	1	63985	1600	—	

ASSEMBLY

The JUGGERNAUT that awaits atop the Wall poses by far the biggest threat you've had to contend with thus far, so much of your assembly should be focused on making the battle against it as easy as possible. COAM is still quite limited at this point in the game (unless you've been replaying missions), so you should sell off any parts you're not using to amass enough funds to put together a build that gives you the best chance at victory. Keep in mind that you sell parts for the same amount they cost, so you're not losing any COAM by doing this.

Your bazooka and pulse blade will serve you well, because you need hard-hitting weapons that deal as much damage and impact as possible, regardless of your distance from the boss. Jumping over the boss and staying airborne is highly advisable in this battle, so swapping to the KASUAR/42Z reverse-joint legs will allow you to easily shift to aerial combat at no EN cost, thanks to their increased jump height. Using those legs does come at a price in terms of your AP and defenses, but the VP-44S head unit will allow you to recoup some of those specs.

While you can use them whenever you get behind the JUGGERNAUT, the BML-G1/P20MLT-04 missile launchers are not ideal for this boss encounter. You're much better served purchasing a set of vertical missile launchers, which can fire directly onto the boss from above, bypassing its frontal shield. The BML-G1/P03VTC-08 delivers more damage and impact, but the Vvc-70VPM plasma missile launchers will strain the JUGGERNAUT's ACS even if they hit the shield, while also taking advantage of its huge weakness against energy damage.

01	R-ARM UNIT | BAZOOKA	DF-BA-06 XUAN GE	P.56
02	L-ARM UNIT | PULSE BLADE	HI-32: BU-TT/A	P.65
03	R-BACK UNIT | PLASMA MISSILE LAUNCHER	Vvc-70VPM	P.74
04	L-BACK UNIT | PLASMA MISSILE LAUNCHER	Vvc-70VPM	P.74
05	HEAD | —	VP-44S	P.78
06	CORE | —	CC-2000 ORBITER	P.81
07	ARMS | —	AC-2000 TOOL ARM	P.83
08	LEGS | REVERSE JOINT	KASUAR/42Z	P.86
09	BOOSTER | —	BST-G2/P10	P.88
10	FCS | —	FCS-G2/P10SLT	P.90
11	GENERATOR | —	AG-J-098 JOSO	P.91

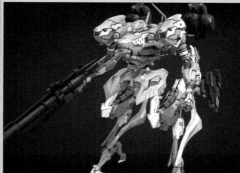

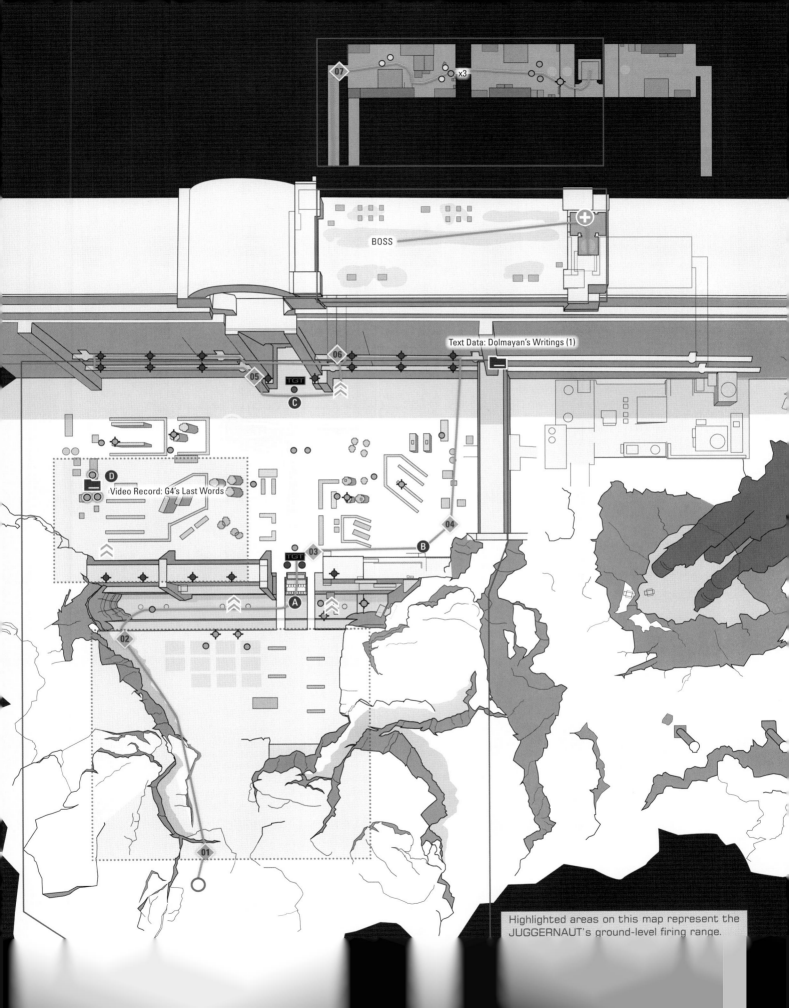

07 x3

BOSS ✚

Text Data: Dolmayan's Writings (1)

06

05

TGT
C

D
Video Record: G4's Last Words

04

B

03
TGT
A

02

01

Highlighted areas on this map represent the
JUGGERNAUT's ground-level firing range.

JUGGERNAUT FIRE

As soon as you progress past the edge of the cliff where you begin, you'll enter the sights of the JUGGERNAUT sitting atop the Wall, and it will begin targeting you relentlessly with explosive shells capable of depleting thousands of AP per shot. Evading these shells should be your primary concern at the start of the mission, so listen for the attack indicator, stay mobile with plenty of changes to your altitude, and use Quick Boosts to help avoid the large blast radius they create. Due to its elevation, the JUGGERNAUT only has a line of sight over the first half of the area (and some of the western side of the city when you're on the ground), so reaching its blind spots as quickly as possible will make things much easier.

OBJECTIVE

Destroy the City Gatling Cannon and Tetrapod MT

01 ◈ From the edge of the cliff here, you'll be able to overlook the besieged outskirts of the base below and can see the towering Wall ahead. The two gatling cannons you need to destroy are on the opposite side of a small bridge spanning a deep divide that splits the area into two distinct halves. Taking a direct route to the gatling cannons and dealing with them head on would put you under fire from both the JUGGERNAUT and the other enemies in the area, so skirting around the battlefield is the safest option. When you're ready, line yourself up such that you can Assault Boost over the section of cliff that juts out between you and the divide and land on the other side of it. From there, boost along the bottom of the cliff and drop into the divide, using your missiles to take out any bipedal MTs that enter your view.

Steer clear of JUGGERNAUT's explosive rounds as you make your way to the Wall.

You'll want to Quick Boost forward as soon as you clear the top of the divide to get behind the gatling cannons before they can fire on you.

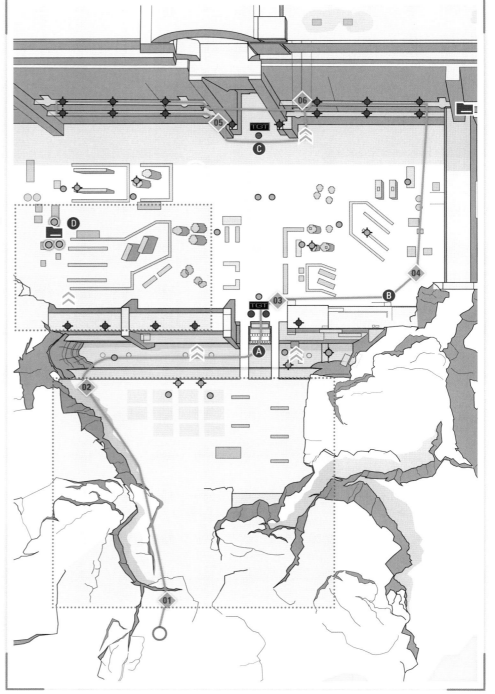

02 ◈ Drop down into the divide once you reach it, and from here, start making your way along it toward **Position A**. Enemy units within the divide are fewer and less hazardous than those outside, and you'll be out of the JUGGERNAUT's line of fire, but many of the bipedal MTs down here are equipped with high-impact missiles that are capable of straining your ACS very quickly. Due to the potential threat they pose if you're targeted by a group of them at once, go slowly, and take them out as you encounter them so that you can safely prepare for your ascent.

Once you reach **Position A**, you'll be directly below the gatling cannons and can ascend the ledges to face them. They're front-shielded, so you'll need to quickly maneuver behind them or use your plasma missiles to take them out. Keep in mind that while the artillery emplacements along the Wall can't reach you, there are other bipedal MTs in the surrounding area that can—stay ready to Quick Boost at a moment's notice if you hear any attack indicators.

03 From your position near the destroyed gatling cannons, you'll have a clear view of the rows of artillery emplacements strategically placed along the Wall's ledges. You're currently outside their effective range, but moving further toward the Wall will cause them to track you with a red targeting laser and open fire. Given the amount of artillery defending the Wall, a less direct route offers a much safer means of reaching your destination; use the city's buildings for cover and start following the road to **Position B**.

04 Once past all of the buildings, you'll have a straight shot to the bottom of the Wall, so when you're ready, Assault Boost directly toward it to remain protected from incoming artillery fire. Along both sides of the Wall are two levels of walkways, each containing three sniper cannon artillery units, with an additional two overlooking the tetrapod MT at **Position C**. Fighting the tetrapod MT while the artillery are still active makes the battle far more risky than it needs to be, so it's recommended that you destroy them before engaging it. The best way to accomplish that is to jump to the upper level and position yourself along the outer edge of it so that you can target the artillery on both levels at the same time. When you reach the central columns, jump out and boost around them so you land on the other side and continue destroying the artillery there.

Text Data Log
DOLMAYAN'S WRITINGS (1)

As you scale the outside of the Wall to destroy the artillery, it's worth taking a quick detour to the edge of the combat zone so that you can grab the data log that's nestled away in a corner behind a large column.

05 After clearing out the artillery units and any bipedal MTs in the immediate area, it's time to face the tetrapod MT. As long as you've remained high on the Wall while destroying the artillery, you shouldn't have alerted it, allowing you to take advantage of the surprise attack impact bonus with your first strike. The tetrapod MT is outfitted with gatling guns and a powerful 9-shot bazooka that are more suited to close- or medium-range encounters, and it even has the ability to boost toward you and fire a barrage of bazooka shells, which can be extremely dangerous and makes fighting it from this elevated location your safest option.

At this range, the tetrapod MT will only use its gatling guns. Because you're outside of their effective range, you'll only take negligible damage if they hit you. You can freely fire your missiles and bazooka at it—although it will occasionally attempt to dodge your bazooka, the elevated position usually ensures that your shot hits close enough to deal damage. You can even walk backward out of sight for a while until it loses track of you, at which point it will become unaware again and reset its position, allowing for another surprise attack with your bazooka.

Bronze Combat Log + Video Record
G4'S LAST WORDS

The area should be significantly safer now, making this a good time to head over to **Position D**, where you'll be able to obtain three bronze combat logs by defeating a group of bipedal MTs. There's also a data log that you can acquire by scanning G4 Volta's wreck once the nearby enemies have been defeated.

| OBJECTIVE | Penetrate the Wall and Reach the Top |

06 The doors leading to the interior of the Wall will open once the tetrapod MT has been destroyed, finally giving you a route to the top, where the JUGGERNAUT awaits. There's an access door on both of the levels you previously cleared the artillery from, and you can use either of these to continue forward. Be warned, however: once you enter the Wall, you won't be able to return outside. So make sure you've collected everything, including your fill of bonus pay, before you enter.

Make sure to keep scanning as you follow the road near **Position B**, because there are numerous bipedal MTs among the buildings that you should try to destroy as you pass by.

Even if you're confident you could defeat the tetrapod MT without destroying the artillery, the amount of bonus pay you'll earn in the process makes them worthwhile targets.

If you choose to fight the tetrapod MT on the ground, you'll want to stay as mobile as possible, sticking to its sides to keep clear of the gatling guns. If you get in trouble, use the vertical catapult to escape.

Infiltrating the Wall from the bottom entrance pits you against two guard mechs on the way through.

Using the top entrance allows you to easily skip the encounter, as long as you boost ahead.

07 ◈ Be ready to engage a batch of guard mechs once you enter this room. When you near the opposite side, the connecting door will open and a small group of bipedal MTs will advance on you. These enemies are tightly grouped, so a well placed shot from your bazooka can make quick work of them. There's another group of bipedal MTs in the adjacent room, so enter with caution. One of these is atop a higher platform at the back, and equipped with a high-impact grenade cannon; this enemy should be your priority target, so it's worth flying past the initial group with an Assault Boost to quickly destroy it. Proceed through the door near that bipedal MT, and then use the elevator on the other side to reach the top of the Wall, where you'll be able to call in a supply sherpa. Make sure to take advantage of its services, because once you exit the nearby door, you'll immediately begin the fight with the HA-T-102 JUGGERNAUT. ▶ A

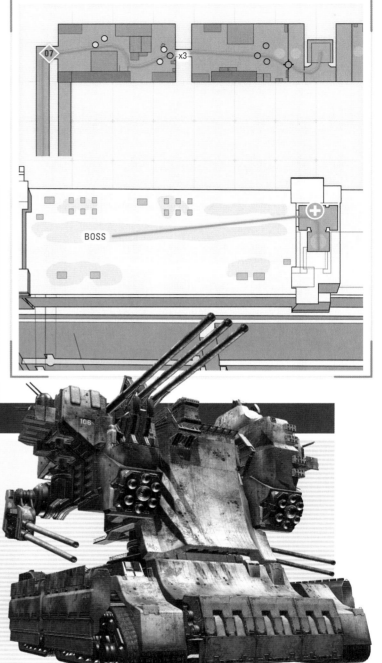

HA-T-102

JUGGERNAUT

The front of the JUGGERNAUT is impervious to damage due to its thick armor plating, so your only option for dealing damage and overloading its ACS is to circle around it and attack from the sides or the rear, with its exposed thrusters being the main weak spot. You'll be accompanied by V.IV Rusty during the first phase of this fight, and since he'll draw a lot of the JUGGERNAUT's attention, use that time to accustom yourself to maneuvering around it and finding opportunities to get a shot in.

The top section of the Wall where the fight takes place is lengthy and flat, with only a few small destructible obstacles to impede your movement. If you ever feel overwhelmed, remember that you can drop to a lower ledge on either side of the combat zone to shield yourself from incoming fire. However, be aware that hiding will cause the JUGGERNAUT to return to the center of the area and face your position, so this isn't an advantageous location from which to directly attack the boss.

BASIC SPECS

AP	63985
Attitude Stability	1600
Anti-Kinetic Defense	1210
Anti-Energy Defense	176
Anti-Explosive Defense	361
Elec. Discharge Tolerance	999
Shock Resistance	0%
ACS Anomaly Tolerance	999
Heat Resistance	0%

■ **OBJECTIVE**

Destroy JUGGERNAUT Heavy
Mobile Artillery Platform

The JUGGERNAUT always begins the fight by attempting to ram your AC with its crashing charge. This collision is potentially enough to overload your ACS; mastering the use of Quick Boosts to jump away when the JUGGERNAUT charges is crucial to victory.

PHASES

1 Take some time during this opening phase to observe how the JUGGERNAUT uses its crashing charge, and the type of attacks that follow it—mastering these patterns is the key to defeating this behemoth. If it charges evasively to create distance, it will typically follow up with either its auxiliary cannon or missile salvo. When it charges directly at you, however, you should always expect the 3-shot grenade cannon to follow—as soon as you evade the charge, listen for an attack indicator and be ready to avoid the incoming projectiles. These explosive rounds not only inflict a great deal of impact, but they also create a large explosion upon detonation; if you're on the ground, even a well-timed Quick Boost might not be enough to clear their blast radius. Jumping and maneuvering in the air is generally the safest way to avoid JUGGERNAUT's explosive rounds.

While you're in front of the JUGGERNAUT, you should be constantly moving and firing your plasma missiles to build up ACS strain while you attempt to get an angle on its blind spot. The easiest way to do that is to toggle Target Assist to focus your view on JUGGERNAUT, then jump over it and move toward its rear until the camera automatically spins around to face it again. At this point, your bazooka should fire directly into the exposed thrusters instead of at a downward angle—where it risks clipping the frontal shield—which is likely to happen if you fire while above the boss.

If you're close enough after firing your bazooka—and depending on the JUGGER-NAUT's current ACS strain—you may want to follow up with a pulse blade combo. The bazooka and plasma missiles should be your primary means of straining its ACS in an effort to stagger it, whereas your pulse blade has the highest direct hit value and will deal the most damage after it has been staggered; if the boss is close to staggering after your bazooka shot, hold off on using your pulse blade until after you've staggered it to ensure you can use it straight away. Be prepared to immediately Quick Boost to either side after your attacks, however, because the JUGGERNAUT can respond by quickly charging in reverse, which would apply heavy strain to your ACS and high AP damage if it hits you.

2 After losing 40% of its AP, the JUGGERNAUT will begin deploying large numbers of landmines whenever it repositions with a crashing charge or quick turn. Individual landmines can deal significant damage and impact when stepped on, but the combined impact of multiple mines in quick succession is the real threat, as this will overload your ACS and leave you open to direct hits.

At this point, Rusty will receive a call from his superiors ordering him to exit the battle. Try to land as many solid hits as possible and stagger the JUGGERNAUT one more time before Rusty leaves, because you'll be forced to handle the rest of the fight alone once he's gone. The strategies you've been using up until this point still apply, but without Rusty there to draw some of the boss's attention, your evasive skills and timing will need to be that much sharper to stay alive and create openings.

There's little room for you to move cautiously around JUGGERNAUT, as its increased mobility gives you fewer chances to get behind it. Beyond launching constant volleys of plasma missiles, you'll need to try to match its speed and shift to aerial combat more often in order to hit its blind spot. Looking for opportunities to land bazooka or pulse blade hits should still be your priority, but given the amount of attack opportunities you're likely to have, staggering JUGGERNAUT again can be extremely difficult. Keep in mind that while you won't deal any damage or additional ACS buildup when hitting its frontal shield, doing so will stop its ACS from recovering, and taking the occasional shot at it will go a long way toward an eventual stagger.

JUGGERNAUT ATTACKS

CRASHING CHARGE

DESCRIPTION Revs its wheels in place for a brief moment and quickly charges toward your AC. It can either move forward or backward depending on your position.

EVASION Quick Boost to either side of the JUGGERNAUT.

QUICK TURN

DESCRIPTION Revs its treads similarly to if it was about to charge but will instead spin in place.

EVASION Evade backward or keep your distance from the frame of the JUGGERNAUT.

MULTI MISSILE LAUNCHER

DESCRIPTION Releases a high volume of low-impact missiles with limited homing capabilities.

EVASION Quick Boost to either side of the salvo.

AUXILIARY CANNON

DESCRIPTION Opens fire with one or both kinetic rifles simultaneously. Deals heavy AP damage and high ACS strain.

EVASION Jump and Quick Boost to either side of the shot.

3-SHOT GRENADE CANNON ▼

DESCRIPTION Fires a burst of three high-impact grenades in a tight pattern or fanning spread. Shots can be aimed either horizontally or vertically.

EVASION Signaled by attack indicators around the cannons. Stay mobile and visually track the rounds, then jump, use boost movement, or Quick Boost to avoid them.

LANDMINE THROWER   PHASE 2

DESCRIPTION Releases a trail of explosive landmines in its wake during crashing charge; can also deploy mines while spinning during quick turn.

EVASION The landmines are timed explosives as well as proximity detonating, so be vigilant and maneuver around them until they explode.

RETRIEVE COMBAT LOGS

*"I'm a Coral Warrior, just like the others!
And I will not give in!"*

—Little Ziyi

Having themselves failed to reach the top of the Wall, Balam is seeking information about the Vesper who partnered with you in your successful assault: V.IV Rusty. To this end, they're tasking you with retrieving at least five (but potentially up to eight) data logs scattered around the map relating to him and his AC, STEEL HAZE. To avoid clashing with incoming Arquebus reinforcements, you'll only have four minutes to complete this job. If you have at least five logs when the time runs out, the mission will be counted as a success, and collecting all eight will end the mission immediately. Keep this in mind as there's an optional AC fight that rewards you with a combat log, and it's easy to accidentally end the mission before defeating it if you're not keeping count.

The only other enemies in the mission are some bipedal MTs and guard mechs, but the area is expansive so you can't afford to stop and fight if you want to retrieve all of the logs. Acquiring all of them is highly recommended because while your base pay is only 10,000 COAM, you earn extra bonus pay for each log, up to a total of 123,100 COAM for all of them. None of the enemies give bonus pay, so you only need to focus on defeating the ones that pose an immediate threat.

ASSEMBLY

As you're racing against the clock in this mission, it's advisable to assemble a frame that prioritizes speed over survivability. The HI-32: BU-TT/A gives you a light but high-damage option, which is especially useful if you intend on fighting the AC YUE YU for the combat log: if you don't, then you may want to swap it for an additional machine gun so that you never need to stop moving. Without compromising your speed, you can get a big bump to your defensive specs with the VP-40S core, which will help you absorb incoming damage as you're moving between scanning locations.

The BST-G2/P04 booster gives you a nice increase to your overall boost and Quick Boost speed, which will make it easier to hit all of the objective locations in time, and going back to the DF-GN-02 LING-TAI will make sure your EN comes back as fast as possible. If you've already completed the "Investigate BAWS Arsenal No. 2" mission and have unlocked the Arena, you may want to consider earning some OST Chips and installing Access Speed – Optimization to greatly reduce the time it takes to access the wrecks.

01	R-ARM UNIT | MACHINE GUN MG-014 LUDLOW	P.53
02	L-ARM UNIT | PULSE BLADE HI-32: BU-TT/A	P.65
03	R-BACK UNIT | MISSILE LAUNCHER BML-G1/P20MLT-04	P.69
04	L-BACK UNIT | MISSILE LAUNCHER BML-G1/P20MLT-04	P.69
05	HEAD | — VP-44S	P.78
06	CORE | — VP-40S	P.80
07	ARMS | — AC-2000 TOOL ARM	P.83
08	LEGS | BIPEDAL NACHTREIHER/42E	P.85
09	BOOSTER | — BST-G2/P04	P.88
10	FCS | — FCS-G2/P10SLT	P.90
11	GENERATOR | — DF-GN-02 LING-TAI	P.91

MISSION OBJECTIVE

Retrieve Combat Logs from Wrecks

MISSION INFO

Combat Zone	Central Belius—Arquebus Survey Base "The Wall"
Client	Balam Industries
Reward	10,000
Max Bonus Pay	123,100
Completion Unlocks	OS Tuning, Arena (If completed before "Investigate BAWS Arsenal No. 2")
Combat Logs	Gold x1
Data Logs	8
Part Containers	—

ENEMY DATA

	No.	AP	AS	Bonus Pay	Analysis
● MT-T-026 Guard Mech (Rifle)	8	102	121	—	P.310
● CD-J-098 Quad Drone (Transport Hangar)	4	302	310	—	P.312
● MT-E-104 BAWS Bipedal MT (Missile Launcher)	10	470	364	—	P.316
● MT-E-104 BAWS Bipedal MT (Grenade Cannon)	4	470	364	—	P.316
◉ AC YUE YU / Little Ziyi	1	11420	1620	—	

Text Data: The Well Dries

System Log: One-Sided Engagement

Video Record: BAWS Arsenal No. 2

Video Record: STEEL HAZE

System Log: The Deserter

Comms Record: Rusty's Encoded Comms

Video Record: Communication Attempt

Comms Record: Friendly Comms

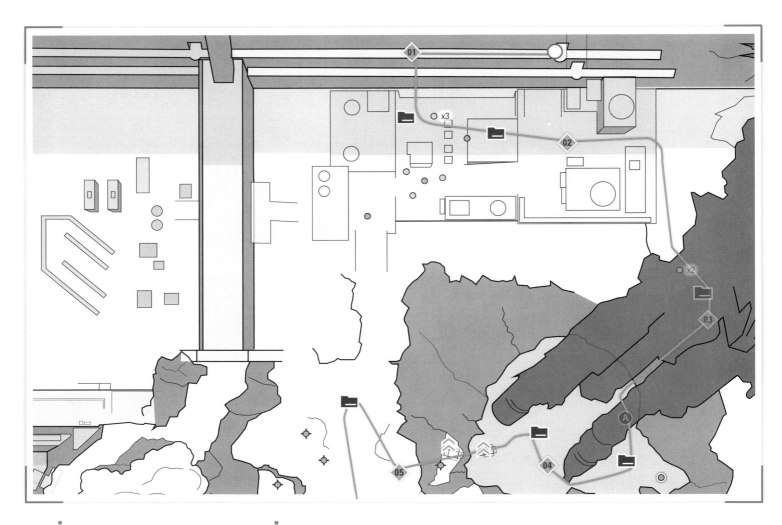

COAM TRADER

Through both earned income and selling parts you've acquired, you should now have access to a large enough working pool of funds to assemble any combination of currently available parts and create a build to suit any mission. As such, you'll see our build recommendations incorporate a wider variety of parts from this point onward to keep pace with the increasing complexity and difficulty of the missions.

OBJECTIVE | Retrieve Combat Logs from Wrecks

01 Text Data   The Well Dries (1,000 COAM)
      System Log   One-Sided Engagement (5,000 COAM)

There are two logs in the building complex directly below your starting position, and to avoid backtracking, you should boost along the ledge you start on until you're above the furthest of the two. From there, you can drop down to it while using your missiles to destroy the guard mechs and begin accessing it when you land. A bipedal MT on a nearby rooftop may fire at you, so listen for the alert indicator and dodge as necessary, then use your missiles to take it out. Once you've acquired the first log, ascend to the rooftop where that bipedal MT was standing and grab the second one.

02 Video Record   BAWS Arsenal No. 2 (50,000 COAM)

The fastest way to reach the next log is to turn toward coordinates 270 and continue along the roof of the building you're on until you find yourself underneath the large wreckage covering much of the area, then drop to the right once you reach the end. You'll soon see the next wreck ahead of you—this one defended by two guard mechs—so boost toward it while using multi-lock missiles to destroy both of the mechs so that you can safely retrieve the log.

03 Comms Record   Rusty's Encoded Comms (35,000 COAM)

From the previous log, start descending into the large crater nearby, and then cut underneath part of it once you reach **Position A**. You should see the next smoldering wreck on the ground just ahead of you, but be careful as you approach it because a hostile AC, YUE YU, will attack you from the top of the surrounding cliffs once you move closer. If you don't want to engage this opponent, use the wreck for cover and keep moving around until access is complete. However, it's highly recommended that you destroy this AC to obtain the gold combat log it holds.

Look for a burning plume of smoke to quickly identify wrecks you haven't collected yet. If you stay close to a wreck while accessing it, you can freely boost and continue fighting around it without interrupting the data retrieval.

A yellow reinforcement indicator signals YUE YU's arrival on your HUD, so you'll receive some warning to help avoid her opening salvo.

AC // YUE YU

YUE YU is equipped with dual IRIDIUM grenade launchers which it will use to rapidly fire grenades with large area of effects at you, and a SI-29: SU-TT/C pulse buckler for defense. The grenades won't home in on you, but they'll deal significant ACS strain and AP damage even if you don't get hit directly, so aerial evasion is highly recommended. Your attacks will apply less ACS strain while YUE YU's shield is active, but it won't completely negate the buildup. Remember that you can use your pulse blade to quickly disrupt the shield if you're close enough.

YUE YU has relatively low AP, but it's highly mobile and will attempt to constantly move around and keep you at mid range if you approach or move away. Even though its movement speed is YUE YU's greatest strength, given the time constraints of the mission, you'll need to take a very aggressive approach to the fight, and staying close to it so you can use your pulse blade is still the shortest path to victory. The pulse buckler's Initial Guard is when it is at its most efficient, so try to bait YUE YU into using it with your missiles and machine gun, and then use your pulse blade shortly afterward to destroy it and continue your offense.

BASIC SPECS

AP	11420
Attitude Stability	1620
Anti-Kinetic Defense	1228
Anti-Energy Defense	1083
Anti-Explosive Defense	1310
Elec. Discharge Tolerance	490
Shock Resistance	-32%
ACS Anomaly Tolerance	490
Heat Resistance	-32%

04 ◆ System Log   The Deserter (100 COAM)

The next log is only a short distance away from the previous one, and if you destroyed YUE YU, it may look like it's completely unguarded. When you approach it, however, a bipedal MT with a grenade launcher high above you will start firing down, so you'll need to retrieve the log while evading its shots. Once it's yours, use the nearby vertical catapult to reach the ledge with the bipedal MT and destroy it, and then use the vertical catapult on that ledge to get out of the crater.

05 ◆ Video Record   STEEL HAZE (10,000 COAM)

While you're in the air from the vertical catapult, you'll get targeted by a group of bipedal MTs on the cliffs ahead, so quickly Assault Boost toward them and use your missiles to take them out one at a time as they enter your range. Trying to retrieve the log in this area while those enemies are still around can be very difficult and likely lead to you taking a lot of damage, so destroying them as you approach is the much quicker and safer option.

06 ◆ Comms Record   Friendly Comms (2,000 COAM)
     ◆ Video Record   Communication Attempt (20,000 COAM)

If you set your heading to 340 from the previous log, you'll see the billowing smoke from the wrecks of the final two in the distance. Between you and the first one is another group of bipedal MTs, so Assault Boost toward them and use your missiles to start picking them off as you approach, and if anything survives, finish it off quickly with your pulse blade before starting to retrieve the log. Like the log in the crater, the final log here too looks to be completely unguarded, but when you get near, a group of four bipedal MTs will enter from outside the area behind it. Since the mission will end upon retrieving this last log, simply take cover behind the wreck to avoid getting hit until the scan and the mission are complete.

Positioning yourself so that YUE YU backs into a cliff wall as it attempts to move away from you will make closing in and landing pulse blade combos much easier.

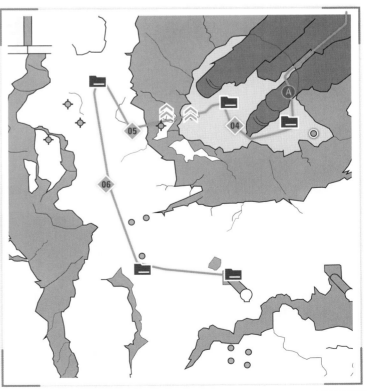

If the bipedal MTs start firing on you while you're closing in, remember that you can still dodge laterally during an Assault Boost to avoid the incoming shots.

//05-B
INVESTIGATE BAWS ARSENAL NO. 2

> *"...Some advice before you go, 621. 'Expect the unexpected.'"*
>
> —Handler Walter

Despite partaking in several sorties against them, the RLF has decided to seek your aid in investigating an important BAWS facility that has gone mysteriously quiet. You'll only encounter a handful of enemies in this mission, but these are a new variant and they're much more capable than the previous enemies you've tackled. They're known as GHOSTs, and you'll have to contend with both long-range and melee specialist variants of them. Scanning is by far your most valuable tool in this mission, because as fearsome as their offensive capabilities are, the GHOSTs' greatest trick is that they're virtually invisible, and only through either scanning or vigilantly watching for where they're attacking from—in conjunction with using your compass—will you be able to discern their location.

MISSION INFO

Combat Zone	Northern Belius—BAWS Arsenal No. 2
Client	Rubicon Liberation Front
Reward	180,000
Max Bonus Pay	—
Completion Unlocks	OS Tuning, Arena (If completed before "Retrieve Combat Logs")
Combat Logs	—
Data Logs	2
Part Containers	—

MISSION OBJECTIVE

Survey the Arsenal Interior

ENEMY DATA

	No.	AP	AS	Bonus Pay	Analysis
IA-27: GHOST (Sniper Type)	7	3820	1066	—	P.343
IA-27: GHOST (Melee Type)	3	3820	1066	—	P.343
IA-27: GHOST (Pulse Armor)	1	4775	1066	—	P.343

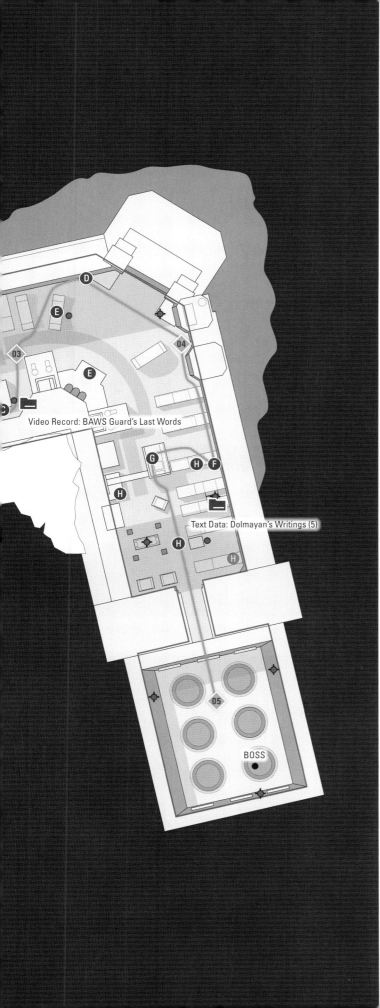

Video Record: BAWS Guard's Last Words

Text Data: Dolmayan's Writings (5)

05

BOSS

ASSEMBLY

The GHOSTs you face in this mission deal primarily energy damage, and are weak to explosive weaponry; creating a build that takes advantage of both of those traits will put you in good stead. Their weakness to explosive damage is so great that you can easily kill them with a volley of missiles followed by two shots from the DF-BA-06 XUAN-GE bazookas, so dual-wielding these weapons in addition to a single BML-G1/P20MLT-04 lets you destroy most of the enemies quickly once you've located them. The VP-422 legs are a solid bipedal option, since they too provide a decent amount of energy defense. For a slightly different playstyle, it's also worth considering the VP-424 tetrapod legs, which allow you to fire the bazookas while hovering, eliminating recoil and staying out of harm's way.

The SI-29: SU-TT/C pulse buckler can help you mitigate some of the damage from long-range sniper shots when you're dealing with multiple enemies. Watch for attack indicators and deploy your shield to perform an Initial Guard whenever you aren't in a position to Quick Boost out of the way. Just remember to keep an eye on the shield's heat gauge and allow it to cool down between activations.

01	R-ARM UNIT | BAZOOKA **DF-BA-06 XUAN GE**	P.56
02	L-ARM UNIT | BAZOOKA **DF-BA-06 XUAN GE**	P.56
03	R-BACK UNIT | MISSILE LAUNCHER **BML-G1/P20MLT-04**	P.69
04	L-BACK UNIT | PULSE BUCKLER **SI-29: SU-TT/C**	P.76
05	HEAD | — **VP-44S**	P.78
06	CORE | — **VP-40S**	P.80
07	ARMS | — **VP-46S**	P.83
08	LEGS | BIPEDAL **VP-422**	P.85
09	BOOSTER | — **BST-G2/P04**	P.88
10	FCS | — **FCS-G2/P05**	P.89
11	GENERATOR | — **VP-20S**	P.92

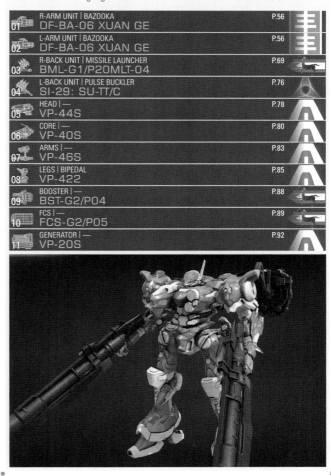

OBJECTIVE	Survey the Arsenal Interior

01 ◆ Begin with an Assault Boost from your starting position to the top of the wall overlooking the interior of the BAWS facility. While it may appear desolate, remember to heed the words of Walter and expect the unexpected. Be ready to evade as soon as you pass over the third road bridge, because a GHOST with a laser gun will start firing on you from its position underneath a crane at **Position A**. Use lateral dodges during an Assault Boost to evade the shots—or deploy your shield if you think you won't make it—then once you get close, use your scanner to reveal its location.

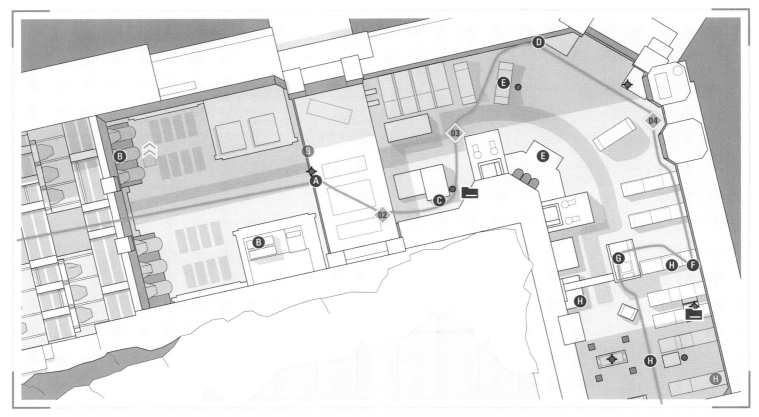

You'll need to act quickly upon revealing the GHOST, otherwise it will vanish from sight and reappear in a different location (indicated by the **Position B** markers on the map). The moment you're locked on to a GHOST, launch a missile volley while simultaneously firing one of your bazookas to instantly overload its ACS and set it up for a direct hit with the other bazooka. It's important to introduce a brief delay before firing a second bazooka shot, however, because the first will knock the GHOST backward, which can throw off the aim of your second shot if you fire again immediately. To prevent this from happening, wait until the GHOST stops reeling and quickly fire your second shot to finish it off before it can escape.

02 ◈ There are a lot more buildings that you can use as cover in the next part of the facility, but there are also significantly more GHOSTs that are laying in wait to take advantage of any wrong step you take. With the right approach and use of your scan, however, it's possible for you to catch many of them unaware. From here, you can see the sparking of a wreck containing the Video Record: BAWS Guard's Last Words data log, but there's also a GHOST nearby that will ambush you if you were to access it straight away. Instead, head to **Position C** near the corner of the building, use your scan to reveal the GHOST, then move out quickly and finish it off with a couple of bazooka shots.

03 ◈ There's a melee-type GHOST hiding near some scaffolding on the opposite side of the area that you can sneak up on, though doing so exposes you to a sniper-type GHOST on a nearby rooftop. Instead, cross the room until you're behind the support structure. Use your scan to reveal the location of the melee-type GHOST, then boost over behind the building at **Position D**. From there, you'll be out of the sniper GHOST's line of fire and can get clear bazooka shots on the still unaware melee-type GHOST. After defeating that enemy, ascend and Assault Boost over to the sniper GHOST until you can destroy it too. If these GHOSTs vanish, they'll typically reappear at one of the **Position E** locations.

04 ◈ One final group of GHOSTs has taken up ambush positions defending the entrance to the interior of the facility, and while you can't reverse the situation and ambush all of them, it's still possible to make the encounter significantly easier than if you were to head straight in. Boost along the wall of the facility until you reach the platform at **Position F**, then use a scan to reveal the location of a sniper-type GHOST on a rooftop in front of you; fire off your missiles and bazookas to destroy it.

If you get into open combat with the melee-type GHOST, keep in mind that their whips have deceptive range, so always stay further back than you might think.

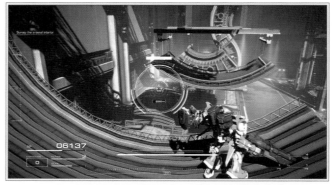

If the final ghost relocates, it'll reappear at one of the **Position H** locations, and your scan radius should be large enough to find it from this central position.

This will alert the other two, and the melee-type GHOST will start closing in on you; the second sniper GHOST can't hit you from its starting location, so you won't need to worry about it. Use your scan to keep track of the melee GHOST as it approaches and fire at it when you have a clear shot. If it gets close to the base of the platform you're on, it will try to jump up, which just makes it easier to hit. The final sniper GHOST is located on the opposite side of the area, so if you backtrack slightly and jump onto the central structure at **Position G**, you can get a clear shot on it. Once you've secured the area, access the doors at the back and enter the Arsenal to continue the investigation.

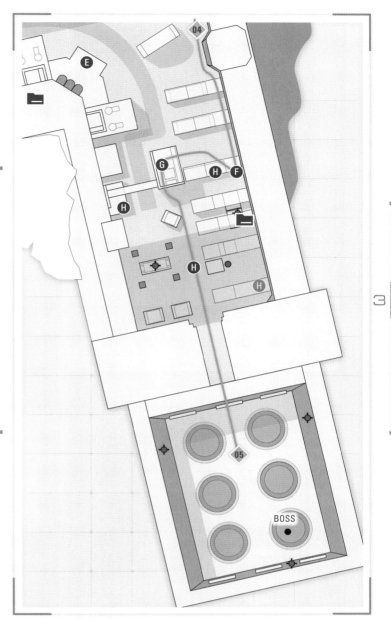

Text Data Log
DOLMAYAN'S WRITINGS (5)

Before moving inside the facility, be sure to scale the various structures in the area to get to the top of one of the cranes, where you'll find another wreck that you can access for a data log.

05 ◇ Upon reaching the bottom of this large chamber, you'll get an update from Walter (and a very welcome checkpoint), shortly after which you'll get attacked by a squad of four GHOSTs, consisting of three sniper types and a more advanced melee type unit that can use pulse armor. Attempting to fight this GHOST while evading shots from the three ranged ones positioned high on the walls around the room can be very difficult. An easier approach is to stay airborne and mobile as much as possible to keep away from the pulse armor GHOST while making your way around the room taking out the ranged ones.

It still only takes two bazooka shots to defeat these ranged GHOSTs, but you'll need slightly different timing due to their positions on the walls. When you hit one with a bazooka shot, it will fall to the ground, so immediately engage Target Assist to keep it within view. Wait until it has nearly landed before firing your second shot to minimize the chances of it missing. If any of the ranged ghosts vanish on you in this room, they can reappear at various locations along each of the walls, so you'll need to quickly but meticulously scan as you work your way around the room to locate them, using your compass for directional guidance. If you see a GHOST firing at you, quickly Assault Boost in its direction and take it out.

The pulse armor GHOST here is equipped with the same laser whip as the previous two melee units, however, its attack pattern is altered. Depending on its proximity, this GHOST can jump and crash the whip down vertically, perform a quick linear thrust, a singular horizontal sweep, or perform long combos that string some of these attacks together. It also has pulse armor that it can regenerate during the encounter, and you'll need to deplete that before you can either damage it or begin straining its ACS. All of these factors can lead to a problematic battle, given how highly mobile this enemy is. It will often dodge your bazooka shots unless you use missiles first and hit it after it evades. Aim to stay above it as much as possible to negate its powerful whip attacks and force it to use its plasma gun instead. As soon as the final enemy is destroyed, the mission will be complete.

If you see the pulse armor GHOST spin its whip briefly like this, it means the next attack string it uses will end with an energy explosion.

"Have we... made Contact?"

—Ayre

Walter has communicated a personal request with you to infiltrate the PCA Watchpoint and destroy the sensor valve at its core. While his motivation for sending you there remains a mystery, your job is clear: fight through multiple squads of Subject Guard MTs backed up by heavy artillery, take on a hostile AC, and then destroy the imposing PCA SP autonomous craft BALTEUS. The terrain in this combat zone varies greatly over the course of the mission, alternating between industrial structures and wide open spaces, so you'll need a versatile build to handle the shifting conditions. It should also be noted that while you'll earn 100,000 COAM in bonus pay, this is not awarded on a per-enemy destroyed basis, and is instead just a single payout upon completion.

MISSION OBJECTIVES

Annihilate the SG Squad in Sector 1

Annihilate the SG Squad in Sector 2

Head for Sector 3

Destroy the AC of Unknown Affiliation

Infiltrate Control Center and Destroy Target Device

Destroy the PCA SP Autonomous Craft BALTEUS

MISSION INFO

Combat Zone	Northern Belius - Watchpoint Delta
Client	Handler Walter
Reward	380,000
Max Bonus Pay	100,000
Completion Unlocks	E-Rank Arena targets, Parts Shop Update 4
Combat Logs	Gold x1
Data Logs	2
Part Containers	—

ENEMY DATA

	No.	AP	AS	Analysis
● AM14: Subject Guard SENTRY MT (Missile Launcher)	9	437	310	P.320
○ Artillery (Laser Cannon)	4	1131	—	P.329
◎ AC ENTANGLE / Sulla	1	10640	1761	—
■ Sensor Valve	1	1300	—	—
● AAP07: BALTEUS	1	36290	1550	—

BOSS

06

05
Monitoring Station—Exterior

04

B

C

02

Comms Record: Independent Merc Comms

A

01

03
Observation Data: Wave Mutation Detected

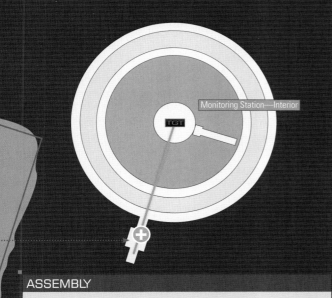

Monitoring Station—Interior

TGT

ASSEMBLY

Similar to Operation Wallclimber, your build should be geared around defeating the boss at the end of this mission, as well as the difficult AC battle just before it. Both use a lot of explosive weaponry, so the full MELANDER frame is a good choice, providing the best explosive resistance for a medium-weight frame. BALTEUS is especially weak against energy damage and has a strong pulse armor, so your complement of weapons should lean toward being able to deplete the pulse armor while dealing good damage and ACS strain—a full suite of plasma weapons fills that role nicely.

Firing down on these enemies to catch them within the blast radius of your plasma weapons is one of the most effective ways of dealing with them, so depending on your preferred playstyle, you may want to swap the LG-011 MELANDER legs for the VP-424 tetrapod legs. These legs have excellent defensive values and can facilitate extended periods of aerial bombardment, and the VP-20D generator gives you plenty of spare EN capacity to help speed up your EN recovery, regardless of which legs you choose. Since you now have access to the Arena, it's highly recommended that you attempt to defeat all of the F-rank enemies and use the OST Chips to unlock some very useful upgrades.

01	R-ARM UNIT | PLASMA RIFLE Vvc-760PR	P.60
02	L-ARM UNIT | PLASMA RIFLE Vvc-760PR	P.60
03	R-BACK UNIT | PLASMA MISSILE LAUNCHER Vvc-70VPM	P.74
04	L-BACK UNIT | PLASMA MISSILE LAUNCHER Vvc-70VPM	P.74
05	HEAD | — HD-011 MELANDER	P.77
06	CORE | — BD-011 MELANDER	P.80
07	ARMS | — AR-011 MELANDER	P.82
08	LEGS | BIPEDAL LG-011 MELANDER	P.84
09	BOOSTER | — BST-G2/P04	P.88
10	FCS | — FCS-G2/P05	P.89
11	GENERATOR | — VP-20D	P.92

01 ◆ The area ahead is vast and features various heights of sub- and super-structure, providing plenty of places for you to seek cover. This will be important going forward, because the SG squad stationed here has taken positions around the area that give them excellent fields of view, and they're all equipped with long-range weaponry. Of even greater danger are the two artillery installations that use high-impact laser cannons, capable of tracking you anywhere atop the buildings. Boosting straight in and dodging all of the incoming fire while picking off the enemies is possible, but it's highly dangerous and requires exceptional movement skills. Thankfully, the varying terrain height allows you to take a tactical, and more importantly, safe approach. You can reach this point safely without alerting any enemies, and then use your scanner and missiles to pick off the three nearby SG units while using the wall of the building for cover.

02 ◆ The first artillery installation should be your next target—take advantage of the fact that you can safely traverse through the water by dropping down and boosting around the structure, emerging in this location. From here, two uncharged shots from your plasma rifles are sufficient to destroy the artillery. Drop down again and continue around the side of the structure until you're behind the next artillery installation, and then destroy it too before ascending to **Position A**. From here, you can dispatch the nearby SG unit, then Assault Boost across the area to target another SG unit with your missiles as you pass over it. To clear the area, quickly destroy the final SG unit on the other side with your plasma rifles once you're within range.

Thanks to the vertical trajectory of your plasma missiles, you don't need a direct firing line. All you need to do is jump up between artillery shots so you can target the SG units, fire your missiles, and then drop back down to safety.

Comms Record
INDEPENDENT MERC COMMS

Before moving to the next part of the area, drop down to the water level next to the second artillery installation to find a wreck containing a data log.

<table>
<tr><td>OBJECTIVE</td><td>Annihilate the SG Squad in Sector 2</td></tr>
</table>

03 Instead of heading directly for the next objective marker, head back to the second artillery installation, and from there, use your Assault Boost to reach this elevated location atop the nearby tower. Much like the first part of the mission, this courtyard is defended by a squad of SG units and two artillery installations, so effective use of the environment is once again called for. From here, Assault Boost down toward **Position B** so that you're behind the first artillery installation and can destroy it easily with your plasma rifles. You'll need to cross the area to reach the remaining targets, and if you Assault Boost over to **Position C**, you can use the rooftop there to provide cover. The SG units can be picked off from here with your missiles; once they've been destroyed, move up a bit and take out the remaining artillery with your plasma rifles.

<table>
<tr><td>OBJECTIVE</td><td>Head for Sector 3</td></tr>
</table>

04 Proceed to this location after clearing out all of the defenses and you'll get an update from Walter directing you toward the structure housing the sensor valve in the distance. Note that once you move past this area, you cannot return, so make sure to collect any data logs you may have missed up to this point.

<table>
<tr><td>OBJECTIVE</td><td>Destroy the AC of Unknown Affiliation</td></tr>
</table>

05 After crossing a bridge toward the monitoring station, you'll be met by Sulla, piloting the AC ENTANGLE. Walter informs you that Sulla is a first-gen augmented human, three generations your augmentation elder, and an independent mercenary that you'll need to defeat in order to reach your main target. Sulla is by far the most skilled AC pilot you've come up against thus far, and his aggressive combat style coupled with the range of munitions at his disposal allows him to very quickly apply strain to your ACS.

Make sure to retrieve the "Observation Data: Wave Mutation Detected" data log from the nearby wreck after ascending on top of the tower.

If you ever need cover to give your ACS a chance to reset, move around the bridge's support columns rather than fighting Sulla in the open water.

If you've equipped the assault armor Core Expansion, save it for when Sulla attempts a Boost Kick so you can deliver a deadly counterattack and avoid taking damage.

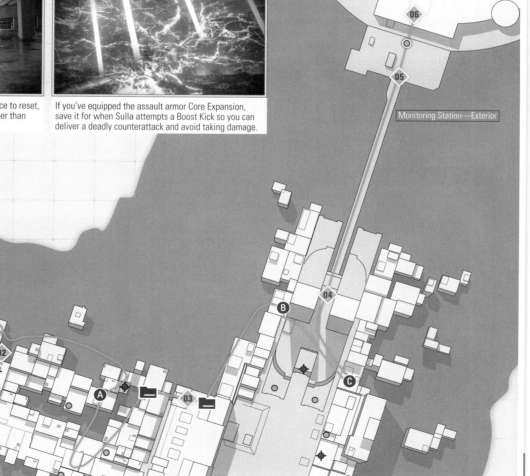

BOSS

Monitoring Station—Exterior

AC // ENTANGLE

Sulla is packing explosive and plasma weapons on his AC, meaning many of his attacks have a large effect radius and leave behind lingering areas of damage. This means that staying mobile and off the ground is crucial against him. Always try to lead with your missiles, since they have the strongest homing capabilities. While Sulla is getting hit by your missiles—or using all of his EN to evade them—charge up and fire your plasma rifles at him from above. The area of effect from your missiles combined with the charged plasma rifle shots makes it almost impossible for him to escape unscathed. Keep moving around the area while firing at him, and watch for when he begins to fire from his right arm; the JVLN ALPHA equipped to that arm causes him to stop moving, giving you a brief but consistent opportunity to attack him. Once you've lowered Sulla's AP below 40%, he will use a repair kit to recover a portion of his AC's durability. This can be a challenging fight, so don't worry about using your own repair kits, since you'll be able to resupply immediately after winning the duel.

BASIC SPECS

AP	10640
Attitude Stability	1761
Anti-Kinetic Defense	1178
Anti-Energy Defense	1261
Anti-Explosive Defense	1135
Elec. Discharge Tolerance	490
Shock Resistance	0%
ACS Anomaly Tolerance	490
Heat Resistance	0%
Repair Kits	1

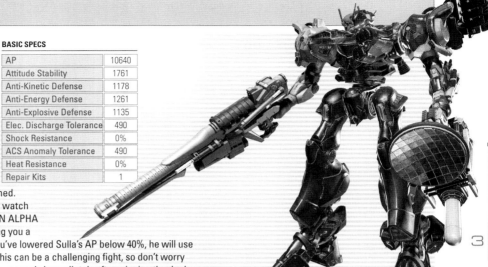

ENTANGLE / SULLA ATTACKS

BOOST KICK

DESCRIPTION Sulla will rush in and attempt to kick your AC. He'll most frequently use this attack when your ACS is either close to or already overloaded.

EVASION Quick boost away from ENTANGLE.

44-141 JVLN ALPHA ▼

DESCRIPTION Can be used at any time or range, and upon impact will cause a short chain of explosions, further increasing its effective range.

EVASION Use a carefully timed Quick Boost to either side once the shell has fired. Evade too soon and the shot will adjust its trajectory to match; too late and you'll get caught in the blast.

HI-18: GU-A2

DESCRIPTION This pulse gun shoots bursts of pulse energy that favor speed over pinpoint accuracy, causing the projectiles to spread into a frontal cone pattern.

EVASION Strafe or Quick Boost away from the direction Sulla is firing in, or jump and ascend above the stream.

Vvc-703PM

DESCRIPTION A volley of three plasma missiles with aggressive homing capabilities that create lingering damage fields upon impact.

EVASION Jump and Quick Boost away to avoid being caught in the damage fields.

45-091 JVLN BETA ▼

DESCRIPTION The missile releases a cord behind itself and moves relatively slowly through the air, capable of multiple changes in direction. Upon impact, in addition to the explosion from the missile itself, the cord will also detonate, creating a chain of explosions toward its release point.

EVASION Boosting above the trajectory of the missile or using a Quick Boost to either side will most effectively avoid it and its subsequent explosions.

OBJECTIVE

Infiltrate Control Center and Destroy Target Device

06 After defeating Sulla, you'll be able to access the bulkhead at the base of the control center building. Once you're inside, move through the vestibule and into the control center, descending to the very bottom of the monitoring station. Destroying the device at the bottom triggers a cutscene during which a Coral flow engulfs you, and you make telepathic Contact with a Rubiconian named Ayre. Your meeting with Ayre is cut short, however, by the arrival of a hostile craft that you'll first have to defeat before you can begin to unravel what may have just transpired.

Make sure to use the supply sherpa here, because you're going to need to be in top shape for the upcoming fight.

BALTEUS

BASIC SPECS

AP	40110
Attitude Stability	1900
Anti-Kinetic Defense	1210
Anti-Energy Defense	854
Anti-Explosive Defense	1000
Elec. Discharge Tolerance	500
Shock Resistance	35%
ACS Anomaly Tolerance	500
Heat Resistance	20%
Pulse Armor Resilience	5500

OBJECTIVE

Destroy the PCA SP Autonomous Craft BALTEUS

BALTEUS comes to this fight equipped with a large array of weaponry and defensive capabilities, and not since the JUGGERNAUT will you have had to face such a difficult enemy. One of its most notable abilities is its pulse armor, which negates all incoming damage—this must be fully disrupted before you can deal even a single point of AP damage. Thankfully, depleting it is guaranteed to stagger the boss, so aim to have your highest direct hit attacks ready to go as soon as that happens. After recovering from the stagger, BALTEUS will not have its pulse armor active for a while and you can begin straining its ACS. If left unstaggered for long enough, it will regenerate the armor and you'll have to deplete it again. BALTEUS tends to stick to medium or long ranges, since that's where its missile attacks are most effective. To facilitate this, you'll sometimes see it start to rev its thrusters up, indicating that it's about to move either behind you or to the opposite side of the area. Because of the effectiveness of its missile salvos over long distances, playing aggressively while sticking as close to it as possible will give you the best chance of success.

PHASES

1 In this phase of the fight, your primary concern will be BALTEUS's various missile salvos, especially its tri-directional and spread missile salvos. Due to the sheer volume of missiles released in both of these attacks, it can prove difficult to entirely evade them, so your goal should be to minimize damage by recognizing them quickly and getting into position to avoid as many as possible while also moving into range to launch your own attacks. Use your missiles whenever they become available as you're moving around, while taking uncharged shots with your plasma rifles whenever you get the opportunity. Due to the amount of time you're going to spend moving and repositioning, using uncharged shots will allow you to hit the boss far more frequently and deal more damage than if you were waiting for the perfect time to unleash charged shots.

Play aggressively, but somewhat safely while you're trying to deplete its pulse armor. The instant it breaks and the boss is staggered, you should go on full offensive. With good positioning and timing of your attacks, it's possible to stagger BALTEUS several times before its armor regenerates, which will significantly reduce the number of missiles you'll need to evade in this phase.

2 Shortly after you've depleted around 50% of its AP, you'll hear Ayre over the comms telling you to get clear, signifying the start of this phase. Heed her advice and make sure you're well clear of BALTEUS so you don't get caught in the explosion—if it hits you, it'll instantly overload your ACS. The flame attacks that BALTEUS has access to in this phase can build up an ACS anomaly gauge if they hit you; if this gauge fills up, it'll inflict a status effect that makes it significantly easier for BALTEUS to stagger you. You'll also have to start dealing with flame-based melee attacks that have deceptively long range. While these may seem daunting at first, they shouldn't deter you from trying to stay close to the boss. Sticking near it will ensure it uses more of its close-range attacks, meaning you'll have less to think about and can concentrate on using Quick Boosts to get past most of them and returning fire afterward. Continue to emphasize offense in this phase and BALTEUS will have little time to use its longer-lasting combos.

3 This phase begins when you hear Ayre over the comms once again, this time letting you know that the enemy can't take much more, which happens when BALTEUS has roughly a third of its AP left. The only new attack it gains in this phase is its variable extreme-heat burner, but if you've recently depleted its pulse armor and are keeping up the aggressive missile barrages and plasma rifle shots, it's possible to finish it off entirely before you have to contend with that attack. Defeat BALTEUS and you'll complete the mission and progress to Chapter 2.

BALTEUS always starts the encounter with its tri-directional missile salvo; it will be stationary during this attack, so Assault Boost toward it while evading, and try to deal as much damage as possible to its pulse armor.

If you've installed the assault armor Core Expansion, you can trigger it when you see BALTEUS use one of its melee attacks to simultaneously negate the damage and retaliate with a powerful attack.

TRI-DIRECTIONAL MISSILE SALVO

DESCRIPTION Fires a salvo of missiles from its multi missile launcher in two waves. The missiles themselves are not very quick, and the focus of the attack itself is volume.

EVASION Assault Boost toward BALTEUS along a slightly upward diagonal trajectory to avoid most of the missiles.

SIDE-FACING MISSILE SALVO

DESCRIPTION Faces one side of its multi missile launcher toward you and unleashes a small salvo of missiles horizontally.

EVASION Quick Boost away from the direction of the missiles.

FANNING MISSILE SALVO

DESCRIPTION After boosting away from you, it can fire eight higher-impact and faster-moving missiles from its multi missile launcher that have no homing capabilities

EVASION Jump and ascend above the salvo.

VERTICAL MISSILE SALVO

DESCRIPTION Locks its multi missile launcher vertically and fires an overhead salvo with a delayed release.

EVASION Quick Boost to either side of the salvo just before the missiles are about to hit.

HORIZONTAL MISSILE SALVO

DESCRIPTION Locks its ring horizontally and fires two salvos of missiles in a pincer pattern with a staggered release.

EVASION Jump and Quick Boost directly toward BALTEUS to avoid a large amount of these missiles.

SPREAD MISSILE SALVO

DESCRIPTION Fires its 156-shot missile launcher creating a spherical pattern. This particular attack is also signaled by a unique audio cue.

EVASION Create as much distance as possible to allow the missiles to begin converging and then Assault Boost diagonally toward BALTEUS once they begin impacting at your position.

GRENADE CANNON ▼

DESCRIPTION Fires a high-velocity direct explosive shot.

EVASION Quick Boost to either side of the shot immediately as it fires.

3-SHOT GATLING GUN

DESCRIPTION Drifts around your AC while firing a gatling gun. It may follow this with a shotgun blast.

EVASION Quick Boost in the opposite direction that BALTEUS is drifting in.

4-SHOT SHOTGUN

DESCRIPTION Fires its shotgun three times; the first two back-to-back, then a brief pause before the third.

EVASION Quick Boost twice to avoid the shots then pause briefly before using another Quick Boost.

PULSE ARMOR   PHASE 2

DESCRIPTION This attack is unique to the beginning of Phase 2 and involves BALTEUS briefly charging up and unleashing a massive explosion.

EVASION Immediately create as much distance as possible between you and BALTEUS.

HIGH VERTICAL MISSILE SALVO   PHASES 2/3

DESCRIPTION Similar to the normal vertical missile salvo, but travels much higher before breaking toward you.

EVASION Use lateral Quick Boosts as soon as the missiles begin impacting your position.

SINGLE SLASH   PHASES 2/3

DESCRIPTION Quickly drifts toward you and slashes at a slight downward angle. Can use the variable extreme-heat burner on either its left or right arm.

EVASION Quick Boost past BALTEUS toward the side it's not striking from.

DOUBLE SLASH   PHASES 2/3

DESCRIPTION Continuation from the single slash using the variable extreme-heat burner on the opposite arm.

EVASION Quick Boost past BALTEUS toward the side it's not striking from.

CROSS SLASH   PHASES 2/3

DESCRIPTION Brings both variable extreme-heat burner blades together horizontally, where they'll remain active and drawn for a brief period of time.

EVASION Jump into the air above BALTEUS, making sure to stay clear of the blades.

UPPERCUT SLASH   PHASES 2/3

DESCRIPTION Uppercut swipe with either arm against your AC as a standalone hit when you're in melee range.

EVASION Quick Boost past BALTEUS toward the side it's not striking from.

SPINNING SLASH   PHASES 2/3

DESCRIPTION Utilizes both variable extreme-heat burner blades to perform a spinning slash toward your AC, covering a tremendous amount of ground.

EVASION Quick Boost away from BALTEUS as quickly as possible until the attack ceases.

AREA BLAST   PHASES 2/3

DESCRIPTION Creates an explosion that scorches a large portion of the ground in front of it.

EVASION Quickly jump and hover over the explosion and lingering flames.

FOUR-ATTACK COMBO   PHASES 2/3

DESCRIPTION Slashes with one of its blades, then fires a high vertical missile salvo, followed by a side-facing missile salvo, and finally rushes toward you with another slash using the opposite arm.

EVASION The blade slashes are the most crucial attacks to evade, so jump in the air and boost away to create as much distance as possible.

EIGHT-ATTACK COMBO   PHASES 2/3

DESCRIPTION Begins with firing its gatling gun, then a single slash from the variable extreme-heat burner, a spread missile salvo, a double shotgun blast, followed by both a high vertical and regular vertical missile salvos before finishing off with a single slash and spinning slash.

EVASION Prioritize creating distance on the ground to ensure you don't run out of EN prematurely. Continuously move away from BALTEUS, putting the highest priority on evading the slashes.

VARIABLE EXTREME-HEAT BURNER ▼   PHASE 3

DESCRIPTION Shoots flames with both arms while sweeping toward you. If you're in the air, it can aim upward, and if you're on the ground, the attack will leave residual flames.

EVASION Jump into the air and hover while moving away from the flames.

Comms Record: Doser Ravings

MISSION OBJECTIVES

Reach Center of Grid 086's Lower Level

Annihilate the MT Squad

Destroy the Autonomous Heavy SMART CLEANER

HC-3000 WRECKER (Head)

CC-3000 WRECKER (Core)

Video Record: The Collector's Last Words

AC-3000 WRECKER (Arms)

MISSION INFO

Combat Zone	Western Belius - Grid 086
Client	Ayre
Reward	160,000
Max Bonus Pay	617,200
Completion Unlocks	—
Combat Logs	Bronze x5, Silver x3, Gold x1
Data Logs	2
Part Containers	4

ENEMY DATA

	No.	AP	AS	Bonus Pay	Analysis
MT-T-026 Guard Mech (Rifle)	31	102	121	800	P.310
MT-E-104 Bipedal MT (Missile Launcher)	4	470	364	2400	P.316
MT-E-104 Bipedal MT (Dual Machine Gun)	10	470	364	2400	P.316
MT-E-104 Bipedal MT (Grenade Cannon)	3	470	364	2400	P.316
MB-0100 CLUTCH Crawler MT (Electro Saw)	32	650	364	5600	P.319
MB-0100 CLUTCH Crawler MT (Heavy Rocket Launcher)	9	650	364	5600	P.318
MB-0100 CLUTCH Crawler MT (Stun Plug)	4	650	364	5600	P.319
Artillery (Vertical Missile Array)	2	202	105	4000	P.328
MT-J-048 Tetrapod MT (Laser Blade)	2	13370	2200	24000	P.322
MB-0202 TOYBOX MT	7	1848	1053	12800	P.325
MT-J-048 Tetrapod MT (3-Shot Bazooka)	1	13370	2200	24000	P.323
AC MAD STOMP / "Invincible" Rummy	1	10670	1669	30000	—
AC BITTER PROMISE / Nosaac	1	10290	1576	40000	—
EC-0804 SMART CLEANER	1	48705	2600	60000	—

"I don't owe you a damn thing. You've made a big mistake coming here!"

—Nosaac

Grid 086 is a large, sprawling factory superstructure under the control of the RaD group and occupied by a band of outlaws known as "Dosers." Primarily designed for the production of MTs, the cargo launcher within it used to distribute those MTs happens to be just what you need to cross the ice field. The locals, however, will do everything in their power to stop you from reaching it. The openness and intricate nature of the facility means there are multiple routes that you can take through it, and within its walls are many secrets to uncover if you're willing to explore it thoroughly. The route provided here will take you through many of those optional areas, and approach them from advantageous positions to make the encounters you find there as easy as possible.

Nearly all of the enemies you face in this mission grant you bonus pay, so even outside of the data logs and part containers, going out of your way to destroy them all is highly recommended. This does mean, however, that ammunition counts will be a major concern throughout the mission, and you'll need to make sure every shot counts to avoid running out. Before all of that COAM can be secured, though, you'll also need to contend with the SMART CLEANER boss, a monstrous machine covered in thick armor with very few weakpoints; like previous similarly dangerous boss encounters, make sure your build is geared toward it above all else in this mission.

ASSEMBLY

Since this is a long mission, you'll need tools for taking out both weaker enemies and tough opponents, such as ACs. Dual HML-G2/P19MLT-04 missile launchers in your arm slots give you more than enough ammo for dealing with most enemies without sacrificing homing capabilities by going with weapons like assault rifles or machine guns. The SMART CLEANER's weakpoints are also very susceptible to energy damage, and since you'll need some precision to accurately hit those spots, weapons like the VP-60LCS laser cannon will be ideal. No weakpoint is more apparent than the opening in the furnace exhaust on the back of the SMART CLEANER, and to reliably target that you're going to want to spend as much time as possible airborne—the VP-424 tetrapod legs make that relatively easy to accomplish.

The rest of your frame should be comprised of parts with good anti-explosive and anti-kinetic defenses, both of which the MELANDER parts provide, and the DF-HD-08 TIAN-QIANG head offers excellent anti-explosive defense while also keeping your weight down. Your booster and generator should be geared toward getting you into the air and letting you stay there for as long as possible; the BST-G2/P04 and VP-20D fit that mandate nicely, and the FCS-G2/P10SLT pairs well with the dual hand missile launchers, since it greatly reduces the time required for them to lock onto enemies.

01	R-ARM UNIT | MISSILE LAUNCHER HML-G2/P19MLT-04	P.61
02	L-ARM UNIT | MISSILE LAUNCHER HML-G2/P19MLT-04	P.61
03	R-BACK UNIT | LASER CANNON VP-60LCS	P.67
04	L-BACK UNIT | LASER CANNON VP-60LCS	P.67
05	HEAD | — DF-HD-08 TIAN-QIANG	P.77
06	CORE | — BD-011 MELANDER	P.80
07	ARMS | — AR-011 MELANDER	P.82
08	LEGS | TETRAPOD VP-424	P.86
09	BOOSTER | — BST-G2/P04	P.88
10	FCS | — FCS-G2/P10SLT	P.90
11	GENERATOR | — VP-20D	P.92

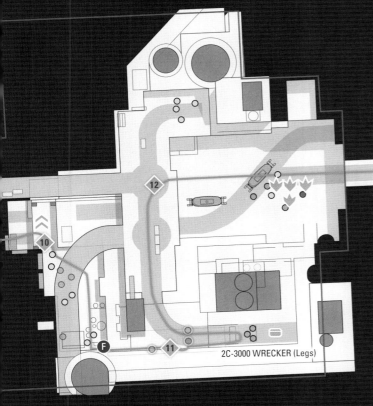

2C-3000 WRECKER (Legs)

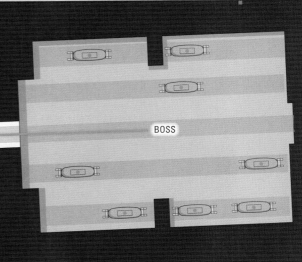

BOSS

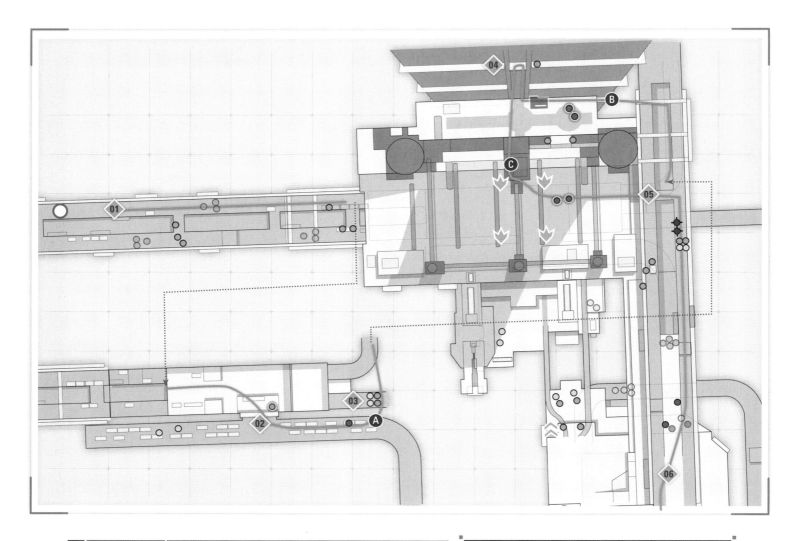

Reach Center of Grid 086's Lower Level

01 ◇ You'll begin on the upper deck of a long bridge within the Grid, directly facing your first objective, and will have to contend with small groups of crawler MTs as you proceed. There are multiple groups on the same level of the bridge as you, but most of them are hanging from the underside of the bridge and will remain in their dormant state unless you drop down. Whether you just want to press on toward the objective, or drop down and destroy the crawler MTs on the lower level of the bridge, it's worth taking out the ones on top first so that you don't end up in a battle against two groups at once. It takes a full volley from one of the HML-G2/P19MLT-04 missile launchers to destroy one of these enemies, so rather than using multi-lock to target groups of them, fire each volley individually at a single enemy. A combat zone border will appear behind you as soon as you jump up to the large hangar at the end of the bridge, and you'll be locked into a mandatory encounter with MAD STOMP. ▶ A

DORMANT CRAWLERS

You'll encounter large numbers of RaD crawler MTs throughout this mission, many of which will be clinging to walls or ceilings in a dormant state, scanning for intruders. While in this state, crawler MTs can't be locked on to and will drop down to ambush you if you move close enough. However, your scanner is powerful enough to pinpoint their location and render them targetable by your FCS, so it's a good idea to thoroughly scan your surroundings as you proceed through this mission.

To conserve ammo, Boost Kick is also quite effective for dealing with crawler MTs if you have it equipped.

AC // MAD STOMP

Piloted by "Invincible" Rummy, MAD STOMP is equipped with a shotgun and a chainsaw, and due to the nature of his arsenal, Rummy will constantly attempt to stick close to you and land a blow with his deadly chainsaw. You can use this to your advantage in the fight if you're equipped with the recommended tetrapod legs. With these, you can easily position yourself as high as possible in the hangar and constantly move around to stay as far away as possible. This will cause Rummy to waste a lot of EN trying to reach you, making it difficult for him to evade your attacks. Lead with your missile launchers, and stick to uncharged shots with the laser cannons while he's falling back down after spending all of his EN, and you should be able to destroy him without expending too many resources.

BASIC SPECS

AP	11670
Attitude Stability	1839
Anti-Kinetic Defense	1197
Anti-Energy Defense	1060
Anti-Explosive Defense	1282
Elec. Discharge Tolerance	490
Shock Resistance	-27%
ACS Anomaly Tolerance	490
Heat Resistance	-27%

02 ◈ Upon defeating Rummy, a door up high at the rear of the hangar will open, allowing access deeper into the facility. Turn left as soon as you reach this point, and proceed through the tunnel carefully, because near the end of the cargo trolleys is the first of many TOYBOX MTs in the area. These enemies are initially curled up in a heavily armored ball form, and will break out of it once activated, allowing you to deal damage to them. If you're quick, you can get behind the TOYBOX before it activates, and easily land a couple of charged shots with your laser cannons to finish it off while it's in the process of transitioning into its active combat mode. Head to **Position A** after dispatching the TOYBOX MT, then look down over the edge of the tracks to locate the enemy group on another set of tracks below you; use your missile launchers to safely target and destroy them from this vantage point before dropping down. ▶ B

03 ◈ These lower tracks offer a particularly worthwhile detour: they lead to some well-hidden enemies for more bonus pay, and you'll also emerge above the area with the two tetrapod MTs, making them much easier to deal with. Jump over to the adjacent set of tracks and follow them until you're parallel with the wall near the combat zone border, then jump across to **Position B** on the narrow walkway running along that wall. Proceed along the ledge (making sure to access the data log along the way), and board the elevator once it reaches the bottom. Start charging both of your laser cannons once the lift begins to rise again, because it will shortly reach a platform where two more TOYBOX MTs are waiting to attack you. If you have both cannons primed, you can use a salvo from one of your missile launchers and a shot from a charged cannon to dispatch each of them quickly for their combat logs. ▶ C

04 ◈ Jump back over to the elevator once the area is clear and use it to reach the upper walkway, where you'll then have to destroy a few more crawler MTs. After destroying them, jump over to the roof of a small tower at **Position C**, from which you'll be able to observe the two tetrapod MTs patrolling the floor below you. Their patrol route takes them past a number of large explosive tanks, and if you time it right, you can use a shot from one of your laser cannons to detonate the tanks and inflict huge amounts of damage to those enemies (potentially even destroying them) without them becoming aware of your presence. You can repeat the process at each of the tank locations to further cripple them, after which you can drop down and finish them off quickly with some charged laser cannon shots, rewarding you with another pair of combat logs and a large amount of bonus pay. ▶ D

05 ◈ To the side of the area where you faced the tetrapod MTs is another large bridge that connects to the area you need to head to for the objective, so jump up there and be ready to face the enemies defending it. The immediate threats are some bipedal and crawler MTs, so use your missiles to destroy them, then take out the turrets so that you can move around freely. Another group of crawler MTs will start making their way down the tracks to attack you while you're dealing with the initial threats, so keep an eye out for them and engage them once they're within range.

TOYBOX MTs are highly aggressive and attack frequently once they're fully active, so destroying them the instant they emerge is the best way to deal with them.

You'll need to jump onto the elevator to avoid falling through the gap between it and the walkway.

You can easily target the tanks if you have Manual Aiming installed in OS Tuning, otherwise you might need to boost high enough to aim at them without locking onto either of the enemies.

06 ◇ Push along the bridge toward the seemingly unguarded refinery door that you'll need to open. Stay alert, because as soon as you start accessing the door, two TOYBOX MTs will drop down behind you. One drops down slightly before the other, so you should try to destroy it as quickly as possible to avoid having to contend with both at the same time. Like the previous two, one charged laser cannon shot and salvo from a missile launcher is enough to get the job done. After destroying them both, resume accessing the door and push on into the refinery.

07 ◇ The interior of the refinery is a maze of platforms and tight corridors, so it's highly recommended that you make liberal use of your scanner to locate the part containers hidden in this area and avoid being ambushed by the crawler MTs that are hidden away in corners. The tight spaces mean you won't have a lot of room to maneuver, and you should be mindful of your positioning to avoid having your missiles impact surfaces before they can strike enemies. Jump up to the sub-floor and proceed along it toward a hole at the end, taking out the crawler MT along the way; when you reach the hole, use your missiles to destroy another crawler MT below you and drop down. Proceed through the tunnel leading out of this room, but charge one of your laser cannons, because when you near the end of it, another TOYBOX MT will drop down. Once it's safe to do so, jump up to the floor above using the opening the enemy dropped through. ▶A

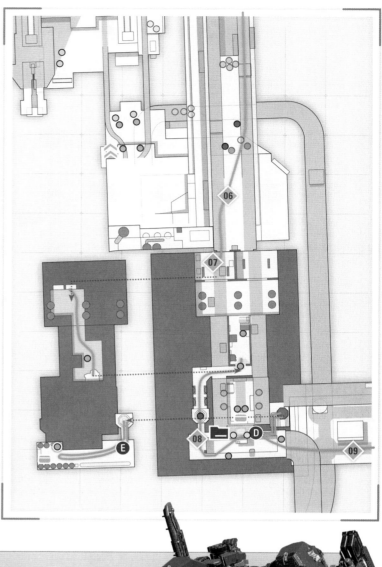

After dropping down, turn around and head to the back of the room to find the first hidden part container.

NOSSAC

AC // BITTER PROMISE

After entering the empty pipe in the smelting area and dropping into the optional room at Position E, you'll immediately notice a part container out in the open. Resist the urge to head straight for it, however, because Nosaac is waiting in ambush directly to the right in his AC, BITTER PROMISE. The room you'll fight him in is fairly large, but it has a low ceiling, so this is one fight where the tetrapod legs' aerial advantage is somewhat nullified. Advance slowly using your scanner until you locate him, and then start charging your laser cannons; try to land both shots the instant he comes into view to hit him before he starts moving.

Nosaac's AC is equipped with a pulse shield, so you'll need to watch out for when he deploys it and make sure you only fire your laser cannons when it's not active. He also has a spread bazooka, so try to keep your distance from him to avoid taking the full brunt of that attack. Fortunately, it's relatively easy to overload his ACS and stagger him if you time your attacks well. If you need to create some breathing room, you can retreat back out the way you came with no risk of him following you. Once Nosaac has been neutralized, make sure to open the part container, then head back and access the door leading into the next section of the refinery.

BASIC SPECS

AP	10290
Attitude Stability	1576
Anti-Kinetic Defense	1199
Anti-Energy Defense	1200
Anti-Explosive Defense	1127
Elec. Discharge Tolerance	490
Shock Resistance	10%
ACS Anomaly Tolerance	490
Heat Resistance	10%

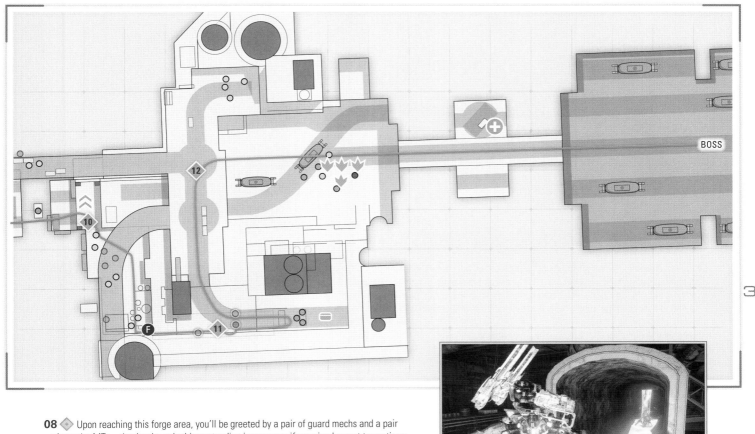

08 ◆ Upon reaching this forge area, you'll be greeted by a pair of guard mechs and a pair of crawler MTs—they're the only things standing in your way if you simply want to continue through the area by accessing the door on the opposite side. Before doing so, however, it's worth taking some time to explore this room, because it holds a number of optional secrets to uncover. To begin with, pass through the area with the molten metal to reach the opposite side of the room, where you'll need to defeat a large number of crawler MTs so that you can open the part container sitting on the floor.

The molten metal will damage you if you move through it, so make sure to jump or hover over it to avoid taking unnecessary damage. With the contents of the part container now yours, head back toward the smelting area, but this time, enter the pipe at **Position D** and follow it to reach a hidden room at **Position E**, containing another part container, and a battle against AC BITTER PROMISE. ▶ B

09 ◆ Jump across the chasm and make your way up the ledges until you reach the area with the vertical catapult. From there, you can use this catapult to continue directly toward the objective. Alternatively, you can take another detour for more bonus pay and items, which is where the recommended route will be heading.

10 ◆ You'll see a few guard mechs patrolling this area when you first head in this direction, but as soon as you close in to engage them, a large number of crawler MTs will drop down to attack you. To avoid getting overwhelmed, try to pick them off as they appear. After clearing them out, approach the corner at **Position F** and peer around it to see another crawler MT and a TOYBOX MT in its armored ball form. What you won't see are two more crawler MTs waiting to ambush you if you close in to attack the other enemies. ▶ C

Instead, charge one of your laser cannons, and then round the corner and use one missile salvo to destroy the crawler, and another in conjunction with your laser cannon to destroy the TOYBOX MT once it breaks out of its armored ball form. If done quickly enough, you can destroy both of these enemies before the other crawlers appear, which makes dealing with them much easier, and nets you another three combat logs.

11 ◆ There's a final part container on the floor directly above this location, so after destroying the previous enemy group, go to the outside edge of this floor and ascend to the floor above you. There are three crawler MTs near the part container: one active and two hanging from a beam. If you use your missiles to destroy the active one without getting too close, you can scan to make the other two targetable, then destroy them with more missiles before they become a threat. After claiming the contents of the final part container, follow the tracks around to the objective location. ▶ D

The pipe directly opposite **Position D** has a data log hidden within it; just remember to hover above the molten metal while scanning it or you'll take a lot of damage in the process.

You can use the various protruding wall sections and the lower ledges around the area for cover to avoid taking too much damage in this encounter.

By following the different tracks near the objective marker during Step Point 11, you can find a few additional groups of enemies to destroy for bonus pay along with a part container.

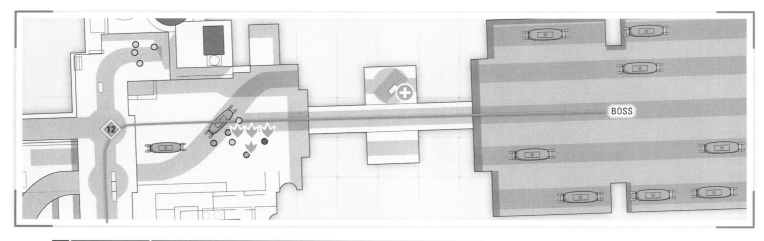

BOSS

OBJECTIVE	Annihilate the MT Squad

12 ◆ Upon reaching the objective marker, you'll be tasked with destroying a formidable MT squad in the large room nearby. Thankfully, there are a few elements here that you can take advantage of to even the odds. Carla has secured large explosive canisters to the beams above the room, which she intends to drop onto you the moment you head down and engage the enemies. It's possible to turn the tables on her little surprise, however, by shooting either the canisters themselves or the couplings that they're attached to. There are four in total to exploit in this manner, and doing so will destroy every enemy except the tetrapod MT, making things significantly easier for you. ▶ A

If you're using the tetrapod legs, you can now hover above the room while constantly moving to the side to evade all of the tetrapod MT's attacks. Since there's a supply sherpa coming up, unload everything you have to finish it off. Carla will automatically open the large hangar doors at the back of the room when the last enemy has been destroyed. Head through them, resupply at the sherpa, and then continue along the tracks to face the autonomous heavy SMART CLEANER.

If you opt to fight the tetrapod MT guarding the gate head on, be mindful of the shield it can use both for defense and as part of a highly damaging attack.

EC-0804

SMART CLEANER

OBJECTIVE
Destroy the Autonomous Heavy SMART CLEANER

BASIC SPECS

AP	48705
Attitude Stability	2600
Anti-Kinetic Defense	930
Anti-Energy Defense	361
Anti-Explosive Defense	1000
Elec. Discharge Tolerance	999
Shock Resistance	0%
ACS Anomaly Tolerance	999
Heat Resistance	0%

SMART CLEANER is a gigantic industrial machine with huge arms that can cover a vast amount of area in a single attack. Its arms are lined with grinders that can rev up to deal continuous damage for as long as they're in contact with you, even if the arms aren't moving. Much like to JUGGERNAUT, SMART CLEANER also begins the encounter with a charging attack, during which it will slam both of its grinder arms together, so be ready to evade the instant the fight begins.

Attacking this boss anywhere other than the furnace exhaust on its back or furnace intake at the front will deal damage and ACS strain, but at such a reduced rate that it's a waste of ammunition. Many of SMART CLEANER's most dangerous attacks also originate from the front of the boss, so try to stay above it as much as possible while hovering using the tetrapod legs fire directly down into the exhaust. If you have to land to recover EN, make sure you're either behind it, or at its side.

STAGGERING SMART CLEANER

SMART CLEANER only has two areas that aren't covered in heavy armor: the small furnace intake between its grinder arms and the protruding furnace exhaust on the top of its frame. Both the damage and ACS strain you inflict are the same whether you hit one or the other, but the most convenient point of attack will be the exhaust, since it's easier to hit and is more safely targeted from the air while avoiding SMART CLEANER's attacks. Once staggered, it will drop its head to the ground for an extended period, during which it's safe to land and attack the frontal weakpoint. Molten metal will be expelled from the furnace intake when you stagger the boss, but it won't damage you; just be sure to move out of harm's way the instant SMART CLEARNER recovers.

PHASES

1 After the boss opens with its cross swing, it will base its offense around your proximity and altitude, allowing you to somewhat dictate which attacks you'll have to deal with by positioning yourself accordingly. The most effective position to fight this boss from is high above the furnace exhaust, so that you can fire directly down into it. This is also a strong defensive position, since you'll effectively dodge all of its melee options, whether they're charges or swings with its grinder arms.

In this phase, you should place a high priority on becoming accustomed to how long your EN lasts while you're airborne above the exhaust, always ensuring that you have enough for an emergency Quick Boost should the need arise. It's important to be mindful of the timing of your attacks, because any missiles fired while moving are likely to miss their target, given that it's a fairly small weakpoint.

Similarly, stick to uncharged shots with your laser cannons; the resulting loss of ammo if you do miss is not as severe as if you were using charged shots, and the cooldown time from the charged shots can cost you precious damage-dealing seconds when SMART CLEANER is staggered. ▶ B

2 This phase begins when you hear Ayre over your comms telling you to watch out, because the SMART CLEANER's behavior has changed—take this as a warning that you'll need to watch out for its quick magma and debris toss attack. While the boss becomes a bit faster and more aggressive in this phase, and gains access to that attack, its general patterns do not change, and thus your overall strategy should also remain the same. If you've reached this point relatively unscathed, it can be worth staying a bit closer to the exhaust, even when it expels debris, so that you can bring the fight to an end sooner. Destroy the SMART CLEANER and the mission will be complete. ▶ C

When you see SMART CLEANER start to recover from a stagger, quickly Assault Boost in, use a Boost Kick, then follow up with assault armor for a big chunk of damage.

If you notice SMART CLEANER starting to use its quick magma and debris toss attack at the start of phase two, keep in mind that you can hover between its grinder arms as it comes toward you for a few easy shots into its exhaust.

AUTONOMOUS HEAVY SMART CLEANER ATTACKS

CROSS SWING

DESCRIPTION Grinder arms extend outward and the boss will charge at you, bringing both arms together. Always used as an opening attack.

EVASION Jump and ascend high enough above the boss that the charge and both arm swings miss you.

ARM CHARGE

DESCRIPTION One grinder arm is placed on the ground and the boss charges at you.

EVASION Quick Boost toward the side of the unused arm or boost above the boss.

ARM SWEEP

DESCRIPTION One grinder arm is placed on the ground and then swept across a frontal arc, ending in a release of missiles. Can chain two hits.

EVASION Quick Boost toward the side of the unused arm or boost vertically above the boss.

BODY CHARGE

DESCRIPTION The boss will boost into you with its body or crush you with its underside grinder if you're close to it.

EVASION Quick Boost to either side.

SWEEPING MAGMA TOSS

DESCRIPTION Releases a stream of molten metal in a semi-circle around the front of its body.

EVASION Quick Boost directly away from the boss to get out of range.

EVASIVE MAGMA TOSS

DESCRIPTION Releases molten metal while boosting backward if you're close to it.

EVASION Quick Boost to either side of the molten metal without following the boss when it moves.

DEBRIS TOSS ▼

DESCRIPTION Molten debris is expelled from the boss's furnace exhaust if you hover over it; the trajectory of the debris is random.

EVASION Aerial Quick Boost directly away from the furnace exhaust.

2-SHOT GRENADE CANNON

DESCRIPTION Fires a small salvo of rapid, head-on grenades with no homing capacity

EVASION Quick Boost to either side away from where the boss is facing, or boost vertically above the boss.

QUICK MAGMA AND DEBRIS TOSS ▼ | PHASE 2

DESCRIPTION Both grinder arms are held out in front of the boss, throwing molten metal, followed by a single expulsion of debris. Always begins Phase 2 with this attack.

EVASION Continue to move to either side of the boss or be prepared to aerially Quick Boost to evade the debris if you're above the furnace exhaust.

EXTENDED MAGMA AND DEBRIS TOSS ▼ | PHASE 2

DESCRIPTION Both grinder arms will raise and throw molten metal across a semi-circle in front of the boss, while debris is expelled from the chimney.

EVASION Move away from the front of the boss, or be prepared to aerially Quick Boost to evade the debris if you're above the furnace exhaust.

ELIMINATE THE DOSER FACTION

"They might be a pack of dumb animals, but at least they know quality workmanship..."

—"Cinder" Carla

Your sole objective in this mission is to help "Cinder" Carla by destroying several squads of MTs and agile custom guard mechs that are under the control of the Junker Coyotes, a rival band of Dosers that have moved into Grid 086 thanks to your previous efforts there. The enemy units are equipped with multiple weapon types, the most dangerous of which are their high-volume or high-impact missiles. Due to the nature of the locations you'll encounter them in, you'll need to contend with these enemies at various ranges, so this mission will be a test of your ability to quickly and evasively move between targets to stop them from grouping up on you.

MISSION OBJECTIVE

Eliminate the Coyotes MT Squad

MISSION INFO

Combat Zone	Western Belius - Grid 086
Client	RaD
Reward	65,000
Max Bonus Pay	63,000
Completion Unlocks	—
Combat Logs	—
Data Logs	—
Part Containers	—

ENEMY DATA

	No.	AP	AS	Bonus Pay	Analysis
MT-T-026-RC2 KICKER Guard Mech	4	504	418	3400	P.311
MT-T-026-RC1 PUNCHER Guard Mech	3	459	351	3400	P.311
MB-0100 CLUTCH Crawler MT (Enclosure Shield)	1	650	364	5600	P.319
MB-0100 CLUTCH Crawler MT (Heavy Rocket Launcher)	6	650	364	5600	P.318

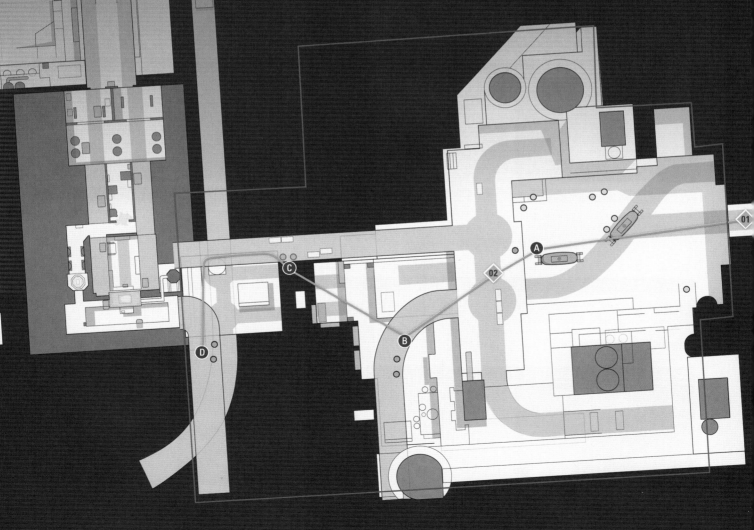

ASSEMBLY

Your defensive specs should be geared toward anti-explosive here; your best defenses in this mission, however, should be speed and evasion, because avoiding getting hit by missiles is paramount. While your head, core, and arms can focus on actual defensive specs, your legs should favor movement speed, making the NACHTREIHER/42E legs an ideal choice. Because you're dealing with large numbers of smaller enemies, a Double Trigger setup with a pair of MG-014 LUDLOW machine guns is perfect for hitting targets on the move. You'll also face groups of enemies, and the large area of effect and lingering damage fields of the Vvc-703PM plasma missiles will let you clear them out quickly and efficiently.

01	R-ARM UNIT | MACHINE GUN MG-014 LUDLOW	P.53
02	L-ARM UNIT | MACHINE GUN MG-014 LUDLOW	P.53
03	R-BACK UNIT | PLASMA MISSILE LCHR. Vvc-703PM	P.73
04	L-BACK UNIT | PLASMA MISSILE LCHR. Vvc-703PM	P.73
05	HEAD | — DF-HD-08 TIAN-QIANG	P.77
06	CORE | — BD-011 MELANDER	P.80
07	ARMS | — AR-011 MELANDER	P.82
08	LEGS | BIPEDAL NACHTREIHER/42E	P.85
09	BOOSTER | — ALULA/21E	P.88
10	FCS | — FCS-G2/P10SLT	P.90
11	GENERATOR | — VP-20S	P.92

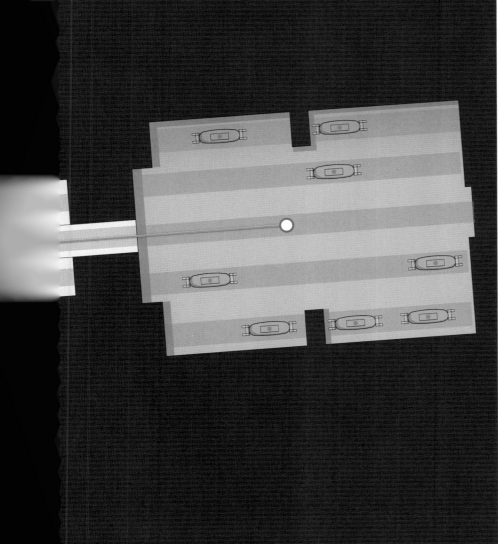

01 ◈ The first group of enemies you need to clear out occupy the large area originally guarded by the shielded tetrapod MT during the previous mission. Sadly, there are no explosives to aid you this time, and there's a combat zone border locking you in with the Junker Coyote assailants who soon make their entrance by jumping down into the arena. The custom PUNCHER and KICKER guard mechs that are prevalent in this mission are enemies you haven't encountered before, but you should resist the urge to focus on them, because by far the biggest threat in this room is the shielded crawler MT at the back near **Position A**. Its powerful missiles, coupled with the shield it can deploy, make it troublesome to deal with while contending with the other enemies, so the best option is to try to destroy it first.

The other enemies start on the outskirts of the room, so if you're quick, you can make it to the back before most of them jump into the area, at which point you can quickly destroy the crawler MT with a volley from both missile launchers and a few machine gun shots. For the remaining enemies, take advantage of their lack of strong homing attacks and the wide-open nature of the room by continuously boosting around the outskirts of it, while using multi-lock with your plasma missile launchers to destroy enemies that are grouped up. While they're reloading, pick off any stragglers with your machine guns. As long as you keep moving around the room, you should be able to defeat them relatively unscathed. ▶ A

A

02 ◈ The combat zone border surrounding the room will drop when the entire first group of enemies has been destroyed, but as soon as you jump and boost out, six crawler MTs will start firing missiles at you from various locations on the surrounding train tracks. Much like before, movement will be your best defensive option here; never stop boosting as you move around the area. The pair at **Position B** is closest, so Assault Boost toward them and jump so that you have a clear line of sight and can destroy them quickly.

When you land, Assault Boost directly to the pair on the lower section of the tracks at **Position C** and destroy them once they're within range. The support columns here provide plenty of cover to protect yourself from incoming missiles, so travel along this lower section until you're parallel to the final pair of enemies at **Position D**, then jump up and destroy them to complete the mission.

"You know the cargo launcher's strictly for cargo, right?"

—"Cinder" Carla

The PCA has trained its array of orbital laser satellites on the top of Grid 086, and they'll destroy anything caught trespassing. Attempting to pass through any area under the watchful eyes of the satellites is likely to lead to a hasty demise, so you'll need to employ a stealthy approach to this mission and make use of any and all available cover to reach the cargo launcher in one piece.

The only regular enemies you'll encounter throughout the mission are squid-like PCA WATCHER drones that deploy floating mines and also have the ability to charge directly at you and explode; use frequent scans to locate and keep track of them to ensure none of them get close enough to detonate. The final hurdle you need to clear before you can use the cargo launcher is the towering IA-13: SEA SPIDER boss. This relic from Rubicon's past utilizes Coral-based weaponry, against which there is no defensive spec to protect you.

MISSION OBJECTIVES

Reach the Center of Grid 086's Upper Level

Destroy the Drones in the Vicinity

Destroy the C-Weapon SEA SPIDER

Board the Container on the Cargo Launcher

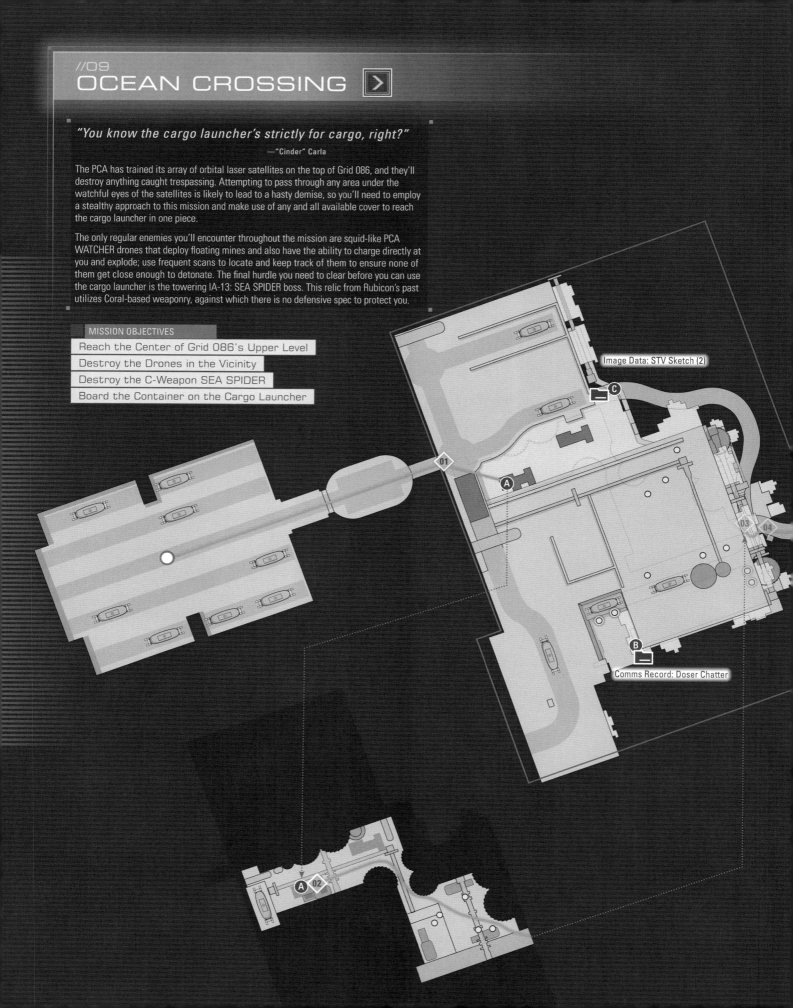

Image Data: STV Sketch (2)

Comms Record: Doser Chatter

MISSION INFO

Combat Zone	Western Belius - Upper Grid 086, Outer Shell
Client	Ayre
Reward	330,000
Max Bonus Pay	—
Completion Unlocks	D-Rank Arena targets, Parts Shop Update 5, Access Granted: Nest
Combat Logs	Bronze x4
Data Logs	2
Part Containers	0

ENEMY DATA

	No.	AP	AS	Bonus Pay	Analysis
● AM06: WATCHER	31	101	175	—	P.338
● IA-13: SEA SPIDER	1	76400	3550		

BOSS

06

D

05

ASSEMBLY

You'll need to plan your build around dealing with the PCA satellites as well as the IA-13: SEA SPIDER boss. The various platforms and parts of the sub-structure throughout Grid 086 provide plenty of overhead cover that you can use to safely pass through areas guarded by the satellites; to make that as easy as possible, the extended hovering capabilities of tetrapod legs are highly recommended. This leg type also works well against the IA-13: SEA SPIDER, since it employs a lot of melee strikes that you can evade by hovering high above it. This means the booster and generator you pick should be geared toward extending your hover time. While the VP-20D does have a higher capacity, the DF-GN MING-TANG gives you much faster EN recovery rates and only slightly less capacity, so it's a safer option for when you need to land.

Your weaponry should reflect the encounters against groups of drones as well as the boss fight, and a full contingent of missiles can serve you well in both capacities. Salvos of multi-lock missiles will make short work of the drones, and their effectiveness at long range works well with the strategy of staying high above the IA-13: SEA SPIDER. If you're going to use all missile launchers, an FCS that gives you the lowest possible lock-on times is a good pairing, and that points to the FCS-G2/P10SLT as the ideal candidate.

01	R-ARM UNIT | MISSILE LAUNCHER	HML-G2/P19MLT-04	P.61
02	L-ARM UNIT | MISSILE LAUNCHER	HML-G2/P19MLT-04	P.61
03	R-BACK UNIT | MISSILE LAUNCHER	BML-G2/P05MLT-10	P.69
04	L-BACK UNIT | MISSILE LAUNCHER	BML-G2/P05MLT-10	P.69
05	HEAD | —	DF-HD-08 TIAN-QIANG	P.77
06	CORE | —	BD-011 MELANDER	P.80
07	ARMS | —	04-101 MIND ALPHA	P.84
08	LEGS | TETRAPOD	VP-424	P.86
09	BOOSTER | —	BST-G2/P04	P.88
10	FCS | —	FCS-G2/P10SLT	P.90
11	GENERATOR | —	DF-GN-06 MING-TANG	P.91

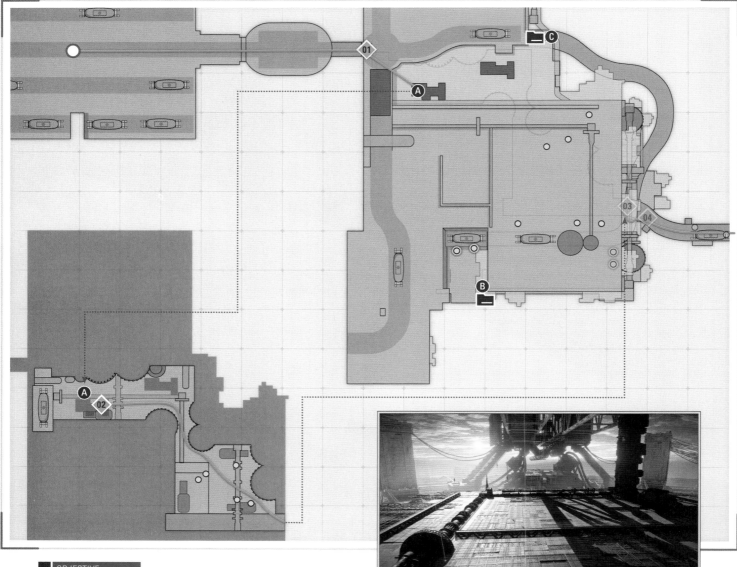

OBJECTIVE

Reach the Center of Grid 086's Upper Level

01 ◇ You'll begin facing a large elevator that takes you to the outer shell of the Grid. On the way there, Carla informs you that the Planetary Closure Administration keeps watch of the outer shell using satellites, which turns out to be accurate intel. From your vantage point just outside the elevator, you'll be able to see the lasers constantly scanning the top of the area for targets, so your primary goal should be staying clear of their watchful eyes, which means using gaps in the floor to reach a maintenance area below.

There's a large enough hole for you to fit through just down and to the right of your vantage point at **Position A**, so quickly Assault Boost down into it away from the opening so the satellites lose track of you. You'll hear a warning sound accompanied by an on-screen alert if a satellite does target you. It will still take a few seconds before they fire at that point, so don't stray from your path trying to dodge them; just keep going until you're safe beneath the floor.

02 ◇ Make sure to stick to the sides of the room here, because the satellites can still target you through the hole in the roof. With that in mind, proceed until you reach a narrow opening surrounded by large gears. Proceed through it slowly and make sure to use your scan, because there's a large number of WATCHER drones in the latter half of the room, and if you're quick you can target most of them with your missiles and destroy them before they charge at you. If you need to, retreat back through the narrow opening and funnel the remaining drones through it to make them easier to deal with.

The position of the satellite targeting beams does not reflect their detection area; if you step anywhere out in the open, they will quickly lock onto you, regardless of how close to a beam you were.

03 ◇ You can see the objective location clearly ahead of you from the exit of this room, but attempting a straight shot toward it is just begging to obliterated by the PCA's satellites. Instead, if you turn to the right you'll see another pair of WATCHERs that you can destroy for two combat logs, and beneath them is a lower track that you can safely drop onto. From there, you can either take a detour to gather the remaining combat logs and pair of data logs, or continue towards the objective. ▶ A

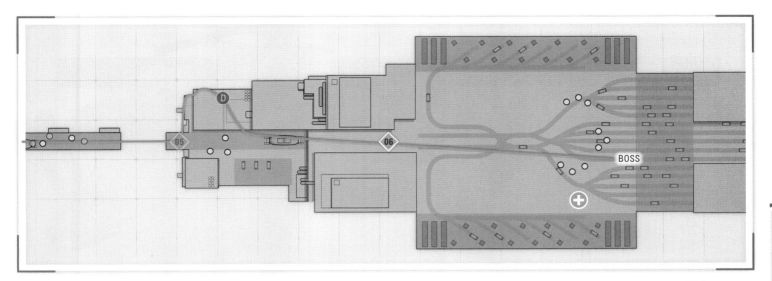

LOG CLEANUP

The tunnel near where you land on the lower tracks will allow you to reach another group of WATCHERs, two of which contain combat logs. If you then continue out the other end, you'll find a wreck that you can access for a data log at **Position B**.

Return where you first dropped down onto the lower tracks now. If you look through to the opposite side of the upper track, you should just about be able to see a small maintenance conduit in the side of the structure that is just large enough for you to fit into. When you're in that conduit, you cannot be targeted by the satellites, so boost over and enter it. Then, follow it along around the structure until you reach the end. The next data log at **Position C** should be clearly visible through the grating at that point, so quickly exit the conduit and boost around to access it, then re-enter the conduit and make your way back to where you started to continue toward the objective.

04 ◈ Since the top of the bridge leading to the objective location is so dangerous, the best way across is to travel underneath it. If you have the tetrapod legs equipped, you can easily make it to the end of the track without landing; simply drop down below it and start hovering along slowly, making sure to destroy the drones quickly as you reach them. For other leg types, you'll need to be extremely careful and try to land on the narrow ledges between the beams positioned along the tracks to recharge your EN. Once you see open sky above you, activate Assault Boost to reach the safety of a small ledge below the floor of your objective.

05 ◈ From this point, you can go in either direction to reach the floor above you, but since there's far more cover to the left as you look toward the objective marker (coordinate 290), that's the recommended approach. If you look out in that direction, you'll see another small ledge on the corner of the building that has some cover. Assault Boost over to that, then drop down onto the narrow ledge below it and round the corner. Once you're around the corner, you can boost upward and out slightly—making sure not to drift so far out that the satellites can target you—and land on the floor above at **Position D**. ▶ B-C

There's a roof above this floor, so you're safe from the satellites. However, another group of WATCHER drones will attack you when you land, so be ready to fire your missiles at them straight away. If you move to the opposite side of this covered area, you'll be able to get a clear view of the platform by the objective marker. Since there's no cover available along the way, you'll have to Assault Boost toward it to get there unscathed.

OBJECTIVE	Destroy the Drones in the Vicinity

06 ◈ Once you reach this point, you'll be safe from the satellites for the remainder of the mission, but a large number of WATCHER drones have formed a blockade on the opposite side of the room. You'll need to break through it in order to proceed. Make sure not to rush in recklessly, because it can be difficult to evade the sheer number of explosions if you get caught in a group of drones. If you approach slowly, you can target nearly the entire blockade thanks to the multi-lock capabilities of your missile launchers. Wait for the smoke and explosions to clear after your first volley before advancing, then pick off any stragglers that remain.

Carla will give you the all-clear to approach the cargo launcher once all of the drones have been destroyed, but a supply sherpa appears as you get close to it, which should be a clue that trouble is on the horizon. Be sure to make use of the sherpa's services, because attempting to access the container will trigger the enormous IA-13: SEA SPIDER C-Weapon to leap into the combat zone looking for a fight. ▶ D

IA-13

SEA SPIDER

BASIC SPECS

AP	76400
Attitude Stability	3550
Anti-Kinetic Defense	859
Anti-Energy Defense	854
Anti-Explosive Defense	1135
Elec. Discharge Tolerance	999
Shock Resistance	45%
ACS Anomaly Tolerance	999
Heat Resistance	60%

OBJECTIVE

Destroy the C-Weapon SEA SPIDER

Board the Container on the Cargo Launcher

SEA SPIDER is your first encounter with Coral weaponry and, like plasma weapons, it can leave residual damage fields behind on impact, although they tend to have a shorter duration. SEA SPIDER is a large, slow-moving enemy, which means you have more control over positioning than in some other encounters. While most of the environment is empty and easy to move around in, you should remain aware of the cargo containers and gates dotted around the room at the start of the battle, since getting caught up on one of them could be fatal. As the fight progress, the SEA SPIDER is likely to destroy most of these obstacles, turning the arena into a completely open space that you can boost around in.

PHASES

1 Provided you followed the recommended build, you should be able to out-range the boss's melee strikes by staying far away from it in this phase. Stay in the air and maintain maximum effective range while watching out for the boss leaping or boosting toward you in an attempt to land a melee strike. Once it does, Quick Boost away to avoid the hit before circling around it and creating distance yet again. From this range, you can evade most of the boss's other attacks by simply moving laterally around them, firing your missiles the entire time as soon as they finish reloading. ▶A

2 With around a third of its AP remaining, SEA SPIDER will jump off the ground and begin sustained hovering for the remainder of the battle. None of its attacks

from the first phase are used while it's airborne, so you'll have to contend with an entirely new suite of attacks, the most dangerous of which are a new variation of its main Coral cannon and its Coral explosion. Due to its new positioning, however, you'll be able to get a bit of advanced warning that it's about to use one of those attacks because you'll be able to see its thorax glow. ▶B

Keep hovering around while staying away as much as possible, firing missiles off. Be aware that if you manage to stagger the boss in this phase, it will not fall to the ground. If you're utilizing a full complement of missile launchers, then that's not much of a problem, but if you're using a melee weapon, you'll need to very quickly boost up to its aerial position. Due to the attacks it uses in this phase, there's less of an immediate threat if you do find yourself close to it. Additionally, if you do find yourself low on ammo by the end of the fight it is advisable to make use of your Boost Kick if you have it unlocked to deal damage to the boss.

Upon destroying the SEA SPIDER, you'll need to once again attempt to board the cargo launcher. Keep in mind that you won't get a checkpoint at this time, so if you accidentally restart from the last checkpoint, you'll have to go through the fight again. After accessing the launcher, you'll be safely fired across the ice field and will have completed both the mission and the chapter.

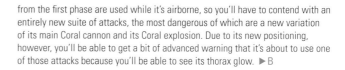

The SEA SPIDER doesn't move right away after making its entrance, so take advantage of the situation by inflicting as much damage and ACS strain as possible.

SEA SPIDER is impervious to all damage from when it begins the transition into Phase 2 until it has established its aerial position.

If the SEA SPIDER uses the leaping slam while you're hovering, you'll be able to Quick Boost a greater distance away from this attack.

While SEA SPIDER is charging its horizontal sweeping beam, you have a good opportunity to get close and deal extreme damage with your weaponry.

While the tetrapod legs are an excellent option in this fight, be mindful of running out of EN while you're hovering.

SEA SPIDER ATTACKS

AUXILIARY CORAL GUN | PHASE 1

DESCRIPTION Auxiliary Coral gun shots fired in quick succession from either side of boss's frame.

EVASION Quick Boost away from the origin point of the shots.

LEAPING SLAM | PHASE 1

DESCRIPTION Leaps in your direction with frontal legs raised and leg-mounted Coral oscillators extended before slamming down with both legs to release a Coral explosion.

EVASION Immediately begin Quick Boosting directly away from the boss.

VERTICAL CORAL MISSILES | PHASE 1

DESCRIPTION Uses vertical Coral missile launcher to release a low or high volume of Coral missiles in an overhead trajectory.

EVASION Quick Boost toward the boss, or Quick Boost laterally multiple times.

CORAL CANNON BLASTS ▼ | PHASE 1

DESCRIPTION Fires two powerful shots in quick succession from main Coral cannon. Shot detonate on impact, creating a large blast radius and lingering damage fields.

EVASION Boost vertically, and Quick Boost in the opposite direction of current trajectory when shot was fired.

HORIZONTAL SWEEPING BEAM | PHASE 1

DESCRIPTION Coral beam that sweeps horizontally across the area, leaving a trail of lingering damage fields behind it. Beam can also slightly track you vertically.

EVASION Boost into the air until the beam has passed beneath you.

VERTICAL SWEEPING BEAM | PHASE 1

DESCRIPTION Fires a beam aimed at the nearby ground with main Coral cannon, then sweeps the beam vertically toward you, leaving a trail of lingering Coral damage fields in its wake.

EVASION Quick Boost to either side of the beam as it approaches you.

CORAL EXPLOSION WAVE ▼ | PHASE 2

DESCRIPTION Charges up main Coral cannon and releases a large explosive shot aimed at the ground below, creating an enormous Coral wave surrounding the impact site.

EVASION Immediately ascend into the air and create distance from the boss.

MULTI-ANGLE CORAL MISSILES | PHASE 2

DESCRIPTION Combination of overhead and lateral missile salvos from vertical Coral missile launcher.

EVASION Quick Boost or Assault Boost toward the boss.

CORAL SHOTGUN | PHASE 2

DESCRIPTION Release two shotgun blasts from auxiliary Coral gun at close range.

EVASION Immediately boost into the air and create distance from the boss

SPINNING BLADES | PHASE 2

DESCRIPTION Activates Coral oscillators on all legs and angles itself toward the ground as it spins rapidly in your direction. Releases several waves of Coral bullets as it stops.

EVASION Quick Boost laterally away from the boss's path or ascend above it as it travels along the ground.

CONTROLLED CORAL LASER | PHASE 2

DESCRIPTION Amplified beam from main Coral cannon that's guided freely along the ground, leaving a trail of lingering damage fields in its wake.

EVASION Create distance from the boss in order to track where it's leading the beam, and Quick Boost as needed to stay away from it.

STEAL THE SURVEY DATA

*"Looks like we got a little too eager, 621...
Us and the corporations both."*

—Handler Walter

Arquebus survey drones have gathered some important data regarding the presence of Coral in this region, so Balam Industries has tasked you with investigating the area and securing this intel. Arquebus units and a PCA squad, headed up by a AS07: HEAVY WARSHIP, have other plans, however, so you'll need to contend with them along the way if you want to get the data back safely.

The initial area features some locations that are very wide and open, and others where numerous buildings can be used for cover. You can attempt to access the survey drones in this location in any order you wish. As you advance through the mission, there will be progressively less cover available and you'll need to rely on your aerial maneuverability for survival. The PCA forces are comprised of a mix of unit types, most of which grant bonus pay if you destroy them.

Observation Data: Installations Survey

Observation Data: Terrain Survey

Observation Data: Coral Density Survey

MISSION OBJECTIVES
Retrieve Coral Survey Data Collected by Drones
Prevent Delivery of the Observational Data
Intercept the PCA Enforcement Squad

MISSION INFO

Combat Zone	Central Ice Field—Hjalmar Mine
Client	Balam Industries
Reward	100,000
Max Bonus Pay	227,200
Completion Unlocks	—
Combat Logs	Silver x1
Data Logs	4
Part Containers	—

ENEMY DATA

	No.	AP	AS	Bonus Pay	Analysis
MT-T-026 Guard Mech (Rifle)	17	102	121	800	P.310
CD-E-086 Aerial Defense Drone (Mini Gatling Gun)	2	40	—	800	P.308
CH-T-025 Attack Helicopter (Anti-Tank Cannon)	8	28	—	800	P.309
TH-E-012 Transport Helicopter	4	750	486	10000	P.314
MT-E-104 Bipedal MT (Hand Rocket Launcher)	7	470	364	2400	P.317
MT-E-104 Bipedal MT (Missile Launcher)	14	470	364	2400	P.316
MT-E-104 Bipedal MT (Shotgun)	1	470	364	2400	P.317
MT-E-104 Bipedal MT (Dual Machine Gun)	9	470	364	2400	P.316
MT-E-104 Bipedal MT (Grenade Cannon)	5	470	364	2400	P.316
AM14: SENTRY SG MT (Missile Launcher)	24	437	310	—	P.320
Artillery (Missile Array)	2	202	150	4000	P.328
Artillery (Grenade Cannon)	2	470	150	4000	P.326
MT-J-048 Tetrapod MT (Grenade Cannon)	1	13370	2200	24000	P.324
MT-J-048 Tetrapod MT (9-Shot Bazooka)	2	13370	2200	24000	P.323
AA18: LIGHT CAVALRY (Enforcement Officer Spec)	1	8595	1750	—	P.331
AA18: LIGHT CAVALRY (Sniper Type)	2	1075	1750	—	P.332
AS07: HEAVY WARSHIP	1	2688	—	—	P.341
AS07: HEAVY WARSHIP (Drone Units)	10	350	351	—	P.341

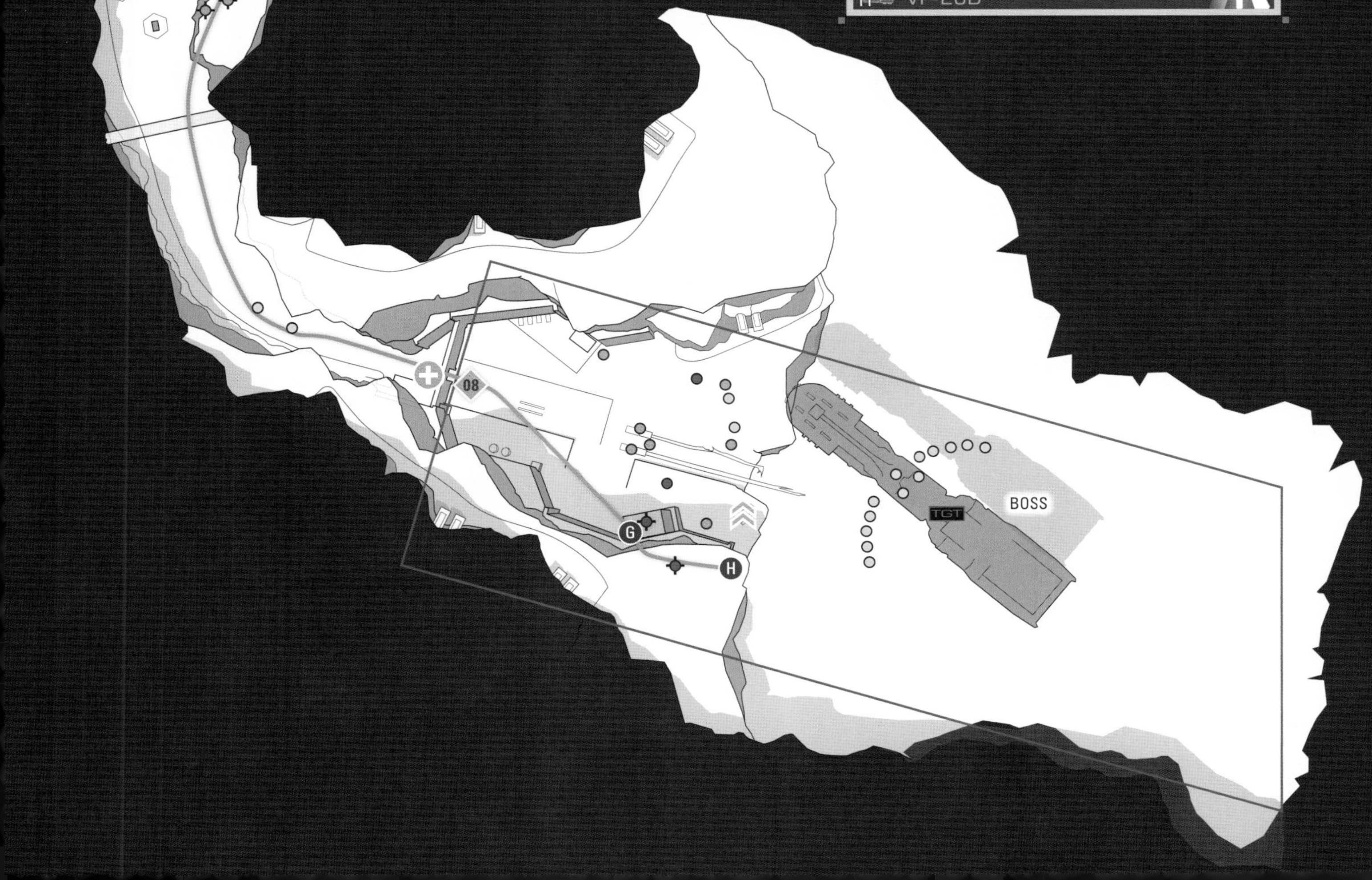

Observation Data: Offshore Survey

06

x2

x2

F

07

BOSS

TGT

G

H

08

ASSEMBLY

The defensive specs of your frame parts for this mission should prioritize anti-explosive first, followed by anti-energy, because most of the enemies you'll encounter use explosive munitions. A heavier frame with high AP and attitude stability is recommended to help manage the impact of these weapons, so the TIAN-QIANG line of parts should be strongly considered. Aerial mobility is also a consideration, since a lot of enemies remain airborne—tetrapod legs like the VP-424 give you both the mobility you need and excellent defensive specs. Bringing a melee weapon with you will help with tackling the stronger enemies and allow you to conserve some ammo if you're going for maximum bonus pay. You'll also want a potent ranged option such as a bazooka for the stronger enemies, and some missile launchers with multi-lock capabilities to help dispatch the groups of weaker enemies.

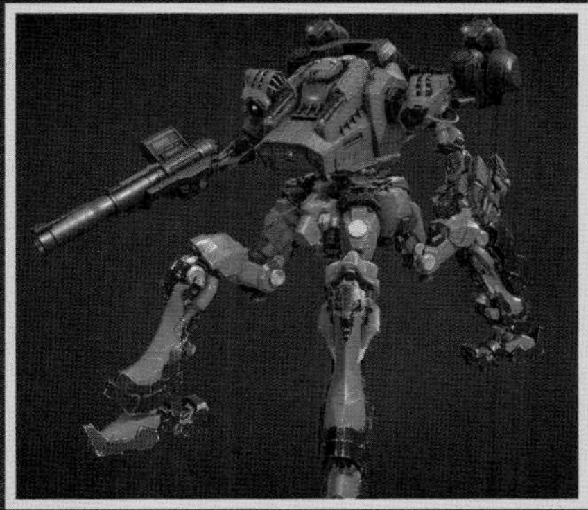

01	R-ARM UNIT | BAZOOKA MAJESTIC	P.56	ELINITE
02	L-ARM UNIT | PULSE BLADE HI-32: BU-TT/A	P.65	
03	R-BACK UNIT | PLASMA MISSILE LAUNCHER Vvc-70VPM	P.74	
04	L-BACK UNIT | PLASMA MISSILE LAUNCHER Vvc-70VPM	P.74	
05	HEAD | — DF-HD-08 TIAN-QIANG	P.77	
06	CORE | — DF-BD-08 TIAN-QIANG	P.80	
07	ARMS | — 04-101 MIND ALPHA	P.84	
08	LEGS | TETRAPOD VP-424	P.86	
09	BOOSTER | — BST-G2/P04	P.88	
10	FCS | — FCS-G2/P12SML	P.90	
11	GENERATOR | — VP-20D	P.92	

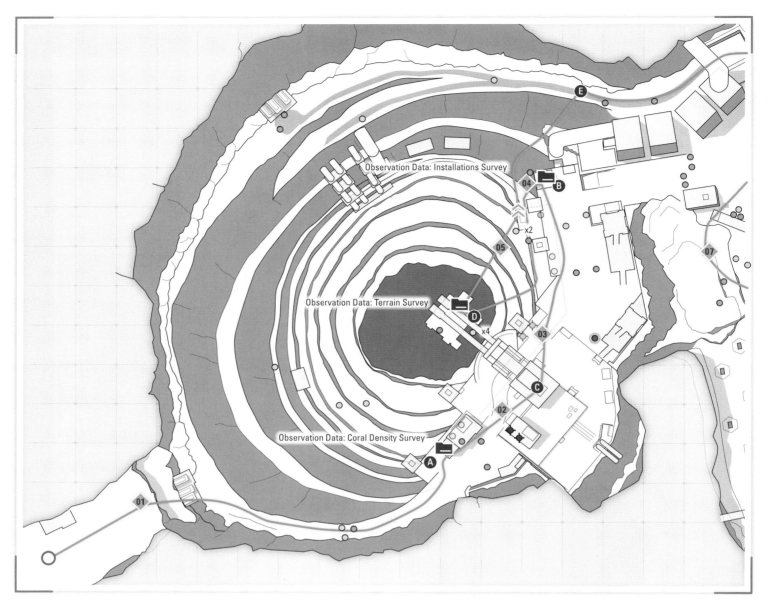

Observation Data: Installations Survey

Observation Data: Terrain Survey

Observation Data: Coral Density Survey

Retrieve Coral Survey Data Collected by Drones

01 ◈ When you reach the vantage point atop the cliff here, the locations of the four data logs you need to retrieve will be marked for you, and while you can access them in any order, there's an optimal route that we'll follow. The first survey drone is located at **Position A**, so drop down to the road below and start heading toward it. There's an Arquebus squad patrolling the road between you and your destination, and a second squad, including some artillery installations, defending the data itself. Since they're not expecting you, many of them are in an unaware state. Where you encounter these enemies is entirely dependent on how fast you initially start, but there's a good chance the patrol group will be moving away from you, and you'll be able to catch them unaware.

Approach the camp slowly and stop as soon as you can target the first enemies; as long as you stay back from the edge of the camp, the artillery won't be able to target you. You'll also be out of effective range for most of the other enemy attacks, allowing you to fairly safely destroy all of the bipedal MTs in the area. When only the artillery remains, Assault Boost down behind the building the drone is on, then peek out quickly so your missiles can lock onto them, open fire, and get back behind cover. One salvo to each is enough to destroy them, after which you can access the data log safely. ▶ A

The wall of the building the first survey drone is on at **Position A** makes perfect cover to protect you from the incoming artillery fire while you launch your missiles at them.

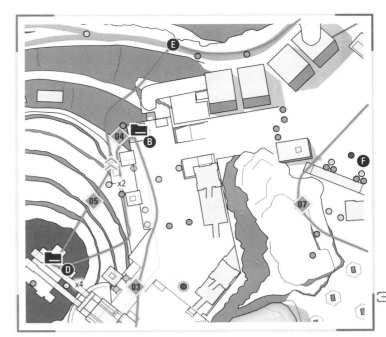

02 ◈ While the data log on the suspended platform above the pit is technically the closest one, there are a large number of enemies positioned along the different levels within the pit, and making your way up through all of them can be difficult. A safer option is to continue around the top of the pit toward the data log at **Position B**, and then fight your way down into the pit so you have the advantage.

There are a lot of enemies along the way, and by far the most dangerous of them is the tetrapod MT with a combat log; it too is unaware, however, meaning you can dictate where and when the fight starts. If you jump up to the back of the large yellow crane at **Position C**, you'll have a clear line of sight down to the tetrapod MT without it detecting you. Most of its attacks won't be able to reach you here, and you can engage it without alerting the other nearby enemies. When you're ready, launch your missiles, and then immediately fire your bazooka to get the impact bonus from hitting an unaware enemy. Keep firing off your missiles and bazooka from your safe perch until it's destroyed, and then continue up the path ahead.

03 ◈ There are still a few enemies to contend with on the way to the data log. If you Assault Boost down from your perch on the crane to the top of the road here, you can pick them off with your missiles as they come into range while you make your way to access the data log. ▶ B

04 ◈ It's now time to start clearing the enemies out from the various levels of the pit, so that you can safely retrieve the log in the middle of it. From the previous data log, if you walk to the edge of the building overlooking the pit you should be able to target and destroy a couple of the flying drones with your missiles. Drop down from the rooftop and use a scan to locate the bipedal MT near the support column of the building you were on, then use your pulse blade to make short work of it. From here, you can walk out onto a small protruding ledge and use your bazooka to destroy another bipedal MT standing on top of a storage area, next to the vertical catapult. ▶ C

Drop down again to where the vertical catapult is, and follow the path in front of the storage areas. There's a guard mech on top of another storage area just past the one with the previous bipedal MT that you can locate with your scanner and destroy with some missiles. If you continue past it, you'll be able to destroy two more bipedal MTs with your bazooka, and a squadron of helicopters hovering above the pit. The only enemy left at this point should be the bipedal MT on the suspended platform with the data log, so use your bazooka to destroy it and boost over to access the data at **Position D**. ▶ D-E

05 ◈ The direct path to the final piece of survey data is defended by a bipedal MT blockade and artillery installations, but there's an old mining road that you can use to circumvent their defensive efforts. Return to the vertical catapult and use it to land on the rooftop with the previous drone, and then jump up past the nearby large pipe to reach the road at **Position E**. Follow the road toward the survey drone until you reach the end and start picking off the enemies behind the artillery and near the drone, but don't access it yet. ▶ F

As soon as you access the final piece of data, two transport helicopters carrying a large group of enemies will come flying in and attempt a drop-off near **Position F**. To make dealing with those enemies easier, work your way back down through the area, destroying the artillery and bipedal MT blockade from behind. Head back to the drone and access the data once you've cleared out the area.

Stay close to the mine as you approach the next data log, as a large group of bipedal MTs positioned at the top of the ramp adjacent to it will start attacking if you move too close to that side of the area.

There's a barely visible bipedal MT that you can destroy with your bazooka from your position on the rooftop at **Position B**, even though you can't lock onto it.

Destroying the enemies along this path will ensure you can access the next data log safely.

The data log on the central platform will now only be protected by four helicopters and one bipedal MT.

There are a couple of patrolling bipedal MTs on this road just past **Position E**. Try to destroy them before you proceed so that they don't catch you unaware later.

Prevent Delivery of the Observational Data

06 ◈ You can simply boost past the enemies that were dropped off by the helicopters, but it's worth taking them out for the additional bonus pay. The rooftop with the survey drone on it is a perfect place to engage them from, because the tetrapod MT cannot reach you there and you have plenty of cover to use. ▶ A

07 ◈ To reach your next destination you'll need to proceed through a small wind farm flanked on either side by bipedal MTs. Begin your approach along the cliffs here and use the terrain to block the shots of the bipedal MTs as you use your

missiles to destroy them. There are more bipedal MTs on the opposite side of the wind turbines, but the turbines' blades can block both your progress and your shots, so it's best to cross to the left side of the ravine and navigate past the turbines along the rocky outcroppings at the base of the high cliff until you're within range to destroy the bipedal MTs. Continue along the road until you reach the supply sherpa, and make sure to resupply before jumping over the road, so you're fully prepared for the encounter ahead. ▶ B

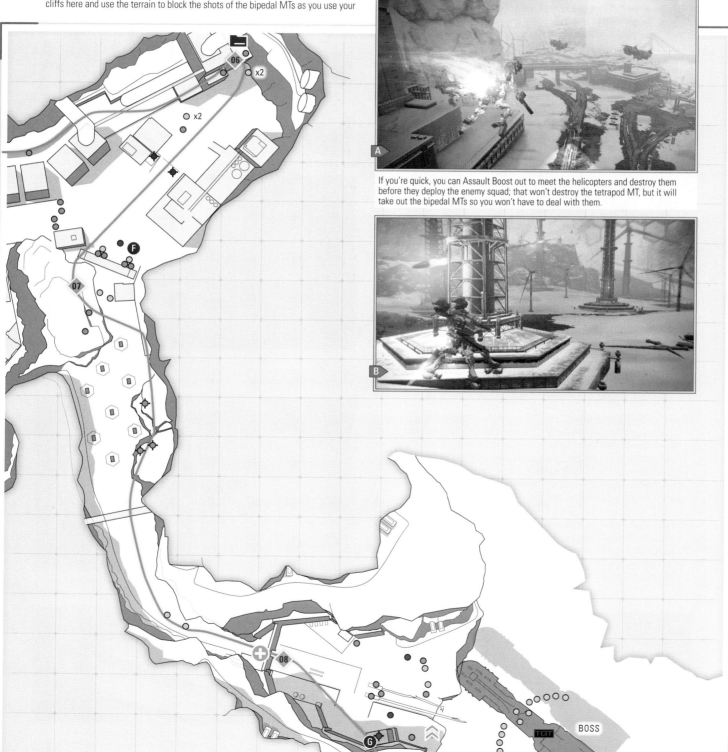

If you're quick, you can Assault Boost out to meet the helicopters and destroy them before they deploy the enemy squad; that won't destroy the tetrapod MT, but it will take out the bipedal MTs so you won't have to deal with them.

Intercept the PCA Enforcement Squad

08 ♦ There's a large contingent of Arquebus forces in this area, but it's recommended that you don't directly engage them. Instead, Assault Boost straight past them up to a rooftop at **Position G**. ▶ C

Shortly after you land on this rooftop, a massive PCA attack vessel, the AS07: HEAVY WARSHIP, will fly into the area and lay waste to the entire Arquebus force with heavy laser fire. The ship's bow lasers will travel toward you, but there's enough room on the rooftop to move between the beams. The main threat here is the PCA light cavalry (LC) squad that it deploys, along with a few support units. An LC is a piloted mech that has more mobility and improved firepower compared to a bipedal MT, and while not quite on the same level as an AC, they're still extremely dangerous. One of the LCs lands on the same rooftop you're on, so quickly use your pulse blade to destroy it before it moves away. ▶ D

Fighting the remainder of the enemies from the rooftop position can be difficult, so jump across to the nearby cliffs and fight them from **Position H**. The location's elevation means the other LCs have to ascend to reach you, and while they're boosting up you can fire at them with your missiles and bazooka—if any get close enough, switch to the pulse blade. Try to focus on the two rifle LCs first from medium-to-long range, as they have less AP than the one with the shield. When only the shield-wielding LC remains, switch to a close-range approach and rely heavily on your pulse blade to deal with its shield. Speed is somewhat of the essence, because the warship will begin another strafing run above the area after a short period, this time focused on you. If that happens, listen out for Ayre's warnings, because the focused shot the warship fires from its keel rail cannon is fast and has precise targeting. ▶ E

C

The rooftop here allows you to safely wait for the warship without having to engage the enemies below.

D

As the warship flies overhead you can target the heavy missile launchers on its underside to reduce the number of missiles it fires at you.

E

After destroying the LC on the rooftop, jumping onto the cliffs behind you quickly enough can allow you to destroy a second LC before it attacks you.

AS07

HEAVY WARSHIP

After firing a few opening shots from its keel rail cannon directly at you, the warship will settle into a static position, launching a swarm of drone units armed with laser guns as it prepares to engage with closer-range weaponry. From your position up on the cliff, you should be safe from most of its attacks. Watch for its port and starboard bays to open when it launches the drones, and keep your reticle trained on them so you can multi-lock with both missile launchers to eliminate the entire group as soon as they become targetable.

You can destroy most of the weapon emplacements on the warship, but doing so provides no bonus pay and only prolongs the encounter.

BASIC SPECS

AP	2688
Attitude Stability	—
Anti-Kinetic Defense	1210
Anti-Energy Defense	854
Anti-Explosive Defense	1000
Elec. Discharge Tolerance	—
Shock Resistance	—
ACS Anomaly Tolerance	—
Heat Resistance	—

A target marker will appear above the heavy warship's bridge when it comes to a stop, informing you of the precise weak point on which you should direct your fire. The safest approach is to simply Assault Boost toward the bridge and unload your bazooka and missiles once within range, then continue closing in until you can finish off the warship with your pulse blade. It will still attempt to fire at you as it goes down in flames, so retreat to the area next to the vertical catapult until the warship crashes to the ground, bringing the mission to an end.

ATTACK THE REFUELING BASE

"We won't fail this time. The System gave its verdict—immediate termination."

—PCA SP 2nd Lieutenant

Balam recently lost this survey base to the PCA suppression fleet, and now Arquebus is eager for you to make your way to the energy refinery in the rear of the area and destroy it. The area you'll be moving through is expansive with multiple levels, but it's a predominantly linear path so it's easy to keep track of where you need to go. The only enemies that are mandatory to destroy in this mission are the two bosses at the end, but since you'll get bonus pay for every other enemy you destroy, it can be a very lucrative mission. Enemies are not the only thing that you can earn bonus pay for here; 12 green fuel tanks can be found throughout the mission, each of which will grant you 10,000 COAM if you destroy them. Our route for this mission will take you through all of the fuel tank locations, a majority of the enemy groups along the way, and to all of the collectibles. It will not pass the location of every enemy, however, so if you want the maximum bonus pay, you'll need to branch off it periodically.

Fuel Storage Tanks x2

TGT

05

Fuel Storage Tanks x4

TGT

Fuel Storage Tanks x4

TGT

B

02

D

01

A

04

Comms Record: Enforcement Squad Comms

03

C

MISSION OBJECTIVES

Destroy the Energy Refinery Plant

Destroy the PCA SP EKDROMOI Craft

MISSION INFO

Combat Zone	Central Ice Field—Jorgen Refueling Base
Client	Arquebus Corporation
Reward	240,000
Max Bonus Pay	432,600
Completion Unlocks	—
Combat Logs	Bronze x2
Data Logs	2
Part Containers	—

ENEMY DATA

	No.	AP	AS	Bonus Pay	Analysis
MT-T-026 Guard Mech (Laser Gun)	16	102	121	800	P.310
MT-T-026 Guard Mech (Missile Launcher)	3	102	121	800	P.310
CD-J-098 Quad Drone (Laser Cannon)	6	302	310	3200	P.312
TH-E-012 Transport Helicopter	4	750	486	10000	P.314
AM14: SENTRY SG MT (Missile Launcher)	23	437	310	3400	P.320
AM14: SENTRY SG MT (Stun Gun)	8	437	310	3400	P.320
Artillery (Missile Array)	6	202	150	4000	P.328
Artillery (Gatling Gun)	2	403	150	4000	P.328
AA18: LIGHT CAVALRY (Enforcement Officer Spec)	1	8595	1750	30000	P.331
AA18: LIGHT CAVALRY (Sniper Type)	4	1075	837	6000	P.332
Energy Refinery Plant	1	1000	—	—	—
AAS03: EKDROMOI PG / PCA SP Chief Sergeant 1st Cls	1	15280	1550	—	—
AAS03: EKDROMOI EP / PCA SP 2nd Lieutenant	1	15280	1550	—	—
Fuel Storage Tanks	16	100	—	10000	

01 The location of the refinery you're tasked with destroying is clearly marked directly ahead of you in the distance from where you start, and it's possible to avoid all of the other enemies along the way by skirting around the outside edge of the area. Doing so loses you a lot of bonus pay, however, so instead, destroy the pair of guard mechs at the entrance to the facility. Then, hover over toward **Position A**, using your gatling guns to take out the Subject Guard MTs as they come into range. Continuing directly toward the objective from here would put you right in the crosshairs of some artillery installations. Thankfully, the first group of fuel storage tanks is off to the side at **Position B**, and heading for them will let you initiate a flanking maneuver to get around behind the artillery.

02 There are a couple of Subject Guard MTs defending the fuel tanks, so make sure you destroy them before the tanks. This will avoid having to contend with their attacks and to remain grounded while you're in this area, because the artillery can hit you if you're airborne. There's a large pipe just beyond the fuel tanks; follow the outside edge of it around until you reach the point where it turns downwards. If you look beneath it, you'll spot a powerful enforcement spec LC on the other side, unaware of your presence. Fully charge your laser cannons and stagger the LC using your gatling gun fire, before unloading your laser blasts in its vulnerable state for a quick kill. ▶A

Following this pipe will ensure you reach a vantage point from where you can get a tactical advantage against the LC below

03 Walter will update your objective marker around this time, and will pinpoint the location of the reactor you are to destroy as being within the large dome in the distance, on the other side of a wide ravine. Spanning the ravine is a bridge that's heavily defended by various enemies, along with a pair of gatling gun artillery installations that have thick frontal armor. Thankfully, the surrounding terrain offers plenty of alternative routes and opportunities for bonus pay and combat logs. If you boost over toward **Position C** from here, the artillery installations on the bridge will be able to target you briefly, but you'll soon be out of their firing range once you land. Continue along to the end of the ledge and you'll have a clear firing angle on an unaware sniper-type LC standing below the lower of the two narrow bridges; stagger it with your gatling guns before decimating it with your laser cannons to claim your combat log reward.

Image Data: STV Sketch (6)

Fuel Storage Tanks x6
TGT
TGT
BOSS
BOSS
H
07
G

ASSEMBLY

This mission contains a gauntlet of highly mobile enemies featuring a mixture of kinetic and energy damage vulnerabilities. Dual gatling guns allow you to mitigate this evasiveness as well as counter the LCs susceptible to kinetic damage, while the paired laser cannons serve as heavy hitters against the EKDROMOI special forces crafts. The EKDROMOI are your deadliest opponents this mission, boasting an intimidating arsenal of energy weaponry. As such, your frame parts should prioritize anti-energy defense first and anti-explosive defense second, while still supporting a heavy maximum load and EN load.

01	R-ARM UNIT | GATLING GUN DF-GA-08 HU-BEN	P.53
02	L-ARM UNIT | GATLING GUN DF-GA-08 HU-BEN	P.53
03	R-BACK UNIT | LASER CANNON VP-60LCS	P.67
04	L-BACK UNIT | LASER CANNON VP-60LCS	P.67
05	HEAD | — VP-44S	P.78
06	CORE | — VP-40S	P.80
07	ARMS | — NACHTREIHER/46E	P.80
08	LEGS | TETRAPOD RC-2000 SPRING CHICKEN	P.86
09	BOOSTER | — BUERZEL/21D	P.88
10	FCS | — FCS-G2/P05	P.89
11	GENERATOR | — VP-20D	P.92

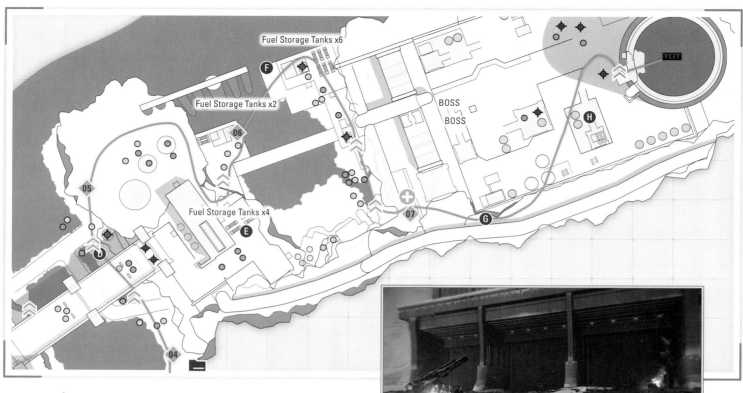

04 ◆ Drop down to the bottom of the ravine and start working your way along it underneath the main bridge, destroying the quad drones and Subject Guard MTs as you go. When you're under the bridge you'll encounter another sniper LC with a combat log; destroying it should be your focus over the other enemies, and if needed, make use of the large bridge support columns for cover. Once the area is clear, use the vertical catapult at **Position D** to reach the top of the ravine again. ▶ A

There are quite a few enemies in this area, but they are easy prey for your gatling guns. The transport helicopters in the area provide some handy temporary cover, which you can then destroy for some bonus pay. Next, move around behind the large building and destroy the fuel tanks at **Position E**, then drop down over the edge of the cliff and destroy the guard mechs defending another pair of fuel tanks and take cover behind the small building.

06 ◆ The final fuel tanks are just across the water at coordinate 165, and are heavily defended by a large group of enemies including sniper LCs—approaching them directly would lead to you getting attacked from all sides. If you instead boost out and along the water to **Position F**, you can start systematically destroying the enemies from the perimeter. The two LCs are the biggest threat, but if you reach this area carefully, you can usually catch the one above the fuel tanks unaware and destroy it quickly with suppressive gatling gun fire and charged laser cannons. The different floors of the buildings and fuel tank supports make excellent cover, which you'll need while dispatching the other nearby enemies, because the remaining LC will start firing at you.

After clearing out the other enemies, wait behind cover for the LC to fire, and then quickly Assault Boost toward it and use the same tactic as for the other LC to destroy it. The vertical catapults nearby lead you back up to the top of the cliffs, but before using them you might want to venture out across the inlet to destroy the patrolling enemies there, including some guard mechs and quad drones along the various ledges for extra bonus pay.

07 ◆ The first thing you should do here is take advantage of the supply sherpa's services to refill your ammunition and resources, because there's a tough battle against a pair of formidable EKDROMOI special forces crafts coming up. Before you face them, however, you'll need to get close to the reactor, and it's guarded by four vertical missile artillery installations. Since their missiles fire directly down at you, most of the buildings in the area do not provide as much cover as you might think. The best option is to jump over the wall and up the ledge at **Position G**, and once you're within range of the first artillery installation, jump out and hover

While you're near the narrow bridges here, make sure to access the wreck for the "Comms Record: Enforcement Squad Comms" data log hidden below one of them.

so that you can launch missiles at both the artillery and Subject Guard MTs as you constantly boost around the area in the air. ▶ B

After laying waste to everything, use the vertical catapult to propel you up to an opening in the dome, through which you can finally attack the heart of the plant and destroy it. Destroying the plant satisfies the mission objective, but you'll then be attacked by two PCA officers and have to fight your way through them.

You can destroy the plant without dealing with the enemies and artillery in the area, but they'll vanish when the EKDROMOI appear, so if you want maximum bonus pay you'll need to destroy them first.

Data Log
IMAGE DATA: STV SKETCH (6)

After using the vertical catapult to reach the opening leading to the reactor, you can enter a narrow gap between the walls and follow it around to find another data log. Make sure to access the data log before destroying the plant, because you'll be unable to reach this part of the area afterward.

EKDROMOI EP / PCA SP 2ND LIEUTENANT &
EKDROMOI PG / PCA SP CHIEF SERGEANT 1ST CLS

OBJECTIVE

Destroy the PCA SP
EKDROMOI Craft

BASIC SPECS (BOTH MODELS)

AP	15280
Attitude Stability	1550
Anti-Kinetic Defense	1140
Anti-Energy Defense	700
Anti-Explosive Defense	1135
Elec. Discharge Tolerance	500
Shock Resistance	0%
ACS Anomaly Tolerance	500
Heat Resistance	0%

After the arrival of the two EKDROMOI, the area of operation will shift and you won't be able to access the plant or the vertical catapult in front of it, so you'll only be able to use the surrounding buildings for cover during the engagement. The EP is a close-quarters variant, equipped with a machine gun, and more notably, a very dangerous energy pile bunker, with which it utilizes different variations of stabbing and slashing attacks. The PG is a ranged variant that attacks with charged plasma shots that leave behind lingering damage fields, and a unique missile salvo that can be very difficult to evade. Although the PG's attacks can cause you some issues, the EP is by far the more dangerous of the two, as it will attempt to constantly close in on you while the PG shoots from afar, which means that the EP should be your primary target.

It's best to separate these foes as much as possible, so that you only have to contend with the attacks of one of them at a time, and the easiest way to do that is to make use of the building at **Position H**. This building is one of the few parts of the area that has walls solid enough to use for cover, and is open enough so that you can maneuver around it as needed to obstruct the PG's line of sight. As you move around the building, attack with your gatling guns while the EP is mobile, and as soon as it staggers, use your charged laser cannons to inflict massive damage. Boost Kick is also extremely useful here if you have it unlocked, because you can use it against the charging EP to knock it back slightly and open it up for a barrage of gatling gun rounds.

The EP is generally too evasive to be caught off guard by your laser cannons, so these should be saved for when a stagger occurs. Due to the EP's aggressiveness, keeping on top of it with your gatling guns is simple enough, with the only major issue being how belligerent the PG is at the time. You can retreat around the building to help cut off some of the EP's charges, but it's so aggressive that it can sometimes catch up to you. If that happens, don't be afraid to Assault Boost away and rest a bit before returning to the building.

The same approach applies even more so to the less active PG variant. The distance this enemy naturally creates means you want to be the aggressor and stay as close to it as possible, constantly pressuring it with your heavy munitions and Boost Kicks. It tends to move less erratically than the EP variant, which means you can dictate a lot of the positioning and try to push it into a wall or corner so that it can't escape. Destroy EKDROMOI and the mission will be complete.

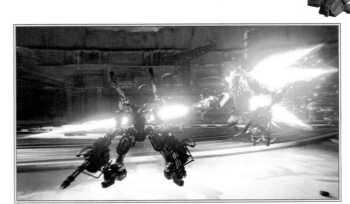

Be especially careful if you see the EP begin to charge up its pile bunker, because shortly afterward it will rapidly dash toward you for a grab attack. The speed of the attack makes it particularly difficult to evade, so as soon as the charge begins, immediately begin boosting away and create as much distance as possible.

The PG's missiles hover in the air briefly after release before breaking toward you, making the evasion timing very different and awkward, especially if you're dealing with a plasma shot or the second EKDROMOI at the same time.

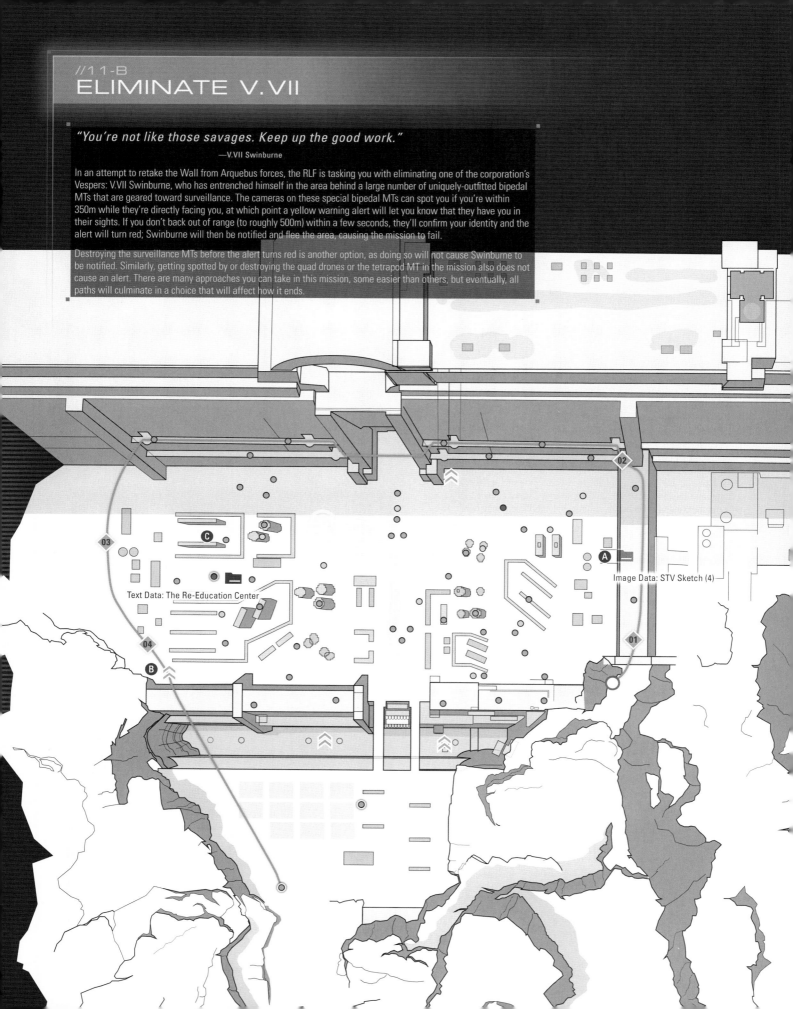

ELIMINATE V.VII

"You're not like those savages. Keep up the good work."

—V.VII Swinburne

In an attempt to retake the Wall from Arquebus forces, the RLF is tasking you with eliminating one of the corporation's Vespers: V.VII Swinburne, who has entrenched himself in the area behind a large number of uniquely-outfitted bipedal MTs that are geared toward surveillance. The cameras on these special bipedal MTs can spot you if you're within 350m while they're directly facing you, at which point a yellow warning alert will let you know that they have you in their sights. If you don't back out of range (to roughly 500m) within a few seconds, they'll confirm your identity and the alert will turn red; Swinburne will then be notified and flee the area, causing the mission to fail.

Destroying the surveillance MTs before the alert turns red is another option, as doing so will not cause Swinburne to be notified. Similarly, getting spotted by or destroying the quad drones or the tetrapod MT in the mission also does not cause an alert. There are many approaches you can take in this mission, some easier than others, but eventually, all paths will culminate in a choice that will affect how it ends.

Text Data: The Re-Education Center

Image Data: STV Sketch (4)

ASSEMBLY

While there are a large number of enemies to tackle in this mission, it's the battle against one—or potentially two—ACs, that are the most dangerous encounters, so it's these that you should build around. Jump distance and height, along with a generally fast Quick Boost-focused build are the recommendations for both navigating the mission and dealing with the ACs. Getting your anti-explosive spec as high as possible, with as much anti-energy as you can without greatly increasing your weight should be your priority defensively, and the AH-J-124 BASHO provides the highest anti-explosive and AP specs of any head you currently have access to.

The RC-2000 SPRING CHICKEN legs have the kind of mobility that you're looking for, and what the NACHTREIHER/46E arms lack in defensive specs, they more than make up for with their firearm specialization. That comes into play with the dual ZIMMERMAN shotguns that are recommended for using against the ACs, along with a grenade cannon to use while they're staggered. The Vvc-703PM plasma missile launcher has the ideal mix of range and damage for taking out the drones and bipedal MTs you'll encounter. Given that you're using a mix of both long- and close-range weaponry, an FCS with a good balance of assist for both ranges is required, and the FCS-G2/P05 is the recommended choice.

01	R-ARM UNIT | SHOTGUN SG-027 ZIMMERMAN	P.54
02	L-ARM UNIT | SHOTGUN SG-027 ZIMMERMAN	P.54
03	R-BACK UNIT | GRENADE CANNON SONGBIRDS	P.66
04	L-BACK UNIT | PLASMA MISSILE LAUNCHER Vvc-703PM	P.73
05	HEAD | — AH-J-124 BASHO	P.77
06	CORE | — VP-40S	P.80
07	ARMS | — NACHTREIHER/46E	P.83
08	LEGS | REVERSE JOINT RC-2000 SPRING CHICKEN	P.86
09	BOOSTER | — ALULA/21E	P.88
10	FCS | — FC-006 ABBOT	P.90
11	GENERATOR | — VP-20S	P.92

MISSION OBJECTIVES

Reach the Destination

Eliminate V.VII Swinburne

Defeat Rokumonsen of the Rubicon Liberation Front

MISSION INFO

Combat Zone	Central Belius—Arquebus Survey Base "The Wall"
Client	Rubicon Liberation Front
Reward	200,000
Max Bonus Pay	270,000
Completion Unlocks	Completed After "Attack the Refueling Base" & "Tunnel Sabotage": Arena: C Rank Mercenary Registration
Combat Logs	Gold x2 (cannot be retrieved in one playthrough), Silver x1
Data Logs	2
Part Containers	—

ENEMY DATA

	No.	AP	AS	Bonus Pay	Analysis
CD-J-098 Quad Drone (Laser Cannon)	10	302	310	—	P.312
MT-E-104 Bipedal MT (Capture Camera)	47	470	364	—	P.318
MT-J-048 Tetrapod MT (3-Shot Bazooka)	2	13370	2200	—	P.323
AC GUIDANCE / V.VII Swinburne	1	11880	2333	—	—
AC SHINOBI / Rokumonsen	1	9500	1590	—	—

HIDE & SNEAK

Due to the fact that you'll instantly fail the mission upon detection, the opening section is heavily reliant on stealth, and more importantly, keeping your distance from enemies. If you see the yellow warning icon above a camera MT it means they've been alerted to your presence. If you move out of their line of sight again, they'll eventually return back to their unaware state and the icon will disappear. It can take a short period of time for them to abandon their search, but having a bit of patience in these situations will increase the chances of making it through undetected.

OBJECTIVE	Reach the Destination

Data Log
IMAGE DATA: STV SKETCH (4)

Before attempting to traverse the surveillance zone, it's worth taking some time to access a nearby wreck for a data log, to avoid having to reach it later from a more difficult location. If you look along the base of the ramparts next to where you start, you'll be able to spot a ramp leading down to a sealed parking garage at **Position A**; the log is at the bottom of that ramp. Drop down there and access it, and then return to the starting position atop the cliff.

01 ◈ The highest concentration of enemies, and thus the highest likelihood you'll get detected, is in the middle portion of the area, so skirting along the perimeter of the Wall is one of the simpler routes you can take to minimize the chances of that happening. Start by jumping onto the ramparts here, then boost along them while using your missiles to destroy the two bipedal MTs along the way. ▶ A

02 ◈ While it may be tempting, it's important not to take any shortcuts by jumping across diagonally to the Wall, because that's likely to get you spotted. Only once you reach this point should you jump up to the higher of the two ledges on the Wall. Another bipedal MT will be in range when you land, so use your missiles again to destroy it, and then quickly move into the nearby alcove. A second MT further along the ledge will become alerted from the destruction of the previous one, but if you stay in the alcove it will shortly return to an unaware state and you can move along the ledge and destroy it when it's within range. ▶ B

From the end of that ledge, you'll be able to target and destroy another drone, after which you can safely Assault Boost out and around the central opening in the

Wall. Another bipedal MT will be very close when you land, so destroy it with your missiles as soon as you can target it to ensure it doesn't detect you. Continue along this ledge and destroy the remaining bipedal MT, then you can safely descend to the objective area, since there are no other enemies close enough to spot you. ▶ C

03 ◈ Upon reaching this point, you'll see and hear signs of an intense battle in the distance, and you'll now need to head over there and investigate. There are still surveillance bipedal MTs in this area, including one you should be able to target from here, so you'll need to be careful when moving around until you reach your destination. The vertical catapult at **Position B** will take you to where you need to go, and you can reach it fairly safely as long as you stick to the outside of the area. If you want to obtain more of the collectibles, though, you'll need to venture inwards and contend with some of the enemies there.

Silver Combat Log + Data Log
ON THE HUNT FOR LOGS

The biggest threat in attempting to acquire this combat log is not the tetrapod MT that bears it, but the likelihood of the surveillance bipedal MTs that surround it detecting you if you get into open combat before dealing with them. If you move toward **Position C** you can destroy one of the bipedal MTs, and then move to the end of the building and jump up to fire your missiles at the one close to the tetrapod MT. You'll lose the element of surprise doing this, but eliminating the risk of instantly failing the mission is worth the cost.

When it comes to dealing with the tetrapod MT, it carries a heavy shield that will nullify much of your shotgun's potency, but your grenade cannon can still deliver enough impact to cause a stagger. You can also jump over the tetrapod MT and use your shotguns when above or behind it, which—combined with your grenade cannon—will make short work of it. Once it's destroyed, make sure to access the wreck in the area for the final data log of the mission.

OBJECTIVE	Eliminate V.VII Swinburne

04 ◈ Your objective will update as you get close to the vertical catapult, but you won't activate a checkpoint until you use it, so in the meantime you'll need to remain cautious and keep an eye out for patrolling surveillance bipedal MTs. Upon landing on top of the ramparts you'll see the result of Swinburne's attack; the only thing left is to Assault Boost down and meet him on the battlefield. ▶ D-E

You can also destroy one of the laser cannon quad drones flying above the area when you near the end of this section, which will make the next part slightly easier.

As long as you don't jump down in front of them, the bipedal MTs on the ledge below you won't detect you as you move above them.

If you watch the movement of the bipedal MT below you can time your descent when it's moving away for additional safety.

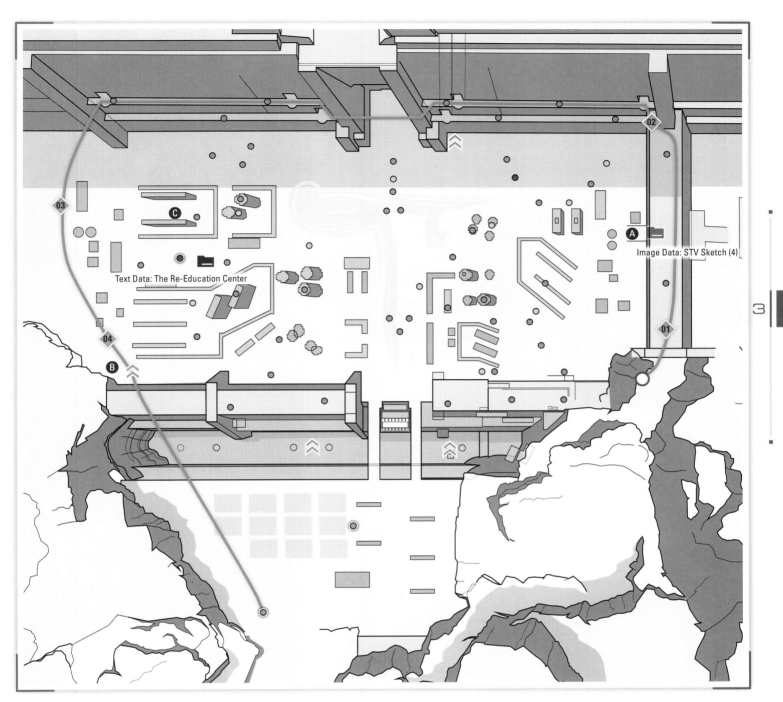

Image Data: STV Sketch (4)

Text Data: The Re-Education Center

The top of this wall is your destination, but make sure to clean up any collectibles left in the area before using the vertical catapult.

From the top of the ramparts you finally get a clear view of the destruction wrought by Swinburne, and all that's left is to Assault Boost down to meet him in battle.

AC // GUIDANCE

Swinburne does not immediately become hostile as you approach, because he believes you to be an Arquebus pilot. This gives you an opportunity to land a preemptive strike while he's in an unaware state, but if you wait too long or move too close he'll become hostile, so you only have a small window within which to take advantage.

BASIC SPECS

AP	10380
Attitude Stability	2308
Anti-Kinetic Defense	1174
Anti-Energy Defense	1255
Anti-Explosive Defense	1165
Elec. Discharge Tolerance	490
Shock Resistance	0%
ACS Anomaly Tolerance	490
Heat Resistance	0%
Repair Kits	3

Since your grenade cannon can take the biggest advantage of the impact bonus against an unaware enemy, that should be your opening shot against Swinburne.

AC GUIDANCE has two particularly dangerous weapons: an EARSHOT grenade cannon and a VP-67EB stun baton. The baton builds up your AC's electrical discharge gauge and deals heavy AP damage if it strikes you. The EARSHOT is not too dissimilar to other weapons you've faced off against, but its high impact and damage can very quickly put you in a dangerous position; pay close attention to the alert indicator for this attack, and when you hear it, immediately prepare to Quick Boost away, rather than continuing with any other action.

Swinburne will usually try to keep away from you; his AC is equipped with tetrapod legs, which he'll use to hover above you in an attempt to place you in an unfavorable position. The shield his AC is equipped with makes overloading his ACS somewhat difficult, and you'll need to rely on good movement to get around it, or be patient enough to concentrate on attacking only when it's lowered. He does still take some impact damage, so as long as you're landing your shots and have the ammunition to spare, simply attacking his shield directly can be an option.

One of the best opportunities to land a clean hit is during his melee attacks, because he'll lower his shield and get close to you when using them. He can perform a string of attacks with the baton, but it has limited range, so with good movement you can evade all of the hits while landing some of your own. Partway through the fight, Swinburne will realize things aren't going in his favor and will attempt to bargain his way out of the engagement. If you choose to spare Swinburne, he'll thank you and leave, but in his place—upset at your betrayal of the RLF—Rokumonsen will enter the area in AC SHINOBI and attempt to defeat you in his stead.

SWINBURNE'S OFFER

Before you're able to defeat him, Swinburne proclaims that he controls the purse strings for the Vespers, and thus can give you a large sum of money (270,000 COAM) in exchange for his life. You'll then be given the choice to either accept his offer or decline it, and while accepting does grant you some bonus pay, it also brings with it a financial penalty of 200,000 COAM for deviating from your assigned mission, resulting in a net increase of only 70,000 COAM. This choice affects the outcome of this mission, but does not affect the story moving forward in any significant way, although sparing him does get you an Arquebus emblem.

If you deny his offer, the fight will continue as normal until he's defeated. However, if you accept his offer and wait until the AP gauge disappears from above his AC, and then attack him, he'll immediately be defeated. This strategy bypasses any additional combat required to destroy his AC, and you'll still receive his combat log. Since the mission ends with Swinburne's defeat, you won't be able to obtain the combat log from AC SHINOBI and will need to replay the mission and choose not to defeat Swinburne instead.

AC GUIDANCE ATTACKS

HML-G2/P19MLT-04

DESCRIPTION Fires four missiles with high homing capabilities.

EVASION Quick Boost away from the missiles as close to the moment of impact as possible.

VP-67EB

DESCRIPTION Multi-hit stun baton that inflicts shock buildup, eventually triggering an electrical discharge.

EVASION Quick Boost away from the short range of the weapon.

EARSHOT ▼

DESCRIPTION High-impact, high-damage grenade cannon which creates a large explosion on impact.

EVASION Quick Boost to either side immediately once the grenade fires. At range the shot can be more easily avoided in the air.

VP-61PS

DESCRIPTION Energy shield which heavily mitigates incoming fire during its Initial Guard.

EVASION Not used offensively.

PULSE ARMOR

DESCRIPTION Spherical pulse barrier that covers AC GUIDANCE and absorbs damage until drained.

EVASION Allow the shield to degrade naturally or damage it until it depletes.

AC // SHINOBI

BASIC SPECS

AP	9500
Attitude Stability	1590
Anti-Kinetic Defense	1134
Anti-Energy Defense	1093
Anti-Explosive Defense	1056
Elec. Discharge Tolerance	490
Shock Resistance	-1%
ACS Anomaly Tolerance	490
Heat Resistance	-1%
Repair Kits	2

OBJECTIVE

Defeat Rokumonsen of the Rubicon Liberation Front

SHINOBI is one of the more difficult AC encounters up to this point in the game, especially if you expended a lot of ammunition when fighting Swinburne. Rokumonsen is a dangerous pilot whose aggressive fighting style and weaponry can easily strain your ACS and apply consistent, heavy AP damage, making it a struggle to land shots of your own. SHINOBI is equipped with a shotgun and a burst assault rifle, but the deadliest tools in its arsenal are its detonating missile launcher and a melee weapon that Rokumonsen likes to use when your ACS is overloaded.

You'll need to be constantly on the move and evading during this encounter in an attempt to mitigate as much damage as possible, regardless of the range you're at. With the recommended assembly, your goal should be to take the fight to Rokumonsen, rather than letting him dictate the pace. This means staying up close with your shotguns and grenade cannon.

Due to AC SHINOBI's frame, you can strain his ACS very quickly and consequently deal heavy AP damage while it is staggered, although it doesn't take long to recover. Try to stay as close to Rokumonsen as possible, and ideally above him, so that you can mitigate his evasiveness with the area of effect caused by your grenade cannon and plasma missiles whenever he's on the ground. Defeating AC SHINOBI will bring the slightly extended version of the mission to an end.

ROKUMONSEN FIGHT FAILURE

If you lose the fight with Rokumonsen, you'll be placed back at your checkpoint before engaging with Swinburne, so be prepared to fight both of them again.

Like Swinburne, at the right range, you can bait Rokumonsen into using his melee attack, and then move out of range and punish him with an attack of your own.

AC SHINOBI ATTACKS

BOOST KICK

DESCRIPTION Rokumonsen will use this to either rush you down or to damage you near or at ACS overload.

EVASION Quick Boost away from AC SHINOBI.

SG-026 HALDEMAN

DESCRIPTION Fires a wide cone of shots that leads to heavy ACS strain at close range.

EVASION Quick Boost away from the direct center of its firing pattern.

44-143 HMMR

DESCRIPTION Swings a plasma blade at the end of a plasma whip.

EVASION Quick Boost away or boost above Rokumonsen.

45-091 JVLN BETA ▼

DESCRIPTION The missile releases a cord behind itself and moves relatively slowly through the air, capable of multiple changes in direction. On impact, in addition to the explosion from the missile itself, the cord will also detonate, creating a chain of explosions toward its release point.

EVASION Boosting above the trajectory of the missile or using Quick Boosts to either side will most effectively avoid it and its subsequent explosions.

MA-J 201 RANSETSU-AR

DESCRIPTION A three-round burst of a higher-impact kinetic weapon, often fired in quick succession.

EVASION Quick Boost away from the direction that Rokumonsen is firing toward.

PULSE ARMOR

DESCRIPTION Spherical pulse barrier that covers AC SHINOBI and absorbs damage until drained.

EVASION Allow the shield to degrade naturally or damage it until it depletes.

//11-C
TUNNEL SABOTAGE

"Raven... Must you always put your life on the line?"

—Ayre

The Engebret Tunnel is home to a derelict PCA base containing a sensor device that Balam wants you to destroy to prevent its repair by the PCA—they hope this will create a distraction to lure PCA forces away from another area of operation. However, things do not go according to plan, and you'll have to make a hasty escape upon destroying the device. The tunnel you'll traverse has various ledges along the walls and bridges connecting them, but for vast stretches of it, there's no floor present, so you'll always need to be mindful of your surroundings. In preparation for the impending restoration of the base, a standard contingent of PCA units comprised of REPAIRER mechs, Subject Guard MTs, and a couple of LCs are stationed within the tunnel, all of which will do their best to stop you from destroying your target.

MISSION INFO

Combat Zone	Central Ice Field—Engebret Tunnel
Client	Balam Industries
Reward	130,000
Max Bonus Pay	113,600
Completion Unlocks	If completed after "Attack the Refueling Base" & "Eliminate V.VII": C Rank Mercenary Registration
Combat Logs	Bronze x1
Data Logs	—
Part Containers	1

MISSION OBJECTIVES

Destroy the Old Device in the Facility's Center

Escape the Underground Tunnel

ENEMY DATA

	No.	AP	AS	Bonus Pay	Analysis
● AM01: REPAIRER (Worker Type)	10	51	—	400	P.313
● AM01: REPAIRER (Guard Type)	13	51	—	400	P.313
● AM01: REPAIRER (Stun Smog)	7	51	—	400	P.314
● CD-J-098 Quad Drone (Laser Cannon)	2	302	310	3200	P.312
● AM14: SENTRY SG MT (Electrothermo Cutter)	8	437	310	3400	P.321
● AM14: SENTRY SG MT (Missile Launcher)	10	437	310	3400	P.320
◎ AA18: LIGHT CAVALRY (Sniper Type)	1	1075	1750	6000	P.332
● AA18: LIGHT CAVALRY (Support Type)	1	5730	1066	22000	P.332
■ Old Device	1	300	—	—	—

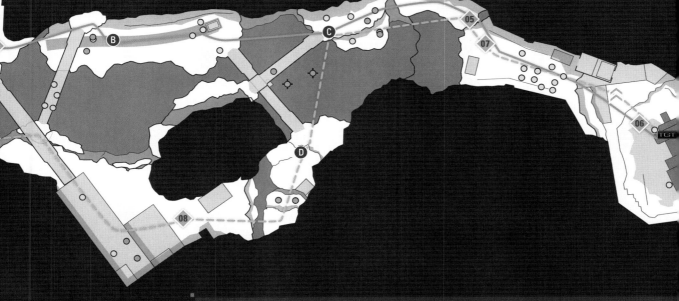

ASSEMBLY

For much of this mission, you'll be jumping between ledges along the tunnel, and being able to do so with minimal EN cost will make things significantly easier. Mobility—particularly the ability to Assault Boost for extended periods of time—is of a high priority in this mission, so a pair of reverse joint legs such as the RC-2000 SPRING CHICKEN, and a lighter, more nimble frame are recommended. Defensively, anti-energy should be your priority, and the VP series of parts offers a respectable level of it, while still allowing for the weight and mobility you're looking for.

Double Trigger machine guns give you a good amount of up-close damage output, while allowing you to stay mobile, and the reliable Vvc-703PM plasma missiles are ideal for destroying groups of enemies from a distance. If you want to use different missile launchers, be sure to keep in mind their launch trajectories and avoid any that either launch vertically or have a wide horizontal spread, because they're likely to end up hitting the tunnel walls unless you constantly account for their trajectory.

01	R-ARM UNIT | MACHINE GUN MG-014 LUDLOW	P.53	
02	L-ARM UNIT | MACHINE GUN MG-014 LUDLOW	P.53	
03	R-BACK UNIT | PLASMA MISSILE LAUNCHER Vvc-703PM	P.73	
04	L-BACK UNIT | PLASMA MISSILE LAUNCHER Vvc-703PM	P.73	
05	HEAD | — VP-44S	P.78	
06	CORE | — VP-40S	P.80	
07	ARMS | — VP-46S	P.83	
08	LEGS | REVERSE JOINT RC-2000 SPRING CHICKEN	P.86	
09	BOOSTER | — ALULA/21E	P.88	
10	FCS | — FCS-G2/P12SML	P.90	
11	GENERATOR | — VP-20S	P.92	

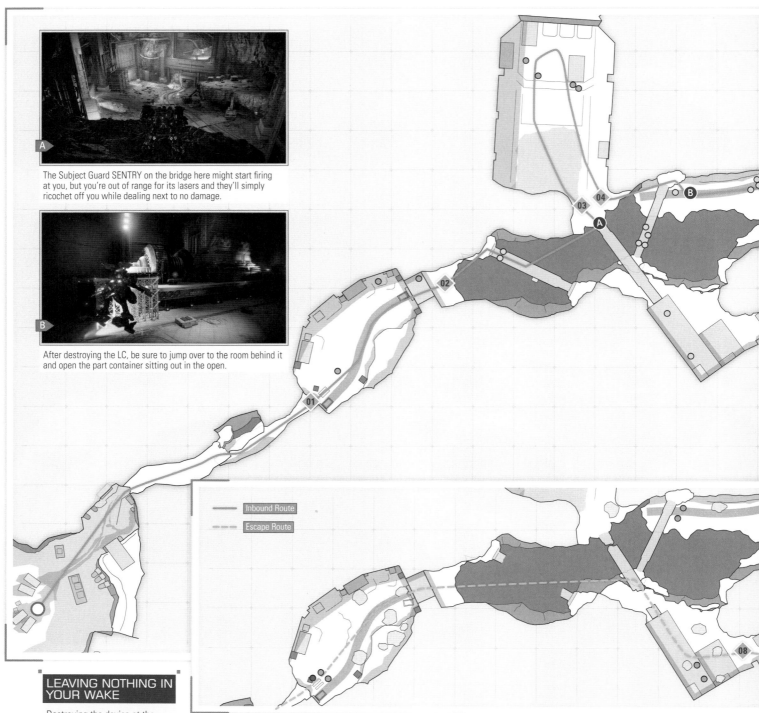

The Subject Guard SENTRY on the bridge here might start firing at you, but you're out of range for its lasers and they'll simply ricochet off you while dealing next to no damage.

After destroying the LC, be sure to jump over to the room behind it and open the part container sitting out in the open.

Inbound Route

Escape Route

LEAVING NOTHING IN YOUR WAKE

Destroying the device at the end of the tunnel will trigger an escape sequence, during which new enemies will appear in the tunnel. They do not replace the enemies on the way in, however, so anything that you didn't destroy on the way in will still be there, making your escape even more difficult. To prevent that, try to destroy as many enemies as possible on the way in, netting yourself a nice amount of bonus pay in the process.

| OBJECTIVE | Destroy the Old Device in the Facility's Center |

01 ◇ Proceed into the narrow tunnel until you reach this ledge, overlooking a room containing three Subject Guard MTs. You should be able to target and destroy two of them from here with your missiles, after which you can move forward a bit and eliminate the third one on the bridge at the opposite end of the room. The tunnel opens up a bit from that point on, so remember to watch your step and keep an eye on your EN supply when boosting between areas of solid ground. ▶ A

02 ◇ Jump over to the narrow bridge ahead of this ledge. From there, you'll see two ways to proceed: an upper

bridge and a lower one. Both routes eventually lead to your destination, but it's recommended to first enter an optional branching path from the upper bridge to get a combat log and part container—along with some additional bonus pay—and then return and take the lower path. The entrance to the room is at **Position A**, and you can reach it easily with an Assault Boost from the bridge you're standing on.

03 ◇ There are four Subject Guard MTs and a sniper LC in this room, but the LC never moves, so the MTs should be your initial targets. Enter the room and immediately use multi-lock

On top of the normal Coral energy, you'll also have to contend with strong Coral currents that can inflict large amounts of AP damage if you attempt to move through them.

If you want to destroy the final two Subject Guard MTs in the cave, drop down from the bridge before using Assault Boost to head to the exit and you'll find them on the ledge below.

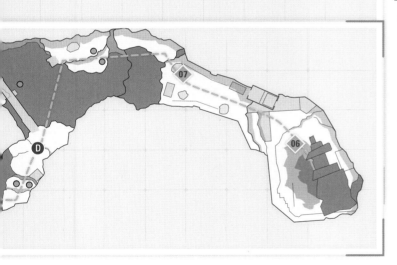

05 Continue through the tunnel until you reach this point, and then come to a stop, because there's an ambush waiting for you up ahead. On the ground are three clearly visible REPAIRER mechs, but if you look up to the ceiling of the cave and use your scanner, you'll reveal a huge number of REPAIRERs just waiting to drop down on you, many of which release a stun smog. From this ledge, you can use your scanner to target the REPAIRER mechs, then destroy most of them with your missiles, after which you can advance and pick off any that remain, before entering the room at the end of the tunnel. The device is behind a pulse shield, but all you need to do to bypass it is to walk through and destroy the target.

OBJECTIVE

Escape the Underground Tunnel

EN ANOMALY

The Coral surge is partially sustaining your EN output during this section of the mission, meaning you'll have additional EN and can Assault Boost and Quick Boost more than you normally could.

---

06 Destroying the sensor triggered a large Coral response in the cave, causing the area to be flooded with Coral energy that constantly damages your AC. Time is of the essence now, because you need to escape the tunnel before your AP runs out; remember to use your repair kits if needed to buy yourself some more time. You can get a bit of a head start by moving toward the exit before the Coral response begins, so head for the vertical catapult as soon as you destroy the device and use it to leave the room. ▶ C

07 Although you'll be taking constant damage as you try to escape, it's still worth trying to destroy as many enemies as you can for some extra bonus pay—thankfully, most of them are along the main path and you'll only need a slight detour if you want to get them all. These enemies will also be taking damage from the Coral surge, however, so you'll need to be quick if you want the credit for destroying them. When you reach this point you'll be able to see three Subject Guard MTs, so when you jump up to the ledge ahead, use multi-lock with your missiles to destroy them all. Instead of proceeding back the way you came, Assault Boost over toward the opening at **Position D** and start making your way up the ledges, destroying a pair of Subject Guard MTs along the way.

08 Another two Subject Guard MTs are moving along the bridge above this point—jump up there and use missiles to destroy them quickly, so that you can continue along the bridge before you Assault Boost toward the exit. The final room has another pair of Subject Guard MTs and a support-type LC, but if you're running low on AP it's advisable that you simply Assault Boost straight past them to exit the tunnel and complete the mission. If you have the AP to spare, however, the 22,000 COAM bonus pay for the LC makes it a very tempting target. ▶ D

The easiest way to deal with the encounter is to use your missiles to destroy the two Subject Guard MTs from the entrance of the room first, and then focus all of your attention on the LC. The agility of the LC can make it difficult to keep track of, so try to avoid the middle of the room and stick to the sides to cut down on the places it can move to, all while using your full arsenal to try and destroy it as quickly as possible. When you eventually exit the tunnel, the mission will end. be complete.

to destroy two of the Subject Guard MTs, and then keep boosting further into the room and veer to the side slightly so that you can use the crane near the back of the room to block the LC's incoming shots. Once your plasma missiles have reloaded, destroy the remaining Subject Guard MTs, and then jump up and fire on the LC between its shots until it's destroyed and you get the combat log. ▶ B

04 Upon returning to the entrance of the room, drop down to **Position B** and start destroying the REPAIRER mechs as you proceed, until you reach an open cargo container at the end of the tracks. A pair of quad drones will open fire on you with their lasers, so use the container for cover and peek out between their shots to destroy them safely. Move forward past the container once it's safe, and you should be able to target and destroy the REPAIRER mechs and Subject Guard MTs over at **Position C**. The Subject Guard MTs might start boosting toward you, but you can easily destroy them before they get close.

SURVEY THE UNINHABITED FLOATING CITY

"You've come a long way since your crash landing on Rubicon—show them."

—Handler Walter

In an effort to gain the upper hand in identifying the location of the Coral convergence, Walter is sending you on a mission to disable the electronic countermeasure fog-generating devices that are making surveys of Xylem city impossible. The navigational suppressing effect in the area means that your normal compass will be inoperable while the fog is present, and your only aid will come from the flashing beacons left behind by a drone on a failed previous survey attempt. Also hidden within the fog are hostile forces, both new and familiar, and while their numbers may not be as high as some other missions, the fact that your targeting systems are affected by the fog makes them a lot more dangerous than they normally would be.

MISSION OBJECTIVES

Shut Down All ECM Fog Control Devices (1)

Engage the Hostile Machines

Shut Down All ECM Fog Control Devices (2)

Destroy the PCA Enforcement Squad

MISSION INFO

Combat Zone	Alean Ocean—Xylem, the Floating City
Client	Handler Walter
Reward	380,000
Max Bonus Pay	—
Completion Unlocks	—
Combat Logs	Silver x1
Data Logs	2
Part Containers	1

ENEMY DATA

	No.	AP	AS	Bonus Pay	Analysis
● CD-E-086 Drone (Self-Destructing)	11	40	—	—	P.308
● IA-24: KITE (Wing Laser Blades)	6	840	486	—	P.342
● IA-24: KITE (Plasma Cannon)	2	840	486	—	P.342
◐ AA18: LIGHT CAVALRY (Sniper Type)	4	1075	1750	—	P.332
◔ IA-27: GHOST (Melee Type)	3	3820	1066	—	P.343
● AH12: HC HELICOPTER	1	38200	3000	—	—

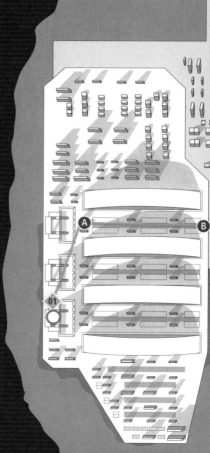

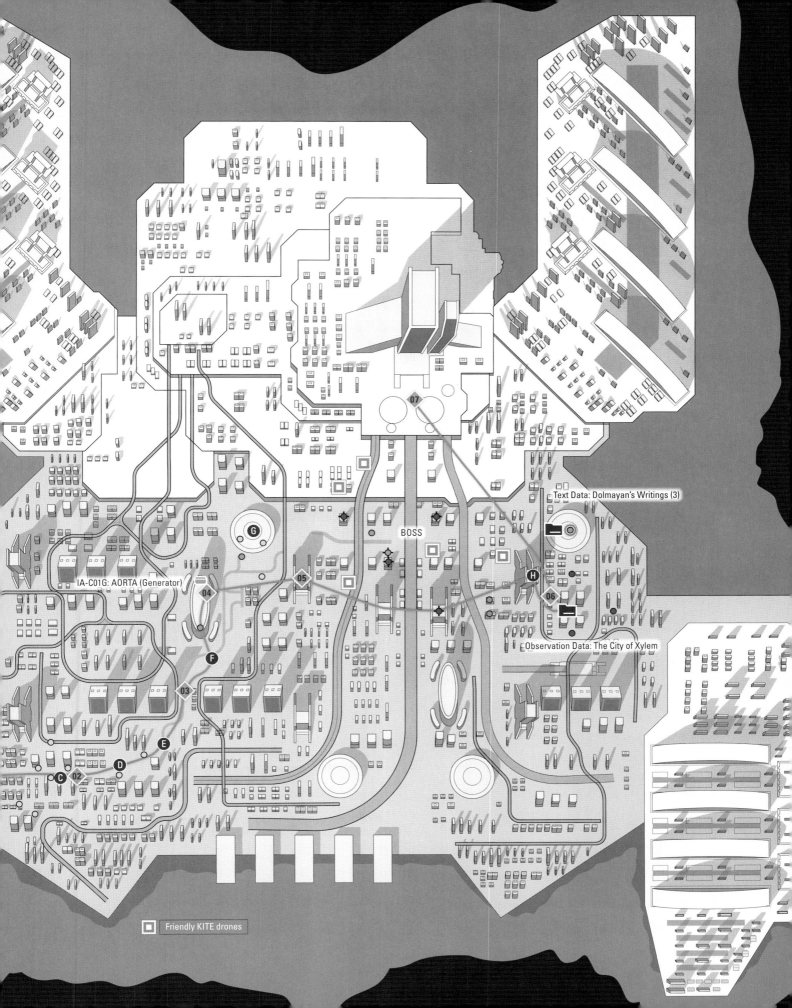

07

Text Data: Dolmayan's Writings (3)

G

BOSS

IA-C01G: AORTA (Generator)

H

05

04

06

F

Observation Data: The City of Xylem

03

E

C 02 D

Friendly KITE drones

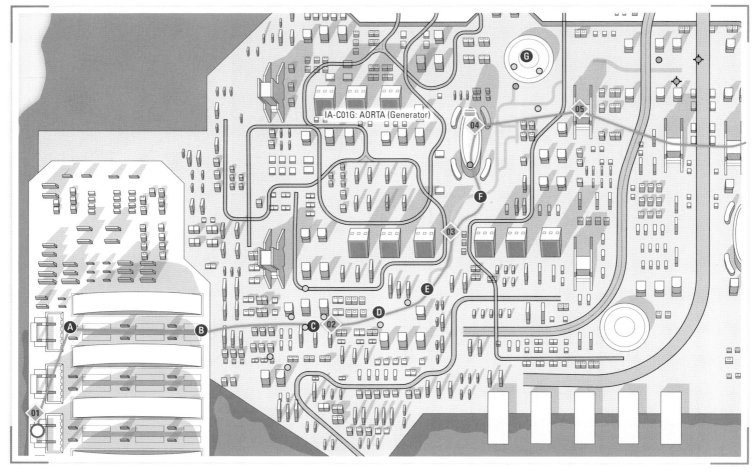

IA-C01G: AORTA (Generator)

The self-destructing aerial defense drones in this area are proximity activated and will fly toward you before blowing up if they detect you. Either destroy them at a distance, or Quick Boost away from the blast to save ammo.

The fog generators are illuminated with a blue light which helps distinguish them from anything else in the area.

Shut Down All ECM Fog Control Devices (1)

01 From where you start, the first of many red flashing beacons that will aid you in navigating your way through the fog is clearly visible down on the street at **Position A**, so jump down toward it. Once you've gotten close to a beacon, Ayre will keep track of the most recent beacon position and place a yellow alert indicator on it that you'll be able to use to guide yourself back if needed. You'll see the next beacon on the opposite side of the bridge at **Position B**; boost over to it and you'll be able to see the third beacon at **Position C**.

The city's automated defenses will detect you as soon as you drop down from the wall near the second beacon, which means the swarm of self-destructing aerial defense drones will start flying toward you until they're close enough to explode. Scanning your surroundings can detect the drones before they detect you, allowing you to down them with a multi-lock missile salvo. ► A

02 The fourth beacon is further along the same street you've been following at **Position D**, and it's right next to the first fog generator you need to disable. Destroy the self-destructing drone as you approach the beacon, then access the fog generator to disable it, before following the street around to the next two beacons at **Positions E** and then **F**. ► B

03 Use your scanner to investigate the buildings ahead once you reach this point, because a KITE drone will launch from the top of one of them and start firing at you. It launches a missile salvo on its approach, and once it's close, it'll switch to a combination of wing laser blade slashes and close-range energy blasts; take cover behind the nearby buildings to block the missiles, and then retaliate with your own missiles once the drone is close enough for you to target. ► C

ASSEMBLY

The mandatory encounter with the GHOSTs and LCs in this mission, not to mention the various defense drones that you'll have to contend with, means your defensive specs should lean toward anti-energy first, closely followed by anti-explosive. The MIND ALPHA series parts have very respectable defensive specs in both categories, but especially anti-energy. As the city is blanketed with ECM fog, the VP-44S head assists with scanning enemies undetected by your targeting systems. With all of the buildings and structures throughout the city, you'll want a set of legs that excel at jumping, which makes the RC-2000 SPRING CHICKEN a good choice.

Most of the enemies you'll face need to be destroyed quickly, and often from long range, while under less-than-ideal targeting circumstances. Mixing a pair of missile launchers with the destructive power and large blast radius of some grenade cannons gives you a very potent combination that can deal with anything this mission has to offer.

01	R-ARM UNIT | MISSILE LAUNCHER HML-G2/P19MLT-04	P.62
02	L-ARM UNIT | MISSILE LAUNCHER HML-G2/P19MLT-04	P.62
03	R-BACK UNIT | GRENADE CANNON SONGBIRDS	P.66
04	L-BACK UNIT | GRENADE CANNON SONGBIRDS	P.66
05	HEAD | — VP-44S	P.77
06	CORE | — 07-061 MIND ALPHA	P.81
07	ARMS | — 04-101 MIND ALPHA	P.84
08	LEGS | REVERSE JOINT RC-2000 SPRING CHICKEN	P.86
09	BOOSTER | — BST-G2/P04	P.88
10	FCS | — FCS-G2/P10SLT	P.90
11	GENERATOR | — VP-20C	P.92

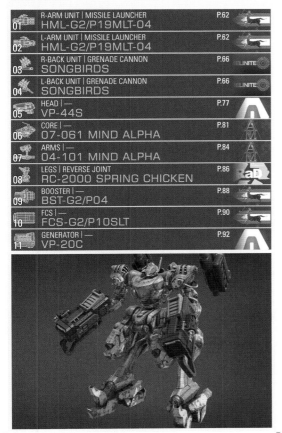

04 Jump onto the roof of the building that the KITE drone attacked you from and walk over to the opposite side of it to open the part container. From there, you can see the next beacon, and another fog-generating machine on top of a dome at **Position G**, but also hidden within the fog are a couple of self-destructing drones and another KITE drone. Although you won't be able to target it from this range, your scan has enough range to detect the dormant KITE drone; manually fire your grenade cannon to destroy it before it activates. Assault Boost down to the fog generator after destroying the KITE drone, taking out the two self-destructing drones as you approach, and access it once you land. ▶ D

05 You'll see another beacon down the road from the fog generator you just deactivated, but the next section of the area is best handled by deviating from the beacons. There's another group of KITE drones—two of which are equipped with high-power plasma cannons—waiting with direct line of sight over the street, and the easiest way to get past them is to go over and around them via the rooftops of some of the tall buildings. There's a series of four uniquely-shaped buildings with rectangular rooftops visible through the fog, starting from the one here that you can Assault Boost between until you reach the final one at **Position H**, bypassing some of the enemies below.

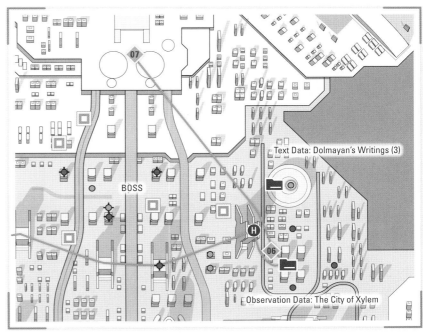

Silver Combat Log + Data Log
TEXT DATA: DOLMAYAN'S WRITINGS (3)

From the top of the building at **Position H**, you can see another dome-shaped building below and the sparking from a wreck on it. There's also a KITE drone in the middle of that dome that has a combat log, and from this location, you can easily fire down on it with a grenade cannon and destroy it without having to engage it properly. After destroying it, make sure to jump down and access the data log.

The KITE drone can clearly be seen perched atop the building as you approach this area, so keep a watchful eye on it so you know when to start taking cover.

Getting close to the edge of the building will cause you to get detected by the self-destructing drones; be ready to Quick Boost away if you notice them starting to move.

OBJECTIVE

Engage the Hostile Machines

06 ◈ While you're on the rooftop, you should be able to see some bright blue sparks coming from between a group of four buildings; this is the wreck of the survey drone that deployed the beacons you've been taking advantage of. Drop down and start accessing the drone, but be ready for a fight, because as soon as you finish retrieving the data, a group of three GHOSTs will ambush you. The easiest way to deal with them is to jump up to the roof of the tallest of the group of four buildings and fight them from there; the GHOSTs will attempt to boost up and attack but are largely unsuccessful. You can see them moving around in the fog, and can also scan to reveal them, letting you easily hit them with all of your weaponry. ▶ A

If you choose to fight the GHOSTs on the street and haven't destroyed all of the KITE drones on the way here, try to keep the fight in roughly the same area in which it begins to avoid attracting some of the KITEs here as well.

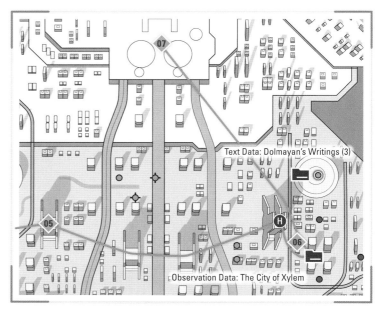

Text Data: Dolmayan's Writings (3)

Observation Data: The City of Xylem

OBJECTIVE

OBJECTIVE Shut Down All ECM Fog Control Devices (2)

07 ◈ The downed drone has the location of the final fog-generating device, so after accessing it, Ayre will mark the location for you. Accessing it will clear out the fog and enable your navigational and targeting systems to function normally. Once the fog has dissipated, four long-range LCs will immediately attack you, shortly followed by a heavy combat helicopter boss. ▶ B

AH12

HC HELICOPTER (ENFORCEMENT SCOUT)

BASIC SPECS

AP	38200
Attitude Stability	3000
Anti-Kinetic Defense	1301
Anti-Energy Defense	1029
Anti-Explosive Defense	1283
Elec. Discharge Tolerance	999
Shock Resistance	40%
ACS Anomaly Tolerance	999
Heat Resistance	35%

OBJECTIVE

Destroy the PCA Enforcement Squad

You're quite exposed at the start of the fight, so your first course of action should be to seek cover beneath the bridges leading to the building you're standing in front of. All four LCs and the helicopter have to be destroyed in order to complete the mission, and it's recommended that you deal with the LCs first. The location of the first couple of drones you'll be able to access is near one of the bridges you can use for cover, so you should operate within that area while you're waiting for the drones to come online.

Three of the LCs are close enough to target with your weapons from beneath the bridge near those drones, and you can get clear lines of sight on them by briefly jumping out so you're at their level before firing. Either a shot from one of your grenade cannons or a volley from both missile launchers will suffice to destroy an LC, so begin picking them off while evading incoming fire. As long as you don't stay in the air too long, the LCs' shots should miss as you fall back to the ground.

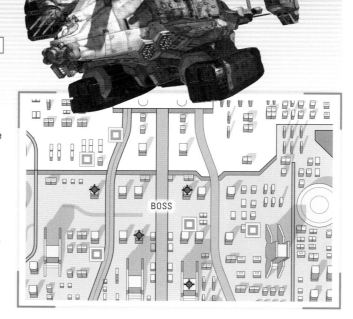

BOSS

GRENADE CANNON ▼

DESCRIPTION Head-on volley of high-impact grenades launched from underside grenade cannon. No homing capabilities but large blast radius upon detonation.

EVASION Take cover behind a building or Quick Boost away from the salvo.

MULTI MISSILE LAUNCHER

DESCRIPTION Releases a high volume of low-impact missiles with high homing capacity. Can either fire from one or both sides simultaneously.

EVASION Quick Boost to either side of the salvo or boost into the air.

GATLING GUNS

DESCRIPTION Deals heavy AP damage at medium range and inflicts severe strain on your ACS. Can either fire from one or both sides simultaneously.

EVASION Quickly take cover behind a building or place yourself underneath the boss.

FLARES

DESCRIPTION Non-damaging flares released to disrupt missile homing. Can also happen while firing at the LCs if the helicopter is close enough.

EVASION Match the altitude of the helicopter or force it to use the flares against one missile salvo and fire another soon after.

◻ FRIENDLY KITE DRONES

Shortly after getting attacked by the boss and accompanying LCs, you'll get notified that there are a number of KITE drones in the area that you can access and gain control of to fight on your behalf. They won't deal a lot of damage to the boss, but can deal respectable damage to the LCs, and more importantly, enemies tend to focus on targeting them more than you, making the fight much easier to manage. Your positioning will be important while attempting to access the drones, since the process takes a few seconds. All of the enemies will be focused on you initially, so try and stay as close to any surrounding cover as possible. The drones are visible before the fight begins, so you can make a mental note of their positions, but you won't be able to access them until after the fight has started.

The best time to activate a friendly drone is after the helicopter finishes an attack, as it will often momentarily pause or reposition allowing you a brief respite.

Even if you managed to destroy most of the LCs before you're able to access the drones, it's still highly recommended that you activate them when they're available, because they'll keep the boss distracted long enough for you to heavily damage it. The boss itself is almost the same as the one you face during the "Illegal Entry" prologue mission, but with the addition of flares that it uses as a countermeasure to your missiles. While it's distracted by the friendly drones, you can easily find openings to jump and fire missiles, while also unloading your grenade cannons constantly, since that's where the bulk of your damage comes

Try not to get too close to the LCs when attacking them or they'll dodge your fire or reposition entirely, prolonging the fight.

from. The safest place to fight the helicopter from is down on the streets, so that you can use the bridges for cover. If you see it focusing on the drones, it can be worth jumping the rooftops so that you're above the height at which it can effectively use its flares, allowing you to constantly fire your missiles without further jumping. Destroy all of the enemies here and the area will be clear for surveys to resume, completing the mission. ▶ C

HEAVY MISSILE LAUNCH SUPPORT

*"Here come the fireworks! Enjoy...
Scumbags!"*

—"Cinder" Carla

Carla is once again having problems with the Coyotes, who are now operating on behalf of the PCA, and she needs your help to defend the launch site of some "fireworks" that she's prepared to dissuade them from encroaching on her territory. She needs five minutes to prepare for the launch, during which time you'll have to defend the missiles against increasingly difficult waves of enemies that are approaching from multiple fronts. Ayre will notify you of the direction they're coming from, but if you see any of the missiles taking damage, you'll know something has slipped through and may need to use your scan to locate the enemy. The center missile is the only one you need to protect for the sake of mission completion, but there's a bonus objective to keep the left and right sub-missiles from being destroyed, granting you an additional 80,000 COAM for each one that survives to the conclusion.

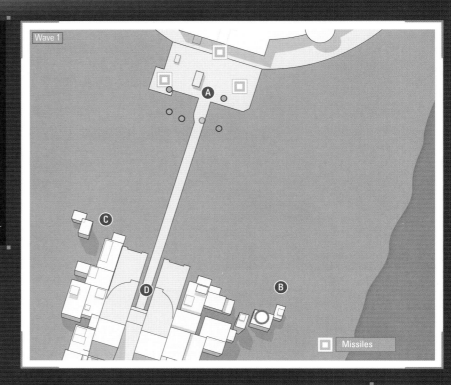

Wave 1

□ Missiles

MISSION OBJECTIVE

Eliminate the Coyotes MT Squad

MISSION INFO

Combat Zone	Northern Belius—Watchpoint Delta
Client	RaD
Reward	160,000
Max Bonus Pay	160,000
Completion Unlocks	—
Combat Logs	—
Data Logs	—
Part Containers	—

ENEMY DATA

	No.	AP	AS	Bonus Pay	Analysis
● TH-E-012 Transport Helicopter	7	750	—	—	P.314
● MT-E-104 Bipedal MT (Missile Launcher)	24	470	364	—	P.316
● MT-E-104 Bipedal MT (Cluster Gun)	30+ (Variable)	470	364	—	P.317
● MT-E-104 Bipedal MT (Grenade Cannon)	8	470	364	—	P.316
○ MB-0202 TOYBOX	4	1848	1053	—	P.325
○ AS07: HEAVY WARSHIP	1	2688	—	—	P.341
○ AS07: HEAVY WARSHIP (Turrets)	10	90	—	—	—

ASSEMBLY

Your weapon loadout for this mission should account for destroying groups of enemies very quickly while moving between multiple locations, which makes a full suite of missiles your best option. With that much multi-lock capability you'll have no trouble with the groups—after firing a salvo at some enemies, you can already be moving to the next group without having to wait for impact. A mixture of explosive missiles for their damage, and plasma missiles for the additional area of effect radius is an ideal balance.

Speed and maneuverability should also be prioritized over defensive specs; for your frame parts, using a lighter frame so you can move between enemy groups as quickly as possible is recommended.

Enemies will often target the missiles, so your own defensive specs are not as important as they usually are, although some anti-explosive spec can be helpful. The NACHTREIHER/42E legs are some of the lightest available, though such a lightweight build will mean that your choice of core is somewhat constrained, since you'll need a very light one to stay under the limit. Your two main options, the NACHTREIHER/40E and EL-TC-10 FIRMEZA are both light enough, but the FIRMEZA has better defensive specs, so it's the recommended choice.

01	R-ARM UNIT | MISSILE LAUNCHER HML-G2/P19MLT-04	P.62
02	L-ARM UNIT | MISSILE LAUNCHER HML-G2/P19MLT-04	P.62
03	R-BACK UNIT | PLASMA MISSILE LAUNCHER Vvc-703PM	P.73
04	L-BACK UNIT | PLASMA MISSILE LAUNCHER Vvc-703PM	P.73
05	HEAD | — DF-HD-08 TIAN-QIANG	P.77
06	CORE | — EL-TC-10 FIRMEZA	P.81
07	ARMS | — 04-101 MIND ALPHA	P.84
08	LEGS | BIPEDAL NACHTREIHER/42E	P.85
09	BOOSTER | — ALULA/21E	P.88
10	FCS | — FCS-G2/P10SLT	P.90
11	GENERATOR | — VP-20C	P.92

OBJECTIVE

Eliminate the Coyotes MT Squad

Wave 1 Bipedal MT x6
Countdown Uninitiated

A group of Coyote bipedal MTs will already be on the scene when you arrive, so you should Assault Boost over toward **Position A** and start taking them out with your missiles. Carla has two artillery installations set up in front of the missiles that are capable of destroying a few of the enemies, but you should try to destroy them as quickly as possible to minimize the damage they deal to the missiles before the countdown even begins.

Wave 2 4:50 Transport Helicopter x3
(w/ Bipedal MT x4)

ROAMING REINFORCEMENTS

From this wave onwards you'll also start having to contend with additional groups of three bipedal MTs wielding cluster guns that periodically appear from either **Position B**, **C**, or **D** and will make their way toward the missiles. The main enemies within each wave should still be your priority, but as soon as they're dealt with you should destroy these roaming enemies to keep their numbers in check. The easiest way to spot and keep track of them is to look for the red enemy indicators on your compass.

The transport helicopters that appear in this wave approach from **Position E**, and you should take all possible measures to destroy them before they can deploy the bipedal MTs they're carrying. Doing so will also destroy the bipedal MTs, saving you ammunition, time, and potential damage to the missiles. The easiest way to accomplish this is to start boosting toward **Position E** as soon as you've finished dealing with the previous enemies, so that you can start destroying them as soon as they appear. It only takes a volley from one pair of missile launchers to destroy a helicopter, so make sure you only target one with the right amount of missiles to destroy it and save the rest for the next target.

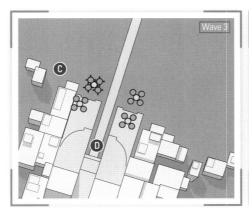

Wave 3 3:55 Transport Helicopter
(w/ Bipedal MT x4) x4

This group of helicopters starts flying in from **Position D** straight along the bridge, and shortly after they appear they'll split off into pairs and move toward separate drop-off points on either side of the bridge. As before, if you're quick enough, it's possible to destroy them all before they release their cargo, but the most important thing is to ensure that you at least destroy one of the pairs before they split, so you don't have to end up moving between the two drop-off locations.

Wave 4 3:05 TOYBOX MT x1
Bipedal MT x3

TOYBOX DEFENSES

The TOYBOX MTs drop down in their defensive configuration, so attacking them before they unfurl themselves is a waste of both ammunition and time. Watch them carefully, and time your attacks for the instant they open up, because they'll begin their assault shortly afterward and are capable of inflicting huge amounts of damage to the missiles.

Wave 4 introduces a TOYBOX MT that drops in at **Position D**. These units are capable of both rapid kinetic fire and high-volume missile salvos, and by themselves can easily deplete half of the AP of one of the missiles if allowed to unleash their missile salvo. Like the transport helicopters, regardless of whether or not there are some remaining reinforcements, the TOYBOX MT needs to be your priority target. A volley from both plasma missile launchers is enough to destroy one of them, but you'll need a couple of volleys from your hand missile launchers to get the job done.

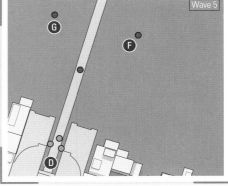

Wave 5 2:20 TOYBOX MT x3
Bipedal MT x3

This wave is arguably the most difficult if your goal is to prevent either of the sub-missiles from being destroyed. Three TOYBOX MTs will drop in simultaneously at **Positions D**, **F**, and **G**. Depending on the current state of your missiles and relative location, it can be beneficial to prioritize the TOYBOX MT that would target the missile with the lowest AP. If you've been clearing the other waves quickly, however, you should wait near **Position D** for the TOYBOX MTs to drop, and then quickly destroy the one on the bridge once it unfurls with a volley from two of your missile launchers. This leaves your other two missile launchers free to quickly target and destroy one of the remaining TOYBOX MTs before it can advance on the missiles. The final one will no doubt be speeding toward the missile by this time, so you'll need to quickly Assault Boost toward it and destroy it before it can deal too much damage.

Wave 6 1:15 PCA Heavy Warship x1
Bipedal MT x3

The PCA heavy warship is the primary target in this wave, sporting heavy lasers capable of destroying all of the missiles in a single laser sweep if you let it get into a firing position. The warship flies in from **Position B**, and unlike the other enemies in previous waves, it will immediately fire both its lasers and missiles directly at you, so use the bridge for cover until its initial barrage is over. The mission will complete upon either the warship being destroyed or the timer running down, but given the potential for it to destroy your missiles, the safest option is to bring down the warship. Once it's within range, Assault Boost above it, ignoring all of the defensive turrets, and focus all of your missiles on the command deck to destroy it, then sit back and enjoy the fireworks.

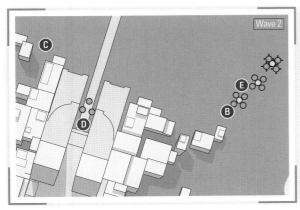

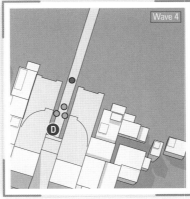

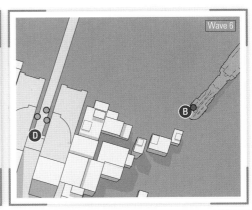

ELIMINATE THE ENFORCEMENT SQUADS

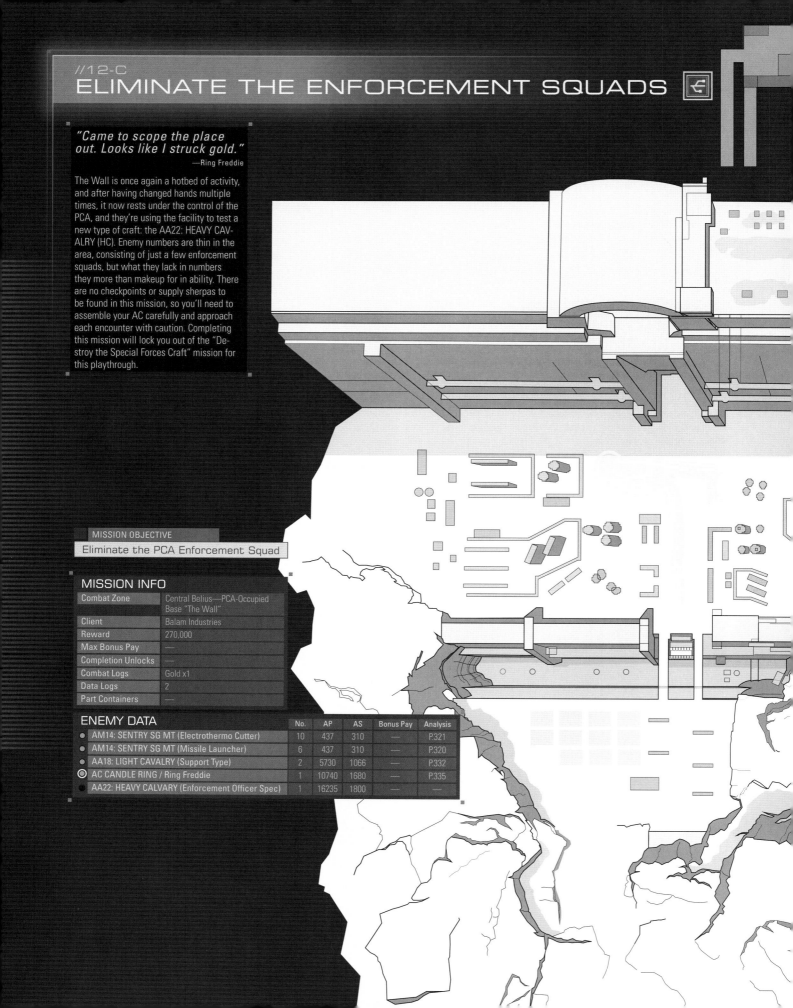

> *"Came to scope the place out. Looks like I struck gold."*
> —Ring Freddie

The Wall is once again a hotbed of activity, and after having changed hands multiple times, it now rests under the control of the PCA, and they're using the facility to test a new type of craft: the AA22: HEAVY CAVALRY (HC). Enemy numbers are thin in the area, consisting of just a few enforcement squads, but what they lack in numbers they more than makeup for in ability. There are no checkpoints or supply sherpas to be found in this mission, so you'll need to assemble your AC carefully and approach each encounter with caution. Completing this mission will lock you out of the "Destroy the Special Forces Craft" mission for this playthrough.

MISSION OBJECTIVE
Eliminate the PCA Enforcement Squad

MISSION INFO

Combat Zone	Central Belius—PCA-Occupied Base "The Wall"
Client	Balam Industries
Reward	270,000
Max Bonus Pay	—
Completion Unlocks	—
Combat Logs	Gold x1
Data Logs	2
Part Containers	—

ENEMY DATA

	No.	AP	AS	Bonus Pay	Analysis
● AM14: SENTRY SG MT (Electrothermo Cutter)	10	437	310	—	P.321
● AM14: SENTRY SG MT (Missile Launcher)	6	437	310	—	P.320
● AA18: LIGHT CAVALRY (Support Type)	2	5730	1066	—	P.332
◉ AC CANDLE RING / Ring Freddie	1	10740	1680	—	P.335
● AA22: HEAVY CALVARY (Enforcement Officer Spec)	1	16235	1800	—	—

BOSS

03

Image Data: STV Sketch (1)

B

02

01

A

Video Record: Rubiconian Invective

ASSEMBLY

The primary threats you'll need to contend with are the SONGBIRDS that Ring Freddie uses, and the laser rifle utilized by the HC at the end, meaning that your defensive specs should be a mix of both anti-explosive and anti-energy; parts like the BASHO head and TIAN-QIANG core offer a balance of both. A more attitude stability-focused build is recommended for this mission over something more maneuverable, and the VP-424 legs give you plenty of both, along with the ability to hover out of harm's way if needed.

Dual gatling guns excel at staggering evasive foes and mopping up weaker enemies, but you'll need some heavy firepower to deal with CANDLE RING and the HC at the end. The SONGBIRDS fill this role nicely and pair well with the ability to hover above enemies and fire down onto them.

01	R-ARM UNIT | GATLING GUN DF-GA-08 HU-BEN	P.53	
02	L-ARM UNIT | GATLING GUN DF-GA-08 HU-BEN	P.53	
03	R-BACK UNIT | GRENADE CANNON SONGBIRDS	P.66	ELINITE
04	L-BACK UNIT | GRENADE CANNON SONGBIRDS	P.66	ELINITE
05	HEAD | — AH-J-124 BASHO	P.77	BAWS
06	CORE | — DF-BD-08 TIAN-QIANG	P.80	
07	ARMS | — NACHTREIHER/46E	P.83	
08	LEGS | TETRAPOD VP-424	P.86	
09	BOOSTER | — BST-G2/P04	P.88	
10	FCS | — FCS-G2/P05	P.89	
11	GENERATOR | — DF-GN-06 MING-TANG	P.91	

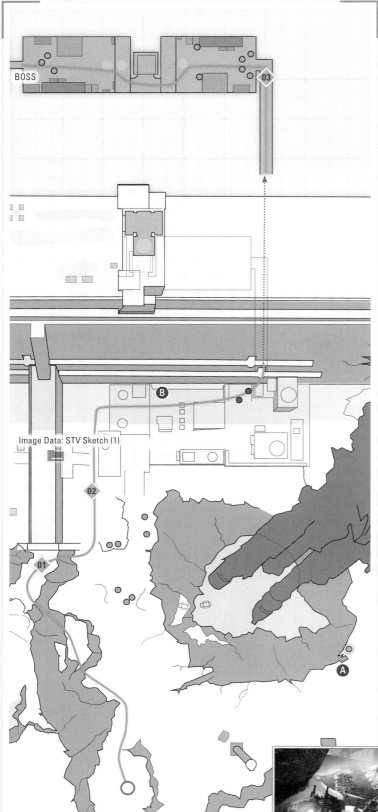

BOSS

03

Image Data: STV Sketch (1)

02

01

B

A

AC // CANDLE RING

Before progressing with the mission objective, it's recommended that you take a detour to **Position A** and fight this optional enemy for the combat log you'll obtain for defeating him. Ring Freddie is a skilled pilot, so this can be a dangerous fight, and tackling it straight away means you can go in with full supplies and be able to gauge afterward if you have enough left to complete the mission. ▶ A

BASIC SPECS

AP	10740
Attitude Stability	1630
Anti-Kinetic Defense	1095
Anti-Energy Defense	1043
Anti-Explosive Defense	1030
Elec. Discharge Tolerance	490
Shock Resistance	-1%
ACS Anomaly Tolerance	490
Heat Resistance	-1%

AC CANDLE RING is outfitted with the EL-TL-11 FORTALEZA tank legs, which are some of the highest mobility and fastest legs in the game. Ring Freddie makes full use of these legs and will move constantly, always trying to circle around your AC to make it difficult to fire on him. To get around that, either try to use the hover capabilities of the tetrapod legs to remain above him, or stay far enough away to easily compensate for his movement. Alternatively, keep the cliffs behind you, so he has nowhere to go—just make sure you're not too close to them, or you'll likely get caught in the blasts from his weapons. CANDLE RING is equipped with two HML-G2/P19MLT-04 missile launchers and two SONGBIRDS grenade cannons, so it has a lot of firepower at its disposal, which is very dangerous given how fast it can move.

Your main advantage in this fight comes from Ring Freddie's initial starting location. He's behind a small cliff at **Position A**, waiting to ambush anyone that attempts to access the nearby data log. If you scan or move into view he'll become hostile and deliver a unique line about you discovering his hiding place, but the best way to begin the encounter is to drop down as close as possible in front of him. This lets you box him in and severely limit his movement options, and he'll be close enough that you can unleash all your firepower before he has a chance to react, if not outright eliminate him.

In the event CANDLE RING survives your initial onslaught, how you proceed will entirely depend on your positioning relative to his own. If Ring Freddie is still boxed in, then it's worth pressing your advantage and trying to finish him off, but if he escaped, you'll want to take to the air to minimize the effectiveness of his SONGBIRDS and maximize the effectiveness of your own. After defeating him and acquiring the combat log, make sure to access the nearby data log before getting back to the mission.

A

Ambushing Ring Freddie with a double SONGBIRDS salvo guarantees an instant ACS overload, which you can follow up with assault armor or gatling gun fire to shred his AP with direct hits.

B

Just past the PCA squad blockade you can find a data log hidden away in a small entrance at the base of the Wall.

Eliminate the PCA Enforcement Squad

01 ◈ From your starting position, you'll be able to see two PCA squads directly ahead of you on the slopes leading up to the base of the Wall. Heading straight for them would allow the farther group to rain their grenades down on you while you're engaging the closer group, but if you skirt around the cliffs to the side of the slope you can get behind the closer group and take on the farther group instead. By adopting this strategy, you'll be able to use the natural terrain to block most of the incoming fire, while you pop out and use grenade cannons to destroy the enemies. The Subject Guard MTs from the lower group will jump up to try to reach you, but that puts them in the perfect position to mow them down with your gatling guns. ▶ B

02 ◈ When you enter the compound here, two support-type LCs will be called in an attempt to stop you from accessing the Wall, and their hit-and-run style attacks can be difficult to deal with in open combat. The LCs will land at **Position B**, and provided you hurry, you can meet them here as they touch down. Unload your gatling guns into one LC to stagger it upon landing, and use your grenade cannons to dispatch it for good. The remaining solo LC can easily be staggered by sustained gatling gun fire and dispatched similarly to the first.

03 ◈ A group of Subject Guard MTs armed with electrothermo cutters will ambush you as soon as you finish accessing the door into the room here, so retreat back down the tunnel to let them group up and destroy them with a grenade cannon shot. Two more Subject Guard MTs will hang back at the opposite end of the room, but these are easily eliminated with gatling gun fire. You'll be able to access a small doorway leading to an adjacent room once all of the Subject Guard MTs are destroyed, and there will be another group of MTs waiting for you in that room. If you move too far into the room you'll be attacked by the AA22: HEAVY CAVALRY, so pick off all targets using more grenade cannon shots. Destroying that final Subject Guard MT will then cause the AA22: HEAVY CAVALRY to enter the room, and it has orders to eliminate you.

NO SAFETY NET

There's no checkpoint before this final encounter, so keep in mind that failure to defeat the HC will result in playing through the entire mission again.

AA22

HEAVY CALVARY/ PCA WARRANT OFFICER

The AA22: HEAVY CAVALRY (Enforcement Officer Spec) is a highly specialized PCA craft with strong defenses and predictive fire capabilities, and isn't lacking in mobility or firepower, making it a particularly dangerous threat. The HC is equipped with two multi-missile launchers, a laser rifle, and a pulse shieldbasher, which it will charge at you with in lieu of a traditional melee weapon from close proximity, inflicting huge amounts of ACS strain in the process. It will typically stay airborne while firing its weapons and using its shield to greatly reduce both the damage and impact from your shots, so for that reason, it's recommended that you play aggressively and overload its ACS using your gatling guns.

BASIC SPECS

AP	16235
Attitude Stability	1800
Anti-Kinetic Defense	1060
Anti-Energy Defense	1413
Anti-Explosive Defense	1305
Elec. Discharge Tolerance	500
Shock Resistance	15%
ACS Anomaly Tolerance	500
Heat Resistance	10%

The assault armor Core Expansion is the ideal option for starting this fight. Meeting the HC in the middle of the room and unleashing an assault armor usually results in the HC staggering, at which point you can switch to your gatling guns. Gatling guns are particularly effective in this encounter because the overwhelming hail of bullets will regularly hit the HC around the sides of its shield. This builds ACS strain surprisingly fast, and you can often stagger the HC before overheating the gatling guns. Exploit the ACS overload window with direct hits from your grenade cannons and gatling guns if they've cooled down, and repeat the process until the HC falls.

The HC itself is highly mobile and can traverse the room with ease, so be mindful if you need to retreat to allow your gatling guns to cool down. This boss is best fought at medium range, just outside of its shield being a melee threat while maintain your gatling guns' efficacy. As well, you want to stay airborne with your tetrapod legs as much as possible, as this mitigates the HC's ability to bombard you with attacks from above. If you can maintain aggression and keep staggering this elite PCA enforcer, it will quickly fall and the mission will be complete.

The charged laser rifle shot deals devastating damage if it connects, but is forgivingly simple to avoid with a Quick Boost as soon as you hear the audio attack indicator.

HEAVY CALVARY ATTACKS

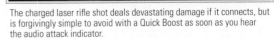

MISSILE LAUNCHERS	ENERGY RIFLE ▼ (CHARGED)	ENERGY SHIELD BASH
DESCRIPTION Four-missile salvos are released from launchers on both shoulders of the HC.	**DESCRIPTION** Rifle which fires energy shots; has two firing modes.	**DESCRIPTION** The HC will raise its shield and Quick Boost toward you, attempting to strike you with the shield.
EVASION Quick Boost to either side of the projectiles as close to when they reach you as possible.	**EVASION** Quick Boost away from the shots or seek cover behind the objects present in the room.	**EVASION** Quick Boost away from the HC.

DESTROY THE SPECIAL FORCES CRAFT

"I don't know who you are, but you're dead!"

—PCA SP Captain

The task given to you by the RLF is a straightforward one: destroy the AAS02: CATAPHRACT. Newly created by the PCA, the threat this weapon would pose if either of the corporations got their hands on it is significant, and it's your job to ensure that doesn't happen. Similar to the JUGGERNAUT, the CATAPHRACT can only be effectively hit from a specific spot on its frame, and due to it being stationed in the open desert, you'll need to rely on your evasive skills rather than cover when battling it. Completing this mission will lock you out of the "Eliminate the Enforcement Squads" mission for this playthrough.

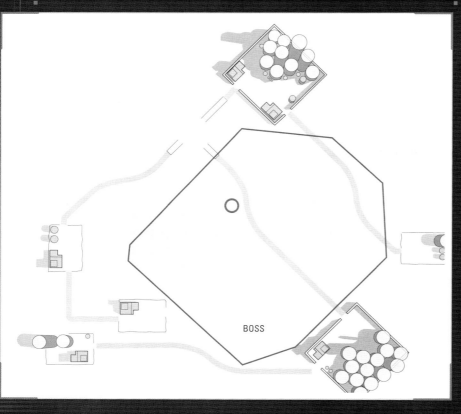

MISSION OBJECTIVE

Destroy the PCA SP Craft CATAPHRACT

MISSION INFO

Combat Zone	Central Ice Field—Old Bertram Spaceport Environs
Client	Rubicon Liberation Front
Reward	300,000
Max Bonus Pay	—
Completion Unlocks	—
Combat Logs	—
Data Logs	—
Part Containers	—

ENEMY DATA

	No.	AP	AS	Bonus Pay	Analysis
AAS02: CATAPHRACT / PCA SP Captain	1	38200	1500	—	—

ASSEMBLY

Your choice of weaponry is important for this fight, because the CATAPHRACT needs to be damaged in a specific way; weapons that fire in an arc or require close proximity may be either ineffectual or simply more hazardous to you than to the CATAPHRACT. High-impact direct weapons such as the MAJESTIC bazooka will heavily strain the boss's ACS, overloading it in just two hits, so pairing them up gives you an extremely potent combination. Combine those bazookas with similarly direct weapons that you can fire rapidly, like the VP-60LCS laser cannons, and you can inflict a lot of damage in a short amount of time.

An alternative recommendation instead of a second back unit weapon would be the VP-61PB pulse buckler, because a properly timed Initial Guard can greatly reduce the damage from many of the boss's attacks, making the encounter safer, even though it may take slightly longer. Between all of its attacks, CATAPHRACT can inflict every damage type, but the most dangerous are energy-based, so anti-energy should be the primary defensive spec you're looking for.

Both of the ALLMIND frame parts offer the highest anti-energy defense you have access to at this point, and have appropriate weight for you to be able to use the RC-2000 SPRING CHICKEN legs; jumping and Quick Boosts are the best evasive options in the fight, both of which these legs excel at.

01	R-ARM UNIT	BAZOOKA MAJESTIC	P.56	ELINITE
02	L-ARM UNIT	BAZOOKA MAJESTIC	P.56	ELINITE
03	R-BACK UNIT	LASER CANNON VP-60LCS	P.67	
04	L-BACK UNIT	LASER CANNON VP-60LCS	P.67	
05	HEAD	AH-J-124 BASHO	P.77	AWS
06	CORE	07-061 MIND ALPHA	P.81	
07	ARMS	04-101 MIND ALPHA	P.84	
08	LEGS	REVERSE JOINT RC-2000 SPRING CHICKEN	P.86	BaD
09	BOOSTER	ALULA/21E	P.88	
10	FCS	FCS-G2/P12SML	P.90	
11	GENERATOR	VP-20C	P.92	

CATAPHRACT

BASIC SPECS

AP	38200
Attitude Stability	1500
Anti-Kinetic Defense	1165
Anti-Energy Defense	889
Anti-Explosive Defense	1283
Elec. Discharge Tolerance	999
Shock Resistance	40%
ACS Anomaly Tolerance	999
Heat Resistance	40%

CATAPHRACT SEGMENTS

The CATAPHRACT can move its treads independently from its "upper body," with both segments containing different weapons. This means the boss can turn some of its weapons toward you regardless of the orientation of its treads, the main exception being its gatling grenade launchers which fire entirely based on the tread direction.

OBJECTIVE

Destroy the PCA SP Craft CATAPHRACT

The CATAPHRACT is highly mobile, very aggressive, and comes equipped with a large arsenal. In addition, you cannot damage or strain its ACS if you hit anything other than the exposed MT that's been integrated within the tank frame. Your windows of opportunity to deal damage are narrow, and even when you do stagger the boss, it recovers very quickly, so making the most of every chance to deal direct damage is critical for success.

You'll face the CATAPHRACT in a large area, but it can close in on you in far less time than you can create space, so don't let yourself get pushed to the edges of the combat zone, or you'll severely limit your evasive options. The easiest times to hit it are when it's facing directly toward you, so look for those moments to strike, and try not to waste all of your EN circling around it.

Certain attacks will leave the CATAPHRACT in a favorable position for you to attack it from, so the key to victory is understanding and reacting to these attacks in time to capitalize on them. Its gatling grenade launchers won't give you an audio alert indicator, just a visual one, but this is the main attack you're looking for. When it uses those turrets it will sometimes jump to orientate itself, but depending on your positioning, it may stay in place and move the treads to face or advance toward you slightly. If you jump early enough in anticipation of the grenades, you can get a clear and prolonged window of opportunity to fire at the boss.

A similar, albeit much smaller window also presents itself when the CATAPHRACT is revving up to use its rushing charge. During that attack, it will face you directly, and depending on both the proximity and your weapon loadout, it can be possible to shoot the exposed MT and still have enough time to Quick Boost out of the way of the attack. This is quite a risky move, however, so it's only really recommended if the shots you take during the rushing charge will stagger the boss and interrupt it.

PHASES

1 The CATAPHRACT enters the area from a considerable distance away and begins the fight by firing its double gatling cannons while moving toward you. It always opens the fight in this manner, so if you're fast enough you can take a clear shot for an early hit and begin straining the boss's ACS. From that point on the CATAPHRACT will largely react to the distance at which you try to fight it from: if you stay far away, it will rush toward you, but stay very close for too long and it will attempt to distance itself from you. This constant movement is what makes strafing around the boss to get into a favorable firing position where it's directly facing you difficult and time consuming.

2 When you've depleted roughly 50% of its AP, the CA SP Captain of the CATAPHRACT will put out a request over the comms for more information about you, and that signifies the transition to the second phase of the fight. Most of the CATA-PHRACT behavior doesn't change in this phase, but it does gain access to its extremely dangerous spiral laser attack. This attack is more dangerous and difficult to evade than the shotgun laser, as it retains its efficacy over long distances, so you'll need to pay even more attention to whether or not CATAPHRACT is charging its variable laser cannon at all times. Remember that your lasers fire faster than your bazookas, so unless you're sure the bazooka shots will land, you're better off using the lasers, especially since you can fire them simultaneously. Continue looking for your openings and taking full advantage of them when they present themselves until the boss is defeated and the mission is complete.

AAS02: CATAPHRACT ATTACKS

VERTICAL MISSILE SALVO

DESCRIPTION Releases a large salvo of overhead missiles from its multi-shot suppressive missile launcher.

EVASION Quick Boost to the side as the salvo begins to land and continue to either boost or Quick Boost in that direction until all of the missiles have been evaded.

RUSHING CHARGE

DESCRIPTION Revs its wheels before attempting to charge directly into you.

EVASION Quick Boost to either side or jump over it during its approach.

MORTAR TURRETS ▼ (VISUAL INDICATOR ONLY)

DESCRIPTION A string of gatling grenade launcher rounds are released at slightly variable front-facing positions which increases their horizontal range. Explosions can obscure vision.

EVASION Jump above the lines of fire as they are being released or Quick Boost to either side if there's a wide enough space to allow for the boss to move while it uses this attack.

HEAD-ON MISSILE SALVO

DESCRIPTION Releases one or two densely packed multi-shot suppressive missile launcher salvos in quick succession that fly straight toward you.

EVASION Quick Boost away from the salvo shortly before they reach you.

SHOTGUN LASER ▼

DESCRIPTION A charged, horizontal wave of lasers from its variable laser cannon that fan outward. High-damage attack that can be used at any range.

EVASION Jump into the air as soon as the alert indicator activates or if you are in the air already, immediately drop down.

DOUBLE GATLING CANNONS

DESCRIPTION Highly predictive double gatling guns that can be used at any range with sustained periods of firing. Always starts the fight with this attack.

EVASION Determine the direction the rounds are firing toward and dodge away from them; do not try to outpace the fire in the direction it is moving.

SPIRAL LASER ▼   PHASE 2

DESCRIPTION A charged, single shot of energy is released at high speed. Deals extremely high damage and can be used at any range.

EVASION At the moment of release, Quick Boost in the opposite direction to which you had been moving.

ATTACK THE OLD SPACEPORT

"I've got your back, buddy. Hope you've got mine."

—V.IV Rusty

The old spaceport is being used by the PCA to house its suppression fleet, and as part of a two-pronged attack on PCA facilities, Arquebus wants you to infiltrate the base and destroy all of the warships berthed there. V.IV Rusty will join you partway through the mission, and you'll need the backup because even though the warships are berthed, their weapon systems are still active, and there are numerous PCA units in the area to defend them. You don't have to destroy them all to complete your objectives, but since you'll be able to claim some bonus pay for each that you do, a methodical and thorough sweep through the area is recommended. In a final attempt to put a stop to your trail of destruction around the base, the PCA will then send in a pair of their new experimental craft that you'll battle with Rusty's help.

MISSION OBJECTIVES

- Destroy all Berthed Heavy Warships
- Prepare for Enemy Reinforcements
- Intercept Enemy Reinforcements
- Destroy the HC and high-mobility LC
- Identify Signal Approaching From Underground

MISSION INFO

Combat Zone	Central Ice Field—Old Bertram Spaceport
Client	Arquebus Corporation
Reward	320,000
Max Bonus Pay	370,400
Completion Unlocks	Arena: B Rank Mercenary Registration
Combat Logs	Silver x3
Data Logs	—
Part Containers	—

ENEMY DATA

		No.	AP	AS	Bonus Pay	Analysis
●	MT-T-026 Guard Mech (Laser Gun)	4	102	121	800	P.310
●	CH-T-025 Attack Helicopter (Laser Gun)	5	28	—	800	P.308
●	AS07: HEAVY WARSHIP (Turrets)	40	90	—	—	—
●	AS07: HEAVY WARSHIP (Cannons)	18	134	—	—	—
●	AM14: SENTRY SG MT (Missile Launcher)	16	437	310	3400	P.320
●	AM14: SENTRY SG MT (Electrothermo Cutter)	10	437	310	3400	P.321
●	AM14: SENTRY SG MT (Grenade Cannon)	4	437	310	3400	P.321
○	Artillery (Pulse Cannon)	4	246	—	4000	P.330
●	Artillery (Plasma Missile Launcher)	3	280	—	4000	P.330
●	AS07: HEAVY WARSHIP (Berthed)	5	1344	—	—	—
●	AS07: HEAVY WARSHIP	2	2688	—	—	P.341
●	AA18: LIGHT CAVALRY (Support Type)	5	5730	1066	22000	P.332
○	AA18: LIGHT CAVALRY (Enforcement Officer Spec)	1	8595	1750	30000	P.331
◇	AA18: LIGHT CAVALRY (Sniper Type)	4	1075	837	6000	P.332
●	AA22: HEAVY CAVALRY / PCA Captain	1	16235	1800	50000	—
●	AA18A: LIGHT CAVALRY HM / PCA 1st Lieutenant	1	15758	1750	40000	—

ASSEMBLY

This mission takes place in a large area with a particularly high number of enemies throughout it, and a significant amount of them are tough opponents. Because of that, it's recommended that you choose your weaponry to suit multiple one-on-one encounters rather than groups. The ZIMMERMAN shotguns can destroy a Subject Guard MT in a single shot and pack enough of a punch to also be useful against sturdier enemies, and the consistently deadly dual SONGBIRDS grenade cannons are a good choice for your heavy hitters.

Mobility, both for getting around the area quickly and to help with evasion against the HC and LCs, should be a factor you strongly consider for your frame. With that in mind, it's recommended to use the RC-2000 SPRING CHICKEN legs for their mix of good mobility specs and respectable load limit that allows for the recommended choice of weaponry. If you're using the SG-027 ZIMMERMAN shotguns, you'll be spending a lot of time at close or medium range, so the FCS you equip should reflect that, and the FC-008 TALBOT has the best ratings in both that you can get at the moment.

01	R-ARM UNIT	SHOTGUN SG-027 ZIMMERMAN	P.54	
02	L-ARM UNIT	SHOTGUN SG-027 ZIMMERMAN	P.54	
03	R-BACK UNIT	GRENADE CANNON SONGBIRDS	P.66	ELINITE
04	L-BACK UNIT	GRENADE CANNON SONGBIRDS	P.66	ELINITE
05	HEAD	— AH-J-124 BASHO	P.77	AWS
06	CORE	— 07-061 MIND ALPHA	P.81	
07	ARMS	— 04-101 MIND ALPHA	P.84	
08	LEGS	REVERSE JOINT RC-2000 SPRING CHICKEN	P.86	RaD
09	BOOSTER	— BST-G2/P04	P.88	
10	FCS	— FC-008 TALBOT	P.90	
11	GENERATOR	— VP-20C	P.92	

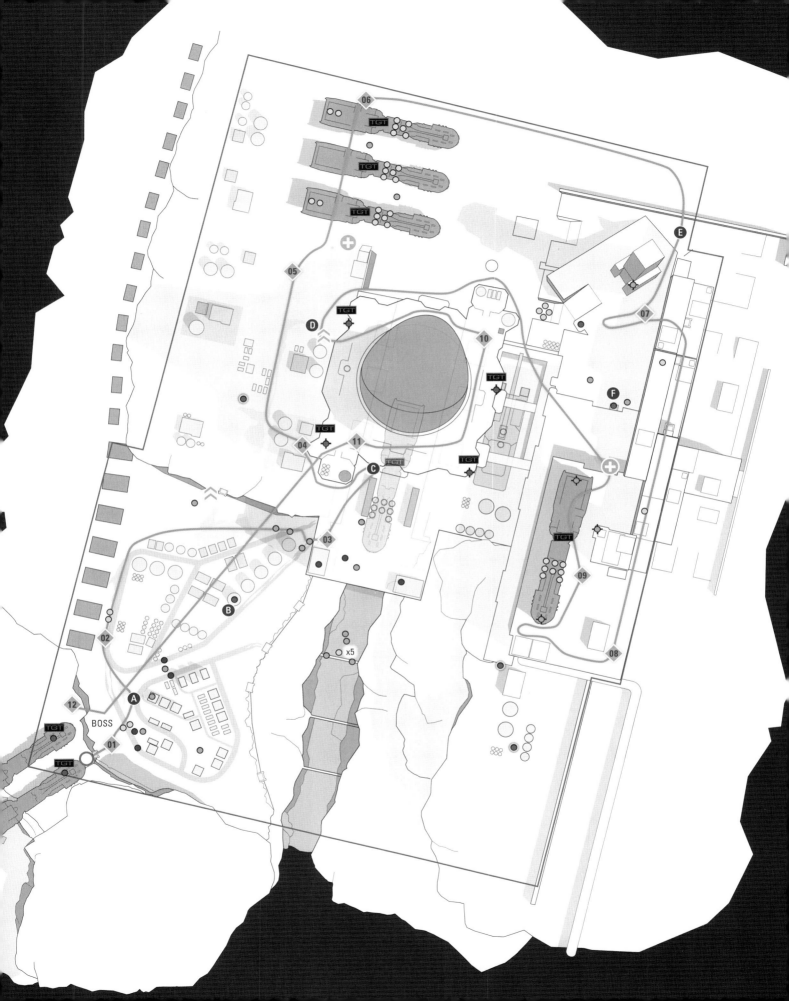

BONUS PAYDAY

The locations of the berthed warships will be placed on your HUD as soon as the mission starts, so the main thing you need to consider is your route to them. You can head straight for them, boosting past all of the other enemies, but doing so will cost you a considerable amount of bonus pay; this route through the mission is based on racking up an optimal amount of bonus pay while progressing toward the main objectives.

01 ◈ From your starting position atop the cliff, you'll be able to see a group of enemies directly below you that includes a couple of pulse cannon artillery installations capable of firing high-damage pulse blasts. To avoid having to deal

with them and the enemies below at the same time, destroy them both with a shot from your grenade cannons. Doing so will alert all of the other enemies to your presence, so quickly drop down and begin using your shotguns to take them out while taking cover behind the concrete barricades. There are a lot of buildings in the area, so use your scanner periodically to ensure that there are no enemies left hidden behind one of them before you proceed

Once the first group has been destroyed, move around the corner slightly at **Position A** so that you can get an angle to destroy the next two artillery installations and Subject Guard MTs. Make sure not to get too close to them, because proceeding past that point will cause the LC perched on a rooftop at **Position B** to come boosting toward you, and you'll want to have everything else destroyed before that happens. When you're ready, move forward until you see the LC take off, and then get into a good position to attack it once it's within range. ▶ A

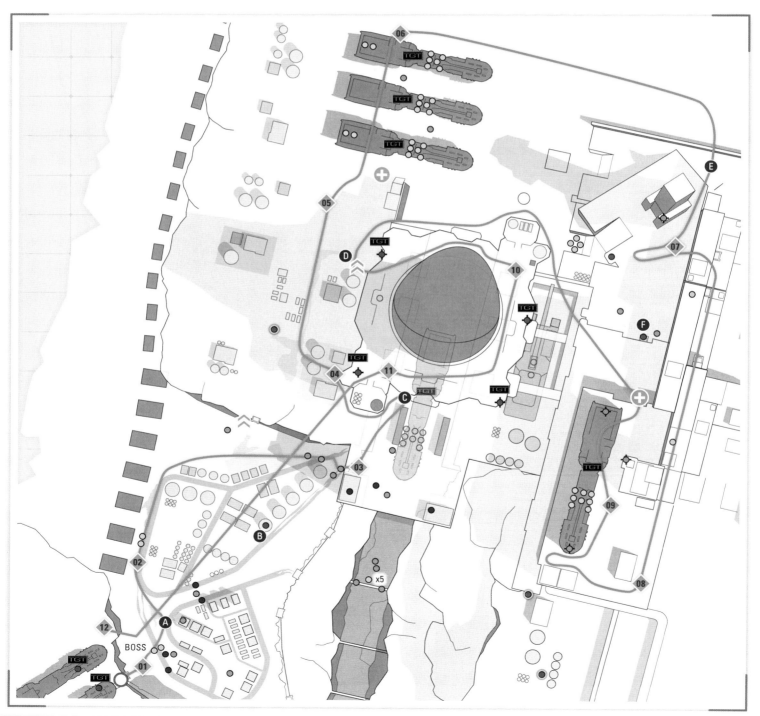

Blast the LC at point blank with both shotguns to stagger it, then unload all of your weapons for a quick kill. If you catch it while it's boosting in, you can destroy it before it starts attacking.

02 ◈ The warship in the underground hanger is the closest, so that should be your first target, but rather than going directly toward it, take the outside road around the area so that you can destroy a few more enemies along the way. Be careful when you reach the group of Subject Guard MTs just outside the hangar, because the warship inside will open fire on you when you're within range; use the hangar walls or storage tanks outside for cover while you deal with the Subject Guard MTs so that none of the warship's attacks hit you.

03 ◈ When the area outside the hangar is clear, instead of heading straight in, boost up on top of it and destroy the artillery installations and enemies up there. You can then go along the roof until you reach an opening at **Position C** and drop down onto the warship you need to destroy; you'll be behind all of its defenses and can safely fire on the command center to destroy it. ▶ B

04 ◈ Jump back up through the opening you dropped through and this time go around the rooftop to this location, from which you should be able to see another LC—this one with a combat log—just past some storage containers. This LC is equipped with a shield which, in conjunction with its maneuverability, can make it difficult to hit in open combat; try to Assault Boost up to it quickly when it's facing the opposite direction to catch it unaware and unload your shotguns to stagger it before it moves, then fire with everything you have for an easy victory.

05 ◈ The next three warships you need to destroy should be clearly visible at the back of the area, so start heading toward them. Once you're within range, Assault Boost up behind the command center of the closest one to minimize the effectiveness of their turrets. From there you can easily destroy the first warship, and then jump over to the next two, destroying each one as you go. ▶ C

TIME SENSITIVE

Depending on which warship you destroy last, the single supply sherpa in this mission will appear in one of two places. Destroy the warship in the hangar or the rear set of warships last and it'll appear near **Position D**, but if you destroy the side ship (at Step Point 09) last then it will appear closer to that ship. Once the supply sherpa arrives, you'll only have a very limited window within which to make use of its services. Once the reinforcements turn up it will disappear, along with some of the remaining LCs, potentially costing you a good deal of bonus pay. Take care of any cleanup before you destroy the last of the five warships.

06 ◈ There are many more opportunities for bonus pay in the mission, so the recommended approach is to continue past the previous warships until you reach the combat zone border, and then follow it along to the opposite side of the area. By taking this route you can flank around behind a lot of the enemies on this side of the area and put yourself in a better position to attack them from.

Jumping over the wall at **Position E** will trigger an alert, but only the Subject Guard MTs will investigate, so if you're quick, you can jump up and destroy the Subject Guard MT on the nearby building, and then wait behind it while two more from further down the area close in. When they're in range, destroy them without venturing out, so that the nearby LC doesn't spot you. The LC will hear the explosion and turn to look at it, so peek around the corner and wait until it turns

After destroying the first warship, make sure to descend into the ravine and destroy the patrolling group of enemies down there for more bonus pay.

back around, and then Assault Boost over to it and use your shotguns to stagger it before finishing it off in the same manner as the previous LCs.

07 ◈ The LC at **Position F** should still be unaware, but since it's looking in your direction, a quick detour is in order to ensure you get an early advantage. Jump onto the buildings here and move along the outside of the rooftops until you're behind the LC, and then boost down and blast it with your shotguns it before it can take off to safely destroy it as usual. Jump back up to the rooftops and continue along them, taking out the guard mechs and Subject Guard MTs along the way, including those on top of the warship, so that you can reap the bonus pay from them.

08 ◈ There are still two more LCs left at this point, both of which have combat logs, and you should attempt to destroy them first before the warship so that you get the maximum benefit from the supply sherpa that arrives once the warship has been destroyed. If you drop down to this point you can cross in front of the warship until you're behind the first LC and easily catch it unaware with your shotguns. The next LC is likely to be alerted by the fighting in the area, so try to destroy the first one as quickly as possible and catch the second one while it's still near the large storage tanks, so that its maneuverability is limited.

There are Subject Guard MTs and guard mechs defending these warships, but you should ignore them until after you've destroyed the warships, since those are the biggest threat.

| OBJECTIVE | Prepare for Enemy Reinforcements |

09 ◈ With all of the other enemies destroyed, turn your sights to the warship and Assault Boost up over it so that you can target the command center with your grenade cannon to quickly destroy it. Take advantage of the supply sherpa's facilities when it arrives nearby, and then start heading back over to the vertical catapult at **Position D** and use it to reach the top of the large central structure, so that you can get into position for when the reinforcements arrive.

10 ◈ The reinforcements that arrive are two pairs of sniper LCs on the top of this structure, all equipped with laser sniper rifles. Thankfully, however, these LCs are significantly less durable than the other ones you encountered in this mission, and their weaponry requires them to be stationary to fire, which also makes them easy targets for your shotguns. There's plenty of cover to use up here if needed, so just move around the rooftop destroying the LCs as you encounter them.

Intercept Enemy Reinforcements

11 ◈ Shortly after the LCs arrive, you'll hear the PCA over your comms demanding your surrender as two of their warships fly into the area from near where you started the mission. They'll begin quite high and approach the central structure while firing their lasers, but there's plenty of cover that you can use to keep safe. Once they get close to this area, they'll descend slightly and start firing on you with their turrets, and that's when you should make your move. The first warship can be easily destroyed from here with your grenade cannons, but to reach the second one you'll need to Assault Boost down toward it first. Destroying the second warship triggers a cutscene during which a pair of high-ranking PCA officers will boost into the area as a last-ditch attempt to defend the spaceport, but thankfully, V.IV Rusty is finished with his other responsibilities and will join you for the fight. ▶ A

The two PCA officers begin the fight next to each other, but you should try to separate them as quickly as possible.

AA22/AA18A

HEAVY CAVALRY / PCA CAPTAIN & LIGHT CAVALRY HM / PCA 1ST LIEUTENANT

BASIC SPECS

	LC	HC
AP	15758	16235
Attitude Stability	1750	1800
Anti-Kinetic Defense	1000	1060
Anti-Energy Defense	1375	1413
Anti-Explosive Defense	1260	1305
Elec. Discharge Tolerance	500	500
Shock Resistance	0%	15%
ACS Anomaly Tolerance	500	500
Heat Resistance	0%	10%

Destroy the HC and high-mobility LC

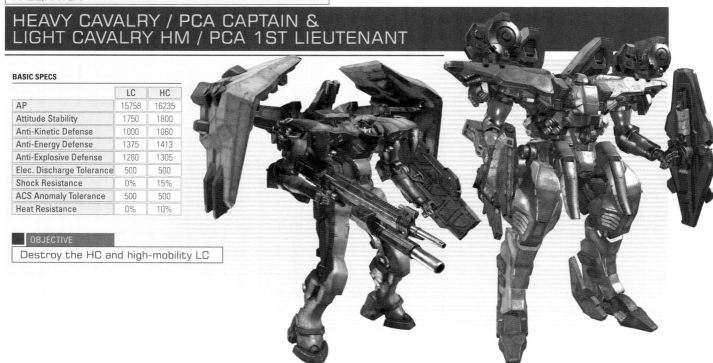

GOT MY BACK, BUDDY?

The enemies in this battle are capable of inflicting a lot of damage, and if left alone, Rusty can easily sustain critical damage, causing him to leave the battlefield. If that happens you'll have to contend with both enemies at once, making the fight significantly harder, so helping Rusty out is in your best interests; if you notice him in trouble, quickly boost over and try to take some of the heat off him.

The pilots for both of these units are significantly more skilled than any PCA pilots you've previously encountered and their attacks are much more difficult to evade, especially those from the HC. Because of how aggressive and dangerous this HC is, it's recommended that you take it on first and allow Rusty to keep the LC busy, so that you don't have to worry about getting shot from behind. The HC is primarily a melee-focused unit, although it does have some ranged capabilities, and that means you'll be engaging it predominantly at close range, putting a lot of pressure on your movement skills. This battle is the main reason for equipping the reverse-joint legs, so that you can take full advantage of the extended Quick Boost distance, and the extra jumping height to facilitate firing down on the HC with your grenade cannons.

Rusty will engage the enemies first, since you'll need to jump over the wreckage of the warship to reach them, but even though you want to keep him away from the HC for most of the fight, at the start it's worth waiting for a second or two so that the HC targets Rusty. With it distracted, you're free to quickly get into optimal range to deliver a powerful opening attack with all of your weapons, inflicting huge amounts of ACS strain and hopefully staggering it. Keeping up the pressure will ensure that the HC is on the back foot and reacting to you rather than being able to mount its own offense. If you do need to evade any of its attacks with a Quick Boost, try to retaliate with a Boost Kick or Quick Boost back into close range again and use your shotguns as quickly as possible. ▶ B

The high-mobility LC will largely spend most of the fight hovering above the battlefield trying to fire at either you or Rusty, but if you're staying mobile and keeping the fight with the HC away from it, Rusty should keep it busy until you're ready to face it. Hitting the HM LC can be difficult given how fast it moves, so try to position yourself such that there's something in the environment behind it to limit its movement options. Similarly, pay close attention to when it moves and only attack it when it comes to a stop, because anything else is likely to just be a waste of ammo. It will attempt to create some distance for some of its more dangerous attacks, so if you see it boost away, seek cover until the attack is over and then resume your normal offensive until it's defeated.

LIGHT CAVALRY HM / PCA 1ST LIEUTENANT ATTACKS

SHIELD

DESCRIPTION Armored shield that the HM LC will raise when it hovers, usually while firing its kinetic rifle.

EVASION Not used offensively.

ASSAULT RIFLE

DESCRIPTION Fires an assault rifle at you from any range. Can be used while boosting toward you.

EVASION Quick Boost away from the direction in which the HM LC is firing toward.

WING MISSILE LAUNCHER

DESCRIPTION The HM LC will fire off a high-volume missile salvo in front of it. The missiles will rapidly pincer your AC.

EVASION Seek cover behind structures in the environment to help shield from some of the missiles, or Quick Boost directly underneath the HM LC.

MULTI MISSILE LAUNCHER

DESCRIPTION The HM LC will release a lower volume of front-facing missiles; can release the salvo more than once in rapid succession.

EVASION Quick Boost to either side of the missiles.

BAZOOKA

DESCRIPTION Fire a single fast-moving explosive shot with a large blast radius at your AC.

EVASION Immediately jump into the air and boost away from the explosive, ensuring it doesn't hit the ground and create an explosion.

HEAVY CAVALRY / PCA CAPTAIN ATTACKS

PULSE SHIELD

DESCRIPTION Pulse shield that it can charge at you with.

EVASION Quick Boost to either side of the charge.

PULSE SALVO

DESCRIPTION Large salvo of pulse orbs that are fired in a wide cone. Used at close range.

EVASION Can either be jumped over, or create enough distance to render the effects of the orbs negligible.

TWIN PULSE BURSTS INTO CHARGING DOWNWARD SLASH ▼

DESCRIPTION Large bursts of pulse energy that will sometimes be followed by a downward slash from midair.

EVASION Create distance and boost into the air.

LARGE HORIZONTAL SWEEP

DESCRIPTION The HC will charge its pulse blade above its head briefly and come in with a far-reaching and almost 360-degree horizontal sweep.

EVASION Quick Boost immediately away when you see it charging its pulse blade.

HEAVY DOWNWARD SLASH

DESCRIPTION HC will jump in the air for a brief period and charge its pulse blade, after which it will Quick Boost at you and swing the blade in a downward, diagonal swing.

EVASION Quick Boost underneath the HC if you're close, or away out of range.

HEAVY UPPERCUT

DESCRIPTION Follow-up to the heavy downward slash depending on your proximity.

EVASION Quick Boost directly past the HC or away from it depending on your distance.

FAST DOWNWARD SLASH

DESCRIPTION Lower-impact but faster version of the heavy downward slash used at medium range.

EVASION Quick Boost away.

While it is preferable for Rusty to distract the HM LC, it may happen that he instead focuses on the HC.

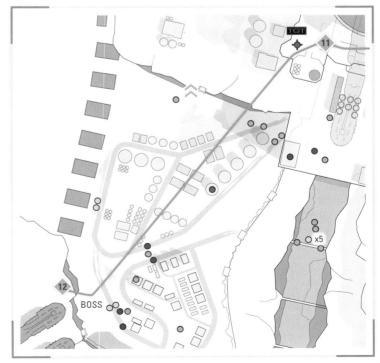

OBJECTIVE

Identify Signal Approaching From Underground

12 ◆ Quickly boost up to the elevated ridge in front of you once the two PCA officers have been defeated, because the PCA will authorize the use of an autonomous C-Weapon that will soon burst into the area below, and if you're still down there at that point it can very easily damage you. From your vantage point up you'll be able to safely watch as the C-Weapon demolishes much of the area surrounding the spaceport before leaving, at which point the mission is complete.

ELIMINATE "HONEST" BRUTE

"Ah, my new friend! You're here at last!"
—"Honest" Brute

Your objective is to retrieve a weapon needed to destroy the ICE WORM, which was stolen from Carla by a RaD defector named "Honest" Brute. The objective may be simple, but reaching him is anything but. To get there you'll need to make your way across the ancient Grid 012 area that's comprised almost entirely of half-collapsing small platforms suspended below the newer sections of the Grid above. "Honest" Brute has a lot of Doser hardware in the area for backup, and since Carla is willing to pay handsomely for each one that you defeat, the numerous part containers and logs should not be the only things motivating you to explore the entire area.

MISSION OBJECTIVES

Reach Center of Grid 012's Collapsed Area

MISSION INFO

Combat Zone	Contaminated Zone—Grid 012
Client	"Cinder" Carla / RaD
Reward	50,000
Max Bonus Pay	500,400
Completion Unlocks	Complete Before "Defend the Old Spaceport" & Historic Data Recovery": RaD Emblem. Completed After "Defend the Old Spaceport" & Historic Data Recovery": RaD Emblem, VE-60SNA Stun Needle Launcher, Arquebus Advanced Development Division Emblem
Combat Logs	Platinum x1, Silver x1, Bronze x3
Data Logs	2
Part Containers	3

PRACTICE MAKES PERFECT

Normally you don't get to preview what a boss fight will be like beforehand, but this mission is one of the rare occasions where you can. At the end of this mission, you'll face off against AC MILK TOOTH, who also happens to be the final B-rank opponent in the Arena, which you unlocked upon completing the previous mission. If you want to see how your build will do against MILK TOOTH, then take it into the Arena and see how you fare, then make any changes before attempting the mission itself.

Comms Record: Coyote Chatter

WB-0010 DOUBLE TROUBLE

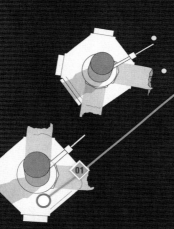
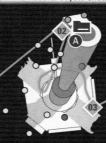
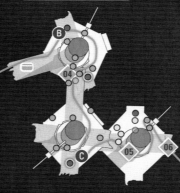

ENEMY DATA

	No.	AP	AS	Bonus Pay	Analysis
AM06: WATCHER	17	101	175	—	P.338
MB-0202 TOYBOX	6	1848	1053	19200	P.325
MB-0100 CLUTCH Crawler MT (Heavy Rocket Launcher)	32	650	364	8400	P.318
MB-0100 CLUTCH Crawler MT (Electro Saw)	3	650	364	8400	P.319
MB-0100 CLUTCH Crawler MT (Stun Plug)	2	650	364	8400	P.319
MT-J-048 Tetrapod MT (Grenade Cannon)	1	13370	2200	36000	P.324
MT-E-104 Bipedal MT (Missile Launcher)	8	470	364	3600	P.316
MT-E-104 Bipedal MT (Grenade Cannon)	2	470	364	3600	P.316
MB-0202 TOYBOX (Pulse Protection)	1	1848	1053	19200	P.325
AC MILK TOOTH / "Honest" Brute	1	11320	1797	—	—

BC-0600 12345

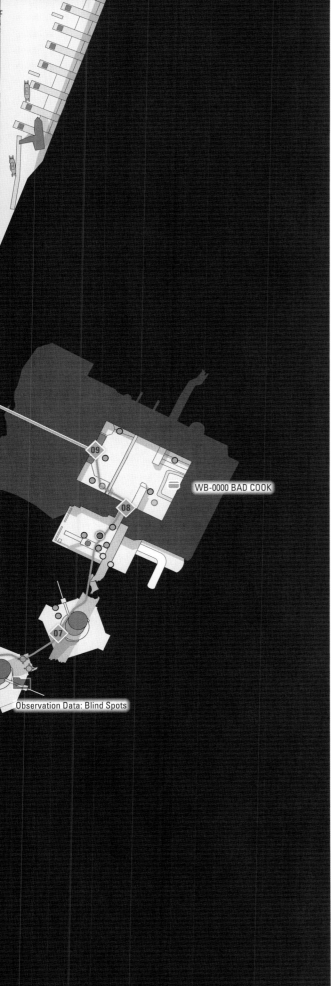

WB-0000 BAD COOK

Observation Data: Blind Spots

01 For the majority of your time in this area, you'll be descending along a series of large platforms, and the elevation changes in conjunction with all of the debris can make backtracking both confusing and difficult to attempt. If you want to destroy all of the enemies for bonus pay and collect everything in the mission, then it's best to take a slow approach and clear each section as you come to it. Before beginning your descent, however, you should bypass the nearest platform below you and instead Assault Boost over to a small platform halfway up an adjacent support pillar at **Position A**.

02 It's a vast gap to cover, and the recommended setup should just about get you to the ledge below the platform, and from there you can jump up and destroy the pair of crawler MTs before accessing the data log. Start making your way down the pillar now, but be careful as you do so, because the numerous WATCHER drones hovering in the vicinity will start charging toward you and detonating once they're within range. It can be easy to lose track of them due to the angles of the ledges as you descend, so try to use the pillar itself for cover and move around it while dropping down. You'll find two TOYBOX MTs on this platform, but they won't be active until you get near them, so you can take them on one at a time with your pulse blade the instant they activate.

LASER SENSORS

From here, you'll be able to see the strong defensive blockade on the series of three linked platforms below you, the key component of which are the laser sensors equipped to a special crawler MT variant. These crawler MTs emit a red laser from a static position while being in a semi-powered-down state. They will not move or attack unless something either passes through their beam or damages them, without destroying them. If they are disturbed or damaged, however, not only will the crawler MT that made the initial detection fire off a large salvo of missiles, but all of the other crawler MTs near it will do the same. While you might evade one salvo, evading 10 is a very different story. In their powered-down state, your systems cannot target these crawler MTs, but you can manually aim at them or scan to make them targetable if you're within range.

03 In order to descend to the next platform safely you're going to have to do some careful navigating while slowly descending and using hover, if necessary, to make sure you're aligned between the lasers before dropping down again. The initial landing spot you should aim for is to the side

of the part container, which you can then access if you don't get too close. From that landing spot, move closer to the pillar ahead and use your laser cannon to pick off the two crawler MTs just to the right of it, but make sure not to hit the TOYBOX MT on that side yet. Instead, move around to **Position B** and destroy the TOYBOX MT there first, followed by the two crawler MTs on that side of the pillar. Continue around the pillar and pick off the last remaining crawler MT on this platform, after which you can boost underneath the laser emanating from the adjacent platform and destroy the other TOYBOX MT for its combat log. ▶ A

04 To continue clearing out the enemies, jump up onto the broken tracks directly above where the second TOYBOX MT was and destroy the crawler MT nearby. Work your way around this platform carefully picking off the crawler MTs as you reach them, making sure to destroy as many as possible before you reach the opposite side at **Position C**, so you can get the combat log from the TOYBOX MT there without worrying about tripping a laser.

05 There should only be a few crawler MTs and a final TOYBOX MT left in the area by this point. Jump across to the narrow ledge running around the pillar here, and circle around it, so you can get a clear shot at the crawler MT sitting on the platform on the opposite side. From there you can drop down and use your laser cannons to destroy the two crawler MTs from far enough away so you don't activate the TOYBOX MT, and then boost over and use your pulse blade to destroy it to fully clear the area.

ASSEMBLY

The threat of falling is constant throughout this mission, so equipping a pair of tetrapod legs for their hover capabilities is highly recommended, as is pairing them with a booster like the BUERZEL/21D to facilitate the need to Assault Boost across open spaces. Having good anti-explosive defense is also important, partly due to the number of TOYBOX MTs you're going to face, but mainly because MILK TOOTH has some particularly deadly explosive attacks; thankfully, the VP-424 legs shine in that department too.

A lot of burst damage is recommended for your weapon selection, because one of the best ways to deal with MILK TOOTH is to attack aggressively. A shotgun is a good choice for a close-range weapon, as it allows you to pick off most of the enemies you'll encounter in a single shot; anything that survives can be finished off quickly with the pulse blade, which is also one of the best weapons to help finish off MILK TOOTH. To round out your weapon loadout, it's recommended to take a pair of laser cannons to give you a strong ranged option that you can easily weave into your close-range offense when needed.

01	R-ARM UNIT | SHOTGUN **SG-027 ZIMMERMAN**	P.54
02	L-ARM UNIT | PULSE BLADE **HI-32: BU-TT/A**	P.65
03	R-BACK UNIT | LASER CANNON **VP-60LCS**	P.67
04	L-BACK UNIT | LASER CANNON **VP-60LCS**	P.67
05	HEAD | — **VP-44S**	P.78
06	CORE | — **DF-BD-08 TIAN-QIANG**	P.80
07	ARMS | — **EL-TA-10 FIRMEZA**	P.83
08	LEGS | TETRAPOD **VP-424**	P.86
09	BOOSTER | — **BUERZEL/21D**	P.88
10	FCS | — **FC-008 TALBOT**	P.90
11	GENERATOR | — **VP-20D**	P.92

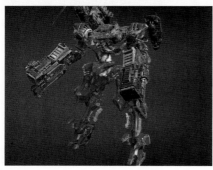

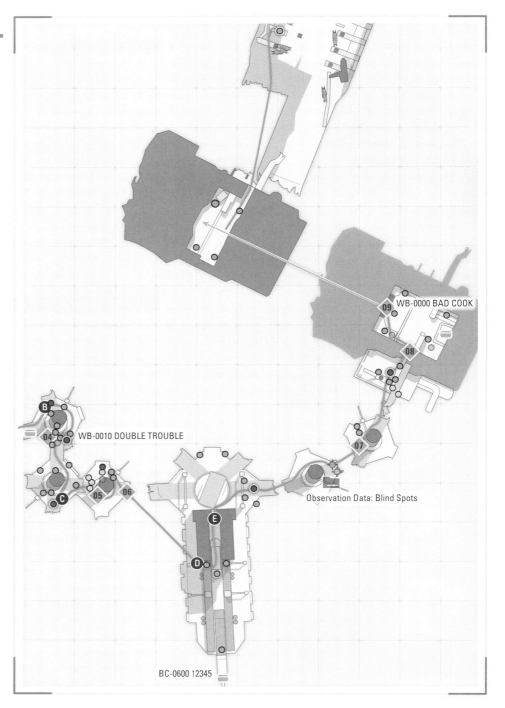

WB-0000 BAD COOK

WB-0010 DOUBLE TROUBLE

Observation Data: Blind Spots

BC-0600 12345

06 ◈ A dangerous tetrapod MT can be seen on the platform below from here, but what you can't see is the group of crawler MTs laying in ambush to the side of the platform close to it. Dealing with all of those enemies in a direct attack can be very dangerous, so instead, Assault Boost over to the opposite side of the pillar to **Position D** and destroy the crawler MTs on top of the crane there. Now you can drop down beneath the crane and use the tracks to reach the other side of the central pillar, at which point the crawler MTs will spring their ambush. By taking this approach, you'll have plenty of cover available and can easily pick them off as they appear. ▶ A

The tetrapod MT will typically stay in place, attempting to fire at you with its missile launcher as long as you don't venture out too far. If it does approach, you can simply retreat further back beneath the crane or jump up to some of the ledges on either side. Make sure to destroy all of the crawler MTs before you start your attack on the tetrapod MT, so that you only have to focus on it. When you're ready to attack it, keep in mind that it's strongest at range, so your best bet is to Assault Boost toward it as quickly as possible and try to pressure it with your shotgun and pulse blade. By rushing it down in that manner you should be able to quickly stagger it and finish it off.

07 ◈ Descend along the next platforms to reach this point and destroy the pair of bipedal MTs standing guard when you land. The entrance to a facility can be found on the next platform down, but as soon as you approach, the enemies defending it will deploy a large pulse barrier, making an attack from the outside all but impossible. There are a number of enemies within the barrier, but the biggest threat as always is the special TOYBOX MT generating the barrier, so try to locate it, then Assault Boost straight through the shield and destroy it as quickly as possible. The other enemies won't give you any time to rest, but each of them can be quickly destroyed by a single hit from any of your weapons, so boost around while picking them off before jumping up and taking out the missile-launching crawler MT last. ▶ B

08 ◈ Head through the narrow passage to enter the facility, but stop at the end of it before dropping down into the room, because there are numerous crawler MTs with laser sensors positioned around it. If you look down to the left from the end of the passage you'll be able to see one of those crawler MTs on a small ledge, so drop down and destroy it, then use your laser cannons to destroy the bipedal MTs below and the crawler MT on a ledge opposite you. Now you can drop down and work your way around the room destroying the remaining crawler MTs before accessing the part container once it's safe.

09 ◈ Use the opening in the floor here to reach a small ledge below, from which you'll be able to see the lasers from four more crawler MTs. Carefully drop down and hover toward the two at the back of the room and destroy them from above, after which you can land and easily take out the remaining two. No other enemies remain, so exit the room and finally begin your confrontation with "Honest" Brute.

The "Observation Data: Blind Spots" data log in this area is hidden at the base of the pillar in a small alcove, and to reach it you'll need to descend carefully and maneuver inside. To get back, Assault Boost up while taking a wide, steep angle so you don't hit the bottom of the platform.

"HONEST" BRUTE

AC // MILK TOOTH

MILK TOOTH is a dangerous AC with high-impact attacks and a flame-thrower that sees almost constant use, to the point where between the various environmental objects and the sea of flames in front of you, it can be very easy to lose track of where you and your opponent are. While the flamethrower is active, "Honest" Brute will still use some of the other attacks at his disposal, and they can be very difficult to evade when you can't see them coming. If you can locate the epicenter of the flames, then it can be effective to fire straight into them, because you'll either hit "Honest" Brute or force him to evade, which will give you a brief, flame-free moment to re-orientate yourself.

Using Assault Boost to create space can be effective if you need to reset and make a new approach, but generally you'll want to stay close to "Honest" Brute, because playing aggressively at close range is the best way to defeat him. Trying to play defensively will just lead to you getting hit by his flamethrower too much, and if your ACS anomaly gauge fills because of the flames, then the rest of the fight will be that much harder. Try to remain close to one of his sides to reduce the effectiveness of his flamethrower, or alternatively, use something in the environment to block it so that you can see where to go and make your move.

MILK TOOTH can be staggered reasonably easily if you land a few good hits and an attack with your pulse blade, but due to the nature of the constant movement and changing height levels in the fight, even once you've caused a stagger it can be difficult to capitalize on it. Try to orientate yourself beforehand so that you know where you're going the instant you stagger it, to ensure you deal the most damage possible. Brute does have access to repair kits, so try to maintain the pressure if you gain the advantage, and don't let up until he's defeated.

BASIC SPECS

AP	12320
Attitude Stability	1857
Anti-Kinetic Defense	1250
Anti-Energy Defense	1086
Anti-Explosive Defense	1268
Elec. Discharge Tolerance	490
Shock Resistance	-25%
ACS Anomaly Tolerance	490
Heat Resistance	-25%
Repair Kits	2

Instead of heading for the objective marker, you can skirt the left side of the room to get behind "Honest" Brute; He'll detect you as soon as he comes into view, but you can still get into position to launch an attack and gain an early advantage.

AC MILKTOOTH ATTACKS

WB-0000 BAD COOK

DESCRIPTION Flamethrower with particularly long range and extended usage that can be fired in any direction. Causes heat buildup and can inflict ACS anomaly.

EVASION Quick Boost to either side of the stream.

WB-0010 DOUBLE TROUBLE

DESCRIPTION Chainsaw melee weapon that Brute will attempt to rush you down with. Blades remain active for extended periods of time.

EVASION Quick Boost away from Brute as he charges at you.

BML-G2/P19SPL-12

DESCRIPTION Brute will fire two missiles that split apart into six micro missiles. These volleys have a high homing capacity.

EVASION Quick Boost to either side of the split missiles as close to when they reach you as possible.

SB-033M MORLEY ▼

DESCRIPTION Spread bazooka that can deal significant AP damage and high ACS strain at close range.

EVASION At close range, this weapon can be difficult to effectively evade. Create immediate distance and attempt to move to either the left or right.

DEFEND THE OLD SPACEPORT

"Let's see how far they can fly... on borrowed wings."

—Raven's Operator

While initially called in to protect the Old Bertram Spaceport from the PCA forces trying to recapture it, you find the battle already decided—but not in favor of either side you had been told to expect. The AC pilot, Raven, is standing as the lone survivor of an encounter likely between himself and both the PCA and Arquebus pilots. His attention is now turned toward you, the one who stole his name, and the ensuing battle will decide who will carry the moniker going forward.

MISSION OBJECTIVE
Defeat the Independent Mercenary Raven

MISSION INFO

Combat Zone	Central Ice Field—Old Bertram Spaceport
Client	Arquebus Corporation
Reward	200,000
Max Bonus Pay	—
Completion Unlocks	Completed Before "Eliminate "Honest" Brute & "Historic Data Recovery": AC NIGHTFALL Emblem Completed After "Eliminate "Honest" Brute & "Historic Data Recovery": AC NIGHTFALL Emblem, VE-60SNA Stun Needle Launcher, Arquebus Advanced Development Division Emblem
Combat Logs	Platinum x1
Data Logs	—
Part Containers	—

ENEMY DATA

	No.	AP	AS	Bonus Pay	Analysis
◉ AC NIGHTFALL / Raven	1	10569	1604	—	—

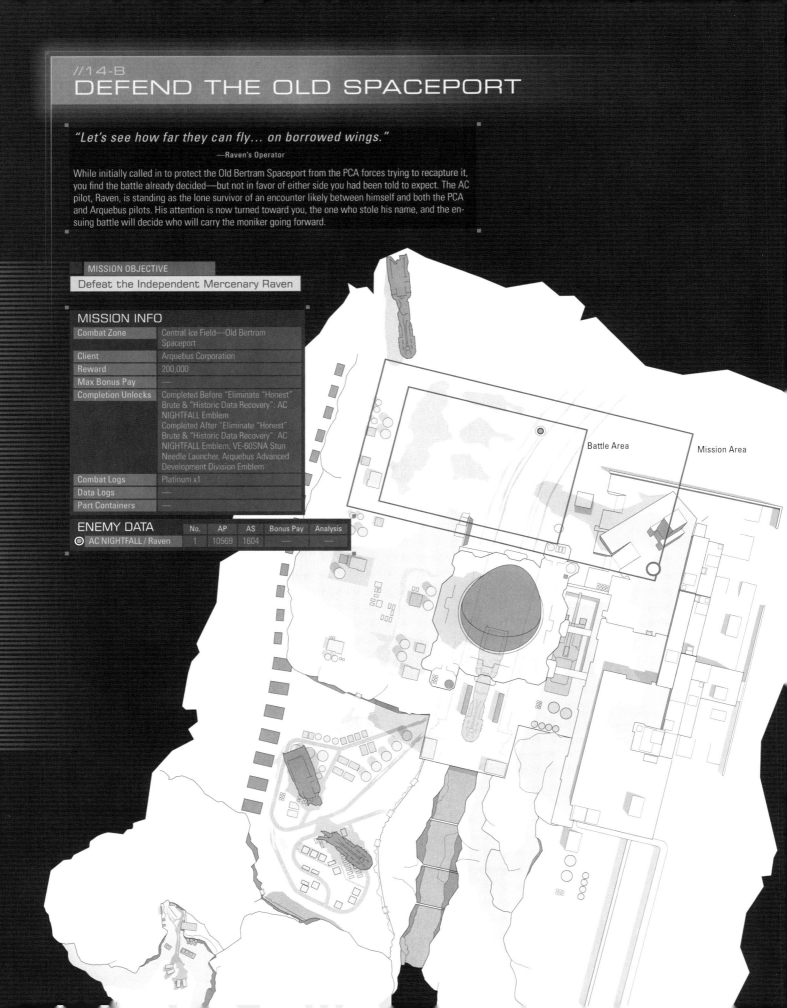

Battle Area

Mission Area

ASSEMBLY

With only one fight to consider, you can fully tailor your build toward dealing with Raven, and that means having as much attitude stability and anti-explosive defense as possible to mitigate the effectiveness of his SONGBIRDS. Reinforcing the defensive approach with your MIND ALPHA and BASHO frame parts gives you a strong enough foundation to mount an aggressive offense. Being able to Assault Boost through some of Raven's attacks without taking too much damage or accruing a lot of ACS strain is key to mounting the close-range offense that is recommended against him. Few weapons are as strong or versatile at that range as the dual ZIMMERMAN shotguns, and pairing them with dual SONGBIRDS grenade cannons allow you to very quickly stagger Raven, stopping him from mounting his own offensive.

01	R-ARM UNIT | SHOTGUN SG-027 ZIMMERMAN	P.54
02	L-ARM UNIT | SHOTGUN SG-027 ZIMMERMAN	P.54
03	R-BACK UNIT | GRENADE CANNON SONGBIRDS	P.66
04	L-BACK UNIT | GRENADE CANNON SONGBIRDS	P.66
05	HEAD | — AH-J-124 BASHO	P.77
06	CORE | — 07-061 MIND ALPHA	P.81
07	ARMS | — 04-101 MIND ALPHA	P.84
08	LEGS | TETRAPOD VP-424	P.86
09	BOOSTER | — ALULA/21E	P.88
10	FCS | — FC-008 TALBOT	P.90
11	GENERATOR | — VP-20C	P.92

AC // NIGHTFALL

BASIC SPECS

AP	9190
Attitude Stability	1654
Anti-Kinetic Defense	1100
Anti-Energy Defense	1059
Anti-Explosive Defense	1101
Elec. Discharge Tolerance	490
Shock Resistance	20%
ACS Anomaly Tolerance	490
Heat Resistance	20%
Repair Kits	3

You'll need to be ever mindful of your attack timing against Raven, because he's a skilled pilot and can easily evade poorly executed attacks. By far his most dangerous weapons are his SONGBIRDS and ASHMEAD pile bunker; whenever you're out of his melee range you need to always be prepared to Quick Boost the instant you hear the alert indicator in order to evade a shot from his SONGBIRDS. If you're within melee range and notice him begin charging toward you, it's possible to turn the tables on him by boosting backward out of range and counterattacking with your own grenade cannons.

Raven will constantly try to suppress you by boosting around while firing his SCUDDER assault rifle and missiles, and will typically try to position himself above or behind you in an attempt to fire down on you with his SONGBIRDS. Don't let him dictate the pace of the fight by reacting and trying to evade; instead, just charge straight toward him until you're within range to use your shotguns.

When you're further away, it can be worth using your grenade cannons knowing that Raven will evade them, just so you can create an opening to Assault Boost toward him and either Boost Kick him or use your shotguns. Although Raven likes to stay in the air, he doesn't have the EN to sustain it for very long, and if you have tetrapod legs, you can use that to your advantage by hovering above him, reducing the effectiveness of his SONGBIRDS while greatly increasing the effectiveness of yours. Defeat Raven to complete the mission and solidify your right to carry on the name.

After reducing NIGHTFALL's AP to around 50%, Raven will often use the assault armor Core Expansion.

AC NIGHTFALL ATTACKS

RF-025 SCUDDER

DESCRIPTION Assault rifle which Raven will use often throughout the fight.

EVASION Quick Boost in the opposite direction in which Raven is firing.

PB-033M ASHMEAD

DESCRIPTION Heavy-impact melee weapon with two stages of attack.

EVASION Quick Boost to either side of Raven when he comes in for the strike.

SONGBIRDS ▼

DESCRIPTION High-impact grenade cannon which fires two shots per attack.

EVASION Chain Quick Boosts to avoid both shots; Raven will not fire the second shot directly behind the first.

BML-G1/P32DUO-03

DESCRIPTION Three missiles fire to the left and three missiles to the right.

EVASION Quick Boost away as close to the moment of impact as possible.

ASSAULT ARMOR

DESCRIPTION AC NIGHTFALL charges energy and releases it as a large burst around itself.

EVASION Rapidly create distance from NIGHTFALL.

CHAPTER 3　MISSION INTEL　199

HISTORIC DATA RECOVERY

"Thank you for doing this for me... Raven."

—Ayre

Your previous trip into the Engebret Tunnel forced you to make a very hasty retreat, but now Ayre wants you to return and conduct a survey looking for historical relics from Rubicon's past before the tunnel is shut down for good. The information you're looking for is found on various wrecks throughout the tunnel that you'll need to reach and access, and there are also some non-mission critical PCA wrecks that you can obtain data from to sell for a hefty sum of bonus pay. A skeleton crew of PCA forces still remains in the tunnel, however, and you'll have to contend with them while you scout the area.

MISSION OBJECTIVE
Retrieve Data From Wrecks

MISSION INFO

Combat Zone	Central Ice Field—Engebret Tunnel
Client	Ayre
Reward	0
Max Bonus Pay	215,000
Completion Unlocks	Completed After "Eliminate "Honest" Brute & "Defend the Old Spaceport": VE-60SNA Stun Needle Launcher, Arquebus Advanced Development Division Emblem
Combat Logs	—
Data Logs	3
Part Containers	—

ENEMY DATA

	No.	AP	AS	Bonus Pay	Analysis
CD-E-086 Drone (Mini Gatling Gun)	2	40	—	—	P.308
AM01: REPAIRER (Worker Type)	17	51	—	—	P.313
AM01: REPAIRER (Guard Type)	4	51	—	—	P.313
AM01: REPAIRER (Stun Smog)	3	51	—	—	P.314
AM14: SENTRY SG MT (Flamethrower)	8	437	310	—	P.321
AM14: SENTRY SG MT (Missile Launcher)	2	437	310	—	P.320

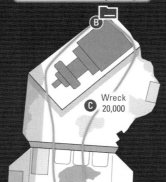

Text Data: Professor Nagai's Log (4)

B

C Wreck 20,000

Wreck 38,000 **F**

03

Wreck 85,000

02

D

Text Data: Dolmayan's Writings (2)

A Wreck 12,000

01

ASSEMBLY

The majority of the enemies you encounter on this mission are Subject Guard MTs or generic weaponry, so your weapon loadout should focus on multi-lock capabilities to facilitate the quick destruction of groups. With a full missile loadout and no difficult enemies you need to account for, a nimble frame comprised of lightweight parts that lets you move between objective locations as quickly as possible is recommended.

01	R-ARM UNIT | MISSILE LAUNCHER HML-G2/P19MLT-04	P.62	
02	L-ARM UNIT | MISSILE LAUNCHER HML-G2/P19MLT-04	P.62	
03	R-BACK UNIT | PLASMA MISSILE LAUNCHER Vvc-703PM	P.73	
04	L-BACK UNIT | PLASMA MISSILE LAUNCHER Vvc-703PM	P.73	
05	HEAD | — DF-HD-08 TIAN-QIANG	P.77	
06	CORE | — EL-TC-10 FIRMEZA	P.81	
07	ARMS | — 04-101 MIND ALPHA	P.84	
08	LEGS | BIPEDAL NACHTREIHER/42E	P.85	
09	BOOSTER | — ALULA/21E	P.88	
10	FCS | — FCS-G2/P10SLT	P.90	
11	GENERATOR | — VP-20C	P.92	

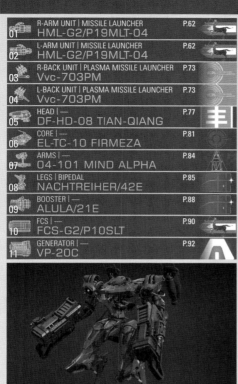

Wreck
60,000

Text Data: Professor Nagai's Log (2)

HUNTING FOR WRECKS

The wrecks in this mission do not have the usual tell-tale sparking effect that they often feature when there's data to be obtained from them. The specific wrecks containing the data logs are all clearly marked as objectives, but if you're looking for the ones with information to sell for bonus pay, you'll need to get close enough for the access prompt to appear before you can be certain it contains something valuable.

01 The basic terrain within the tunnel is the same as when you were here previously, but the Coral surge has caused significant damage to the PCA infrastructure inside, so you'll need to navigate through contorted bulkheads and half-destroyed walkways, much of which is still on fire. Proceed through the tunnel until you reach the ledge overlooking the first room once again, and then use a salvo of plasma missiles to destroy both of the crawler MTs inside, so that you can access the wreck at **Position A** for some bonus pay.

02 Ayre will update you with three locations that are likely to contain wrecks with the data you're looking for. The closest one is at **Position B**, and you can just about reach the opening of the room leading to it with an Assault Boost from here. Upon landing, immediately start using your multi-lock to target the crawler MTs and drones in the room, aiming to destroy most of them before they start attacking. One of the Subject Guard MTs is equipped with a flamethrower, so if it wasn't destroyed in your initial attack, make sure it's the priority target for the next salvo, so that you can destroy it before building up too much ACS anomaly. There are no enemies in the next section of the room, so after clearing the initial area, boost over and access the wreck at **Position B** for the data log, and the other wreck at **Position C** for some more bonus pay.

03 Return to the entrance of the room, and then Assault Boost over to the opposite side of the tunnel. Here, you can retrieve the second piece of data from the wreck at **Position D**, just at the entrance of the narrow section of the tunnel. Drop down the nearby ledges, but stop just before you reach the bottom, because if you turn around and look over the ledge into the dark hole at **Position E** you'll be able to spot a faint light coming from a wreck on a ledge below. This wreck offers the highest bonus payout in the mission, so drop down and access it before continuing down the ledges and across the bridge to **Position F** for another bonus pay wreck. ▶ A

04 Boost through the tunnel until you reach this point and try to fire a salvo of missiles at the Subject Guard MT standing near the ledge before it notices you, so you can destroy it easily. Drop down to the ledge below, and you'll be able to destroy the Subject Guard MT equipped with a laser rifle on an adjacent ledge; doing that will alert the remaining MTs in the room and they'll converge on you, so pick them off as they come into view. There are no enemies left after that, so you can safely retrieve the last piece of data from the wreck at **Position G**—just make sure you've accessed all of the bonus pay wrecks first, because once you have the final piece of data, the mission will come to an end.

The large number of REPAIRER drones on the way to **Position D** are not as passive as the other ones in the mission. If you linger in the area they'll release a cloud of stun smog that can rapidly build up your electrical discharge gauge.

15

DESTROY THE ICE WORM >

"Just so happens, the Redguns have a saying for this...
'You beg for your mother, we'll give you another!'"

—G1 Michigan

With the prototype weaponry given to you by Arquebus, and the Overed Rail Cannon developed by "Cinder" Carla of RaD, you just might have a fighting chance of destroying the C-Weapon IA-02: ICE WORM that was released by the PCA at the end of the "Attack the Spaceport" mission. You're the lynch-pin of the corporate coalition that was formed with the express purpose of waging war against the PCA and destroying this massive machine. Both corporations provide additional ACs to aid in its destruction, but with only one stun needle launcher, they're restricted to a supportive role and you'll need to take the lead and create the opportunities to deal a massive blow to the PCA and bring the ICE WORM down once and for all.

MISSION OBJECTIVE

Destroy the C-Weapon ICE WORM

MISSION INFO

Combat Zone	Central Ice Field—Unobservable Area
Client	Balam/Arquebus Joint-Operation
Reward	420,000
Max Bonus Pay	—
Completion Unlocks	Arena: A Rank Mercenary Registration, Parts Shop Update 6
Combat Logs	—
Data Logs	—
Part Containers	—

ENEMY DATA

	No.	AP	AS	Bonus Pay	Analysis
○ IA-02: ICE WORM (Drones)	12	224	175	—	—
● IA-02: ICE WORM	1	210000	4250	—	—

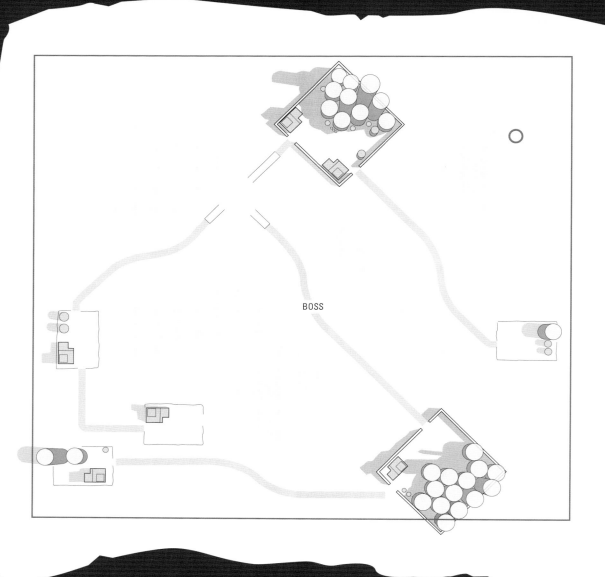

BOSS

ASSEMBLY

The VE-60SNA is all but essential for this mission, because without it the fight will take significantly longer and put you at greater risk, but the rest of your weapon slots are fairly flexible. Other than the ICE WORM, the only other enemies that you'll need to contend with are the drones that it releases at the start of Phase 2, so your weapons need to be able to easily destroy multiple enemies, but also deal enough damage to the ICE WORM to progress the fight quickly each time you bring it down. Missiles give you plenty of flexibility, since you can lock onto multiple enemies and fire them off while moving around.

All of the ICE WORM's attacks are Coral-based, and since none of your defenses can mitigate that damage type, focusing on speed to help you evade the attacks is a better choice. This frame gives you a lot of maneuverability and agility, while still having a decent amount of anti-energy defense to help against the EN lasers that the drones employ.

01	R-ARM UNIT | MISSILE LAUNCHER HML-G2/P19MLT-04	P.62
02	L-ARM UNIT | MISSILE LAUNCHER HML-G2/P19MLT-04	P.62
03	R-BACK UNIT | STUN NEEDLE LAUNCHER VE-60SNA	P.67
04	L-BACK UNIT | PLASMA MISSILE LAUNCHER Vvc-703PM	P.73
05	HEAD | DF-HD-08 TIAN-QIANG	P.77
06	CORE | EL-TC-10 FIRMEZA	P.81
07	ARMS | 04-101 MIND ALPHA	P.84
08	LEGS | REVERSE JOINT 06-042 MIND BETA	P.86
09	BOOSTER | — ALULA/21E	P.88
10	FCS | — FCS-G2/P10SLT	P.90
11	GENERATOR | — VP-20C	P.92

ICE WORM

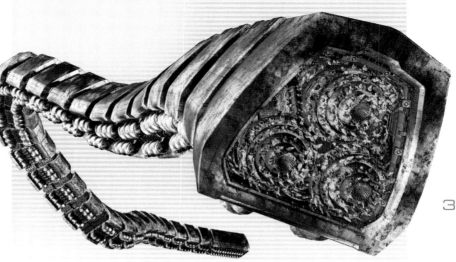

BASIC SPECS

AP	210000
Attitude Stability	—
Anti-Kinetic Defense	1257
Anti-Energy Defense	923
Anti-Explosive Defense	1411
Elec. Discharge Tolerance	—
Shock Resistance	—
ACS Anomaly Tolerance	—
Heat Resistance	—

ALLIES

AC	Pilot
HEAD BRINGER	G5 Iguazu
OPEN FAITH	V.II Snail
CIRCUS	"Chatty" Stick

OBJECTIVE   Destroy the C-Weapon ICE WORM

DISRUPTION OF DIALOGUE

At certain points during the fight against the ICE WORM, your allies will communicate specific lines of dialogue that you can use as audio cues to let you know that an opportunity to land a shot with your stun needle launcher is about to present itself. If one of your allies goes down before the point at which they should deliver their normal line, then you'll hear their defeat dialogue instead; however, even though the lines may change, the timing of events in the fight do not, so you can always use the dialogue as a guidepost.

Although there are multiple phases to this fight, the basic loop remains the same in each of them: you use the stun needle launcher to destroy the primary shield, then V.IV Rusty will use the rail cannon to destroy the secondary shield, after which the boss will be staggered. Staggering the boss causes it to collapse onto the ground, at which point you can damage it until it recovers. If you deal enough damage you'll push into the next phase of the fight; otherwise, you'll need to repeat the cycle until you can once again damage it. The thresholds for reaching the next phases of the fight occur at roughly every third of the boss's total AP that you deplete, and you'll know you're moving into a new phase because the ICE WORM will release an explosion when it rears up after recovering from the stagger.

Keeping track of the ICE WORM's location is one of the main things you need to contend with in the fight, because you'll only have very small windows within which you can land a clean shot to its head-mounted grinder with the stun needle. One of the best ways to keep track of it is by using your compass—it can track the signal of the ICE WORM and will always show you the direction in which you need to look to face it. Also keep in mind that just because the area the fight is taking place in is huge, it doesn't mean you need to constantly move around and try to get in front of the ICE WORM. In fact, for the first two phases, it can be very beneficial not to move at all unless you have to move out of the ICE WORM's way, because it often approaches along the same vector, and if you stick to facing toward coordinate 280, you'll usually be able to get clear shot opportunities.

PHASES

1 Your most convenient opportunity to shoot at the ICE WORM within Phase 1 comes almost immediately at the start of the fight. Begin with an Assault Boost toward the ICE WORM with your allies, and then come to a stop just before you run out of EN and listen for Snail to comment on the mission participants "Acting like a professional outfit…," at which point—if you're facing roughly coordinate 260—you'll see the ICE WORM rear up and give you a clear line of sight to its head-mounted grinder. If you manage to land your stun needle shot, wait for it to stagger after Rusty lands the rail cannon shot, and then unload all of your weapons, including the stun needle launcher, into it, you should be able to deal enough to damage to move to the next phase.

Miss that early opportunity and you'll need to be patient and wait for another one to present itself, and the most important thing to keep in mind is the timing of your shot. The stun needle launcher has a fairly slow firing speed, and a long reload time, so you need to fire it slightly ahead of when you think the ICE WORM's head-mounted grinder will come into view; if you wait until it's looking right at you, your shot will likely miss, and due to the reload time, you won't get a second shot and will have to wait for another opportunity. Keep your sights trained in the general direction of coordinate 280 as often as possible, and you shouldn't have to wait long before you can take another shot.

The main thing to watch out for during this phase is the position of the ICE WORM itself, because it incidentally hitting you while moving around is enough to inflict a significant amount of AP damage. Its burrowing missile launcher can be equally deadly because the Coral torpedoes it contains are released in large numbers and if you're not constantly keeping the ICE WORM in your sights to see when they get released, they can sneak up on you and are difficult to evade at the last moment; keep alert, and if you see the torpedos coming, make sure to jump and stay airborne until their explosions have dissipated.

2 The ICE WORM opens this phase by releasing a swarm of drones onto the battlefield, and while they can fire on you, try not to focus on them too much and keep your sights on the main target. Your allies will often take the lead against the drones and deal with most of them for you. If any do get past them, quickly destroy them with your missiles, because while they don't pose much of a threat, having additional targets on your compass makes keeping track of the ICE WORM more difficult. The general movement and stun needle shot opportunities remain largely the same in this phase as the first, so take your shots when they present themselves, and after damaging it enough, get ready for the transition into the final and most dangerous phase of the fight. ▶ A

There is a guaranteed opportunity similar to Phase 1 in which you can easily disrupt the ICE WORM's shield. Listen for the line "Sure is an honor to be praised by the Redguns' 'Hell on Four Legs'… but I'll pass." The ICE WORM will then rear up toward coordinate 290 giving you a clear shot, just be sure to move out of the way quickly afterward.

ONE LAST SHOT

In previous phases, if you didn't deal enough damage to progress to the next phase during a single shield disruption, then you'd be able to disrupt it again and deal more damage. In this phase, however, if you do not defeat the ICE WORM after the first time you disrupt its shield you will not get a second chance. The surging Coral response from the ICE WORM gains so much strength that it permanently puts the rail cannon out of commission, and with no other means of disrupting the inner shield, the mission is a failure and you'll have to begin the battle all over again.

3 The ICE WORM becomes overcharged with Coral at the start of this phase, making it much more aggressive and erratic. It also gains access to a slew of new, and highly-damaging attacks which, coupled with the fact that you'll now need to land two shots with the stun needle launcher to disrupt its primary shield, makes this portion of the fight much harder than the previous phases. Whereas in the previous phases you'd naturally be presented with clear shots to fire off the stun needle, such opportunities are much rarer in this phase, so you should try to be a bit more active and put yourself in the position to land a shot based on what attack the ICE WORM is using.

The coral flash wave and coral shockwave are both good examples of attacks that you should be looking for, because both of them have extended windows within which the ICE WORM's head-mounted grinder is exposed enough to hit. Similarly, if you can position yourself in front of the boss before it initiates its sweeping strike attack, you can also get a clear shot at its head, but your priority with that attack should be identifying it fast enough so that you can get clear of it; merely brushing past you with this attack will likely destroy your AC, regardless of your assembly. Because of all of the Coral energy coming off the ICE WORM's body, you'll want to stay further away from it than you might have done previously, and keep on the move to ensure that you maintain that distance at all times. Continue looking for your moments to fire, and after disrupting its shield for a third time, don't hold anything back and keep firing until it's destroyed.

GROUND SPIKE

DESCRIPTION Rears up, pauses briefly, and quickly comes back down head first to dig into the ground.

EVASION Quick Boost away from the impact point.

CORAL MISSILES

DESCRIPTION Volley of large, low-impact, overhead missiles fired from its back-mounted multi missile launcher. Leaves behind a lingering damage field.

EVASION Chain Quick Boosts to avoid the impact and the damage fields.

CORAL TORPEDOES

DESCRIPTION Volleys of missiles from its burrowing missile launcher that plant themselves into the ground and travel quickly toward you. They have homing capacities and spread over a wide area.

EVASION Jump into the air to see them as they approach and Quick Boost away from them.

DRONE UNITS — PHASE 2

DESCRIPTION Autonomous drones released over a wide area that shoot energy-based beams. Always begins Phase 2 with this attack.

EVASION Destroy the drones as they come into range.

PHASE SHIFT CORAL EXPLOSION — PHASE 3

DESCRIPTION The ICE WORM begins Phase 3 by charging and releasing a massive Coral energy explosion over a wide area.

EVASION Create as much distance as possible to get out of range.

LIMITED CORAL EXPLOSION ▼ — PHASE 3

DESCRIPTION A smaller version of the Coral explosion it released upon entering Phase 3.

EVASION Create distance between yourself and the ICE WORM.

CORAL FLASH WAVE ▼ — PHASE 3

DESCRIPTION The ICE WORM will rear up and release a wave of Coral in front of itself in a downward arc. It follows this up by dropping to the ground with its head exposed and charges toward you.

EVASION First Quick Boost away from the head of the ICE WORM to avoid the Coral, then Quick Boost to either side as it charges at you.

CORAL ERUPTION — PHASE 3

DESCRIPTION When the ICE WORM emerges from beneath the ground in this phase it will cause an eruption of Coral energy around the exit point.

EVASION Watch your compass to know roughly where the boss is while it's underground and Quick Boost away from its point of emergence.

CORAL SHOCKWAVE ▼ — PHASE 3

DESCRIPTION ICE WORM rears up before slamming down onto the ground releasing a shockwave of Coral energy followed by subsequent releases of Coral energy as it drags its head along the ground.

EVASION Quick Boost away from the head of the ICE WORM and jump above the shockwaves.

SWEEPING STRIKE ▼ — PHASE 3

DESCRIPTION The ICE WORM will emerge out of the ground and lay flat momenterily before sweeping its body in one direction across the ground while releasing Coral energy. Can be done twice in alternating directions.

EVASION Position yourself infront of the boss and far away so that the sweep passes in front of you.

16

UNDERGROUND EXPLORATION – DEPTH 1

"You're the only one who can do this. I'm counting on you to reach the Coral."

—Handler Walter

Before you can continue the exploration of Watchpoint Alpha, you'll need to make it past the first line of autonomous defenses and navigate your way down the vertical shaft that makes up Depth 1. Most of the defenses should be familiar to you, but the massive energy weapon at the bottom of the shaft, the NEPENTHES, is something entirely new and deadly. To get past the constant barrages of laser beams and missiles, you'll need to make use of various platforms and walkways, timing your movement to coincide with the brief periods during which the NEPENTHES recharges between shots.

AC ASSEMBLY

Your biggest priority here should be to increase your anti-energy defense as much as possible, to help mitigate some of the damage from NEPENTHES during your descent. A heavier build is also recommended, since a great deal of maneuvering isn't necessary, and the extra AP will help a lot in the event that you take a few hits; a mix of Arquebus and ALLMIND parts tick all of those boxes and are highly recommended. Most of the enemies in the mission are resistant to energy damage, so sticking to kinetic and explosive is a good choice, and you'll want a mix of close-range for heavy damage and multi-lock capabilities to deal with the different enemy types. One thing that can make your descent much safer is a shield, since you'll be able to use it to mitigate a lot of the damage from NEPENTHES's lasers, and the SI-27:SU-R8 has one of the best damage mitigation specs available.

No.	Part	Name	Page
01	R-ARM UNIT | SHOTGUN	SG-027 ZIMMERMAN	P.54
02	L-ARM UNIT | SHOTGUN	SG-027 ZIMMERMAN	P.54
03	R-BACK UNIT | MISSILE LAUNCHER	BML-G2/P03MLT-06	P.69
04	L-BACK UNIT | PULSE SHIELD	SI-27:SU-R8	P.76
05	HEAD | —	VE-44A	P.78
06	CORE | —	07-061 MIND ALPHA	P.81
07	ARMS | —	VE-46A	P.83
08	LEGS | TETRAPOD	VP-424	P.86
09	BOOSTER | —	ALULA/21E	P.88
10	FCS | —	FCS-G2/P10SLT	P.90
11	GENERATOR | —	VP-20C	P.92

MISSION OBJECTIVES

Reach the End of Depth 1

Destroy the NEPENTHES Artillery Platform

MISSION INFO

Combat Zone	Watchpoint Alpha—Depth 1
Client	Arquebus Corporation
Reward	250,000
Max Bonus Pay	—
Completion Unlocks	—
Combat Logs	—
Data Logs	—
Part Containers	1

IA-C01L: EPHEMERA (Legs)

ENEMY DATA

		No.	AP	AS	Analysis
●	AM06: WATCHER	8	101	175	P.338
●	AM02: DENOISER (Melee Type)	4	1254	783	P.339
○	AM02: DENOISER (Sniper Type)	3	1254	783	P.339
●	AB08: NEPENTHES	1	4480	—	—

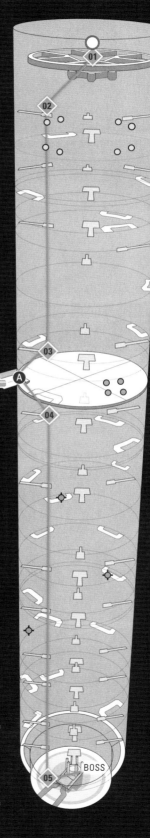

BOSS

01 ◈ At the top of the Depth 1 shaft, you'll find yourself standing on a large industrial elevator and are instructed by Walter to use it to reach the bottom. The access point is in the middle of the elevator, but almost immediately after using it, the enforcement system will recognize the infiltration and shut the

elevator down. A number of PCA WATCHER drones will attempt to encircle you at this point, so quickly move to the side of the shaft so they're all in front of you, allowing you to multi-lock with your missiles to destroy them all quickly. With the elevator out of commission, you'll need to rely on gravity to reach the bottom, and that means contending with the defense system that's responsible for wiping out large numbers of Balam forces, the NEPENTHES.

AB08

NEPENTHES

At the bottom of the Depth 1 part of the facility is the autonomous enforcement artillery platform NEPENTHES, which primarily attacks with its 6-shot laser cannon array capable of firing diffuse and heavy laser blasts through the entire height of the vertical shaft. It's also outfitted with a container plasma missile launcher that comes into play as you descend further. From this point on in the mission, you'll need to dodge its attacks while you continue your descent, something its target tracking systems won't make easy for you.

BASIC SPECS

AP	4480
Attitude Stability	—
Anti-Kinetic Defense	930
Anti-Energy Defense	1375
Anti-Explosive Defense	1000
Elec. Discharge Tolerance	500
Shock Resistance	0%
ACS Anomaly Tolerance	500
Heat Resistance	0%

AB08: NEPENTHES ATTACKS

DIFFUSE LASER BLASTS ▼   PHASE 1

DESCRIPTION The NEPENTHES can diffuse its energy into six laser blasts that are fired in rapid succession. The pattern of the blasts is in short bursts of three lasers at a time from its left to its right side.

EVASION Raise your shield and find cover beneath you.

HEAVY LASER BLASTS ▼

DESCRIPTION These focused laser blasts are slower than the diffuse shots, but significantly more powerful and can strain and overload your ACS quickly.

EVASION Raise your shield and find cover beneath you.

Even glancing blows from the lasers can inflict a lot of AP damage, and as you get closer to the bottom, NEPENTHES will begin using plasma missiles, alternating between them and its lasers and forcing you to change how you defend or move through the area. Between these attacks, you'll have small windows of opportunity to safely descend out in the open, but the various platforms and walkways can be used to provide additional cover and speed up your descent.

PLASMA MISSILES   PHASE 2

DESCRIPTION A high-volume volley of plasma missiles that leave behind lingering damage fields. The missiles themselves are large compared to your AC, but they are not high impact.

EVASION Raise your shield and find cover beneath you.

PLASMA WARHEADS   PHASE 2

DESCRIPTION Three large container plasma missiles are released from its center. These are very slow-moving projectiles that are fired in conjunction with the missiles.

EVASION Raise your shield and find cover beneath you.

02 ◈ Since you're going to be under almost constant fire from NEPENTHES as you descend, minimizing the amount of time you spend without one of the various platforms and walkways scattered along the shaft directly below you is crucial. There are three main types of platforms: long walkways that extend from the side of the shaft toward the center, smaller c-shaped platforms, and even smaller standalone platforms that can also be found along the side wall.

The long walkways that stick out from various points around the shaft offer you one of the easiest and safest methods for descending, because they appear directly under each other. That allows you to use them for cover while you descend by positioning yourself directly above them as you drop down, causing them to block most if not all of the lasers. When you land on one, simply wait for an opening between laser barrages to step off the side and drop down far enough to move back in slightly so you're above the net walkway below you, and repeat. Any time spent moving laterally increases the number of attacks that you'll have to contend with, and this approach minimizes that. To start your descent, simply look down from the elevator to locate the closest walkway, Assault Boost over to it, and then drop off the side when it's safe.

03 ◈ After descending for a while, a large partition will seal the shaft and prevent you from descending any further. A small squad of melee PCA DENOISER drones will take advantage of the situation and attempt to ambush you, but if you've been using the walkways for cover while descending, you should safely be standing on top of one, well out of their effective range.

Dropping down to face them directly can be quite dangerous, due to their strong melee attacks, but if you stay up on the walkway, they'll take turns trying to boost up to your position. Use your scan to locate them and pick them off with your

shotgun as they do, or peek over the edge and fire some missiles down at them. If you want to be a bit more proactive, you can make use of the tetrapod legs to move out from your cover and hover above them, so that you can attack more frequently. After clearing the room, you'll be directed to the partition controls at **Position A**, and if you boost over there and access them, the partition will open up and you can continue your descent. Make sure to access the part container in the back of the control room before moving on.

04 ◈ Resume descending using the walkways, which will still serve as good cover even after NEPENTHES starts launching plasma missiles. You can make slight adjustments to your descent angle as you fall to increase the number of missiles that hit the walkway. There are a few sniper DENOISERs on small platforms along the side of the shaft, but as long as you keep descending you'll easily avoid their shots.

Destroy the NEPENTHES Artillery Platform

05 ◈ The lower you get, the easier it will be to see NEPENTHES's attacks coming, since you'll actually be able to see the laser cannons themselves. Just keep in mind that it can angle its cannons, so it doesn't necessarily become easier to evade the lasers if you're out in the open. You can, however, use their charge time to your advantage once you're close to the bottom; you can forgo cover somewhat and just keep dropping, since you only have to get below the laser cannon array—not reach the bottom of the shaft—before the lasers can no longer hit you. The plasma missiles, however, can still hit you, so once you're at the bottom, quickly boost over close to the neck joint so that you can unload your shotguns into it and destroy the troublesome machine for good.

17

UNDERGROUND EXPLORATION – DEPTH 2

"Let's go, Raven. This is where the survey begins in earnest."

—Ayre

Depth 2, the second section of the Watchpoint Alpha complex, is a sprawling subterranean facility comprised of narrow tunnels and cramped rooms, forcing you to battle predominantly in close quarters. Enemies will often use this environment to their advantage by hiding around bends in tunnels or in corners of interconnected rooms, so you'll need to be prepared for combat at all times unless you're diligently scanning as you proceed.

The path through the facility is fairly linear, so you'll never have to venture far off the main path to find the collectibles or some extra enemies for bonus pay, making a high payout at the end of the mission all but a certainty. As long as you proceed cautiously, you'll rarely find yourself in multi-enemy encounters, but you'll still have to contend with a dangerous AC battle and boss at the end if you wish to continue your exploration of the complex.

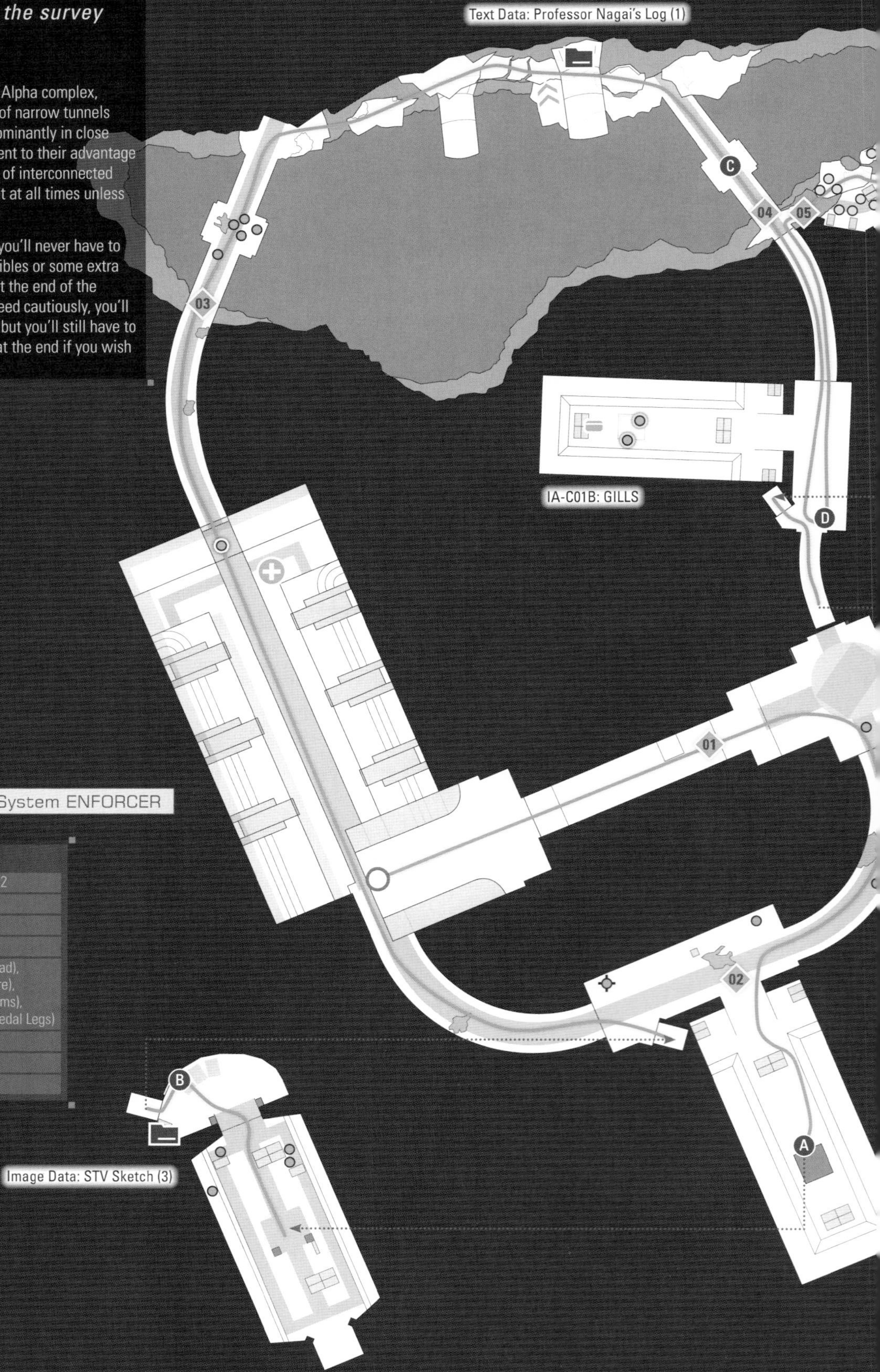

Text Data: Professor Nagai's Log (1)

C

04 05

03

IA-C01B: GILLS

D

01

MISSION OBJECTIVES

Reach the End of Depth 2 (1)

Defeat G5 Iguazu

Reach the End of Depth 2 (2)

Destroy the Automated Defense System ENFORCER

MISSION INFO

Combat Zone	Watchpoint Alpha—Depth 2
Client	Arquebus Corporation
Reward	300,000
Max Bonus Pay	218,200
Completion Unlocks	HD-012 MELANDER C3 (Head), BD-012 MELANDER C3 (Core), AM-012 MELANDER C3 (Arms), LG-012 MELANDER C3 (Bipedal Legs)
Combat Logs	Bronze x2, Gold x1
Data Logs	2
Part Containers	2

02

B

Image Data: STV Sketch (3)

A

IA-C01A: EPHEMERA

BOSS

ENEMY DATA	No.	AP	AS	Bonus Pay	Analysis
● AM01: REPAIRER (Worker Type)	8	51	—	800	P.313
● AM01: REPAIRER (Guard Type)	8	51	—	800	P.313
● AM01: REPAIRER (Stun Smog)	6	51	—	800	P.314
● MT-E-104 Bipedal MT (Dual Machine Gun)	6	470	364	2400	P.316
● MT-E-104 Bipedal MT (Cluster Gun)	3	470	364	2400	P.317
● AM02: DENOISER (Melee Type)	9	1254	783	9000	P.339
● AM02: DENOISER (Support Type)	4	1254	783	9000	P.340
● AM02: DENOISER (Sniper Type)	1	1254	783	9000	P.340
◎ AC HEAD BRINGER / G5 Iguazu	1	9690	1584	45000	—
● AAP03: ENFORCER / Enforcement System	1	10280	1598	72000	—

01 ◈ Your continued exploration of the Depth picks up exactly where you left off after destroying NE-PENTHES. The door leading further into the complex can now be accessed, so make your way through it and follow the tunnel down, destroying the DENOIS-ER at the bottom with your shotguns. Continue along the only open tunnel and dispatch the next enemy in the same manner, but when the tunnel opens up ahead, slow down and hug the inside wall to mask your approach from the two enemies. Use your scanner to locate the one closest to you, then boost and destroy it while using the debris in the area for cover against the incoming fire from the sniper DENOISER, which you can then boost over and finish off while it reloads. ▶ A

02 ◈ Attempt to access the partition leading further into the facility, and Ayre will tell you that the power to it is down and needs to be reconnected. The controls you need are on a lower floor. To reach that area, you'll need to head into the nearby room and drop through the hole at **Position A**. Be ready for combat as soon as you land, because there's a small group of bipedal MTs waiting below, but they only require a single shot from any of your weapons to destroy, so you can take them all out quickly without waiting to reload by using each of your weapons once.

The power controls are located at **Position B** just outside of the room, so head over and access them to restore the power to both the partition you need to open and the nearby elevator that takes you back up, right next to that door. Go through the partition and the next one to reach the heat exchange room, where G5 Iguazu is blocking your path; only by defeating him will you be able to delve deeper. ▶ B

Regularly use your scanner when moving through the narrow tunnels to avoid being caught unaware.

Before taking the elevator up out of this area, be sure to access the wreck hidden behind a concrete barricade for a data log.

AC ASSEMBLY

Given the close-quarters nature of many of the encounters in this mission, a heavier build that focuses on high AP and attitude stability is recommended to give yourself a bit of a cushion in case you get caught off guard or out of position. Many of the enemies, including the boss, make use of energy-based attacks, so when you're looking at defensive specs on parts, anti-energy should be the priority. A mix of mainly Arquebus and ALLMIND frame parts is recommended, but to come in underweight when you factor in the weapon suggestions, you'll need to use a lighter set of arms. For maximum close-range combat efficiency, dual ZIMMERMAN shotguns, and dual diffuse laser cannons are hard to beat and will give you more than enough firepower to overcome any foe that you encounter, though swapping one of the shotguns out for a melee weapon is also a good option.

01	R-ARM UNIT | SHOTGUN **SG-027 ZIMMERMAN**	P.54
02	L-ARM UNIT | SHOTGUN **SG-027 ZIMMERMAN**	P.54
03	R-BACK UNIT | DIFFUSE LASER CAN. **VP-60LCD**	P.67
04	L-BACK UNIT | DIFFUSE LASER CAN. **VP-60LCD**	P.67
05	HEAD | — **VE-44A**	P.78
06	CORE | — **07-061 MIND ALPHA**	P.81
07	ARMS | — **NACHTREIHER/46E**	P.85
08	LEGS | TETRAPOD **VP-424**	P.86
09	BOOSTER | — **ALULA/21E**	P.88
10	FCS | — **FC-008 TALBOT**	P.90
11	GENERATOR | — **VP-20D**	P.92

AC // HEAD BRINGER

HEAD BRINGER is not a particularly fast AC, but Iguazu is a smart pilot and will make use of the environment by constantly moving around behind cover or hovering in difficult-to-see positions. He'll also make efficient use of his weapons' ranges to maintain pressure on you regardless of where he is, and his aggressiveness means he can strain your ACS very quickly, so pay close attention and disengage to seek cover if needed.

BASIC SPECS

AP	9980
Attitude Stability	1704
Anti-Kinetic Defense	1208
Anti-Energy Defense	1153
Anti-Explosive Defense	1200
Elec. Discharge Tolerance	490
Shock Resistance	6%
ACS Anomaly Tolerance	490
Heat Resistance	6%
Repair Kits	1

OBJECTIVE

Defeat G5 Iguazu

There are numerous environmental obstacles in the room you're fighting in, which—coupled with Iguazu's evasive style—means you'll need to maintain your Target Assist and use your scanner as much as possible to keep track of him. Most of the fight will take place at close range, because even though the room is large, the structures within it often block most of the longer sight lines. Thankfully, that's the range at which the recommended loadout shines, so even if the bout comes down to trading blows, you should easily come out on top. You can afford to be a bit more reckless and not worry so much about conserving ammo, because as soon as you defeat Iguazu a supply sherpa appears, allowing for a handy restock. ▶ A

Iguazu will not wait for you to approach and will begin the fight as soon as you access the partition.

AC HEAD BRINGER ATTACKS

LR-036 CURTIS ▼ (CHARGED)

DESCRIPTION Kinetic linear rifle capable of rapid uncharged shots or a powerful charged shot.

EVASION Quick Boost to either side of the shots.

BML-G1/P20MLT-04

DESCRIPTION Launcher that releases four missiles with high coming capabilities.

EVASION Quick Boost to either side of the missiles as close to when they reach you as possible.

MG-014 LUDLOW

DESCRIPTION Rapid-firing machine gun capable of quickly straining your ACS.

EVASION Create distance so that the shots ricochet off you or Quick Boost to either side of the shots.

45-091 ORBT

DESCRIPTION Autonomous drone that hovers around Iguazu and fires laser bursts; can target your AC even if Iguazu himself is not directly facing you.

EVASION Strafe or Quick Boost away from the shots once you see the ORBT has been deployed.

HEAD BRINGER's most dangerous weapon is his linear rifle, with the highly damaging charged version being even deadlier; make sure to listen out for the alert indicator on the charged version and evade accordingly.

Take care approaching the end of the tunnel as the PCA ENFORCER will fire upon you the moment the door opens.

While you're making your way toward the Enforcement System you can jump on top of the large pipe above it and access a wreck for a data log.

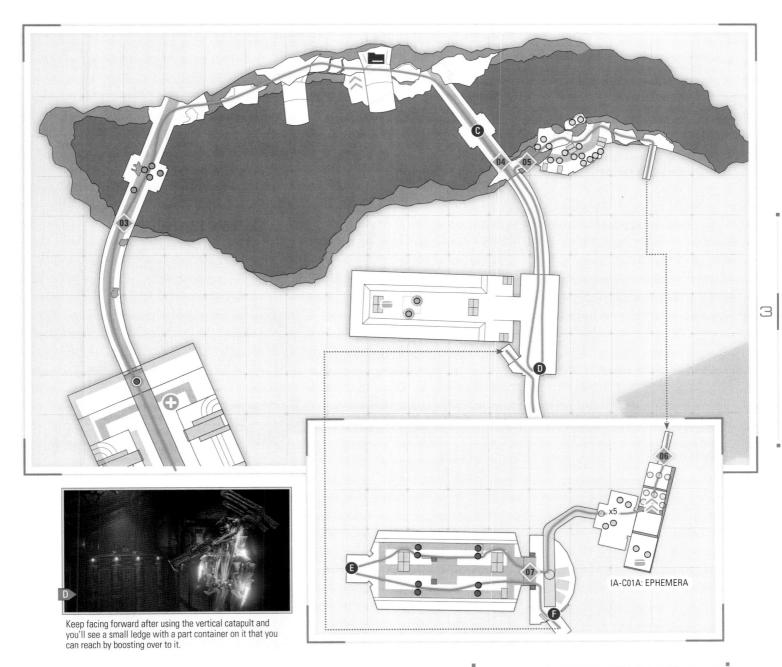

Keep facing forward after using the vertical catapult and you'll see a small ledge with a part container on it that you can reach by boosting over to it.

IA-C01A: EPHEMERA

▶ B

▶ C

▶ D

OBJECTIVE	Reach the End of Depth 2 (2)

03 After defeating Iguazu and moving into the next section, you'll have your first encounter with the PCA ENFORCER as the tunnel opens up. It drops in and destroys a group of bipedal MTs standing on a bridge. As soon as you see it, make sure to move back into the tunnel and use the inside wall for cover, so that you don't get hit by its lasers. It will then move to **Position C** on a bridge in the distance. As soon as you move out of the tunnel, it will begin firing its laser cannon at you. ▶ B

You'll need to move toward the ENFORCER, since it's guarding the entrance to the next part of the facility, but the elevation difference means that you can use the terrain to block the laser as long as you hug the cave wall while moving between the ledges along it. It will also start firing missiles at you once you get closer, but the terrain can block them as long as you stay back from the edge of the ledges. The ENFORCER will relocate once again when you get close to the bridge, so it's advisable to boost across the ledges as quickly as possible, so that it moves away before you begin exploring. ▶ C

04 Proceed into the tunnel here, but do so very carefully because the ENFORCER is waiting at **Position D** and will fire its laser at you as soon as you round the corner; hug the inside wall and move back slightly as soon as you see the alert indicator to avoid the incoming shots. It will then retreat back through another partition, locking it in the process, so now you'll need to find the control room to unlock it.

Bronze Combat Log
LOG HUNT

Unlike the previous time you had to open a partition, the way forward is not through a hole in the floor of the side room here, but that doesn't mean it's not worth a quick detour. The two DENOISER drones in there both contain combat logs that are easily obtained by boosting in while they're unaware and destroying them before they can retaliate. Once the room is clear, you can then open the part container for a new Booster part before continuing through the facility. ▶ D

05 The route down to the control room begins just outside the tunnel here. If you look down, you'll be able to see a small rocky ledge with some REPAIRER mechs on it. Drop down onto that ledge, and then follow the series of ledges down, destroying the REPAIRER mechs along the way for some easy bonus pay. Once you reach the bottom, use the large ventilation pipe to reach the interior of the complex once again.

06 ◇ Approach the end of the ventilation pipe carefully and don't drop down into the room beyond it straight away, because a large group of REPAIRER mechs will spring an ambush and drop down while releasing a large cloud of stun smog. If you get caught amongst them, you'll quickly incur enough shock buildup to trigger an electrical discharge. So pick off the first mechs from the exit of the pipe, and then enter the room and boost straight up so you can start destroying the larger group on the platform ahead. Use the vertical catapult once the stun smog has dissipated and destroy the next group of mechs on the platform above to clear the way for entering the pipe above them.

07 ◇ Drop down through the hole near the end of the pipe and enter the nearby room, but do not head straight to **Position E** and access the control panel yet. If you use your scanner, you'll notice that there are a large number of inactive DENOISER drones hanging from the ceiling. If you were to start accessing the control panel, they would all drop down and attack you. You can, however, freely destroy them while they're hanging to negate their trap and rack up a sizable amount of bonus pay. When you're ready to proceed, access the control panel to restore power and use the elevator at **Position F** to get back up to the partition, which you can now access. There's another supply sherpa just past the partition— make use of its services, because after you pass through the next door you'll be locked into a final encounter with the AAP03: ENFORCER.

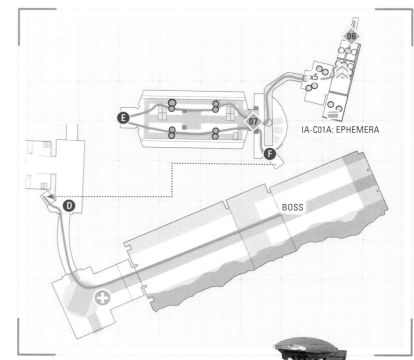

IA-C01A: EPHEMERA

BOSS

AAP03

ENFORCER / ENFORCEMENT SYSTEM

PHASES

1 In this phase, the ENFORCER will mostly make use of its ranged options while keeping its shield up as much as possible, so closing the gap and getting through the shield will be the biggest obstacle to get around. Depending on how far away from it you are, if you see its shield up, you may want to focus on evading attacks and repositioning yourself so that as soon as the shield drops you can close in and unleash your weapons on it. Generally, try to stay at medium range as much as possible, because that gives you enough room to evade some of the boss's dangerous melee attacks, and you'll be close enough for your weapons to apply continuous ACS strain. Then, just before the boss is about to stagger, close in and inflict as much damage as possible before moving back out to medium range just after it recovers to avoid getting hit with a nasty melee counterattack.

2 At around 50% remaining AP, the ENFORCER will release its limiters, gaining new attacks and becoming more aggressive for the remainder of the fight. Even

BASIC SPECS

AP	52525
Attitude Stability	2200
Anti-Kinetic Defense	1257
Anti-Energy Defense	923
Anti-Explosive Defense	1413
Elec. Discharge Tolerance	500
Shock Resistance	15%
ACS Anomaly Tolerance	500
Heat Resistance	33%

OBJECTIVE

Destroy the Autonomous
Defense Weapon ENFORCER

with the addition of those new attacks, your general approach should remain much the same: build up ACS strain at mid-range, and then close in when it's about to stagger so you can inflict as much damage as possible. Once you destroy the ENFORCER, the mission will be complete and you can move even deeper into Watchpoint Alpha.

Make sure to only hit one of the DENOISER drones at a time to ensure you destroy them; if you partially damage one it will activate.

The ENFORCER will begin the fight by charging its rifle from afar.

The ENFORCER will always leap in for its shockwave attack at the start of Phase 2.

PULSE SHIELD

DESCRIPTION Large pulse shield deployed from pulse gunshield, capable of covering the entire front of the boss's frame.

EVASION Not used offensively.

PAIRED MISSILE VOLLEY

DESCRIPTION Six pairs of missiles are released from its variable missile launcher; missiles have high homing capabilities.

EVASION Quick Boost away from the missiles close to their moment of impact.

SPLIT MISSILE VOLLEY

DESCRIPTION Two volleys of six missiles splitting to the left and right released from its variable missile launcher; missiles have high homing capabilities.

EVASION Quick Boost away from the missiles close to their moment of impact.

FANNING MISSILE VOLLEY

DESCRIPTION Twelve missiles are released from its variable missile launcher, fanning outward and homing in; missiles have low homing capabilities.

EVASION Quick Boost away from the missiles close to their moment of impact.

PULSE BLASTS

DESCRIPTION Rapidly releases pulse blasts from its pulse gunshield that can neutralize a shield if you have one equipped, as well as dealing damage and straining your ACS; can release longer or shorter streams.

EVASION Strafe or Quick Boost away from the blasts.

LASER SHOT (CHARGED) ▼

DESCRIPTION The boss will rear its arm back and raise its shield, charging and releasing a single, powerful laser shot. It will always begin the fight with this attack.

EVASION Strafe to one side, and at the moment you're alerted to the attack, Quick Boost in the opposite direction.

LASER SHOT (UNCHARGED)

DESCRIPTION Quick shot with the pulse gunshield that can be fired twice, or sometimes followed up with by the pulse blasts. It can also fire this weapon while the pulse shield is active.

EVASION Position yourself on the elevated part of the area so the ENFORCER effectively fires below you or Quick Boost away from the shots.

PIERCING THRUST

DESCRIPTION Charges its variable high-power laser pile bunker and boosts at you while piercing through your AC. This is a high-impact strike and can deal thousands of AP damage; can use this attack by itself or follow it up with another thrust attack or a left-facing downward slash.

EVASION Depending on proximity you can either rapidly Quick Boost away from the boss or directly past it.

LEFT-FACING DOWNWARD SLASH

DESCRIPTION The ENFORCER will bring its variable high-power laser pile bunker down on you after lifting it up and dashing toward you. This attack will often follow its thrust and can easily destroy your AC if both hits connect.

EVASION Depending on proximity you can either rapidly Quick Boost away from the boss or directly past it.

RIGHT-FACING DOWNWARD SLASH

DESCRIPTION Similar to the left-facing version of the swing, this slash can instantly overload your ACS and deal high AP damage and may be followed up with further swings of the ENFORCER's pile bunker.

EVASION Depending on proximity, you can either rapidly Quick Boost away from the boss or directly past it.

GRAB ATTACK   PHASE 2

DESCRIPTION If you remain close to it, the boss will charge its pile bunker and attempt to hook your AC. The visual queue of this attack is a dark energy being emitted from the ENFORCER's pile bunker.

EVASION Similar range and striking pattern to the piercing thrust; due to your likely proximity it's advisable to Quick Boost past the boss.

TWO-HIT COMBO   PHASE 2

DESCRIPTION The boss will charge at you with an overhead strike, spin around, then charge and slash with a horizontal sweep.

EVASION If unstaggered, you have an opportunity to Quick Boost after the first hit, otherwise a Quick Boost away from both hits is crucial.

SHOCKWAVE COMBO   PHASE 2

DESCRIPTION The boss will attack you with a quick piercing thrust and then smash its pile bunker into the ground. After a brief pause an eruption of energy will spread in a circle outward from the boss, breaking into points with gaps in between.

EVASION Quick Boost away from its piercing thrust and immediately begin boosting into the air and away from the boss to evade the energy wave.

UNDERGROUND EXPLORATION – DEPTH 3

"Walter... It's like he already knows where the Coral convergence is."

—Ayre

In order to access the greater depths below Watchpoint Alpha, you'll need to remove a barrier that's preventing any access, which means destroying a large reactor core and cutting off its power supply. The very large and open reactor area is heavily defended by extremely long-range beam laser artillery installations and enemies that will fire on you from well outside of the range of any weaponry available to you; careful planning and excellent movement skills will be required to make it to the core safely. Getting there is only half the battle, however, because blocking your escape is an autonomous AC that you'll need to defeat in a limited amount of time if you're to escape the area in one piece.

MISSION INFO

Combat Zone	Watchpoint Alpha—Depth 3
Client	Arquebus Corporation
Reward	270,000
Max Bonus Pay	386,600
Completion Unlocks	Arena: S Rank Mercenary Registration
Combat Logs	Silver x2, Gold x1
Data Logs	2
Part Containers	2

MISSION OBJECTIVES

Infiltrate the Core of the Depth 3 Reactor

Destroy the Pressure Chamber

Escape from the Reactor Core (1)

Destroy the Automated Defense System ENFORCER

Escape from the Reactor Core (2)

ENEMY DATA

		No.	AP	AS	Bonus Pay	Analysis
●	AM01: REPAIRER (Worker Type)	22	51	—	800	P.313
●	AM01: REPAIRER (Guard Type)	13	51	—	800	P.313
○	Artillery (Beam Laser)	12	302	—	8000	P.329
●	AM02: DENOISER (Melee Type)	4	1254	783	9000	P.339
●	AM02: DENOISER (Support Type)	8	1254	783	9000	P.340
●	AM02: DENOISER (Sniper Type)	3	1254	783	9000	P.339
●	AM02: DENOISER (Heavy Firepower)	4	4775	1600	18000	P.340
■	Generator	1	700	—	—	—
◎	IA-C01: EPHEMERA / Enforcement System	1	10280	1598	72000	—

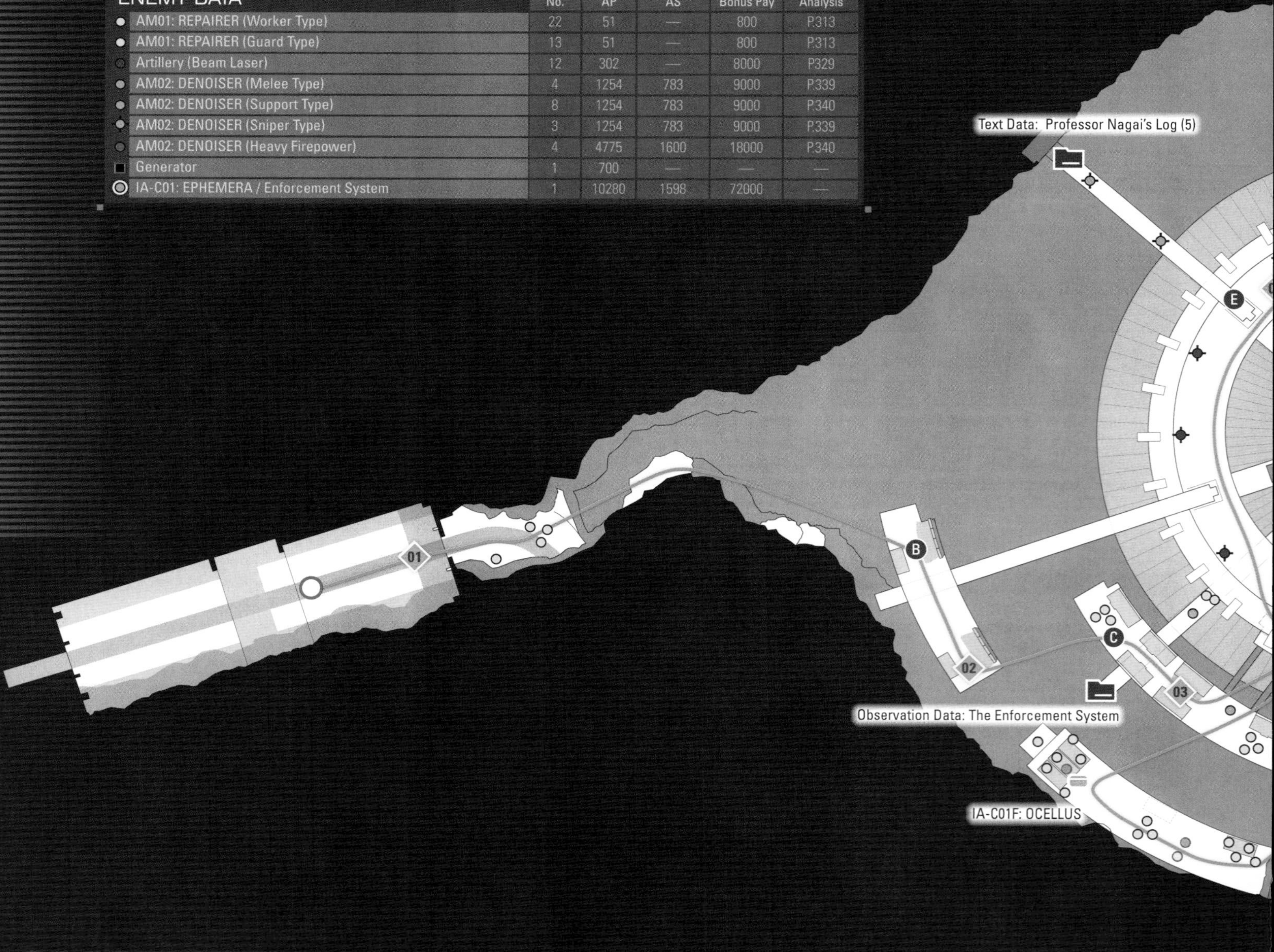

Text Data: Professor Nagai's Log (5)

E

B

C

02

03

Observation Data: The Enforcement System

IA-C01F: OCELLUS

01

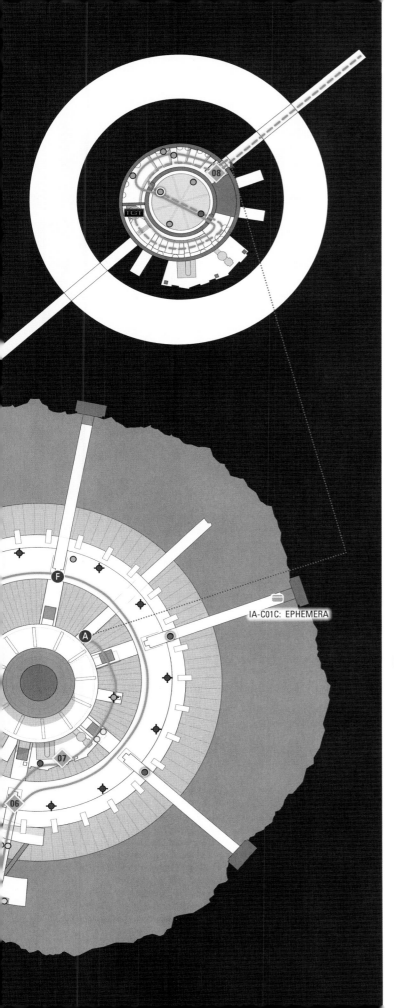

IA-C01C: EPHEMERA

Infiltrate the Core of the Depth 3 Reactor

01 ◈ Your continued exploration of the Watchpoint Alpha complex picks up in the room where the AAP03: ENFORCER was bested in the previous mission. From there, you need to access the door in front of you to enter the massive cavern containing the core. Follow the path along until you reach the end of it, and then boost over to the small ledge along the cavern wall, from which you'll be able to take in the sheer scale of the structure being housed here.

From up here, the area looks quiet. Dotted along the outer ring are numerous beam laser artillery batteries that will commence firing upon you as soon as you begin your descent. DENOISER drones have also taken up strategic positions along key bridges. The entrance to the interior part of the core is on the opposite side of the facility at **Position A**, so begin your descent with an Assault Boost down to the platform at **Position B**, where you can use the barricades to shield you from the artillery.

02 ◈ Unlike previous artillery batteries, the ones here do not fire single shots from their beam lasers, but rather produce a sustained beam that deals constant damage as long as it's in contact with you. If you're caught out in the open and hit with multiple beams, the damage can accumulate very quickly. Taking a brief hit from a single beam, however, isn't instantly devastating like it is from the single-shot cannons, so don't be afraid of quickly moving through their fields of fire if needed.

The other thing to keep in mind with these artillery installations is that—unlike most other forms of artillery—they can swivel a full 360-degrees and can do so very quickly, so the usual approach of just getting behind them isn't as effective. If they're unaware of you, however, it is possible to destroy them from behind without them firing on you, a fact that's very important if you want to explore the area to acquire all of the logs and parts, not to mention accrue as much bonus pay as possible. To start working your way down and around behind them, move to this point, and then Assault Boost down to the platform below at **Position C**. ▶ A

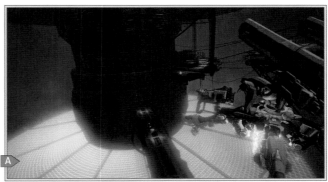

Drop off the platform at **Position C** to ambush the DENOISER below you. Access the wreck at the other end of the bridge for a data log before using an Assault Boost to get back up to the platform at **Position D**.

03 ◈ REPAIRER mechs will also start firing when you land on this platform, so destroy them quickly, but try not to advance too far along the platform in the process to avoid being detected by the DENOISER up ahead. The artillery can't reach you down here, so simply Assault Boost over and use your diffuse laser cannons to quickly destroy the DENOISER. If you now want to head straight for the entrance, then you can drop down to **Position D** and cross over to the platforms surrounding the base of the core and follow them around. There's plenty of bonus pay and items still to be had in the area, however, and this is an excellent place from which to begin acquiring it all.

04 ◈ You'll need to deal with the artillery installations next, but now that you're low enough, you can Assault Boost over to this point on the ring just below them quite safely. Once here, you can jump up and destroy the nearby artillery, and then boost to the same level as them and move around the ring clockwise, destroying them as you go.

AC ASSEMBLY

The majority of the enemies in this mission, including the autonomous AC, use energy weapons almost exclusively, so prioritizing defense against that damage type is recommended. Much of the build from the previous mission is still extremely effective here because a heavier build with high AP and attitude stability can help soften the blows from the long-range defenses if you happen to get hit, and also help you against some of the tougher enemies and the autonomous AC. Staying close to many of those enemies is still a big advantage for you, so the shotguns and diffuse laser cannons continue to be excellent options. It can be worth swapping out one of the shotguns for a missile launcher, however, to both help with softening up tougher enemies as you approach, and for using multi-lock against some of the weaker enemies.

01	R-ARM UNIT | SHOTGUN **SG-027 ZIMMERMAN**	P.54
02	L-ARM UNIT | MISSILE LAUNCHER **HML-G2/P19MLT-04**	P.62
03	R-BACK UNIT | DIFFUSE LASER CANNON **VP-60LCD**	P.67
04	L-BACK UNIT | DIFFUSE LASER CANNON **VP-60LCD**	P.67
05	HEAD | — **VE-44A**	P.78
06	CORE | — **07-061 MIND ALPHA**	P.81
07	ARMS | — **NACHTREIHER/46E**	P.83
08	LEGS | TETRAPOD **VP-424**	P.86
09	BOOSTER | — **BC-0600 12345**	P.88
10	FCS | — **FC-008 TALBOT**	P.90
11	GENERATOR | — **VP-20D**	P.92

Support beams around the area provide sufficient cover to prepare a surprise attack.

Only grab the data log at the end of **Position E** after eliminating the four adjacent turrets.

The platform with this part container is infested with REPAIRER mechs; eliminate them before collecting your reward.

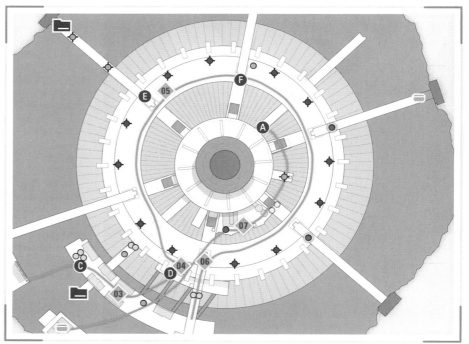

When you arrive at **Position E**, resist the urge to destroy the two sniper DENOISERs as soon as you reach the bridge they're on; instead, continue around the ring and destroy the next couple of artillery installations. Once the artillery is out of the way, you can Assault Boost along the bridge and use your diffuse laser cannons to destroy each of the drones quickly as you go, and then access the wreck at the other end for the data log. ▶ A

05 ◆ Be a bit more cautious from this point on, because although the next DENOISER has the same strength as the ones you've encountered previously in this mission and can be dispatched quickly, the two after that are considerably stronger. Once you reach **Position F**, proceed slowly and use your missiles to destroy the artillery so you can stay further back, all the while keep an eye on the DENOISER on the bridge ahead.

These heavy firepower DENOISERs have better detection systems than other versions and can spot you from long distances. Since they're the greatest threat at the moment, it's recommended that you destroy them before proceeding to eliminate the artillery installations. Wait for them to be moving away from you along the bridges, and then quickly Assault Boost in and destroy them before they can retaliate. If you get spotted before you're in position, drop onto the small ledges on the interior of the ring and stay out of sight until they become unaware again.

06 ◆ Continue around the ring, completing your loop of the facility by destroying the final artillery installations on your way to this point. The final part container is on the highest platform along the outer wall of the cavern, and now that all of the artillery installations have been destroyed, reaching it is a much safer proposition. Start your approach to it along this bridge, destroying the REPAIRER mechs along the way, and then Assault Boost over to the platform the container is on, clearing out all of the mechs first so that you can open it safely. With the detour now complete, Assault Boost back down to the platform at **Position D**. From there, continue to the inner platforms at the base of the core facility. ▶ B

07 ◆ The DENOISER on this platform is one of the stronger variants; try to use the support column for cover while you Assault Boost into range to destroy it quickly with your shotgun and diffuse laser cannons. With that enemy down, follow the platforms around the base of the facility, destroying the remaining few enemies as you go. Finally, access the door at **Position A** to gain entry to the core. ▶ C

Destroy the Pressure Chamber / Escape From the Reactor Core (1)

08 The inside of the reactor is a significantly more cramped space. You'll have limited room to move and will need to rely on speed and overwhelming force to deal with enemies, rather than finesse. There are three more DENOISER drones in this outer section of the core: one on a beam and two on the platforms below it. Hover over to the one on the beam and destroy it first, before dropping down and dealing with the other two. Continue around this maintenance section until you reach the hatch leading to the central area, but do not enter straight away.

There are three more DENOISERs inside, one of which is the heavy firepower variant. If you peek through the hatch opening, you can use your missiles to get an early attack on one of them. They'll then converge near the hatch opening without leaving the room, and you'll only have to cover a very short distance before you can get into optimal range to destroy them. With the room now clear, access the hatch on the opposite wall to the one you entered through, and follow the passage along to reach your target and destroy it. The chain reaction caused by the destruction of the pressure chamber will immediately start bringing the entire facility down, so quickly retrace your steps and start making your way back out. In a last-ditch effort to stop you, however, the PCA closes the hatch and locks you in with one of their autonomous ACs—the only way out is through it.

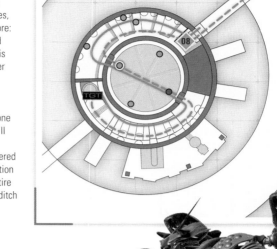

IA-C01

EPHEMERA / ENFORCEMENT SYSTEM

AC EPHEMERA would be a difficult enough opponent under the best of circumstances, but to complicate things here, the impending destruction of the facility means you're also up against the clock. A two-minute countdown timer will appear on your screen shortly after the fight begins. If you don't complete the fight and escape the reactor in time, the mission will fail.

BASIC SPECS

AP	9880
Attitude Stability	1638
Anti-Kinetic Defense	1011
Anti-Energy Defense	1186
Anti-Explosive Defense	1144
Elec. Discharge Tolerance	490
Shock Resistance	32%
ACS Anomaly Tolerance	490
Heat Resistance	32%
Repair Kits	2

Destroy the Autonomous Defense AC EPHEMERA / Escape From the Reactor Core (2)

The limited time and space here means that you can't safely engage from a distance, so the only recourse is to play extremely aggressively and try to take control of the fight. Even though space is limited, positioning is still important; you'll want to limit EPHEMERA's movement as much as possible by trying to keep it pinned near one of the walls.

Careful positioning will help to keep track of EPHEMERA, since it moves around a lot and will hover for extended periods of time—the less you have to move your camera to keep up with it, the better. Though time is limited, pick your moments to fire wisely, because time spent reloading after a miss can be more significant than waiting to land a clean shot. Upon destroying EPHEMERA, you'll be able to access the hatch and continue your escape. Once you've exited the core and made it a safe distance across the bridge, the mission will be complete.

EPHEMERA / ENFORCEMENT SYSTEM ATTACKS

IA-C01W1: NEBULA ▼ CHARGED

DESCRIPTION Pulse rifle with charged and uncharged modes; leaves a lasting damage field from either mode.

EVASION Quick Boost to either side of the shots.

IA-C01W2: MOONLIGHT

DESCRIPTION Melee weapon that releases a wave of energy per swipe; swipes twice per use.

EVASION Create distance so that the swipes do not impact you and strafe or Quick Boost away from the energy waves produced.

IA-C01W3: AURORA (RIGHT)

DESCRIPTION Light wave cannon that fires a salvo of eight energy projectiles with homing capabilities.

EVASION Quick Boost to either side of the projectiles as close to when they reach you as possible.

IA-C01W3: AURORA (LEFT)

DESCRIPTION Light wave cannon that fires a salvo of eight energy projectiles with homing capabilities.

EVASION Quick Boost to either side of the projectiles as close to when they reach you as possible.

PULSE ARMOR

DESCRIPTION Coral barrier that gradually degrades and absorbs damage until depleted.

EVASION Not used offensively.

INTERCEPT THE REDGUNS

> *"Maggots! Do you read me? You can tell this to posterity: mean old Michigan died of a bad fall!"*
>
> —G1 Michigan

Siding with Arquebus at this juncture will lead you into a battle against the remaining Balam forces that survived the descent through the depths, including the leader of the elite Redguns, G1 Michigan. The battle takes place at the bottom of Depth 1, around the wreckage of the NEPENTHES. There, you'll need to fight your way through waves of Balam forces until Michigan turns up to put a stop to you. He won't go down easy, and with no checkpoints or supply sherpas, managing your ammo and resources will be crucial.

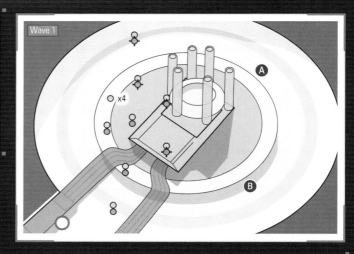

Wave 1

MISSION OBJECTIVES

Intercept Balam's Main MT Force

Defeat G1 Michigan and Balam's Main MT Force

MISSION INFO

Combat Zone	Watchpoint Alpha—Depth 1
Client	Arquebus Corporation
Reward	400,000
Max Bonus Pay	290,000
Completion Unlocks	—
Combat Logs	Platinum x1
Data Logs	—
Part Containers	—

ENEMY DATA

		No.	AP	AS	Bonus Pay	Analysis
Wave 1	CD-E-086 Aerial Defense Drone (Mini Gatling Gun)	4	40	—	400	P.304
Wave 1	CD-J-098 Quad Drone (Transport Hangar)	8	302	310	1600	P.312
Wave 1	MT-E-104 Bipedal MT (Dual Machine Gun)	4	470	364	1200	P.316
Wave 1	MT-E-104 Bipedal MT (Grenade Cannon)	4	470	364	1200	P.316
Wave 2	CD-J-098 Quad Drone (Transport Hangar)	4	302	310	1600	P.312
Wave 2	TH-E-012 Transport Helicopter	1	750	—	5000	P.314
Wave 2	CD-J-098 Quad Drone (Cluster Missile Launcher)	2	302	310	1600	P.312
Wave 2	MT-E-104 Bipedal MT (Missile Launcher)	4	470	364	1200	P.317
Wave 2	MT-E-104 Bipedal MT (Shotgun)	4	470	364	1200	P.317
Wave 3	CD-E-086 Aerial Defense Drone (Mini Gatling Gun)	8	40	—	400	P.308
Wave 3	CD-J-098 Quad Drone (Transport Hangar)	4	302	310	1600	P.312
Wave 3	TH-E-012 Transport Helicopter	1	750	—	5000	P.314
Wave 3	MT-E-104 Bipedal MT (Hand Rocket Launcher)	4	470	364	1200	P.317
Wave 3	MT-E-104 Bipedal MT (Cluster Gun)	4	470	364	1200	P.317
Wave 3	MT-J-048 Tetrapod MT (Grenade Cannon)	1	13370	2200	12000	P.324
Wave 4	CD-J-098 Quad Drone (Transport Hangar)	8	302	310	1600	P.312
Wave 4	MT-E-104 Bipedal MT (Shotgun)	8	470	364	1200	P.317
Wave 4	AC LIGER TAIL / G1 Michigan	1	13420	2340	200000	—
Wave 5	CD-J-098 Quad Drone (Transport Hangar)	8	302	310	1600	P.312
Wave 5	MT-E-104 Bipedal MT (Missile Launcher)	4	470	364	1200	P.316
Wave 5	MT-E-104 Bipedal MT (Grenade Cannon)	4	470	364	1200	P.316
Wave 5	MT-E-104 Bipedal MT (Grenade Cannon)	1	13370	2200	12000	P.324

AC ASSEMBLY

This mission features multiple enemy types of various strengths, a large number of which are wielding shields, so you're going to need some versatile weapons. Ammo count, the ability to keep moving and firing, and some area of effect damage are also worth keeping in mind. One weapon that ticks all of those boxes is the WB-0000 BAD COOK flamethrower. Its ability to deal constant damage to multiple enemies without having to reload—and the fact that it can deal with shields quickly—makes it hard to beat in this mission, so it's recommended to equip two of them.

That leaves your back units free for high damage explosive weapons, to help against the tougher units; a pair of laser cannons or SONGBIRDS are good choices, but dual stun needle launchers are the prevailing recommendation. To provide the option of hovering in the air and keep moving, while also ensuring that ground-based movement remains manageable, it's recommended to use tetrapod legs with this assembly. For the rest of your frame parts, it's worth trying to focus on getting your anti-kinetic and explosive specs as high as possible to protect against the most common damage types.

01	R-ARM UNIT	FLAMETHROWER	WB-0000 BAD COOK	P.54
02	L-ARM UNIT	FLAMETHROWER	WB-0000 BAD COOK	P.62
03	R-BACK UNIT	STUN NEEDLE LAUNCHER	VE-60SNA	P.67
04	L-BACK UNIT	STUN NEEDLE LAUNCHER	VE-60SNA	P.67
05	HEAD	—	AH-J-124 BASHO	P.77
06	CORE	—	CC-3000 WRECKER	P.81
07	ARMS	—	IA-C01A: EPHEMERA	P.84
08	LEGS	TETRAPOD	LG-033M VERRILL	P.86
09	BOOSTER	—	ALULA/21E	P.88
10	FCS	—	FC-008 TALBOT	P.90
11	GENERATOR	—	VP-20D	P.92

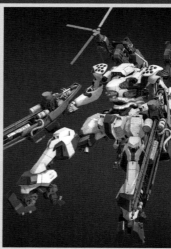

PREPARATION

Unlike some of the other wave-based missions, this one has no timer. Instead of beginning at specific times, most of the waves in this mission are triggered by defeating a certain number of enemies from the previous wave. Walter will give you an audible warning over comms just before a new wave of enemies appears, and when they do, many will display a yellow warning indicator to let you know where they are. New waves of enemies don't appear immediately after you've destroyed a sufficient number from the previous wave, so if you're fast, it's possible to fully clear a wave of enemies before the next appears.

While this makes time less of a factor, it also means you need to place greater emphasis on target selection; taking out the priority targets in each wave should be your focus. Weaker enemies such as drones should be left for last, to minimize the number of dangerous threats you have to contend with at any given time. All of the MTs that you'll face in this mission are deployed via either drone or helicopter. While the drones deploy the MTs at such a pace that they're almost impossible to destroy beforehand, taking out helicopters carrying groups of MTs is key to keeping things manageable.

Nowhere is this more important than in the lead-up to Michigan's appearance in Wave 4 and shortly after. If you destroy the wrong targets here, you can easily end up facing Michigan and two tetrapod MTs simultaneously—a situation that should be avoided at all costs. Every enemy will be gunning for you as soon as they appear, because destroying you is the sole goal of the Balam forces. So, while you won't have to go far to find a fight, try to use cover to mask your approach, and aim to have plenty of AP and repair kits left for the showdown with Michigan.

OBJECTIVE
Intercept Balam's Main MT Force

Wave 1   Aerial Defense Drone (Mini Gatling Gun) x4
Quad Drone (w/ Dual Machine Gun Bipedal MT x1) x4
Quad Drone (w/ Grenade Cannon Bipedal MT x1) x4

The first wave of enemies will be upon you the instant the mission begins, and Wave 2 enemies will be deployed automatically after a brief period of time, regardless of how many enemies from the first wave have been destroyed. That being the case, your goal should be to get into position to deal with the main threat in the second wave: the transport helicopter carrying four bipedal MTs. It descends on the opposite side of the room, near **Position A**, and if you're quick, it's possible to destroy all of the current enemies before it appears. Your flamethrowers are all you should need this round, so boost forward until you're within range of the initial enemies, and start firing on both of them. Jump onto the NEPEN-THES wreck and take out the enemies there, then drop down to the side and systematically work your way around the room using your flamethrower.

Wave 2   Transport Helicopter (w/ Shotgun Bipedal MT x4) x1
Quad Drone (Cluster Missile Launcher) x2
Quad Drone (w/ Missile Launcher Bipedal MT x1) x4

Transport hangar drones will deploy some MTs before the transport helicopter enters your weapon range. While you're waiting near **Position A** for the helicopter to arrive, destroy any nearby MTs to make the area a little safer. Periodically check on the helicopter; once it's low enough that you can jump and fire at it with your stun needle launchers, do so to practically halve the number of enemies you'll need to face in this wave. Rather than resuming your offense against the remaining MTs once the helicopter is down, turn your attention skyward once again and destroy the two cluster missile drones. These drones will constantly bombard you with highly damaging missiles that can be tough to avoid when there are more enemies in the area, so it's best to deal with them now.

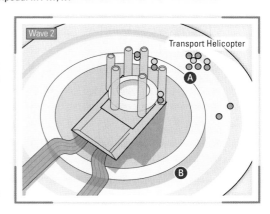

Wave 3   Transport Helicopter (w/ Cluster Gun Bipedal MT x4) x1
Aerial Defense Drone (Mini Gatling Gun) x8
Quad Drone (w/ Hand Rocket Launcher Bipedal MT x1) x4
Tetrapod MT (Grenade Cannon) x1

Unlike the previous wave, the transport helicopter that arrives in this one does so straight away. If you move around to **Position B** after the previous wave ends, you can boost into the air immediately to destroy it. The other major threat in this wave is the tetrapod MT. It'll be one of the last enemies to appear, so until you see the warning icon letting you know that it has arrived, focus on destroying bipedal MTs in the area. When it comes time to face the tetrapod MT, a constant barrage from your flamethrowers and stun needle launchers can make fairly short work of it, especially since it's not the most agile unit and typically won't evade your stun needle shots.

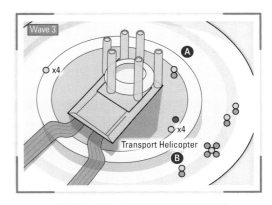

OBJECTIVE
Defeat G1 Michigan and Balam's Main MT Force

Wave 4   Quad Drone (w/ Shotgun Bipedal MT x1) x8
AC LIGER TAIL / G1 Michigan

Michigan is this wave's obvious headliner. Once he arrives, he'll command a lot of your attention, but you can use the small window before he reaches you to make things a bit easier. The shotgun-wielding bipedal MTs that accompany him in this wave are all carrying shields. Their primary role is to box you in and reduce your maneuverability, which can be deadly with a skilled pilot like Michigan on the field. They will also make it more difficult to keep your weapons trained on Michigan, so thinning them out is crucial.

Thankfully, the flamethrowers are quite effective at dealing with these shielded enemies. If you begin this wave again near **Position B**, you should have just about enough time to destroy all of the bipedal MTs in the immediate area. It might be tempting to destroy the rest of them, but doing so would trigger the next enemy wave, and you'll want to have Michigan defeated before that happens.

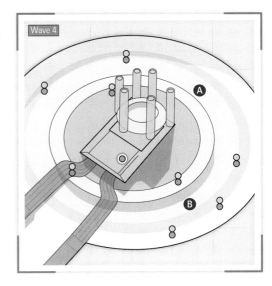

AC // LIGER TAIL

Despite not appearing at the conclusion of the fight, G1 Michigan is effectively the boss of this mission and by far the most difficult foe. He'll often make use of his AC's tetrapod legs by hovering during the fight, causing you to choose between keeping track of him or the other enemies on the ground, adding an extra layer of difficulty to the fight. The constant elevation changes and quick maneuvers he makes use of also means that firing at him with conventional weapons can be difficult, but since the area is quite small, you can use your own movement to try and keep him pinned near a wall to make it a bit easier to line up shots.

BASIC SPECS

AP	13420
Attitude Stability	2340
Anti-Kinetic Defense	1275
Anti-Energy Defense	1139
Anti-Explosive Defense	1220
Elec. Discharge Tolerance	490
Shock Resistance	7%
ACS Anomaly Tolerance	490
Heat Resistance	7%
Repair Kits	2

LIGER TAIL has particularly high attitude stability, so if you let Michigan move around the way he wants, overloading his ACS can be very difficult. One of his most common tactics is to Quick Boost directly at you and then jump over you, all while firing his gatling gun and explosive thrower. If you identify that quickly enough, you can either Quick Boost backward yourself so he can't get over you, or move toward the center of the area, so you can use the change in ground height to block some of his shots, which is a useful tactic in general against him.

For the majority of the fight, you should be constantly firing at him with your flamethrowers, and as long as you keep him in the general vicinity of your reticle, you should be hitting him. Whenever you do get a clear shot, depending on how much ACS strain you've already built up, unleash one or both stun needles to stagger him. If you only fired off one stun needle to stagger him, fire off the other one straight away to deal huge amounts of damage, and then repeat the process until he's defeated.

AC LIGER TAIL ATTACKS

DF-GA-08 HU-BEN

DESCRIPTION Gatling gun that Michigan uses as his primary weapon; fires near-continuous kinetic shots.

EVASION Quick Boost to either side of the shots.

DF-ET-09 TAI-YANG-SHOU

DESCRIPTION This explosive thrower tosses out a high volume of small grenades within close proximity to Michigan; can be charged to throw the grenades vertically instead of its base horizontal pattern.

EVASION Quick Boost away from Michigan to avoid the blast from the explosives.

BML-G2/P17SPL-16

DESCRIPTION This split missile launcher fires two volleys of eight missiles which come out in a diamond pattern and have minimal homing capabilities.

EVASION The missiles converge as they approach, making one Quick Boost enough to evade them.

SONGBIRDS

DESCRIPTION Fires two high-impact grenades and can be used at any range.

EVASION Chain Quick Boosts to either side of Michigan as soon as you hear the alert indicator.

PULSE PROTECTION

DESCRIPTION Fixed-location spherical barrier that Michigan will deploy at around 50% remaining AP.

EVASION Enter the barrier to attack Michigan or retreat and use the environment for cover until it dissipates.

Wave 5 Quad Drone (w/ Missile Launcher Bipedal MT x1) x4
Quad Drone (w/ Grenade Cannon Bipedal MT x1) x4
Tetrapod MT (Grenade Cannon) x1

The tetrapod MT in this wave drops down near **Position A**. If you're still near **Position B** after destroying Michigan, start by heading toward the NEPENTHES wreck to destroy the bipedal MTs that make their descent there, using the wreck as cover. Once those enemies have been destroyed, drop down and start making your way around the room, destroying more bipedal MTs as you come to them. When you reach the tetrapod MT, it should be your focus. As with the previous one, apply constant pressure with your flamethrowers and keep unloading your stun needle launchers as soon as they've finished reloading to destroy it quickly. Track down and destroy remaining enemies and the mission will be complete, dealing a crippling blow to Balam's interests in the area.

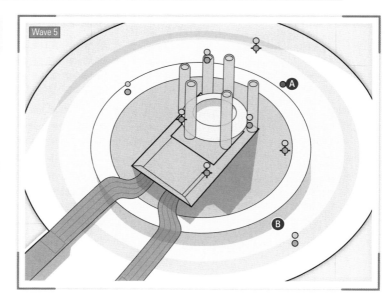

//19-B
AMBUSH THE VESPERS

"We're war buddies now. Maybe I'll find a comrade in you yet."

—Middle Flatwell

If you choose to side with the RLF by accepting this mission, you'll be tasked with dealing a crippling blow to Arquebus by ambushing and destroying two of their high-ranking Vespers: V.VIII Pater and V.V Hawkins. The ambush takes place in the same room in which you faced the AAP03: ENFORCER at the end of your initial Depth 2 exploration, and the layout hasn't changed for this encounter. You begin on a platform above the room and will be accompanied by Middle Flatwell, the commander of the Rubicon Liberation Front, making this a two-on-two AC fight.

Your two targets enter the room unaware of your ambush, so you're free to listen to their conversation for a while. If you let it go on for too long, they'll eventually become suspicious and notice you. Flatwell will prompt you when he thinks the time is right to attack, and whether you listen to him or not, as well as how you initiate the fight, will affect his dialogue once the fight starts; this of course has

no impact on the mission or its outcome. Depending on the weapons you have equipped though, you may find it better to jump across to the adjacent platform in front of your starting position, because from there you can drop directly down onto either of your targets.

Who you choose to target first is up to you, but it's worth keeping in mind that Pater's lightweight frame has much lower AP and is also easier to stagger. Defeating him quickly means you'll only have to contend with one foe for the remainder of the fight, whereas tackling Hawkins first will mean fighting both enemies together for longer. Whichever you decide to engage though, try to only hit that enemy, because Flatwell will often pick up the other target. As long as you don't hit the alternate target, you'll typically only have to worry about keeping out of the way of errant shots, rather than evading any specific attacks from that AC.

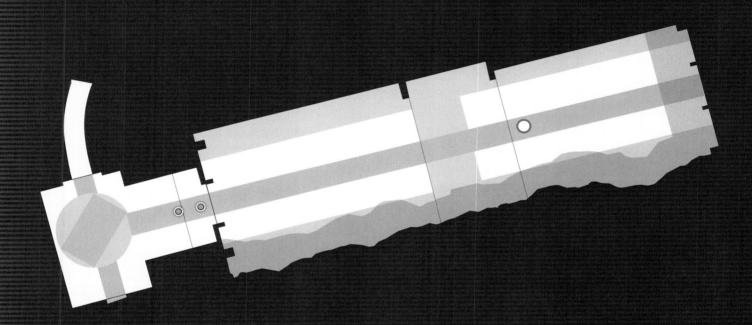

MISSION INFO

Combat Zone	Watchpoint Alpha—Depth 2
Client	Rubicon Liberation Front
Reward	180,000
Max Bonus Pay	—
Completion Unlocks	—
Combat Logs	Gold x2
Data Logs	—
Part Containers	—

MISSION OBJECTIVE

Defeat V.V Hawkins / V.VIII Pater

ENEMY DATA

	No.	AP	AS	Bonus Pay	Analysis
⊙ AC RECONFIG / V.V Hawkins	1	13010	2265	—	—
⊙ AC DUAL NATURE / V.VIII Pater	1	8690	1314	—	—

AC ASSEMBLY

Both enemy ACs make potent use of primarily energy-based weaponry, including their melee weapons, so prioritizing defense against that damage type is recommended. The potential for taking a big hit from the melee weapons of either enemy is quite high given the chaotic nature of the fight, so it's worth putting together an AC with high AP and attitude stability to help absorb some of those potential blows. Those specs will also allow you to be a bit more aggressive and fight both enemies at close range to try and finish one of them off quickly, so to help further facilitate that, close-range weaponry that specializes in one-on-one encounters is recommended. The ZIMMERMAN shotguns can very quickly and heavily strain the ACS of either AC, so are a good choice for creating your openings to deal heavy damage, which is something that a weapon like the MORLEY spread bazooka excels at.

01	R-ARM UNIT | SHOTGUN **SG-027 ZIMMERMAN**	P.54
02	L-ARM UNIT | SHOTGUN **SG-027 ZIMMERMAN**	P.54
03	R-BACK UNIT | SPREAD BAZOOKA **SB-033M MORLEY**	P.66
04	L-BACK UNIT | SPREAD BAZOOKA **SB-033M MORLEY**	P.66
05	HEAD | — **VE-44A**	P.78
06	CORE | — **07-061 MIND ALPHA**	P.81
07	ARMS | — **IA-C01A: EPHEMERA**	P.84
08	LEGS | TETRAPOD **VP-424**	P.86
09	BOOSTER | — **ALULA/21E**	P.88
10	FCS | — **FC-008 TALBOT**	P.90
11	GENERATOR | — **VP-20C**	P.92

AC // DUAL NATURE

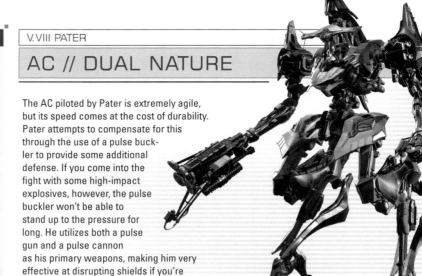

The AC piloted by Pater is extremely agile, but its speed comes at the cost of durability. Pater attempts to compensate for this through the use of a pulse buckler to provide some additional defense. If you come into the fight with some high-impact explosives, however, the pulse buckler won't be able to stand up to the pressure for long. He utilizes both a pulse gun and a pulse cannon as his primary weapons, making him very effective at disrupting shields if you're using one, but if your anti-energy spec is high enough, those shots will deal little AP damage and only moderate ACS strain, so you're better off without one.

BASIC SPECS

AP	8690
Attitude Stability	1431
Anti-Kinetic Defense	1005
Anti-Energy Defense	1098
Anti-Explosive Defense	977
Elec. Discharge Tolerance	490
Shock Resistance	54%
ACS Anomaly Tolerance	490
Heat Resistance	54%
Repair Kits	2

Pater's mobility makes slower munitions less effective, since he'll often Quick Boost away from incoming fire. However, because his AC has relatively low attitude stability, you don't need to land as many shots as you would against other ACs before causing a stagger. DUAL NATURE'S low AP also means that you only need a couple of staggers to be able to deal enough damage to destroy it, and that can happen very quickly if you aggressively stick to him and try to position yourself around him, limiting his movement by forcing him into walls or corners. Keep in mind, however, that he will activate the terminal armor Core Expansion once during the fight upon taking lethal damage, so don't let up after depleting his AP, because you're going to need to land a few more shots to finish him off for good.

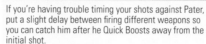

If you're having trouble timing your shots against Pater, put a slight delay between firing different weapons so you can catch him after he Quick Boosts away from the initial shot.

Pater's terminal armor will interrupt your combat flow. If he has an unused repair kit, he will always use it once his terminal armor is activated.

AC DUAL NATURE ATTACKS

HI-16: GU-Q1

DESCRIPTION Pulse gun that shoots out quick but inaccurate bursts of pulse energy that spread in a cone-shaped pattern at range.

EVASION Quick Boost to either side of the shots.

HI-32: BU-TT/A

DESCRIPTION Pulse blade with a moderate range that he'll swing twice with when used.

EVASION Quick Boost away from Pater to avoid the swipes.

KRANICH/60Z

DESCRIPTION Pulse cannon that fires bursts of pulse energy with much greater accuracy than the pulse gun.

EVASION Quick Boost to either side of the shots.

VP-61PB

DESCRIPTION Pater will use his pulse buckler when attacked, and will often use his other pulse munitions simultaneously.

EVASION Not used offensively.

TERMINAL ARMOR

DESCRIPTION Once AC DUAL NATURE's AP has taken a lethal hit, it will utilize its Core Expansion to deploy an extremely durable barrier. If Pater has any repair kits remaining, he'll use one here, otherwise his AC will be brought to 1 AP.

EVASION Not used offensively.

AC // RECONFIG

In stark contrast to DUAL NATURE, AC RECONFIG, piloted by Hawkins, is a heavily armored behemoth with defensive specs that make him resistant to all damage types. Despite using a defensive frame, however, Hawkins tends to operate at mid range, where he'll attempt to constantly barrage you with an array of plasma weapons, forcing you to also contend with trying to maneuver around the lingering damage fields they leave behind.

Due to the considerable number of damage fields he creates, attempting to fight Hawkins at his preferred range can be extremely difficult, so you should either try to outrange him or get in close. The high AP and attitude stability of RECONFIG means it's going to be difficult to strain its ACS and will take some time to destroy it, so unless your own defensive specs can match, trading blows will not be a viable approach and you'll need to be very precise with your evasion.

Thanks to its tetrapod legs, Hawkins will often try to hover above you in AC RECONFIG to increase the effectiveness of its plasma munitions. Your best defense against this is to try to match or exceed his altitude, something which will be much easier if you're also using tetrapod legs. If you can stay at that altitude and get around him, you'll often find openings to land solid hits against him. Unlike Pater, Hawkins will periodically stop moving, leaving himself open to attack.

BASIC SPECS

AP	11510
Attitude Stability	2295
Anti-Kinetic Defense	1214
Anti-Energy Defense	1303
Anti-Explosive Defense	1230
Elec. Discharge Tolerance	490
Shock Resistance	17%
ACS Anomaly Tolerance	490
Heat Resistance	17%
Repair Kits	2

AC RECONFIG ATTACKS

Vvc-760PR

DESCRIPTION Plasma rifle with two firing modes: quick shot and charged. The beam from both modes creates a lingering damage field upon making contact with anything, but the charged version produces three simultaneous, outward-fanning beams instead of just one.

EVASION Evade the beams by boosting to the side, and then immediately jump into the air to avoid the lingering damage fields.

Vvc-770LB

DESCRIPTION This laser blade is Hawkins's answer for when you get too close; can be charged to extend the range and hit twice.

EVASION Quick Boost away from Hawkins to get out of the weapon's range.

VP-60LCS

DESCRIPTION High-damage energy beam that travels quickly through the air. This weapon is often used in conjunction with the Vvc-760PR.

EVASION Quick Boost away from the shot the moment it fires.

PULSE ARMOR

DESCRIPTION Pulse barrier that covers AC RECONFIG and absorbs damage until you exceed its durability.

EVASION Not used offensively.

Vvc-706PM

DESCRIPTION Plasma missile launcher that releases six front-facing missiles that leave a lingering damage field at their point of impact. They have limited homing capabilities and are often fired while Hawkins is strafing or about to use another attack.

EVASION At close proximity, these missiles are difficult to evade, but taking an aerial position will help limit the effectiveness of the lingering damage fields. At range, they can be jumped over or evaded with Quick Boosts.

Try to pay attention to the trajectory of Hawkins's plasma shots so that you can judge where the lingering damage field will be and can stay clear of it.

*"Hate to say it, but... Rubicon still needs me.
So, buddy... Who needs you?"*

—V.IV Rusty

The final leg of your journey to explore the Depths beneath Watchpoint Alpha leads you to an area that the PCA has attempted to keep hidden from the other factions on the planet. With the laser barrier that was blocking entry to this area now disabled, their secret is exposed and you're free to explore and attempt to uncover what they've been hiding: the location of the Coral convergence. This cave system starts off very open, but as you descend below the reactor, you'll find that it quickly turns into a series of narrow tunnels and cramped rooms, filled with swarms of natural inhabitants. These mealworms serve more as obstacles than opponents, and since there's no purpose in killing them unnecessarily, doing so is simply a waste of ammunition, and something you can't afford to do, because the real crux of the mission is the showdown with your former ally at the end.

AC ASSEMBLY

Rusty's primary weapons deal kinetic and energy damage, so you'll want to focus all of your defensive attention on those areas, with kinetic being the highest priority. The fight against him takes place in a relatively enclosed area that doesn't offer you much room to move around, making a heavier build with high AP and attitude stability the recommended approach, so that you can use brute force rather than finesse to deal with him. Conversely, AC STEEL HAZE has relatively low defensive specs, so in keeping with the theme of a close-range fight, weapons such as shotguns can be extremely devastating to its AP. Since it's particularly weak to explosive damage, the MORLEY spread bazookas are also very effective and are the perfect accompaniment to the ZIMMERMAN shotguns

01	R-ARM UNIT | SHOTGUN	P.54	
	SG-027 ZIMMERMAN		
02	L-ARM UNIT | SHOTGUN	P.54	
	SG-027 ZIMMERMAN		
03	R-BACK UNIT | SPREAD BAZOOKA	P.66	
	SB-033M MORLEY		
04	L-BACK UNIT | SPREAD BAZOOKA	P.66	
	SB-033M MORLEY		
05	HEAD |	P.77	
	AH-J-124 BASHO		BAWS
06	CORE |	P.79	
	CC-3000 WRECKER		RaD
07	ARMS |	P.84	
	IA-C01A: EPHEMERA		RI
08	LEGS | TETRAPOD	P.86	
	LG-033M VERRILL		
09	BOOSTER |	P.88	
	ALULA/21E		
10	FCS |	P.90	
	FC-008 TALBOT		
11	GENERATOR |	P.92	
	VP-20D		

MISSION OBJECTIVES

Reach the Heart of the Unknown Territory (1)
Defeat V.IV Rusty
Reach the Heart of the Unknown Territory (2)

MISSION INFO

Combat Zone	Watchpoint Alpha—Unknown Territory
Client	Arquebus Corporation
Reward	260,000
Max Bonus Pay	—
Completion Unlocks	Rubicon III Research Institute Emblem
Combat Logs	Platinum x1
Data Logs	—
Part Containers	1

ENEMY DATA

	No.	AP	AS	Bonus Pay	Analysis
● Mealworm	38	339	—	—	—
◎ AC STEEL HAZE / V.IV Rusty	1	10725	1482	—	—

IA-C01H: EPHEMERA

01 You begin on a bridge leading to the reactor you destroyed in a previous mission, and while you're free to explore the area, there's nothing to collect, so you can simply drop off the side and descend toward the tunnel opening far below you. The Coral in the cave will begin to interfere with your systems when you approach the opening, and from that point onward you'll lose access to your compass. Thankfully, the tunnel you're entering is fairly linear so you won't need your compass for navigation, and the only enemies you'll encounter are local fauna called mealworms.

02 After following the tunnel down for a while you'll eventually emerge onto a ledge overlooking a wide chasm, and you'll need to be mindful of your EN when attempting to cross it, because it's bottomless; if you run out of EN partway and drop below the lower altitude limit you'll cost yourself a portion of your AP right before a difficult encounter. When you reach the back of the room on the opposite side of the chasm, you'll finally find out just who it was that's been tailing you, and with no other choice, you're forced into a confrontation with your old buddy, V.IV Rusty.

HIDDEN IN PLAIN SIGHT

There's a part container tucked away next to the tunnel wall just after a short drop, and it can be easy to miss while you're quickly moving through the area trying to avoid the blasts from the mealworms. If you reach the large chasm with the breeding pods and haven't yet opened the container, backtrack slightly to retrieve its contents before you cross the gap.

V.IV RUSTY

AC // STEEL HAZE

Having proven to be too dangerous and effective to both be left alive, Arquebus has attempted to set you and Rusty up, creating a showdown between you from which only one will get out alive. After the cutscene in which STEEL HAZE reveals itself, you'll immediately be in combat with it in the center of the small room you pass through. There's very little effective cover to use, and most of the objects in the room serve more to impede your movement than help you escape incoming fire, but the same is true for your opponent. With some smart positioning, you can often use the high mobility of STEEL HAZE to your advantage by making it trap itself against the wall while trying to evade one of your attacks, making it much easier to land your subsequent ones.

Rusty tends to prefer keeping a moderate distance from you while trying to use the mobility of STEEL HAZE to constantly move around while firing his kinetic weapons. While that might be an effective strategy in many encounters, the environment is not in his favor here. Trying to stay at range just plays into his hand, but thankfully, the small room makes it very easy for you to cut off his movement, allowing you to easily move in and pressure him with your close-range weaponry. With its main advantage nullified, the low AP and attitude stability of STEEL HAZE won't be able to stand up to the power of your weapons. When the AP of his AC reaches critical levels, Rusty will leave the battlefield, wounded but still alive and vowing to return.

BASIC SPECS

AP	8580
Attitude Stability	1499
Anti-Kinetic Defense	1001
Anti-Energy Defense	1057
Anti-Explosive Defense	976
Elec. Discharge Tolerance	490
Shock Resistance	-8%
ACS Anomaly Tolerance	490
Heat Resistance	-8%
Repair Kits	3

AC STEEL HAZE ATTACKS

BOOST KICK

DESCRIPTION Rusty will Assault Boost toward you and attempt to kick your AC.

EVASION Quick Boost to either side as he approaches you.

MA-E-211 SAMPU

DESCRIPTION Burst handgun that Rusty will use as his primary weapon; deals limited damage but can quickly strain your ACS.

EVASION Has particularly short range and can be easily out-spaced.

Vvc-774LS

DESCRIPTION Rusty will often use this laser slicer when your ACS is strained, attempting to overload it and deal heavy direct damage. The weapon's blades will spin in a circular pattern dealing multiple hits for a period of time, concluding with a large horizontal slash downward.

EVASION Chain Quick Boosts away from Rusty as he uses the weapon; can lead to opportunities to counterattack him.

Vvc-703PM

DESCRIPTION Releases three plasma missiles with a slow break that leave lingering damage fields on impact.

EVASION Chain Quick Boosts away from the missiles to ensure you escape both their initial detonations and lingering damage fields.

MA-J-200 RANSETSU-RF

DESCRIPTION Low-damage burst rifle that Rusty fires alongside his SAMPU to try and quickly strain your ACS.

EVASION Quick Boost away from the stream of kinetic rounds.

03 Once the fight is over, continue down the tunnel a small distance and drop down into the deep crevasse on the opposite side of the room. Following a lengthy drop, you'll reach your destination and complete the mission.

REACH THE CORAL CONVERGENCE

"I'll see that the arrogant dog is punished and brought to heel..."

—V.II Snail

Although you were responsible for wresting the path to Insitute City from the PCA's grasp, the corporations, and especially Arquebus, still think they're in charge and want you to cease any further action in the area so that they can claim the Coral for themselves. The PCA and RLF also have some forces in the area, and while the two Arquebus ACs pose the biggest immediate threat, there are far more dangerous foes that await you at the Coral convergence.

Many of the enemies you encounter here are ones you haven't faced before, so even though you have access to a supply sherpa later in the mission, don't engage recklessly or underestimate your opponents until you've become familiar with their attack patterns. You will need to face off against many of those dangerous foes if you want to obtain the large number of combat logs available, but the huge boost to your Hunter Class upon completing the mission will make it worth the effort. The city itself is broken up into different districts comprised of terrains varying from destroyed cityscapes to large open bodies of shallow water, but one thing they all have in common is that there's always plenty of cover available if you're paying attention to the environment.

MISSION OBJECTIVES

Defeat V.VI Maeterlinck / G3 Wu Huahai

Reach the Coral Convergence

Destroy the Ibis Series CEL 240

MISSION INFO

Combat Zone	Rubicon Research Institute City
Client	Handler Walter
Reward	520,000
Max Bonus Pay	—
Completion Unlocks	—
Combat Logs	Gold x2, Silver x2, Bronze x9
Data Logs	2
Part Containers	2

IA-C01W2: MOONLIGHT

04

03

Image Data: STK Sketch

B Video Record: The Fires of Ibis

02

01

A IA-C01W3: AURORA

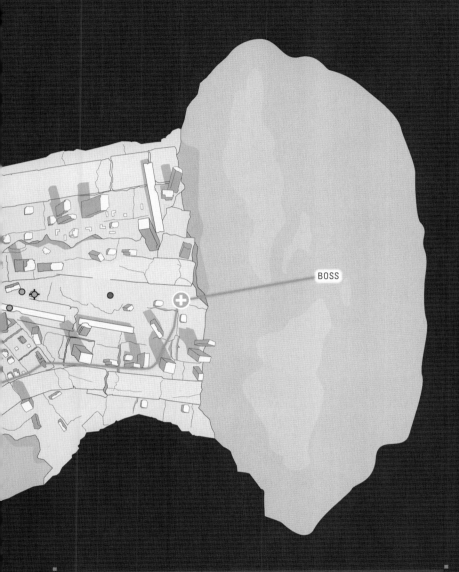

BOSS

AC ASSEMBLY

Despite the fact that you'll be encountering a high volume of enemies throughout this mission, a suite of weapons that specializes in single-target damage will serve you much better due to the difficulty of the ACs and the boss you'll need to contend with. The reliability of the paired gatling guns for pinning down fast-moving opponents while inflicting significant ACS strain is effective at combating the speed of the ACs and boss. This configuration is supplemented with dual spread bazookas to inflict lethal damage on most staggered targets.

CEL 240 uses Coral-based weaponry so there's no defensive spec to help mitigate its damage, but most of the other enemies use either explosive or energy weapon types, so you should factor those defenses into your assembly. The frame parts recommended here give you a balance of both of those defensive specs, but if you're finding one damage type harming you more than the other, you might want to swap some parts around to better suit your requirements. Most leg types can work well in this mission, but it is recommended to go with the tetrapod legs, because the HELIANTHUS are much easier to deal with from the air.

No.	Part	Name	Page
01	R-ARM UNIT	GATLING GUN	DF-GA-08 HU-BEN	P.53
02	L-ARM UNIT	GATLING GUN	DF-GA-08 HU-BEN	P.53
03	R-BACK UNIT	SPREAD BAZOOKA	SB-033M MORLEY	P.66
04	L-BACK UNIT	SPREAD BAZOOKA	SB-033M MORLEY	P.66
05	HEAD	—	HD-033M VERRILL	P.77
06	CORE	—	VE-40A	P.81
07	ARMS	—	VP-46S	P.83
08	LEGS	TETRAPOD	LG-033M VERRILL	P.86
09	BOOSTER	—	FLUEGEL/21Z	P.88
10	FCS	—	FC-008 TALBOT	P.90
11	GENERATOR	—	VP-20C	P.92

ENEMY DATA

	No.	AP	AS	Bonus Pay	Analysis
MT-E-104 Bipedal MT (Grenade Cannon)	2	470	364	—	P.316
AM14: SENTRY SG MT (Missile Launcher)	2	437	310	—	P.320
AC INFECTION / V.VI Maeterlinck	1	9570	1598	—	—
AC LI LONG / G3 Wu Huahai	1	13530	2139	—	—
AM02: DENOISER (Support Type)	4	1254	783	—	P.340
AM02: DENOISER (Sniper Type)	4	1254	783	—	P.339
IE-09: HELIANTHUS	9	2800	1053	—	P.344
IA-05: WEEVIL (Cluster Missile Launcher)	1	9550	1600	—	P.344
IA-05: WEEVIL (Detonating Cannon)	1	9550	1600	—	P.345
AM02: DENOISER (Melee Type)	2	1254	783	—	P.339
AM02: DENOISER (Heavy Firepower)	1	4775	1600	—	P.340
IB-01: CEL 240	1	42020	1700	—	—

Defeat V.VI Maeterlinck / G3 Wu Huahai

01 ◈ Upon first touching down in the city, you'll be able to see signs of an intense battle off in the distance involving the corporations and PCA forces. The two corporation ACs are your main targets, and depending on how you want to handle the fight against them, you can either wait until the battle has concluded or dive straight in and try to take advantage of the chaos. Waiting for the fight to end does mean the ACs are likely to have less AP when you fight them and you won't have to contend with any of the PCA forces, but reaching the site of the conflict as soon as possible is the recommended approach. Engaging the ACs while they're distracted by the other enemies makes it much easier for you to land your shots and less likely that they'll target you; you'll be able to separate them and concentrate your efforts on destroying them one at a time.

Begin your approach by heading around the buildings so that you emerge behind the corporation forces, trapping them between you and the PCA units. From there, identify which of the corporation ACs either has the lowest AP or is closest to being staggered, and focus all of your attention on it. If either their positioning doesn't allow for that, or if there isn't much of a difference between their ACS strain, then it's recommended that you focus on V.VI Maeterlinck first, since her AC has lower AP and defensive specs.

Land a good opening barrage and it's possible to finish either of the ACs off very quickly. If your initial target survives, however, try to position yourself so that if it moves, it does so into one of the buildings or away from the other enemies, separating it from nearby support units. The ACs should be your primary focus, so ignore all of the other enemies until both of them have been destroyed. If you notice them targeting you while you're fighting the ACs, try to use the environment for cover until you're ready to take them on.

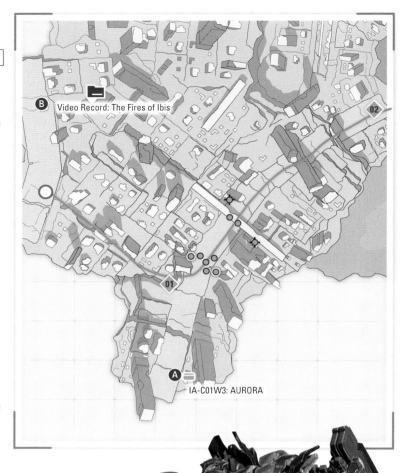

B Video Record: The Fires of Ibis

A IA-C01W3: AURORA

V.VI MAETERLINCK

AC // INFECTION

V.VI Maeterlinck pilots a midweight AC build that focuses on streams of shots from its pulse gun to suppress your AC before releasing a high-impact charge shot from its plasma cannon. She'll try to use her pulse shield to mitigate damage, but if you keep her between you and the PCA forces you can all but remove its defensive abilities from the fight; she'll constantly turn to block either your or their shots, opening her up to attacks from both sides. If she takes some extra hits from the PCA, she can prove to be a relatively easy target, thanks to how quickly you can strain INFECTION's ACS with the recommended assembly.

BASIC SPECS

AP	9570
Attitude Stability	1698
Anti-Kinetic Defense	1136
Anti-Energy Defense	1183
Anti-Explosive Defense	1070
Elec. Discharge Tolerance	490
Shock Resistance	-8%
ACS Anomaly Tolerance	490
Heat Resistance	-8%
Repair Kits	1

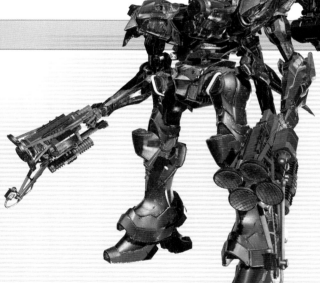

AC INFECTION ATTACKS

VP-61PS

DESCRIPTION Pulse shield which Maeterlinck will use as she moves around the battlefield.

EVASION Not used offensively.

HI-16: GU-Q1 (X2)

DESCRIPTION Pulse gun that shoots out quick but inaccurate bursts of pulse energy that spread in a cone-shaped pattern at range.

EVASION Quick Boost or jump away from the bursts.

FASAN/60E

DESCRIPTION This plasma cannon fires a fast, high-impact shot with a large lingering damage field.

EVASION Quick Boost toward Maeterlinck at an angle to avoid the shot itself, which should also limit your exposure to the damage field.

AC // LI LONG

Despite being a heavy build, LI LONG does not come equipped with heavy or high-impact munitions and tends to favor either a close-range aggressive style, or a more mid-range aerial dominance tactic through sustained damage and ACS strain. Wu Huahai will attempt to make good use of LI LONG's tetrapod legs by hovering above the battlefield, firing barrages of missiles and streams of bullets at you. Both of those attacks can be difficult to evade in the narrow streets if you position yourself poorly and end up boosting into the side of a building, so always be mindful of the space around you while keeping your focus on your target.

BASIC SPECS

AP	11930
Attitude Stability	2249
Anti-Kinetic Defense	1264
Anti-Energy Defense	1152
Anti-Explosive Defense	1268
Elec. Discharge Tolerance	490
Shock Resistance	-27%
ACS Anomaly Tolerance	490
Heat Resistance	-27%
Repair Kits	1

Like INFECTION, LI LONG also has a pulse buckler that it will use while continuing to fire, so depending on how long it took you to destroy INFECTION, you may or may not be able to use the PCA forces to help you bypass the defensive measure and will need to rely on brute force or wait for an opening. Overwhelming fire from your gatling guns will quickly overcome the shield, so sticking close to him and playing aggressively while forcing him back into a wall is the recommended approach.

AC LI LONG ATTACKS

MG-014 LUDLOW

DESCRIPTION Machine gun that fires low-impact kinetic rounds at high speed to quickly strain your ACS.

EVASION Quick Boost away from the bullets.

HML-G3/P08SPL-06

DESCRIPTION Split missile launcher that launches one pod which breaks into six missiles.

EVASION Quick Boost to either side of the pattern of missiles.

BML-G2/P19SPL-12

DESCRIPTION Three-cell split missile launcher that is used at range. These missiles have a fast break after splitting from their initial pod.

EVASION Missiles are nearly head-on and at range can be evaded by strafing while boosting or with a Quick Boost.

SI-24: SU-Q5

DESCRIPTION Heavy pulse buckler that Wu Huahai will use as he moves around the battlefield.

EVASION Not used offensively.

ASSAULT ARMOR

DESCRIPTION Core Expansion that produces a pulse shockwave around LI LONG.

EVASION Quick Boost away as it charges the energy.

A — This part container can be found atop a small building located behind the skyscrapers near the road's end.

B — The wreck containing this data log sits high above the battlefield.

C — You can easily pick out the functioning WEEVIL drones from the destroyed ones by the glowing sensors on the front of their heads.

DATA LOG / PART CONTAINER

While you can acquire the data log and open the part container before you engage the enemies in this area, it's worth waiting until they've all been destroyed so that you can get the most benefit from both groups fighting each other. After that, simply boost down the road behind where the ACs were making their stand to find a part container on a low rooftop at **Position A**. The data log is on the opposite side of the area, and the easiest way to reach it is to make your way back up to the road near where you started and follow it along until you reach **Position B**. Look to the side of the road from there and you'll be able to see a very tall building with two other smaller ones leaning against it; the data log is atop the tall building, so just Assault Boost straight up there to find the wreck which contains it. ▶ A-B

OBJECTIVE	Reach the Coral Convergence

02 ◇ Upon reaching the end of the road, you'll be able to look out over a wide, shallow-water chasm, with a bridge spanning the open area between here and the objective location on the opposite side. Look down to the waters below and you'll see a large number of HELIANTHUS units rolling around, each of which you

can obtain a combat log from if you destroy them. There are even more combat logs and other collectibles to acquire in this area if you're will to risk exploring.

The HELIANTHUS are dangerous foes that can inflict huge amounts of damage very quickly by rolling into you with their grinders, but if you've equipped the recommended tetrapod legs, you can spend most of your time hovering above them to nullify that attack. Their speed makes them difficult to hit if they gain distance on you, however, so only fire on them when they're rolling beneath you. Another effective strategy is to drop to the ground and bait the HELIANTHUS to charge you, then fire both spread bazookas when it enters range, though this should only be attempted when a single HELIANTHUS is present.

There are two groups of HELIANTHUS: one near the start of the bridge and another near the opposite end. Avoid engaging both groups at once, as the sheer number of missiles they fire will swiftly overwhelm you. When you're engaged with the group on the opposite side of the lake, make sure not to cross beneath the bridge, or you might drag the two WEEVILs into the fight with an errant shot. ▶ C

03 ◈ Make sure to open the part container after destroying all of the HELIANTHUS, and then make your way over to this area near the data log, which at first glance appears safe. You can freely move around without any risk, but the instant you finish scanning the data log, two WEEVILs that were lying in wait will spring into action and ambush you. These enemies are extremely tough and are equipped with some dangerous weaponry, which makes fighting them in open combat a risky proposition. You can, however, attack them before you access the data log, and attacking one of them will not cause the other to become active, allowing you to pick them off one at a time. If you attack them in their dormant state with full barrages from all of your weapons, it's possible to destroy them before they can return fire, allowing you to access the data log unscathed.

PROCEED WITH CAUTION

There has been no additional checkpoint since you emerged from the engagement with the two ACs. This means that if you're defeated in this section, you'll have to reobtain all logs and parts you've collected, so proceed with caution.

04 ◈ The final stretch before you reach the Coral convergence has you once again moving through the destroyed cityscape above the lake, and in a last-ditch effort to stop you from reaching it, the PCA has deployed a large number of their DENOISER drones to the area. Their sniper units hold elevated positions that make a frontal approach dangerous. Since there's nothing to be gained from destroying them, it's best to sneak around them by skirting the edge of the combat zone until you reach the objective, where a supply sherpa awaits. This is your last chance to prepare, so be sure to make use of the sherpa's services. Once you descend into the giant crater filled with Coral, you'll be attacked by the extremely dangerous IB-01: CEL 240 C-Weapon.

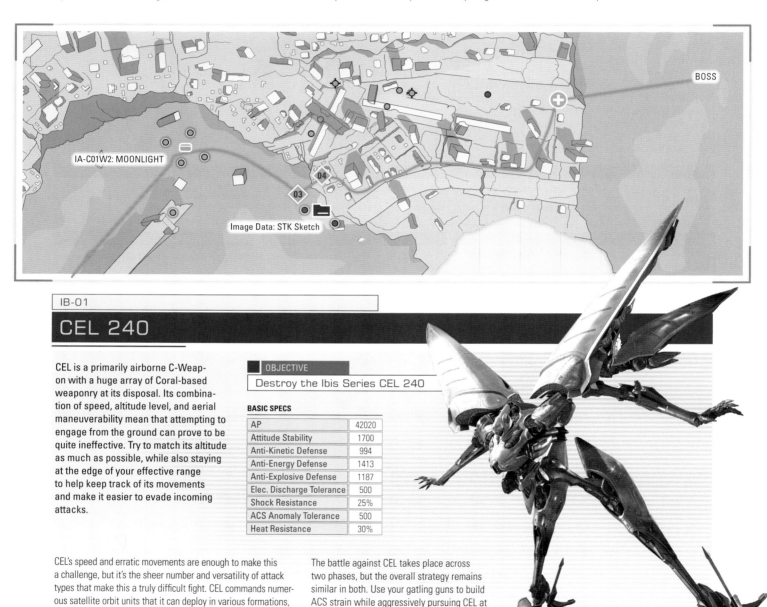

BOSS

IA-C01W2: MOONLIGHT

04

03

Image Data: STK Sketch

IB-01

CEL 240

CEL is a primarily airborne C-Weapon with a huge array of Coral-based weaponry at its disposal. Its combination of speed, altitude level, and aerial maneuverability mean that attempting to engage from the ground can prove to be quite ineffective. Try to match its altitude as much as possible, while also staying at the edge of your effective range to help keep track of its movements and make it easier to evade incoming attacks.

OBJECTIVE

Destroy the Ibis Series CEL 240

BASIC SPECS

AP	42020
Attitude Stability	1700
Anti-Kinetic Defense	994
Anti-Energy Defense	1413
Anti-Explosive Defense	1187
Elec. Discharge Tolerance	500
Shock Resistance	25%
ACS Anomaly Tolerance	500
Heat Resistance	30%

CEL's speed and erratic movements are enough to make this a challenge, but it's the sheer number and versatility of attack types that make this a truly difficult fight. CEL commands numerous satellite orbit units that it can deploy in various formations, either away from or directly in front of your AC, allowing it to fire Coral beams at you from a multitude of different angles. In addition to those, CEL can generate Coral blades using its arm-mounted Coral oscillator. These appear either directly on its arms, or autonomously around its frame, and it can use them for direct melee attacks, or even as ranged attacks, thanks to the energy waves they can produce.

The battle against CEL takes place across two phases, but the overall strategy remains similar in both. Use your gatling guns to build ACS strain while aggressively pursuing CEL at close range; Target Assist is excellent for tracking its chaotic movements. Depending on the phase, there are certain attacks where you will want to back off and remain defensive, but succeeding in staggering CEL lets you decimate its AP with your spread bazookas at point blank.

PHASES

1 CEL always opens this phase with a v-pattern combo. This attack has a lengthy recovery period where CEL remains stationary—a huge opportunity for you to inflict ACS strain.

In general, any attack where CEL creates Coral blades precludes CEL standing still, sometimes for several seconds. Your goal in this phase is to pursue CEL closely, identify these Coral blade attacks, and dodge appropriately before building ACS strain. You can usually cause ACS overload before overheating both your gatling guns, then blast CEL with your spread bazookas for massive direct hit damage. Your build is quite heavy, so Boost Kicks are also a good way to keep hammering the boss before it recovers.

If you see CEL instead deploy lasers via its long-range Coral orbits, it's time to go on the defensive and give the boss some space. Don't worry about doing damage or building ACS strain during these attacks, as it's simply going to get you caught in the middle of CEL's Coral orbit beams. Maintain a distance of around 300m and wait for the hail of beams to clear before re-engaging the boss. After depleting its AP, CEL will briefly shut down before rebooting into phase two.

2 CEL begins this phase with an impressive light show of Coral explosions and beams. Unfortunately, you can't damage it until its name and filled AP gauge reappear, so all you can do is watch the fireworks. This beam barrage will damage you, however, so maintain a distance of around 400m and continuously move to evade the Coral projectiles.

Phase two retains the same general attack patterns and rules from phase one: build ACS strain during Coral blade attacks, and play defensive during Coral orbit attacks. The main differences are CEL is faster and gains a slightly augmented move set in this phase.

The unique attacks CEL uses in Phase 2 frequently involve sweeping Coral blades that skim the floor of the arena. This requires you to be prepared to jump or remain airborne at times; tetrapod legs make timing these jumps easier, and give you some additional aerial mobility if you need to make a hasty retreat. The battle against CEL is one of the most challenging you will experience, but if you remain persistent, this Rubiconian relic will soon meet the same doomed fate as its masters.

IB-01: CEL 240 ATTACKS

V-FORMATION COMBO   PHASE 1

DESCRIPTION Orbits take on a v-formation and rain Coral energy down on you. After the orbits, CEL brandishes its blade before flying toward you while performing a slash that also produces an energy wave. Always begins the fight with this attack.

EVASION Jump into the air and boost upward and away from CEL.

CLUSTER FORMATION COMBO ▼   PHASE 1

DESCRIPTION CEL places the orbits in a cluster before releasing their energy and slashing at you with its blade from a distance. It will then position its orbits in another cluster to release another wave of lasers; will sometimes slash first then release two volleys of lasers.

EVASION Jump into the air and boost upward and away from CEL.

ORBIT QUICK BURSTS   PHASE 1

DESCRIPTION Three Coral orbits that release Coral energy.

EVASION Chain Quick Boosts to avoid the three shots.

CHARGED BEAM BARRAGE ▼   PHASE 1

DESCRIPTION CEL takes a static position at long range and begins charging a series of high-impact Coral shots with its chest-mounted Coral cannon.

EVASION Strafe to one side as CEL charges the shots and then Quick Boost in the other direction as the shot is released.

CROSS SLASH ▼   PHASE 1

DESCRIPTION CEL adopts a similar position to its beam barrage but will brandish its arm-mounted Coral oscillators in a cross-pattern before slashing with them, releasing waves of Coral energy.

EVASION Quick Boost away from CEL and jump into the air, ready to aerially Quick Boost.

THREE-HIT COMBO ▼   PHASE 1

DESCRIPTION CEL quickly charges its blades before releasing a three-hit ranged slash combo. The first two slashes release quickly, but the third strike has a slight delay; will sometimes only slash twice.

EVASION Quick Boost to whichever side of the energy wave requires the least boost distance to evade it. Make sure to pause after the second slash in order to have a properly timed Quick Boost for the third slash.

CONTINUOUS BEAM BARRAGE   PHASE 2

DESCRIPTION CEL will place all of its long-range Coral orbits in front of you and release a much higher-volume version of its beam barrage.

EVASION The duration of the attack will necessitate longer evasion time than the shorter Phase 1 version, but you can use a combination of your Quick Boost and normal boosting while strafing to evade them.

TRIPLE ORBIT QUICK BURSTS   PHASE 2

DESCRIPTION This version of Phase 1's orbit quick burst is amplified by an additional two rounds of beams. The orbits will be placed in different locations for each burst.

EVASION Wait until the orbits appear in front of you and then Quick Boost away. If this would drain too much EN then it is advisable to strafe continuously to one side and away from CEL.

OVERHEAD SLAM   PHASE 2

DESCRIPTION CEL produces three large blades above its head and brings them down on you. The blades are stacked behind each other.

EVASION Quick Boost to either side of the blades.

ENCLOSING SLASH   PHASE 2

DESCRIPTION CEL produces a number of blades around itself and keeps them drawn for a brief moment before drawing them inward, enclosing them around your AC. Each blade can hit you individually.

EVASION Chain uses of your Quick Boost away from CEL before it can draw the blades in.

DOWNWARD SLASH   PHASE 2

DESCRIPTION CEL will produce a fan of oscillator blades and slash downward at you with them. These blades have a long reach and come down at a diagonal angle. Each blade can hit you individually.

EVASION Quick Boost toward and past CEL if at close range; Quick Boost away if at mid or long-range.

DIVE COMBO   PHASE 2

DESCRIPTION CEL masks itself in Coral energy and rushes toward you three times. For the first two strikes, it will move along the ground diagonally, with one wing in the ground and the other in the air. It will then place itself flush with the ground for the third strike, which has more range than the previous two.

EVASION Chain Quick Boosts directly away from CEL for the first two strikes and jump over it for the third.

22

ESCAPE

"The Coral must be burned, 621. Even if that means reigniting the fire that scorched the stars."

—Handler Walter

After the vicious Arquebus ambush at the end of the previous mission, you now find yourself in the tunnels below the city with your usual AC destroyed, forcing you to pilot an old cobbled-together AC that was left here by Walter. This AC is unsuitable for heavy combat, so you should try to avoid unnecessary engagements and only take on single targets or small groups. Ideally, however, you should sneak around enemies as much as possible if you want to get through the city in one piece. Thankfully, most of the enemies are standard bipedal MTs. Once you're out of the tunnels, the cityscape provides you plenty of avenues for stealth or cover. Just be sure to diligently use your scan, so you can spot enemies and plan your route around them.

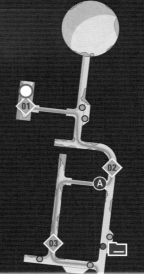

Video Record: Testing New Components

MISSION INFO

Combat Zone	Institute City
Client	Handler Walter
Reward	—
Max Bonus Pay	—
Completion Unlocks	AH-J-124/RC JAILBREAK (Head), AC-J-120/RC JAILBREAK (Core), AA-J-123/RC JAILBREAK (Arms), AL-J-121/RC JAILBREAK (Legs), Parts Shop Update 7
Combat Logs	—
Data Logs	1
Part Containers	—

MISSION OBJECTIVES

Reach the Destination

Reach the Rendezvous Point

Annihilate the Arquebus MT Squad

ENEMY DATA

	No.	AP	AS	Bonus Pay	Analysis
CD-J-098 Quad Drone (Cluster Missile Launcher)	8	302	310	—	P.312
TH-E-012 Transport Helicopter	2	750	—	—	P.314
MT-E-104 Bipedal MT (Dual Machine Gun)	7	470	364	—	P.316
MT-E-104 Bipedal MT (Cluster Gun)	23	470	364	—	P.317
MT-E-104 Bipedal MT (Shotgun)	1	470	364	—	P.317
MT-E-104 Bipedal MT (Grenade Cannon)	13	470	364	—	P.316
MT-J-048 Tetrapod MT (3-Shot Bazooka)	1	13370	2200	—	P.323
MT-J-048 Tetrapod MT (9-Shot Bazooka)	1	13370	2200	—	P.323

AC ASSEMBLY

Your assembly for this mission is predetermined, since you don't have access to the Garage. This means you won't be able to use the Assembly to change any of the parts on the mission fail screen. AC JAILBREAK is what you're piloting, and the parts it comes equipped with are listed here so that you know what you're working with. Your overall mobility, firepower, defensive specs, and AP are all very low, so you'll want to take a cautious approach during the mission; the purpose of this AC is simply to provide you a means of evading capture and making it to the extraction point in one piece, which is made much easier the fewer enemies you encounter. That said, at very close ranges the MORLEY is a potent option and will destroy any of the bipedal MTs you encounter in a single shot. The reload, however, is very slow, and it loses its destructive potential very quickly the further you are from the target, so you can get into trouble very quickly against multiple opponents.

UNATTAINABLE ASSEMBLY

Despite this being an AC for which you are given the frame parts, AC JAILBREAK's Booster, FCS, and Generator are unique to this mission, so you cannot replicate the full assembly anywhere else.

01	R-ARM UNIT | MACHINE GUN **MG-014 LUDLOW**	P.53
02	L-ARM UNIT | JAMMING BOMB LA. **MA-T-223 KYORIKU**	P.57 *AWS*
03	R-BACK UNIT | —	
04	L-BACK UNIT | SPREAD BAZOOKA **SB-033M MORLEY**	P.66
05	HEAD | — **AH-J-124/RC JAILBREAK**	P.77 *AWS*
06	CORE | — **AC-J-120/RC JAILBREAK**	P.80 *AWS*
07	ARMS | — **AA-J-123/RC JAILBREAK**	P.82 *AWS*
08	LEGS | BIPEDAL **AL-J-121/RC JAILBREAK**	P.84 *AWS*
09	BOOSTER | —	
10	FCS | —	
11	GENERATOR | —	

OBJECTIVE
Reach the Destination

01 Although made of low-grade parts with no real aptitude for combat or stealth, the AC you start with is your only lifeline. You can avoid combat entirely for most of the mission, but if you do find yourself up against an opponent, your best option is to get close enough to use your spread bazooka on them. Scanning at every turn is also crucial; it'll let you see which way they're facing so you know how to sneak around them.

When you're ready to start making your escape, jump into the small tunnel just ahead of you, but come to a stop about halfway along it. From there, you'll be able to see two patrolling bipedal MTs. If you want to destroy them, wait until they stop moving, at which point you can boost up behind one of them and destroy it with your spread bazooka, then fire a jamming bomb at the other enemy to give you time to reload your explosive and use it again. Alternatively, if you're quick, you can catch them both in a single jamming bomb and then simply boost straight past them; they won't pursue you.

02 Upon rounding the corner here, you'll be able to see the menacing red glint from the sensor on a tetrapod MT at the opposite end of the tunnel. With your current AC, attempting to take it on is a very risky proposition. Fire a jamming bomb up the tunnel to mask your presence, and then quickly boost into the branching path at **Position A**. ▶A

03 There are three more bipedal MTs in the tunnel just beyond this point, and it's highly recommended that you take the time to destroy them, because you'll have to traverse a lengthy section of tunnel. If you get caught by them and the tetrapod MT, they can easily overwhelm you. Use your scan as you approach the junction so that you can locate the closest one, and then quickly boost out and destroy it with your spread bazooka.

The sound will usually get the attention of the other two, but if you retreat back up the tunnel slightly they'll lose track of you and become unaware again, at which point you can repeat the process of scanning, boosting out to destroy one, then retreating back into the tunnel until all three have been destroyed. With the immediate area clear, you can move along to the junction near the tetrapod MT, fire another jamming bomb into the area to disrupt its sensors, and then either quickly access the wreck it's guarding for a data log or boost out through the opening in the tunnel and up to street level at **Position B**.

04 The streets of the city are lined with Arquebus forces searching for you, but with some smart use of shadows and rooftops, it's possible to evade them all and reach your destination safely. Ahead of where you land, you'll see quad drones flying overhead, sweeping specific parts of the area with searchlights. If they spot you, all nearby enemies will be drawn to your location, so stay clear of their light beams at all costs. To start your stealth route, boost over to the right side of the tunnel entrance and make your way between the buildings until you reach the cliff face. Your goal is to reach the vertical catapult at **Position C**, and if you stick to the shadows, move slowly, and scan often to keep track of enemies, you can make it there undetected. ▶B

Once you've reached that vertical catapult, use it, and then at the apex, Assault Boost over the nearby enemies toward another vertical catapult directly ahead at **Position D**. Use that catapult to reach the rooftop of the tall building directly next to it, and from there you can continue to utilize your Assault Boost from rooftop to rooftop in order to reach the wreck at **Position E**.

Arguably the most useful part of your temporary AC, the jamming bomb can briefly disrupt enemy targeting systems, buying you a few seconds of unrelenting fire or a quick escape.

A constant challenge in this mission is the terrain; the scrap AC barely has enough propulsion to clear simple jumps, and it will feel more like hopping around rather than flying.

OBJECTIVE
Reach the Rendezvous Point

05 Accessing the wreck releases an emergency beacon that lets your allies at RaD know where you are, and they'll designate a rendezvous point that you need to reach so they can pick you up. Unfortunately, that rendezvous point happens to be on the other side of an Arquebus blockade, which means you'll need to find a safe way around it. Start by facing the rendezvous location and dropping off the rooftop, so you land between the buildings. From there, advance into the area where the road has collapsed and flank outward until you reach the combat zone border. If you follow the boundary, you can use the buildings to keep you hidden from the enemy blockade until you're behind them, and can safely reach the rendezvous point.

OBJECTIVE
Annihilate the Arquebus MT Squad

06 Reaching the rendezvous point triggers an unavoidable ambush by a large number of Arquebus bipedal MTs. While it may seem like impossible odds given your current AC, you'll only have to hold out for a few precious seconds before help arrives. As soon as the ambush is sprung, quickly retreat back behind the large building here; not only does it make for excellent cover, but the narrow street between the buildings serves as a choke point, so that the enemies can only approach you single-file. Use your jamming bombs to further hinder their ability to target you, and if any of the enemy units gets close to the corner of the building, quickly pop out and use your spread bazooka to destroy them.

After a short period of time, Carla will join you and unleash a barrage of missiles that makes all of the enemies focus on her. All of the ambushing enemies need to be destroyed, but Carla is more than capable of doing that herself. If your AC is a little worse for wear, you can just duck behind one of the buildings to wait it out. Once the MT squad has been fully cleared, the mission will be complete and you can once again return to the safety of the Garage and your personal AC.

23

TAKE THE UNINHABITED FLOATING CITY

"The Observers fear the Coral, and want only to eradicate it."

—Ayre

In order to unlock the secrets hidden within the floating city of Xylem, RaD hackers are going to attempt to breach the systems contained inside the central control tower. Once they begin, Arquebus forces will close in quickly to investigate and attempt to put a stop to it, so Carla needs you to act as a last line of defense to stop them and protect the tower at all costs. Similar to the "Heavy Missile Launch Support" mission back in Chapter 2, you'll need to defend a single location on the map for five minutes, during which time Arquebus will send six waves of units at set intervals.

The majority of the units Arquebus sends at you will be smaller drones or bipedal MTs, but there are also some very dangerous LCs capable of rapid, high-damage outputs that you need to be wary of. Whether you choose to engage them near the building or venture out to intercept them is up to you, but the pair of artillery installations that serve as your backup can only hold the enemies off for so long if some slip past you; good compass awareness is a key component of this mission for finding and engaging enemies as quickly as possible. The control tower has a shield to help defend itself, and your potential bonus pay is tied directly to it. If the shield is still operational at the mission's end, regardless of how low its durability is, you'll receive the full 200,000 COAM. However, if it gets destroyed, you can only receive a maximum bonus of 120,000 COAM.

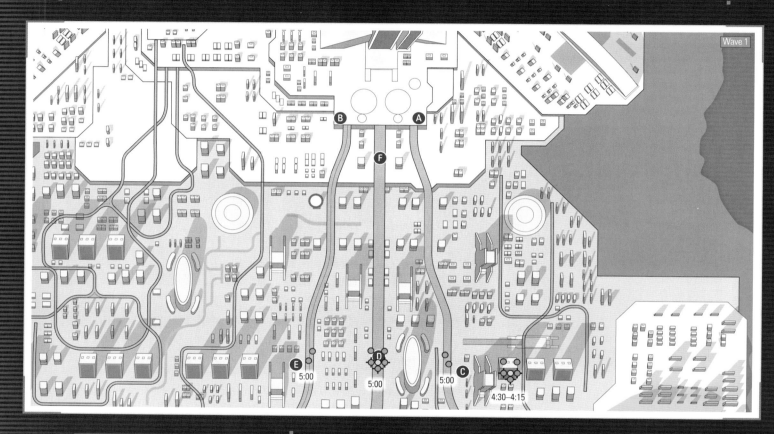

MISSION OBJECTIVE

Defend the Xylem's Control Tower

MISSION INFO

Combat Zone	Alea Ocean—Xylem, the Floating City
Client	"Cinder" Carla / Overseer
Reward	385,000
Max Bonus Pay	200,000
Completion Unlocks	—
Combat Logs	—
Data Logs	—
Part Containers	—

ENEMY DATA

		No.	AP	AS	Bonus Pay	Analysis
Wave 1	CD-J-098 Quad Drone (Cluster Missile Launcher)	4	302	310	—	P.312
Wave 1	TH-E-012 Transport Helicopter	2	750	—	—	P.314
Wave 1	MT-E-104 Bipedal MT (Cluster Gun)	4	470	364	—	P.317
Wave 1	MT-E-104 Bipedal MT (Grenade Cannon)	6	470	364	—	P.316
Wave 2	CD-J-098 Quad Drone (Cluster Missile Launcher)	2	302	310	—	P.312
Wave 2	TH-E-012 Transport Helicopter	2	750	—	—	P.314
Wave 2	MT-E-104 Bipedal MT (Cluster Gun)	7	470	364	—	P.317
Wave 2	MT-E-104 Bipedal MT (Grenade Cannon)	6	470	364	—	P.316
Wave 3	AA18: LIGHT CAVALRY (Sniper Type)	7	1075	837	—	P.332
Wave 4	Suicide Drones	8	102	—	—	—
Wave 5	CD-J-098 Quad Drone (Transport Hangar)	2	302	310	—	P.312
Wave 5	MT-E-104 Bipedal MT (Grenade Cannon)	8	470	364	—	P.316
Wave 5	AA18C: LIGHT CAVALRY HF	1	8595	1750	—	P.334
Wave 5	MT-E-104 Bipedal MT (Cluster Gun)	6	470	364	—	P.317
Wave 5	TH-E-012 Transport Helicopter	2	750	—	—	P.314
Wave 6	CD-J-098 Quad Drone (Transport Hangar)	4	302	310	—	P.312
Wave 6	MT-E-104 Bipedal MT (Grenade Cannon)	4	470	364	—	P.316
Wave 6	MT-E-104 Bipedal MT (Cluster Gun)	8	470	364	—	P.317

AC ASSEMBLY

Since enemies will prioritize hitting the tower rather than you, putting together an assembly that's focused more on speed and maneuverability to enable you to move between groups of enemies faster is recommended. The EPHEMERA core and arms, along with the BASHO head unit, give you the lightweight attributes you want, and a good mix of defensive specs just in case an enemy does turn their attention toward you. A set of reverse-joint legs is essential for meeting the level of movement you want, and pairing them with the FLUEGEL/21Z booster will allow you to gain a lot of height very quickly, something that will come in handy for one particular wave of enemies.

Equipping the pulse protection Core Expansion if you have it will also make dealing with that wave of troublesome enemies much easier, and can often be the difference between getting maximum bonus pay or not. For weaponry, multi-lock capabilities and short reload times should be at the forefront of your mind so that you can quickly destroy multiple groups of enemies; a combination of explosive and plasma missiles is ideal since it gives you a good mix of damage and area coverage.

01	R-ARM UNIT | MISSILE LAUNCHER **HML-G2/P19MLT-04**	P.62
02	L-ARM UNIT | MISSILE LAUNCHER **HML-G2/P19MLT-04**	P.62
03	R-BACK UNIT | PLASMA MISSILE LAUNCHER **Vvc-706PM**	P.73
04	L-BACK UNIT | PLASMA MISSILE LAUNCHER **Vvc-706PM**	P.73
05	HEAD | — **AH-J-124 BASHO**	P.77
06	CORE | — **IA-C01C: EPHEMERA**	P.81
07	ARMS | — **IA-C01A: EPHEMERA**	P.84
08	LEGS | REVERSE-JOINT **06-042 MIND BETA**	P.86
09	BOOSTER | — **FLUEGEL/21Z**	P.88
10	FCS | — **FCS-G2/P10SLT**	P.90
11	GENERATOR | — **VP-20C**	P.92

PREPARATION: XYLEM DEFENSES

You'll have access to two artillery installations in front of the control tower: one on the left at **Position A** and one on the right at **Position B**. Unlike similar artillery, these are not active at all times and instead need to be accessed first to start them up, after which they'll fire for a brief period before deactivating again. You can only use them once in the entirety of the mission and so must make strategic use of them to ensure they're active when you need them most. Factoring their activation and start-up duration into your planning is a crucial part of the mission, to ensure you're not out of position when the time comes to use them. ▶ A

Xylem City is effectively one large rectangular space with two levels and buildings of variable sizes on which enemies will take up positions. The three bridges in front of the tower are the primary routes the enemies take while getting into position, so those should be key focal points throughout the mission. You can't stop the enemies from appearing or skip any waves, so understanding where they'll appear and using that knowledge to ensure you're in the right position to instantly attack them is key to keeping the tower safe.

Enemies will focus on getting into range or firing on the tower over attacking you, and while that does make it easier to preserve your own AP or move between enemies, it also means that the tower will be targeted from multiple locations at all times. They'll typically appear at roughly the same distance from the tower, either near **Position C** on the left bridge, **Position D** on the central bridge, and **Position E** on the bridge to the right if you're looking out at them with your back to the tower. ▶ B

The number of enemies you'll have to contend with at any given time can be overwhelming, but prioritizing targets based on how much damage they could potentially deal to the shield will allow you to systematically work through them in an orderly manner. In general, if there's an LC on the field you should forgo any other enemies and focus on it immediately until it's destroyed, as they are by far the biggest threat. After that is destroying transport helicopters before they can deploy the units they're carrying, as that goes a long way to making the fights more manageable, and then finally mop up any bipedal MTs. It should also be noted that the timing for when the different waves appear can vary slightly depending on how quickly you defeat the enemies of the previous wave.

OBJECTIVE	Reach the Rendezvous Point

Wave 1
5:00-4:15

Quad Drone (Cluster Missile Launcher) x4
Bipedal MT (Cluster Gun) x4
Transport Helicopter (w/ Grenade Cannon Bipedal MT x3) x2

To keep things manageable, the transport helicopters carrying the bipedal MTs need to be your priority in this wave. After moving to the starting location, quickly boost straight along the middle toward **Position D** so that you're ready to fire when they appear. Use your missiles to take out the helicopter and bipedal MTs accompanying it, then move straight to **Position E** to head off another pair of bipedal MTs traveling along that bridge. The remaining enemies all appear near **Position C**, so Assault Boost over there, take out the pair of bipedal MTs traveling along that bridge, and stay in the area so that you can destroy the final helicopter and accompanying units once it's within range.

The artillery installations you can activate sport impressive range, damage, and accuracy. It is recommended to save their activation for a later wave such as the sniper LCs.

Like in many other wave-based defense missions, enemy reinforcements are not always indicated by a yellow warning icon. Be sure to check your compass regularly and scan for new threats.

Wave 2
4:05

Bipedal MT (Cluster Gun) x7
Quad Drone (Cluster Missile Launcher) x2
Transport Helicopter (w/ Grenade Cannon Bipedal MT x3) x2

If you stay near **Position C** after clearing Wave 1, you can catch the two bipedal MTs that approach along that bridge as soon as they appear, and then quickly make your way across the area between **Positions D** and **E**, destroying the groups of enemies as you reach them. The group at **Position D** is quite large and will require most of your missiles, so take a little bit of time to ensure everything is destroyed before moving on.

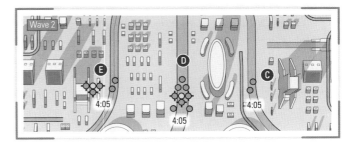

Wave 3 2:55-2:20   LC (Sniper Type) x7

The sniper LCs that you'll have to contend with during this wave fly in and take up positions on rooftops between the three bridges, before firing extremely powerful long-range laser shots at the shield. They can destroy the shield very quickly if given the chance, and since they don't have to get as close as the other enemies, you'll have very limited time to destroy them. A good option is to stay on or near the central bridge as much as possible, about halfway along it just before you reach the tall buildings. From there, you should be able to target all of the LCs as they come boosting in—thanks to the excellent range of your missile launchers— just remember to keep your reticle trained on your targets after releasing your missiles to ensure they hit their mark. It takes a volley from two launchers to destroy one of these LCs, meaning you can alternate between pairs to always ensure one pair is reloaded for the next target.

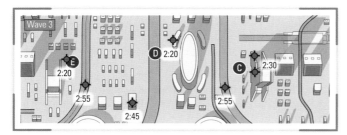

Wave 4 1:50   Suicide Drone x8

There are no regular enemies to contend with in this wave, but it's one of the most difficult waves to defend against fully. The suicide drones move extremely quickly, so they're difficult to target and for your missiles to catch, and can collectively deal enough damage to decimate the shield. By far the easiest and safest method is to make use of the pulse protection Core Expansion to deploy a static shield in the flight path of the drones, destroying them all as they hit it. The wave appears along the central bridge, so as soon as they appear on the horizon, boost up into the air until you're at an altitude of roughly 330, and then activate pulse protection. If done correctly, all of the drones should be destroyed. ▶ A

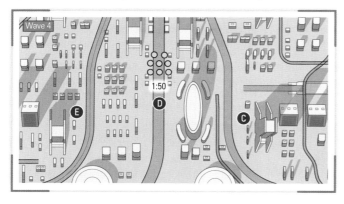

When simply trying to clear the mission, it won't be catastrophic if most of the suicide drones collide with the tower. If you've done a good job cleaning up prior waves, this won't cause the Xylem shield to fail.

Wave 5 1:30   Quad Drone (w/ Grenade Cannon Bipedal MT x1) x7
LC (High Firepower) x1 Bipedal MT (Cluster Gun) x6
Transport Helicopter (w/ Grenade Cannon Bipedal MT x3) x2

The high-firepower LCs in this wave is the most dangerous single enemy in the mission, and unlike the previous LCs, this one will require multiple volleys of missiles from both of your launchers to destroy, which means you'll need to be focused on it for a while. Since there'll be a lot of other enemies arriving simultaneously, it's highly recommended that as soon as the suicide drones have been destroyed in the previous wave, head back to the tower and activate both artillery batteries to give you some additional support. Once the LC has been destroyed, quickly locate any targets that have survived the artillery's onslaught, focusing particularly on the transport helicopters and MT-carrying quad drones if any remain; use your Assault Boost to get into range and destroy them as quickly as possible so you're not overwhelmed when the next wave starts rolling in.

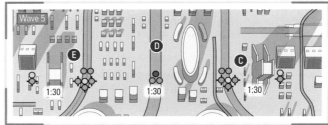

Wave 6 1:00-0:30   Bipedal MT (Cluster Gun) x8
Quad Drone (w/ Grenade Cannon Bipedal MT x1) x4

Although enemies approach from all three of the major routes for this final wave, it's actually best if you take a central position near the front of the tower at **Position F** to deal with them all. The MT-carrying quad drones move extremely quickly, so if you move out to engage them on one side, there's a good chance the ones on the other side would have deployed their units by the time you reach them. A central position allows you to fire on them quickly enough to destroy them on both sides before they can deploy their MTs, and allows you to target and destroy all of the other bipedal MTs that approach along the bridges. You don't need to destroy all of the enemies to complete the mission, just ensure the tower survives until the timer expires and the hacking attempt is successful.

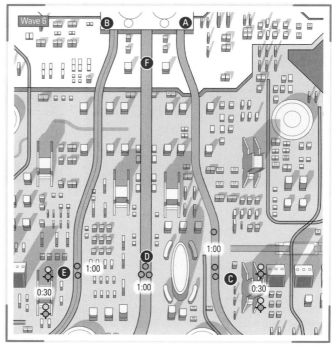

INTERCEPT THE CORPORATE FORCES

"Let's get this trash out of the way."

—V.I Freud

Arquebus forces using stolen PCA tech, led by V.I Freud, are attempting to capture the Xylem to further their own interests, and if you decide to aid Carla, you'll be helping to repel the corporations and keep the city out of their hands. The part of the city you need to purge of enemy units is narrow, but it's worth exploring the area thoroughly, because there are pockets of hidden enemies to find that can increase the total bonus payout for the mission. You'll need to be careful when exploring, however, as many of the enemy units are ranged experts, which means you'll need to make use of the buildings lining the streets for cover as you close in on them.

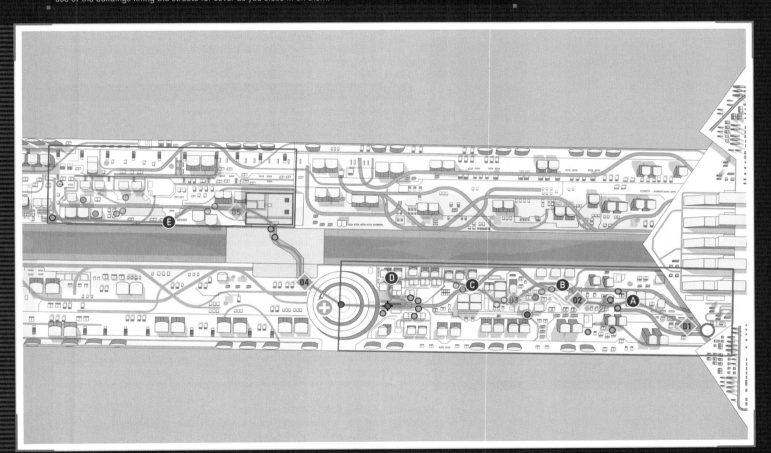

MISSION OBJECTIVES

Eliminate the Assimilated Corporate Craft

Go to "Chatty" Stick's Rescue

Defeat V.I Freud

MISSION INFO

Combat Zone	Troposphere—Xylem Upper Districts
Client	"Cinder" Carla / Overseer
Reward	440,000
Max Bonus Pay	427,800
Completion Unlocks	Overseer Emblem
Combat Logs	Platinum x1, Silver x1
Data Logs	—
Part Containers	—

ENEMY DATA

	No.	AP	AS	Bonus Pay	Analysis
MT-T-026 Guard Mech (Rifle)	2	102	121	800	P.310
CD-J-098 Quad Drone (Cluster Missile Launcher)	2	302	310	3200	P.312
CD-J-098 Quad Drone (Laser Cannon)	2	302	310	3400	P.312
CD-J-098 Quad Drone (Pulse Protection)	3	302	310	3400	P.312
AM14: SENTRY SG MT (Missile Launcher)	9	437	310	3400	P.320
AM14: SENTRY SG MT (Electrothermo Cutter)	6	437	310	3400	P.321
AA18: LIGHT CAVALRY (Support Type)	1	5730	1066	22000	P.332
AA18: LIGHT CAVALRY (Sniper Type)	1	1075	837	6000	P.332
AA18A: LIGHT CAVALRY HM	1	15758	1750	40000	P.333
AA18C: LIGHT CAVALRY HF	2	8595	1750	34000	P.334
AA22: HEAVY CAVALRY (Arquebus Remodel)	1	16235	1800	50000	—
AC LOCKSMITH / V.I Freud	1	10460	1719	180000	—

AC ASSEMBLY

It's best to focus your choice of munitions on the mission's major single-target threats; you'll not only have to contend with V.I Freud, but also some strong LC and HC units that are ranged specialists, and the quicker you can dispatch each of them, the better. When it comes to close-range burst damage, it's hard to find a stronger combination than dual ZIMMERMAN shotguns and dual diffuse laser cannons. Your foes will tend to use energy and explosive weaponry, so tailoring your defensive specs to prioritize those will go a long way toward ensuring you emerge victorious.

01	R-ARM UNIT	SHOTGUN SG-027 ZIMMERMAN	P.54
02	L-ARM UNIT	SHOTGUN SG-027 ZIMMERMAN	P.54
03	R-BACK UNIT	DIFFUSE LASER CANNON VP-60LCD	P.67
04	L-BACK UNIT	DIFFUSE LASER CANNON VP-60LCD	P.67
05	HEAD	— VE-44A	P.78
06	CORE	— 07-061 MIND ALPHA	P.81
07	ARMS	— IA-C01A: EPHEMERA	P.84
08	LEGS	TETRAPOD VP-424	P.86
09	BOOSTER	— BST-G2/P06SPD	P.88
10	FCS	— IB-C03F: WLT 001	P.90
11	GENERATOR	— VP-20D	P.92

01 You'll begin the mission overlooking the city, where a pitched battle is taking place between Carla's forces and those of the corporations. Without your assistance, the corporations will undoubtedly be victorious. While you don't need to destroy every enemy you encounter, doing so makes things much safer and increases bonus pay, so it's the recommended approach. The first group of enemies in your path is comprised of quad drones and Subject Guard MTs and it's much easier to fight them from an elevated position, so Assault Boost over to the rooftops at **Position A** and destroy them all from there.

02 Drop down to the road and continue along it until you reach the group of buildings here; you should be able to see an enemy LC with backup from a pair of laser cannon-wielding MTs. If you peek out from behind the building just enough so that the LC spots you, it will boost straight toward you. Use your scan to keep an eye on it, and hit it with your weapons as soon as it tries to move around the building. One decent blast from all of your weapons can destroy it. If it survives, make sure to stick behind the buildings while you finish it off, to avoid being hit by the MTs further ahead. When you're ready, boost around to the side of the road at **Position B** and use the buildings to provide cover while you get into range. ▶ A

COMBAT LOG OPPORTUNITY

Before moving on from this point, you can make your way up onto the large glass ceiling covering this entire section of the city by using your Assault Boost to climb to the roof of one of the nearby buildings. Up there you'll be able to fight an AA18A: LIGHT CAVALRY HM, similar to the one you faced in the "Attack the Old Spaceport" mission. This LC has much higher AP and defensive specs than normal LCs. When you land on the glass rooftop it will release a large volley of missiles, and if you Assault Boost directly at it you can take advantage of the fact that it's stationary to inflict a decent amount of damage. For the remainder of the fight, it will hover a lot, so pick your moments and avoid wasting ammunition. Destroying it will award you 40,000 bonus pay and the combat log.

03 Cut through the buildings to reach the slightly elevated area here, where there's a pair of guard mechs to destroy. Next, head back toward the road at **Position C** and take out the pair of Subject Guard MTs there. You'll be able to see signs of battle just ahead of those enemies, and while you can head straight there and capitalize on the chaos, taking the time to flank around behind the enemies is wiser; use the buildings to the side for cover until you reach **Position D**.

If you reach this position undetected, you can quickly boost inside the pulse protection barrier and destroy the LC before it can fire at you, and then destroy the drone generating the barrier. The other MTs in the area will start firing at you, so make use of the barricades and buildings for cover while you get close enough to destroy each of them. Once the area is clear, use the door at the bottom of the ramp to enter the dome and face off against the AA22: HEAVY CALVARY.

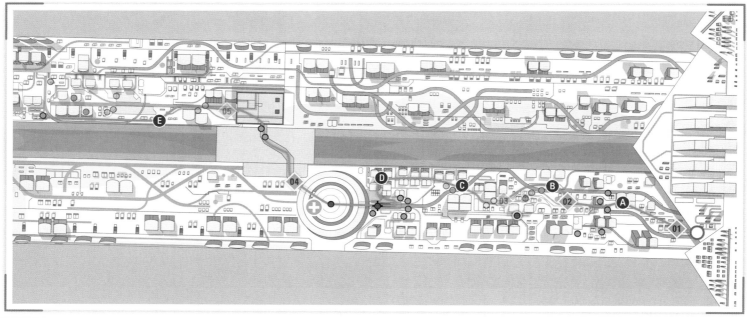

HEAVY CALVARY / ARQUEBUS MAIN SQUAD MEMBER

This Arquebus Remodel HC tends to keep its distance from you while raining down missiles and laying down suppressive fire with its plasma rifle, a feat that's made much safer by the pulse shieldbasher that it can deploy while firing. The key to the fight is making sure you capitalize on opportunities when its shield isn't deployed, but there's no getting around the fact that you're going to be shooting into that shield for some of the time.

BASIC SPECS

AP	16235
Attitude Stability	1800
Anti-Kinetic Defense	1060
Anti-Energy Defense	1413
Anti-Explosive Defense	1305
Elec. Discharge Tolerance	500
Shock Resistance	15%
ACS Anomaly Tolerance	500
Heat Resistance	10%

With some very careful positioning, it's possible to increase your opportunities to land some clean hits; if you move close enough, you can bait the HC into using its shield bash, and if you dodge it, you'll have time to retaliate. If you fight aggressively and try to box it against the walls of the dome so it can't get away from you, it's possible to destroy the HC fairly quickly. There's a supply sherpa after the fight, so there's no need to conserve your ammo.

AA22: HEAVY CALVARY ATTACKS

PULSE SHIELD

DESCRIPTION This pulse shieldbasher will be raised for the majority of the encounter, and the HC can fire its pulse rifle and missiles from behind it.

EVASION Not used offensively.

SHIELD BASH

DESCRIPTION The HC uses its shield as a melee weapon. A high-impact hit, but it does not deal high AP damage. No audible alert, but the HC readies its shield briefly before use.

EVASION Quick Boost to either side of the HC.

PLASMA RIFLE ▼ CHARGED

DESCRIPTION Fires either a volley of uncharged shots at you or charges the weapon to increase its impact and create a lingering damage field where the shot lands.

EVASION Strafe or Quick Boost around regular shots. Immediately jump into the air when attack indicator signals charged shot.

SPIDER MISSILES

DESCRIPTION Releases a volley of four or eight energy missiles. They can stop in mid-air and change directions, only to fly straight at your AC again.

EVASION Evade these missiles while remaining grounded, as if they pass you in the air they'll likely redirect. Quick Boost directly toward the HC causes the missiles to fly straight over you.

OBJECTIVE Go to "Chatty" Stick's Rescue

04 ◇ After using the supply sherpa you'll get an update on the battle from "Chatty" Stick; things are not looking good for him, so you'll need to reach his location and even the odds. Continue along the path and destroy the two Subject Guard MTs when you reach them—making sure not to let them get too close to you, since they're both equipped with melee weapons—and then access the door at the opposite end of the tunnel to reach the outside once again.

05 ◇ There are a pair of Subject Guard MTs just outside the hangar as you exit, and if you're quick, you can close in and destroy them while they are distracted fighting friendly units. The enemies have set up a strong blockade further along the street, with the major threat coming from LCs operating within pulse protection barriers, similar to the one you encountered on the way into the dome. The HF variants of LC you face here are much more of a threat than the sniper variant you've previously faced, so you'll need to be even more careful in your approach. ▶ B

"Chatty" does a good job of drawing the enemies' attention by bombarding them with missiles, and while they will target you if they spot you, they'll resume firing at him when you're out of sight again. Use this to flank around the front of the blockade by heading to **Position E** and boosting behind the buildings until you emerge behind the enemies. Once you're there, wait until you see the closest LC target "Chatty," then jump up right next to it and unload your weapons, which will usually knock it off the rooftop it's standing on.

Drop down to the streets and finish it off, then remain among the buildings and wait for the next one to drop down near you and quickly destroy it. Disabling the pulse protection barriers should be your next priority, while "Chatty" helps pick off the remaining enemies in the area. When the final enemy in the blockade has been destroyed, V.I Freud will fly into the area to finish you off personally.

The main weakness of HF LCs is their lack of mobility; they're limited to short boosts, making them easy prey up close.

The pulse protection drones are high priority targets as they serve to hinder you from engaging the significantly more dangerous LCs from afar.

AC // LOCKSMITH

The arrival of V.I Freud—the leader of Arquebus's Vesper military forces and the number one ranked AC pilot—shows how serious the corporations are about taking the city, and he wastes no time establishing his dominance by destroying "Chatty" in his opening salvo. "Chatty" does get a few hits in before he goes down, and if you Assault Boost toward him as soon as the fight starts you can get close enough to hit Freud so that his sacrifice isn't in vain. You'll need every advantage you can get, because Freud is ignoring the goal of his corporation, and is now solely focused on having a battle with one of Walter's hounds.

BASIC SPECS

AP	10460
Attitude Stability	1589
Anti-Kinetic Defense	1200
Anti-Energy Defense	1196
Anti-Explosive Defense	1138
Elec. Discharge Tolerance	490
Shock Resistance	10%
ACS Anomaly Tolerance	490
Heat Resistance	10%
Repair Kits	3

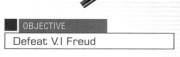

OBJECTIVE

Defeat V.I Freud

The weaponry on Freud's AC will allow him to apply pressure with constant shots from either his rifle or drones. This sets you up for big damage from his melee weapon or spread bazooka, which can destroy your AC in a single shot if you take the full brunt of it. Simply trying to evade Freud is not an effective tactic, since the drones will keep following you regardless. That being the case, an aggressive approach works best; aim to keep him staggered as much as possible, because drawing the fight out works in his favor.

Freud will attempt to change ranges often based on how you react; if you approach him too quickly, he'll back away, but that can work in your favor if it means he backs himself up against the area barrier or a building. Once you have him cornered, constantly rotate through your weapons to ensure that you're always inflicting huge amounts of damage and keeping him almost perpetually staggered. If he does get away, one of the best openings to regain control is when you see him use his laser blade; after the second swipe, he'll stand still for a moment and you'll be able to regain control. Defeating Freud will secure the city for now and bring the mission to an end.

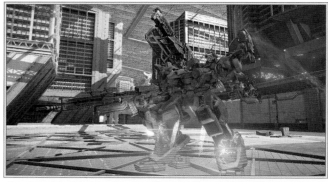

One of the main challenges of dealing with Freud is how quickly he will retaliate from ACS overload. He recovers and repositions extremely quickly, often deploying pulse armor or a repair kit in the process.

AC LOCKSMITH ATTACKS

RF-024 TURNER

DESCRIPTION This kinetic rifle is Freud's main weapon throughout the fight, firing it at a near-constant rate from any distance.

EVASION Do not be led into the shots and instead attempt to strafe or Quick Boost away from where Freud is placing the rounds.

BOOST KICK

DESCRIPTION Freud will Assault Boost toward you in an attempt to Boost Kick you.

EVASION Quick Boost in either direction away from him.

SB-033M MORLEY

DESCRIPTION Fires five bazooka rounds that fan outward at random trajectories. Extremely powerful weapon and can easily overload your ACS or destroy your AC if all shots connect.

EVASION Jump up and Quick Boost away as soon as you hear the alert.

VVC-770LB

DESCRIPTION Freud holds the laser blade out briefly, after which it produces two long-range spinning sweeps. He uses this weapon at close proximity, especially if your AC is staggered.

EVASION If your ACS is overloaded you cannot evade these strikes. Otherwise, Quick Boost away from Freud, or if he's above you, Quick Boost underneath him.

PULSE ARMOR

DESCRIPTION Core Expansion that produces a shield to mitigate all damage until depleted.

EVASION Not used offensively.

VVC-700LD

DESCRIPTION Freud will release six laser drones that follow your AC around the battlefield. These drones last for a while and cannot be interacted with. They have two firing patterns: a laser barrage with low-impact shots and a double shot of combined higher-impact lasers.

EVASION Do not stop moving once these drones are released unless there's cover protecting you; strafe or Quick Boost when the drones halt to fire.

//24-B
ELIMINATE "CINDER" CARLA

"Well hi, tourist. How much did Arquebus pay you?!"

—'Cinder' Carla

If you choose to side with Ayre and the Rubiconians, your mission will be to infiltrate the city. You'll take advantage of the chaos caused by the corporations fighting with Carla's forces to locate and wrest control of the city from her and the Overseer group, by any means necessary. To reach her you'll need to navigate the city's streets, and since there's no bonus pay to be had, partaking in the battles that rage upon them is entirely optional. Keep in mind, however, that the mission culminates in a tough fight against two skilled pilots, for which you'll want to have as much AP and ammunition as possible.

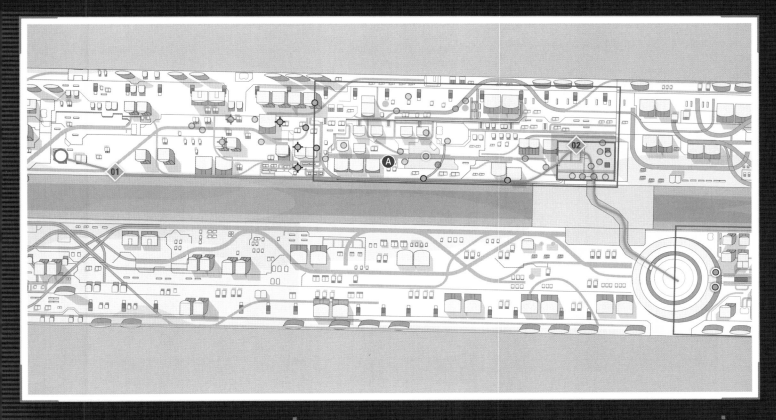

MISSION OBJECTIVE

Eliminate "Cinder" Carla

MISSION INFO

Combat Zone	Troposphere—Xylem Upper Districts
Client	Ayre
Reward	81,000
Max Bonus Pay	—
Completion Unlocks	—
Combat Logs	Platinum x2, Gold x1
Data Logs	—
Part Containers	—

ENEMY DATA

	No.	AP	AS	Bonus Pay	Analysis
AM01: REPAIRER (Stun Smog)	4	51	—	—	P.314
MT-E-104 Bipedal MT (Grenade Cannon)	2	470	364	—	P.316
MT-E-104 Bipedal MT (Missile Launcher)	1	470	364	—	P.316
MT-E-104 Bipedal MT (Dual Machine Gun)	1	470	364	—	P.316
MT-E-104 Bipedal MT (Cluster Gun)	2	470	364	—	P.317
MB-0100 CLUTCH Crawler MT (Heavy Rocket Launcher)	9	650	364	—	P.318
MB-0100 CLUTCH Crawler MT (Electro Saw)	6	650	364	—	P.319
AM14: SENTRY SG MT (Grenade Cannon)	4	437	310	—	P.321
AM14: SENTRY SG MT (Missile Launcher)	4	437	310	—	P.320
AM14: SENTRY SG MT (Electrothermo Cutter)	3	437	310	—	P.321
MB-0202 TOYBOX MT	1	1848	1053	—	P.325
AC OPEN FAITH / V.II Snail	1	14040	1911	—	—
AC FULL COURSE / "Cinder" Carla	1	12700	2014	—	—
AC CIRCUS / "Chatty" Stick	1	13040	1724	—	—

AC ASSEMBLY

Both "Chatty" and Carla make heavy use of explosive munitions that are very dangerous and hard to effectively evade, so having a decent amount of anti-explosive spec will help considerably against them. There's also an optional encounter against V.II Snail; his weaponry is primarily energy-based, so if you plan on facing him you'll want to incorporate some defense against that damage type. Since your focus is on these three fights, utilizing weaponry that will allow you to pressure single targets at close range is recommended—which the pairing of ZIMMERMAN shotguns and diffuse laser cannons are perfectly suited for.

01	R-ARM UNIT | SHOTGUN SG-027 ZIMMERMAN	P.54
02	L-ARM UNIT | SHOTGUN SG-027 ZIMMERMAN	P.54
03	R-BACK UNIT | DIFFUSE LASER CANNON VP-60LCD	P.67
04	L-BACK UNIT | DIFFUSE LASER CANNON VP-60LCD	P.67
05	HEAD | — VE-44A	P.78
06	CORE | — 07-061 MIND ALPHA	P.81
07	ARMS | — IA-C01A: EPHEMERA	P.84
08	LEGS | TETRAPOD VP-424	P.86
09	BOOSTER | — BST-G2/P06SPD	P.88
10	FCS | — IB-C03F: WLT 001	P.90
11	GENERATOR | — VP-20D	P.92

If you're not particularly interested in optional combat, including V.II Snail, you can bypass most of the firefight by hugging the right side of the Xylem.

Take heed of incoming explosive artillery if you make your way rightward toward the partition.

OBJECTIVE — Eliminate "Cinder" Carla

01 ◇ The siege of the Xylem by the corporations' assimilated forces is underway when the mission begins, with Carla's forces holding them at bay, for now. To take control of the Xylem for the Rubiconians, you'll need to reach the reservoir dome at the opposite end of this section of the city, where Carla and "Chatty" have taken positions to make their last stand. Fighting both of them simultaneously is tough, and any resources you expend along the way will only make it more difficult.

The safest approach is to bypass the raging battle in the streets completely, since there's no bonus pay to be gained from it. From where you begin, head to this point on the side of the street, and then simply follow the area barrier along the edge of the city until you reach the hangar. Along the way, you'll encounter V.II Snail taking on a group of Carla's units, and depending on where he is at the time, he may or may not see you as you boost past the area. Fighting him is completely optional, so if you just want to progress, you can keep going to the hangar. If you want the combat log, however, you'll need to take a quick detour to battle him. ▶ A-C

The opening to V.II Snail's encounter can vary drastically. Sometimes he is so preoccupied with the other enemies that he doesn't even notice your approach, and sometimes he will even disengage you to battle stragglers.

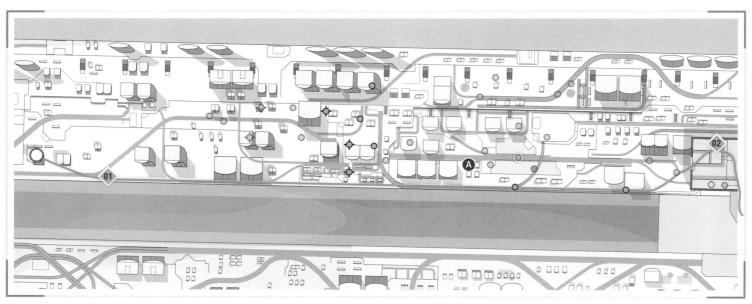

AC // OPEN FAITH

Snail's AC, OPEN FAITH, is a heavy build with strong resistance to most damage types, so this can be a lengthy fight. Snail tends to stick to close range and will use deadly melee attacks often, so try to position yourself slightly away from him, so that you have time to react and evade the melee attacks; just inside the range of your shotguns is ideal. Similarly, try to always be moving laterally if you're in the open. This will increase the likelihood of his melee attacks missing, and if you're near the buildings, hovering above him while weaving between them can also be an effective countermeasure to his melee attempts.

BASIC SPECS

AP	13240
Attitude Stability	1791
Anti-Kinetic Defense	1285
Anti-Energy Defense	1406
Anti-Explosive Defense	1287
Elec. Discharge Tolerance	490
Shock Resistance	4%
ACS Anomaly Tolerance	490
Heat Resistance	4%
Repair Kits	2

SITUATIONAL AWARENESS

Snail will often be engaged in combat when you reach him, and depending on how fast you get there and how that fight is going, you can use the situation to your advantage. Carla's forces in the area will usually prioritize Snail if they have line of sight on him. If they hit him, he'll often move to retaliate, giving you a window within which to land some attacks. Those same units can sometimes target you, which can make fighting Snail more difficult. Judge the situation as it plays out, and if needed, destroy the other units so you can focus on Snail.

The other corporation forces will also fire on you given the chance, so you'll either need to fight Snail in areas where they can't hit you, or destroy them first. By far the biggest threats to eliminate are the two Subject Guard MTs near **Position A**, because their long-range attacks can inflict a lot of damage while you're dealing with Snail.

The longer the fight goes on, the more likely it is he'll tag you with a melee strike, so try to remain aggressive and end the fight as quickly as possible. Thankfully, while his melee attack is dangerous, if you successfully evade one he'll be left open for a brief period of time afterward. If you have Boost Kick unlocked, you should always follow a stagger with an Assault Boost and Boost Kick while your weapons reload—just make sure to move away again quickly.

Even if V.II Snail manages to see you and engage, he's still very much an optional battle, so don't feel obligated to stay and oblige him.

AC OPEN FAITH ATTACKS

VE-67LLA

DESCRIPTION This melee weapon strikes twice. The first is quick and capable of crossing large distances. The second will likely overload your ACS and deal heavy direct damage.

EVASION These are head-on attacks, and while dodging the first strike may prove difficult, you can Quick Boost past the second strike toward Snail to evade it and position yourself behind him for a counterattack.

VE-60SNA ▼

DESCRIPTION Fires a high-velocity bolt that releases an active damage field where it lands. The impact and explosion deal direct damage, and large amounts of shock buildup.

EVASION The shot is very quick and you'll only have a brief window of time to react to the alert indicator and Quick Boost to the side.

VP-66EG

DESCRIPTION Fires a series of quick-moving shots that both strain your ACS and inflict shock buildup.

EVASION Quick Boost in the opposite direction Snail is firing toward.

VVC-70VPM

DESCRIPTION Vertical plasma missiles that leave a lingering damage field upon impact.

EVASION Find cover between buildings or chain Quick Boosts as soon as the volley begins landing.

ASSAULT ARMOR

DESCRIPTION After bringing AC OPEN FAITH's AP down to almost zero, Snail will use his Core Expansion in desperation.

EVASION This attack can easily overload your ACS, so anticipate Snail using it based on his remaining AP and Quick Boost away from him.

02 ◈ Shortly after you enter the hangar leading to the dome, Carla will close the partition doors, trapping you inside with a large number of drones and MTs. These particular drones release a stun smog that causes shock buildup and can trigger an electrical discharge if you remain in it. All of the enemies are on the middle and lower levels of the room, and if you drop down to face them you can quickly get disoriented in the stun smog and take unnecessary damage. A safer method is to remain on the upper platforms and simply fire down from there. None of the enemies can reach you, and one or two shots from your shotguns is sufficient to destroy each of them. Once the room is clear, Ayre will unlock the partition and you can continue into the dome and face off against Carla and "Chatty." ▶A

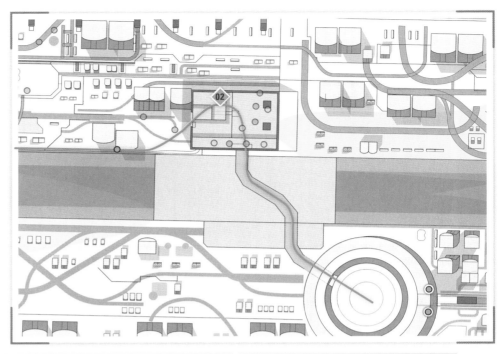

When Carla traps you in the room prior to her encounter, keep the high ground to avoid being overwhelmed by electrical discharge and enemy gunfire. You can slowly pick off enemies from above before proceeding.

One of "Chatty's" favorite habits is to perch on the upper rings of the arena and pepper you with projectiles, particularly at the start. This gives you even more incentive to just chase after Carla instead.

Your movement is paramount in this fight, as the overwhelming explosive arsenals of Carla and "Chatty" can overload your ACS and shred your AP if they catch you stationary.

"CINDER" CARLA

AC // FULL COURSE

"CHATTY" STICK

AC // CIRCUS

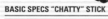

Carla is your target, but she'll be fighting alongside her trusty compatriot, "Chatty" Stick. Carla's AC, FULL COURSE, is a heavy build with high defensive specs against all damage types, whereas "Chatty's" AC CIRCUS has much lower defenses, but much higher AP, and utilizes the FORTALEZA tank legs, giving it very high mobility.

BASIC SPECS "CINDER" CARLA	
AP	12700
Attitude Stability	2014
Anti-Kinetic Defense	1306
Anti-Energy Defense	1348
Anti-Explosive Defense	1282
Elec. Discharge Tolerance	490
Shock Resistance	-7%
ACS Anomaly Tolerance	490
Heat Resistance	-7%
Repair Kits	2

BASIC SPECS "CHATTY" STICK	
AP	13040
Attitude Stability	1724
Anti-Kinetic Defense	1261
Anti-Energy Defense	1118
Anti-Explosive Defense	1176
Elec. Discharge Tolerance	490
Shock Resistance	-16%
ACS Anomaly Tolerance	490
Heat Resistance	-16%
Repair Kits	1

Though she has high defensive specs, Carla tends to stay around medium range, frequently hovering above you so that she's in a prime position to fire off missiles. "Chatty" will be constantly boosting around the dome, hardly ever stopping, and he can do so at a pace that lets him out-run many of your projectiles if you simply fire at him head on. The difficulty of landing clean hits makes him the more challenging of your two opponents, so it's best to engage Carla first.

Quickly reducing the number of ACs you have to contend with is the key to victory, so focus on FULL COURSE as much as possible, keeping an eye on where CIRCUS is on the battlefield so that you know which direction its attacks will come from. Of particular danger are the attacks from "Chatty's" LITTLE GEM and IRIDIUM weapons, because both attacks can be used at any distance, travel relatively fast, and fire off high-impact explosives that deal high AP damage. ▶ B-C

While not as immediately dangerous, the vertical missiles from "Chatty's" BML-G1 launcher will affect how you fight Carla the most. They are difficult to evade, and even under the best of circumstances you'll be limiting the number of missiles that hit you, rather than completely avoiding them.

Pressuring Carla can be relatively easy, because she'll often end up positioning herself up against a wall. This creates the ideal situation for your close-range weaponry, and also means that the SOUP missiles she fires will impact the wall, reducing the number that you'll need to evade. Her APERITIF missiles are still a threat in this situation, but knowing that they're the main attack you need to watch out for makes it easier for you to evade them. While you're pressuring Carla, make sure to keep facing her while moving around to help with avoiding missiles from "Chatty."

"Chatty" spends most of the time on one of the dome's upper rings, and only occasionally will he hover out into the open. When it's time to face him, position yourself on the inside of that ring so that he has to travel a greater distance around it, making it easier for you to keep up with him. There are support columns around the walls, and luring him near one of these will let you land a number of quick hits before he gets away again. If you're using the primarily close-range suggested loadout, hold your fire when he hovers above the dome—he can't stay there for long and will land back on the ring, at which point you can close in and resume your offense. The mission is complete when both ACs have been defeated.

AC FULL COURSE ATTACKS

BOOST KICK

DESCRIPTION Carla will boost toward you and attempt to strike you with a Boost Kick. She always uses this attack after firing an initial volley of missiles at the start of the fight.

EVASION Quick Boost to either side of Carla.

WS-5000 APERITIF (X2)

DESCRIPTION Missile launcher with a unique firing pattern. The missiles release and briefly hover before flying at your AC. They have a relatively head-on approach and limited homing capacities.

EVASION Anticipate when they'll break towards you after hovering and Quick Boost as they approach you.

WS-5001 SOUP (X2)

DESCRIPTION The SOUP missile launcher releases two simultaneous volleys of high-volume missiles from both left and right back units. These missiles approach in a split pattern.

EVASION Quick Boost toward Carla, causing the majority of missiles to pass over your AC.

ASSAULT ARMOR

DESCRIPTION Carla uses this Core Expansion aggressively to start the fight. After charging your AC and using a Boost Kick she'll immediately utilize this attack.

EVASION Quick Boost away from Carla as she charges the attack.

AC CIRCUS ATTACKS

IRIDIUM

DESCRIPTION This grenade launcher fires a high-impact round without alert indicators, so it can be easy to be caught off guard when "Chatty" fires it.

EVASION Often fired while he's in midair; you can either preempt the attack and boost under "Chatty," or Quick Boost away from the likely impact point of the explosive.

WR-0999 DELIVERY BOY ▼

DESCRIPTION This back missile fires out a siege warhead that breaks apart to unleash a series of missiles along a linear path.

EVASION The warhead fires along a linear path, so move far away from its vector to avoid it and the missiles raining down.

LITTLE GEM ▼

DESCRIPTION "Chatty" often fires this bazooka when he's in close proximity to your AC.

EVASION Quick Boost to either side of the explosive as soon as it's fired, or jump over it if your legs have enough jump height.

BML-G1/P07VTC-12

DESCRIPTION A high-volume volley of missiles that release overhead. The missiles also have aggressive homing capacities, making them difficult to evade.

EVASION If you cannot account for them directly due to the height they fly to, begin strafing on their release and Quick Boost as soon as they begin to impact you or the ground next to you.

//25-A
BREACH THE KÁRMÁN LINE

"Let's get our laughs while we can."

—"Cinder" Carla

The Xylem is on its final approach to destroy the Coral, and due to both their previous efforts failing to stop you, and their lack of control over the PCA satellite weapons, Arquebus—in a last-ditch effort to destroy the city—have sent in their interceptor fleet of warships. The fleet is your primary target at the onset of the mission, and engaging them will require a lot of airborne combat and traversal across large open spaces, given the distance between each of the ships. As luck would have it, the area you're operating in is highly charged with Coral, causing an EN anomaly that gives you unlimited EN. If you survive the fleet, an old buddy will make a return in an upgraded AC for one final showdown to decide the fate of the city.

MISSION INFO

Combat Zone	Mesosphere—Xylem Upper Districts
Client	"Cinder" Carla / Overseer
Reward	470,000
Max Bonus Pay	—
Completion Unlocks	EL-PH-00 ALBA (Head), EL-PC-00 ALBA (Core), EL-PA-00 ALBA (Arms), EL-PL-00 ALBA (Bipedal Legs)
Combat Logs	—
Data Logs	—
Part Containers	—

MISSION OBJECTIVES

Destroy the Arquebus Interceptor Fleet

Eliminate the Interceptor Fleet in the Sector Ahead

Defeat Rusty

ENEMY DATA

	No.	AP	AS	Bonus Pay	Analysis
AS07: HEAVY WARSHIP (Arquebus Interceptor)	10	2688	—	—	P.341
AS07: HEAVY WARSHIP (Cannon)	25	134	—	—	—
AS07: HEAVY WARSHIP (Turret)	28	90	—	—	—
AC STEEL HAZE ORTUS / Rusty	1	9050	1591	—	—

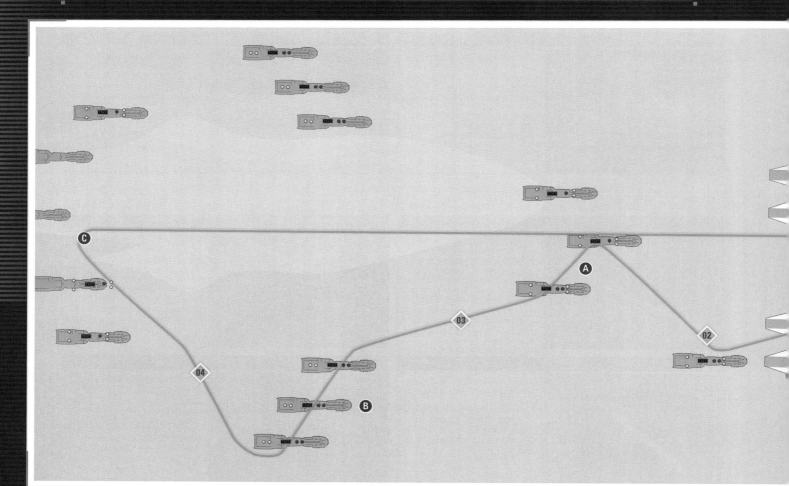

AC ASSEMBLY

This build is primarily designed to counter Rusty's advanced AC, while still having enough directed firepower to easily take down the Arquebus interceptor fleet. Dual handguns are effective at keeping pace with Rusty's quick movements and hammering his ACS, and once he's staggered, you can unload with the twin laser cannons mounted on your back units. Rusty's evasiveness is further combated by arms and an FCS which provide excellent close-range target tracking.

The infinite EN caused by the anomaly in this mission has a major influence on the rest of this build. The VE-20C generator is selected purely to augment your laser cannons, but the remainder of the frame parts and boosters are chosen to optimize the speed and reload time of your Quick Boosts, allowing you to match Rusty's evasiveness in your duel with him.

01	R-ARM UNIT | HANDGUN HG-003 COQUILLETT	P.54
02	L-ARM UNIT | HANDGUN HG-003 COQUILLETT	P.54
03	R-BACK UNIT | LASER CANNON VP-60LCS	P.54
04	L-BACK UNIT | LASER CANNON VP-60LCS	P.54
05	HEAD | — HD-033M VERRILL	P.77
06	CORE | — 07-061 MIND ALPHA	P.81
07	ARMS | — NACHTREIHER/46E	P.83
08	LEGS | BIPEDAL VP-422	P.85
09	BOOSTER | — ALULA/21E	P.88
10	FCS | — IA-C01F: OCELLUS	P.90
11	GENERATOR | — VE-20C	P.92

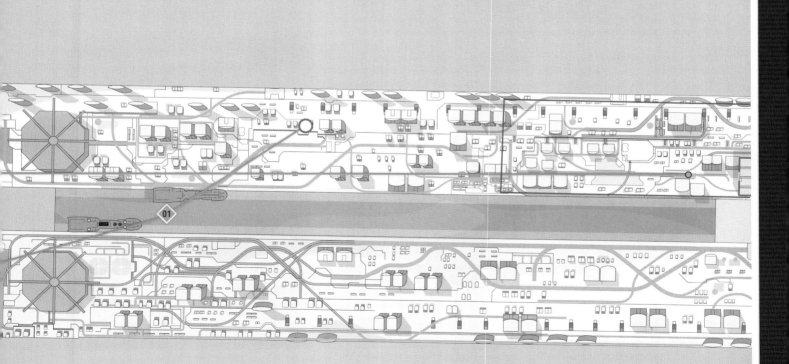

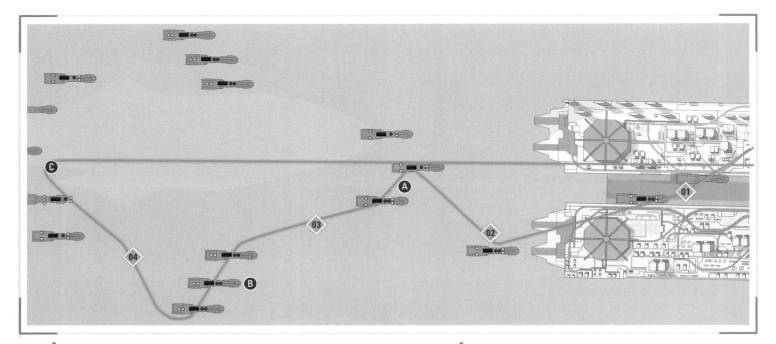

TIME IS NOT OF THE ESSENCE

The Arquebus fleet has formed a blockade and is utilizing long-range bombardments to attack the Xylem, so other than the first few warships, the rest will maintain their positions and not actually approach. That means you have more time than you might think and do not have to rush when moving between targets—from that range the city can withstand their attacks.

OBJECTIVE   Intercept the Arquebus Interceptor Fleet

01 ◈ Carla takes the lead at the start of the mission and will destroy the warship closest to the city, after which the next two get marked as targets for you to destroy. Thanks to the anomaly granting you unlimited EN, you'll have far more freedom of movement than you normally would, so although the warships are far away, you can easily Assault Boost over to them. Similarly, you don't lose any EN when you Quick Boost, so you can easily evade any incoming fire on your way to them.

Start by activating your Assault Boost toward the ship closest to you, just close enough that your laser cannons are within range of the warship's command center. Simultaneous regular shots from both your laser cannons will be enough to down a heavy warship, after which you can locate the next ship and Assault Boost onward to destroy it.

OBJECTIVE   Eliminate the Interceptor Fleet in the Sector Ahead

02 ◈ Carla highlights another group of warships at **Position A** as your next target, and since you'll have a fairly large distance to travel, you'll need to be mindful of your positioning when trying to evade their lasers. The beams come from below you and fan outward, so it can be difficult to judge your relative position while you're moving; keep the camera trained down slightly to provide a better view until you become accustomed to that attack. Although there are three warships in the group, Carla will destroy one of them, so you'll only need to destroy two. As before, you can largely ignore their close-range missiles once you're within range of them and instead head straight for the command center to destroy the ship quickly. ▶ A-B

03 ◈ The next group of warships you need to destroy is at **Position B**, and this time you'll need to destroy all three of them. This particular group is outfitted with additional long-range weaponry, however, and they'll start firing large volleys of highly damaging missiles at you during your approach. These missiles are far more deadly than the other warship attacks up to this point, especially since they have decent homing capabilities for such long-range missiles, and you'll have to contend with volleys from all three ships simultaneously.

Due to the ranges the missiles are fired from, you'll hear the audible alert indicator long before the missiles actually reach you, so you'll need to watch them as they approach and time your lateral movement to evade them just before they strike. Once you get close to a warship, it will stop using this attack and switch to its normal missiles, but the other warships can still use theirs if they're far enough away. ▶ C

Once you're close enough to the warships to fire, just prioritize the bridge and ignore the turrets. You'll make quick work of the warships before the turrets can properly retaliate.

Though they can look intimidating from afar, squeezing in between the gaps of the warships' bow lasers is easy if you juke left or right to adjust your position during an Assault Boost.

You'll get the indicator of the warships' missiles appearing long before they actually reach you, so you'll need to evade quite late.

04 ◈ One final group of five interceptors approaches the city from near **Position C**. Carla will destroy two while you're on your way to them, though, leaving only the remaining three for you to contend with. Similar to the previous group, these ones have additional weaponry, but this time they're equipped with high-power rail cannons that travel much faster than the long-range missiles. When approaching what remains of the Arquebus fleet with an Assault Boost, you'll want to juke sideways to avoid incoming rail cannon shots whenever your system alerts you that a warship is about to open fire. Destroying the final warship here will put an end to their assault, but the threat to the city is not over; you'll automatically be brought back to Xylem to deal with the appearance of an unknown AC attempting to destroy the city. This turns out to be your old buddy Rusty, albeit with significant upgrades since the last time you met. ▶ D-F

Carla and the Xylem are completely capable of handling themselves; the Xylem cannot be destroyed and will often take out its targets faster than you eliminate your own.

Railgun fire from the warships is best avoided by repeatedly using your Quick Boost to the side; the tolerance on this is very generous due to your infinite energy.

You fortunately don't have to Assault Boost all the way back to the Xylem to engage the interloper, as you will be automatically transported there after a few seconds.

RUSTY

AC // STEEL HAZE ORTUS

Rusty's ORTUS model is drastically enhanced compared to the original STEEL HAZE. Whereas he previously utilized primarily kinetic burst rifles, here he's equipped with an autonomous drone and two versions of needle launchers; only his melee weapon and Core Expansion remain unchanged. Defensively, AC STEEL HAZE ORTUS retains Rusty's preference for high mobility, lightweight assemblies, meaning that while it's fast, it also has fairly low defensive specs and AP.

BASIC SPECS

AP	9050
Attitude Stability	1591
Anti-Kinetic Defense	1062
Anti-Energy Defense	1062
Anti-Explosive Defense	1062
Elec. Discharge Tolerance	490
Shock Resistance	11%
ACS Anomaly Tolerance	490
Heat Resistance	11%
Repair Kits	2

OBJECTIVE

Defeat Rusty

Rusty's extreme speed coupled with the infinite EN reservoir makes him considerably difficult to pin down, so make sure to use Target Assist for this fight. Your goal is to stagger him quickly before using high-powered weapons to do significant AP damage. Keep at close range and pressure Rusty with your handguns to rapidly build up ACS strain; at the same time, charge your laser cannons and unleash them as soon as his AC staggers. Assault armor is also excellent for pushing Rusty into a stagger, especially if you've already landed a few shots.

In between successive staggers, take care to fully reload your handguns and allow your laser cannons to recharge while you focus on being defensive. Most of Rusty's attacks can be dodged by chaining backward Quick Boosts in a zig-zag pattern. You'll need to repeat this process a few times, including when Rusty's terminal armor activates in a last-ditch effort to prevail. With Rusty vanquished for good, the mission ends with the Xylem subject to a different danger.

Rusty's most dangerous weapon is the VVC-774LS, but its long animation means you can punish it with your handguns if you dodge away.

AC STEEL HAZE ORTUS ATTACKS

BOOST KICK

DESCRIPTION Rusty quickly approaches your AC and attempts to kick you. He can use this attack at any time, but it is most often used after he's staggered you.

EVASION Quick Boost away from Rusty as he approaches.

EL-PW-00 VIENTO

DESCRIPTION Needle guns that fire kinetic rounds.

EVASION Create space between yourself and STEEL HAZE ORTUS to get out of their effective range and cause the rounds to ricochet.

VVC-774LS

DESCRIPTION Rusty's melee weapon produces a four-point energy chakram that spins, hitting multiple times and ending with a high-impact slash.

EVASION Chain Quick Boosts away from Rusty as he uses the weapon.

EL-PW-01 TRUENO ▼

DESCRIPTION High-impact kinetic needle launcher that fires a two-round volley and can be effectively utilized at a greater distance than its arm-unit counterpart.

EVASION Create space between yourself and STEEL HAZE ORTUS to get out of their effective range or Quick Boost away from the shots.

BO-044 HUXLEY

DESCRIPTION Autonomous drone that rapidly fires kinetic rounds and is used in conjunction with Rusty's other weapons.

EVASION Create space between yourself and the drone to get out of its effective range.

TERMINAL ARMOR

DESCRIPTION Rusty's terminal armor creates a barrier that deploys automatically upon his AC taking lethal damage, leaving it with 1 AP. If he has any remaining repair kits he will use one at this point as well.

EVASION Not used offensively.

DESTROY THE DRIVE BLOCK

"You are vermin. And I will be rid of you!"

—V.II Snail

As her final act, Carla sabotaged the Xylem locking everyone out of its systems and setting it on a collision course with the Coral stream. The only way to stop it from crashing into the Coral and igniting it is to destroy the skyrmion generators that are powering the engines, causing the Xylem to fall before it reaches the Coral. To locate them, you'll need to traverse maze-like interior sections of the Xylem and contend with heavy cannon fire whenever you have to venture outside, all while fighting your way past forces still loyal to Carla and Overseer, including another encounter with SMART CLEANER.

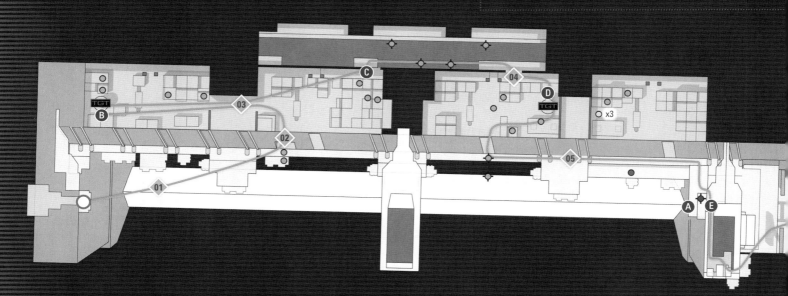

MISSION OBJECTIVES

Destroy All Large Skyrmion Generators

Escape From the Drive Block

Defeat V.II Snail

MISSION INFO

Combat Zone	Stratosphere—Xylem Drive Block
Client	Ayre
Reward	630,000
Max Bonus Pay	—
Completion Unlocks	—
Combat Logs	—
Data Logs	—
Part Containers	—

ENEMY DATA

		No.	AP	AS	Bonus Pay	Analysis
■	Skyrmion Generator	4	700	—	—	—
●	CD-E-086 Aerial Defense Drone (Mini Gatling Gun)	7	40	—	—	P.308
●	CD-J-098 Quad Drone (Laser Cannon)	6	302	310	—	P.312
●	MT-E-104 Bipedal MT (Dual Machine Gun)	7	470	364	—	P.316
●	MT-E-104 Bipedal MT (Missile Launcher)	2	470	364	—	P.316
●	MT-E-104 Bipedal MT (Shotgun)	2	470	364	—	P.317
●	MT-E-104 Bipedal MT (Grenade Cannon)	1	470	364	—	P.316
●	MT-E-104 Bipedal MT (Hand Rocket Launcher)	3	470	364	—	P.317
●	MB-0100 CLUTCH Crawler MT (Stun Plug)	2	650	364	—	P.319
●	MB-0100 CLUTCH Crawler MT (Electro Saw)	7	650	364	—	P.319
●	MB-0100 CLUTCH Crawler MT (Heavy Rocket Launcher)	2	650	364	—	P.318
◇	Artillery (Plasma Cannon)	1	672	—	—	P.330
●	MT-J-048 Tetrapod MT (Laser Blade)	1	13370	2200	—	P.322
●	MB-0202 TOYBOX MT	2	1848	1053	—	P.325
●	EC-0804 SMART CLEANER	1	48705	2600	—	—
●	AAP07A: ARQUEBUS BALTEUS / V.II Snail	1	40110	1900	—	—

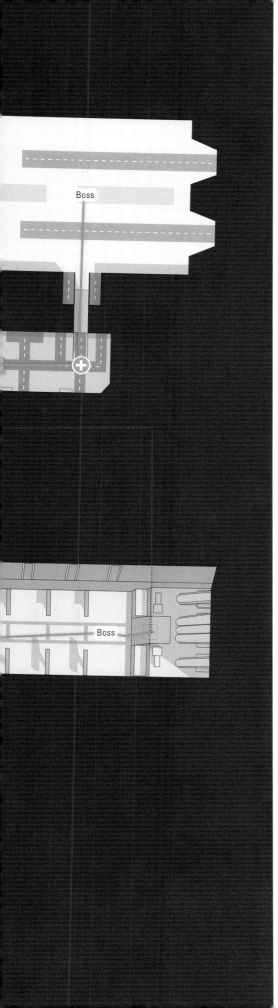

Boss

Boss

AC ASSEMBLY

You'll be encountering a large variety of enemies during this mission, including a couple of very tough encounters, so defensively it's prudent to cover as many bases as possible with your frame parts. A mix of Arquebus, ALLMIND, and Rubicon Research Institute parts gives you a nice spread of defensive specs, and since you'll be facing SMART CLEANER again, equipping tetrapod legs is recommended for the ability to easily hover above it.

In terms of offense, you'll be getting up close and personal with the more challenging foes. Dual shotguns and diffuse laser cannons act as an ad-hoc quadruple shotgun build, allowing for alternating shots to tear through enemy shields and AP.

01	R-ARM UNIT | SHOTGUN SG-027 ZIMMERMAN	P.54
02	L-ARM UNIT | SHOTGUN SG-027 ZIMMERMAN	P.54
03	R-BACK UNIT | DIFFUSE LASER CANNON VP-60LCD	P.67
04	L-BACK UNIT | DIFFUSE LASER CANNON VP-60LCD	P.67
05	HEAD | — VE-44A	P.78
06	CORE | — 07-061 MIND ALPHA	P.81
07	ARMS | — IA-C01A: EPHEMERA	P.84
08	LEGS | TETRAPOD VP-424	P.86
09	BOOSTER | — BST-G2/P06SPD	P.88
10	FCS | — IB-C03F: WLT 001	P.90
11	GENERATOR | — VE-20C	P.92

OBJECTIVE

Destroy All Large Skyrmion Generators

01 ◈ You begin the mission on a small platform looking out along the Xylem with Rusty in his upgraded STEEL HAZE ORTUS AC at your side. The generators you need to destroy are hidden away in the Xylem's interior, and while the path toward the door leading inside may appear clear, there are hidden dangers waiting for you to make a move. Toward the opposite end of the area at **Position A**, there's a plasma cannon artillery battery that will open fire on you as soon as it has a clear line of sight. The safest approach is to Assault Boost toward the opening while maintaining the same height level of the starting platform, until you're directly above it, then drop straight down and move inside. ▶ A

02 ◈ The locations of two generators will be marked as targets when you enter this room, and Rusty will typically take the lead by immediately engaging any enemy forces he spots, leaving you free to deal with the generators. Head toward the generator at **Position B** first, since it's the closest, taking out the bipedal MTs in the area along the way if Rusty hasn't already done so. ▶ B

03 ◈ Destroy the generator, and then start heading toward **Position C**, where you can use a service area to reach the adjacent room in which the second generator is housed, and that's where the access point is. When you reach the opening, peek around the corner to get the attention of the drones defending the area and move back behind the wall so that they slowly emerge, allowing you to easily and safely pick them off one at a time.

04 ◈ The generator at **Position D** is clearly visible as soon as you enter this room, so destroy it immediately. You should then move around the outskirts of the room behind the generator, destroying the bipedal MTs standing guard in there, with the aid of Rusty. You'll need to head back outside again to proceed, but there's another pair of drones hovering just outside, so either close in quickly and destroy them, or simply let Rusty take them out.

The plasma artillery cannon at the far side of the catwalk will harass you as soon as the mission starts; fortunately, there is plenty of cover to allow your approach.

The generators are nestled in close-quarters areas flanked by groups of enemies, a situation where your dual shotguns shine.

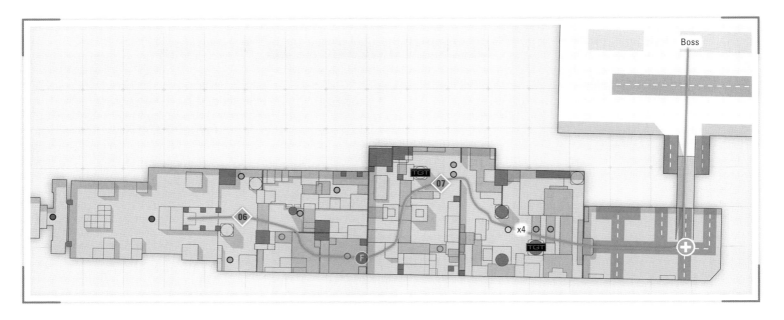

Boss

05 ◈ You'll come under fire from the artillery once you're back outside, so make use of the pillars on the side of the wall for cover as you make your way along the area toward it. Between you and the artillery is a tetrapod MT, but Rusty should take the lead and draw its attention. You should focus only on the artillery, because fighting the tetrapod MT while dodging artillery fire can be very dangerous. When you run out of cover, Assault Boost toward the open door just past the tetrapod MT, so you can use the room for cover, making sure to evade any artillery shots fired your way. There are enemies inside the room, so don't venture too far into it, or you'll get drawn into an unnecessary battle.

From there, you can quickly boost up to the side of the artillery installation and destroy it. Once it's destroyed, drop back down and help Rusty out with the tetrapod MT, if it's still active. Boost down there and unload all of your weapons into it while it's distracted, which will easily stagger it and allow for an easy victory. With the area clear, you can make your way up to **Position E** above the platform the artillery was on, and use the hallway there to reach a large open area where you'll once again need to battle a SMART CLEANER. ▶ A

The second encounter with the SMART CLEANER is significantly easier, primarily because Rusty is there to provide a distraction while you pummel the boss.

EC-0804 SMART CLEANER

A CLEAN SWEEP

This SMART CLEANER is identical to the one you faced during the "Infiltrate Grid 086" mission back in Chapter 2, so for a full breakdown of its specs and attacks, refer to its entry on P.144.

Like the previous battle with a SMART CLEANER, hovering above its furnace exhaust and firing down into the opening is still by far the best way of dealing damage and staggering it. Once it's staggered, drop down and shoot it in the furnace intake so that you can let your EN recharge, then switch back to hovering when it recovers. Avoid charging your diffuse laser cannons; simply shooting them provides higher damage output over time. Destroying SMART CLEANER enables you to continue toward the next generator. You'll have to bid farewell to Rusty, because he'll get called away to take care of an enemy fleet, so from this point onward, your're on your own. Access the door at the opposite end of the room and drop down the shaft beyond it when you're ready to continue.

| OBJECTIVE | Escape from the Drive Block |

06 ◈ This drive block core area is protected by a large number of crawler MTs that can be hard to locate among all of the machinery—be sure to rely on your scan to keep track of them. They can be destroyed fairly easily if you're quick, just make sure to hit them before they get too close, because their attacks can be difficult to evade in this cramped environment. The next generator is in an adjacent room, and to reach it you'll need to make your way through the room to a small opening at **Position F**, and then make your way up and across the various platforms on the other side.

07 ◈ You'll encounter more crawler MTs in this room, but you can safely destroy them from the platform the generator is on. After taking them out, drop down and go through the large opening they were patrolling. The final generator is up high in the opposite corner of the next room, guarded by a number of drones and crawler MTs. If you approach along the ground, you can make use of the corner just before the generator comes into view to block the MTs' attacks while you pick off the drones.

Once the drones are down, Assault Boost up to the crawler MTs to destroy them quickly and then turn your attention to the final generator. Destroying this generator will trigger a chain reaction causing the drive block to blow, but you're not under any time constraints, so there's no need to rush. The way out is through a small opening in the wall near the generator, which leads you down to a small garage area, where you'll find a supply sherpa that you can use, before heading down the ramp and facing the final obstacle in the way of your escape: V.II Snail.

AAP07A ARQUEBUS BALTEUS

BASIC SPECS

AP	40110
Attitude Stability	1900
Anti-Kinetic Defense	1089
Anti-Energy Defense	1529
Anti-Explosive Defense	1616
Elec. Discharge Tolerance	500
Shock Resistance	35%
ACS Anomaly Tolerance	500
Heat Resistance	20%
Pulse Armor Resilience	6050

OBJECTIVE
Defeat V.II Snail

PHASES

1 Having taken on the new Arquebus BALTEUS weapons platform, your fight with V.II Snail will be more in line with the fight against the original BALTEUS in Chapter 1 than a traditional AC battle. In this first phase of the fight, your main concern should be anticipating and evading Snail's extremely dangerous spiral energy cannon; the further you are away from this attack the easier it is to evade, but once you become familiar with its timing pattern, you can lead the shot and dodge away from it at any distance, giving you a brief window to land your own shots if you're close enough. Snail will sometimes use this attack consecutively, however, to try and catch you by surprise, so you'll need to be careful.

The close-range build that is recommended will require you to chase Snail around a bit until you manage to break through his pulse armor. Once that happens, you'll be able to inflict huge amounts of AP damage, so the effort is worth it. Alternate shots from your dual shotguns and dual diffuse laser cannons rhythmically, and avoid charging the latter as they once again shred through the boss faster un-charged. If you are pressuring Snail well, this strategy requires breaking his shield twice to reach the next phase.

2 Ayre will remark that BALTEUS's energy is increasing once you've depleted roughly half of its AP, which is the signal that you're transitioning into the second phase of the fight. During this phase, it's advisable that you attempt to pressure Snail to the absolute fullest extent of your ability, because the laser attacks he starts using are among the deadliest attacks in the game, and if you give him an opening, he can finish you off very quickly. Your movement abilities will be put to the test to keep up with him while evading his attacks, but anything other than an aggressive approach to end the fight as quickly as possible will just lead to it lasting longer, putting you in more danger. Make sure you're hovering as much as possible during this phase, so you can fire your diffuse laser cannons while moving, because being stationary can quickly be lethal.

AAP07A: ARQUEBUS BALTEUS / V.II SNAIL ATTACKS

PULSE ARMOR
DESCRIPTION Shield that absorbs all damage until depleted. Will regenerate after a short period of time after being broken.

EVASION Not used offensively.

MISSILES
DESCRIPTION Volley of eight total explosive missiles fired from both multi-missile launchers; the volleys can be stacked either vertically or horizontally.

EVASION These are direct missiles with limited homing capabilities, so you can simply Quick Boost away from them.

SPIRAL ENERGY BLAST ▼
DESCRIPTION Charges a large orb of swirling energy before condensing it down and releasing it as a high-impact shot that leaves a lingering damage field on impact.

EVASION Strafe to one side as the shot charges, and then Quick Boost in the opposite direction as it fires.

PLASMA SHOT
DESCRIPTION Rapid-fire volley of shots fired from plasma rifle that travel quickly through the air and leave lingering damage fields.

EVASION Quick Boost away from the shots and jump to avoid the lingering damage field.

CHARGED PLASMA SHOT
DESCRIPTION Charged plasma rifle shot that releases two projectiles that leave large lingering damage fields behind.

EVASION As soon as you see the pulse rifle begin charging, jump into the air and Quick Boost away from the shots.

PULSE SHOCK STREAM
DESCRIPTION Two streams of pulse energy that get fired toward your AC. The strike diffuses outward from the point of release creating a cone of energy.

EVASION Chain uses of your Quick Boost away from the streams but toward BALTEUS to avoid the wider arc of energy.

PULSE SHOTGUN ▼
DESCRIPTION Lateral wave of pulse energy which consists of eight shots that fan outward. Inner-most shots converge while the rest move outward.

EVASION Jump and boost upward toward BALTEUS.

PULSE GUN
DESCRIPTION Sustained wave of pulse energy that is more accurate the closer you are to the boss.

EVASION Quickly create distance between yourself and BALTEUS while chaining uses of your Quick Boost away from the shots.

PULSE EXPLOSION — PHASE 2
DESCRIPTION Gathers a large volume of pulse energy into its frame and releases it back outward as a large explosion. Always begins Phase 2 with this attack.

EVASION Chain Quick Boosts away from BALTEUS when its AP is reduced to half in anticipation of this attack.

PULSE ANTI-LOCK FIELD — PHASE 2
DESCRIPTION Releases a field of pulse energy that will interfere with the lock-on capacities of some types of munitions.

EVASION Not used offensively.

TRIPLE PULSE SHOTGUN ▼ — PHASE 2
DESCRIPTION Stronger version of Phase 1's pulse shotgun in which three waves of more condensed pulse shots are released.

EVASION Jump and boost away from BALTEUS.

DIFFUSE PLAMSA BEAM COMBO — PHASE 2
DESCRIPTION Creates two plasma beams facing outward from its plasma rifles and sweeps them across the area while spinning.

EVASION Back away until you're out of range of the beams, and then keep moving back as it spins toward you; can interrupt the attack by causing a stagger or breaking the shield.

CONDENSED PLASMA BEAM COMBO — PHASE 2
DESCRIPTION Plasma beam is amplified and brought down on you from above BALTEUS, then swept back and forth. This version of the attack leaves a large amount of lingering damage fields where the beam travels.

EVASION Quick Boost laterally to avoid the overhead slam and then jump over the beam as it's swept back and forth and move toward BALTEUS while in the air to avoid the damage fields.

SHUT DOWN THE CLOSURE SATELLITES

"You and I... could have walked together."

—Ayre

Ayre accepts that you've made your own choices and are now on a different path, but for the sake of the Rubiconians, she must try to stop Overseer and the Xylem. That means you'll need to oppose her in one final battle to see the job through. Your goal is to ensure that the Xylem reaches the vascular plant and collides with it to ignite the Coral. Ayre is integrated with a highly mobile and dangerous C-Weapon with powerful attacks that can easily destroy the few objects that resemble cover on this circular platform, meaning you'll have nowhere to hide. This climactic battle will be the ultimate test of your piloting skills, and you'll need to pull together everything that you've learned along the way if you wish to emerge victorious.

AC ASSEMBLY

Ayre's attacks deal exclusively Coral damage, and since there's no spec to help you mitigate it, it's recommended that you focus on AP, attitude stability, and mobility on the ground. The FORTALEZA tank legs are an great choice for these purposes, and allow you to build a surprisingly durable AC from the legs up. For weaponry, Ayre is extremely fast and weak to energy damage, but you'll need to punch through her Coral shield first. This combination of challenges is overcome by pairing kinetic and energy handguns, with diffuse laser cannons providing decisive blows when Ayre staggers.

01	R-ARM UNIT	LASER HANDGUN VP-66LH	P.59
02	L-ARM UNIT	HANDGUN HG-003 COQUILLETT	P.54
03	R-BACK UNIT	DIFFUSE LASER CANNON VP-60LCD	P.67
04	L-BACK UNIT	DIFFUSE LASER CANNON VP-60LCD	P.67
05	HEAD	— VE-44A	P.78
06	CORE	— VE-40A	P.81
07	ARMS	— NACHTREIHER/46E	P.83
08	LEGS	TANK EL-TL-11 FORTALEZA	P.87
09	BOOSTER	— 	—
10	FCS	— IB-C03F: WLT 001	P.90
11	GENERATOR	— VE-20C	P.92

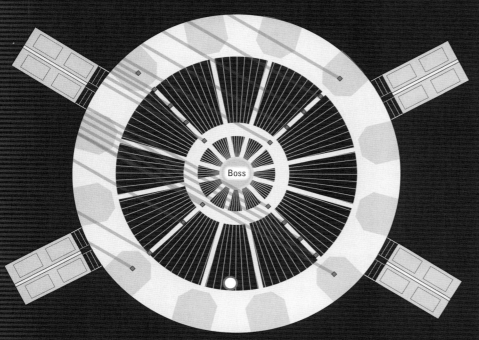

MISSION OBJECTIVE

Defeat Ayre

MISSION INFO

Combat Zone	Exosphere—LOC Station 31
Client	"Cinder" Carla / Overseer
Reward	550,000
Max Bonus Pay	—
Completion Unlocks	—
Combat Logs	—
Data Logs	—
Part Containers	—

ENEMY DATA

	No.	AP	AS	Bonus Pay	Analysis
IB-07: SOL 644 / Ayre	1	42020	1750	—	—

IB-07

SOL 644 / AYRE

BASIC SPECS

AP	42020
Attitude Stability	1750
Anti-Kinetic Defense	1280
Anti-Energy Defense	1090
Anti-Explosive Defense	1326
Elec. Discharge Tolerance	500
Shock Resistance	20%
ACS Anomaly Tolerance	500
Heat Resistance	30%
Pulse Armor Resilience	4500

OBJECTIVE
Defeat Ayre

PHASES

1 Ayre begins phase one in the middle of the platform, passive and slow. You have a few moments to get your bearings before her all-out assault commences, so retreat to the arena boundary. By fighting at the boundary, you limit Ayre's rapid repositioning abilities and force her to attack you from a limited number of angles. This also hampers some of her more intense combos in later phases.

Your efforts in Phase 1 should be spent remaining close to Ayre; this is where your handguns are at their strongest. Aggressively punish Ayre at the end of her melee attacks and avoid becoming too passive; you should rapidly accumulate massive hits to her Coral armor. Meanwhile, charge your diffuse laser cannons and fire them as soon as her shield depletes.

This phase is unsurprisingly the simplest and most forgiving of the battle, and is a good primer for upcoming phases due to some similarities. You'll need to be mindful when she repositions and identify if she is using a melee or ranged attack, but her ranged attacks in this phase are simple enough to evade with a Quick Boost or just a strafe, thanks to your tank legs' speed. Even if these attacks connect, they aren't particularly damaging, unlike her second phase variations.

2 Ayre gains access to a slew of new attacks in this phase, and she adopts a far more aggressive attack pattern, so even more so than in the first phase, it's important to limit the amount of time she spends attacking by constantly pressuring her with your own offense. Your overall strategy remains largely the same: deplete her shield, and then inflict as much damage as possible while she's staggered. However, while attempting to do that, you'll need to be extra mindful and watch closely for her transformations, as they signal her most deadly attacks.

AYRE'S DIVE COMBO

During this attack, Ayre will fly higher above the ground than normal, then attempt to bombard you with Coral lasers as she flies by, before sending four clones at you. When these clones impact the ground, they'll create large explosions in their wake, during which Ayre transforms into her cannon frame and fires a sustained Coral beam. That beam has an audible alert indicator, and evading both it and the clones that precede it is of the utmost importance due to the huge amount of damage those parts of the attack inflicts. As soon as the clones appear, Assault Boost toward Ayre so that you move past the explosions; this should get you close enough to Ayre that you can boost underneath her to evade the Coral beam. From that distance, you'll be able to fire at her for the duration of the beam, which is one of the largest attack opportunities you'll get in the fight.

3 The start of this phase is accompanied by a cinematic slow-motion effect, similar to when you destroy a boss or AC. Unfortunately, Ayre will still have roughly 50% of her AP remaining. However, she no longer utilizes her Coral barrier, meaning your energy weapons become even more potent.

Ayre's melee options in phase three remain largely the same as phase two, meaning your options for punishing her will remain similar as well. Her ranged attack options are now even further augmented and can be extremely lengthy and highly damaging if you get caught in them. Avoiding pursuing her away from the arena boundary is paramount now, as you can easily lose track of her and be caught by a devastating ranged attack. Remain patient in this phase and continue to counterattack Ayre's melee options, and she will quickly expire.

IB-07: SOL 644 / AYRE ATTACKS

CORAL ARMOR   PHASES 1, 2

DESCRIPTION Barrier that absorbs all damage until depleted, which then causes an instant stagger. Regenerates after a short while.

EVASION Not used offensively.

CORAL BEAM RIFLE (BURST FIRE)

DESCRIPTION Arm-mounted Coral oscillator can fire three bursts or double-shot round. Fewer bursts are fired if used in conjunction with another attack.

EVASION Quick Boost away from the shots.

CORAL BEAM RIFLE (QUICK MULTI-SHOT)

DESCRIPTION Coral oscillator fires two bursts of lighter but faster-moving shots than her standard double-shot bursts. This attack will be used after Ayre attempts to dodge your own attacks.

EVASION Quick Boost away from the shots.

CORAL SPIDER MISSILES (FULL RELEASE)

DESCRIPTION Large volley of split-pattern missiles with staggered momentum fired from back-mounted Coral missile launcher.

EVASION Quick Boost while on the ground or the missiles may be able to course correct midair and return to you.

CORAL BLADE SWEEP — PHASES 1, 2

DESCRIPTION Limited range, rushing singular blade slash from arm-mounted Coral oscillator.

EVASION Quick Boost away from Ayre if you are at mid or long-range, otherwise Quick Boost toward her and away from the blade's direction.

CORAL SPIDER MISSILES (QUICK-RELEASE) — PHASE 2

DESCRIPTION Partial volley of four spider missiles that are often fired while defensively boosting.

EVASION Quick Boost while on the ground, or the missiles may be able to course correct midair and return to you.

CORAL EXTENDED BLADE COMBO — PHASE 2

DESCRIPTION Coral blade string comprised of a quick slash, followed by one or two slow extended blade sweeping attacks.

EVASION When Ayre boosts toward you to position herself at an appropriate range for the strikes, immediately Quick Boost away from the quick slash and then behind her to best avoid the extended blade.

CORAL BLADE CROSS SLASH COMBO — PHASE 2

DESCRIPTION Extremely powerful Coral blade string comprised of two quick slashes followed by a heavily staggered cross slash.

EVASION When Ayre boosts toward you to position herself at an appropriate range for the strikes, immediately Quick Boost behind and to her left side. If at range then chain Quick Boosts away.

DIVE ATTACK ▼ — PHASE 2

DESCRIPTION Ayre's frame transforms into a winged ship and enshrouds itself in Coral energy before flying at you for a grab attack with her wing Coral blade; releases a high volume of Coral beams in her wake.

EVASION Once Ayre transforms and begins to move downward, you can jump and boost straight up to avoid being caught.

SUSTAINED CORAL BEAM ▼ — PHASE 3

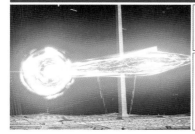

DESCRIPTION Ayre's frame transforms into a quadrupedal cannon before charging and releasing a high-impact sustained Coral beam.

EVASION At long-range, you can watch for the alert indicator after she fully transforms and Quick Boost to either side of the beam. At mid-range or close-range, try to get under her using an Assault Boost or Quick Boost respectively.

CORAL CLONE COMBO (VER. A) — PHASE 3

DESCRIPTION Ayre releases one clone in front of her that comes in for a single slash, after which she also unleashes a single slash.

EVASION As soon as the clone appears, jump and boost upward as you move toward Ayre. The clone and Ayre should strike beneath you.

MULTI-BURST BEAM ▼ — PHASE 2

DESCRIPTION After flying into the air, a beam of Coral energy is released from shoulder-mounted Coral cannons, warping the space around it, causing explosions after a brief time.

EVASION The direction of the beam is head-on toward you, so you can Quick Boost away and to the side of it to avoid both the beam and the ensuing explosions.

CORAL SHOTGUN ▼ — PHASES 2, 3

DESCRIPTION High-impact, shotgun-like blast of Coral beams fired out from shoulder-mounted Coral cannons that fan outward slightly.

EVASION Quick Boost underneath the shots as they appear; this will cause a majority to pass over your head.

CORAL CLONE COMBO (VER. D) — PHASE 3

DESCRIPTION Ayre releases a clone that performs two quick slashes simultaneously with her before she performs a cross slash, and after a brief delay, the clone also cross slashes.

EVASION Either Quick Boost away from Ayre or jump above her.

CORAL CLONE COMBO (VER. B) — PHASE 3

DESCRIPTION Ayre releases one clone immediately behind her, slashes once, and then the clone also slashes once.

EVASION Either chain Quick Boosts away from Ayre or jump above her.

CORAL CLONE COMBO (VER. C) — PHASE 3

DESCRIPTION Releases a clone in front of her that uses a double slash. She'll then use a delayed single slash follow-up before backing off and creating another clone, after which she and the clone rush back in and each perform a final slash.

EVASION As soon as the clone appears, jump and boost upward as you move toward Ayre. The clone and Ayre should strike beneath you.

CORAL CLONE COMBO (VER. E) — PHASE 3

DESCRIPTION Ayre releases two clones at long range that rush toward you and perform a single slash, after which she follows up with her own single slash.

EVASION As soon as the clones appear, jump and boost upward as you move toward Ayre. The clone and Ayre should strike beneath you.

CORAL CLONE COMBO (VER. F) ▼ — PHASE 3

DESCRIPTION Ayre releases a clone that slashes once, followed by quickly coming in for a single slash. She then quickly transforms and releases a sustained Coral beam that can sweep across the area.

EVASION As soon as the clone appears, jump and boost upward as you move toward Ayre. The clone and Ayre should strike beneath you. Quick Boost past Ayre as she fires the Coral beam.

CORAL CLONE COMBO (VER. G) ▼ — PHASE 3

DESCRIPTION Ayre releases two clones sequentially each rushing in with a cross slash. She then comes in for a single slash before quickly transforming and releasing a sustained Coral beam that can sweep across the area.

EVASION As soon as the clone appears, jump and boost upward as you move toward Ayre. The clone and Ayre should strike beneath you. Quick Boost past Ayre as she fires the Coral beam.

CORAL BOMBARDMENT DIVE COMBO ▼ — PH 3

DESCRIPTION Ayre performs a diving attack while raining down Coral beams. She'll then create clones that impact the ground and explode, before she transforms again and releases a sustained Coral beam.

EVASION Jump to evade her dive attack, and then begin strafing to match her position. Assault Boost toward her once the clones begin to fly at you, so that you end up underneath her while she fires the Coral beam.

BRING DOWN THE XYLEM >

"They... 621... I have to... dispose of you."

—Handler Walter

Even after all of your sabotage attempts, the Xylem is still on course to hit the plant and ignite the Coral. The only remaining course of action is to destroy the ramjet engines that are propelling it, to bring the city down for good. After ensuring the safety of the planet below and the Rubiconians that inhabit it, one final showdown with the person who first set you on the mercenary path will need to be overcome before you can rest.

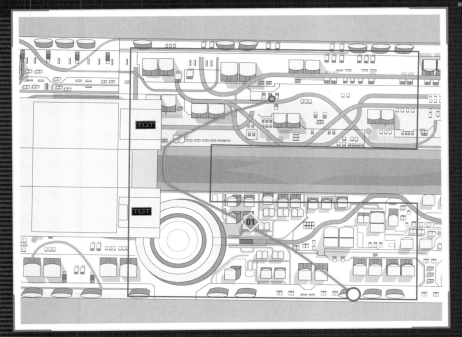

MISSION OBJECTIVES

Destroy the Ramjet Engines

Defeat Handler Walter

MISSION INFO

Combat Zone	Exosphere—Xylem Upper Districts
Client	Ayre
Reward	340,000
Max Bonus Pay	—
Completion Unlocks	IB-C03H: HAL 826 (Head) IB-C03C: HAL 826 (Core) IB-C03A: HAL 826 (Arms) IB-C03L: HAL 826 (Bipedal Legs)
Combat Logs	—
Data Logs	—
Part Containers	—

ENEMY DATA

	No.	AP	AS	Bonus Pay	Analysis
■ Ramjet Engine	2	400	—	—	—
● AC IB-C03: HAL 826 / Handler Walter	1	10810	1742	—	—

AC ASSEMBLY

The HAL 826 piloted by Walter is the only enemy you'll face in this mission, so your entire assembly can be tailored toward fighting it. Unfortunately, the damage from his Coral weaponry cannot be mitigated by your specs, so how you approach him will come down to whether you prefer lightweight movement-based builds or slower builds with high AP and attitude stability. The recommended build below is designed around tetrapod legs for their relatively high AP and attitude stability, while still maintaining a decent amount of movement speed.

Like many single-target encounters, the HAL 826 is best fought using close-range weaponry with high-impact burst damage, since that allows you to play aggressively and dictate the pace of the fight, rather than simply reacting from range. The reliable combo of ZIMMERMAN shotguns and diffuse laser cannons are among the best options to fulfill this role.

01	R-ARM UNIT | SHOTGUN SG-027 ZIMMERMAN	P.54	
02	L-ARM UNIT | SHOTGUN SG-027 ZIMMERMAN	P.54	
03	R-BACK UNIT | DIFFUSE LASER CANNON VP-60LCD	P.67	
04	L-BACK UNIT | DIFFUSE LASER CANNON VP-60LCD	P.67	
05	HEAD | — VE-44A	P.78	
06	CORE | — 07-061 MIND ALPHA	P.81	
07	ARMS | — IA-C01A: EPHEMERA	P.84	
08	LEGS | TETRAPOD VP-424	P.86	
09	BOOSTER | — BST-G2/P06SPD	P.88	
10	FCS | — IB-C03F: WLT 001	P.90	
11	GENERATOR | — VE-20C	P.92	

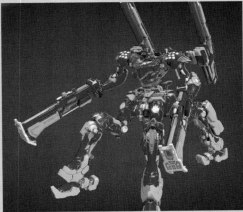

01 ◈ The ramjets you need to destroy are directly ahead of you in the middle of the Xylem when you begin the mission. There's nothing else in your way, so you can just Assault Boost toward them. There's a small platform just in front of each engine. If you land on that, you'll have a stable place with a clear view of the engine to fire from. A cutscene plays out once the second engine has been destroyed, after which you'll immediately enter combat against Handler Walter atop the Xylem, as it plummets toward the planet.

HANDLER WALTER

AC // IB-C03 HAL 826

BASIC SPECS

AP	10810
Attitude Stability	1742
Anti-Kinetic Defense	1204
Anti-Energy Defense	1279
Anti-Explosive Defense	1230
Elec. Discharge Tolerance	490
Shock Resistance	25%
ACS Anomaly Tolerance	490
Heat Resistance	25%

■■ OBJECTIVE | Defeat Handler Walter

The fight against Walter only consists of a single phase, so he has access to all of his attacks from the onset. This means you don't have to worry about any potentially dangerous phase transition attacks. He'll typically attempt to stay at roughly medium range from you. If you pressure him, he'll make use of his quick melee attacks to force you to back off, so he can Quick Boost either away from or behind you.

Walter has a number of dangerous attacks, but the most important ones to watch out for are his sustained Coral laser, missiles, and drone. His Coral laser does trigger an audible alert indicator from your systems, but it can be used at any range so it's difficult to anticipate. It also fires very quickly, so you won't have a lot of time to react, and the continuous beam damages your AC and strains your ACS

for as long as it's in contact with you. Regardless of what you're doing at the time, your priority should be to move safely away from it.

He'll use his missiles in conjunction with his drone, but the missiles travel fairly slowly, while the drone moves quickly. This means you can end up in overwhelming situations in which you're forced to evade multiple staggered attacks, while Walter is also repositioning for another attack. These situations can only arise if he has time to create them, which is why an aggressive approach where you attempt to effectively shut down his ability to use many of his attacks, is one of the best strategies here. There's no cover to speak of in the area, so the fight essentially comes down to evading his attacks until you can get close enough to use your weapons. Once you're close, try to stay there, and constantly rotate through your weapons to ensure he's kept on the back foot.

IB-C03: HAL 826 / HANDLER WALTER ATTACKS

IB-C03W4: NGI 028

DESCRIPTION Walter is shielded by a Coral barrier for the majority of the fight, dampening the efficacy of your shots so they inflict less ACS strain and AP damage to his AC. He will occasionally lower the shield, but he'll raise it again intermittently throughout the fight.

EVASION Not used offensively.

IB-C03W1: WLT 011 (CHARGED) ▼

DESCRIPTION Coral rifle shot that releases a high-impact shot and creates a larger, more hazardous lingering damage field in its wake. Walter can delay the release of the shot after it's charged while he repositions himself.

EVASION It's difficult to anticipate the release of the shot, but you can boost into the air to evade it, which has the added benefit of making it not hit a surface to create the damage field.

IB-C03W1: WLT 011 (UNCHARGED)

DESCRIPTION Quick rifle shot that inflicts damage both from the initial hit and the lingering damage field it creates.

EVASION Difficult to evade if at close or mid-range, but chaining uses of your Quick Boost can evade the shots.

BOOST KICK

DESCRIPTION Walter will Assault Boost toward you and performs a Boost Kick.

EVASION Quick Boost to either side of the HAL 826.

IB-C03W3: NGI 006 (UNCHARGED) ▼

DESCRIPTION High-impact missile that moves slowly through the air and can make sharp midair maneuvers to better home in on you; creates a lingering damage field on impact.

EVASION Evade while on the ground if possible, otherwise it can easily circle back on you. Quick Boost away from it until it eventually impacts the ground.

IB-C03W3: NGI 006 (CHARGED)

DESCRIPTION Semiautonomous drone that has a secondary function as a lower-impact missile. Primarily this drone chases your AC while releasing constant streams of Coral energy waves.

EVASION Chain Quick Boosts to avoid both the drone and its lasers.

IB-C03W1: WLT 011 (FULLY CHARGED) ▼

DESCRIPTION Walter charges his Coral rifle and uses it to produce a sustained appendage-like beam of energy which he'll either sweep horizontally or shoot straight with. This beam is capable of a degree of movement independent of the gun's own movement in Walter's hand.

EVASION Quick Boost to either side of the beam but make sure to move some additional distance to account for the beam's movement.

IB-C03W2: WLT 101 (SWEEP) ▼ (AUDIO ONLY)

DESCRIPTION Walter forms a large Coral blade with his melee attachment and sweeps it horizontally toward you. This strike is slow, but Walter is capable of directing the strike at an angle.

EVASION Chain uses of your Quick Boost backward, or if at close range, Quick Boost past Walter.

IB-C03W2: WLT 101 (QUICK SLASH)

DESCRIPTION Walter charges at your AC and releases a quick, overhead slash. This strike can be used in conjunction with his missile or drone, making it an effective tactic for pressuring you up-close.

EVASION Quick Boost away from Walter as he approaches or past him if at close range.

ASSAULT ARMOR

DESCRIPTION Coral-based version of this Core Expansion that produces a large Coral explosion in place of pulse energy.

EVASION Quick Boost away from Walter as he charges the Coral energy.

ATTACK THE DAM COMPLEX (ALT)

"Iguazu! How many ranks below you is G13?
You can count, right?"

—G1 Michigan

In a repeat of your first visit to the Gallia Dam Complex, you'll accompany Balam Redguns G4 Volta and G5 Iguazu with intent to cripple the RLF's source of energy, supplied via generators placed throughout the complex. Be attentive of the branching point you'll soon encounter, because this mission presents you with a choice that sets the stage for the remainder of your playthrough, and must be accepted. Shortly after destroying the second generator, you'll be contacted by the RLF and offered double the pay to betray the allies who contracted you; if you accept, you'll soon find yourself in a face-to-face battle against them.

This alternate mission largely plays out the same way it did on your first visit, so your strategy for destroying the first two generators is unchanged. Let your allies engage RLF defenses out in the open, while you dispatch distracted opponents from the sidelines. Once you accept the offer to join the other side of the conflict, the Redguns will be sitting ducks, too occupied with proceeding to the next generator to realize the betrayal. The accessible area gives you the option of engaging in combat with the Redguns either in the tight mountain corridor where you meet them, or on the expansive ice sheet that you passed right before it.

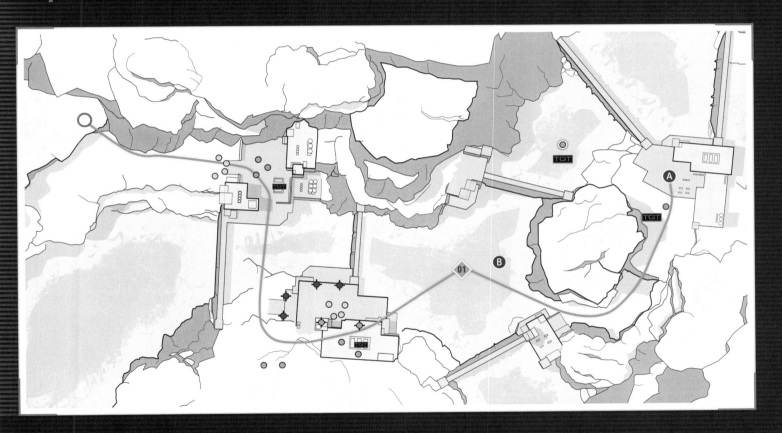

MISSION INFO

Combat Zone	Southern Belius—Gallia Dam Complex
Client	Balam Industries / Rubicon Liberation Front
Reward	190,000
Max Bonus Pay	190,000 (Necessary expense penalty of 190,000 applied to bonus pay)
Completion Unlocks	—
Combat Logs	Gold x1
Data Logs	—
Part Containers	—

MISSION OBJECTIVE
Defeat G4 Volta/G5 Iguazu

ENEMY DATA*

	No.	AP	AS	Bonus Pay	Analysis
◎ AC CANNON HEAD / G4 Volta	1	16940	2466	—	—
● AC HEAD BRINGER / G5 Iguazu	1	9690	1704	—	—

*For additional enemy data, see P.208

DECISION TIME

It's important to note that if you refuse the RLF's offer of double pay for turning on the Redguns and conclude the mission as normal, nothing will change moving forward. You must choose to take the alternate mission objective and complete the mission to proceed along an alternate path in NG+. You cannot make up for this in Replay Mission mode, but if you accidentally refuse the offer, you can quit the mission and start from the beginning for another chance to accept. Upon accepting, all of the RLF units will immediately turn non-hostile and cease firing on you, allowing you to focus on the two Redguns.

AC ASSEMBLY

This time, you'll craft your assembly with Volta and Iguazu in mind, rather than the RLF artillery you'll encounter before them. It's recommended to build for attitude stability, with anti-explosive defense as your primary defensive spec and anti-kinetic as your secondary focus. A heavy build including RaD, Dafeng, and Balam parts will offer the required defensive specs for this mission, including the Balam tank legs with their extreme attitude stability.

Your munitions should focus on high-impact energy damage output, as both Iguazu and Volta are susceptible to energy-based attacks. A fully charged shot from a pair of VP-60LCS laser cannons is capable of instantly destroying Iguazu's AC if you hit it when it's staggered, and will deal significant damage to Volta's AC as well, making them ideal after overloading their ACS with your shotguns.

01	R-ARM UNIT | SHOTGUN **SG-027 ZIMMERMAN**	P.54
02	L-ARM UNIT | SHOTGUN **SG-027 ZIMMERMAN**	P.54
03	R-BACK UNIT | LASER CANNON **VP-60LCS**	P.67
04	L-BACK UNIT | LASER CANNON **VP-60LCS**	P.67
05	HEAD | — **HC-3000 WRECKER**	P.79
06	CORE | — **DF-BD-08 TIAN-QIANG**	P.80
07	ARMS | — **DF-AR-09 TIAN-LAO**	P.82
08	LEGS | TANK **LG-022T BORNEMISSZA**	P.87
09	BOOSTER | —	
10	FCS | — **IB-C03F: WLT 001**	P.90
11	GENERATOR | — **VE-20C**	P.92

01 ◈ After destroying the two generator targets, you'll be contacted by the RLF with an offer for you to direct your hostilities toward your Redgun escorts rather than pursue your original objective, and you'll be unable to proceed in the mission until you make a choice. By the time you accept the RLF's offer, Volta and Iguazu have already split up and advanced toward the generator near **Position A**. This is to your benefit, as it allows you to easily get the jump on either of the two Redguns. Given HEAD BRINGER's relatively weaker defensive stats, it's recommended you target Iguazu first by engaging him in the narrow mountain pass. A solid opening strike is crucial to ending this fight quickly, because as soon as you initiate hostilities, Volta will start closing in on you.

If you defeat Iguazu quickly, you can choose to either engage Volta in the same area and attempt to use the surrounding terrain to your advantage, or fall back to **Position B** on the ice field, where you'll have more room to evade his attacks. Iguazu can use repair kits, so if he manages to use one before you destroy his AC you'll end up having to fight both of them simultaneously. If this occurs, falling back is recommended, since you'll need the room to maneuver.

G5 IGUAZU

AC // HEAD BRINGER

Assault Boost toward Iguazu while he's distracted and line up a perfect opening blast with your shotguns once you're in range. Keep firing them, but charge your laser cannons ahead of time when Iguazu is close to staggering, then release them as soon as his ACS overloads. This will either defeat Iguazu immediately or bring his AP just low enough for quick cleanup with the shotguns. If he somehow manages to survive and use a repair kit, he'll attempt to fight you from mid range using his MG-014 LUDLOW and LR-036 CURTIS. If given the chance, he can stagger you fairly quickly, so aim to close in and overload his ACS first, which shouldn't take long.

BASIC SPECS

AP	9690
Attitude Stability	1704
Anti-Kinetic Defense	1202
Anti-Energy Defense	1105
Anti-Explosive Defense	1187
Elec. Discharge Tolerance	490
Shock Resistance	6%
ACS Anomaly Tolerance	490
Heat Resistance	6%
Repair Kits	2

An Assault Boost into a couple of well-placed shotgun rounds is a good way to strain Iguazu's ACs.

AC HEAD BRINGER ATTACKS

LR-036 CURTIS ▼ (CHARGED)

DESCRIPTION Kinetic linear rifle capable of rapid uncharged shots, or a powerful charged shot.

EVASION Quick Boost to either side of the shot(s).

BML-G1/P20MLT-04

DESCRIPTION Launcher that releases four missiles with high homing capabilities.

EVASION Quick Boost to either side of the missiles as close to when they reach you as possible.

SI-27: SU-R8

DESCRIPTION Energy shield that Iguazu will often raise in defense.

EVASION Not used offensively.

MG-014 LUDLOW

DESCRIPTION Rapid-firing machine gun capable of quickly straining your ACS.

EVASION Create distance so that the shots ricochet off you, or Quick Boost to either side of the shots.

G4 VOLTA

AC // CANNON HEAD

CANNON HEAD's extraordinarily high AP, defenses, and attitude stability make Volta the more dangerous of the two Redguns that you'll be facing. If possible, deal with Iguazu first, so that when the time comes you can focus solely on Volta. On top of his massive defensive specs, Volta's AC is equipped with high-impact explosive and kinetic weaponry that can easily overload your ACS if his shots connect. Despite his heavy bulk, Volta will easily Quick Boost away from your shots if you attempt to confront him from a distance.

BASIC SPECS

AP	16940
Attitude Stability	2466
Anti-Kinetic Defense	1315
Anti-Energy Defense	1164
Anti-Explosive Defense	1312
Elec. Discharge Tolerance	490
Shock Resistance	-27%
ACS Anomaly Tolerance	490
Heat Resistance	-27%
Repair Kits	2

Due to the nature of explosive weaponry, Volta's range is very high, and he'll have no trouble straining your ACS from afar. Staying directly in front of him at close range can prove equally costly, due to his shotgun and grenade launcher. Fighting him effectively will come down to your positioning and movement; you'll want to be close enough that you can hit him effectively, but also give yourself enough room to move around him constantly, to ensure that he can't land any clean hits on you.

The ice at **Position B** is a spacious arena in case you need more room to dodge Volta's explosive shells.

AC CANNON HEAD ATTACKS

DF-GR-07 GOU-CHEN ▼

DESCRIPTION Fast-firing grenade launcher that releases an explosive that moves quickly through the air.

EVASION Quick Boost to either side to avoid its head-on pattern.

BML-G2/P19SPL-12

DESCRIPTION Fires two cells of a split missile, resulting in 12 sub-missiles. These do not have highly aggressive homing capacity.

EVASION Quick Boost as the missiles converge on you to limit the distance you need to evade.

SG-027 ZIMMERMAN

DESCRIPTION Shotgun that has a longer effective range than others in its class.

EVASION Continuously strafe around Volta to best avoid being hit flush by the shotgun.

SONGBIRDS ▼

DESCRIPTION High-impact grenade cannon that fires two shots per attack.

EVASION Chain Quick Boosts to avoid both shots; Volta will not fire the second shot directly behind the first.

PRISONER RESCUE

"You... you don't know what you're saying, girl...
There'll be nothing left... but dying embers..."

—Thumb Dolmayan

Impressed with your performance at the Gallia Dam, the RLF is recruiting you again. They want your aid in the extraction of three RLF prisoners, by protecting a transport helicopter as it navigates the contaminated city in Southern Belius. Fortunately, many enemies are in positions easily reached by pacing ahead of the helicopter. An awareness of enemy positions combined with munitions capable of swift destruction from afar will allow you to intercept unaware enemies here before they can become a threat. Look out for opponents that enter from outside of the area—they'll be marked with warning indicators. Depending on your build, you can take advantage of the city's terrain for cover between encounters, or leverage aerial superiority over your foes. Your bonus pay here is dependent upon the damage sustained by the helicopter; the more damage it takes, the lower your reward.

MISSION OBJECTIVES

Assist POW Rescue Mission and Escort Helicopter

Escort Helicopter Until it Exits Zone / Defeat G2 Nile/Balam MT Squad

MISSION INFO

Combat Zone	Southern Belius—Contaminated City
Client	Rubicon Liberation Front
Reward	250,000
Max Bonus Pay	190,000
Completion Unlocks	—
Combat Logs	Platinum x1, Silver x1
Data Logs	—
Part Containers	—

ENEMY DATA

	No.	AP	AS	Bonus Pay	Analysis
MT-T-026 BAWS Guard Mech (Rifle)	11	102	121	—	P.310
CH-T-025 Attack Helicopter (Anti-Tank Cannon)	2	28	—	—	P.309
CD-J-098 Quad Drone (Transport Hangar)	7	302	310	—	P.312
CD-J-098 Quad Drone (Laser Cannon)	3	302	310	—	P.312
TH-E-012 Transport Helicopter	6	750	—	—	P.314
MT-E-104 Bipedal MT (Dual Machine Gun)	12	470	364	—	P.316
MT-E-104 Bipedal MT (Cluster Gun)	8	470	364	—	P.317
MT-E-104 Bipedal MT (Hand Rocket Launcher)	8	470	364	—	P.317
MT-E-104 Bipedal MT (Missile Launcher)	3	470	364	—	P.316
MT-E-104 Bipedal MT (Grenade Cannon)	6	470	364	—	P.316
Artillery (Gatling Gun)	2	403	—	—	P.328
Artillery (Vertical Missile Launcher)	4	202	—	—	P.328
MT-J-048 Tetrapod MT (9-Shot Bazooka)	1	13370	2200	—	P.323
AC DEEP DOWN / G2 Nile	1	12510	1813	—	—

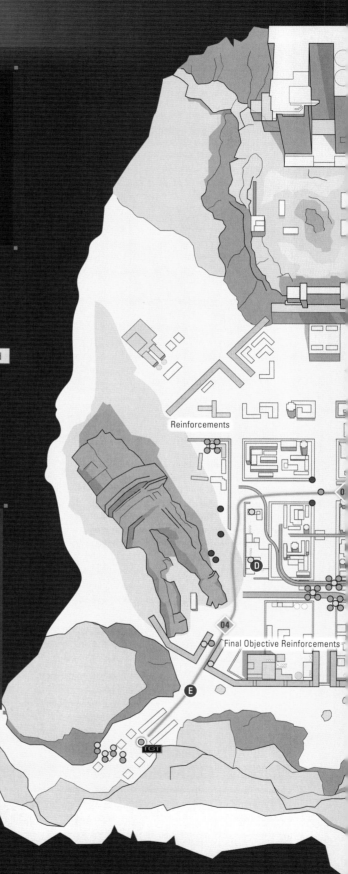

Reinforcements

Final Objective Reinforcements

AC ASSEMBLY

The recommended build for this mission uses tetrapod legs to rain destruction on enemies from above, creating a safe corridor for the rescue helicopter to fly through. Enemies deal a combination of kinetic and explosive damage, but this build prioritizes explosive defense. Mobility is also prioritized over AP and attitude stability, to help you intercept enemies before the helicopter is anywhere near them. With that in mind, fast-moving munitions that cover long distances are recommended. The goal is to dispatch opposing units before they become a threat, which is where the dual HML-G2/P19MLT-04 missile launchers come in. There are a couple of encounters where you'll need something that packs more of a punch, such as the fight against Nile, and for those, dual diffuse laser cannons are recommended.

01	R-ARM UNIT | MISSILE LAUNCHER HML-G2/P19MLT-04	P.62
02	L-ARM UNIT | MISSILE LAUNCHER HML-G2/P19MLT-04	P.62
03	R-BACK UNIT | DIFFUSE LASER CANNON VP-60LCD	P.67
04	L-BACK UNIT | DIFFUSE LASER CANNON VP-60LCD	P.67
05	HEAD | — HD-033M VERRILL	P.77
06	CORE | — IA-C01C: EPHEMERA	P.81
07	ARMS | — NACHTREIHER/46E	P.83
08	LEGS | TETRAPOD VP-424	P.86
09	BOOSTER | — BST-G2/P06SPD	P.88
10	FCS | — FCS-G2/P10SLT	P.90
11	GENERATOR | — VE-20C	P.92

OBJECTIVE

Assist POW Rescue Mission and Escort Helicopter

01 ◈ You'll need to rescue POWs from three locations, with enemy units mobilizing as the helicopter approaches their positions. It's recommended to move ahead of the helicopter to dispose of enemies lying in wait before they have a chance to damage the helicopter. At certain points during the mission, enemy units will close in on the helicopter from outside of the area, but their arrival is clearly marked with warning indicators. Prioritize enemy transport helicopters as well as artillery, as these pose the biggest threats to your rescue effort. To reach the first group of POWs, you'll need to fight through a group of enemy units. Among these is a pair of bipedal MTs with grenade launchers; these should be prioritized, due to the damage they can inflict on the helicopter.

The best practice during this mission is to prioritize any unit that triggers your AC's warning indicators. Upon reaching **Position A**, warning indicators alert you to two incoming transport helicopters, preparing to drop squads of two bipedal MTs each—all armed with bazookas. The ideal way to deal with this is by not giving the bipedal MTs a chance to become a problem and destroying the transport helicopters right away. After the helicopter lands at **Position A** and retrieves Little Ziyi, it will continue along its flight path.

SILVER COMBAT LOG

While you're near the helipad at **Position B**, look toward coordinate 220 and boost up the cliff to find a tetrapod MT bearing a combat log at **Position C**. It will be unaware at first, which gives you a chance to quickly strain its ACS. You'll have to be quick about destroying it, as the mission carries on regardless of your actions, so make sure you're well ahead of the helicopter when you take this detour.

02 ◈ En route to the second helipad at **Position B**, you'll find a row of unaware enemies awaiting the escort helicopter's approach. When the rescue helicopter is roughly 1,000 meters from the next objective, a squad of three transport quad drones bolts into the area, ready to deploy bipedal MTs equipped with grenade cannons. If you pushed forward to engage the back-most enemies ahead of the helicopter, you should double back at this point to eliminate the marked MTs. While it is possible to intercept the drones before they drop the bipedal MTs, it's advisable to target the MTs when they hit the field instead. ▶ A

When the rescue helicopter reaches **Position B**, a new squad of enemy units will close in from outside of the area. Marked with warning indicators, the three quad drones that appear—each equipped with laser cannons—will be the most significant threat to the helicopter thus far. Despite their massive damage output, their defensive spec totals are low, meaning the drones are disposed of quickly when prioritized appropriately. After the rescue helicopter has extracted the second POW, it will move on toward **Position D**.

03 ◈ On the way to the next pickup, the helicopter will travel a path guarded by a single bipedal MT and—more disconcertingly—two gatling gun artillery. The two artillery, marked with warning indicators, must be destroyed quickly, as their rapid-fire kinetic rounds can quickly decimate the rescue helicopter and your ACS. Take care to approach the artillery from behind, using the surrounding buildings for cover as you approach. ▶ B

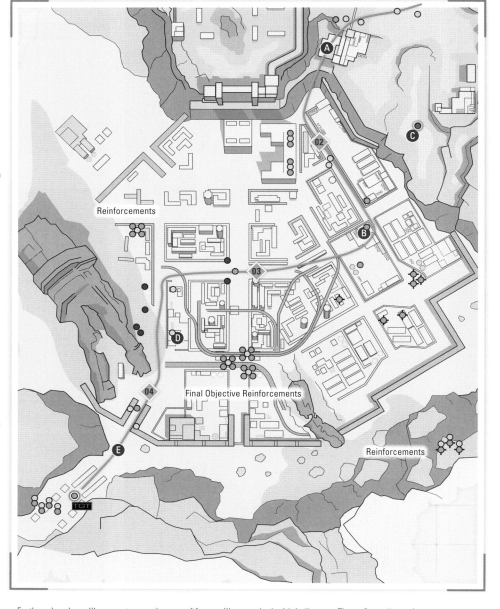

Further ahead, you'll encounter another set of four artillery marked with indicators. These fire volleys of over-head missiles from long range. Unlike the gatling gun artillery, they are unshielded with low AP, making them easy to destroy with a multi-lock sweep with your missile launchers. Once the helicopter approaches **Position D**, a transport helicopter will appear from outside the area carrying four bipedal MTs, each equipped with dual machine guns. Removing the transport helicopter from battle before it can deploy should not prove difficult, but prioritize the artillery if any are left. Once the rescue helicopter has safely extracted Father Dolmayan, it will advance a final time toward the exit point at **Position E**.

OBJECTIVE

Escort Helicopter Until it Exits Zone / Defeat G2 Nile/Balam MT Squad

04 ◈ Once the rescue helicopter reaches the edge of the area, dialogue and warning indicators alert you to the approach of AC DEEP DOWN piloted by G2 Nile. Nile will be accompanied by four transport drones carrying bipedal MTs with dual machine guns. Given the spacing of the MTs once deployed, it's recommended you focus your efforts on Nile, who will begin attacking the helicopter and poses the most significant threat to it.

Periodically, from the point Nile enters the combat zone, a series of enemy transport helicopters will appear. These helicopters offload squads of four dual machine gun MTs each, but as always, it's possible to dispose of the transport helicopter before the MTs are deployed. Keep in mind that the first transport helicopter will appear regardless of whether Nile and his companions are on the field. If the fight with Nile drags on long enough, however, it's possible for more transport helicopters to appear—up to five in total. Once the combat zone is cleared of all threats, the rescue helicopter will finally make its exit, ending the mission.

A

B

AC // DEEP DOWN

Nile opens the fight with his attention turned to the escort helicopter so it's important to intercept his assault quickly, but this also gives you an opportunity to initiate your assault unobstructed. Nile will attack you if actively engaged but will turn his attention back to the helicopter periodically. He generally positions himself close to the helicopter, making the task of closing in or pulling away that much easier, and the confined area makes it relatively easy to make short of work him using your laser cannons.

BASIC SPECS

AP	12510
Attitude Stability	1813
Anti-Kinetic Defense	1330
Anti-Energy Defense	1181
Anti-Explosive Defense	1271
Elec. Discharge Tolerance	490
Shock Resistance	15%
ACS Anomaly Tolerance	490
Heat Resistance	15%
Repair Kits	1

AC DEEP DOWN ATTACKS

HML-G2/P19MLT-04

DESCRIPTION This missile launcher releases a stream of four low-impact missiles and fires more quickly than his other explosives.

EVASION Immediately Quick Boost and strafe after the missiles are fired.

LR-037 HARRIS

DESCRIPTION Kinetic linear rifle capable of rapid uncharged shots or a single charged shot that Nile can hold for any amount of time.

EVASION Difficult to evade at close range, but a Quick Boost works best.

BML-G3/P05ACT-02

DESCRIPTION Releases two high-impact missiles that move slowly through the air, making them difficult to evade.

EVASION Quick Boost to evade them until they impact objects in the environment.

BML-G1/P07VTC-12

DESCRIPTION This missile launcher releases a high volume of overhead missiles.

EVASION Quick Boost away as soon as you see the missiles beginning to impact around you.

STOP THE SECRET DATA BREACH

"Anyway, did I mention that this is all your fault?"

—"Cinder" Carla

Your previous efforts have created an opening for the Junker Coyotes to gain control of Grid 086, to Carla's great displeasure. Five hacking drones placed throughout the facility are actively decrypting sensitive data held by "Cinder" Carla, and will be successful in their theft if you don't step in. It's easy to lose yourself if you venture off the beaten path, but even though time is of the essence (indicated by the gradually decreasing progress bar at the top of your HUD), if you take an efficient route, it's possible to do a bit of log hunting and still have time to foil the Coyotes' plans for piracy. Be aware that there is a penalty based on how much of Carla's data is leaked; the longer you spend destroying all five drones, the higher your penalty will be.

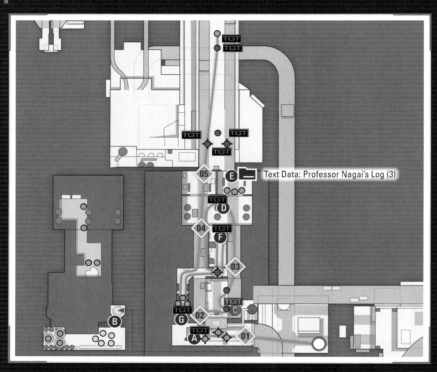

Text Data: Professor Nagai's Log (3)

AC ASSEMBLY

Your assembly for this mission should focus on anti-explosive and especially anti-energy defenses to help protect you against the GHOSTs' aggressive use of energy whips. Dual SG-027 ZIMMERMAN shotguns perform exceptionally well in the facility's cramped corridors, since most encounters are restricted to close ranges. Even when you're placed outside for the final battle against Iguazu and the GHOST squad, shotguns provide a reasonable response to their aggression by staggering them as quickly as possible before their offense gets into a rhythm. Dual diffuse laser cannons are recommended for use during direct hit windows, and are exceptionally powerful if charged beforehand.

01	R-ARM UNIT | SHOTGUN SG-027 ZIMMERMAN	P.54	
02	L-ARM UNIT | SHOTGUN SG-027 ZIMMERMAN	P.54	
03	R-BACK UNIT | DIFFUSE LASER CANNON VP-60LCD	P.67	
04	L-BACK UNIT | DIFFUSE LASER CANNON VP-60LCD	P.67	
05	HEAD | — VE-44A	P.78	
06	CORE | — 07-061 MIND ALPHA	P.81	
07	ARMS | — IA-C01A: EPHEMERA	P.83	
08	LEGS | TETRAPOD VP-424	P.86	
09	BOOSTER | — BST-G2/P06SPD	P.88	
10	FCS | — IB-C03F: WLT 001	P.90	
11	GENERATOR | — VE-20C	P.92	

MISSION OBJECTIVES

Destroy All Hacking Drones

Intercept Reinforcements

Defeat G5 Iguazu/Craft of Unknown Affiliation

MISSION INFO

Combat Zone	Western Belius—Grid 086
Client	"Cinder" Carla
Reward	380,000
Max Bonus Pay	—
Completion Unlocks	—
Combat Logs	Silver x1, Bronze x3
Data Logs	1
Part Containers	—

ENEMY DATA

	No.	AP	AS	Analysis
■ Hacking Drone	5	700	—	—
● CD-J-098 Quad Drone (Laser Cannon)	3	302	310	P.312
● CD-E-086 Aerial Defense Drone (Self-Destructing)	5	40	—	P.308
● MB-0100 CLUTCH RaD Crawler MT (Electro Saw)	12	650	364	P.319
● MB-0100 CLUTCH RaD Crawler MT (Enclosure Shield)	1	650	364	P.319
● MB-0202 TOYBOX MT	2	1848	1053	P.325
◇ MT-J-048 Tetrapod MT (Laser Blade)	1	13370	2200	P.322
● IA-27: GHOST (Sniper Type)	2	3820	1066	P.343
● IA-27: GHOST (Pulse Armor)	2	4775	1066	P.343
● AC HEAD BRINGER / G5 Iguazu	1	9690	1584	—

01 ◈ It can be difficult to keep track of where you've been once you start wandering around, so keep an eye out for clues the area leaves for you. It's just as easy to get back on the right path if you remember that your next target is always positioned close to your current one, and there will usually be a door you'll need to access. Make generous use of your scanner during the mission to pinpoint both enemies and hacking drones to make navigation even easier.

The first hacking drone is found directly ahead and below the point where you enter the facility. Clear the room of laser cannon quad drones before dipping down to the floor below, and then look for your first target. You'll find it partially obscured by a fuel container at **Position A**. After you destroy the drone, open the door on the opposite side of the room to proceed.

TRIPLE LOG

If you're confident in your offensive capabilities, you can save yourself some back-tracking by accessing a hidden area now, in order to obtain three combat logs. There's an inactive side of the forge above the room with the first hacking drone, and you can enter and follow the tunnel along and drop down at the end to reach the room at **Position B**. There's a large number of self-destructing drones and a trio of crawler MTs—including a heavier, shielded variant—awaiting you in the room. Enter carefully and try to use the walls to block the drones, so they don't hit you. Two of the crawler MTs can be quickly dispatched with your shotguns, but the shielded variant will require a couple of shots. You can still complete this side area and have plenty of time to destroy all of the hacking drones afterward, but you can also return here once all of the drones have been dealt with if you think time will be tight.

The opening of the inactive forge pipe can be hard to spot, but the tetrapod legs' hover capabilities will make finding and entering it much easier.

02 ◈ Like the previous target, the second hacking drone is found on the floor below the one you entered on. Drop down and head to the right-hand side of the room to find the target hidden behind a set of containers at **Position C**, but be ready to counter a pair of TOYBOX MTs that reveal themselves for a surprise attack. This encounter is optional; they won't follow you if you destroy the target quickly and move on. Once you've eliminated or evaded the threat, head back up to the floor above and proceed through the next door. ▶ A

03 ◈ The hallway revealed leads to the next hacking drone, which is nestled up against the back wall of the room ahead, at **Position D**. On your way there, a nearby door will open up and a group of crawler MTs will attack you. If you enter the room, another batch will plunge from the ceiling in an attempt to get the drop on you. A single shotgun blast is all that's needed to destroy each of them, so clear the area quickly before destroying the hacking drone. ▶ B

03 ◈ Head down this corridor now, but stick to the left-hand side of it, because a tetrapod MT will move across the area at the opposite end. If you use the fuel tank for cover, you can zip out at the last second to catch it unaware. An opening barrage from all of your weapons will instantly stagger your foe, and then a second round will finish it off, netting you an easy combat log. Now that the area is clear, head around the corner to the left to reach another room, at the back of which you'll find the next drone at **Position F**. Two more crawler MTs will drop down through a hole in the ceiling when you attempt to leave, so be ready to take them out on your way to the next target at **Position G**. Another squad of crawler MTs awaits you in front of that drone; dispatch them, and then destroy the drone to put an end to the time-sensitive portion of the mission.

Intercept Reinforcements /
Defeat G5 Iguazu/Craft of Unknown Affiliation

05 ◈ The reinforcements arrive on the opposite side of the area, so make your way to this point and access the door to face them. You'll be met by Iguazu piloting AC HEAD BRINGER, with an assembly identical to the one found in the mission "Attack the Dam Complex (Alt)." Iguazu begins the fight alone, but you won't have long before a squad of four GHOSTs drops in to crash the party. Ideally, you'll wear Iguazu down a little before the GHOSTs show up, and that means playing aggressively to get through his shield. Remember to start charging your diffuse laser cannons before the direct hit window opens up, and hit him with everything you've got when you get the chance. Regardless of the outcome, once the GHOSTs show up, Iguazu will turn his attention to them for the most part. ▶ C

The squad of GHOSTs—identical to those you met in the mission "Investigate BAWS Arsenal No. 2"—is made up of two sniper GHOSTs and two pulse armor GHOSTs. If possible, target the sniper GHOSTs first, since they're quicker to defeat due to their lack of pulse shielding. Use the same strategy of building up ACS strain with your shotguns, charging your diffuse laser cannons in anticipation of the direct hit window, and then letting rip when it's time—this will destroy the standard GHOSTs almost immediately.

The pulse armor GHOSTs put up more of a fight with their pulse shielding, but go down just as easily once they're finally staggered. Remember to keep moving as you engage all four GHOSTs; their energy whips and sniper shots all deal incredible damage, and you don't have a lot of environmental protection, outside of a couple of containers that make you vulnerable to sniper blasts if occupied for too long. If Iguazu is still around when the final GHOST goes down, he'll turn his attention back to you, picking up where things left off. Otherwise, the mission ends when the field is cleared of all opponents.

It's not essential to destroy these TOYBOX MTs, but doing so makes things simpler.

If you're log hunting, check the room the crawler MTs emerged from to find a wreck holding the data log "Text Data: Professor Nagai's Log (3)" in the back, at **Position E**.

Iguazu's shield is the main thing preventing a swift victory, but even it can't withstand sustained offense from your shotguns for long.

PREVENT CORPORATE SALVAGE OF NEW TECH

"System verdict... 'Continue.' Gladly...! I'll teach you to defy the law, interloper!"

—PCA 2nd Lieutenant

You're approached by Middle Flatwell—de facto leader of the RLF—with a request to attack the Arquebus survey camp near Hjalmar Mine. You'll need to defeat two LCs and one new-model HC deployed by the PCA, before they're captured by the corporations to be used for their own gain. Set in the Central Ice Field, a mountainous valley path ends at a fork in the road, leading into two separate encounters. Unlike most missions, standard enemy units here can prove to be threats when mingled in with the mission's primary foes.

The area features a number of alternating platform heights as well as cliffs, buildings and other man-made structures to act as cover for both yourself and your enemies. You have the choice of which encounter to tackle first, but the location you start will likely be where the mission ends, as any units still unengaged will head for you as soon as you've made your decision.

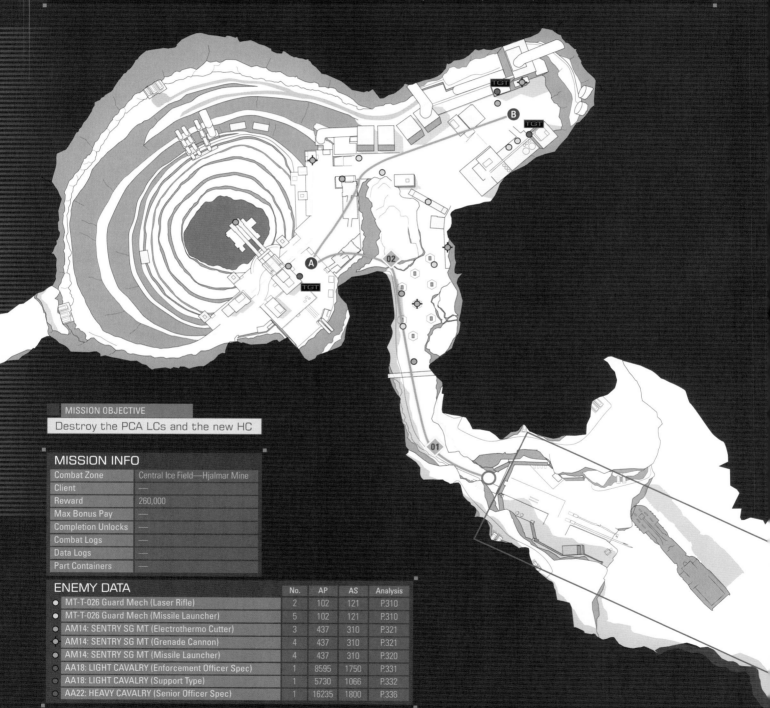

MISSION OBJECTIVE

Destroy the PCA LCs and the new HC

MISSION INFO

Combat Zone	Central Ice Field—Hjalmar Mine
Client	—
Reward	260,000
Max Bonus Pay	—
Completion Unlocks	—
Combat Logs	—
Data Logs	—
Part Containers	—

ENEMY DATA

	No.	AP	AS	Analysis
MT-T-026 Guard Mech (Laser Rifle)	2	102	121	P.310
MT-T-026 Guard Mech (Missile Launcher)	5	102	121	P.310
AM14: SENTRY SG MT (Electrothermo Cutter)	3	437	310	P.321
AM14: SENTRY SG MT (Grenade Cannon)	4	437	310	P.321
AM14: SENTRY SG MT (Missile Launcher)	4	437	310	P.320
AA18: LIGHT CAVALRY (Enforcement Officer Spec)	1	8595	1750	P.331
AA18: LIGHT CAVALRY (Support Type)	1	5730	1066	P.332
AA22: HEAVY CAVALRY (Senior Officer Spec)	1	16235	1800	P.336

Upon reaching the end of the windmills, you can choose which of the upcoming enemies you'll face first. This choice will dictate the how the following encounters play out.

AC ASSEMBLY

Weapon choice for this mission should revolve around building ACS strain as quickly as possible. While there is benefit to long-range and multi-lock weaponry to clear out drones and mechs, such options may drag out your battles with the mission's primary opponents. Both the HC and the two LCs have kinetic as their weakest defensive spec, so dual gatling guns and MORLEY spread bazookas will prove efficient in these fights.

You'll be up against a combination of energy and explosive weaponry. Stray explosive rounds from standard mechs—both en route to the target and during combat—have to be considered to conserve precious AP for the battle ahead. Your biggest threat will be the HC's energy-based melee and ranged damage.

01	R-ARM UNIT | GATLING GUN DF-GA-08 HU-BEN	P.53
02	L-ARM UNIT | GATLING GUN DF-GA-08 HU-BEN	P.53
03	R-BACK UNIT | SPREAD BAZOOKA SB-033M MORLEY	P.66
04	L-BACK UNIT | SPREAD BAZOOKA SB-033M MORLEY	P.66
05	HEAD | — IA-C01H: EPHEMERA	P.79
06	CORE | — 07-061 MIND ALPHA	P.81
07	ARMS | — NACHTREIHER/46E	P.83
08	LEGS | BIPEDAL DF-LG-08 TIAN-QIANG	P.85
09	BOOSTER | — BST-G2/P06SPD	P.88
10	FCS | — IB-C03F: WLT 001	P.90
11	GENERATOR | — VE-20C	P.92

01 ◈ The mission begins at the end of the valley corridor that you traveled along toward the end of "Steal the Survey Data." The windfarm area is now defended by PCA Subject Guard MTs that are a significant step up from the BAWS bipedal models you previously encountered here, but the narrow ledge along the left side of the cliff edge still provides a fairly safe path to follow. Your gatling guns will make short work of them if need be, but you should try to conserve as much ammo as possible for the upcoming encounter against some of the more dangerous PCA units. ▶ A

02 ◈ Your choice of battlefield should take a number of factors into consideration: the pace at which you can defeat your chosen targets, the environment's room for movement and cover, and the accompanying enemies in the area. If you keep encounters brief, there is no wrong choice. You may find it easier to go for the HC at **Position A** first, as the strategic clifftop location leading to the encounter allows you room to pick off Subject Guard MTs from a distance, before engaging the HC itself. The area with the two LCs at **Position B** offers more cover, but with more powerful enemies and a higher likelihood of being caught in pincer formation by the LCs.

Regardless of your choice, once you engage in combat with either side, remaining units will quickly be on their way. With little time to neutralize your chosen threat, your best move is to stagger your target as early as possible. Firing your gatling guns during an Assault Boost will quickly open the direct hit window, with the MORLEYs inflicting massive damage afterwards. The direct hit windows of all three enemies are lengthy, so depleting their low AP values is not particularly difficult if you maintain offensive pressure. The mission ends after all three targets are defeated.

AA22

HEAVY CAVALRY / PCA 2ND LIEUTENANT

BASIC SPECS

AP	16235
Attitude Stability	1800
Anti-Kinetic Defense	1060
Anti-Energy Defense	1413
Anti-Explosive Defense	1305
Elec. Discharge Tolerance	500
Shock Resistance	15%
ACS Anomaly Tolerance	500
Heat Resistance	10%
Repair Kits	—

▇ OBJECTIVE

Destroy the PCA LCs and the new HC

The cutting-edge HC you encounter at Position A specializes in close-range combat and is identical to the one you've faced off against at the end of "Attack the Old Spaceport." If you choose to approach this HC as your first target, it will be undergoing maintenance in a hangar bay, which you can use to your advantage by landing a powerful opening bazooka salvo to overload its ACS before it becomes operational.

HEAVY CAVALRY / PCA 2ND LIEUTENANT ATTACKS

PULSE SHIELD

DESCRIPTION Pulse shield that it can charge at you with.

EVASION Quick Boost to either side of the charge.

PULSE SALVO

DESCRIPTION Large salvo of pulse orbs that are fired in a wide cone. Used at close range.

EVASION Can either be jumped over, or create enough distance to render the effects of the orbs negligible.

TWIN PULSE BURSTS INTO CHARGING DOWNWARD SLASH ▼

DESCRIPTION Large bursts of pulse energy that will sometimes be followed by a downward slash from midair.

EVASION Create distance and boost into the air.

LARGE HORIZONTAL SWEEP

DESCRIPTION The HC will charge its pulse blade above its head briefly and come in with a far-reaching and almost 360-degree horizontal sweep.

EVASION Quick Boost immediately away when you see it charging its pulse blade.

HEAVY DOWNWARD SLASH

DESCRIPTION HC will jump in the air for a brief period and charge its pulse blade, after which it will Quick Boost at you and swing the blade in a downward, diagonal swing.

EVASION Quick Boost underneath the HC if you're close, or away out of range.

HEAVY UPPERCUT

DESCRIPTION Follow-up to the heavy downward slash depending on your proximity.

EVASION Quick Boost directly past the HC or away from it depending on your distance.

FAST DOWNWARD SLASH

DESCRIPTION Lower-impact but faster version of the heavy downward slash used at medium range.

EVASION Quick Boost away.

AA18

LIGHT CAVALRY / PCA CHIEF SERGEANT 1ST & 2ND CLS

BASIC SPECS

	1ST CLS	2ND CLS
AP	8595	5730
Attitude Stability	1750	1066
Anti-Kinetic Defense	930	859
Anti-Energy Defense	1375	1260
Anti-Explosive Defense	1135	1135
Elec. Discharge Tolerance	500	500
Shock Resistance	0%	0%
ACS Anomaly Tolerance	500	500
Heat Resistance	0%	0%

PCA CHIEF SERGEANT 1ST CLS ATTACKS

KINETIC SHIELD

DESCRIPTION The LC is equipped with a kinetic shield on its left arm. This shield will effectively increase the craft's attitude stability, but its ACS will still be strained while it is active.

EVASION Not used offensively.

SHOULDER MISSILES

DESCRIPTION The LC can fire four head-on explosive missiles from its shoulder. These missiles have a slow break meaning they will not home in aggressively on your AC.

EVASION Strafe or Quick Boost to the side as the missiles approach you.

KINETIC RIFLE

DESCRIPTION Rifle with extended effective range which the LC is capable of firing while behind its shield.

EVASION Use cover to block the shots or Quick Boost away from them.

UNDER-BARREL GRENADE LAUNCHER ▼

DESCRIPTION The LC is equipped with a grenade attachment to its kinetic rifle. The grenade it fires will fly through the air with a slight arc.

EVASION Boost into the air to avoid the explosion of the grenade and use Quick Boosts to either side.

PCA CHIEF SERGEANT 2ND CLS ATTACKS

SCATTER BAZOOKA

DESCRIPTION Bazooka blast that quickly spilts into a hexagonal spread.

EVASION Stay at medium range and strafe. At close range you'll need to use a predictive Quick Boost.

VERTICAL MISSILE LAUNCHER

DESCRIPTION Fires its back-mounted vertical missile launcher. Missiles have a high arc and impact after 2-3 seconds.

EVASION Watch for the vertical fire, keep moving and Quick Boost 2 seconds later.

DEFEND THE DAM COMPLEX

"This isn't right... You're just a Gen Four!
You belong in a museum, not an AC!"

—Chartreuse

The Gallia Dam Complex is under siege by two PCA mercenaries. The RLF won't hold for long, which is where you come in. Your battle at the dam against two foes ultimately becomes three, as an unexpected visitor arrives. The area you fight in is a series of alternating-height frozen beds of water, with dam walls and buildings offering cover for both sides of the conflict.

AC ASSEMBLY

Your weaponry will focus on high-impact, high-damage output, ideal for removing individual ACs from the battlefield as efficiently as possible, to avoid being tag teamed by multiple adept mercenaries. Dual spread bazookas and a laser lance provide uncompromising damage against staggered foes, with a laser shotgun entering the mix to further exploit energy weaknesses. Defensively, an assembly of frame parts from Arquebus, ALLMIND, and Rubicon Research Institute provide the necessary anti-explosive and anti-energy defenses for the attack types used against you. Tetrapod legs are here for their aerial maneuverability and altitude capabilities, as well as their attitude stability.

01	R-ARM UNIT | LASER SHOTGUN **WUERGER/66E**	P.59	
02	L-ARM UNIT | LASER LANCE **VE-67LLA**	P.64	
03	R-BACK UNIT | SPREAD BAZOOKA **SB-033M MORLEY**	P.66	
04	L-BACK UNIT | SPREAD BAZOOKA **SB-033M MORLEY**	P.66	
05	HEAD | — **HC-3000 WRECKER**	P.79	
06	CORE | — **07-061 MIND ALPHA**	P.81	
07	ARMS | — **AA-J-123 BASHO**	P.82	
08	LEGS | TANK **EL-TL-11 FORTALEZA**	P.87	
09	BOOSTER | —	—	
10	FCS | — **IA-C01F: OCELLUS**	P.90	
11	GENERATOR | — **VE-20C**	P.92	

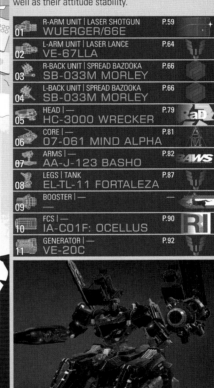

MISSION OBJECTIVES

Defeat the Independent Mercenaries King/Chartreuse

Defeat Raven and the Other Independent Mercenaries

MISSION INFO

Combat Zone	Southern Belius—Gallia Dam Complex
Client	Rubicon Liberation Front
Reward	450,000
Max Bonus Pay	—
Completion Unlocks	—
Combat Logs	Platinum x2
Data Logs	—
Part Containers	—

ENEMY DATA

	No.	AP	AS	Analysis
◎ AC UMBER OX / Chartreuse	1	15270	1748	—
◎ AC ASTER CROWN / King	1	12010	2321	—
• AC NIGHTFALL / Raven	1	9190	1604	—

01 ◈ The mission begins at an overlook ahead of the dam complex, where battle is already underway between a squad of friendly MTs and your two targets: King and Chartreuse. Boost over to the cliff at **Position A** and decide which mercenary to engage first. Starting with either is viable, but King is the defensively weaker of the two, making him the recommended initial target. Closing in on either mercenary will alert both to your presence, and draw them to you. Friendly MTs on the field will continue to divert the attention of your opponents periodically, giving you a chance to get in a few easy hits. You should aim to defeat your chosen target quickly, as full attention will be on you once your ally MTs fall. Be aware that the third AC will eventually enter combat, regardless of whether or not King and Chartreuse are still in the battle. The AC's approach distance of over 2000 meters does give you extra time to wrap up your initial conflict, however. ▶ A

The choice of initial encounter is yours between King on the left, and Chartreuse on the right.

KING

AC // ASTER CROWN

King—piloting the medium-weight tetrapod AC ASTER CROWN—is defensively the most fragile of the initial opponents, making him the recommended first target. ASTER CROWN will attempt to rush you down with a combination of kinetic and energy attacks, which you'll find are easy to Quick Boost away from. Your strategy should be to pull in close, to more easily build ACS strain and prevent King from deploying his pulse shield.

BASIC SPECS

AP	10410
Attitude Stability	2321
Anti-Kinetic Defense	1182
Anti-Energy Defense	1091
Anti-Explosive Defense	1132
Elec. Discharge Tolerance	490
Shock Resistance	28%
ACS Anomaly Tolerance	490
Heat Resistance	28%
Repair Kits	1

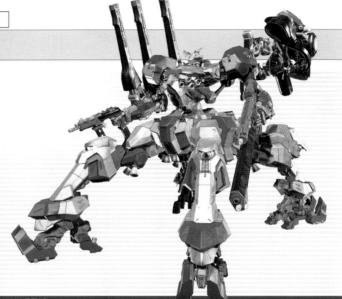

AC ASTER CROWN ATTACKS

MA-E-211 SAMPU

DESCRIPTION Burst handgun with limited range, which is used to strain your ACS.

EVASION Shots can be out-distanced or Quick Boosted away from.

VE-60LCA ▼

DESCRIPTION Triple-barrel laser cannon which can be charged to produce a shot capable of instantly destroying your AC.

EVASION The shot covers a relatively wide area. It is advisable to strafe in one direction as it is alerted, and Quick Boost to the opposite direction the moment it fires.

LR-037 HARRIS

DESCRIPTION Linear rifle shot, which is often used along with SAMPU fire to quickly strain your ACS.

EVASION Shots can be out-distanced, but it is advisable to attempt a Quick Boost in order to avoid them.

VE-61PSA

DESCRIPTION This pulse scutum has extremely high damage mitigation and impact dampening. The tradeoff is that the scutum has a weak Initial Guard.

EVASION Not used offensively.

CHARTREUSE

AC // UMBER OX

Chartreuse pilots the defensively tankier AC UMBER OX, capable of being effective at longer ranges than ASTER CROWN. Her strategy against you is to either attack from distance or hover over you in order to line up a barrage of explosive munitions. Meeting her altitude with the recommended tetrapod's hover mode diminishes her advantage over you. When UMBER OX's AP is low enough, Chartreuse will deploy her pulse armor, mitigating damage from further attacks while simultaneously clearing her ACS strain. Her barrier will be broken after enough damage is dealt to it, however.

BASIC SPECS

AP	15270
Attitude Stability	1778
Anti-Kinetic Defense	1238
Anti-Energy Defense	1338
Anti-Explosive Defense	1220
Elec. Discharge Tolerance	490
Shock Resistance	17%
ACS Anomaly Tolerance	490
Heat Resistance	17%
Repair Kits	1

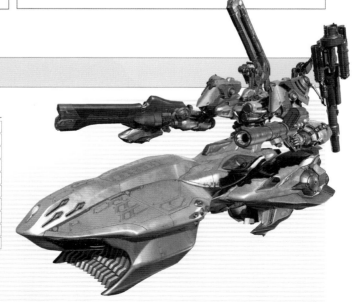

VE-66LRB

DESCRIPTION This laser rifle fires as a dual beam of energy and travels through the air quickly. Chartreuse will fire this weapon as a single shot, but can quickly follow up another attack with it.

EVASION Strafe or Quick Boost away from the shots.

MAJESTIC ▼

DESCRIPTION The MAJESTIC fires a high-impact explosive projectile and can be used at any range. The shot is fired toward the direction you are moving prior to its release.

EVASION Strafe to one side and then Quick Boost in the opposite direction as soon as the explosive is released.

EARSHOT ▼

DESCRIPTION The EARSHOT releases a single, quick moving grenade. The impact and damage output of this weapon is one of the highest of any of Chartreuse's munitions, along with her diffuse laser cannon at close range.

EVASION At mid or close-range it is advisable to avoid letting Chartreuse get above you. The best way to avoid the EARSHOT is to be in the air either above or at least at the same level as Chartreuse.

VP-60LCD ▼

DESCRIPTION Diffuse laser cannon that fires two vertical beams of energy that fan outward from the point of release.

EVASION At medium and long-range this attack becomes less effective, as the beams separate. At close-range it's best to Quick Boost to either side of Chartreuse to avoid the weapon's point of release.

PULSE ARMOR

DESCRIPTION This Core Expansion generates a shield which naturally depletes in energy over time, but any damage afflicted to it will further diminish it.

EVASION Not used offensively.

OBJECTIVE | Defeat Raven and the Other Independent Mercenaries

02 ◈ King and Chartreuse won't be the only AC pilots you encounter on this mission. Ayre will eventually alert you to the approach of a third pilot—none other than Raven. Raven enters combat immediately after the two mercenaries go down, or after enough time has passed. Be aware that you won't receive a checkpoint upon Raven's arrival. The mission ends when the field is clear of all three opponents. ▶ B

RAVEN

AC // NIGHTFALL

Raven—piloting AC NIGHTFALL—is similarly aggressive to King, but tends to stay slightly further away. Raven will use his assault rifle to advance your ACS strain meter, while occasionally leaping overhead to strike you from above with rounds from his grenade cannon. His bipedal build puts him at a disadvantage with keeping airborne, however. Defensively, Raven is the weakest of the three, meaning you can safely continue your match with King or Chartreuse, should they still be on the field at this point.

BASIC SPECS

AP	9190
Attitude Stability	1654
Anti-Kinetic Defense	1100
Anti-Energy Defense	1059
Anti-Explosive Defense	1101
Elec. Discharge Tolerance	490
Shock Resistance	20%
ACS Anomaly Tolerance	490
Heat Resistance	20%
Repair Kits	2

AC NIGHTFALL ATTACKS

BOOST KICK

DESCRIPTION Raven will Assault Boost toward you in an effort to kick your AC.

EVASION Quick Boost to either side of NIGHTFALL.

RF-025 SCUDDER

DESCRIPTION Assault rifle that Raven will use often throughout the fight.

EVASION Quick Boost in the opposite direction in which Raven is firing.

PB-033M ASHMEAD

DESCRIPTION Heavy-impact melee weapon with two stages of attack.

EVASION Quick Boost to either side of Raven when he comes in for the strike.

SONGBIRDS ▼

DESCRIPTION High-impact grenade cannon that fires two shots per attack.

EVASION Chain Quick Boosts to avoid both shots; Raven will not fire the second shot directly behind the first.

BML-G1/P32DUO-03

DESCRIPTION Fires three missiles to the left and three missiles to the right.

EVASION Quick Boost away as close to the moment of impact as possible.

ASSAULT ARMOR

DESCRIPTION NIGHTFALL charges energy and releases it as a large burst around itself.

EVASION Rapidly create distance from NIGHTFALL.

UNDERGROUND EXPLORATION – DEPTH 2 (ALT)

"Ah, it comes... The Inevitable..."
—Coldcall

Mission objectives for your repeat visit to Depth 2 are largely the same as they were the first time around. The difference in this version is that your encounter with G5 Iguazu is exchanged for a fight with the gun-for-hire Coldcall and his AC, DEADSLED. Coldcall is functionally similar to Iguazu, and will aggressively pursue you if you attempt to pull back. This essentially means that you can employ the strategy that got you through the fight with Iguazu.

Be aware that every enemy—with the exceptions of DEADSLED and the ENFORCER—award bonus pay. Most are found along the way, but a few can be discovered tucked away in optional areas. Feel free to go all out for the extra COAM, as there are multiple sherpas to get you through this extensive mission.

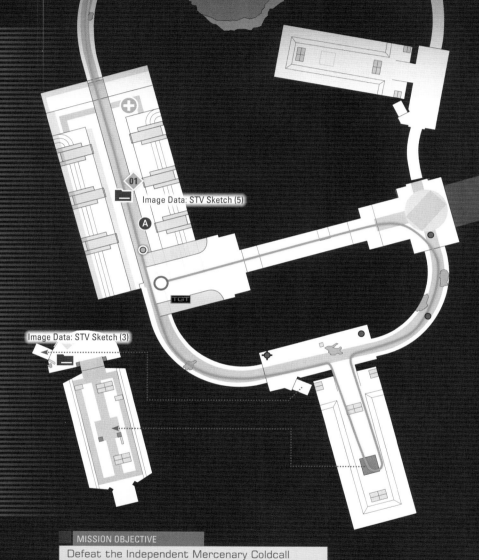

Image Data: STV Sketch (5)

01

A

TGT

Image Data: STV Sketch (3)

AC ASSEMBLY

Your Assembly for this alt mission is a behemoth with no compromise to energy damage output, perfect for dispatching DEADSLED and the ENFORCER. Unlike Iguazu, Coldcall employs some heavy-duty energy-based weaponry that you'll want to steel yourself against. The seemingly dangerous corridor you're locked into combat within provides convenient opportunity to pin Coldcall against walls to then spike his ACS strain gauge with dual shotguns. With missiles, laser cannons, and a laser lance capable of skewering unfortunate targets, you'll find yourself utterly dominating the opposition.

01	R-ARM UNIT | SHOTGUN SG-027 ZIMMERMAN	P.54	
02	L-ARM UNIT | LASER LANCE VE-67LLA	P.64	
03	R-BACK UNIT | LASER CANNON VE-60LCA	P.67	
04	L-BACK UNIT | PLASMA MISSILE LAUNCHER Vvc-706PM	P.73	
05	HEAD | — HS-5000 APPETIZER	P.79	
06	CORE | — 07-061 MIND ALPHA	P.81	
07	ARMS | — VP-46S	P.83	
08	LEGS | BIPEDAL 2S-5000 DESSERT	P.85	
09	BOOSTER | — BC-0600 12345	P.88	
10	FCS | — IA-C01F: OCELLUS	P.90	
11	GENERATOR | — VE-20C	P.92	

MISSION OBJECTIVE

Defeat the Independent Mercenary Coldcall

MISSION INFO

Combat Zone	Watchpoint Alpha—Depth 2
Client	Arquebus Corporation
Reward	320,000
Max Bonus Pay	—
Completion Unlocks	—
Combat Logs	Platinum x1
Data Logs	1
Part Containers	—

ENEMY DATA*

	No.	AP	AS	Bonus Pay	Analysis
◉ AC DEADSLED / Coldcall	1	10380	1513	—	

*For additional enemy data, see P.208

01 Before the fight with Coldcall, you have a chance to retrieve a data log directly in front of you at **Position A** as you enter the room. You aren't in danger of ambush as you approach the log, so feel free to grab it right away. Coldcall appears after you reach the end of the ramp, when Ayre remarks that you're alone.

COLDCALL

AC // DEADSLED

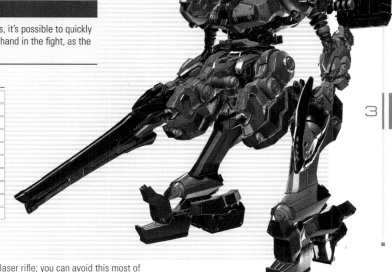

COLDCALL'S ENTRY

Coldcall appears from the tunnel you had just come from, and if you can anticipate this, it's possible to quickly double back and intercept him before he enters the room. This can give you the upper hand in the fight, as the cramped tunnel limits his evasiveness.

DEADSLED—piloted by Coldcall—is a highly aggressive and agile foe. Coldcall will respond to attempts to create distance by closing in, in order to be in effective range for his laser shotgun. DEADSLED's reverse-joint legs are the source of his mobility and ability to reposition himself without exhausting EN. Your best chance at opening the window of opportunity is to bait Coldcall into unintentionally pinning himself to the wall with his own evasive maneuvers. When this happens, be ready to unload with the full force of your weaponry.

BASIC SPECS

AP	10380
Attitude Stability	1613
Anti-Kinetic Defense	1190
Anti-Energy Defense	1103
Anti-Explosive Defense	1183
Elec. Discharge Tolerance	490
Shock Resistance	12%
ACS Anomaly Tolerance	490
Heat Resistance	12%
Repair Kits	2

From longer ranges, Coldcall will pressure you with a combination of missiles and his laser rifle; you can avoid this most of the time with Quick Boosts or taking cover underneath the ramp. At close range, Coldcall will either attempt to leap over you to fire his laser shotgun, or Assault Boost toward you for the added impact to his shot. He only breaks his movement voluntarily to release charge shots; if you can anticipate these shots, you have opportunity for a counterattack. After Coldcall goes down, you'll proceed through the mission normally until the end.

AC DEADSLED ATTACKS

BOOST KICK

DESCRIPTION Coldcall will Assault Boost toward you in an effort to kick your AC.

EVASION Quick Boost to either side of DEADSLED.

VE-66LRA ▼ CHARGED

DESCRIPTION Laser rifle shots will be used to suppress you the entire fight. These are not high-impact shots, but are fast moving and can steadily build up AP damage.

EVASION Place cover between yourself and Coldcall to evade the shots, or Quick Boost away from them.

WUERGER/66E ▼ CHARGED

DESCRIPTION Laser shotgun used often at mid and close range. Releases a cone of beams that fan out. If charged, the beams are compressed into a single shot.

EVASION At mid and long range this attack becomes less effective, as the beams separate. At close-range it is advisable to Quick Boost to either side of Coldcall to best avoid the weapon's point of release. The charged shot can be laterally evaded.

BML-G3/P04ACT-01

DESCRIPTION This launcher produces a single high-impact missile. The missile moves particularly slowly through the air, which can make it uniquely difficult to evade.

EVASION The missile can easily alter directions without impacting the ground, so it can be simpler to lead it into a wall or other cover object to evade the impact.

BML-G1/P20MLT-04

DESCRIPTION This launcher releases a single cell of four low-impact missiles. These are head-on missiles, so it is less likely that they will hit a wall or a ceiling than other firing patterns.

EVASION Either Quick Boost away from the missiles, or lead them into a wall or other cover object to avoid the impact.

UNKNOWN TERRITORY SURVEY (ALT)

"Rusty... That pilot's more than just a hound. You don't see the potential!"

—Middle Flatwell

This alternate version of "Unknown Territory Survey" is almost entirely the same as the original mission, with the exception of the fight with Rusty. What is usually a solo encounter becomes a battle against two, as Middle Flatwell enters the ring after Rusty has taken a bit of damage. When both pilots go down, the mission will conclude as it did before.

MISSION OBJECTIVES

Reach the Heart of the Unknown Territory

Defeat V.IV Rusty/Middle Flatwell

MISSION INFO

Combat Zone	Watchpoint Alpha—Unknown Territory
Client	Arquebus Corporation
Reward	260,000
Max Bonus Pay	100,000
Completion Unlocks	—
Combat Logs	Gold x1
Data Logs	1
Part Containers	—

ENEMY DATA*

	No.	AP	AS	Bonus Pay	Analysis
◎ AC TSUBASA / Middle Flatwell	1	8480	1545	—	—

*For additional enemy data, see P.224

AC ASSEMBLY

Your fight with Rusty will be the same as before, meaning a similar build to the original mission is still recommended. Though Flatwell packs explosives in his artillery, his kinetic pressure will be the greater threat overall. On that note, both Flatwell and Rusty are weakest to explosive damage, making the SONGBIRDS a reliable option for exploiting their fragile attitude stabilities, and dealing large chunks of damage with your direct hits.

01	R-ARM UNIT | SHOTGUN	P.54	
	SG-027 ZIMMERMAN		
02	L-ARM UNIT | SHOTGUN	P.54	
	SG-027 ZIMMERMAN		
03	R-BACK UNIT | GRENADE CANNON	P.66	MELINITE
	SONGBIRDS		
04	L-BACK UNIT | GRENADE CANNON	P.66	MELINITE
	SONGBIRDS		
05	HEAD | —	P.78	
	VE-44A		
06	CORE | —	P.81	
	07-061 MIND ALPHA		
07	ARMS | —	P.84	
	IA-C01A: EPHEMERA		
08	LEGS | TETRAPOD	P.86	
	VP-424		
09	BOOSTER | —	P.88	
	BST-G2/P06SPD		
10	FCS | —	P.90	
	IB-C03F: WLT 001		
11	GENERATOR | —	P.92	
	VE-20C		

IA-C01H: EPHEMERA

Comms Record: Message for Uncle

A

01

TGT

02

B

OBJECTIVE	Reach the Heart of the Unknown Territory

01 ◈ As you descend into the inert Coral to make your way through the mission, you'll find one new item stashed in the area: a data log. When you land, check the wreckage to the right of the doorway at **Position A** to obtain "Comms Record: Message for Uncle." Other than this, the path is unchanged, so continue forward to **Position B** for the fight with Rusty.

OBJECTIVE	Defeat V.IV Rusty/Middle Flatwell

02 ◈ After dealing enough damage to Rusty, Middle Flatwell will join the fray. You'll be taking both of them on simultaneously, to Flatwell's displeasure. You can defeat these ACs in any order, and the mission won't prove much more difficult, despite the appearance of Flatwell. Unlike your first adventure through the Unknown Territory, the cavern descent following the match won't occur, and the mission ends immediately after defeating both pilots. ▶ A

MIDDLE FLATWELL

AC // TSUBASA

On top of being similarly agile as Rusty, Flatwell prefers to keep moderate distance to pressure you with TSUBASA's kinetic weaponry. Unfortunately, you won't find much in the way of cover within this limited arena, with environmental features serving more as obstacles to get you stuck should you hang too close to the edges while maneuvering. Fortunately, those same obstacles can be used to set Flatwell up for an appointment with shotgun and grenade cannon rounds in the event that evasion action doesn't go his way.

BASIC SPECS

AP	8480
Attitude Stability	1545
Anti-Kinetic Defense	1078
Anti-Energy Defense	998
Anti-Explosive Defense	986
Elec. Discharge Tolerance	490
Shock Resistance	-1%
ACS Anomaly Tolerance	490
Heat Resistance	-1%
Repair Kits	—

TSUBASA enters the match at half AP and has no repair kits, making him your logical first target if Rusty has restored himself. Flatwell occasionally takes to the air, which is easily countered by meeting his altitude with your AC's tetrapod legs. When Flatwell is back on the ground, take the opportunity to leverage the blast radius of your SONGBIRDS and Flatwell's frail defenses to put him into ACS overload immediately.

AC TSUBASA ATTACKS

MA-J 200 RANSETSU-RF ▼

DESCRIPTION Kinetic burst rifle that briefly charges and releases a triple-round burst.

EVASION Chain Quick Boosts away from Flatwell.

BML-G1/P20MLT-04

DESCRIPTION This missile launcher releases a stream of four low-impact missiles.

EVASION Quick Boost away from the missiles as close to their point of impact as possible.

PULSE PROTECTION

DESCRIPTION Fixed-location shield that Flatwell places after damage is applied to him.

EVASION Not used offensively.

MA-E-210 ETSUJIN

DESCRIPTION The ETSUJIN fires a rapid string of kinetic rounds. The weapon has a limited effective range, but its near-continuous fire can work to apply a steady strain on your ACS.

EVASION Out-distance the effective range of the weapon or Quick Boost to either side of TSUBASA.

LITTLE GEM ▼

DESCRIPTION Bazooka that shoots a high-impact explosive. Due to the slow projectile speed it can be awkward to evade in conjunction with TSUBASA's other faster-moving munitions.

EVASION By itself you can jump over the projectile or Quick Boost from it.

ESCORT THE WEAPONIZED MINING SHIP

"Wh- What is that thing?!"
—RLF Mining Ship Crew

The RLF has mobilized STRIDER, their weaponized mining ship and key military asset, amid conflicting requests sent your way to either destroy or escort the Coral extraction craft. Shortly after accepting the RLF's offer to protect the carrier, responsibility for the objective is plucked directly from your hands as a sharp turn of events leads to your deployment becoming a mission of self-preservation instead. Three waves of enemy units comprised of HELIANTHUS and WEEVILs descend upon you, showing little mercy as they attempt to overwhelm you with sheer numbers.

The area ahead of the STRIDER is expansive, and its natural terrain unfortunately offers little opportunity for cover. It's recommended to let the distance be your advantage, as waves arrive in staggered numbers that you can more easily pick apart one by one. Your bonus pay of 340,000 COAM will be canceled out by a penalty of the same amount for failing to protect the STRIDER; your only earnings will be what you earn for completion of the mission itself.

AC ASSEMBLY

You'll be up against a combination of kinetic and explosive damage in the waves ahead. Your parts should prioritize anti-explosive defense, with anti-kinetic defense being secondary. Given the extreme threat introduced by your foes' explosive pressure, speed and mobility are the focus, but not at the expense of of additional attitude stability.

It's best to tackle this mission with a build that offers extreme mobility. This not only helps avoid the HELIANTHUS, but allows you to better exchange fire with the WEEVIL drones as well. EL-TL-11 FORTALEZA tank legs accomplish this task, while the rest of your AC parts also have decent anti-explosive defense and a respectable amount of attitude stability.

A full loadout of explosive weaponry can manage the long distances that the majority of your shots require against these aggressively mobile units. Both HML-G2/P19MLT-04 hand missile launchers are able to pursue moving targets after achieving homing lock, while the twin BML-G2/P05MLT-10 mounted on your shoulders can help finish off the enemy you were targeting.

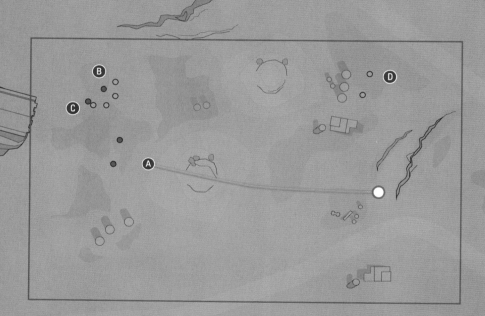

01	R-ARM UNIT | MISSILE LAUNCHER HML-G2/P19MLT-04	P.62	
02	L-ARM UNIT | MISSILE LAUNCHER HML-G2/P19MLT-04	P.62	
03	R-BACK UNIT | MISSILE LAUNCHER BML-G2/P05MLT-10	P.69	
04	L-BACK UNIT | MISSILE LAUNCHER BML-G2/P05MLT-10	P.69	
05	HEAD | — DF-HD-08 TIAN-QIANG	P.77	
06	CORE | — CS-5000 MAIN DISH	P.81	
07	ARMS | — DF-AR-09 TIAN-QIANG	P.82	
08	LEGS | TANK EL-TL-11 FORTALEZA	P.87	
09	BOOSTER | — —	—	
10	FCS | — FCS-G2/P10SLT	P.90	
11	GENERATOR | — VE-20B	P.92	

MISSION OBJECTIVES

Head Out to Rescue Weaponized Mining Ship STRIDER

Annihilate Enemy Craft of Unknown Affiliation

MISSION INFO

Combat Zone	Western Belius—Bona Dea Dunes
Client	Rubicon Liberation Front
Reward	500,000
Max Bonus Pay	—
Completion Unlocks	—
Combat Logs	—
Data Logs	—
Part Containers	—

ENEMY DATA

	No.	AP	AS	Bonus Pay	Analysis
IA-05: WEEVIL (Grenade Cannon)	4	9550	1600	—	P.345
IE-09: HELIANTHUS	6	2800	1053	—	P.344

Head Out to Rescue Weaponized Mining Ship STRIDER / Annihilate Enemy Craft of Unknown Affiliation

Head to **Position A** but avoid getting too close to the edge of the combat zone. You'll want as much of an open area as you can get for this fight, and it's best to avoid the impact crater as it can make this fight more difficult. Anything on the field that makes the plain uneven can become a hindrance for your weaponry, as your missiles can instead hit objects that are near the enemies that you're firing at. This location also allows you to view all of the enemies that get deployed in this area, which will provide you an opportunity to eliminate them quickly. The strategy through this mission is to initiate Target Assist on an enemy, then circle around it while firing your weaponry. The tank legs make navigating around the enemies and any necessary evasive maneuvers much easier to perform. ▶ A

IA-05: WEEVIL (GRENADE CANNON) ATTACKS

LEAPING KICK

DESCRIPTION At close range, the WEEVIL can briefly jump into the air and launch itself at you while kicking. This kick propels the WEEVIL rapidly and will land it behind you.

EVASION Quick Boost to either side or jump above the enemy.

KINETIC TURRET

DESCRIPTION The WEEVIL will fire its kinetic turret to assist it in covering large distances. The weapon will fire in bursts of two shots and can be fired multiple times repeatedly.

EVASION The shots can be out-spaced to where they ricochet on impact, otherwise it is advisable to Quick Boost to evade them.

Wave 1   WEEVIL (Grenade Cannon) x2

Two WEEVIL C-Weapons approach you from over 1,000 meters away after destroying the STRIDER, closing the gap quickly toward **Position A** after Walter alerts you to their presence. Wave 1 is not timed, so you can take your time fighting the two WEEVILs. Pick off both of them one at a time using your HML-G2/P19MLT-04 to strain their ACS, and following up with the BML-G2/P05MLT-10 to finish them off. Because these enemies are even more mobile than you are, they may have a bit of AP remaining. If you're close enough to them, a Boost Kick should finish them off. ▶ B-C

Wave 2   HELIANTHUS x4

The second wave brings a group of four HELIANTHUS in direct approach from the edge of the area near **Position B**, and can be swiftly destroyed with the MLT-04. They'll primarily attempt to ram into you at ground level with their multi-hit spinning attack, so take to the air before any of them can reach you. Depending on the distance, you may still be within range of their flamethrower attacks, which can leave you susceptible to ACS anomaly if you aren't careful. Fortunately, HELIANTHUS are defensively fragile and go down in a couple of missile volleys, but if they're still alive from the hand missile launchers, the BML-G2/P05MLT-10 will certainly finish them off. Take care to clean up this wave as quickly as possible, because you only have around 45 seconds from the time Walter alerts you to the beginning of Wave 2 before Wave 3 begins.

Wave 3   WEEVIL (Grenade Cannon) x2
HELIANTHUS x2

The third and final wave is a combination of the two enemy types you encountered before, with no notable differences. The four of them enter from **Position C** and **D**, allowing you extra time to complete Wave 2, in case you're still engaged at this point. Given their speed, it's likely the two HELIANTHUS will reach you first, and you should prioritize them due to their frail defenses. Unlike the previous wave, the wave concluding the mission is not timed, meaning no additional enemies enter the field if the encounter drags on. Once you've defeated all standing enemies, the mission ends.

A

The barren terrain may lack any real form of cover, but the open space lets you take full advantage of the tank leg's excellent mobility.

MISSILE VOLLEY

DESCRIPTION The WEEVIL can release a high-volume, low-impact missile salvo; fans slightly to the left and right. Missiles have limited homing capabilities.

EVASION Pick one side and Quick Boost once or twice to that side depending on proximity from enemy.

GRENADE CANNON ▼

DESCRIPTION The grenade will fly in a long arc when fired. While the weapon does have range, it will become less effective over distances. The munition is high-impact and can easily overload your ACS.

EVASION Jump into the air and Quick Boost away from the explosive, avoiding its direct impact and explosion.

B

C

Try to avoid fighting on uneven ground, like the crater impact. Enemies can easily circumvent your missiles, and you'll lose visibility if they leave the impact.

OBSTRUCT THE MANDATORY INSPECTION

"We'll meet again."
—Kate Markson

BAWS needs a few good mercenaries to interrupt the inspection in progress by the PCA squads deployed into their facility. Independent mercenary Kate Markson requests you to accompany her. You'll ambush a total of three vanguard squads along the way before you rendezvous with Kate to face off against a team of high-profile PCA enemies outside the facility. The area is made up largely of open space, save for the section in which you face the first squad. Variable-height platforms are available during combat, but you'll largely rely on grounded or aerial evasive maneuvers.

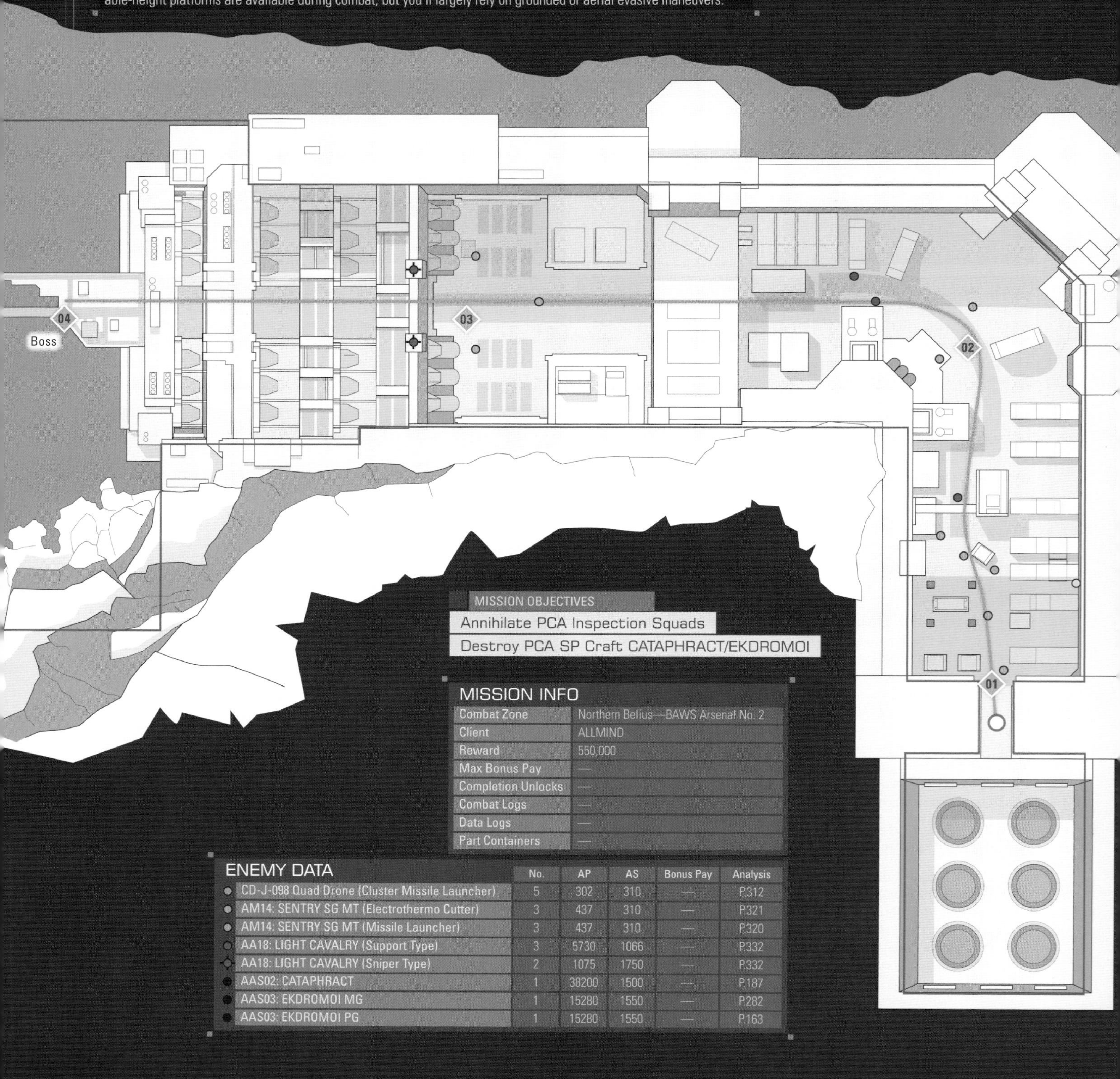

04
Boss

03

02

01

MISSION OBJECTIVES
Annihilate PCA Inspection Squads

Destroy PCA SP Craft CATAPHRACT/EKDROMOI

MISSION INFO

Combat Zone	Northern Belius—BAWS Arsenal No. 2
Client	ALLMIND
Reward	550,000
Max Bonus Pay	—
Completion Unlocks	—
Combat Logs	—
Data Logs	—
Part Containers	—

ENEMY DATA

	No.	AP	AS	Bonus Pay	Analysis
CD-J-098 Quad Drone (Cluster Missile Launcher)	5	302	310	—	P.312
AM14: SENTRY SG MT (Electrothermo Cutter)	3	437	310	—	P.321
AM14: SENTRY SG MT (Missile Launcher)	3	437	310	—	P.320
AA18: LIGHT CAVALRY (Support Type)	3	5730	1066	—	P.332
AA18: LIGHT CAVALRY (Sniper Type)	2	1075	1750	—	P.332
AAS02: CATAPHRACT	1	38200	1500	—	P.187
AAS03: EKDROMOI MG	1	15280	1550	—	P.282
AAS03: EKDROMOI PG	1	15280	1550	—	P.163

AC ASSEMBLY

The primary focus here is put on the five-party brawl at the end of the mission. The three PCA SP units both deal and take massive amounts of energy damage, so this build revolves around energy damage both offensively and defensively. The addition of a spread bazooka provides ample blast radius to catch the skittish EKDROMOI and allows you to follow up with even more energy damage.

01	R-ARM UNIT | LASER HANDGUN VP-66LH	P.59
02	L-ARM UNIT | LASER HANDGUN VP-66LH	P.59
03	R-BACK UNIT | SPREAD BAZOOKA SB-033M MORLEY	P.66
04	L-BACK UNIT | LASER CANNON VP-60LCS	P.67
05	HEAD | — IA-C01H: EPHEMERA	P.79
06	CORE | — 07-061 MIND ALPHA	P.81
07	ARMS | — IA-C01A: EPHEMERA	P.84
08	LEGS | BIPEDAL 2S-5000 DESSERT	P.85
09	BOOSTER | — BC-0600 12345	P.88
10	FCS | — IB-C03F: WLT 001	P.90
11	GENERATOR | — VE-20C	P.92

<table>
OBJECTIVE

Annihilate PCA Inspection Squads

01 You'll face a total of three PCA squads on your way out of the BAWS facility. Squads contain a variety of unit types, with LCs being the biggest threat. Your encounter with the first squad provides ample opportunity for cover, while the remaining battles are fought in more spacious settings.

The first squad is encountered immediately following your exit from the elevator, where you'll have the opportunity to approach an unaware Subject Guard MT from behind. This squad is made up of a few more Subject Guard MTs and lead by an LC. Your biggest threat here will be the rifle-wielding MT and the LC, so be ready to take cover when your warning indicator signals an incoming attack. Make use of your scanner to keep track of remaining enemy units during this encounter, as it's likely they'll be employing nearby cover. ▶ A

02 The second squad you encounter doubles the LC count, and these are accompanied by two Subject Guard MTs carrying laser guns. Laser shots will cause your AC the most AP damage, so make MTs your primary target and boost up to the one on top of the building before turning your attention to the other on the ground. By this point, the LCs will have closed in to engage you, so focus on whichever of the two is closest. Take care when meeting these LCs in close quarters, as you'll be within effective range of their spread bazookas.

03 The third and final squad is comprised of two sniper-type LCs, and three quad drones with cluster missile launchers. The LCs aren't immediately present, so take the opportunity to Assault Boost toward the two closest quad drones in order to begin thinning the numbers of the opposition. By the time you've engaged the third drone, the LCs will be active, but their shots won't be able to reach you from the downward angle, due to where you're positioned. Make your way upward with either of the two vertical catapults in the area and allow yourself to fall rather than boost; this will lead to the LCs missing their shots on you as you move to match their altitude. After clearing the area, proceed to meet with Kate in preparation for the final encounter.

OBJECTIVE

Destroy PCA SP Craft CATAPHRACT/EKDROMOI

04 Shortly after meeting up with Kate, you'll be alerted to the approach of three PCA units in the shallow waters outside the BAWS facility: two EKDROMOI units closely followed by the CATAPHRACT. Kate proves herself a valuable ally during the fight as she often tends to build significant ACS strain, and sometimes even staggers units entirely on her own. She also provides enough distraction to free you up to focus on any of the three in combat, of which you should put your immediate focus on the EKDROMOI PG, as it can most easily overload your ACS. Afterward, point your attention toward the EKDROMOI MG, before taking on the CATAPHRACT, since it's not actually the greatest threat here.

Opportunities for cover in this combat zone are limited. A bridge is available, but it only provides a temporary safeguard that CATAPHRACT will tear down early in the encounter. If you need a breather to use a repair kit or cool down your weapons, disengaging your target can be a good way to get Kate to distract them instead, awarding you a sneak attack. Try to avoid changing targets yourself, as it's most important to take bosses off the battlefield as quickly as possible.

EKDROMOI PG / PCA SP WARRANT OFFICER

Make the Warrant Officer your first target, if possible. His plasma gun, which is often charged before use and fired from mid-air, makes him too great a threat to leave standing during the encounter. The blast radius of his plasma gun shots will likely catch you if you're caught unaware and will build significant ACS strain. If you spot the warning indicator for an incoming blast, Quick Boost toward him to close in for a counterattack. Attacking the Warrant Officer can be tricky due to his mobility, but continue trying to stagger him with your handguns, then you'll often kill him in one burst of your shoulder weapons.

BASIC SPECS

AP	15280
Attitude Stability	1550
Anti-Kinetic Defense	1140
Anti-Energy Defense	700
Anti-Explosive Defense	1135
Elec. Discharge Tolerance	500
Shock Resistance	0%
ACS Anomaly Tolerance	500
Heat Resistance	0%

AAS03: EKDROMOI EP / PCA SP WARRANT OFFICER ATTACKS

PLASMA BLAST ▼ CHARGED

DESCRIPTION Plasma gun capable of charge attacks; leaves lasting damage field on impact.

EVASION Quick Boost away from the shots; stay airborne.

DUAL MISSILE VOLLEY

DESCRIPTION The Warrant Officer can release a dual volley of low-impact missiles from its multi-missile launchers.

EVASION Chain Quick Boosts away from the Warrant Officer.

EKDROMOI MG / PCA SP CHIEF SERGEANT 2ND CLS

Compared to the Warrant Officer, the Chief Sergeant engages at close-range, and uses a set of dual machine guns as his primary damage source. He'll occasionally leap at you while kicking in order to close the gap and get within effective range. If you've defeated the Warrant Officer beforehand, it's likely Kate will be keeping the Chief Sergeant busy enough for you to position yourself for attack. The EKDROMOI MG is highly mobile and often makes aerial maneuvers, necessitating a patient approach. Once staggered, your laser weapons should deal heavy AP damage to the MG.

BASIC SPECS

AP	15280
Attitude Stability	1550
Anti-Kinetic Defense	1140
Anti-Energy Defense	700
Anti-Explosive Defense	1135
Elec. Discharge Tolerance	500
Shock Resistance	0%
ACS Anomaly Tolerance	500
Heat Resistance	0%

AAS03: EKDROMOI PG / PCA SP CHIEF SERGEANT 2ND CLS ATTACKS

LEAPING KICK

DESCRIPTION Leaps toward you while kicking to reposition itself; also used when your ACS is overloaded.

EVASION Quick Boost to either side of the Chief Sergeant.

DUAL MACHINE GUNS

DESCRIPTION Kinetic machine guns which the Chief Sergeant will use primarily as his damage source.

EVASION Escape the effective range, or Quick Boost away.

DUAL MISSILE VOLLEY

DESCRIPTION Releases a dual volley of missiles from its scatter missile launcher.

EVASION Chain Quick Boosts away from the Chief Sergeant.

CATAPHRACT / PCA SP 1ST LIEUTENANT

This is the same craft that you faced in the mission "Destroy the Special Forces Craft." Even with the addition of two partners, this encounter proves a lot simpler than the solo version. Kate often keeps it busy as you work on the two EKDROMOI, and tends to draw its attention long enough for you to position yourself for attack or use a repair kit. She'll apply some ACS strain, but the job will largely be on you.

You can either fight at close or long range against CATAPHRACT, but playing closer allows your handguns to once rack up AP damage swiftly. Your build is sufficiently mobile to keep up with CATAPHRACT's erratic movements, allowing you to remain aggressive and wrap up this battle quickly.

NG++ //06-B
ATTACK THE WATCHPOINT (ALT)

"Handler Walter... Forget about the hound..."

—Sulla

This alternate version of your initial assault on the Watchpoint plays out nearly identically to the original, with the exception of one encounter. While Sulla is normally fought by himself at the monitoring station before the fight with BALTEUS, it's revealed here that he's cooperating with the GHOST mechs, so there will be four of them accompanying him. This adds an additional element of pressure during the fight, but there are no further differences in this mission. You'll receive a flat bonus payout of 100,000 COAM for completing the job.

MISSION OBJECTIVE
Annihilate Enemy AC / Craft of Unknown Affiliation

MISSION INFO

Combat Zone	Northern Belius—Watchpoint Delta
Client	Handler Walter
Reward	380,000
Max Bonus Pay	160,000
Completion Unlocks	—
Combat Logs	—
Data Logs	—
Part Containers	—

AC ASSEMBLY

Paired pulse cannons are the star of this build, capable of shredding BALTEUS's pulse shield and easily cutting down the more generic enemies. This build's movement is unparalleled, allowing rapid Quick Boosts and excellent melee capability; this accommodates a powerful laser lance, which decimates both BALTEUS and Sulla. Finally, a handheld bazooka covers distant targets like turrets or GHOSTs.

01	R-ARM UNIT | BAZOOKA	MAJESTIC	P.56
02	L-ARM UNIT | LASER LANCE	VE-67LLA	P.64
03	R-BACK UNIT | PULSE CANNON	KRANICH/60Z	P.68
04	L-BACK UNIT | PULSE CANNON	KRANICH/60Z	P.68
05	HEAD | —	IB-C03H: HAL 826	P.79
06	CORE | —	EL-TC-10 FIRMEZA	P.81
07	ARMS | —	AA-J-123 BASHO	P.82
08	LEGS | BIPEDAL	IB-C03L: HAL 826	P.86
09	BOOSTER | —	ALULA/21E	P.88
10	FCS | —	IA-C01F: OCELLUS	P.90
11	GENERATOR | —	VP-20C	P.92

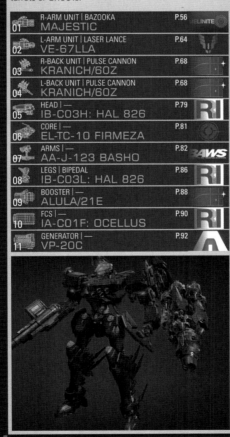

BOSS

ENEMY DATA

	No.	AP	AS	Bonus Pay	Analysis
IA-27: GHOST (Sniper Type)	4	3820	1066	—	P.343
AC ENTANGLE / Sulla	1	10640	1836	—	—

OBJECTIVE
Annihilate Enemy AC / Craft of Unknown Affiliation

Rather than engaging Sulla in a solo confrontation, he'll be accompanied by a squad of GHOSTs. Four in total are positioned around the battlefield—two on the buildings behind you, and two on the edge of the platform in front of the monitoring station. ▶ A

Sulla hasn't changed since your first encounter with him in the original mission, so it's recommended you target the GHOST mechs first, as their high-impact lasers are difficult to evade and place heavy strain on your ACS. As soon as the battle starts, immediately turn the way you entered and Assault Boost directly toward the two GHOSTs firing at you, making sure to strafe out of the way of incoming lasers. GHOSTs are invisible until you approach them, but using your scanner can help keep them in your sights once engaged. GHOSTs require more effort to defeat compared to weaker MTs, but can be wiped out with a single bazooka shot followed by a stab of your lance.

After defeating the first two GHOST mechs, make your way back to the monitoring station to engage the remaining two. The long distance of the return trip gives them plenty of opportunity to fire at you, which can be mitigated by using the bridge as cover. At this point, if the GHOSTs have obscured their location, then fight with Sulla until you've gained your bearings, but make the remaining GHOSTs your primary target as soon as you're aware of their whereabouts. Once all five enemies have been defeated, you'll proceed through the remainder of the mission with no alternative conditions. ▶ B-C

A

B

C

SURVEY THE UNINHABITED FLOATING CITY (ALT)

> *"'Coral, abide with Rubicon. Coral, endure within us all, for none of us shall cast the die.'"*
>
> —Thumb Dolmayan

The only difference between the Alt and original versions of this mission is a special guest showing up during its final encounter. Normally, you're matched up against four LCs and the HC HELICOPTER, but instead you'll be facing off against Thumb Dolmayan piloting AC ASTGHIK. A bonus payout of 150,000 COAM is given for completion of this Alt mission and you'll automatically obtain the data log "Text Data: Dolmayan's Writings (4)."

MISSION OBJECTIVES

Shut Down All ECM Fog Control Devices (1)

Access the Wrecked Survey Drones

Engage the Hostile Machines

Shut Down All ECM Fog Control Devices (2)

Defeat Thumb Dolmayan of the RLF

MISSION INFO

Combat Zone	Alean Ocean—Xylem, the Floating City
Client	Handler Walter
Reward	380,000
Max Bonus Pay	150,000
Completion Unlocks	—
Combat Logs	Platinum x1
Data Logs	1
Part Containers	—

ENEMY DATA

	No.	AP	AS	Bonus Pay	Analysis
◎ AC ASTGHIK / Thumb Dolmayan	1	11420	1670	150000	—

AC ASSEMBLY

The strategy for this mission is tweaked from its original counterpart due to the presence of an enemy AC, a much smaller and faster target than the original PCA helicopter. ASTGHIK is susceptible to energy weaponry, and the build reflects this accordingly.

One notable choice is the inclusion of a flamethrower. This handily dispatches the KITE drones and other smaller enemies in a few bursts, and has the added bonus of subjecting ASTGHIK to ACS anomaly.

01	R-ARM UNIT | FLAMETHROWER WB-0000 BAD COOK	P.58	
02	L-ARM UNIT | PULSE BLADE HI-32: BU-TT/A	P.65	
03	R-BACK UNIT | DIFFUSE LASER CANNON VP-60LCD	P.67	
04	L-BACK UNIT | DIFFUSE LASER CANNON VP-60LCD	P.67	
05	HEAD | — HD-033M VERRILL	P.77	
06	CORE | — 07-061 MIND ALPHA	P.81	
07	ARMS | — VP-46S	P.83	
08	LEGS | BIPEDAL 2S-5000 DESSERT	P.85	
09	BOOSTER | — ALULA/21E	P.88	
10	FCS | — IB-C03F: WLT 001	P.90	
11	GENERATOR | — VE-20C	P.92	

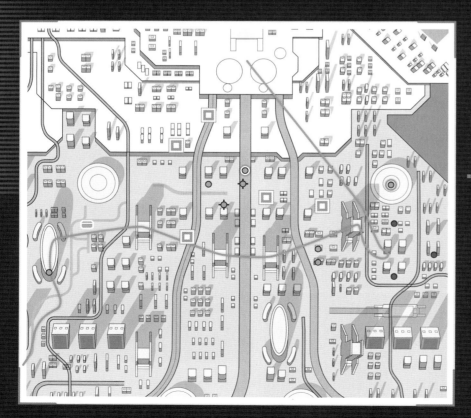

⬜ Friendly KITE drones

AC // ASTGHIK

The appearance of the AH12: HC HELICOPTER is abruptly cut short by Thumb Dolmayan's arrival. Dolmayan proceeds to eliminate this powerful craft before you can even make a dent in it. Facing off against Dolmayan is this mission's only alternate condition, and the mission will end after the conclusion of the battle.

BASIC SPECS

AP	11420
Attitude Stability	1670
Anti-Kinetic Defense	1196
Anti-Energy Defense	1083
Anti-Explosive Defense	1275
Elec. Discharge Tolerance	490
Shock Resistance	-16%
ACS Anomaly Tolerance	490
Heat Resistance	-16%
Repair Kits	3

OBJECTIVE

Defeat Thumb Dolmayan of the RLF

Dolmayan pilots ASTGHIK, an aggressive bipedal AC, and often attempts to position himself at medium range to best set up a counter-attack with his pulse blade. Just as you'll be making extensive use of the cover available to you, so will your opponent, as you both look for opportunities to exploit openings. The biggest threat you'll face will be Dolmayan's KYORAI napalm bomb launcher, which he'll use to set most of the terrain ablaze, causing heat buildup that edges you closer to ACS anomaly as you maneuver around the hazardous flames. Be especially careful when engaging ASTGHIK in close quarters, because falling victim to a direct impact from one of his napalm rounds can be lethal. As the two of you make your way in and out of cover, remember to use your scan—whenever it's not on cooldown—to better track Dolmayan's movement. He's a tough opponent, but once he goes down, the mission draws to a close.

Avoid fighting ASTGHIK on the raised platform where you disabled the ECM fog control device. Instead, drop below, where you can use the numerous buildings as cover.

AC ASTGHIK ATTACKS

MA-J 200 RANSETSU-RF ▼ CHARGED

DESCRIPTION This burst rifle can place a high strain on your ACS, especially if charged. More often, however, Dolmayan will opt to use its single-shot firing type at moderate distance.

EVASION Quick Boost away from the shots or place yourself behind cover.

HI-32: BU-TT/A

DESCRIPTION A pulse blade attack, which is used to slash twice at mid or close range.

EVASION Quick Boost away from Dolmayan for both hits.

MA-T-222 KYORAI ▼

DESCRIPTION Napalm bomb launcher which releases three exploding canisters that deal impact damage, and leave behind a lasting fire effect on any surface they touch.

EVASION Boost into the air to avoid the impact of the canisters, and focus on avoiding the fire they leave behind.

HML-G2/P19MLT-04

DESCRIPTION This hand launcher fires out a stream of four head-on, low-impact missiles.

EVASION Quick Boost away from the missiles, or place yourself behind cover.

ASSAULT ARMOR

DESCRIPTION Dolmayan only makes use of his AC's assault armor during his entrance to destroy the helicopter. It is worth noting that if you attempt to intercept him, you can be hit by this attack.

EVASION Do not rapidly approach him while he is above the helicopter, and instead wait for him to destroy it.

CORAL EXPORT DENIAL

> *"...No...choice...?"*
> —Ayre

The events at Watchpoint Delta have led to a series of Coral upsurges that the corporations are naturally attempting to capitalize upon, with transport carriers exporting substantial quantities from the Jorgen Refueling Base. ALLMIND is prepared to sacrifice Coral orphaned from the main population, and as such, you're being recruited to eliminate all transports attempting to depart from the facility. Bonus pay is awarded based on how few transport helicopters you allow to leave the combat zone, as well as the number of Coral storage tanks destroyed. Each helicopter destroyed awards 10,000 COAM, while losing a helicopter loses you 60,000. A total of five Coral storage tanks planted around the facility grant you an additional 8,000 COAM each.

MISSION OBJECTIVE

Destroy All Coral Transports

MISSION INFO

Combat Zone	Central Ice Field—Jorgen Refueling Base
Client	Rubicon Liberation Front
Reward	110,000
Max Bonus Pay	500,000
Completion Unlocks	—
Combat Logs	—
Data Logs	—
Part Containers	—

ENEMY DATA

	No.	AP	AS	Bonus Pay	Analysis
☐ Coral Storage Tank	5	—	—	8000	—
● MT-T-026 Guard Mech (Laser Gun)	3	102	121	—	P.310
● CD-J-098 Quad Drone (Laser Cannon)	2	302	310	—	P.312
● CD-J-098 Quad Drone (Cluster Missile Launcher)	2	302	310	—	P.312
● TH-E-012 Transport Helicopter	36	750	—	10000	P.314
● AM14: SENTRY SG MT (Missile Launcher)	8	437	310	—	P.320
● AM14: SENTRY SG MT (Grenade Cannon)	9	437	310	—	P.321
● AA18: LIGHT CAVALRY (Sniper Type)	4	1075	1750	—	P.332

Wave 1

ALT-180

AC ASSEMBLY

Transport helicopters in this mission will not attack you, but the high volume of enemies accompanying them will attempt to put you down with a combination of energy and explosive damage, so it's recommended to defend against both. It's also a good idea to build your frame with sustained EN usage and additional EN capacity, due to the amount of Quick Boosts and Assault Boosts required. Their improved jumping ability makes reverse-joint legs an excellent choice. They will make moving between ground level and the bridges above much easier when eliminating the final wave of transports. Weapons should focus on multi-lock, range, and homing ability. To that end, dual HML-G2/P19MLT-04 missile launchers and dual BML-G2/P05MLT-10 missile launchers are recommended, for their combination of high damage output and quick reload times.

01	R-ARM UNIT | MISSILE LAUNCHER **HML-G2/P19MLT-04**	P.62
02	L-ARM UNIT | MISSILE LAUNCHER **HML-G2/P19MLT-04**	P.62
03	R-BACK UNIT | MISSILE LAUNCHER **BML-G2/P05MLT-10**	P.69
04	L-BACK UNIT | MISSILE LAUNCHER **BML-G2/P05MLT-10**	P.69
05	HEAD | — **DF-HD-08 TIAN-QIANG**	P.77
06	CORE | — **NACHTREIHER/40E**	P.80
07	ARMS | — **AA-J-123/RC JAILBREAK**	P.82
08	LEGS | REVERSE JOINT **KASUAR/42Z**	P.86
09	BOOSTER | — **BC-0600 12345**	P.88
10	FCS | — **FCS-G2/P10SLT**	P.90
11	GENERATOR | — **DF-GN-06 MING-TANG**	P.91

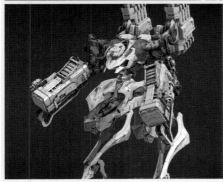

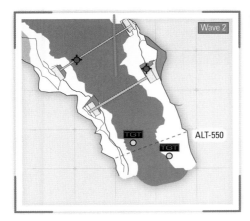

Wave 2

ALT-550

TGT

TGT

---

01 ◈ The most important thing to remember during this mission is that if five transport helicopters leave the battlefield, you'll immediately fail. Fortunately, all transports are marked targets, making it unlikely to lose track of them. Bear in mind, however, that there will be no supply sherpas or checkpoints. Conserve your ammunition for transport helicopters as best you can, but do catch enemies in your way via multi-lock to thin the numbers of the opposing force. When transports are flying directly next to each other, you'll likely only need to destroy one, as the explosion generated by the sacrificed Coral will be enough to destroy the adjacent craft.

CORAL CARRIERS

These transports are carrying volatile containers of pure Coral, and as such, they will explode when you destroy the transports. If you are within range of the explosion, your AC will take high amounts of AP damage.

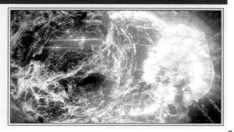

At **Position A**, you'll encounter a total of six transport helicopters; four immediately active, with the last two mobilizing only after the first squad has been destroyed. Laser cannon quad drones will likely deal the most damage to you over time, so you should spare the ammunition necessary to destroy them. The fifth and sixth transports are present in the area from the very beginning, but it's not advisable to target them right away while the first four are attempting to make their getaway.

After taking out the fourth transport, immediately turn back toward your starting position, where you'll find the remaining two helicopters attempting to leave the area. Once destroyed, make your way over to **Position B** for the next group of departing transports.

02 ◈ **Position B** also contains a total of six transport helicopters. Your first targets should be the two helicopters directly below you as you make your way over the cliff. Descend and immediately rush for the furthest target, as it will be the one closest to leaving the area at this point. The remaining targets will fly almost directly above you from the point you destroyed the first transport. After clearing out **Position B**, the events at **Position C** will not trigger right away, giving you time to backtrack to destroy the Coral storage tanks. Vertical catapults are located at both ends of the gorge, allowing you to either quickly return to **Position A** or continue to **Position C**.

03 ◈ The waves encountered at **Position C** will be the most difficult by far. Unlike **Position A**, where all transports were immediately present, these ones fly in from outside of the area, necessitating urgent interception. You'll need to move between two heights—ground level and bridge height—using the vertical catapults near the edge of the combat area, or your own vertical thrust. Destroy the additional enemy units between waves if possible—not just for your own safety, but to reduce the number of unintended targets which receive homing fire meant for a transport helicopter.

Wave 1	Transport Helicopter x2 Subject Guard MT (Grenade Cannon) x2

Wave 1 occurs at ground level, and is comprised of two transports accompanied by one SENTRY Subject Guard MT each. Immediately following the end of this wave, make your way to the vertical catapults and get to bridge height. ▶ A

Wave 2	Transport Helicopter x2 Subject Guard MT (Grenade Cannon) x2

Wave 2 occurs at bridge height, and is comprised of two transports accompanied by one SENTRY Subject Guard MT each. After taking down the transports, immediately return to ground level and approach the helicopter entry point. ▶ B

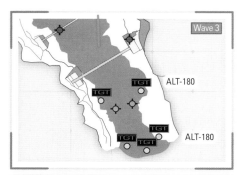

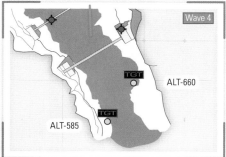

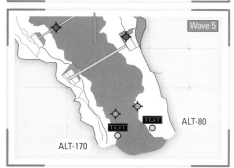

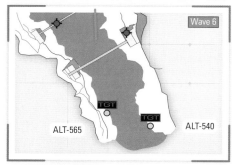

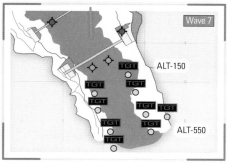

Wave 3 Transport Helicopter x5
Subject Guard MT (Grenade Cannon) x2

Wave 3 occurs at ground level, comprised of five transport helicopters accompanied by two Subject Guard MTs. The five transports are split; two at the front, and three in the back. Once you've destroyed the five transports, quickly return to bridge height. ▶ A

Wave 4 Transport Helicopter x2

Wave 4 occurs at bridge height, comprised of two unaccompanied transports. The two helicopters are not flying apace, but instead in a linear formation, paced a few hundred meters apart. After you've taken the two transports down, return to ground level. ▶ B

Wave 5 Transport Helicopter x2
Subject Guard MT (Grenade Cannon) x2

Wave 5 occurs at ground level, comprised of two transports at variable altitudes accompanied by one Subject Guard MT each. Wave 6 follows almost immediately after, requiring an especially quick return to bridge height in anticipation. ▶ C

Wave 6 Transport Helicopter x2
Subject Guard MT (Grenade Cannon) x2

Wave 6 occurs at bridge height, comprised of two transports accompanied by a total of three Subject Guard MTs. The transports departing are heavily staggered by nearly 700 meters of distance. The first transport appears quickly following the end of Wave 5, with the transports after allowing a more relaxed window of time to capture them. Once these transports are destroyed, return to ground level. ▶ D

Wave 7 Transport Helicopter x9
Subject Guard MT (Grenade Cannon) x2

The seventh and final wave occurs at both ground level and bridge height. Starting at ground level, you'll encounter four transports accompanied by three Subject Guard MTs. Enemies accompanying the transport helicopters can easily steal the lock-on from your intended target, so destroy them if needs be. As the helicopters approach you from their point of entry, it's recommended to move with them at ground level, in order to reach the vertical catapult quickly after destroying unless you can rapidly reach bridge height. ▶ E

Immediately behind the first squad of transports you destroyed will be five more helicopters accompanied by two Subject Guard MTs. This will likely be the most difficult squad of all to destroy without any leaving the combat zone. By the time you've reached bridge level from the vertical or your own boost, it's likely these transports have already arrived at the bridge, leaving little time to destroy them. Depending on your performance before now, as long as no more than four transports escape, then Kate will take care of the rest, and the mission will end when the final wave is cleared. ▶ F

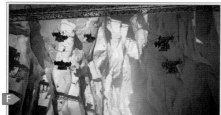

ELIMINATE V.III

> *"Shovel down your bland rations. Slurp your coffee-flavored sludge. Sure, it sucks—but that's being human."*
>
> —O'Keeffe

Your objective in this mission is simple; remove V.III O'Keeffe from Rubicon. As he is the only enemy encountered here, you are free to take up any position within the area. However, it is recommended that you stay on the large, circular platform on which you begin the mission, otherwise O'Keeffe may take to the skies, with massive drops below. This can make him a tricky target to pin down, and knowing where the ground beneath you is at all times will ensure that you can retreat to safety when necessary. The combat zone is expansive, and unless you go with a tetrapod assembly, it can be difficult to maneuver across the gaps that stretch between some sections and pursue O'Keeffe.

AC ASSEMBLY

O'Keeffe uses a combination of all three damage types, so it will help to have your defenses reflect this. His RANSETSU and Vvc-760PR plasma rifle in particular are his most dangerous weapons, so prioritizing anti-energy defense followed by anti-kinetic should be your plan here. O'Keeffe will often hover in the air, which can put him in an advantageous position over you. It's almost always recommended to fight tetrapods with tetrapods, to even the playing field and attempt to gain an aerial advantage. The VP-424 legs will provide this hovering capacity, as well as allowing you to retain speed better than your other option.

It's also advisable to choose weapons that you can use from long distances, due to the massive size of the combat zone. Dual HML-G2/P19MLT-04 hand missile launchers and dual Vvc-706PM plasma missile launchers will provide high ACS strain capability, and deal high direct hit damage once BARREN FLOWER is staggered.

01	R-ARM UNIT	MISSILE LAUNCHER **HML-G2/P19MLT-04**	P.62
02	L-ARM UNIT	MISSILE LAUNCHER **HML-G2/P19MLT-04**	P.62
03	R-BACK UNIT	PLASMA MISSILE LAUNCHER **Vvc-706PM**	P.73
04	L-BACK UNIT	PLASMA MISSILE LAUNCHER **Vvc-706PM**	P.73
05	HEAD	**VE-44A**	P.78
06	CORE	**IB-C03C: HAL 826**	P.81
07	ARMS	**IA-C01A: EPHEMERA**	P.84
08	LEGS	TETRAPOD **VP-424**	P.86
09	BOOSTER	**BST-G2/P06SPD**	P.88
10	FCS	**FCS-G2/P10SLT**	P.90
11	GENERATOR	**VE-20C**	P.92

MISSION OBJECTIVE
Eliminate V.III O'Keeffe

MISSION INFO

Combat Zone	Watchpoint Alpha—Depth 3
Client	ALLMIND
Reward	320,000
Max Bonus Pay	—
Completion Unlocks	—
Combat Logs	Platinum x1
Data Logs	—
Part Containers	—

ENEMY DATA

	No.	AP	AS	Bonus Pay	Analysis
AC BARREN FLOWER / V.III O'Keeffe	1	10210	2127	—	

01 ◆ You'll begin the mission facing the bridge at **Position A**, where O'Keeffe is positioned. There are no other enemy units in the area and you are free to engage with O'Keeffe on any of the surrounding platforms.

V.III O'KEEFFE

AC // BARREN FLOWER

BARREN FLOWER is a medium weight AC with evenly balanced resistances, high attitude stability and a good amount of AP. O'Keeffe will attempt to keep a moderate distance from you, as all of his weapons function best at medium to long ranges. If you aggressively approach him, he'll often attempt to gain elevation and hover almost directly over you. This can make his container missile launcher less effective, but his plasma rifle significantly more effective, due to the plasma explosions the shots cause. It is advisable to limit the efficacy of his plasma rifle as best you can, since it's easily O'Keeffe's most dangerous weapon.

BASIC SPECS

AP	10210
Attitude Stability	2127
Anti-Kinetic Defense	1155
Anti-Energy Defense	1199
Anti-Explosive Defense	1147
Elec. Discharge Tolerance	490
Shock Resistance	9%
ACS Anomaly Tolerance	490
Heat Resistance	9%
Repair Kits	3

O'Keeffe is not a particularly aggressive pilot and while BARREN FLOWER can prove to be a dangerous threat at close range, O'Keeffe tends to approach slowly and cautiously. While he does have weaponry capable of homing in on you from a distance, it's recommended to match his own strategy of using your weapons at their maximum effective range and simply outpacing his damage. He will attempt to evade shots, but will often be too slow to avoid many of them, especially if your time your shots at a steady pace to keep a continuous barrage assaulting him from a distance. Defeating O'Keeffe will bring the mission to a close.

Alternate your shots to keep constant pressure on O'Keeffe. It won't be long until his AC staggers.

AC BARREN FLOWER ATTACKS

BML-G1/P29CNT ▼

DESCRIPTION This container missile launcher releases a pod from which numerous micro-missiles release in an unbroken stream.

EVASION Until the pod has exhausted its supply of micro-missiles or it impacts you or a surface, it is recommended to move in the air and strafe backward and away from the missiles as they approach.

VVC-760PR ▼ CHARGED

DESCRIPTION Depending on your proximity to O'Keeffe and whether he is positioned in the air above you, the charged shot—which releases a triple-round that leaves large lingering damage fields behind—can result in high AP damage.

EVASION Keep in the air as much as possible, allowing you to attempt to evade the shot(s), as well as the lingering damage field or fields left behind.

MA-J-200 RANSETSU-RF ▼ CHARGED

DESCRIPTION This burst rifle can place a high strain on your ACS, especially if charged.

EVASION Quick Boost away from the shots, or place yourself behind cover.

VVC-70VPM

DESCRIPTION This plasma missile launcher releases a volley of five overhead missiles.

EVASION It is difficult to keep track of these missiles once released, but you can anticipate their approach by continuing to strafe or Quick Boost once you see them impacting your position.

PULSE ARMOR

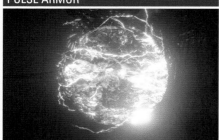

DESCRIPTION This barrier makes BARREN FLOWER completely immune to damage, but that decays over time and can be damaged to further diminish it.

EVASION Not used offensively.

REACH THE CORAL CONVERGENCE (ALT)

> *"Augmented human C4-621—Raven. Well done. Now, you are one with us. Welcome to ALLMIND."*
>
> —ALLMIND

The difference between this Alt mission and its standard counterpart is more significant than most others. You will be directed to a different location within the city to complete an entirely different task, namely the elimination of V.II Snail and subsequently G5 Iguazu. You will still encounter Maeterlinck and Wu Huahai to begin the mission, and once that objective has been completed, the Alt mission will clearly present itself.

There's a bonus payout of 330,000 COAM for completing this Alt mission, but you'll also be hit with a hefty 520,000 COAM penalty for disobeying Walter. Fortunately, the base pay for this mission is particularly high, and will offset the negative value from the bonus.

MISSION OBJECTIVES

Defeat V.VI Maeterlinck / G3 Wu Huahai

Secure the Area

Eliminate V.II Snail

Eliminate V.II Snail / G5 Iguazu

MISSION INFO

Combat Zone	Institute City
Client	ALLMIND
Reward	850,000
Max Bonus Pay	330,000 (Necessary penalty of 520,000)
Completion Unlocks	—
Combat Logs	—
Data Logs	—
Part Containers	—

ENEMY DATA

		No.	AP	AS	Bonus Pay	Analysis
●	MT-E-104 Bipedal MT (Grenade Cannon)	2	470	364	—	P.316
●	MT-E-104 Bipedal MT (Cluster Gun)	7	470	364	—	P.317
●	AM14: SENTRY SG MT (Missile Launcher)	2	437	310	—	P.320
●	AM02: DENOISER (Support Type)	2	1254	783	—	P.339
●	AM02: DENOISER (Sniper Type)	2	1254	783	—	P.339
◉	AC INFECTION / V.VI Maeterlinck	1	9570	1698	—	—
◉	AC LI LONG / G3 Wu Huahai	1	11930	2249	—	—
●	AC OPEN FAITH / V.II Snail	1	14040	1911	—	—
●	AC HEAD BRINGER / G5 Iguazu	1	9980	1704	—	—

G5 Iguazu (Reinforcements)

AC ASSEMBLY

This mission is a gauntlet of hostile AC encounters accompanied by smaller, weaker foes. Each of these ACs comes equipped with repair kits and Core Expansions, so ideally you'll aim to wipe them out before they can use either. The WB-0010 DOUBLE TROUBLE guarantees a stagger on any enemy AC if you can land a charged attack; follow this up with your spread bazookas to make a devastating dent in enemy ACs, if not destroy them outright. Your frame parts are highly mobile to allow this aggressive, melee-based combat style.

01	R-ARM UNIT | SHOTGUN SG-027 ZIMMERMAN	P.54	
02	L-ARM UNIT | CHAINSAW WB-0010 DOUBLE TROUBLE	P.63	aD
03	R-BACK UNIT | SPREAD BAZOOKA SB-033M MORLEY	P.66	
04	L-BACK UNIT | SPREAD BAZOOKA SB-033M MORLEY	P.66	
05	HEAD | — IA-C01H: EPHEMERA	P.79	R||
06	CORE | — EL-TC-10 FIRMEZA	P.81	
07	ARMS | — AA-J-123 BASHO	P.82	AWS
08	LEGS | BIPEDAL IB-C03L: HAL 826	P.86	R||
09	BOOSTER | — BST-G2/P06SPD	P.88	
10	FCS | — IA-C01F: OCELLUS	P.90	R||
11	GENERATOR | — VP-20C	P.92	A

01 ◇ Once V.VI Maeterlink and G3 Wu Huahai have been defeated, ALLMIND will come over the comms to redirect your focus away from the regular path of the mission, and give the order to take V.II Snail down. Instead of heading toward the riverbed as you would in the original mission, you'll instead need to head into the underground sewer system at **Position A**. ▶A

You'll encounter Arquebus bipedal MTs as you proceed through the tunnels, but these should offer little resistance. There are no new collectibles to be found in this mission, so just focus on making your way through the tunnels. Ayre will remark that you have the opportunity for a surprise attack, so utilize this chance by first scanning the area below to reveal the enemies, and then pick out Snail. Once you reach the objective marker, you'll be locked in the combat zone, but have access to a checkpoint.

Proceed to the tunnel to hunt down Snail.

V.II SNAIL

AC // OPEN FAITH

After entering the room with Snail and his accompanying squad of four bipedal MTs, you'll initially fight him by yourself. It's advisable to quickly destroy the bipedal MTs, because they can both potentially damage you with their grenades, and get in the way of your lock-on, including your shots targeting Snail. Shortly after engaging with Snail, you'll both be attacking by Iguazu, resulting in a "Mission Update" alert.

BASIC SPECS

AP	14040
Attitude Stability	1791
Anti-Kinetic Defense	1285
Anti-Energy Defense	1406
Anti-Explosive Defense	1287
Elec. Discharge Tolerance	490
Shock Resistance	10%
ACS Anomaly Tolerance	490
Heat Resistance	10%
Repair Kits	2

AC OPEN FAITH ATTACKS

VP-66EG

DESCRIPTION Fires a series of quick-moving shots that both strain your ACS and build up the Shock status abnormality on your AC.

EVASION Quick Boost in the opposite direction Snail is firing toward.

VE-67LLA

DESCRIPTION This melee weapon strikes twice, the first is very quick and capable of crossing large distances. The second strike will likely overload your ACS if it connects, and deals heavy direct damage.

EVASION These are head-on attacks, and while dodging the first strike may prove difficult, you can dodge into Snail on the second strike to not only evade it but position yourself behind him for a counterattack.

VE-60SNA ▼	VVC-70VPM	ASSAULT ARMOR

DESCRIPTION Fires a high-velocity bolt that releases a powerful lingering damage field where it lands. If hit, you'll take damage from the impact, the explosion, and will instantly have the Shock abnormality applied to your AC.

EVASION The shot is very quick, and you'll only have a very small window of time in which to react to the alert indicator and Quick Boost to the side to evade it.

DESCRIPTION Vertical plasma missiles that leave a lingering damage field on impact.

EVASION Chain Quick Boosts as soon as the volley begins landing.

DESCRIPTION After bringing OPEN FAITH's AP down to almost zero, Snail will use his core expansion in desperation.

EVASION This attack can easily overload your ACS so anticipate Snail using it based on his remaining AP and Quick Boost away from him.

OBJECTIVE	Eliminate V.II Snail / G5 Iguazu

02 ◆ Normally, seeing indicators for two priority targets on your HUD would mean that you have allies, but this battle is an exception. You'll need to defeat both Snail and Iguazu to end the mission, but Iguazu intends to defeat you both, making this is a three-way fight.

It's unlikely that you'll have significantly damaged Snail by the point at which Iguazu enters the fight, and once this becomes a three-way standoff, your best bet is to eliminate Iguazu first. Iguazu has a frustrating habit of tag-teaming you along with Snail, and he can place you in ACS overload faster than you might expect, leaving you easy prey for Snail. After knocking Iguazu out, Snail is fairly manageable on his own. He may have the most durable AC in this mission, but you can repeatedly stagger him and quickly burn through his repair kits, ending the fight.

Snail and Iguazu will briefly turn their attention away from you to fight each other

---

G5 IGUAZU

AC // HEAD BRINGER

Iguazu is your main priority in this brawl, primarily due to his habit of targeting you instead of Snail and how unrelenting he is with his attacks. Focus on landing a charged attack with your chainsaw. When you're successful, the guaranteed stagger will lead to massive damage, forcing him to use a repair kit if he doesn't die instantly. HEAD BRINGER's assembly here is the same as in the mission "Underground Exploration - Depth 2," which means instead of a shield, he'll have the 45-091 ORBT laser drone in his L-Back unit slot. Beyond this, he doesn't have any fancy tricks or surprises for you. Once both ACs have been defeated, the mission draws to a close.

BASIC SPECS

AP	9980
Attitude Stability	1704
Anti-Kinetic Defense	1208
Anti-Energy Defense	1153
Anti-Explosive Defense	1200
Elec. Discharge Tolerance	490
Shock Resistance	-1%
ACS Anomaly Tolerance	490
Heat Resistance	-1%
Repair Kits	2/3

AC HEAD BRINGER ATTACKS

LR-036 CURTIS ▼ CHARGED

DESCRIPTION Kinetic linear rifle capable of rapid uncharged shots, or a powerful charged shot.

EVASION Quick Boost to either side of the shot(s).

45-091 ORBT

DESCRIPTION Autonomous drone that hovers around Iguazu and fires laser bursts; can target your AC even if Iguazu himself is not directly facing you.

EVASION Strafe or Quick Boost away from the shots once you see the ORBT has been deployed.

BML-G1/P20MLT-04

DESCRIPTION Launcher that releases four missiles, each with fast breaks and high homing capacities.

EVASION Quick Boost to either side of the split missiles as close to when they reach you as possible.

MG-014 LUDLOW ▼

DESCRIPTION Rapid-firing machine gun capable of quickly straining your ACS.

EVASION Create distance, so that the shots ricochet off you, or Quick Boost to either side of the shots.

MIA

"Once you reach the rendezvous point... No one will be able to threaten you anymore."

—ALLMIND

ALLMIND has extended an offer to guarantee your safety, but only if you successfully reach the rendezvous point at the end of Depth 2. By the time you've deployed, ALLMIND will have already begun an assault on the corporations, resulting in the chaos you'll make your way through as you push ahead. Enemies encountered include SENTRY Subject Guard MTs, LCs wielding laser rifles, an optional encounter with G6 Red, and ultimately a fight with V.III Pater. You've traveled this route in a previous mission, but this time you're heading in the opposite direction and much of the area is engulfed in flame; the threat of ACS Failure will be ever present and only some careful navigating will keep you safe.

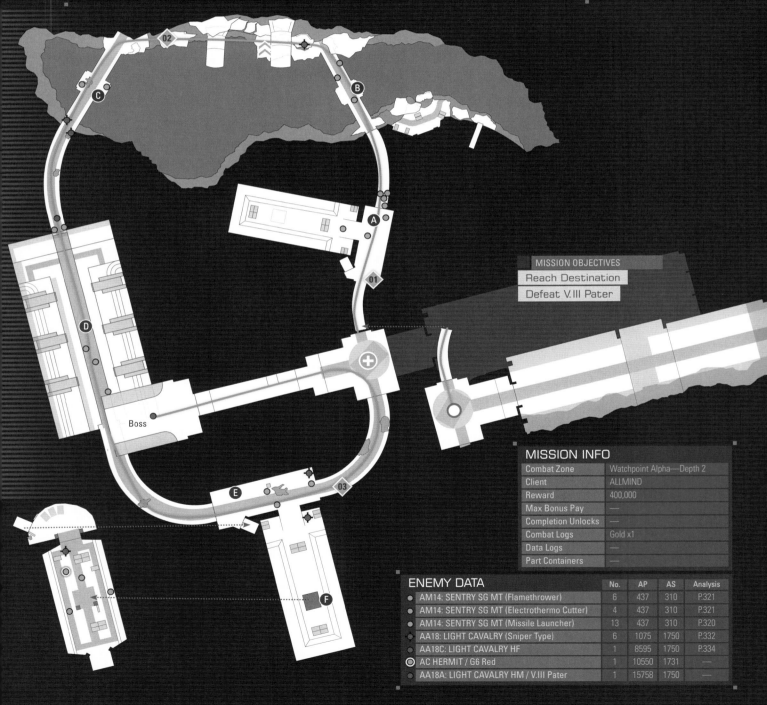

MISSION OBJECTIVES

Reach Destination

Defeat V.III Pater

MISSION INFO

Combat Zone	Watchpoint Alpha—Depth 2
Client	ALLMIND
Reward	400,000
Max Bonus Pay	—
Completion Unlocks	—
Combat Logs	Gold x1
Data Logs	—
Part Containers	—

ENEMY DATA

	No.	AP	AS	Analysis
AM14: SENTRY SG MT (Flamethrower)	6	437	310	P.321
AM14: SENTRY SG MT (Electrothermo Cutter)	4	437	310	P.321
AM14: SENTRY SG MT (Missile Launcher)	13	437	310	P.320
AA18: LIGHT CAVALRY (Sniper Type)	6	1075	1750	P.332
AA18C: LIGHT CAVALRY HF	1	8595	1750	P.334
AC HERMIT / G6 Red	1	10550	1731	—
AA18A: LIGHT CAVALRY HM / V.III Pater	1	15758	1750	—

AC ASSEMBLY

The turmoil that has engulfed Watchpoint Alpha has resulted in a series of fiery infernos blocking your escape. Tetrapod legs help you avoid the fire to begin with, and your head provides excellent system recovery should you be grazed by a flame.

The majority of this mission is fought in close quarters, so handguns are a natural and light choice for staggering enemies. Paired with two grenade launchers, this allows you to saturate indoor areas in large blasts of flame to dispatch staggered foes. This strategy also translates well to eliminating the two unique encounters in this mission: G6 Red and V.III Pater.

01	R-ARM UNIT | HANDGUN HG-003 COQUILLETT	P.54
02	L-ARM UNIT | HANDGUN HG-003 COQUILLETT	P.54
03	R-BACK UNIT | GRENADE CANNON EARSHOT	P.66
04	L-BACK UNIT | GRENADE CANNON EARSHOT	P.66
05	HEAD | — IA-C01H: EPHEMERA	P.79
06	CORE | — VE-40A	P.81
07	ARMS | — NACHTREIHER/46E	P.83
08	LEGS | TETRAPOD LG-033M VERRILL	P.86
09	BOOSTER | — BC-0600 12345	P.88
10	FCS | — IB-C03F: WLT 001	P.90
11	GENERATOR | — VE-20C	P.92

01 You'll be moving backward through Depth 2 to the chamber that housed NEPENTHES. The access point at **Position A** leads you into a battle between ALLMIND's forces and the corporations'. Mechs under ALLMIND are friendly, and won't engage you, but the three Subject Guard MTs equipped with flamethrowers will damage the both of you until dealt with. ▶ A

When you open the next partition, you're quickly met by an additional four Subject Guard MTs—two equipped with flamethrowers and two wielding cutters. Do your best to keep at least one of ALLMIND's units protected during these initial encounters, as they will keep the corporations' forces occupied while you're at range. ▶ B

Once the two squads have been defeated, head out from the cavern onto the bridge at **Position B**, where you'll encounter Subject Guard MTs equipped with laser rifles, along with a similarly equipped LC on a platform further out at a higher altitude. By allowing the ALLMIND units to exit the tunnel ahead of you, they will draw the enemies' fire. First target the LC, who may take to the air, and then clear out the remaining MTs. Use the nearby vertical catapult and scale the walls leading to the bridge at **Position C**.

02 A battle is in progress at **Position C** between two LCs and two ALLMIND units that won't last long, as an explosion will soon consume both LCs. The blast can reach you as well, impacting your ACS anomaly meter, so do your best to move out of harm's way when Ayre gives the warning. ▶ C

Take care not to linger in open flames while passing through the tunnel, as those will additionally contribute to heat buildup. Enter the room at **Position D**—the former battleground where you faced Iguazu or Coldcall—and engage the group of three Subject Guard MTs. After you've cleared the threat and have access to the partition, you'll be ambushed from behind by a much more threatening squad of two Subject Guard MTs and one HF LC. Quickly take cover, as they approach, only revealing yourself to take fire upon the nearest opponent. Make use of your scanner during this encounter to help uncover any enemies that have obscured themselves. ▶ D

Approach the adjoining hallway at **Position E** with caution; a squad of two Subject Guard MTs and two sniper type LCs are ahead, and they'll have an easy time targeting you from the narrow corridor that you enter from, with little room to evade. Two ALLMIND units are also present, so take the opportunity to thin the enemy's ranks before they turn their attention back to you.

G6 RED

Instead of moving through the partition to the objective marker, you can head into the room directly next to it and drop into the opening at **Position F** for an encounter with G6 Red, piloting AC HERMIT.

AC // HERMIT

You'll initially find Red engaged in combat with an Arquebus squad of three Subject Guard MTs and one LC, and he'll request your assistance dealing with them. Red's gratitude quickly fades, however, as he takes up arms against you. G6 Red is an aggressive foe, utilizing kinetic and high-impact explosive rounds at close range, easily overloading your ACS if you play to his advantage. It's recommended to match his aggression with unrelenting pressure from your handguns, and a stagger will often result in nearly killing him with two grenade cannon blasts. Pillars in the room's center offer the only true cover available within this cramped combat zone. Once G6 Red is down, continue toward the objective marker.

BASIC SPECS

AP	10550
Attitude Stability	1731
Anti-Kinetic Defense	1227
Anti-Energy Defense	1105
Anti-Explosive Defense	1194
Elec. Discharge Tolerance	490
Shock Resistance	15%
ACS Anomaly Tolerance	490
Heat Resistance	15%

AC HERMIT ATTACKS

HG-003 COQUILLETT

DESCRIPTION This handgun has a limited effective range, but within close proximity it can quickly strain your ACS.

EVASION Place yourself behind cover, out-distance the effective range of the weapon, or Quick Boost away from the shots.

DF-BA-06 XUAN-GE

DESCRIPTION Bazooka which fires a high-impact explosive that can apply high strain to your ACS, as well as heavy AP damage.

EVASION Place yourself behind cover or attempt to Quick Boost away to avoid the direct impact of the explosive.

BML-G2/P03MLT-06

DESCRIPTION This missile launcher fires a stream of six low-impact missiles.

EVASION Due to the limited space you have to evade, it may be difficult to entirely avoid these missiles so you should have the center column between you and Red as much as possible during the fight.

BML-G2/P16SPL-08

DESCRIPTION This split missile launcher will fire a pod from which eight micro-missiles release to home in on you. They will break immediately and converge on your position simultaneously, making it more akin to evading a single strike.

EVASION Use the room's central column as cover against and Red as much as possible to block these missiles.

OBJECTIVE Defeat V.III Pater

03 ◈ The partition leading away from **Position E** will bring you to a room with a supply sherpa. The following hallway leads you to the rendezvous point, where ALLMIND is prepared to retrieve you—but not before V.III Pater comes crashing in, piloting the AA18A: LIGHT CAVALRY HM. Identical to the LC encountered in the mission "Attack the Old Spaceport," you'll be taking on the LC in a solo encounter this time around.

Pater's LC is capable of remaining airborne throughout the entire fight, and covers enormous distances quickly. Don't allow Pater to position himself directly above you, as tracking him to land shots will become incredibly difficult if you do. The flames atop the platform Pater destroyed will cause heat buildup, but the sides of the platform, along with the beams surrounding it, can provide cover if necessary. If using the recommended build, meet his altitude with your tetrapod's hover mode while pelting him with handgun fire. As Pater succumbs to ACS overload, blast him with both grenade cannons for huge direct hit damage. It should only take a couple of rounds of direct hit attacks to conclude the battle. Once Pater is defeated, the mission ends. ▶ A

Due to the flames, staying airborne as much as possible prevents accidental ACS anomaly buildup.

REGAIN CONTROL OF THE XYLEM

*"You've come... tourist. Got a message from the chief for you.
'Sorry, but I'm not laughing this time.'"*

—"Chatty" Stick

Ending Overseer's efforts to lock the Xylem onto a collision course with the Vascular Plant calls for the destruction of six parasite modules scattered throughout its interior. Up against you are numerous KITEs and GHOSTs—not to mention the disorienting labyrinth that is the Xylem itself; this is the same area you navigated in "Destroy the Drive Block." Keep your eyes peeled for the part containers that appear toward the end of the mission.

IB-C03W4: NGI 028

IB-C03W3: NGI 006

MISSION INFO

Combat Zone	Mesosphere—Xylem Drive Block
Client	ALLMIND
Reward	380,000
Max Bonus Pay	—
Completion Unlocks	—
Combat Logs	—
Data Logs	—
Part Containers	2

MISSION OBJECTIVES

Destroy All Parasite Modules

Stop the Lockout Activation Sequence

ENEMY DATA

		No.	AP	AS	Bonus Pay	Analysis
■	Parasite Module	6	700	—	—	
◆	IA-24: KITE (Plasma Cannon)	10	840	486	—	P.342
◆	AM01: REPAIRER (Guard Type)	19	51	—	—	P.313
◆	AM01: REPAIRER (Stun Smog)	2	51	—	—	P.314
◆	IA-27: GHOST (Sniper Type)	3	3820	1066	—	P.343

AC ASSEMBLY

The interior of the Xylem is a cramped, multi-layered labyrinth of small enemies that find their strength in numbers. Close range and medium range options are both important, so your issued build makes use of the Weapon Bay unlock from OS Tuning.

Dual shotguns allow you to shred through closer enemies with ease, while paired bazookas allow you the option to snipe a distant target instead. Your frame parts are focused on speed and mobility, rather than excessive durability, as this mission has no traditional boss or powerful combatant at the end.

01	R-ARM UNIT | BAZOOKA	MAJESTIC	P.56
02	L-ARM UNIT | BAZOOKA	MAJESTIC	P.56
03	R-BACK UNIT | SHOTGUN	SG-027 ZIMMERMAN	P.54
04	L-BACK UNIT | SHOTGUN	SG-027 ZIMMERMAN	P.54
05	HEAD | —	IB-C03H: HAL 826	P.79
06	CORE | —	IA-C01C: EPHEMERA	P.81
07	ARMS | —	NACHTREIHER/46E	P.83
08	LEGS | REVERSE JOINT	06-042 MIND BETA	P.86
09	BOOSTER | —	ALULA/21E	P.88
10	FCS | —	IB-C03F: WLT 001	P.90
11	GENERATOR | —	VE-20C	P.92

GHOST SCANNING

Each area of the Xylem houses GHOSTs that, if eliminated early enough, reveal the locations of modules to be destroyed. Scanning, or moving close enough, reveals hidden GHOSTs, but the most important encounters are marked on the map and noted below.

01 The mission begins atop a walkway inside the Xylem. Not all of its interior is available at all times; most areas are blocked off until modules in your current vicinity have been destroyed. The first module is located fairly close to your stating position, at **Position A** on the floor below, and destroying it triggers a four-minute countdown timer. Within meters of module 1, a GHOST can be found hiding at **Position B**, which reveals the location of module 2 at **Position C** on the floor above. After destroying these two modules, drop down to the floor below and follow the objective marker to the adjacent room. ▶ A

02 This second room is more maze-like than the first, so it's recommended to hunt down its GHOST mech as early as possible. Thrust upward to locate and destroy the GHOST at **Position D** and reveal the locations of both obscured modules. Module 3 is found on the floor below at **Position E**, a short distance from the GHOST's hiding place. From here, point the camera upward in the direction of **Position F** to find module 4 on the highest platform in the room. Once these modules are down, an objective marker at **Position G** points to the newly opened room. Ascend toward the opposite side of the room from where you found module 4, hover over the platforms and then drop down in the corner to reach the opening. ▶ B

03 The third and final GHOST doesn't reveal itself until after destroying the fifth module; it will appear in the open area in front of the sixth module. Upon entering the room, boost in the direction of **Position H**. Prioritize destroying module 5, which is found nestled away among the highest elevated platforms in the room, past a group of generic weaponry.

PART CONTAINER

From module 5, you can retrieve a part from a container at **Position I**. However it's recommended to instead move directly to module 6, as the timer ends after it's destroyed.

Head toward the end of the room at **Position J**. By the time you've arrived, the room's GHOST will have finally revealed itself to you. Destroy it to reveal the location of the final module, atop the platform behind you. Destroying the sixth module ends the timer, giving you an opportunity to pick up the collectibles you may have left behind. When you're ready, access the door at the objective marker and drop down the chute to reach the mission's final objective.

04 "Chatty" contacts you to inform you that he's controlling a lockout sequence indicated by a rapidly incrementing bar at the top of your screen. If the bar is completely filled, lockout completes and you'll fail the mission. Each generator disabled reduces this meter, buying more time to continue the lockout sequence. The control module is protected by a shield produced by the eight generators surrounding the room. Following a brief dialogue, these generators become targetable and need to be disabled before the central control module is accessible.

One generator is active at a time, with the next appearing at the side of the room opposite to you, assisting you in anticipating how best to position yourself behind the central terminal to avoid the incoming pulse shot. The rhythm of the fight is as follows: hover behind the control module at the same level as the eyes of the generators between waves, watch for the alert indicator revealing the now-active generator, protect yourself from the incoming pulse shot, and then Assault Boost to the generator to access it. This same sequence follows for each generator until you're granted access to the control module in the center of the room, which finally ends the lockout sequence. Once disabled, the mission ends. ▶ C

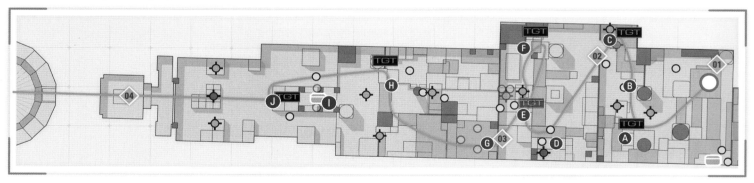

Use your scanner from the location of the first module to find the GHOST hiding at **Position B**.

Scanning from the upper elevation of the second room will reliably reveal the GHOST at **Position D**.

Bear in mind that an Assault Boost strafe is also a viable evasive maneuver if you're fast enough.

XYLEM LOCKOUT PROGRESS DEFENSIVE PROTOCOLS

STATIC ENERGY BEAM

DESCRIPTION The eyes of the inactive generators release a sustained energy beam at random angles across the room, creating an environmental hazard.

EVASION Simply do not hit the beams where they rest, or at least do not stand or hover in them.

GUIDED ENERGY BEAM

DESCRIPTION The eye of the active generator will produce an energy laser that tracks your AC as you approach it.

EVASION Hover at generator-eye level until after the pulse shot is released, and then Assault Boost at a downward angle toward the generator to shut it down. The laser will track you but it will be above your AC.

CHARGED PULSE SHOT ▼

DESCRIPTION The eye of the active generator will charge briefly and release a highly-damaging pulse shot, which leaves a lasting damage field.

EVASION Anticipate the side of the room from which the shot is coming and hide behind the control module to block the shot and the lasting damage field.

CORAL RELEASE ▷

"...I'm with you, Raven. Now... I can fight by your side."

—Ayre

Your sole objective in this mission is to defeat ALLMIND. With almost everyone else either dead or assimilated, you're potentially the last person who's capable of putting its systems down before Coral Release is achieved. Accompanying ALLMIND at different points in the fight are numerous enemy units, AC drones, and ORBIT units that it has taken direct control over, making an already difficult encounter that much harder.

You can let these extra units distract you, or you can continue to focus on the main body. None of the subordinates are as dangerous as their builds suggest, and will go down fairly quickly, so taking them out can relieve some of the pressure if the pace of the fight is proving troublesome. The arena is a large circular platform and there's no cover to assist you, so your only option here is to fight. Be aware that even if you destroy ALLMIND's subordinates, it is not alone...

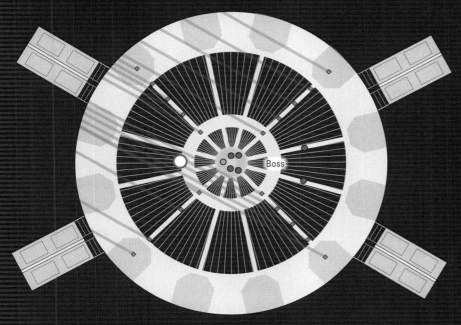

Boss

MISSION OBJECTIVE

Defeat ALLMIND

MISSION INFO

Combat Zone	Exosphere—LOC Station 31
Client	ALLMIND
Reward	660,000
Max Bonus Pay	—
Completion Unlocks	—
Combat Logs	—
Data Logs	—
Part Containers	—

ENEMY DATA

	No.	AP	AS	Bonus Pay	Analysis
○ ALLMIND (1st Phase)	1	10260	1566	—	—
○ ALLMIND (Melee AC Unit)	2	3000	1614	—	—
○ ALLMIND (Support AC Unit)	2	3000	1614	—	—
● ALLMIND (2nd Phase)	1	58255	2050	—	—
○ ALLMIND ORBIT	2	28650	1500	—	—

AC ASSEMBLY

In all phases of this fight, energy damage is the biggest threat, with only a small handful of attacks being either kinetic or explosive, meaning you should prioritize getting your anti-energy spec as high as possible. Any defense against the other types should be considered a bonus. A combination of Arquebus, ALLMIND, and Rubicon Research Institute frame parts will give you just the right balance of defensive specs that you're looking for.

Additionally, while it's recommended to focus on ALLMIND during these phases, it's worth considering the use of tetrapod legs for their hover mode during the phase involving the Sea Spider drones, because they're much easier to fight if you can match their altitude. Your weaponry should reflect a mission that revolves heavily around one-on-one combat, and as such, the SG-027 ZIMMERMAN shotguns and dual diffuse laser cannons are once again solid choices here.

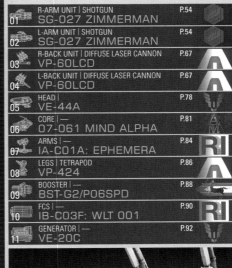

01	R-ARM UNIT | SHOTGUN SG-027 ZIMMERMAN	P.54	
02	L-ARM UNIT | SHOTGUN SG-027 ZIMMERMAN	P.54	
03	R-BACK UNIT | DIFFUSE LASER CANNON VP-60LCD	P.67	
04	L-BACK UNIT | DIFFUSE LASER CANNON VP-60LCD	P.67	
05	HEAD | VE-44A	P.78	
06	CORE | — 07-061 MIND ALPHA	P.81	
07	ARMS | — IA-C01A: EPHEMERA	P.84	
08	LEGS | TETRAPOD VP-424	P.86	
09	BOOSTER | — BST-G2/P06SPD	P.88	
10	FCS | — IB-C03F: WLT 001	P.90	
11	GENERATOR | — VE-20C	P.92	

ALLMIND (PHASE 1)

BASIC SPECS

AP	10260
Attitude Stability	1566
Anti-Kinetic Defense	1183
Anti-Energy Defense	1239
Anti-Explosive Defense	1205
Elec. Discharge Tolerance	490
Shock Resistance	16%
ACS Anomaly Tolerance	490
Heat Resistance	16%

OBJECTIVE

Defeat ALLMIND

ALLMIND starts the encounter with four subordinate ALLMIND AC drones; two of these are ranged variants, and the other two are focused on melee attacks. These enemies use MIND frames, but they have significantly reduced attitude stability and AP, and only have access to two weapons and the assault armor Core Expansion. The support AC is equipped with two back unit missile launchers that it will use from range, rather than trying to get close to you. If you're planning on destroying the subordinates, it's recommended that you destroy this variant first, because their missiles are both more damaging and more difficult to evade than the melee attacks of the other variant.

The melee subordinate moves much more aggressively than the missile launcher variant, and will use its burst machine gun to fire on you while closing into range to use its laser dagger. Because they have to be close to be effective, as long as you stay out of range of their attacks they pose little threat, and you can simply move around the area to destroy the missile launcher variants while staying out of their attack range. This variant also has access to the assault armor Core Expansion so if they get close enough to attack, you're a lot more likely to be caught within the blast radius, unless you react quickly enough to escape.

ALLMIND is piloting AC MIND GAMMA, which is a midweight bipedal AC carrying a combination of energy and kinetic weapons. At the start of the fight, it will always use a charge shot from its multi-energy rifle, so be prepared to move out of the way immediately. For most of this phase, ALLMIND will attempt to keep a moderate distance from you rather than closing in, a tactic made easier to employ by the additional pressure applied by its subordinates.

If you attempt to approach ALLMIND, it will continuously move away from you, usually with its shield raised for safety, or while using the LUDLOW for suppressing fire while the subordinates attack you. Getting around the shield will be one of the biggest hurdles during the fight, because its entire purpose is to prolong the encounter and increase the likelihood that you'll eventually make a mistake. This can be a very chaotic fight, since you'll be dealing with five enemies at once, so try to keep ALLMIND in view while you quickly destroy the subordinates. Using Target Assist to keep your reticule trained on ALLMIND is all but essential, and although it keeps moving away, your best option is to keep trying to get into range to hit it with your shotguns, and only use your diffuse laser cannons if you're sure it'll remain in place for long enough.

What their laser daggers lack in range, they make up for in speed and number of attacks, providing they get close enough to use them.

If you manage to defeat ALLMIND before destroying the subordinate AC drones, any that remain will be removed during ALLMIND's transition into its next form.

ALLMIND (SUPPORT AC UNIT) ATTACKS

BML-G1/P32DUO-03

DESCRIPTION Two volleys of three missiles fired in a pincer pattern.

EVASION The firing pattern places missiles to both sides, instead of just on one side, but a Quick Boost near the point of impact is still effective.

VVC-703PM

DESCRIPTION This plasma missile launcher fires three head-on missiles that leave a lingering damage field.

EVASION Missiles have limited homing capacity and you can easily Quick Boost away from them.

ASSAULT ARMOR

DESCRIPTION A large, damaging pulse explosion that can easily overload your ACS.

EVASION Maintain distance when targeting these AC drones.

ALLMIND (MELEE AC UNIT) ATTACKS

MA-E-210 ETSUJIN

DESCRIPTION This burst machine gun is low-impact and will not deal high AP damage.

EVASION Shots can be out-distanced, or Quick Boost away from them.

VP-67LD

DESCRIPTION This laser dagger strikes three times in a string and cannot be canceled by the subordinate. Can be charged for a longer, single slash.

EVASION Quick Boost away from the subordinate.

ASSAULT ARMOR

DESCRIPTION A large, damaging pulse explosion that can easily overload your ACS.

EVASION Maintain distance when targeting these AC drones.

ALLMIND (1ST PHASE) ATTACKS

44-142 KRSV ▼ CHARGED

DESCRIPTION Pulse rifle capable of uncharged or charged shots. When firing the charged shot, ALLMIND will often jump into the air. Leaves lingering damage field.

EVASION Quick Boost away from the uncharged shots, jump into the air preceding a charged shot and boost away.

MG-014 LUDLOW

DESCRIPTION Machine gun with a high rate of fire, used to strain your ACS.

EVASION Create distance to move out of the effective range of the rounds, or Quick Boost away from them.

45-091 ORBT

DESCRIPTION Autonomous drone that fires energy beams. Not constantly active but can be redeployed after a short cooldown period.

EVASION Quick Boost away from the drone's shots.

SI-27: SU-R8

DESCRIPTION ALLMIND can raise this pulse shield while firing its multi-energy rifle, and while the ORBT drone fires as well.

EVASION If ALLMIND gets close to you, Quick Boost away if its swings the shield.

ALLMIND (PHASE 2)

At the beginning of this phase, ALLMIND will be accompanied by two ORBITs. These are similar to the SEA SPIDER from the mission "Ocean Crossing," but have limited attacks and strictly remain airborne. They are still dangerous, however, and in addition to a more aggressive version of ALLMIND, can pose a significant threat. Their considerable AP reserves and ability to remain at high altitudes make fighting the ORBITs difficult, and attempting to do so will likely put you in a bad situation with ALLMIND. If you do choose to fight them, use Assault Boosts to get into range, so that you can attack them somewhat effectively. Try to focus your attacks on one of them to overload its ACS, to both stop it from attacking and give you an opportunity to deal some powerful direct hit damage.

BASIC SPECS

AP	58255
Attitude Stability	2050
Anti-Kinetic Defense	1268
Anti-Energy Defense	1265
Anti-Explosive Defense	1370
Elec. Discharge Tolerance	500
Shock Resistance	20%
ACS Anomaly Tolerance	500
Heat Resistance	30%

ALLMIND ORBIT ATTACKS

SPIRAL LASER CANNON ▼

DESCRIPTION Charges its main laser cannon to release a highly damaging blast that causes a fanning wave of energy along the ground after impact.

EVASION Boost into the air and move in one direction as the shot charges, then Quick Boost in the opposite direction as it releases.

OVERHEAD PLASMA MISSILE SALVO

DESCRIPTION Release three overhead salvos of high-volume plasma missiles. These missiles function similarly to grenades, falling and impacting the ground almost immediately.

EVASION The homing capacity of the missiles is limited so evading aerially will cause them to miss.

VERTICAL LASER SWEEP ▼

DESCRIPTION Charges its main laser cannon and releases the energy as a vertical sweeping laser; leaves lingering damage fields.

EVASION Quick Boost directly away from the arc of the laser.

LASER SHOTGUN BLAST

DESCRIPTION A high-volume shotgun blast from the unit's auxiliary laser gun; lasers converge as they move toward you.

EVASION Quick Boost to either side of the lasers just before they would impact you.

SPINNING BLADE STRIKE

DESCRIPTION Produces its leg-mounted laser blade and subsequently spinning at an angle and sweeping across the battlefield. It will alter its angle at the end of the sweep to boost back upwards above you.

EVASION Jump into the air and boost above the ORBIT as it passes below you.

After defeating the MIND GAMMA AC, ALLMIND will discard that body in favor of a brand new, larger frame, with entirely different weaponry and attack patterns. Its mobility is significantly improved, to the point of almost instant teleportation at times. It will begin weaving in and out of close quarters, deftly mixing long-range and melee attacks. The most dangerous of these are the two varieties of leg-mounted laser cannon attacks, and the claw strikes from its variable multi-energy unit.

Thankfully, this new frame is no longer equipped with the shield that AC MIND GAMMA had, so you'll be able to deal full damage whenever you hit it. Finding openings still won't be easy, however, due to the two ORBITs that appear to fight alongside ALLMIND. Piloting the powerful AC ECHO, Ayre will boost in and join you for this part of the fight, which can help split the focus of the enemies and allow you to keep your attention on ALLMIND. Unlike the previous phase, though the battle can still be chaotic, focusing solely on ALLMIND is recommended here.

At the beginning of this phase, it's likely that ALLMIND will immediately target you. Allow Ayre to either distract one or both of the ORBIT units or assist with your fight against ALLMIND. Doing that while keeping track of where the ORBITs are—and who they're attacking—can be difficult, but the longer the fight goes on the more you're putting yourself at risk. Once you deplete roughly half of ALLMIND's AP in this phase, Iguazu releases a pulse that doesn't affect you, but silences the voices of all AI in the area, ALLMIND included. This pulse instantly destroys Ayre's AC, as well as any ORBITs that are still active, so by focusing on ALLMIND you can save a lot of ammunition, not to mention AP, that you would have lost in the process of destroying the two support units.

Once ALLMIND fires off its spiral laser it can freely aim it to track your movements.

Watch out for ALLMIND's efforts to get close and attack you within melee range.

ALLMIND (2ND PHASE) ATTACKS

SWEEPING SPIRAL LASER ▼ — PHASE 2

DESCRIPTION The leg-mounted laser cannon charges to produce a highly damaging sweeping beam. This version of the laser lasts less time but covers a wide area.

EVASION Strafe to one side as the beam charges, and Quick Boost to the opposite side as it releases. Boosting into the air is also recommended.

SUSTAINED SPIRAL LASER ▼ — PHASE 2

DESCRIPTION The leg-mounted laser cannon charges to produce a highly damaging beam. ALLMIND remains still for its duration.

EVASION Strafe to one side as the beam charges and Quick Boost to the opposite direction as it releases. Rapidly ascending can also evade this attack.

BOOST SLASH COMBO — PHASE 2

DESCRIPTION Charges its variable-energy blades and unleashes heavy, high-impact strikes. It will boost quickly toward you from the air and strike at a slight downward angle; Can follow up with cross slash.

EVASION Chain Quick Boosts away from ALLMIND or Quick Boost past it if you're close enough.

CROSS SLASH — PHASE 2

DESCRIPTION Brandishes both variable-energy blades and executes a heavy cross slash.

EVASION The attack has limited range, so Quick Boost directly away from ALLMIND.

VARIABLE-ENERGY GATLING GUN — PHASES 2, 3

DESCRIPTION Fires one or both variable multi-energy units.

EVASION Quick Boost away from the direction in which ALLMIND is firing.

CHARGED LASER SHOT — PHASES 2, 3

DESCRIPTION Charged variable multi-energy unit shot that fires without warning and travels quickly.

EVASION At close range, you can Quick Boost to either side of ALLMIND, at long range, react to the laser and move away.

CLAW SLASH — PHASES 2, 3

DESCRIPTION Uses a variable-energy claw for a single quick slash. This is a higher-impact strike than the pulse blade and has a wider swing.

EVASION Quick Boost past ALLMIND if at close range, otherwise Quick Boost away.

QUICK SLASH — PHASES 2, 3

DESCRIPTION ALLMIND will use its blade to slash at you. This is a quick and low-impact slash but can be used in rapid succession with other attacks.

EVASION If ALLMIND uses the attack at close range, Quick Boost past it. Otherwise, Quick Boost away from it.

ALLMIND (PHASE 3)

After reducing ALLMIND's AP to 50% in the second phase, Iguazu completely hijacks control of the ALLMIND body and retains control of it for the remainder of the battle. Iguazu favors the variable-energy claws over the blade, so expect to see more attacks with that weapon in this phase, including many new ones. Staying on the ground during this phase makes you extremely vulnerable to those attacks, so it's advised that you take an aerial position as much as possible, while maintaining a safe distance. EN management will be crucial with this tactic, because dropping down just as Iguazu launches an attack could be devastating. Wait until just after Iguazu has finished an attack and then land before your EN runs out to give yourself a bit of a buffer.

Iguazu will no longer use the leg-mounted laser cannon during this phase. He does gain access to a new and very dangerous ranged attack, however, in the form of a triple energy wave. This can be released after his claw boost sweep, so learning the visual cue for that attack will go a long way to keeping you safe in the air. Unlike the previous phases of this fight, there are no additional units to worry about, which means you can focus all of your attention on Iguazu, making evading and countering attacks much easier. While you remain airborne, the recommended approach is to stay within your effective range and try to pressure Iguazu by playing aggressively to rapidly apply ACS strain. Maintaining this range actually makes it easier to deal with his attacks, because he's capable of moving extremely quickly to cover long distances or to get into range for a melee attack, the speed of which can easily catch you off guard.

Iguazu seizes control of ALLMIND, which disables the ORBITS and Ayre.

Iguazu prefers things to be up close and personal, using a set of brutally powerful and fast variable-energy claws that can hit from a number of angles.

ALLMIND (3RD PHASE) NEW ATTACKS

MIND PULSE — PHASE 3

DESCRIPTION Resonance pulse that acts as an EMP blast. This attack does not affect you, but instead allows Iguazu total control of the ALLMIND body and creates interference with Ayre's connection to her AC, removing her from the fight.

EVASION Not used offensively.

CLAW TWO-HIT COMBO — PHASE 3

DESCRIPTION Two quick claw strikes comprised of a slightly charged uppercut slash followed by a piercing strike.

EVASION Remain on the ground and Quick Boost away from Iguazu for the first strike, then past him for the second strike.

HEAVY CLAW STRIKE — PHASE 3

DESCRIPTION Charge his variable-energy claw to strike with additional impact.

EVASION Quick Boost past Iguazu, who will likely move past you while striking.

HEAVY FOUR-HIT CLAW COMBO — PHASE 3

DESCRIPTION Two quick slashes followed by a jump into the air for two heavy strikes.

EVASION Quick Boost directly away from Iguazu to evade the two quick strikes, then underneath him while he's in the air for the first heavy strike, and finally away again to evade the final hit.

CLAW BOOST THRUST — PHASE 3

DESCRIPTION Charges the claw, before rapidly boosting toward you along the ground with a heavy piercing strike.

EVASION Quickly boost into the air.

CLAW BOOST SWEEP — PHASE 3

DESCRIPTION Iguazu will position himself away from you and boost in a large arc with his claw charged. He'll then slash the claw through the air and release an energy wave from each prong of the claw.

EVASION Create distance from Iguazu so that his slash misses you, and then jump between the energy waves as they fan outward.

CHAPTER 4 ENEMY ANALYSIS

Each faction battling for control of Rubicon builds their own armies of factory-manufactured mechs to aid in their search for Coral. Due to the intensity of the arms race you find yourself in, powerful weapon platforms are in high demand, and the threats you'll face will only escalate as corporations battle to gain a foothold on the planet. This chapter will analyze each of these threats and detail their vulnerabilities, allowing a skilled pilot to reduce even the deadliest of them to smoking piles of scrap.

USING THIS CHAPTER

This chapter covers all of the standard enemy types in the game. Since many bosses are inseparable from the missions they appear in, you'll find them all covered as part of the Mission Intel chapter. Arena battles against ACs are covered in the Arena Guide chapter, starting on P.346, and many ACs also appear as featured enemies in missions, which means that additional strategies for fighting them are provided throughout the Mission Intel chapter.

The overall format used for entries in this chapter is very straightforward, but there are some details that are worth explaining here to ensure that all elements are clearly understandable.

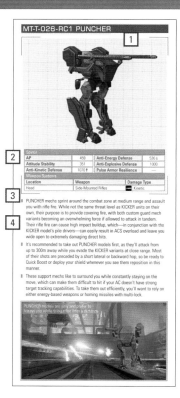

1 Enemy Name/Model

This tells you the enemy's name and specific model, which is usually denoted by their primary weapon type, and appears in parenthesis after the name.

2 Specs

This chart shows the enemy's basic specs, including their total AP, attitude stability, and defense ratings. Enemies often share specs with other models of their type, and in these cases, the chart will only appear once, near the enemy group's description. Enemies using pulse armor (that can be canceled with attacks) will also have this barrier's durability listed here. The defensive specs of enemies function similarly to those of your own AC: 1000 serves as the baseline, with higher values indicating resistance to that damage type and lower values indicating vulnerability

3 Weapon Systems

This small chart lists all of the weaponry the enemy can wield, and tells you exactly where on their frame each weapon is located, which can make identifying them easier during battle. Each weapon's damage type is also listed, so you can easily discern their level of threat to your current build.

4 Enemy Intel

For each enemy model, we've provided some information that's useful to know when tackling them. This text analyzes their capabilities and aspects of their behavior to ensure that you know exactly what you're dealing with in each case.

ENEMY BEHAVIOR

In their passive state before entering combat, enemies can exhibit a few possible behaviors. Stationary enemies such as artillery,, as well as some mobile units, will simply maintain one position indefinitely. Other mobile enemies patrol a prescribed route, which they will not deviate from unless provoked. Regardless of this behavior, it's rare to find entirely isolated enemies; the corporate and native enemy forces find their strength in their numbers and organization.

Detection

Combat usually is preceded by enemies being alerted to your presence, either through direct line of sight or by noise you make. Their visual detection range can vary, but for most enemies you can assume they'll detect you from around 450m

when approached from the front. Enemies that spot you via line of sight will immediately stop their passive routines and open fire. Sound detection is slightly more technical; enemies will leave their post or patrol route to approach the source of the noise (such as a gunshot, footsteps, or bullet impact) in an attempt to locate the perpetrator. At this point, they'll either detect you via line of sight, or if they fail to find anything anomalous, will simply return to their original position or patrol route.

Surprise Attacks

If you manage to move into lock-on range without being detected by an enemy, it will be marked as "unaware" on your HUD. The first attack that connects against an unaware target deals an additional 20% impact, so it's worth taking the time to line up your highest impact weapon to take advantage of this bonus. This can even combo with the impact bonus from attacking during an Assault Boost, should you manage to surprise an enemy in this way. Only the first hit you land will benefit from the impact bonus, though; in the case of something like a shotgun blast, any projectiles that connect at the same time receive the impact bonus. Getting a head start on straining an enemy's ACS is a major advantage at the beginning of a fight, so flanking around opponents and hitting them with a surprise attack is a tactic you should employ whenever possible. Retreating to an undetectable position can even cause enemies to lose track of you completely, putting them back into the unaware state.

Combat Ranges

Much like your own approach to combat—as defined in the System Guide chapter on P.20—enemy actions can be categorized as "close-range," "medium-range," and "long-range" combat routines. Simpler enemies tend to only be effective within a single combat range, whereas complex enemies will often exhibit varied behaviors based on their distance to you. A massive component of engaging with targets is knowing how a particular enemy will behave within each combat range, and more importantly, which ranges are its most and least effective. Units such as artillery and rifle-wielding LCs are superior at combat over long ranges, and can often attack before you even see them on the horizon. Conversely, these same enemies will recognize their disadvantage and, if possible, reposition if you engage them at close range. Many enemy types display similar patterns based on ranges; keep this in mind when engaging hostiles to ensure the quickest fight possible.

Target Tracking

Enemies wielding grenade cannons, rifles, and other non-homing projectile weaponry will frequently track your movements and lead their shots, firing slightly ahead of your position with an estimation based on your speed and trajectory. For this reason, it's important to consider your movement in combat and avoid moving in straight lines or predictable patterns for too long. Switching directions with a Quick Boost just before an enemy opens fire is key to fooling their target tracking systems.

ENEMY SPECS

When looking at an enemy's specs, keep in mind that each particular model shares the same AP, attitude stability, and defense ratings across every mission where it can be encountered. This means that enemy types, like BAWS bipedal MTs, won't become stronger as you progress. The lack of scaling is sometimes compensated for by weaker enemies appearing in larger groups during later missions, and tougher enemy types being deployed more frequently.

BOSSES & ACS

SPOILER ALERT: To the right, you'll find lists of all ACs and bosses, including page references for in-depth information and strategies on each encounter. If you haven't completed a playthrough of the game yet, be aware that these lists contain major potential spoilers.

AC

AC Name	Pilot Name	Mission Ref.	Arena Ref.
MAD STOMP	"Invincible" Rummy	P.141	P.351
BURN PICKAXE	Index Dunham	P.113	P.352
HERMIT	G6 Red	P.296	P.353
BITTER PROMISE	Nosaac	P.142	P.354
INFECTION	V.VI Maeterlinck	P.228	P.355
YUE YU	Little Ziyi	P.127	P.356
GUIDANCE	V.VII Swinburne	P.168	P.357
LI LONG	G3 Wu Huahai	P.229	P.358
CANDLE RING	Ring Freddie	P.184	P.359
RECONFIG	V.V Hawkins	P.223	P.360
HEAD BRINGER	G5 Iguazu	P.210 / 260 / 293	P.361
SHINOBI	Rokumonsen	P.169	P.362
CANNON HEAD	G4 Volta	P.261	P.363
DUAL NATURE	V.VIII Pater	P.222	P.364
ENTANGLE	Sulla	P.135	P.365
CIRCUS	"Chatty" Stick	P.244	P.366
TSUBASA	Middle Flatwell	P.277	P.367
BARREN FLOWER	V.III O'Keeffe	P.290	P.368
FULL COURSE	"Cinder" Carla	P.244	P.369
DEADSLED	Coldcall	P.275	P.370
STEEL HAZE	V.IV Rusty	P.225	P.371
MILK TOOTH	"Honest" Brute	P.197	P.372
DEEP DOWN	G2 Nile	P.265	P.373
OPEN FAITH	V.II Snail	P.243	P.374
UMBER OX	Chartreuse	P.272	P.375
ASTGHIK	Thumb Dolmayan	P.285	P.376
ASTER CROWN	King	P.272	P.377
LIGER TAIL	G1 Michigan	P.220	P.378
LOCKSMITH	V.I Freud	P.240	P.379
MIND ALPHA	Integration Subject 51-001 K	—	P.380
TRAINER	Analysis Subject 51-011 AL	—	P.381
TESTER	Analysis Subject 51-012 AL	P.109	P.382
MIND BETA	Integration Subject 51-002 K	—	P.383
CORPORATION	Analysis Subject 51-013 BE	—	P.384
RUBICONIAN	Analysis Subject 51-014 BE	—	P.385
MIND GAMMA	Integration Subject 51-003 K	—	P.386
INSTITUTE	Analysis Subject 51-015 GA	—	P.387
NIGHTFALL	Raven / Analysis Subject 51-016 GA	P.199 / 273	P.388
STEEL HAZE ORTUS	Rusty / Classified Subject 51-101 R	P.249	P.389
IB-C03: HAL 826	Handler Walter / Classified Subject 51-201 W	P.258	P.390
ECHO	Ayre / Classified Subject ------ -	P.255	P.391

BOSSES

Name	Mission Reference
AH12: HC HELICOPTER	P.101
EB-0309 STRIDER	P.117
HA-T-102 JUGGERNAUT	P.122
AAP07: BALTEUS	P.136
EC-0804 SMART CLEANER	P.144 / 252
IA-13: SEA SPIDER	P.152
AAS03: EKDROMOI (Energy Pile Bunker)	P.163
AAS03: EKDROMOI (Dual Machine Gun)	P.282
AAS03: EKDROMOI (Plasma Gun)	P.163 / 282
AH12: HC HELICOPTER (Enforcement Scout)	P.178
AAS02: CATAPHRACT	P.187 / 282
IA-02: ICE WORM	P.203
IA-02: ICE WORM (Drone Unit)	P.204
AB08: NEPENTHES	P.207
AAP03: ENFORCER	P.212
IB-01: CEL 240	P.230
AAP07A: ARQUEBUS BALTEUS	P.253
IB-07: SOL 644 / Ayre	P.255
ALLMIND (1st Phase)	P.300
ALLMIND (Melee Drone AC)	P.301
ALLMIND (Support Drone AC)	P.300
ALLMIND (2nd Phase)	P.302

GENERIC WEAPONRY

Generic weaponry encompasses various classes of slow, fragile enemies typically used to support primary MT forces in combat. These foes are among the most common types of military hardware you'll encounter, often as the enemy's vanguard on the battlefield. While not individually threatening to an AC when compared to more advanced crafts and weapon systems, they have strength in numbers and can swarm you if you're careless.

AERIAL DEFENSE DRONES

These small, single-rotor aerial drones are not built for intense combat. They are unmanned and usually found in groups of four or more drones patrolling small areas or hovering on standby, waiting to support larger units. Aerial defense drones are extremely fragile and will go down quickly; a well-orchestrated multi-lock missile swarm is especially effective against them.

Specs	
AP	40
Attitude Stability	—
Anti-Kinetic Defense	1070 ↑
Anti-Energy Defense	536 ↓
Anti-Explosive Defense	1000
Pulse Armor Resilience	—

CD-E-086 (MINI GATLING GUN)

Weapon Systems		
Location	Weapon	Damage Type
Undercarriage	Mini Gatling Gun	Kinetic

▌ Aerial defense drones tend to zip around once they've targeted you, in an attempt to disorient you. They'll need to come to a stop before firing their gatling gun, however.

▌ Aerial defense drones lose effectiveness at mid range, with their shots ricocheting at roughly 150m and targeting system reaching its limit around 200m. Picking them off at any range beyond that will ensure a safe way to dispatch large groups.

CD-E-086 (SELF-DESTRUCTING)

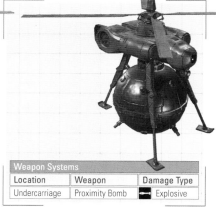

Weapon Systems		
Location	Weapon	Damage Type
Undercarriage	Proximity Bomb	Explosive

Self-destructing drones will overwhelm you if you encounter a large number of them in the ECM fog. Be careful to not alert too many at a time.

▌ This uncommon model of aerial defense drone carries a powerful explosive payload and operates as a mobile mine, destroying itself to eliminate intruders. Self-destructing drones remain immobile until a target is acquired and will fly directly at you before blowing up, inflicting severe damage and ACS strain; getting caught off guard by multiple blasts in quick succession will usually be enough to overload the ACS of most builds.

▌ These drones blink red and emit high-pitched beeping as they make their approach, so back away accordingly. Deal with them from a distance before they notice you, as they can lock on from about 250m away. Scanning can help you spot them and safely eliminate them.

▌ ECM fog accompanies these drones in the "Survey the Uninhabited Floating City" mission, scrambling your compass. The fog also reduces your lock-on range by roughly 50%, so if detected, you'll have to shoot them out of the sky as they make their approach, get behind cover, or use a well-timed Quick Boost at the last second to evade them.

ATTACK HELICOPTERS

Equipped with more conventional armaments than aerial defense drones, these assault crafts are primarily built for close-range combat and cannot take many hits from AC weaponry. They appear in groups of four or five, and are easy targets for multi-lock missiles at long range. Attack helicopters are fragile enough that simply flying into them, even at low speeds, will send them spiraling to the ground, saving you some ammo in the process.

Specs	
AP	28
Attitude Stability	—
Anti-Kinetic Defense	1070 ↑
Anti-Energy Defense	536 ↓
Anti-Explosive Defense	1000
Pulse Armor Resilience	—

CH-T-025 (ANTI-TANK CANNON)

Weapon Systems

Location	Weapon	Damage Type
Undercarriage	Anti-Tank Cannon	▰ Kinetic
Nose	Machine Gun	▰ Kinetic

▮ The machine gun outfitted on these helicopters is exclusively used at close range, with the rounds it fires losing all power beyond 95m. Within that range, however, groups of them can inflict a surprising amount of damage.

▮ Attack helicopters can also fire relatively weak shells from their anti-tank cannons at close range, which remain effective up to a distance of 160m. Moving beyond this point will cause them to cease firing entirely.

CH-T-025 (LASER GUN)

Weapon Systems

Location	Weapon	Damage Type
Undercarriage	Laser Gun	▰ Energy

▮ Exclusive to the "Attack the Old Spaceport" mission, this special model appears in a squadron of five helicopters and rapidly fires energy shots from its laser gun. Its damage output is similar to the more common kinetic counterpart, but the removal of the anti-tank cannon makes this rare variant exclusively suited for close-range assaults. These choppers will attempt to fire upon you from up to 170m, but their laser guns won't inflict any damage until you're within their 95m effective range.

Given their ability to fire two weapons simultaneously when within their effective range, groups of these helicopters should be dispatched quickly.

Attack helicopters equipped with laser guns lack the secondary armament of the standard model, but compensate for it with an improved rate of fire.

Attack helicopters can congregate in groups of four or five. Weapons that support the multi-lock functionality make quick work of these squads.

Due to their weapons being installed on their underside, attacking from above is an excellent way to deal with these enemies, as this prevents them from firing at you.

The small size of attack helicopters relative to your AC can make them difficult to spot in certain environments, so highlighting them with your scanner can help.

BAWS GUARD MECHS

Mass-produced by BAWS in their arsenal facilities and sold to various factions waging war on Rubicon, these rudimentary bipedal mechs offer only the most basic combat capabilities. Incapable of swift movement or engaging in aerial combat, guard mechs are strictly ground-based support units. They can come equipped with every type of common weaponry, making them versatile defensive troops. Often found patrolling in pairs, these foes can be easily dispatched from any range, but are particularly vulnerable at longer distances.

Specs	
AP	102
Attitude Stability	121
Anti-Kinetic Defense	1070 ↑
Anti-Energy Defense	536 ↓
Anti-Explosive Defense	1000
Pulse Armor Resilience	—

MT-T-026 (RIFLE)

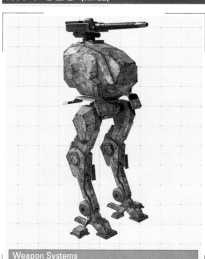

Weapon Systems		
Location	Weapon	Damage Type
Head	Rifle	▬ Kinetic

- Firing in bursts of two or three rounds, the head-mounted rifle equipped on these mechs deals modest damage from close range, and stops being effective at roughly 120m

- The primary threat these guard mech models pose is their tendency to appear in large numbers, working together to keep your ACS from cooling down, and giving their stronger allies the opportunity to slowly build up strain until they can overload you.

Rifle guard mechs can pose a marginal threat if they catch you off guard at close range, but are fragile enough that a single melee strike or Boost Kick will instantly take them out of action.

MT-T-026 (LASER GUN)

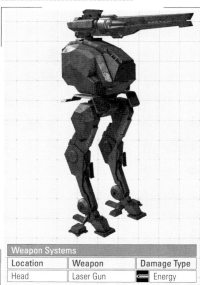

Weapon Systems		
Location	Weapon	Damage Type
Head	Laser Gun	▬ Energy

- Guard mechs outfitted with laser guns focus on dealing energy damage, but are otherwise functionally identical to the rifle-wielding variant. Their laser guns have greater attack power than the standard model's kinetic rounds, but with lower impact, which makes them less likely to overload your ACS.

- Despite the greater range typically with lasers, this model's effective range remains the same at roughly 120m, meaning you can safely deal with them from medium or long ranges.

Like their kinetic counterparts, laser gun guard mechs won't be a threat if you keep some distance since their shots will ricochet and lose all effectiveness.

MT-T-026 (MISSILE LAUNCHER)

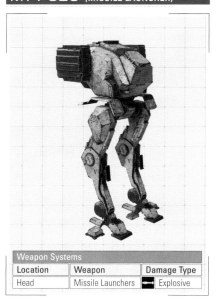

Weapon Systems		
Location	Weapon	Damage Type
Head	Missile Launchers	▬ Explosive

- This model of guard mech focuses on improved performance when fighting at range. Equipped with twin missile launchers and tasked with defending key choke points or locations, missile guard mechs fire two missiles at a time as their only form of offensive engagement. As long as you're inside their detection range, these variants pose a threat on the battlefield.

- Their missiles can deal substantial AP damage as well as high impact that puts a lot of strain on your ACS, potentially leaving you in a compromised position if they're allowed to continue attacking while you deal with other threats. Due to their ranged capabilities, missile guard mechs should be considered higher priority targets than the other models.

Unlike other BAWS guard mechs, the missile launcher variant remains a threat even at long range.

CUSTOM GUARD MECHS

Custom RaD designs purchased on the black market by rival Dosers, these souped-up guard mechs are in no way comparable to the disposable commercially produced models. They're surprisingly mobile and capable combat units, even warranting the use of Target Assist to help keep up with their dizzying movement patterns. As the Junker Coyotes' surprise attack force, the aptly named PUNCHER and KICKER MTs are exclusively fought during the "Eliminate the Doser Faction" mission.

MT-T-026-RC1 PUNCHER

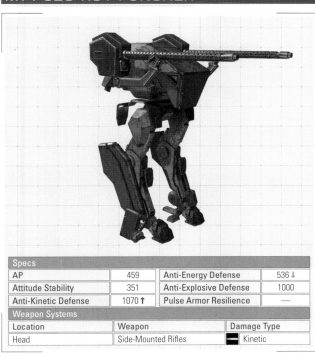

Specs			
AP	459	Anti-Energy Defense	536 ↓
Attitude Stability	351	Anti-Explosive Defense	1000
Anti-Kinetic Defense	1070 ↑	Pulse Armor Resilience	—

Weapon Systems		
Location	Weapon	Damage Type
Head	Side-Mounted Rifles	▮ Kinetic

▮ PUNCHER mechs sprint around the combat zone at medium range and assault you with rifle fire. While not the same threat level as KICKER units on their own, their purpose is to provide covering fire, with both custom guard mech variants becoming an overwhelming force if allowed to attack in tandem. Their rifle fire can cause high impact buildup, which—in conjunction with the KICKER model's pile drivers—can easily result in ACS overload and leave you wide open to extremely damaging direct hits.

▮ It's recommended to take out PUNCHER models first, as they'll attack from up to 300m away while you evade the KICKER variants at close range. Most of their shots are preceded by a short lateral or backward hop, so be ready to Quick Boost or deploy your shield whenever you see them reposition in this manner.

▮ These support mechs like to surround you while constantly staying on the move, which can make them difficult to hit if your AC doesn't have strong target tracking capabilities. To take them out efficiently, you'll want to rely on either energy-based weapons or homing missiles with multi-lock.

PUNCHER models are wily and prefer to harass you while firing rifles from a distance.

MT-T-026-RC2 KICKER

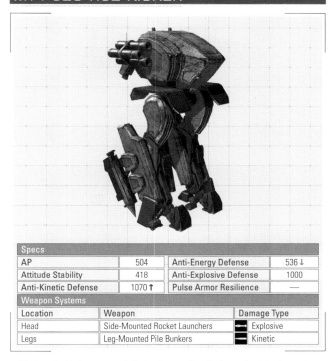

Specs			
AP	504	Anti-Energy Defense	536 ↓
Attitude Stability	418	Anti-Explosive Defense	1000
Anti-Kinetic Defense	1070 ↑	Pulse Armor Resilience	—

Weapon Systems		
Location	Weapon	Damage Type
Head	Side-Mounted Rocket Launchers	▮ Explosive
Legs	Leg-Mounted Pile Bunkers	▮ Kinetic

▮ Equipped with leg-mounted pile bunkers and explosive rocket launchers, the KICKER models are all about dishing out damage with melee attacks and over-whelming your ACS. Their primary combat routine is to get within 100m while firing rockets before hitting you with a powerful lunging kick.

▮ KICKER variants are also able to leap high into the air and perform a long-range diving kick from up to 250m away, so it's important to keep track of them to avoid getting blindsided. Their enhanced kicks have extremely high attack power and impact, which means they can quickly stagger you and leave you vulnerable to follow-up direct hits. Staying airborne is the best way to remove the threat posed by custom guard mechs, as both the KICKER and PUNCHER models struggle to fight back when you shift to aerial combat. They're likely to cluster tightly together while attempting to chase you, so blasting them with plasma rifles or plasma missile launchers can quickly thin the herd.

Avoid staying on the ground whenever possible, since the KICKER units can use their pile-bunker dive kicks from surprising distances.

QUAD DRONES

Autonomous aerial combat and support units capable of filling multiple roles on the battlefield, the versatile quad drones are significantly bigger and more robust than aerial defense drones or attack helicopters. Their distinct quad-rotor design increases load capacity, making it possible to outfit them with heavier weaponry or hangars used to transport MT troops into combat zones. Their range of movement can often be greater than other generic aerial weaponry, though quad drones appear in smaller groups.

Specs	
AP	302
Attitude Stability	310
Anti-Kinetic Defense	790 ↓
Anti-Energy Defense	1135 ↑
Anti-Explosive Defense	1000
Pulse Armor Resilience	Unlimited*

*Pulse protection model only

CD-J-098 (CLUSTER MISSILE LAUNCHER)

Weapon Systems		
Location	Weapon	Damage Type
Undercarriage	Cluster Missile Launcher	■ Explosive

▌ These quad drones fire a cluster missile that sheds more explosives along its flight path, leaving a large trail of explosions. They are most effective from medium- to long-range, as their missiles won't splinter when too close—once you're within 175m of these drones, they'll stop firing entirely.

▌ If you're outside of the 175m range, these missiles have exceptional tracking capabilities, even tracking above you if you take flight. Cluster missiles pick up speed after they're launched, making their path somewhat hard to gauge.

▌ Quad drones try to maintain distance by slowly fleeing until they regain a position from which they can fire their missiles. Your safest option for evading these missiles is to time a Quick Boost to the left or right as they approach you, or Assault Boost toward the quad drones to remove their range advantage. This can be followed up by a Boost Kick to instantly destroy them.

CD-J-098 (LASER CANNON)

Weapon Systems		
Location	Weapon	Damage Type
Undercarriage	Laser Cannon	■ Energy

▌ This variant fires a high-power energy beam in single shots, operating as a sniper. Their laser will significantly lower your AP if it hits you, but will deal little impact. Using a pulse shield can help you to safely get close enough to destroy these long-range threats.

▌ Effective at all distances, laser cannon drones will begin charging a shot the moment you enter their detection range of 450m. AC builds with high anti-energy defense can mitigate how dangerous they are at extremely long ranges, but expect their laser cannons to always be potent within 300m.

▌ Their laser shots are telegraphed by alert indicators, but can be difficult to evade due to how fast the beam travels. Agile ACs can reliably dodge these lasers by waiting a split second after the alert indicator finishes flashing before using a lateral Quick Boost.

CD-J-098 (TRANSPORT HANGAR)

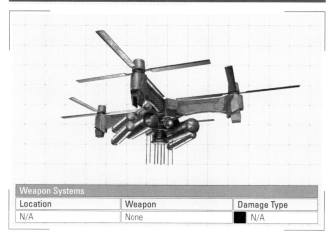

Weapon Systems		
Location	Weapon	Damage Type
N/A	None	■ N/A

▌ A non-combat quad drone model capable of transporting individual MT units to a battlefield. Destroying these drones before they can complete their mission also destroys the MT that's being carried. MT transport drones will always retreat once their delivery is complete.

▌ They often enter the combat zone slowly from high above, stopping for a brief period to deploy MTs close to the ground. Transport drones approaching from a low altitude are able to airdrop the MTs mid-flight without stopping.

CD-J-098 (PULSE PROTECTION)

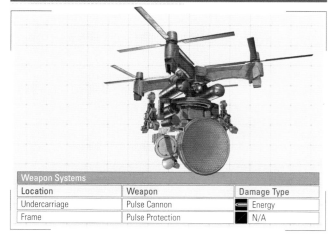

Weapon Systems		
Location	Weapon	Damage Type
Undercarriage	Pulse Cannon	■ Energy
Frame	Pulse Protection	■ N/A

▌ Hovering in place, these defensive quad drones project an invincible spherical pulse protection barrier around them, shielding any enemies within a 110m radius of the barrier from attacks.

▌ The only way to disable this barrier is to enter its radius, which causes the quad drone to retract it in favor of defending itself with its pulse cannon. Rushing in and taking out these support drones should always be your top priority, as they will otherwise hinder your efforts.

CV-T-020 COMBAT VEHICLE

Slow-moving, ground combat vehicles frequently deployed by the RLF. Although they have limited combat abilities, they're often encountered as a first line of defense protecting vital structures and choke points.

- These combat vehicles fire a single, non-homing shell at a time, and while capable of movement, they'll only travel small distances to reorient themselves.

- Their shells are able to deal damage over longer ranges; however, they'll lose velocity and begin to drop off at around 300m, making them less likely to hit. From this distance, the vehicles also stop firing, and will slowly move to re-enter their combat range.

Stay out of the CV-T-020's line of fire and be evasive as you approach it. Its weaknesses are its lack of mobility and easily avoidable shots.

Specs			
AP	73	Anti-Energy Defense	536 ↓
Attitude Stability	—	Anti-Explosive Defense	1000
Anti-Kinetic Defense	1070 ↑	Pulse Armor Resilience	—

Weapon Systems		
Location	Weapon	Damage Type
Overhead	Anti-Tank Gun	▮ Kinetic

PCA REPAIR MECHS

Bug-like mechs purpose-built for repair and maintenance of underground facilities. Though not threatening on their own—and occasionally passive—wherever you find REPAIRER mechs, PCA personnel are likely also not far. Often encountered clinging to walls or ceilings, they'll sometimes drop down and ambush you. Repair mechs appear in large groups, but passive worker types are frequently accompanied by hostile guard models, and are best picked off one by one.

Specs	
AP	51
Attitude Stability	—
Anti-Kinetic Defense	1070 ↑
Anti-Energy Defense	536 ↓
Anti-Explosive Defense	1000
Pulse Armor Resilience	—

AM01: REPAIRER (WORKER TYPE)

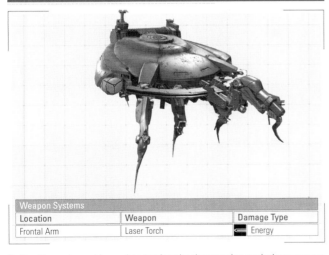

Weapon Systems		
Location	Weapon	Damage Type
Frontal Arm	Laser Torch	◣ Energy

- Usually passive and focused on repair tasks, these worker mechs become more aggressive the further down you descend into the Depths. They're able to jump and chase you over short distances, and once they catch up to you, they'll attack at close range with their laser torch. Even when aggressive, they approach very slowly and only attack within a range of 20m, which is among the shortest attack ranges of any enemy you'll encounter.

- Worker repair mechs are easily evaded and their attacks deal insignificant damage. Their laser torch can take you by surprise if you're busy fighting other enemies, but it still won't pose any real threat to an AC.

AM01: REPAIRER (GUARD TYPE)

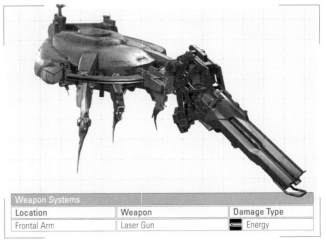

Weapon Systems		
Location	Weapon	Damage Type
Frontal Arm	Laser Gun	◣ Energy

- These more offense-oriented guard models come armed with a rifle, and are capable of firing in three-shot bursts at ranges of up to 310m. Their shots deal only light energy damage to your AP and insignificant impact.

- Their slow movement speed means that even if they crawl toward you, they cannot hope to keep up with an AC's movement and are easily outmaneuvered.

AM01: REPAIRER (STUN SMOG)

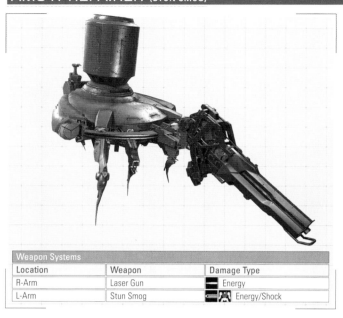

- The electric coil mounted on top of this special variant allows them to generate a persistent stun smog field within a 70m radius surrounding their bodies, capable of inflicting shock buildup that quickly results in electrical discharge.

- Stun smog fields can overlap, multiplying their effectiveness and making them a legitimate threat, especially since these repair mechs often cling to ceilings in large groups waiting to ambush you. It's best to always destroy them before you get stuck in their smog, but equipping a head part with a high System Recovery spec can reduce the risk of electrical discharge.

Multiple repair mechs releasing overlapping stun smog clouds at once can be surprisingly dangerous. Act swiftly if they catch you off guard.

Weapon Systems

Location	Weapon	Damage Type
R-Arm	Laser Gun	▬ Energy
L-Arm	Stun Smog	⬛🔲 Energy/Shock

TH-E-012 TRANSPORT HELICOPTER

These huge four-rotor helicopters are capable of transporting cargo that the smaller quad drones are unable to hoist. The nature of your assignments means you'll often encounter these helicopters in the process of being loaded, refueled or repaired.

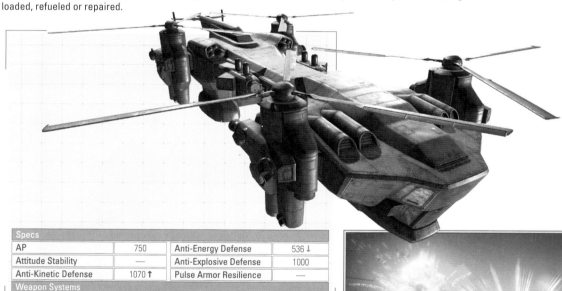

Specs

AP	750	Anti-Energy Defense	536 ↓
Attitude Stability	—	Anti-Explosive Defense	1000
Anti-Kinetic Defense	1070 ↑	Pulse Armor Resilience	—

Weapon Systems

Location	Weapon	Damage Type
N/A	None	⬛ N/A

- Transport helicopters are non-combat aerial units, typically used to transport four MTs at a time. These helicopters are often used for extraction, and will be encountered carrying mission-critical cargo. Be careful of those that transport Coral in the "Coral Export Denial" mission, as the volatile substance can cause large explosions when the helicopters are destroyed.

- Much like the transport quad drones, destroying these vehicles will immediately destroy any cargo they're carrying, MTs included. This means they should be considered high priority targets whenever you spot them entering an area.

Destroy transport helicopters before they can drop off their cargo to take out any MTs they might be carrying.

LIGHT MTS

Mass-produced main combat units, these enemies are much more modular than generic weaponry. Light MTs are capable of wielding a variety of weapons and can equip shields for defensive assignments without giving up mobility. As primary infantry units, they'll often work in squads with allied MTs. Their multi-purpose design has led to many factions operating on Rubicon building their own custom light MT forces.

BAWS BIPEDAL MTS

Specs	
AP	470
Attitude Stability	364
Anti-Kinetic Defense	1070 ↑
Anti-Energy Defense	536 ↓
Anti-Explosive Defense	1000
Pulse Armor Resilience	—

Abundant on the battlefield, bipedal MTs are widely used across Rubicon, coming equipped with either kinetic or explosive weaponry. They'll often remain grounded, but are capable of short boosts and can jump to reach elevated positions. While their armor is thicker than that of generic weaponry, it proves to be no match for an AC's weaponry, meaning that your shots are far less likely to ricochet even at range. Bipedal MTs are also susceptible to energy weaponry, taking significantly more damage than from other sources.

MT-E-104 (MACHINE GUN)

Weapon Systems		
Location	Weapon	Damage Type
R-Arm	Machine Gun	Kinetic
L-Arm (Optional)	Shield	N/A

▌ These are the most generic of bipedal MTs, featuring all of their type's general characteristics, such as slowly walking or boosting around. They employ their single machine guns at medium- to close-range to deal kinetic damage, and can boost within 25m of you while shooting, but they'll quickly retreat before attacking again.

▌ At close range, most of their machine gun shots will hit you, and sustained fire will cause substantial ACS strain. Their impact falls off significantly at medium range, where they'll struggle to hit you if you remain mobile. Despite their most effective range being inside 100m, these MTs will typically boost away from you, maintaining a fighting distance of 100-150m.

▌ If multiple machine gun bipedal MTs are encountered at once, it's best to take to the air. They lack aerial combat capability, and you'll find it easier to maintain the range needed to avoid their machine gun fire.

The inaccuracy of machine gun-wielding MTs means that they don't pose much of a threat from a distance.

ARMORED SHIELDS

Bipedal MTs equipped with either a machine gun, rifle, or shotgun are sometimes outfitted with a shield that mitigates direct frontal damage. The most efficient way to deal with shields is to destroy them using melee weaponry, but staggering the MT is another option. This will occur when you deal enough impact to its shield, and will open it up to direct hits.

It's also possible to attack a shielded MT from above or behind, though there's no guarantee that you'll be able to eliminate it before it can turn around, especially if you're trying to fend off multiple MTs at once. If you avoid detection, surprise attacks against unaware shielded MTs can allow you to dispatch them before they can raise their defenses.

Breaking a bipedal MT's shield will trigger an ACS overload and give you a clear opportunity to take it out. After recovering, shielded variants will behave like standard MTs and can be dispatched in the same manner.

MT-E-104 (DUAL MACHINE GUN)

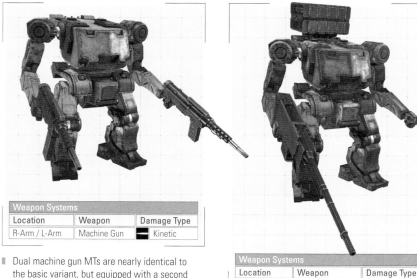

Weapon Systems		
Location	Weapon	Damage Type
R-Arm / L-Arm	Machine Gun	▉ Kinetic

▌ Dual machine gun MTs are nearly identical to the basic variant, but equipped with a second machine gun for increased firepower. These MTs are more likely to boost around the battlefield at close range, where they're a slightly greater threat than their single machine gun-wielding counterparts.

▌ The augmented firepower of dual machine gun MTs can rapidly cause high ACS strain, overloading your systems and opening you up to even greater potential damage. These enemies are capable of continuous machine gun fire, and will begin to engage targets from 360m. They're best taken care of before entering this range if possible, but they'll remain relatively ineffective until you get within 100m of them.

▌ Much like the basic model, the spread of this MT's weaponry is its most glaring weakness. Mobility and aerial combat will again prove to be the best countermeasures.

Dual machine gun light MTs will boost toward you in combat to maintain their most effective range.

This MT will never alternate its weapons when firing, so both of its machine guns will need to reload at once.

MT-E-104 (MISSILE LAUNCHER)

Weapon Systems		
Location	Weapon	Damage Type
R-Arm	Rifle	▉ Kinetic
Back	Missile Launcher	▉ Explosive

▌ While sharing similarities with machine gun MTs, this model's back-mounted missile launcher makes them a greater threat. These MTs prefer to operate at medium range, where they will alternate between shooting their rifles and launching missiles. They can move while firing their rifles, but will try to gain some distance to deal more damage with their missiles.

▌ Missile launcher MTs only boost to maintain appropriate combat distance, and won't do so to evade attacks.

▌ At longer ranges, missile launcher MTs will rely solely on their missiles and will boost toward you until they get back within their rifle's ideal range.

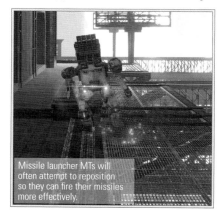

Missile launcher MTs will often attempt to reposition so they can fire their missiles more effectively.

Using Quick Boosts is a great way to evade a bipedal MT's incoming missiles at close proximity.

MT-E-104 (GRENADE CANNON)

Weapon Systems		
Location	Weapon	Damage Type
R-Arm	Machine Gun	▉ Kinetic
Back	Grenade Cannon	▉ Explosive

▌ Due to its back-mounted grenade cannon, this model presents the greatest long-range threat among bipedal MTs. Much like an artillery unit, grenade cannon MTs can lock onto you before you even notice they're on the battlefield. You'll often be alerted by your systems as one of these MTs primes a grenade, well before you've managed to spot them.

▌ These MTs use predictive fire when launching their grenades, so be ready to take evasive action once a grenade is let loose. Their grenades are most easily evaded by approaching the MT directly, and using a lateral Quick Boost or juking mid Assault Boost once they fire.

▌ Once you get within 160m, these artillery-like MTs will begin alternating between firing their machine guns and grenade cannons. While their machine guns are capable of sustained fire, their accuracy is poor, and most shots will miss from outside close range.

▌ The grenade cannon MTs' machine guns are only a major threat if your ACS strain is high. If they manage to overload you, they will take full advantage and switch to their grenade cannons for direct damage.

Grenade cannon light MTs are highly dangerous at long range, so take them out quickly.

MT-E-104 (SHOTGUN)

Weapon Systems		
Location	Weapon	Damage Type
R-Arm	Shotgun	Kinetic
L-Arm	Shield	N/A

▍ A close-range variant of bipedal MT, shotgun MTs will steadily advance with shield and kinetic shotgun in hand, firing broad shots that can deal high impact from up close.

▍ Shotgun MTs can perform a gap-closing boost immediately followed by a shotgun blast from 120m away or more. Their weapon's spread causes shotgun-wielding MTs to lose effectiveness from a distance, and their shots will barely graze you from 250m or more.

▍ Inflicting ACS overload on a shotgun bipedal MT will cause them to lower their shield, leaving them defenseless. Using a melee attack to break the shield is another option that leads to the same result. They'll still be a threat once they recover, so prioritize dispatching them quickly when they're vulnerable.

Shotguns won't pose much of a threat from a distance; their bullets will spread out considerably and only some will graze your AC.

MT-E-104 (HAND ROCKET LAUNCHER)

Weapon Systems		
Location	Weapon	Damage Type
R-Arm	Machine Gun / Rifle	Kinetic
L-Arm	Hand Rocket Launcher	Explosive

▍ Bipedal MTs that are equipped with rocket launchers and either a machine gun or rifle in their right hand. Their rockets allow them to deal potent explosive damage and can quickly strain your ACS gauge. These MTs will use suppressive fire from their right hand weapon while reloading their hand rocket launcher.

▍ Their rockets are telegraphed by an AC system alert, which is your cue to Quick Boost. You can visually identify when they're preparing to fire, as they ready their launcher at a clear upward angle.

▍ These MTs' rockets have no homing properties, and instead rely on predictive fire to follow your trajectory in a straight line. If a rocket hits you, the MTs may use the opportunity to perform a short boost toward you to deal additional damage with their machine guns or rifles. The rifle variant is also capable of performing a jumping rocket launcher shot, increasing the effectiveness of the explosive shell.

▍ Rockets, like grenades, are capable of hitting from long distances. These projectiles are easy to sidestep or boost around, however, which reduces their threat when at range. Rifle variants tend to be more dangerous from a distance, but are still easily picked off unless encountered in large groups.

If a rocket launcher light MT fires a shell from the air, it has a greater chance to hit the ground around you and cause splash damage.

MT-E-104 (CLUSTER GUN)

Weapon Systems		
Location	Weapon	Damage Type
R-Arm	Rifle	Kinetic
L-Arm	Cluster Gun	Explosive

▍ These variants approach slowly and use a combination of rifle and cluster gun to deal both kinetic and explosive damage. These bipedal MTs will primarily focus on their rifle fire, launching cluster grenades only sparingly.

▍ While their rifles feature moderate attack power, they can't match the firing rate of the machine gun-wielding models; it's their lesser-used cluster grenades you'll need to worry about, though they feature an obvious telegraph—they will always perform a boost to the side and rapidly fire two shots from their rifle, before launching four grenades at you. These grenades travel in an arc, landing on the ground around you, making them very dangerous if you're using Quick Boosts carelessly.

▍ These MTs are able to ascend and fire their grenades while airborne, resulting in a greater spread when they hit the ground. They won't launch grenades at ranges farther than 225m, and will instead boost forward to close the gap. Long-range weaponry such as laser rifles will let you safely take care of cluster gun MTs with little risk. Due to their explosive potential destroying these MTs should be high priority.

Cluster grenades have a long range and cause large explosions, making them surprisingly difficult to escape.

MT-E-104 (CAPTURE CAMERA)

Weapon Systems

Location	Weapon	Damage Type
R-Arm	Rifle	▬ Kinetic
R-Back	Capture Camera	◣ N/A

▎ Encountered only in the "Eliminate V.VII" mission, capture camera MTs are armed with rifles and cameras that will expose your position. Their searchlights illuminate the ground, allowing you to avoid their line of sight. Beware of surveillance MTs perched in elevated positions, as they're often not easily spotted and benefit from increased peripheral vision.

▎ With an exceptional targeting distance of 350m, capture camera MTs can be incredibly difficult to avoid. If you stay within their camera's range for too long, a warning indicator will appear above the MT that spots you, resulting in a failed mission if it alerts its allies. Destroying it quickly will stop the alert, but you'll have less than five seconds to achieve this, and doing so may alert other MTs in the vicinity.

▎ Usually, your best option will be to stay mobile and hide behind cover the moment you're spotted. Attempting to destroy surveillance MTs that spot you can easily lead to a chain of alerts among other MTs in the vicinity.

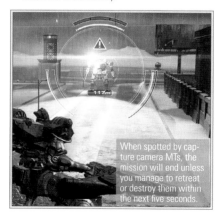

When spotted by capture camera MTs, the mission will end unless you manage to retreat or destroy them within the next five seconds.

RAD CRAWLER MTS

RaD crawlers are unique spider-like MTs used by various Doser factions operating in the Grids of Rubicon. Built with a stocky, low profile, these MTs are designed to overwhelm their targets with high impact explosive and kinetic weaponry. Crawlers of all kinds can be found waiting on walls, ceilings, and other structures, dormant and ready for an ambush. Scan regularly when you're up against factions that deploy these MTs, as prone crawlers can be difficult to identify, and you won't be able to target them unless they're picked up by your systems.

Specs

Specs	
AP	650
Attitude Stability	364
Anti-Kinetic Defense	1140 ↑
Anti-Energy Defense	700 ↓
Anti-Explosive Defense	1000
Pulse Armor Resilience	—

MB-0100 CLUTCH (HEAVY ROCKET LAUNCHER)

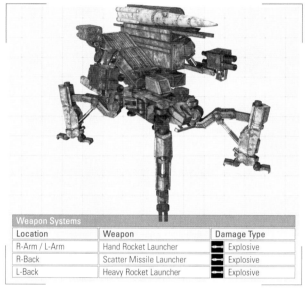

Weapon Systems

Location	Weapon	Damage Type
R-Arm / L-Arm	Hand Rocket Launcher	▬ Explosive
R-Back	Scatter Missile Launcher	▬ Explosive
L-Back	Heavy Rocket Launcher	█ Explosive

▎ These crawlers perform short, quick scurries to avoid incoming fire and tend to stay at a distance. They'll barrage you with rockets and homing missiles, which can lead to fighting them becoming disorienting as explosions begin to overwhelm you. Each hand rocket can cause high ACS build-up, leading to an overload in just a few hits.

▎ At medium range and closer, their most devastating weapon is their hand rocket launcher, which they can fire up to eight shells from in quick succession, sometimes accompanied by a barrage of eight additional winding homing missiles. At long range, the accuracy of their hand rockets drops off considerably, making this the ideal range to

deal with them. Their shells can still hit, however, and their homing missiles remain a threat past this range.

▎ They can fire their huge, back-mounted rockets from medium to long ranges. This rocket is launched alongside an unyielding volley of homing missiles and hand rockets, so it can be hard to notice it being fired. You'll be alerted by your AC once they're preparing to fire the missile, but it's extraordinarily slow to launch so you won't need to take any immediate action.

▎ Despite how threatening their heavy rocket seems, it won't deal any damage unless it hits directly, and it tends to miss if you've been pushed back by a prior explosion. If it does hit, it won't inflict much more damage than a regular hand rocket.

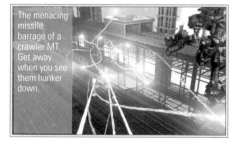

The menacing missile barrage of a crawler MT. Get away when you see them hunker down.

LASER SENSOR VARIANT

This rare variant is only encountered in the "Eliminate 'Honest' Brute" mission during Chapter 3. Laser sensor crawlers are passive and lie dormant until you activate them by tripping their laser sensors. They can be attacked and destroyed before activating, but behave like regular RaD crawlers once active. Scan them before attacking to lock on to any in the area. Be careful, as tripping one sensor can activate multiple crawlers in the area.

MB-0100 CLUTCH (ELECTRO SAW)

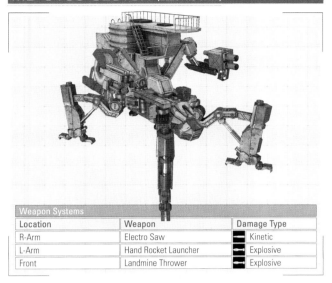

Weapon Systems

Location	Weapon		Damage Type
R-Arm	Electro Saw		Kinetic
L-Arm	Hand Rocket Launcher		Explosive
Front	Landmine Thrower		Explosive

▌ This variant comes armed with electro saw blades, rockets, and mines, giving them access to short-range kinetic damage and long-range explosive damage. They tend to fall back and fire their powerful rocket launchers, causing ACS overload quickly if their shots land. They can then combo this into melee attacks with their electro saw for incredible damage.

▌ Occasionally, these crawlers will throw out numerous timed landmines in the area in front of them. While individually weak, these mines are an additional source of damage you should be careful of when fighting them.

▌ They can perform a quick, horizontal swipe with their electro saw that has a range of 50m in front of them. Their electro saw charge, however, features deceptively long range—hitting from over 100m away— and deals heavy damage while temporarily stopping your movement.

▌ These crawler models can leap into the air at the end of their saw charge for a devastating saw dive, making them tricky to predict. Never underestimate the danger they pose at close range; if they combo into the saw dive after overloading your ACS, you can take over 5000 AP in damage from a single attack.

MB-0100 CLUTCH (ENCLOSURE SHIELD)

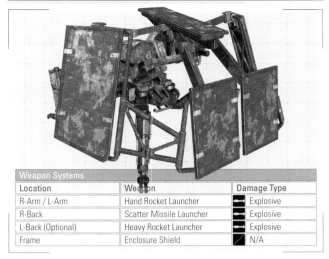

Weapon Systems

Location	Weapon		Damage Type
R-Arm / L-Arm	Hand Rocket Launcher		Explosive
R-Back	Scatter Missile Launcher		Explosive
L-Back (Optional)	Heavy Rocket Launcher		Explosive
Frame	Enclosure Shield		N/A

▌ The shielded variant has similar behavior to regular crawlers, but can retreat into its shields for extra protection, while unleashing numerous explosives. This makes them a particularly potent threat, as they're able to provide effective cover for their comrades with a barrage of rockets and missiles, while remaining defensive.

▌ They're particularly weak from behind while in their shielded configuration, and their shields can be quickly destroyed by melee weapons. Once their shields are broken, they act like the unshielded crawlers, but tend to fire their rockets far more erratically and aggressively, and use their missiles more frequently.

Enclosure shield crawlers act just like the base versions, but with far better defenses that cover their entire front.

MB-0100 CLUTCH (STUN PLUG)

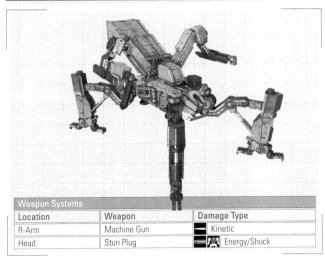

Weapon Systems

Location	Weapon		Damage Type
R-Arm	Machine Gun		Kinetic
Head	Stun Plug		Energy/Shock

▌ This model's stun plug provides it with a very unique attack. Your AC will alert you when they lower their back section, at which point they'll release a shock blast in a short cone of about 110m in front of them—pay attention to the attack indicator to know where it's coming from. Once they unleash this shock blast, they'll need to cool down for about five seconds, leaving them vulnerable.

▌ Unlike other crawler MTs, their danger lies less in their individual damage potential, than in the ability of their machine guns and stun plug to disrupt you; if they cause an electrical discharge while you fight more threatening units, you'll quickly lose control of the situation.

The cone of a stun plug crawler's shock blast is tight, but can be hard to escape if they attack in groups.

▌ Stun plug crawler MTs primarily attack with their machine gun, which deals low damage but rapidly builds impact, quickly leading to ACS overload.

The rank-and-file troops of the PCA's planetside force, Subject Guard MTs are much quicker and more aerially adept than the other bipedal MTs. Focusing on long-range, energy-based weaponry, they'll often attack from farther away and reposition when they're in danger. Certain models come equipped with kinetic and explosive weapons, so a good spread of defensive specs will pay off when engaging Subject Guard MTs.

Specs	
AP	437
Attitude Stability	310
Anti-Kinetic Defense	859 ↓
Anti-Energy Defense	1260 ↑
Anti-Explosive Defense	1000
Pulse Armor Resilience	—

AM14: SENTRY (MISSILE LAUNCHER)

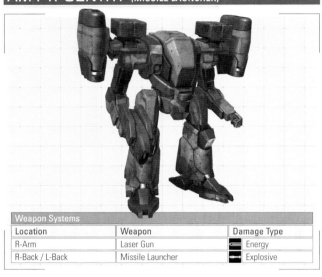

Weapon Systems		
Location	Weapon	Damage Type
R-Arm	Laser Gun	Energy
R-Back / L-Back	Missile Launcher	Explosive

- Missile launcher-wielding Subject Guard MTs prefer to attack with their energy-based laser guns from long distance, and will do so the moment they spot you—often from a high vantage point. For added firepower and versatility, these foes can fire two sets of back-mounted dual missiles without interrupting their laser gun assault, dealing sudden explosive damage.

- Their laser gun is typically fired in bursts of three or four shots, and four-shot bursts can be followed by a fifth charged shot that's also accompanied by missiles. This five-shot burst is telegraphed by the MT taking an extra second to ready its gun before firing. They can also loose a volley of more than five shots, though this won't be followed up with a charged shot.

- This model's missiles complement their laser guns, providing them with a well-rounded arsenal. Their rifles lose effectiveness against mobile targets, but the missiles can compensate by pinning you down. This can cause some unexpected damage if you try to fight up close, so it's wiser to create some distance to avoid dodging into missiles or laser fire.

- ACs with high anti-energy defense will have an easier time approaching these MTs, as their laser fire will begin to ricochet at much shorter distances compared to ACs that eschew anti-energy defense. As with all explosive weaponry, their missiles remain effective at any range, regardless of defenses.

- Pulse shields can allow you to safely close the distance on them, though be wary; nearby enemies in the area can attack you from the sides. If you get too close, Subject Guard MTs will attempt to reposition themselves by jumping to an elevated position or quickly retreating a good distance.

Watch their barrels; missile launcher Subject Guard MTs can charge up a powerful shot in the midst of their laser flurries.

AM14: SENTRY (STUN GUN)

Weapon Systems		
Location	Weapon	Damage Type
R-Arm	Machine Gun	Kinetic
L-Arm	Stun Gun	Energy/Shock

- Stun gun-wielding MTs are proficient in aerial combat, and will spend their time either boosting and strafing on the ground, or peppering you with machine gun fire while airborne.

- Their machine guns can deliver consistent damage, and lack the spread of lesser MTs' machine guns, so you'll need to stay mobile or the continuous damage can quickly become dangerous.

- Compared to the basic bipedal light MT machine guns, Subject Guard machine guns will begin to ricochet off even the lightest and lowest defense ACs at 440m. Don't expect this to mean they're best fought at this range, however, as they'll have plenty of time to close that distance while keeping up the pressure.

- Once within 250m, they'll begin to ready their stun guns, firing off single shots in a parabolic arc. The stun grenade will explode in mid-air and create a forward-moving electrical projectile that inflicts shock buildup and can quickly trigger an electrical discharge. Since these MTs need to stop boosting to fire their stun grenades, and cannot fire them while airborne, you'll have a window in which to deal damage, though you'll need to watch for incoming stun grenades.

When a stun gun MT aims its stun gun toward the sky, it's preparing to fire a stun grenade.

AM14: SENTRY (ELECTROTHERMO CUTTER)

Weapon Systems

Location	Weapon		Damage Type
R-Arm	Machine Gun		Kinetic
L-Arm	Electrothermo Cutter		Kinetic/Incendiary

▮ Equipped with a custom electrothermo cutter, these MTs will gun you down from range with kinetic rounds and then rush in to deal heavy damage with melee attacks. Possessing extreme agility, their attacks tend to reposition them suddenly, so use Target Assist to keep track of them.

▮ While the emphasis is on their melee capabilities, this is another highly mobile Subject Guard model, capable of prolonged aerial combat. From the air, they'll strafe past you with machine gun fire. Once grounded, however, they're more likely to use their electrothermo cutter, which inflicts heat buildup capable of triggering an ACS anomaly.

▮ Beware that these foes have a few unique attacks with their electrothermo cutter, the first of which is a jumping horizontal slash. This attack will be preceded by a forward boost to close distance if you're far enough away, or executed without a boost if you're within 50m. Once in the air, this attack has a brief moment of wind-up, allowing you to prepare an evade—a forward Quick Boost will cause the MT to miss you completely. If it hits, it will deal moderate AP damage, but high impact and heat buildup.

▮ One of the more menacing attacks used by these MTs is a quicker, back-handed horizontal swing. This swing isn't any more powerful than the jumping slash, and shares the same boost telegraphs, but is executed much faster. They can also use this attack while airborne, which can lead to confusion if you're not expecting it.

Electrothermo cutter Subject Guards can execute a jumping melee slash, which can cause heavy ACS strain.

AM14: SENTRY (GRENADE CANNON)

Weapon Systems

Location	Weapon		Damage Type
R-Arm	Laser Gun		Energy
R-Back / L-Back	Grenade Cannon		Explosive

▮ This variant can fire two powerful explosive grenade rounds at once, giving them high damage and ACS strain potential. As is typical for grenades, they can be fired over long distances, from well outside your own lock-on range.

▮ Functionally similar to an artillery unit, these variants are often perched in high positions, where they're either accompanied by direct combat units, or stationed to cover an objective. They'll remain generally immobile, only turning occasionally to adjust their aim. Because grenade cannon Subject Guard MTs are usually positioned on high ground, their grenades' explosive radius can inflict unexpected splash damage.

▮ You'll often first be notified of this model's presence by red attack indicators and audio warnings before you're able to target them. Since their cannons fire extremely slowly, it's best to match their firing timing with a dodge, then Quick Boost in to destroy them while they reload.

Be sure to close the gap as quickly as possible against grenade cannon Subject Guards. You'll be at a disadvantage at longer distances.

AM14: SENTRY (FLAMETHROWER)

Weapon Systems

Location	Weapon		Damage Type
R-Arm	Flamethrower		Explosive/Incendiary

▮ Often attacking in groups, these incendiary MTs will focus on overwhelming you and obscuring your view with flames. This can inflict ACS anomaly, and make it difficult for you to regenerate

ACS strain. Add their aerial capabilities into the mix, and you have a foe that is hard to keep track of, and capable of attacking from all angles.

▮ This model can perform a wide, sweeping flamethrower burst after a boost, and will tend to sweep their flamethrowers back and forth across large areas. Beware that they're also capable of doing this in mid-air, spreading their flames all over the ground beneath them.

▮ While their flamethrower's range is relatively short—with their flames largely losing effectiveness past close range—their power is not to be underestimated. Even a single flamethrower unit can deal severe AP damage and quickly cause ACS anomaly. Groups of these units are not to be taken lightly, and should be prioritized above almost any other threat nearby.

Their mid-air sweep can be extremely dangerous in close quarters, coating the battlefield in flames.

HEAVY MTS

This category includes some of the heaviest hitters that most factions have access to on the battlefield. They're a noticeable upgrade from light MTs, with stronger frames capable of carrying greater firepower, making them attractive combat platforms for many of the corporations and factions fighting on Rubicon. While not as commonly deployed as light MTs, you can expect to see these hulking tetrapod models acting as a last line of defense in key facilities and disputed areas.

BAWS TETRAPOD MTS

These heavily armed tetrapod MTs can remain highly mobile while launching a powerful offensive. Despite their size, they're able to jump and boost to gain a better angle of attack. Due to their high bulk, attempting to overload their ACS and attacking while they're staggered is the optimal way of dealing with them.

Specs	
AP	13370
Attitude Stability	2200
Anti-Kinetic Defense	1210 ↑
Anti-Energy Defense	854 ↓
Anti-Explosive Defense	1135 ↑
Pulse Armor Resilience	—

MT-J-048 (LASER BLADE)

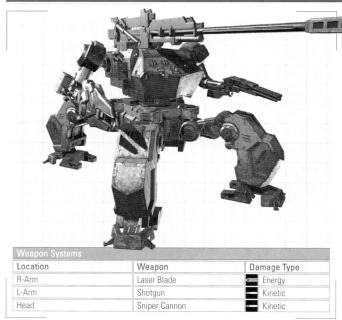

Weapon Systems		
Location	Weapon	Damage Type
R-Arm	Laser Blade	Energy
L-Arm	Shotgun	Kinetic
Head	Sniper Cannon	Kinetic

▌ Massive and versatile, laser blade heavy MTs will use their shotgun and sniper cannon at longer ranges, ready to unleash a laser blade if you get too close.

▌ Your systems will often warn you of incoming sniper fire before you fully engage with these MTs. Their sniper rounds deal high AP damage and severe ACS strain. Lighter ACs can avoid this with a well-timed Quick Boost—time your Quick Boost about a second after the system alert.

▌ Once you're within close combat range, laser blade MTs will begin using their shotgun, though this presents little threat on its own. This weapon fires three shots at once in a wide spread, dealing minor damage to your AP with moderate ACS strain; however, these blasts become more dangerous when followed up by a laser blade attack.

▌ Their laser blades have surprising range that can catch you off guard. Once they fold their sniper cannon barrels back, they're able to jump and launch a 300m diagonal laser blade slash. This attack is used to cover any remaining distance between you and the MTs, and it deals high damage to your AP. It also causes significant ACS strain, but your AC will recover from it before you're in any danger of being hit with a follow-up attack. You can dodge this attack by using a forward Quick Boost to slip underneath them after they execute their jump.

▌ Once within 250m, blade-wielding tetrapod MTs will stop attempting their jumping slash, and instead advance on you using serpentine-like movements, while integrating close-range slashes and stabs. They'll also gain a close-range boosting diagonal slash, similar to their jumping slash, which can be followed up with a second diagonal slash. If you're hit by both, expect high AP damage and a potential ACS overload. Laser blade MTs can easily escape melee range with a boost that sends them 200m backward; they'll follow this up with an attack from their sniper cannon. They're likely to do this if any of their close-range attacks stagger you, allowing for massive follow-up damage.

▌ They'll sometimes strafe in a circular arc while using covering shotgun fire—this signals the launch of a forward stab attack directly in front of them. The stab deals greater damage than their other blade attacks, but can be blocked with a shield or avoided with any lateral Quick Boost. Close-range builds that rely on staggering them and dealing direct hit damage will find squaring off with these MTs in melee range precarious. If you're within 60m when they recover from a stagger, laser blade MTs will execute a powerful, swift horizontal blade swipe. You can avoid this by staying out of this range, or attacking the MTs from their flank or rear while staggered.

MT-J-048 (9-SHOT BAZOOKA)

fires all rounds at once in a massive area, and in two sequential bursts, consisting of four rounds and then five in quick succession, in an attempt to get you to Quick Boost into the second volley. These bursts are always preceded by an alert indicator from your AC's systems, so be ready to react accordingly.

▌ They also have a unique attack, in which they'll combine their gatling and missile fire into a single salvo. This attack is telegraphed by them rooting themselves to the ground and firing in a wide arc with their gatling guns, before firing their bazooka mid-way through the sweep. The gatling fire can be easily avoided by any AC with strong aerial capabilities, or by jumping over the barrage with reverse-joint assemblies; the follow-up bazooka attack is not so easily avoided, however. It's unlikely to hit if you move in the opposite direction of the gatling gun sweep, but can still pose a threat. Once you're comfortable dodging this attack, it'll offer an opportunity to retaliate.

▌ These MTs might not be highly mobile, but they can Quick Boost suddenly, which in conjunction with missile volleys, can result in some unpredictable behavior and unexpected damage. They have limited aerial capability, but can Quick Boost in the air for a short period, which makes it harder to track them.

Watch out when this tetrapod MT fires its 9-shot bazooka; the variety of its patterns can catch you off guard if you wait too long to get out of the way.

| Weapon Systems | | |
Location	Weapon	Damage Type
R-Arm / L-Arm	Gatling Gun	Kinetic
Head	9-Shot Bazooka	Explosive

▌ Armed with two gatling guns and a bazooka capable of firing a volley of nine missiles in a straight line, this heavy MT variant can deal continuous kinetic damage and abrupt explosive damage.

▌ This model will fire a barrage of bullets at you as long as you're within 300m, and they're capable of causing significant ACS strain if they stay trained on you for too long, which will open you up to a devastating hit from its missiles.

▌ Their bazookas are as dangerous as their gatling guns. They deal high AP damage and even just a few missiles can cause significant stress on your AC's systems. Their shells can be fired in two configurations: a shotgun-like blast that

MT-J-048 (3-SHOT BAZOOKA)

▌ This model of heavy MT often fires its machine gun from behind the cover of its shield, and can fire three shells at once from its 3-shot bazookas. Its machine gun deals low damage and ACS strain, but they risk little in using it, as they can remain mobile and fire continuous bursts without having to drop their shields. They can boost and strafe while firing their machine guns, and even perform short boosts for dodging, but tend to spend most of their time in battle walking with their shield up. This approach makes them nearly impervious from the front, so you may need to take to the air to reach an exposed portion of their frame.

▌ If you take to the sky or attack from ranges past 150m, shield-wielding tetrapod MTs will begin using their bazooka more frequently. They'll fire in one of two distinct patterns: three shells all at once, or three in quick succession, and when firing from ground to air, they'll always opt for the latter pattern. Their bazooka shells will be indicated by an alert from your AC's systems, and can deal heavy damage and ACS strain.

▌ Shield-wielding heavy MTs can employ a hover boost attack, which they'll use to either counter your aerial efforts, or gain an advantageous position by flanking you or attacking you from behind. This hovering attack will end in a shell volley while the MTs is still airborne, which can catch you from behind if they manage to get directly above you.

| Weapon Systems | | |
Location	Weapon	Damage Type
R-Arm	Machine Gun	Kinetic
L-Arm	Shield	N/A
Head	3-Shot Bazooka	Explosive

- From close range, these heavy MTs are capable of performing a devastating boosted shield bash. This deals heavy ACS strain, and can be followed up with three shots from their bazookas, dishing out severe damage. The shield bash triggers an audible alert from your systems, and can be most effectively dodged by boosting into the air, or with a quick jump from reverse-joint legs.

- ACs with moderate boosting or aerial capabilities shouldn't have too much trouble fighting this heavy MT. Their attacks aren't fast enough to hit strafing targets, and they struggle against airborne opponents. If you're having trouble getting past their shields, their slow turning speed makes circling them in boost mode viable at extremely close ranges—they'll have little recourse to defend themselves. Be prepared to jump or use Quick Boosts at a moment's notice, since their shield bash attack poses a real threat at this range. After overloading its ACS, this MT will retaliate with grenade fire upon recovering.

Overloading this tetrapod MT's ACS will always shatter its shield, leaving it wide open for the rest of the fight and much easier to finish off.

MT-J-048 (9-Shot Bazooka)

MT-J-048 (3-Shot Bazooka)

MT-J-048 (Grenade Cannon)

MT-J-048 (GRENADE CANNON)

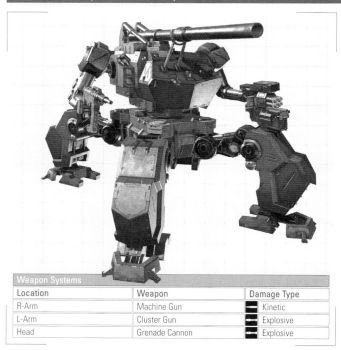

- Similar to the laser blade variants, when this model prepares to fire its grenade cannon you'll hear an audible alert, but the shell that's fired moves slower and is much easier to dodge. Grenade variants also don't lose access to their grenade cannon at close range, making the threat of severe damage and ACS strain constant during any encounter with them.

- These MTs can fire their cluster guns vertically into the air, causing them to arc back down on you if you're within about 230m. These cluster grenades deal moderate damage to your AP and ACS strain, but their wide coverage and the explosive splash along the ground can make evasion at the ground level precarious. Cluster grenades trigger an audible alert from your systems, and you'll have some advance visual warning if you notice them raise their left arm into the air before firing. Just make sure you have room to maneuver once the cluster grenades begin raining down upon you.

- Though a rarely used ability, these MTs can boost into the air and fire cluster grenades down at the ground, creating a large explosion that's difficult to evade. This ability makes them hard to predict in combat, but if you see them boost upward, take to the sky yourself and be ready to evade just in case

Weapon Systems

Location	Weapon	Damage Type
R-Arm	Machine Gun	Kinetic
L-Arm	Cluster Gun	Explosive
Head	Grenade Cannon	Explosive

- Grenade cannon heavy MTs focus their offense around their machine guns, and come equipped with an explosive cluster gun and back-mounted grenade cannon for explosive damage.

- Behaving similar to other tetrapod MTs you've encountered, these MTs mainly rely on their machine gun while strafing—much like the shield-wielding heavy MTs—but are more agile and boost more frequently, similarly to pulse blade or gatling gun heavy MTs. Like the shield-wielding heavy MTs, their machine gun isn't intended to be a major threat on its own, but grenade cannon variants lack the defensive options to compensate.

This heavy MT fires volleys of cluster grenades, which can cause heavy, unexpected damage if they land near your AC.

RAD TOYBOX MTS

One of "Cinder" Carla's most eccentric creations, these heavy MTs are loaded to the gills with weapons, and deployed by her RaD group as heavy fire or support units. Initially rolled up into seemingly innocuous balls, TOYBOX MTs spring to life once alerted, delivering a deadly surprise to any hostiles unfortunate enough to be nearby.

Specs	
AP	1848
Attitude Stability	1053
Anti-Kinetic Defense	1070 ↑
Anti-Energy Defense	854 ↓
Anti-Explosive Defense	1000
Pulse Armor Resilience	—

MB-0202 TOYBOX

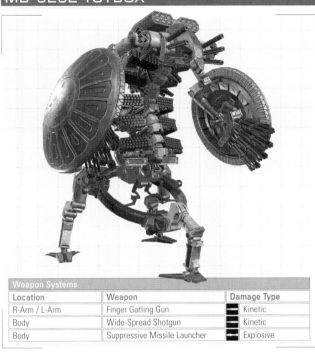

Weapon Systems

Location	Weapon	Damage Type	
R-Arm / L-Arm	Finger Gatling Gun	▬	Kinetic
Body	Wide-Spread Shotgun	▬	Kinetic
Body	Suppressive Missile Launcher	◀▬	Explosive

▌ These heavy MTs can roll into a ball and attack with rapid-fire finger gatling guns equipped to their outer casing, as well as homing missiles that are released from their abdomen.

▌ Their finger gatling guns aren't a massive threat if you stay mobile, though their damage and ACS strain will ramp up very quickly if they manage to land sustained fire on you. Once they have you in their sights, keep up a steady boost strafe to avoid most incoming fire.

▌ TOYBOX MTs can easily hit moving targets with their homing missiles, though these missiles don't pose a significant threat on their own. The real danger comes from volleys launched when you're staggered; if they're able to tag you while you're in this state, they'll deal significant AP damage.

▌ Their last major attack is a close-range shotgun blast that's initiated after they roll toward you. This attack covers an extremely wide area and can be difficult to avoid; your AC's systems will provide an audible alert to ensure you have plenty of time to react to it. The extreme ACS strain dealt by this attack can be fatal if you take the brunt of it followed by a volley of missiles. Thankfully, they have no tracking capabilities during the initial roll, so either boost strafe or Quick Boost around them, or even jump over them if you're close enough.

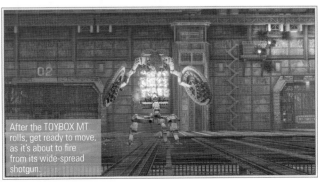

After the TOYBOX MT rolls, get ready to move, as it's about to fire from its wide-spread shotgun.

MB-0202 TOYBOX (PULSE PROTECTION)

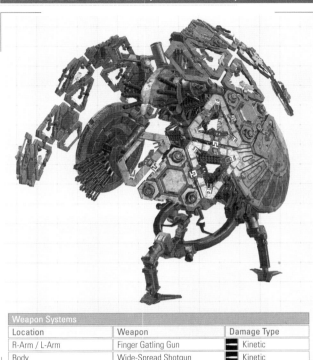

Weapon Systems

Location	Weapon	Damage Type	
R-Arm / L-Arm	Finger Gatling Gun	▬	Kinetic
Body	Wide-Spread Shotgun	▬	Kinetic
Body	Suppressive Missile Launcher	◀▬	Explosive
R-Back / L-Back	Pulse Protection	▮	N/A

▌ A unique TOYBOX MT encountered in the "Eliminate 'Honest' Brute" mission that can emit a large pulse shield in a 200m radius, centered on its position. This barrier blocks all incoming damage, but does not prevent other units from entering within its radius.

▌ Due to this MT's positioning, you can easily enter its shield and destroy every MT inside without much difficulty. Though be aware that the Pulse Protection TOYBOX will lower its barrier and spring into action, fighting just like a regular TOYBOX MT as long as you stay within the range of its pulse barrier. You can destroy the TOYBOX to get rid of the barrier, making it the highest priority target in the area.

TOYBOX MT's pulse protection shield can't be canceled and provides a large area of protection for your enemies. Get inside the bubble and eliminate the MT that generates it.

ARTILLERY

Artillery are long-range defensive batteries installed at key locations all over Rubicon. Designed to inflict substantial damage from a distance, they're often positioned at elevated vantage points to maximize their reach. Artillery units are less effective at close range and can be easily outmaneuvered and destroyed once you reach their blind spots. Many types of artillery can come in shielded and non-shielded variants, making them more difficult to overcome from a distance.

ARTILLERY (GRENADE CANNON)

Focus on avoiding incoming grenades, then take advantage of their slow reload time to close the gap and destroy them.

▌ Many grenade cannon emplacements are protected by shielded armor plating that completely negates damage from frontal attacks. Their turret can only swivel up to 180-degrees, however, leaving them entirely defenseless if you manage to get behind them.

Some attacks, like vertical missiles or charged plasma rifle shots, can be used to bypass the frontal shield of artillery emplacements without the need to maneuver behind them.

Specs			
AP	470	Anti-Energy Defense	536 ↓
Attitude Stability	—	Anti-Explosive Defense	1000
Anti-Kinetic Defense	1070 ↑	Pulse Armor Resilience	—

Weapon Systems		
Location	Weapon	Damage Type
Turret	Grenade Cannon	Explosive
Turret (Optional)	Frontal Shield	N/A

▌ An artillery cannon that fires a long-range explosive grenade in an arcing trajectory, causing a large blast upon detonation. Due to the nature of the grenade's firing arc, even shots that don't connect directly can cause serious damage if they hit close enough for you to get caught in their blast radius. To counteract this, the safest bet is to approach from the air.

▌ Be vigilant, as grenade cannons will instantly open fire once you're within their line of sight, with an alert often being the first warning sign that you've been targeted.

Pay attention to the arc of artillery shells; it's not a straight line, so anticipate shots with that in mind.

ARTILLERY (SNIPER CANNON)

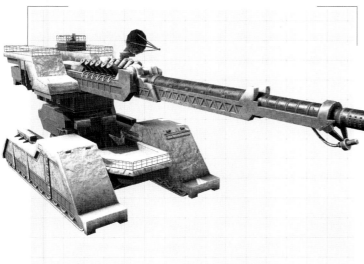

- This artillery cannon fires a long-range kinetic shot, dealing heavy damage and ACS strain. Sniper cannons will often spot you well before you're even aware of their presence, and once they do, you'll see their targeting laser tracking your movement. Be prepared to take evasive maneuvers the instant you hear the audible alert indicator warning you that they're about to fire.

- These emplacements are extremely dangerous and can immediately put defensively weak ACs into ACS overload. Their shots travel at extremely high velocity, and can be difficult to dodge with a lateral Quick Boost, especially if your attention is on other threats in the area. Always consider them a top priority and take them out as quickly as possible.

- Shielded variants must be dealt with by flanking and attacking their blind spots. These cannons have a wide turning radius, but will have a hard time keeping up with you at ranges of less than 100m; move inside this range and flank the artillery in either direction.

Be ready to move when you find yourself tracked by a laser sight.

Specs

AP	437	Anti-Energy Defense	536 ↓
Attitude Stability	—	Anti-Explosive Defense	1000
Anti-Kinetic Defense	1070 ↑	Pulse Armor Durability	—

Weapon Systems

Location	Weapon	Damage Type	
Turret	Sniper Cannon	▬	Kinetic
Turret (Optional)	Frontal Shield	◤	N/A

ARTILLERY (BAZOOKA)

- Similar to sniper cannons, bazooka artillery fire single explosive shells. These rounds only inflict moderate AP damage, but will cause significantly greater ACS strain.

- Their shells can hit from extremely long range, and without the arcing trajectory of a grenade. You'll be alerted by your AC's systems as a shell is being fired—look for red visual warnings and audio indicators.

- Bazooka artillery rounds aren't capable of homing in on you. Instead, they use predictive fire to calculate your current range and directional movement and fire their shells in a straight line to hit where you're most likely to be. Any deviation from your flight path after the alert indicator will therefore cause the shot to miss.

Immediately change course when these artillery installations fire on you; their shots are aimed to intercept you along your current movement path.

Specs

AP	269	Anti-Energy Defense	536 ↓
Attitude Stability	—	Anti-Explosive Defense	1000
Anti-Kinetic Defense	1070 ↑	Pulse Armor Resilience	—

Weapon Systems

Location	Weapon	Damage Type	
Turret	Bazooka	▬	Explosive

ARTILLERY (GATLING GUN)

- Capable of dealing great kinetic damage, gatling artillery will fire their four gatling guns from behind the protection of a shield. Despite most rapid-fire gatling shots having a tendency to spread out over longer distances, gatling artillery units are highly precise from long range, just like the other artillery variants.

- Their volleys of fire can quickly overwhelm you and lead to an ACS overload, so mobile ACs will be at an advantage when facing these emplacements.

- Even the most defensively sturdy ACs won't survive a direct assault when two or more of these artillery units are locked on at once. You'll need to either get behind one quickly and eliminate it, or flank them by moving behind cover. They do have a moderate reload phase, which can give you a chance to quickly get behind cover.

- Like all shielded artillery, gatling cannon variants are immune to damage from the front, but vulnerable from behind and above. Your approach through the area will need to be based on a combination of their positioning and the available cover.

Even the bulkiest of builds will fold quickly against a pair of gatling guns if a frontal assault is attempted.

Specs			
AP	403	Anti-Energy Defense	536 ↓
Attitude Stability	—	Anti-Explosive Defense	1000
Anti-Kinetic Defense	1070 ↑	Pulse Armor Resilience	—

Weapon Systems		
Location	Weapon	Damage Type
Turret	Gatling Gun	Kinetic
Turret	Frontal Shield	N/A

ARTILLERY (MISSILE ARRAY)

Specs			
AP	202	Anti-Energy Defense	536 ↓
Attitude Stability	—	Anti-Explosive Defense	1000
Anti-Kinetic Defense	1070 ↑	Pulse Armor Durability	—

- These missile artillery units fire sixteen missiles per volley, and if even a few missiles hit, they'll cause significant explosive damage. Missile arrays can appear in three distinct configurations:

  - A forward multi-missile array, which fire their missiles sequentially, directly in their line of sight. Agile ACs will have an easier time avoiding these missiles with mid-air Quick Boosts than heavier builds.

  - A vertical array that fires missiles directly upward into the air, causing them to fall back down on your position, dealing splash damage along the ground.

  - A horizontal array that fires missiles all at once in a wide line, making it easiest to dodge them up close by moving vertically, which reverse-joint legs are best suited for. These missiles lose formation and begin to bunch together at range, making them easier to dodge in any direction.

- Unlike many other artillery units, missile arrays will give no warning when they have you targeted, nor when they are about to fire upon you. You can hear the rapid firing of their missiles, but you should keep an eye on the artillery to know for sure when you're in danger, especially against the horizontal array.

Weapon Systems		
Location	Weapon	Damage Type
Turret	Missile Array	Explosive

Multi-Missile Array

Horizontal Missile Array

Vertical Missile Array

ARTILLERY (LASER CANNON)

- Found in the "Attack the Watchpoint" mission, laser cannon artillery will charge up a large, devastating energy shot that covers huge distances. They will fire three shots at a slow pace before entering a long cooldown period.

- Incoming lasers cause heavy ACS strain and can stop your AC dead in its tracks, leaving you vulnerable to follow-up shots from other laser cannon artillery. Getting hit by multiple laser shots sequentially is extremely dangerous.

- There's a brief pause between your AC's alert indicators signaling a shot, and the shot occurring. Laser cannon shots are also deceptively broad and travel quite fast, which means that each beam requires strict timing to dodge.

- Besides their cooldown period, the laser cannon artillery's biggest weakness is their combination of a 180-degree targeting radius and slow turning speed. Getting behind them will leave them completely ineffective, though you'll need to be mindful of additional laser artillery that can cover blind spots.

- Destroying them should be your top priority on the battlefield, doubly so if there are multiple present. They are best tackled using a pulse shield—along with any cover available—to bait their attacks, and then retaliating between their shots.

Laser Cannon artillery has to go through a long venting period to cool down after three shots. This is an ideal time to take them out safely.

Specs			
AP	1131	Anti-Energy Defense	1260 ↑
Attitude Stability	—	Anti-Explosive Defense	1000
Anti-Kinetic Defense	859 ↓	Pulse Armor Durability	—

Weapon Systems		
Location	Weapon	Damage Type
Turret	Laser Cannon	Energy

ARTILLERY (BEAM LASER)

- Like sniper cannon artillery, these installations has extreme range and can use their targeting laser to track you well beyond your own range. Once targeted, you'll have a few seconds to break their line of sight; their accurate tracking means Quick Boosts will not be a reliable way to avoid damage.

- Their beams can deal significant damage to AP and ACS if they maintain contact for too long, especially if multiple beam lasers are able to lock onto you at once. It's best to take cover in the environment, and reach a position below each of them. They're capable of swiveling a complete 360-degrees around themselves, but cannot aim at a significant downward angle.

- A viable strategy is to come into the mission with a pulse shield like the VP-61PS, and approach the central structure with your shield deployed. Move toward the beam laser and descend until they cannot target you. Once they're no longer a threat, approach and land on the platform below the nearest beam laser.

- Each beam laser has a small platform directly below it, which offers you a safe position from which to eliminate them. There are 12 beam lasers across the plate, segmented off in pairs that will cover each other as you try to take them out. You can safely take each pair out without having to worry about the rest.

Specs			
AP	302	Anti-Energy Defense	1135 ↑
Attitude Stability	—	Anti-Explosive Defense	1000
Anti-Kinetic Defense	790 ↓	Pulse Armor Durability	—

Weapon Systems		
Location	Weapon	Damage Type
Turret	Beam Laser	Energy

- Beam laser artillery are found accompanying PCA forces in the "Underground Exploration – Depth 3" mission, and can deal severe energy damage. They can lock onto you from long range and fire a steadily tracking energy beam, dealing damage over time. Their beams last about five seconds, and the beam lasers will suffer a heavy cooldown period after each shot.

The platforms just below the beam lasers are a major blind spot, and offer you complete cover around the central platform of the area.

ARTILLERY (PLASMA MISSILE LAUNCHER)

Specs			
AP	280	Anti-Energy Defense	1135 ↑
Attitude Stability	—	Anti-Explosive Defense	1000
Anti-Kinetic Defense	790 ↓	Pulse Armor Durability	—

Weapon Systems		
Location	Weapon	Damage Type
Turret	Plasma Missile Launcher	Energy

▌ Among the most dangerous artillery units, plasma missile artillery are found exclusively in the "Attack the Old Spaceport" mission. They fire six plasma missiles at a time, dealing energy damage, and are deployed in a three-unit formation.

▌ Much like the missile arrays, plasma missile launcher artillery volleys aren't telegraphed with an alert indicator. Their missiles deal extremely high AP damage, track your movement, and leave respectably-sized explosions when they hit. They have an approximately seven second cooldown period between volleys.

▌ As with most tracking artillery, plasma missile artillery struggle to hit aerial targets, and staying airborne will help you avoid their missiles. Stay attentive, however, as their missiles can explode mid-air and clip you if they get too close.

▌ Engaging these artilleries in the air at ranges of greater than 350m allows you ample time to react to their missiles. It also causes them to spread quite a bit, lessening their effectiveness and lowering the risk of getting hit by them.

ARTILLERY (PLASMA CANNON)

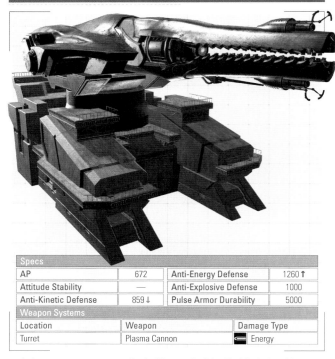

Specs			
AP	672	Anti-Energy Defense	1260 ↑
Attitude Stability	—	Anti-Explosive Defense	1000
Anti-Kinetic Defense	859 ↓	Pulse Armor Durability	5000

Weapon Systems		
Location	Weapon	Damage Type
Turret	Plasma Cannon	Energy

▌ A plasma cannon encountered in the "Destroy the Drive Block" mission, this artillery fires two long-range explosive energy shots in quick succession. You'll be targeted the moment you're spotted—even from kilometers away—giving this emplacement some of the longest range among all enemies. Your only warning will be a red visual indicator and audio alert, signaling that you are about to be fired upon.

▌ Its beam is fast, deals heavy damage and leaves a large plasma field wherever it hits. This unit fires off 10 shots before going through a long cool-down process.

▌ Your best strategy to avoid damage is to use the environment as cover while making your approach to an opening leading inside the Xylem, but a pulse shield can also help mitigate most of the risk.

▌ The cannon is protected from the front by a pulse shield that can be worn down or bypassed by simply attacking from the artillery's flank or from above. Due to how long it takes to destroy the shield—and since doing so won't stagger the cannon or disrupt its firing—it's best to flank it rather than attempt to destroy its shield.

ARTILLERY (PULSE CANNON)

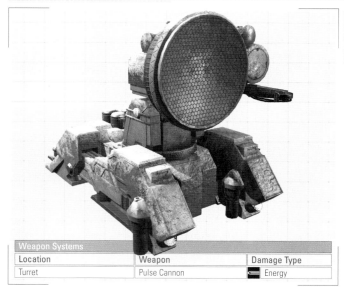

Specs			
AP	246	Anti-Energy Defense	1135 ↑
Attitude Stability	—	Anti-Explosive Defense	1000
Anti-Kinetic Defense	790 ↓	Pulse Armor Durability	—

▌ Exclusively encountered in the "Attack the Old Spaceport" mission, pulse cannon artillery will unleash a volley of pulse blasts at close- to medium-range. Pulse artillery deal energy damage that can disrupt shields and quickly lead to ACS overload, so avoid blocking their onslaught or tackling them head-on while other threats are around.

▌ Pulse blasts will dissipate from around 360m, so you should try to engage them at long range, with a kinetic or laser rifle. Pulse artillery only appear in groups of two in a small area, positioned so that they can cover each other, which means you'll need to make a careful approach.

▌ Eliminating pulse artillery is of low urgency—prioritize taking out surrounding enemies first, then pick off each artillery one-by-one from just outside of their range.

Weapon Systems		
Location	Weapon	Damage Type
Turret	Pulse Cannon	Energy

LIGHT CAVALRY

Agile, well-rounded bipedal mechs, light cavalry are designed to go toe-to-toe with ACs. More specialized in mobile combat than MTs, these are battle-hardened PCA soldiers that demand your full attention wherever they appear. They'll employ advanced combat tactics, frequently taking to the air or strafing along the ground to flank you and exploit your blind spots.

AA18: LIGHT CAVALRY (ENFORCEMENT OFFICER SPEC)

- This powerful LC model designed for higher-ranking PCA officers is capable of dealing kinetic damage alongside bursts of explosive damage. Their range of weaponry makes them a genuine threat at all distances. They'll spend much of their time in battle airborne, repositioning to attack you from various angles, and will back away if you approach them. Their rifle shots don't deal high damage, but can whittle you down as you try to close the gap.

- These LCs can be seen loading their under-barrel bazookas prior to firing them, and your AC's systems will issue a warning indicator before they fire it. These are their most dangerous attacks, dealing moderate AP damage and causing high ACS strain. If the shell connects, make every effort to avoid subsequent hits from the LC or other enemies to give your ACS time to recover.

- In addition to persistent rifle fire and bazooka bombardment, enforcement officer LCs will sometimes use missiles, which they can launch without indication. These missiles track your movement, but can be dodged with boost strafing.

- Enforcement officer PCA LCs can come equipped with shields to block incoming fire as they gain distance. Their shields aren't as robust as those of MTs, and LCs will frequently drop their guard, such as when they boost or fire their bazookas. They can still be effective at guarding your attacks, and bypassing them by breaking their guard with high impact weaponry remains a viable strategy.

Specs			
AP	8595	Anti-Energy Defense	1375 ↑
Attitude Stability	1750	Anti-Explosive Defense	1135 ↑
Anti-Kinetic Defense	930 ↓	Pulse Armor Resilience	—

Weapon Systems		
Location	Weapon	Damage Type
R-Arm	Rifle & Bazooka	Kinetic/Explosive
L-Arm	Shield	N/A
R-Back	Multi-Missile Launcher	Explosive

Letting LCs maintain an aerial position will put you at a disadvantage. Don't let yourself get cornered.

AA18: LIGHT CAVALRY (SNIPER TYPE)

Specs

AP	1075	Anti-Energy Defense	1260 ↑
Attitude Stability	837	Anti-Explosive Defense	1135 ↑
Anti-Kinetic Defense	859 ↓	Pulse Armor Resilience	—

can effectively dodge their attacks with a jump, boost strafe, or Quick Boost the moment the warning stops flashing.

■ These LCs will remain stationary at long range, but will retreat to the air and reposition if you get within 200m. Once sniper type LCs begin repositioning, they'll pull out their backup assault rifles for close combat, firing in short, three-round bursts that deal light damage to your AP and don't accumulate ACS strain to any notable degree. Given enough distance, they will eventually return to their perch and resume sniping duty.

■ Cornered LCs can take to the air, which will make them harder to hit, but their aerial attack options are limited. These LCs are more fragile compared to the other LCs and not built for prolonged encounters. They will struggle in quick, up-close engagements, so focus on closing the gap and dodging their laser rifle fire.

Weapon Systems

Location	Weapon	Damage Type	
R-Arm	Laser Sniper Rifle & Assault Rifle		Energy/Kinetic

■ Sniper-type LCs always strike from afar, often from an elevated position, targeting you from a position safe from retaliation. These LCs deal high damage with their energy-based weaponry, and can switch to kinetic rifles at closer ranges.

■ Keep an eye out for targeting lasers tracking your movement when these foes are around; your AC's danger indicators will alert you to incoming shots the instant before they fire, at which point they'll lock onto your present position. You

Expect to be picked off at extremely long range if sniper type LCs are on the field. Close in and deal with them quickly.

AA18: LIGHT CAVALRY (SUPPORT TYPE)

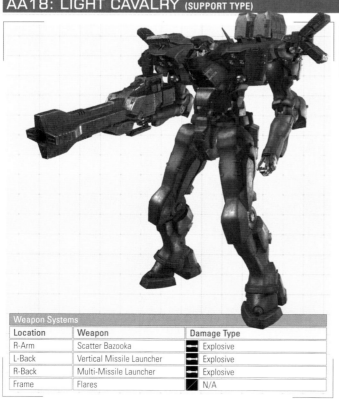

Specs

AP	5730	Anti-Energy Defense	1260 ↑
Attitude Stability	1066	Anti-Explosive Defense	1135 ↑
Anti-Kinetic Defense	859 ↓	Pulse Armor Resilience	—

■ These LCs focus on explosive blasts from their scatter bazookas at close range, firing a shell that bursts into shotgun-like slugs after a short distance. Their secondary fire remains similar to other LCs, with access to missiles to pin you down.

■ Support-type LCs primarily fire their bazookas at close- and medium-range. Their shots spread very quickly, but fire in a consistent hexagonal pattern,

Support LCs can use flares to disrupt homing missiles, making missiles impractical when fighting them.

Weapon Systems

Location	Weapon	Damage Type	
R-Arm	Scatter Bazooka		Explosive
L-Back	Vertical Missile Launcher		Explosive
R-Back	Multi-Missile Launcher		Explosive
Frame	Flares		N/A

which can give them surprising coverage from a distance. However, these shots individually don't pose any real threat if you stay mobile to avoid taking direct hits—this is especially true for builds with high anti-explosive defense. Remain vigilant, however, as their bazookas can serve to distract you from descending missile volleys.

▌ If you rely on missiles heavily, support LCs can launch flares to disrupt their homing capabilities. Their flares have about a ten second cooldown period, but it's not wise to use your missiles in an attempt to bait them; even without the flares, the mobility of the LC allows it to dodge missiles with ease. They cannot fire flares while staggered, however, so missiles remain viable during ACS overload.

▌ The best option for fighting this LC is to stay mobile. Their shots may clip you, but the damage will be negligible if you're not hit with a full blast, and it will help you avoid abrupt missile fire.

AA18A: LIGHT CAVALRY HM

Specs			
AP	15758	Anti-Energy Defense	1375 ↑
Attitude Stability	1750	Anti-Explosive Defense	1260 ↑
Anti-Kinetic Defense	1000	Pulse Armor Resilience	—

Weapon Systems		
Location	Weapon	Damage Type
R-Arm	Rifle & Bazooka	Kinetic/Explosive
L-Arm	Shield	N/A
R-Back	Multi-Missile Launcher	Explosive
High-Mobility Gear	Wing Missile Launcher	Explosive

▌ Be careful if HM LCs suddenly charge in front of you, as they may be attempting a close-range bazooka shot, which will require a tightly timed lateral Quick Boost to effectively dodge. If the shot hits, it will deal moderate AP damage, but high ACS strain on your systems.

▌ Missiles are these LCs' primary damage source, and they have light tracking abilities, but can be fired from various angles and in many configurations. They'll most frequently fire a small cluster of four missiles, as they can do this without interrupting their movements. If these missiles hit you, they'll deal light damage to your AP and won't cause significant ACS strain, but the constant pressure they present with the rest of this LC's arsenal will keep you moving throughout the fight. This high-mobility model is designed to primarily wear you down through attrition, rather than trying to end the fight in a few powerful hits.

▌ High-mobility LCs can perform a sweeping dive, telegraphed by them either raising their boosters and accelerating with their back to you, or with an aerial backflip. They can also fire larger clusters of missiles during it; they'll release six at a time rather than four, and they're capable of loosing up to three sets per dive. Furthermore, they may load a shell into the attachment on their rifle and launch it at you once they come to a stop. If you've been hit by missiles during this dive, a hit from the bazooka shell may be enough to overload your ACS, so listen for the alert and prioritize dodging or blocking the shell.

▌ This advanced LC's most notable and most effective attack is initiated by a charge directly toward you, covered by assault rifle fire. They'll make a short stop right in front of you, followed by a sharp, 90-degree boost around you. All of the high-mobility LCs missile launchers will open when they stop, unleashing a massive salvo of several dozens of missiles. Do not stop moving at any point during this attack, as any hesitation can lead to a severely overwhelming amount of damage to your AP, rapidly overloading your systems.

▌ Your safest option for fighting these foes is to stay mobile, and launch counterattacks when they drop their shields during grenade fire. None of their attacks are particularly fast, and all can be reliably dodged by boost strafing. Your biggest opportunity will be during their missile salvo attack. Builds with high anti-kinetic defense will be able to safely trade damage during the assault rifle charge portion of this attack, potentially interrupting the attack if you cause a stagger. The missile salvo also leaves them vulnerable, giving mobile ACs their own opportunity to launch a counteroffensive.

▌ Extremely agile units that fight exclusively in the air with the aid of their shoulder-mounted boosters. These foes jet around quickly, carpeting the battlefield with their back-mounted missiles, assault rifle fire, and bazooka shells. Additionally, they come equipped with a shield that provides extra protection while they fire their assault rifle, but staggering them will instantly break this shield and permanently weaken their defense.

▌ While high-mobility LCs are covering themselves with their shield, they tend to fire their rifles in short bursts as they strafe through the air. Though these shots deal low damage, they allow the HM LC to stay defensive, and with additional cover from their missiles, they can be extremely difficult to pin down.

▌ Once these targets drop their shields, they'll likely fire from the bazooka attachment on their rifles. Incoming shells will set off your system's alerts, giving you a short period to dodge the shot. This shell will arc, allowing you to avoid it with a Quick Boost toward the HM LC once you hear the alert. Dodging in this way also gives you an opportunity to launch a counterattack; a rare window of opportunity while fighting high-mobility units.

The missile salvo of a High Mobility unit will be extremely dangerous. Stop your assault and focus on retreating.

Specs			
AP	8595	Anti-Energy Defense	1375 ↑
Attitude Stability	1750	Anti-Explosive Defense	1260 ↑
Anti-Kinetic Defense	1000	Pulse Armor Resilience	—

Weapon Systems		
Location	Weapon	Damage Type
R-Arm	Grenade Launcher	Explosive
L-Arm	Scatter Bazooka	Explosive
R-Back	Multi-Missile Launcher	Explosive
High-Firepower Gear	6-Shot Grenade Cannon	Explosive
High-Firepower Gear	Split Missile Launcher	Explosive

▎ A powerful LC remodeled by Arquebus that sacrifices mobility for the sake of overwhelming offensive capability. Compared to other LCs, high-firepower variants stick to fighting on the ground, and will rarely boost to dodge attacks. Armed with a shotgun-like scatter bazooka, homing spread missiles, and grenade launcher, this LC is designed to deal high explosive damage in a large area.

▎ HF LCs scarcely use their bazookas, which function similarly to those used by support-type LCs, with similar damage potential. These scatter bazookas still pose a threat up close, but glancing shots will deal light damage.

▎ Other than the scatter bazooka, all of the HF LC's explosive attacks deal high damage and will overload your ACS easily if you're not equipped with high anti-explosive defense. The grenade cannons equipped on their backs are especially potent; they're capable of firing six grenades at a time, and dealing severe damage to your AP and your systems.

▎ These LCs are able to fire 20 missiles at once, which they can do while boosting along the ground. If a majority of these hit, they'll deal severe damage and can cause significant system instability. They only have light homing capabilities, and can be dodged laterally if you see them coming, but high-firepower variants can fire them off in quick succession and they can be hard to spot, so stay alert.

▎ One of their most dangerous weapons is the grenade launcher in their right hand. Once a high-firepower LC comes to a stop, you'll get a system alert, notifying you that a grenade is coming. While slow moving, HF LCs have good predictive aiming capabilities, and will track your movements. In addition, these grenades cause large explosions that can easily catch you. Be careful, as like a lot of their arsenal, these grenades deal high damage and can overload your systems, especially if you're still recovering from other attacks. Once you notice a warning indicator appear over their right hand, change the direction of your movement to avoid the coming grenade.

▎ HF LCs can huddle down and perform an explosive boost charge, which is their most dangerous attack. Once you're at medium range or further, they'll begin using this boost charge, during which they can quickly fire their entire arsenal. An overwhelming barrage of bazooka shells, missiles, and grenades can all make their way toward you. Each one of these boosts will be capped off by an instantaneous flurry of grenade shots from their back mounted cannons, which will be signaled by a warning from your AC's systems. Their lateral boosts can be dodged in much the same way as the rest of their arsenal. Change directions for the grenades fired from their hand, and strafe or Quick Boost to dodge everything else. Be very careful if they perform a forward boost, as this will be initiated surprisingly fast, and begin with them firing a grenade in close proximity. If you get hit with this and are staggered, you will get hit by the follow-up attack from their grenade cannons, which can easily remove 50% or more of your AC's AP unless your assembly features a good deal of anti-explosive defense.

▎ Staying in mid-air can mitigate a lot of their explosive weaponry's splash damage, which is a legitimate threat while fighting high-firepower LCs Lighter, agile ACs will have an easier time dodging all of their attacks, but will be at greater risk of ACS overload if any explosions clip your AC. Don't expect an AC with high anti-explosive defense to be able to ignore the damage of these LCs, as they're still a major threat.

Thankfully, these high-firepower LCs can't make full use of their weaponry while mobile.

Stay vigilant at medium to long range, since high-firepower LCs can charge in while firing all of their weaponry in rapid succession.

HEAVY CAVALRY

Heavy cavalry units are the most elite mechs that the PCA can field, and are exclusively reserved for use by their highest-ranking officers. While every bit as agile and versatile as light cavalry, these units are a step up in both offensive firepower and defensive capability. The deployment of cutting-edge HCs is a certain indicator that the battle's outcome is critical to the PCA's goals; they will only use these units as a last resort, when throwing everything they have at the situation is worth the potential cost.

AA22: HEAVY CAVALRY (ENFORCEMENT OFFICER SPEC)

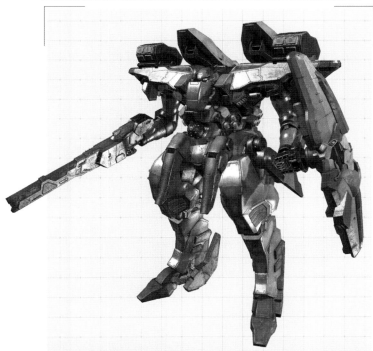

■ This HC, encountered in the "Eliminate the Enforcement Squads" mission, comes equipped with a laser rifle, pulse shield, and shoulder-mounted missiles. It is highly mobile, boosting around—whether in mid-air or on the ground—while alternating between rapidly firing its laser rifle and using missiles for cover fire.

■ This model will usually engage you with its shield raised, pelting you with quick laser rifle fire. Each shot deals low damage, but over time they'll whittle away at you while the HC evades or blocks your shots. This is compounded by how robust their pulse shieldbasher is—it blocks all damage from the front and unlike physical shields, can't be easily broken by melee attacks.

■ When the HC's barrel begins to glow and you hear energy crackling, expect a powerful laser shot to follow. It can charge this shot indefinitely, often waiting to unleash it until you're in a vulnerable position. The HC will drop its shield, and you will receive a warning as it's being launched. This beam travels swiftly, but won't track you and can be dodged if you time a Quick Boost to your left or right as the indicator disappears. Avoid staying within 50m of them, however, as the timing to dodge this beam becomes tighter the closer you get. If it hits, it will cause significant AP damage and high impact build-up. The HC can charge this shot up rapidly, so avoid getting hit by them in succession.

■ If you're piloting a heavy AC and are having trouble timing your boosts correctly, stay close to crates or scaffolding to use them as cover. Due to the mobility of the HC, you cannot rely on any one piece of cover for long, so try to plan out your movements around the area. The laser is also fast enough that you can effectively Initial Guard the charged shot by raising a shield right as the indicator fades.

■ This HC complements its rifle fire with homing missiles, which it can fire without missing a step. Each shoulder can fire up to four missiles at a time, and often both will fire at once. Their tracking abilities aren't high, so using Quick Boosts or boost strafing will be enough to avoid these missiles. Much like the laser shots, these missiles don't deal significant damage, but the passive threat they pose can eventually wear you down.

■ These HC models can perform a pulse shield bash, which deals moderate damage but high impact damage. They only do this within around 50m, but they're capable of performing a Quick Boost to get inside this range, and will follow up forward boosts with this shield bash. If this overloads your ACS, the HC can immediately follow with a charged laser shot, dealing extremely high AP damage. Avoid this attack at all costs, and spend as little time up close with these fearsome HCs as possible, even in the air.

Specs			
AP	16235	Shock Limit	500
Attitude Stability	1800	Shock Resistance	15%
Anti-Kinetic Defense	1060 ↑	ACS Failure Limit	500
Anti-Energy Defense	1413 ↑	Incendiary Resistance	10%
Anti-Explosive Defense	1060 ↑	Pulse Armor Resilience	—

Weapon Systems			
Location	Weapon		Damage Type
R-Arm	Laser Rifle		Energy
L-Arm	Pulse Shieldbasher		Energy
R-Back	Multi-Missile Launcher		Explosive
L-Back	Multi-Missile Launcher		Explosive

- The enforcement officer HC's most unique attack is initiated via a diagonal boost through the air. For a brief moment, the HC will drop its shield and lean into a wide, arcing boost, followed by a rapid volley of rifle fire. Eventually, the HC reaches your flank, ready to fire a charged shot. There's a brief window to get your bearings before the warning for this shot fires, so don't panic and boost into its rifle fire.

- While its shield blocks most damage from the front, the HC will disable it when it fires its charged laser shot. This provides a good opportunity to retaliate but isn't without risks, as you'll need to time your boosts well. Its diagonal aerial boost also leaves it vulnerable; don't waste ammo trying to anticipate this, however, unless you have options like homing missiles available. Outside of these brief openings, persistent attacks will deplete the shield's energy and overload the HC, leaving it open for heavy damage. If you feel confident in your abilities to get away from the HC, a Boost Kick is an effective tool for dealing with its shield. you to conserve ammo. Four or five rounds of depleting its shield should be enough to put the HC down.

This HC can boost while holding a charged laser rifle shot, turning one of the rare windows of opportunity to retaliate into an extremely risky gamble.

AA22: HEAVY CAVALRY (SENIOR OFFICER SPEC)

Specs			
AP	16235	Shock Limit	500
Attitude Stability	1800	Shock Resistance	15%
Anti-Kinetic Defense	1060 ↑	ACS Failure Limit	500
Anti-Energy Defense	1413 ↑	Incendiary Resistance	10%
Anti-Explosive Defense	1305 ↑	Pulse Armor Resilience	—

Weapon Systems		
Location	Weapon	Damage Type
R-Arm	Laser Blade	Energy
L-Arm	Pulse Shield	N/A
R-Back	Pulse Cannon	Energy
L-Back	Pulse Cannon	Energy

- This close-range-focused HC comes equipped with a laser blade, pulse shield, and pulse cannon on its back, exclusively dealing energy damage.

- Its laser blade has a wide range of attacks, which can make it hard to predict. It's capable of horizontal, diagonal, and vertical slashes, as well as forward boost stabs, which it can string together in combos of up to three hits. Each blade attack deals high damage to your AP, and moderate impact, but getting caught in a flurry can quickly overload your ACS, and your only escape is a well-timed Quick Boost. Perform a lateral boost if it pulls its right arm straight back, as that's the signal for a forward stab, which can catch you at around 100m if you're attempting to dodge blade attacks with a backward Quick Boost.

- A lone boost stab performed outside of a combo can reach you up to 300m away, so be ready to perform a lateral Quick Boost if you attempt to fight from range. Additionally, this HC is capable of performing jumping boosts into horizontal, vertical, and diagonal slashes, which add about 75-100m to the blade's effective range.

- Pay close attention to the blade in combat. Beyond the usual attacks, it's capable of charging up its laser blade for a massive sweep that extends its reach to just under 100m. This laser blade attack will deal about 2.5x the damage of a normal blade attack and deals higher impact, so stay vigilant while engaging this enemy.

- Senior officer spec HCs are able to perform these same maneuvers in the air, and don't require the same jumping telegraphs for attacks such as its vertical slash. If the HC takes to the air, be prepared to use more lateral dodges, constant strafing, and avoid attempting aerial combat.

- While the laser attacks are its primary offensive option, it can also fire moderately damaging pulse blasts from its back. These are not nearly as threatening as the blade attacks and dissipate after about 160m, but serve to further discourage close range combat. They also use shields as an effective tool for blocking blade attacks, as the combination of the two will break your guard quickly.

- It is capable of firing these pulse blasts in a few configurations: a steady stream of shots, a broad wall of shots directly in front of the HC and as a particularly damaging double shot from each gun. This double shot deals much higher AP damage and has effectively unlimited range. The only audible system alerts during this fight will occur when this double shot is about to be fired, and thankfully, it can be easily strafed around.

- Fighting with this HC involves a lot of push and pull. Unlike the enforcement officer variant, the senior officer spec HC offers far more openings to retaliate. All of its laser blade attacks leave it open for counterattacks, and attacking while retreating will be an important tactic during this fight, though proper Quick Boost timing is vital. Since all of this HC's attacks deal energy damage, anti-energy AC parts will help considerably.

Be extremely cautious when you see this HC overcharging its laser blade, as this amplifies its range and power by a significant amount.

Watch for the senior officer spec HC's shield to disengage while fighting; this is a telegraph that it may be attempting to slash you with its laser blade.

Despite being heavy cavalry, they are still incredibly mobile, so be prepared to deal with their aggressive speed.

AA22: HEAVY CAVALRY (ARQUEBUS REMODEL)

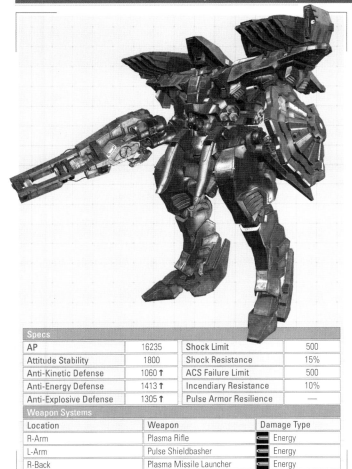

▌ A threat at both close and long ranges, the Arquebus remodel HC will engage you with plasma blasts from a distance, and attempt to bash you with its shield if you manage to close in. The shield bash deals negligible damage, but causes considerable ACS strain.

▌ The most difficult aspect of dealing with this foe is that its shield will remain active nearly the entire battle; this model can use its plasma rifle and fire missiles even with its shield raised. The majority of this fight revolves around finding openings to bypass the shield.

▌ Its shield is effective at reducing impact, and unless you have weapons that continuously from all four units, it's recommended to wait for an opening, which usually occurs when it needs to charge its plasma rifle.

▌ The plasma rifle it uses can fire singular shots that can be dangerous, but its greatest threat by far is from its charged shots, which it takes every opportunity to unleash. You can suffer extreme AP loss if a charged shot directly hits you, so your best bet against this HC is to remain mobile.

▌ One possible strategy if you are piloting a close-range AC is to deliberately close in on the HC and bait the shield bash. This attack requires the HC to briefly lower its shield, allowing for a well-timed counterattack.

▌ If you are piloting a long-range AC, a better option is to remain mobile to evade plasma shots and missiles and slowly chip away at the HC with explosive damage or rapid-firing weapons that can hit it in areas not covered by the shield.

Specs			
AP	16235	Shock Limit	500
Attitude Stability	1800	Shock Resistance	15%
Anti-Kinetic Defense	1060 ↑	ACS Failure Limit	500
Anti-Energy Defense	1413 ↑	Incendiary Resistance	10%
Anti-Explosive Defense	1305 ↑	Pulse Armor Resilience	—

Weapon Systems		
Location	Weapon	Damage Type
R-Arm	Plasma Rifle	Energy
L-Arm	Pulse Shieldbasher	Energy
R-Back	Plasma Missile Launcher	Energy
L-Back	Plasma Missile Launcher	Energy

Prepare to Quick Boost or deploy your shield whenever this HC charges up its plasma rifle.

▌ An extremely defense-oriented heavy cavalry variant, this Arquebus remodel dishes out energy damage using its plasma rifle, pulse shieldbasher, and dual back-mounted plasma missile launchers.

▌ This enemy is exclusively encountered in the "Intercept the Corporate Forces" mission, serving as a unique opponent standing in the way of your objective. Interestingly, you'll first encounter this HC obliterating two of "Cinder" Carla's TOYBOX MTs with its shieldbasher, giving you a taste of its formidable power.

PCA WEAPONRY

This class designates various specialized weapon platforms utilized by the Planetary Closure Administration—and anyone who can salvage their tech. From WATCHER units deployed to monitor critical infrastructure to DENOISER enforcement drones tasked with safeguarding Rubicon's long-buried secrets, all the way to massive space-faring warships that serve as the executors of the System's verdict and a symbol of the PCA's dominion.

AM06: WATCHER

▌ Autonomous seek-and-destroy drones often found in groups floating above the ground, extending out their limbs and releasing aerial mines. These mines aren't particularly damaging, but will be slow to detonate unless you make direct contact with one. Additionally, WATCHER drones closer to the ground or in enclosed spaces can fire a five-round laser burst. These bursts are similar to the mines, and aren't particularly dangerous, but they can make it hard to keep an eye on other drones in the vicinity.

▌ WATCHER drones can also be found monitoring the Grids or Depths, hovering in place until a threat gets within their range. This range is considerable, and they'll lock on, close their propellers, and begin to accelerate quickly toward their target. Upon collision, they'll explode in a fiery explosion, dealing high damage and ACS strain. They frequently appear in large groups, and because they can close in on you from so far away, it can be difficult to effectively evade them all, so try and shoot them down as they approach. Your systems will not pick up on them once they target you, however. It's best to approach areas monitored by these drones slowly, and deal with them as they appear in front of you to limit the chances that you'll be caught off guard by swarms of them at once.

A pair of watchers en route to collide with an AC. Once they collide, they'll deal heavy damage.

Specs			
AP	101	Anti-Energy Defense	1135 ↑
Attitude Stability	175	Anti-Explosive Defense	1000
Anti-Kinetic Defense	790 ↓	Pulse Armor Resilience	—
Weapon Systems			

Location	Weapon	Damage Type	
Frame	Laser Gun		Energy
Frame	Floating Mines		Explosive

AM02: DENOISER (MELEE TYPE)

AM02: DENOISER (SNIPER TYPE)

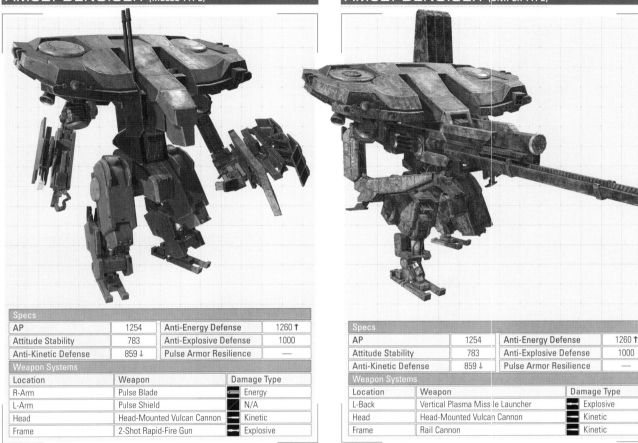

Specs

AP	1254	Anti-Energy Defense	1260 ↑
Attitude Stability	783	Anti-Explosive Defense	1000
Anti-Kinetic Defense	859 ↓	Pulse Armor Resilience	—

Weapon Systems

Location	Weapon		Damage Type
R-Arm	Pulse Blade		Energy
L-Arm	Pulse Shield		N/A
Head	Head-Mounted Vulcan Cannon		Kinetic
Frame	2-Shot Rapid-Fire Gun		Explosive

Specs

AP	1254	Anti-Energy Defense	1260 ↑
Attitude Stability	783	Anti-Explosive Defense	1000
Anti-Kinetic Defense	859 ↓	Pulse Armor Resilience	—

Weapon Systems

Location	Weapon		Damage Type
L-Back	Vertical Plasma Missile Launcher		Explosive
Head	Head-Mounted Vulcan Cannon		Kinetic
Frame	Rail Cannon		Kinetic

- ▌ DENOISER drones are assigned by the Enforcement System to defend the Depths that extend deep into the bowels of Rubicon. This model specializes in close combat, with a well-rounded arsenal that gives them access to all damage types.

- ▌ Outside of close range, expect them to keep their shields up, pestering you with vulcan cannon fire and explosive rounds. Their 2-shot rapid-fire guns cause your systems to issue an audible attack indicator, after which a lateral Quick Boost will reliably evade the attack.

- ▌ As they approach, they'll charge at you with horizontal blade swipes. These blades have a two-hit combo that can deal heavy damage and a boost charge that can catch you off guard with its reach of about 80m. Their boost attacks can be followed up with a second swipe that can clip you if you attempt to evade with a Quick Boost. Dodging with a jump can help, but be aware of your surroundings, as you may not get enough altitude in areas with low ceilings.

- ▌ Melee-type DENOISER drones are best fought in the air, as they lack aerial capabilities and will not be able to rely on their powerful blade attacks. Their machine guns can be easily evaded while strafing in the air, but beware crossing the 100m range, as they can start mixing in their missiles more frequently.

- ▌ Sniper-type DENOISER drones are noticeably different than the others in that kinetic weaponry is their primary source of damage, with energy weaponry being secondary. Their plasma missiles will be in play at any range, however, launching three homing missiles at a time.

- ▌ A slower model of DENOISER, this variant is less prone to fast movements; instead, they slowly walk around, occasionally performing short boosts to reposition or dodge attacks, and will hunch down to remain immobile while firing their rail cannons. At ranges past 200m, listen for an audible attack indicator to let you know that they're about to fire a shot from their rail cannon after briefly charging up. Within 200m, they're a lot more likely to use their vulcan cannons in an attempt to quickly stagger you.

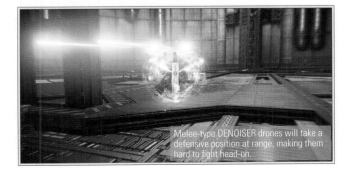

Melee-type DENOISER drones will take a defensive position at range, making them hard to fight head-on.

DENOISE drones outfitted with rail cannons excel at long-distance sniping, and can target you well beyond your maximum lock-on range.

AM02: DENOISER (SUPPORT TYPE)

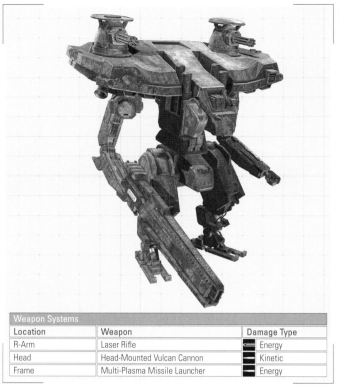

Specs			
AP	1254	Anti-Energy Defense	1260 ↑
Attitude Stability	783	Anti-Explosive Defense	1000
Anti-Kinetic Defense	859 ↓	Pulse Armor Resilience	—

▌ Designed to lay down suppressive fire and support other DENOISER types in battle, this variant will launch volleys of dual plasma missiles from a distance. The twin head-mounted vulcan cannons can fire without warning, but their target tracking systems will struggle to hit mobile ACs, so it's essential to stay mobile while engaging these enemies.

▌ Their laser rifles only fire one shot at a time, but can be charged up to release a rapid-fire volley of shots, telegraphed by a blue glow emanating from the barrel of the rifle.

▌ Support-type DENOISERs can perform multiple evasive boosts in succession, making them challenging to track unless you enable Target Assist. Focus on isolating these enemies so you can take them out without other distractions.

After charging its laser rifle, this variant will unleash a rapid volley of shots.

Weapon Systems		
Location	Weapon	Damage Type
R-Arm	Laser Rifle	◀ Energy
Head	Head-Mounted Vulcan Cannon	▬ Kinetic
Frame	Multi-Plasma Missile Launcher	◀ Energy

AM02: DENOISER (HEAVY FIREPOWER)

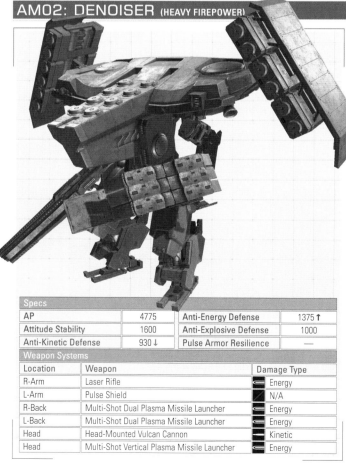

▌ Heavy firepower DENOISER models share some behavior and weaponry with the support types but are far better equipped, coming with a pulse shield, extra plasma missiles, and over 4x the AP of the standard variants.

▌ They can fire plasma missiles in three distinct patterns: eight forward-facing missiles from their head, two groups of six fired from the missile launchers on their shoulders, and a combined barrage that fires all 20 missiles at once, which can deal colossal damage.

At ranges of 75m or closer, missiles fired from their shoulders will arc around you if you're directly in front of the drone; however, their blast radius can still hit you at ranges beyond 65m once they hit the ground—this is when they can switch to their vulcan cannons as a secondary offensive option.

▌ Finally, this heavy firepower variant comes with a pulse shield that blocks damage from the front. They typically only deploy this shield while boosting, and will become more passive while doing so, firing only single shots from their laser rifles or using their vulcan cannons at close range.

The full plasma missile barrage of a heavy firepower DENOISER homing in on your position is a sight to behold, and a clear warning that you should seek cover or prepare to Quick Boost.

Specs			
AP	4775	Anti-Energy Defense	1375 ↑
Attitude Stability	1600	Anti-Explosive Defense	1000
Anti-Kinetic Defense	930 ↓	Pulse Armor Resilience	—

Weapon Systems		
Location	Weapon	Damage Type
R-Arm	Laser Rifle	◀ Energy
L-Arm	Pulse Shield	◢ N/A
R-Back	Multi-Shot Dual Plasma Missile Launcher	◀ Energy
L-Back	Multi-Shot Dual Plasma Missile Launcher	◀ Energy
Head	Head-Mounted Vulcan Cannon	▬ Kinetic
Head	Multi-Shot Vertical Plasma Missile Launcher	◀ Energy

AS07: HEAVY WARSHIP

▌ These flying behemoths are equipped with several cannons and turrets to protect the generator on the ship's main deck. This means that approaching the ship from the bow or side is the safest option, despite leaving you exposed to some of its weaponry.

▌ The most serious threats as you make your approach are the eight-pronged bow lasers these warships are typically equipped with, and the huge volley of missiles that can be fired from their hull. A unique variant in the "Steal the Survey Data" mission is also able to deploy ten quad-laser drones from its port and starboard sides, and comes equipped with a massive, long-range rail cannon on its keel. Destroying a warship's bridge will instantly bring down the entire ship, weaponry included, so that should always be your main target.

▌ Positioned along the decks of the warship are two large, double-barreled cannons, each capable of firing two shells that deal high damage and impact; these can be deadly if you get hit multiple times. The cannons will trigger an audible attack indicator, so be prepared to evade them while making your approach. They fire infrequently, however, so quickly destroying them between their blasts is the best way to deal with them.

▌ The turning speed of their cannons is very slow. This means that if you approach the bridge from the bow of the ship, you can fly over the cannons and destroy the bridge without having to worry about them. If they do manage to stagger you while you're heading to the bridge, however, you'll be in a very bad position, so be vigilant while boosting past them.

▌ Each warship also comes equipped with, at minimum, six double-barreled turrets—three on the port and three on the starboard sides of the ship. Active warships can be armed with an additional four turrets on the hull of the ship, deterring approaches from beneath. These turrets fire in extremely short bursts, so they're not overwhelming, but they can inflict a lot of impact and can potentially knock you out of the sky before you can reach the ship's deck.

Specs			
AP	2688	Anti-Energy Defense	854 ↓
Attitude Stability	—	Anti-Explosive Defense	1000
Anti-Kinetic Defense	1210 ↑	Pulse Armor Resilience	—

Weapon Systems		
Location	Weapon	Damage Type
Bow	Bow Laser	Energy
Underside (Optional)	Keel Rail Cannon	Kinetic
Deck	Heavy Missile Launcher	Explosive
Deck	Cannons	Kinetic
Deck	Turrets	Kinetic
Deployment Bays (Optional)	Drone Units	Energy

ARQUEBUS INTERCEPTOR FLEET

Warships hijacked by Arquebus are functionally very similar to the PCA heavy warships, and come equipped with a single cannon and a set of turrets to protect the generator on the ship's deck. Take full advantage of the EN anomaly providing your AC with unlimited EN in "Breach the Kármán Line," but be ready to dodge during frontal assaults, as each of these ships is equipped with bow lasers and a keel rail cannon.

AS07: HEAVY WARSHIP (DRONE UNITS)

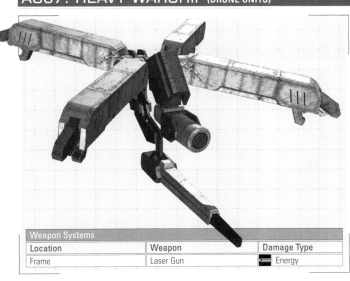

Specs			
AP	350	Anti-Energy Defense	700 ↓
Attitude Stability	351	Anti-Explosive Defense	1000
Anti-Kinetic Defense	1140 ↑	Pulse Armor Resilience	—

▌ These support units originate from heavy warships, and are independently controlled drones that employ energy lasers. They can use two different attacks: a singular beam that is shot at your position, and a triad of lasers that fire at you simultaneously.

▌ Since they congregate and focus on you, they can be dangerous if you aren't careful. Builds in the lower ranges of energy resistance can find these an even larger threat.

▌ Though you may encounter large numbers of these drones, they go down easily, even with weaker weaponry. The biggest concern is that they can continue to fire at you even when the warship has been eliminated. In situations where it's essential to eliminate them, using weapons that support multi-lock such as missiles or plasma missiles will make quick work of them.

Weapon Systems		
Location	Weapon	Damage Type
Frame	Laser Gun	Energy

RUBICON INSTITUTE WEAPONRY

This collection of mysterious and deadly units make use of "forgotten" technology that has lain dormant since the era of the Rubicon Research Institute. For autonomous combat units, their capability in battle is unrivaled, hinting at the true potential of weaponized Coral. As the conflict spreads, you'll encounter these seemingly unaffiliated units in many abandoned parts of Rubicon that have yet to be claimed by the major factions.

IA-24: KITE (WING LASER BLADES)

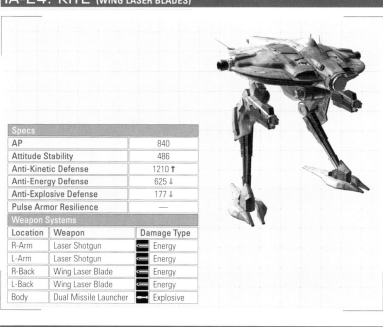

Specs	
AP	840
Attitude Stability	486
Anti-Kinetic Defense	1210 ↑
Anti-Energy Defense	625 ↓
Anti-Explosive Defense	177 ↓
Pulse Armor Resilience	—

Weapon Systems		
Location	Weapon	Damage Type
R-Arm	Laser Shotgun	Energy
L-Arm	Laser Shotgun	Energy
R-Back	Wing Laser Blade	Energy
L-Back	Wing Laser Blade	Energy
Body	Dual Missile Launcher	Explosive

▌ Extremely agile unmanned drones that defend the Xylem with their specialized form of aerial combat. While not particularly durable, KITE drones are practically unmatched in aerial combat, and can take to the air to bolster their offense—making use of Target Assist can help ensure they don't exploit your blind spots, though be careful when tackling them in ECM fog.

▌ As they fly high into the air, they'll deploy their wing laser blades and execute a powerful dive attack. These dives usually happen two at a time, and are their main offensive option. They deal high AP damage and ACS strain, but also provide the best opportunity to strike the drones with energy or explosive weaponry. Kinetic weapons that deal concentrated bursts of damage also work particularly well.

▌ If you try to meet them in the air, these KITE models are more likely to use their laser shotguns, which can fire two shotgun blasts in quick succession, and fire six homing plasma missiles as they fly through the air between aerial dives.

▌ They'll occasionally land on the ground, at which point they lose their laser blades as a source of damage. You can force them to the ground if you shoot them out of the air by overloading their ACS. Scan them to keep a visual on them in the uninhabited city's ECM fog, and nail them down with fast homing missiles.

IA-24: KITE (PLASMA CANNON)

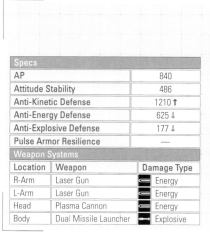

Specs	
AP	840
Attitude Stability	486
Anti-Kinetic Defense	1210 ↑
Anti-Energy Defense	625 ↓
Anti-Explosive Defense	177 ↓
Pulse Armor Resilience	—

Weapon Systems		
Location	Weapon	Damage Type
R-Arm	Laser Gun	Energy
L-Arm	Laser Gun	Energy
Head	Plasma Cannon	Energy
Body	Dual Missile Launcher	Explosive

▌ A long-range variant of the KITE drone, this model spends less time in the air in favor of firing high-powered sniper shots at you from elevated positions. Their primary plasma attacks deal significant AP damage.

▌ You'll be alerted of their presence by your system's warning indicators before you get a chance to lock on to them. As you approach, they'll take to the air, and fire weaker plasma blasts or rapid laser shots, and use the same missiles as the laser blade variants.

▌ While airborne, they'll be just as agile as the wing laser blade models and will dodge your shots, but their offensive abilities are reduced. Destroy them in the same manner as the wing laser drones, by pelting them with explosive and energy damage or shotguns. Unless you have manual aiming unlocked, engaging these enemies at long range is ineffective due to the rampant ECM fog.

IA-27: GHOST (SNIPER TYPE)

Specs	
AP	3820
Attitude Stability	1066
Anti-Kinetic Defense	1210 ↑
Anti-Energy Defense	625 ↓
Anti-Explosive Defense	177 ↓
Pulse Armor Resilience	—

Weapon Systems		
Location	Weapon	Damage Type
R-Arm	Laser Gun	Energy
L-Back	ECM Mines	Explosive
R-Back	ECM Mines	Explosive

- GHOST are agile mechs with Monitor Display Deception jamming tech that can render them invisible to AC sensors; this variant capitalizes on this cloaking ability by remaining practically invisible at long range, sniping you with their laser gun when they have a clear shot.

- Pay attention to your systems, because the audible alert indicator caused by their shots will often be your first indication that a sniper GHOST is in the area. These shots deal high AP damage and moderate ACS strain.

- This variant will do everything to avoid direct combat, and when they lose stealth they'll jump back to escape and reappear elsewhere. This often puts them very far away from their original position, and since they'll be cloaked again, you'll have to use your scan to find them, or wait for them to fire and appear on the compass.

- Uniquely, they're capable of hanging from high walls to gain a vantage point, from which they can fire from, and tracing the origin of their shot is often your best means of discerning their location. Make sure you unload all of your weapons on them after finding them, because your aim should be to destroy them before they can reposition. Explosive weapons will handle GHOST quickly.

IA-27: GHOST (MELEE TYPE)

Specs	
AP	3820
Attitude Stability	1066
Anti-Kinetic Defense	1210 ↑
Anti-Energy Defense	625 ↓
Anti-Explosive Defense	177 ↓
Pulse Armor Resilience	—

Weapon Systems		
Location	Weapon	Damage Type
L-Arm	Laser Whip	Energy
L-Back	ECM Mines	Explosive
R-Back	ECM Mines	Explosive

- Melee Type GHOST are nimble and like to hop and boost around before retreating back into stealth. They attack with a medium-to-close-range laser whip, which can catch you off guard with deceptive ranged attacks, dealing light AP damage, but heavy ACS strain.

- They're capable of both vertical lashes and wide horizontal sweeps, which can reach up to 130m directly in front of them. Past this range, they'll precede this sweep with a hop that will add about 40m of range, but regardless of where they initiate it from, it's relatively easy to evade by jumping over it.

- Their vertical attacks can also include a short 40m hop, out of which they can unleash a series of lashes followed by a damaging high-jump attack. All vertical attacks are best avoided by lateral Quick Boosts.

- They can release ECM mines that release an explosive blast cloud, which is always preceded by a boost jump.

- When this GHOST model enters stealth again, they don't retreat very far, and as such are much easier to find again by scanning the environment. You can quickly counterattack as they retreat, and a volley of explosive rounds makes quick work of these targets.

IA-27: GHOST (PULSE ARMOR)

Specs	
AP	4775
Attitude Stability	1066
Anti-Kinetic Defense	1210 ↑
Anti-Energy Defense	625 ↓
Anti-Explosive Defense	177 ↓
Pulse Armor Resilience	4500

Weapon Systems		
Location	Weapon	Damage Type
L-Arm	Laser Whip	Energy
R-Arm	Plasma Gun	Energy
L-Back	ECM Mines	Explosive
R-Back	ECM Mines	Explosive

- Pulse armor GHOST can fire their plasma rifles in single shots, or charge their shots for a stronger attack with a large explosive radius. They'll continue to use this at close range and will use it in conjunction with their melee whip attacks.

- Their shields can be overloaded with consistent damage, especially energy, leading to a prolonged stagger. Dispatch them in this staggered state with a volley of explosive or energy rounds.

- As with the melee variants, this model's vertical melee attacks are best dodged by lateral Quick Boosts, while their horizontal attacks can be dodged by jumping. They have an extended melee move set, and can combo their whip attacks beyond the single attacks of the melee variant. They can also change their attack direction mid-combo, so you'll need to dodge multiple times to be safe, even if you avoid the first attack.

Pulse shield GHOST models can suddenly swap to their plasma rifle as a primary damage source, giving them a lot of mix-up potential.

IE-09: HELIANTHUS

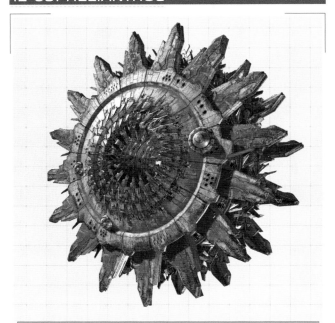

Specs			
AP	2800	Anti-Energy Defense	1806 ↑
Attitude Stability	1053	Anti-Explosive Defense	177 ↓
Anti-Kinetic Defense	1560 ↑	Pulse Armor Resilience	—

Weapon Systems		
Location	Weapon	Damage Type
Body	Ray Floret Cutters	Kinetic
Body	Disk Flamethrower	Explosive /Incendiary
Body	Side-Mounted Multi-Missile Launcher	Explosive

▌ HELIANTHUS are huge, autonomous grinder wheels that roll around the battlefield at high speeds attempting to ram you. They will either launch missiles while they close in, or spit fire from their core if they come to a sudden halt.

▌ HELIANTHUS' most dangerous attack is their ramming charge, during which any contact with their ray floret cutters causes immense AP damage and extremely rapid ACS strain. Avoid this devastating attack by using lateral Quick Boosts, or better yet, by jumping and shifting to aerial combat.

▌ Once these enemies slow down and their core begins to glow, they'll spit fire at you, causing ACS anomaly, which increases incoming impact. This can be avoided by boost strafing around them as they grind to a halt, but you'll need to keep track of the other HELIANTHUS in the area, as it's easy to accidentally strafe into them.

▌ The missile launchers on their sides fire six missiles as they begin to make their approach. These missiles are easy to dodge with a Quick Boost, but mostly serve as a distraction to catch you off guard while you're focused on the HELIANTHUS itself.

▌ The high speed of HELIANTHUS grinder wheels makes them difficult to hit and keep track of, so scanning them can help to maintain visual detection as they move around. Trying to hit them from long range is futile due to their speed; wait for them to stop and change directions before unloading powerful explosive attacks on their core.

▌ Attacking them while airborne is extremely effective, as they have little recourse beyond missiles to defend themselves. This allows you to get close to them while eliminating the threats in their arsenal. Flamethrowers are extremely effective at dealing with HELIANTHUS due to their sustained explosive damage, so consider equipping one if you're struggling with these enemies.

IA-05: WEEVIL (CLUSTER MISSILE LAUNCHER)

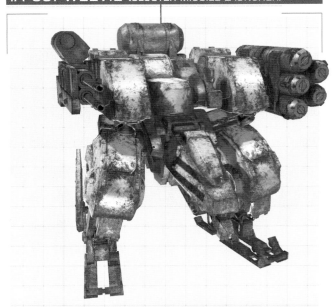

Specs			
AP	9550	Anti-Energy Defense	1806 ↑
Attitude Stability	1600	Anti-Explosive Defense	177 ↓
Anti-Kinetic Defense	1560 ↑	Pulse Armor Resilience	—

Weapon Systems		
Location	Weapon	Damage Type
R-Arm	2-Shot Rapid-Fire Gun	Kinetic
L-Arm	Cluster Missile Launcher	Explosive
L-Back	Scatter Missile Launcher	Explosive
R-Back	Scatter Missile Launcher	Explosive

▌ Ancient, powerful autonomous drones designed by the Rubicon Research Institute, WEEVILs come in several configurations, but all models are well equipped and carry a unique weapon in their left-arm slot. They are reclusive and dormant, but will activate if they sense threats to the Coral. They are highly mobile combatants, capable of boost strafing while firing their weapons, and performing devastating kicks.

▌ While their rapid-fire guns deal moderate to low damage, they'll use them to box you in to facilitate the use of their specialized, powerful vertical cluster missiles as their primary source of damage. As such, avoid being overly aggressive with these targets and pick them off one by one from a respectable distance. As such, avoid being overly aggressive with these targets and pick them off one by one from a respectable distance.

▌ Their forward-facing scatter missiles are their most common attack, available at all ranges, without a warning. These missiles do not deal significant damage outside of 150m, and their true danger comes from multiple WEEVIL drones cornering you, so avoid getting caught between a group of them.

▌ These drones will more frequently use their vertical cluster missiles at ranges of 150m or farther. Their missiles will be highlighted by your system's alerts, and will be fired in groups of five that split on their way down. While they don't cause large explosions or significant splash damage, you'll need to stay mobile to avoid damage, as they arc downward to carpet the ground.

▌ Keep an eye on their movements, as their most powerful attacks are kicks, and these models are good at obscuring these attacks with their missiles. Their kicks are telegraphed by a short jump and have a range of around 200m. If you see a WEEVIL jump, prepare to Quick Boost to the side and counterattack as it lands.

▌ WEEVIL drones are best handled using explosive weaponry due to their severe lack of defense against that damage type and extreme resistance to kinetic and energy weapons. Staggering them first can make your other weaponry more effective, but blasting them with explosives is the most efficient way to take them out. Always consider bringing an explosive weapon or two when dealing with these dangerous threats.

IA-05: WEEVIL (GRENADE CANNON)

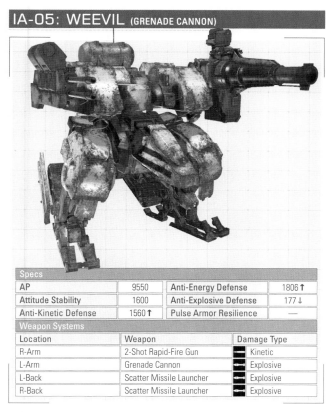

Specs				
AP	9550	Anti-Energy Defense	1806 ↑
Attitude Stability	1600	Anti-Explosive Defense	177 ↓
Anti-Kinetic Defense	1560 ↑	Pulse Armor Resilience	—

Weapon Systems		
Location	Weapon	Damage Type
R-Arm	2-Shot Rapid-Fire Gun	Kinetic
L-Arm	Grenade Cannon	Explosive
L-Back	Scatter Missile Launcher	Explosive
R-Back	Scatter Missile Launcher	Explosive

▌ This model is equipped with entirely forward-facing weaponry, including a single, powerful grenade cannon on its left arm. Like their cluster missile counterpart, they are particularly weak to explosive damage.

▌ The major difference the grenade cannon brings to the table when compared to the detonating cannon variant lies in the nature of grenade fire. This variant's grenades travel faster than the detonating cannon variant's shells with a large explosive radius, so always remain on the move and give these enemies a bit of space to inherently avoid the cannon.

▌ These enemies show up in two groups of two in the "Escort the Weaponized Mining Ship" mission. Alone they may seem trivial, but working as a pair allows their weapons to shine; due to the large blasts they can cause, letting one out of your sight can be dangerous. That said, you can approach them like the encounter with the missile and detonating cannon variants: focus your fire on one at a time, keeping at medium range while not letting the other too far out of sight, while being ready to dodge when you hear a system alert.

The grenade cannon WEEVIL drones are especially deadly in pairs, as they tend to alternate their cannon shots in an attempt to fake you out.

IA-05: WEEVIL (DETONATING CANNON)

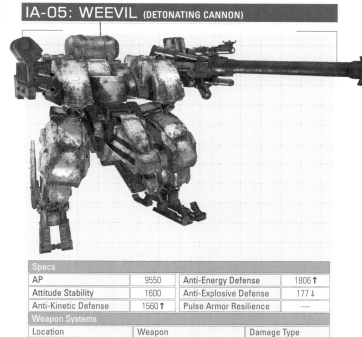

Specs				
AP	9550	Anti-Energy Defense	1806 ↑
Attitude Stability	1600	Anti-Explosive Defense	177 ↓
Anti-Kinetic Defense	1560 ↑	Pulse Armor Resilience	—

Weapon Systems		
Location	Weapon	Damage Type
R-Arm	2-Shot Rapid-Fire Gun	Kinetic
L-Arm	Detonating Cannon	Explosive
L-Back	Scatter Missile Launcher	Explosive
R-Back	Scatter Missile Launcher	Explosive

▌ Compared to the cluster missile variant, this model's detonating cannon doesn't work quite as harmoniously with the WEEVIL drone's basic abilities, so it relies more heavily on it to deal damage. Since all of its attacks are forward-facing, it's much easier to keep track of where they're going to fire; watch their movements and dodge accordingly with Quick Boosts.

▌ Their detonating cannon deals heavy damage, and—much like a kick—can instantly stagger fragile AC builds, leading to potentially massive damage from follow-up kicks. Their grenades are aimed with predictive firing and will track your movements, so be ready to change direction once an audible warning alerts you to a grenade. Sometimes they will perform a short hop before shooting, directing the explosive into the ground, but this will also be avoided if you change directions and Quick Boost appropriately.

▌ Unlike the cluster missile variant, this MT is best fought from an extremely long range. Without the looming threat of vertical missiles, all of their attacks can be avoided by boost strafing at long range. Missiles may pose a minor threat at this distance, but their most dangerous attacks can be easily avoided once beyond 200m, and you can retaliate either with missiles, or by sniping them as they attempt a jumping attack.

▌ As this model appears alongside the cluster missile variant in "Reach the Coral Convergence," it'll be an easier encounter if you focus on the missile-wielding WEEVIL at close range, while attempting to avoid the slow-moving projectiles from the detonating cannon model. Just as with the other WEEVIL drones, the detonating cannon variant is weak to explosive damage

Grenade cannon models can fire grenades suddenly in mid air, making the resulting explosion more likely to hit.

CHAPTER 5 ARENA GUIDE

The Arena is both a critical part of your journey as a pilot—aiding in the experimentation process that inches you closer to fully understanding your AC's abilities—and a central component of the machinations that have consumed Rubicon. As you take on simulated opponents of varying skill levels and tastes in AC design, this chapter will guide you through the process of carefully adjusting your own assembly and applying the most tactically sound approaches to each of the battles you'll face.

ABOUT THIS CHAPTER

The Arena is a key part of progression in Armored Core VI, and its one-on-one battles provide short bursts of pure action that perfectly leverage the game's core combat mechanics. This chapter will cover each Arena battle in the order of your opponents' ranks, from lowest to highest.

The format used for entries throughout this chapter is very straightforward, but we'll explain each element here to ensure that everything is clear:

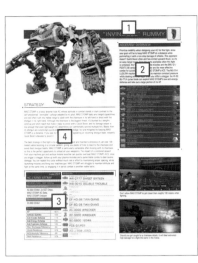

[1] Opponent Name

This tells you the name of the enemy pilot and shows their emblem.

[2] Recommended Assembly

This is the AC build we recommend you use against the opponent. We've taken care to ensure that all parts are accessible from the earliest point at which each Arena battle can be unlocked.

[3] Opponent Details

Here you'll find the opponent's assembly, key specs and rewards, along with which combat zone the battle takes place in. If you're unsure about what any of the stats means, they are all explained in full in the Assembly & Specs section, starting on P.28.

[4] Strategy

For each Arena battle, we've provided key strategies to help you defeat the opponent using our recommended build.

ARENA BASICS

Designed by ALLMIND for data gathering and training purposes, the Arena sits alongside the story missions as a core component of the game. Duels in the Arena take place in a virtual environment, pitting you against AI-controlled simulations of every registered mercenary operating on Rubicon. After completing either "Retrieve Combat Logs" or "Investigate BAWS Arsenal No. 2," you'll unlock the ability to access the Arena from the Garage menu. Upon entering the Arena, you'll be presented with a roster of all currently available opponents including their ranks, and since you're just getting started, you'll be ranked dead last.

You can then begin working your way through the ranks of ALLMIND's database, with higher ranks featuring progressively more challenging opponents. Bouts take place in a handful of small virtual combat zones specifically assigned to each battle, so once you've seen a combat zone, you won't have to familiarize yourself with it again when fighting a different opponent there. However, be mindful of how simulated Arena fights differ from confrontations against the real version of these pilots that can occur during missions. While mission encounters with rival AC pilots can sometimes be lengthy, brutal affairs, fights in the Arena are designed to be quick and to the point, often taking less than a minute to get through. You'll be stripped of your repair kits for these simulation battles, but otherwise retain access to your AC's full suite of capabilities.

Rewards
With each victory in the Arena, you'll be rewarded with OST Chips, which can be used in the OS Tuning menu to unlock powerful limited-use abilities for your AC called Core Expansions, along with other upgrades and abilities that can help give

you an edge in battle. Additional info on OST Chips and OS Tuning can be found on P.32. You'll also unlock your opponent's AC Data and their emblem for use in the AC Design menu. Loading this data lets you build the exact ACs piloted by these mercenaries and test them out for yourself, provided you have the parts available or the necessary funds to purchase them. Finally, the Arena can be a major source of COAM—each rank's battles offer progressively higher payouts. As this is a virtual program, you won't have to pay for your ammunition or repair costs, so the reward that's displayed is the exact amount you'll get for defeating that opponent.

Additional Tips

» *The builds we recommend are just examples of approaches that work and are intended to encourage experimentation; many other build types can also prove successful in each battle.*

» *The Arena is an ideal place to test out AC parts and builds in real-time combat against realistic opponents on an even playing field.*

» *Building ACS strain, causing stagger, and dealing high burst damage with direct hits will form the core of every fight.*

» *Aim to complete each set of battles as soon as possible to quickly unlock more OST Chips and upgrade your AC.*

Battles in the Arena are tactical and intense, usually culminating in quick bursts of actions.

MERCENARY LORE

Each opponent that you can face in the Arena has an accompanying text entry that details some of their personal history and motivations. These are well worth reading through for anyone interested in learning about the game's world, characters, and factions. If you're looking for info on how to fight the real version of each ranked AC pilot, turn to P.307, where you'll find a full list of encounters with links to missions where they make an appearance.

RANKS & CATEGORIES

Arena fights are organized into multiple letter-graded ranks and split across two distinct categories: Records and Analysis. You'll initially only have access to the Records category, consisting of 29 simulated opponents based on real AC pilots. Winning every match within your current rank (F -> S) is necessary to advance to the next, but you'll also have to progress through the story to unlock higher ranks. The Analysis category only becomes available after progressing through Chapter 1 on NG+, and consists of multiple phases (α -> δ) of virtual test subjects. Unlocking some of the later Analysis phases will require you to reach NG++; however, note that the δ phase is unique, in that proceeding to a new game cycle after clearing NG++ will lock these opponents out until the conditions are met again.

Check the charts on the right to learn when you'll be able to access each rank or phase. Assuming you clear each set of opponents as soon as they become available, you can expect to unlock new Arena battles throughout the three playthroughs required to achieve all endings. It's possible to tackle the Arena whenever you want, but we recommend climbing the ranks as early as possible to upgrade your AC. The number of OST Chips listed here represents how many you'll unlock when first defeating each opponent in that rank, for a total of 197 OST Chips.

RECORD

Rank	Unlock Condition	OST Chips
29-27/F	Complete "Retrieve Combat Logs" or "Investigate BAWS Arsenal No. 2"	2
26-23/E	Complete "Attack the Watchpoint"	2
22-18/D	Complete "Ocean Crossing"	3
17-13/C	Complete "Attack the Refueling Base," "Tunnel Sabotage," and "Eliminate V.VII"	3
12-08/B	Complete "Attack the Old Spaceport"	4
07-04/A	Complete "Destroy the Ice Worm"	4
03-01/S	Complete "Underground Exploration – Depth 3"	6

ANALYSIS

Phase	Unlock Condition	OST Chips
α-1-3	Complete "Attack the Watchpoint" in NG+	8
β-1-3	Complete "Attack the Refueling Base" in NG+	10
γ-1-3	Complete "Destroy the Ice Worm" in NG+	15
δ-1	Complete "Ocean Crossing" in NG++	—
δ-2	Complete "Survey the Uninhabited City (Alt)," "Heavy Missile Support Launch," and "Eliminate the Enforcement Squads" or "Destroy the Special Forces Craft" in NG++	—
δ-3	Complete "Underground Exploration – Depth 2" in NG++	—

COMBAT ZONES

Arena encounters are set in a variety of familiar combat zones, most of which are based on locations from the main story missions. Learning to use the geography of each map to your advantage is one of the keys to success—whether you're taking cover from enemy fire, or pressuring the opponent into a tight corner with little room to escape your incoming onslaught. See the descriptions below for a preview of where you'll be spending your time climbing the Arena ranks. If you're struggling in a particular battle, it's worth checking to see if there's anything in the combat zone that could help to even the odds a little.

Legend Player Starting Location   Opponent Starting Location

COMBAT ZONE: TEST ARENA

This box-shaped virtual arena has a flat surface and high ceiling, with no cover whatsoever to retreat to or hide behind. The only spatial advantages you will be able to leverage here are keeping your distance from the opponent, ascending to attack from above, or pressuring them into a corner.

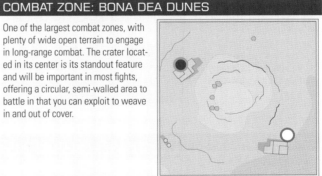

COMBAT ZONE: CONTAMINATED CITY

A larger combat zone with a few structures to potentially utilize for cover. Scanning will be helpful if obstacles get in the way, but it's ultimately best to stay out in the open where you can take advantage of your AC's mobility. Be careful not to get caught on buildings while boosting, as this will slow you down and potentially leave you open to attacks.

COMBAT ZONE: BONA DEA DUNES

One of the largest combat zones, with plenty of wide open terrain to engage in long-range combat. The crater located in its center is its standout feature and will be important in most fights, offering a circular, semi-walled area to battle in that you can exploit to weave in and out of cover.

COMBAT ZONE: BAWS ARSENAL NO. 2

Aerial builds capable of avoiding the circular depressions on the floor will be at an advantage in this combat zone, as opponents will be sure to punish any ACs that get caught in the terrain. Because of the dim lighting and low visibility, you'll want to scan often and activate Target Assist whenever you're struggling to keep track of the opponent.

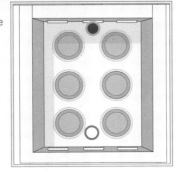

COMBAT ZONE: THE WALL

An expansive combat zone, with a mix of open spaces and city blocks across both sides of its central divide. Once you've engaged the opponent, you'll want to fight primarily in the main open strip between your starting locations, though you may find the buildings and walls useful for cover while your weapons reload.

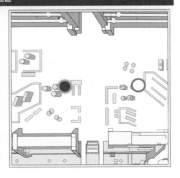

COMBAT ZONE: GALLIA DAM COMPLEX

This combat zone is an open ice field at the center of the Gallia dam complex. It's possible to scale the walls and cliff sides along the perimeter, but it's easier to meet opponents in the central area since this provides plenty of room to maneuver. Scaling the rocky cliffs along coordinates 115 can allow you to break line of sight if you feel overwhelmed.

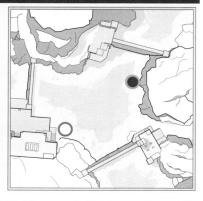

COMBAT ZONE: WATCHPOINT DELTA

Battles in this combat zone take place atop the Watchpoint Delta building where you were ambushed by AAP07: BALTEUS. It's a large, flat, circular area with a few minor obstacles along its perimeter, but they're insignificant and don't offer any real strategic advantage or disadvantage.

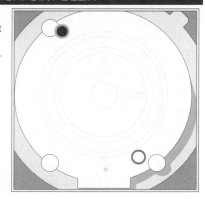

COMBAT ZONE: GRID 086 OUTER SHELL

There are multiple steel structures and train cars that can serve as cover if you need to recover EN during battles taking place in this combat zone. Circling around environmental obstacles like train cars makes it easy to avoid incoming projectiles, but can also limit opportunities to retaliate with attacks of your own.

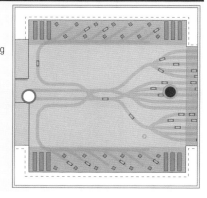

COMBAT ZONE: JORGEN REFUELING BASE

This combat zone is located in a multi-layered courtyard with plenty of tall buildings and towers that allow you to gain a positional advantage and strike from a high vantage point. This degree of verticality doesn't always play in your favor, however, as it can also easily be exploited by your opponent.

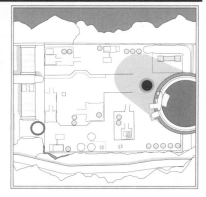

COMBAT ZONE: GRID 086

This area's low ceiling sets it apart from other open combat zones. Connecting with vertical missile launchers may become an issue if you're trying to primarily maneuver in the air, as your missiles will hit the ceiling before they can arc back down toward the enemy. There are explosive tanks dotted throughout the area, but they cannot be used to harm any combatants.

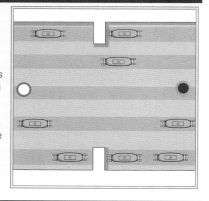

COMBAT ZONE: XYLEM, THE FLOATING CITY

There's a large, circular structure with a slight elevation close to your opponent's starting location. This dome serves as the ideal space to battle but presents a noted lack of cover. You can stick by any of the surrounding buildings as safety in case you need to get out of a tight space quickly. If the AC you're dueling gets cornered within the numerous buildings of the Xylem, capitalize on it.

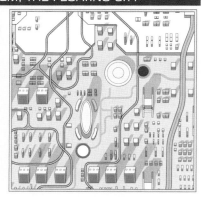

COMBAT ZONE: GRID 012

The wide, open field here allows freedom of mobility, but it's not without unique features to exploit in your favor. Notice the two trenches in the central ring of the battlefield; if used to your advantage, you can easily pin the opponent in a corner to then set them up for tons of direct hit damage. Just be careful not to get yourself caught up on the lips of either trench.

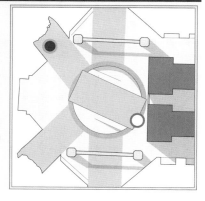

COMBAT ZONE: OLD BERTRAM SPACEPORT

This battlefield is littered with wreckage, which can easily get you in trouble if you're not careful. Always keep some EN on standby in your gauge so you can boost upward and avoid accidentally circling into a pile of scrap. If you're lucky enough to see the opponent corner itself instead, then be sure to react quickly and capitalize on the opportunity.

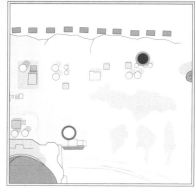

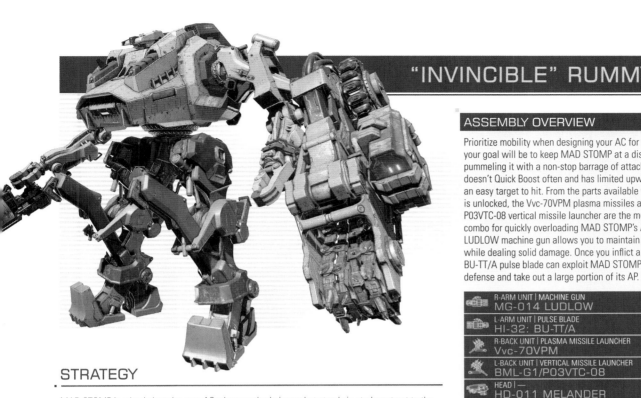

"INVINCIBLE" RUMMY

ASSEMBLY OVERVIEW

Prioritize mobility when designing your AC for this fight, since your goal will be to keep MAD STOMP at a distance while pummeling it with a non-stop barrage of attacks. This opponent doesn't Quick Boost often and has limited upward thrust, so it's an easy target to hit. From the parts available when this fight is unlocked, the Vvc-70VPM plasma missiles and the BML-G1/P03VTC-08 vertical missile launcher are the most effective combo for quickly overloading MAD STOMP's ACS. The MG-014 LUDLOW machine gun allows you to maintain constant pressure while dealing solid damage. Once you inflict a stagger, the HI-32: BU-TT/A pulse blade can exploit MAD STOMP's low anti-energy defense and take out a large portion of its AP.

R-ARM UNIT | MACHINE GUN	MG-014 LUDLOW
L-ARM UNIT | PULSE BLADE	HI-32: BU-TT/A
R-BACK UNIT | PLASMA MISSILE LAUNCHER	Vvc-70VPM
L-BACK UNIT | VERTICAL MISSILE LAUNCHER	BML-G1/P03VTC-08
HEAD | —	HD-011 MELANDER
CORE | —	BD-011 MELANDER
ARMS | —	AR-011 MELANDER
LEGS | BIPEDAL	LG-011 MELANDER
BOOSTER | —	ALULA/21E
FCS | —	FCS-G2/P05
GENERATOR | —	VP-20D
EXPANSION | —	—

STRATEGY

MAD STOMP is a basic brawler-type AC whose aptitude in combat stands in stark contrast to the self-proclaimed "invincible" callsign adopted by its pilot. Lacking any real offensive options at range, it will often rush in your direction to slash with the chainsaw mounted on its left arm or blast you with the high-impact shotgun wielded in its right hand. Although the chainsaw is the biggest threat, it's blunted by a lengthy wind-up and short reach that make it easy to avoid with a Quick Boost, and its damage output is low enough that even lightweight AC assemblies can comfortably survive multiple hits. Blasts from its shotgun are surprisingly fast and can be tricky to dodge, but are mitigated by keeping MAD STOMP at a distance. If you see its right hand lift up, signaling an incoming shotgun blast, instantly Quick Boost sideways to avoid it.

The best strategy in this fight is to activate Target Assist and maintain a distance of just over 100 meters while boosting in a circular pattern, giving you plenty of time to react to the chainsaw and avoid most shotgun blasts. MAD STOMP is particularly vulnerable after missing with its chainsaw, so this is the perfect opportunity to unload all your weaponry. The impact of a combined assault from your machine gun and vertical missile launcher can quickly overload MAD STOMP's ACS; once you trigger a stagger, follow up with your plasma missiles and a pulse blade combo to deal severe damage. You can repeat this cycle without much risk or effort by maintaining proper spacing, while launching missiles and firing your machine gun. MAD STOMP will struggle to maintain altitude and fight at the same time, so engaging it in aerial combat is another viable tactic.

Don't allow MAD STOMP to get closer than roughly 100 meters when fighting.

Getting caught by a fully revved up chainsaw attack after an ACS overload can deal serious damage if you aren't careful.

RANK 29/F	ASSEMBLY	
AC // MAD STOMP	R-ARM UNIT | SHOTGUN	WR-0777 SWEET SIXTEEN
	L-ARM UNIT | CHAINSAW	WB-0010 DOUBLE TROUBLE
COMBAT ZONE: TEST ARENA	R-BACK UNIT | —	—
Rewards (1st Victory)	L-BACK UNIT | —	—
35,000 COAM, 2x OST Chips, MAD STOMP AC Data, MAD STOMP Emblem	HEAD | —	DF-HD-08 TIAN-QIANG
Reward (Replay)	CORE | —	DF-BD-08 TIAN-QIANG
17,500 COAM	ARMS | —	AC-3000 WRECKER
	LEGS | BIPEDAL	2C-3000 WRECKER

SPECS				
AP	11670		BOOSTER | —	BC-0600 12345
Attitude Stability	1839		FCS | —	FCS-G1/P01
Anti-Kinetic Defense	1197		GENERATOR | —	AG-J-098 JOSO
Anti-Energy Defense	1060		EXPANSION | —	—
Anti-Explosive Defense	1282			
Elec. Discharge Tolerance	490			
Shock Resistance	-27%			
ACS Anomaly Tolerance	490			
Heat Resistance	-27%			

INDEX DUNHAM

ASSEMBLY OVERVIEW

Builds that worked in the last battle will largely prove effective against BURN PICKAXE. This opponent will also suffer from limited mobility, but has greater ranged capabilities. Despite this, its weaponry isn't a major threat to any moderately agile AC that can boost strafe around the battlefield. The second Vvc-70VPM plasma missile equipped to your shoulder unit will provide extra damage here, as BURN PICKAXE is most susceptible to energy weaponry. The higher damage during the opponent's ACS overload window will make the HI-32:BU-TT/A pulse blade important for ending the fight quickly. Don't be concerned if you don't get any plasma missiles off when your opponent is vulnerable during overload, as your pulse blade will still be dealing the bulk of the damage in this fight.

R-ARM UNIT | MACHINE GUN	MG-014 LUDLOW
L-ARM UNIT | PULSE BLADE	HI-32: BU-TT/A
R-BACK UNIT | PLASMA MISSILE LAUNCHER	Vvc-70VPM
L-BACK UNIT | PLASMA MISSILE LAUNCHER	Vvc-70VPM
HEAD | —	HD-011 MELANDER
CORE | —	BD-011 MELANDER
ARMS | —	AR-011 MELANDER
LEGS | BIPEDAL	LG-011 MELANDER
BOOSTER | —	ALULA/21E
FCS | —	FCS-G2/P05
GENERATOR | —	VP-20D
EXPANSION | —	—

STRATEGY

Much like MAD STOMP, BURN PICKAXE will try to maintain a minimum distance between the two of you. Though you can try to capitalize on the cover that's placed around the map, this opponent's missiles fire straight into the air and will home in on you, making this a potentially detrimental tactic. Close-range evasive maneuvers will be key here, and a constant boost strafe will keep you safe from falling missiles. This AC's most dangerous weapon is its bazooka, which can be hard to avoid depending on how close BURN PICKAXE gets before it launches a shell. Your AC's systems will warn you with an attack indicator before a shell is fired, and a well-timed Quick Boost will be needed. Aerial Quick Boosts can prove useful if explosions keep clipping your AC on the ground.

An efficient way to dispatch this opponent is to close in and suffocate its ACS with your machine gun. While you're doing this, supplement your kinetic fire with the plasma missiles equipped on your shoulder units. BURN PICKAXE has to come to a stop to fire its bazooka, but you should prioritize using Quick Boosts to dodge the shell, rather than attempting a counter attack. Once staggered, close in with your pulse blade and unleash your plasma missiles after they've cooled down.

RANK 28/F		ASSEMBLY	
AC // BURN PICKAXE		R-ARM UNIT | BURST MACHINE GUN	MA-E-210 ETSUJIN
		L-ARM UNIT | BAZOOKA	LITTLE GEM
COMBAT ZONE: CONTAMINATED CITY		R-BACK UNIT | VERTICAL MISSILE LAUNCHER	BML-G1/P01VTC-04
Rewards (1st Victory)		L-BACK UNIT | —	—
37,000 COAM, 2x OST Chips, BURN PICKAXE AC Data, BURN PICKAXE Emblem		HEAD | —	AH-J-124 BASHO
Reward (Replay)		CORE | —	AC-J-120 BASHO
18,500 COAM		ARMS | —	AA-J-123 BASHO
		LEGS | BIPEDAL	AL-J-121 BASHO
SPECS		BOOSTER | —	AB-J-137 KIKAKU
AP	11420	FCS | —	FCS-G1/P01
Attitude Stability	1670	GENERATOR | —	AG-J-098 JOSO
Anti-Kinetic Defense	1196	EXPANSION | —	—
Anti-Energy Defense	1083		
Anti-Explosive Defense	1275		
Elec. Discharge Tolerance	490		
Shock Resistance	-16%		
ACS Anomaly Tolerance	490		
Heat Resistance	-16%		

Watch out for attack indicators, as BURN PICKAXE's bazooka is far and away its most dangerous weapon.

A few well-placed attacks will make this a brief fight.

ASSEMBLY OVERVIEW

This assembly emphasizes taking an elevated position over HERMIT, and hitting it with energy damage. The VP-424 legs will be the first tetrapod legs you'll have access to, granting you the ability to hover. Hovering will keep your AC airborne while consuming little EN, and trivializes explosions from explosive weapons. The Vvc-760PR plasma rifle and Vvc-70VPM plasma missiles will create plasma explosions when fired from above, cornering HERMIT. These will whittle the enemy AC down very quickly, and box it in effectively. TIAN-QIANG head and core pieces will offer you the best combination of high anti-explosive and anti-kinetic defense, significantly dulling HERMIT's offensive potential.

	R-ARM UNIT | PLASMA RIFLE Vvc-760PR	
	L-ARM UNIT | PLASMA RIFLE Vvc-760PR	
	R-BACK UNIT | PLASMA MISSILE LAUNCHER Vvc-70VPM	
	L-BACK UNIT | PLASMA MISSILE LAUNCHER Vvc-70VPM	
	HEAD | — DF-HD-08 TIAN-QIANG	
	CORE | — DF-BD-08 TIAN-QIANG	
	ARMS | — AR-011 MELANDER	
	LEGS | TETRAPOD VP-424	
	BOOSTER | — BST-G2/P04	
	FCS | — FCS-G2/P10SLT	
	GENERATOR | — VP-20S	
	EXPANSION | — —	

STRATEGY

As the top pilot in F rank, G6 Red will be your first tough fight in the Arena, and sports a powerful set of weaponry. HERMIT starts the battle closer to the central hill, so you will want to meet it at the top before it can begin attacking from above to prevent its missiles from causing numerous explosions on the ground below. Attack indicators from your AC's systems will alert you to an incoming bazooka shell, which can easily overload you. This will be the first opponent to really take advantage of overloading your ACS in the Arena, so be ready to Quick Boost once warned. HERMIT's explosive weapons excel at mid-range, and it will try to maintain a distance from which it can effectively utilize them. As a result, closing in will cause it to retreat and rely on its weaker handgun until it gets back to its ideal range. You can exploit this to keep HERMIT from being too elusive, as it will usually prioritize retreating over evading.

You'll want to attack aggressively, taking to the air, hovering and firing from above. The plasma rifles will deal considerable damage and slowly accumulate ACS strain, leaving HERMIT particularly vulnerable to your rifle fire and missiles. You can charge one rifle for higher damage once you've inflicted ACS overload, but constant fire from both plasma rifles will be important for keeping your opponent pinned down. Stay airborne unless it's strictly necessary to recover your EN. Should this happen, trace the perimeter of the crater in the middle of the map, using ridges for cover if necessary. Once your EN is full, take to the air again, and repeat the process until HERMIT goes down.

You can use the ridge of the crater for cover when needed.

HERMIT will often use its handgun to cover itself as it retreats.

RANK 27/F	ASSEMBLY	
AC // HERMIT	R-ARM UNIT | HANDGUN HG-003 COQUILLETT	
	L-ARM UNIT | BAZOOKA DF-BA-06 XUAN-GE	
COMBAT ZONE: BONA DEA DUNES	R-BACK UNIT | MISSILE LAUNCHER BML-G2/P03MLT-06	
Rewards (1st Victory)	L-BACK UNIT | SPLIT MISSILE LAUNCHER BML-G2/P16SPL-08	
40,000 COAM, 2x OST Chips, HERMIT AC Data, HERMIT Emblem	HEAD | — HD-011 MELANDER	
	CORE | — BD-011 MELANDER	
Reward (Replay)	ARMS | — AR-011 MELANDER	
20,000 COAM	LEGS | BIPEDAL LG-011 MELANDER	
	BOOSTER | — BST-G2/P04	
SPECS	FCS | — FC-006 ABBOT	
AP	10550	GENERATOR | — DF-GN-02 LING-TAI
Attitude Stability	1731	EXPANSION | — —
Anti-Kinetic Defense	1227	
Anti-Energy Defense	1105	
Anti-Explosive Defense	1194	
Elec. Discharge Tolerance	490	
Shock Resistance	15%	
ACS Anomaly Tolerance	490	
Heat Resistance	15%	

NOSAAC

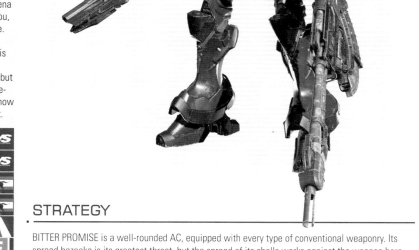

ASSEMBLY OVERVIEW

Due to your enemy's lackluster anti-explosive defense, you'll want a build geared toward explosive weaponry. MA-T-222 KYORAI napalm bomb launchers will deal high damage and engulf the arena in flames, triggering ACS anomaly. These flames won't harm you, and will make the area harder for BITTER PROMISE to navigate. BML-G1/P31DUO-02 dual missile launchers provide a strong source of damage while your MA-T-222 KYORAIs reload. As this is heavy weaponry, you'll want to go with heavy arms, a heavy core and legs with a high load limit. This lowers your mobility, but provides the bulk necessary to trade with and outpace your enemy's damage output. Consider this fight an opportunity to see how tank legs like the LG-022T BORNEMISSZA can shine in combat.

R-ARM UNIT | NAPALM BOMB LAUNCHER MA-T-222 KYORAI		BAWS
L-ARM UNIT | NAPALM BOMB LAUNCHER MA-T-222 KYORAI		BAWS
R-BACK UNIT | DUAL MISSILE LAUNCHER BML-G1/P31DUO-02		
L-BACK UNIT | DUAL MISSILE LAUNCHER BML-G1/P31DUO-02		
HEAD | — VP-44S		
CORE | — DF-BD-08 TIAN-QIANG		
ARMS | — DF-AR-08 TIAN-QIANG		
LEGS | TANK LG-022T BORNEMISSZA		
BOOSTER | —		
FCS | — FCS-G2/P05		
GENERATOR | — DF-GN-06 MING-TANG		
EXPANSION | — TERMINAL ARMOR		

STRATEGY

BITTER PROMISE is a well-rounded AC, equipped with every type of conventional weaponry. Its spread bazooka is its greatest threat, but the spread of its shells works against the weapon here, as it's unlikely that enough will hit for them to cause significant harm. Its laser handgun and burst rifle will deal very little damage to the recommended AC assembly. However, its laser handgun can be charged up for rapid fire shots that can deal a respectable portion of damage. Notably, this is the first Arena combatant to come equipped with a shield. This pulse shield will dampen most incoming damage from the front, making frontal assaults difficult. Large explosions from your dual missile launchers and the fire from your napalm bomb launchers will get around this shield and deal substantial impact.

You can corner BITTER PROMISE against the buildings in the area, which will make explosive weapons more effective. Keeping up an unrelenting barrage of missiles and bombs will safely wear the opponent down, but you'll have few windows of opportunity for dealing heavy damage. Both its spread bazooka and charged up laser handgun shots will be forewarned by your AC's systems, but BITTER PROMISE will need to drop its shield to fire. While risky, waiting to fire all of your weaponry once you are warned of incoming danger will be effective here; it'll be a trade you will handily win.

RANK 26/E	ASSEMBLY	
AC // BITTER PROMISE	R-ARM UNIT | LASER HANDGUN VP-66LH	
COMBAT ZONE: THE WALL	L-ARM UNIT | BURST RIFLE MA-J-200 RANSETSU-RF	
Rewards (1st Victory)	R-BACK UNIT | SPREAD BAZOOKA SB-033M MORLEY	
43,000 COAM, 2x OST Chips, BITTER PROMISE AC Data, BITTER PROMISE Emblem	L-BACK UNIT | PULSE SHIELD VP-61PS	
Reward (Replay)	HEAD | — HD-011 MELANDER	
21,500 COAM	CORE | — VP-40S	
	ARMS | — AR-011 MELANDER	
SPECS	LEGS | BIPEDAL VP-422	
AP	10290	BOOSTER | — FLUEGEL/21Z
Attitude Stability	1706	FCS | — FCS-G2/P10SLT
Anti-Kinetic Defense	1199	GENERATOR | — VP-20S
Anti-Energy Defense	1200	EXPANSION | — —
Anti-Explosive Defense	1127	
Elec. Discharge Tolerance	490	
Shock Resistance	15%	
ACS Anomaly Tolerance	490	
Heat Resistance	15%	

Use your napalm bomb launchers to corner BITTER PROMISE.

Don't stop if the first shot of the charged laser handgun lands, as you'll have further shots to dodge.

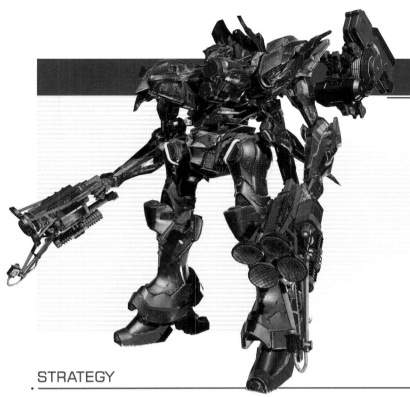

ASSEMBLY OVERVIEW

High anti-energy defense is a must here, and these parts will grant you the best defense available. The ever-versatile VP-424 tetrapod legs will also mitigate the obstacles provided by the uneven terrain in the area. On the offensive end, front-facing missile units with moderate reload speeds like the BML-G1/P20MLT-04 missile launcher and BML-G2/P16SPL-08 split missile launcher equipped on your back will be your most reliable weapons in this fight. The HI-16: GU-Q1 pulse gun will disrupt your enemy's shields and the MA-J-201 RANSETSU-AR assault rifle will keep the pressure up while your missiles reload.

R-ARM UNIT | BURST ASSAULT RIFLE	MA-J 201 RANSETSU-AR	BAWS
L-ARM UNIT | PULSE GUN	HI-16: GU-Q1	
R-BACK UNIT | MISSILE LAUNCHER	BML-G1/P20MLT-04	
L-BACK UNIT | SPLIT MISSILE LAUNCHER	BML-G2/P16SPL-08	
HEAD | —	VP-44S	
CORE | —	DF-BD-08 TIAN-QIANG	
ARMS | —	04-101 MIND ALPHA	
LEGS | TETRAPOD	VP-424	
BOOSTER | —	ALULA/21E	
FCS | —	FCS-G2/P05	
GENERATOR | —	DF-GN-06 MING-TANG	
EXPANSION | —	TERMINAL ARMOR	

STRATEGY

INFECTION is a nimble, evasive AC, often boosting through the air. Most of your attacks will be met with Quick Boosts or Initial Guards through quick pulse shield deployments. It will fire a high volume of pulse gun shots while swiftly moving around the Arena. These shots are difficult to avoid for long, and trying to Quick Boost away from them will only waste energy. Their impact accumulation is negligible, but the damage to your AP will quickly add up, leading to a dire situation if you cannot land your shots. INFECTION's plasma cannon is a much more immediate threat, inflicting heavy damage. You'll be warned by your systems, but the real power of these shots lies in the resulting explosion; leave the blast zone immediately if you get by the initial shot.

Maneuvering around this arena may be tricky due to its layout, but hovering will help bypass these obstacles. Launching an assault from above gives the added benefit of removing most of the threat of the pulse cannon. Balancing offense and defense against such a mobile combatant can make dealing damage with missiles difficult if you fire carelessly—focus on using them when the opponent is inflicted with ACS overload and staggered. You can accomplish this by using your opponent's shield against it. Your pulse gun will rapidly cause strain, and when combined with assault rifle fire to bait use of the shield, can open up INFECTION. Maintain steady hits with the pulse gun and assault rifle fire from above, and be ready to launch missiles once its ACS strain begins to climb. As fast and aggressive as INFECTION is, it's the most fragile AC you've faced yet, and can't withstand timed volleys for long.

Your own pulse gun will rapidly disrupt INFECTION's shield.

Glancing blows from INFECTION's plasma rifle can lead to greater damage, even in the air.

	RANK 25/E
AC // INFECTION	

COMBAT ZONE: BAWS ARSENAL NO.2	
Rewards (1st Victory)	
45,000 COAM, 2x OST Chips, INFECTION AC Data, INFECTION Emblem	
Reward (Replay)	
22,500 COAM	

SPECS	
AP	9570
Attitude Stability	1698
Anti-Kinetic Defense	1136
Anti-Energy Defense	1183
Anti-Explosive Defense	1070
Elec. Discharge Tolerance	490
Shock Resistance	-8%
ACS Anomaly Tolerance	490
Heat Resistance	-8%

ASSEMBLY	
R-ARM UNIT | PULSE GUN	HI-16: GU-Q1
L-ARM UNIT | PULSE GUN	HI-16: GU-Q1
R-BACK UNIT | PLASMA CANNON	FASAN/60E
L-BACK UNIT | PULSE SHIELD	VP-61PS
HEAD | —	NACHTREIHER/44E
CORE | —	VP-40S
ARMS | —	NACHTREIHER/46E
LEGS | BIPEDAL	VP-422
BOOSTER | —	ALULA/21E
FCS | —	FCS-G2/P05
GENERATOR | —	VE-20C
EXPANSION | —	

LITTLE ZIYI

ASSEMBLY OVERVIEW

For this fight, you'll want to focus on pairing a fast, hard-hitting energy weapon with a shotgun to deal major damage during the right moments. YUE YU is a slow, heavy build, and with this assembly, you'll be able to dance around it while dealing high damage incredibly quickly. Like the last few fights, you'll be dealing with a pulse shield, or in this case, pulse buckler. Bucklers function similarly to shields, but mitigate more impact. Regardless of the differences, the HI-16: GU-Q1 pulse gun and Vvc-70VPM plasma missile launchers will give you the offensive edge. Your shotgun will deal incredible damage to an overloaded YUE YU, or deal high ACS strain during regular combat. Just remember to close the distance prior to firing to ensure maximum effectiveness.

	R-ARM UNIT | SHOTGUN	
	SG-026 HALDEMAN	
	L-ARM UNIT | PULSE GUN	
	HI-16: GU-Q1	
	R-BACK UNIT | PLASMA MISSILE LAUNCHER	
	Vvc-70VPM	
	L-BACK UNIT | PLASMA MISSILE LAUNCHER	
	Vvc-70VPM	
	HEAD | —	
	DF-HD-08 TIAN-QIANG	
	CORE | —	
	VP-40S	
	ARMS | —	
	NACHTREIHER/46E	
	LEGS | BIPEDAL	
	VP-422	
	BOOSTER | —	
	ALULA/21E	
	FCS | —	
	FCS-G2/P05	
	GENERATOR | —	
	DF-GN-06 MING-TANG	
	EXPANSION | —	
	TERMINAL ARMOR	

STRATEGY

YUE YU is fairly docile, and comes equipped with two grenade launchers that will deal massive damage if the grenades hit. If they do, don't panic, as their substantial reload times result in infrequent bursts of damage. Even with the fragile nature of the suggested assembly, YUE YU will take a considerable amount of time to bring you down, and will struggle to capitalize after causing a stagger. Grenade fire will always follow a sudden Quick Boost from this AC, and staying airborne makes it easy to avoid incoming grenades without even having to spend EN on a Quick Boost. You can also deal reliable damage with repeated shots from your plasma missiles and shotgun from the air while avoiding grenades.

While YUE YU is reloading, it will often slowly boost around with its pulse buckler up, making it an easy target for your pulse gun. Whenever your opponent is in this position, begin unloading your pulse gun; combined with your plasma missiles, you'll be able to quickly inflict ACS overload. Move in and unload your shotgun once YUE YU is staggered to deal severe AP damage. Don't worry about missing this shot if YUE YU recovers from stagger, as you'll have multiple opportunities to do this. This AC is passive and slow enough that it won't be hard to keep pressuring it. Using your shotgun even while your enemy isn't overloaded will wear it down considerably.

AC // YUE YU	RANK 24/E

COMBAT ZONE: GALLIA DAM COMPLEX	
Rewards (1st Victory)	

47,000 COAM, 2x OST Chips,
YUE YU AC Data, YUE YU Emblem

Reward (Replay)

23,500 COAM

SPECS	
AP	11420
Attitude Stability	1670
Anti-Kinetic Defense	1196
Anti-Energy Defense	1083
Anti-Explosive Defense	1275
Elec. Discharge Tolerance	490
Shock Resistance	-16%
ACS Anomaly Tolerance	490
Heat Resistance	-16%

ASSEMBLY

R-ARM UNIT | GRENADE LAUNCHER	**IRIDIUM**
L-ARM UNIT | GRENADE LAUNCHER	**IRIDIUM**
R-BACK UNIT | —	
L-BACK UNIT | PULSE BUCKLER	**SI-29: SU-TT/C**
HEAD | —	**AH-J-124 BASHO**
CORE | —	**AC-J-120 BASHO**
ARMS | —	**AA-J-123 BASHO**
LEGS | BIPEDAL	**AL-J-121 BASHO**
BOOSTER | —	**AB-J-137 KIKAKU**
FCS | —	**FCS-G1/P01**
GENERATOR | —	**AG-E-013 YABA**
EXPANSION | —	

Shotguns will devastate an ACS overloaded YUE YU.

Watch out if YUE YU Quick Boosts abruptly; a grenade is likely to follow.

ASSEMBLY OVERVIEW

As this will be a long fight, you'll need an AC that can go the distance. This assembly offers the bulk you need to outlast GUIDANCE, with the VP-424 tetrapod legs giving you the mobility needed to fight the enemy on an even playing field. Your assault armor, in conjunction with the SG-026 HALDEMAN shotgun, will be an additional source or damage, especially if you can corner the enemy and intercept attempts to retreat. As with the previous E-Rank fights, use your pulse gun when you see the shield. You'll want to use your missiles liberally throughout the fight. GUIDANCE has high AP, and you won't be able to reliably cause ACS overload, so missiles should be considered a regular damage source for this fight.

R-ARM UNIT	SHOTGUN	**SG-026 HALDEMAN**	
L-ARM UNIT	PULSE GUN	**HI-16: GU-Q1**	
R-BACK UNIT	MISSILE LAUNCHER	**BML-G1/P20MLT-04**	
L-BACK UNIT	SPLIT MISSILE LAUNCHER	**BML-G2/P16SPL-08**	
HEAD	—	**VP-44S**	
CORE	—	**DF-BD-08 TIAN-QIANG**	
ARMS	—	**DF-AR-09 TIAN-LAO**	
LEGS	TETRAPOD	**VP-424**	
BOOSTER	—	**ALULA/21E**	
FCS	—	**FC-008 TALBOT**	
GENERATOR	—	**DF-GN-06 MING-TANG**	
EXPANSION	—	**ASSAULT ARMOR**	

STRATEGY

Your first tetrapod opponent in the Arena will showcase how difficult they can be to fight against. GUIDANCE has a shield like the rest of the E-Rank opponents, making it harder to bring it down. In conjunction, this AC has well rounded defenses and a respectably high AP value. All in all, this is likely to be the longest fight you've had in the Arena so far. GUIDANCE's missiles come with no warning, but the grenades will be preceded by a system alert. Both will deal high AP damage and impact, even against the recommended assembly. It also has a kinetic stun baton in its arsenal; when used, it will be telegraphed by a small wind-up, or quick lunge, leading into a flurry of blows or a charged stab attack that inflicts shock buildup. This fight is also the first instance where you'll come across an enemy who frequently uses Boost Kicks to get in close and deal additional damage.

As GUIDANCE prefers the air, you should make the effort to meet it there and bring it down. As you approach, it will try to retreat; use this to corral the enemy toward a corner of the arena. Once cornered, it will struggle to escape your attacks, and you can close in to use assault armor, causing significant damage and ACS strain. Unload your pulse gun when you see the pulse shield, and complement this with your shotgun and missiles. Your chances of dealing heavy damage during ACS overload will be too precarious to be reliable. Consider it a bonus if all of your weapons are ready to fire during this window—dealing continuous damage will be more important during this fight. This will be a war of attrition and you'll need to press every advantage.

Maintain an aerial advantage over GUIDANCE while pressuring it into a corner.

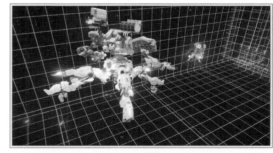

Keep an eye out for sudden stun baton attacks.

	RANK 23/E
AC // GUIDANCE	

COMBAT ZONE: TEST ARENA	
Rewards (1st Victory)	
50,000 COAM, 2x OST Chips, GUIDANCE AC Data, GUIDANCE Emblem	
Reward (Replay)	
25,000 COAM	

SPECS	
AP	10380
Attitude Stability	2308
Anti-Kinetic Defense	1174
Anti-Energy Defense	1255
Anti-Explosive Defense	1165
Elec. Discharge Tolerance	490
Shock Resistance	0%
ACS Anomaly Tolerance	490
Heat Resistance	0%

ASSEMBLY	
R-ARM UNIT	MISSILE LAUNCHER	**HML-G2/P19MLT-04**
L-ARM UNIT	STUN BATON	**VP-67EB**
R-BACK UNIT	GRENADE CANNON	**EARSHOT**
L-BACK UNIT	PULSE SHIELD	**VP-61PS**
HEAD	—	**VP-44D**
CORE	—	**VP-40S**
ARMS	—	**VP-46S**
LEGS	TETRAPOD	**VP-424**
BOOSTER	—	**FLUEGEL/21Z**
FCS	—	**FCS-G2/P10SLT**
GENERATOR	—	**VP-20C**
EXPANSION	—	**PULSE ARMOR**

G3 WU HUAHAI

ASSEMBLY OVERVIEW

While previous assemblies have focused on using a combination of pulse guns, explosives, and plasma missiles to bypass pulse shields, this assembly will focus exclusively on plasma weaponry. Area of effect weapons are always effective against such ACs, as they'll cause explosions that can bypass their shields, and plasma missiles like the Vvc-70VPM will track the enemy in the air. Coupled with Vvc-760PR plasma rifles, you'll have two angles of attack to combat LI LONG, which will prove effective whether it's on the ground or in the air. Your AC itself will need a high load limit and EN capacity, while also maintaining a good balance of mobility with anti-kinetic and anti-explosive defenses. As LI LONG is a tetrapod assembly, you may find it helpful to go with a tetrapod build yourself, but it's not necessary for this fight.

	R-ARM UNIT | PLASMA RIFLE	Vvc-760PR
	L-ARM UNIT | PLASMA RIFLE	Vvc-760PR
	R-BACK UNIT | PLASMA MISSILE LAUNCHER	Vvc-70VPM
	L-BACK UNIT | PLASMA MISSILE LAUNCHER	Vvc-70VPM
	HEAD | —	EL-TH-10 FIRMEZA
	CORE | —	BD-011 MELANDER
	ARMS | —	04-101 MIND ALPHA
	LEGS | BIPEDAL	DF-LG-08 TIAN-QIANG
	BOOSTER | —	ALULA/21E
	FCS | —	FCS-G2/P05
	GENERATOR | —	VP-20C
	EXPANSION | —	TERMINAL ARMOR

STRATEGY

As the first D-Rank pilot, LI LONG shares a few similarities with your previous tetrapod fight; though this AC tends to alternate being in the air and on the ground more frequently, rather than sticking to just aerial combat. Offensively, the opponent comes with a rapid-fire kinetic machine gun and multi-hit, homing explosive missiles that can quickly cause ACS overload, especially if you're not quick enough with your dodges. As none of these attacks are telegraphed by your systems, you'll have to rely on learning the proper timing to evade. Both split missiles can be effectively dodged if you change your direction of movement with a Quick Boost once you see them split. This will be difficult if LI LONG fires them from the air, but the missiles are only a significant threat if multiple hit you in a short period. Its machine gun can be safely avoided by maintaining a circular boost strafe.

You can begin this fight by charging up both of your plasma rifles as you approach the enemy. Once within range, begin firing missiles and unload with your rifles when they're fully charged. Don't be concerned if the hits don't connect; LI LONG's pulse shield will mitigate a lot of damage, but provides little in the way of impact dampening. Ultimately your goal here is to never let up on your offense, and back your enemy into a corner. After inflicting ACS overload, your weapons will deal significant damage to the enemy's AP. LI LONG is not a highly-evasive AC, and will crumple under pressure.

RANK 22/D	ASSEMBLY	
AC // LI LONG	R-ARM UNIT | MACHINE GUN	MG-014 LUDLOW
	L-ARM UNIT | SPLIT MISSILE LAUNCHER	HML-G3/P08SPL-06
COMBAT ZONE: TEST ARENA	R-BACK UNIT | SPLIT MISSILE LAUNCHER	BML-G2/P19SPL-12
Rewards (1st Victory)	L-BACK UNIT | PULSE SHIELD	SI-24: SU-Q5
52,000 COAM, 3x OST Chips,	HEAD | —	DF-HD-08 TIAN-QIANG
LI LONG AC Data,	CORE | —	DF-BD-08 TIAN-QIANG
LI LONG Emblem	ARMS | —	AR-011 MELANDER
Reward (Replay)	LEGS | TETRAPOD	LG-033M VERRILL
26,000 COAM	BOOSTER | —	BST-G2/P04
	FCS | —	FCS-G2/P12SML
	GENERATOR | —	DF-GN-06 MING-TANG
	EXPANSION | —	ASSAULT ARMOR

SPECS	
AP	11930
Attitude Stability	2249
Anti-Kinetic Defense	1264
Anti-Energy Defense	1152
Anti-Explosive Defense	1268
Elec. Discharge Tolerance	490
Shock Resistance	-27%
ACS Anomaly Tolerance	490
Heat Resistance	-27%

Plasma weapons will be able to catch LI LONG, even in the air.

Get ready to move once the enemy begins to hover above you.

ASSEMBLY OVERVIEW

Winning this fight will be easy with an AC assembly with high anti-explosive defense and explosive weaponry that can catch fast opponents. Actually building such a specific AC is easier said than done, however. HML-G2/P19MLT-04 Missile Launchers will be your most reliable choice for arm weapons, giving you a solid, homing missile option, but your BML-G1/P32DUO-03s dual missile launchers will be the star here. These will launch a set of homing pincer missiles, which will be vital for tagging erratic opponents like CANDLE RING. Defensively, you won't need to account for anything but explosive weapons here, so this assembly will focus on high anti-explosive defense and high attitude stability. The VP-424 tetrapod legs make a return, to increase the effectiveness of your arm weapons, as shots fired from above will have a greater chance of clipping CANDLE RING.

R-ARM UNIT | MISSILE LAUNCHER	HML-G2/P19MLT-04
L-ARM UNIT | MISSILE LAUNCHER	HML-G2/P19MLT-04
R-BACK UNIT | DUAL MISSILE LAUNCHER	BML-G1/P32DUO-03
L-BACK UNIT | DUAL MISSILE LAUNCHER	BML-G1/P32DUO-03
HEAD | —	AH-J-124 BASHO
CORE | —	DF-BD-08 TIAN-QIANG
ARMS | —	AC-3000 WRECKER
LEGS | TETRAPOD	VP-424
BOOSTER | —	BUERZEL/21D
FCS | —	FCS-G2/P10SLT
GENERATOR | —	VP-20D
EXPANSION | —	TERMINAL ARMOR

5

STRATEGY

CANDLE RING is an extremely quick opponent, with the capacity to overwhelm you and deal high damage in a very short period if you're not careful. Its grenade cannons have among the highest impact you'll encounter, each firing two grenades in quick succession. It won't take many hits to overload your ACS, and your AC's systems will warn you prior to the cannons firing. Be sure to watch for attack indicators, as both grenade cannons can fire at once, resulting in four grenades being launched simultaneously. A single one of these can cause substantial impact, so be ready to Quick Boost away from multiple grenades. If your ACS gets overloaded, follow-ups from CANDLE RING's other grenades or missile launchers will cause high AP damage and wear you down very quickly.

If you stick to the ground, the terrain will be a detriment. You'll need to keep CANDLE RING in your sights at all times, and letting it get away can result in your missiles missing and the enemy potentially blindsiding you. Stay in the air, just above the buildings, and directly above the enemy. This will keep all of your weapons effective and make it difficult for your foe to escape their explosions. CANDLE RING is a fragile AC, and a single successful volley from your weapons can easily overload its ACS. Watch out for its pulse armor; CANDLE RING tends to use it whenever it's being overwhelmed, and it can disrupt your tactics briefly.

RANK 21/D		ASSEMBLY	
AC // CANDLE RING		R-ARM UNIT | MISSILE LAUNCHER	HML-G2/P19MLT-04
		L-ARM UNIT | MISSILE LAUNCHER	HML-G2/P19MLT-04
COMBAT ZONE: CONTAMINATED CITY		R-BACK UNIT | GRENADE CANNON	SONGBIRDS
Rewards (1st Victory)		L-BACK UNIT | GRENADE CANNON	SONGBIRDS
54,000 COAM, 3x OST Chips, CANDLE RING AC Data, CANDLE RING Emblem		HEAD | —	EL-TH-10 FIRMEZA
		CORE | —	EL-TC-10 FIRMEZA
Reward (Replay)		ARMS | —	EL-TA-10 FIRMEZA
27,000 COAM		LEGS | TANK	EL-TL-11 FORTALEZA
		BOOSTER | —	

SPECS	
AP	10740
Attitude Stability	1630
Anti-Kinetic Defense	1095
Anti-Energy Defense	1043
Anti-Explosive Defense	1030
Elec. Discharge Tolerance	490
Shock Resistance	-1%
ACS Anomaly Tolerance	490
Heat Resistance	-1%

FCS | —	FCS-G2/P10SLT
GENERATOR | —	AG-E-013 YABA
EXPANSION | —	PULSE ARMOR

CANDLE RING won't be able to run away from missiles for long, so keep firing if it tries to retreat.

Watch the enemy, as its goal is to get behind you and hit you where you can't easily return fire.

V.V HAWKINS

ASSEMBLY OVERVIEW

As your options for anti-energy defense are initially limited, this assembly will focus on supplementing what you lack with mobility. This combination of head, core, arm, and leg parts will provide a good mix of anti-energy defense without sacrificing mobility. A pair of SG-027 ZIMMERMAN shotguns will give you a large spread, and deal extremely high damage against overloaded enemies. BML-G2/P05MLT-10 missile launchers will deliver the impact and ACS strain needed to quickly open up RECONFIG to high damage from your shotguns. A build with VP-424 legs and the VP-20C generator can let you meet the enemy AC in the air, but that assembly will sacrifice some anti-energy defense and ground mobility, which may not be ideal for a prolonged battle.

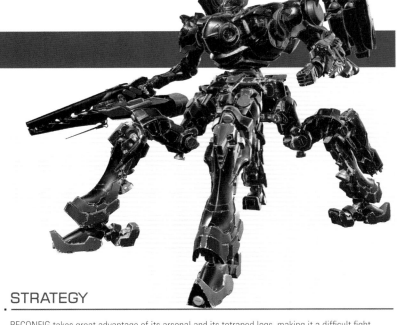

R-ARM UNIT | SHOTGUN SG-027 ZIMMERMAN	
L-ARM UNIT | SHOTGUN SG-027 ZIMMERMAN	
R-BACK UNIT | MISSILE LAUNCHER BML-G2/P05MLT-10	
L-BACK UNIT | MISSILE LAUNCHER BML-G2/P05MLT-10	
HEAD | — VP-44S	
CORE | — VP-40S	
ARMS | — 04-101 MIND ALPHA	
LEGS | BIPEDAL 06-041 MIND ALPHA	
BOOSTER | — ALULA/21E	
FCS | — FC-008 TALBOT	
GENERATOR | — DF-GN-06 MING-TANG	
EXPANSION | — ASSAULT ARMOR	

STRATEGY

RECONFIG takes great advantage of its arsenal and its tetrapod legs, making it a difficult fight. Armed with a plasma rifle and plasma missiles, it's equipped to handle targets on the ground with area-of-effect pressure. While hovering from above, any near-misses can tag opponents. If you get hit with either its laser cannon or laser blade while you're overloaded, they'll deal massive damage, likely removing thousands of your AP at once. However, with your assembly's respectable anti-energy defense and effective Quick Boosts, you should rarely feel cornered by plasma weaponry. Keep moving and don't stay in place for too long, and you should only ever take glancing blows. RECONFIG won't use its laser blade unless your systems are overloaded, so you can stay close to it while avoiding rifle shots and missiles. It can still use its laser cannon while you're not overloaded, so watch for system alert indicators.

Without the worry of its laser blade, you can get up close and begin laying into RECONFIG with your missiles and shotguns. You may take hits if you can't consistently dodge its plasma attacks, but it's necessary to force this opponent back to the ground. A relentless assault will cause RECONFIG to continuously Quick Boost. This will quickly deplete its EN, grounding it and leaving it a sitting duck for heavy damage. Try not to get overzealous, as this AC is equipped with pulse armor, and can use it to recover its energy if it finds itself in a compromised position. If you have an opportunity when the enemy is downed, hit it with assault armor for a massive spike of damage and impact. Diligently keep up your attack, and try to line up your shotgun reloads with the enemy's ACS overload. If timed properly, you should be able to get two shots from each shotgun during this opportunity.

RANK 20/D	ASSEMBLY	
AC // RECONFIG	R-ARM UNIT | PLASMA RIFLE Vvc-760PR	

COMBAT ZONE: WATCHPOINT DELTA	L-ARM UNIT | LASER BLADE Vvc-770LB
Rewards (1st Victory)	R-BACK UNIT | LASER CANON VP-60LCS
56,000 COAM, 3x OST Chips, RECONFIG AC Data, RECONFIG Emblem	L-BACK UNIT | PLASMA MISSILE LAUNCHER Vvc-706PM
Reward (Replay)	HEAD | — VP-44S
28,000 COAM	CORE | — VE-40A

SPECS		ARMS | — VP-46S
AP	11510	LEGS | TETRAPOD VP-424
Attitude Stability	2295	BOOSTER | — BUERZEL/21D
Anti-Kinetic Defense	1214	FCS | — VE-21A
Anti-Energy Defense	1303	GENERATOR | — VP-20D
Anti-Explosive Defense	1230	EXPANSION | — PULSE ARMOR
Elec. Discharge Tolerance	490	
Shock Resistance	17%	
ACS Anomaly Tolerance	490	
Heat Resistance	17%	

This will be a tough opponent to pin down in the air; focus on wearing it out and forcing it to the ground.

RECONFIG will take advantage of your staggered status to launch a laser blade attack.

G5 IGUAZU

ASSEMBLY OVERVIEW

Few assemblies will efficiently dismantle a specific opponent quite like this one. The HI-18: GU-A2 pulse gun is a marked improvement over the HI-16: GU-Q1 pulse gun used in the prior Arena ranks. Beyond being an effective shield breaker, it will be a sufficiently reliable, powerful weapon in its own right when used against ACs with low anti-energy defense. A pair of these will quickly put down any enemy trying to defend themselves with a shield. To complement this, VP-60LCS laser cannons, with their high attack power rating, will deal extreme damage to overloaded enemies. This assembly will give you a dominating offense, which can be emphasized further with a high mobility AC that can quickly close the gap on the enemy.

R-ARM UNIT | PULSE GUN	HI-18: GU-A2
L-ARM UNIT | PULSE GUN	HI-18: GU-A2
R-BACK UNIT | LASER CANNON	VP-60LCS
L-BACK UNIT | LASER CANNON	VP-60LCS
HEAD | —	HD-011 MELANDER
CORE | —	BD-011 MELANDER
ARMS | —	DF-AR-08 TIAN-QIANG
LEGS | REVERSE JOINT	RC-2000 SPRING CHICKEN
BOOSTER | —	BC-0400 MULE
FCS | —	FCS-G2/P05
GENERATOR | —	VP-20D
EXPANSION | —	TERMINAL ARMOR

STRATEGY

The fight against HEAD BRINGER is one of the more straightforward AC fights you'll have experienced in this stretch of Arena battles. Its weaponry provides a fairly standard mix of kinetic and explosive damage. Its most dangerous weapon will be its linear rifle, which can be quickly charged up and fired for heavy damage. You will know when it's charged when the barrel of the rifle is emanating an orange, electric glow. Right before the shot fires, you'll get a warning from your systems. Should you get hit, the shot will deal solid AP damage and moderate impact, capable of sending you into ACS overload if you've accumulated enough strain. Even with this in mind, HEAD BRINGER's offenses are limited, and it cannot quickly deal significant damage.

HEAD BRINGER's pulse shield can pose a problem, but it's possible to use this against your opponent. Once you've made it to the open strip and the enemy is in sight, begin charging a single laser cannon, while firing alternating single shots from your pulse guns. They will slowly begin to build ACS strain on HEAD BRINGER when its shield is down, but will almost immediately cause ACS overload if it attempts to block any shots. The moment you inflict overload, fire your charged cannon, and begin alternating fire with both of your cannons once you recover from the recoil. With this method, HEAD BRINGER can be brought down in a single round of ACS overload.

RANK 19/D	ASSEMBLY	
AC // HEAD BRINGER	R-ARM UNIT | LINEAR RIFLE	LR-036 CURTIS
	L-ARM UNIT | MACHINE GUN	MG-014 LUDLOW
COMBAT ZONE: THE WALL	R-BACK UNIT | MISSILE LAUNCHER	BML-G1/P20MLT-04
Rewards (1st Victory)	L-BACK UNIT | PULSE SHIELD	SI-27: SU-R8
58,000 COAM, 3x OST Chips,	HEAD | —	HD-012 MELANDER C3
HEAD BRINGER AC Data,	CORE | —	BD-012 MELANDER C3
HEAD BRINGER Emblem	ARMS | —	AR-012 MELANDER C3
Reward (Replay)	LEGS | BIPEDAL	LG-012 MELANDER C3
29,000 COAM	BOOSTER | —	BST-G2/P04
	FCS | —	FC-008 TALBOT
	GENERATOR | —	DF-GN-06 MING-TANG
	EXPANSION | —	—

SPECS	
AP	9690
Attitude Stability	1704
Anti-Kinetic Defense	1202
Anti-Energy Defense	1105
Anti-Explosive Defense	1187
Elec. Discharge Tolerance	490
Shock Resistance	6%
ACS Anomaly Tolerance	490
Heat Resistance	6%

Unload on HEAD BRINGER the moment you see its shield.

Charge rifle attacks will deal high damage, so get moving once attack indicators flash up on screen.

ROKUMONSEN

ASSEMBLY OVERVIEW

This is another assembly designed to catch a fast opponent; you'll be facing the quickest opponent you've fought yet, and you'll need an AC to match. Few legs will give you the agility on the ground that the EL-TL-11 FORTALEZA tank legs give you, which will be vital when SHINOBI begins to Assault Boost toward you. Use these tank legs, which allow for omni-directional movement without breaking lock-on, to focus on retreating without sacrificing offense. Homing missiles of all kinds will be solid weapons for catching the enemy when it slips up, and the front-facing HML-G2/P19MLT-04s on your arms and pincer BML-G1/P32DUO-03 dual missile launchers on your back will provide you many angles to attack from. Be sure to save this assembly in your AC Data, as it will be important going forward.

R-ARM UNIT | MISSILE LAUNCHER	
HML-G2/P19MLT-04	
L-ARM UNIT | MISSILE LAUNCHER	
HML-G2/P19MLT-04	
R-BACK UNIT | DUAL MISSILE LAUNCHER	
BML-G1/P32DUO-03	
L-BACK UNIT | DUAL MISSILE LAUNCHER	
BML-G1/P32DUO-03	
HEAD | —	
AH-J-124 BASHO	RAWS
CORE | —	
BD-011 MELANDER	
ARMS | —	
DF-AR-08 TIAN-QIANG	
LEGS | TANK	
EL-TL-11 FORTALEZA	
BOOSTER | —	
FCS | —	
FCS-G2/P10SLT	
GENERATOR | —	
VP-20C	
EXPANSION | —	
TERMINAL ARMOR	

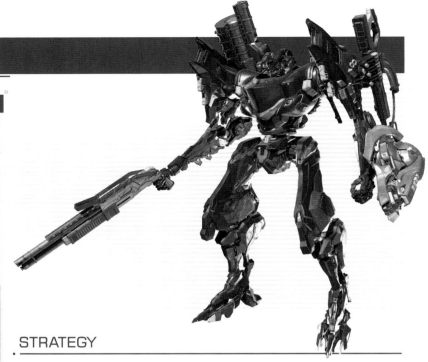

STRATEGY

SHINOBI is the quickest opponent you've faced, with excellent aerial capabilities. It's a close-range specialized AC, equipped with a plasma thrower that acts as an exploding plasma whip, as well as a shotgun. Getting hit with either of these will cause heavy AP damage. Boosting around and baiting the enemy's ranged options is the best way to put yourself on the offensive with missiles. SHINOBI isn't helpless from a distance, since it can swap its plasma thrower for a burst assault rifle. Your systems will alert you when it fires a detonating missile—a single missile that leaves a trail of explosions behind it once it detonates. Boosting into this trail will cause heavy damage. Beware staying at longer ranges for too long, as the enemy will perform an Assault Boost if you maintain distance. It will then execute a Boost Kick once it reaches you, causing quite a bit of ACS strain. Be ready to Quick Boost away from its aggressive charges.

Hitting SHINOBI can be difficult, but it's only a matter of time before you land devastating blows. Alternate your missile fire, using only one of your weapons at a time, then firing another quickly after. Trying to land all of your shots at once will waste ammo, and result in the enemy dodging multiple times. Keeping up a steady stream of missile fire will minimize downtime, and prevent you needing to reload while your opponent is staggered and overloaded. Stay mobile, keep your distance, and be deliberate with your attacks, and SHINOBI will go down quickly.

	RANK 18/D
AC // SHINOBI	

COMBAT ZONE: GALLIA DAM COMPLEX
Rewards (1st Victory)
60,000 COAM, 3x OST Chips, SHINOBI AC Data, SHINOBI Emblem
Reward (Replay)
30,000 COAM

SPECS	
AP	9500
Attitude Stability	1590
Anti-Kinetic Defense	1134
Anti-Energy Defense	1093
Anti-Explosive Defense	1056
Elec. Discharge Tolerance	490
Shock Resistance	-1%
ACS Anomaly Tolerance	490
Heat Resistance	-1%

ASSEMBLY

R-ARM UNIT | SHOTGUN	
SG-026 HALDEMAN	
L-ARM UNIT | PLASMA THROWER	
44-143 HMMR	
R-BACK UNIT | DETONATING MISSILE LAUNCHER	
45-091 JVLN BETA	
L-BACK UNIT | BURST ASSAULT RIFLE	
MA-J 201 RANSETSU-AR	
HEAD | —	
EL-TH-10 FIRMEZA	
CORE | —	
07-161 MIND ALPHA	
ARMS | —	
EL-TA-10 FIRMEZA	
LEGS | BIPEDAL	
EL-TL-10 FIRMEZA	
BOOSTER | —	
BST-G2/P06SPD	
FCS | —	
FCS-G2/P05	
GENERATOR | —	
DF-GN-06 MING-TANG	
EXPANSION | —	
PULSE ARMOR	

Stay alert if SHINOBI begins to charge you suddenly, especially if you're being trailed by a homing missile.

Detonating missiles can be used to deter your offense or corner you, so keep your distance from the missile's trail.

ASSEMBLY OVERVIEW

Your weapon options have not changed since the last time you fought a heavy, offensively-built AC with low anti-energy defense. As such, plasma rifles and plasma missiles remain reliable, and will serve you well here. This fight also takes place on rough, uneven terrain, making the VP-424 tetrapod legs your best option for maintaining line of sight on the enemy. Since you'll be taking to the sky here, either the Vvc-703PM or Vvc-70VPM plasma missiles will work as auxiliary weaponry, but the Vvc-703PMs will allow more frequent, direct damage when fired from above. Your head, core, and arm parts will all be geared toward high anti-explosive defense, high anti-kinetic defense, and attitude stability in the off chance that you get pressured in this fight

R-ARM UNIT | PLASMA RIFLE	Vvc-760PR
L-ARM UNIT | PLASMA RIFLE	Vvc-760PR
R-BACK UNIT | PLASMA MISSILE LAUNCHER	Vvc-703PM
L-BACK UNIT | PLASMA MISSILE LAUNCHER	Vvc-703PM
HEAD | —	AH-J-124 BASHO
CORE | —	DF-BD-08 TIAN-QIANG
ARMS | —	AA-J-123 BASHO
LEGS | TETRAPOD	VP-424
BOOSTER | —	ALULA/21E
FCS | —	FCS-G2/P05
GENERATOR | —	VP-20D
EXPANSION | —	TERMINAL ARMOR

5

STRATEGY

CANNON HEAD lives up to its name as another offensively-oriented assembly, and one of the more durable opponents you've faced so far. Equipped with a grenade launcher, shotgun, split missile launcher, and grenade cannon, this AC is packing a lot of power onto its frame. The grenade launcher and grenade cannon in particular will have your AC's alerts ringing very often, and with missiles also being loosed throughout the fight, it can even be hard to discern whether the opponent is firing its grenade cannon or grenade launcher. As long as you stay airborne, constantly staying above the enemy and circling it in the air, it will struggle to land any heavy blows on you. Its shotgun shouldn't be ignored, either; while it will be harder to avoid in this position than either grenade weapon, it can pose a major threat if CANNON HEAD decides to use it liberally.

As with any tank leg enemy, CANNON HEAD will struggle to defend against aerial opponents. With its weakest attribute being its anti-energy defense, the enemy has no answer for plasma weaponry. Its primary goal will be to close the gap between the two of you, which will frequently keep it below you, in a vulnerable position. Stay aerial, continue moving, and don't get close, and you shouldn't have to worry about being staggered. Keep up your own offense, and it'll only be a matter of time before you wear down CANNON HEAD's thick armor.

RANK 17/C	ASSEMBLY	
AC // CANNON HEAD	R-ARM UNIT | GRENADE LAUNCHER	DF-GR-07 GOU-CHEN
	L-ARM UNIT | SHOTGUN	SG-027 ZIMMERMAN
COMBAT ZONE: BONA DEA DUNES	R-BACK UNIT | SPLIT MISSILE LAUNCHER	BML-G2/P19SPL-12
Rewards (1st Victory)	L-BACK UNIT | GRENADE CANNON	SONGBIRDS
62,000 COAM, 3x OST Chips, CANNON HEAD AC Data, CANNON HEAD Emblem	HEAD | —	DF-HD-08 TIAN-QIANG
Reward (Replay)	CORE | —	DF-BD-08 TIAN-QIANG
31,000 COAM	ARMS | —	DF-AR-08 TIAN-QIANG
	LEGS | TANK	LG-022T BORNEMISSZA

SPECS		BOOSTER | —
AP	16940	—
Attitude Stability	2466	FCS | —
Anti-Kinetic Defense	1315	FC-008 TALBOT
Anti-Energy Defense	1164	GENERATOR | —
Anti-Explosive Defense	1312	DF-GN-06 MING-TANG
Elec. Discharge Tolerance	490	EXPANSION | —
Shock Resistance	-27%	—
ACS Anomaly Tolerance	490	
Heat Resistance	-27%	

Your opponent will try, and fail, to keep up with you in the air.

CANNON HEAD can simultaneously utilize all of its explosives to gain a momentary advantage.

V. VIII PATER

ASSEMBLY OVERVIEW

The assembly you used against SHINOBI will be your go-to for fighting quick, brittle close-range opponents like DUAL NATURE. Each assembly will require small tweaks specifically catered toward your current opponent, but the fundamentals and general setup will be very similar. Heavy weaponry like the HML-G2/P19MLT-04 and BML-G1/P32DUO-03 missile launchers will be extremely effective at dealing high damage and boxing opponents in. On the defensive end, you'll want to go all in on anti-energy defense, with the MIND ALPHA and VP series equipment being among your best options. The EL-TL-11 FORTALEZA tank legs will be your only sub-optimal equipment in this regard, but the extra mobility to avoid DUAL NATURE's pulse weaponry will make up for any extra damage an attack may end up causing. Do not bring any sort of pulse shield or pulse buckler into this fight, as you will be fighting exclusively pulse weaponry, which would quickly compromise your ACS.

R-ARM UNIT | MISSILE LAUNCHER HML-G2/P19MLT-04	
L-ARM UNIT | MISSILE LAUNCHER HML-G2/P19MLT-04	
R-BACK UNIT | DUAL MISSILE LAUNCHER BML-G1/P32DUO-03	
L-BACK UNIT | DUAL MISSILE LAUNCHER BML-G1/P32DUO-03	
HEAD | — VP-44S	
CORE | — 07-161 MIND ALPHA	
ARMS | — 04-101 MIND ALPHA	
LEGS | TANK EL-TL-11 FORTALEZA	
BOOSTER | — —	
FCS | — FCS-G2/P10SLT	
GENERATOR | — VP-20C	
EXPANSION | — TERMINAL ARMOR	

STRATEGY

DUAL NATURE's methods are fairly unique compared to the opponents you've faced so far. It wants to wear you down with its pulse gun and pulse cannon, chipping away at you until it can land a heavy blow with its pulse blade. With your high anti-energy defense assembly, this will end up taking a while, but the relentless nature of pulse guns can still cause significant accumulation of ACS strain. In conjunction with this, the pulse cannon on DUAL NATURE's shoulder acts similarly to a pulse gun, firing a fully-automatic salvo of pulse blasts, further emphasizing how important mobility is for this fight. Try to limit your movement to the flat areas surrounding the water reservoirs, as the terrain there won't impede your movements. If you get stuck, you can find yourself quickly overwhelmed. Should you corner yourself and let the enemy AC get within melee distance, it will use its pulse blade, causing severe damage.

If you can maintain distance, you should be able to recover quickly if you ever feel pressured. Your missiles will reliably deal damage if you alternate your fire to keep DUAL NATURE moving, draining its EN. The terminal armor expansion is worth mentioning here, since it offers your opponent five seconds of near invincibility after taking a fatal blow. You're unlikely to break this armor within those five seconds, but keep up the pressure to ensure you get the final blow as soon as possible.

	RANK 16/C
AC // DUAL NATURE	

COMBAT ZONE: BAWS ARSENAL NO.2
Rewards (1st Victory)
64,000 COAM, 3x OST Chips, DUAL NATURE AC Data, DUAL NATURE Emblem
Reward (Replay)
32,000 COAM

SPECS	
AP	8690
Attitude Stability	1431
Anti-Kinetic Defense	1005
Anti-Energy Defense	1098
Anti-Explosive Defense	977
Elec. Discharge Tolerance	490
Shock Resistance	54%
ACS Anomaly Tolerance	490
Heat Resistance	54%

ASSEMBLY	
R-ARM UNIT | PULSE GUN HI-16: GU-Q1	
L-ARM UNIT | PULSE BLADE HI-32: BU-TT/A	
R-BACK UNIT | PULSE CANNON KRANICH/60Z	
L-BACK UNIT | PULSE BUCKLER VP-61PB	
HEAD | — VE-44B	
CORE | — NACHTREIHER/40E	
ARMS | — VP-46D	
LEGS | REVERSE JOINT KASUAR/42Z	
BOOSTER | — ALULA/21E	
FCS | — FCS-G2/P05	
GENERATOR | — VP-20D	
EXPANSION | — TERMINAL ARMOR	

Don't let DUAL NATURE's Terminal Armor throw off your offense.

Be careful to not get caught on the walls while quickly moving around the stage; your enemy can easily capitalize on this.

STRATEGY

This is the same AC you fought in the "Attack the Watchpoint" mission. There are fewer obstructions, with no repair kits available, meaning it won't be as lengthy a battle as it was then. That said, ENTANGLE is an AC with no glaring weaknesses, meaning it's going to take some extra effort to take down. Coming in hot with a detonating bazooka and a detonating missile launcher, the opponent has incredible offensive power. Both weapons are signaled by warning indicators, but fire extremely quickly, and they can easily overload your ACS within a shot or two. You can mitigate this by jumping high above ENTANGLE and maintaining a moderate distance, giving you more time to react. Chances are still high that you will take some brutal hits here; be careful if you get too close to the enemy, as it can quickly unleash a Boost Kick, further causing strain on your systems

The optimal approach is to outpace the opponent's damage, avoiding its weaponry as much as possible, and not panicking if the situation seems dire. Your grenade cannons should allow you to deal devastating damage, easily winning any trade with the enemy. ENTANGLE is a very aerial AC, but tends to stay grounded if you jump over it. When your grenade cannons are fully loaded, jump directly over ENTANGLE, firing one grenade cannon as you're directly above the enemy. Fire the second cannon immediately after the first ejects its second grenade. Keep firing one machine gun to continue building ACS strain while your missiles reload, then switch to firing the other machine gun as the active one runs low on ammo.

ASSEMBLY OVERVIEW

This assembly will be geared toward high-risk, high-reward tactics. As your opponent will be a balanced AC, it might be difficult to rely on a straightforward strategy to combat it. MG-014 LUDLOW machine guns will primarily be used to exert pressure on ENTANGLE, with SONGBIRDS grenade cannons pushing it toward ACS overload. When fired from above, less agile opponents will have a difficult time avoiding four consecutive grenades, often trying to Quick Boost away from the initial grenade, and right into one of the following three. Reverse-joint legs will facilitate this, letting you swiftly leapfrog your opponent, and making quick hit-and-run tactics in the air feasible. Despite facing a pulse gun, you won't need to be concerned with the minimal damage it deals. Instead, focus on anti-explosive defense equipment, to mitigate hits from the enemy's far deadlier detonating weapons.

R-ARM UNIT | MACHINE GUN	**MG-014 LUDLOW**	
L-ARM UNIT | MACHINE GUN	**MG-014 LUDLOW**	
R-BACK UNIT | GRENADE CANNON	**SONGBIRDS**	MELINITE
L-BACK UNIT | GRENADE CANNON	**SONGBIRDS**	MELINITE
HEAD | —	**AH-J-124 BASHO**	BAWS
CORE | —	**AC-J-120 BASHO**	BAWS
ARMS | —	**AA-J-123 BASHO**	BAWS
LEGS | REVERSE JOINT	**RC-2000 SPRING CHICKEN**	RaD
BOOSTER | —	**BUERZEL/21D**	
FCS | —	**FC-008 TALBOT**	
GENERATOR | —	**VP-20C**	
EXPANSION | —	**TERMINAL ARMOR**	

Utilize the splash damage of your grenades, and pace your attacks well to snuff out ENTANGLE.

	RANK 15/C
AC // ENTANGLE	

COMBAT ZONE: WATCHPOINT DELTA
Rewards (1st Victory)
66,000 COAM, 3x OST Chips, ENTANGLE AC Data, ENTANGLE Emblem
Reward (Replay)
33,000 COAM

SPECS	
AP	10640
Attitude Stability	1836
Anti-Kinetic Defense	1178
Anti-Energy Defense	1261
Anti-Explosive Defense	1135
Elec. Discharge Tolerance	490
Shock Resistance	0%
ACS Anomaly Tolerance	490
Heat Resistance	0%

ASSEMBLY	
R-ARM UNIT | DETONATING BAZOOKA	**44-141 JVLN ALPHA**
L-ARM UNIT | PULSE GUN	**HI-18: GU-A2**
R-BACK UNIT | PLASMA MISSILE LAUNCHER	**Vvc-703PM**
L-BACK UNIT | DETONATING MISSILE LAUNCHER	**45-091 JVLN BETA**
HEAD | —	**VP-44D**
CORE | —	**VP-40S**
ARMS | —	**VP-46S**
LEGS | BIPEDAL	**06-041 MIND ALPHA**
BOOSTER | —	**BST-G2/P06SPD**
FCS | —	**FCS-G2/P05**
GENERATOR | —	**VP-20C**
EXPANSION | —	—

ENTANGLE will frequently use its own explosions as a mask to launch a Boost Kick.

"CHATTY" STICK

ASSEMBLY OVERVIEW

The AC you'll be facing off against in this fight is a sturdy assembly with solid defenses. Its one weak link will be its anti-energy defense, meaning you'll be relying on a pair of energy weapons that have proven reliable thus far: the Vvc-760PR plasma rifle and Vvc-703PM plasma missiles. To top this off, these weapons are ideal for dealing with zippy opponents like CIRCUS. However, even with this loadout, the enemy's sheer bulk means that it can still take a while to put down, so you can't afford to neglect your defenses. As the enemy only has explosive weaponry, you should exclusively build toward anti-explosive defense. The AH-J-124 BASHO and HC-3000 WRECKER heads have greater stats in this regard, but will overburden this assembly. This could be avoided by swapping out for tank legs, but aerial suppression will be a huge boon during this fight.

R-ARM UNIT | PLASMA RIFLE	Vvc-760PR	
L-ARM UNIT | PLASMA RIFLE	Vvc-760PR	
R-BACK UNIT | PLASMA MISSILE LAUNCHER	Vvc-703PM	
L-BACK UNIT | PLASMA MISSILE LAUNCHER	Vvc-703PM	
HEAD | —	DF-HD-08 TIAN-QIANG	
CORE | —	DF-BD-08 TIAN-QIANG	
ARMS | —	DF-AR-09 TIAN-LAO	
LEGS | TETRAPOD	VP-424	
BOOSTER | —	BUERZEL/21D	
FCS | —	FCS-G2/P10SLT	
GENERATOR | —	VP-20C	
EXPANSION | —	TERMINAL ARMOR	

STRATEGY

From a distance, CIRCUS will rely primarily on its back weapons. Vertical missiles will be the trickiest weapons in its arsenal, firing 12 missiles directly in the air that will come back down after a short period. On their own, they're non-threatening if you keep mobile, but trying to avoid other explosives can make it easy to accidentally Quick Boost into them. Cluster missiles are designed to do precisely this, unleashing a large volume of sub-missiles, following the trajectory of the main missile. Any sudden Quick Boosts should be executed with care to avoid dodging toward the direction you were previously moving. Your systems will alert you when a cluster missile is being fired, so plan accordingly. If CIRCUS begins closing in on you, take to the sky; this usually means it's about to fire its arm weapons, often both at the same time. Even with this assembly, they cause high damage, and can potentially overload your ACS if both hit at the same time.

CIRCUS doesn't have a way of defending itself against energy weapons. Having tank legs, it also can't defend itself very well against area-of-effect weapons fired from above. As with similar fights, you should spend as much time airborne as possible, firing without relent. All of your weapons will cause minor ACS strain, which can make timing bursts of damage difficult. This will be another fight where persistent damage is more vital to success than aiming for bursts of high damage.

AC // CIRCUS	RANK 14/C

COMBAT ZONE: GRID 086 OUTER SHELL

Rewards (1st Victory)

68,000 COAM, 3x OST Chips,
CIRCUS AC Data,
CIRCUS HEAD Emblem

Reward (Replay)

34,000 COAM

SPECS	
AP	13040
Attitude Stability	1724
Anti-Kinetic Defense	1261
Anti-Energy Defense	1118
Anti-Explosive Defense	1176
Elec. Discharge Tolerance	490
Shock Resistance	-16%
ACS Anomaly Tolerance	490
Heat Resistance	-16%

ASSEMBLY	
R-ARM UNIT | GRENADE LAUNCHER	IRIDIUM
L-ARM UNIT | BAZOOKA	LITTLE GEM
R-BACK UNIT | CLUSTER MISSILE LAUNCHER	BM-0999 DELIVERY BOY
L-BACK UNIT | VERTICAL MISSILE LAUNCHER	BML-G1/P07VTC-12
HEAD | —	AH-J-124 BASHO
CORE | —	CC-3000 WRECKER
ARMS | —	AC-2000 TOOL ARM
LEGS | TANK	EL-TL-11 FORTALEZA
BOOSTER | —	—
FCS | —	FCS-G2/P10SLT
GENERATOR | —	AG-T-005 HOKUSHI
EXPANSION | —	—

Stay mobile to avoid CIRCUS's overwhelming explosives.

CIRCUS is wide open when firing all of its missiles at once.

ASSEMBLY OVERVIEW

Your opponent here is almost identical to SHINOBI, being assembled from most of the same parts. Even TSUBASA's offensive output is similar, having a mix of explosive and kinetic weaponry. With no newly relevant equipment being available to you, your assembly from that fight will be just as effective here. You'll have the missile launchers and dual missile launchers that hit from many angles, and the EL-TL-11 FORTALEZA legs for high ground mobility.

R-ARM UNIT | MISSILE LAUNCHER HML-G2/P19MLT-04		
L-ARM UNIT | MISSILE LAUNCHER HML-G2/P19MLT-04		
R-BACK UNIT | DUAL MISSILE LAUNCHER BML-G1/P32DUO-03		
L-BACK UNIT | DUAL MISSILE LAUNCHER BML-G1/P32DUO-03		
HEAD | — AH-J-124 BASHO		BAWS
CORE | — BD-011 MELANDER		
ARMS | — DF-AR-08 TIAN-QIANG		
LEGS | TANK EL-TL-11 FORTALEZA		
BOOSTER | —		
FCS | — FCS-G2/P10SLT		
GENERATOR | — VP-20S		
EXPANSION | —		

STRATEGY

As mentioned, TSUBASA's assembly is nearly identically to SHINOBI's; built for offense, with a lightweight, fast AC design. However, while the previous fight was about aggressive, close-range combat, the enemy AC here is built for mid range. It likes to stay airborne while pelting you with its missiles and kinetic weaponry from a safe distance, dealing continuous damage and ACS strain if you don't remain mobile. It'll occasionally Assault Boost toward you and follow up with a Boost Kick, but it does this infrequently. While it may be appealing to try to close the distance on this AC, that's where its most dangerous weapon functions best. TSUBASA can swap between having its burst machine gun and bazooka in its right hand on the fly, giving it unexpected mix-up potential. You'll get a warning when it fires, but it's quick enough that it becomes difficult to Quick Boost away at close range. If it hits, it'll be by far the most devastating attack in its arsenal.

Your strategy for assaulting TSUBASA will be simple. Maintain a moderate distance, alternating your missile shots to ensure a constant barrage of missiles. Quick hops and firing at a downward angle will give your missiles added coverage, making them even harder to avoid. Even with its high mobility, your enemy will have a hard time escaping your assault for extended periods, and will

quickly be worn down with significant pressure. TSUBASA can use pulse protection, creating a pulse dome for cover. This is a relatively bad Core Expansion for highly mobile ACs, as they'll move out of it almost immediately after using it. It can be destroyed, but you should ignore it, treating it as a minor annoyance that shouldn't slow you down.

RANK **13/C**	ASSEMBLY
AC // TSUBASA	R-ARM UNIT | BURST MACHINE GUN MA-E-210 ETSUJIN
COMBAT ZONE: TEST ARENA	L-ARM UNIT | BURST RIFLE MA-J 200 RANSETSU-RF
Rewards (1st Victory)	R-BACK UNIT | BAZOOKA LITTLE GEM
70,000 COAM, 3x OST Chips, TSUBASA AC Data, TSUBASA Emblem	L-BACK UNIT | MISSILE LAUNCHER BML-G1/P20MLT-04
	HEAD | — EL-TH-10 FIRMEZA
Reward (Replay)	CORE | — EL-TC-10 FIRMEZA
35,000 COAM	ARMS | — EL-TA-10 FIRMEZA
	LEGS | REVERSE JOINT EL-TL-10 FIRMEZA

SPECS	
AP	8480
Attitude Stability	1545
Anti-Kinetic Defense	1078
Anti-Energy Defense	998
Anti-Explosive Defense	986
Elec. Discharge Tolerance	490
Shock Resistance	-1%
ACS Anomaly Tolerance	490
Heat Resistance	-1%

BOOSTER \| —
BC-0200 GRIDWALKER

FCS \| —
FCS-G2/P05

GENERATOR \| —
AG-E-013 YABA

EXPANSION \| —
PULSE PROTECTION

Corner TSUBASA by unloading your missiles when they're ready and loaded.

If you slow down, TSUBASA will use its speed to hit you from multiple angles.

V.III O'KEEFFE

ASSEMBLY OVERVIEW

If you haven't been able to yet, this fight will be a good opportunity to test out the Weapon Bay OS Tuning option. As you've seen in a few fights, this allows an AC to swap between arm weapons on the same side while sacrificing a back weapon. In this case, you'll want a HI-32: BU-TT/A pulse blade equipped to your L-Back Unit slot. This will be your primary damage dealer for the fight, but you need your dual SG-027 ZIMMERMAN shotguns and BML-G1/P32DUO-03 dual missile launcher to wear down BARREN FLOWER, overloading it and making it vulnerable. It's a particularly evasive aerial AC, so you likely won't regret losing a back weapon with a slow projectile for this fight. You'll also be encountering all weapon types here, with the most dangerous of them all being a plasma rifle, so you'll want an assembly with balanced defenses and a slight bias toward anti-energy defense.

R-ARM UNIT | SHOTGUN	**SG-027 ZIMMERMAN**
L-ARM UNIT | SHOTGUN	**SG-027 ZIMMERMAN**
R-BACK UNIT | DUAL MISSILE LAUNCHER	**BML-G1/P32DUO-03**
L-BACK UNIT | PULSE BLADE	**HI-32: BU-TT/A**
HEAD | —	**VP-44S**
CORE | —	**07-161 MIND ALPHA**
ARMS | —	**EL-TA-10 FIRMEZA**
LEGS | BIPEDAL	**06-041 MIND ALPHA**
BOOSTER | —	**BST-G2/P06SPD**
FCS | —	**FC-008 TALBOT**
GENERATOR | —	**VP-20C**
EXPANSION | —	**ASSAULT ARMOR**

STRATEGY

BARREN FLOWER is one of the most versatile ACs you've fought so far. Its defenses aren't great, but it makes up for this with high attitude stability. While not the most agile AC, its airborne capabilities make it hard to hit with many projectiles. It also doesn't possess overwhelming offense, but it has energy, kinetic, and explosive weapons. This jack-of-all-trades approach will make this one of the harder opponents to plan around from the most recent sets of Arena opponents. BARREN FLOWER's burst rifle and container missiles are easy to avoid, but its plasma missiles are good at dealing continuous damage, and its plasma rifle should be considered a major threat. The regular plasma shots will deal similar damage to its missiles, but if you see it begin to charge and glow purple, stop your offense and retreat. This charge attack can deal extreme damage if it connects, and will cause substantial ACS strain. You will be warned with an indicator and safest at a distance.

You'll spend much of this fight in the air, aiming to bring the enemy down. Alternating shots with your shotguns and peppering in missiles will deal gradual AP damage, and quickly cause ACS strain. To compound this, as the enemy focuses on aerial combat, constant firing will force it to use Quick Boosts and leave it unable to regenerate EN. Eventually, it will fall to the ground, being unable to dodge for a short period. This will be your signal to unload and push for ACS overload with your assault armor. Once overload has been inflicted, quickly swap your left shotgun to your pulse blade and perform a two-hit combo. After two rounds of this, BARREN FLOWER will go down.

	RANK 12/B
AC // BARREN FLOWER	

COMBAT ZONE: TEST ARENA
Rewards (1st Victory)
72,000 COAM, 4x OST Chips, BARREN FLOWER AC Data, BARREN FLOWER Emblem
Reward (Replay)
36,000 COAM

SPECS	
AP	10210
Attitude Stability	2127
Anti-Kinetic Defense	1155
Anti-Energy Defense	1199
Anti-Explosive Defense	1147
Elec. Discharge Tolerance	490
Shock Resistance	9%
ACS Anomaly Tolerance	490
Heat Resistance	9%

ASSEMBLY	
R-ARM UNIT | BURST RIFLE	**MA-J 200 RANSETSU-RF**
L-ARM UNIT | PLASMA RIFLE	**Vvc-760PR**
R-BACK UNIT | CONTAINER MISSILE LAUNCHER	**BML-G1/P29CNT**
L-BACK UNIT | PLASMA MISSILE	**Vvc-70VPM**
HEAD | —	**20-081 MIND ALPHA**
CORE | —	**NACHTREIHER/40E**
ARMS | —	**VE-46A**
LEGS | TETRAPOD	**VP-424**
BOOSTER | —	**FLUEGEL/21Z**
FCS | —	**FCS-G1/P01**
GENERATOR | —	**VE-20C**
EXPANSION | —	**PULSE ARMOR**

Swap to your pulse blade to deal severe damage once BARREN FLOWER is staggered from ACS overload.

BARREN FLOWER will often close the gap before firing its charged plasma rifle.

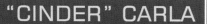

ASSEMBLY OVERVIEW

This assembly aims to go tit for tat with your opponent. FULL COURSE is an extremely durable opponent, being able to take hits from all types of weaponry. Its lowest defensive attribute is its anti-explosive defense, so that's the hole in its armor that you'll want to continually drill at, using all of your weaponry liberally throughout the fight. HML-G2/P19MLT-04s remain a reliable arm weapon option for sustainable explosive damage. When these are combined with SONGBIRDS and EL-TL-11 FORTALEZA legs, a new staple build for certain types of Arena battles begins to emerge. Much like your assembly, FULL COURSE deals explosive damage exclusively, so your assembly will specifically build toward anti-explosive defense.

R-ARM UNIT | MISSILE LAUNCHER GML-G2/P19MLT04	BAWS
L-ARM UNIT | MISSILE LAUNCHER GML-G2/P19MLT04	
R-BACK UNIT | GRENADE CANNON SONGBIRDS	MELINITE
L-BACK UNIT | GRENADE CANNON SONGBIRDS	MELINITE
HEAD | — AH-J-124 BASHO	BAWS
CORE | — DF-BD-08 TIAN-QIANG	
ARMS | — AA-J-123 BASHO	
LEGS | TANK EL-TL-11 FORTALEZA	
BOOSTER | — ALULA/21E	
FCS | — FCS-G2/P12SML	
GENERATOR | — VP-20S	
EXPANSION | — TERMINAL ARMOR	

STRATEGY

Carla has outfitted her AC much like her right hand Chatty has, with an emphasis on explosive weapons. FULL COURSE can be a bit harder to avoid, as its four siege missile launchers can fire a staggering number of explosives in short order. To illustrate this, the fight begins with all four missile launchers firing at once, unleashing a massive salvo from all sides. Stay focused while avoiding these missiles, as this is largely a smoke screen to hide FULL COURSE's Assault Boost, which will be followed by a Boost Kick. You can disrupt this by firing off all of your weaponry before you perform a lateral Quick Boost, forcing the enemy to either dodge or take the hits head on. Beyond this, a constant boost strafe around the combat zone will consistently keep you safe from any missiles fired your way.

Due to FULL COURSE's high defense and attitude stability, you won't find any prime opportunities to return volleys. Instead, you should launch an even flow of missiles and grenades toward the enemy. Firing missiles as often as possible will keep this AC on its toes, while slowly whittling away at its AP. To complement this, it will struggle to continuously dodge your grenades if you alternate firing them. Keep your distance, as FULL COURSE can detonate its assault armor, causing heavy damage. You'll have a lot on your plate when dealing with this robust AC, but keep cooking it with explosives and you'll soon savor its defeat.

Keep your distance and beware of FULL COURSE's assault armor.

	RANK 11/B
AC // FULL COURSE	

COMBAT ZONE: GRID 086
Rewards (1st Victory)
74,000 COAM, 4x OST Chips, FULL COURSE AC Data, FULL COURSE Emblem
Reward (Replay)
37,000 COAM

SPECS	
AP	12700
Attitude Stability	2014
Anti-Kinetic Defense	1306
Anti-Energy Defense	1348
Anti-Explosive Defense	1282
Elec. Discharge Tolerance	490
Shock Resistance	-7%
ACS Anomaly Tolerance	490
Heat Resistance	-7%

ASSEMBLY	
R-ARM UNIT | SIEGE MISSILE LAUNCHER WS-5000 APERITIF	
L-ARM UNIT | SIEGE MISSILE LAUNCHER WS-5000 APERITIF	
R-BACK UNIT | SIEGE MISSILE LAUNCHER WS-5001 SOUP	
L-BACK UNIT | SIEGE MISSILE LAUNCHER WS-5001 SOUP	
HEAD | — HS-5000 APPETIZER	
CORE | — CS-5000 MAIN DISH	
ARMS | — AS-5000 SALAD	
LEGS | BIPEDAL 2S-5000 DESSERT	
BOOSTER | — AB-J-137 KIKAKU	
FCS | — FCS-G2/P10SLT	
GENERATOR | — AG-T-005 HOKUSHI	
EXPANSION | — ASSAULT ARMOR	

Use FULL COURSE's attempts to Assault Boost as an opportunity to hit it with a few grenades.

COLDCALL

ASSEMBLY OVERVIEW

Your worst enemy in this fight will be the terrain. The arena is an open, multi-level area with plentiful obstacles and walls to get caught on if you don't plan ahead. This means either tetrapod or reverse-joint legs will best facilitate traversal, but only tetrapod legs give you the aerial superiority needed to gain the edge over the opponent, letting you soar high in the sky. The BC-0400 MULE booster hinders your boost speed, but has the lower upward EN consumption of any available booster, letting you ascend with little impact to your EN. DEADSLED has middling defenses all around, but is weakest to energy. Additionally, it's an extremely mobile reverse-joint AC, so fast weaponry that can cause damage in an area will be preferred here. The always-reliable plasma rifle and plasma missiles work as well as ever.

R-ARM UNIT | PLASMA RIFLE
Vvc-760PR

L-ARM UNIT | PLASMA RIFLE
Vvc-760PR

R-BACK UNIT | PLASMA MISSILE LAUNCHER
Vvc-703PM

L-BACK UNIT | PLASMA MISSILE LAUNCHER
Vvc-703PM

HEAD | —
HC-3000 WRECKER

CORE | —
07-161 MIND ALPHA

ARMS | —
EL-TA-10 FIRMEZA

LEGS | TETRAPOD
VP-424

BOOSTER | —
BC-0400 MULE

FCS | —
FCS-G2/P05

GENERATOR | —
VE-20A

EXPANSION | —
TERMINAL ARMOR

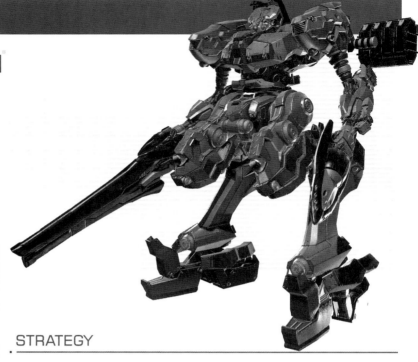

STRATEGY

Immediately after the match begins, DEADSLED will charge at you. This can be advantageous, as you will start at an elevated position with room to engage your enemy. You'll have a much easier fight if you wait to move until the enemy is closer, and stay overhead. If you're the one being pressed from above, you'll be met with a flurry of lasers and missiles. DEADSLED's laser weapons aren't particularly dangerous, but don't brush them off while trying to avoid the much deadlier active homing missile. Once launched, evading it should be your top priority, as it will deal massive AP damage and cause ACS overload if it hits. This shouldn't be difficult if you stay airborne and strafe, as the missile is quite slow, but watch your EN as you evade; a sudden drop can get you hit.

Once DEADSLED has had a second or two to advance, head toward the center of the map, and hover as you leave the building that acts as your starting position. So long as you keep up an assault with your plasma weaponry, you'll have the advantage throughout this entire fight. DEADSLED can still dodge your weaponry quite adeptly, but it will only be a matter of time before it's overwhelmed and gets caught on the terrain. Once that happens, DEADSLED will be dead in the water.

RANK 10/B	
AC // DEADSLED	

COMBAT ZONE: JORGEN REFUELING BASE
Rewards (1st Victory)
76,000 COAM, 4x OST Chips, DEADSLED AC Data, DEADSLED Emblem
Reward (Replay)
38,000 COAM

SPECS	
AP	10380
Attitude Stability	1613
Anti-Kinetic Defense	1190
Anti-Energy Defense	1103
Anti-Explosive Defense	1183
Elec. Discharge Tolerance	490
Shock Resistance	12%
ACS Anomaly Tolerance	490
Heat Resistance	12%

ASSEMBLY

R-ARM UNIT | LASER RIFLE
VE-66LRA

L-ARM UNIT | LASER SHOTGUN
WUERGER/66E

R-BACK UNIT | ACTIVE HOMING MISSILE LAUNCHER
BML-G3/P04ACT-01

L-BACK UNIT | MISSILE LAUNCHER
BML-G1/P20MLT-04

HEAD | —
HD-033M VERRILL

CORE | —
BD-011 MELANDER

ARMS | —
AC-2000 TOOL ARM

LEGS | REVERSE JOINT
RC-2000 SPRING CHICKEN

BOOSTER | —
BST-G2/P04

FCS | —
FC-008 TALBOT

GENERATOR | —
DF-GN-06 MING-TANG

EXPANSION | —
ASSAULT ARMOR

Take advantage of openings created by the enemy cornering itself.

Don't forget to keep track of any active homing missiles fired your way.

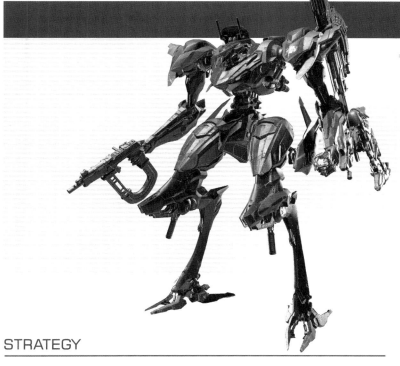

ASSEMBLY OVERVIEW

Assemblies that can catch quick, evasive ACs will work here. The setup of missile launchers and dual missile launchers will be just as potent as it's ever been against fragile ACs. STEEL HAZE will be coming in with a mixture of kinetic and energy weaponry. This assembly will be built toward anti-kinetic defense, as your goal should be to always dodge any energy attacks in this fight, which should be easier than it sounds. You'll need to constantly hound STEEL HAZE, and keeping up with such an agile AC will mean you have to be quite fast yourself. Despite their weakness in the air, the EL-TL-11 FORTALEZA legs will shine here, allowing you to weave around plasma missiles and pressure your opponent across the arena.

R-ARM UNIT | MISSILE LAUNCHER	HML-G2/P19MLT-04	
L-ARM UNIT | MISSILE LAUNCHER	HML-G2/P19MLT-04	
R-BACK UNIT | DUAL MISSILE LAUNCHER	BML-G1/P32DUO-03	
L-BACK UNIT | DUAL MISSILE LAUNCHER	BML-G1/P32DUO-03	
HEAD | —	HC-3000 WRECKER	RaD
CORE | —	CC-3000 WRECKER	RaD
ARMS | —	DF-AR-08 TIAN-QIANG	
LEGS | TANK	EL-TL-11 FORTALEZA	
BOOSTER | —		
FCS | —	FCS-G2/P10SLT	
GENERATOR | —	VP-20C	
EXPANSION | —	TERMINAL ARMOR	

STRATEGY

In the same vein as prior enemies like SHINOBI, STEEL HAZE is quick, offensively oriented, and frail. You'll want to engage in combat in the middle of the city, near the large circular structure. As you start heading toward the center, you'll find that your opponent will also be heading for you. Once you pass the buildings on the right, STEEL HAZE will be ready, potentially getting the drop on you. At the range where you'll meet each other, none of its weapons will pose a threat. STEEL HAZE's burst handgun and burst rifle will struggle to deal significant damage, and you can easily avoid plasma missiles if you keep moving. Its most dangerous weapon is its laser slicer, which enables a devastating multi-hit combo. This can be avoided by engaging at medium- to close-range, where it will only keep its burst rifle in its left hand.

At mid-range, you'll have an extreme edge when it comes to offense. Your missiles will have greater range than anything your enemy has in its arsenal besides plasma missiles, and the greater the area STEEL HAZE has to move around in, the more likely it is to crash into buildings. Despite the aerial advantage and incredible boosting abilities that its reverse-joint legs provide, buildings will humble this AC very quickly. Alternate your shots until STEEL HAZE gets cornered, then unload on it with everything you've got to put it down.

Keep a safe distance, and avoid STEEL HAZE's attempts to rush you down.

RANK 09/B	ASSEMBLY	
AC // STEEL HAZE	R-ARM UNIT | BURST HANDGUN	MA-E-211 SAMPU
	L-ARM UNIT | LASER SLICER	Vvc-774LS
COMBAT ZONE: XYLEM, THE FLOATING CITY	R-BACK UNIT | PLASMA MISSILE LAUNCHER	Vvc-703PM
Rewards (1st Victory)	L-BACK UNIT | BURST RIFLE	MA-J 200 RANSETSU-RF
78,000 COAM, 4x OST Chips, STEEL HAZE AC Data, STEEL HAZE Emblem	HEAD | —	NACHTREIHER/44E
	CORE | —	NACHTREIHER/40E
Reward (Replay)	ARMS | —	NACHTREIHER/46E
39,000 COAM	LEGS | REVERSE JOINT	NACHTREIHER/42E

SPECS			BOOSTER | —	ALULA/21E
AP	8580		FCS | —	FC-006 ABBOT
Attitude Stability	1499		GENERATOR | —	AG-T-005 HOKUSHI
Anti-Kinetic Defense	1001		EXPANSION | —	ASSAULT ARMOR
Anti-Energy Defense	1057			
Anti-Explosive Defense	976			
Elec. Discharge Tolerance	490			
Shock Resistance	-8%			
ACS Anomaly Tolerance	490			
Heat Resistance	-8%			

Quickly capitalize on moments when the enemy crashes into a building.

"HONEST" BRUTE

ASSEMBLY OVERVIEW

High mobility and anti-explosive defense should be your priority here, with the VP-44S head helping to mitigate MILK TOOTH's flames. This AC won't prove too dangerous regardless of which approach you favor, but its unique and domineering arsenal will mean that it's better to play safe. The RC-2000 SPRING CHICKEN legs will be able to bear heavy equipment without compromising mobility. Additionally, the topography of the arena can make it easy to get caught in dips and gaps, which you can quickly escape from with reverse-joint legs. MILK TOOTH is bulky, but highly susceptible to energy weapons. It also jumps around a lot, meaning your plasma rifles won't be as effective as they usually are. That said, they'll still be your most reliable arm weapons, due to how quickly they can cause ACS strain. Your goal here is to land direct hits with the laser cannon and end this fight before it becomes overwhelming.

R-ARM UNIT | PLASMA RIFLE	Vvc-760PR
L-ARM UNIT | PLASMA RIFLE	Vvc-760PR
R-BACK UNIT | PLASMA MISSILE LAUNCHER	Vvc-70VPM
L-BACK UNIT | LASER CANNON	VP-60LCS
HEAD | —	VP-44S
CORE | —	BD-011 MELANDER
ARMS | —	NACHTREIHER/46E
LEGS | REVERSE JOINT	RC-2000 SPRING CHICKEN
BOOSTER | —	FLUEGEL/21Z
FCS | —	FCS-G2/P05
GENERATOR | —	VP-20C
EXPANSION | —	TERMINAL ARMOR

STRATEGY

Your enemy in this fight is a very unique AC. Laying on constant pressure with its flamethrower is MILK TOOTH's primary tactic. Not only does this weapon remain a constant threat and obscure your vision, it is the first weapon in the Arena to cause the ACS anomaly effect. This heat overload reduces your stability, making you vulnerable to stagger. This can make MILK TOOTH a very difficult AC to engage with, which means that—without even addressing the chainsaw equipped in its left hand or its explosive assault armor—close range isn't advisable for this fight. The constant flames can make it hard to tell if MILK TOOTH is revving its chainsaw, which will deal heavy damage if it hits. It's better to stay at a distance, using Quick Boosts to escape the flames and dodge explosives.

MILK TOOTH will struggle against energy weapons. As long as you've come properly equipped, you'll be dealing solid damage throughout the fight. Your opponent can be a surprisingly jumpy AC, and landing hits may be difficult, but persistent attacks are bound to wear it down. Its charged chainsaw attack is a prime opportunity to land some counter hits, due to that weapon's long recovery period. Keep your laser cannon charged while using plasma missiles and plasma rifle fire. Once you've inflicted ACS overload, release your laser cannon charge—you should be able to take down MILK TOOTH after only one or two cycles.

	RANK 08/B
AC // MILK TOOTH	

COMBAT ZONE: JORGEN REFUELING BASE
Rewards (1st Victory)
80,000 COAM, 4x OST Chips, MILK TOOTH AC Data, MILK TOOTH Emblem
Reward (Replay)
40,000 COAM

SPECS	
AP	12320
Attitude Stability	1857
Anti-Kinetic Defense	1250
Anti-Energy Defense	1086
Anti-Explosive Defense	1268
Elec. Discharge Tolerance	490
Shock Resistance	-25%
ACS Anomaly Tolerance	490
Heat Resistance	-25%

ASSEMBLY	
R-ARM UNIT | FLAMETHROWER	WB-0000 BAD COOK
L-ARM UNIT | CHAINSAW	WB-0010 DOUBLE TROUBLE
R-BACK UNIT | SPLIT MISSILE LAUNCHER	BML-G2/P19SPL-12
L-BACK UNIT | SPREAD BAZOOKA	SB-033M MORLEY
HEAD | —	HC-3000 WRECKER
CORE | —	CC-3000 WRECKER
ARMS | —	AC-3000 WRECKER
LEGS | BIPEDAL	2C-3000 WRECKER
BOOSTER | —	BC-0400 MULE
FCS | —	FCS-G1/P01
GENERATOR | —	DF-GN-06 MING-TANG
EXPANSION | —	ASSAULT ARMOR

Avoiding MILK TOOTH's chainsaw gives you ample time to lay into it with everything you've got.

Stay on the move to keep flames from engulfing you and obscuring MILK TOOTH's attacks.

ASSEMBLY OVERVIEW

Now that you've finally gotten some new toys to play with, the Arena will be a good place to test them out. The VE-66LRA laser rifle functions very similarly to the VP-66LR, but packs a greater punch. The same can be said of the BML-G3/P05ACT-02 active homing missile launcher compared to the BML-G3/P04ACT-01, the difference being that the P05ACT-02 variant fires two missiles at once. This vastly increases its usability when fighting ACs, forcing them to either dodge two devastating missiles or concede at least one hit. You'll need an AC with a large equip load to carry these heavy weapons. DEEP DOWN is similarly packing heavy weapons, requiring you to also gear toward mobility without compromising your offense.

R-ARM UNIT | LASER RIFLE	VE-66LRA	
L-ARM UNIT | LASER RIFLE	VE-66LRA	
R-BACK UNIT | ACTIVE HOMING MISSILE LAUNCHER	BML-G3/P05ACT-02	
L-BACK UNIT | ACTIVE HOMING MISSILE LAUNCHER	BML-G3/P05ACT-02	
HEAD | —	HC-3000 WRECKER	
CORE | —	BD-011 MELANDER	
ARMS | —	VE-46A	
LEGS | REVERSE JOINT	RC-2000 SPRING CHICKEN	
BOOSTER | —	ALULA/21E	
FCS | —	FCS-G2/P10SLT	
GENERATOR | —	VP-20C	
EXPANSION | —	TERMINAL ARMOR	

STRATEGY

Your opponent is designed to down you in as few shots as possible. Equipped with many homing missiles and a lightning-quick linear rifle, DEEP DOWN will keep you on your toes. With an active homing missile launcher in its arsenal, you'll be hounded for an extended period, forced to move whenever these missiles are launched. Throughout the entire fight, DEEP DOWN will periodically charge up its linear rifle, which presents a looming threat; a single shot can easily put you in ACS overload. If you're hit by the linear rifle while being tracked by missiles, you can find yourself at an almost insurmountable disadvantage for the rest of the fight. When the linear rifle's barrel begins to glow orange, be ready to perform a Quick Boost once you're alerted by your systems. Even if you end up dodging into missiles, that will be preferable to taking a hit from the linear rifle.

Your counter offense should take place from an elevated position. Reverse-joint legs should make it easy to always stay above DEEP DOWN, where your active homing missiles will be particularly effective, making them harder to avoid. They'll be key for causing ACS strain, and the more consistently they hit, the quicker this fight will go. Once you're close to inflicting ACS overload, begin charging both of your rifles. Their high attack power will make them your primary source of damage during this window, and charged shots amplify their potency. DEEP DOWN comes with two charges of pulse armor, however, so don't expect it to go down easy.

Taking a direct hit from DEEP DOWN's linear rifle is not advisable; avoid it at all costs.

Pulse armor will give your opponent some breathing room, but keep up your attacks.

RANK 07/A		ASSEMBLY	
AC // DEEP DOWN		R-ARM UNIT | MISSILE LAUNCHER	HML-G2/P19MLT-04
		L-ARM UNIT | LINEAR RIFLE	LR-037 HARRIS
COMBAT ZONE: GRID 012		R-BACK UNIT | ACTIVE HOMING MISSILE LAUNCHER	BML-G3/P05ACT-02
Rewards (1st Victory)		L-BACK UNIT | VERTICAL MISSILE LAUNCHER	BML-G1/P07VTC-12
83,000 COAM, 4x OST Chips, DEEP DOWN AC Data, DEEP DOWN Emblem		HEAD | —	HD-011 MELANDER
		CORE | —	BD-011 MELANDER
Reward (Replay)		ARMS | —	DF-AR-09 TIAN-LAO
41,500 COAM		LEGS | BIPEDAL	DF-LG-08 TIAN-QIANG

SPECS			
AP	12510	BOOSTER | —	BST-G2/P04
Attitude Stability	1813	FCS | —	FCS-G2/P10SLT
Anti-Kinetic Defense	1330	GENERATOR | —	DF-GN-08 SAN-TAI
Anti-Energy Defense	1181	EXPANSION | —	PULSE ARMOR
Anti-Explosive Defense	1271		
Elec. Discharge Tolerance	490		
Shock Resistance	15%		
ACS Anomaly Tolerance	490		
Heat Resistance	15%		

V.II SNAIL

ASSEMBLY OVERVIEW

OPEN FAITH is a resilient AC, with high AP and good defenses. It's especially resistant to energy weapons, giving you two offensive options for an effective assembly. Keeping the combat zone's layout in mind, fast, linear weaponry will be the safest bet, giving kinetic weapons the edge. With the newly available VE-60SNA stun needle launcher, you have access to a powerful kinetic back weapon, and two of them will be put to good use against OPEN FAITH. The LR-037 HARRIS complements them well, and will help strain this AC's systems, swiftly overloading it. Closing in while it's overloaded and scoring a direct hit from the PB-033M ASHMEAD will punch a hole right through your opponent. As long as your AC is assembled for anti-energy defense, with a head like the KASUAR/44Z to mitigate Shock buildup from OPEN FAITH's stun weapons, there won't be any significant danger in close combat.

R-ARM UNIT | LINEAR RIFLE	**LR-037 HARRIS**
L-ARM UNIT | PILE BUNKER	**PB-033M ASHMEAD**
R-BACK UNIT | STUN NEEDLE LAUNCHER	**VE-60SNA**
L-BACK UNIT | STUN NEEDLE LAUNCHER	**VE-60SNA**
HEAD | —	**KASUAR/44Z**
CORE | —	**VE-40A**
ARMS | —	**VP-46S**
LEGS | TANK	**EL-TL-11 FORTALEZA**
BOOSTER | —	—
FCS | —	**FCS-G2/P05**
GENERATOR | —	**VP-20C**
EXPANSION | —	**TERMINAL ARMOR**

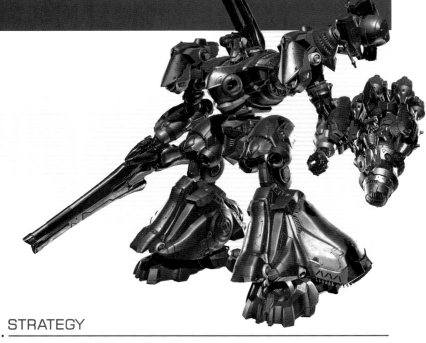

STRATEGY

OPEN FAITH is another close- to mid-range AC, and is a slow and resilient combatant. If you get too close, you open yourself up to attacks from its left-handed laser lance. This can catch you by surprise, but will deal little AP damage to the recommended assembly; however, it can cause swift ACS strain, so be ready to Quick Boost if you're staggered. OPEN FAITH also has a right-handed stun gun, which causes shock and can deal substantial damage if allowed to build up. The stun gun is avoidable by keeping your distance and retreating, but it's used infrequently, so you can stay in the fight relatively safely. It also frequently fires plasma missiles, which can be largely avoided if you stay on the move. This ultimately leaves its stun needle launcher as the only threat in its arsenal, so Quick Boost once you're warned by your systems. In the event that you get overloaded, stay calm; OPEN FAITH lacks the means to capitalize on moments of vulnerability.

Utilize the space of the Arena, aiming to stay at mid-range, and lay into OPEN FAITH with your linear rifle and stun needles, alternating fire. As its ACS stress begins to climb, close in on the opponent. It won't be able to reasonably maintain any sort of assault if you overpower it. Once you've pushed it into overload, hit it with an uncharged pile bunker, and watch OPEN FAITH's AP vanish. It is equipped with assault armor, however, so retreat back to mid range if it recovers.

	RANK 06/A
AC // OPEN FAITH	

COMBAT ZONE: OLD BERTRAM SPACEPORT
Rewards (1st Victory)
85,000 COAM, 4x OST Chips, OPEN FAITH AC Data, OPEN FAITH Emblem
Reward (Replay)
42,500 COAM

SPECS	
AP	14040
Attitude Stability	1911
Anti-Kinetic Defense	1285
Anti-Energy Defense	1406
Anti-Explosive Defense	1287
Elec. Discharge Tolerance	490
Shock Resistance	10%
ACS Anomaly Tolerance	490
Heat Resistance	10%

ASSEMBLY	
R-ARM UNIT | STUN GUN	**VP-66EG**
L-ARM UNIT | LASER LANCE	**VE-67LLA**
R-BACK UNIT | STUN NEEDLE LAUNCHER	**VE-60SNA**
L-BACK UNIT | PLASMA MISSILE LAUNCHER	**Vvc-70VPM**
HEAD | —	**VE-44A**
CORE | —	**VE-40A**
ARMS | —	**VE-46A**
LEGS | BIPEDAL	**VE-42A**
BOOSTER | —	**BUERZEL-21D**
FCS | —	**VE-21B**
GENERATOR | —	**VE-20C**
EXPANSION | —	**ASSAULT ARMOR**

Everyone has a plan until they take a pile bunker to the Core.

OPEN FAITH will most commonly try to wear you down with plasma missiles.

ASSEMBLY OVERVIEW

No matter how you assemble your AC, this is going to be one of the longest fights in the entire Arena. UMBER OX is another tank AC that'll dominate the ground if you let it, with a small twist in the form of its VE-42B legs, which are tank legs designed around aerial combat. On your end, you'll need steady, reliable damage, likely in the form of explosive weapons with a large blast radius. A combination of LITTLE GEM bazookas and SONGBIRDS grenade cannons will allow you to launch a steady stream of high power explosives with alternating fire, or up to six at once with the right opportunity. You'll want to constantly stay above UMBER OX, using the recoil from your weapons to keep you afloat, with AC parts that can withstand occasional energy and explosive attacks.

R-ARM UNIT | BAZOOKA LITTLE GEM		MELINITE
L-ARM UNIT | BAZOOKA LITTLE GEM		MELINITE
R-BACK UNIT | GRENADE CANNON SONGBIRDS		MELINITE
L-BACK UNIT | GRENADE CANNON SONGBIRDS		MELINITE
HEAD | — AH-J-124 BASHO		BAWS
CORE | — VE-40A		
ARMS | — 04-101 MIND ALPHA		
LEGS | REVERSE JOINT RC-2000 SPRING CHICKEN		RaD
BOOSTER | — BC-0600 12345		RaD
FCS | — FCS-G2/P05		
GENERATOR | — VP-20C		
EXPANSION | — TERMINAL ARMOR		

STRATEGY

UMBER OX is much like its namesake: a bulky, aggressive assembly. It will already be launching volleys at you before you can get close to it. Despite being a tank-legged assembly, the VE-42B legs actually facilitate verticality, and your opponent will spend much of the match in the air. It's wise to stick to the air yourself, avoiding the splash damage from its explosive weapons. You will be vulnerable to the laser rifle and diffuse laser cannon, so don't get complacent. If an explosive hits you head on, the effectiveness of your opponent's energy weapons will be magnified. The diffuse laser cannon in particular can be a domineering threat if you get too close, acting like a laser shotgun, and dealing heavy damage if you're overloaded. It'll also charge its laser rifle, signified by a blue glow around the barrel. Aside from regular laser rifle fire, all of UMBER OX's weapons will cause alerts from your systems; be ready to Quick Boost to avoid shells and grenades.

You'll want to gain the aerial advantage over UMBER OX as soon as you can. Once you meet near the middle of the arena, leap and continue to boost into the air. At the point where you're at mid range, begin firing your grenade cannons and bazookas in an alternating pattern. You can sustain your EN purely from the recoil of your weapons, making aerial Quick Boosts possible when needed. Maintain your assault from above; this will be the longest fight yet—even without considering the brief moment of invulnerability granted by its pulse armor—but stealing UMBER OX's aerial advantage will only make it a matter of time.

RANK 05/A		ASSEMBLY	
AC // UMBER OX		R-ARM UNIT | LASER RIFLE VE-66LRB	
		L-ARM UNIT | BAZOOKA MAJESTIC	
COMBAT ZONE: WATCHPOINT DELTA		R-BACK UNIT | DIFFUSE LASER CANNON VP-60LCD	
Rewards (1st Victory)		L-BACK UNIT | GRENADE CANNON EARSHOT	
87,000 COAM, 4x OST Chips, UMBER OX AC Data, UMBER OX Emblem		HEAD | — VP-44S	
		CORE | — VP-40S	
Reward (Replay)		ARMS | — VE-46A	
43,500 COAM		LEGS | TANK VE-42B	
SPECS		BOOSTER | — —	
AP	15270	FCS | — VE-21A	
Attitude Stability	1778	GENERATOR | — VE-20C	
Anti-Kinetic Defense	1238	EXPANSION | — PULSE ARMOR	
Anti-Energy Defense	1338		
Anti-Explosive Defense	1220		
Elec. Discharge Tolerance	490		
Shock Resistance	17%		
ACS Anomaly Tolerance	490		
Heat Resistance	17%		

UMBER OX will have a hard time avoiding attacks from above, and even more so if they're explosives.

Diffuse laser cannons function like shotguns, and can catch you at close range if you're not quick to dodge.

THUMB DOLMAYAN

ASSEMBLY OVERVIEW

The opponent comes equipped with every type of conventional weaponry, but this assembly features high defenses and can shrug off many incoming attacks. Additionally, this is a fight where there's a high potential for the combat zone to get covered in napalm and flames, so hovering with a pair of tetrapod legs will be extremely useful for avoiding heat buildup and ACS anomaly. The usual suspects for plasma weapons will make their appearances here, with numerous plasma explosions being the best ways to leave a dent in ASTGHIK's otherwise thick armor.

R-ARM UNIT | PLASMA RIFLE	Vvc-760PR
L-ARM UNIT | PLASMA RIFLE	Vvc-760PR
R-BACK UNIT | PLASMA MISSILE LAUNCHER	Vvc-706PM
L-BACK UNIT | PLASMA MISSILE LAUNCHER	Vvc-706PM
HEAD | —	HD-033M VERRILL
CORE | —	DF-BD-08 TIAN-QIANG
ARMS | —	DF-AR-09 TIAN-LAO
LEGS | TETRAPOD	LG-033M VERRILL
BOOSTER | —	BC-0400 MULE
FCS | —	FCS-G2/P10SLT
GENERATOR | —	VP-20C
EXPANSION | —	TERMINAL ARMOR

STRATEGY

ASTGHIK can be a crafty opponent. Rather than going in with a full loadout of two arm weapons and two back weapons, it comes in with two arm weapons ready to go, and two arm weapons equipped to the back, which it can swap between on the fly. This makes your opponent particularly unpredictable, as the range it's most effective at will change suddenly. On the other hand, it limits the AC's offensive capabilities to using only two weapons at a time. Its most dangerous weapons are the pulse blade and napalm bomb launcher, which means shields aren't ideal for this fight. When it's using its napalm bomb launcher, make sure to stay airborne to avoid the flames on the ground of the arena. If you remain at long range, it will more often rely on its burst rifle and missile launcher, making it easier to deal with. As long as you circle the air above ASTGHIK, it will struggle to maintain any sort of consistent damage.

Your best option is to stay high and assault the enemy with plasma weapons. ASTGHIK can hop around the arena, effectively avoiding attacks as long as it has the EN to do so. It cannot keep this up for long against plasma weaponry, with plasma missiles in particular making the battlefield hazardous for opponents. With two Vvc-706PMs, you'll be able to fire a series of 12 plasma missiles at once, which can effectively corner ASTGHIK even in the middle of the arena. Don't expect high ACS strain or ACS overload to open windows of opportunity for you in this fight; this is a battle that will largely be won by whittling down the opponent with persistent damage. With this in mind, you should still be able to take out the enemy fairly easily, without even needing to leave the air.

RANK 04/A	
AC // ASTGHIK	

ASSEMBLY	
R-ARM UNIT | BURST RIFLE	MA-J 200 RANSETSU-RF
L-ARM UNIT | PULSE BLADE	HI-32: BU-TT/A
R-BACK UNIT | NAPALM BOMB LAUNCHER	MA-T-222 KYORAI
L-BACK UNIT | MISSILE LAUNCHER	HML-G2/P19MLT-04
HEAD | —	AH-J-124 BASHO
CORE | —	AC-J-120 BASHO
ARMS | —	AA-J-123 BASHO
LEGS | BIPEDAL	AL-J-121 BASHO
BOOSTER | —	AB-J-137 KIKAKU
FCS | —	FCS-G2/P05
GENERATOR | —	IA-C01G: AORTA
EXPANSION | —	ASSAULT ARMOR

COMBAT ZONE: TEST ARENA

Rewards (1st Victory)

90,000 COAM, 4x OST Chips, ASTGHIK AC Data, ASTGHIK Emblem

Reward (Replay)

45,000 COAM

SPECS	
AP	11420
Attitude Stability	1670
Anti-Kinetic Defense	1196
Anti-Energy Defense	1083
Anti-Explosive Defense	1275
Elec. Discharge Tolerance	490
Shock Resistance	-16%
ACS Anomaly Tolerance	490
Heat Resistance	-16%

ASTGHIK will eventually run out of steam as it attempts to escape your plasma explosions.

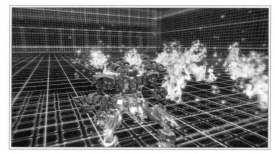

This opponent can control the battlefield from a distance by covering it in napalm if you stay grounded.

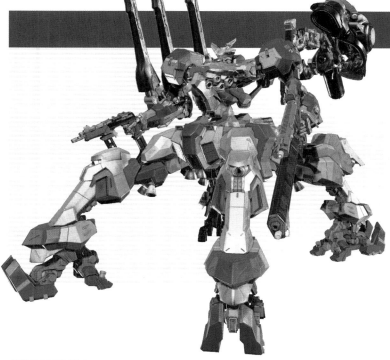

ASSEMBLY OVERVIEW

Despite not using any strictly close-range weaponry, this assembly should effectively be viewed as a close-quarters build. You'll want to be capable of closing in and staying with your opponent. This will make your weapons more effective, and eliminate some of the threat posed by the opposition's weaponry. While tetrapod builds usually have an advantage on neutral terrain like the empty virtual arena, ASTER CROWN isn't outfitted with weapons that take advantage of its hovering capabilities. Your assembly should have high anti-kinetic defense to be able to take hits from its LR-037 HARRIS linear rifle, which will usually be its most dangerous weapon. On your end, a pair of pulse guns will be vital for quickly shredding through the pulse scutum, which will otherwise provide ASTER CROWN with a nearly impenetrable defense. SONGBIRDS will be a perfect follow-up once the enemy is staggered, capable of dealing massive damage in brief windows.

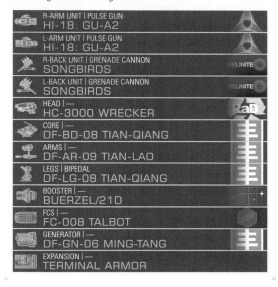

	R-ARM UNIT | PULSE GUN	
	HI-18: GU-A2	
	L-ARM UNIT | PULSE GUN	
	HI-18: GU-A2	
	R-BACK UNIT | GRENADE CANNON	MELINITE
	SONGBIRDS	
	L-BACK UNIT | GRENADE CANNON	MELINITE
	SONGBIRDS	
	HEAD | —	RaD
	HC-3000 WRECKER	
	CORE | —	
	DF-BD-08 TIAN-QIANG	
	ARMS | —	
	DF-AR-09 TIAN-LAO	
	LEGS | BIPEDAL	
	DF-LG-08 TIAN-QIANG	
	BOOSTER | —	
	BUERZEL/21D	
	FCS | —	
	FC-008 TALBOT	
	GENERATOR | —	
	DF-GN-06 MING-TANG	
	EXPANSION | —	
	TERMINAL ARMOR	

STRATEGY

Without explosive weaponry to carpet the ground, this is more straightforward than previous tetrapod fights in the Arena. Instead of trying to match it in the sky, stay under ASTER CROWN when it hovers. Within about 20 meters, it'll struggle to strike beneath itself, and spend most of its time evading and retreating to a distance where its weapons will be effective. It's slightly more effective on the ground, but will struggle to maintain consistent damage as it tries to regain an aerial position. Its burst handgun will deal moderate AP damage and ACS strain, but high anti-kinetic defense will mitigate its effectiveness. Charged laser cannon and linear rifle shots present a greater threat, and will set off your AC's alerts, so be ready to evade once you see barrels glowing. ASTER CROWN is unlikely to use charge attacks at close range, instead using its linear rifle to force you to retreat. Be careful of its assault armor if you choose to engage at close range.

With mediocre defenses across the board, your enemy primarily relies on its pulse scutum for damage mitigation. You can easily turn this back on the opponent by pounding it with pulse guns, quickly shattering its ACS and staggering it. Once overloaded, ASTER CROWN will take massive damage from close range grenades. With additional help from the pulse guns, you should find it quite effective to exploit overload windows, whether ASTER CROWN is in the air or on the ground.

ASTER CROWN's biggest blind spot is the space immediately below it.

RANK 03/S		ASSEMBLY	
AC // ASTER CROWN			R-ARM UNIT | BURST HANDGUN
			MA-E-211 SAMPU
COMBAT ZONE: TEST ARENA			L-ARM UNIT | LINEAR RIFLE
Rewards (1st Victory)			LR-037 HARRIS
			R-BACK UNIT | LASER CANNON
95,000 COAM, 6x OST Chips,			VE-60LCA
ASTER CROWN AC Data,			L-BACK UNIT | PULSE SCUTUM
ASTER CROWN Emblem			VE-61PSA
Reward (Replay)			HEAD | —
			KASUAR/44Z
47,500 COAM			CORE | —
			EL-TC-10 FIRMEZA

SPECS		ARMS | —
		AR-011 MELANDER
AP	10410	LEGS | TETRAPOD
Attitude Stability	2321	LG-033M VERRILL
Anti-Kinetic Defense	1182	BOOSTER | —
Anti-Energy Defense	1091	BC-0200 GRIDWALKER
Anti-Explosive Defense	1132	FCS | —
Elec. Discharge Tolerance	490	FC-006 ABBOT
Shock Resistance	28%	GENERATOR | —
ACS Anomaly Tolerance	490	VP-20D
Heat Resistance	28%	EXPANSION | —
		ASSAULT ARMOR

This AC's burst handgun will ricochet at even moderate distances in this fight, making the weapon largely superfluous.

G1 MICHIGAN

ASSEMBLY OVERVIEW

Airspace control is vital for getting through this fight comfortably. LIGER TAIL hits extremely hard, making retaliation difficult if you let it reach an elevated position uncontested. Unlike some other tetrapod opponents, your foe here will always attempt to rise above you; this is where a specific booster will save the day. The BC-0400 MULE is always a good partner for tetrapod legs, as it boasts extremely good EN efficiency, keeping you airborne for long periods of time. In this fight, even if you're challenged for aerial supremacy, you will almost always come out on top with this booster. LIGER TAIL comes equipped with powerful explosive weaponry, and a DF-GG-08 HU-BEN that can be problematic at close range, making it important that you stay far above it whenever possible. With high defenses and reliable energy weapons for aerial combat, such as the Vvc-760PR plasma rifle and Vvc-706PM plasma missile, your assembly should give you dominance over LIGER TAIL in the air.

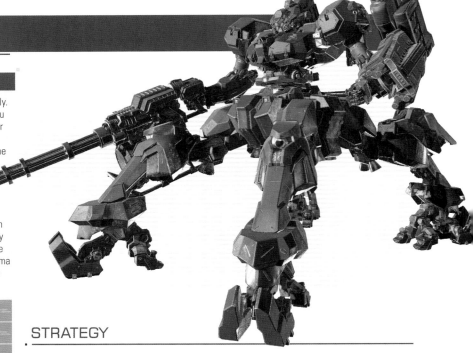

R-ARM UNIT | PLASMA RIFLE	Vvc-760PR
L-ARM UNIT | PLASMA RIFLE	Vvc-760PR
R-BACK UNIT | PLASMA MISSILE LAUNCHER	Vvc-706PM
L-BACK UNIT | PLASMA MISSILE LAUNCHER	Vvc-706PM
HEAD | —	AH-J-124 BASHO
CORE | —	DF-BD-08 TIAN-QIANG
ARMS | —	DF-AR-09 TIAN-LAO
LEGS | TETRAPOD	LG-033M VERRILL
BOOSTER | —	BC-0400 MULE
FCS | —	FCS-G2/P05
GENERATOR | —	VP-20C
EXPANSION | —	TERMINAL ARMOR

STRATEGY

LIGER TAIL is built similarly to the previous opponent, but fights more typically for a tetrapod—it will take to the air more often, and rain down explosives. Before you can even get close to this AC, you'll be facing gatling gun fire and missiles. And if you get too close, you'll be hit with a fistful of compact explosives, courtesy of its left-hand explosive thrower. You'll generally want to stick to mid range, and hover above LIGER TAIL to help neutralize its explosive damage potential. You'll need to stay as high as possible for much of this fight, and your safest opportunity for doing so is as soon as the match starts. It'll attempt to close in on you and hit you with grenades and explosives, which are all capable of overloading and staggering you quickly. Watch out for attack indicators, as they'll warn you of incoming grenades. You will take damage in this fight, but the ultimate winner here will be the one who can stay airborne longer.

As long as you can at least maintain an even playing field, LIGER TAIL will be susceptible to energy weaponry. Even in the sky, plasma explosions are effective at catching opponents, causing large areas of damage. Don't surrender this advantage, as you'll have a much harder time hitting your shots while grounded, leaving you open. Just maintain a steady stream of plasma rifle shots and plasma missiles to deplete LIGER TAIL's EN, and send it back down to the floor. It can use pulse protection to try to force you to back off or to rush in close. The barrier will run out eventually, so don't let it throw you off.

RANK 02/S	ASSEMBLY	
AC // LIGER TAIL	R-ARM UNIT | GATLING GUN	DF-GA-08 HU-BEN
	L-ARM UNIT | EXPLOSIVE THROWER	DF-ET-09 TAI-YANG-SHOU
COMBAT ZONE: TEST ARENA	R-BACK UNIT | SPLIT MISSILE LAUNCHER	BML-G2/P17SPL-16
Rewards (1st Victory)	L-BACK UNIT | GRENADE CANNON	SONGBIRDS
97,000 COAM, 6x OST Chips, LIGER TAIL AC Data, LIGER TAIL Emblem	HEAD | —	HD-033 VERRILL
	CORE | —	BD-011 MELANDER
Reward (Replay)	ARMS | —	AR-011 MELANDER
48,500 COAM	LEGS | TETRAPOD	LG-033M VERRILL
	BOOSTER | —	BST-G2/P04

SPECS		
AP	11820	
Attitude Stability	2340	FCS | — FCS-G2/P05
Anti-Kinetic Defense	1275	
Anti-Energy Defense	1139	GENERATOR | — DF-GN-08 SAN-TAI
Anti-Explosive Defense	1220	
Elec. Discharge Tolerance	490	EXPANSION | — PULSE PROTECTION
Shock Resistance	12%	
ACS Anomaly Tolerance	490	
Heat Resistance	12%	

This match will likely come down to who can maintain air dominance.

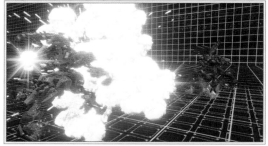

If you rush in carelessly, expect to be met with a fistful of bombs.

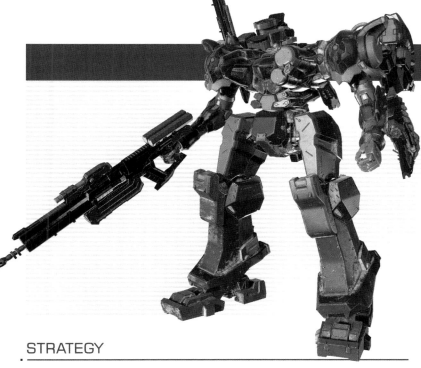

ASSEMBLY OVERVIEW

LOCKSMITH is an incredibly wily, well-rounded AC, and getting the best of it can be tricky if you can't hit it from all angles. With a missile launcher on your arm, complemented by vertical and dual missile launchers, you'll have a method to attack from every angle. LOCKSMITH can still slip through your salvos, but it can't run forever. You'll want to keep your linear rifle in your back pocket for the fight, waiting to unload when you see an opening. Utilize the distance Quick Boosts grant you with reverse-joint legs to weave in and out of a comfortable distance in combat. Despite the fact that you'll encounter every type of weapon, you'll only have to regularly worry about its Vvc-770LB laser blade and BC-033M MORELY spread bazooka, so higher anti-energy and anti-explosive defense should be the priority.

R-ARM UNIT | LINEAR RIFLE **LR-037 HARRIS**	
L-ARM UNIT | MISSILE LAUNCHER **HML-G2/P19MLT-04**	
R-BACK UNIT | VERTICAL MISSILE LAUNCHER **BML-G1/P03VTC-08**	
L-BACK UNIT | DUAL MISSILE LAUNCHER **BML-G1/P32DUO-03**	
HEAD | — **HD-033M VERRILL**	
CORE | — **07-161 MIND ALPHA**	
ARMS | — **VP-46S**	
LEGS | REVERSE JOINT **RC-2000 SPRING CHICKEN**	
BOOSTER | — **BST-G2/P06SPD**	
FCS | — **FCS-G2/P10SLT**	
GENERATOR | — **VP-20C**	
EXPANSION | — **TERMINAL ARMOR**	

STRATEGY

Here you are, at the top of the Arena. One last AC sits in front of you. If its assembly looks familiar, you're not imagining things: LOCKSMITH is essentially a tuned-up version of the AC you crash-landed on Rubicon in, at least in terms of its arsenal. A right-arm assault rifle, a left-arm laser blade and a right back explosive launcher. The most obvious addition Freud has made to his AC are the laser drones, which act as missiles that can continuously fire lasers at you. Before the drones are fired, you'll get an attack indicator, despite them not posing an immediate threat. If you notice that your ACS strain is accumulating, generally after taking hits from the spread bazooka, retreat. LOCKSMITH's most dangerous weapon is its laser blade, which it saves almost exclusively for when your AC is staggered after an overload. If this connects, it will deal severe AP damage, making it a weapon that can quickly change the pace of the match, even if you've had the edge up until that point.

Missile launchers are great options for trapping and staggering LOCKSMITH. They'll provide an overwhelming offense, bound to catch the enemy eventually, especially if fired mid jump. On top of dealing consistent strain, your missile launchers will be reliable for dealing damage all throughout the fight. Use them as much as possible, saving your linear rifle for select moments. The first time you're close to inflicting ACS overload, LOCKSMITH is likely to use its pulse armor. Despite how logical it seems to charge your linear rifle for an overload, it's more economical to keep it uncharged, ready to fire at a moment's notice. You don't want to find yourself in a situation where your enemy is vulnerable, but your linear rifle is cooling down.

RANK 01/S	ASSEMBLY	
AC // LOCKSMITH	R-ARM UNIT | ASSAULT RIFLE **RF-024 TURNER**	
COMBAT ZONE: TEST ARENA	L-ARM UNIT | LASER BLADE **Vvc-770LB**	
Rewards (1st Victory)	R-BACK UNIT | SPREAD BAZOOKA **SB-033M MORLEY**	
100,000 COAM, 6x OST Chips, LOCKSMITH AC Data and Emblem, Vvc- 700LD (R-Back Unit: 247,000 COAM)	L-BACK UNIT | LASER DRONE **Vvc-700LD**	
	HEAD | — **HD-011 MELANDER**	
Reward (Replay)	CORE | — **VP-40S**	
50,000 COAM	ARMS | — **VP-46S**	
	LEGS | BIPEDAL **LG-011 MELANDER**	
SPECS		BOOSTER | — **FLUEGEL/21Z**
AP	10460	
Attitude Stability	1719	FCS | — **FC-006 ABBOT**
Anti-Kinetic Defense	1200	
Anti-Energy Defense	1196	GENERATOR | — **VE-20A**
Anti-Explosive Defense	1138	
Elec. Discharge Tolerance	490	EXPANSION | — **PULSE ARMOR**
Shock Resistance	15%	
ACS Anomaly Tolerance	490	
Heat Resistance	15%	

Missiles can continue to safely whittle down LOCKSMITH throughout this duel.

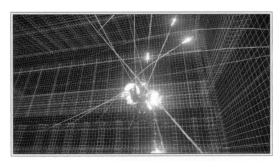

Laser drones will hound you for a large portion of this fight.

INTEGRATION SUBJECT 51-001 K

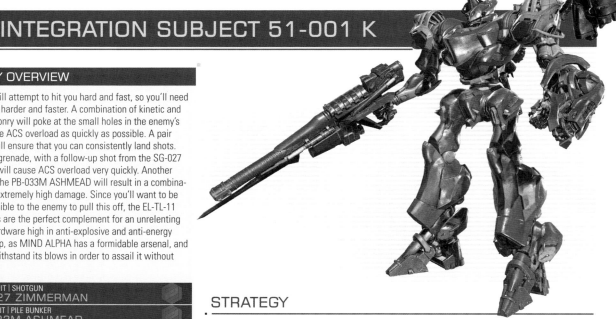

ASSEMBLY OVERVIEW

MIND ALPHA will attempt to hit you hard and fast, so you'll need to be able to hit harder and faster. A combination of kinetic and explosive weaponry will poke at the small holes in the enemy's frame, and cause ACS overload as quickly as possible. A pair of EARSHOTs will ensure that you can consistently land shots. Each individual grenade, with a follow-up shot from the SG-027 ZIMMERMAN, will cause ACS overload very quickly. Another follow-up from the PB-033M ASHMEAD will result in a combination that deals extremely high damage. Since you'll want to be as close as possible to the enemy to pull this off, the EL-TL-11 FORTALEZA legs are the perfect complement for an unrelenting offense. Any hardware high in anti-explosive and anti-energy defense will help, as MIND ALPHA has a formidable arsenal, and you'll need to withstand its blows in order to assail it without pause.

R-ARM UNIT | SHOTGUN	**SG-027 ZIMMERMAN**
L-ARM UNIT | PILE BUNKER	**PB-033M ASHMEAD**
R-BACK UNIT | GRENADE CANNON	**EARSHOT**
L-BACK UNIT | GRENADE CANNON	**EARSHOT**
HEAD | —	**HC-3000 WRECKER**
CORE | —	**VE-40A**
ARMS | —	**IA-C01A: EPHEMERA**
LEGS | TANK	**EL-TL-11 FORTALEZA**
BOOSTER | —	
FCS | —	**FC-008 TALBOT**
GENERATOR | —	**VP-20S**
EXPANSION | —	**ASSAULT ARMOR**

STRATEGY

Welcome to the Integration Program fights. While these are their own class of Arena battles, they operate identically to the ranked battles. To showcase this, you'll be fighting in the empty virtual arena. MIND ALPHA has some unique tricks to bring to this introductory fight; its laser orbit weapon enables it to passively target and pester you throughout the entire fight without having to actively engage you, and it likes to take advantage of this. The enemy will often boost into the air, hang back, and let the laser orbits do the work, while firing explosive rounds and bazooka shells. The laser orbits don't deal high damage, and trying to dodge them will only waste your energy. If you maintain a minimal distance between you and MIND ALPHA, it'll use its plasma thrower frequently.

So long as your assembly is sufficiently built for anti-energy and anti-explosive defense, you'll win battles with MIND ALPHA at close range. Assault Boost toward it as soon as the match starts, performing lateral boosts to avoid missiles. Once you close in, it will likely take to the air. Stop once you're right below it, and begin firing a volley of shotgun blasts and grenades. A single grenade and shotgun slug will cause enough strain to overload your opponent's ACS. Just one assault armor blast will also do the trick at close range. As long as you're as close to the enemy as possible, it will be within pile bunker distance once overloaded. The timing will be tight, so don't attempt a charged hit. The range is shorter compared to uncharged, and the enemy can recover from stagger during the charge time. Stick to MIND ALPHA like glue, and it will go down in three rounds of overload.

RANK α-1	ASSEMBLY	
AC // MIND ALPHA	R-ARM UNIT | DETONATING BAZOOKA	**44-141 JVLN ALPHA**
	L-ARM UNIT | PLASMA THROWER	**44-143 HMMR**
COMBAT ZONE: TEST ARENA	R-BACK UNIT | LASER ORBIT	**45-091 ORBT**
Rewards (1st Victory)	L-BACK UNIT | DETONATING MISSILE LAUNCHER	**45-091 JVLN BETA**
60,000 COAM, 8x OST Chips, MIND ALPHA AC Data, MIND ALPHA Emblem	HEAD | —	**20-081 MIND ALPHA**
Reward (Replay)	CORE | —	**07-161 MIND ALPHA**
30,000 COAM	ARMS | —	**04-101 MIND ALPHA**
	LEGS | BIPEDAL	**06-041 MIND ALPHA**

SPECS	
AP	11000
Attitude Stability	1744
Anti-Kinetic Defense	1233
Anti-Energy Defense	1291
Anti-Explosive Defense	1220
Elec. Discharge Tolerance	490
Shock Resistance	9%
ACS Anomaly Tolerance	490
Heat Resistance	9%

BOOSTER | —	**BST-G2/P06SPD**	
FCS | —	**FCS-G2/P05**	
GENERATOR | —	**VP-20C**	
EXPANSION | —	—	

Use assault armor if MIND ALPHA manages to escape your attack.

The plasma thrower is hard to evade and can attack from many angles.

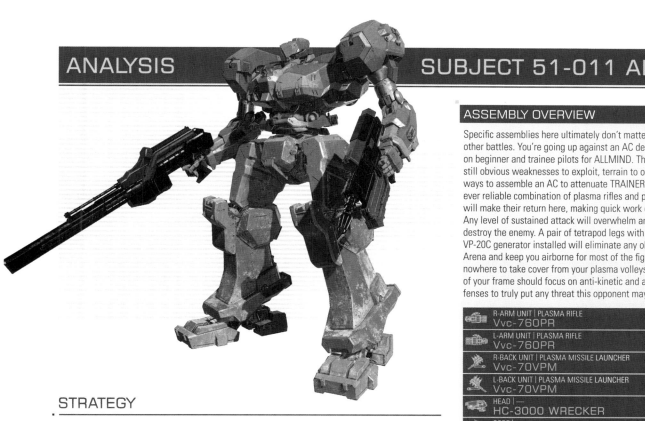

ANALYSIS

SUBJECT 51-011 AL

STRATEGY

Don't be mistaken; TRAINER is as weak as it looks. ALLMIND isn't throwing you a curveball with this fight. This is simply a fight meant to gather data, using an AC designed to train new pilots. Obviously this doesn't apply to you, so this isn't meant to be a challenge like MIND ALPHA or the high-ranked Arena fights. As such, you are more than well equipped to deal with an AC that is outfitted with dependable, but low-performance parts and weapons. TRAINER doesn't even have a full set of weapons, with an empty back left weapon slot. Nothing in its arsenal will be a considerable threat to you.

Approach this fight as you have previous battles in which you aimed to gain an aerial advantage. As you reach the top of the hill, you will be hit with machine gun fire, but this will deal negligible damage. Make contact with the enemy at the top of the hill, then immediately go into hover mode. TRAINER may dodge a few shots, but it cannot keep it up for long. Don't stop firing on it, and this will be one of, if not the single quickest fight you've had in the Arena.

ASSEMBLY OVERVIEW

Specific assemblies here ultimately don't matter as much as in other battles. You're going up against an AC designed to get data on beginner and trainee pilots for ALLMIND. That said, there are still obvious weaknesses to exploit, terrain to overcome, and ways to assemble an AC to attenuate TRAINER's weaponry. The ever reliable combination of plasma rifles and plasma missiles will make their return here, making quick work of the opponent. Any level of sustained attack will overwhelm and eventually destroy the enemy. A pair of tetrapod legs with the high-capacity VP-20C generator installed will eliminate any obstructions in the Arena and keep you airborne for most of the fight, giving TRAINER nowhere to take cover from your plasma volleys. Finally, the rest of your frame should focus on anti-kinetic and anti-explosive defenses to truly put any threat this opponent may pose in the dirt.

R-ARM UNIT | PLASMA RIFLE	Vvc-760PR
L-ARM UNIT | PLASMA RIFLE	Vvc-760PR
R-BACK UNIT | PLASMA MISSILE LAUNCHER	Vvc-70VPM
L-BACK UNIT | PLASMA MISSILE LAUNCHER	Vvc-70VPM
HEAD | —	HC-3000 WRECKER
CORE | —	EL-TC-10 FIRMEZA
ARMS | —	AC-3000 WRECKER
LEGS | TETRAPOD	VP-424
BOOSTER | —	BC-0400 MULE
FCS | —	FCS-G2/P05
GENERATOR | —	VP-20C
EXPANSION | —	TERMINAL ARMOR

	RANK α-2
AC // TRAINER	

COMBAT ZONE: BONA DEA DUNES
Rewards (1st Victory)
66,000 COAM, 8x OST Chips, TRAINER AC Data, TRAINER Emblem
Reward (Replay)
33,000 COAM

SPECS	
AP	10550
Attitude Stability	1731
Anti-Kinetic Defense	1227
Anti-Energy Defense	1105
Anti-Explosive Defense	1194
Elec. Discharge Tolerance	490
Shock Resistance	15%
ACS Anomaly Tolerance	490
Heat Resistance	15%

ASSEMBLY	
R-ARM UNIT | LINEAR RIFLE	LR-036 CURTIS
L-ARM UNIT | MACHINE GUN	MG-014 LUDLOW
R-BACK UNIT | MISSILE LAUNCHER	BML-G1/P20MLT-04
L-BACK UNIT |	
HEAD | —	HD-011 MELANDER
CORE | —	BD-011 MELANDER
ARMS | —	AR-011 MELANDER
LEGS | BIPEDAL	LG-011 MELANDER
BOOSTER | —	BST-G2/P04
FCS | —	FC-008 TALBOT
GENERATOR | —	AG-E-013 YABA
EXPANSION | —	—

At this point in your mercenary career, any approach you take will best TRAINER.

TRAINER will have a brief height advantage at the start of the match.

ANALYSIS SUBJECT 51-012 AL

ASSEMBLY OVERVIEW

You're facing off against another AC designed to put new pilots to the test. TESTER is a hardier AC than TRAINER, and has some weapons that can deal hefty damage if you're not careful. This will mainly be an issue if its BML-G3/P05ACT-02 active homing missiles catch you. Because of that, you should go for high anti-explosive defense, which will help if a missile manages to connect. You'll want to keep your plasma weapons from the last match, as well as the same leg and booster to increase your defense and reduce the chances of a hit from TESTER's HI-32 BU-TT/A.

R-ARM UNIT | PLASMA RIFLE	Vvc-760PR	
L-ARM UNIT | PLASMA RIFLE	Vvc-760PR	
R-BACK UNIT | PLASMA MISSILE LAUNCHER	Vvc-70VPM	
L-BACK UNIT | PLASMA MISSILE LAUNCHER	Vvc-70VPM	
HEAD | —	AH-J-124 BASHO	BAWS
CORE | —	DF-BD-08 TIAN-QIANG	
ARMS | —	AA-J-123 BASHO	BAWS
LEGS | TETRAPOD	VP-424	
BOOSTER | —	BC-0400 MULE	RaD
FCS | —	FCS-G2/P05	
GENERATOR | —	VP-20C	
EXPANSION | —	TERMINAL ARMOR	

STRATEGY

TESTER follows TRAINER very closely, and similarly, it doesn't come in with a full kit. It's outfitted with one burst assault rifle, one pulse blade, and one active homing missile launcher. This is another combatant that prefers to stay grounded and has mediocre anti-energy defense. All this means that you can rely on a similar build to the one used in the previous battle, but your approach should be made with more attentiveness. TESTER most frequently relies on its burst assault rifle, its weakest weapon. Its active homing missiles are more threatening; it fires two at once, and they will slowly track your movements, trailing behind you. If both hit you, it can put you in ACS overload, leaving you open to a successive attack from its pulse blade. This one-two punch can result in your AC taking a startling amount of damage from such an unassuming opponent.

Staying airborne will generally keep you safe. You'll be able to avoid the missiles if you stay moving in the air. And, as always, an aerial approach increases your plasma weapons' offensive capabilities. Stay airborne, stay mobile, and lay into TESTER. Despite having stronger weaponry and extra bulk, it won't last much longer than TRAINER did.

	RANK α-3
AC // TESTER	

COMBAT ZONE: CONTAMINATED CITY	
Rewards (1st Victory)	
72,000 COAM, 8x OST Chips, TESTER AC Data, TESTER Emblem	
Reward (Replay)	
36,000 COAM	

SPECS	
AP	12200
Attitude Stability	1761
Anti-Kinetic Defense	1289
Anti-Energy Defense	1210
Anti-Explosive Defense	1308
Elec. Discharge Tolerance	490
Shock Resistance	-27%
ACS Anomaly Tolerance	490
Heat Resistance	-27%

ASSEMBLY	
R-ARM UNIT | BURST ASSAULT RIFLE	MA-J-201 RANSETSU-AR
L-ARM UNIT | PULSE BLADE	HI-32: BU-TT/A
R-BACK UNIT | —	—
L-BACK UNIT | ACTIVE HOMING MISSILE LAUNCHER	BML-G3/P05ACT-02
HEAD | —	DF-HD-08 TIAN-QIANG
CORE | —	DF-BD-08 TIAN-QIANG
ARMS | —	DF-AR-08 TIAN-QIANG
LEGS | BIPEDAL	DF-LG-08 TIAN-QIANG
BOOSTER | —	BC-0600 12345
FCS | —	FC-006 ABBOT
GENERATOR | —	DF-GN-02 LING-TAI
EXPANSION | —	—

You can comfortably smother TESTER with little worry for retaliation.

TESTER's active homing missiles will trail you for quite a while.

MIND BETA

STRATEGY

The fight against MIND BETA is much like the fight against MIND ALPHA. This latest iteration keeps its predecessor's pestering orbit laser, but swaps out the rest of its weapons. It comes equipped with a powerful 44-142 KRSV multi energy rifle in its right hand, which acts like a plasma rifle and explodes on contact. This rifle can cause subtle ACS buildup and damage if you aren't moving quickly enough. The rifle can also be fully charged up to two stages to fire an extremely powerful plasma shot, which will deal substantial damage if it lands. If it begins to glow, be ready to receive a warning indicator from your systems, which is your cue to get moving and be prepared to Quick Boost. If MIND BETA is allowed to overwhelm you and inflict ACS overload, it'll close in and perform a powerful three-hit attack with its laser dagger.

MIND BETA's defenses are the same as MIND ALPHA's, but it covers itself with a pulse shield. Countering it with a pulse gun any time you see its shield will be a major boon in this fight, and your primary source of inflicting strain. It won't take long to bring its shield down, leaving it open to massive damage from your grenades. To increase the chances of all of your grenades landing, keep MIND BETA within about 100 meters for as long as you can. It's not a particularly hardy AC, and won't be able to withstand a few well placed grenades.

ASSEMBLY OVERVIEW

With MIND BETA being a slightly adjusted MIND ALPHA, your assembly here will largely follow the same template as your assembly from that fight. The major differences come as a direct response to the adjustments ALLMIND has made. BETA's core build is identical, but with a VP-61PS pulse shield in tow, you'll need a weapon with high PA interference like a pulse gun, making its biggest defensive change a weakness. It will be best to swap out the PB-033M ASHMEAD for the HI-18: GU-A2 pulse gun, as you can focus on using the pulse gun to stagger this AC, giving you three grenades to launch when its exposed. Beyond this, MIND BETA is lacking any of the explosive weapons its last iteration had, meaning you can build your AC exclusively with anti-energy defense in response.

R-ARM UNIT | GRENADE LAUNCHER	DIZZY
L-ARM UNIT | PULSE GUN	HI-18: GU-A2
R-BACK UNIT | GRENADE CANNON	EARSHOT
L-BACK UNIT | GRENADE CANNON	EARSHOT
HEAD | —	IA-C01H: EPHEMERA
CORE | —	VE-40A
ARMS | —	IA-C01A: EPHEMERA
LEGS | TANK	EL-TL-11 FORTALEZA
BOOSTER | —	
FCS | —	FC-008 TALBOT
GENERATOR | —	VP-20S
EXPANSION | —	TERMINAL ARMOR

Be extremely wary when MIND BETA has its multi energy rifle primed and glowing like this, and prepare to take immediate evasive action.

Your offenses should easily overwhelm MIND BETA's defensive capabilities.

	RANK β-1
AC // MIND BETA	

COMBAT ZONE: BAWS ARSENAL NO.2
Rewards (1st Victory)
80,000 COAM, 10x OST Chips, MIND BETA AC Data, MIND BETA Emblem
Reward (Replay)
40,000 COAM

SPECS	
AP	11000
Attitude Stability	1744
Anti-Kinetic Defense	1233
Anti-Energy Defense	1291
Anti-Explosive Defense	1220
Elec. Discharge Tolerance	490
Shock Resistance	9%
ACS Anomaly Tolerance	490
Heat Resistance	9%

ASSEMBLY	
R-ARM UNIT | MULTI ENERGY RIFLE	44-142 KRSV
L-ARM UNIT | LASER DAGGER	VP-67VLD
R-BACK UNIT | LASER ORBIT	45-091 ORBT
L-BACK UNIT | PULSE SHIELD	VP-61PS
HEAD | —	20-081 MIND ALPHA
CORE | —	07-161 MIND ALPHA
ARMS | —	04-101 MIND ALPHA
LEGS | BIPEDAL	06-041 MIND ALPHA
BOOSTER | —	BST-G2/P06SPD
FCS | —	FCS-G2/P05
GENERATOR | —	VP-20C
EXPANSION | —	PULSE ARMOR

ANALYSIS SUBJECT 51-013 BE

ASSEMBLY OVERVIEW

CORPORATION is able to bully landlocked ACs in this arena, so your strategy should be to get above it and outlast it with a tetrapod assembly of your own. Your opponent has weak defenses, so this can be a fight to test out any weaponry that's caught your eye. That being said, you'll need something that can catch CORPORATION and deal damage consistently, as it's a highly mobile aerial build. For that purpose, a pair of HML-G3/P08SPL siege missile launchers and a pair of BM-0999 DELIVERY BOY cluster missile launchers will be ideal. This combination of missile launchers will absolutely suffocate the opposition, never giving it a chance to escape your unrelenting barrage. As these both splinter into smaller missiles, most of your projectiles will miss, but it's a near guarantee that a significant amount will hit with each salvo. Gear out your AC with a BC-0400 MULE to minimize EN consumption when gaining altitude, and you'll have your bases covered.

R-ARM UNIT | SPLIT MISSILE LAUNCHER HML-G3/P08SPL-06	
L-ARM UNIT | SPLIT MISSILE LAUNCHER HML-G3/P08SPL-06	
R-BACK UNIT | CLUSTER MISSILE LAUNCHER BM-0999 DELIVERY BOY	
L-BACK UNIT | CLUSTER MISSILE LAUNCHER BM-0999 DELIVERY BOY	
HEAD | — HD-033M VERRILL	
CORE | — 07-161 MIND ALPHA	
ARMS | — AS-5000 SALAD	
LEGS | TETRAPOD LG-033M VERRILL	
BOOSTER | — BC-0400 MULE	
FCS | — FCS-G2/P10SLT	
GENERATOR | — VP-20S	
EXPANSION | — TERMINAL ARMOR	

STRATEGY

CORPORATION is a very well-rounded, offensively tuned AC. It shouldn't be anything beyond your abilities if you've made it this far, but it has the hallmarks of an oppressive tetrapod build: a powerful back-mounted vertical missile launcher to keep you pinned with explosive damage, and a respectable combo of a machine gun, laser rifle, and laser turret, which give it a very domineering presence in this fight if it can corner you on the ground. As per usual in this arena, take to the sky immediately after leaving your starting platform, and maintain altitude the whole fight. As long as you circle CORPORATION like a vulture, it will struggle to land any meaningful blows. Watch out for charged laser rifle shots, as they'll have the greatest potential to cause harm here—dodge them when your systems warn you.

From the air, fire your missiles individually in sequence. Once one of your missile launchers is done firing, fire the next missile launcher. Doing this will ensure that there are always missiles raining down on CORPORATION, dealing persistent damage, causing ACS strain, and never giving it any room to breathe. Once it's in a vulnerable state, whether it be through stagger, or pinned against a wall on the ground after running out of EN, fire all of your missiles that are currently loaded. Doing so will cause extreme damage, bringing CORPORATION down quickly.

AC // CORPORATION		RANK β-2

COMBAT ZONE: JORGEN REFUELING BASE	
Rewards (1st Victory)	
86,000 COAM, 10x OST Chips, CORPORATION AC Data, CORPORATION Emblem	
Reward (Replay)	
43,000 COAM	

SPECS	
AP	9310
Attitude Stability	1939
Anti-Kinetic Defense	1104
Anti-Energy Defense	1100
Anti-Explosive Defense	1135
Elec. Discharge Tolerance	490
Shock Resistance	-27%
ACS Anomaly Tolerance	490
Heat Resistance	-27%

ASSEMBLY

R-ARM UNIT | MACHINE GUN DF-MG-02 CHANG-CHEN	
L-ARM UNIT | LASER RIFLE VP-66LR	
R-BACK UNIT | VERTICAL MISSILE LAUNCHER BML-G1/P03VTC-08	
L-BACK UNIT | LASER TURRET VP-60LT	
HEAD | — DF-HD-08 TIAN-QIANG	
CORE | — NACHTREIHER/40E	
ARMS | — AR-011 MELANDER	
LEGS | TETRAPOD VP-424	
BOOSTER | — ALULA/21E	
FCS | — FCS-G2/P12SML	
GENERATOR | — VP-20D	
EXPANSION | — PULSE ARMOR	

Once you find a rhythm with your missiles, the constant bombardment will eventually consume CORPORATION and take it down.

CORPORATION will be able to dominate if it gets above you.

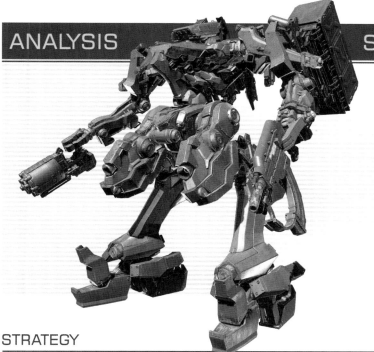

STRATEGY

This is a typical fight against a kinetic/explosive assembly. Its WS-1200 THERAPIST stun bomb launcher can cause shock buildup and trigger electrical discharges, something you can only partly mitigate by upping your System Recovery spec. However, it's an arm weapon bayed on its back, and due to the effectiveness of the shotgun, which it shares a weapon slot with, it won't swap to its stun bomb launcher if you stay close. RUBICONIAN can't keep up with you if you stick close to it and hammer away. The shotgun and burst machine gun will still be a threat up close, but they're minor compared to the potential threat of its other weaponry. If you're built for anti-kinetic defense, you can relentlessly hound RUBICONIAN unabated at close range. Its reverse-joint legs will give it the ability to briefly escape, but with a pair of your own, it can't run for long.

Your arsenal won't have high impact outside your assault armor charges, and will likely not be able to overload RUBICONIAN's systems frequently. Even landing assault armor can be tricky if the enemy hops away when you get into melee range. With this context, you're free to use all of your weapons without having to worry about specific windows of opportunity. The laser dagger may look peculiar here, due to the tendency for melee weapons to have long cooldown periods, but its cooling is the highest in its class, meaning you should be using it as a primary damage source for this fight. Your plasma cannons and shotguns will be your main weapons whenever RUBICONIAN is slightly out of range of your laser dagger.

ASSEMBLY OVERVIEW

Your assembly here will be blunt and to the point. The main priority, defensively, should be to completely shut down the danger RUBICONIAN's kinetic weaponry poses. You're going to be spending the entire fight as close as possible to the enemy, so mitigating the impact of its weaponry will be important in pulling this off. As it's particularly weak to energy damage, plasma and laser weapons work wonders. Close-range arm weapons like the VP-66LS laser shotgun and VP-67LD laser dagger will be constant sources of damage here, even without the ability to reliably put the opponent in ACS overload. A pair of FASAN/60E plasma cannons are also effective here, but will be important in tagging RUBICONIAN if it attempts to jump away. Should this happen, a set of RC-2000 SPRING CHICKEN legs on your AC will ensure that you're never far behind.

R-ARM UNIT | LASER SHOTGUN	VP-66LS	
L-ARM UNIT | LASER DAGGER	VP-67LD	
R-BACK UNIT | PLASMA CANNON	FASAN/60E	
L-BACK UNIT | PLASMA CANNON	FASAN/60E	
HEAD | —	HC-3000 WRECKER	
CORE | —	DF-BD-08 TIAN-QIANG	
ARMS | —	AA-J-123 BASHO	
LEGS | REVERSE JOINT	RC-2000 SPRING CHICKEN	
BOOSTER | —	BC-0600 12345	
FCS | —	IB-C03F: WLT 001	
GENERATOR | —	VP-20D	
EXPANSION | —	ASSAULT ARMOR	

Make liberal use of your laser dagger; its brief cooldown gives you a very reliable melee weapon here.

AC // RUBICONIAN	RANK β-3

COMBAT ZONE: THE WALL	
Rewards (1st Victory)	
92,000 COAM, 10x OST Chips, RUBICONIAN AC Data, RUBICONIAN Emblem	
Reward (Replay)	
46,000 COAM	

SPECS	
AP	9860
Attitude Stability	1466
Anti-Kinetic Defense	1164
Anti-Energy Defense	1033
Anti-Explosive Defense	1164
Elec. Discharge Tolerance	490
Shock Resistance	-16%
ACS Anomaly Tolerance	490
Heat Resistance	-16%

ASSEMBLY

R-ARM UNIT | SHOTGUN	WR-0777 SWEET SIXTEEN	
L-ARM UNIT | BURST MACHINE GUN	MA-E-210 ETSUJIN	
R-BACK UNIT | STUN BOMB LAUNCHER	WS-1200 THERAPIST	
L-BACK UNIT | CLUSTER MISSILE LAUNCHER	BM-0999 DELIVERY BOY	
HEAD | —	AH-J-124 BASHO	
CORE | —	EL-TC-10 FIRMEZA	
ARMS | —	AC-3000 WRECKER	
LEGS | REVERSE JOINT	RC-2000 SPRING CHICKEN	
BOOSTER | —	BC-0200 GRIDWALKER	
FCS | —	FCS-G1/P01	
GENERATOR | —	AG-E-013 YABA	
EXPANSION | —	—	

Rely on your reverse-joint legs to pursue RUBICONIAN relentlessly.

INTEGRATION SUBJECT 51-003 K

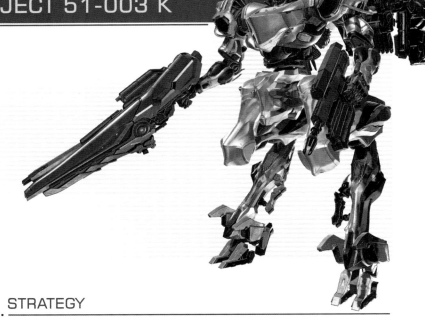

ASSEMBLY OVERVIEW

MIND GAMMA is similar to the previous two models, but different enough to warrant changes to your own AC for this fight. It carries a pulse shield, much like MIND BETA, giving you a target to watch out for to tear away at and cause near-immediate ACS overload with a pair of pulse guns. It's also vulnerable to explosives, making high-powered weapons like the EARSHOT grenade cannons highly effective. GAMMA's most apparent change compared to ALPHA and BETA are the 6-042 MIND BETA legs, so you'll want to take its aerial superiority away from it. Compounded with the fact that explosives will be your primary damage source for this fight, tetrapod legs are the best fit for this assembly. Despite the safety you'll have in the sky, you'll be facing off against another 44-142 KRSV multi energy rifle, which can be extremely dangerous. High anti-energy defense parts will be your safest option.

R-ARM UNIT | PULSE GUN	HI-18: GU-A2	
L-ARM UNIT | PULSE GUN	HI-18: GU-A2	
R-BACK UNIT | GRENADE CANNON	EARSHOT	MELINITE
L-BACK UNIT | GRENADE CANNON	EARSHOT	MELINITE
HEAD | —	IA-C01H: EPHEMERA	RI
CORE | —	07-161 MIND ALPHA	A
ARMS | —	VP-46S	A
LEGS | TETRAPOD	VP-424	RI
BOOSTER | —	IB-C03B: NGI 001	RI
FCS | —	IB-C03F: WLT 001	RI
GENERATOR | —	IB-C03G: NGI 000	RI
EXPANSION | —	TERMINAL ARMOR	

STRATEGY

MIND GAMMA switches things up from the rest of its ilk. The common thread between the three is the laser orbit back weapon, so approach knowing it will be around to badger you for much of the fight. That aside, this iteration tends to have a more balanced build than the others. It likes to keep its distance and guard with its pulse shield, letting its machine gun and laser orbit keep you at a distance while charging up its multi energy rifle. Watch out for switch-ups from your opponent, as once its rifle is charged, MIND GAMMA is capable of charging you with a Boost Kick, and then dealing heavy damage with its rifle once it has you staggered. It tends to do this more often and more successfully if you get close, so hang back and attack from range. If you've assembled your AC for anti-energy defense, you'll remove some of it's rifle's bite, but it can still deal surprising damage if it successfully staggers you with a kick and lands a fully charged shot.

Much like with BETA, you can largely disrupt its tactics with the usual pulse shield strategy; causing substantial ACS overload with pulse guns and dealing splash damage with explosive weaponry. GAMMA has different parts than ALPHA and BETA, giving it slightly higher anti-energy defense, meaning you'll want to stop the pulse shots once its shield has been disrupted. Stay above MIND GAMMA in the air, from a reasonable distance away, breaking its shield when it comes up, and firing both grenades at once when it has been staggered.

RANK γ-1	ASSEMBLY	
AC // MIND GAMMA	R-ARM UNIT | MULTI ENERGY RIFLE	44-142 KRSV
	L-ARM UNIT | MACHINE GUN	MG-014 LUDLOW
COMBAT ZONE: WATCHPOINT DELTA	R-BACK UNIT | LASER ORBIT	45-091 ORBT
Rewards (1st Victory)	L-BACK UNIT | PULSE SHIELD	SI-27: SU-R8
100,000 COAM, 15x OST Chips, MIND GAMMA AC Data, MIND GAMMA Emblem	HEAD | —	20-082 MIND BETA
	CORE | —	07-161 MIND ALPHA
Reward (Replay)	ARMS | —	04-101 MIND ALPHA
50,000 COAM	LEGS | REVERSE JOINT	06-042 MIND BETA
	BOOSTER | —	BST-G2/P06SPD

SPECS	
AP	10260
Attitude Stability	1666
Anti-Kinetic Defense	1183
Anti-Energy Defense	1239
Anti-Explosive Defense	1205
Elec. Discharge Tolerance	490
Shock Resistance	16%
ACS Anomaly Tolerance	490
Heat Resistance	16%

FCS | —	FCS-G2/P05	
GENERATOR | —	VP-20C	
EXPANSION | —	PULSE ARMOR	

Your pulse guns will also deal substantial damage to MIND GAMMA's pulse armor.

The 44-142 KRSV's full-charge attack will be hard to avoid, even with proper Quick Boost timing.

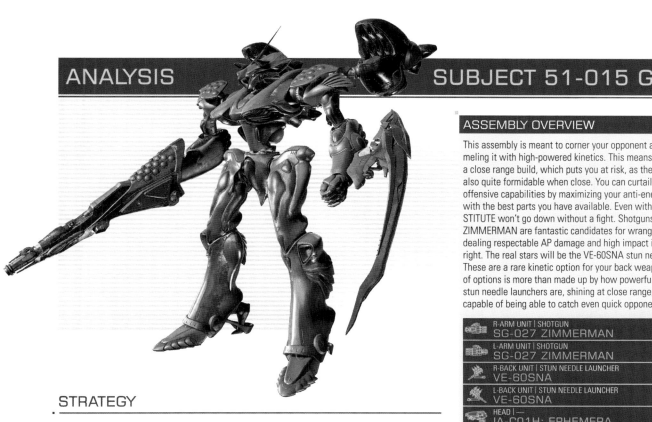

ANALYSIS

SUBJECT 51-015 G

ASSEMBLY OVERVIEW

This assembly is meant to corner your opponent and keep pummeling it with high-powered kinetics. This means it's also largely a close range build, which puts you at risk, as the opponent is also quite formidable when close. You can curtail INSTITUTE's offensive capabilities by maximizing your anti-energy defense with the best parts you have available. Even with this in mind, INSTITUTE won't go down without a fight. Shotguns like the SG-027 ZIMMERMAN are fantastic candidates for wrangling the enemy, dealing respectable AP damage and high impact in their own right. The real stars will be the VE-60SNA stun needle launchers. These are a rare kinetic option for your back weapons. Your lack of options is more than made up by how powerful and quick these stun needle launchers are, shining at close range, while also capable of being able to catch even quick opponents at mid range.

R-ARM UNIT | SHOTGUN **SG-027 ZIMMERMAN**	
L-ARM UNIT | SHOTGUN **SG-027 ZIMMERMAN**	
R-BACK UNIT | STUN NEEDLE LAUNCHER **VE-60SNA**	
L-BACK UNIT | STUN NEEDLE LAUNCHER **VE-60SNA**	
HEAD | — **IA-C01H: EPHEMERA**	RI
CORE | — **VE-40A**	
ARMS | — **AS-5000 SALAD**	
LEGS | BIPEDAL **VE-42A**	
BOOSTER | — **IB-C03B: NGI 001**	RI
FCS | — **IB-C03F: WLT 001**	RI
GENERATOR | — **IB-C03G: NGI 000**	RI
EXPANSION | — **PULSE ARMOR**	

STRATEGY

INSTITUTE is probably the stiffest challenge you've had in the Integration Program so far. This AC's parts give it long lock-on range, allowing it to snipe at you with its powerful plasma rifle and dual light wave cannons, which act like quick-firing homing lasers fired from the back. To make matters worse, at close to mid range, its light wave blade comes into play. This is a melee weapon that can fire a ranged blade attack to hit you from a distance, and it covers a wide area, making it hard to effectively dodge. INSTITUTE can cause a lot of damage very quickly if you're not diligent.

One of the best options at your disposal is one that's easy to overlook: the Boost Kick. It's a viable option any time INSTITUTE starts to build distance between the two of you. With a preemptive Pulse Armor charge, you'll have a safe, effective approach. Since your opponent has dismal anti-kinetic defense, following a Boost Kick up with close-range weaponry like shotguns is a strong choice. This will build up ACS very quickly, leaving it open for extreme damage from your stun needle launchers when overloaded. Fire both at once, and should they land, you'll effectively have this match in the bag. Don't celebrate if it seems like you've won, however, as INSTITUTE has terminal armor up its sleeve, allowing it to withstand a fatal attack.

RANK γ-2	ASSEMBLY	
AC // INSTITUTE	R-ARM UNIT | PLASMA RIFLE **IA-C01W1: NEBULA**	
	L-ARM UNIT | LIGHT WAVE BLADE **IA-C01W2: MOONLIGHT**	
COMBAT ZONE: GRID 012	R-BACK UNIT | LIGHT WAVE CANNON **IA-C01W3: AURORA**	
Rewards (1st Victory)	L-BACK UNIT | LIGHT WAVE CANNON **IA-C01W3: AURORA**	
110,000 COAM, 15x OST Chips, INSTITUTE AC Data, INSTUTUTE Emblem	HEAD | — **IA-C01H: EPHEMERA**	
Reward (Replay)	CORE | — **IA-C01C: EPHEMERA**	
55,000 COAM	ARMS | — **IA-C01A: EPHEMERA**	

SPECS		LEGS | BIPEDAL **IA-C01L: EPHEMERA**
AP	9880	BOOSTER | — **IA-C01B: GILLS**
Attitude Stability	1638	
Anti-Kinetic Defense	1011	FCS | — **IA-C01F: OCELLUS**
Anti-Energy Defense	1186	
Anti-Explosive Defense	1144	GENERATOR | — **IA-C01G: AORTA**
Elec. Discharge Tolerance	490	
Shock Resistance	32%	EXPANSION | — **TERMINAL ARMOR**
ACS Anomaly Tolerance	490	
Heat Resistance	32%	

Make sure the Boost Kick is a part of your kit for this fight, and never give INSTITUTE an opportunity to retreat.

Light wave cannons will fire unpredictable beams, which can be hard to avoid if you slow down at all.

5

ANALYSIS SUBJECT 51-016 GA

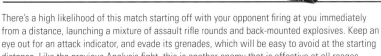

ASSEMBLY OVERVIEW

This assembly is the first in a while that focuses on beating the opponent reliably, as opposed to doing it in as few shots as possible. Your opponent is a slippery AC with mediocre defenses, and trying to take it out with big, slow weaponry won't be ideal. Hence, slightly weaker weapon options that can fire more frequently are preferable to their more powerful siblings. The IA-C01W1: NEBULA is a weaker plasma rifle than the Vvc-760PR, but takes almost twice as long to overheat. The SONGBIRD is a weaker grenade cannon than the EARSHOT, but fires two grenades at once. NIGHTFALL may dodge an attack or two, but it won't be able to evade your shots for long. And as these are weapon types with a prominent blast radius, firing them from above will increase your chances of clipping NIGHTFALL's wings.

R-ARM UNIT | PLASMA RIFLE	IA-C01W1: NEBULA	RI
L-ARM UNIT | PLASMA RIFLE	IA-C01W1: NEBULA	RI
R-BACK UNIT | GRENADE CANNON	SONGBIRDS	MELINITE
L-BACK UNIT | GRENADE CANNON	SONGBIRDS	MELINITE
HEAD | —	AH-J-124 BASHO	BAWS
CORE | —	CC-3000 WRECKER	RaD
ARMS | —	VE-46A	
LEGS | TETRAPOD	LG-033M VERRILL	
BOOSTER | —	BC-0400 MULE	RaD
FCS | —	IB-C03F: WLT 001	RI
GENERATOR | —	IB-C03G: NGI 000	RI
EXPANSION | —	TERMINAL ARMOR	

STRATEGY

There's a high likelihood of this match starting off with your opponent firing at you immediately from a distance, launching a mixture of assault rifle rounds and back-mounted explosives. Keep an eye out for an attack indicator, and evade its grenades, which will be easy to avoid at the starting distance. Like the previous Analysis fight, this is another enemy that is effective at all ranges, though NIGHTFALL isn't quite as effective at long distances. Its weaponry is most problematic at mid- to close-range, so keep your distance. To make things even worse, it can activate its assault armor at close range, which will likely put you into ACS overload. This is compounded by this AC's most effective weapon being its pile bunker, which can deal respectable damage and high impact. If NIGHTFALL is able to combo its assault armor into a pile bunker hit, you can end up losing nearly half of your AP. Stay airborne, and avoid getting close to this opponent.

NIGHTFALL suffers from a general lack of bulk, having one of the worst AP values in the Arena, and all-around poor defenses. Try as it may, it won't last very long if you continue laying into it with your weaponry. You'll want your grenade cannons to function as your source of ACS strain in this fight. They'll consistently hit, and cause high buildup throughout the fight, often only requiring you to fire them two or three times before staggering the enemy, and less if your plasma rifle shots hit frequently. This match can turn into one where hard swings in offensive momentum can happen, so keep hammering away if things don't get off to a great start. Once NIGHTFALL succumbs to ACS overload, all of your weapons will deal high damage, and it will fall quickly.

RANK γ-3	
AC // NIGHTFALL	

COMBAT ZONE: TEST ARENA
Rewards (1st Victory)
120,000 COAM, 15x OST Chips, NIGHTFALL AC Data, NIGHTFALL Emblem, HC-2000/BC SHADE EYE
Reward (Replay)
60,000 COAM

SPECS	
AP	9190
Attitude Stability	1654
Anti-Kinetic Defense	1100
Anti-Energy Defense	1059
Anti-Explosive Defense	1101
Elec. Discharge Tolerance	490
Shock Resistance	20%
ACS Anomaly Tolerance	490
Heat Resistance	20%

ASSEMBLY	
R-ARM UNIT | ASSAULT RIFLE	RF-025 SCUDDER
L-ARM UNIT | PILE BUNKER	PB-033M ASHMEAD
R-BACK UNIT | GRENADE CANNON	SONGBIRDS
L-BACK UNIT | DUAL MISSILE LAUNCHER	BML-G1/P32DUO-03
HEAD | —	HC-2000/BC SHADE EYE
CORE | —	CC-2000 ORBITER
ARMS | —	AC-2000 TOOL ARM
LEGS | BIPEDAL	2C-2000 CRAWLER
BOOSTER | —	BST-G1/P10
FCS | —	FC-006 ABBOT
GENERATOR | —	DF-GN-02 LING-TAI
EXPANSION | —	ASSAULT ARMOR

NIGHTFALL can be hard to pin down, but your SONGBIRDS are one of the best weapons in your arsenal to exploit its weaknesses.

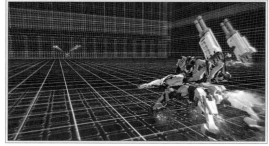

From the outset, NIGHTFALL will demand a response with its aggressive attacks.

CLASSIFIED

SUBJECT 51-101 R

ASSEMBLY OVERVIEW

As far as weapon damage goes, everything hits your opponent with equal efficacy, so your choices are vast, though this is an extremely quick AC that will be hard to nail down. The deciding factor should be how dependably your weaponry connects with the enemy. Missile launchers that fire sequentially are a great choice as always, to ensnare ACs that are prone to Quick Boost like this one. The more angles you can utilize to achieve this, the better. STEEL HAZE ORTUS heavily favors kinetic weaponry, and optimizing your AC for anti-kinetic defense can shut down the enemy so completely that most of its shots will begin to ricochet at medium range. Removing the ability for STEEL HAZE ORTUS to cause significant impact with its kinetics has the knock-on effect of eliminating overload windows, where its Vvc-774LS laser slicer will be most dangerous. Just install a pair of fast legs to be able to keep your distance, and you'll be set to tackle this fight.

R-ARM UNIT | MISSILE LAUNCHER	HML-G2/P19MLT-04
L-ARM UNIT | MISSILE LAUNCHER	HML-G2/P19MLT-04
R-BACK UNIT | PLASMA MISSILE LAUNCHER	Vvc-70VPM
L-BACK UNIT | DUAL MISSILE LAUNCHER	BML-G2/P08DUO-03
HEAD | —	HC-3000 WRECKER
CORE | —	CC-3000 WRECKER
ARMS | —	VE-46A
LEGS | TANK	EL-TL-11 FORTALEZA
BOOSTER | —	
FCS | —	FCS-G2/P10SLT
GENERATOR | —	VE-20A
EXPANSION | —	TERMINAL ARMOR

STRATEGY

This battle exemplifies the ultimate culmination of the quick and heavy-hitting AC archetypes. And like a lot of fast ACs, STEEL HAZE ORTUS is primarily focused on staggering you and getting in close for a powerful combo from its laser slicer. Should you allow it to succeed, it can take a severe amount of AP from you very quickly. Ultimately, the best way to avoid this is to just stay moving. None of your opponent's weapons are particularly intimidating on their own—it's only when it's allowed to combo them all together that it becomes a problem. Staying light on your feet is the best way to ensure ACS overload doesn't occur abruptly. Since all of STEEL HAZE ORTUS's weapons are kinetic—other than its laser slicer—high anti-kinetic defense and high attitude stability will more than carry you through this fight, as long as you don't try to engage at close range.

As STEEL HAZE ORTUS focuses entirely on attack power, it is quite fragile. It relies on its speed to cover for its low AP and poor defenses. It tends to hop around and perform short jumps, but isn't an aerial AC by any means. Even with the tank legs recommended for this fight, short hops of your own will increase the chances of you tagging STEEL HAZE ORTUS with your homing missiles. Explosives and plasma weapons fired from above have always been a good method for pinning elusive opponents, and this fight is no different. Alternate firing your missile launchers, and no matter how many miss, the ones that land will hit hard.

Be extremely careful of STEEL HAZE ORTUS's laser slicer; letting it get close can be fatal.

RANK δ-1	ASSEMBLY	
AC // STEEL HAZE ORTUS	R-ARM UNIT | NEEDLE GUN	EL-PW-00 VIENTO
	L-ARM UNIT | LASER SLICER	Vvc-774LS
COMBAT ZONE: TEST ARENA	R-BACK UNIT | NEEDLE MISSILE LAUNCHER	EL-PW-01 TRUENO
Rewards (1st Victory)	L-BACK UNIT | BULLET ORBIT	BO-044 HUXLEY
135,000 COAM, STEEL HAZE ORTUS AC Data and Emblem, EL-PW-01 TRUE-NO (R-Back Unit: 271,000 COAM)	HEAD | —	EL-PH-00 ALBA
	CORE | —	EL-PC-00 ALBA
Reward (Replay)	ARMS | —	EL-PA-00 ALBA
75,000 COAM	LEGS | BIPEDAL	EL-PL-00 ALBA
	BOOSTER | —	BST-G2/P04

SPECS	
AP	9050
Attitude Stability	1591
Anti-Kinetic Defense	1062
Anti-Energy Defense	1062
Anti-Explosive Defense	1062
Elec. Discharge Tolerance	490
Shock Resistance	11%
ACS Anomaly Tolerance	490
Heat Resistance	11%

FCS | —	FC-006 ABBOT
GENERATOR | —	AG-T-005 HOKUSHI
EXPANSION | —	TERMINAL ARMOR

As STEEL HAZE ORTUS is the truest embodiment of the glass cannon ACs, it can be taken down fairly quickly.

CLASSIFIED SUBJECT 51-201 W

ASSEMBLY OVERVIEW

All of IB-C03: HAL 826's weapons are Coral-based, which means that you cannot defend against them. This is both a blessing and a curse, as this is the first assembly where your defense values ultimately don't matter. Your only priority should be a mix of mobility and enough equip load to carry your loadout. IB-C03: HAL 826 is most dangerous at close range, but 06-042 MIND BETA legs are a good option for getting in and out of close range very quickly, maximizing your damage potential. Your most viable weapon options here will be kinetic weapons. As VE-60SNA stun needle launchers will be far and away the most potent kinetic back weapons, you'll have to compromise a bit with arm options. The HM-0777 SWEET SIXTEEN shotgun isn't a particularly deadly shotgun, but it's light, and serves its purpose of maintaining ACS strain while your primary weaponry reloads.

R-ARM UNIT | SHOTGUN	WR-0777 SWEET SIXTEEN
L-ARM UNIT | SHOTGUN	WR-0777 SWEET SIXTEEN
R-BACK UNIT | STUN NEEDLE LAUNCHER	VE-60SNA
L-BACK UNIT | STUN NEEDLE LAUNCHER	VE-60SNA
HEAD | —	EL-PH-00 ALBA
CORE | —	EL-TC-10 FIRMEZA
ARMS | —	EL-PA-00 ALBA
LEGS | REVERSE JOINT	06-042 MIND BETA
BOOSTER | —	BST-G2/P06SPD
FCS | —	FC-008 TALBOT
GENERATOR | —	VP-20C
EXPANSION | —	—

STRATEGY

This is perhaps the strangest fight in the Arena's Integration Program. Your opponent sports a wholly unique loadout, with a Coral rifle that sits somewhere between a plasma and laser rifle in utility, but features a second charge stage that fires a large, sweeping beam. It also uses a Coral missile launcher, which fires a winding homing missile that creates a massive explosion if it connects, a Coral oscillator that deals incredible damage up close, and a Coral shield, which reduces damage taken and decreases ACS build-up. All taken together, this can make IB-C03: HAL 826 seem more alarming than it is, since despite all of these oddities, it still functions like all other ACs. Coral rifle aside, all of its attacks are easy to Quick Boost away from, as long as you keep a respectable distance. Be on your guard when you close the gap to land some extra damage; in addition to its deadly Coral oscillator, IB-C03: HAL 826 can also activate assault armor.

IB-C03: HAL 826 has average defenses, with its anti-kinetic defense being the weakest link in its armor. To offset this, it often relies on its Coral shield, which it can use sporadically to mitigate all damage and impact sent its way. When IB-C03: HAL 826 has a red electric field around it, it'll be harder to harm. Despite this, your stun needle launchers can still make quick work of your enemy, providing your attacks hit. This is where weaving in and out of close range with your reverse-joint legs will be extremely advantageous. Hop within mid to close-range, fire your stun needle launchers, then hop backward. Whenever they're reloading, substitute your shotguns or use assault armor to keep the pressure up.

RANK δ-2	ASSEMBLY	
AC // IB-C03: HAL 826	R-ARM UNIT | CORAL RIFLE	IB-C03W1: WLT 011
	L-ARM UNIT | CORAL OSCILLATOR	IB-C03W2: WLT 101
COMBAT ZONE: TEST ARENA	R-BACK UNIT | CORAL MISSILE LAUNCHER	IB-C03W3: NGI 006
Rewards (1st Victory)	L-BACK UNIT | CORAL SHIELD	IB-C03W4: NGI 028
150,000 COAM, IB-C03: HAL 826 AC Data and Emblem, IB-C03W1: WLT 011 (L-Arm Unit: 335,000 COAM)	HEAD | —	IB-C03H: HAL 826
	CORE | —	IB-C03C: HAL 826
Reward (Replay)	ARMS | —	IB-C03A: HAL 826
85,000 COAM	LEGS | BIPEDAL	IB-C03L: HAL 826
	BOOSTER | —	IB-C03B: NGI 001

SPECS	
AP	10810
Attitude Stability	1742
Anti-Kinetic Defense	1204
Anti-Energy Defense	1279
Anti-Explosive Defense	1230
Elec. Discharge Tolerance	490
Shock Resistance	25%
ACS Anomaly Tolerance	490
Heat Resistance	25%

FCS | —	IB-C03F: WLT 001
GENERATOR | —	IB-C03G: NGI 000
EXPANSION | —	ASSAULT ARMOR

IB-C03: HAL 826's wide-sweeping attacks can be extremely powerful, and cover a significant portion of the Arena.

Alongside its Coral oscillator, IB-C03: HAL 826's Coral rifle is capable of firing a massive beam that can change direction.

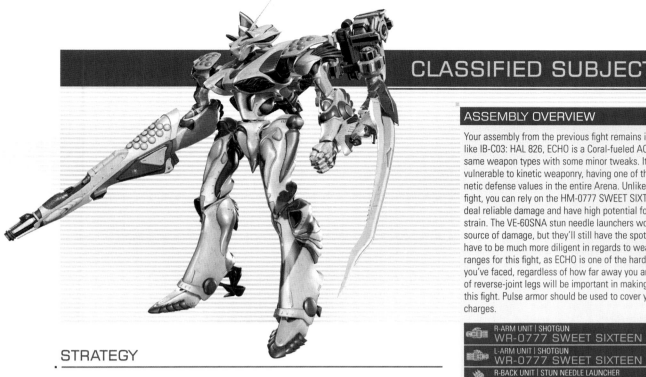

CLASSIFIED SUBJECT

ASSEMBLY OVERVIEW

Your assembly from the previous fight remains ideal here. Much like IB-C03: HAL 826, ECHO is a Coral-fueled AC, sporting the same weapon types with some minor tweaks. It's also specifically vulnerable to kinetic weaponry, having one of the lowest anti-kinetic defense values in the entire Arena. Unlike with the previous fight, you can rely on the HM-0777 SWEET SIXTEEN shotguns to deal reliable damage and have high potential for building ACS strain. The VE-60SNA stun needle launchers won't be your sole source of damage, but they'll still have the spotlight here. You'll have to be much more diligent in regards to weaving through the ranges for this fight, as ECHO is one of the hardest-hitting ACs you've faced, regardless of how far away you are. Full utilization of reverse-joint legs will be important in making it through this fight. Pulse armor should be used to cover your aggressive charges.

	R-ARM UNIT	SHOTGUN	
	WR-0777 SWEET SIXTEEN	
	L-ARM UNIT	SHOTGUN	
	WR-0777 SWEET SIXTEEN	
	R-BACK UNIT	STUN NEEDLE LAUNCHER	
	VE-60SNA	
	L-BACK UNIT	STUN NEEDLE LAUNCHER	
	VE-60SNA	
	HEAD	—	
	EL-PH-00 ALBA	
	CORE	—	
	EL-TC-10 FIRMEZA	
	ARMS	—	
	EL-PA-00 ALBA	
	LEGS	REVERSE JOINT	
	06-042 MIND BETA	
	BOOSTER	—	
	BST-G2/P06SPD	
	FCS	—	
	FC-008 TALBOT	
	GENERATOR	—	
	VP-20C	
	EXPANSION	—	
	PULSE ARMOR	

STRATEGY

Ayre will be piloting her own AC against you in what is potentially the hardest fight against an AC that you'll experience. ECHO is exceptionally well built, and utilizes all of its equipment for maximum potency. As a build, ECHO sits somewhere between INSTITUTE and IB-C03: HAL 826, coming in with most of INSTITUTE's frame, and IB-C03: HAL 826's Coral shield and Coral missile launcher. Ayre's biggest threats are her unique REDSHIFT weapons. Her right-handed weapon is another Coral rifle, but acts more like a traditional energy rifle, and can deal high damage and impact, accumulating ACS strain surprisingly quickly. Even more dangerous is her left-handed Coral oscillator. It can strike from a long distance, and will eviscerate your AP if it hits you after a charge. If you see this weapon glowing red and receive an attack indicator, immediately get some distance between you and her. If you can't and aren't ready to jump or Quick Boost, you're at risk of losing several thousand AP in a single hit.

You'll win this fight by out-damaging Ayre. While she is much more aggressive and dangerous, the flow can feel very similar to the previous fight. The same back weapons, a right-handed Coral rifle, and a left-handed weapon that encourages you to keep your distance. You'll want to jump in and out of close-range frequently, staying at mid- to long-range for most of the fight until your weapons are loaded. Ayre has an opening that is risky to try to exploit, but will give you the best opportunity to deal heavy damage if you can time it right. After swinging her Coral oscillator, she'll be stationary for a brief moment, making it a perfect time to hit her with your stun needle launchers. Take note of her pulse protection, however. With her Coral-powered generator, it will glow red, much like her Coral shield, so don't panic if it seems like she's stopped taking damage suddenly.

Among all of Ayre's oppressive weaponry, it's imperative that you are always ready to dodge her charged Coral oscillator.

	RANK δ-3
AC // ECHO	

COMBAT ZONE: TEST ARENA
Rewards (1st Victory)
170,000 COAM, ECHO AC Data and Emblem, IA-C01W6: NB-REDSHIFT (L-Arm Unit: 312,000 COAM), IA-C01W7: ML-REDSHIFT
Reward (Replay)
100,000 COAM

SPECS	
AP	9880
Attitude Stability	1638
Anti-Kinetic Defense	1011
Anti-Energy Defense	1186
Anti-Explosive Defense	1144
Elec. Discharge Tolerance	490
Shock Resistance	32%
ACS Anomaly Tolerance	490
Heat Resistance	32%

ASSEMBLY	
R-ARM UNIT	CORAL RIFLE	
IA-C01W6: NB-REDSHIFT	
L-ARM UNIT	CORAL OSCILLATOR	
IA-C01W7: ML-REDSHIFT	
R-BACK UNIT	CORAL MISSILE LAUNCHER	
IB-C03W3: NGI 006	
L-BACK UNIT	CORAL SHIELD	
IB-C03W4: NGI 028	
HEAD	—	
IA-C01H: EPHEMERA	
CORE	—	
IA-C01C: EPHEMERA	
ARMS	—	
IA-C01A: EPHEMERA	
LEGS	BIPEDAL	
IA-C01L: EPHEMERA	
BOOSTER	—	
IA-C01B: GILLS	
FCS	—	
IA-C01F: OCELLUS	
GENERATOR	—	
IB-C03G: NGI 000	
EXPANSION	—	
PULSE PROTECTION	

Stay mobile in this fight, and pick your moments to retaliate carefully.

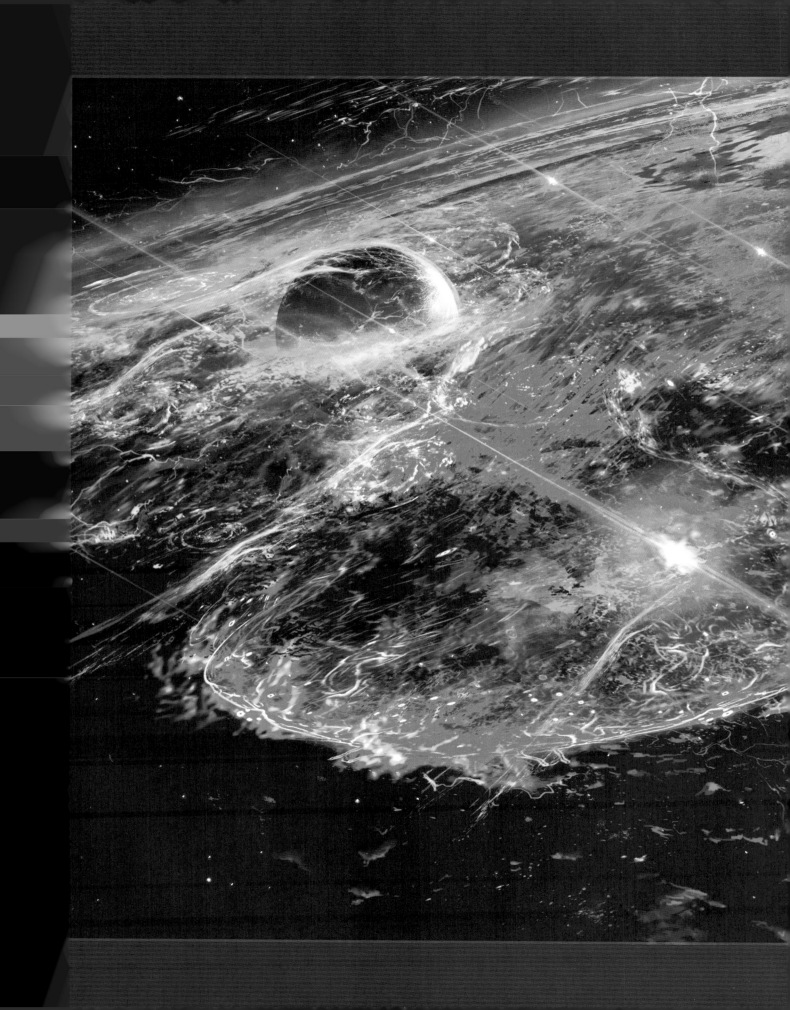

CHAPTER 6 EXTRA INTEL

The surface of Rubicon has suffered extended periods of conflict and disaster, as a network of factions and key players have struggled for dominance. Those seeking to piece together the records of the conflict will find help in this chapter, along with guidance on acquiring all parts and achieving the highest rankings and rewards from missions.

THE ARCHIVE

This section covers all of the various collectibles and rewards that you can unlock while playing the game. The lists here will point you to the locations of all combat logs, data logs and part containers on the maps in the Mission Intel chapter. If you play through the game three times following the Progression Guide on P.398 while using each of these as check-lists—and purchase everything available from the Parts Shop—you'll end up acquiring every single weapon and part, and will have a complete Archive in your Mercenary License menu.

PART CONTAINERS

Part containers are the first and most straightforward source of non-purchasable weapons and parts. There are a total of 19 part containers in the game, each appearing in fixed locations within specific missions. Part containers will show up when scanned, so it's worth equipping a head with decent scanning-related specs and scanning often during missions to find them. In case you're looking for a specific part container, the chart here lists them all, with references to the maps in the Mission Intel chapter to easily locate each one.

PART CONTAINERS

Mission	Part	Type	Ref.
Infiltrate Grid 086	HC-3000 WRECKER	Head	P.136
Infiltrate Grid 086	CC-3000 WRECKER	Core	P.136
Infiltrate Grid 086	AC-3000 WRECKER	Arms	P.136
Infiltrate Grid 086	2C-3000 WRECKER	Legs	P.136
Tunnel Sabotage	IA-C01W1: NEBULA	Plasma Rifle	P.170
Eliminate "Honest" Brute	BC-0600 12345	Booster	P.195
Eliminate "Honest" Brute	WB-0000 BAD COOK	Flamethrower	P.195
Eliminate "Honest" Brute	WB-0010 DOUBLE TROUBLE	Chainsaw	P.195
Underground Exploration – Depth 1	IA-C01L: EPHEMERA	Legs	P.206
Underground Exploration – Depth 2	IA-C01B: GILLS	Booster	P.208
Underground Exploration – Depth 2	IA-C01A: EPHEMERA	Arms	P.208
Underground Exploration – Depth 3	IA-C01C: EPHEMERA	Core	P.214
Underground Exploration – Depth 3	IA-C01F-OCELLUS	FCS	P.214
Unknown Territory Survey	IA-C01H: EPHEMERA	Head	P.224
Reach the Coral Convergence	IA-C01W2: MOONLIGHT	Light Wave Blade	P.226
Reach the Coral Convergence	IA-C01W3: AURORA	Light Wave Cannon	P.226
Survey the Uninhabited Floating City	IA-C01G: AORTA	Generator	P.174
Regain Control of the Xylem	IB-C03W3: NGI 006	Coral Missile Launcher	P.297
Regain Control of the Xylem	IB-C03W4: NGI 028	Coral Shield	P.297

TRAINING PROGRAM REWARDS

Completing most training programs will reward you with a weapon or part for your collection. The chart below lists each of these rewards, and directs you to the relevant page in the Assembly chapter for their specs.

TRAINING PROGRAM REWARDS

Mission	Part	Type	Ref.
Beginner Trainer 1: Basic Controls (Complete "Illegal Entry")	MG-014 LUDLOW	Machine Gun	P.53
Beginner Trainer 2: Combat Fundamentals (Complete "Destroy Artillery Installations" or "Grid 135 Cleanup")	LR-036 CURTIS	Linear Rifle	P.51
Intermediate Support 1: Assembling an AC (Complete "Attack the Dam Complex" & "Destroy the Weaponized Mining Ship")	ALULA/21E FC-006 ABBOT VP-20S	Booster FCS Generator	P.88 P.90 P.92
Intermediate Support 2: Reverse-Jointed ACs (Complete "Attack the Dam Complex" & "Destroy the Weaponized Mining Ship")	VP-66LH	Laser Handgun	P.59
Intermediate Support 3: Tetrapod ACs (Complete "Operation Wallclimber")	DF-GR-07 GOU-CHEN	Grenade Launcher	P.57
Intermediate Support 4: Tank ACs (Complete "Operation Wallclimber")	BML-G1/P01VTC-04	Vertical Missile Launcher	P.71

HUNTER CLASS

Your Hunter Class is visible in the Mercenary License profile. There are 15 ranks, and your current rank is entirely determined by the amount of combat logs you've managed to acquire. These logs are carried by specific—and often very challenging—opponents, encountered across a wide variety of missions. Each combat log you acquire falls into one of four tiers: bronze, silver, gold or platinum, with each tier offering more points toward your Hunter Class. You can track your combat logs by looking at missions on the Replay Mission screen. The chart here shows how many points each tier is worth:

Bronze	Silver	Gold	Platinum
1	2	3	4

A highlighted combat log icon and filled checkbox on the Replay Mission screen means you have all of the combat logs in the mission.

An unhighlighted combat log icon and unfilled checkbox means you do not have all of the combat logs in the mission.

Every time you gain a rank, you'll be rewarded with an exclusive part or weapon that you can equip in the Assembly. To reach the highest rank—Hunter Class 15—you'll need 175 points, which requires you to collect every combat log in the game. You'll find all of the Hunter Class rewards listed in the chart here, again with references to their specs in the Assembly chapter.

HUNTER CLASS

Rank	PTS.	Reward	Type	Ref.
1	8	04-101 MIND ALPHA	Arms	P.84
2	16	44-141 JVLN ALPHA	Detonating Bazooka	P.56
3	25	06-041 MIND ALPHA	Legs	P.86
4	34	45-091 JVLN BETA	Detonating Missile Launcher	P.56
5	44	07-061 MIND ALPHA	Core	P.81
6	54	44-143 HMMR	Plasma Thrower	P.64
7	65	06-042 MIND BETA	Legs	P.86
8	76	45-091 ORBT	Laser Orbit	P.74
9	88	IB-C03G: NGI 000	Generator	P.92
10	100	20-081 MIND ALPHA	Head	P.79
11	113	IB-C03F: WLT 001	FCS	P.90
12	127	44-142 KRSV	Multi Energy Rifle	P.61
13	142	IB-C03B: NGI 001	Booster	P.89
14	158	20-082 MIND BETA	Head	P.79
15	175	IB-C03W2: WLT 101	Coral Oscillator	P.65

ARENA REWARDS

Defeating a few of the later virtual opponents in the Arena will reward you with some of the final pieces of unique and powerful weaponry and parts, all of which are listed in the chart here.

ARENA REWARDS

Rank	Reward	Type	Ref.
01/S	Vvc-700LD	Laser Drone	P.75
γ-3	HC-2000/BC SHADE EYE	Head	P.78
δ-1	EL-PW-01 TRUENO	Needle Missile Launcher	P.73
δ-2	IB-C03W1: WLT 011	Coral Rifle	P.60
δ-3	IA-C01W6: NB-REDSHIFT	Coral Rifle	P.60
δ-3	IA-C01W7: ML REDSHIFT	Coral Oscillator	P.65

COMBAT LOGS

Acquiring combat logs is a matter of finding and defeating the specific opponents within missions that award them. If you play through each mission while destroying every enemy you come across, you're likely to end up acquiring a lot of combat logs. Many are carried by some of the toughest AC pilots you'll encounter—these foes will tend to have the gold and platinum logs—but some are found only by defeating enemies in out-of-the-way locations that can be easily missed. Acquiring all 82 combat logs will unlock unique weapons by increasing your Hunter Class, as well as the "Combat Log Collector" Trophy/Achievement and the "Medal: Elite Hunter" emblem.

Below is the full list of combat logs you'll need to track down, ordered by mission. Following the references will take you to maps of their precise locations in the Mission Intel chapter. The colored dots here reflect an enemy's relative strength according to the categorization used on the maps, which is defined on P.97.

The combat log icon on the upper left of the reticule shows you the log's tier.

MISSION	Tier	Enemy	Ref.
Destroy the Transport Helicopters	Silver	BAWS Tetrapod MT (Laser Blade)	P.106
Destroy the Tester AC	Silver	TESTER AC / Dafeng Student Pilot	P.108
Attack the Dam Complex	Silver	BAWS Tetrapod MT (Laser Blade)	P.110
Attack the Dam Complex	Gold	Index Dunham	P.110
Operation Wallclimber	Bronze	MT-E-104 BAWS Bipedal MT (Missile Launcher)	P.118
Operation Wallclimber	Bronze	MT-E-104 BAWS Bipedal MT (Missile Launcher)	P.118
Operation Wallclimber	Bronze	MT-E-104 BAWS Bipedal MT (Machine Gun)	P.118
Retrieve Combat Logs	Gold	Little Ziyi	P.124
Attack the Watchpoint	Gold	Sulla	P.132
Infiltrate Grid 086	Silver	"Invincible" Rummy	P.136
Infiltrate Grid 086	Silver	BAWS Tetrapod MT (Laser Blade)	P.136
Infiltrate Grid 086	Silver	BAWS Tetrapod MT (Laser Blade)	P.136
Infiltrate Grid 086	Bronze	MB-0202 RaD TOYBOX MT	P.136
Infiltrate Grid 086	Bronze	MB-0202 RaD TOYBOX MT	P.136
Infiltrate Grid 086	Gold	Nosaac	P.136
Infiltrate Grid 086	Bronze	MB-0100 CLUTCH RaD Crawler MT (Electro Saw)	P.136
Infiltrate Grid 086	Bronze	MB-0100 CLUTCH RaD Crawler MT (Electro Saw)	P.136
Infiltrate Grid 086	Bronze	MB-0202 RaD TOYBOX MT	P.136
Ocean Crossing	Bronze	AM06: WATCHER	P.148
Ocean Crossing	Bronze	AM06: WATCHER	P.148
Ocean Crossing	Bronze	AM06: WATCHER	P.148
Ocean Crossing	Bronze	AM06: WATCHER	P.148
Steal the Survey Data	Silver	MT-J-048 BAWS Tetrapod MT (Grenade Cannon)	P.154
Attack the Refueling Base	Bronze	AA18: LIGHT CAVALRY (Sniper Type)	P.160
Attack the Refueling Base	Bronze	AA18: LIGHT CAVALRY (Sniper Type)	P.160
Eliminate V.VII	Silver	MT-J-048 BAWS Tetrapod MT (3-Shot Bazooka)	P.164
Eliminate V.VII	Gold	V.VII Swinburne	P.164
Eliminate V.VII	Gold	Rokumonsen	P.164
Tunnel Sabotage	Bronze	AA18: LIGHT CAVALRY (Sniper Type)	P.170
Survey the Uninhabited Floating City	Silver	IA-24: KITE (Plasma Cannon)	P.174
Eliminate the Enforcement Squads	Gold	Ring Freddie	P.182
Attack the Old Spaceport	Silver	AA18: LIGHT CAVALRY (Support Type)	P.188
Attack the Old Spaceport	Silver	AA18: LIGHT CAVALRY (Support Type)	P.188
Attack the Old Spaceport	Silver	AA18: LIGHT CAVALRY (Enforcement Officer Spec)	P.188
Defend the Old Spaceport	Platinum	Raven	P.198
Eliminate "Honest" Brute	Bronze	MB-0202 RaD TOYBOX MT	P.195
Eliminate "Honest" Brute	Silver	MT-J-048 BAWS Tetrapod MT (Grenade Cannon)	P.195
Eliminate "Honest" Brute	Bronze	MB-0202 RaD TOYBOX MT	P.195
Eliminate "Honest" Brute	Bronze	MB-0202 RaD TOYBOX MT (Pulse Protection)	P.195
Eliminate "Honest" Brute	Platinum	"Honest" Brute	P.195
Underground Exploration – Depth 2	Gold	G5 Iguazu	P.208

MISSION	Tier	Enemy	Ref.
Underground Exploration – Depth 2	Bronze	AM02: DENOISER (Melee Type)	P.208
Underground Exploration – Depth 2	Bronze	AM02: DENOISER (Melee Type)	P.208
Underground Exploration – Depth 3	Silver	AM02: DENOISER (Heavy Firepower)	P.214
Underground Exploration – Depth 3	Silver	AM02: DENOISER (Heavy Firepower)	P.214
Underground Exploration – Depth 3	Gold	IA-C01: EPHEMERA / Enforcement System	P.214
Intercept the Redguns	Platinum	G1 Michigan	P.218
Unknown Territory Survey	Platinum	V.IV Rusty	P.224
Reach the Coral Convergence	Gold	V.VI Maeterlinck	P.226
Reach the Coral Convergence	Gold	G3 Wu Huahai	P.226
Reach the Coral Convergence	Bronze	IE-09: HELIANTHUS	P.226
Reach the Coral Convergence	Bronze	IE-09: HELIANTHUS	P.226
Reach the Coral Convergence	Bronze	IE-09: HELIANTHUS	P.226
Reach the Coral Convergence	Bronze	IE-09: HELIANTHUS	P.226
Reach the Coral Convergence	Bronze	IE-09: HELIANTHUS	P.226
Reach the Coral Convergence	Bronze	IE-09: HELIANTHUS	P.226
Reach the Coral Convergence	Bronze	IE-09: HELIANTHUS	P.226
Reach the Coral Convergence	Bronze	IE-09: HELIANTHUS	P.226
Reach the Coral Convergence	Silver	IA-05: WEEVIL (Cluster Missile Launcher)	P.226
Reach the Coral Convergence	Silver	IA-05: WEEVIL (Detonating Cannon)	P.226
Eliminate "Cinder" Carla	Platinum	V.II Snail	P.241
Eliminate "Cinder" Carla	Platinum	"Cinder" Carla	P.241
Eliminate "Cinder" Carla	Gold	"Chatty" Stick	P.241
Attack the Dam Complex (Alt)	Gold	G4 Volta	P.259
Prisoner Rescue	Platinum	G2 Nile	P.262
Prisoner Rescue	Silver	MT-J-048 BAWS Tetrapod MT (9-Shot Bazooka)	P.262
Defend the Dam Complex	Platinum	Chartreuse	P.271
Defend the Dam Complex	Platinum	King	P.271
Underground Exploration – Depth 2 (Alt)	Platinum	Coldcall	P.274
Ambush the Vespers	Gold	V.VIII Pater	P.221
Ambush the Vespers	Gold	V.V Hawkins	P.221
Unknown Territory Survey (Alt)	Gold	Middle Flatwell	P.276
Intercept the Corporate Forces	Silver	AA18A: LIGHT CAVALRY HM	P.237
Intercept the Corporate Forces	Platinum	V.I Freud	P.237
Stop the Secret Data Breach	Bronze	MB-0100 CLUTCH RaD Crawler MT (Electro Saw)	P.266
Stop the Secret Data Breach	Bronze	MB-0100 CLUTCH RaD Crawler MT (Electro Saw)	P.266
Stop the Secret Data Breach	Bronze	MB-0100 CLUTCH RaD Crawler MT (Shield)	P.266
Stop the Secret Data Breach	Silver	MT-J-048 BAWS Tetrapod MT (Laser Blade)	P.266
Survey the Uninhabited Floating City (Alt)	Platinum	Thumb Dolmayan	P.284
Eliminate V.III	Platinum	V.III O'Keeffe	P.289
MIA	Gold	G6 Red	P.294

DATA LOGS

Data logs are encoded records of past events and conversations, stored digitally in various formats. As you explore the combat zones of certain missions, you'll occasionally come across wrecks that have an access point, and scanning these will lead to acquiring a data log. The log's contents are displayed on-screen at the time you collect it. If you'd rather read them after the mission ends, then you'll find all of those you've collected in the Archives section of your Mercenary License menu.

You'll obtain quite a few data logs naturally while completing mission objectives, and collecting your first 10 will unlock the "Data Log Collector" Trophy/Achievement. There are a total of 50 data logs to collect, and finding all of them will unlock the "Medal: Omniscience" emblem. All of them are listed in the chart below in their in-game order to make it easy to find ones you're missing, with page references to the maps in the Mission Intel chapter.

DATA LOGS

Data Log	Mission	Ref.
License Code: Raven	"Illegal Entry"	P.98
License Code: Thomas Kirk	"Illegal Entry"	P.98
License Code: Monkey Gordo	"Illegal Entry"	P.98
License Code: G7 Hakra	"Illegal Entry"	P.98
System Log: One-Sided Engagement	"Retrieve Combat Logs"	P.124
System Log: The Deserter	"Retrieve Combat Logs"	P.124
Video Record: STEEL HAZE	"Retrieve Combat Logs"	P.124
Video Record: Communication Attempt	"Retrieve Combat Logs"	P.124
Video Record: BAWS Arsenal No. 2	"Retrieve Combat Logs"	P.124
Video Record: Rubiconian Invective	"Eliminate the Enforcement Squads"	P.182
Video Record: G4's Last Words	"Operation Wallclimber"	P.118
Video Record: BAWS Guard's Last Words	"Investigate BAWS Arsenal No. 2"	P.128
Video Record: The Collector's Last Words	"Infiltrate Grid 086"	P.136
Video Record: Testing New Components	"Escape"	P.232
Video Record: The Fires of Ibis	"Reach the Coral Convergence"	P.226
Comms Record: Friendly Comms	"Retrieve Combat Logs"	P.124
Comms Record: Rusty's Encoded Comms	"Retrieve Combat Logs"	P.124
Comms Record: Message for Uncle	"Unknown Territory Survey (Alt)"	P.276
Comms Record: Doser Ravings	"Infiltrate Grid 086"	P.136
Comms Record: Doser Chatter	"Ocean Crossing"	P.148
Comms Record: Coyote Chatter	"Eliminate 'Honest' Brute"	P.195
Comms Record: Independent Merc Comms	"Attack the Watchpoint"	P.132
Comms Record: Enforcement Squad Comms	"Attack the Refueling Base"	P.160
Observation Data: Coral Density Survey	"Steal the Survey Data"*	P.154
Observation Data: Installations Survey	"Steal the Survey Data"*	P.154
Observation Data: Offshore Survey	"Steal the Survey Data"*	P.154
Observation Data: Terrain Survey	"Steal the Survey Data"*	P.154
Observation Data: The City of Xylem	"Survey the Uninhabited Floating City"	P.174
Observation Data: Wave Mutation Detected	"Attack the Watchpoint"	P.132
Observation Data: Blind Spots	"Eliminate 'Honest' Brute"	P.195
Observation Data: The Enforcement System	"Underground Exploration - Depth 3"	P.214
Text Data: Dolmayan's Writings (1)	"Operation Wallclimber"	P.118
Text Data: Dolmayan's Writings (2)	"Historic Data Recovery"	P.200
Text Data: Dolmayan's Writings (3)	"Survey the Uninhabited Floating City"	P.174
Text Data: Dolmayan's Writings (4)	Complete "Survey the Uninhabited Floating City (Alt)"	P.284
Text Data: Dolmayan's Writings (5)	"Investigate BAWS Arsenal No. 2"	P.128
Text Data: Professor Nagai's Log (1)	"Underground Exploration – Depth 2"	P.208
Text Data: Professor Nagai's Log (2)	"Historic Data Recovery"	P.200
Text Data: Professor Nagai's Log (3)	"Stop the Secret Data Breach"	P.266
Text Data: Professor Nagai's Log (4)	"Historic Data Recovery"	P.200
Text Data: Professor Nagai's Log (5)	"Underground Exploration – Depth 3"	P.214
Text Data: The Well Dries	"Retrieve Combat Logs"	P.124
Text Data: The Re-education Center	"Eliminate V.VII"	P.164
Image Data: STV Sketch (1)	"Eliminate the Enforcement Squads"	P.182
Image Data: STV Sketch (2)	"Ocean Crossing"	P.148
Image Data: STV Sketch (3)	"Underground Exploration – Depth 2"	P.208
Image Data: STV Sketch (4)	"Eliminate V.VII"	P.164
Image Data: STV Sketch (5)	"Underground Exploration – Depth 2 (Alt)"	P.274
Image Data: STV Sketch (6)	"Attack the Refueling Base"	P.160
Image Data: STK Sketch	"Reach the Coral Convergence"	P.226

Tied to Mission Progress/Objectives   *Scan survey drone during the mission.

EMBLEMS

Emblems are preset decals that can either be loaded from the Decals menu and placed on any part of your AC, or assigned to your Mercenary License as your main visual identifier. When playing with other players online, your emblem will appear on their HUD. Many decals/emblem images are available by default (including all of those in Presets 1 and 5), but as you progress through the game and reach certain milestones or defeat specific opponents, additional images will be added to your collection. Detailed below are all of the ones you'll have unlocked by default, along with the unlock conditions for all of the additional images.

PRESET 1

	Lizard
	Cat
	Knight
	Flora
	Shattered Planet
	Spider
	Panther
	Unicorn
	Ammonite
	Shark
	Pawn
	Soldier
	Grenade
	Bullets
	Sights

PRESET 2

G13	Unlocked by default with pre-order DLC, or clear the mission "Attack the Dam Complex."
G6 Red	Defeat G6 Red in the Arena.
G5 Iguazu	Defeat G5 Iguazu in the Arena.
G4 Volta	Defeat G4 Volta in the Arena.
G3 Wu Huahai	Defeat G3 Wu Huahai in the Arena.
G2 Nile	Defeat G2 Nile in the Arena.
G1 Michigan	Defeat G1 Michigan in the Arena.
V.VIII Pater	Defeat V.VIII Pater in the Arena.
V.VII Swinburne	Defeat V.VII Swinburne in the Arena.
V.VI Maeterlinck	Defeat V.VI Maeterlinck in the Arena.
V.V Hawkins	Defeat V.V Hawkins in the Arena.
V.IV Rusty	Defeat V.IV Rusty in the Arena.
V.III O'Keeffe	Defeat V.III O'Keeffe in the Arena.
V.II Snail	Defeat V.II Snail in the Arena.
V.I Freud	Defeat V.I Freud in the Arena.
Index Dunham	Defeat Index Dunham in the Arena.
Little Ziyi	Defeat Little Ziyi in the Arena.
Ring Freddie	Defeat Ring Freddie in the Arena.
Middle Flatwell	Defeat Middle Flatwell in the Arena.
Thumb Dolmayan	Defeat Thumb Dolmayan in the Arena.
Rokumonsen	Defeat Rokumonsen in the Arena.
Rusty	Defeat Classified Subject: 51-101 R in the Arena.

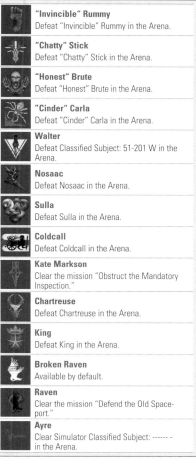

"Invincible" Rummy
Defeat "Invincible" Rummy in the Arena.

"Chatty" Stick
Defeat "Chatty" Stick in the Arena.

"Honest" Brute
Defeat "Honest" Brute in the Arena.

"Cinder" Carla
Defeat "Cinder" Carla in the Arena.

Walter
Defeat Classified Subject: 51-201 W in the Arena.

Nosaac
Defeat Nosaac in the Arena.

Sulla
Defeat Sulla in the Arena.

Coldcall
Defeat Coldcall in the Arena.

Kate Markson
Clear the mission "Obstruct the Mandatory Inspection."

Chartreuse
Defeat Chartreuse in the Arena.

King
Defeat King in the Arena.

Broken Raven
Available by default.

Raven
Clear the mission "Defend the Old Space-port."

Ayre
Clear Simulator Classified Subject: ------ - in the Arena.

PRESET 3

Balam Industries
Clear the mission "Retrieve Combat Logs."

Dafeng Core Industry
Available by default.

Redguns
Clear the mission "Intercept the Redguns."

Arquebus Corporation
Clear the mission "Destroy the Weaponized Mining Ship."

Arquebus Advanced Development Division
Immediately before the mission "Destroy the Ice Worm" (Complete the 3 missions before "Destroy the Ice Worm").

Schneider
Available by default.

VCPL
Available by default.

Vespers
Accept Swinburne's offer during 'Eliminate V.VII' and defeat Rokumonsen.

Furlong Dynamics
Available by default.

Melinite
Available by default.

Takigawa Harmonics
Available by default.

BAWS
Available by default.

Elcano Foundry
Available by default.

Rubicon Liberation Front
Refuse Swinburne's offer and defeat him during the "Eliminate V.VII" mission.

RaD
Clear the mission "Eliminate "Honest" Brute."

Rubicon III Research Institute
Clear the mission "Unknown Territory Survey."

Overseer
Clear the mission "Intercept the Corporate Forces."

ALLMIND
Clear the mission "Eliminate V.VIII."

PRESET 4

Integration: MIND ALPHA
Defeat Integration Subject 51-001 K in the Arena.

Integration: MIND BETA
Defeat Subject 51-002 K in the Arena.

Integration: MIND GAMMA
Defeat Subject 51-003 K in the Arena.

Analysis: TRAINER
Defeat Analysis Subject 51-011 AL in the Arena.

Analysis: TESTER
Defeat Analysis Subject 51-012 AL in the Arena.

Analysis: CORPORATION
Defeat Analysis Subject 51-013 BE in the Arena.

Analysis: RUBICONIAN
Defeat Analysis Subject 51-014 BE in the Arena.

Analysis: INSTITUTE
Defeat Analysis Subject 51-015 G in the Arena.

Analysis: NIGHTFALL
Defeat Analysis Subject 51-016 GA in the Arena.

Classified: STEEL HAZE ORTUS
Defeat Classified Subject: 51-101 R in the Arena.

Classified: HAL 826
Defeat Classified Subject: 51-201 W in the Arena.

Classified: Unknown Sample
Defeat Classified Subject: ------ - in the Arena.

Medal: Advanced Mercenary
Complete the "Advanced Mercenary Certification" Training Program.

Medal: Evaluation Complete
Reach rank 1 in the Arena.

Medal: Elite Hunter
Reach Hunter Class 15.

Medal: Omniscience
Obtain all data logs.

Medal: Analysis Complete
Clear all of the Analysis Arena matches.

Medal: Stargazer
Complete all missions.

Medal: Perfect Mercenary
Obtain an S-Rank rating on all missions.

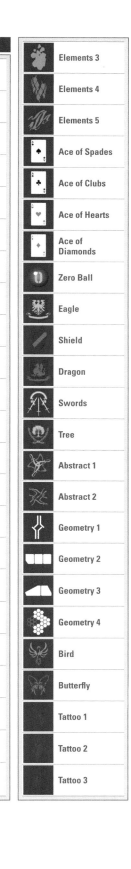

PRESET 5

Crossbones
Clawmark
Skull 1
Skull 2
Skull 3
Fossil 1
Fossil 2
Triple Scorpion
Fishbones 1
Fishbones 2
Bullet Holes
Missiles
Helmets
Parachutes
Target
Shark 1
Shark 2
Beast 1
Beast 2
Smile
Wink
Elements 1
Elements 2

Elements 3
Elements 4
Elements 5
Ace of Spades
Ace of Clubs
Ace of Hearts
Ace of Diamonds
Zero Ball
Eagle
Shield
Dragon
Swords
Tree
Abstract 1
Abstract 2
Geometry 1
Geometry 2
Geometry 3
Geometry 4
Bird
Butterfly
Tattoo 1
Tattoo 2
Tattoo 3

6

PROGRESSION GUIDE

Armored Core VI requires a minimum of three playthroughs to access all of its missions and see all endings. Below is our suggested roadmap for how to best approach the game's missions and Arena fights. By following it, you'll have all 59 missions completed by the end of your third playthrough, and will have cleared all of the Arena simulations. It's worth noting that you'll naturally revisit most missions over the course of your three playthroughs; the key to clearing all 59 missions is to always make alternate choices when a Decision arrives. The mission selection here is based on the path of least resistance, while accommodating early access to Arena fights and missions. For your first playthrough, simply follow the recommended path as shown here, including timely completion of Arena fights to continually upgrade your AC's abilities.

The choices you make within a mission can have a permanent effect on your current playthrough; choose carefully.

NEW GAME

| Progression Chart Legend | Mission Chosen | Mission Not Chosen | **Newly Available Mission** | Ending |

Here you'll find our recommended order for your initial playthrough. Immediately tackling each set of Arena battles as you unlock them will allow you to make your AC more powerful, and provide additional options in combat. You'll begin to be offered "Decisions" in Chapter 3, which give you the option to choose which mission to complete. Your choice in the final Decision of Chapter 5 will dictate which ending you receive. It's recommended to pursue the Liberator of Rubicon ending, as doing so is much easier than attempting the Fires of Raven ending on your first playthrough.

Chapter 1

[00]	Illegal Entry	P.98
[01-A]	Destroy Artillery Installations	P.102
[01-B]	Grid 135 Cleanup	P.104
[02-A]	Destroy the Transport Helicopters	P.106
[02-B]	Destroy the Tester AC	P.108
[03-A]	Attack the Dam Complex	P.110
[03-B]	Destroy the Weaponized Mining Ship	P.114
[04]	Operation Wallclimber	P.118
[05-A]	Retrieve Combat Logs	P.124
[05-B]	Investigate BAWS Arsenal No.2	P.128
Arena	Defeat all Rank F opponents	P.351
[06-A]	Attack the Watchpoint	P.132

Chapter 2

Arena	Defeat all Rank E opponents.	P.354
[07]	Infiltrate Grid 086	P.136
[08-A]	Eliminate the Doser Faction	P.146
[09]	Ocean Crossing	P.148

Chapter 3

Arena	Defeat all Rank D opponents.	P.358
[10]	Steal the Survey Data	P.154
[11-A]	Attack the Refueling Base	P.160
[11-B]	Eliminate V.VII	P.164
[11-C]	Tunnel Sabotage	P.170
Arena	Defeat all Rank C opponents.	P.363
[12-A]	Survey the Uninhabited Floating City	P.174
[12-B]	Heavy Missile Launch Support	P.180
[12-C]	Eliminate the Enforcement Squads	P.182
[12-D]	Destroy the Special Forces Craft (Save for NG+)	P.186
[13]	Attack the Old Spaceport	P.188
Arena	Defeat all Rank B opponents.	P.368
[14-A]	Eliminate "Honest" Brute	P.195
[14-B]	Defend the Old Spaceport	P.198
[14-C]	Historic Data Recovery	P.200
[15]	Destroy the Ice Worm	P.202

Chapter 4

Arena	Defeat all Rank A opponents.	P.373
[16]	Underground Exploration - Depth 1	P.206
[17-A]	Underground Exploration - Depth 2	P.208
[18]	Underground Exploration - Depth 3	P.214
Arena	Defeat all Rank S opponents.	P.377
[19-A]	Intercept the Redguns (Save for NG+)	P.218
[19-B]	Ambush the Vespers	P.221
[20-A]	Unknown Territory Survey	P.224
[21-A]	Reach the Coral Convergence	P.226

Chapter 5

[22-A]	Escape	P.232
[23-A]	Take the Uninhabited Floating City	P.234
[24-A]	Intercept the Corporate Forces (Save for NG+)	P.237
[24-B]	Eliminate "Cinder" Carla	P.241
[25-B]	Destroy the Drive Block	P.250
[26-B]	Bring Down the Xylem	P.257
	[Ending: Liberator of Rubicon]	

FARMING COAM

Since COAM is used to buy new parts and reset OS upgrades, you may find yourself in situations where you'll want a little extra to expand your parts collection or tune your AC's performance. Even after completing three full playthroughs worth of jobs, you won't have earned enough COAM to purchase all parts available in the shop unless you've also been supplementing your income by replaying missions or Arena duels.

Luckily, there's a simple early-game mission that offers an exceptional COAM payout: "Destroy the Tester AC." With an optimized loadout capable of quickly eliminating the Tester AC, you can earn over 500,000 COAM in roughly 10 minutes. The recommended build for that mission in the S Rank Guide (on P.404) provides a good assembly to rely on here. "Destroy the Special Forces Craft" (P.424) is a more lucrative but slightly more challenging alternative; defeat the CATAPHRACT quickly and you can accrue over 1,000,000 COAM every 10 minutes.

Lastly, the most efficient option for players much farther in the game is "Shut Down the Closure Satellites." Using the method provided in the S Rank Guide (on P.443), you can earn over 2,000,000 COAM within 10 minutes of play. However, it's worth noting that if you're pursuing clearing all missions with an S Rank, you'll likely be able to afford all of the parts naturally.

With his back to you on your approach, the Dafeng Student Pilot leaves himself vulnerable to a strong opening attack.

NEW GAME+

For each Decision in your second playthrough, you'll be selecting the opposing choices to your initial ones. New Game+ will introduce you to Alt missions; these initially play out the same, but have alternative elements and new scenarios that were not present in the original versions of these missions. In order to access all of the new content within this playthrough, you'll need to select the "Accept" option when a choice is offered to you in Attack the Dam Complex. The game doesn't immediately designate what is or isn't an Alt mission until you view the Replay Mission screen, but we've labeled them as such here. You won't need to complete the prologue mission again on subsequent playthroughs, and from this point on—and well into New Game ++—there will also be exclusive missions available.

NEW GAME++

If you've made all of the right choices, this should be your final playthrough, and it includes new exclusive missions and Arena fights. New Game++ also features an exclusive ending; making the wrong Decision in Chapter 1 can lock you out of this ending, so it's vital to carefully follow the recommended order. Not completing the last available Arena missions in this playthrough will result in you losing access to those simulations until you enter your fourth playthrough. For this playthrough, the order assumes that you refuse the RLF's offer in "Attack the Dam Complex (Alt)." You can accept the offer, but doing so will mean playing through some NG+ missions during Chapters 1, 2 and 3. Because you've played out both scenarios from Attack the Dam Complex, your choice in this playthrough has no real impact.

S RANK GUIDE

This section is for those who want to take on the game's greatest challenge: achieving the coveted S-Rank rating on all 59 missions. On the following pages we'll explain how mission ranking works and provide strategies for obtaining an S Rank on every mission in the game.

RANKING OVERVIEW

When you're starting your S Rank completion journey, the most important thing you need to know is that resuming from a past checkpoint, either by doing so manually or upon mission failure, will instantly lock you out of obtaining one. While that's often one of the biggest considerations, avoiding restarting from a checkpoint will by no means guarantee you an S Rank—there are other factors to consider, which we'll outline here. Once you obtain an S Rank in a mission, it's locked in and saved, so even if you play the mission again and get a lower rank, the S Rank you previously achieved will still be displayed and counted.

Throughout this section, we'll sometimes recommend parts that cannot be obtained until you've completed the game at least once, or have met other requirements. Those parts, while not strictly necessary, do make obtaining an S Rank easier. Pursuing S Ranks is best left until you've unlocked all of the missions and seen all of the endings, as you'll have access to a wide selection of weapons and parts as well as all OS Tuning upgrades. You can, of course, tackle the S Ranks in order as you complete missions normally. If you save them for last, however, both your mechanical proficiency and mission knowledge will be vastly superior, which will greatly increase the likelihood of getting your desired rank.

REWARDS

There is one small in-game reward to signify that you've earned an S Rank in every mission: the "Perfect Mercenary" Emblem. There's also a Trophy/Achievement related to completing this feat, which will likely be the last such accolade you unlock, since this is no small undertaking. The reflexes you've developed, the build theories you've tested, and the parts you've collected, will be put to their full use in surmounting this challenge.

RANKING SYSTEM

The following are the contributing factors that you'll need to keep in mind while playing through a mission with the goal of obtaining an S-Rank rating at the end.

1. Damage Taken

Each point of AP you lose will count against your rank. The more damage you take, the lower the chance that you'll achieve an S Rank.

2. Ammunition Expended

Every weapon that has a "Total Rounds" value in its "Part Specs" information costs COAM to use in missions, and any ammo it uses counts against your rating in the ranking system. Only ammo used counts here; rounds "discarded" through manual reloading have no effect. Similarly, using a melee weapon has no associated cost in the ranking system. Ammo is always the lowest contributing factor to your overall rank, and while it does have an impact, your pursuit of an S Rank should prioritize the other three contributing elements; just avoid liberally using ammo with no purpose.

3. Clear Time

Every second that ticks by counts against your rank, so you'll need to factor expediency in a lot of the missions in order to earn your S Rank. It's worth noting that the only point at which the timer is not ticking, is when you're watching a non-interactive cutscene, including those that occur mid-mission. This means that whenever you're in control of your AC, time is being weighed against you. Even if you've completed the mission objective and are getting a debrief through dialogue, these moments still count against your time.

4. Enemies Defeated

Every enemy you defeat within a mission is factored into your overall rating at the end. This includes boss encounters and other ACs that you fight. Because each enemy varies wildly in how much they contribute, the S Rank walkthroughs that follow will sometimes single out those that should get priority. Rarely will it be advised to eliminate every enemy within a mission, beyond the ones that inherently require you to do that.

MISSION-SPECIFIC RATINGS

There's no way to view your current rank while in a mission, so not until you complete it and receive the final judgment will you truly know how well you did. Each mission also weighs the different ranking factors slightly differently, so doing well and getting an S Rank on one mission does not automatically mean you'll be able to do the same on another. Because of this, each mission has its own specific strategy regarding what you should prioritize within it, which extends to the loadout that best suits the challenges it presents.

USING THE S RANK GUIDE

1 Difficulty

We use this four-point scale to represent the relative difficulty of earning the S-Rank rating in each mission. This doesn't appear anywhere in the game; we've included it here to provide some guidance on difficulty.

2 Assembly

We've assembled and tested the specified build to try to make earning the S-Rank rating as easy and approachable as possible. The text here explains why certain parts are recommended.

3 Strategy

A summarization of the mission and what to do and prioritize to ensure an S-Rank rating. This will also include screenshots of key moments within the mission. Naturally, not all missions are equally complex or require similar effort to earn their S-Rank ratings, so some will offer less guidance than others.

4 Map

Most missions have the route described in the text plotted on a map, which will usually appear on the same page. Some maps cater to more than one mission, in which case each route and key positions will have it's own color and be clearly labeled with the mission's name.

Difficulty Ratings

Rating	Total Missions	Description
	10	Easy: Minimal effort and strategy
	29	Medium: Some effort and strategy
	14	Hard: Moderate effort and strategy
	6	Extreme: Serious effort and strategy required

ILLEGAL ENTRY

Despite being the prologue mission, most enemies present here are optional. None of the enemies are worth going out of your way for, but destroying those along the mission's main path can give you some buffer to help with your rank, especially the group of four bipedal MTs near the city outskirts. The boss doesn't count toward enemies defeated, and losing too much AP against it is the biggest threat to your S Rank. Outside of that, aim to finish the mission in under six minutes while taking less than two repair kits worth of damage.

Strategy

▌ Begin by clearing out the group of guard mechs and bipedal MTs defending the large warehouse on your way to the catapult. Maintaining your distance and being evasive will be key here, as there are many more enemies to dispatch later in the mission. When you've catapulted to the contaminated city, destroy the group of four bipedal MTs on your way to the first site at **Position A**. ▶ A

▌ Every MT you come across on the way to each mercenary license should be destroyed, including the MTs by the vertical catapult right before the boss fight. The guard mechs will hardly impact your score, so only eliminate them if they're near bipedal MTs.

▌ Make your way to **Position B** then **C** while eliminating the bipedal MTs along your path. It's worth noting that the enemies taken out by the AH12: HC HELICOPTER near **Position B** still count toward your score, so keep a safe distance to capitalize on this event. ▶ B

▌ There are plenty of hostiles guarding the wreck at **Position C**, so use your missiles and assault rifle to destroy them as you approach. This will minimize the damage you take while accessing the data—once it's yours, make your way to the vertical catapult and use it to reach **Position D**.

▌ All that's left is to destroy the AH12: HC HELICOPTER. Stay underneath and toward the rear of the chopper to avoid getting hit by its arsenal. Constantly fire your missiles and assault rifle while you boost close enough to use your pulse blade, but watch the boss's ACS, because you want to make sure your pulse blade is available for use the instant it's staggered. Since most of your damage comes from landing pulse blade strikes, pay close attention to how the boss is moving—if it flies out of the area boundary it can remain outside your melee range for a while. Sticking to the middle of the area as much as possible is the best way to avoid this scenario. ▶ C

ASSEMBLY

You're unable to modify your AC in this mission, so the build shown here is the default assembly available at the start of the game.

R-ARM UNIT	RF-024 TURNER
L-ARM UNIT	HI-32: BU-TT/A
R-BACK UNIT	BML-G1/P20MLT-04
L-BACK UNIT	—
HEAD	HC-2000 FINDER EYE
CORE	CC-2000 ORBITER
ARMS	AC-2000 TOOL ARM
LEGS	2C-2000 CRAWLER
BOOSTER	BST-G1/P10
FCS	FCS-G1/P01
GENERATOR	AG-J-098 JOSO
EXPANSION	—

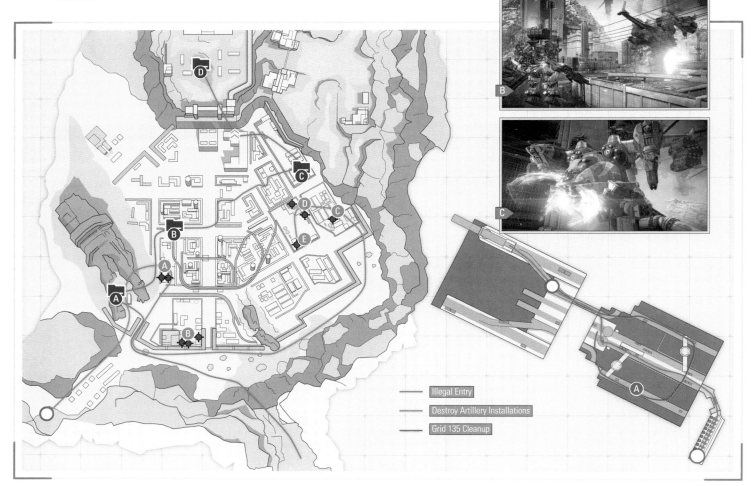

Illegal Entry

Destroy Artillery Installations

Grid 135 Cleanup

DESTROY ARTILLERY INSTALLATIONS

CH01 [01-A]

For this S Rank, all you need to concern yourself with is destroying the artillery installations as quickly as possible. Although taking out other enemies will add to your rating, speed is much more important. If you ignore all enemies, it's possible to complete the mission in under two minutes. The requirements are quite lenient, however, and you can finish in around three minutes while taking some damage and destroying no additional enemies.

Strategy

▌ Make your way toward **Position A**, sticking to the left as much as possible to avoid the enemies along the way, and going through the wreckage to quickly and safely get behind the artillery. ▶ D
As soon as you have the installations in your sights, fire off a salvo from one missile launcher at each of them to destroy them, then head back toward the city entrance.

▌ Follow the outside of the city wall until you reach **Position B**, and fire missile salvos at two of the installations there while you use your machine guns on the third one. Once they've been destroyed, Assault Boost along the city outskirts toward **Position C**.

▌ Jump over the wall once you're behind **Position C** and fire off a missile salvo to destroy the artillery there while you Assault Boost toward **Position D**. ▶ E There are a few enemies in the area, so if you're having trouble targeting the artillery installations, use multi-lock and finish them off with your machine guns. All that's left is to Assault Boost over toward **Position E** and use a final missile salvo to destroy the last artillery installation and complete the mission. ▶ F

ASSEMBLY

This build is designed with the goal of destroying the artillery installations as quickly and easily as possible, while also offering extreme mobility. The mobility advantage this AC offers is largely down to the generator's fast cooling speed, and the ability to gain a lot of altitude without sacrificing too much EN. The vertical missile launchers allow you to destroy the artillery installations without stopping or worrying about their frontal armor if you get out of position. The LUDLOW's give you a solid backup to finish off anything in your way

R-ARM UNIT	MG-014 LUDLOW
L-ARM UNIT	MG-014 LUDLOW
R-BACK UNIT	BML-G1/P01VTC-04
L-BACK UNIT	BML-G1/P01VTC-04
HEAD	VP-44D
CORE	NACHTREIHER/40E
ARMS	04-101 MIND ALPHA
LEGS	KASUAR/42Z
BOOSTER	BST-G1/P10
FCS	FCS-G2/P10SLT
GENERATOR	DF-GN-06 MING-TANG
EXPANSION	PULSE ARMOR

GRID 135 CLEANUP

CH01 [01-B]

This straightforward mission consists of only a single area, defended by a group of enemies that must all be destroyed (except for the hidden GHOST) to complete the job. Achieving an S-Rank rating is on the lower end of the difficulty range, and your primary concern should be your clear time. Damage taken is the second priority, and you're able to essentially ignore ammunition expenditure and use it liberally.

Strategy

▌ Time is a critical factor in attaining this S Rank, so Assault Boost toward the access bulkhead at the start of the mission. Try to keep your momentum up while working your way clockwise around the room full of enemies, so that you don't lose any time. Only Assault Boost if you have a considerable distance to travel to the next enemy group, however, because you'll need a bit of time for your multi-lock to acquire their targets, and boosting past them will slow you down overall.

▌ Work your way between the enemy groups using multi-lock to destroy multiple enemies at a time; use your hand missile launchers if the group is small, and the launchers on your back for larger groups or tougher enemies.

▌ When you reach the shield-wielding bipedal MTs near **Position A**, use a Boost Kick to break through their shields quickly before finishing them off with some missiles

▌ The final wave of enemies is capable of inflicting a decent amount of damage if you're reckless. Keep your distance while locking onto them, so that you don't lose your S Rank right at the end.

ASSEMBLY

This build is focused on mid-range combat, with weaponry and systems designed to maximize multi-lock capabilities for destroying groups of enemies as quickly as possible.

R-ARM UNIT	HML-G2/P19MLT-04
L-ARM UNIT	HML-G2/P19MLT-04
R-BACK UNIT	BML-G2/P05MLT-10
L-BACK UNIT	BML-G2/P05MLT-10
HEAD	DF-HD-08 TIAN QIANG
CORE	NACHTREIHER/40E
ARMS	AA-J-123/RC JAILBREAK
LEGS	NACHTREIHER/42E
BOOSTER	IB-C03B: NGI 001
FCS	FCS-G2/P12SML
GENERATOR	DF-GN-06 MING-TANG
EXPANSION	PULSE ARMOR

DESTROY THE TRANSPORT HELICOPTERS

The main challenge in earning an S-Rank rating here lies in destroying a sufficient number of enemies while quickly moving between the transport helicopter locations; the faster you are, the fewer enemies you'll need to destroy to get an S Rank.

Strategy

▌ Assault Boost toward **Position A** and slow down once the bipedal MTs are within range, so that you can multi-lock them all and destroy them while you land near the helicopter. Shotgun the helicopter—and any other enemies that are close enough—but don't waste any time here, because you'll want to Assault Boost toward **Position B** as soon as possible. ▶ A

▌ On your way to the helicopter at **Position B**, be sure to use multi-lock to destroy enemies at the blockade, including the last of the artillery sites, since they count more toward your rank than the other enemies.

▌ Assault Boost up the cliff after destroying the second helicopter and move between the buildings until you reach the third set of helicopters at **Position C**, then use your shotguns to quickly eliminate them. ▶ B

▌ While crossing the open ground toward the final set of helicopters, use your missiles to destroy the bipedal MTs as they attempt to close in on you, and evade any incoming fire from the tetrapod MT. Destroy the final helicopter at **Position D** once you're close enough, and then jump over the nearby wall until the mission ends to avoid taking any unnecessary damage. ▶ C

ASSEMBLY

This build is focused on using multi-lock missile launchers to destroy as many enemies as possible in a single salvo, as you boost past them on your way to the helicopters. The shotguns can deal with the helicopters in a single shot, which again, allows you to move between targets quickly. They also give you some extra punch in case other enemies get too close.

R-ARM UNIT	SG-027 ZIMMERMAN
L-ARM UNIT	SG-027 ZIMMERMAN
R-BACK UNIT	BML-G2/P05MLT-10
L-BACK UNIT	BML-G2/P05MLT-10
HEAD	HD-033M VERILL
CORE	BD-012 MELANDER C3
ARMS	AS-5000 SALAD
LEGS	RC-2000 SPRING CHICKEN
BOOSTER	BST-G2/P06SPD
FCS	FCS-G2/P10SLT
GENERATOR	VP-20C
EXPANSION	PULSE ARMOR

DESTROY THE TESTER AC

The Tester AC that the Redguns are interested in acquiring doesn't put up much of a fight, thanks to it being piloted by a rookie that does not use any repair kits. This battle shouldn't last very long at all and is one of the simpler S Ranks to obtain.

Strategy

▌ With quick initial positioning, it's possible to catch the Tester AC unaware to put you in good stead for a quick victory. Assault Boost toward **Position A**, getting close to the combat zone boundary, so you're behind the Tester AC. ▶ D

▌ Close in until you're at around 180m away from it—any closer and it will detect you—and then activate your pulse armor, before ascending to get a clear shot on your unsuspecting target. A clean hit from both grenade cannons will easily stagger it; once you fire them, Assault Boost in and Boost Kick it before unloading your shotguns until it's destroyed. ▶ E

▌ The battle can become frantic if the Tester AC gets a chance to move. If it survives past your opening attack, try to box it in against one of the walls while staying close. It might retaliate with a melee attack but your build can easily absorb it. It's worth taking the hit if it means you can finish the Tester AC off.

ASSEMBLY

Overwhelming offense is the key to getting an S Rank in this mission. That means staggering the Tester AC as quickly as possible and inflicting huge amounts of damage before it recovers, which this selection of weaponry allows for. The tetrapod legs help with getting into position initially, and the use of pulse armor gives you a nice buffer period where you don't have to worry about taking damage.

R-ARM UNIT	SG-027 ZIMMERMAN
L-ARM UNIT	SG-027 ZIMMERMAN
R-BACK UNIT	EARSHOT
L-BACK UNIT	EARSHOT
HEAD	VP-44D
CORE	07-061 MIND ALPHA
ARMS	AS-5000 SALAD
LEGS	LG-033M VERRILL
BOOSTER	ALULA/21E
FCS	FC-008 TALBOT
GENERATOR	DF-GN-08 SAN-TAI
EXPANSION	PULSE ARMOR

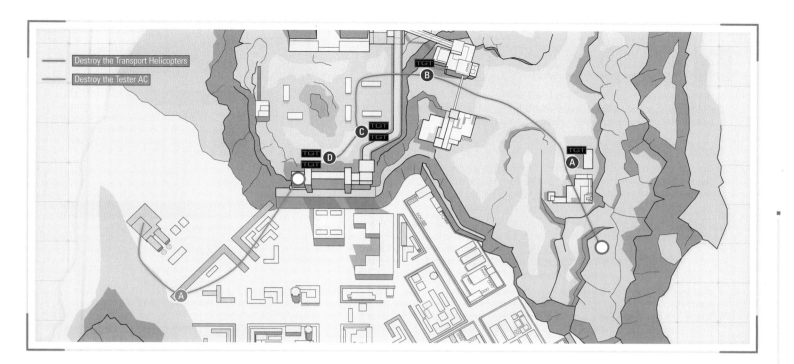

Destroy the Transport Helicopters

Destroy the Tester AC

CH01 [03-A] ATTACK THE DAM COMPLEX

Your main priority when storming the dam complex will be to eliminate both the optional tetrapod MT and AC BURN PICKAXE. A secondary focus should be to complete the mission as fast as possible, which is easily manageable using the recommended AC configuration. Enemies killed by your allies count toward your score, but you shouldn't rely on them to kill everything on their own, and should take the lead as much as possible.

Strategy

▌ Begin with an Assault Boost toward the first generator at **Position A**, using multi-lock with your missile launchers to destroy most of the enemies along the way. If any survive, mop them up with your shotguns and destroy the generator.

▌ Hug the lower dam on your way toward the second generator at **Position B**, to make it much harder for the artillery installations near it to lock onto you. As soon as you can target them, use your multi-lock missiles again to destroy them and any nearby enemies, while flanking around behind to deal with the enemies on the cliffs. Push down toward the generator and destroy it and any remaining enemies.

▌ You'll now need to face the tetrapod MT at **Position C**, so Assault Boost along the cliffs until you reach the dam behind it and destroy the two bipedal MTs that are defending your target. Now's a good time to activate pulse armor if you have it, then you can boost straight down toward the tetrapod MT while firing your missiles without having to worry about evading attacks. Once you're up close, constant fire from your shotguns will keep it off balance and unable to attack until it's destroyed. ▶ F

▌ The enemies around the third generator at **Position D** do not need to be destroyed for you to proceed, so you can ignore them all and just Assault Boost up and destroy the target while evading incoming fire.

▌ Start heading toward **Position E**, where BURN PICKAXE awaits you. Before engaging it, destroy all of the other MTs in the area to get a sizable boost toward your rank, while reducing the amount of incoming fire you have to contend with. BURN PICKAXE is quite agile, so use your missiles first and time your shotgun shots for when Index Dunham tries to evade them.

▶ G If you play aggressively, victory won't take long, especially with the help of your allies. Once BURN PICKAXE has been destroyed, use the nearby vertical catapult to reach the final generator and destroy it to complete the mission. There are enemies near the generator, so while Walter congratulates you, destroy them to solidify your S Rank.

ASSEMBLY

This build offers good mobility to cover a lot of the mission area, as well as having the EN supply to travel to all sites and points of interest easily. The weaponry is focused on dispatching multiple light MTs and generic weaponry efficiently, while also giving you the close-range damage needed to destroy the priority targets quickly.

R-ARM UNIT	SG-027 ZIMMERMAN
L-ARM UNIT	SG-027 ZIMMERMAN
R-BACK UNIT	BML-G2/P05MLT-10
L-BACK UNIT	BML-G2/P05MLT-10
HEAD	VP-44D
CORE	07-061 MIND ALPHA
ARMS	AC-2000 TOOL ARM
LEGS	RC-2000 SPRING CHICKEN
BOOSTER	IB-C03B: NGI 001
FCS	FC-008 TALBOT
GENERATOR	DF-GN-08 SAN-TAI
EXPANSION	PULSE ARMOR

F

G

ATTACK THE DAM COMPLEX (ALT)

Both Redguns are dangerous, but G4 Volta will be the greatest threat to your S Rank. Dealing with him can be tricky, especially if he intercepts your fight with G5 Iguazu; defeating both of them as quickly as possible without sustaining too much damage will be required to secure the S Rank.

Strategy

▌ The start of the mission plays out the same as in the original version; destroy both of the first generators and the enemies near them as quickly as possible. Your weapons are strong enough to destroy any of these enemies in a single hit—as long as you rotate through them you can clear out groups fairly quickly.

▌ After you've accepted the RLF's offer, pursue Iguazu toward **Position A**. G5 Iguazu is much easier to eliminate than Volta, and while he's on his own you can afford to be very aggressive with only minimal evasion. While he's unaware of your betrayal, quickly get into position to land a clean blast with all of your weapons and try to stagger him before he can retaliate. ▶ A He can use repair kits, but if you're quick enough, it's possible to defeat him before he has the chance to use one. If Iguazu is still around when Volta turns up, it's worth using your pulse armor so you can focus on defeating him without wasting time evading.

▌ Next is G4 Volta, who's packing much more serious firepower, which you'll need to be ready to evade at a moment's notice when you hear the attack indicator. The recommended build can take a bit of a beating, so try to stay as close to him as possible and take advantage of the fact that he's not as evasive as Iguazu to constantly pummel him with attacks. ▶ B His AC's high AP pool means this fight can take a while even with a strong selection of weapons, so make sure you pay close attention to his ACS gauge and have as many weapons as possible ready to fire the instant you stagger him. If you end up fighting Iguazu and Volta together, you may want to move to **Position B**, to give yourself more room to maneuver and evade the duo's attacks.

■ SPECIAL OBJECTIVE

Eliminate the Redguns

In order to be eligible for the S Rank in this mission, you need to accept the RLF's offer to betray the Redguns. It is impossible to get the S Rank for this Alt mission under the original mission's circumstance.

ASSEMBLY

The build required for this mission is in almost complete contrast to the one for the original version; it's entirely designed around inflicting as much close-range damage as possible to your two priority targets. Being that close to dangerous foes brings inherent risks, but this selection of parts gives you the defensive specs to be able to withstand a lot of punishment.

R-ARM UNIT	SG-027 ZIMMERMAN
L-ARM UNIT	SG-027 ZIMMERMAN
R-BACK UNIT	VP-60LCD
L-BACK UNIT	VP-60LCD
HEAD	20-082 MIND BETA
CORE	CC-3000 WRECKER
ARMS	NACHTREIHER/46E
LEGS	LG-022T BORNEMISSZA
BOOSTER	—
FCS	FC-006 ABBOT
GENERATOR	VP-20D
EXPANSION	PULSE ARMOR

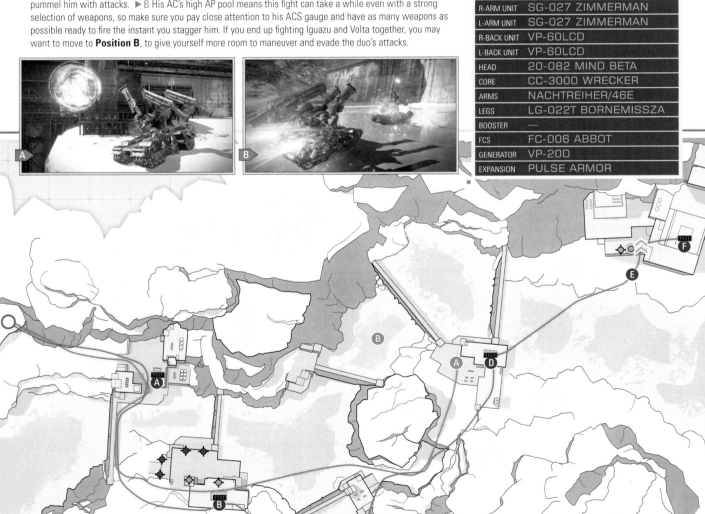

Attack the Dam Complex

Attack the Dam Complex (ALT)

DESTROY THE WEAPONIZED MINING SHIP

Speed is essentially the only metric that matters when it comes to getting an S Rank on this mission. Familiarity with the locations of the generators—and how to quickly reach them—will go a long way toward your goal here. You can ignore all of the other MTs in the area and the turrets on the mining ship, but once you reach the Eye, it needs to rapidly be destroyed before you flee the area.

Strategy

▌ The basic approach to this mission is identical to the approach detailed in the walkthrough on P.114. Start with an Assault Boost along the side of the area until you're behind the STRIDER, so you won't need to worry about its lasers. ▶ C Destroy the leg joint when you reach it, and eliminate the bipedal MTs in the area while the STRIDER collapses.

▌ Make your way up the STRIDER as usual and begin destroying the generators, starting with the one underneath at **Position A** first, then the far side one at **Position B**, near side one at **Position C**, and finally the top one at **Position D**.

▌ Start your assault on the Eye by heading straight to the small side platform at **Position E**, from where you can use your medium-range machine guns and grenade cannons in safety. ▶ D If you're confident in your evasion skills, you can stay in front of the Eye the entire time you're fighting it. If you complete the other parts of the mission fast enough, however, you can use the safe platform and still get the S Rank.

▌ When you notice the Eye power down briefly, jump out and aggressively attack, aiming to finish it off before it recovers. Once it's destroyed, immediately Assault Boost out to the rally point in the desert, rather than waiting for the prompt from Walter, to ensure you finish as quickly as possible. ▶ E

ASSEMBLY

This build is primarily focused on mobility, so that you can get to and move between objectives as quickly as possible. Then, once you reach the Eye, the dual SONGBIRDS have the necessary damage to finish it with time to spare.

R-ARM UNIT	MG-014 LUDLOW
L-ARM UNIT	MG-014 LUDLOW
R-BACK UNIT	SONGBIRDS
L-BACK UNIT	SONGBIRDS
HEAD	DF-HD-08 TIAN-QIANG
CORE	EL-TC-10 FIRMEZA
ARMS	EL-TA-10 FIRMEZA
LEGS	KASUAR/42Z
BOOSTER	BC-02000 GRIDWALKER
FCS	FC-008 TALBOT
GENERATOR	DF-GN-06 MING-TANG
EXPANSION	PULSE ARMOR

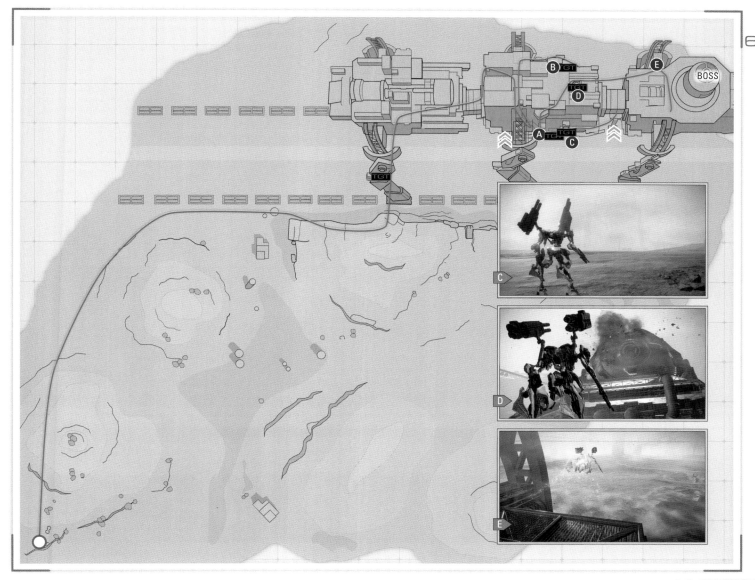

ESCORT THE WEAPONIZED MINING SHIP

This can be a very challenging S Rank to acquire, because you're dealing with incredibly agile and powerful enemies, all of which need to be destroyed. Surviving is not enough, however, because you'll need to come out of the fight relatively unscathed; having to use even one repair kit can be an indicator that you've missed out on the S Rank.

Strategy

▌ Speed is of the essence in this mission, and while you're somewhat restricted by the periods between enemy waves, you'll need that time to destroy the enemies at hand before the next ones appear. The speed of the enemies you'll face in this mission provides much of the challenge. If you're patient, however, small windows of opportunity will present themselves, and you need to be ready to strike with everything you have.

▌ Try to keep the battle near the crater at **Position A**, because it gives you some solid cover to use if needed. Your hand missiles release faster than the back ones, so for most of the fight those should be your lead weapon—only unleash your back missiles when you see a clear opening. ▶ A

▌ You're exclusively fighting WEEVILs and HELIANTHUS enemies, with waves comprised of two WEEVILs, followed by a large group of HELIANTHUS, and then a combined group at the end. These HELIANTHUS use their missiles frequently, so the usual tactic of staying above them is not as effective. Jumping over them when they charge at you, however, still offers a good opportunity to land some hits. ▶ B

▌ When facing the group of HELIANTHUS or the combined group, be sure to use your pulse armor for some extra protection. If you have multiple charges of pulse armor, using them during both of those encounters can make the difference toward getting the S Rank. ▶ C

ASSEMBLY

The goal of this build is to enable you to maintain a lot of distance from the enemies. This will help with evading their attacks while sending as many missiles at them as possible, with the knowledge that a number of them will miss due to their evasiveness. Since the enemies are also attempting to do the same to you, use of the FORTALEZA legs is recommended, to help evade incoming attacks.

R-ARM UNIT	HML-G2/P19MLT-04
L-ARM UNIT	HML-G2/P19MLT-04
R-BACK UNIT	BML-G2/P05MLT-10
L-BACK UNIT	BML-G2/P05MLT-10
HEAD	HD-033M VERRILL
CORE	BD-011 MELANDER
ARMS	AS-5000 SALAD
LEGS	EL-TL-11 FORTALEZA
BOOSTER	—
FCS	FCS-G2/P12SML
GENERATOR	DF-GN-06 MING TANG
EXPANSION	PULSE ARMOR

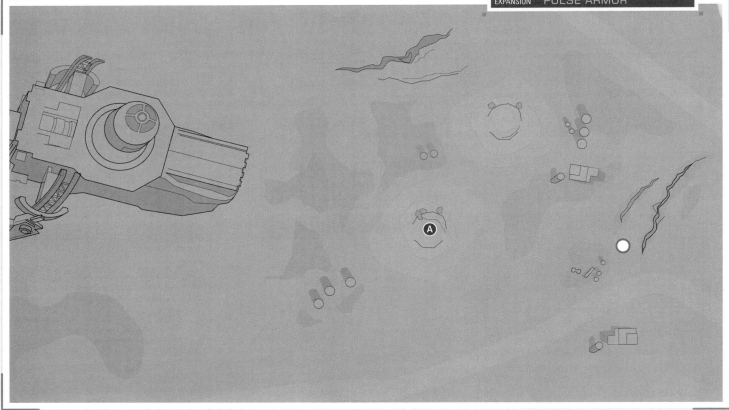

OPERATION WALLCLIMBER

Clear time is by far the highest priority for this mission, though most of its requirements are fairly lenient, especially when it comes to number of enemies defeated. You can ignore most enemies—other than those required to progress—but taking out a few extra along the way will help with your score. Ammo cost is hardly a factor, so don't feel the need to be conservative. There is no penalty for using the supply sherpa before the boss fight.

Strategy

▌ Ignore all of the enemies while you Assault Boost toward **Position A**, and drop down into the safety of the divide. Follow it along and boost up to **Position B**, so you can get behind the artillery and destroy both it and the nearby bipedal MT. ▶ D

▌ Assault Boost over to the nearby buildings and use them for cover from the artillery on the wall, while you approach the tetrapod MT at **Position C**. You'll have to cross some open space here, so you might want to activate pulse armor for this section to ensure you don't take any damage. Once you're within range of the tetrapod MT, lead with your missiles as you close in, and then unload with your shotguns. Keep firing your weapons as they become available, and it won't last long against this configuration. ▶ E

▌ Assault Boost up to the access door and enter the Wall. While you make your way through the interior, destroy all of the enemies to give your score a boost.

▌ Make sure to access the supply sherpa after using the elevator, and then commence the fight with the JUGGERNAUT. With your weaponry and build, you're able to safely hover above the JUGGERNAUT and attack while you're airborne, making the fight significantly easier. Your missiles alone will be nearly enough to stagger it—once you land a couple of shotgun shots on it, you can keep it perpetually staggered if you time your attacks well. ▶ F

6

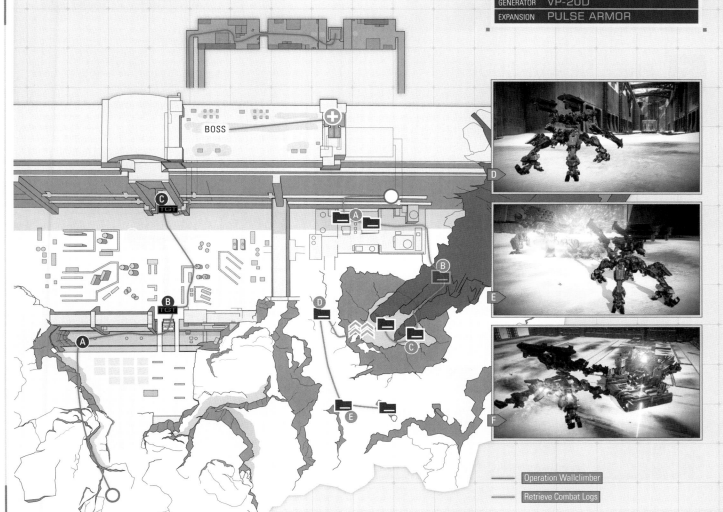

BOSS

Operation Wallclimber

Retrieve Combat Logs

RETRIEVE COMBAT LOGS

Speed is essential for this mission because not only do you need to get all eight of the combat logs, you have to do so well before the mission timer would typically expire.

Strategy

- Since you need to remain somewhat stationary while accessing the combat logs, use the time to destroy any enemies in the vicinity, as this will help increase your rank. Assault Boost down to **Position A**, where you'll find the first two logs near each other, with a few guard mechs and bipedal MTs nearby to destroy. The next log you should go for is the one at **Position B**, under the wreckage, so head there as fast as possible and destroy the enemies as you close in on the wreck.

- **Position C** is the location of the fourth log, and while accessing it you'll get ambushed by Little Ziyi in AC YUE YU. ▶ A It's not essential to fight her, but your arsenal lets you deal with her fairly quickly, and eliminating her will help solidify your S Rank.

- After defeating Little Ziyi, access the combat log at the bottom of the crash site, and then use the nearby vertical catapults to ascend out of the crater. Assault Boost toward **Position D** once you're high enough, since that's where the next log is, and use your missiles to destroy the sniper enemies along the way.

- All that's left now is a quick Assault Boost toward **Position E** to secure that log, before heading to the final log site nearby. ▶ B Additional enemies will arrive on the scene, but your S Rank should already be secure, so eliminating them is optional.

Recover All Eight Combat Logs

In order to be eligible for the S Rank in this mission you need to retrieve all eight combat logs. Make retrieving them your first priority, with speed being a close second.

ASSEMBLY

While focused on mobility, this build also offers decently powerful weaponry to ensure that none of the fights the mission throws at you will slow you down.

R-ARM UNIT	SG-027 ZIMMERMAN
L-ARM UNIT	SG-027 ZIMMERMAN
R-BACK UNIT	BML-G2/P05MLT-10
L-BACK UNIT	BML-G2/P05MLT-10
HEAD	DF-HD-08 TIAN-QIANG
CORE	EL-TC-10 FIRMEZA
ARMS	AS-5000 SALAD
LEGS	06-042 MIND BETA
BOOSTER	BST-G1/P10
FCS	VE-21A
GENERATOR	DF-GN-06 MING-TANG
EXPANSION	PULSE ARMOR

PRISONER RESCUE

Though clear time is an important factor here, you can't affect the speed of the RLF Helicopter as it picks up its allies—you can only protect it. You can, however, move ahead and eliminate threats before the helicopter passes through an area. The number of threats and ambushes to deal with makes keeping the helicopter above the AP threshold extremely difficult, so you'll need to be very efficient.

Strategy

- Don't wait for the helicopter to start heading for the first pickup at **Position A**. Instead, Assault Boost ahead of it and begin clearing the path of enemies, all the way up to second pickup at **Position B**. If you're quick enough, you can also venture over toward its third stop at **Position C**, so you can take out the artillery along the road and the installations on the cliffs. ▶ C-D

- Drones carrying bipedal MTs will ambush the helicopter when it nears **Position B**, so make sure you're back there in time to destroy them all quickly—they can make short work of the helicopter if left alone. It's worth keeping an eye on the helicopter's AP, to ensure you'll notice if it starts taking damage, and react in time. ▶ E

- Once G2 Nile shows up, be sure to prioritize him and draw his fire away from the helicopter. ▶ F Things can get chaotic at this point, so it's worth deploying the pulse protection Core Expansion around the helicopter to mitigate the damage it takes. The area is fairly cramped, so Nile doesn't have a lot of room to evade your attacks. He can still take a while to defeat, and you'll need to remain mobile while battling him. During this time, a transport helicopter will attempt to deploy bipedal MT reinforcements; try to destroy it before it has a chance to do so. Once Nile has been defeated, deal with any remaining enemies to complete the mission.

Ensure the RLF's Helicopter's Sustainability

To be eligible for the S Rank, you need to ensure that the RLF helicopter reaches the end of the mission with at least 80% of its AP remaining.

ASSEMBLY

G2 Nile is the biggest threat in the mission, so much of this build is designed to make that encounter as easy as possible, while providing multi-lock capabilities to quickly dispatch other groups of enemies.

R-ARM UNIT	SG-027 ZIMMERMAN
L-ARM UNIT	HML-G2/P19MLT-04
R-BACK UNIT	VP-60LCD
L-BACK UNIT	VP-60LCD
HEAD	VP-44D
CORE	BD-012 MELANDER C3
ARMS	EL-PA-00 ALBA
LEGS	VP-424
BOOSTER	BST-G1/P10
FCS	FCS-G2/P12SML
GENERATOR	VE-20C
EXPANSION	PULSE PROTECTION

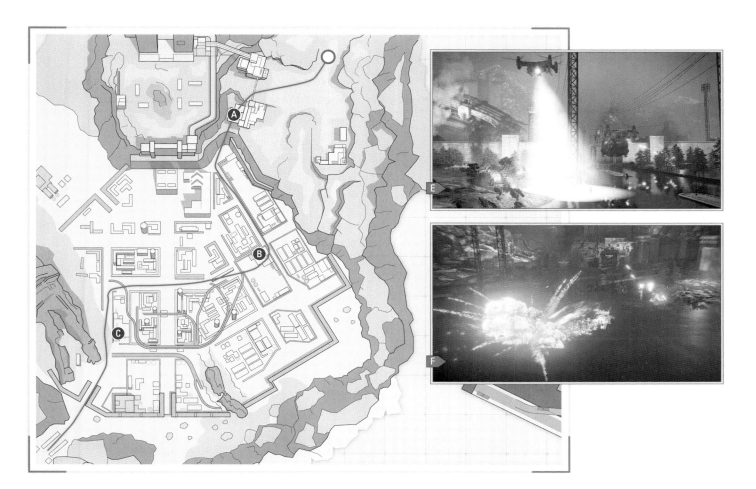

CH01 [05-B]
INVESTIGATE BAWS ARSENAL NO. 2

Speed and damage taken are your two main concerns for this S Rank. While the recommended assembly can take out the GHOSTs fairly quickly, one mistake can lead to enough damage to knock you out of eligibility. Memorizing the locations of the GHOSTs will go a long way here—it will minimize time spent scanning, and reduce the likelihood of them detecting you and repositioning.

Strategy

▓ A salvo from both hand missile launchers is sufficient to destroy a GHOST, so your aim should be to Assault Boost into firing range and destroy the GHOST without letting it reposition. The GHOST at **Position A** will fire on as you approach, but it doesn't reposition, so you can evade its shots and destroy it once you're close enough. ▶ G

▓ You can get the drop on the GHOSTs at **Positions B** and **C** to destroy them easily. The GHOST at **Position D** will also fire on you, so you'll need to evade the shots and close in quickly to destroy it before it disappears.

▓ If you follow along the wall from there, you can also fire on the GHOST at **Position E** without being detected, leaving only the final two to destroy before you enter the partition. ▶ H

▓ When fighting the group of GHOSTs at the end, prioritize the pulse armor variant first, since it poses the biggest threat; use all of your missiles against it, while staying out of its melee range. ▶ I While fighting it, try to identify the position of the three sniper GHOSTs clinging to the walls—once the pulse armor GHOST has been destroyed, you'll need to Assault Boost to the sniper variants to quickly get within range and fire your missiles at them.

ASSEMBLY

The damage from the missiles, coupled with the mobility of the build, lets you destroy the GHOSTs and move between targets extremely quickly, which is necessary for this S Rank.

R-ARM UNIT	HML-G2/P19MLT-04
L-ARM UNIT	HML-G2/P19MLT-04
R-BACK UNIT	BML-G2/P05MLT-10
L-BACK UNIT	BML-G2/P05MLT-10
HEAD	VE-44B
CORE	IA-C01C: EPHEMERA
ARMS	VP-46D
LEGS	06-042 MIND BETA
BOOSTER	BST-G2/P06SPD
FCS	FCS-G2/P10SLT
GENERATOR	DF-GN-08 SAN-TAI
EXPANSION	PULSE ARMOR

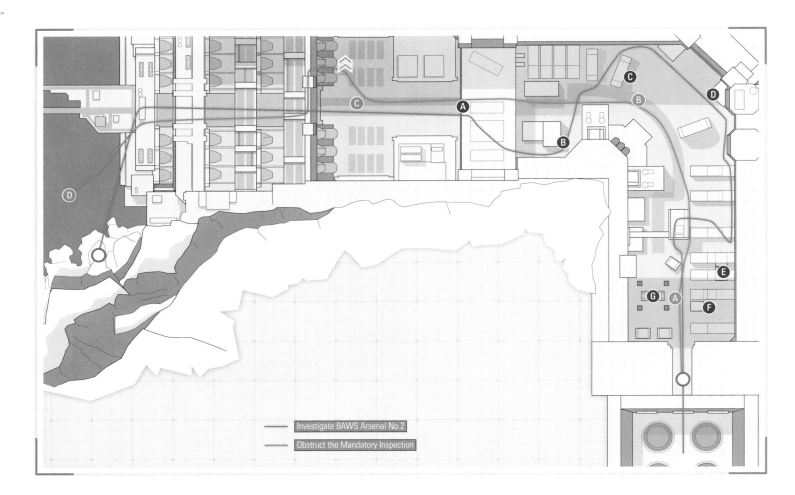

Investigate BAWS Arsenal No.2

Obstruct the Mandatory Inspection

OBSTRUCT THE MANDATORY INSPECTION

The damage your AC sustains is the largest factor in this mission's S Rank grading. You'll also need to destroy every enemy and get through the mission quickly, which means both your skills and arsenal of weapons will be pushed to their limits.

Strategy

▌ Eliminate the first group of Subject Guard MTs and quad drones around **Position A** as quickly as possible. The LC takes a little while to turn up, so this is your chance to clear the battlefield. If there are other enemies left when it arrives, finish them off before tackling the LC. ▶ A

▌ The next group of enemies are at **Position B**, and you'll want to once gain destroy the Subject Guard MTs before dealing with the two LCs. Given their speed and aerial maneuverability, stick to using your shotguns until you stagger them, and only then fire the diffuse laser cannons.

▌ Assault Boost out over the area at **Position C**, so that you can quickly take out the quad drones, and then use the vertical catapult to reach the area with the two sniper LCs. ▶ B This type is much weaker than the previous variants, and a double shotgun blast is sufficient to dispatch them.

▌ At **Position D**, allow the bosses to begin focusing on Kate, so that you can pick your targets. You should aim to destroy the two EKDROMOI before moving on to the CATAPHRACT. The CATAPHRACT should still be fighting Kate when you defeat the other bosses, providing an opportunity to stagger it with a full blast from all of your munitions. Even after that, the boss will often turn its attention back to Kate—if you notice that happening, be sure to take advantage of the situation. ▶ C

ASSEMBLY

This build is focused on providing plenty of anti-explosive and energy defense, in case things go awry. It also offers enough single-target damage to get through the enemies in the time required.

R-ARM UNIT	SG-027 ZIMMERMAN
L-ARM UNIT	SG-027 ZIMMERMAN
R-BACK UNIT	VP-60LCD
L-BACK UNIT	VP-60LCD
HEAD	HD-033M VERRILL
CORE	07-061 MIND ALPHA
ARMS	IA-C01A: EPHEMERA
LEGS	VP-424
BOOSTER	BST-G2/P06SPD
FCS	FC-008 TALBOT
GENERATOR	VE-20C
EXPANSION	TERMINAL ARMOR

ATTACK THE WATCHPOINT

This is a fairly long mission, featuring two mandatory fights before a pair of boss battles. Ammo cost and damage taken are of little concern, so capitalize on this with an AC focused on extremely high damage output. The most difficult part of the mission is the battle against Sulla; he's incredibly mobile, and while your weaponry is effective against him, hitting him can prove challenging.

Strategy

▌ Your first priority is to destroy the two artillery installations at **Positions A** and **B**, before dealing with the other enemies. ▶ D If you fly down and around the outside of the structure, you can get behind them and pop up to destroy them with a quick shotgun blast. You can then Assault Boost around the area doing the same to the other enemies.

▌ The same plan should be used for the second area. Destroy the two artillery installations at **Positions C** and **D** first, before doing a lap and eliminating the remaining enemies as quickly as possible.

▌ Sulla is your next target at **Position E**, and the best way to deal with him is through overwhelming offense to negate his constant movement. ▶ E Try to position him near a wall, and throw your entire arsenal at him— including Boost Kicks while you're reloading—to stagger him quickly, then deal extreme amounts of damage with your diffuse laser cannons before he recovers.

▌ The fight with BALTEUS is similar to the one with Sulla, since you'll need to take some risks with your offense to end the fight quickly. ▶ F Stay close and constantly use all of your weapons to deplete BALTEUS's shield and start dealing damage. Stand your ground against attacks you might usually retreat from, and keep firing to try to stagger it again, knocking it out of whichever attack it was about to use; with this weapon loadout, it shouldn't have many opportunities to retaliate.

ASSEMBLY

The two mandatory enemy encounters can be very difficult, so despite the variety of enemies, the focus here is on single-target burst damage, to end the fights as quickly as possible.

R-ARM UNIT	SG-027 ZIMMERMAN
L-ARM UNIT	SG-027 ZIMMERMAN
R-BACK UNIT	VP-60LCD
L-BACK UNIT	VP-60LCD
HEAD	HD-033M VERRILL
CORE	07-061 MIND ALPHA
ARMS	IA-C01A: EPHEMERA
LEGS	VP-424
BOOSTER	BST-G2/P06SPD
FCS	FC-008 TALBOT
GENERATOR	VE-20C
EXPANSION	TERMINAL ARMOR

Attack the Watchpoint & ALT Version

ATTACK THE WATCHPOINT (ALT)

The only difference between this mission and the standard version is that Sulla is accompanied by four sniper GHOSTs. All of the strategies that you utilized in the standard mission apply here, but you'll need to be just a little faster and more careful to get the S Rank.

Strategy

▓ Proceed through the mission as before until you reach Sulla at **Position A**. He should be your initial focus, because if you go after the GHOSTs he'll aggressively intercept you. The GHOSTs are a lot more dynamic at close range, making both fights more difficult. While fighting Sulla, you'll need to evade incoming shots from two sniper GHOSTs at **Positions B** and **C**. ▶ A Depending on where you end up fighting him, there should be cover available, which you can use to avoid having to worry about the GHOSTs. ▶ B

▓ After defeating Sulla, travel back toward the GHOSTs, using the cover of the road bridge for protection, and then Assault Boost up and destroy them individually. This GHOST variant is quite sturdy, so give them everything you have to finish them off before they disappear. When the first two have been defeated, another two appear at **Positions D** and **E**—handle them in the same manner .

▓ After defeating Sulla and the GHOSTs, resume the mission as normal and employ the same tactics as used to get the S Rank on the regular version of this mission ▶ C

ASSEMBLY

Again focused on single-target damage, this is the same build used for the standard version of the mission.

R-ARM UNIT	SG-027 ZIMMERMAN
L-ARM UNIT	SG-027 ZIMMERMAN
R-BACK UNIT	VP-60LCD
L-BACK UNIT	VP-60LCD
HEAD	HD-033M VERRILL
CORE	07-061 MIND ALPHA
ARMS	IA-C01A: EPHEMERA
LEGS	VP-424
BOOSTER	BST-G2/P06SPD
FCS	FC-008 TALBOT
GENERATOR	VE-20C
EXPANSION	TERMINAL ARMOR

INFILTRATE GRID 086

The number of enemies defeated and your clear time are the biggest contributing factors toward getting this S Rank, with the two ACs and final boss having the biggest impact.

Strategy

▓ To get through this mission in the required time, you'll want to be firing while moving as much as possible. Head toward **Position A**, where "Invincible" Rummy awaits, destroying the enemies along the way. His AC MAD STOMP lacks ranged weapons, so hover above him while firing until you stagger him, then drop down and keep firing until he's destroyed. ▶ D

▓ Head up to the tracks to destroy some extra enemies on the way to the door, and then make sure to defeat all of the crawler MTs in the foundry, before following the pipe down to Nosaac at **Position B**. He starts in a corner, so simply boost around and unleash your full arsenal on him to destroy him before he can move. ▶ E

▓ When you reach the ambush point at **Position C**, drop down and start destroying enemies, but back away as soon as the explosives drop to avoid taking damage. If the tetrapod MT survives, hover above it and fire down to bypass its shield for a quick victory.

▓ When fighting the SMART CLEANER at the end, hover above and fire down into its chimney to get a quick initial stagger, and then drop down in front of it and fire into the opening. Keep firing even as it recovers, and you should be able to stagger it again before it attacks for an easy victory. ▶ F

ASSEMBLY

This build is focused on swiftly eliminating enemies, and dealing damage against the SMART CLEANER. Since this mission has mandatory fights prior to fighting the boss, it's best to focus only on the enemies along the way, with Nosaac as the sole exception.

R-ARM UNIT	SG-027 ZIMMERMAN
L-ARM UNIT	SG-027 ZIMMERMAN
R-BACK UNIT	SONGBIRDS
L-BACK UNIT	SONGBIRDS
HEAD	HC-2000/BC SHADE EYE
CORE	EL-TC-10 FIRMEZA
ARMS	VP-46D
LEGS	VP-424
BOOSTER	BST-G2/P06SPD
FCS	FC-006 ABBOT
GENERATOR	DF-GN-08 SAN-TAI
EXPANSION	TERMINAL ARMOR

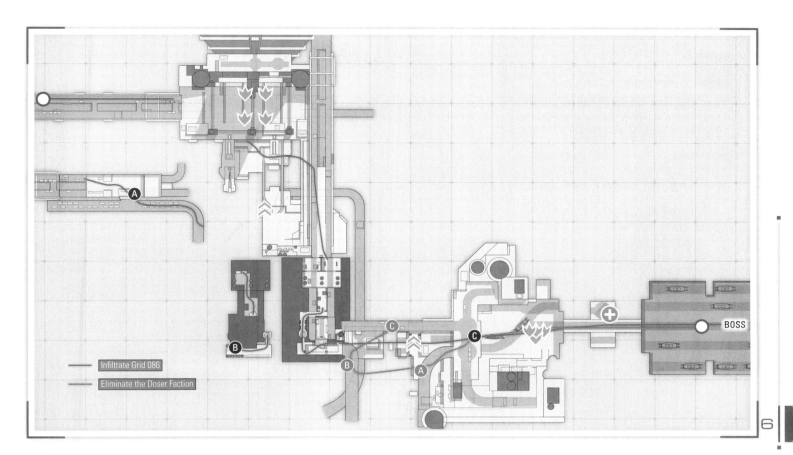

CH02 [08-A] ELIMINATE THE DOSER FACTION

Speed is by far the biggest contributing factor toward attaining an S Rank in this mission. You'll need to destroy every enemy, and your movement and accuracy will be put to the test in order to complete the mission in time. Aiming to defeat all of the enemies within around 90 seconds will put you in good stead. To achieve that, you'll need to miss very few shots, and not get hit by anything that causes you to stop moving. Taking damage can have a fairly negative impact on your rank, but if you're destroying enemies fast enough, they shouldn't be able to hit you at all.

Strategy

▌ Assault Boost up to the bulkhead to get there quickly. Once Carla opens up, Assault Boost again toward the rear of the room ahead and target the enemies with your shotguns as they're jumping in. Activate your orbits as you land, and they'll damage the enemies around you while you stay mobile, destroying the KICKERs as quickly as possible. Once all of the KICKERs have been finished off, deal with the crawler MT.

▌ As soon as you're able, Assault Boost up and out of the room toward **Position A**, then destroy both of the crawler MTs with a single shotgun blast each. ▶ G

▌ Next, Assault Boost toward **Position B**, being mindful to evade any incoming missiles. Finish off the two enemies when you land, before straight away using another Assault Boost, this time to **Position C** to destroy the final two enemies. ▶ H-I

ASSEMBLY

This build is focused on maneuverability and expediency. The shotguns can dispatch all of the enemies in this mission very quickly while staying mobile, and the orbits give you passive damage to pick off enemies other than the one you're focused on, which can speed you up considerably in the first room.

R-ARM UNIT	SG-027 ZIMMERMAN
L-ARM UNIT	SG-027 ZIMMERMAN
R-BACK UNIT	45-091 ORBT
L-BACK UNIT	45-091 ORBT
HEAD	DF-HD-08 TIAN QIANG
CORE	NACHTREIHER/40E
ARMS	EL-TA-10 FIRMEZA
LEGS	NACHTREIHER/42E
BOOSTER	BST-G1/P10
FCS	FCS-G2/P10SLT
GENERATOR	VP-20C
EXPANSION	PULSE ARMOR

STOP THE SECRET DATA BREACH

Memorizing the location of the hacking drones is crucial here, since time is by far the biggest contributing factor to your rank. Damage taken and enemies defeated are also strong considerations, but if you're fast enough, you can offset a lot of their impact.

Strategy

▌ Follow the same route through the drones as normal, starting with the first one at **Position A** and working your way around to **Position E**. ▶ A-B

▌ Ignore as many enemies as possible while moving between the drones, with the exception of the tetrapod MT on the way to **Position D**. Destroying this enemy is worthwhile, since it contributes a lot toward your rank, and you can defeat it fast enough to be worth it.

▌ Once you reach Iguazu, jump up and fire your SONGBIRDS down at him, to attempt to mitigate the effectiveness of his evasion. Follow up by using your shotguns as you land, and once they've reloaded you can repeat the process.

▌ If Iguazu is still alive when the GHOSTs show up, you can take advantage of the chaos to pick the GHOSTs off while they're attacking him, which will make finishing him off much easier. ▶ C

ASSEMBLY

You'll need all-out offense to defeat Iguazu and the GHOSTs in time, and this weapon loadout lets you accomplish that. It also provides plenty of defense, so you can afford to be a little reckless with your offense.

R-ARM UNIT	SG-027 ZIMMERMAN
L-ARM UNIT	SG-027 ZIMMERMAN
R-BACK UNIT	SONGBIRDS
L-BACK UNIT	SONGBIRDS
HEAD	VP-44D
CORE	DF-BD-08 TIAN-QIANG
ARMS	VP-46D
LEGS	LG-033M VERRILL
BOOSTER	BST-G2/P06SPD
FCS	FC-006 ABBOT
GENERATOR	DF-GN-08 SAN-TAI
EXPANSION	TERMINAL ARMOR

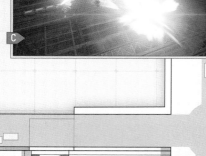

OCEAN CROSSING

This mission can be tough to S Rank, primarily due to the SEA SPIDER's huge AP pool and how much damage it can inflict. Both time and damage taken are the major contributing factors to your rank in this mission, so getting an S Rank essentially boils down to how safely and quickly you can defeat the boss.

Strategy

▌ You can take the usual route through the mission, dropping down into the interior of the Grid and traveling beneath the bridge to safely evade the lasers. The main difference here is that you'll need to Assault Boost as much as possible and ignore all of the enemies to get to the boss quickly.

▌ Destroy the drones when you reach the boss area; they do contribute a little toward your rank and the large group of them can be eliminated very quickly. Use the supply sherpa if you need it, and then investigate the crate to begin the fight with the SEA SPIDER. ▶ D

▌ While you're waiting for the SEA SPIDER to arrive, charge your diffuse laser cannons and direct them full force the instant the boss can be targeted. As with other bosses, aggressive play is called for and you'll need to throw everything at it—including Boost Kicks—to defeat it swiftly enough. Constantly fire while boosting around it to evade some of its attacks. If you time your attacks well and maximize the damage dealt during staggers, it's possible to defeat the SEA SPIDER before it can transition into its second phase. You can still get the S Rank if it does, you'll just need to boost up to it and hover nearby while continuing to fire on it. ▶ E

▌ After the SEA SPIDER has been eliminated, immediately head to the end of the area, where "Cinder" Carla wants you to evacuate, instead of waiting for the objective marker to show up. ▶ F

ASSEMBLY

The tetrapod legs' hover mode can help with both navigating the early portion of the mission safely and quickly, and for fighting the boss at the end, so they're strongly recommended. Since the boss is the only enemy you need to concern yourself with, maximum close-range damage is called for, which this loadout has in spades.

R-ARM UNIT	SG-027 ZIMMERMAN
L-ARM UNIT	SG-027 ZIMMERMAN
R-BACK UNIT	VP-60LCD
L-BACK UNIT	VP-60LCD
HEAD	VP-44D
CORE	DF-BD-08 TIAN-QIANG
ARMS	VP-46D
LEGS	LG-033M VERRILL
BOOSTER	BST-G2/P06SPD
FCS	FC-006 ABBOT
GENERATOR	VE-20C
EXPANSION	TERMINAL ARMOR

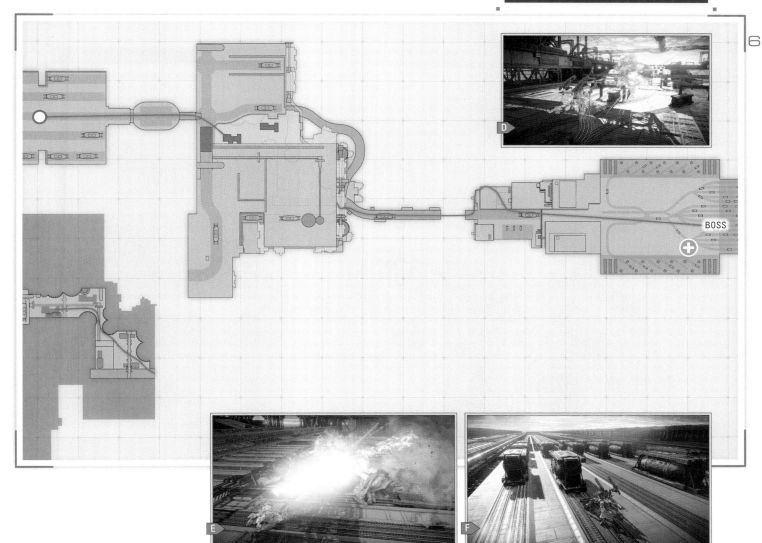

BOSS

STEAL THE SURVEY DATA

Clear time is your primary concern for this S Rank, and although defeating enemies does help, it's not worth going too far out of your way to destroy any that are optional.

Strategy

- For the initial part of the mission, you'll need to visit the data locations at **Positions A, B, C,** and **D** as quickly as possible, destroying any enemies along your path. Use the time spent accessing the data to destroy any nearby enemies before moving on.

- After leaving the final data location, head for **Position E**. Take a moment to destroy the two incoming transport helicopters as you leave, because doing so will contribute a decent amount toward your rank.

- Once you reach the final area, destroy all of the enemies quickly before the warship arrives. Make sure to focus on the tetrapod MT first, then boost up to the rooftop at **Position E**.

- When the LCs arrive, one will land on this roof, and you can destroy it instantly with your laser cannons. Next, jump up to the cliff behind you to destroy the one that lands there, before turning your attention to the sturdier enforcement officer spec variant.

- As soon as the warship arrives, Assault Boost toward it and destroy the command center to finish it off quickly, Finally, Assault Boost back and take cover to avoid taking damage from the drones.

ASSEMBLY

A combination of multi-lock missiles and hard-hitting weapons are required for this mission. This will allow you to quickly dispatch enemies while remaining mobile, and to deal with tougher enemies without running out of ammo.

R-ARM UNIT	HML-G2/P19MLT-04
L-ARM UNIT	HML-G2/P19MLT-04
R-BACK UNIT	VP-60LCD
L-BACK UNIT	VP-60LCD
HEAD	HD-033M VERILL
CORE	07-061 MIND ALPHA
ARMS	IA-C01A: EPHEMERA
LEGS	VP-424
BOOSTER	BST-G2/P06SPD
FCS	FC-008 TALBOT
GENERATOR	VE-20C
EXPANSION	PULSE ARMOR

PREVENT CORPORATE SALVAGE OF NEW TECH

Destroying the three mandatory PCA targets should be your sole focus in this mission, so ignore all other enemies and simply try to accomplish that goal as quickly as possible.

Strategy

- The HC at **Position A** should be your first target. If you boost along the narrow canyon ledge you can reach the area above it without having to deal with the other enemies. Once you can see it below you, simply drop down and start firing on it the instant you're within range. With the recommended loadout, it's possible to destroy it before it can even move.

- As soon as that target is down, head toward the small rooftop at **Position B**, by going up and over the cliffs. The two LCs will start advancing on you shortly after you get there, and if you stay behind the pillar on the rooftop, they'll get close enough for you to pop out and attack them. Target the support type first, since it's much easier to destroy, and then go for the senior officer spec—it has much higher AP and is more maneuverable, but shouldn't last long if you can stay near it. ▶ A-B

ASSEMBLY

This build is focused on eliminating the three mandatory enemies as swiftly and easily as possible, while also getting to each location without losing much time.

R-ARM UNIT	SG-027 ZIMMERMAN
L-ARM UNIT	SG-027 ZIMMERMAN
R-BACK UNIT	VP-60LCD
L-BACK UNIT	VP-60LCD
HEAD	HD-033M VERILL
CORE	07-061 MIND ALPHA
ARMS	IA-C01A: EPHEMERA
LEGS	VP-424
BOOSTER	BST-G2/P06SPD
FCS	FC-008 TALBOT
GENERATOR	VE-20C
EXPANSION	TERMINAL ARMOR

Steal the Survey Data

Prevent the Corporate Salvage of New Tech

ATTACK THE REFUELING BASE

The S Rank for this mission requires that you move quickly along a concise path while destroying enemies as you progress, along with most of the secondary objective fuel tanks. There are high-priority targets—such as the LCs and artillery—which, when you factor in the dual EKDROMOI at the end, makes AP management a strong factor in this mission. If you assemble your frame properly, it will mitigate a large amount of the incoming damage, but you'll need to have a clear idea of the enemies along the path and how best to handle the bosses at the end of the stage.

Strategy

▮ Head straight through the compound toward the LC at **Position A**, ignoring the fuel tanks, but destroying any bipedal MTs or artillery that you encounter along the way. Next, destroy the LC and Assault Boost down below the bridge. ▶ C

▮ Take out the quad drones as you cross the ravine, since they can prove too hazardous to ignore, and then destroy the sniper LC at **Position B**, before using the vertical catapult.

▮ Destroy the artillery at **Position C** and continue toward the fuel tanks at **Position D**. Unlike the previous tanks, be sure to destroy these ones and the ones in the area below. Next, you'll want to cross over the ice toward **Position E** and eliminate the LC there, so you can safely destroy the nearby fuel tanks. There's a final LC at **Position F** that you should destroy, along with any other enemies on your way to it. ▶ D

▮ Use the vertical catapults to get back up to the top of the cliffs again, destroying the quad drones as you go. Make use of the supply sherpa if you need it, and then head into the compound and destroy all of the MTs and artillery within it, before taking out the target.

▮ After the cutscene, use the building at **Position G** for cover and try to split up the EKDROMOI, because the PG will often stay further back, while the EP is more aggressive. Use a combination of missiles, Boost Kicks, and your diffuse laser cannons to quickly destroy the EP, before venturing out and applying the same tactics to the PG. ▶ E

ASSEMBLY

This is a heavier frame with good anti-energy and explosive defense, in consideration of how many enemies you'll encounter throughout the mission. You do not need to destroy every enemy, but having an AP cushion to absorb hits as you focus your fire on the important targets will assist you toward the S Rank. Dual MLT-04 missile launchers provide you with multi-lock and quick reload capabilities, making them a versatile option for dealing with enemies in a timely fashion. The dual VP-60LCD diffuse laser cannons are for when you need to inflict some big damage, or strain the ACS of priority targets.

R-ARM UNIT	HML-G2/P19MLT-04
L-ARM UNIT	HML-G2/P19MLT-04
R-BACK UNIT	VP-60LCD
L-BACK UNIT	VP-60LCD
HEAD	VE-44A
CORE	07-061 MIND ALPHA
ARMS	IA-C01A: EPHEMERA
LEGS	VP-424
BOOSTER	BST-G2/P06SPD
FCS	FC-008 TALBOT
GENERATOR	VE-20C
EXPANSION	TERMINAL ARMOR

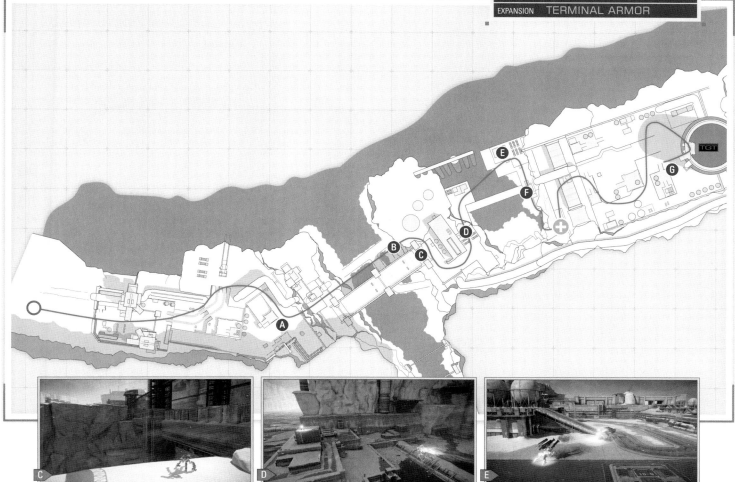

TUNNEL SABOTAGE

Speed is all that matters here, which makes it a relatively simple mission to S Rank. You don't need to destroy any enemies before reaching the target generator at the back of the tunnel, after which your only concern will be to return to the entrance as quickly as possible.

Strategy

- Immediately Assault Boost into the tunnel, and try to keep your boost active as you fall and move throughout the area. ▶ A

- Destroy any bipedal MTs in your path while maintaining as much forward momentum as possible, and make sure to destroy the quad drones at **Position A**, since they're especially dangerous to your light frame.

- The group of repair drones that drop down at **Position B** should also be destroyed before you head down to the generator. This will ensure that they don't inflict shock on you, which would result in a big hit to your AP.

- Destroy the generator and immediately turn around and use the vertical catapult. Use Assault Boosts, only pausing for EN recovery when you've gained some distance to the nearest groups of enemies. ▶ B

- Ignore the bipedal MTs and the LC in the final room, and simply escape through the mouth of the tunnel. The LC may land some of the missiles from its salvo, but if your momentum is adequate you should not take significant AP damage. ▶ C

Although you'll want to prioritize speed and mobility over defense for this mission, it's worth trying to get as much anti-energy spec as you can. Reverse-joint legs—especially the KASUAR/42Z—are helpful for Quick Boost and jump mobility. The recommended booster and generator facilitate extended Assault Boosts before and during the anomaly, when your EN output potential is even further augmented. The dual LUDLOWS are light and effective at clearing the path as you go, with the plasma missiles giving you a bit of additional offense if you need it. Finally, the shield can give you a bit of protection while you're getting your EN back between Assault Boosts.

R-ARM UNIT	MG-014 LUDLOW
L-ARM UNIT	MG-014 LUDLOW
R-BACK UNIT	Vvc-706PM
L-BACK UNIT	SI-24: SU-Q5
HEAD	DF-HD-08 TIAN-QIANG
CORE	IA-C01C: EPHEMERA
ARMS	NACHTREIHER/46E
LEGS	KASUAR/42Z
BOOSTER	BST-G2/P06SPD
FCS	IB-C03F: WLT 001
GENERATOR	VE-20B
EXPANSION	TERMINAL ARMOR

A

B

C

ELIMINATE V. VII

The toughest part of this mission is not being detected. If you follow this simple route fast enough, you'll only have to destroy six bipedal MTs and Swinburne at the end to get the S Rank.

Strategy

▌ Immediately after beginning the mission, turn to the right and jump up to **Position A**. Boost along the top of the wall, destroying the two bipedal MTs with your missiles as you go. ▶ D

▌ Once you're directly below the Wall, jump to the upper ledge and boost along it. There are two bipedal MTs on this ledge, and when you destroy the first, the second will turn to investigate. The trick to getting past them is to get close to the second very quickly, and fire your missiles at it before the first has finished blowing up.

▌ After jumping out and around the central break in the Wall, you'll need to take out another two bipedal MTs in the same manner as the previous two. ▶ E

▌ Assault Boost down to the objective marker once it's directly below you, and—once the objective has updated—head toward Swinburne at **Position B**. Rather than using the vertical catapult to get over the lower section of the Wall, simply Assault Boost up and over it to save time.

▌ Assault Boost straight at Swinburne and start the fight with a Boost Kick, then unload with all of your weapons. If you hit him cleanly with everything, you can defeat him before the end of the dialog. ▶ F

ASSEMBLY

Defensively, you should focus primarily on anti-explosive, with anti-energy as a secondary priority. However, the recommended frame is built for speed and jumping, rather than defensive capabilities. Sustained EN output for both Quick Boosts and Assault Boosts is valuable in this mission, because you'll be moving quickly along straight paths, and your booster and generator should reflect this. It is crucial to have a long-range option, and the MLT-04 missile launcher is a good choice, with three high-impact and high-damage weapons to quickly overload Swinburne's ACS and destroy his AC.

R-ARM UNIT	SG-027 ZIMMERMAN
L-ARM UNIT	HM-G2/P19MLT-04
R-BACK UNIT	VP-60LCD
L-BACK UNIT	VP-60LCD
HEAD	DF-HD-08 TIAN-QIANG
CORE	IA-C01C: EPHEMERA
ARMS	NACHTREIHER/46E
LEGS	06-042 MIND BETA
BOOSTER	BST-G2/P06SPD
FCS	VE-21B
GENERATOR	VE-20C
EXPANSION	TERMINAL ARMOR

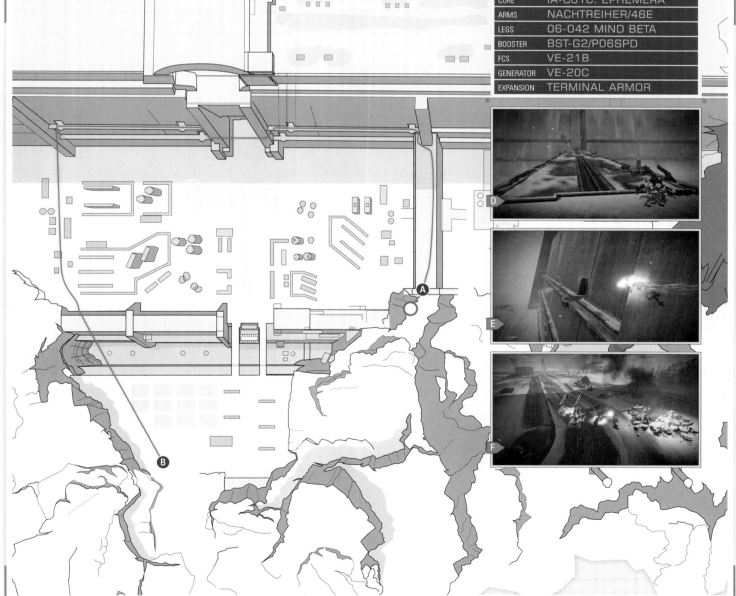

SURVEY THE UNINHABITED FLOATING CITY

Your priority in this mission is a fast completion time. The mandatory encounters with the GHOSTs, LCs and HC HELICOPTER—in conjunction with a handful of other enemies—will be enough to secure the S Rank. Given the presence of the EM fog, familiarizing yourself with the location of the control devices and downed drone is necessary, to ensure you can move between them fast enough.

Strategy

▮ From the starting point, Assault Boost straight ahead until you reach the area boundary, and then follow it along until you're parallel with the first control device at **Position A**, before veering toward it. Taking this route should let you bypass all of the initial drones, so you can safely access the device.

▮ Start heading toward the next device at **Position B**. Along the way, fire your bazooka at the KITE on the roof of the building, and then at the one near the dome to take them out before they become a problem.

▮ Take a wide, flanking route from there, toward the downed drone at **Position C**, so that you don't have to engage the other KITEs.

▮ As soon as you finish accessing the drone, boost upward and hover high above the ground to evade the ambushing GHOSTs. From this vantage point, you should be safe from their attacks and can destroy them quickly. If you lose track of them, remember to use a scan to reveal their locations. ▶ A

▮ To initiate the final encounter, Assault Boost straight to the final device at **Position D**. The LCs on the rooftops should be your first targets, and you should try to take them out from as far away as possible, so they don't reposition. Next, turn your attention to the HC HELICOPTER, and try to stay beneath it and as close as you can, so that you can attack without worrying about its missiles; with the arsenal you're carrying, you should bring it down fairly quickly. ▶ B

ASSEMBLY

Mobility is important here, since the mission involves using Assault Boosts over long stretches, and quickly gaining altitude.

While the tetrapod legs do not excel at gaining altitude, they'll be useful in some of the encounters, and the BC-0200 GRIDWALKER booster can help provide a bit of extra upward thrust. By utilizing this selection of explosive and energy weapons, your munitions should cover the mission's combat requirements.

R-ARM UNIT	HML-G2/P19MLT-04
L-ARM UNIT	MAJESTIC
R-BACK UNIT	FASAN/60E
L-BACK UNIT	FASAN/60E
HEAD	VE-44A
CORE	IB-C03C: HAL 826
ARMS	IA-C01A: EPHEMERA
LEGS	VP-424
BOOSTER	BC-0200 GRIDWALKER
FCS	VE-21B
GENERATOR	VE-20C
EXPANSION	TERMINAL ARMOR

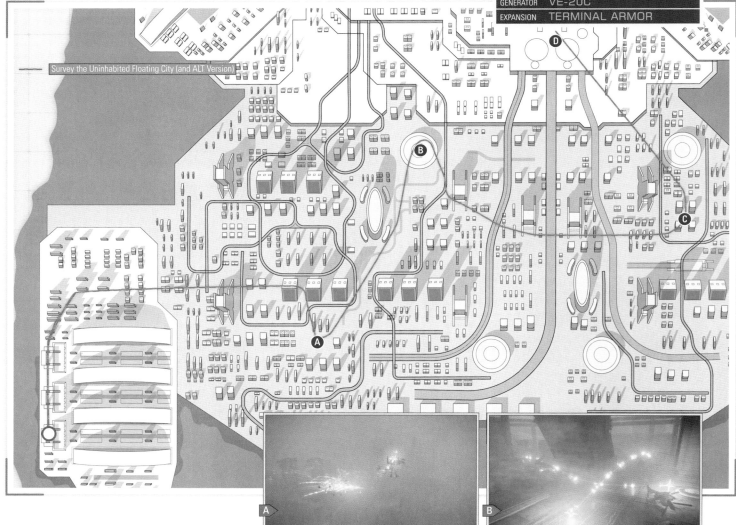

Survey the Uninhabited Floating City (and ALT Version)

CH03 [12-E]
SURVEY THE UNINHABITED FLOATING CITY (ALT)

This mission closely resembles the standard version, but instead of fighting the AH12: HC HELICOPTER and squad of LCs, you'll battle AC ASTGHIK, piloted by Thumb Dolmayan. The same overall strategy can be followed, including the prioritization of clear time.

Strategy

▌ After accessing the final control device, head down the central bridge straight away, so that you can begin the fight with Dolmayan as soon as possible.

▌ Defeating Dolmayan quickly is the key to success here; the damage you take is less important, so trading blows with him is not likely to cost you the S Rank. It's advisable to aggressively chase him when he hides behind the surrounding buildings, and to make constant use of Boost Kicks to interrupt his movement. He can heal up to three times, but your powerful energy weaponry should make quick enough work of him.

ASSEMBLY

There are a few key differences here, compared to the standard version of the mission. The booster, FCS and a more close-range focused selection of weapons have been chosen to hasten the fight with AC ASTGHIK.

R-ARM UNIT	HML-G2/P19MLT-04
L-ARM UNIT	SG-027 ZIMMERMAN
R-BACK UNIT	VP-60LCD
L-BACK UNIT	VP-60LCD
HEAD	VE-44A
CORE	07-061 MIND ALPHA
ARMS	IA-C01A: EPHEMERA
LEGS	VP-424
BOOSTER	BST-G2/P06SPD
FCS	FC-008 TALBOT
GENERATOR	VE-20C
EXPANSION	TERMINAL ARMOR

CH03 [12-C]
ELIMINATE THE ENFORCEMENT SQUADS

Speed and damage taken are the two key factors in this mission. Since you'll be facing some very evasive and powerful enemies, the best course of action is to destroy them before they become a problem.

Strategy

▌ Ignore Ring Freddie in the distance and carefully destroy the seven bipedal MTs directly in front of you; your multi-lock missiles can easily destroy two at a time.

ASSEMBLY

Maneuverability and speed are less of a factor in this mission, so opting for a heavier build with plenty of anti-energy and explosive spec is recommended. The use of tetrapod legs gives you decent aerial mobility, which can help against the bipedal MTs and HC at the end. The single HML-G2/P19MLT-04 comes in very handy for quickly dispatching the bipedal MTs. When it comes to dealing with the LCs and HC as quickly as possible, dual MORLEYs are hard to beat—as long as you remain close enough that their spread doesn't become a factor.

R-ARM UNIT	HML-G2/P19MLT-04
L-ARM UNIT	SG-027 ZIMMERMAN
R-BACK UNIT	SB-033M MORLEY
L-BACK UNIT	SB-033M MORLEY
HEAD	VE-44A
CORE	07-061 MIND ALPHA
ARMS	IA-C01A: EPHEMERA
LEGS	VP-424
BOOSTER	ALULA/21E
FCS	FC-008 TALBOT
GENERATOR	VE-20C
EXPANSION	TERMINAL ARMOR

▌ Remain in hover mode to have the clearest line-of-sight and make it easy to evade the rockets being fired at you.

▌ When you reach the LCs at **Position A**, focus on one at a time. Boost Kick into it, then unload all of your weapons; a few clean hits are more than enough to destroy it. Do the same thing to the second one, and then enter the Wall.

▌ Scan the room as you access the door at **Position B**, so you know the location of the ambushing enemies on the other side. Destroy the initial pair that are right in front of the door, and then Assault Boost to the opposite end of the room and turn around, so that you have an easier time targeting the remaining enemies.

▌ When you enter the final room, quickly use your missiles to destroy the two bipedal MTs that approach you. Next, boost over toward **Position C** and finish off the third one as quickly as possible.

▌ The recommended flow of combat against the HC is to Assault Boost immediately for a Boost Kick, then simply attack as aggressively as possible while trying to remain close. Boost Kick often and ensure that your MORLEYs are ready to fire as soon as you stagger it, so you can deal the maximum possible direct damage. You will likely need to overload its ACS at least twice.

6

HEAVY MISSILE LAUNCH SUPPORT

Your only real concern is ensuring the missiles take as little damage as possible. The easiest way to do that is to familiarize yourself with both the arrival locations and enemies that appear in each wave, so that you're always in the best place to destroy them instantly

Strategy

▌ The enemies in this mission are primarily focused on damaging the missiles, which means that you can move around the area without fear of taking damage. Your goal should be to get to where a group of enemies appears as quickly as possible by using Assault Boosts, and then using multi-lock to target and destroy the entire group in one salvo. The last thing you want to do is be chasing stragglers. ▶ A

▌ The TOYBOX MTs in waves four and five present the biggest threat, since they can inflict huge amounts of damage to the missiles very quickly. They all appear around **Position A**, so wait there for them, and try to preemptively fire your missiles so they connect the instant the TOYBOX MTs break out of their containers.

▌ Before the warship arrives in the final wave, move to **Position B** up on the rooftops, so that you can easily Assault Boost above it. Land on it, then destroy the command center before it can hit the missiles with its lasers. ▶ B

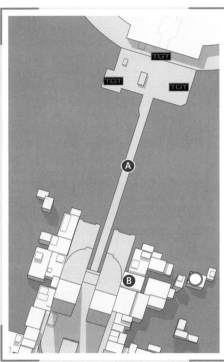

SPECIAL OBJECTIVE

Defend the Missiles

To be eligible for the S Rank, you'll need to ensure the missiles retain most of their AP

ASSEMBLY

By going with a full suite of missile launchers, you can easily target and destroy entire groups of enemies from range, and a lightweight frame is essential for moving between those groups as quickly as possible.

R-ARM UNIT	HML-G2/P19MLT-04
L-ARM UNIT	HML-G2/P19MLT-04
R-BACK UNIT	Vvc-706PM
L-BACK UNIT	Vvc-706PM
HEAD	DF-HD-08 TIAN QIANG
CORE	NACHTREIHER/40E
ARMS	EL-TA-10 FIRMEZA
LEGS	06-042 MIND BETA
BOOSTER	BST-G2/P06SPD
FCS	FCS-G2/P10SLT
GENERATOR	VE-20C
EXPANSION	PULSE ARMOR

DESTROY THE SPECIAL FORCES CRAFT

Your only concern in this mission is destroying the CATAPHRACT. Prioritizing speed above the preservation of your AP is the key to getting an S Rank here.

Strategy

▌ The CATAPHRACT always appears from the same location, and charges directly at you while firing its gatling turrets. If you can get into position quickly, you can fire on it as it moves past you.

▌ Look for openings, such it remaining stationary after using its energy shotgun, to launch your offense. Take every such chance to strike, even if that means getting partially hit by its attacks; as long as the CATAPHRACT doesn't overload your ACS, this strategy will prove effective.

▌ Your bazooka shots can be worthwhile even if they don't directly impact the MT itself—their explosions will build up ACS strain if they reach the CATAPHRACT's exposed body. This means firing down at it from above, or firing at its base, can be effective if those are the only openings you have. ▶ C

▌ Be aggressive in pursuing the boss; if you can fully capitalize after staggering it, you should only need to overload its ACS two or three times. You can achieve this very quickly if you time your attacks well, and can remain in front of it. ▶ D

ASSEMBLY

The CATAPHRACT's energy attacks are its most dangerous. If you have enough defense to effectively withstand its energy shotgun attack, then the fight will be much easier. The SPRING CHICKEN legs are selected for their evasive advantages here, while the dual LITTLE GEM bazookas can quickly overload the boss's ACS, and the dual VP-60LCD diffuse laser cannons will deal fast, direct damage.

R-ARM UNIT	LITTLE GEM
L-ARM UNIT	LITTLE GEM
R-BACK UNIT	VP-60LCD
L-BACK UNIT	VP-60LCD
HEAD	HC-2000/BC SHADE EYE
CORE	IB-C03C: HAL 826
ARMS	IA-C01A: EPHEMERA
LEGS	RC-2000 SPRING CHICKEN
BOOSTER	ALULA/21E
FCS	IB-C03F: WLT 001
GENERATOR	VE-20C
EXPANSION	TERMINAL ARMOR

ATTACK THE OLD SPACEPORT

Speed is once again the primary concern for your rank in this mission. Though destroying enemies does help your rank—particularly so in the case of the LCs—you can ignore most of them if you're fast enough.

Strategy

▍ Begin by skirting the edge of the area, bypassing the group of enemies below you unscathed, and then cross over the bridge. Next, Assault Boost up to the warship at **Position A** and destroy it.

▍ Quickly move below the main spaceport building, so you can drop down and destroy the next warship at **Position B**. From there, head up the rear ramp and take out the final three warships at **Position C**. ▶ E

▍ Spend some time destroying the bipedal MTs in this area, because you'll want to use the supply sherpa when it becomes available. After resupplying, use the vertical catapult at **Position D** to reach the top of the spaceport, where you can engage the LCs as each one arrives. Your weapons will make short work of these sniper variants at close range. ▶ F

▍ Wait on top of the spaceport until the two warships get close enough, then Assault Boost toward them and destroy them. ▶ G

▍ When fighting the PCA officers near **Position E**, focus your attention on the captain first and let Rusty take the attention of the lieutenant. Fight these two officers aggressively and do not concern yourself taking damage—ending the battle quickly is far more important. A combination of Boost Kicks and your heavier munitions will stagger these foes. As soon as both of them are down, Boost up to the cliff where you began the mission. Wait here to avoid taking damage from the Ice Worm until the mission ends.

ASSEMBLY

Due to the expansiveness of the combat zone in this mission, utilizing a build that's focused on speed and mobility rather than survivability is all but a requirement for finishing quickly enough. Thankfully, since you'll only likely be attacking a limited number of solo enemies, focusing your weapons on single-target damage can help get through the mission's encounters swiftly.

R-ARM UNIT	SG-027 ZIMMERMAN
L-ARM UNIT	SG-027 ZIMMERMAN
R-BACK UNIT	VP-60LCD
L-BACK UNIT	VP-60LCD
HEAD	DF-HD-08 TIAN-QIANG
CORE	IA-C01C: EPHEMERA
ARMS	NACHTREIHER/46E
LEGS	06-042 MIND BETA
BOOSTER	BST-G2/P06SPD
FCS	FC-008 TALBOT
GENERATOR	VE-20C
EXPANSION	TERMINAL ARMOR

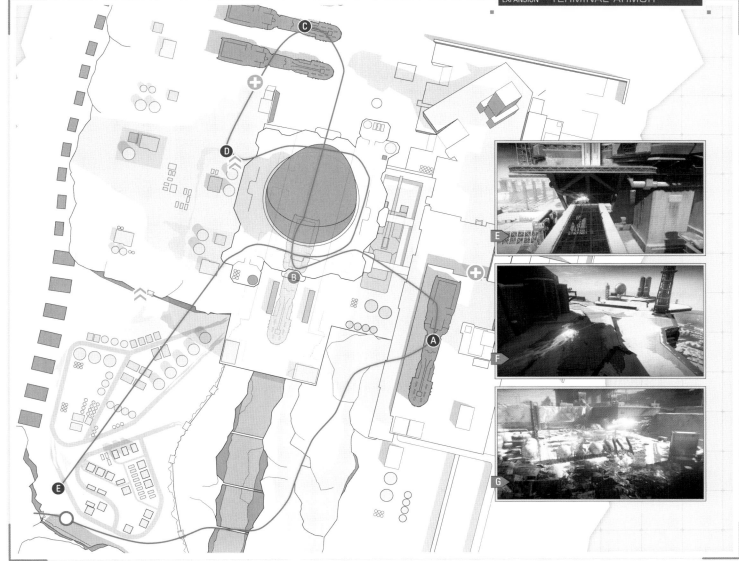

DEFEND THE OLD SPACEPORT

Your only objective in this mission is to defeat AC NIGHTFALL. This means the only important factor for the S Rank is to defeat him quickly, which a powerful assembly can easily accomplish.

Strategy

▌ Clear time is the most crucial ranking factor here, so Assault Boost your way to the objective marker immediately to trigger the cutscene.

▌ As soon as the cutscene is over, Assault Boost toward NIGHTFALL and attempt a Boost Kick. Alternate using Boost Kicks and your shotguns to strain NIGHTFALL's ACS, and then follow up with your diffuse laser cannons after its ACS has been overloaded.

▌ AC NIGHTFALL will use assault armor more than once throughout the fight—along with multiple repair kits—but if you keep up an aggressive assault, you'll end the fight quickly. Just keep in mind that damage taken is a limited factor compared to your completion time.

ASSEMBLY

The recommended build is designed for high attitude stability and anti-explosive defense, without sacrificing much maneuverability. Your goal is to trade blows with Raven and simply out-damage him. With that in mind, the choice of weaponry should reflect a very close-range encounter.

R-ARM UNIT	SG-027 ZIMMERMAN
L-ARM UNIT	SG-027 ZIMMERMAN
R-BACK UNIT	VP-60LCD
L-BACK UNIT	VP-60LCD
HEAD	AH-J-124 BASHO
CORE	07-061 MIND ALPHA
ARMS	NACHTREIHER/46E
LEGS	VP-424
BOOSTER	BST-G2/P06SPD
FCS	FC-008 TALBOT
GENERATOR	VE-20C
EXPANSION	TERMINAL ARMOR

ELIMINATE "HONEST" BRUTE

Finishing the mission quickly is once again your highest priority here. The open nature of the environment will help you—some creative boosting allows you to traverse nearly the entire area in safety.

Strategy

▌ The quickest way through this area is to bypass most of the suspended platforms entirely. Assault Boost as high as possible until you run out of EN, then use your boosters while falling until your EN regenerates and you can Assault Boost again. ▶ A

▌ From the starting point, you can reach the large central platform at **Position A** within a couple of Assault Boosts, providing you start off high enough. With a good angle you can land on the upper section of this platform, so you won't have to worry about any of the enemies below you. After briefly touching down, you can then use another couple of Assault Boosts to reach the platform at **Position B**, where you can head inside. ▶ B

▌ Try to avoid the targeting lasers in the interior section as you drop down. If you do pass through one, as long as you Assault Boost out of the room quickly enough once you reach the bottom, you can escape before the enemies attack.

▌ When you enter the room with "Honest" Brute, instead of heading along the crane and intercepting his ambush, head around the side of the room to get the drop on him with an opening blast from all of your weapons. Constantly pressure him after that with a combination of Boost Kicks and shotguns, then unleash your diffuse laser cannons once you stagger him—this should make short work of the fight.

ASSEMBLY

You'll be avoiding every enemy in the mission other than "Honest" Brute. This means you'll want to tailor your defensive specs for that fight, which requires anti-explosive defense. He tends to stay above you and will move around a lot, so reverse-joint legs can help you to keep up with him, as well as evading his flamethrower. As is often the case when chasing S Ranks, a strong close-range loadout will be required to end the fight as quickly as possible.

R-ARM UNIT	SG-027 ZIMMERMAN
L-ARM UNIT	SG-027 ZIMMERMAN
R-BACK UNIT	VP-60LCD
L-BACK UNIT	VP-60LCD
HEAD	DF-HD-08 TIAN-QIANG
CORE	IA-C01C: EPHEMERA
ARMS	NACHTREIHER/46E
LEGS	06-042 MIND BETA
BOOSTER	BST-G2/P06SPD
FCS	FC-008 TALBOT
GENERATOR	VE-20C
EXPANSION	TERMINAL ARMOR

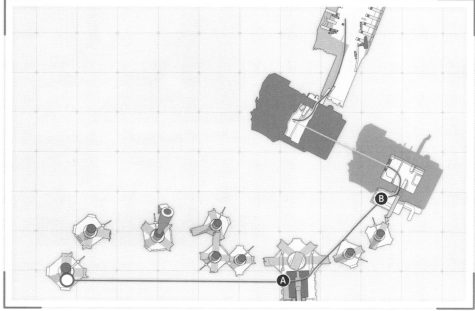

CORAL EXPORT DENIAL

Clear time and damage taken are both crucial in this mission. Unless you're waiting for helicopters or moving between locations, you can largely ignore the bipedal MTs. This leaves the helicopters as the greatest threat to you; their volatile Coral cargo creates large explosions when destroyed, and if you're anywhere in the vicinity, they can inflict a lot of damage.

Strategy

▐ The helicopters transporting Coral will not wait for you—you'll need to quickly plot a course through the locations they take off from. The helicopters at **Positions A** and **B** should be your first destinations, before crossing the area to **Position C**, where you'll see a large number of helicopters taking off. You'll need to hit the helicopters taking off from **Positions D** and **E** almost immediately afterward, so you might want to use multi-lock to speed things up .

▐ After destroying all of the helicopters fleeing within the compound, large numbers of them will start attempting to leave the area along the ravine. Make your way up to the large bridge, and then out to the narrow bridge at **Position F**—this is where you'll make your stand. Some of the nearby bipedal MTs will have direct line of fire on you, so try to destroy them before the helicopters show up. From your position on the bridge, you can target the helicopters that fly low along the ravine as well as those that attempt to take a high route. The reverse-joint legs let you elevate enough to target them without having to use the vertical catapults, and if you drop off the bridge, getting back up again is easy. ▶ C

▐ For the final part of the mission, you'll want to stay on or near the bridge at **Position F**. This will help you to destroy the helicopters that are above and below you. It also allows you to remain at high altitude without having to rely on the vertical catapults that are close to the helicopters' evacuation points. ▶ D

▐ Despite Kate Markson handling up to four of the transport helicopters herself, a single ship leaving the combat zone will eliminate the possibility of an S Rank. Though damage taken and clear time are a concern, make sure that your primary objective is to eliminate all transport helicopters.

SPECIAL OBJECTIVE

Destroy all Transport Helicopters Exporting the Coral

To be eligible for the S Rank in this mission, you'll need to ensure that every transport helicopter has been destroyed, avoiding Kate Markson having to clean up the remains. If you see one escape, you'll need to restart the mission.

ASSEMBLY

Using missiles to destroy the helicopters enables you to fire from further away, which can make a real difference here. A single salvo from an MLT-04 can destroy a helicopter, and this loadout lets you easily target individual helicopters, or multiple at once if needed. Occasionally you'll need to reach great heights to target them, and for that reason, reverse-joint legs are all but essential.

R-ARM UNIT	HML-G2/P19MLT-04
L-ARM UNIT	HML-G2/P19MLT-04
R-BACK UNIT	BML-G2/P05MLT-10
L-BACK UNIT	BML-G2/P05MLT-10
HEAD	VE-44B
CORE	EL-TC-10 FIRMEZA
ARMS	EL-TA-10 FIRMEZA
LEGS	06-042 MIND BETA
BOOSTER	BC-0200 GRIDWALKER
FCS	FCS-G2/P10SLT
GENERATOR	DF-GN-08 SAN-TAI
EXPANSION	PULSE ARMOR

DEFEND THE DAM COMPLEX

Clear time has the biggest impact on your rank once again. The time limit is extreme here, however; as long as you defeat the ACs quickly enough, you can use all of your repair kits in the process.

Strategy

▮ Your first target should be King in AC ASTER CROWN, initially located on a ridge fighting your allies at **Position A**. You'll need to cover a large distance to reach him, so pay attention to the environment while using Assault Boosts. Try to plan where you want to touch down to recharge EN, rather than letting it run out entirely.

▮ ASTER CROWN's shield can absorb a lot of damage, but if you make effective use of Boost Kicks and your shotguns, you can get through it fairly quickly. King will often attempt to hover above you, so try to match his altitude, attack aggressively, and aim to finish the fight before Chartreuse can join. ▶ A

▮ Chartreuse in UMBER OX starts at **Position B**. As soon as you engage ASTER CROWN, she'll head to its aid, so where you end up fighting her will depend on how quickly you deal with King. UMBER OX has high defense and some dangerous weaponry, and—while it lacks ASTER CROWN's shield—it's far more mobile and will attempt to stay airborne. Use Boost Kicks to chase it while evading incoming attacks, however, and your weaponry can make short work of it. ▶ B

▮ AC NIGHTFALL will eventually enter the area from **Position C**. As soon as you've dealt with ASTER CROWN AND UMBER OX, you should begin moving to intercept it, regardless of whether or not the cutscene has played out.

▮ NIGHTFALL is identical to the version you battled in the "Defend the Old Spaceport" mission (P.198), though he has one less repair kit available here. Using the same tactics as employed against the other ACs in this mission, you should be able to make short work of it.

ASSEMBLY

Each of the three ACs you'll fight here have different builds with different weaponry, so a well-rounded defensive build is appropriate. Your goal should be to limit the fights to one AC at a time. This lets you trade blows and withstand their attacks, while you out-damage them, and is the key to getting through the mission quickly.

R-ARM UNIT	SG-027 ZIMMERMAN
L-ARM UNIT	SG-027 ZIMMERMAN
R-BACK UNIT	VP-60LCD
L-BACK UNIT	VP-60LCD
HEAD	AH-J-124 BASHO
CORE	07-061 MIND ALPHA
ARMS	NACHTREIHER/46E
LEGS	VP-424
BOOSTER	BST-G2/P06SPD
FCS	FC-008 TALBOT
GENERATOR	VE-20C
EXPANSION	TERMINAL ARMOR

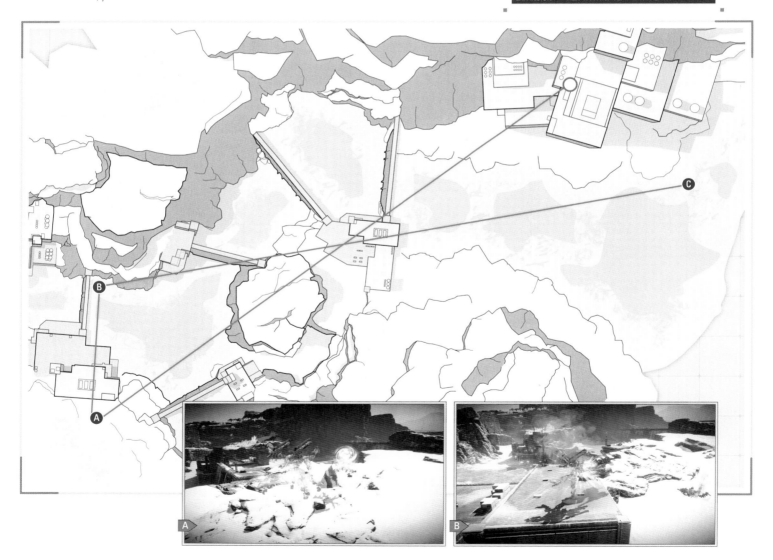

HISTORIC DATA RECOVERY

You can safely ignore most enemies in this mission. There's also no need to access any of the optional logs, because all that matters is accessing the three mandatory ones as quickly as possible to get the S Rank.

Strategy

▌ Boost straight into the tunnel, then Assault Boost over the enemies in the first room and move as quickly as possible toward the first log at **Position A**. When you reach the room preceding the log, use your missiles to thin out some of the enemies as you boost over them, to make your exit a bit smoother.

▌ When you're heading toward **Position B** for the second log, make sure to keep your speed up after crossing the bridge so that you can get past the drone ambush cleanly.

▌ After dropping down the ledges near the second log, Assault Boost and you can make it all the way to the final log very quickly. Just as with the first log, it's worth using your missiles to destroy the enemies in that room as you boost over them, since they do contribute to your rank and will help offset any shortcomings in your completion time. ▶ C

ASSEMBLY

A lightweight and highly mobile build is in order for this mission, since combat encounters are few and far between. You may want to clear out a few enemies near the data logs, and a full complement of missile launchers will let you dispatch them all quickly while you keep moving.

R-ARM UNIT	HML-G2/P19MLT-04
L-ARM UNIT	HML-G2/P19MLT-04
R-BACK UNIT	Vvc-703PM
L-BACK UNIT	Vvc-703PM
HEAD	DF-HD-08 TIAN-QIANG
CORE	NACHTREIHER/40E
ARMS	EL-TA-10 FIRMEZA
LEGS	06-042 MIND BETA
BOOSTER	BST-G2/P06SPD
FCS	FCS-G2/P10SLT
GENERATOR	VE-20C
EXPANSION	PULSE ARMOR

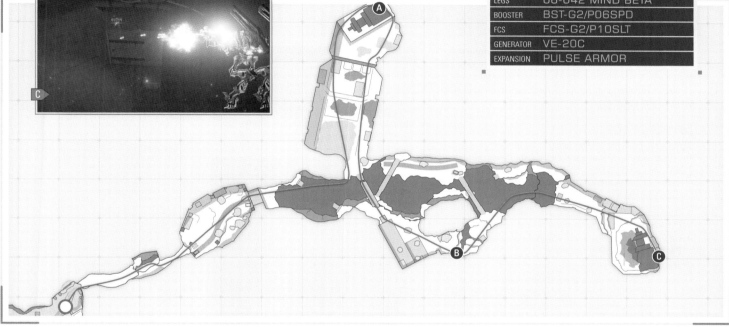

DESTROY THE ICE WORM

Damage taken will have the largest impact on your rank here, making it one of the more challenging missions to S Rank. While your focus should be on avoiding taking damage, you must take clean shots during the first two phases to allow for the difficulty in hitting the required shots in Phase 3.

Strategy

▌ Upon starting the mission, move ahead with your allies until after Iguazu says "Who does that creep think he is?," at which point the ICE WORM will be in position for you to fire your first stun needle shot. Be careful not to miss this chance, otherwise you'll effectively void the S Rank attempt.

ASSEMBLY

The ICE WORM utilizes Coral-based damage against which there is no specific defense. A set of legs like the SPRING CHICKEN will make using Quick Boosts to get away from both the body of the worm and its attacks much easier. Increasing your anti-energy spec is still worthwhile, since it will be beneficial against the drones in phase 2 of the fight. The use of two VE-60SNA stun needle launchers won't instantly bring the Ice Worm's shield down in phase 3, but by staggering your shots with two of them you'll give yourself a second chance of landing a shot if the first misses. Given how chaotic the final phase can be, using pulse armor to defend against either missiles or torpedoes could save a crucial amount of AP.

R-ARM UNIT	SG-027 ZIMMERMAN
L-ARM UNIT	SG-027 ZIMMERMAN
R-BACK UNIT	VE-60SNA
L-BACK UNIT	VE-60SNA
HEAD	AH-J-124 BASHO
CORE	07-061 MIND ALPHA
ARMS	NACHTREIHER/46E
LEGS	RC-2000 SPRING CHICKEN
BOOSTER	BST-G2/P06SPD
FCS	IB-C03F: WLT 001
GENERATOR	VE-20C
EXPANSION	PULSE ARMOR

- After Rusty brings it down, quickly boost up to the Ice Worm's head, so you can deal enough damage to initiate the next phase of the fight.

- The Ice Worm will release drones at the start of the second phase, and while your allies will start picking them off, you should help destroy them to avoid taking any unnecessary damage. When Rusty says "Sure is an honor to be praised by the Redguns' 'Hell on Four Legs'... but I'll pass," the Ice Worm will rear up and be in position for your shot. ▶ A

- After bringing it down and dealing sufficient damage, you'll enter the final phase of the fight, which is the most critical part of the mission. Not only does the Ice Worm move around a lot faster, but it also releases missiles and torpedoes

that you'll need to evade. Since you need to bring it down twice in this phase, missing even a single opportunity to hit it with a stun needle can cost you the time required for an S Rank. ▶ B

- You'll need to deal more damage to the Ice Worm once Rusty brings it down for the final time in this phase. Try to reach its head as quickly as possible, and fire at it until you're victorious.

CH04 [16] UNDERGROUND EXPLORATION – DEPTH 1

If you're out of position even briefly time at the wrong moment, the NEPENTHES is capable of inflicting huge amounts of damage. Since both damage taken and clear time are important requirements for this S Rank, one misstep is all it takes to end an attempt.

Strategy

- Since time is of the essence, drop off the elevator as soon as you active it, so that you can descend faster. Using the long walkways extending out from the edge of the area for cover is the safest and fastest way of descending, so keep your shield up and try to keep one of them below you as much as possible.

- Once the partition closes, you'll have to take out the four DENOISERS as usual. Hover above them and pick them off as quickly as possible, so you can access the partition controls at **Position A** and resume descending.

- When the partition opens, continue your descent as before, using your shield as much as possible for an extra layer of protection. When you get closer to the bottom, activate your pulse armor if you've taken a few hits and notice your ACS is about to overload, since it can protect you from additional hits before breaking. ▶ C

- Once you have reached the bottom, maneuver yourself close to the neck of the NEPENTHES and destroy it as quickly as possible. ▶ D

ASSEMBLY

This build's high attitude stability will allow you to take a few hits from NEPENTHES without getting staggered, possibly providing enough time to get behind cover. A shield is highly recommended to further protect you during the descent, while the rest of your weapons should be geared toward eliminating the mandatory enemies quickly.

R-ARM UNIT	SG-027 ZIMMERMAN
L-ARM UNIT	SG-027 ZIMMERMAN
R-BACK UNIT	SONGBIRDS
L-BACK UNIT	VE-61PSA
HEAD	20-082 MIND BETA
CORE	CS-5000 MAIN DISH
ARMS	VP-46S
LEGS	LG-033M VERRILL
BOOSTER	BST-G2/P06SPD
FCS	FC-008 TALBOT
GENERATOR	VP-20D
EXPANSION	PULSE ARMOR

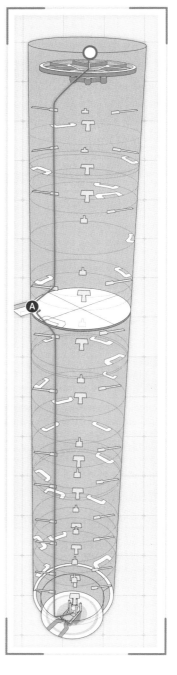

UNDERGROUND EXPLORATION – DEPTH 2 (& ALT VERSION)

For both of these missions, number of enemies defeated has the biggest impact on your ranking, and can easily offset a slow clear time. The standard and Alt versions of the mission are almost identical, with the only difference being that in the Alt version you'll fight Coldcall in AC DEADSLED, instead of Iguazu in AC HEAD BRINGER.

Strategy

▌ All of the enemies you need to destroy for the S Rank are encountered along the main path, so take out everything you see on your way to **Position A**. Once there, you'll face either Iguazu or Coldcall—depending on which version of the mission you're playing—but the tactics remain the same for either: use a combination of Boost Kicks and your shotguns to stagger them, then unload your diffuse laser cannons to deal extreme damage.

▌ Once the enemy AC is down, start heading toward **Position B**, where the ENFORCER destroys the enemies on the bridge. Stay above it once it relocates, and activate your pulse armor if you need to, so that you can keep advancing on it until it relocates again.

▌ When you enter the room near **Position C** to activate the generator, use your scanner to highlight all of the dormant MTs hanging from the ceiling. Destroy each of them individually with a blast from both shotguns before turning on the power. This lets you take them all out safely before they activate, and they still contribute toward your rank . ▶ E

▌ The same approach that you used against the enemy AC is applicable against the ENFORCER at **Position D**. Constant pressure with Boost Kicks and your shotguns can strain its ACS very quickly, and the faster you can stagger it the less you'll have to worry about its attacks. Even if you end up taking a decent amount of damage in the process, between the enemies you destroyed along the way and the boss, it's difficult to lose your S Rank. ▶ F

ASSEMBLY

Speed isn't as much of a factor in this mission, so a heavier build with close-range weaponry is best. This lets you go toe-to-toe with the boss and enemy AC and quickly come out on top.

R-ARM UNIT	SG-027 ZIMMERMAN
L-ARM UNIT	SG-027 ZIMMERMAN
R-BACK UNIT	VP-60LCD
L-BACK UNIT	VP-60LCD
HEAD	20-082 MIND BETA
CORE	CC-3000 WRECKER
ARMS	VP-46S
LEGS	LG-033M VERRILL
BOOSTER	BST-G2/P06SPD
FCS	FC-006 ABBOT
GENERATOR	VP-20D
EXPANSION	TERMINAL ARMOR

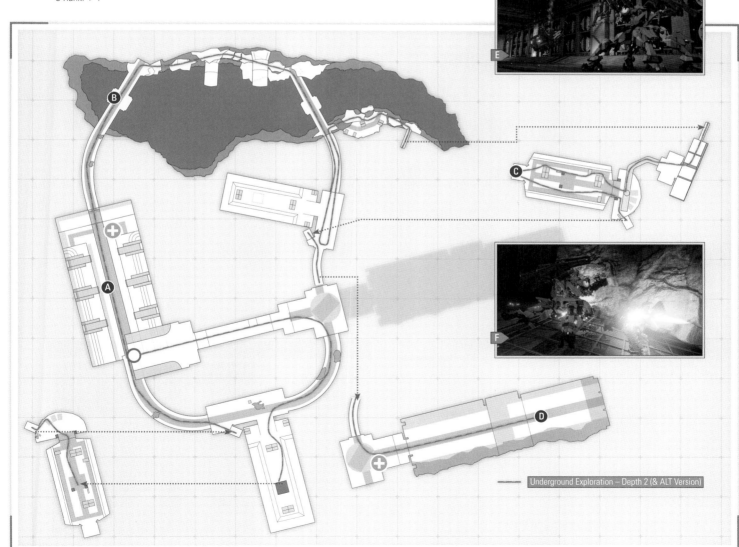

Underground Exploration – Depth 2 (& ALT Version)

UNDERGROUND EXPLORATION – DEPTH 3

Attaining an S Rank here depends on a combination of a quick clear time and a decent number of enemies being destroyed. It's worth going out of your way for a few extra enemies, as doing so can make the time requirements a little easier to meet.

Strategy

▌ As fast as you can, head straight toward **Position A**, ignoring all of the enemies along the way. Next, activate your pulse armor and Assault Boost down to the lower level of the ring around the facility, so you're below the artillery.

▌ While not strictly necessary to achieve an S Rank, taking a bit of time to destroy all of the artillery installations—along with any DENOISERs that are close to them—contributes so much toward your rank that it will offset any time lost in the fight against the EPHEMERA. ▶ A

▌ The group of DENOISERs you fight at **Position B** can quickly overwhelm you if you're not careful. As soon as you enter the room, fire off your grenade cannons at the one directly ahead of you and Assault Boost over to quickly finish it off, making the rest of the fight much simpler.

▌ The EPHEMERA should be treated like any other AC battle. Constantly pressure it with Boost Kicks and shotgun blasts to strain its ACS, and only use your grenade cannons during a clear opening or while it's staggered. ▶ B

Not only do you have the S Rank time constraints to contend with her, you'll also have to destroy IA-C01: EPHEMERA before the facility blows up. Doing so is going to require some serious firepower, so we're going with shotguns and diffuse laser cannons once again.

R-ARM UNIT	SG-027 ZIMMERMAN
L-ARM UNIT	SG-027 ZIMMERMAN
R-BACK UNIT	VP-60LCD
L-BACK UNIT	VP-60LCD
HEAD	20-082 MIND BETA
CORE	CC-3000 WRECKER
ARMS	VP-46S
LEGS	LG-033M VERRILL
BOOSTER	BST-G2/P06SPD
FCS	FC-006 ABBOT
GENERATOR	VP-20D
EXPANSION	PULSE ARMOR

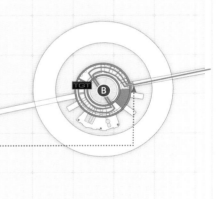

ELIMINATE V.III

This mission is focused on V.III, O'Keeffe. Despite being exclusive to New Game ++, it isn't very difficult. Your foe largely remains in the air, however, and will easily evade your missiles.

Strategy

▌ When you begin the mission, Assault Boost to O'Keeffe at **Position A** and begin straining his ACS with your shotguns.

▌ O'Keeffe remains airborne throughout the battle, but tetrapod legs allow you to match his altitude by hovering. Once he's been staggered, use your diffuse laser cannons. He can use up to three of his repair kits, but that shouldn't keep him alive long enough to stop you from getting an S Rank.

▌ Avoid being staggered in mid-air, and if you're running out of EN, ground yourself to regain it. One major threat to your S Rank is the amount of AP lost from falling outside of the combat area, so avoid that at all costs.

Since the mission is essentially a single encounter, this build was designed for quickly straining BARREN FLOWER's ACS. Once the enemy AC is staggered, it will enable you to follow up with an extreme burst of damage from your diffuse laser cannons.

R-ARM UNIT	SG-027 ZIMMERMAN
L-ARM UNIT	SG-027 ZIMMERMAN
R-BACK UNIT	VP-60LCD
L-BACK UNIT	VP-60LCD
HEAD	20-082 MIND BETA
CORE	CC-3000 WRECKER
ARMS	VP-46S
LEGS	LG-033M VERRILL
BOOSTER	BST-G2/P06SPD
FCS	FC-006 ABBOT
GENERATOR	VP-20D
EXPANSION	PULSE ARMOR

INTERCEPT THE REDGUNS

Damage taken and clear time are your biggest areas of focus during this mission. It's easy to get over-whelmed by Balam's infantry, so accomplishing those goals will be no small task.

Strategy

▪ Assault Boost straight toward the enemies at the start, using your flamethrowers as you pass them by on your way toward **Position A**. In the earlier waves, it's crucial to destroy the quad drones transporting large numbers of bipedal MTs before they can be deployed. These appear at either **Position A** or **B** depending on the wave, and as long as you're close enough, they're fairly easy to eliminate.

▪ Try to thin out as many enemies as possible before Michigan arrives. Once he does, focus on him with Boost Kicks and your flamethrowers until he's staggered, and then use your diffuse laser cannons. ▶ C

▪ Your highest priority is defeating Michigan before the tetrapod MT enters the battle in the final wave (at **Position A**). If both of them are on the field together, the likelihood they'll be able to land enough damage to rule out your S Rank is quite high. ▶ D

ASSEMBLY

Due to the confined area you're fighting in, and the sheer number of enemies present, close-range weapons that excel at hitting multiple targets are a necessity. Few weapons can match the power of a pair of flamethrowers under these circumstances. Having plenty of AP and attitude stability will allow you to absorb hits while moving between targets. Finally, you'll want a couple of hard hitting back weapons, like the diffuse laser cannons, to help make short work of G1 Michigan.

R-ARM UNIT	WB-0000 BAD COOK
L-ARM UNIT	WB-0000 BAD COOK
R-BACK UNIT	VP-60LCD
L-BACK UNIT	VP-60LCD
HEAD	VE-44B
CORE	CC-2000 ORBITER
ARMS	EL-TA-10 FIRMEZA
LEGS	LG-033M VERRILL
BOOSTER	BST-G1/P10
FCS	FCS-G2/P10SLT
GENERATOR	VP-20D
EXPANSION	PULSE ARMOR

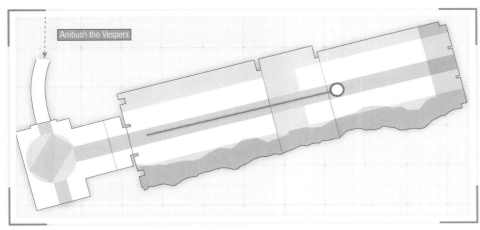

Ambush the Vespers

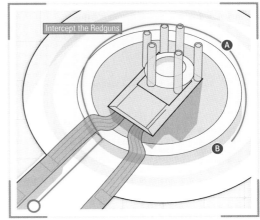

Intercept the Redguns

AMBUSH THE VESPERS

Considering how durable your configuration is, as well as how fragile the enemy ACs are, you and Middle Flatwell should have no trouble eliminating the Vespers fast enough for an S Rank.

Strategy

▪ When you start the mission, head toward the partition from which the ACs emerge, and hover above it. You should attack Hawkins first, since his AC is the easiest to destroy. The instant you see him, drop down and start attacking with all of your weapons. Try to pin him where he emerges—the low ceiling and confined area make it much easier to keep track of him. Switch to Boost Kicks while you reload, and repeat until you've destroyed his AC.

▪ Middle Flatwell will likely be focusing on Pater, so join their fight as soon as you've finished with Hawkins. Capitalize on Flatwell's distraction by slamming Pater with a Boost Kick first, then firing on him. Use the same tactics that you employed against Hawkins, and Pater will go down just as quickly.

ASSEMBLY

You'll need to be capable of dealing extreme damage at close range while simultaneously absorbing incoming damage here. This will leave you free to focus almost entirely on offense. Both of the enemy ACs can use repair kits, but with this build and the aid of Middle Flatwell, it's quite likely they won't get an opportunity to use them.

R-ARM UNIT	SG-027 ZIMMERMAN
L-ARM UNIT	SG-027 ZIMMERMAN
R-BACK UNIT	VP-60LCD
L-BACK UNIT	VP-60LCD
HEAD	20-082 MIND BETA
CORE	CC-3000 WRECKER
ARMS	VP-46S
LEGS	LG-033M VERRILL
BOOSTER	BST-G2/P06SPD
FCS	FC-006 ABBOT
GENERATOR	VP-20D
EXPANSION	TERMINAL ARMOR

UNKNOWN TERRITORY SURVEY (& ALT VERSION)

The main fight in this mission is against V.IV Rusty (alongside Middle Flatwell in the Alt version). Ignore the mealworms throughout the mission, as they'll hardly add anything to your score.

Strategy

▌ Immediately Assault Boost down through the network of tunnels once the mission begins. The tunnels are home to numerous mealworms, but slowing down to kill them contributes nothing toward your rank, and will likely lead to you getting caught in a Coral explosion.

▌ The main difficulty in this fight comes from actually trying to hit Rusty— whom you'll encounter at **Position A**—since he's very mobile. Try to stay close to him as much as possible, using Boost Kicks and positioning to back him into a wall. Unless he's recovering after using an attack he's typically too fast to hit with your diffuse laser cannons, so stick to Boost Kicks and your shotguns until he's staggered. Even though he's liberal with his repair kit usage, the damage output of this build can still bring him down quickly enough for an easy S Rank. Once he's destroyed, you'll need to progress through the next cave to complete the mission.

▌ In the Alt version, Middle Flatwell will show up in a damaged AC shortly after you initiate the fight with Rusty. Both ACs going after you can be chaotic, so prioritize Middle Flatwell first, as he goes down much easier, before turning your attention once again on Rusty. Defeating both ACs ends the Alt mission immediately—you won't need to continue through the tunnels. ▶ A

ASSEMBLY

V.IV Rusty—along with Middle Flatwell in the Alt version of the mission—are the only opponents you need to concern yourself with. This means it's best to go with a heavy build, designed overpower ACs at close range.

R-ARM UNIT	SG-027 ZIMMERMAN
L-ARM UNIT	SG-027 ZIMMERMAN
R-BACK UNIT	VP-60LCD
L-BACK UNIT	VP-60LCD
HEAD	20-082 MIND BETA
CORE	CC-3000 WRECKER
ARMS	VP-46S
LEGS	LG-033M VERRILL
BOOSTER	BST-G2/P06SPD
FCS	FC-006 ABBOT
GENERATOR	VP-20D
EXPANSION	PULSE ARMOR

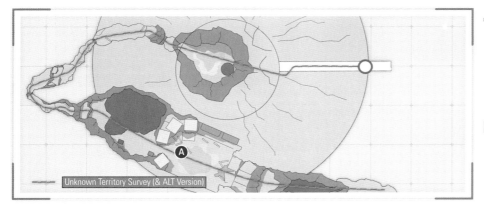

Unknown Territory Survey (& ALT Version)

REACH THE CORAL CONVERGENCE (& ALT VERSION)

Getting the S Rank on either of these missions is extremely challenging. Destroying enemies has a major impact on your rank, so it's highly recommended that you take out every enemy you can.

Strategy

▌ Begin by heading toward **Position A** and engaging the two ACs. Focus on V.VI Maeterlinck, and then G3 Wu Huahai, using Boost Kicks and shotguns to stagger them, before unloading your grenade cannons. After clearing the area, go to **Position B** and destroy all of the HELIANTHUS while hovering above them, as well as the two WEEVILs at **Position C** before they fully activate. Continue up to the clifftop, destroying all of the DENOISERs on the way to the supply sherpa; make use of its services before descending into the lake.

▌ The IB-01: CEL 240 always starts the fight with the same attack, so hold your ground in anticipation and activate Target Assist. Once it gets closer to you, fire both EARSHOTs, which will stagger it, then close the distance and start using your shotguns and Boost Kicks to quickly end the phase.

▌ Remember not to waste any ammo firing until its AP fully restores. This phase consists of using your grenade cannons when you have definite openings to deal large amounts of damage, between which you should squeeze in Boost Kicks or attacks with your shotguns. If you eliminated all of the previous enemies, you should be safe to take this slow and still emerge with an S Rank.

▌ In the Alt version, after destroying the two ACs and the multiple MTs, you'll get a transmission from ALL-MIND to intercept Snail. Make your way to **Position D** and proceed through the tunnel toward **Position E**. Fire your grenade cannons at Snail to catch him by surprise; this can also eliminate some of the MTs in the immediate area.

▌ Fight Snail until Iguazu shows up, and then switch focus to Iguazu. He's more mobile than previous appearances so you'll need to pressure him aggressively while trying to evade Snail's attacks. Once Iguazu is down, finish off Snail; he can use up to three repair kits, and has a very powerful AC so fighting him is a test of your persistence and ability to consistently evade dangerous attacks.

ASSEMBLY

A combination of close- and long-range damage is required for both versions of this mission. Dual SG-027 ZIMMERMANs are hard to beat at close range—they give you a solid option to use against both the basic MTs and the tougher enemies. To help catch some of the evasive enemies, and also deal huge amounts of long-range damage to those that are staggered, we recommend bringing along a pair of EARSHOTs.

R-ARM UNIT	SG-027 ZIMMERMAN
L-ARM UNIT	SG-027 ZIMMERMAN
R-BACK UNIT	EARSHOT
L-BACK UNIT	EARSHOT
HEAD	HD-033M VERRILL
CORE	CS-5000 MAIN DISH
ARMS	EL-TA-10 FIRMEZA
LEGS	LG-033M VERRILL
BOOSTER	BC-0200 GRIDWALKER
FCS	FC-006 ABBOT
GENERATOR	VP-20D
EXPANSION	TERMINAL ARMOR

ESCAPE

Memorizing the route through the city once you emerge from the tunnels is one of the most important factors for getting an S Rank on this mission, because you'll need to move quickly. Time spent getting in unnecessary fights can mean the difference between getting an S Rank or not.

Strategy

▌ Your EN output is limited in this mission, so make careful use of your booster and ignore the enemies while escaping the underground section. Once you reach the city, boost over the pipe to the right at **Position A**. ▶ B

▌ Continue up the hill until you reach the sheer raise in the terrain and ascend a level. There's one quad drone that flies toward your location, but heads up to a level further above you and can be ignored. Face toward coordinate 0 and continue forward.

▌ When you reach a sheer drop with a squad of bipedal MTs and a quad drone ahead of you, turn roughly toward coordinate 55 and make your way to the vertical catapult at **Position B**. Ideally, use the vertical catapult when the quad drone is moving away and—more importantly—when the bipedal MT is facing away from you. Scan the area to determine the direction they're facing and use the vertical catapult when it's safe, then Assault Boost toward the next catapult.

▌ After touching down on the elevated section of the city, scan the area to locate the surrounding enemies while facing toward the objective. The safest route to the objective is along the roofs of buildings that form a row leading toward it. ▶ C

▌ As soon as you finish accessing the beacon on the roof, immediately head toward your next objective; you do not need to be stationed at the beacon during the dialogue with "Chatty." Face toward coordinate 0 and jump down, so you can start heading toward **Position C** near the final objective.

▌ Once the MTs begin appearing, you should take cover behind the buildings on the sides of the area. From here you can pick them as they come into view, and avoid taking unnecessary damage.

▌ Carla will arrive after a short while, and that'll be your signal to start attacking the enemy units a bit more aggressively, because they all need to be destroyed to complete the mission. If you traversed the city section fast enough, you can afford to take some hits in this fight and still get an S Rank.

ASSEMBLY

Piloting AC JAILBREAK, your most powerful tool is the MORLEY spread bazooka launcher, which can easily destroy the Light MTs you encounter in the mission.

R-ARM UNIT	MG-014 LUDLOW
L-ARM UNIT	MA-T-223 KYORIKU
R-BACK UNIT	—
L-BACK UNIT	SB-033M MORLEY
HEAD	AH-J-124/RC JAILBREAK
CORE	AC-J-120/RC JAILBREAK
ARMS	AA-J-123/RC JAILBREAK
LEGS	AL-J-121/RC JAILBREAK
BOOSTER	BST-G1/P10
FCS	—
GENERATOR	—
EXPANSION	—

Reach the Coral Convergence
Reach the Coral Convergence (ALT Version)
Escape

MIA

This mission and your path through it are fairly straightforward. Your shotguns can quickly take out the enemies in your way, but you'll need to steer clear of the numerous environmental hazards. The optional fight with AC HERMIT can contribute a lot toward your rank, and even with this detour you can still finish the mission fast enough for the S Rank.

Strategy

▮ Move forward and dispatch the initial group of bipedal MTs as quickly as possible, but don't storm ahead once you get outside. It can be difficult to get past the combination of bipedal MTs—and the LC above them—without taking damage, so allow the friendly MTs to catch up. They'll draw some of the enemy fire, while you move around picking them off.

▮ Once you reach the next bridge at **Position A**, be sure you're not standing on it when ALLMIND causes the large explosion that wipes out all of the enemy units. Wait for the flames to dissipate before continuing forward or you'll be at risk of ACS anomaly. ▶ A

▮ Head into the next room at **Position B**, and—after destroying the initial enemies—attempt to access the door, springing the LC's ambush. Quickly drop off the side of the ramp and stand underneath it so they don't spot you, then use a scan to determine their locations and take out the closest enemy before they can react. Next, finish off the rest and press onward.

▮ Continue through the door and down the hallway, clearing out the encounter with the LCs and MTs at the end. Instead of directly heading through the door, venture into the nearby room and drop down to face G6 Red, piloting AC HERMIT at **Position C**; defeating him will help a good deal toward the S Rank. Once you're done, jump back up and continue on toward **Position D**, where you'll face Pater. ▶ B

▮ You can attempt to meet Pater in the air, but he starts particularly high, so you're better off waiting in the tunnel for him to descend. Forcing him into the tunnel during the fight will make things much easier, since it will severely limit his aerial maneuverability. You can be fairly aggressive in the fight against him—as long as you defeat him quickly, taking some damage in the process won't adversely affect your rank too much. ▶ C

ASSEMBLY

The greatest threats here are the explosive munitions of the LC HF, and the energy weapons of the Subject Guard. Assemble your AC with defense against those damage types in mind. The recommended build is geared toward maneuverability, however, as time to completion is prioritized over survivability. This should not be difficult to manage, as long as you're aware of the threats each section will throw at you. The ZIM-MERMANs are capable of easily destroying the MTs and LCs you encounter, while the diffuse laser cannons make quick work of the LC HF, Red and Pater.

R-ARM UNIT	SG-027 ZIMMERMAN
L-ARM UNIT	SG-027 ZIMMERMAN
R-BACK UNIT	VP-60LCD
L-BACK UNIT	VP-60LCD
HEAD	DF-HD-08 TIAN-QIANG
CORE	IA-C01C: EPHEMERA
ARMS	NACHTREIHER/46E
LEGS	06-042 MIND BETA
BOOSTER	BST-G2/P06SPD
FCS	FC-008 TALBOT
GENERATOR	VE-20C
EXPANSION	TERMINAL ARMOR

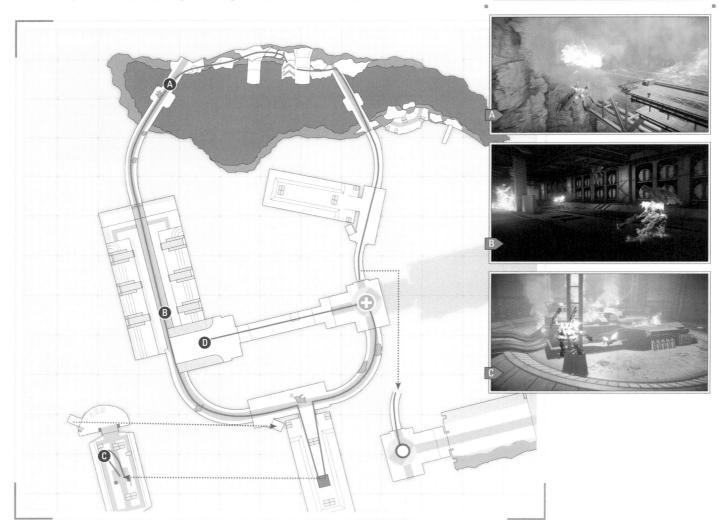

TAKE THE UNINHABITED FLOATING CITY

It is recommended that you refer to the Mission Intel chapter (P.234) for full details on the timing and composition of each wave. The goal for this S Rank is to be as efficient in intercepting the waves as possible, and to protect the shield from incoming damage. Certain waves are more critical to be prepared for than others, and your choice of when to use the defense cannons is also important.

Strategy

▌ The first couple of waves consist mostly of bipedal MTs, that appear from either **Position A**, **B**, or **C**. The greatest threats, however, are the transport helicopters, because destroying them will make things much easier to manage. After those waves are complete, get onto one of the buildings near **Position A**, so that you're ready for the next enemies.

▌ Wave 3 introduces the laser rifle LCs (seven in total), which are the first real threat to the objectives. They appear in fixed locations on rooftops, starting near **Positions A** and **C**, and then on other roofs between them, so you'll need to reposition quickly and often. If possible, launch your missiles at them before they land, as this will save precious time and ensure they don't get a shot off. ▶ D

▌ When the timer reaches 1:50, the 4th wave of enemies will arrive, this time comprised of a large group of suicide drones. The best way to handle them is to quickly move to a central position and boost up to an altitude of 330. Then, as soon as the drones start flying toward the objective, activate pulse protection so they all crash into it. When you land, activate both defense cannons in anticipation of the next enemy wave.

▌ At around 1:30, the LC and a large group of enemies will arrive. While the cannons help thin these enemies out, move to **Position B** to head off the LC. This enemy needs to be destroyed quickly, so that you can fend off everything else; make heavy use of your Boost Kick and diffuse laser cannons. The remaining enemies are all bipedal MTs, so quickly use your missiles during boost movement to take them out before the timer expires. ▶ E

SPECIAL OBJECTIVE

Defend the Xylem

In order to be eligible for the S Rank in this mission, you must defend the Xylem Shield from being destroyed. Some damage is allowed, but the more AP the shield has by the end, the better your chances at the S Rank will be.

ASSEMBLY

You'll be defending a location against enemies that are not focused on you and approach from different vectors, so the build is assembled with maneuverability in mind to help you intercept them. The GRIDWALKER booster is especially important, as it will allow you to easily reach the suicide drones' altitude, making deploying the pulse protection simpler. The MLT-04 missile launchers, matched with the VE-21B FCS, allow for maximum distance and multi-lock. Finally, you'll need something that packs a punch, like the diffuse laser cannons, to defeat the LC quickly.

R-ARM UNIT	HML-G2/P19MLT-04
L-ARM UNIT	HML-G2/P19MLT-04
R-BACK UNIT	VP-60LCD
L-BACK UNIT	VP-60LCD
HEAD	DF-HD-08 TIAN-QIANG
CORE	IA-C01C: EPHEMERA
ARMS	NACHTREIHER/46E
LEGS	06-042 MIND BETA
BOOSTER	BC-0200 GRIDWALKER
FCS	VE-21B
GENERATOR	VE-20C
EXPANSION	PULSE PROTECTION

6

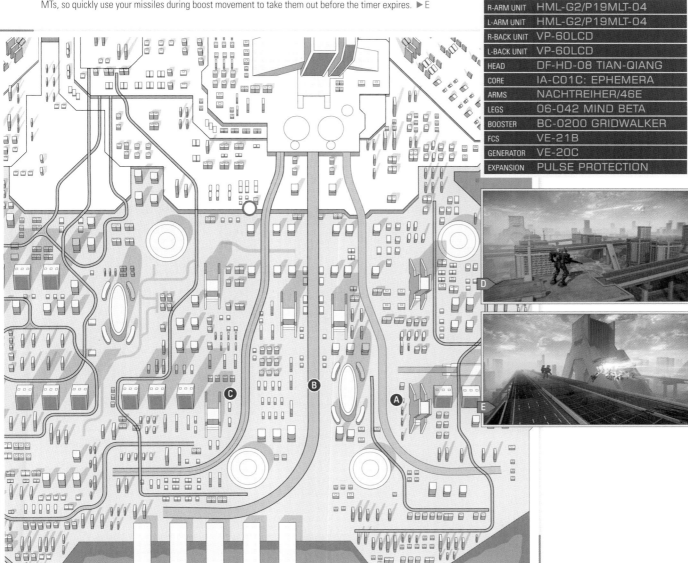

INTERCEPT THE CORPORATE FORCES

Speed is once again the key factor for achieving an S Rank here. There are a lot of enemies to contend with, but you only need to concern yourself with the ones directly in your path. You have a large area to cover, but you can afford to take a reasonable amount of damage while simply using Assault Boosts to fly past most enemies.

Strategy

▧ Stay high and move along the rooftops while advancing to the first objective, so that you can avoid the enemies below until you're within range of the LC at **Position A**. Ignore everything else and destroy the LC. Next, cross over to the opposite side of the area to avoid more enemies, while you advance on **Position B**. ▶ A

▧ It's possible to ignore the LC inside the pulse protection barrier, but since the door takes some time to open, it's safer to destroy it quickly. Once the door opens, head inside to **Position C**, where you'll face the HC.

▧ This is one of the more dangerous encounters in the mission, but as long as you destroy it quickly enough, taking some damage in the process is worth it. Positioning is crucial, so avoid letting it remain above you, where it's likely to break your Target Assist and can potentially catch you with its grab attack. Try to catch it with a Boost Kick while it's focusing on your allied units, and stay aggressive with constant use of shotguns and Boost Kicks to stagger it and create openings for your diffuse laser cannons. ▶ B

▧ Make use of the supply sherpa, and then head for the exterior, straight toward **Position D**. Ignore the bipedal MTs near "Chatty," and Assault Boost straight into the pulse protection fields. Destroy the drones generating the fields, and then turn your attention on the two LC HFs. Use your scanner to keep track of them if they drop down between the buildings, and try to isolate them. Use cover to block the incoming fire from the one you're not actively attacking.

▧ Once Freud appears in AC LOCKSMITH, Assault Boost over to him and begin the fight quickly. If you arrive swiftly enough, you can Boost Kick him before he turns to focus on you. With a strong enough opening, it's possible to defeat him before he has an opportunity to repair or activate his pulse armor. If you miss that opportunity, you'll need to chase him down as aggressively as possible, while using all of your weapons to strain LOCKSMITH's ACS. Speed is the priority here—not safety—because your weapons are capable of out-damaging his. Despite Freud's use of repair kits and pulse armor making this a lengthy battle, it's still entirely possible to get an S Rank if things don't go entirely in your favor. ▶ C

Your focus in this mission should be quickly reaching and destroying the HC, AC and all of the LCs. To facilitate this, you'll need a build that's both light and fast. You'll also want high enough anti-energy and anti-explosive defense specs to allow you to go toe-to-toe with them, while using powerful close-range weaponry to end the fights quickly.

R-ARM UNIT	SG-027 ZIMMERMAN
L-ARM UNIT	SG-027 ZIMMERMAN
R-BACK UNIT	VP-60LCD
L-BACK UNIT	VP-60LCD
HEAD	DF-HD-08 TIAN-QIANG
CORE	IA-C01C: EPHEMERA
ARMS	NACHTREIHER/46E
LEGS	06-042 MIND BETA
BOOSTER	BST-G2/P06SPD
FCS	FC-008 TALBOT
GENERATOR	VE-20C
EXPANSION	TERMINAL ARMOR

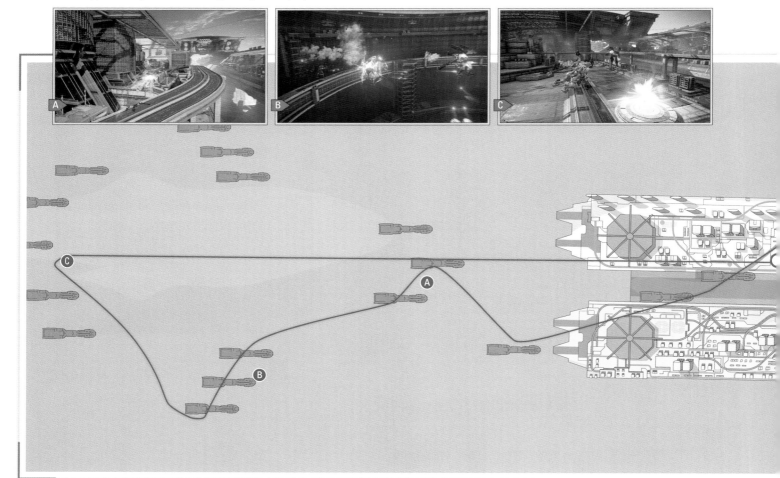

ELIMINATE "CINDER" CARLA

While defeating enemies, including Snail, can have a positive impact on your rank, speed is by far the biggest contributing factor. Getting through the mandatory encounters quickly is your best route toward an S Rank

Strategy

- The right-hand side of the area offers a significantly safer route, so head there straight away and hug the boundary all the way down to **Position A**. Defeating Snail quickly without incurring a significant AP or ammunition cost can have a positive impact on your rank, but this will rarely be enough to move you from an A to an S Rank, so skipping him is recommended. ▶ D-E

- Once inside, wait for the partition to close and destroy the enemies in the room carefully. The grenade cannons that the MTs are equipped with can easily overload your ACS, and—since your own munitions are all close range—you'll need to take some risks and be aggressive.

- The fight with Carla and "Chatty" takes place inside the dome at **Position B**. It's recommended that you take on Carla first, since she closes in on you at the start of the fight. She always begins with a Boost Kick and assault armor follow-up. Evade these, and then begin attacking her aggressively, using Boost Kicks to create openings to fire your weapons.

- If "Chatty" is still on the upper floor when Carla is defeated, don't wait for him to head back down. Instead, Assault Boost straight up to him to save time. Try to pin him against the wall, and attack him in the same manner you did Carla until he too is defeated. ▶ F

ASSEMBLY

Since you'll likely be skipping the fight with Snail, you can focus on increasing your anti-explosive spec. This will greatly reduce the threat from the enemies you do need to engage. Tetrapod legs will also be very useful in these mandatory fights, because you'll be able to hover above the repair drones in the ambush, and keep up with "Chatty," who likes to remain airborne.

R-ARM UNIT	SG-027 ZIMMERMAN
L-ARM UNIT	SG-027 ZIMMERMAN
R-BACK UNIT	VP-60LCD
L-BACK UNIT	VP-60LCD
HEAD	AH-J-124 BASHO
CORE	07-061 MIND ALPHA
ARMS	IA:C01A: EPHEMERA
LEGS	VP-424
BOOSTER	BST-G2/P06SPD
FCS	FC-008 TALBOT
GENERATOR	VE-20C
EXPANSION	TERMINAL ARMOR

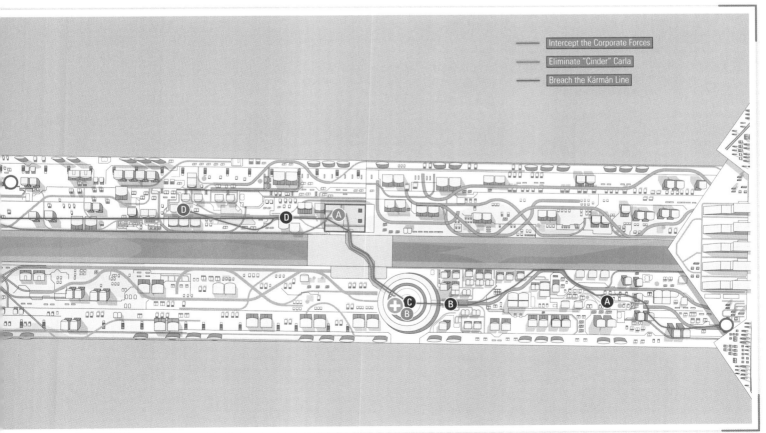

Intercept the Corporate Forces

Eliminate "Cinder" Carla

Breach the Kármán Line

CH05 [25-A] BREACH THE KÁRMÁN LINE

Enemies defeated is not a contributing factor to your rank in this mission. Instead, you're graded on clear time and damage taken, which means you'll need to be efficient when eliminating the warships.

Strategy

▌ Assault Boost your way toward each warship that Carla designates for elimination. Be sure to take full advantage of your infinite EN, using plenty of lateral dodges to evade incoming fire. Fly above the warships once you're within range; fire directly at their command centers to destroy them instantly, then move onto the next target.

▌ You'll first need to destroy the warships at **Position A** and **B**, followed by the group way out at **Position C**. As you progress through the warship groups, they'll use increasingly dangerous and more frequent attacks, so vary your trajectory often to evade them.

▌ Once they're eliminated, you'll be brought back to the Xylem, and will face off against Rusty at **Position D**.

▌ Once Rusty engages you, begin straining his ACS gauge with your shotguns and Boost Kicks. Remember that you have functionally unlimited EN, so you can afford to be very liberal with your Boost Kick attempts. After staggering him, use your diffuse laser cannons, and then repeat the process until he's defeated.

ASSEMBLY

The warships can be easily destroyed by firing on their command centers with most weapons. This means we've prioritized a generator and booster that lets you move between the warships quickly, and a suite of strong close-range weaponry to use against Rusty.

R-ARM UNIT	SG-027 ZIMMERMAN
L-ARM UNIT	SG-027 ZIMMERMAN
R-BACK UNIT	VP-60LCD
L-BACK UNIT	VP-60LCD
HEAD	DF-HD-08 TIAN-QIANG
CORE	IA-C01C: EPHEMERA
ARMS	NACHTREIHER/46E
LEGS	06-042 MIND BETA
BOOSTER	BST-G2/P06SPD
FCS	FC-008 TALBOT
GENERATOR	VE-20C
EXPANSION	TERMINAL ARMOR

CH05 [26-B] BRING DOWN THE XYLEM

The restrictions for getting an S Rank against Walter are nowhere near as strict as they are in the other ending missions. As long as you play smartly and quickly, attaining it shouldn't be too much trouble.

Strategy

▌ Immediately make your way to the engines at **Positions A** and **B**, and destroy each of them; a single shot from one of you shotguns is sufficient to get the job done. Once they're both down, head toward **Position C**, where you'll do battle with Walter

▌ Walter uses a Coral shield that will deflect a lot of your weaponry. Once you break his shield, he'll stagger immediately, leaving him open for a Boost Kick and a follow-up barrage from your weapons. Walter's AC is very mobile, and allows him to remain airborne throughout the fight. This can make it difficult to stay close to him, but attempting to do so is still the fastest way to deal with him.

▌ He has access to three repair kits, which he'll use liberally, so it can be tricky to defeat him before he has the opportunity to use all of them. As long as you keep up the offensive pressure, you should still be able to defeat him in time for the S Rank. ▶ A

ASSEMBLY

Walter is the only threat in this mission, and the recommended configuration here will aid in bringing him down quickly and easily.

R-ARM UNIT	SG-027 ZIMMERMAN
L-ARM UNIT	SG-027 ZIMMERMAN
R-BACK UNIT	VP-60LCD
L-BACK UNIT	VP-60LCD
HEAD	HD-033M VERRILL
CORE	BD-011 MELANDER
ARMS	IA-C01A: EPHEMERA
LEGS	LG-033M VERRILL
BOOSTER	BST-G1/P10
FCS	FC-006 ABBOT
GENERATOR	AG-T-005 HOKUSHI
EXPANSION	TERMINAL ARMOR

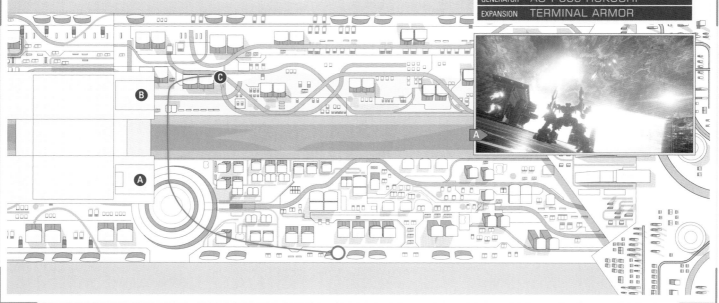

DESTROY THE DRIVE BLOCK

Clear time is once again your number one priority here, but—with the correct choice of weaponry—the battles against the SMART CLEANER and BALTEUS can be quick affairs. Boosting past enemies will help, but memorizing the route between the generators to avoid getting lost in the interiors will save you the most time.

Strategy

▌ Start heading straight toward the first generator at **Position A**. Make sure the artillery cannon at **Position B** doesn't have a line of fire on you—stay at the starting altitude until you're ready to drop down and go inside.

▌ Destroy the first generator, then go through the maintenance area toward the second generator at **Position C**, destroying any quad drones you encounter along the way. Head outside again, and Assault Boost past the artillery, reach the SMART CLEANER at **Position D**. ▶ B

▌ You'll begin above the SMART CLEANER, so it's easy to get into position to fire into its chimney. Once you've staggered it, drop down and attack it from the front. Your weapons are powerful enough to defeat it before it can fully recover. Once Rusty has left, access the door and continue to the next generator. ▶ C

▌ The third generator is at **Position E** in the second room you enter, so Assault Boost through the first room, completely ignoring the enemies until you're within range to destroy it. The final generator can be found nearby, at **Position F** in the adjacent room. Once it's gone, access the supply sherpa and head outside to fight BALTEUS.

▌ Your main concern is bringing BALTEUS's barrier down; doing this just once can potentially be enough. Take care to avoid its spiral laser cannon, and aggressively pursue it with Boost Kicks to deplete the barrier and stagger it. It will recover its ACS before you can defeat it, but a combination of Boost Kicks and shotgun blasts will overload it again before the barrier regenerates. ▶ D

ASSEMBLY

You'll need to forgo destroying most enemies for the sake of speed. Some of them, however, such as the laser cannon quad drones and the artillery installation, can deal heavy damage as you boost past them. This means having a decent amount of anti-energy spec can help a lot. The added defensive specs from tetrapod legs will also help, and will make the fight against the SMART CLEANER significantly easier. For weaponry, a high-damage single-target loadout is recommended, as that will be most effective against the bosses.

R-ARM UNIT	SG-027 ZIMMERMAN
L-ARM UNIT	SG-027 ZIMMERMAN
R-BACK UNIT	VP-60LCD
L-BACK UNIT	VP-60LCD
HEAD	VE-44A
CORE	07-061 MIND ALPHA
ARMS	IA:C01A: EPHEMERA
LEGS	VP-424
BOOSTER	BST-G2/P06SPD
FCS	FC-008 TALBOT
GENERATOR	VE-20C
EXPANSION	TERMINAL ARMOR

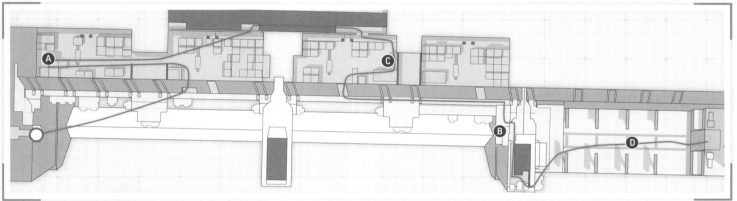

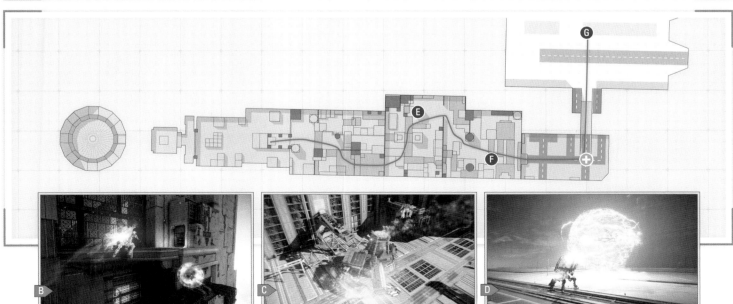

REGAIN CONTROL OF THE XYLEM

A combination of clear time, number of enemies defeated and damage received all contribute highly toward your rank. You'll need to know how to get to the modules quickly, and being familiar with the order in which the panels appear in the final room will dramatically improve your chances of attaining an S Rank.

Strategy

▓ Quick Boost to the edge of the starting platform and hover above the two KITE drones. Eliminate them quickly, before destroying the first module at **Position A**. Take out any of the repair drones in the area that block your path, but don't go out of your way for them.

▓ Quickly turn and start heading toward the second module at **Position B**. Make sure you destroy the GHOST in this room on the way to the module. More KITE drones will drop down nearby; eliminate them before dropping down and moving to the next room.

▓ Destroy the GHOST at **Position C** in this room before proceeding further, so that you can deal with it without interference from the other enemies. Use your scanner if you're having trouble locating it. ▶ A

▓ Head to the ground level and destroy the module at **Position D**. Use your scanner again here to reveal the location of the KITE drones, so you can destroy them if they come within rage. Boost back up toward **Position E** and destroy the module there, then make your way back across and enter the next room.

▓ The GHOST in the third room is located toward the opposite side. Prioritize destroying the module at **Position F** before concerning yourself with it or the nearby KITE drones.

▓ Assault Boost toward the final module at **Position G**, taking care to avoid the plasma shots from the KITE drones. Scan the area to locate the GHOST, but destroy the module first, because you'll need to wait for some dialogue to complete before you can progress further. Move near the exit door and can hide behind the wall there. This will force the enemies to come closer, making it easier to destroy them. Try to eliminate the GHOST and any nearby KITES before the door is fully opened; once it opens, drop down to the final area at **Position H**. ▶ B

▓ You need to access a number of panels in this room while navigating static security lasers. Tracking lasers will fire at you constantly from above the panel you need to reach, until you start accessing the panel below them. Learning the order of the panels is the key to getting through this section smoothly. The best way to deal with the tracking laser is to use the central device as a shield, by hovering behind it. You can only do that, however, when you know where the next laser will come from. Use your shield if you're unsure, since it will help mitigate some of the damage. When advancing on the panels, Assault Boost toward them at a slightly downward angle—so that the laser fires above you—then pop up and Quick Boost toward it at the last second. Once you begin accessing the panel, the laser will stop. Repeat this until you can access the central device, ending the mission. ▶ C

ASSEMBLY

A few strong close-range weapons are enough to deal with the enemies you'll need to defeat in this mission. It's highly recommended that you bring a shield to help deal with the lasers in the final encounter. On that same note, the anti-energy spec is a priority, as it will mitigate the risk from the lasers, and help defend against the energy attacks that the enemies employ. The ability to stay behind the central device at the end will keep you safe, and for that reason, tetrapod legs are recommended.

R-ARM UNIT	SG-027 ZIMMERMAN
L-ARM UNIT	SG-027 ZIMMERMAN
R-BACK UNIT	VP-60LCD
L-BACK UNIT	IB-C03W4: NGI 028
HEAD	VE-44A
CORE	IB-C03C: HAL 826
ARMS	NACHTREIHER/46E
LEGS	VP-424
BOOSTER	IB-C03B: NGI 001
FCS	IB-C03F: WLT 001
GENERATOR	VE-20C
EXPANSION	PULSE ARMOR

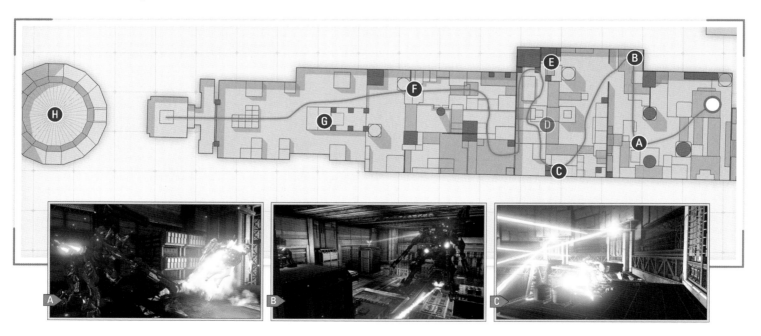

SHUT DOWN THE CLOSURE SATELLITES

As with other missions that feature single bosses, clear time—and especially damage taken—will have the biggest impact on your rank. This places the emphasis on ensuring a quick, clean fight.

Strategy

▌ Begin working on Ayre's barrier with your shotguns while circling around her to evade her attacks. She'll stagger the instant the barrier breaks, and you'll want to time a Boost Kick immediately after that happens. If you mistime your strike, she'll recover and evade your attacks, costing you an opportunity to deal serious damage. ▶ D

▌ During the second phase of the fight, you'll need to focus on extended periods of evasion, especially when she unleashes consecutive attacks. Pick your moments to attack carefully, and make sure you fully capitalize when you stagger her. Ayre can deal huge amounts of damage, so keep moving and remain patient. Remember that, while clear time is important, taking as little damage as possible is even more so. ▶ E

ASSEMBLY

Quickly strafing around Ayre is a very effective strategy against her. Basing your assembly around tank legs will enable you to do that much more effectively, and keep you in position for a close-range offense.

R-ARM UNIT	SG-027 ZIMMERMAN
L-ARM UNIT	SG-027 ZIMMERMAN
R-BACK UNIT	VP-60LCD
L-BACK UNIT	VP-60LCD
HEAD	HD-033M VERRILL
CORE	BD-011 MELANDER
ARMS	IA-C01A: EPHEMERA
LEGS	EL-TL-11 FORTALEZA
BOOSTER	—
FCS	FC-006 ABBOT
GENERATOR	VP-20C
EXPANSION	TERMINAL ARMOR

CORAL RELEASE

Coral Release features only the battle against ALLMIND. With the right AC configuration, it offers up a quick and easily attained S Rank.

Strategy

▌ The easiest way to achieve an S Rank in this mission is to eliminate the four AC subordinates in the first phase, and the two SEA SPIDERs in the second. Their contribution toward you rank will give you a huge margin for error in terms of both speed and damage received, though expediency shouldn't be an issue. ▶ F-G

▌ ALLMIND always begin the fight with the same attack; learn the timing to evade it, because getting hit straight away will put you on the back foot before the battle even begins. Using Target Assist to fix your camera, and then perform a jump, hover and Quick Boost to reliably get away from the attack. Turn your attention to the subordinates immediately afterward—Assault Boost straight up to them and use your shotguns to dispatch each of them quickly.

▌ When only ALLMIND is left, attack it aggressively with Boost Kicks and your shotguns until its staggered. Fire off everything at it, and attempt another Boost Kick before it recovers to maximize the damage you deal. Repeat this tactic until the first phase ends

▌ In the second phase, immediately focus on the two SEA SPIDERs and eliminate them both. Start hovering once you've reached their altitude and use all of your weaponry to finish them off as quickly as possible. You can use Boost Kicks against them, but it's best to conserve your EN. Once both SEA SPIDERs have been eliminated, focus on ALLMIND again until the third phase begins.

▌ Stay close to ALLMIND in this phase and use your entire arsenal—including Boost Kicks—to stagger it as quickly as possible. You'll need to go through a few damage cycles to finish it off, due to the amount of AP it has. The key to this phase will be getting familiar enough with its attacks that you can easily evade them; if you're constantly getting hit, the likelihood of getting an S Rank is slim. ▶ H

ASSEMBLY

Staying close to both ALLMIND and its subordinates is the easiest and quickest way to find openings to deal damage. A combination of high-impact weapons and an FCS that can keep up with their movement will allow you to fully capitalize on these openings when they arise.

R-ARM UNIT	SG-027 ZIMMERMAN
L-ARM UNIT	SG-027 ZIMMERMAN
R-BACK UNIT	VP-60LCD
L-BACK UNIT	VP-60LCD
HEAD	HD-033M VERRILL
CORE	BD-012 MELANDER C3
ARMS	VE-46A
LEGS	LG-033M VERRILL
BOOSTER	BC-0600 12345
FCS	IA-C01F: OCELLUS
GENERATOR	VE-20C
EXPANSION	TERMINAL ARMOR

TROPHY/ACHIEVEMENT GUIDE

There are a total of 30 Trophies/Achievements that can be unlocked in the game, many of which are awarded naturally as you complete missions. Not all of these can be obtained in a single playthrough, however. Some of them are related to the game's various endings and you'll need to complete the game at least three times in order to obtain them all. This section will detail how to unlock all of the Trophies/Achievements, often linking to other parts of the book for full details. For ease of use, we've grouped them into the following categories:

SPOILERS

Due to the nature of many of these Trophies/Achievements, major spoilers are possible here. Proceed with caution if you haven't yet completed the game at least once.

PROGRESSION

Trophies/Achievements that are unlocked upon completing specific missions.

EXPLORATION/COLLECTIBLE

Each of these will unlock when obtaining all of the collectibles in any given category, most of which are entirely optional and off the mission-critical path.

COMPLETIONIST

These are awarded for completing some of the more difficult challenges the game has to offer.

PROGRESSION

The Fires of Raven

To reach this ending, you'll need to complete the "Shut Down the Closure Satellites" mission. To reach it, choose the "Intercept the Corporate Forces" mission instead of "Eliminate 'Cinder' Carla" in Chapter 5. See P.254 for more information on "Shut Down the Closure Satellites."

Liberator of Rubicon

The Liberator of Rubicon Ending is achieved by completing "Bring Down the Xylem" as your final mission. To reach it, choose "Eliminate 'Cinder' Carla" instead of "Intercept the Corporate Forces" during Chapter 5. The walkthroughs for those missions can be found on P.241 and P.257, respectively.

Alea Iacta Est

This ending requires you to complete "Coral Release," which can only be reached by first having seen the other two endings. On NG++, you'll need to select the missions shown in the Progression Guide on P.398 that result in accepting the "Coral Release" mission. If you want to read up on "Coral Release," head over to P.299.

MIA

This Trophy/Achievement unlocks when you complete the mission "MIA" in Chapter 5. This mission does not become available until you're on NG++, and are following the path toward the Alea Iacta Est ending. To read more about this mission, flip to P.294.

The Fires of Raven Reached ending: "The Fires of Raven."	30 Ⓖ	**A New Threat** Cleared mission: "Attack the Old Spaceport." 15 Ⓖ
Liberator of Rubicon Reached ending: "Liberator of Rubicon."	30 Ⓖ	**Ayre and the Coral** Cleared mission: "Destroy the Ice Worm." 15 Ⓖ
Alea Iacta Est Reached ending: "Alea Iacta Est."	30 Ⓖ	**Into Unknown Territory** Cleared mission: "Underground Exploration - Depth 3." 15 Ⓖ
Illegal Entry Cleared mission: "Illegal Entry."	15 Ⓖ	**Re-education** Cleared mission: "Reach the Coral Convergence." 15 Ⓖ
Operation Wallclimber Cleared mission: "Operation Wallclimber."	15 Ⓖ	**The Floating City** Cleared mission: "Take the Uninhabited Floating City." 15 Ⓖ
Contact Cleared mission: "Attack the Watchpoint."	15 Ⓖ	**MIA** Cleared mission: "MIA." 15 Ⓖ
Ocean Crossing Cleared mission: "Ocean Crossing."	15 Ⓖ	

EXPLORATION/COLLECTIBLE

Asset Holder

This will likely be one of the final Trophies/Achievements you unlock. It requires you to obtain every part in the game, which can't be done until you're on NG++. Head to the Archives section on P.394 for lists of everything you'll need to do, which includes reaching Hunter Class 15, finding all part containers, completing all missions (including training missions), completing all Arena fights (including the "Analysis" portion from NG+ and onward), and purchasing everything in the Parts Shop. If you're working toward this you'll also end up unlocking the Weapon Collector, External Parts Collector, Internal Parts Collector, Expansion Collector, and Combat Log Collector Trophies/Achievements along the way. You can also check the Parts Catalogue, starting on P.50, for info on specific parts.

Asset Holder Obtained all parts.	70 Ⓖ	**Expansion Collector** Obtained all Core Expansions. 30 Ⓖ
Weapon Collector Obtained all weapon parts.	30 Ⓖ	**Combat Log Collector** Obtained all combat logs. 30 Ⓖ
External Parts Collector Obtained all frame parts.	30 Ⓖ	**Data Log Collector** Obtained 10 data logs. 30 Ⓖ
Internal Parts Collector Obtained all inner parts.	30 Ⓖ	

Data Log Collector

Mission Name	No. Logs
Illegal Entry	4
Operation Wallclimber	2
Retrieve Combat Logs	8

Data logs can be collected throughout various missions in the game, and are obtained by accessing the wrecks of broken-down ACs. There are 50 in total, but you will only need to find 10 of them for this particular trophy, which you'll accomplish naturally while playing through the game. Head to P.396 for the full list of these logs and the missions in which they appear.

Combat Log Collector

There are a total of 98 combat logs within the game that you can obtain from defeating specific enemies within some missions, and you'll need all of them to unlock this Trophy/Achievement. After completing a mission, you can check the Replay Mission screen to see if that mission has any combat logs to obtain, and whether or not you've acquired them all. If you missed one or more combat logs within a mission, you can simply replay it to look for them.

It's important to note that whenever the same combat log is available in both a mission's original and Alt versions, obtaining it in one of the versions of the mission will make it unavailable in the other. Sometimes combat logs are only available in one version of the mission, due to different enemies appearing. In these cases, it's best to use the confirmation check mark in the Replay Mission screen to know if you have them all or not. Or, you can consult the chart on P.395 that lists all of the missions and enemies that contain combat logs to make tracking them all down easier.

COMPLETIONIST

The Perfect Mercenary

Getting a highly coveted S-Rank rating on a mission is no easy feat, and doing so for every mission in the game will require you to truly become the perfect mercenary. You'll need to attain S-Ranks for every Alt mission as well, since they're counted separately from their original counterparts, as are both missions that are involved in Decision conflicts. This means unlocking this Trophy/Achievement won't be possible until you finish NG++. Mission ranks are unlocked only when replaying missions through the Replay Mission screen, so even though you'll naturally play missions multiple times as you progress through NG+ cycles, you won't receive any grading for regular play. For more information on the ranking systems, and full strategies for how to S-Rank each mission, please refer to the S-Rank Guide section, starting on P.401.

Armored Core VI	Unlocked all achievements.	140 ⓖ	**Testing Complete** — Cleared all combat aptitude evaluation programs in the Arena.	30 ⓖ
The Perfect Mercenary	Cleared all missions with an S-Rank rating.	70 ⓖ	**Training Complete** — Cleared training: "Advanced Mercenary Certification."	15 ⓖ
Stargazer	Cleared all missions.	70 ⓖ	**Hardware Engineer** — Assembled an AC.	15 ⓖ
Master of Arena	Cleared all Arena programs.	70 ⓖ	**Software Engineer** — Upgraded your AC's OS.	15 ⓖ
Tuning Expert	Performed all OS upgrades.	70 ⓖ	**Graphic Designer** — Changed the colors of your AC.	15 ⓖ

Stargazer

Unlocking this Trophy/Achievement requires you to complete at least three playthroughs of the game, since some missions are exclusive to NG+ and NG++. You'll need to keep track of which Decisions you made on previous playthroughs, and make sure that you make different choices on subsequent ones. This includes the final choice in Chapter 5, which dictates which ending you'll get. For an easy-to-follow route to unlocking all of the missions and endings, head over to our Progression Guide on P.398—this will ensure you unlock this Trophy/Achievement in the least number of playthroughs.

Master of Arena

The virtual battlefields in the Arena offer some of the greatest tests of your skills as a pilot. You'll need to climb the Arena's ranks and emerge victorious in all regular 29 Arena encounters to reach the number one spot and unlock this Trophy/Achievement. There's no way to circumvent the order in which you face specific opponents along the way, so you'll need to plan for each opponent individually and battle each of them in turn. It should be noted that to unlock this Trophy/Achievement, you just have to reach Rank 1 in the Arena, which means you won't have to complete any of the Analysis encounters that ALLMIND offers you in NG+ and NG++. The Arena Guide chapter starting on P.346 includes full strategies and recommended builds for every opponent you'll need to defeat.

Testing Complete

This is one of two Trophies/Achievements tied to ALLIMND's virtual training programs. You'll automatically unlock training missions as you progress through the game, and to unlock this Trophy/Achievement, you'll need to complete all them. Completing the programs brings with it additional rewards such as unique parts, so going through them is highly recommended, even if you're already familiar with the concepts they cover. Consult the chart here for unlocking all training missions, and head to P.394 for a full list of training mission rewards.

Tuning Expert

Similar to the "Master of Arena" Trophy/Achievement, to unlock this one, you'll also need to progress deep into the Arena. Acquiring all of the upgrades available through OS Tuning requires 197 OST Chips. The order in which you unlock OS Tuning options doesn't matter, so you're free to choose whichever best suits your build as you progress. Resetting them also won't affect this Trophy/Achievement. To acquire all 197 OS Chips, you'll need to defeat the additional "Analysis" Arena opponents that are unlocked during your NG+ playthrough. NG++ Arena opponents no longer award OS Chips, so you won't need to defeat those.

UNLOCKING TRAINING MISSIONS

Mission Completion Requirement	Training Mission Unlocked
Illegal Entry	Beginner Training 1: Basic Controls
Destroy Artillery Installations or Grid 135 Cleanup	Beginner Training 2: Combat Fundamentals
Attack the Dam Complex & Destroy the Weaponized Mining Ship	Intermediate Support 1: Assembling an AC
Attack the Dam Complex & Destroy the Weaponized Mining Ship	Intermediate Support 2: Reverse-Jointed ACs
Operation Wallclimber	Intermediate Support 3: Tetrapod ACs
Operation Wallclimber	Intermediate Support 4: Tank ACs

Training Complete

After completing all of the previous training programs, you'll unlock the "Advanced Mercenary Certification" program. Upon completing that, you'll be rewarded with this Trophy/Achievement.

Armored Core VI features a huge selection of missions, enemies, mechanics and general topics that you might want to know more about. The index on these pages allows for easy search and reference of any such entry in the entire book. For missions and ACs, white text entries will lead to the Mission Intel chapter, while references in red text will lead to the S-Rank Guide and the Arena Guide, respectively.

INCOMING CREDITS & THANKS

ARMORED CORE VI FIRES OF RUBICON OFFICIAL PILOT'S MANUAL

A *FUTUREPRESS* GAME GUIDE

Created and published by
Future Press Verlag & Marketing GmbH
Mansteinstr. 52, 20253 Hamburg, Germany

■ FUTURE PRESS

MANAGING DIRECTORS	Frank Glaser
	Jörg Kraut
EDITOR-IN-CHIEF	Wil Murray
EDITORS	Bruce Byrne
	Jonathan Gagné
AUTHORS	Christopher Honard
	Dylan Hirtler
	Grant (Glance)
	Nehemiah Wesley Ramazanov
	Sam Maxwell Gordenier
LAYOUT	Jörg Kraut
	Sven Kanth
ASSET TRANSLATION	Leuca Hache

■ STAY IN TOUCH future-press.com // support@future-press.com
■ TWITTER/X/FACEBOOK/YOUTUBE /futurepress
■ INSTAGRAM /futurepressbooks

■ THANKS TO OUR FAMILY & FRIENDS

Luke Doherty, Ryan Payton, David Waybright, Björn Hammarstroem, Anwar Hassan, Lyne & Serge Gagné and Fran Smyth, Annette Byrne, Kathleen & Patrick Murray, Ulrike, Jim and Caitlin Murray, Grit, Jil & Emmie Preuss, Katja, Lea & Alex Glaser

ISBN 9783869931272 // Printed in Germany.

■ BANDAI NAMCO ENTERTAINMENT AMERICA INC.

ARMORED CORE VI FIRES OF RUBICON GAME TEAM

PRODUCER	Amanda Khoury Ruscher
DIRECTOR, BRAND	Adrian Chen
SENIOR BRAND MANAGER	Raymond So
BRAND MANAGERS	David Alonzo, Sam Wilkinson
ASSOCIATE BRAND MANAGERS	Carolyn Chang, Savannah Ho
QUALITY ASSURANCE PROJECT MANAGER	Keith Kit Alorro

CORPORATE DEVELOPMENT

SENIOR VICE PRESIDENT, CORPORATE DEVELOPMENT	Karim Farghaly
MANAGER, LICENSING & BUSINESS STRATEGY	Yu Sugimoto
SENIOR DIRECTOR, LICENSING	Linh Forse
DIRECTOR, LICENSING	Daphine Carrillo

■ GLOBALSTEP (MONTREAL)

QUALITY ASSURANCE PROJECT MANAGER	Tyler Tizard
QUALITY ASSURANCE	Jean-Sébastien Laganière, Marc-André Brière, Sherman Fong, Joshua Melanson, Elijah Salcedo

MARKETING & PUBLIC RELATIONS

DIRECTOR, SOCIAL MARKETING AND COMMUNITY MANAGEMENT	Erin Berkenmeier
SOCIAL MARKETING MANAGER	Samantha Reinert
ASSOCIATE COMMUNITY MANAGER, SOCIAL MARKETING	Tanner Levine
SOCIAL MARKETING & COMMUNITY MANAGER, COMPETITIVE GAMES	Rose Renzelman
SPECIALIST, SOCIAL & DIGITAL CONTENT	Krista De Guzman
SENIOR MANAGER, CRM	Michael C. Lee
ASSOCIATE CRM MANAGER	Josiah Rodriguez Beke

■ BANDAI NAMCO ENTERTAINMENT EUROPE S.A.S

ARMORED CORE VI FIRES OF RUBICON GAME TEAM

PRODUCER	Bertrand Mangin
BRAND CORE TEAM	Nazim Doualane

MARKETING AND COMMUNICATIONS

EMEA PRODUCT MANAGER	Charlotte Latil
SOCIAL MEDIA MANAGER	Elissa Dukes
COMMUNITY SPECIALIST	Théo Rusé-Cartereau
EMEA PR & COMMUNICATIONS MANAGER	Steven Favret
CREATIVE PROJECT MANAGER	Etienne Viriot
CREATIVE SPECIALIST	Stella Neang
WEB MARKETING SPECIALIST	Tatjana Gouin
WEB ASSISTANT	Erine Peyronie

LICENSING & BUSINESS STRATEGY

DIRECTOR OF LICENSING & BUSINESS STRATEGY	Aâdil Tayouga
LICENSING AND BUSINESS STRATEGY MANAGER	Kazuki Ikeda
LICENSING AND TRANSMEDIA PARTNERSHIPS SENIOR MANAGER	Clémence Oliviero

■ BANDAI NAMCO ENTERTAINMENT INC.

ARMORED CORE VI FIRES OF RUBICON GAME TEAM

GLOBAL LOCALIZATION COORDINATION & ENGLISH LOCALIZATION	Jeremy Clark, Hiroki Saito
GLOBAL MARKETING	Shuhei Hokari, Eshley Gao, Marina Komatsu, Masami Ozaki
ASSISTANT PRODUCERS	Yuta Kamio, Kohei Sugihara
CHIEF PRODUCER	Atsuo Yoshimura

■ FROMSOFTWARE, INC.

ARMORED CORE VI FIRES OF RUBICON GAME TEAM